Lecture Notes in Computer Science 12607

Founding Editors

Gerhard Goos, Germany
Juris Hartmanis, USA

Editorial Board Members

Elisa Bertino, USA
Wen Gao, China
Bernhard Steffen⬤, Germany

Gerhard Woeginger⬤, Germany
Moti Yung, USA

Advanced Research in Computing and Software Science
Subline of Lecture Notes in Computer Science

Subline Series Editors

Giorgio Ausiello, *University of Rome 'La Sapienza', Italy*
Vladimiro Sassone, *University of Southampton, UK*

Subline Advisory Board

Susanne Albers, *TU Munich, Germany*
Benjamin C. Pierce, *University of Pennsylvania, USA*
Bernhard Steffen⬤, *University of Dortmund, Germany*
Deng Xiaotie, *Peking University, Beijing, China*
Jeannette M. Wing, *Microsoft Research, Redmond, WA, USA*

More information about this subseries at http://www.springer.com/series/7407

Tomáš Bureš · Riccardo Dondi ·
Johann Gamper · Giovanna Guerrini ·
Tomasz Jurdziński · Claus Pahl ·
Florian Sikora · Prudence W. H. Wong (Eds.)

SOFSEM 2021:
Theory and Practice
of Computer Science

47th International Conference on Current Trends
in Theory and Practice of Computer Science, SOFSEM 2021
Bolzano-Bozen, Italy, January 25–29, 2021
Proceedings

 Springer

Editors
Tomáš Bureš
Charles University
Prague, Czech Republic

Riccardo Dondi
University of Bergamo
Bergamo, Italy

Johann Gamper 🆔
Free University of Bozen-Bolzano
Bolzano, Italy

Giovanna Guerrini
University of Genoa
Genoa, Italy

Tomasz Jurdziński
University of Wroclaw
Wroclaw, Poland

Claus Pahl
Free University of Bozen-Bolzano
Bolzano, Italy

Florian Sikora 🆔
University Paris Dauphine
Paris, France

Prudence W. H. Wong
University of Liverpool
Liverpool, UK

ISSN 0302-9743   ISSN 1611-3349   (electronic)
Lecture Notes in Computer Science
ISBN 978-3-030-67730-5   ISBN 978-3-030-67731-2   (eBook)
https://doi.org/10.1007/978-3-030-67731-2

LNCS Sublibrary: SL1 – Theoretical Computer Science and General Issues

This Springer imprint is published by the registered company Springer Nature Switzerland AG
The registered company address is: Gewerbestrasse 11, 6330 Cham, Switzerland

Preface

This volume contains the invited and contributed papers selected for presentation at SOFSEM 2021, the 47th International Conference on Current Trends in Theory and Practice of Computer Science, which was held online during January 25–29, 2021, hosted by the Free University of Bozen-Bolzano, Italy.

SOFSEM (originally SOFtware SEMinar) is an annual international winter conference devoted to the theory and practice of computer science. Its aim is to present the latest developments in research for professionals from academia and industry working in leading areas of computer science. While being a well-established and fully international conference, SOFSEM also maintains the best of its original Winter School aspects, such as a high number of invited talks, in-depth coverage of selected research areas, and ample opportunity to discuss and exchange new ideas. SOFSEM 2021 was organized around the following four tracks:

- Foundations of Computer Science (chairs: Tomasz Jurdziński and Prudence W. H. Wong)
- Foundations of Data Science and Engineering (chair: Giovanna Guerrini)
- Foundations of Software Engineering (chair: Tomáš Bureš)
- Foundations of Algorithmic Computational Biology (chairs: Riccardo Dondi and Florian Sikora)

With these tracks, SOFSEM 2021 covered the latest advances in both theoretical and applied research in leading areas of computer science.

An integral part of SOFSEM 2021 was the traditional Student Research Forum (chairs: Anton Dignös, Nabil El Ioini, Bruno Rossi) organized with the aim of giving students feedback both on the originality of their scientific results and on their work in progress.

The SOFSEM 2021 Program Committee (PC) consisted of 91 international experts from 28 countries across the 4 tracks, representing the track areas with outstanding expertise. Another 62 external reviewers contributed as well. The committee undertook the task of assembling a scientific program for the SOFSEM audience by selecting from 100 submissions from 31 countries entered in the EasyChair system in response to the call for papers. The submissions were carefully reviewed with at least 3 reviews per paper and thoroughly discussed. Following strict criteria of quality and originality, 33 papers were accepted for presentation as regular research papers, as well as 7 papers for presentation as short papers. These 40 papers were contributed by authors from 26 countries. Thus, the acceptance ratio for regular papers was 33%, plus another 7% for short papers.

As editors of these proceedings, we are grateful to everyone who contributed to the scientific program of the conference. We would like to thank the invited speakers:

- Thomas Erlebach (University of Leicester, UK)
- Renée Miller (Northeastern University, USA)

- Merav Parter (Weizmann Institute of Science, Israel)
- Jiří Wiedermann (Academy of Sciences, Czech Republic)
- Jan van Leeuwen (Utrecht University, The Netherlands)
- Celine Scornavacca (CNRS, Université de Montpellier, France)

for presenting their work to the audience of SOFSEM 2021. We thank all authors who submitted their papers for consideration. Many thanks are due to the PC members, and to all external referees, for their precise and detailed reviewing of the submissions. The work of the PC was carried out using the EasyChair system, and we gratefully acknowledge this contribution.

Special thanks are due to the SOFSEM Steering Committee, headed by Július Štuller, for its support throughout the preparation of the conference.

January 2021

Tomáš Bureš
Riccardo Dondi
Johann Gamper
Giovanna Guerrini
Tomasz Jurdziński
Claus Pahl
Florian Sikora
Prudence W. H. Wong

Organization

General Chairs

Johann Gamper	Free University of Bozen-Bolzano, Italy
Claus Pahl	Free University of Bozen-Bolzano, Italy

Program Committee Chairs

Tomasz Jurdziński	University of Wrocław, Poland
Prudence W. H. Wong	University of Liverpool, UK
Tomáš Bureš	Charles University, Czech Republic
Giovanna Guerrini	University of Genoa, Italy
Riccardo Dondi	University of Bergamo, Italy
Florian Sikora	Université Paris-Dauphine, France

Steering Committee

Július Štuller (Chair)	Academy of Sciences, Czech Republic
Barbara Catania	University of Genoa, Italy
Miroslaw Kutylowski	Wrocław University of Technology, Poland
Tiziana Margaria-Steffen	University of Limerick, Ireland
Branislav Rovan	Comenius University in Bratislava, Slovakia
Petr Saloun	Technical University of Ostrava, Czech Republic
Jan van Leeuwen	Utrecht University, The Netherland

Program Committee

Foundations of Computer Science

Leonid Barenboim	Open University of Israel, Israel
Marie-Pierre Béal	Université Paris-Est Marne-la-Vallée, France
Marcin Bieńkowski	University of Wrocław, Poland
Shantanu Das	Aix-Marseille University, France
Gianluca De Marco	University of Salerno, Italy
Martin Dietzfelbinger	Technische Universität Ilmenau, Germany
György Dósa	University of Pannonia, Hungary
Leszek Gąsieniec	University of Liverpool, UK; Augusta University, USA
Lucjan Hanzlik	Stanford University, USA
Markus Holzer	Justus Liebig University Giessen, Germany
Christos A. Kapoutsis	Carnegie Mellon University in Qatar, Qatar
Jarkko Kari	University of Turku, Finland
Rastislav Královič	Comenius University in Bratislava, Slovakia

Orna Kupferman	The Hebrew University of Jerusalem, Israel
Mirosław Kutyłowski	Wrocław University of Science and Technology, Poland
Alexei Lisitsa	University of Liverpool, UK
Hsiang-Hsuan Liu	Utrecht University, The Netherland
Euripides Markou	University of Thessaly, Greece
Miguel A. Mosteiro	Pace University, USA
František Mráz	Charles University, Czech Republic
Kim Thang Nguyen	IBISC, Univ. Évry, Université Paris-Saclay, France
Alexander Okhotin	St. Petersburg State University, Russia
Solon P. Pissis	CWI, The Netherland
Alexandru Popa	University of Bucharest, Romania
Tomasz Radzik	King's College London, UK
Dror Rawitz	Bar-Ilan University, Israel

Foundations of Software Engineering

Apostolos Ampatzoglou	University of Macedonia, Greece
Paolo Arcaini	National Institute of Informatics, Japan
Francesca Arcelli Fontana	University of Milano-Bicocca, Italy
Steffen Becker	University of Stuttgart, Germany
Stefan Biffl	Vienna University of Technology, Austria
Jalil Boudjadar	Aarhus University, Denmark
Premek Brada	University of West Bohemia, Czech Republic
Federico Ciccozzi	Mälardalen University, Sweden
Marios Fokaefs	École Polytechnique de Montréal, Canada
Ilias Gerostathopoulos	Vrije Universiteit Amsterdam, The Netherland
Petr Hnétynka	Charles University, Czech Republic
Clemente Izurieta	Montana State University, USA
Johan Jeuring	Utrecht University and Open University, The Netherland
Anne Koziolek	Karlsruhe Institute of Technology, Germany
Maurizio Leotta	Università di Genova, Italy
Raffaela Mirandola	Politecnico di Milano, Italy
Jerzy Nawrocki	Poznań University of Technology, Poland
Fabio Palomba	University of Salerno, Italy
Patrizia Scandurra	DIIMM - University of Bergamo, Italy
Valentino Vranić	Slovak University of Technology in Bratislava, Slovakia
Danny Weyns	Katholieke Universiteit Leuven, Belgium
Manuel Wimmer	Johannes Kepler University Linz, Austria
Wolf Zimmermann	Martin Luther University Halle-Wittenberg, Germany

Foundations of Data Science and Engineering

| Nikolaus Augsten | University of Salzburg, Austria |
| Ladjel Bellatreche | LIAS/ENSMA, France |

Michela Bertolotto	University College Dublin, Ireland
Mária Bieliková	Slovak University of Technology in Bratislava, Slovakia
Stéphane Bressan	National University of Singapore, Singapore
Davide Buscaldi	LIPN, Université Sorbonne Paris Nord, France
Barbara Catania	University of Genoa, Italy
Johann Eder	Alpen-Adria-Universität Klagenfurt, Austria
Floris Geerts	University of Antwerp, Belgium
Ernesto Jiménez-Ruiz	City, University of London, UK
Georgia Koutrika	Athena Research Center, Greece
Sebastian Link	The University of Auckland, New Zealand
Marco Mesiti	University of Milan, Italy
Paolo Missier	Newcastle University, UK
Kostas Stefanidis	Tampere University, Finland
Ernest Teniente	Universitat Politècnica de Catalunya, Spain
Martin Theobald	University of Luxembourg, Luxembourg
Maurice van Keulen	University of Twente, The Netherland
Panos Vassiliadis	University of Ioannina, Greece
Robert Wrembel	Poznań Unviersity of Technology, Poland

Foundations of Algorithmic Computational Biology

Guillaume Blin	Université de Bordeaux, France
Edouard Bonnet	ENS Lyon, CNRS, France
Broňa Brejová	Comenius University in Bratislava, Slovakia
Laurent Bulteau	CNRS - Université Paris-Est Marne-la-Vallée, France
Zhi-Zhong Chen	Tokyo Denki University, Japan
Peter Damaschke	Chalmers University of Technology, Sweden
Mohammed El-Kebir	University of Illinois at Urbana-Champaign, USA
Nadia El-Mabrouk	Université de Montréal, Canada
Pawel Gorecki	University of Warsaw, Poland
Jesper Jansson	The Hong Kong Polytechnic University, Hong Kong
Minghui Jiang	Utah State University, USA
Iyad Kanj	DePaul University, USA
Christian Komusiewicz	Philipps-Universität Marburg, Germany
Manuel Lafond	Université de Sherbrooke, Canada
Zsuzsanna Liptak	University of Verona, Italy
Neeldhara Misra	Indian Institute of Science, India
Nadia Pisanti	University of Pisa, Italy
Alberto Policriti	University of Udine, Italy
Eric Rivals	Université de Montpellier, France
Marinella Sciortino	University of Palermo, Italy
Mathias Weller	CNRS, Université Paris-Est Marne-la-Vallée, France
Meirav Zehavi	Ben-Gurion University of the Negev, Israel

Additional Reviewers

Abhinav Srivastav
Aleksi Saarela
Alexander Melnikov
Anna Lauks-Dutka
Arnaud Labourel
Basile Couëtoux
Carla Selmi
Christoph Dürr
Claudio Antares Mezzina
Dana Pardubská
Daniel Gibney
Daniel Průša
Dariusz Dereniowski
Dariusz Kowalski
Dominique Perrin
Erik Jan van Leeuwen
Evangelos Bampas
Evangelos Kranakis
Fedor Sandomirskiy
Fu-Hong Liu
Henning Fernau
Ian McQuillan
Istvan Estelyi
Ján Mazák
Jérémie Chalopin
Jesper Nederlof
Leizhen Cai
Loukas Georgiadis
Lu Dong
Lukasz Kowalik
Luke Mathieson

Marinella Sciortino
Martin Böhm
Martin Kutrib
Maxime Crochemore
Mikhail Volkov
Nicola Prezza
Patrick Brosi
Patryk Stopyra
Paula Medina
Paweł Schmidt
Peter Auer
Peter Høyer
Philipp Kindermann
Razvan Vasile
Rod Downey
Rogério Reis
Ronny Hänsch
Samuel Pecár
Sankardeep Chakraborty
Sarah Christensen
Sebastian Ordyniak
Sergey Verlan
Stefan Dobrev
Stefan M. Moser
Tami Tamir
Thierry Lecroq
Thomas Kesselheim
Tomohiro Koana
Valia Mitsou
Vincent Chau
Wiktor Zuba

Reconstructing Phylogenetic Networks from Sequences: Where We Stand and What to Do Next (Abstract of Invited Paper)

Celine Scornavacca

IISEM, Univ. Montpellier, CNRS, IRD, EPHE, 34095 Montpellier, France
celine.scornavacca@umontpellier.fr
http://celine.scornavacca.org

Abstract. Phylogenetics is the field of evolutionary biology that studies evolutionary relationships among species through the analysis of molecular data. Graphs are used to depict the relatedness and shared history of multiple species. Traditionally, these graphs are rooted leaf-labelled trees. These trees are devised to represent evolutionary histories in which the main events are specifications (at the internal nodes of the tree) and descent with modification (along the branches of the tree). However, the last few years have witnessed a growing appreciation of reticulate evolution – that is, events causing inheritance from more than one ancestor. Classic examples of such events are hybrid speciation, horizontal gene transfer and recombination. Such events cannot be represented on trees, and in these cases using rooted leaf-labelled DAGs is more appropriate. There remains a strong demand for practical algorithms to reconstruct such DAGs from genomic data, mainly due to the fact that existing methods can only be used on a small number of taxa. In this talk, I will present several recent progresses towards efficient and scalable algorithms for the task.

Keywords: Phylogenetic network · Maximum parsimony · Maximum likelihood · NP-hardnes · Fixed-parameter tractability

Contents

Foundations of Data Science and Engineering – Short Papers

Foundations of Algorithmic Computational Biology – Full Papers

Invited Papers

Algorithms that Access the Input via Queries

Thomas Erlebach[(✉)]

School of Informatics, University of Leicester, Leicester, England
`te17@leicester.ac.uk`

Abstract. Problems where an algorithm cannot simply access the whole input but needs to obtain information about it using queries arise naturally in many settings. We discuss different aspects of models where an algorithm needs to query the input, and of how the performance of algorithms for such models can be measured. After that, we give some concrete examples of algorithmic settings and results for scenarios where algorithms access the input via queries. Finally, we discuss recent results for the setting of computing with explorable uncertainty with parallel queries and with untrusted predictions.

Keywords: Explorable uncertainty · Query-competitive algorithm

1 Introduction

In classical algorithms research, it is typically assumed that the full input of a problem is provided to an algorithm at the start of its execution, and the algorithm can freely access the input or any parts of it. Another model is the setting of online computation, where the input is provided to an algorithm over time, and irrevocable decisions need to be made without knowledge of future parts of the input. There is also the model of streaming algorithms, where algorithms can only read the input linearly (one or several times) and must compute results while using only a small amount of working memory (much smaller than the size of the input).

In all these settings, the algorithm has no control over how the input is presented to it. The situation changes substantially when an algorithm is given the chance to actively ask about parts of the input. We will refer to the operation that an algorithm can execute in order to learn a specific piece of information about the input as a *query*. Depending on the context, such queries are sometimes also called *probes* or *oracle accesses*. For example, a query could correspond to simply looking up the element in a certain position of a large matrix (e.g., the adjacency matrix of the input graph), or to a comparison between two input elements that returns which of the two elements is smaller, or to determining whether a given point lies inside a convex input object or not. In settings where the algorithm accesses the input via queries, one often considers the goal of solving the given problem using a minimum number of queries.

Supported by EPSRC grant "Algorithms for Computing with Uncertainty: Theory and Experiments" (EP/S033483/1).

T. Bureš et al. (Eds.): SOFSEM 2021, LNCS 12607, pp. 3–12, 2021.
https://doi.org/10.1007/978-3-030-67731-2_1

The consideration of problem settings where algorithms access the input via queries is often motivated by application scenarios that naturally lead to the notion of queries, but sometimes it is also useful to consider a model with queries in order to derive lower bounds on the running-time of algorithms that solve a problem using a certain type of operations. For example, lower bounds on the number of comparison queries that a sorting algorithm needs to perform lead to lower bounds on the running-time of comparison-based sorting algorithms, and lower bounds on the number of demand queries needed for bipartite maximum matching yield lower bounds on the running-time of certain types of matching algorithms [20].

In this paper, we will first discuss the different aspects of models where an algorithm needs to query the input, and of how algorithms for such models can be analyzed. Then, we will give some examples of algorithmic settings and results for scenarios where algorithms access the input via queries. After that, we will discuss recent results for the setting of computing with explorable uncertainty. In that setting, the input contains uncertain elements – these are elements for which only a set containing the precise value is known, but not the precise value itself. A query of an element returns its precise value. For example, an uncertain input element may be given as the open interval $(2, 4)$, and a query of the element may reveal that its precise value is 3.7.

2   Modeling and Analyzing a Problem with Queries

The basic ingredients that are needed to specify an algorithmic problem where the algorithm accesses the input via queries (and how we want to measure the performance of the algorithm) are as follows: What information is provided to the algorithm in advance, and what kind of queries is the algorithm allowed to make to obtain further information? Does the algorithm make the queries sequentially (i.e., can it use the answers of all previous queries to determine what next query it will make), or must it make all queries simultaneously, or can it make queries in rounds, where the queries in each round must be made simultaneously? (We consider sequential queries for now and will discuss parallel queries briefly at the end of this section.) What is the algorithm required to output? Is our goal to use as few queries as possible, or are we also interested in the running-time of other operations that the algorithm executes? If our goal is to minimize the number of queries, are we aiming for an absolute bound on the number of queries (e.g., as a function of the input size), or do we want to compare the number of queries that the algorithm makes for the given instance with the best possible number of queries for that same instance? Furthermore, queries could be associated with costs, and we might be interested in minimizing the total cost of the queries the algorithm makes, instead of just the number of queries.

It is worth discussing briefly the notion of the *best possible number of queries* for a given input, as this notion sometimes causes confusion. It refers to the size of a *smallest feasible query set*, i.e., to the minimum number of queries that allow an algorithm to obtain sufficient information to be able to output a provably correct solution.

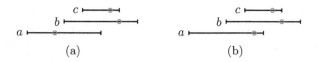

Fig. 1. Two example instances of the minimum problem with uncertainty.

The problem of computing the best possible number of queries, given full information about the input (including the answers to all possible queries), is also called the *verification problem*. The set of queries that form a solution to the verification problem is also referred to as the *offline optimum*, and its cardinality is usually denoted by OPT. An algorithm is ρ-*query competitive* if, on any input, it makes at most $\rho \cdot OPT$ queries.

For example, consider the problem of having to determine which of the three elements a, b, c has the smallest value, where initially we are given only intervals I_a, I_b, I_c containing their precise values, see Fig. 1. If the precise values are as indicated by the little circles in Fig. 1(a), the minimal feasible query sets are $\{a\}$ and $\{b, c\}$, so the smallest feasible query set is $\{a\}$, and we have $OPT = 1$. If the precise values are as shown in Fig. 1(b), the only minimal feasible query set is $\{b, c\}$, and we have $OPT = 2$.

Apart from the model with sequential queries, which is called the *adaptive* query model, it is also interesting to consider models where queries can or must be made simultaneously. The extreme case is where all queries must be made simultaneously and the algorithm must guarantee that, no matter what the answers to the queries are, it will have sufficient information to output a provably correct solution to the problem. This is called the *non-adaptive* query model.

An intermediate model allows an algorithm to make several rounds of queries. The queries in each round are made in parallel, and the results of the queries of all previous rounds can be taken into account when determining the queries to be made in the next round. The two most natural models in this setting are the model where the number of rounds is fixed in advance, and the goal is to minimize the number of queries made in total [4,19]; and the model where the number of queries that can be made in each round is bounded, and the goal is to minimize the number of query rounds [8].

3   A Small Sample of Query Models and Results

In this section, we briefly touch upon a number of examples of existing models that fit into the general theme of algorithms that ask queries, and of results for these models. Our aim is to give a glimpse of the wide range of existing models and results, without any attempt to achieve complete coverage. The amount of work that will not be mentioned far exceeds the amount presented, and we apologize in advance to all authors whose work is not covered here.

An area that has been studied extensively and for which a plethora of results have been obtained is **property testing** [9], which considers sublinear algorithms for decision problems. The task is to decide whether the input satisfies a certain property P or is ε-far from having that property. The algorithm is typically randomized, and it must output YES with probability at least $2/3$ (or with probability 1 if the algorithm has *one-sided error*) if the input has the property P, and NO with probability at least $2/3$ if the input is ε-far from having the property P. As an example, consider the problem of checking whether a given undirected graph with n vertices, represented by an adjacency matrix whose entries can be accessed via queries, is bipartite or ε-far from being bipartite. Here, a graph is ε-far from being bipartite if one has to remove at least εn^2 edges to make the graph bipartite. A randomized property tester with one-sided error for bipartiteness that makes $O(\text{poly}(1/\varepsilon))$ queries (note that this number is independent of the size of the graph) can be obtained by sampling vertices, checking if the subgraph induced by those vertices is bipartite, and outputting YES if it is, and NO otherwise. Hence, bipartiteness can be checked with a constant number of non-adaptive queries, for every fixed $\varepsilon > 0$. In general, however, adaptivity can have a significant impact on the number of queries needed in property testing [4].

The **graph reconstruction** problem is the problem of reconstructing the edge set of a hidden graph by asking queries. Initially, the vertex set V of the graph is known, and the goal is to determine all its edges. Graph reconstruction has been studied for many different query models. Some examples are as follows. *Additive queries* specify a subset S of the vertex set V and return the number of edges in the subgraph induced by S. Mazzawi gave a polynomial-time constructive algorithm that solves this problem using a number of queries that matches the information-theoretic lower bound [17]. Furthermore, the algorithm asks its queries in a logarithmic number of rounds. *Layered-graph queries* specify a vertex v and return the set of all edges that lie on at least one shortest path between v and any another vertex, i.e., the union of all shortest-path trees rooted at v. Beerliova et al. [3] gave a randomized $O(\sqrt{n \log n})$-query-competitive algorithm (also for the case of *all-distance queries*, where a query at v returns the distances from v to all other vertices), and Sen and Muralidhara [23] gave an improved $O(\log^2 n)$-query competitive Monte Carlo randomized algorithm. Kannan et al. [16] study network discovery using distance queries and shortest-path queries: *Distance queries* specify a pair (u, v) of vertices and return the number of edges on a shortest path between u and v. *Shortest-path queries* specify a pair (u, v) of vertices and return the edge set of an arbitrary shortest path between u and v.

The problem of **edge estimation**, i.e., estimating the number m of edges of a hidden graph with vertex set V, was studied by Beame et al. [2]. They consider *independent set queries* (specified by a subset S of V, and returning whether the subgraph induced by V contains at least one edge) and *bipartite independent set queries* (specified by two disjoint subsets A and B of V, and returning whether the graph contains at least one edge between a vertex in A

and a vertex in B). Considering randomized algorithms that output an estimate that lies within a factor of $1+\varepsilon$ of m with high probability, they give an algorithm that uses polylog(n) bipartite independent set queries and an algorithm that uses $n^{2/3} \cdot$ polylog(n) independent set queries.

Minimum cut problems for a hidden graph with vertex set V were studied by Rubinstein et al. [22]. They consider *cut queries*, which specify a subset S of V and return the size of the cut between S and $V \setminus S$. They present randomized algorithms that compute, with high probability, a minimum s-t-cut using $\tilde{O}(n^{5/3})$ queries and a global minimum cut using $\tilde{O}(n)$ queries.

Recently, a **demand query model** (motivated by demand queries that were previously considered in economic settings) was studied for the bipartite matching problem by Nisan [20]. We are given the vertex set of a bipartite graph, with n left vertices and n right vertices. A *demand query* specifies a left vertex v and an order σ of the right vertices. The answer to the query is the first right vertex w in the order σ that is adjacent to v (or 0 if no such vertex exists). A demand query can be simulated by $\log_2(n+1)$ OR-queries, where an OR query specifies a left vertex v and a subset S of the right vertices, and returns whether there exists a vertex in S that is adjacent to v. Therefore, lower bounds on the number of OR queries translate into lower bounds on the number of demand queries, up to logarithmic factors. Nisan shows that a deterministic algorithm that runs in $n^{o(1)}$ rounds, where each round can make at most $n^{1.99}$ demand queries, cannot find a matching whose size is within a $n^{o(1)}$ factor of the maximum matching size. This is in contrast to the existence of a randomized algorithm that produces a $(1 - \varepsilon)$-approximate maximum matching in $O(\frac{1}{\varepsilon^2} \log n)$ rounds of n demand queries each [5].

Taking a broader view, other problem areas where algorithms ask queries about the input are geometric algorithms in combinatorial optimization (where convex bodies are presented via separation oracles) [11], black-box optimization (where the goal is to find the maximum or the minimum of a function that is given via an oracle that can be used to query the value of the function for given values of its parameters) [1,10] and query-based learning (a field of machine learning where the learner is active and has a dialogue with the teacher) [14].

4   Explorable Uncertainty

As already discussed in the introduction, explorable uncertainty refers to settings where only uncertain information about some elements of the input is initially available, while precise information can be obtained via queries. For sequential queries, one is usually interested in query-competitive algorithms, as for most problems one cannot hope for non-trivial absolute bounds on the number of queries. Kahan's pioneering work [15] studied query-competitive algorithms for the problems of computing the maximum, the median, or the closest pair of a given set of uncertain values.

A problem that has been widely studied in this setting is the minimum spanning tree problem with edge uncertainty (MST-U) [13]: We are given a connected, undirected graph $G = (V, E)$ together with an interval I_e for each edge

$e \in E$. Each of these intervals I_e can be either an open interval $I_e = (L_e, U_e)$ or a singleton set $I_e = \{w_e\}$. The precise weight of the edge e is a value w_e that is guaranteed to lie in I_e, but initially unknown to an algorithm (except in the case where I_e is a singleton interval). Querying an edge e (or querying the interval I_e) is an operation that returns the precise value w_e. The goal is to compute the edge set of a minimum spanning tree of G with respect to the edge weights w_e, after making as few queries as possible. It was shown in [13] that a deterministic 2-query-competitive algorithm for MST-U can be obtained by repeatedly identifying a *witness set* of size 2 and querying both its elements. Here a witness set is a set W of uncertain elements with the property that it is impossible to identify a provably correct minimum spanning tree without querying at least one of the elements of W. Algorithms that repeatedly identify and query a witness set are also called *witness set algorithms*. It is known that query-competitive ratio 2 is best possible for deterministic algorithms for MST-U. Randomization makes it possible to improve the competitive ratio at least to $1 + 1/\sqrt{2} \approx 1.707$ [18].

We refer to [6] for a survey of work on explorable uncertainty until 2015, including results for non-adaptive query models. In the rest of this section, we discuss our recent work on explorable uncertainty with parallel queries [7], and on explorable uncertainty with untrusted predictions [8].

4.1   Parallel Queries

While sequential query models allow the algorithm to benefit immediately from the result of each query, a very natural question is how the situation changes if a number of queries can be made in parallel. This is desirable in many application settings because making queries in parallel can save time, and often there are sufficient resources available to execute a certain number of queries simultaneously. Let us assume that we are allowed to make up to k queries in parallel in each round, and that our goal is to minimize the number of query rounds we need until we have obtained sufficient information to solve the given problem.

Denote by OPT_1 the best possible number of queries for the given instance of the problem, and by OPT_k the best possible number of query rounds. It is clear that $OPT_k = \lceil OPT_1/k \rceil$, because the OPT_1 queries can be distributed arbitrarily into rounds of up to k queries. Let ALG_k be the number of query rounds of an algorithm ALG. Then the algorithm is called *ρ-round-competitive* for a problem if $ALG_k \leq \rho \cdot OPT_k$ for all instances of the problem.

While the witness set concept has been hugely successful for designing query-competitive algorithms for sequential query models, it is not sufficient for designing algorithms for the parallel query model if k is much larger than the size of the witness sets. One might wish to add different witness sets to a query round until the round is full, but the problem is that the identity of further witness sets may depend on the results of queries made for the first witness set. Therefore, new ideas are needed for the parallel query model.

In joint work with Hoffmann and de Lima [7], we considered the problem of determining the minimum value of each of a number of possibly overlapping sets of uncertain elements. More formally, we are given a ground set $\mathcal{I}$ of n uncertain values represented by intervals I_i (which can be open intervals or singleton sets) for $1 \leq i \leq n$, and a family $\mathcal{S}$ of non-empty subsets of $\mathcal{I}$. Let w_i denote the precise value of I_i. Querying I_i returns w_i. The problem we want to solve is to find for each set $S \in \mathcal{S}$ the element of S with minimum precise value, together with its precise value.

If $\mathcal{S}$ consists of a single set S, then it is easy to show that querying the intervals in order of non-decreasing left endpoints is an optimal query strategy in the sequential model. This query strategy can be easily adapted to rounds with k queries: We simply query in each round the k intervals with smallest left endpoints, until we have obtained sufficient information to identify the minimum element and its value.

The problem becomes more difficult if $\mathcal{S}$ contains multiple sets and if these sets may have elements in common. Call a set in $\mathcal{S}$ *unsolved* if the precise value of its minimum element cannot be identified yet. It is clear that querying the interval with smallest left endpoint in each unsolved set is necessary, but what if these queries are not enough to fill a round of k queries? How should the remaining queries that we can make in the round be distributed to all the unsolved sets? In [7] we propose an algorithm that is inspired by how some primal-dual algorithms work, although no linear program features in the analysis. Each unsolved set is given a budget, initially zero. Then the budgets of all sets are grown at the same rate. When the budgets of the unsolved sets that have the same interval I_i as the interval with smallest endpoint, among the unqueried intervals of the set that have not yet been added to the current query round, add up to 1, these sets 'buy' a query for I_i, their budgets are reset to 0, and the query is added to the current round. This repeats until the round is full. We can show that the number of query rounds that this algorithm needs is at most

$$(2 + \varepsilon) \cdot OPT_k + O\left(\frac{1}{\varepsilon} \cdot \log m\right)$$

for every $0 < \varepsilon < 1$, where m denotes the number of sets in $\mathcal{S}$. The execution of the algorithm does not depend on ε, so the bound holds simultaneously for all $0 < \varepsilon < 1$.

We also show that for arbitrarily large m there are instances with $k > m$ and $OPT_k = 1$ for which every deterministic algorithm ALG requires

$$\Omega\left(\frac{\log \min\{k, m\}}{\log \log \min\{k, m\}}\right)$$

queries. Thus, the additive term of the upper bound cannot be completely avoided. The lower bound holds even for instances where the sets in $\mathcal{S}$ are pairwise disjoint. For that special case we show that distributing the queries in a balanced way among all unsolved sets yields an $O(\log \min\{k, m\} / \log \log \min\{k, m\})$-round-competitive algorithm. We also give 2-round competitive algorithms for sorting multiple sets (by adapting ideas from previous work on sorting with uncertainty [12, 19]) and for determining the i-th smallest value (and all elements whose value is equal to that value) of a single set.

An interesting open problem for explorable uncertainty with parallel queries is what round-competitive ratio can be achieved for MST-U in this model.

4.2   Untrusted Predictions

The impressive successes in machine learning that have been achieved in recent years have motivated the study of online problems where the algorithm is provided with *predictions* for aspects of the problem instance or solution that would otherwise only be revealed over time as further parts of the input are given to the algorithm [21]. It is assumed that the predictions could be provided by a machine learning algorithm that has been trained on past instances. One expects that such predictions may often be very good, but could also be completely wrong in some cases. One is therefore interested in algorithms that benefit if the predictions are good, but whose performance does not deteriorate too much even if the predictions are completely wrong. The extreme cases are when the predictions are fully accurate, and when the predictions are arbitrarily wrong. An algorithm is said to be α-*consistent* and β-*robust* if it is α-query-competitive in the case where the predictions are fully accurate, and β-query-competitive no matter how wrong the predictions are. Ideally, one would additionally like the query-competitive ratio to degrade smoothly from α to β as the prediction error increases, for a suitable measure of how wrong the predictions are. Furthermore, one would like β to be equal to (or not much larger than) the best possible query-competitive ratio that can be achieved without predictions.

The incorporation of untrusted predictions also leads to interesting problems in the context of explorable uncertainty. In the following, we discuss our results obtained in joint work with Hoffmann, de Lima, Megow, and Schlöter [8]. We consider the following problems: Determining the minimum element (but not necessarily its value) of each set in a given family $\mathcal{S}$ of subsets of a ground set of uncertain values, sorting each set in a given family $\mathcal{S}$ of subsets of a ground set of uncertain values, and computing the edge set of a minimum spanning tree in a connected graph with uncertain edge weights. In each of these problems, for each uncertain element e we are given an interval I_e and a predicted value $\overline{w}_e \in I_e$. The true value of I_e is denoted by $w_e \in I_e$ and can be obtained by a query of I_e. Let us assume that each interval I_e is either an open interval or a singleton set. (The results for sorting apply to a more general setting.) Without predictions, the best possible query-competitive ratio that can be achieved for these problems is 2: A lower bound of 2 can be shown for determining the minimum of just two uncertain values with overlapping intervals, and ratio 2 can be achieved using witness set algorithms.

The problem of sorting multiple sets is a special case of the problem of determining the minimum elements of multiple sets, as sorting a set is equivalent to determining for each pair of given elements which of the two is smaller.

For sorting a single set of uncertain values, we obtain the best possible result that one can hope for, an algorithm that is 1-consistent, 2-robust, and whose performance degrades smoothly with the number of prediction errors: The algorithm makes at most $\min\{OPT + \kappa, 2 \cdot OPT\}$ queries, where κ is one of three prediction error measures: the number $\kappa_{\#}$ of inaccurate predictions, the hop distance κ_h between the predictions and the true values (where we count for each interval I_e the number of interval endpoints that lie between $\overline{w}_e$ and w_e), and the mandatory query distance κ_M (the number of intervals that are in every feasible query set if the predicted values are correct but not in every feasible query set with respect to the true values, and vice versa).

For the minimum problem with overlapping sets, for sorting overlapping sets, and for MST-U, we give algorithms that are 1.5-consistent and 2-robust. We also explore the trade-off between consistency and robustness, showing that consistency closer to 1 can be achieved at the cost of an increase in the robustness. For example, we achieve $(1+\frac{1}{\gamma})$-consistency and γ-robustness for the minimum problem with overlapping sets for every $\gamma \geq 2$. The performance of our algorithms degrades smoothly with κ_h for all problems, and with κ_M for the minimum problem (and therefore also the sorting problem) with overlapping sets.

References

1. Audet, C.: A survey on direct search methods for Blackbox optimization and their applications. In: Pardalos, P.M., Rassias, T.M. (eds.) Mathematics Without Boundaries, pp. 31–56. Springer, New York (2014). https://doi.org/10.1007/978-1-4939-1124-0_2
2. Beame, P., Har-Peled, S., Ramamoorthy, S.N., Rashtchian, C., Sinha, M.: Edge estimation with independent set oracles. ACM Trans. Algorithms 16(4), 52:1–52:27 (2020). https://doi.org/10.1145/3404867
3. Beerliova, Z., et al.: Network discovery and verification. IEEE J. Sel. Areas Commun. 24(12), 2168–2181 (2006). https://doi.org/10.1109/JSAC.2006.884015
4. Canonne, C.L., Gur, T.: An adaptivity hierarchy theorem for property testing. Comput. Complex. 27(4), 671–716 (2018). https://doi.org/10.1007/s00037-018-0168-4
5. Dobzinski, S., Nisan, N., Oren, S.: Economic efficiency requires interaction. Games Econ. Behav. 118, 589–608 (2019). https://doi.org/10.1016/j.geb.2018.02.010
6. Erlebach, T., Hoffmann, M.: Query-competitive algorithms for computing with uncertainty. Bulletin EATCS 116, 22–39 (2015). http://bulletin.eatcs.org/index.php/beatcs/article/view/335
7. Erlebach, T., Hoffmann, M., de Lima, M.S.: Round-competitive algorithms for uncertainty problems with parallel queries (2020), unpublished manuscript
8. Erlebach, T., Hoffmann, M., de Lima, M.S., Megow, N., Schlöter, J.: Untrusted predictions improve trustable query policies. CoRR abs/2011.07385 (2020). https://arxiv.org/abs/2011.07385
9. Goldreich, O.: Introduction to Property Testing. Cambridge University Press, Israel (2017). https://doi.org/10.1017/9781108135252
10. Graur, A., Pollner, T., Ramaswamy, V., Weinberg, S.M.: New query lower bounds for submodular function minimization. In: Vidick, T. (ed.) 11th Innovations in Theoretical Computer Science Conference (ITCS 2020). LIPIcs, vol. 151, pp. 64:1–64:16. Schloss Dagstuhl - Leibniz-Zentrum für Informatik (2020). https://doi.org/10.4230/LIPIcs.ITCS.2020.64
11. Grötschel, M., Lovász, L., Schrijver, A.: Geometric Algorithms and Combinatorial Optimization, Algorithms and Combinatorics, vol. 2. Springer, Berlin (1988). https://doi.org/10.1007/978-3-642-97881-4

12. Halldórsson, M.M., de Lima, M.S.: Query-competitive sorting with uncertainty. In: Rossmanith, P., Heggernes, P., Katoen, J. (eds.) 44th International Symposium on Mathematical Foundations of Computer Science (MFCS 2019). LIPIcs, vol. 138, pp. 7:1–7:15. Schloss Dagstuhl - Leibniz-Zentrum für Informatik (2019). https://doi.org/10.4230/LIPIcs.MFCS.2019.7

13. Hoffmann, M., Erlebach, T., Krizanc, D., Mihalák, M., Raman, R.: Computing minimum spanning trees with uncertainty. In: Albers, S., Weil, P. (eds.) 25th Annual Symposium on Theoretical Aspects of Computer Science (STACS 2008). LIPIcs, vol. 1, pp. 277–288. Schloss Dagstuhl - Leibniz-Zentrum für Informatik, Germany (2008). https://doi.org/10.4230/LIPIcs.STACS.2008.1358

14. Jain, S., Stephan, F.: Query-based learning. In: Sammut, C., Webb, G.I. (eds.) Encyclopedia of Machine Learning and Data Mining, pp. 1044–1047. Springer, Berlin (2017). https://doi.org/10.1007/978-1-4899-7687-1_694

15. Kahan, S.: A model for data in motion. In: Koutsougeras, C., Vitter, J.S. (eds.) 23rd Annual ACM Symposium on Theory of Computing (STOC 1991), pp. 265–277 (1991). https://doi.org/10.1145/103418.103449

16. Kannan, S., Mathieu, C., Zhou, H.: Graph reconstruction and verification. ACM Trans. Algorithms **14**(4), 40:1–40:30 (2018). https://doi.org/10.1145/3199606

17. Mazzawi, H.: Optimally reconstructing weighted graphs using queries. In: Charikar, M. (ed.) 21st Annual ACM-SIAM Symposium on Discrete Algorithms (SODA 2010), pp. 608–615. SIAM (2010). https://doi.org/10.1137/1.9781611973075.51

18. Megow, N., Meißner, J., Skutella, M.: Randomization helps computing a minimum spanning tree under uncertainty. SIAM J. Comput. **46**(4), 1217–1240 (2017). https://doi.org/10.1137/16M1088375

19. Meißner, J.: Uncertainty Exploration: Algorithms, Competitive Analysis, and Computational Experiments. Ph.D. thesis, Technische Universität Berlin (2018). https://doi.org/10.14279/depositonce-7327

20. Nisan, N.: The demand query model for bipartite matching. CoRR abs/1906.04213 (2019). http://arxiv.org/abs/1906.04213, to appear in SODA 2021

21. Purohit, M., Svitkina, Z., Kumar, R.: Improving online algorithms via ML predictions. In: Bengio, S., Wallach, H.M., Larochelle, H., Grauman, K., Cesa-Bianchi, N., Garnett, R. (eds.) Advances in Neural Information Processing Systems 31: Annual Conference on Neural Information Processing Systems 2018 (NeurIPS 2018), pp. 9684–9693 (2018). http://papers.nips.cc/paper/8174-improving-online-algorithms-via-ml-predictions

22. Rubinstein, A., Schramm, T., Weinberg, S.M.: Computing exact minimum cuts without knowing the graph. In: Karlin, A.R. (ed.) 9th Innovations in Theoretical Computer Science Conference (ITCS 2018), LIPIcs, vol. 94, pp. 39:1–39:16. Schloss Dagstuhl - Leibniz-Zentrum für Informatik (2018). https://doi.org/10.4230/LIPIcs.ITCS.2018.39

23. Sen, S., Muralidhara, V.N.: The covert set-cover problem with application to network discovery. In: Rahman, M.S., Fujita, S. (eds.) WALCOM 2010. LNCS, vol. 5942, pp. 228–239. Springer, Heidelberg (2010). https://doi.org/10.1007/978-3-642-11440-3_21

Towards Knowledge Exchange: State-of-the-Art and Open Problems

Bahar Ghadiri Bashardoost[1](iD), Kelly Lyons[1](iD), and Renée J. Miller[2](✉)(iD)

[1] University of Toronto, Toronto, ON, Canada
{ghadiri,klyons}@cs.toronto.edu
[2] Northeastern University, Boston, USA
miller@northeastern.edu

Abstract. We discuss our experience in bringing data exchange to knowledge graphs. This experience includes the development of Kensho, a tool for generating mapping rules and performing knowledge exchange between two Knowledge Bases (KBs). We highlight the challenges addressed in Kensho, including managing the rich structural complexity of KBs and the need to handle incomplete correspondences between property paths. We use Kensho to highlight many open problems related to knowledge exchange including how knowledge translation can inform the task of KB integration and population.

Keywords: Knowledge exchange and translation · Data exchange · Mapping generation

1 Introduction

Knowledge-rich applications can see significant performance improvements by using domain-specific Knowledge bases (KBs). Populating and enriching these KBs has, thus, become an important challenge. Many KB population methods use Information Extraction (IE) techniques in order to harvest facts from unstructured and semi-structured corpora. While very useful, the extracted information can be inaccurate, requiring careful curation to produce high-quality knowledge. In this work, we examine a complementary and powerful approach for KB expansion that is based on knowledge exchange, the process of translating knowledge from one KB to another, even when these KBs use very different concepts, properties, and graphs to represent their knowledge. We consider how to lift knowledge from KBs (such as upper ontologies or hand-curated domain-specific KBs) to expand other KBs. We explore the state-of-the-art in creating KB mappings and using them for knowledge translation. We discuss how this work has implications for using relational or other structured data sources for both KB expansion and for automating mapping creation in OBDA (Ontology-based Data Access).

This research was funded in part by an NSERC Strategic Partnership Grant.

T. Bureš et al. (Eds.): SOFSEM 2021, LNCS 12607, pp. 13–27, 2021.
https://doi.org/10.1007/978-3-030-67731-2_2

Recent advances have made the discovery of desirable structured sources of knowledge more and more feasible. While these advances help data engineers explore and discover related knowledge to enrich a KB, translating and integrating the newly discovered knowledge into the KB remains challenging. Data exchange [27] is a prominent approach for data translation within and among relational and nested relational databases and thus, it makes sense to investigate how data exchange solutions can be applied to knowledge base exchange. In the data exchange problem, data that is structured under a source schema is transformed into an instance of a target schema. This is accomplished using a set of rules (called mapping rules or a schema mapping) that specify the relationship between the source and target schemas.

Fagin et al. [27] laid the theoretical foundation for data exchange over relational data and identified important data exchange tasks, namely materializing a target instance and answering queries. Target materialization focuses on problems such as determining whether a target instance (i.e., a solution) exists for a given source instance and accompanying set of mapping rules and, if so, how to generate solutions efficiently. Since there can be more than one solution that satisfies the given set of mapping rules, another important problem is to determine whether there exists a preferred solution(s) and if so, whether a preferred solution can be created with reasonable complexity. Having multiple possible solutions raises another challenge. The main goal of data exchange is to allow queries to be answered over a target instance in a way that is consistent with the data stored in the source; however, the query result might differ, depending on the target solution over which the query is evaluated. Research on query answering in data exchange investigates which query answer is the most desirable. In practical applications of data exchange, another important challenge is identifying mapping rules using automated or semi-automated techniques.

To date, data exchange literature has primarily focused on relational or nested relational source and target settings with less work dedicated to data exchange in KBs. In this paper, we present some current work in KB exchange and highlight challenges and open problems for future research.

2   Knowledge Exchange: Where Are We Now

Researchers have begun the systematic investigation of exchanging data among KBs [9–12]. In recent work, Arenas et al. [10] proposed a formal framework for exchanging knowledge between two KBs that are expressed using $DL\text{-}Lite_R$. In this work, three main types of solutions were investigated that potentially have desirable characteristics for materialization and query answering.

Another important challenge that needs to be addressed in order to make knowledge exchange possible is identifying a set of mapping rules that correctly describes the relationship between the source and the target. When dealing with KBs, several languages [14, 24, 55, and others] and frameworks [24, 66] have been proposed to facilitate the manual generation of these rules. In addition, there are a few pioneering KB schema mapping generation tools (KMGT), including

Mosto [59,62] and a system by Qin et al. [58] that automatically create mappings given a set of correspondences. In this direction, we have recently proposed Kensho [35] which improves upon the first generation mapping tools by taking into consideration the lessons learned from traditional (nested) relational data exchange and mapping tools (MGT) [16] and extends these, taking into account the unique characteristics of KBs. Kensho can produce mapping rules even in the presence of cycles, incompleteness in the source, and in settings with missing or unknown correspondences between properties or property paths. In addition, Kensho performs knowledge translation using value invention to preserve the proper grouping of data in the target KB.

Usually, the first step in data sharing tasks is alignment (a.k.a., matching). The output of this step is a set of correspondences each expressing a relationship among a (set of) resource(s) in the source and a (set of) resource(s) in the target. For instance, in Fig. 1, the output of the first step (the alignment task) is the red and blue lines, that indicate the concept *Person* in the source corresponds to concept *Person* in the target, and similarly, *workAddress* in the source corresponds to *address* in the target. Note that if one uses only the information provided through correspondences for translating knowledge from source to target, some of the information in the source might not be transferred to the target. For instance, in this example, while people and their addresses may be copied over to target, people will not be associated with their own work address in the target. In addition, looking more closely at the structure of the target, one might notice that two people in the target are associated using a relationship called *related*. Thus a desirable solution for the exchange might be a target instance in which the *related* property is also populated using some/all of the possible relationships between people in the source. For instance, depending on the semantics of the target, if two people work on a project in the source, it may be desirable to model those people as *related* in the target. Alternatively, if one person is related to another through *hasSupervisor* in the source, it may be desirable to model these two people as *related* in the target. In fact, both of these relationships may be desirable to model in the target. An important goal of schema mapping creation is to ensure that associations like these between resources are modelled and preserved by the mapping rules.

In traditional data exchange, a large number of tools that automatically generate the mapping rules between a source and a target do so by taking as input a set of correspondences between the source and target (i.e., the alignment), and enriching them with information obtained from the structural characteristics of the source and target. Except for MostoDex [63,64] (see Sect. 3 for more details), all KMGTs, including Kensho, follow the same strategy. Kensho, generates the mapping rules in two main steps: 1) semantic association discovery; and 2) correspondence interpretation. The goal of the first step is to capture all semantic associations between aligned resources of each KB. One key feature of Kensho is that in this phase, it captures all the ways that resources are associated with each other, of course, up to a certain depth (when there are cycles). For instance, two people in the source are associated if they work on a project, or if they have

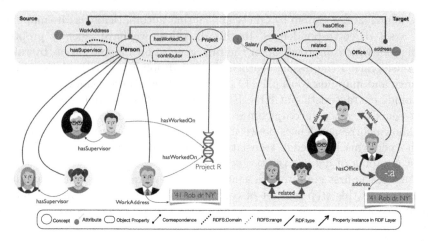

Fig. 1. RDFS and RDF layers of two KBs and correspondences between them. Target KB is populated using source instance.

the same supervisor, or if they are in a supervision chain of a certain length, etc. The goal of the second step is to interpret the set of given correspondences *collectively* using the discovered associations among resources of each KB. To see why this step is necessary, note that in the example of Fig. 1, we will fail to transfer the relationship between people and their work addresses if we consider each correspondence separately and not collectively. Note that the associations among resources that participate in the correspondences provide cues on how to weave these correspondences together to find mapping rules that not only transfer resources that participate in correspondences, but also their relationships with each other.

Most of the advantages of Kensho over previous work stems from the fact that Kensho captures all possible ways that resources of KBs are associated with each other. For instance, in the example of Fig. 1, Kensho will suggest a rule that interprets the two correspondences together since it captures the fact that people and their work addresses are associated in the source and in the target and this provides a cue that this association should be preserved by the mapping. The associations also provide means for proper value invention. For instance, to preserve the association between a person and their work address, for each individual of type *Person* and for each of their work addresses, a new blank node of type *Office* will be created which has the value of the source's *workAddress* as the value of its *address* attribute and participates in a *hasOffice* relation with the transferred individual of the type *Person*. One problem with capturing all associations among resources is that a large number of possible associations may be identified that subsequently have to be considered in the interpretation phase. To address this problem we have used a set of validity and pruning measures to reduce the possible choices that need to be considered as a valid mapping rule [35]. In addition, we have proposed a set of ranking heuristics to help reduce the burden of selecting the best set of mapping rules.

3 Challenges and Opportunities

In this section, we present a vision for some of the most important open problems related to knowledge translation and exchange. Some of the challenges mentioned in this section are already studied in depth in traditional (non-KB) data exchange literature. One goal of this section is to highlight important challenges already identified in the parent field. We establish a call to use lessons learned from the solutions proposed for these challenges to further broaden the research in the KB exchange area. We also talk about some challenges which are more unique to KBs and thus have been studied less in previous work. We consider the evaluation of mapping generation tools which is not a trivial task. Unfortunately most approaches used to evaluate traditional mapping generation tools can not be readily adapted to KBs. We present new evaluation challenges and discuss opportunities for leveraging the Ontology Alignment Evaluation Initiative (OAEI) which provides a series of correspondence discovery tasks [8].

3.1 Mapping Generation: Input Evidence

Metadata Evidence. Mapping generation is carried out using initial evidence about how KBs correspond. In Kensho and other KMGTs [35,58,59,62], this evidence is a set of correspondences. In the ontology alignment literature, correspondences are distinguished as being 1:1, aka simple correspondences (e.g., connecting a source concept with a target concept) or n:m, aka complex correspondences (e.g., connecting a source path/property – and therefore the endpoints of the path – with a target path/property) [25]. Kensho was the first KMGT to consider complex correspondences. An important innovation in Kensho is that it does *not* assume that the set of correspondences is complete. From the given correspondences and KB structure, Kensho can suggest additional possible correspondences that would map more of the source data. One important type of correspondence that, to the best of our knowledge, is not considered in KMGTs is metadata-data (MAD) correspondences [40,51]. Such correspondences articulate the need for a mapping that transforms data values to metadata (e.g., a property name) or vice versa. Arguably, such transformations may be more prevalent in KBs than in relational or semi-structured models. Generating proper mappings from MAD correspondences can be challenging.

Another type of important correspondence which needs further investigation is complex correspondences which indicate that a function can be used to transform a (set of) source value(s) into a (set of) target value(s), or that a filter should be imposed on source values that are being transferred. It is straight forward to extend algorithms in current KMGTs to cover most of these correspondences. However, one advantage that these types of correspondences might bring to the table is in helping to impose some constraints on invented values, which can in turn help improve the query answering capabilities of the materialized target. For instance, imagine that in the example of Fig. 1, there was a correspondence that expresses that if a person supervises another person in the source, their *salary* is greater than $10k. In this case, although the salary of individuals cannot be materialized, a constraint can be added to the target to reflect this fact. Using this added constraint can help in answering queries, for instance, if someone asks for people who earn more than $10k, we know that at least those who were supervisors in the source must be returned as an answer. Of course, studying such correspondences also requires theoretical advances, for example, understanding changes needed in exchange settings so that such constraints can be translated and understanding the effects of doing so on the complexity of the important tasks of materialization and query answering (Afrati et al. [2] discuss some relevant theoretical underpinnings for such tasks in relational data). One other interesting example of such correspondences are those that require aggregation over values in the source. Note that aggregating values is not a trivial task specially in KBs since KBs adhere to an open-world data model [18].

Data Evidence. An alternative to using correspondences to drive mapping generation (sometimes called a schema-driven approach) is to use data. In traditional data exchange, *data-driven* or *example-based* MGTs use source and target data examples. In some approaches, the data is a single full instance of the source schema and the corresponding target instance. In other approaches, smaller sets of example data are used (e.g., a set of source tuples and their corresponding target tuples).

The seminal work of Gottlob and Senellart [37,68] proposed a theoretical framework for the problem of deriving a set of mapping rules from a single ground data example, that is, an instance of the source and an instance of the target schema which do not include nulls. One of the most important contributions of this work is that it casts the problem as an optimization problem by introducing a cost function that expresses how well a rule helps in translating the given source example. Given a *set* of universal examples (pairs of source and target instances where the target instance is a universal solution of the source instance), EIRENE [4] checks whether there exist a set of rules that can fit all the examples, and if so, automatically generates the most general set of rules. In addition, given a set of universal data examples and a membership oracle, ten Cate et al. [19,20] show that a set of mapping rules can be learned in some specific traditional settings. These approaches require very high quality input including examples with certain characteristics (e.g., universal examples). Some of the work in this area can produce mapping rules even when the examples have lower quality (and may even be incorrect) making the approaches more robust if non-experts are providing examples [15,57]. In the future, it is important to understand how data driven approaches can be adopted in KMGTs particularly due to the web scale nature of many KBs making them ideal settings for using data examples.

Mixed Evidence. For KBs, MostoDex [63] uses both an example and a set of source-to-target correspondences. The single example provided to MostoDex must be complete and correct, which puts a large burden on the domain expert. In contrast, for relational exchange, Kimmig et al. [43,44] propose an approach using both data examples and metadata evidence (source-to-target correspondences and source constraints). Importantly in this work, both the data and metadata evidence may be incomplete or incorrect (including schema evidence like correspondences or mined joined paths). They propose Collective Mapping Discovery (CMD) to reason over this possibly inconsistent evidence to produce a schema mapping (a set of mapping rules) that best explain the evidence. An important research direction for KGMTs is mapping generation that can use incomplete or incorrect correspondences and data examples, perhaps leveraging automatically generated examples from the Linked Open Data (LOD) cloud.

Combined Correspondence and Mapping Generation. In the spirit of fully combining logical and statistical reasoning, a KGMT that collectively learns correspondences, examples, and mappings would be an important milestone. Some work including ILIADS [72], PARIS [71], and CODI [41] do this for ontology merging (learning same-as, isa, and equivalent-class axioms to merge two ontologies within a domain), but do not handle deep structural and semantic heterogeneity that cannot be resolved with simple axioms.

3.2 Mapping Refinement

A major challenge in mapping generation is in resolving ambiguity in the relationship between the source and target. Often the evidence provided is not sufficient to select a single definitive semantic interpretation (e.g., does the target *related* property represent a supervision relationship or something else?). Thus, usually mapping generation involves a refinement phase which is often a user-in-the-loop process of eliciting more information to refine the mapping.

Kensho is part of an *integration by example paradigm* [52] in which a domain expert's feedback is used iteratively to refine the mapping rules. A body of traditional data exchange literature is dedicated to investigating the best set of examples to show to domain experts (to resolve ambiguity or choices in mapping creation), ways to automatically generate these examples, show them to the domain experts, and incorporate domain experts' feedback which might be contradictory or wrong [5,23,77, and others]). On the theoretical front, the complexity of the problem of whether a set of mapping rules can be uniquely identified by a set of finite examples has been investigated for various traditional settings with mapping rules in different languages such as GAV and LAV rules [3,6,21]. We are currently working on approaches for interacting with domain experts, by finding examples which are *sufficient illustrations* [77] of rules generated by Kensho and incorporating the feedback to improve and refine the final set of mapping rules which can be used to exchange data between two KBs.

One of the important features of Kensho is that it does not rely on the existence of any constraints other that domain, range, and subsumption. However, if other constructs are contained in the source or target, they can be used in refinement to eliminate (or lower the confidence of) some ambiguous mapping options. For instance, cardinality constraints such as owl:minCardinality, owl:maxCardinality, owl:FunctionalProperty and owl:InverseFunctional Property or disjointness constraints can sometimes help select a property path that best represents the relationship between two concepts. Note that if the KB is already populated with some instances, even if the cardinality constraints are not present, it might be the case that these constraints can still be automatically inferred (e.g., Bühmann and Lehmann [17] provide some examples of this). In general, we feel that KB profiling and mining may be helpful in improving mapping quality, in a similar way that database profiling and dependency mining [1] has been used to mine for join paths or other constraints that can guide mapping generation.

Depending on the problem at hand, instance based methods can be used to help refine possible mapping alternatives. For instance, if we are trying to transfer as much data as possible from source to target, heuristics can be introduced to give higher priority to mapping rules that translate more source data. In the presence of a set of positive (and/or negative) examples, rule mining approaches [31,50,54, and others] can help identify important paths (or rules) that best fit the given examples. In addition, rule mining approaches can help enrich the set of constraints that are used in order to further refine mapping rules. It is interesting to see whether enriching the source/target ontologies with additional induced constraints produced by running a rule mining algorithm can help generate better mapping rules.

3.3   Knowledge Exchange

Of course an important reason to create mappings is to perform knowledge exchange. The goal in MGTs is to produce a *universal* solution [26], as universal solutions are the only solutions that represent the whole space of solutions in a precise sense [27]. It is important to note that early systems did this heuristically because the theory of data exchange had not yet been developed [52,53,56]. The tools motivated the development of the theory so we could formally reason about the solutions the tools produced – and formally prove they were "good" solutions. Later, as the theory progressed, the theory fed back into the tools. Fagin et al. [28] defined *core* solutions as the smallest universal solutions for relational settings and Mecca et al. [49] used this idea to produce mappings that are guaranteed to produce core solutions. Later on Chirkova et al. [22] showed that when the exchange setting consists of nested relational DTDs, materialization of the solution can be reduced to the materialization of a solution in a relational setting and provided an algorithm to do so. One advantage of the Chirkova et al. work is to enable applications to take advantage of theoretical results and efficient algorithms already proposed in relational data exchange even when they are dealing with nested relational settings (++SPICY [48] is an example).

The study of what are the best solutions for KB exchange has been investigated by Arenas et al. [10]. They define a notion of universal solution (for KBs represented in DL-Lite$_R$), but also two related notions of universal UCQ-solutions (a relaxation of the notion of universal solutions) and UCQ-representations. However, their proposed setting is somewhat different than what is considered in current KMGTs that consider target constraints. An important research question is how to use this formal work to guide KMGTs and if we can use the theory to create tools that produce mappings with certain formal properties.

Most MGTs and Kensho assume that the target is not populated with any data. But this might not be the case in real world application. For relational exchange, this problem has been addressed using a *solution-aware chase*, a procedure that adds and merges source data into an existing target instance [30]. An interesting open problem is to understand how to do this in KBs where inference is more complex. In addition, practical solutions will need to use deduplication and record linkage to create links such as same-as and resolve conflicts in values.

3.4   Scalability and Optimization

One of the most important challenges that KMGTs face is the scale of the KBs. Kensho uses a simple method for slicing the KBs in order to be able to deal with larger scale source and target [34]. However, more sophisticated methods such as modularization [36,45,70] or partitioning [38,67,69] can be adopted to help in efficient generation of mapping rules when dealing with large scale KBs.

In Kensho, mapping rules are expressed using SPARQL. However, there are declarative languages specifically designed for expressing the mapping rules proposed in literature. One such language is R2R [14] is a powerful language for representing mapping rules for large KBs. An interesting open question is to study the use of declarative languages like R2R that can perhaps be optimized and then "compiled" into SPARQL or other execution languages.

The performance of the transformation queries or programs generated by MGTs has been an important research problem [42] and will remain so for KMGTs. To handle the open-world nature of KBs, Kensho generates SPARQL queries with many OPTIONAL clauses. Generally, OPTIONAL clauses are processed as left outer joins in most query engines and thus running nested OPTIONAL clauses is expensive. Recently, there has been research on methods for efficient handling of SPARQL OPTIONAL clauses [76], since similar to our approach, OPTIONAL clauses are required for many data integration tasks when dealing with KBs. We believe our approach (as well as many other KB integration approaches) can immensely benefit from research on how to optimize the execution of queries that use SPARQL OPTIONAL clauses.

3.5   Application to Other Integration Problems

We believe the most important application of Kensho is populating an existing domain-specific ontology using other currently available structured data sources. The source of data might not be a KB as long as it can be automatically converted to one. In our evaluation [35], we showed that Kensho can effectively populate a worker expertise KB using open data published by the US Patent and Trademark Office (USPTO). To use the USPTO corpus as our source KB, we started with a subset of the USPTO's patent XML corpus[1] and automatically created a linked data corpus from it using Xcurator [39], and further enriched it using Vizcurator [32].

The ontology based data access initiative (OBDA) [75] aims to facilitate the integrated access of heterogeneous relational data sources using a target KB. OBDA does not require target materialization and instead, uses the KB as a virtual view over the relational source(s). To enable query answering, they use mapping rules to re-write KB queries in order to enable users to access data in the source by querying the target. Thus in these approaches mapping rules need to be created such that they facilitate efficient query re-writing and deal with source and target models with different expressive power. Xiao et al. [75] state that "mapping creation and management is probably the most complicated OBDA design-time task". Additional research is needed on KGMTs to support the unique requirements of OBDA [46].

3.6   Evaluation

Evaluating the effectiveness of mapping rules is not a trivial task. Computing precision and recall is the standard in the literature for comparing different set of correspondences. However, mapping rules are not simple sets. Two sets of different mapping rules may be equivalent, so it is not sufficient to check if a specific syntactic mapping is produced by a KMGT. In addition, testing equivalence of queries and mappings is undecidable in general, and many of the mapping languages used in practice have this property. Hence, over time, tools and benchmarks have been developed to help evaluate the effectiveness of mapping generation tools. STBenchmark [7] was one of the first for MGTs. One of the contributions of this work is a suite of mapping micro scenarios (or mapping patterns) that represents a minimum set of transformations that should be readily supported by mapping tools. This idea was generalized by the meta-data generator iBench [13] that permits the efficient creation of benchmarks with large and complex schemas and data exchange scenarios that require value invention. These tools are designed to evaluate settings that involve relational sources and targets (or in the case of STBenchmark nested relational). DTSBenchmark [60] was the first to devise a set of scenarios when the source and target are both KBs. LODIB [65] refined these scenarios based on patterns that occur often on examples from the LOD Cloud. Later work [61] proposed a framework called MostoBM, which contains the set of scenarios from DTSBenchmark [60] as well as a metadata generator that allows the complexity of the scenarios to be tuned. MostoBM uses a few parameters that can be changed to systematically generate settings with different degrees of complexity, including three schema-level parameters (namely, *depth* of the class relationships, *breadth* of the class relationships, and *the number of attributes*). However, these parameters are not as

---

[1] https://www.google.com/googlebooks/uspto-patents-grants-text.html.

extensive as the iBench parameters and do not control important factors such as the use of value invention and the number of alternative interpretations for a correspondence. To begin to address this, we recently proposed a new set of scenarios for KB exchange that covers settings that require value invention, incomplete source and target KBs, incomplete correspondences, and KBs containing cycles [33], though notably our work does not go as far as providing the KB equivalent of an iBench metadata (exchange scenario) generator.

Real world scenarios play an important role in knowledge exchange and especially in the evaluation of ranking measures in mapping generation tools. Note that all of the mapping rules generated by Kensho are consistent with the correspondences and source/target KBs but, depending on the context, some mappings may be more desirable than others. Returning to our example in Fig. 1, a user must decide if they want the target *related* property left empty, populated with the source *hasSupervisor* property, populated with the *hasWorkedOn/contributor* path, or some combination (union) of these. And of course given cycles, one could also consider the source *hasSupervisor/hasSupervisor* path (to get a person's second-line supervisor) and so on. None of these mappings are wrong based on the structure of the KBs and the given correspondences. The semantics of what *related* means in the target is missing and must be determined by a human, perhaps with the aid of data examples. Situations like these make it important for tools to rank *most-likely* mappings well, so the user is not overwhelmed by options. Such ambiguity is inherent in integration and it poses important evaluation challenges. Currently there are not enough open source real world scenarios that can be used for settings which involve KBs. One resource we used in the evaluation of Kensho was the OAEI corpora which provides a large set of source and target ontologies together with a curated set of *ground-truth* correspondences. We were able to re-purpose the data provided in this initiative to better evaluate our knowledge translation tool in a real world setting. We believe knowledge translation and exchange research can greatly benefit from a community effort which identifies corpora that can be shared to produce comparable evaluations of KGMT. This research can also benefit from initiatives that push for open source settings which are more focused on the challenges specific to this area.

3.7 Evolution

Source and target KBs or schemas may not be static and can change through time. When this happens, mappings may become invalid or inconsistent. Starting the mapping generation from scratch will waste work and can be expensive especially in cases where significant domain expert intervention is required [29]. In addition there is no guarantee that the regenerated mapping rules will reflect the original semantics of the previous mapping and have the same capabilities in query answering [29,74]. Hence, researchers have studied how to *identify inconsistencies* and *adapt mappings* to conform to the new source and target. This has been done in MGTs such as ToMAS [73,74]. ToMAS considers relational and nested-relational schemas and adapts mappings in the face of schema changes (additions or deletions in the schema) as well as semantic and structural changes (such as changes in the schema constraints or nesting structure).

In addition, in traditional data exchange schema mapping evolution has been proposed [29] based on mapping composition and inversion. For OBDA mappings, Lembo et al. [47] introduce two different notions of repair. The first notion, called deletion-based mapping repair, reflects the idea of repairing through a minimal number of deletion of assertions from the original mapping. The second notion, called entailment based mapping repair, aims to preserve the assertions which are implied by the original mapping, as much as possible. Unfortunately, to the best of our knowledge, there is not yet any work in this area for settings which involve source and target KBs. Indeed some of the motivating scenarios used to evaluate KMGTs come from KB evolution (specifically different versions of DBpedia) [62]. This is an issue since often the source KB resides in a dynamic environment such as web with no centralized authority, and thus its structure might change often and without any prior notice. It is important to see how various repair notions proposed in the literature can be used in the context of knowledge translation and to facilitate the mapping adaptation.

4   Conclusions

We have laid out an extensive research agenda for Knowledge Exchange. While we have focused on the development and evaluation of tools that perform mapping discovery and knowledge translation, we believe that as with data exchange, further development of the theory and foundations of knowledge exchange is critical to informing and fueling the development of better, more robust and accurate, tools and algorithms. We also believe the necessity of being able to exchange knowledge between the heterogeneous and ever growing web of knowledge bases will be a catalyst for the development of new mathematical tools and principles for understanding the foundations of knowledge exchange.

References

1. Abedjan, Z., Golab, L., Naumann, F., Papenbrock, T.: Data Profiling. Morgan & Claypool Publishers, Synthesis Lectures on Data Management (2018)
2. Afrati, F., Li, C., Pavlaki, V.: Data exchange in the presence of arithmetic comparisons. In: EDBT, pp. 487–498 (2008)
3. Alexe, B., ten Cate, B., Kolaitis, P.G., Tan, W.C.: Characterizing schema mappings via data examples. TODS 36(4), 1–48 (2011)
4. Alexe, B., ten Cate, B., Kolaitis, P.G., Tan, W.C.: Eirene: interactive design and refinement of schema mappings via data examples. PVLDB 4(12), 1414–1417 (2011)
5. Alexe, B., Chiticariu, L., Miller, R.J., Tan, W.C.: Muse: Mapping understanding and design by example. In: ICDE, pp. 10–19 (2008)
6. Alexe, B., Kolaitis, P.G., Tan, W.C.: Characterizing schema mappings via data examples. In: PODS, pp. 261–272 (2010)

7. Alexe, B., Tan, W.C., Velegrakis, Y.: STBenchmark: towards a benchmark for mapping systems. PVLDB **1**(1), 230–244 (2008)
8. Algergawy, A., et al.: Results of the ontology alignment evaluation initiative 2019. In: OM, pp. 46–85 (2019)
9. Arenas, M., Botoeva, E., Calvanese, D.: Knowledge base exchange. In: DL, **4** (2011)
10. Arenas, M., Botoeva, E., Calvanese, D., Ryzhikov, V.: Knowledge base exchange: the case of OWL 2 QL. Artif. Intell. **238**, 11–62 (2016)
11. Arenas, M., Botoeva, E., Calvanese, D., Ryzhikov, V., Sherkhonov, E.: Exchanging description logic knowledge bases. In: KR (2012)
12. Arenas, M., Pérez, J., Reutter, J.: Data exchange beyond complete data. JACM **60**(4), 28 (2013)
13. Arocena, P.C., Glavic, B., Ciucanu, R., Miller, R.J.: The iBench integration metadata generator. PVLDB **9**(3), 108–119 (2015)
14. Bizer, C., Schultz, A.: The R2R framework: Publishing and discovering mappings on the web. In: COLD, pp. 97–108 (2010)
15. Bonifati, A., Comignani, U., Coquery, E., Thion, R.: Interactive mapping specification with exemplar tuples. In: SIGMOD, pp. 667–682 (2017)
16. Bonifati, A., Mecca, G., Papotti, P., Velegrakis, Y.: Discovery and correctness of schema mapping transformations. In: Schema Matching and Mapping, pp. 111–147 (2011)
17. Bühmann, L., Lehmann, J.: Universal OWL axiom enrichment for large knowledge bases. In: EKAW, pp. 57–71 (2012)
18. Calvanese, D., Kharlamov, E., Nutt, W., Thorne, C.: Aggregate queries over ontologies. In: ONISW, pp. 97–104 (2008)
19. Ten Cate, B., Dalmau, V., Kolaitis, P.G.: Learning schema mappings. In: ICDT, pp. 182–195 (2012)
20. Ten Cate, B., Kolaitis, P.G., Qian, K., Tan, W.C.: Active learning of GAV schema mappings. In: PODS, pp. 355–368 (2018)
21. Ten Cate, B., Kolaitis, P.G., Tan, W.C.: Database constraints and homomorphism dualities. In: PC, pp. 475–490 (2010)
22. Chirkova, R., Libkin, L., Reutter, J.L.: Tractable xml data exchange via relations. In: CIKM, pp. 1629–1638 (2011)
23. Chiticariu, L., Tan, W.C.: Debugging schema mappings with routes. VLDB **6**, 79–90 (2006)
24. Dou, D., McDermott, D.V., Qi, P.: Ontology translation on the semantic web. J. Data Semantics **2**, 35–57 (2005)
25. Euzenat, J., Shvaiko, P.: Ontology Matching. Springer, Heidelberg (2013). https://doi.org/10.1007/978-3-642-38721-0
26. Fagin, R., Haas, L., Hernández, M., Miller, R., Popa, L., Velegrakis, Y.: Clio: Schema mapping creation and data exchange. Conceptual Modeling: Foundations and Applications, pp. 198–236 (2009)
27. Fagin, R., Kolaitis, P.G., Miller, R.J., Popa, L.: Data exchange: semantics and query answering. Theor. Comput. Sci. **336**(1), 89–124 (2005)
28. Fagin, R., Kolaitis, P.G., Popa, L.: Data exchange: getting to the core. ACM Trans. Database Syst. **30**(1), 174–210 (2005)
29. Fagin, R., Kolaitis, P.G., Popa, L., Tan, W.C.: Schema mapping evolution through composition and inversion. In: Schema matching and mapping, pp. 191–222. Springer, Heidelberg (2011). https://doi.org/10.1007/978-3-642-16518-4_7
30. Fuxman, A., Kolaitis, P.G., Miller, R.J., Tan, W.C.: Peer data exchange. ACM Trans. Database Syst. **31**(4), 1454–1498 (2006)

31. Galárraga, L., Teflioudi, C., Hose, K., Suchanek, F.M.: Fast rule mining in onto-logical knowledge bases with AMIE. VLDB J. **24**(6), 707–730 (2015)
32. Ghadiri Bashardoost, B., Christodoulakis, C., Hassas Yeganeh, S., Hassanzadeh, O., Miller, R.J., Lyons, K.: Vizcurator: a visual tool for curating open data. In: WWW Companion, pp. 195–198 (2015)
33. Ghadiri Bashardoost, B., Miller, R.J., Lyons, K.: Towards a benchmark for knowl-edge base exchange. In: DI2KG (2019)
34. Ghadiri Bashardoost, B., Miller, R.J., Lyons, K., Nargesian, F.: Knowledge trans-lation: extended technical report. Technical report, University of Toronto (2019). https://tny.sh/KBTranslation
35. Ghadiri Bashardoost, B., Miller, R.J., Lyons, K., Nargesian, F.: Knowledge trans-lation. PVLDB **13**(11), 2018–2032 (2020)
36. Ghazvinian, A., Noy, N.F., Musen, M.A.: From mappings to modules: using map-pings to identify domain-specific modules in large ontologies. In: K-CAP, pp. 33–40 (2011)
37. Gottlob, G., Senellart, P.: Schema mapping discovery from data instances. J. ACM **57**(2), 6:1–6:37 (2010)
38. Grau, B.C., Parsia, B., Sirin, E., Kalyanpur, A.: Automatic partitioning of OWL ontologies using E-Connections. In: DL **147** (2005)
39. Hassas Yeganeh, S., Hassanzadeh, O., Miller, R.J.: Linking semistructured data on the web. In: WebDB (2011)
40. Hernández, M.A., Papotti, P., Tan, W.C.: Data exchange with data-metadata translations. PVLDB **1**(1), 260–273 (2008)
41. Huber, J., Sztyler, T., Noessner, J., Meilicke, C.: Codi: combinatorial optimization for data integration - results for OAEI 2011. In: OM, pp. 134–141 (2011)
42. Jiang, H., Ho, H., Popa, L., Han, W.: Mapping-driven XML transformation. In: WWW, pp. 1063–1072 (2007)
43. Kimmig, A., Memory, A., Miller, R.J., Getoor, L.: A collective, probabilistic app-roach to schema mapping. In: ICDE, pp. 921–932 (2017)
44. Kimmig, A., Memory, A., Miller, R.J., Getoor, L.: A collective, probabilistic app-roach to schema mapping using diverse noisy evidence. In: TKDE (2018)
45. Konev, B., Lutz, C., Walther, D., Wolter, F.: Model-theoretic inseparability and modularity of description logic ontologies. Artif. Intell. **203**, 66–103 (2013)
46. Lembo, D., Mora, J., Rosati, R., Savo, D.F., Thorstensen, E.: Mapping analysis in ontology-based data access: algorithms and complexity. In: ISWC (2015)
47. Lembo, D., Rosati, R., Santarelli, V., Savo, D.F., Thorstensen, E.: Mapping repair in ontology-based data access evolving systems. In: IJCAI, pp. 1160–1166 (2017)
48. Marnette, B., Mecca, G., Papotti, P., Raunich, S., Santoro, D., et al.: ++Spicy: an open-source tool for second-generation schema mapping and data exchange. PVLDB **19**(12), 1438–1441 (2011)
49. Mecca, G., Papotti, P., Raunich, S.: Core schema mappings. In: SIGMOD, pp. 655–668 (2009)
50. Meng, C., Cheng, R., Maniu, S., Senellart, P., Zhang, W.: Discovering meta-paths in large heterogeneous information networks. In: WWW, pp. 754–764 (2015)
51. Miller, R.J.: Using schematically heterogeneous structures. In: SIGMOD, pp. 189–200 (1998)
52. Miller, R.J., Haas, L.M., Hernández, M.A.: Schema mapping as query discovery. In: VLDB, pp. 77–88 (2000)
53. Miller, R.J., Hernández, M.A., Haas, L.M., Yan, L.L., Ho, C.H., Fagin, R., Popa, L.: The Clio project: managing heterogeneity. SIGMOD Record **30**(1), 78–83 (2001)

54. Ortona, S., Meduri, V.V., Papotti, P.: Robust discovery of positive and negative rules in knowledge bases. In: ICDE, pp. 1168–1179 (2018)
55. Polleres, A., Scharffe, F., Schindlauer, R.: SPARQL++ for mapping between RDF vocabularies. In: OTM, pp. 878–896 (2007)
56. Popa, L., Velegrakis, Y., Hernández, M.A., Miller, R.J., Fagin, R.: Translating web data. In: VLDB, pp. 598–609 (2002)
57. Qian, L., Cafarella, M.J., Jagadish, H.V.: Sample-driven schema mapping. In: SIGMOD, pp. 73–84 (2012)
58. Qin, H., Dou, D., LePendu, P.: Discovering executable semantic mappings between ontologies. In: OTM, pp. 832–849 (2007)
59. Rivero, C.R., Hernández, I., Ruiz, D., Corchuelo, R.: Generating SPARQL executable mappings to integrate ontologies. In: ER, pp. 118–131 (2011)
60. Rivero, C.R., Hernández, I., Ruiz, D., Corchuelo, R.: On benchmarking data translation systems for semantic-web ontologies. In: CIKM, pp. 1613–1618 (2011)
61. Rivero, C.R., Hernandez, I., Ruiz, D., Corchuelo, R.: Benchmarking data exchange among semantic-web ontologies. TKDE **25**(9), 1997–2009 (2012)
62. Rivero, C.R., Hernández, I., Ruiz, D., Corchuelo, R.: Exchanging data amongst linked data applications. Knowl. Inf. Syst. **37**(3), 693–729 (2013)
63. Rivero, C.R., Hernández, I., Ruiz, D., Corchuelo, R.: MostoDEx: a tool to exchange rdf data using exchange samples. J. Syst. Software **100**, 67–79 (2015)
64. Rivero, C.R., Hernández, I., Ruiz, D., Corchuelo, R.: Mapping RDF knowledge bases using exchange samples. Knowl.-Based Syst. **93**, 47–66 (2016)
65. Rivero, C.R., Schultz, A., Bizer, C., Ruiz Cortés, D.: Benchmarking the performance of linked data translation systems. In: LDOW (2012)
66. Schultz, A., Matteini, A., Isele, R., Bizer, C., Becker, C.: Ldif-linked data integration framework. In: COLD, pp. 125–130 (2011)
67. Seidenberg, J., Rector, A.: Web ontology segmentation: analysis, classification and use. In: WWW, pp. 13–22 (2006)
68. Senellart, P., Gottlob, G.: On the complexity of deriving schema mappings from database instances. In: PODS, pp. 23–32 (2008)
69. Stuckenschmidt, H., Klein, M.: Structure-based partitioning of large concept hierarchies. In: ISWC, pp. 289–303 (2004)
70. Stuckenschmidt, H., Parent, C., Spaccapietra, S.: Modular ontologies: concepts, theories and techniques for knowledge modularization, vol. 5445, Springer, Heidelberg (2009). https://doi.org/10.1007/978-3-642-01907-4
71. Suchanek, F.M., Abiteboul, S., Senellart, P.: Paris: probabilistic alignment of relations, instances, and schema. PVLDB **5**(3), 157–168 (2011)
72. Udrea, O., Getoor, L., Miller, R.J.: Leveraging data and structure in ontology integration. In: SIGMOD, pp. 449–460. ACM (2007)
73. Velegrakis, Y., Miller, J., Popa, L.: Preserving mapping consistency under schema changes. VLDB J. **13**(3), 274–293 (2004)
74. Velegrakis, Y., Miller, R.J., Popa, L., Mylopoulos, J.: Tomas: a system for adapting mappings while schemas evolve. In: ICDE, p. 862 (2004)
75. Xiao, G., et al.: Ontology-based data access: a survey. In: IJCAI, pp. 5511–5519 (2018)
76. Xiao, G., Kontchakov, R., Cogrel, B., Calvanese, D., Botoeva, E.: Efficient Handling of SPARQL optional for OBDA. In: ISWC, pp. 354–373 (2018)
77. Yan, L.L., Miller, R.J., Haas, L.M., Fagin, R.: Data-driven understanding and refinement of schema mappings. In: SIGMOD, pp. 485–496 (2001)

Invited Talk: Resilient Distributed Algorithms

Merav Parter[(⊠)]

Weizmann Institute, Rehovot, Israel
`merav.parter@weizmann.ac.il`

Abstract. Following the immense recent advances in distributed networks, the explosive growth of the Internet, and our increased dependence on these infrastructures, guaranteeing the uninterrupted operation of communication networks has become a major objective in network algorithms. The modern instantiations of distributed networks, such as, the Bitcoin network and cloud computing, introduce in addition, new security challenges that deserve urgent attention in both theory and practice.

This extended abstract describes our initial steps towards developing a unified framework for obtaining **fast, resilient** and **secure** distributed algorithms for fundamental graph problems. We will be focusing on two main objectives:

- Initiating and establishing the theoretical exploration of *security* in distributed graph algorithms. Such a notion has been addressed before mainly in the context of secure multi-party computation (MPC). The heart of our approach is to develop new graph theoretical infrastructures to provide graphical secure channels between nodes in a communication network of an arbitrary topology.
- Developing efficient distributed algorithms against various adversarial settings, such as, node crashes and Byzantine attacks.

The main novelty in addressing these objectives is in our approach, which is based on taking a graph theoretic perspective where common notions of resilience requirements will be translated into suitably tailored combinatorial graph structures. We believe that the proposed perspective will deepen the theoretical foundations for resilient distributed computation, strengthen the connections with the areas of fault tolerant network design and information theoretic security, and provide a refreshing perspective on extensively-studied graph theoretical concepts.

Keywords: CONGEST · Resilient computation · Secure computation

1 Introduction and Motivation

In the rapidly growing area of distributed graph algorithms, the communication network is abstracted by a graph with n nodes, each of which represents an individual processor. While the network as a whole can perform nontrivial tasks, each

Supported by grants from the Israel Science Foundation (no. 2084/18) and the European Research Council (ERC-2020-StG, grant agreement No. 949083).

T. Bureš et al. (Eds.): SOFSEM 2021, LNCS 12607, pp. 28–42, 2021.
https://doi.org/10.1007/978-3-030-67731-2_3

individual node usually follows a fairly simple code based on local interactions with its neighbors. The goal of this area is to provide efficient distributed algorithms for various problems, commonly by taking a graph theoretical approach. Distributed networks nowadays have advanced significantly beyond abstract theoretical concept, and rather play a key role in many aspects of life: they are used for storing private medical data, connecting selfish agents with private (and possibly conflicting) utility functions, or managing decentralized digital currencies such as the Bitcoin. These modern instantiations of distributed networks call for a *new kind of distributed graph algorithms* that are not only efficient in time but also protect the users and their sensitive information, and guarantee the uninterrupted operation in the presence of noise, adversarial faults and malicious attacks. An inherent (and unfortunate) property of almost all classical distributed algorithms is that throughout their execution, the nodes get to learn much more than merely their own part in the solution, but rather collect additional information on the input or output of (potentially) many other vertices in the network. This might raise the question of *how can we apply any of the classical distributed algorithms on a network that stores sensitive information?*

Over the years and up to this date, most of the effort in the community of distributed graph algorithms has been usually devoted for optimizing the efficiency of the algorithms in terms of the number of rounds. This has led to a sequence of breakthrough results in the past decade, providing impressive distributed solutions with nearly optimal round complexity for many graph problems. Notwithstanding this, considerably less attention has been devoted for other crucial objectives, such as, the reliability of the computation, and the privacy of users' information. These latter aspects have been studied thoroughly in several other communities, and as a result, the existing body of resilient algorithms do not quite fit into the standard distributed models.

Objective 1: Efficient Secure Algorithms

Our first objective is to introduce security notions for distributed graph algorithms. These aspects have been widely studied in the area of secure multiparty-computation (MPC), where the underlying graph is usually assumed to be the complete graph. They key challenge is to exploit the extensive research on secure MPC protocols to the benefit of secure distributed graph algorithms. It is important to note that the transition from the complete graphs to graphs with general topologies requires some adaptations of the standard security guarantees. Whereas in the MPC model, the secure protocols handle adversaries that corrupt a constant fraction of the nodes, in general graphs that might be impossible. In one of the most seminal works on fault tolerant computation, Dolev [Dol82] showed that the limit on the adversarial collusion is determined by the vertex connectivity of the graph. The goal is to provide secure algorithms that match this upper bound, while taking the *efficiency* aspects of the secure algorithms into consideration (i.e., rather than focusing on feasibility issues).

We focus on the classical resilience notion of *perfect security* which dates back to the earlier work by Yao in the 80's. Roughly speaking, an algorithm is said to be perfectly secure if at the end of the execution, the nodes in the network learn nothing on the private information of the other nodes, rather than their individual outputs. This strong security notion rules out any use of public-key encryption, as the latter are based on computational assumptions. Prefect security has several advantages in our context: (A) it avoids any cryptographic assumptions, (B) it leads to simpler, more elegant and also more efficient solutions compared to those obtained in the computational setting, and (C) it allows one to reduce the computational problem into a clean graph theoretical problem. Within this framework, our work currently only considers the semi-honest model. In this model, nodes are assumed to follow the protocol, and the adversary taking over these nodes will aim at gaining information on the private input of other nodes by analyzing the messages it has observed throughout the simulation. Note that this kind of adversary is passive, and it would not attempt to change the course of the execution. In the more ambitious *malicious* setting, the adversary is *byzantine*, and might actively change the execution to gain more information on other nodes. The goal of the secure simulation is to preserve the correctness (as much as possible) as well as providing security guarantees on the private information of the uncorrupted nodes. The ultimate goal is to fully characterize the *price of security* defined by the ratio in the round complexity between the secure solution and the non-secure solution for the problem. This price might vary between different distributed graph problem. We then aim at bounding this measure for many fundamental graph problems, as a function of the graph parameters (e.g., diameter, maximum degree) and the computational power of the adversary.

Objective 2: Efficient Algorithms Against Byzantine Attacks

Our second objective considers non-cryptographic adversaries. These adversaries aim at interrupting the normal execution of the protocols, e.g., leading to invalid output solutions at the individual nodes. The rapid growth of computer networks and their high vulnerability to byzantine failures pose an acute need to efficient resilient algorithms for distributed networks. Starting with seminal works of Pease et al. [PSL80] and Lamport et al. [LSP82, PSL80], the area of resilient distributed computation has been receiving substantial attention for over the last four decades. Most of the existing work resilient computation usually assumes, as well, that the communication graph is complete (a K_n clique) [BT85, TPS87, GM98, SW89, SW90, SY96, KK06, AD15, AKM20], and much less is known for general graphs. See [Pel96] for a survey on this topic.

The primary goal, in this context, is to provide efficient distributed algorithms for graphs with arbitrary topologies, in the presence of adversarial edges and nodes. The efficiency is measured by the number of rounds in classical message passing models (e.g., the congest model [Pel00]). The common setting studied in the literature assumes a computationally unlimited adversary that manipulates several vertices in the graph. The adversary can see that entire communication graph, the internal randomness of the nodes, and the messages exchanged throughout the execution. In the lack of any round-efficient algorithm for this adversarial setting, we propose to employ a more gradual approach: understanding first *single edge* failures (which are already far from trivial), moving to *multiple* edge failures and ultimately to multiple *vertices*. We also propose to employ techniques that are commonly applied in the area fault tolerant graph algorithms. One of the most useful tools in this area is given by the fault-tolerant sampling technique [WY13, DK11, Par16, Par19]. Informally, this technique allows one to sub-sample a small collection of subgraphs to "cover" the space of all faulty events. Indeed, in our recent work we make an extensive use of this technique for obtaining round-efficient byzantine broadcast algorithms [HP21], and general byzantine simulations of non-resilient algorithms [HP20].

The Distributed Model. The computational model under which we develop our methodologies is the classical congest model [Pel00] of distributed computing. In this model, the network is abstracted by an n-vertex graph, where nodes stand for computational components and edges indicate available communication links. This is a synchronous setting, where in each round each node can send a message of B-bits to each of its neighbors, typically $B = O(\log n)$ bits to allow the unique identifier of a node to fit in a single message. The local computation performed at each node is considered to be negligible, and the primary complexity measure is the number of rounds required to solve the given task.

Overview. The structure of this manuscript is as follows. Section 2 proposes a graph-based simulation methodology for providing resilient and secure distributed algorithms. In the subsequent sections we illustrate the application of this methodology for several adversarial settings. In Sect. 3, we present a recent line of works on distributed algorithms that provide information-theoretic security against semi-honest adversaries. In Sect. 4, we present our recent work on resilient algorithms against adversarial edges. Finally, in Sect. 5 we discuss the setting where the adversary corrupts multiple edges or vertices in the graph. Throughout, we also highlight some open problems and future directions.

2 Graph-Based Resilient Simulation

The lack of round-efficient resilient algorithms for general graphs, already for basic tasks, serves the key motivation for the line of works presented in this manuscript, which share the following high-level objective:

> Provide *fast*, *resilient* and *secure* distributed algorithms for fundamental distributed tasks through a foundational graph theoretical research.

A naïve approach for handling this challenge is to directly implement the complete graph protocols over the input communication graph. While this clearly satisfies the requirements in terms of correctness and resilience guarantees, the overhead with respect to the number of communication rounds might be too large. We therefore need to design novel algorithms based on graph theoretical methodologies.

At the heart of our approach lies in a **Graph-Based Resilient Simulation** (GBRS) methodology described as follows. For a given adversarial setting σ, we will provide a general simulation scheme that takes any r-round distributed algorithm $\mathcal{A}$ and compiles it into an r'-round algorithm $\mathcal{A}'$ that is resilient under

σ. The efficiency of the scheme is measured by the blowup in the number of rounds, r'/r. This simulation is obtained by taking three conceptual steps, which will be illustrated by using the eavesdropper adversary as a running example. In this setting, the eavesdropper adversary is allowed to listen only on one fixed edge in the graph throughout the entire execution. In the resilient simulation, it is required that the adversary learns nothing (in the information theoretic sense) on the input and output of nodes in the graph. This setting is explained in more details in Sect. 3.

- **Step 1: Translating the resilience requirements into a desired graph structure Φ:** The adversarial setting σ implicitly defines a structural requirement Φ for the input graph G. The efficiency of the resilient computation under σ depends on the extent to which this requirement can satisfied by G. E.g., for the eavesdropper setting, the structure Φ corresponds to low-congestion cycle covers, namely, a collection of short and nearly edge-disjoint cycles that cover all graph edges.
- **Step 2: Efficient distributed computation of Φ:** Upon characterizing the desired graph property Φ, its combinatorial properties in general graphs and in specific graph families will be addressed. The combinatorial understanding of the structure will serve the basis for its efficient computation. E.g., we showed a sub-optimal distributed construction of low-congestion cycle covers, with running time and cycle length of $2^{O(\sqrt{\log n})} \cdot D$, and with a total congestion of $2^{O(\sqrt{\log n})}$.
- **Step 3: Resilient simulation of the non-resilient algorithm $\mathcal{A}$ on top of Φ:** This step usually involves two types of algorithms: the (non-resilient) network algorithm $\mathcal{A}$ and a resilient algorithm $\mathcal{R}$ that works for special graph topologies, e.g., cliques or star networks. The efficient emulation of algorithm $\mathcal{R}$ on top of algorithm $\mathcal{A}$ is made possible due to the resilient structure Φ. E.g., every round of $\mathcal{A}$ is simulated using $\widetilde{O}(D)$ rounds by letting each node u split its message to v into two random parts (i.e., secret shares), and sending each part along the two-edge disjoint paths provided by the cycle cover. Using the random delay approach of [LMR94], all these messages can be sent in $\widetilde{O}(D)$ rounds, with high probability.

In [PY19a] and [PY19b] we implemented this GBRS methodology for several adversarial settings (e.g., eavesdropper, Byzantine and semi-honest adversaries) in which at most one edge or vertex are corrupted. Extending this scheme to support multiple corruptions, calls for providing new combinatorial graph structures that exploit the high connectivity of the graph, as discussed in Sect. 5.

3   Algorithms with Information-Theoretic Security

Secure computation, as introduced by Yao [Yao82] allows a collection on n parties connected by a complete graph to compute a joint function of their private input without learning anything on the private input of other parties. Currently, there is an immense gap in the existing knowledge on efficient secure computation between the multi-party setting (which commonly assumes that the network is the **complete** graph) and the distributed setting (which commonly considers **general** graph topologies). Our goal is to narrow this gap, by developing graph theoretical tools for emulating the existing clique-based solutions on general graphs. We will mainly focus on *information theoretic* adversaries. This has the benefit of avoiding cryptographic assumptions, and as we will see, gives raise to clean graph theoretical formulation.

We note that the design of resilient distributed algorithms for graph problems requires some adaptations in the most basic conventions of this area. One such concept concerns the distinction between local and global distributed problems. Roughly speaking, *local problems* correspond to those tasks whose distributed solution can be verified within a constant number of rounds (e.g., MIS, matching, $(\Delta+1)$ coloring). Most of the classical local problems currently admit poly-logarithmic deterministic solutions. *Global problems*, on the other end, correspond to tasks whose distributed verification might require the inspection of a *large* ball around each node (e.g., MST, shortest path). The state-of-the-art upper bounds for classical global problems is $\widetilde{O}(D+\sqrt{n})$ rounds, where D is the diameter of the network, and n is the number of nodes. Another common aspect, to be violated by our resilience notions, concerns the notion of *trivial* upper bounds. In the CONGEST model, for a network with m edges, a round complexity of $O(m)$ is a trivial upper bounds for all computational tasks. The reason is that within this number of rounds, every node can collect the entire graph information, and locally compute its part in the global solution. The framework of *resilient* distributed algorithms might totally change these above mentioned conventions. For example, the resilient computation of a local task such as MIS, might require $\Omega(D)$ rounds where D is the graph diameter, already for simple graph topologies (e.g., the cycle graph). In addition, due to the non-deterministic nature of the adversarial settings, in certain cases even $O(m)$ rounds will not be sufficient for completing the computation. The brute force approach of collecting the entire graph at each node might fail miserably in this context: Since it is required that the nodes' output will be based on a consistent global solution, the uncertainty of the adversarial choices might lead to inconsistent solutions.

Secure Algorithms with an Eavesdropper Adversary. We start by illustrating an implementation of the GBRS methodology on the setting of an eavesdropper adversary. In a simplified form, the eavesdropper adversary is allowed to listen only on one *fixed* edge (unknown to the nodes) throughout the entire execution. Given a non-secure algorithm $\mathcal{A}$, our goal is compile this algorithm into a resilient algorithm $\mathcal{A}'$ such that the adversary listening on edge u-v learns nothing, in the information-theoretic sense, on content of the messages exchanged between the nodes in the original algorithm $\mathcal{A}$. Towards achieving this goal, we took the following steps. First, we characterized the desired **graph structures** that allow simulating a single communication round of algorithm $\mathcal{A}$ in a secure manner. Recall that, public-key encryption should be avoided here. The work by [Kus89] implies that the graph G in such a setting must be two-edge connected. Specifically, for every edge (u, v) on which the (non-resilient) algorithm

$\mathcal{A}$ passes a message, there must be an alternative u-v path in G as otherwise an adversary listening on the edge (u, v) can learn the information sent from u to v. To provide a safe message exchange between every pair of neighbors u, v in the network, it is required to send messages along the two edge disjoint paths connecting u and v. Note that this should be done *simultaneously* for all neighboring pairs $(u, v) \in E(G)$. Since in our model, the bandwidth of each edge is limited, one of the key challenges in efficiently implementing this message exchange is the potentially large overlap between edge-disjoint paths of *different* neighboring pairs.

To circumvent such a scenario, we introduced the concept of **low-congestion cycle covers**. Formally, a (d, c)-cycle cover of a graph G is a collection of cycles in G in which each cycle is of length at most d and each edge participates in at least one cycle and at most c cycles. A-priori, it is not clear that cycle covers that enjoy both a small overlap and a short cycle length even exist, nor if it is possible to efficiently find them. Perhaps quite surprisingly, we show the following:

Theorem 1 (Existentially Optimal Cycle Covers, [PY19b]). *Every two-edge connected graph of diameter D admits a (d, c)-cycle cover where* $d = \widetilde{O}(D)$ *and[a]* $c = \widetilde{O}(1)$.

---

[a] As usual, the $\widetilde{O}(.)$ notation hides polylogarithmic terms in the number of nodes n.

These parameters are existentially tight up to polylogarithmic terms. In a subsequent work [PY19e], we also provided constructions of universally (nearly) optimal cycle covers in which each edge is covered by nearly the shortest possible cycle, and the total congestion is still bounded by a poly logarithmic term.

Finally, the third step concerns with the efficient resilient **simulation** of algorithm $\mathcal{A}$. For every message $M_{u \to v}$ sent in algorithm $\mathcal{A}$, in the resilient compilation, the sender u splits $M_{u \to v}$ into two shares, to be sent to v in parallel on the two edge-disjoint u-v paths provided by the cycle that covers the edge (u, v) in the collection of low-congestion cycle cover. The resilience argument follows by the fact that the adversary listening on a single edge can only gets random partial shares of the information. The efficiency argument follows by the fact that all messages are sent over short and almost edge-disjoint cycles. As a result, we get the following:

Theorem 2 (Compiler for Eavesdropping, [PY19b]). *Assume that* (d, c)-*cycle cover is computed in a preprocessing phase. Then any distributed algorithm $\mathcal{A}$ can be compiled into an $\mathcal{A}'$ algorithm that is resilient to an eavesdropping adversary while incurring an overhead of $\widetilde{O}(d + c)$ in the number of rounds.*

In [PY19b], we also consider a more involved adversarial setting in which the byzantine adversary can corrupt a *single* message in each round, regardless of the number of messages sent over all. The manipulated edge can vary from round to round, and the goal is to preserve the correctness of the distributed computation. This adversarial setting is handled by using a stronger variant of cycle covers in which each edge is covered by *two* edge-disjoint cycles. The latter can be computed using the fault-tolerant sampling technique [WY13].

Secure Algorithms with Semi-honest Adversaries. The main advantage of the complete communication network is in providing *secure* channels between every pair of nodes. As these channels are simply edges, different pairs can exchange information in a secure manner without interfering each other. When handling a general communication network, our approach is based on establishing such secure channels by means of a collection of edge (or vertex) disjoint paths between the communicating endpoints. To allow different pairs to communicate efficiently along these paths, simultaneously, we will aim at minimizing both the length and the overlap between the *secure channels* of different pairs.

In [PY19a], we initiated the study of prefect security with a *semi-honest adversary* that corrupts a single node in the graph. Recall that in the semi-honest setting, all nodes are assumed to follow the protocol and the goal is that each node learns nothing beyond its own output. Our end result is a simulation scheme that takes any *natural*[1] (non-secure) distributed graph algorithms and compiles it into a secure one while paying a multiplicative overhead of $D \cdot \text{poly}(\Delta)$ in the number of rounds, where D is the diameter of the network and Δ is the maximum degree.

Theorem 3 (Secure Simulation, Informal [PY19a]). *Let G be a 2-vertex connected n-vertex graph with diameter D and maximal degree Δ. Let $\mathcal{A}$ be a* natural *distributed algorithm that runs on G in r rounds. Then, $\mathcal{A}$ can be transformed to an equivalent algorithm $\mathcal{A}'$ with perfect privacy which runs in $\tilde{O}(rD \cdot \text{poly}(\Delta))$ rounds.*

The compiler of [PY19a] is somewhat technical and involves tools from the cryptographic world. However, the key challenge is purely graph theoretic. Using the Private Simultaneous Messages (PSM) protocol of [FKN94], the task of designing an efficient and secure compiler boils down into a clean distributed problem:

For each node u in the graph, simultaneously, the neighbors of u are required to exchange a random string R_u that is hidden from u.

This secret (shared random bits) in each neighborhood enables the compiler to securely simulate a single round of the original distributed algorithm. Note that all these secrets (inside each neighborhood) must be exchanged simultaneously. To provide efficient solution for this new distributed graph problem, we introduced the notion of **private neighborhood trees**, namely, a collection of n trees $T(u_1), \ldots, T(u_n)$, one for each vertex $u_i \in V(G)$, such that each tree $T(u_i)$ spans the neighbors of u_i *without going through u_i*. Intuitively, each tree $T(u_i)$ allows all neighbors of u_i to exchange a *secret* that is hidden from u_i, which

---

[1] The term natural refers to distributed algorithms whose local computation (performed at each node) is polynomial in the input size.

is the basic graph infrastructure for our secure compiler. In a (d, c)-private neighborhood trees, each tree $T(u_i)$ has depth at most d, and each edge $e \in G$ appears in at most c different trees. We denote the largest diameter of these trees as the *private diameter* of the graph. The efficiency of the secure simulation depends on the sum of the dilation d (i.e., the time to exchange a secret on a single tree) and the congestion c, i.e., the time it takes to send all messages through the most overloaded edge. Note that for every two vertex-connected graph, it is easy to compute a collection of trees with small depth but the congestion might be arbitrarily bad. Using connections to low-congestion cycle covers, we were able to show the following:

Theorem 4 (Existentially Optimal Private Trees [PY19a]). *Every two vertex-connected graph admits a collection of* (d, c)-*private neighborhood trees with* $d = \widetilde{O}(\Delta \cdot D)$ *and* $c = \widetilde{O}(D)$.

In a subsequent work, we also studied universally optimal constructions of private trees whose d + c bound competes with the best possible for the given input graph. Towards that goal, we introduce a new diameter measure of the graph which we call the *private diameter* of the graph. The *private diameter* of u_i denoted by

$$\mathsf{PrivateDiam}(u_i, G) = \max_{x,y \in \Gamma(u_i)} \mathrm{dist}(x, y, G \setminus \{u_i\})$$

is the maximum distance between u_i's neighbors in $G \setminus \{u_i\}$, where $\Gamma(u_i)$ are the neighbors of u_i in G. The private diameter of G is then defined by

$$\mathsf{PrivateDiam}(G) = \max_{u_i \in V} \mathsf{PrivateDiam}(u_i, G).$$

Letting $\mathsf{OPT_T}(G)$ be the minimum d + c over all (d, c) private trees for G. Since the depth of any tree $T(u_i)$ is at least $\mathsf{PrivateDiam}(u_i, G)$, we get that $\mathsf{OPT_T}(G) \geq \mathsf{PrivateDiam}(G)$.

Theorem 5 ((Nearly) Universally Optimal Private Trees [PY19e], Informal). *For every two vertex-connected graph G, there is a polynomial time algorithm for computing a collection of* (d, c)-*private neighborhood trees with* $d = \widetilde{O}(\mathsf{PrivateDiam}(G)) = \widetilde{O}(\mathsf{OPT_T}(G))$.

These constructions serve the basis for providing secure compilers for the family of distributed algorithms whose local computation can be expressed by read-once symmetric formulas. We believe that for many fundamental graph problems it is very plausible to provide secure simulation with improved bounds than the one obtained by our general compilation results. It would be very interesting to design such algorithms for global graph problems such as minimum spanning tree, shortest paths and minimum cuts.

Moving forward, the future ultimate goal is to *provide general simulation techniques under multiple byzantine corruptions*. Note that in this setting, it is not so clear if one can provide any correctness guarantees. The reason is that the influence of even a single byzantine node might expand to the entire network.

To delve into the byzantine setting, we start by considering the basic broadcast task and only focus on the correctness of the solution (while putting security aspects aside). This is described in the next section which handles non-cryptographic adversaries.

4   Algorithms Against Non-cryptographic Adversaries

In this section, we consider byzantine adversaries that manipulate a bounded collection of vertices or edges in the graph. Our primary goal in this setting is to preserve the correctness of the computation, putting security and privacy issues aside. Many distributed algorithms against various byzantine settings have been provided over the years, mainly for the setting of complete communication graphs. Perhaps surprisingly, there are no round-efficient distributed algorithms, in the congest model, against byzantine adversaries. To fill this gap, in [HP21] we consider the basic broadcast task with adversarial corrupted edges.

Broadcast against Adversarial Edges [HP21]. In *broadcast against adversarial edges problem* given is a source vertex s holding a designated message M. It is desired for all vertices to learn M in the presence of at most $t \geq 1$ adversarial edges $F \subseteq G$. The adversary controlling these edges has a complete knowledge of the graph topology, the internal inputs and outputs of the vertices and an unlimited computational power. The set of manipulated edges F is fixed throughout the execution, but their identity is *unknown* to the vertices in the graph. Following Dolev [Dol82], we also assume that the input graph it $(2t + 1)$-edge connected.

In a recent work[2] [HP21], we present the first round-efficient *algorithm* for the problem for any constant number of corruptions t. For the most basic setting of $t = 1$, we show:

> **Theorem 6** *[Broadcast against a Single Adversarial Edge] Given a D–diameter, 3–edge connected graph G, there exists a randomized Broadcast protocol against a single adversarial edge that runs in $\widetilde{O}(D^2)$ rounds. In addition, at the end of the algorithm, all nodes obtain a linear estimate for the diameter of the graph.*

Interestingly, the round complexity can be improved in several *relaxed* adversarial settings. For example, we show that if all vertices are given access to a shared randomness of $\widetilde{O}(1)$ bits, then the round complexity can be improved to $\widetilde{O}(D)$ rounds. Such an improvement can also be obtained in the setting of *symmetric adversary* in which the adversary is restricted to send the *same* message to both endpoints of the corrupted edge. We also consider the generalization of the problem to handling multiple adversarial edges and vertices. The efficiency of the algorithm scales exponentially with the number of corruptions.

---

[2] Currently under submission.

Theorem 7 *[Broadcast against t-Adversarial Edges and Vertices] Given a D–diameter $(2t+1)$ edge (vertex) connected graph with maximum degree Δ, we have the following:*

(i) *There exists a randomized broadcast algorithm against t adversarial edges (unknown to the nodes) with round complexity of $D^{O(t)} \cdot t^2 \cdot \log n$ rounds.*

(ii) *Provided that the source node is reliable, there exists a randomized broadcast algorithm against t adversarial vertices with round complexity of $D^{O(t)} \cdot t^2 \cdot \Delta \cdot \log n$ rounds.*

The round complexity of $D^{O(t)}$ rounds for handling $t = O(1)$ adversarial edges raises the question of whether such an exponential dependency on t is necessary. We address this question by providing a graph-theoretical characterization of *route-sets* of nodes, namely, a collection of s-v paths of large flow. Intuitively, in order to send a message from s to v in a reliable manner in the presence of t adversarial edges, it is required that the minimum cut of the s-v paths, along which the messages are passed, to be at least $t + 1$. This holds as otherwise, the adversary can manipulate the t cut edges on these paths. We show that in any collection of s-v paths of large flow value either one of the paths has length $D^{\Omega(t)}$, or else there is at least one edge in the intersection of $D^{\Omega(t)}$ paths.

This serves as the basis for providing a lower bound of $(D/t)^{\Omega(t)}$ rounds for the class of store-and-forward algorithms [LMR94]. In this class, all nodes (except for the source node s) act as relay nodes and can only store and forward the messages they receive, possibly with some changes in the header information. In particular, the nodes cannot employ any coding and other manipulations on their received messages. We have:

Theorem 8 (Lower Bound) *For every constant $t \geq 1$, every store and forward algorithm solving the byzantine Broadcast problem with t adversarial edges requires $(D/t)^{\Omega(t)}$ rounds.*

Omitting the restriction to store-and-forward algorithms is one of the most intriguing open problems left by our work. Specifically, it would be interesting to provide a super-linear in D lower-bound in the presence of multiple adversarial edges for any CONGEST algorithm. We also note that in our results for multiple adversarial edges, we did not attempt to optimize for the constants in the exponent (both in the upper and lower bound results).

Resilient Compilers [HP20]. A systemic approach for providing resilient distributed algorithm might be given by providing *general simulation techniques*. The latter will be applied in a black-box manner by compiling any given distributed algorithm $\mathcal{A}$ into an efficient resilient algorithm $\mathcal{A}'$ that performs the same computation as $\mathcal{A}$. The benefit of such a simulation approach is in obtaining a first-order solution for a wide-class of distributed algorithms, rather than handling one specific task.

In [HP20], we present the first steps by providing a resilient simulation in the presence of a single adversarial edge. This general result is based on the notion of *byzantine cycle covers* which extends the basic low-congestion cycle covers to the byzantine setting. Whereas in [PY19b], the cycle covers are computed in a preprocessing step, in this work the computation of these cycles is performed in the distributed byzantine setting, which is considerably more challenging. One of the main obstacles for computing these cycle covers is in covering the corrupted edge itself, i.e., computing a cycle that contains the byzantine edge. The reason is the following. By using the fault-tolerant sampling technique and the standard algorithm for cycle cover computation of [PY19c, PY19d], it is possible to cover fairly easily all edges except for the byzantine one. To cover the byzantine edge e itself (whose identity is a priori, unknown) it is required for the edge e to participate in the (fault-free) cycle cover algorithm, which might be severely corrupted by the activity of the byzantine edge. The crux of our algorithm is a quite delicate cycle verification procedure, which pinpoints at the only uncovered byzantine edge, that can then be covered b a separate procedure.

5 Handling Multiple Corruptions

Our compilers for handling a single corruption are based on the notion of low-congestion cycle covers. The latter, however, are limited to handling the corruption of at most one edge in the network. By Dolev [Dol82], handling a byzantine corruption of t vertices requires $(2t + 1)$ vertex connectivity[3]. To accommodate multiple corporations, one must exploit the high connectivity of the graph. The efficiency of the resilient algorithms depends upon the congestion and dilation values of the highly-connected paths connecting pairs of neighbors in the graph.

A New Perspective on Graph Connectivity. The challenge in designing efficient resilient and secure computation for highly-connected graphs, leads to a new type of questions and objectives in the long-standing and thoroughly studied topic of graph connectivity. Many previous studies on reliable distributed computation have used the fact that in a k-edge (vertex) connected graph, each pair of vertices is connected by k-edge (vertex) disjoint paths. This allows the design of protocols that are resilient to corruption of $\Theta(k)$ edges (vertices) in the graph. The beautiful work of Dolev [Dol82] has numerous algorithmic applications in the setting of resilient computation, but unfortunately it provides no guarantee on the length of the individual vertex-disjoint disjoint paths (between each pair of neighbors), or on their amount of overlap. Specifically, to provide *efficient* computation in the presence of $t/2$ faults in t-vertex connected graph, it is required that (1) each pair of neighboring nodes would be connected by t *short* vertex-disjoint paths and that (2) the total overlap between these paths (over all neighboring pairs) would be small. A key question is determining the extent to which a $2t+1$ vertex connected graph of diameter D can satisfy both of these two

---

[3] We note that it will be then important to extend this result to the setting of edge corruptions.

requirements as a function of the diameter D, the vertex connectivity parameter t, and the number of nodes n. These questions have been recently addressed in [CPT20, HP21]. We next highlight the main results from [CPT20] which already have implications for secure computation against multiple corruptions.

Packing Trees and Cycles [CPT20]. The celebrated *tree packing* theorem of Tutte and Nash-Williams from 1961 states that every k-edge connected graph G contains a collection $\mathcal{T}$ of $\lfloor k/2 \rfloor$ edge-disjoint *spanning* trees, that we refer to as a *tree packing*; the *diameter* of the tree packing $\mathcal{T}$ is the largest diameter of any tree in $\mathcal{T}$. A desirable property of a tree packing, that is both sufficient and necessary for leveraging the high connectivity of a graph in distributed communication networks, is that its diameter is low. Yet, despite extensive research in this area, it is still unclear how to compute a tree packing, whose diameter is sublinear in $|V(G)|$, in a low-diameter graph G, or alternatively how to show that such a packing does not exist. In [CPT20], we provide non-trivial upper and lower bounds on the diameter of the tree packing. For example, we show the following:

Theorem 9 (Low-Diameter Tree Packing, [CPT20]). *Every k-edge connected n-vertex graph G of diameter D, there is a tree packing $\mathcal{T}$ containing $\Omega(k)$ trees, of diameter $O((101k \log n)^D)$, with edge-congestion at most 2.*

On the lower bound side, we show that there is a k-edge connected graph of diameter $2D$, such that any packing of k/α trees with edge-congestion η contains at least one tree of diameter $\Omega\left((k/(2\alpha\eta D))^D\right)$, for any k, α and η. We also show that low-diameter packing can be translated into lead to *highly-connected cycle cover* of small length and congestion. Roughly speaking, in highly-connected cycle cover for k-edge connected graphs, it is required to cover each edge by $\Omega(k)$ cycles (instead of a single cycle, as in the standard definition). Low-diameter packing of trees and cycles have several applications to the setting of secure distributed algorithms in which the adversary is allowed to collide with $\Omega(k/\log n)$ edges in k-edge connected graphs. It is important to note that most of our constructions in [CPT20] are centralized. Providing efficient distributed constructions of (nearly optimal) tree packing highly-connected cycle covers is yet another interesting future direction.

Concluding Remarks. We propose a graph-theoretic approach for designing secure and resilient distributed algorithms for general graphs. Our perspective is mostly inspired by the area of fault-tolerant graph algorithms. There is still an immense gap in the existing knowledge on efficient resilient computation between the complete-graph setting and the general graph topology setting. We hope that this manuscript will spark the interest of algorithm designers and most notably the distributed graph algorithms community, in order to advance these directions considerably further.

References

[AD15]   Abraham, I., Dolev, D.: Byzantine agreement with optimal early stopping, optimal resilience and polynomial complexity. In: Proceedings of the 47th Annual ACM on Symposium on Theory of Computing, STOC 2015, Portland, OR, USA, June 14–17, 2015, pp. 605–614 (2015)

[AKM20] Augustine, J., King, V., Molla, A.R., Pandurangan, G., Saia, J.: Scalable and secure computation among strangers: message-competitive byzantine protocols. In: 34th International Symposium on Distributed Computing, DISC 2020, October 12–16, 2020, Virtual Conference, pp. 1–19 (2020)

[BT85]   Bracha, G., Toueg, S.: Asynchronous consensus and broadcast protocols. J. ACM **32**(4), 824–840 (1985)

[CPT20] Chuzhoy, J., Parter, M., Tan, Z.: On packing low-diameter spanning trees. In: 47th International Colloquium on Automata, Languages, and Programming, ICALP 2020, July 8–11, 2020, Saarbrücken, Germany (Virtual Conference), pp. 1–18 (2020)

[DK11]   Dinitz, M., Krauthgamer, R.: Fault-tolerant spanners: better and simpler. In: Proceedings of the 30th annual ACM SIGACT-SIGOPS symposium on Principles of distributed computing, pp. 169–178. ACM (2011)

[Dol82] Dolev, D.: The byzantine generals strike again. J. Algorithms **3**(1), 14–30 (1982)

[FKN94] Feige, U., Kilian, J., Naor, M.: A minimal model for secure computation (extended abstract). In: STOC (1994)

[GM98]   Garay, J.A., Yoram, M.: Fully polynomial byzantine agreement for n > 3t processors in t + 1 rounds. SIAM J. Comput. **27**(1), 247–290 (1998)

[HP20]   Hitron, Y., Parter, M.: Round-efficient distributed byzantine computation. CoRR, abs/2004.06436 (2020)

[HP21]   Hitron, Y., Parter, M.: Broadcast algorithms against adaptive adversarial edges. In: Under Submission (2021)

[KK06]   Katz, J., Koo, C.-Y.: On expected constant-round protocols for byzantine agreement. In: Dwork, C. (ed.) CRYPTO 2006. LNCS, vol. 4117, pp. 445–462. Springer, Heidelberg (2006). https://doi.org/10.1007/11818175_27

[Kus89] Kushilevitz, E.: Privacy and communication complexity. In: 30th Annual Symposium on Foundations of Computer Science, Research Triangle Park, North Carolina, USA, 30 October–1 November 1989, pp. 416–421. IEEE Computer Society (1989)

[LMR94] Leighton, F.T., Maggs, B.M., Rao, S.B.: Packet routing and job-shop scheduling ino (congestion+ dilation) steps. Combinatorica **14**(2), 167–186 (1994)

[LSP82] Lamport, L., Shostak, R.E., Pease, M.C.: The byzantine generals problem. ACM Trans. Program. Lang. Syst. **4**(3), 382–401 (1982)

[Par16] Parter, M.: Fault-tolerant logical network structures. Bull. EATCS **118** (2016)

[Par19] Parter, M.: Small cuts and connectivity certificates: a fault tolerant approach. In: 33rd International Symposium on Distributed Computing (DISC 2019). Schloss Dagstuhl-Leibniz-Zentrum fuer Informatik (2019)

[Pel96] Pelc, A.: Fault-tolerant broadcasting and gossiping in communication networks. Netw. Int. J. **28**(3), 143–156 (1996)

[Pel00] Peleg, D.: Distributed Computing: A Locality-sensitive Approach. SIAM, Philadelphia (2000)

[PSL80] Pease, M., Shostak, R., Lamport, L.: Reaching agreement in the presence of faults. J. ACM (JACM) **27**(2), 228–234 (1980)

[PY19a] Parter, M., Yogev, E.: Distributed algorithms made secure: a graph theoretic approach. In: Proceedings of the Thirtieth Annual ACM-SIAM Symposium on Discrete Algorithms, SODA 2019, San Diego, California, USA, January 6–9, 2019, pp. 1693–1710 (2019)

[PY19b] Parter, M., Yogev, E.: Low congestion cycle covers and their applications. In: Proceedings of the 30th Annual ACM-SIAM Symposium on Discrete Algorithms, SODA 2019, San Diego, California, USA, January 6–9, 2019, pp. 1673–1692 (2019)

[PY19c] Parter, M., Yogev, E.: Optimal short cycle decomposition in almost linear time (2019). http://www.weizmann.ac.il/math/parter/sites/math.parter/files/uploads/main-icalp-cycles-full.pdf

[PY19d] Parter, M., Yogev, E.: Optimal short cycle decomposition in almost linear time. In: 46th International Colloquium on Automata, Languages, and Programming, ICALP 2019, July 9–12, 2019, Patras, Greece, pp. 1–14 (2019)

[PY19e] Parter, M., Yogev, E.: Secure distributed computing made (nearly) optimal. In: Proceedings of the 2019 ACM Symposium on Principles of Distributed Computing, PODC 2019, Toronto, ON, Canada, July 29 - August 2, 2019, pp. 107–116 (2019)

[SW89] Santoro, N., Widmayer, P.: Time is not a healer. In: Monien, B., Cori, R. (eds.) STACS 1989. LNCS, vol. 349, pp. 304–313. Springer, Heidelberg (1989). https://doi.org/10.1007/BFb0028994

[SW90] Santoro, N., Widmayer, P.: Distributed function evaluation in the presence of transmission faults. In: Asano, T., Ibaraki, T., Imai, H., Nishizeki, T. (eds.) SIGAL 1990. LNCS, vol. 450, pp. 358–367. Springer, Heidelberg (1990). https://doi.org/10.1007/3-540-52921-7_85

[SY96] Shanbhogue, V., Yung, M.: Distributed computing in asynchronous networks with byzantine edges. In: Cai, J.-Y., Wong, C.K. (eds.) COCOON 1996. LNCS, vol. 1090, pp. 352–360. Springer, Heidelberg (1996). https://doi.org/10.1007/3-540-61332-3_169

[TPS87] Toueg, S., Perry, K.J., Srikanth, T.K.: Fast distributed agreement. SIAM J. Comput. **16**(3), 445–457 (1987)

[WY13] Weimann, O., Yuster, R.: Replacement paths and distance sensitivity oracles via fast matrix multiplication. ACM Trans. Algorithms (TALG) **9**(2), 1–13 (2013)

[Yao82] Yao, A.C.: Protocols for secure computations. In: 23rd Annual Symposium on Foundations of Computer Science (SFCS 1982), pp. 160–164. IEEE (1982)

Towards Minimally Conscious Cyber-Physical Systems: A Manifesto

Jiří Wiedermann[1] and Jan van Leeuwen[2(✉)]

[1] Institute of Computer Science of Czech Academy of Sciences and Karel Čapek Center
for Values in Science and Technology, Prague, Czech Republic
jiri.wiedermann@cs.cas.cz
[2] Department of Information and Computing Sciences, Utrecht University,
Utrecht, The Netherlands
J.vanLeeuwen1@uu.nl

Abstract. Incidents like the crash of Lion Air Flight 610 in 2018 challenge the design of reliable and secure cyber-physical systems that operate in the real-world and have to cope with unpredictable external phenomena and error-prone technology. We argue that their design needs to guarantee *minimal machine consciousness*, which expresses that these systems must operate with full awareness of (the state of) their components and the environment. The concept emerged from our recent effort to develop a computational model for conscious behavior in robots, based on the theory of automata. Making systems 'minimal machine conscious' leads to more trustworthy systems, as it strengthens their behavioral flexibility in varying environments and their resilience to operation and cooperation failures of their components and as a whole. The notion of minimal machine consciousness has the potential to become one of the defining attributes of Industry 4.0.

> *"We don't need artificial cognitive agents. We*
> *need intelligent tools."*
>
> D. C. Dennett [4], 2019

Keywords: Automata theory · Cyber-physical systems · Design philosophy · Industry 4.0 · Minimal machine consciousness · SACA loop · Self-control

1 Introduction

Aircraft crashes like that of Lion Air Flight 610 and collisions of self-driving vehicles can often be reduced to combined failures in the hardware and software components of their underlying systems. Incidents like this seriously challenge the design of reliable and secure systems that operate in the real world and can cope with unpredictable external phenomena and error-prone technology. How should one look at the issues at stake here, from a design philosophical viewpoint?

The research of the first author was partially supported by ICS AS CR fund RVO 67985807, programme Strategy AV21 "Hopes and Risks of the Digital Age" and the Karel Čapek Center for Values in Science and Technology (Prague, Czech Republic).

© Springer Nature Switzerland AG 2021
T. Bureš et al. (Eds.): SOFSEM 2021, LNCS 12607, pp. 43–55, 2021.
https://doi.org/10.1007/978-3-030-67731-2_4

Reliability and safety are crucial in *all* cyber-physical systems, not just in the examples we gave. Cyber-physical systems are systems of many components in which computers (processors) are used to govern the behavior of some parts of the physical world. The systems comprise both the computers and the parts of the physical world they govern [1,8]. In fact, one may well see cyber-physical systems as 'generalized robots'. Their development is rapidly progressing with the increasing use of advanced techniques from AI. And yet, incidents like mentioned above continue to occur.

Example 1. Examples of cyber-physical systems are ATM's, heart pacemakers, mobile phones, smart TVs, driverless cars, aircraft, trains, lifts, cranes, power plants, sea walls, ships, hadron colliders, orbital space stations, manufacturing systems, and many other systems. (Cf. [8].)

Generally speaking, one may argue that today's cyber-physical systems still operate as robot 'zombies' when it comes to adjusting to new or varying environments, their 'awareness' of operation and cooperation failures of their components or as a whole, and reacting properly to combined malfunctions of their modules. A natural question is whether the very use of insights from AI could ameliorate this state of affairs, possibly drastically.

From a philosophical perspective, the vulnerability of cyber-physical systems is rooted in their lacking, or limited, cognitive abilities. Even if we do not know how to endow such systems with the facilities of full-blown intelligence or even consciousness, and perhaps we might not even want to build such systems (cf. [4]), one can imagine to equip them with important aspects of awareness and behavioral knowledge of the parts of the world that they perceive via their sensors (cf. [5]).

In this paper we argue that the design of cyber-physical systems must guarantee, what we call, *minimal machine consciousness*, a concept expressing that the systems must operate and act based on, and maintaining, full awareness of (the state of) their components and the situation in their environment. The concept emerged in our recent effort to give a practical model for conscious behaviour in robots, based on the theory of automata [14]. The concept was initially meant to provide an exploratory, theoretical approach to the computational modeling of certain basic aspects of consciousness. However, we will argue that the underlying ideas can *also* be used in industrial applications, in the design of reliable and secure cyber-physical devices operating in the real world.

We contend that designing cyber-physical systems to be minimal machine conscious is the key to obtaining trustworthy systems, as it potentially strengthens their behavioral flexibility in new or varying environments and their resilience to operation or cooperation failures of their components or as a whole. As a design objective, the notion of minimal machine consciousness seems to provide the missing link to obtaining safe cyber-physical systems, and it should therefore be applied wherever possible and appropriate. This is summarized in the following *manifesto*:

All cyber-physical systems operating in a given environment, with or without human aid, must be designed as minimal machine conscious cognitive systems.

In the remainder we discuss the essence of the design philosophy we propose. In Sect. 2 we outline the architectural basis of the cyber-physical systems that may be termed 'cognitive'. Then, in Sect. 3, we define the 'four principles' of minimal machine consciousness, and we argue why cognitive cyber-physical systems have all it takes to satisfy the criteria. The model derives from the general framework in [14] and includes a refinement of the typical operational cycle of robotic systems.

In the subsequent sections we consider why minimal machine consciousness gives us a proper tool for the design challenge we posed. In Sect. 4 we discuss what is typically made possible by minimal machine consciousness. We also discuss the potential for realizing cognitive cyber-physical systems and the potential of minimal machine consciousness for becoming one of the defining system attributes of *Industry 4.0*. Finally, in Sect. 5, we offer some conclusions. For an extended version of this paper, see [15].

2   Cognitive Cyber-Physical Systems

2.1   Architecture

In general, a cyber-physical system is an embedded entity of components that is producing a behavior in some environment, based solely on the inputs from its sensory and motor modules. Some systems also take inputs from human operators. See [1,2] for a general introduction to cyber-physical systems and their foundation.

In cognitive cyber-physical systems, specific conditions are imposed that allow a qualitative assessment of the information obtained from all sources of input and from the appropriate actions that result from it. The architecture of a cognitive cyber-physical system C consists of four main parts: its sensory units, its motor units (or effectors), its finite-state control unit and its dashboard. See Fig. 1 for a typical systems view.

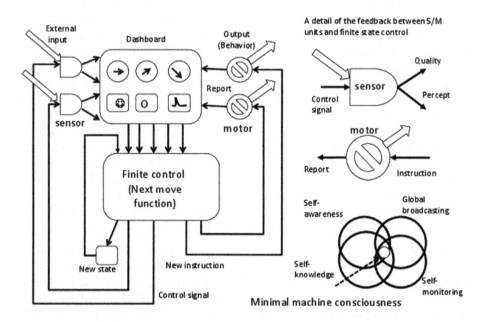

Fig. 1. A schema of a cognitive cyber-physical system

Sensory Units. Sensory units are devices, modules, or subsystems whose purpose is to detect and register events or changes in the system's environment and send the information about them to the control unit of the system. A sensory unit (or sensor) sends both a *representation* of the occurrence of a phenomenon it is specialized to and, depending on the type of sensor, also a feedback signal representing the *accuracy* of the corresponding sensation. The accuracy of a sensation can be graded according to some scale (such as insufficient, low, fair, excellent, and so on) and depends on the nature of that sensation. For example, it can be its magnitude, intensity, frequency, blurriness, etc.etera.

Motor Units. Motor units are devices, modules, or subsystems whose purpose is to perform one or more actions in the environment, seen as components of the system's behavior. Some motor units may serve for the positioning of sensors or of the system as an embodied entity, others may be designed for the manipulation of various effectors of the system. Motor modules send feedback to the control unit in the form of *reports* stating whether, or to what extent, the proposed operation could be realized. The feedback 'accuracy' and the 'reports' together are called the *quality* of the respective feedback. The qualities of the sensations and of the reports from the motor modules provide important feedback information for a system's 'self-monitoring' and 'self-awareness'. The graded responses allow the system to monitor the working of its sensory and motor modules. Clearly, not all effectors must perform mechanical movement. Some of them may be 'transmitters' that just produce internal or external signals of some kind: optical, chemical, acoustic, tactile, visual, radio-magnetic, etc. The emitted signals are used for communication purposes, under the assumption that the system and its environment possess receivers for the respective signals.

Finite-State Control. The finite-state control unit is the *computational* heart of any cognitive cyber-physical system. It acts in a similar fashion as deterministic finite-state automata. The control unit iterates the *operational cycle* of the system (see below). In any iteration, its purpose is to determine the (next) set of actions of the entire system based on four ingredients: the *current state* of the control unit, the current sensations from the sensory modules, the quality of these sensations, and the current reports from the motor modules. Typically, the finite-state control unit will be a *multiprocessor* that is programmed to generate the instructions for the set of actions to follow. States then represent the possible *configurations* of the unit.

Presuming that there is but a finite number of sensory and motor modules and that the control unit can recognize but a finite number of signals of various types received from these modules, a control unit can produce but a finite number of different instructions. Each such instruction states for a specific sensory or motor module what it has to do ('in the next step'). The instructions may require repeating the previous action, or performing a new specific action, or doing nothing at all. The number of different actions can be very large, even exponential in the number of received signals.

Dashboard. The four ingredients on which the control unit operates are jointly called the *dashboard* information of C. (At any time t, this information can be seen as the *instantaneous description* of the system at time t.) We note that all sufficiently complex (cognitive) cyber-physical systems have some form of 'physical' dashboard that has no influence on computation but is only used by a human operator for keeping a system's behavior within reasonable 'boundaries'. This human activity can be partially or fully automated, as we expect it is in self-controlled systems.

Note that in principle, the control unit works orders of magnitude faster than many other modules, especially the mechanical ones, of a cognitive system. Therefore the entire system works in an asynchronous manner.

2.2 Operation

Another characteristic feature of cognitive cyber-physical systems is their particular *operational cycle*. It is a variant of the well-known robotic paradigm, i.e. the *Sense-Think-Act* or *Sense-Plan-Act* cycle, now consisting of four phases that are iterated in sequel: *Sense-Analyze-Compute-Act* (SACA). The 'Analyze-Compute' part may be seen as a refinement of the 'Think' or 'Plan' phase in the standard robotic case. The four phases are distinguished as follows.

Sense. In the first phase ('sense') dashboard information is retrieved, in parallel, by the control unit. The dashboard information must be read in parallel, since the next proceeding of the system must be based on all available information at the time a next iteration cycle begins.

Analyze. In the second step ('analyze'), the dashboard information and its gradings are interpreted and fitted against the state information of the finite control, so as to determine how the system and its actions are progressing internally and, naturally, in the system's environment (as far as it can tell from its sensory input). The phase leads to a decision for a next action.

Compute. In the third step ('compute'), a so-called *transition function* is applied to the dashboard information and the anticipated decision. This is a function that for any given current state, current dashboard information, and the current analysis of it, determines a new state of the control unit and for each sensory and motor module a new action to be realized in this iteration cycle.

Act. Finally, in the fourth step ('act'), the new state of the control unit and the new actions are broadcast to the respective modules in parallel, based on the result of the transition function.

After the modules perform their new operations, a new bundle of data is gathered to refresh the dashboard: new sensations and their qualities from the sensory modules, and new reports from the motor modules. Then the entire operational cycle is repeated.

The *Sense-Analyze-Compute-Act* cycle concept as defined here resembles that of Boyd's *Observe-Orient-Decide-Act* (OODA) loop in operational decision making and the *Monitor-Analyze-Plan-Execute-over-shared-Knowledge* (MAPE-K) loop propagated in the design of self-adaptive *autonomic systems* [10]. The schema of a cognitive cyber-physical system is depicted in Fig. 1. A formal description can be given in a framework like suggested in [1] or in the automata-theoretic framework described in [14].

Definition 1. *A cognitive cyber-physical system is called* complete *if and only if its transition function is defined for all combinations of its inputs.*

A complete cognitive cyber-physical system can, in principle, react differently to different inputs in response to changes in its input parameters.

3   Self-controlled Cognitive Cyber-Physical Systems and Minimal Machine Consciousness

3.1   Minimal Machine Consciousness

Cognitive cyber-physical systems can be adequately self-controlled only when a full 'picture' of itself and its embedding can be derived (implicitly), based on the information from the sensory and motor units and on the potential actions they can initiate at a given time.

Considering the *Sense-Analyze-Compute-Act* paradigm, it makes sense to distinguish four corresponding 'dimensions' that together serve as prerequisites for adequate self-control. This leads to the following 'self-$\star$' properties which one might consider for a cognitive cyber-physical system C:

- *self-knowledge*: C has complete knowledge of its current cognitive state as well as of the data produced by all its sensors (the percepts and their qualities) and motor units (the reports from all of them).
- *self-monitoring*: C is completely informed about the performance and status of its sensory and motor units over time and of its embedding in its environment as it is.
- *self-awareness* (or *self-reflection*): C behaves in a way that unambiguously reflects, resp. is determined by, its current cognitive state and the information gained by its self-knowledge and self-monitoring abilities, and that is 'aware' of the internal and external changes that it causes.
- *self-informing*: C globally broadcasts its cognitive state, to all modules of the system and whenever changes of state occur.

Definition 2. *A cognitive cyber-physical system C is called* minimal machine conscious *(or, MMC) if and only if it is self-monitoring, self-knowledgeable, self-aware, and self-informing.*

There are several reasons for using the term 'minimal machine consciousness' for the collective properties we distinguished. A major reason is that, together, they seem to represent the minimal requirements for a system to respond adequately under all circumstances. Furthermore, a cognitive cyber-physical system was defined as a finite-state system without further resources. Thus, the 'active' memory available to realize any sort of 'conscious behavior' is only assumed to be finite, i.e., 'minimal' when compared to intelligent systems with (potentially) unbounded active memory.

The four principles of self-control are necessarily *informal*. We envision that for any class of cyber-physical systems they are concretized, to the extent that they provide precise requirements for the system designers and are verified for the systems that are claimed to satisfy them.

Example 2. Several disasters of airplanes and space shuttles have been caused by the lack of self-knowledge and self-monitoring qualities, and the absence of cooperation among the modules of the flight-control system. For example, in 1986, the space shuttle Challenger exploded due to an unspotted malfunction of the spacecraft's rubber seals. No one on board survived. The recent crash of Lion Air Flight 610 was caused by a malfunctioning of the flight-control system of a Boeing 737 MAX 8 that should not have happened if it had been a minimal machine conscious system.

Example 3. Cognitive cyber-physical systems that are MMC are not necessarily restricted to having finite memory only. For example, note that a Turing machine can be seen as a cognitive cyber-physical system in which a finite-state control governs a finite set of sensory and motor units, namely the respective read/write heads on its worktapes. Operating over an input stream, the system is seen to be minimal machine conscious. Nevertheless, the work-tapes give it a potentially unbounded memory.

3.2 Self-controlled Cognitive Cyber-Physical Systems Are MMC

The four principles that define minimal machine consciousness (i.e. self-knowledge, self-monitoring, self-awareness and self-informing) correspond precisely to the properties that are required for full and adequate self-control in the various phases of the operational cycle of a cyber-physical system. We formulate this as follows.

Proposition 1. *Self-controlled cognitive cyber-physical systems are necessarily minimal machine conscious.*

In the remainder of this section we expand on our arguments in support of Proposition 1. In Sect. 4 we describe what minimal machine consciousness makes possible.

(a) Self-controlled cognitive cyber-physical systems have self-knowledge
The information needed for self-knowledge includes its current cognitive state and the information produced both by its sensory units (the percepts and their qualities) and its motor modules (the reports from all of them). In a cognitive cyber-physical system, this is the data maintained in the dashboard. It gives the system the possibility to report any information about its functioning, at any time.

(b) Self-controlled cognitive cyber-physical systems are self-monitoring
In the state it is in, the feedback from the sensory and motor modules as it is supplied by the feature of self-knowledge, makes it possible for the system to monitor itself. Namely, from these modules the system gets the data about its current working conditions, and based on this information it can either prolong its functioning without any further special actions or take steps that remedy or adjust its operation. All this confirms the machine's certainty, or errors, in its actions and enables the repair of its own mistakes [3].

(c) Self-controlled cognitive cyber-physical systems are self-aware
The current cognitive state and the information gained by its self-knowledge and self-monitoring abilities, enable a system to determine ('compute') whatever its appropriate next action would be, in the environment in which it operates. The property of self-awareness requires the fulfillment of three conditions:
  – *the capacity of introspection*, i.e. the ability to reflect on one's own mental state (cf. [3]). General mechanisms of introspection seem to be beyond the ability of finite-state devices, as they may require unbounded memory. In the framework of finite-state devices, introspection can be modelled by a finite number of system states. For instance, 'interesting' past states can be stored in the current state, by using the standard automata theory technique of storing data in an automaton's state. In this way, one can even introduce dedicated states of the control unit, so-called *machine qualia states*, in which a system can remember

important past events that still require its ongoing attention (cf. [14]). Machine qualia offer the system a mechanism for remembering certain 'subjective' cognitive states of the system that are bound to certain previous cognitive 'experiences' (states). For instance, a quale state in a mobile phone may keep a remembrance of a recent event when a text message was received. A driverless car can have a quale state regarding a shortage of gas. The qualia states stored in the system's global state can then be broadcast to the entire system as long as a circumstance invoking them persists.

- *the ability to recognize oneself as an individual object separate from the environment and other objects.* This will be implied by a proper selection of sender-receiver modules whose cooperation provides the required effect. There are several modalities of signals that can have a similar effect. For instance, receiving a specific olfactory (or chemosensory), electric, optical, acoustic or haptic return signal may indicate the presence of other instances of the system. Obviously, the absence of such return signals indicates that no similar systems are around. For a similar purpose, in advanced cyber-physical systems a vision system may be available.

- *awareness of changes in the outside world.* The feedback also allows the system to distinguish its actions as registered by its sensory modules from the similarly registered actions performed by other systems. That is to say, in the latter case, the reports from the motor modules do not match the sensations from the sensory modules. Self-awareness thus provides a cognitive system with a rudimentary machine concept of the *self*: the system has information on what goes on in the outside world, what its actions are and what their effects. This information is of the form 'here and now' – it is pertinent to the present position of the system in its environment and the present moment.

(d) *Self-controlled cognitive cyber-physical systems are self-informing*

By the very definition of cognitive cyber-physical systems, the new state of a system and the projected actions are 'broadcast' to all its modules, simultaneously and in parallel. This ensures a synchronization of the actions they need to be synchronized and gives the modules a certain minimal information (namely, that 'stored' in the current state) of what goes on in the entire system. Endowing machines with the possibility of self-informing allows their modules to share information and collaborate to address whatever impending problem (cf. [3]). For example, consider a modern car in which a fuel sensor reports a shortage of gas. If this information is globally available then the navigation system of the car can direct the driver to a nearest gas station [3].

4   A Manifesto on Minimal Machine Consciousness

We claim that minimal machine consciousness is a key criterion for all cognitive cyber-physical systems in practice, to provide them with the necessary abilities for smooth and safe operation. It has important consequences for the engineering of cyber-physical systems. We summarize this in the following assertion.

All cyber-physical systems operating in a given environment, with or without human aid, must be designed as minimal machine conscious cognitive systems.

4.1 What Minimal Machine Consciousness Makes Possible

In Table 1 we list a variety of important abilities which cyber-physical systems should have and the mechanisms that facilitate them if the system is (cognitive and) minimal machine conscious. It shows what is made possible by the combined properties of the architecture and the four principle of minimal machine consciousness.

The feedback from the sensory and motor units brings straightforward benefits for improving system performance. Self-knowledge, self-monitoring, and self-awareness lead to improved decision making and increased detection capabilities. Self-informing enables the cooperation and synchronization of the system's modules. Altogether, minimal machine consciousness enables the system to detect and correct failures that can potentially prevent a possible crash or disaster, and at least diminish the number of false alarms, thus improving the trustability, reliability and safeness of the system under the changing conditions in its environment.

Table 1. Abilities of minimal machine conscious cyber-physical systems and the corresponding mechanisms that realize or facilitate them

Ability	Mechanism
Improved decision making Increased detection capabilities Diminished number of false alarms Failure correction Damage registration Flexibility and improved reliability in varying situations	Graded feedback from sensors and motor units
Interception of adversarial physical actions	Additional sensors
Limited cognitive and calculatory tasks	Finite-state data processing
Attention mechanism	Suppressing disturbing inputs
Limited form of introspection	Cognitive states
Detection of patterns in ongoing processes	Introspection
Recognition of itself as an individual subject, separate from the environment and other systems	Cooperation of send-receive mechanisms
Communication	Send-receive mechanisms
Distinguishing one's own actions from the actions of other systems	Mismatch of motor actions with sensory observations
Reading the intentions of other similar systems (machine empathy)	Situating the system into the position of the other systems
Limited cognitive and calculatory tasks	Finite-state data processing
Subjective machine perception (machine qualia states)	Storing states in states

The detailed mechanisms of self-awareness lead to further potential benefits. For instance, self-awareness requires that the system must be able to distinguish its own movement from any other movement that it can observe in the environment. This property can be used, e.g., by a robotic arm system to intercept a motion (of an 'intruder') within reach of its arm. Another example is collision-free navigation. As an extreme case, a minimal machine conscious system can 'read the mind' of another, similar system by observing its input and by being aware that this is not its input. Namely, thanks to the fact that the observing and the observed systems are of the same construction, the observing system can infer the actions of the observed system.

4.2   Design Considerations

As presented, minimal machine consciousness becomes feasible once a cyber-physical system is, or can be, designed as a *cognitive* system. This follows from the close connection between the four principles of minimal machine consciousness and the necessary features of *self-control* during the consecutive phases of the operational cycle of the system. Minimal machine consciousness enables the system to operate awarely in its environment at any time.

We therefore contend that minimal machine consciousness should be one of the major *design objectives* of any cyber-physical system. Having this is mind, the following bold statement is at the heart of our 'manifesto'.

Claim 1. *Any cognitive cyber-physical system operating in a given environment, with or without human aid, can also be designed as a minimal machine conscious cyber-physical system.*

To see this, consider any cognitive cyber-physical system operating in a given environment that is not minimal machine conscious. This means that the system has knowledge of what behavior must be invoked, based on the inputs from its sensory modules, assuming problem-free operation of both its sensory and motor modules. It should thus be possible to 'redesign' (or, re-program) the system so as to make optimal use of this information and transform it into a system that conforms to the four self-control principles of minimal machine machine consciousness described above. We even *hypothesize* the following, stronger claim:

Claim 2. *All dedicated activities that can be consciously controlled by humans can also be controlled by minimal machine conscious cognitive cyber-physical systems.*

The background for this claim is that, if we take 'conscious control' to mean as much as 'possessing knowledge of how to behave to fulfill a certain task', then one must be close to knowing or discovering the dependencies between various components of behavior and the corresponding inputs from sensory and motor modules. If we accept the cognitive architecture as a *standard*, then the rules and necessary information to drive the operational cycle should be in reach.

The claims can be the starting point for further methodological, or software engineering considerations towards the realization of cyber-physical system as described, for example, in [8] and [9]. Including minimal machine consciousness as a concrete design objective calls for more orderliness and discipline in the design of the system, by insisting on the fulfillment of the four necessary conditions required for this type of 'consciousness'. The benefits are clear.

Example 4. It seems that, currently, no clear-cut example of a deliberately designed minimal machine conscious cyber-physical system exists. The closest example seems to be the modern smartphone. These phones usually have a 'dashboard' in the form of a *status bar* (e.g. along the top of the touchscreen). Here, the statuses of various important sensors, such as the quality of the wifi, mobile network, GPS, the bluetooth signal, battery power, etc.etera, are depicted with the help of the respective icons. At the same time, the icons indicate the quality of the respective signals. This is, in fact, global information describing the current state of the device that is accessible to all modules of the phone, and a witness of the system's self-knowledge and self-monitoring. Last but not least, the system is quite self-aware – it can recognize the incoming calls, send and receive messages, establish the bluetooth connection, identify changes in its location (via GPS), etc. Interestingly, these abilities of smartphones are the result of incremental, technological evolution and the development of user requirements rather than of a purposeful effort to make the devices minimal machine conscious. This only confirms that the idea of minimal machine consciousness is a natural and useful concept that is worth to follow up and exploit as a design objective.

4.3 Minimal Collective Machine Consciousness

Given a number of different cyber-physical systems, there may be considerable potential in combining them into one 'composed system'. This happens, for example, when a complex task must be split over several cyber-physical systems, with each system dedicated to a well-identified subtask. This leads us to consider *networks* of cooperating cyber-physical systems.

If the 'nodes' are all cognitive cyber-physical systems, then one may turn the network into a cognitive cyber-physical 'meta-system' by adding a global finite-control that sees the nodes as sensory/motor units and combines their information into one global operational cycle (which need not be synchronized with the operational cycles of the nodes). This construction is especially interesting when the nodes are all minimal machine conscious.

Example 5. One may think of modern robots as cognitive cyber-physical meta-systems, with subsystems dedicated to specific tasks like vision, motion, sensing, and grasping. More generally, teams of robots, swarms of drones, nano-machines in a bloodstream, etc., also qualify.

To see what sort of additional machine consciousness this may lead to, consider an arbitrary cyber-physical meta-system D. The nature of the information D collects from its nodes may vary widely. It can be data from the specific subtasks of the nodes, statistics related to their activities, reports on the working conditions and cognitive states of the underlying cyber-physical systems, etcetera. Based on this, D can keep track of the part of the 'world' that is registered by its nodes. In particular, if the nodes are minimal machine conscious, D may collect their qualia states. As a result we get a networked cognitive system that is *minimal collective machine conscious.*

With our *manifesto* of cyber-physical system design in mind, one may reformulate both Claims 1 and 2 so as to hold for 'minimally collective machine conscious' cyber-physical meta-systems, and even for *cyber-physical human systems* [13] as well.

4.4 Minimal Machine Consciousness and Industry 4.0

It is a serious challenge to design a specific minimal machine conscious cyber-physical system that can handle all possibilities, in the numerous situations that the system can face. This is well-recognized in the area of software engineering, for embedded systems and cyber-physical systems alike. However, the challenge must be met, as cyber-physical systems are crucial for all enterprises. This is notably expressed in the advanced concepts of smart manufacturing in *Industry 4.0* [7].

In Industry 4.0 it is foreseen that all production processes in factories are automated and computerized, making them flexible and efficient by the use of modern information and communication technologies and intelligent systems and services [12]. The processes will be connected and controlled by smart systems that manage entire production lines and make decisions of their own, in symbiosis with human operators. We refer to [11] for an overview of the technological challenges involved.

The core systems of Industry 4.0 can be recognized to be cyber-physical (human) systems. As we have argued in this manifesto, these systems must be designed so as to be 'cognitive' and, especially, minimal machine conscious. With the testability of the latter in mind [14], this seems certainly achievable as a criterion from the outset. It may be the limit of what current hardware and software engineering methods can do.

Fortunately, a promising technology is emerging that enables both the design and the efficient testing of potentially minimal machine conscious cyber-physical systems: the technology of *digital twins*. In our case, a digital twin would be a digital replica of the physical part of a designated cyber-physical system.

Using a digital twin of (a part of) the given or intended cyber-physical system, one can systematically test whether it will react properly to all external and internal conditions, provided the combinations and scenarios that the system's modules may face can be finitely enumerated. If a system passes such a test, we know that it is complete w.r.t. to all events that can be registered by the system (cf. Definition 1). Of course, if the testing cannot be exhaustive, the system can only be guaranteed as far as the scenarios went.

Digital twin research is a growing and flourishing scientific field (cf. [6]). Its application to the design and testing of minimal machine conscious systems can give further impetus to the research and development of this technology. It is generally accepted that digital twin technology is one of the key enablers of *Industry 4.0*. The concept of minimal machine consciousness has the potential to revolutionize this field further.

5 Conclusion

The main message of our manifesto is the following assertion.

All cyber-physical systems operating in a given environment, with or without human aid, must be designed as minimal machine conscious cognitive systems.

Minimal machine consciousness is not a feature of only highly complex systems, and cannot be achieved by a mere software upgrade. Rather, it requires a different system architecture, and a properly designed operational cycle that can deal with the graded feedbacks from all sensory and motor units.

Minimal machine consciousness has a meaningful purpose, its benefits in industrial applications are substantial and can hardly be obtained differently. What is costly, however, is their development since maximal attention must be paid to their functionality under all possible conditions they can face, be they caused by software or hardware malfunction or unfortunate combinations of adversarial external factors.

When designing new cyber-physical systems, or innovating the existing ones, especially in which risks for human life are at stake, it is a matter of responsible design and ethics to make such systems minimal machine conscious.

References

1. Broy, M.: Engineering cyber-physical systems: challenges and foundations. In: Aiguier, M. et al. (Eds.), Complex Systems Design & Management, Proceedings Third International Conference (CSD&M 2012), Springer, Berlin, Ch. 1, pp. 1–13 (2013)
2. Broy, M., Schmidt, A.: Challenges in engineering cyber-physical systems. IEEE Comput. **47**(2), 70–72 (2014)
3. Dehaene, S., Lau, H., Kouider, S.: What is consciousness, and could machines have it? Science **358**(6362), 486–492 (2017)
4. Dennett, D.C.: What Can We Do? In: Brockman, J. (Ed.), Possible Minds: 25 Ways of Looking at AI, Ch. 5, Penguin Press, London (2019)
5. Eliot, L., Driverless Cars Must Be Self-Aware, A Crucial Missing Ingredient, Medium, May 8, 2019
6. ERCIM: Digital Twins: Special Theme. ERCIM News 115, October 2018. https://ercim-news.ercim.eu/en115
7. i-Scoop: Industry 4.0: the fourth industrial revolution - guide to Industry 4.0, March 2020. https://www.i-scoop.eu/industry-4-0/
8. Jackson, M.: Behaviours as design components of cyber-physical systems. In: Meyer, B., Nordio, M. (eds.) LASER 2014. LNCS, vol. 8987, pp. 43–62. Springer, Cham (2015). https://doi.org/10.1007/978-3-319-28406-4_2
9. Jackson, M.: Behaviours and model fidelity in cyber-physical systems. In: Computability in Europe: Computing with Foresight and Industry (CiE 2019), Special Session: History and Philosophy of Computing, Durham (2019)
10. Kephart, J.O., Chess, D.M.: The vision of autonomic computing. IEEE Comput. **36**(1), 41–50 (2003)
11. Lu, Y.: Industry 4.0: a survey on technologies, applications and open research issues. J. Ind. Inf. Integr. **6**, 1–10 (2017)
12. Rüßmann, M. et al.: Industry 4.0 - the future of productivity and growth in manufacturing industries, report. Boston Consult. Group **9**(1), 54-89 (2015)
13. Sowe, S.K., Simon, E., Zettsu, K., de Vaulx, F.F., Bojanova, I.: Cyber-physical human systems: putting people in the loop. IT Prof. **18**(1), 10–13 (2016)
14. Wiedermann, J., van Leeuwen, J.: Finite state machines with feedback: an architecture supporting minimal machine consciousness. In: Manea, F., Martin, B., Paulusma, D., Primiero, G. (eds.) CiE 2019. LNCS, vol. 11558, pp. 286–297. Springer, Cham (2019). https://doi.org/10.1007/978-3-030-22996-2_25
15. Wiedermann, J., van Leeuwen, J.: Towards Minimally Conscious Cyber-Physical Systems: A Design Philosophy, Technical Report UU-PCS-2020-02, Center for Philosophy of Computer Science, Department of Information and Computing Sciences, Utrecht University, 2020

Foundations of Computer Science – Full Papers

Amnesiac Flooding: Synchronous Stateless Information Dissemination

Volker Turau$^{(\boxtimes)}$ (iD)

Institute of Telematics, Hamburg University of Technology, 21073 Hamburg, Germany
turau@tuhh.de

Abstract. A recently introduced stateless variant of network flooding for synchronous systems is called *amnesiac flooding*. Stateless protocols are advantageous in high volume applications, increasing performance by removing the load caused by retention of session information. In this paper we analyze the termination time of multi-source amnesiac flooding. We provide tight upper and lower bounds for the time complexity.

1 Introduction

The most basic algorithm to disseminate information in a distributed system is deterministic flooding. The originator of the information sends a message with the information to all neighbors and whenever a node receives this message for the first time, it sends it to all its neighbors in the communication graph G. This algorithm uses $2|E|$ messages and terminates after at most $\epsilon_G(v_0) + 1$ rounds, where v_0 is the originating node and $\epsilon_G(v_0)$ is the maximal distance of v_0 to any other node. The flooding algorithm requires each node to maintain for each message a marker that the message has been forwarded. This requires storage per node proportional to the number of disseminated messages. Another issue is how long these markers are kept. Thus, stateful algorithms such as the classic flooding algorithm do not scale well with respect to memory usage.

In *stateless protocols* each message travels on it's own without reference to any previous message. Stateless protocols are very popular in client-server applications because of their high degree of scalability. They simplify the design of the server and require less resources because servers do not need to keep track of session information. In addition they provide fault tolerance after node crashes.

Recently Hussak and Trehan proposed a stateless information dissemination algorithm for synchronous systems called *amnesiac flooding* [7,8]. In this algorithm a node after receiving a message, forwards it to those neighbors from which it did not receive the message in the current round. Obviously, this variant of flooding is stateless and avoids the above mentioned storage issues. It is not obvious that amnesiac flooding terminates since a node can potentially forward the same message several times. Hussak et al. analyzed the termination time of amnesiac flooding with a single originating node v_0 [7,8]. For bipartite graphs amnesiac flooding terminates after $\epsilon_G(v_0)$ rounds, i.e., the same number of rounds as the marker based algorithm. In the non-bipartite case amnesiac

© Springer Nature Switzerland AG 2021
T. Bureš et al. (Eds.): SOFSEM 2021, LNCS 12607, pp. 59–73, 2021.
https://doi.org/10.1007/978-3-030-67731-2_5

flooding requires at least $\epsilon_G(v_0) + 1$ and at most $\epsilon_G(v_0) + Diam(G) + 1$ rounds, where $Diam(G)$ denotes the diameter of G. The proof of this result in [8] is rather technical and does not give much insight into the problem.

The problem of multi-source flooding is motivated by disaster monitoring: A dense distributed monitoring system monitors a geographical region. When several sensors detect an event, they flood this information into the network.

Hussak et al. stated the following open problem: What happens when all nodes of a set S start the flooding process with the same message concurrently? In this paper we give an answer to this problem. The contribution of this paper is twofold. First, we prove that for every non-bipartite graph and every set S there exists a bipartite graph $\mathcal{G}(S)$ such that the execution of amnesiac flooding on both graphs is strongly correlated and termination times coincide. The auxiliary graph $\mathcal{G}(S)$ captures on an intuitive level, what happens during the flooding process. $\mathcal{G}(S)$ considerably simplifies the proof of [8]. It leads to bounds that are independent of the diameter and it allows to determine starting nodes for amnesiac flooding with minimal termination time. Secondly, we give tight lower and upper bounds for the time complexity of amnesiac flooding in special cases.

After introducing our notation and reviewing the state of the art we present in Sect. 4 our implementation $\mathcal{A}_{\mathsf{AF}}$ of amnesiac flooding. Next we summarize our main results. In Sect. 6 we present the construction of the auxiliary graph $\mathcal{G}$ for the case $|S| = 1$ and demonstrate that this graph immediately proves the results of [7,8]. In the next section we reduce the case $|S| > 1$ to the case $|S| = 1$ and prove our main theorems. The full proofs can be found in [11].

2   Notation

In the following $G(V, E)$ is always a finite, connected, undirected, and unweighted graph with $n = |V|$ and $m = |E|$. For a node v, $N(v)$ denotes the set of v's neighbors; v is called *isolated* if $N(v) = \emptyset$. The minimal node degree of G is denoted by δ. For $u, v \in V$ let $d_G(v, u)$ be the *distance* in G between v and u, i.e., the number of edges of a shortest path between v and u. For $U \subseteq V$ and $v \in V$ let $d_G(v, U) = \min\{d_G(v, u) \mid u \in U\}$ and $d_G(U) = \max\{d_G(v, U) \mid v \in V\}$. $G[U]$ denotes the graph induced by U. For $v \in V$ denote by $\epsilon_G(v)$ the *eccentricity* of v in G, i.e., the greatest distance between v and any other node in G, i.e., $\epsilon_G(v) = d_G(\{v\})$. In a few cases we consider disconnected graphs. In this case we define $\epsilon_G(v) = \epsilon_U(v)$, where U is the connected component containing v. The *radius* $Rad(G)$ (resp. *diameter* $Diam(G)$) of G is the minimum (resp. maximum) eccentricity of any node of G. A *central* node in G is a node v with $\epsilon_G(v) = Rad(G)$. An edge $(u, w) \in E$ is called a *cross edge* with respect to a node v_0 if $d_G(v_0, u) = d_G(v_0, w)$. Any edge of G that is not a cross edge with respect to v_0 is called a *forward edge* for v_0.

Let $n \geq k \geq 1$. We call $r_k(G) = \min\{d_G(U) \mid |U| = k\}$ the *k-radius* of G, i.e., $r_1(G) = Rad(G)$. A subset $U \subseteq V$ with $|U| = k$ and $r_k(G) = d_G(U)$ is called a *k-center*. Similarly we call $r_k^{ni}(G) = \min\{d_G(U) \mid |U| = k$ and $G[U]$ contains no isolated node$\}$ the *non-isolated k-radius* of G. Clearly

$r_k(G) \leq r_k^{ni}(G)$. A subset $U \subseteq V$ with $|U| = k$ such that $G[U]$ has no isolated node and $r_k^{ni}(G) = d_G(U)$ is called a *non-isolated k-center*. A *total dominating set* of a connected graph G is a set D of nodes of G such that every node is adjacent to a node in D. The *total domination number* of G, denoted by $\gamma_t(G)$, is the minimum cardinality of a total dominating set of G. Note that a non-isolated k-center with radius 1 is a total dominating set. Thus, $\gamma_t(G) \leq k$ iff $r_k^{ni}(G) = 1$.

In this paper we consider a synchronous distributed system, i.e., algorithms are executed in rounds of fixed length and all messages sent by all nodes in a particular round are received and processed in the next round. An information dissemination algorithm is correct if all nodes receive the information and the algorithm globally terminates. A distributed algorithm has globally terminated if every node locally has terminated and there is no message in transit between nodes. For a discussion of asynchronous amnesiac flooding we refer to [8].

3   State of the Art

Different facets of stateless programming recently received attention: MapReduce framework, and reentrant code [4]. Stateless protocols are popular in client-server applications because of their high degree of scalability. They simplify the design of the server and require less resources because servers do not need to keep track of session information. According to Awerbuch et al. statelessness implies various desirable properties: asynchronous updates and self-stabilization [2].

The classic flooding algorithm, where each node that receives a message for the first time forwards it to all other neighbors, requires in the worst case $Diam(G)$ rounds until all nodes have received the message and uses $O(m)$ messages [10]. This result holds in the synchronous and the asynchronous model. The classic flooding algorithm is a stateful algorithm. Each node needs to maintain for each message a marker that the message has been forwarded. This requires storage per node proportional to the number of disseminated messages. A stateless version of flooding was proposed by Hussak and Trehan [7]. Their algorithm – called amnesiac flooding – forwards every received message to those neighbors from which it did not receive the message in the current round. Amnesiac flooding has a low memory requirement since markers are only kept for one round. Note, that nodes may forward a message more than once. In synchronous networks amnesiac flooding when started by a node v_0 terminates after at most $\epsilon_G(v_0) + Diam(G) + 1$ rounds [8]. The proof is based on an analysis of the forwarding process on a round by round basis, whereas our analysis is based on an auxiliary graph. We believe that our approach opens more possibilities to prove more general results related to amnesiac flooding, such as multi-source flooding. Using this approach Turau proposed a new stateless flooding algorithm $\mathcal{A}_{SF}$ that has the same termination time as the classic flooding algorithm and is thus faster than amnesiac flooding [12].

A problem related to broadcast is rumor spreading that describes the dissemination of information in large and complex networks through pairwise interactions. A simple model for rumor spreading is to assume that in each round, each node that knows the rumor, forwards it to a randomly chosen neighbor. For many network topologies, this strategy is a very efficient way to spread a rumor. With high probability the rumor is received by all vertices in time $\Theta(\log n)$, if the graph is a complete graph or a hypercube [5,6].

4 Amnesiac Flooding: Algorithm $\mathcal{A}_{\mathsf{AF}}$

The goal of amnesiac flooding is to distribute a message – initially stored at all nodes of a set S – to all nodes of the network. In the first round each node of S sends the message to all its neighbors. In each of the following rounds each node that receives at least one message forwards the message to all of its neighbors from which it did not receive the message in this round. Algorithm 1 shows a formal definition of algorithm $\mathcal{A}_{\mathsf{AF}}$. The code shows the handling of a single message m. If several messages are disseminated concurrently, each of them requires its own set M.

Algorithm 1: Algorithm $\mathcal{A}_{\mathsf{AF}}$ distributes a message m in the graph G

---

input : A graph $G = (V, E)$, a subset S of V, and a message m.

In round 1 each node $v \in S$ sends message m to each neighbor in G;
Each node v executes in every round $i > 1$

    $M := N(v)$;
    foreach receive(w, m) **do**
        $M := M \setminus \{w\}$;
    if $M \neq N(v)$ **then**
        forall $u \in M$ **do** send(u, m);

The flow of messages of algorithm $\mathcal{A}_{\mathsf{AF}}$ is illustrated in Fig. 1 (nodes in S are depicted in black). In the first example $\mathcal{A}_{\mathsf{AF}}$ terminates after three rounds and in the second case after five. The last shows an example with $|S| = 2$. In this case the algorithm also terminates after three rounds. These examples demonstrate that the termination time of $\mathcal{A}_{\mathsf{AF}}$ highly depends on S.

Definition 1. *For $S \subseteq V$ denote by $Flood_G(S)$ the number of rounds algorithm $\mathcal{A}_{\mathsf{AF}}$ requires to terminate when started by all nodes in S. For $1 \leq k \leq n$ define*

$$Flood_k(G) = \min\{Flood_G(S) \mid S \subseteq V \text{ with } |S| = k\}.$$

Clearly, $Flood_n(G) = 1$ for any G. If K_n is a complete graph with $n > 2$ then $Flood_i(K_n) = 2$ for $1 < i < n$ and $Flood_1(K_n) = 3$. For a cycle graph C_n we have $Flood_k(C_n) = \lceil n/k \rceil$ if $n \equiv 1(2)$ and otherwise $Flood_k(C_n) = \lceil n/(2k) \rceil$ if $k \leq n/2$, 1 if $k = n$, and 2 otherwise.

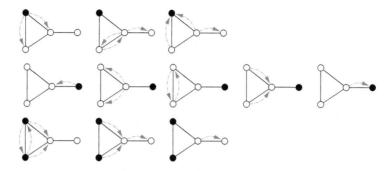

Fig. 1. Three executions (one per row) of algorithm $\mathcal{A}_{AF}$ for different choices of S.

5   The Main Results

Our main contribution is the auxiliary graph that nicely captures on an intuitive level, the operation of the flooding process. This bipartite graph leads to a simple proof that amnesiac flooding terminates when started with more than one initiator. The results of [7,8] are easily derived from this graph. Theorem 1 states that algorithm $\mathcal{A}_{AF}$ is correct. It also summarizes our main result.

Theorem 1. *Let $G = (V, E)$ be a connected graph. For every $S \subseteq V$ there is a bipartite graph $\mathcal{G}(S)$ with a node v^* such that $Flood_G(S) = Flood_{\mathcal{G}(S)}(v^*) - 1 \leq d(S, V) + 1 + Diam(G)$. Algorithm $\mathcal{A}_{AF}$ sends either $|E|$ or $2|E|$ messages.*

Whether $\mathcal{A}_{AF}$ sends $|E|$ or $2|E|$ messages depends on whether $G^*(S)$ is bipartite or not. This graph consists of G and an additional node v^* connected to all nodes of S. The bound $Flood_G(S) \leq d_G(S, V) + 1 + Diam(G)$ coincides with that of [8] for the case $|S| = 1$. To see that the bound is tight consider a graph G with a single cross edge (v, w) such that $d_G(v, S) = d_G(w, S) = Diam(G)$ (see Fig. 2). Apart from proving upper bounds for $Flood_G(S)$ using other graph parameters, we focus on lower bounds for $Flood_k(G)$. The auxiliary graph $\mathcal{G}(S)$ allows to derive upper and lower bounds for $Flood_k(G)$ with respect to $r_k(G)$ and $r_k^{ni}(G)$. Theorem 2 characterizes in addition configurations with short termination times. The stated bounds are tight as demonstrated by examples.

Theorem 2. *Let $G = (V, E)$ be a connected graph.*

1. *If $k > 1$ then $r_k(G) \leq Flood_k(G) \leq r_k^{ni}(G) + 1 \leq r_{\lfloor k/2 \rfloor}(G) + 1$.*
2. *$Flood_k(G) = 1$ iff $n = k$ or G is bipartite with $|V_1| = k$ or $|V_2| = k$.*
3. *$Flood_k(G) \leq 2$ if $k \geq 2n/3$ or $\delta(G) \geq 3$ and $k \geq n/2$.*
4. *$Flood_k(G) \leq 3$ if $k \geq n/2$.*

Amnesiac flooding takes considerably more time when the graph is non-bipartite. Theorem 3 characterizes non-bipartite graphs for which $\mathcal{A}_{AF}$ terminates after two rounds.

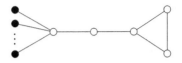

Fig. 2. A graph with $Flood_G(S) = d_G(S, V) + 1 + Diam(G)$ (nodes in S are black)

Theorem 3. *Let* $G = (V, E)$ *be a connected, non-bipartite graph. Then*

1. $Flood_k(G) \geq r_k(G) + 1$.
2. *If* $k > 1$ *then* $Flood_k(G) = 2$ *iff* $r_k^{ni}(G) = 1$.
3. $Flood_k(G) \geq Rad(G)/k + 1/2$ *and* $Flood_{k+1}(G) \leq Flood_k(G)$.

Somehow surprisingly, the termination time on bipartite graphs is at most two rounds more than the k-radius. For $k \leq n/2$ the difference is at most one round. This is an essential difference to the case $k = 1$ where termination time always coincides with the radius. The bounds are tight, see [11] for an example.

Theorem 4. *Let* $G = (V_1 \cup V_2, E)$ *be a connected, bipartite graph. If* $k \geq 1$ *then*

1. $Flood_k(G) = r_k(G)$ *iff* G *has a* k-center S *with either* $S \subseteq V_1$ *or* $S \subseteq V_2$.
2. *If* $k \leq \max(|V_1|, |V_2|)$ *then* $Flood_k(G) - r_k(G) \leq 1$.
3. $Flood_k(G) - r_k(G) \leq 2$.

6   The Case $|S| = 1$

We begin the introduction of the auxiliary graph for the case $|S| = 1$. With the help of a further graph extension technique we will in Sect. 7 reduce the case $|S| > 1$ to this case. Let $S = \{v_0\}$ with $v_0 \in V$. The way messages are forwarded by algorithm $\mathcal{A}_{\mathsf{AF}}$ implies that a message can arrive multiple times at a node. Clearly, the first time that a message arrives at a node is along the shortest path from v_0 to this node. The following lemma is easy to prove.

Lemma 1. *In round* $i > 0$ *of algorithm* $\mathcal{A}_{\mathsf{AF}}$ *each node* v *with* $d_G(v_0, v) = i - 1$ *sends a message to all neighbors* u *with* $d_G(v_0, u) = i$.

Edges that do not belong to a shortest path don't affect the flow of messages along shortest paths, but they can provoke additional messages. Such edges are cross edges with respect to a breadth-first-search starting in v_0. Since bipartite graphs have no cross edges Lemma 1 can be strengthened for bipartite graphs. The proof of the next lemma is by induction on i.

Lemma 2. *Let* G *be a bipartite graph and* v *a node with* $d_G(v_0, v) = i$. *In round* $i + 1$ *of algorithm* $\mathcal{A}_{\mathsf{AF}}$ *node* v *sends a message to all neighbors* u *with* $d_G(v_0, u) = i + 1$ *and to no other neighbor. In all other rounds* v *does not send a message.*

Corollary 1. *If* G *is bipartite then* $Flood_G(v_0) = \epsilon_G(v_0)$ *and* $Flood_1(G) = Rad(G)$.

To analyze the behavior of $\mathcal{A}_{\mathsf{AF}}$ for non-bipartite graphs we introduce the most important concept of this work, the auxiliary graph $\mathcal{G}(v_0)$.

6.1 The Auxiliary Graph $\mathcal{G}(v_0)$

For a given graph G and a starting node v_0 we define the auxiliary graph $\mathcal{G}(v_0)$. The executions of $\mathcal{A}_{\mathsf{AF}}$ on G and $\mathcal{G}(v_0)$ are tightly coupled. Since $\mathcal{G}(v_0)$ is bipartite we can apply Corollary 1 to compute $Flood_G(v_0)$.

Definition 2. *Denote by $\mathcal{F}(v_0)$ the subgraph of G with node set V and all edges of G that are not cross edges with respect to v_0.*

Obviously $\mathcal{F}(v_0)$ is always bipartite. Figure 3 demonstrates this definition.

Fig. 3. On the left the graph G with v_0 marked and $\mathcal{F}(v_o)$ on the right.

Definition 3. *Let $\mathcal{G}(v_0)$ be the graph consisting of two copies of $\mathcal{F}(v_0)$ with node sets V and V' and additionally for any cross edge (u, w) of G the edges (u, w') and (w, u').*

In the following we denote for every $v \in V$ the copy of v in V' by v'. $\mathcal{G}(v_0)$ consists of $2|V|$ nodes and $2|E|$ edges. Every additional edge connects a node from V with a node from V'. Figure 4 demonstrates this construction. For each $v \in V$ we have $deg_G(v) = deg_{\mathcal{G}(v_0)}(v) = deg_{\mathcal{G}(v_0)}(v')$. Also, $d_{\mathcal{G}(v_0)}(v_0, v) = d_{\mathcal{F}(v_0)}(v_0, v) = d_G(v_0, v)$ for $v \in V$.

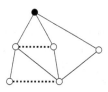 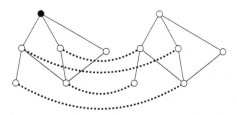

Fig. 4. The graph G (left) has two cross edges (dotted lines), $\mathcal{G}(v_0)$ is on the right.

Lemma 3. $\mathcal{G}(v_0)$ *is bipartite.*

Proof. $\mathcal{G}(v_0)$ consists of two copies of $\mathcal{F}(v_0)$, with node sets V and V'. $\mathcal{F}(v_0)$ is 2-colorable. The cross edges of G are modified so that one end is in V and the other in $V\prime$. We reverse the coloring of the nodes in $V\prime$. Since cross edges are at the same level in G, in $\mathcal{G}(v_0)$ they connect opposite colors. Thus, $\mathcal{G}(v_0)$ is 2-colorable and, hence, bipartite. □

Lemma 2 and 3 yield the following result that is frequently used in this work.

Lemma 4. *Let (u, w') be an edge of $\mathcal{G}(v_0)$ with $u \in V$ and $w' \in V'$. Node w' never sends in $\mathcal{G}(v_0)$ a message to u via edge (u, w') but u sends a message via this edge to w'.*

The last lemma has the following simple corollary.

Corollary 2. *A shortest path in $\mathcal{G}(v_0)$ from v_0 to a node $w' \in V'$ uses exactly one edge from V to V'.*

Fig. 5 depicts an execution of $\mathcal{A}_{\mathsf{AF}}$ on $\mathcal{G}(v_0)$ for the graph of Fig. 4. The next lemma shows the relationship between the execution of $\mathcal{A}_{\mathsf{AF}}$ on G and $\mathcal{G}(v_0)$.

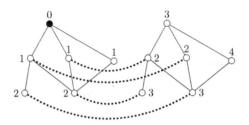

Fig. 5. The nodes' labels denote the round a message is received by the node in $\mathcal{G}(v_0)$.

Lemma 5. *Let $v, w \in V$. Node v receives a message from w in round i in G iff in round i node v receives a message from w in $\mathcal{G}(v_0)$, or v' receives a message from w or from w' in $\mathcal{G}(v_0)$.*

Proof. The proof is by induction on i. The Lemma is true for $i = 1$. Note that from the three conditions for $\mathcal{G}(v_0)$ only the first can occur in round 1. Let $i > 1$.

First suppose that w sends in G a message to v in round i. Then in G in round $i - 1$ node w received a message from a neighbor z with $z \neq v$, i.e., no message from v. By induction in round $i - 1$ in $\mathcal{G}(v_0)$ node v did not send a message neither to w nor to w' and v' did not send a message to w'. Also, in round $i - 1$ in $\mathcal{G}(v_0)$ node z did send a message to w or w' or z' did send a message to w'. Thus, in $\mathcal{G}(v)$ in round i either w sends a message to v or w' sends a message to v or v'.

Conversely suppose that one of the three events happens in $\mathcal{G}(v_0)$ in round i. First assume that in round i node v received a message from w in $\mathcal{G}(v_0)$. By Lemma 4 the message never left $\mathcal{F}(v_0)$, thus the message reached w via a shortest path of G. This yields that in G, node v also received in G message from w.

Next suppose v' receives a message from w in $\mathcal{G}(v_0)$ in round i. Then (v, w) is a cross edge of G. Thus, $d_{\mathcal{G}(v_0)}(v_0, w) = d_{\mathcal{G}(v_0)}(v_0, v) = i - 1$ and hence, $d_G(v_0, w) = d_G(v_0, v) = i - 1$. This implies that v and w do not send messages before round i in G and in round i they send messages to each other in G, i.e., v received in G message from w. Finally suppose v' receives a message from w' in $\mathcal{G}(v_0)$ in round i. By Lemma 2 $i = d_{\mathcal{G}(v_0)}(v_0, v')$ and $d_{\mathcal{G}(v_0)}(v_0, w') = i - 1$. Let P be a shortest path in $\mathcal{G}(v_0)$ from v_0 to w'. By Corollary 2 P uses a single cross edge (x, y'). Thus, x and y receive in G a message in round $d_G(v_0, x)$, but not from each other. Hence, in round $d_G(v_0, x) + 1$ both nodes x and y again receive a message. After another $d_G(y, w)$ rounds, w sends a message to v. Thus, in G node v receives in round $d_G(v_0, x) + 1 + d_G(y, v) = d_{\mathcal{G}(v_0)}(v_0, v') = i$ a message from w. □

The lemma proves that if no node in G receives a message in a specific round then no node in $\mathcal{G}(v_0)$ receives a message in this round and vice versa. This implies the following theorem.

Theorem 5. $Flood_G(v_0) = Flood_{\mathcal{G}(v_0)}(v_0)$ *for every* $v_0 \in V$.

If G is bipartite then $\mathcal{G}(v_0)$ is disconnected and the connected component of $\mathcal{G}(v_0)$ containing v_0 is $\mathcal{F}_{G(v_0)}$, i.e., $\epsilon_{\mathcal{G}(v_0)}(v_0) = \epsilon_{\mathcal{F}_{G(v_0)}}(v_0) = \epsilon_G(v_0)$ in this case. Lemma 3 and Theorem 5 together with Lemma 5 imply the following result.

Theorem 6. *Let* $G(V, E)$ *be a connected graph. Then* $Flood_G(v_0) = \epsilon_{\mathcal{G}(v_0)}(v_0)$. *Algorithm* $\mathcal{A}_{\mathsf{AF}}$ *sends* $|E|$ *messages if* G *is bipartite and* $2|E|$ *otherwise.*

In case G is non-bipartite for some edges messages are sent in both directions, while for other edges two messages are sent in one direction. With the introduced technique the proof of the main result of [8] becomes very simple.

Theorem 7. *(Theorem 10 and 12, [8]) Let* G *be a connected, non-bipartite graph and* $v_0 \in V$. *Then* $Rad(G) < Flood(v_0) \leq \epsilon_G(v_0) + Diam(G) + 1$. *Furthermore,* $Rad(G) < Flood_1(G) \leq Rad(G) + Diam(G) + 1$. $Rad(G) = Flood_1(G)$ *iff* G *is bipartite.*

Proof. Let $u \in V$. Then $d_{\mathcal{G}(v_0)}(v_0, u) \leq Diam(G)$. It suffices to give a bound for $d_{\mathcal{G}(v_0)}(v_0, u')$. Since G is non-bipartite there exist cross edges with respect to v_0. Among all cross edges of G choose (v, w) such that $\min\{d_G(u, v), d_G(u, w)\}$ is minimal. WLOG assume that $d_G(u, v) \leq d_G(u, w)$. Then the shortest path from v to u does not contain a cross edge (by choice of (v, w). Thus, the distance from v' to u' in $\mathcal{G}(v_0)$ is at most $Diam(G)$ and $d_{\mathcal{G}(v_0)}(v_0, u') \leq d_G(v_0, w) + 1 + Diam(G) \leq \epsilon_G(v_0) + Diam(G) + 1$. Hence, Theorem 6 implies the upper bound. Let v be a node with $dist_G(v_0, v) \geq Rad(G)$. Then $d_{\mathcal{G}(v_0)}(v_0, v') \geq Rad(G) + 1$. This yields the lower bound. Since this is true for all $v_0 \in V$ the second statement also holds. Now the last statement follows from Corollary 1. □

The above upper bound is tight as can be seen for $G = C_n$ with $n \equiv 1(2)$. In this case $Rad(C_n) = Diam(C_n) = (n-1)/2$ and $Flood_1(C_n) = n$. Figure 9 shows on the left a non-bipartite graph with $Rad(G) + 1 = Flood_1(G)$.

7   The Case $|S| > 1$

The case $|S| > 1$ requires a slightly different definition of the auxiliary graph $\mathcal{G}$. A virtual source v^* connected by edges to all source nodes in S is introduced. Call this graph $G^*(S)$. Note that even in case G is bipartite $G^*(S)$ is not necessarily bipartite. Figure 6 shows an example for $G^*(S)$. When v^* sends a message to all neighbors, then in the next round all nodes of S send a message to all their neighbors except v^*. Thus, the initial behavior of $\mathcal{A}_{\mathsf{AF}}$ is the same for G with a given set S and for $G^*(S)$ when started by node v^* only. Later the behavior may deviate because nodes of S may send a message to v^*. To eliminate this effect we change the definition of the graph $\mathcal{G}(S)$ as follows. The auxiliary graph $\mathcal{G}(S)$ is the graph $\mathcal{G}(v^*)$ constructed from $G^*(S)$ as in Sect. 6.1 with the only difference that the copy of v^* in the second copy of $\mathcal{F}(S)$ is removed. Figure 7 shows $\mathcal{G}(S)$ where graph G and set S are taken from Fig. 6. More formally.

Fig. 6. On the left a graph with $|S| = 3$; on the right the auxiliary graph $G^*(S)$.

Definition 4. *Let $S \subseteq V$. Denote by $\mathcal{F}_S(v^*)$ the subgraph of $G^*(S)$ with node set $V \cup \{v^*\}$ and all edges of $G^*(S)$ that are not cross edges with respect to v^*. Let $\mathcal{F}'_S(v^*)$ be a copy of $\mathcal{F}_S(v^*)$ without the node v^* and the incident edges. Denote by V' the node set of $\mathcal{F}'_S(v^*)$. Let $\mathcal{G}(S)$ the graph with node set $(V \cup \{v^*\}) \cup V'$ that consists of $\mathcal{F}_S(v^*)$ and $\mathcal{F}'_S(v^*)$ and additionally for any cross edge (u, w) of G the edges (u, w') and (w, u').*

7.1   Proof of Theorem 1 and Theorem 2

Proof. (Theorem 1) Clearly $\mathcal{G}(S)$ is bipartite. We prove by induction on i that the behavior of $\mathcal{A}_{\mathsf{AF}}$ in round i on graph $\mathcal{G}(S)$ when started by the node v^* is the same as that of $\mathcal{A}_{\mathsf{AF}}$ in round $i + 1$ on G when started by the nodes in S. The statement is true for $i = 1$. Let $i > 1$. Note that $Flood_G(S)$ is not in all cases equal to $Flood_{G^*(S)}(v^*) - 1$. In $G^*(S)$ a node in S may send in round $i > 1$ a message to v^* which will cause further messages between nodes in $G^*(S)$ which have no counterpart in G. This only happens if a message has passed a cross edge of $G^*(S)$; consider a graph with a single edge with both end nodes in S. In $\mathcal{G}(S)$ the situation is different. Messages sent via cross edges in G are in $\mathcal{G}(S)$ sent into $\mathcal{F}'_S(v^*)$ and by Lemma 4 they will never leave that component. Since $\mathcal{F}'_S(v^*)$ doesn't contain a copy of v^* the message flow will terminate as in G. Hence, we

Fig. 7. The graph $\mathcal{G}(S)$ for the graph $G^*(S)$ depicted in Fig. 6. Edges connecting $\mathcal{F}_S(v^*)$ and $\mathcal{F}'_S(v^*)$ are displayed as dotted lines.

can repeat the proof of Lemma 5 to show $Flood_G(S) = Flood_{\mathcal{G}(S)}(v^*) - 1$. Since $\mathcal{G}(S)$ is bipartite Corollary 1 implies $Flood_{\mathcal{G}(S)}(v^*) = \epsilon_{\mathcal{G}(S)}(v^*)$. The construction of $\mathcal{G}(S)$ implies $Flood_{\mathcal{G}(S)}(v^*) \leq 1 + d_G(S, V) + 1 + Diam(G)$. Hence, $Flood_G(S) \leq d_G(S, V) + 1 + Diam(G)$. The statement about the number of messages follows immediately from the structure of $\mathcal{G}(S)$: One message is sent over each edge of $\mathcal{F}_S(v^*)$ and $\mathcal{F}'_S(v^*)$ and two messages are sent via each cross edge of G. □

This bound is tight. Figure 8 shows a tree T with $r_4^{ni}(T) = 2$, the black nodes form a non-isolated 4-center of T of minimal radius. Also, $r_7^{ni}(T) = 2$.

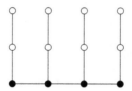

Fig. 8. A bipartite graph G with $Flood_7(G) - r_7(G) = 2$. Furthermore, $r_4(G) + 1 = Flood_4(G) = 2$, $Flood_7(G) = r_7^{ni}(G) + 1 = 3$, $Flood_8(G) = r_4(G) + 1 = 2$, and $Flood_8(G) = Rad(G) + 1 = 2$.

Lemma 6. *Let G be a connected graph and $k \geq n/2$. Then $r_k^{ni}(G) \leq 2$.*

Proof. The proof is by induction on m, the number of edges of G. If $m = n - 1$ then G is a tree and Lemma 20 of [11] yields the result. Let $m > n - 1$. Consider an edge e such that $G \setminus e$ is connected. By induction $r_k^{ni}(G \setminus e) \leq 2$. Since adding an edge does not increase the non-isolated k-radius, the proof is complete. □

Proof. (Theorem 2) (1) Obviously, $r_k(G) \leq Flood_k(G)$. Let S be a non-isolated k-center of G and $v \in V$. Then there exists $u \in S$ such that $d_G(u, v) \leq r_k^{ni}(G)$ and the path from u to v in $G^*(S)$ does not use a cross edge with respect to v^*. Since S contains no isolated node, after the first round each node of V' that is a copy of a node in S receives a message. Thus, there exists $w \in N(u) \cap S$. Hence, the path v^*, w, u' exists in $\mathcal{G}(S)$. Therefore, the distance from v^* to v' in $\mathcal{G}(S)$ is at most $2 + dist_G(u, v)$, i.e., $\epsilon_{\mathcal{G}(S)}(v^*) \leq 2 + r_k^{ni}(G)$. By Lemma 3 and Corollary 1 we have $Flood_{\mathcal{G}(S)}(v^*) \leq 2 + r_k^{ni}(G)$. Theorem 1 proves the first bound.

Let $S \subset V$ with $|S| = \lfloor k/2 \rfloor$ and $d_G(S, V) = r_{\lfloor k/2 \rfloor}(G)$. Obviously, there exists a subset S' of V such that $|\hat{S} \cup S'| = k$ and $G[\hat{S} \cup S']$ has no isolated node. Let $\hat{S} = S \cup S'$. Then, $r_k^{ni}(G) \leq dist(\hat{S}, V) \leq r_{\lfloor k/2 \rfloor}(G)$.

(2) Let $Flood_k(G) = 1$. Then each node $v \in V$ must have all its neighbors in S or none. Let S_1 be the set of nodes that have all their neighbors in S. Let $v \in V \setminus S_1$. Then $N(v) \cap S = \emptyset$. Hence, v does not receive a message in the first round. Since $Flood_k(G) = 1$ and G is connected, we have $v \in S$. Thus $V \setminus S_1 \subseteq S$.

Assume there exists $v \in S_1$ with $N(v) \subseteq S_1$. Then $v \in S$. This yields $N(N(v)) \subseteq S_1$ and consequently $V = S_1$ and thus $V = S$ since G is connected, i.e., $n = k$. Next assume $N(v) \nsubseteq S_1$ for all $v \in S_1$. Thus, for $v_1 \in S_1$ there exits a neighbor v_2 that is not in S_1, i.e., $N(v_2) \cap S = \emptyset$. Then $v_2 \in S$ because $N(v_1) \subseteq S$. If v_1 would be in S, then all neighbors of v_2 would be in S and thus, $v_2 \in S_1$. Thus, $v_1 \notin S$. Hence, $S_1 \cap S = \emptyset$. Therefore, S and S_1 are independent sets. Also $S_1 \cup S = V$. Thus, G is bipartite. Since the opposite direction is trivially true, the proof is complete.

(3) Let S be a minimal total dominating set of G. Then $G[S]$ has no isolated node and $d(S, V) = 1$. Hence, for $k \geq \gamma_t(G)$ we have $r_k^{ni}(G) = 1$. For $k > \gamma_t(G)$ we add $k - \gamma_t(G)$ nodes to S such that the induced subgraph of the resulting set T has no isolated nodes. Obviously, we still have $d(T, V) = 1$. Thus, $Flood_{\mathcal{G}(S)}(v^*) \leq 3$. Now, Theorem 1 yields $Flood_G(T) \leq 2$. There are several upper bounds known for $\gamma_t(G)$. Cockayne et al. proved that $\gamma_t(G) \leq 2n/3$ for a connected graph G with $n \geq 3$ [3]. Archdeacon et al. improved this bound to $n/2$ provided $\delta(G) \geq 3$ [1]. These results complete the proof.

(4) Lemma 6 and Theorem 2 (1) imply the bound.   □

The first bound of Theorem 2 (1) is tight. For C_n with $n \equiv 3(4)$ we have $(n-3)/4 + 1 = Flood_4(C_n) = r_4^{ni}(C_n) + 1$. On the other hand $r_3^{ni}(C_n) - Flood_3(C_n)$ and $Flood_3(C_n) - r_3(C_n)$ with $n \equiv 1(2)$ are unbounded for growing n. All bounds of Theorem 2 (1) are tight, see [11]. Note that $r_k(G) = 1$ for $k \geq n/2$ [9]. Hence, Theorem 2 (4) yields $Flood_k(G) - r_k(G) \leq 2$ if $k \geq n/2$.

The last result does not hold for bipartite graphs as a path P with 12 nodes demonstrates, $Flood_3(P) = 2$ and $r_3^{ni}(P) = 5$. Theorem 2.1 implies that $r_k(G) \in \{1, 2\}$ if G is bipartite and $Flood_k(G) = 2$. Thus, $r_k(G) = 1$ implies $Flood_k(G) \leq 2$. Bipartite graphs with $r_k(G) = 2$ can have $Flood_k(G) > 2$ as the example in Fig. 9 shows.

7.2   Proof of Theorem 3

If G is non-bipartite, then $G^*(S)$ is also non-bipartite. Then $Flood_k(G) \geq r_k(G) + 1$ by Theorem 1. Hence, Theorem 3 (1) holds. In this section we prove a lower bound for $Flood_k(G)$ that depends only on $Rad(G)$ and k.

Lemma 7 ([11]). $kr_k(T) \geq Rad(T) - k/2$ for $k > 0$ and any tree T.

Note that the bound of this lemma is tight. Consider a path P with $k(2c+1)$ nodes for $c > 0$. Then $r_k(P) = c$ and $Rad(P) = k(2c+1)/2$.

Lemma 8 ([11]). Let G be a connected graph. Then there exists a spanning tree T of G such that $r_k(G) = r_k(T)$ for all $k \geq 1$.

The graph shown in Fig. 8 demonstrates that $Flood_k(G)$ is not always decreasing for increasing k: $Flood_5(G) = 1, Flood_6(G) = 3, Flood_7(G) = Flood_8(G) = 2$. Next we show that for non-bipartite graphs these values monotonically decrease.

Lemma 9 ([11]). Let G be a connected non-bipartite graph, $\emptyset \neq S \subset V$, and $v \in V \setminus S$. Then $Flood_G(S \cup \{v\}) \leq Flood_G(S)$.

The reason that Lemma 9 does not hold for a bipartite graph G is that the graph $G^*(S)$ may be bipartite while $G^*(S \cup \{v\})$ is non-bipartite.

Proof. (Theorem 3) (2) If $r_k^{ni}(G) = 1$ then $Flood_k(G) \leq 2$ by Theorem 2 (1) and thus $Flood_k(G) = 2$ by the first part. Next suppose that $Flood_k(G) = 2$ and let S be a subset of V such that $Flood_G(S) = 2$. Assume that $G[S]$ contains an isolated node v. Since G is non-bipartite the shortest path in $\mathcal{G}(S)$ from v^* to v' has length at least 4. Then Theorem 1 implies that $Flood_k(G) \geq 3$. This contradicts the assumption that $Flood_k(G) = 2$. Therefore, $G[S]$ contains no isolated node and hence $r_k(G) = r_k^{ni}(G)$. Since $2 = Flood_k(G) \geq r_k(G) + 1$ we have $r_k^{ni}(G) = 1$.

(3) By Lemma 8 there exists a spanning tree T of G such that $r_k(G) = r_k(T)$. Note that $r_k(G) + 1 \leq Flood_k(G)$. By Lemma 7 $kr_k(T) \geq Rad(T) - k/2$. Hence $kFlood_k(G) \geq kr_k(G) + k = kr_k(T) + k \geq Rad(T) + k/2$ since $Rad(T) \geq Rad(G)$.

Let $S \subset V$ with $|S| = k$ such that $Flood(S) = Flood_k(G)$. Let $v \in V \setminus S$. Then Lemma 9 yields $Flood_{k+1}(G) \leq Flood(S \cup \{v\}) \leq Flood(S) = Flood_k(G)$. □

Theorem 3 (2) does not hold for bipartite graphs as a path P with 12 nodes demonstrates, $Flood_3(P) = 2$ and $r_3^{ni}(P) = 5$. Theorem 2 (1) implies that $r_k(G) \in \{1, 2\}$ if G is bipartite and $Flood_k(G) = 2$. Thus, $r_k(G) = 1$ implies $Flood_k(G) \leq 2$. Bipartite graphs with $r_k(G) = 2$ can have $Flood_k(G) > 2$, see [11] for an example.

7.3   Proof of Theorem 4

For $k = 1$ we have $Flood_1(G) = r_1(G)$ provided G is bipartite and vice versa (Theorem 7, Theorem 11 [8]). For $k > 1$ we have a slightly different situation.

Proof. (Theorem 4) (1) If G has a k-center S contained in V_1 or V_2 then the graph $G^*(S)$ has no cross edge with respect to v^* (nodes with the same distance to v^* are either in V_1 or V_2). Thus, Theorem 1 implies $Flood_k(G) = r_k(G)$.

Next assume that $Flood_k(G) = r_k(G)$. Let $S \subset V$ with $|S| = k$ and $Flood(S) = Flood_k(G)$. Then $r_k(G) \leq d_G(S, V) \leq Flood(S) = r_k(G)$, i.e., $d_G(S, V) = r_k(G)$. Since $Flood_k(G) = r_k(G)$, $G^*(S)$ does not contain a cross edge with respect to v^*. Let $S_i = S \cap V_i$. Denote by V^i the set of nodes that receive a message when $\mathcal{A}_{\mathsf{AF}}$ is executed for set S_i (including S_i). Since there are no cross edges, there exists no edge connecting a node from V^1 with a node from V^2. Since G is connected, either $S_1 = \emptyset$ or $S_2 = \emptyset$. This implies the result.

(2) Let $S \subseteq V = V_1 \cup V_2, E$ with $|S| = k$ such that $d_G(S, V) = r_k(G)$. If $S \subseteq V_1$ or $S \subseteq V_2$ then the result follows from the first part. WLOG assume that $k \leq |V_2|$. Let $S_1 = S \cap V_1$. There exists $T \subseteq V_2$ with $|T| \leq |S_1|$ such that $S_1 \subseteq N(T) \subseteq V_1$. Then $d_G(T \cup (S \cap V_2), V) \leq r_k(G) + 1$. Let $T_r \subseteq V_2$ such if $S_n = T_r \cup T \cup (S \cap V_2)$ then $|S_n| = k$. Clearly, $d_G(S_n, V) \leq r_k(G) + 1$. Obviously, $G^*(S_n)$ does not contain a cross edge, since the graph $G^*(S_n)$ is bipartite. Hence, $Flood_k(G) - r_k(G) \leq 1$ by Theorem 1 and Corollary 1.

(3) If $k \geq n/2$ then $r_k(G) = 1$. Thus, $Flood_k(G) - r_k(G) \leq 2$ by Theorem 2 (4). The case $k < n/2$ is implied by (2).   □

Figure 9 shows on the right a bipartite graph G with $r_2(G) = 2$ and $Flood_2(G) = 3$. Thus, the bound of Theorem 4 (2) is tight. Figure 8 demonstrates that the bound of Theorem 4 (3) is tight.

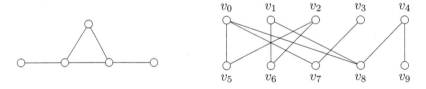

Fig. 9. Left: Non-bipartite graph with $Rad(G) = 2$ and $Flood_1(G) = 3$. Right: Bipartite graph with $r_2(G) = 2$ and $Flood_2(G) = 3$; $d(\{v_0, v_8\}, V) = 2$, $Flood(\{v_0, v_1\}) = 3$.

8   Conclusion and Future Work

In this paper we analyzed amnesiac flooding for a set S of k initiators. The main technical result is the construction of a bipartite graph $\mathcal{G}(S)$ such that the executions of amnesiac flooding on G and $\mathcal{G}(S)$ are equivalent. This allowed us to prove upper and lower bounds for the round complexity of amnesiac flooding.

There are several open problems related to amnesiac flooding. Firstly, we suspect that the first bound stated in Theorem 3 (3) is not tight. Instead we have the following conjecture: If G is connected, non-bipartite then $kFlood_k(G) \geq Rad(G) + k - 1$. If $Flood_k(G) \geq r_k(G) + 2$ then the proof of Theorem 3 (3) can be used to prove this conjecture. Thus, in proving the conjecture one can assume $Flood_k(G) = r_k(G) + 1$. This new bound would be tight, see [11] for an example. Secondly, by Theorem 4 (3) $Flood_k(G)$ assumes one of three values in case G is bipartite. Is it possible to infer from structural parameters of G the value of $Flood_k(G)$?

Denote by $d_r(v, w)$ the number of the round in which node w receives the last message when amnesiac flooding is started in node v. It is straightforward to prove that for non-bipartite graphs this does not define a metric but a meta-metric in the sense of [13]. Hence it it can be used to quantify the importance of a node in a given network, i.e., it defines a centrality index [14]. There are many centrality indices proposed in the literature (degree, closeness, between-ness, eigenvector centrality etc.). The question is whether it coincides with any of the known centrality indices.

Algorithm $\mathcal{A}_{\mathsf{AF}}$ cannot be executed in an asynchronous system. Hussak et al. showed that a simple adaptation of amnesiac flooding to asynchronous systems does not terminate [8]. An interessting question is, whether there exists a stateless asynchronous information dissemination algorithm.

References

1. Archdeacon, D., et al.: Some remarks on domination. J. Graph Theor. **46**(3), 207–210 (2004)
2. Awerbuch, B., Khandekar, R.: Stateless distributed gradient descent for positive linear programs. In: Proceedings 40th Symposium on Theory of Computing, pp. 691–700. ACM (2008)
3. Cockayne, E.J., Dawes, R.M., Hedetniemi, S.T.: Total domination in graphs. Networks **10**(3), 211–219 (1980)
4. Dolev, S., Kahil, R.M., Yagel, R.: Stateless stabilization bootstrap (Extended Abstract). In: Felber, P., Garg, V. (eds.) SSS 2014. LNCS, vol. 8756, pp. 180–194. Springer, Cham (2014). https://doi.org/10.1007/978-3-319-11764-5_13
5. Feige, U., Peleg, D., Raghavan, P., Upfal, E.: Randomized broadcast in networks. In: Asano, T., Ibaraki, T., Imai, H., Nishizeki, T. (eds.) SIGAL 1990. LNCS, vol. 450, pp. 128–137. Springer, Heidelberg (1990). https://doi.org/10.1007/3-540-52921-7_62
6. Frieze, A.M., Grimmett, G.R.: The shortest-path problem for graphs with random arc-lengths. Discrete Appl. Math. **10**(1), 57–77 (1985)
7. Hussak, W., Trehan, A.: Brief announcement: on termination of a flooding process. In: Proceedings ACM Symposium on Principles of Distributed Computing, pp. 153–155 (2019)
8. Hussak, W., Trehan, A.: On the Termination of Flooding. In: Paul, C., Bläser, M. (eds.) 37th Symposium on Theoretical Aspects of Computer Science (STACS), LIPIcs, vol. 154, pp. 17:1–17:13 (2020)
9. Meir, A., Moon, J.W.: Relations between packing and covering numbers of a tree. Pacific J. Math. **61**(1), 225–233 (1975)
10. Peleg, D.: Distributed Computing: A Locality-Sensitive Approach. SIAM Society for Industrial and Applied Mathematics, Philadelphia (2000)
11. Turau, V.: Analysis of Amnesiac Flooding. CoRR abs/2002.10752 (2020). https://arxiv.org/abs/2002.10752
12. Turau, V.: Stateless information dissemination algorithms. In: Richa, A.W., Scheideler, C. (eds.) SIROCCO 2020. LNCS, vol. 12156, pp. 183–199. Springer, Cham (2020). https://doi.org/10.1007/978-3-030-54921-3_11
13. Väisälä, J.: Gromov hyperbolic spaces. Expositiones Mathematicae **23**(3), 187–231 (2005)
14. Zweig, K.A.: Network Analysis Literacy. LNSN. Springer, Vienna (2016). https://doi.org/10.1007/978-3-7091-0741-6

Asymptotic Approximation by Regular Languages

Ryoma Sin'ya[✉]

Akita University, Akita, Japan
ryoma@math.akita-u.ac.jp

Abstract. This paper investigates a new property of formal languages called REG-measurability where REG is the class of regular languages. Intuitively, a language L is REG-measurable if there exists an infinite sequence of regular languages that "converges" to L. A language without REG-measurability has a complex shape in some sense so that it can not be (asymptotically) approximated by regular languages. We show that several context-free languages are REG-measurable (including languages with transcendental generating function and transcendental density, in particular), while a certain simple deterministic context-free language and the set of primitive words are REG-immeasurable in a strong sense.

1 Introduction

Approximating a complex object by more simple objects is a major concept in both computer science and mathematics. In the theory of formal languages, various types of approximations have been investigated (*e.g.*, [5,7,8,10,15,16]). For example, Kappes and Kintala [15] introduced *convergent-reliability* and *slender-reliability* which measure how a given deterministic automaton $\mathcal{A}$ nicely approximates a given language L over an alphabet A. Formally $\mathcal{A}$ is said to accept L convergent-reliability if the ratio $\#\left((L(\mathcal{A})\triangle L)\cap A^n\right)/\#\left(A^n\right)$ of the number of *incorrectly* accepted/rejected words of length n tends to 0 if n tends to infinity, and is said to accept L slender-reliability if the number of incorrectly accepted/rejected words of length n is always bounded above by some constant c: *i.e.*, $\#\left((L(\mathcal{A})\triangle L)\cap A^n\right) \leq c$ for any n. Here $L(\mathcal{A})$ denotes the language accepted by $\mathcal{A}$, $\#\left(S\right)$ denotes the cardinality of the set S, $\overline{L}$ denotes the complement of L and $\triangle$ denotes the symmetric difference. A slightly modified version of approximation is *bounded-ϵ-approximation* which was introduced by Eisman and Ravikumar. They say that two languages L_1 and L_2 provide a bounded-ϵ-approximation of language L if $L_1 \subseteq L \subseteq L_2$ holds and the ratio of their length-n difference satisfies $\#\left((L_2 \setminus L_1)\cap A^n\right)/\#\left(A^n\right) \leq \epsilon$ for every sufficiently large $n \in \mathbb{N}$. Perhaps surprisingly, they showed that no pair of regular languages can provide a bounded-ϵ-approximation of the language $\{w \in \{a,b\}^* \mid w \text{ has more } a\text{'s than } b\text{'s}\}$ for any $0 \leq \epsilon < 1$ [10]. This result

---

The author is also with RIKEN AIP.

T. Bureš et al. (Eds.): SOFSEM 2021, LNCS 12607, pp. 74–88, 2021.
https://doi.org/10.1007/978-3-030-67731-2_6

is a very strong *in*approximable (by regular languages) example of certain non-regular languages. Also, there is a different framework of approximation so-called *minimal-cover* [5,8], and a notion represents some *in*approximability by regular languages so-called REG-*immunity* [12].

A model of approximation introduced in this paper is rather close to the work of Eisman and Ravikumar [10]. Instead of approximating by a *single* regular language, we consider an approximation of some non-regular language L by an *infinite sequence* of regular languages that "converges" to L. Intuitively, we say that L is REG-*measurable* if there exists an infinite sequence of pairs of regular languages $(K_n, M_n)_{n \in \mathbb{N}}$ such that $K_n \subseteq L \subseteq M_n$ holds for all n and the "size" of the difference $M_n \setminus K_n$ tends to 0 if n tends to infinity. The formal definition of "size" is formally described in the next section: we use a notion called *density* *(of languages)* for measuring the "size" of a language.

Although we used the term "approximation" in the title and there are various research on this topic in formal language theory, our work is strongly influenced by the work of Buck [4] which investigates, as the title said, *the measure theoretic approach to density*. In [4] the concept of *measure density* μ of subsets of natural numbers $\mathbb{N}$ was introduced. Roughly speaking, Buck considered an arithmetic progression $X = \{cn + d \mid n \in \mathbb{N}\}$ (where $c, d \in \mathbb{N}$, c can be zero) as a "basic set" whose *natural density* as $\delta(X) = 1/c$ if $c \neq 0$ and $\delta(X) = 0$ otherwise, then defined the *outer measure density* $\mu^*(S)$ of any subset $S \subseteq \mathbb{N}$ as

$$\mu^*(S) = \inf\Big\{\sum_i \delta(X_i) \mid S \subseteq X \text{ and } X \text{ is a finite union of}$$

$$\text{disjoint arithmetic progressions } X_1, \ldots, X_k\Big\}.$$

Then the *measure density* $\mu(S) = \mu^*(S)$ was introduced for the sets satisfying the condition (1) $\mu^*(S) + \mu^*(\overline{S}) = 1$ where $\overline{S} = \mathbb{N} \setminus S$. Technically speaking, the class $\mathcal{D}_\mu$ of all subsets of natural numbers satisfying Condition (1) is the *Carathéodory extension* of the class

$$\mathcal{D}_0 \overset{\text{def}}{=} \{X \subseteq \mathbb{N} \mid X \text{ is a finite union of arithmetic progressions}\},$$

see Section 2 of [4] for more details. Notice that here we regard a singleton $\{d\}$ as an arithmetic progression (the case $c = 0$ for $\{cn + d \mid n \in \mathbb{N}\}$), any finite set belongs to $\mathcal{D}_0$. Buck investigated several properties of μ and $\mathcal{D}_\mu$, and showed that $\mathcal{D}_\mu$ *properly* contains $\mathcal{D}_0$.

In the setting of formal languages, it is very natural to consider the class REG of regular languages as "basic sets" since it has various types of representation, good closure properties and rich decidable properties. Moreover, if we consider regular languages REG_A over a unary alphabet $A = \{a\}$, then REG_A is isomorphic to the class $\mathcal{D}_0$; it is well known that the Parikh image $\{|w| \mid w \in L\} \subseteq \mathbb{N}$ (where $|w|$ denotes the length of w) of every regular language L in REG_A is semilinear and hence it is just a finite union of arithmetic progressions. From this observation, investigating the densities of regular languages and its measure densities (*i.e.*, REG-measurability) for non-regular languages can be naturally considered as an adaptation of Buck's study [4] for formal language theory.

Our Contribution

In this paper we investigate REG-measurability ($\simeq$ asymptotic approximability by regular languages) of non-regular, mainly context-free languages. The main results consist of three kinds. We show that: (1) several context-free languages (including languages with *transcendental generating function* and *transcendental density*) are REG-measurable [Theorem 7–12]. (2) there are "very large/very small" (deterministic) context-free languages that are REG-immeasurable in a strong sense [Theorem 14]. (3) the set of *primitive words* is "very large" and REG-immeasurable in a strong sense [Theorem 15–16]. Open problems and some possibility of an application of the notion of measurability to classifying formal languages will be stated in Sect. 6.

Due to the space limitation, we omit some parts of proofs in Sect. 4 and 5. For detailed proofs we refer the reader to the full version [21] of this paper. We assume that the reader has a basic knowledge of formal language theory.

2   Densities of Formal Languages

For a set S, we write $\#(S)$ for the cardinality of S. The set of natural numbers including 0 is denoted by $\mathbb{N}$. For an alphabet A, we denote the set of all words (resp. all non-empty words) over A by A^* (resp. A^+). We write ε for the empty word and write A^n (resp. $A^{<n}$) for the set of all words of length n (resp. less than n). For a language L, we write $\mathtt{Alph}(L)$ for the set of all letters appeared in L. For word $w \in A^*$ and a letter $a \in A$, $|w|_a$ denotes the number of occurrences of a in w. A word v is said to be a *factor* of a word w if $w = xvy$ for some $x, y \in A^*$, further said to be a *prefix* of w if $x = \varepsilon$. For a language $L \subseteq A^*$, we denote by $\overline{L} = A^* \setminus L$ the complement of L.

A *language class* $\mathcal{C}$ is a family of languages $\{\mathcal{C}_A\}_{A:\text{ finite alphabet}}$ where $\mathcal{C}_A \subseteq 2^{A^*}$ for each A and $\mathcal{C}_A \subseteq \mathcal{C}_B$ for each $A \subseteq B$. We simply write $L \in \mathcal{C}$ if $L \in \mathcal{C}_A$ for some alphabet A. We denote by $\mathrm{REG}, \mathrm{DetCFL}, \mathrm{UnCFL}$ and CFL the class of regular languages, deterministic context-free languages, unambiguous context-free languages and context-free languages, respectively. A language L is said to be $\mathcal{C}$-*immune* if L is infinite and no infinite subset of L belongs to $\mathcal{C}$.

Definition 1. Let $L \subseteq A^*$ be a language. The *natural density* $\delta_A(L)$ of L is defined as

$$\delta_A(L) \overset{\text{def}}{=} \lim_{n \to \infty} \frac{\#(L \cap A^n)}{\#(A^n)}$$

if the limit exists, otherwise we write $\delta_A(L) = \bot$ and say that L does not have a natural density. The *density* $\delta_A^*(L)$ of L is defined as

$$\delta_A^*(L) \overset{\text{def}}{=} \lim_{n \to \infty} \frac{1}{n} \sum_{k=0}^{n-1} \frac{\#(L \cap A^k)}{\#(A^k)}$$

if its exists, otherwise we write $\delta_A^*(L) = \bot$ and say that L does not have a density. A language $L \subseteq A^*$ is called *null* if $\delta_A^*(L) = 0$, and conversely L is called *co-null* if $\delta_A^*(L) = 1$.

Notice that if L has a natural density (*i.e.*, $\delta_A(L) \neq \bot$), then it also has a density and $\delta_A^*(L) = \delta_A(L)$ holds. But the converse is not true in general, *e.g.*, the case $L = (AA)^*$ (see Example 1 below). The following observation is basic.

Claim. Let $K, L \subseteq A^*$ with $\delta_A^*(K) = \alpha, \delta_A^*(L) = \beta$. Then we have: (1) $\alpha \leq \beta$ if $K \subseteq L$. (2) $\delta_A^*(L \setminus K) = \beta - \alpha$ if $K \subseteq L$. (3) $\delta_A^*(\overline{K}) = 1 - \alpha$. (4) $\delta_A^*(K \cup L) \leq \alpha + \beta$ if $\delta_A^*(K \cup L) \neq \bot$. (5) $\delta_A^*(K \cup L) = \alpha + \beta$ if $K \cap L = \emptyset$.

For more properties of δ_A^*, see Chapter 13 of [3].

Example 1. Here we enumerate a few examples of densities of languages.

- For the set $\{a\}A^*$ of all words starting with $a \in A$, we have $\#(\{a\}A^* \cap A^n) / \#(A^n) = \#(aA^{n-1}) / \#(A^n) = 1/\#(A)$. Hence $\delta_A(\{a\}A^*) = 1/\#(A)$.
- The set $(AA)^*$ of all words of even length does not have a natural density, but it have a density $\delta_A^*((AA)^*) = 1/2$.
- The semi-Dyck language

$$\mathsf{D} \stackrel{\mathrm{def}}{=} \{w \in \{a, b\}^* \mid |w|_a = |w|_b \text{ and } |u|_a \geq |u|_b \text{ for every prefix } u \text{ of } w\}$$

is non-regular but context-free. It is well known that the number of words in D of length $2n$ is equal to the n-th Catalan number whose asymptotic approximation is $\Theta(4^n / n^{3/2})$. Thus we have $\delta_A(\mathsf{D}) = 0$, *i.e.*, D is null.

Example 1 shows us that, for some regular language L, its natural density is either zero or one, for some, like $L = \{a\}A^*$ (for $\#(A) \geq 2$), $\delta_A(L)$ could be a real number strictly between zero and one, and for some, like $L = (AA)^*$, a natural density may not even exist. However, the following theorem tells us that all regular languages *do* have densities.

Theorem 1 (*cf.* **Theorem III.6.1 of** [20]). *Let* $L \subseteq A^*$ *be a regular language. Then there is a positive integer* c *such that for all natural numbers* $d < c$, *the limit* $\lim_{n \to \infty} \#(L \cap A^{cn+d}) / \#(A^{cn+d})$ *exists and it is always rational, i.e., the sequence* $(\#(L \cap A^n) / \#(A^n))_{n \in \mathbb{N}}$ *has only finitely many accumulation points and these are rational and periodic.*

Corollary 1. *Every regular language has a density and it is rational.*

Corollary 2. *For any regular language* $L \subseteq A^*$, $\delta_A(L) = 0$ *if and only if* $\delta_A^*(L) = 0$.

Furthermore, for *unambiguous* context-free languages, the following holds.

Theorem 2 (**Berstel** [2]). *For any unambiguous context-free language* L *over* A, *its density* $\delta_A^*(L)$, *if it exists (i.e.,* $\delta_A^*(L) \neq \bot$), *is always algebraic.*

In the next section we will introduce a language with a transcendental density, which should be inherently ambiguous due to Theorem 2.

We conclude the section by introducing the notion called *dense*: a property about some topological "largeness" of a language (*cf.* Chapter 2.5 of [3]).

Definition 2. A language $L \subseteq A^*$ is said to be *dense* if the set of all factors of L is equal to A^*. We say that a word $w \in A^*$ is a *forbidden word* (resp. *forbidden prefix*) of L if $L \cap A^* w A^* = \emptyset$ (resp. $L \cap w A^* = \emptyset$).

Observe that $L \subseteq A^*$ is dense if and only if no word is a forbidden word of L. The next theorem ties two different notions of "largeness" of languages in the regular case.

Theorem 3 (S. [22]). *A regular language is non-null if and only if it is dense.*

The "only if"-part of Theorem 3 is nothing but the well-known so-called *infinite monkey theorem* (which states that L is not dense implies L is null), and this part is true for any (non-regular) languages. But we stress that "if"-part is *not true* beyond regular languages; for example the semi-Dyck language D is null *but dense* (which will be described in Proposition 1). We denote by REG$^+$ the family of non-null regular languages, which is equivalent to the family of regular languages with positive densities thanks to Corollary 1.

3   Approximability and Measurability

Although we will mainly consider REG-measurability of non-regular languages in this paper, here we define two notions approximability and measurability in general setting, with few concrete examples.

Definition 3. Let $\mathcal{C}, \mathcal{D}$ be classes of languages. A language L is said to be $(\mathcal{C}, \epsilon)$-*lower-approximable* if there exists $K \in \mathcal{C}$ such that $K \subseteq L$ and $\delta^*_{\mathrm{Alph}(L)}(L \setminus K) \leq \epsilon$. A language L is said to be $(\mathcal{C}, \epsilon)$-*upper-approximable* if there exists $M \in \mathcal{C}$ such that $L \subseteq M$ and $\delta^*_{\mathrm{Alph}(M)}(M \setminus L) \leq \epsilon$. A language L is said to be $\mathcal{C}$-*approximable* if L is both $(\mathcal{C}, 0)$-lower and $(\mathcal{C}, 0)$-upper-approximable. $\mathcal{D}$ is said to be $\mathcal{C}$-approximable if every language in $\mathcal{D}$ is $\mathcal{C}$-approximable.

The following proposition gives a simple REG-inaproximable example.

Proposition 1. *The semi-Dyck language D is REG-inapproximable.*

Proof. We already mentioned that D is null in Example 1, and thus D is (REG, 0)-lower-approx by $\emptyset \subseteq$ D. One can easily observe that D has no forbidden word: since for any $w \in A^*$ there exists a pair of natural numbers $(n, m) \in \mathbb{N}^2$ such that $a^n w b^m \in$ D. Hence if a regular language L satisfies D $\subseteq L$, L has no forbidden word, too, and thus L is non-null by Theorem 3. Thus by Claim 2, $\delta^*_A(L \setminus D) = \delta^*_A(L) - \delta^*_A(D) = \delta^*_A(L) > 0$, which means that D can not be (REG, 0)-upper-approximable. $\qquad\square$

The proof of Proposition 1 only depends on the non-existence of forbidden words, hence we can apply the same proof to the next theorem.

Theorem 4. *Any null language having no forbidden word is (REG, 0)-upper-inapproximable.*

Because D is deterministic context-free, in our term we have:

Corollary 3. DetCFL *is REG-inapproximable.*

Furthermore, by the combination of Theorem 2 and the next theorem, we will know that there exists a context-free language which can not be approximated by any unambiguous context-free language.

Theorem 5 (Kemp [17]). *Let $A = \{a, b, c\}$. Define*

$$S_1 \overset{\text{def}}{=} \{a\}\{b^i a^i \mid i \geq 1\}^* \qquad S_2 \overset{\text{def}}{=} \{a^i b^{2i} \mid i \geq 1\}^*\{a\}^+,$$

and

$$L_1 \overset{\text{def}}{=} S_1\{c\}A^* \qquad L_2 \overset{\text{def}}{=} S_2\{c\}A^*.$$

Then $K \overset{\text{def}}{=} L_1 \cup L_2$ is a context-free language with a transcendental natural density $\delta_A(K)$.

Corollary 4. CFL *is* UnCFL-*inapproximable.*

We then introduce the notion of C-measurability which is a formal language theoretic analogue of Buck's measure density [4].

Definition 4. Let C, D be classes of languages. For a language L, we define its C-*lower-density* as

$$\underline{\mu}_C(L) \overset{\text{def}}{=} \sup\{\delta_A^*(K) \mid A = \mathtt{Alph}(L), K \subseteq L, K \in C_A, \delta_A^*(K) \neq \perp\}$$

and its C-*upper-density* as

$$\overline{\mu}_C(L) \overset{\text{def}}{=} \inf\{\delta_A^*(K) \mid A = \mathtt{Alph}(L), L \subseteq K, K \in C_A, \delta_A^*(K) \neq \perp\}.$$

A language L is said to be C-*measurable* if $\overline{\mu}_C(L) = \underline{\mu}_C(L)$ holds, and we simply write $\overline{\mu}_C(L)$ as $\mu_C(L)$. D is said to be C-measurable if every language in D is C-measurable.

Definition 5. We call $\overline{\mu}_C(L) - \underline{\mu}_C(L)$ the C-*gap* of a language L. We say that a language L *has full C-gap* if its C-gap equals to 1, i.e., $\overline{\mu}_C(L) - \underline{\mu}_C(L) = 1$.

In the next section, we describe several examples of both REG-measurable and REG-immeasurable languages. The REG-gap could be a good measure how much a given language has a complex shape from the viewpoint of regular languages.

The following lemmata are basic.

Lemma 1. *Let K, L be two languages.*

1. $\overline{\mu}_C(K) \leq \overline{\mu}_C(L)$ *if $K \subseteq L$.*
2. $\overline{\mu}_C(K \cup L) \leq \overline{\mu}_C(K) + \overline{\mu}_C(L)$ *if C is closed under union.*
3. $\overline{\mu}_C(K) = \delta_A^*(K)$ *if $K \in C$ and $\delta_A^*(K) \neq \perp$.*

Lemma 2. *Let C be a language class such that C is closed under complement and every language in C has a density. A language $L \subseteq A^*$ is C-measurable if and only if*

$$\overline{\mu}_C(L) + \overline{\mu}_C(\overline{L}) = 1. \tag{1}$$

Proof. Let L be a language and $A = \text{Alph}(L)$. By definition, L satisfies Condition (1) if and only if

$$\inf\{\delta_A^*(K) \mid L \subseteq K, K \in C\} = 1 - \inf\{\delta_A^*(K) \mid \overline{L} \subseteq K, K \in C\} \tag{2}$$

holds. On the other hand, L is measurable if and only if

$$\inf\{\delta_A^*(K) \mid L \subseteq K, K \in C\} = \sup\{\delta_A^*(K) \mid K \subseteq L, K \in C\}. \tag{3}$$

For any language $K \in C_A$ such that $K \subseteq L$ and $\delta_A^*(K) \neq \perp$, its complement $\overline{K}$ satisfies $\overline{L} \subseteq \overline{K}$ and $\delta_A^*(\overline{K}) = 1 - \delta_A^*(K)$. This means that if C_A is closed under complement then $\sup\{\delta_A^*(K) \mid K \subseteq L, K \in C_A\} = 1 - \inf\{\delta_A^*(K) \mid \overline{L} \subseteq K, K \in C_A\}$, holds, which immediately implies the equivalence of Condition (2) and Condition (3). $\square$

4   REG-Measurability on Context-Free Languages

In this section we examine REG-measurability of several types of context-free languages. The first type of languages (Sect. 4.1) is null context-free languages. Although some null language can have a full REG-gap as stated in the next theorem, we will show that typical null context-free languages are REG-measurable.

Theorem 6. *There is a recursive language L which is null but $\overline{\mu}_{\text{REG}}(L) = 1$.*

Proof. Let A be an alphabet with $\#(A) \geq 2$ and let $(\mathcal{A}_i)_{i \in \mathbb{N}}$ be an enumeration of automata over A such that $\text{REG}_A = \{L(\mathcal{A}_i) \mid i \in \mathbb{N}\}$; we can take such enumeration by enumerating some binary representation of automata via shortlex order $<_{\text{lex}}$. We will construct a null language L such that $\overline{\mu}_{\text{REG}}(L) = 1$, in particular, L is not a subset of every regular co-infinite language.

Consider the following program P which takes an input word w:

Step 1 set $i = 0$ and $\ell = 0$.
Step 2 check $L(\mathcal{A}_i)$ is co-infinite (*i.e.*, the complement $\overline{L(\mathcal{A}_i)}$ is infinite) or not.
Step 3 if $L(\mathcal{A}_i)$ is co-finite, then set $i = i + 1$ and go back to Step 2.
Step 4 otherwise, pick u such that u is the smallest (with respect to $<_{\text{lex}}$) word satisfying $|u| > \ell$ and $u \notin L(\mathcal{A}_i)$ (such u surely exists since $L(\mathcal{A}_i)$ is co-infinite).
Step 5 if $w = u$ then P accepts w and halts.
Step 6 if $w <_{\text{lex}} u$ then P rejects w and halts.
Step 7 if $u <_{\text{lex}} w$ then set $\ell = |u|$, $i = i + 1$ and go back to Step 2.

One can easily observe that all Steps are effective and P ultimately halts for any input word w because the length of the word u in Step 4 is strictly increasing until $u = w$ or $w <_{\text{lex}} u$. Thus the language $L \overset{\text{def}}{=} \{w \in A^* \mid P \text{ accepts } w\}$ is recursive. Moreover, L satisfies the following properties: (1) $L \nsubseteq R$ for any regular co-infinite language because by Step (4–5) P accepts some word $w \notin R$, and (2) $\delta_A(L) = 0$; by Step (5–6) and the length of u is strictly increasing, P rejects every word in A^n except for one single word u, for each n. Clearly, (2) implies $\delta_A(L) = 0$, and (1) implies $\overline{\mu}_{\text{REG}}(L) = 1$ since every language R with $\delta_A^*(R) < 1$ is co-infinite.

The second type of languages (Sect. 4.2) is inherently ambiguous languages and the third type of languages (Sect. 4.3) includes Kemp's language K whose density is transcendental. The last type of languages (Sect. 4.4) is languages with full REG-gap, *i.e.*, strongly REG-immeasurable languages.

4.1 Null Context-Free Languages

First we consider the following language with constraints on the number of occurrences of letters, which is a very typical example of a non-regular but context-free language.

Definition 6. For an alphabet A and letters $a, b \in A$ such that $a \neq b$, we define

$$L_A(a, b) \overset{\text{def}}{=} \{w \in A^* \mid |w|_a = |w|_b\}.$$

Theorem 7. $L_A(a, b)$ is REG-*measurable where* $A = \{a, b\}$.

Proof (sketch). It is enough to show that the complement $L = \overline{L(a,b)}$ satisfies $\underline{\mu}_{\text{REG}}(L) = 1$. For each $k \geq 1$, we define

$$L_k \overset{\text{def}}{=} \{w \in A^* \mid |w|_a \neq |w|_b \mod k\}.$$

Clearly, $L_k \subseteq L$ holds. Each L_k is recognised by a k-states deterministic automaton

$$\mathcal{A}_k = (Q_k = \{q_0, \ldots, q_{k-1}\}, \Delta_k : Q_k \times A \to Q_k, q_0, Q_k \setminus \{q_0\})$$

where

$$\Delta_k(q_i, a) = q_{i+1 \bmod k} \qquad \Delta_k(q_i, b) = q_{i-1 \bmod k} \quad (\text{ for each } i \in \{0, \ldots, k-1\}),$$

q_0 is the initial state, and any other state $q \in Q_k \setminus \{q_0\}$ is a final state. By an analysis of the adjacency matrix of $\mathcal{A}_n$, we can deduce that

$$\#(L_k \cap A^n) = \frac{k-1}{k} 2^n + o(2^n)$$

where $o(2^n)$ means some function such that $\lim_{n \to \infty} o(2^n)/2^n = 0$. Thus we have $\delta_A(L_k) = \frac{k-1}{k}$ for odd $k = 2m + 1$, which tends to 1 if k tends to infinity, *i.e.*, $\mu_{\text{REG}}(L) = 1$. This completes the proof. $\square$

By Theorem 7, it is also true that any subset of $L_{\{a,b\}}(a,b)$ is REG-measurable. In particular, we have:

Corollary 5. *The semi-Dyck language* $\mathsf{D} \subseteq L_{\{a,b\}}(a,b)$ *is REG-measurable.*

The next example is the set of all palindromes.

Theorem 8. $\mathsf{P}_A \stackrel{\text{def}}{=} \{w \in A^* \mid w = \text{rev}(w)\}$ *is REG-measurable.*

Proof (sketch). For each $k \geq 1$, one can easily observe that

$$L_k \stackrel{\text{def}}{=} \{w_1 A^* w_2 \mid w_1, w_2 \in A^k, w_1 \neq \text{rev}(w_2)\}$$

is a proper subset of the complement $\overline{\mathsf{P}_A}$. By an elementary analysis, we can prove $\delta_A(L_k) = 1 - \#(A)^{-k}$ and its tends to 1, *i.e.*, $\mu_{\text{REG}}(\mathsf{P}_A) = 0$.   □

4.2   Some Inherently Ambiguous Languages

There are REG-measurable inherently ambiguous context-free languages. Since every *bounded language* $L \subseteq w_1^* \cdots w_k^*$ is trivially REG-measurable ($\mu_{\text{REG}}(L) = 0$), a typical example of an inherently ambiguous context-free language $\{a^i b^j c^k \mid i = j \text{ or } i = k\}$ is REG-measurable.

Some more complex examples of inherently ambiguous languages are the following languages with constraints on the number of occurrences of letters investigated by Flajolet [13]:

$$\mathsf{O}_3 \stackrel{\text{def}}{=} \{w \in \{a,b,c\}^* \mid |w|_a = |w|_b \text{ or } |w|_a = |w|_c\},$$
$$\mathsf{O}_4 \stackrel{\text{def}}{=} \{w \in \{x, \bar{x}, y, \bar{y}\}^* \mid |w|_x = |w|_{\bar{x}} \text{ or } |w|_y = |w|_{\bar{y}}\}.$$

Theorem 9. O_3 *and* O_4 *are REG-measurable.*

Proof (sketch). Let $A = \{a,b,c\}$. For the case O_3, in a very similar way to Theorem 7, we can construct a sequence of automata $(\mathcal{A}_k^{ab})_{k \in \mathbb{N}}$ such that each automaton $\mathcal{A}_k^{ab}$ satisfies $L(\mathcal{A}_k^{ab}) \subseteq \overline{L_A(a,b)}$ The automaton $\mathcal{A}_k^{ab}$ is obtained by just adding self-loop labeled by c for each state $q \in Q_k$ of $\mathcal{A}_k$ in Theorem 7. This sequence of automata ensures that the language $L_A(a,b)$ is REG-measurable ($\overline{\mu}_{\text{REG}}(L_A(a,b)) = 0$, in particular). The same argument is applicable to the language $L_A(a,c)$, thus these union $\mathsf{O}_3 = L_A(a,b) \cup L_A(a,c)$ is also REG-measurable. The case O_4 can be achieved in the same manner.   □

Next we consider the so-called *Goldstine language*

$$\mathsf{G} \stackrel{\text{def}}{=} \{a^{n_1} b a^{n_2} b \cdots a^{n_p} b \mid p \geq 1, n_i \neq i \text{ for some } i\}.$$

While G can be accepted by a non-deterministic pushdown automaton, its generating function is not algebraic [14] and thus it is an inherently ambiguous context-free language due to the well-known Chomsky–Schützenberger theorem stating that the generating function of every unambiguous context-free language is algebraic [6].

Theorem 10. G *is* REG-*measurable.*

Proof. Let $A = \{a, b\}$. Observe that $G \subseteq A^*b$ and $\overline{\mu}_{\mathrm{REG}}(G) \leq \delta_A(A^*b) = 1/2$. Let
$$L_G = \{u \in A^* \mid uA^*\{b\} \cap \overline{G} = \emptyset\}$$
be the set of all forbidden prefixes of the complement $\overline{G}$. For each $k \geq 1$, we define
$$L_k \overset{\mathrm{def}}{=} \{uA^*\{b\} \mid u \in L_G \cap A^k\}.$$

If a word u is in L_G, then by definition of L_G, uvb is always in G for any word v, thus $L_k \subseteq G$ holds for each k. Any word in $\overline{L_G} = A^* \setminus L_G$ is a prefix of the infinite word $a^{n_1}ba^{n_2}ba^{n_3}b \cdots$ ($n_i = i$ for each $i \in \mathbb{N}$) thus $\#(L_G \cap A^n) = \#(A^n) - 1$ holds for each $n \geq 1$. Hence we have
$$\delta_A(L_k) = \lim_{n \to \infty} \frac{\#(L_k \cap A^n)}{\#(A^n)} = \lim_{n \to \infty} \frac{(\#(A^k) - 1) \cdot \#(A^{n-k-1})}{\#(A^n)}$$
$$= (\#(A)^k - 1) \cdot \#(A)^{-k-1} = 2^{-1} - 2^{-k-1}.$$

This implies that $\delta_A(L_k)$ tends to $1/2$. Thus $\mu_{\mathrm{REG}}(G) = 1/2$.   □

In general, for an infinite word $w \in A^\omega$, the set
$$\mathrm{Copref}(w) \overset{\mathrm{def}}{=} A^* \setminus \{u \in A^* \mid u \text{ is a prefix of } w\}$$

is called the *coprefix language of (w)*. The proof of Theorem 10 uses a key property that G can be characterised by using the coprefix language of the infinite word $w = a^{n_1}ba^{n_2}ba^{n_3}b \cdots$ as $G = \mathrm{Copref}(w) \cap \{a, b\}^*\{b\}$ which was pointed out in [1]. Thus by the same argument, we can say that any coprefix language L is REG-measurable ($\mu_{\mathrm{REG}}(L) = 1$, in particular).

For coprefix languages, the following nice "gap theorem" holds.

Theorem 11 (Autebert–Flajolet–Gabarro [1]). *Let $w \in A^\omega$ be an infinite word generated by an iterated morphism, i.e., $w = h(w) = h^\omega(a)$ for some monoid morphism $h : A^* \to A^*$ and letter $a \in A$. Then for the coprefix language $L = \mathrm{Copref}(w)$ there are only two possibilities:*

1. L is a regular language.
2. L is an inherently ambiguous context-free language.

This means that we can construct, by finding some suitable morphism h, many examples of inherently ambiguous context-free languages.

4.3   K: A Language with Transcendental Density

We now show the fact that the language K defined by Kemp [17] (recall that the definition of K appeared in Theorem 5) is REG-measurable. We will actually show a more general result regarding the following type of languages.

Definition 7. Let $L \subseteq A^*$ be a language and $c \notin A$ be a letter. We call the language $L\{c\}(A \cup \{c\})^*$ over $A \cup \{c\}$ *suffix extension of L by c.*

Theorem 12. *The suffix extension $L' \subseteq (A \cup \{c\})^*$ of any language $L \subseteq A^*$ by $c \notin A$ is REG-measurable.*

Proof. Let $B = A \cup \{c\}$ and $k = \#(B)$. We first show that L' has a natural density. For any words $u, v \in L$ with $u \neq v$, two languages $u\{c\}B^*$ and $v\{c\}B^*$ are disjoint, and clearly

$$\#(u\{c\}B^* \cap B^n) / \#(B^n) = \#(u\{c\}B^{n-|u|-1}) / \#(B^n) = k^{n-|u|-1}/k^n = k^{-(|u|+1)}$$

holds for $n > |u|$ thus $\delta_B(u\{c\}B^*) = k^{-(|u|+1)}$. The natural density of L' is

$$\delta_B(L') = \lim_{n \to \infty} \frac{\#(L' \cap B^n)}{\#(B^n)} = \lim_{n \to \infty} \frac{\#(\bigcup_{w \in L}(w\{c\}B^* \cap B^n))}{\#(B^n)}$$

$$= \lim_{n \to \infty} \frac{\sum_{w \in L} \#(w\{c\}B^* \cap B^n)}{\#(B^n)} = \lim_{n \to \infty} \sum_{w \in (L \cap A^{<n})} k^{-(|w|+1)}. \quad (4)$$

Because the sequence $(\sum_{w \in (L \cap A^{<n})} k^{-(|w|+1)})_{n \in \mathbb{N}}$ is non-decreasing and bounded above by 1, the limit (4) exists, say $\delta_B(L') = \alpha$.

For each $n \in \mathbb{N}$, the language $L_n \stackrel{\text{def}}{=} \bigcup_{w \in L \cap A^{<n}} w\{c\}B^*$ is regular (since $L \cap A^{<n}$ is finite), $L_n \subseteq L'$ and $\delta_B(L_n) = \sum_{w \in (L \cap A^{<n})} k^{-(|w|+1)}$. Hence $\underline{\mu}_{\text{REG}}(L') = \alpha$. By similar argument, for each $n \in \mathbb{N}$, we can claim that the language $K_n \stackrel{\text{def}}{=} B^* \setminus \bigcup_{w \in \overline{L} \cap A^{<n}} w\{c\}B^*$ satisfies $K_n \supseteq L'$ and $\delta_B(K_n)$ tends to α if n tends to infinity. Thus $\mu_{\text{REG}}(L') = \alpha$. $\square$

Since K is the suffix extensions of the union $S_1 \cup S_2$ in Theorem 5, we have:

Corollary 6. K *is REG-measurable.*

Remark 1. Theorem 12 indicates that REG-measurability is a quite relaxed property in some sense: even for a non-recursively-enumerable language, its suffix extension is still non-recursively-enumerable but REG-measurable. Moreover, because the class of recursively enumerable languages is just a countable set, there exist *uncountably many* REG-measurable non-recursively-enumerable languages.

The same proof method works for the *prefix extension* and the *infix extension* (see the full version [21] for details).

4.4   Languages with Full REG-Gap

In Sect. 4.1, we showed that the language $L_{\{a,b\}}(a,b)$ is REG-measurable. On the other hand, by the result of Eisman–Ravikumar [10], we will know that the closely related language

$$\mathsf{M} \stackrel{\text{def}}{=} \{w \in \{a,b\}^* \mid |w|_a > |w|_b\},$$

sometimes called the *majority language*, is not REG-measurable. This contrast is interesting.

Theorem 13 (Eisman–Ravikumar [10,11]**).** *Let* $A = \{a, b\}$ *and* $L \subseteq A^*$ *be a regular language. Then* $\mathsf{M} \subseteq L$ *implies* $\limsup_{n \to \infty} \{\# (\overline{L} \cap A^n) / \# (A^n)\} = 0$.

One can easily observe that $\limsup_{n \to \infty} \{\# (\overline{L} \cap A^n) / \# (A^n)\} = 0$ if and only if $\delta_A(\overline{L}) = 0$, which means that any regular superset of M is co-null. Thus the above theorem implies that both M and $\overline{\mathsf{M}}$ are REG^+-immune, hence we have:

Corollary 7. M *has full* REG*-gap.*

By using the infinite monkey theorem and some probabilistic arguments, we can generalise the previous theorem as follows.

Theorem 14. *For any* $m \geq 1$, *the following language over* $A = \{a, b\}$

$$\mathsf{M}_m \stackrel{\text{def}}{=} \{w \in A^* \mid |w|_a > m \cdot |w|_b\}$$

has full REG*-gap, and* $\delta_A(\mathsf{M}_m) = 1/2$ *if* $m = 1$ *otherwise* $\delta_A(\mathsf{M}_m) = 0$.

Proof (sketch). First we prove that any non-null regular language L can not be a subset of M_m. Let $\eta : A^* \to M$ be the syntactic morphism η and monoid M of L, and let $c = \max_{m \in M} \min_{w \in \eta^{-1}(m)} |w|$ (this is well-defined natural number since M is finite). By the infinite monkey theorem, L is not null implies that L has no forbidden word, and thus for the word b^{2c} there exist two words x and y such that $xb^{2c}y$ is in L. We can assume that $|x|, |y| \leq c$ without loss of generality by the definition of c, which implies $|xb^{2c}y|_a \leq |x| + |y| = 2c \leq |xb^{2c}y|_b$ hence $xb^{2c}y \notin \mathsf{M}_m$. Thus $L \not\subseteq \mathsf{M}_m$ and $\underline{\mu}_{\mathrm{REG}}(\mathsf{M}_m) = 0$. By using same argument, we can prove that $\overline{\mu}_{\mathrm{REG}}(\mathsf{M}_m) = 1$ and hence M_m has full REG-gap.

In the case $m = 1$, $\delta_A(\mathsf{M}_1) = \delta_A(\mathsf{M}) = 1/2$ is obvious. For the case $m \geq 2$, we can prove $\delta_A(\mathsf{M}_m) = 0$ by using the weak law of large numbers (see the full version [21] for details). □

5 REG-Immesurability of Primitive Words

A non-empty word $w \in A^+$ is said to be primitive if $u^n = w$ implies $u = w$ for any $u \in A^+$ and $n \in \mathbb{N}$. The set of all primitive words over A is denoted by Q_A. Because the case $\# (A) = 1$ is meaningless ($\mathsf{Q}_A = A$ in this case), hereafter we always assume $\# (A) \geq 2$. Whether Q_A is context-free or not is a well-known long-standing open problem posed by Dömösi, Horváth and Ito [9]. Reis and Shyr [19] proved $\mathsf{Q}_A^2 = A^+ \setminus \{a^n \mid a \in A, n \neq 2\}$, which intuitively means that every non-empty word w not a power of a letter is a product of two primitive words. From this result one may think that Q_A is "very large" in some sense. Actually, Q_A is somewhat "large" (it is dense in the sense of Definition 2), but we can show more stronger property as follows (see the full version [21] for the proof).

Theorem 15. $\delta_A(Q_A) = 1$.

While Q_A is "very large" (co-null) as stated above, we can also prove that Q_A is REG^+-immune. The proof relies on an analysis of the structure of the syntactic monoid of a non-null regular language. We assume that the reader has a basic knowledge of semigroup theory (*cf.* [18]): Green's relations $\mathcal{J}, \mathcal{R}, \mathcal{L}, \mathcal{H}$ and a direct consequence of Green's theorem (an $\mathcal{H}$-class H in a semigroup S is a subgroup of S if and only if H contains an idempotent), in particular.

Theorem 16. *Any non-null regular language contains infinitely many non-primitive words, and hence* $\mu_{\mathrm{REG}}(Q_A) = 0$.

Proof. Let L be a regular language over A with a positive density $\delta_A(L) > 0$. We consider $\eta : A^* \to M$ the syntactic morphism η and the syntactic monoid M of L, and let S be a subset of M satisfying $\eta^{-1}(S) = L$. L is regular means that M is finite, and hence M has at least one $\leq_{\mathcal{J}}$-minimal element.

We first show that S contains a $\leq_{\mathcal{J}}$-minimal element t. This is rather clear because, for any non-$\leq_{\mathcal{J}}$-minimal element s, its language $\eta^{-1}(s) \subseteq A^*$ is null: s is non-$\leq_{\mathcal{J}}$-minimal means that there is an other element t such that $t <_{\mathcal{J}} s$ (*i.e.*, $MtM \subsetneq MsM$), whence $s \notin MtM$ which implies that any word $w \in \eta^{-1}(t)$ is a forbidden word of $\eta^{-1}(s)$. Thus by the infinite monkey theorem $\eta^{-1}(s)$ is null.

Clearly, we have $t^n \leq_{\mathcal{J}} t$ and thus $t \mathcal{J} t^n$ holds for any $n > 1$ by the $\leq_{\mathcal{J}}$-minimality of t. $t \mathcal{J} t^n$ implies that there is a pair of words x, y such that $xt^n y = t$. Since M is finite, x^m is an idempotent for some $m > 0$ (*i.e.*, $x^{2m} = x^m$). Thus we obtain $t = xt^n y = x(t)t^{n-1}y = x^2(t)(t^{n-1}y)^2 = \cdots = x^m t(t^{n-1}y)^m = x^m x^m t(t^{n-1}y)^m = x^m t$ whence $t = t^n(y(t^{n-1}y)^{m-1})$. It follows that $t \mathcal{R} t^n$. Dually, we also obtain $t \mathcal{L} t^n$ and hence we can deduce that $t \mathcal{H} t^n$ holds. By the finiteness of M, there exists some $n > 0$ such that t^n is an idempotent. Thanks to Green's theorem, the $\mathcal{H}$-equivalent class H_t of t is a subgroup of M with the identity element t^n. Because η is surjective, we can take a word w' from $\eta^{-1}(t)$. Let $t' = \eta(w'a) = t\eta(a)$ for some letter $a \in A$, then by the $\leq_{\mathcal{J}}$-minimality of t, we can take some words $x, y \in A^*$ so that $\eta(xw'ay) = \eta(x)t'\eta(y) = t$. Hence we can deduce that $\eta^{-1}(t)$ contains a non-empty word $w = xw'ay$. Then for any $\varepsilon \neq w \in \eta^{-1}(t)$ and $m \geq 1$, we have

$$\eta(w^{mn+1}) = t^{mn+1} = (t^n)^m \cdot t = t \in S$$

which means that $L \supseteq \eta^{-1}(t)$ contains infinitely many non-primitive words w^{mn+1}. $\qquad\square$

Corollary 8 (of Theorem 15 and 16). Q_A *has full REG-gap.*

Remark 2. We emphasise that the assumption "L is non-null" in Theorem 16 is quite tight, since a slightly weaker assumption "L is of exponential growth" (*i.e.*, $\#(L \cap A^n)$ is exponential for n) does not imply that L contains non-primitive words. A trivial counterexample is $L_0 = \{a, b\}^*c$ over $A = \{a, b, c\}$: $\#(L_0 \cap A^n) = 2^{n-1}$ ($n \geq 1$) is exponential but L_0 only consists of primitive words. L_0 has a cc as a forbidden word, hence it is null by the infinite monkey theorem. Thus L_0 is not a counterexample of Theorem 16.

6 Conclusion and Open Problems

In this paper we proposed REG-measurability and showed that several context-free languages are REG-measurable, excluding M_m. Interestingly, it is shown that, like G and K, languages that have been considered as complex from a combinatorial viewpoint are, actually, easy to asymptotically approximate by regular languages. It is also interesting that a modified majority language M_2 is just a deterministic context-free but it is complex from a measure theoretic viewpoint. Its complement $\overline{M_2}$ is also deterministic context-free, and actually it is co-null but REG$^+$-immune (*i.e.*, has full REG-gap). This means that $\overline{M_2}$ is as complex as Q_A from a viewpoint of REG-measurability.

The following fundamental problems are still open and we consider these to be future work.

Problem 1. Can we give an alternative characterisation of the null (resp. co-null) context-free languages (like Theorem 3)?

Problem 2. Can we give an alternative characterisation of the REG-measurable context-free languages?

Problem 3. Can we find a language class that can "separate" Q_A and CFL? *i.e.*, is there $\mathcal{C}$ such that Q_A has full $\mathcal{C}$-gap but no co-null context-free language has full $\mathcal{C}$-gap, or Q_A is $\mathcal{C}$-immeasurable but any co-null context-free language is $\mathcal{C}$-measurable?

The our results (Theorem 14, 15 and 16) tell us that the class REG of regular languages can not separate Q_A and CFL. However, it is still open whether the situation is the same or not when $\mathcal{C} = \mathrm{DetCFL}, \mathrm{UnCFL}, \mathrm{CFL}$ or other extension of regular languages. Notice that *if* the answer of Problem 3 is "yes", then Q_A is not context-free.

Acknowledgement. The author would like to thank Takanori Maehara (RIKEN AIP) and Fazekas Szilárd (Akita University) whose helpful discussion were an enormous help to me. The author also thank to anonymous reviewers for many valuable comments. This work was supported by JSPS KAKENHI Grant Number JP19K14582.

References

1. Autebert, J.M., Flajolet, P., Gabarro, J.: Prefixes of infinite words and ambiguous context-free languages. Inf. Process. Lett. **25**(4), 211–216 (1987)
2. Berstel, J.: Sur la densité asymptotique de langages formels. In: International Colloquium on Automata. Languages and Programming, pp. 345–358. North-Holland, France (1973)
3. Berstel, J., Perrin, D., Reutenauer, C.: Codes and Automata. Encyclopedia of Mathematics and its Applications. Cambridge University Press, Cambridge (2009)
4. Buck, R.C.: The measure theoretic approach to density. Am. J. Math. **68**(4), 560–580 (1946)

5. Câmpeanu, C., Sântean, N., Yu, S.: Minimal cover-automata for finite languages. Theoret. Comput. Sci. **267**(1), 3–16 (2001)
6. Chomsky, N., Schützenberger, M.: The algebraic theory of context-free languages*. In: Computer Programming and Formal Systems, vol. 35, pp. 118–161. Elsevier (1963)
7. Cordy, B., Salomaa, K.: On the existence of regular approximations. Theoret. Comput. Sci. **387**(2), 125–135 (2007)
8. Domaratzki, M.: Minimal covers of formal languages. Master's thesis, University of Waterloo (2001)
9. Dömösi, P., Horváth, S., Ito, M.: On the connection between formal languages and primitive words, pp. 59–67 (1991)
10. Eisman, G., Ravikumar, B.: Approximate recognition of non-regular languages by finite automata. In: Twenty-Eighth Australasian Computer Science Conference (ACSC 2005), Newcastle, Australia. CRPIT, vol. 38, pp. 219–228. ACS (2005)
11. Eisman, G., Ravikumar, B.: On approximating non-regular languages by regular languages. Fundamenta Informaticae **110**, 125–142 (2011)
12. Flajolet, P., Steyaert, J.M.: On sets having only hard subsets. In: International Colloquium on Automata, Languages and Programming, pp. 446–457. North-Holland (1974)
13. Flajolet, P.: Ambiguity and transcendence. In: Brauer, W. (ed.) ICALP 1985. LNCS, vol. 194, pp. 179–188. Springer, Heidelberg (1985). https://doi.org/10.1007/BFb0015743
14. Flajolet, P.: Analytic models and ambiguity of context-free languages. Theoret. Comput. Sci. **49**(2), 283–309 (1987)
15. Kappes, M., Kintala, C.M.R.: Tradeoffs between reliability and conciseness of deterministic finite automata. J. Autom. Lang. Comb. **9**(2–3), 281–292 (2004)
16. Kappes, M., Nießner, F.: Succinct representations of languages by DFA with different levels of reliability. Theoret. Comput. Sci. **330**(2), 299–310 (2005)
17. Kemp, R.: A note on the density of inherently ambiguous context-free languages. Acta Informatica **14**(3), 295–298 (1980)
18. Pin, J.E.: Mathematical foundations of automata theory (2012)
19. Reis, C., Shyr, H.: Some properties of disjunctive languages on a free monoid. Inf. Control **37**(3), 334–344 (1978)
20. Salomaa, A., Soittola, M.: Automata Theoretic Aspects of Formal Power Series. Springer, New York (1978). https://doi.org/10.1007/978-1-4612-6264-0
21. Sin'ya, R.: Asymptotic approximation by regular languages (full version). http://www.math.akita-u.ac.jp/~ryoma/misc/measure.pdf
22. Sin'ya, R.: An automata theoretic approach to the zero-one law for regular languages: algorithmic and logical aspects. In: Proceedings Sixth International Symposium on Games, Automata, Logics and Formal Verification, GandALF 2015, pp. 172–185 (2015)

Balanced Independent and Dominating Sets on Colored Interval Graphs

Sujoy Bhore[1] , Jan-Henrik Haunert[2] , Fabian Klute[3] , Guangping Li[4(✉)] ,
and Martin Nöllenburg[4]

[1] Université libre de Bruxelles, Brussels, Belgium
sujoy.bhore@gmail.com
[2] Geoinformation Group, University of Bonn, Bonn, Germany
haunert@igg.uni-bonn.de
[3] Department of Information and Computing Sciences, Utrecht University,
Utrecht, The Netherlands
f.m.klute@uu.nl
[4] Algorithms and Complexity Group, TU Wien, Vienna, Austria
{guangping,noellenburg}@ac.tuwien.ac.at

Abstract. We study two new versions of independent and dominating set problems on vertex-colored interval graphs, namely f-*Balanced Independent Set* (f-BIS) and f-*Balanced Dominating Set* (f-BDS). Let $G = (V, E)$ be an interval graph with a *color assignment* function $\gamma \colon V \to \{1, \dots, k\}$ that maps all vertices in G onto k colors. A subset of vertices $S \subseteq V$ is called f-*balanced* if S contains f vertices from each color class. In the f-BIS and f-BDS problems, the objective is to compute an independent set or a dominating set that is f-balanced. We show that both problems are NP-complete even on proper interval graphs. For the BIS problem on interval graphs, we design two **FPT** algorithms, one parameterized by (f, k) and the other by the vertex cover number of G. Moreover, for an optimization variant of BIS on interval graphs, we present a polynomial time approximation scheme (PTAS) and an $O(n \log n)$ time 2-approximation algorithm.

1 Introduction

A graph G is an interval graph if it has an intersection model consisting of intervals on the real line. Formally, $G = (V, E)$ is an interval graph if there is an assignment of an interval $I_v \subseteq \mathbb{R}$ for each $v \in V$ such that $I_u \cap I_v$ is nonempty if and only if $\{u, v\} \in E$. A *proper* interval graph is an interval graph that has an intersection model in which no interval properly contains another [10]. Consider an interval graph $G = (V, E)$ and additionally assume that the vertices of G are k-colored by a *color assignment*[1] $\gamma \colon V \to \{1, \dots, k\}$. We define and study

---

[1] We use the term *color assignment* instead of *vertex coloring* to avoid any confusion with the general notion of vertex coloring; in particular, a color assignment γ can map adjacent vertices to the same color.

© Springer Nature Switzerland AG 2021
T. Bureš et al. (Eds.): SOFSEM 2021, LNCS 12607, pp. 89–103, 2021.
https://doi.org/10.1007/978-3-030-67731-2_7

color-balanced versions of two classical graph problems: maximum independent set and minimum dominating set on vertex-colored (proper) interval graphs. In what follows, we define the problems formally and discuss their underlying motivation.

f-**Balanced Independent Set** (*f*-**BIS**)**:** Let $G = (V, E)$ be an interval graph with a color assignment of the vertices $\gamma \colon V \to \{1, \ldots, k\}$. Find an *f-balanced independent set* of G, i.e., an independent set $L \subseteq V$ that contains exactly f elements from each color class.

The classic maximum independent set problem serves as a natural model for many real-life optimization problems and finds applications across fields, e.g., computer vision [2], information retrieval [18], and scheduling [20]. Specifically, it has been used widely in map-labeling problems [1,4,14,21], where an independent set of a given set of label candidates corresponds to a conflict-free and hence legible set of labels. To display as much relevant information as possible, one usually aims at maximizing the size or, in the case of weighted label candidates, the total weight of the independent set. This approach may be appropriate if all labels represent objects of the same category. In the case of multiple categories, however, maximizing the size or total weight of the labeling does not reflect the aim of selecting a good mixture of different object types. For example, if the aim was to inform a map user about different possible activities in the user's vicinity, labeling one cinema, one theater, and one museum may be better than labeling four cinemas. In such a setting, the *f*-BIS problem asks for an independent set that contains f vertices from each object type.

We initiate this study for interval graphs which is a primary step to understand the behavior of this problem on intersection graphs. Moreover, solving the problem for interval graphs gives rise to optimal solutions for certain labeling models, e.g., if every label candidate is a rectangle that is placed at a fixed position on the boundary of the map [11].

While there exists a simple greedy algorithm for the maximum independent set problem on interval graphs, it turns out that *f*-BIS is much more resilient and NP-complete even for proper interval graphs and $f = 1$ (Sect. 2.1). Then, in Sect. 3, we complement this complexity result with two FPT algorithms for interval graphs, one parameterized by (f, k) and the other parameterized by the vertex cover number. Section 4 introduces a polynomial time approximation scheme (PTAS) and an $O(n \log n)$ time 2-approximation algorithm for an optimization variant (1-MCIS) of BIS on interval graphs.

The second problem we discuss is defined as follows.

f-**Balanced Dominating Set** (*f*-**BDS**)**:** Let $G = (V, E)$ be an interval graphs with a color assignment of the vertices $\gamma \colon V \to \{1, \ldots, k\}$. Find an *f-balanced dominating set*, i.e., a subset $D \subseteq V$ such that every vertex in $V \setminus D$ is adjacent to at least one vertex in D, and D contains exactly f elements from each color class.

The dominating set problem is another fundamental problem in theoretical computer science which also finds applications in various fields of science and engineering [6,12]. Several variants of the dominating set problem have been considered over the years: k-tuple dominating set [7], Liar's dominating set [3], independent dominating set [13], and more. The colored variant of the dominating set problem has been considered in parameterized complexity, namely, red-blue dominating set, where the objective is to choose a dominating set from one color class that dominates the other color class [9]. Instead, our f-BDS problem asks for a dominating set of a vertex-colored graph that contains f vertices of each color class. Similar to the independent set problem, we primarily study this problem on vertex-colored interval graphs, which can be of independent interest. In Sect. 2.2, we prove that f-BDS on vertex-colored proper interval graphs is NP-complete, even for $f = 1$. Due to space constraints, please refer to the appendix for missing proofs and detailed descriptions.

2 Complexity Results

In this section we show that f-BIS and f-BDS are NP-complete even if the given graph G is a proper interval graph and $f = 1$. Our reductions are from restricted, but still NP-complete versions of 3SAT, namely 3-bounded 3SAT [19] and 2P2N-3SAT (hardness follows from the result for 2P1N-SAT [22]). In the former 3SAT variant a variable is allowed to appear in at most three clauses and clauses have two or three literals, in the latter each variable appears exactly four times, twice as positive literal and twice as negative literal.

2.1 f-Balanced Independent Set

We first describe the reduction. Let $\phi(x_1, \ldots, x_n)$ be a 3-bounded 3SAT formula with variables $x_1, \ldots, x_n$ and clause set $\mathcal{C} = \{C_1, \ldots, C_m\}$. From ϕ we construct a proper interval graph $G = (V, E)$ and a color assignment γ of V as follows. We choose the set of colors to contain exactly m colors, one for each clause in $\mathcal{C}$ and we number these colors from 1 to m. We add a vertex $u_{i,j} \in V$ for each occurrence of a variable x_i in a clause C_j in ϕ. Furthermore, we insert an edge $\{u_{i,j}, u_{i,j'}\} \in E$ whenever $u_{i,j}$ was inserted because of a positive occurrence of x_i and $u_{i,j'}$ was inserted because of a negative occurrence of x_i. Finally, we color each vertex $u_{i,j} \in V$ with color j. See Fig. 1 for an illustration. It is clear that the construction is in polynomial time. The graph G created from ϕ is a proper interval graph as it consists only of disjoint paths of length at most three and can clearly be constructed in polynomial time and space.

Theorem 1. *The f-balanced independent set problem on a graph $G = (V, E)$ with a color assignment of the vertices $\gamma \colon V \to \{1, \ldots, k\}$ is NP-complete, even if G is a proper interval graph and $f = 1$.*

Proof. The problem is clearly in NP since for a given solution it can be checked in linear time if it is an independent set and contains f vertices of each color.

We already described the reduction. It remains to argue the correctness. Assume $G = (V, E)$ was constructed as above from a 3-bounded 3SAT formula

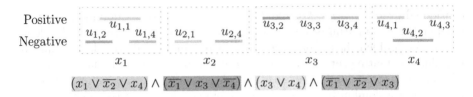

Fig. 1. The graph resulting from the reduction for 1-balanced independent set in Theorem 1 depicted as interval representation with the vertex colors being the colors of the intervals.

$\phi(x_1, \ldots, x_n)$ and let $V' \subseteq V$ be a solution to the 1-balanced independent set problem on G.

We construct a variable assignment for $x_1, \ldots, x_n$ as follows. By definition we find for each color j precisely one vertex $u_{i,j} \in V'$. If $u_{i,j}$ was inserted for a positive occurrence of x_i, then we set x_i to *true* and otherwise x_i to *false*. Moreover, all variables x_i with $i = 1, \ldots, n$ for which we do not find a corresponding interval in V' are also set to *false*. Since V' is an independent set in G this assignment is well defined. Now assume it was not satisfying, then there exists a clause C_j for which none of its literals evaluates to *true*. Hence, none of the at most three vertices corresponding to the literals in C_j is in V'. Recall that there is a one-to-one correspondence between clauses and colors in the instance of 1-balanced independent set we created. Yet, V' does not contain a vertex of that color, a contradiction.

For the opposite direction assume we are given a satisfying assignment of the 3-bounded 3SAT formula $\phi(x_1, \ldots, x_n)$ with clauses $\mathcal{C} = \{C_1, \ldots, C_m\}$. Furthermore let $G = (V, E)$ be the graph with a color assignment of the vertices γ constructed from ϕ as described above. We find a 1-balanced independent set of G from the given assignment as follows. For each clause $C_j \in \mathcal{C}$ we choose one of its literals that evaluates to *true* and add the corresponding vertex $v \in V$ to the set of vertices V'. Since there is a one-to-one correspondence between the colors and the clauses and the assignment is satisfying, V' clearly contains one vertex per color. It remains to show that V' is an independent set of vertices in G. Assume for contradiction that there are two vertices $v_{i,j}, v_{i',j'} \in V'$ and $\{v_{i,j}, v_{i',j'}\} \in E$. Then, by construction of G, we know that $i = i'$ and further that $v_{i,j}, v_{i',j'}$ correspond to one positive and one negative occurrence of x_i in ϕ. By the construction of V' this implies a contradiction to the assignment being satisfying. □

2.2 f-Balanced Dominating Set

We reduce from 2P2N-3SAT where each variable appears exactly twice positive and twice negative. Let $\phi(x_1, \ldots, x_n)$ be a 2P2N-3SAT formula with variables $x_1, \ldots, x_n$ and clause set $\mathcal{C} = \{C_1, \ldots, C_m\}$. For variable x_i in ϕ we denote with $\mathcal{C}_{x_i} = \{C_t^1, C_t^2, C_f^1, C_f^2\}$ the four clauses x_i appears in, where C_t^1, C_t^2 are clauses with positive occurrences of x_i and C_f^1, C_f^2 are clauses containing negative occurrences of x_i.

We construct a graph $G = (V, E)$ from $\phi(x_1, \ldots, x_n)$ as follows. For each variable x_i we introduce six vertices t_1, t_2, f_1, f_2, h_t, and h_f and for each clause C_j with occurrences of variables x_{j_1}, x_{j_2}, and x_{j_3} we add up to three vertices c_k for each $k \in \{j_1, j_2, j_3\}$ (In case a clause has less than three literals we add only one or two vertices). If the connection to the variable is clear, we also write c_t^1, c_t^2, c_f^1, and c_f^2 for the vertices introduced for this variable's occurrences in the clauses C_t^1, C_t^2, C_f^1, and C_f^2, respectively. Furthermore, we add for each variable x_i the edges $\{h_t, t_1\}, \{h_t, t_2\}, \{h_f, f_1\}$, and $\{h_f, f_2\}$, as well as for each clause C_j all possible edges between the three vertices introduced for C_j. For each variable x_i we introduce five colors, namely $z_t^1, z_t^2, z_f^1, z_f^2$, and z_h. We set $\gamma(h_t) = \gamma(h_f) = z_h$. Finally, we set $\gamma(t_1) = \gamma(c_t^1) = z_t^1$. Equivalently for t_2, f_1, and f_2. See Fig. 2 for an example.

In total we create $6n + 3m$ many vertices and $4n + 3m$ many edges, thus the reduction is in polynomial time. All variable and clause gadgets are independent components and only consist of paths of length three and triangles, hence G is a proper interval graph. Furthermore, G can clearly be constructed in polynomial time and space.

To establish the correctness of our reduction for 1-BDS we first introduce a canonical type of solutions for the graphs produced by our reduction. We call V_D canonical, if for each variable x_i we either find $\{h_t, f_1, f_2, c_t^1, c_t^2\} \subset V_D$ or $\{h_f, t_1, t_2, c_f^1, c_f^2\} \subset V_D$. If for a variable $x \in X$ and a 1-balanced dominating set $V_D \subseteq V$ we find one of the two above sets in V_D, we say x is in *canonical form* in V_D. The next lemma shows that if G has a 1-balanced dominating set we can turn it into a canonical one.

Lemma 1. *Let $G = (V, E)$ be a graph generated from a 2P2N-3SAT formula $\phi(x_1, \ldots, x_n)$ with clause set $\mathcal{C} = \{C_1, \ldots, C_m\}$ as above and $V_D \subseteq V$ a 1-balanced dominating set, then V_D can be transformed into a canonical 1-balanced dominating set in $O(|V|)$ time.*

Proof. Let x be not in canonical form in V_D. Since V_D is a 1-balanced dominating set we know that either h_t or h_f of x is in V_D. Without loss of generality assume that $h_t \in V_D$. Consequently, we find that $f_1, f_2 \in V_D$ and $c_f^1, c_f^2 \notin V_D$. Now, we

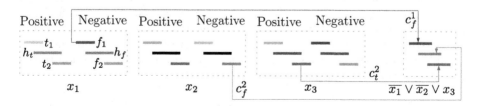

Fig. 2. Illustrations of three variable gadgets and a clause gadget from Theorem 2 as interval representations. Vertex colors correspond to interval colors.

obtain the set V_D' from V_D by removing any occurrence of t_1 or t_2 from V_D and inserting all missing elements of $\{c_t^1, c_t^2\}$. Clearly x is in canonical form in V_D'. We need to show that V_D' is still a 1-balanced dominating set. It is straight forward to verify that every color appears exactly once in V_D' if V_D was 1-balanced. Now assume there was a vertex $u \in V$ that is not dominated by any vertex in V_D'. Yet, we at most deleted t_1 and t_2 in V_D' but since $h_t \in V_D'$ both and all their neighbors are dominated. As our operations only affected vertices introduced for x and occurrences of x we can simply iterate this process for each variable until every variable x_i is in canonical form. $\qquad\square$

Theorem 2. *The f-balanced dominating set problem on a graph $G = (V, E)$ with a color assignment of the vertices $\gamma : V \to \{1, \ldots, k\}$ is NP-complete, even if G is a proper interval graph and $f = 1$.*

Proof. The problem is clearly in NP as we can verify if a given set of vertices is an f-balanced dominating set by checking if it is a dominating set and if it contains f vertices of each color in linear time.

Let $G = (V, E)$ be constructed from a 2P2N-3SAT formula $\phi(x_1, \ldots, x_n)$ with clause set $\mathcal{C} = \{C_1, \ldots, C_m\}$ as above and let V_D be a 1-balanced dominating set of G. By Lemma 1 we can assume V_D is canonical. We construct an assignment of the variables in ϕ by setting x_i to *true* if its $h_t \in V_D$ and to *false* otherwise. Assume this assignment was not satisfying, i.e., there exists a clause $C_j \in \mathcal{C}$ such that none of the literals in C_j evaluates to *true*. For each positive literal of C_j we then get that the corresponding variable x_i was set to *false*. Hence, $h_f \in V_D$ for x_i and consequently $c_t^1, c_t^2 \notin V_D$. Equivalently for each negative literal we find $h_t \in V_D$ and $c_f^1, c_f^2 \notin V_D$. As a result we find that none of the vertices introduced for literals in C_j is in V_D and especially that none of them is dominated as they are each others only neighbors. Yet, V_D is a 1-balanced dominating set by assumption, a contradiction.

In the other direction, assume we are given a satisfying assignment of a 2P2N-3SAT formula $\phi(x_1, \ldots, x_n)$ with clause set $\mathcal{C} = \{C_1, \ldots, C_m\}$. Furthermore, let $G = (V, E)$ be the graph constructed from ϕ as above. We form a canonical 1-balanced dominating set $V_D \subseteq V$ of G in the following way. For every variable x_i that is set to *true* in the assignment we add $\{h_t, f_1, f_2, c_t^1, c_t^2\}$ to V_D and for every variable $x_{i'}$ that is set to *false* we add $\{h_f, t_1, t_2, c_f^1, c_f^2\}$. This clearly is a 1-balanced set and it is canonical. It remains to argue that it dominates G. For the vertices introduced for variables this is clear, since we pick either h_t or h_f, as well as f_1, f_2 or t_1, t_2 for every variable x_i. Now, assume there was a clause $C_j \in \mathcal{C}$ and none of the vertices introduced for literals in C_j was in V_D. Then, by construction of V_D, we find that for any positive (negative) occurrence of a variable x_i in C_j the variable x_i was set to *false* (*true*). A contradiction to the assignment being satisfying. $\qquad\square$

3   Algorithmic Results for the Balanced Independent Set

In this section, we take a parameterized perspective on f-BIS and provide two
FPT algorithms[2] with different parameters. The algorithms described in this
section can be easily generalized to maximize the value of f in f-BIS.

3.1   An FPT Algorithm Parameterized by (f, k)

Assume we are given an instance of f-BIS with $G = (V, E)$ being an interval
graph with a color assignment of the vertices $\gamma \colon V \to \{1, \ldots, k\}$. We can con-
struct an interval representation $\mathcal{I} = \{I_1, \ldots, I_n\}$, $n = |V|$, from G in linear
time [15]. Our algorithm is a dynamic programming based procedure that work
as follows. Firstly, we sort the right end-points of the n intervals in $\mathcal{I}$ in ascend-
ing order. Next, we define a function $prev \colon V \to \{1, \ldots, n\}$. for each interval
$I_i \in I$, the $prev(I_i)$ is the index of the rightmost interval with its right endpoint
left to I_i's left endpoint. If no such interval exists for some interval I_i, we set
$prev(I_i) = 0$.

For each color $\kappa \in \{1, \ldots, k\}$, let $\hat{e}_\kappa$ denote the k-dimensional unit vector
of the form $(0, \ldots, 0, 1, 0, \ldots, 0)$, where the element at the κ-th position is 1
and the rest are 0. For a subset $\mathcal{I}' \subseteq \mathcal{I}$ we define a *cardinality vector* as the
k-dimensional vector $C_{\mathcal{I}'} = (c_1, \ldots, c_k)$, where each element c_i represents the
number of intervals of color i in $\mathcal{I}'$. We say $C_{\mathcal{I}'}$ is *valid* if all $c_i \leq f$ and the set
$\mathcal{I}'$ is independent.

The key observation here is that there are at most $O((f + 1)^k)$ many different valid cardinality vectors as there are only k colors and we are interested in at most f intervals per color. In the following let U_j, $j \in \{1, \ldots, n\}$,
be the union of all valid cardinality vectors of the first j intervals in $\mathcal{I}$. Let
$U_0 = \{(0, \ldots, 0)\}$ in the beginning. To compute an f-balanced independent
set the algorithm simply iterates over all right endpoints of the intervals in
$\mathcal{I}$ and in the i-th step computes U_i as $U_i = \{u + \hat{e}_{\gamma(I_i)} \mid u \in U_{prev(I_i)}$
and $u + \hat{e}_{\gamma(I_i)}$ is a valid cardinality vector$\} \cup U_{i-1}$. Checking if a new cardinality vector is valid can be done easily by remembering for each $u \in U_{i-1}$ one
representative interval set with u as its cardinality vector. Finally, we check the
cardinality vectors in U_n and return *true* in case there is one cardinality vector
$w \in U_n$ with entries being all f and *false* otherwise. Moreover, the representative
interval set of w builds an f-balanced independent set.

Theorem 3. *Let $G = (V, E)$ be an interval graph with a color assignment of
the vertices $\gamma : V \to \{1, \ldots, k\}$. We can compute an f-balanced independent set
of G or determine that no such set exists in $O(n \log n + k(f + 1)^k n)$ time.*

Proof. Let $\mathcal{I} = \{I_1, \ldots, I_n\}$ be an interval representation of G on which we
execute our algorithm. For U_0 the set just contains the valid cardinality vector
with all zeros which is clearly correct. Let U_{i-1} be the set of valid cardinality

---

[2] FPT is the class of parameterized problems that can be solved in time $O(g(k)n^{O(1)})$
for input size n, parameter k, and some computable function g.

vectors computed after step $i - 1$. Now, in step $i \leq n$ we calculate the set U_i as the union of U_{i-1} and the potential new solutions based on independent sets of intervals containing I_i. Assume $\mathcal{I}_x \subseteq \{I_1, \ldots, I_i\}$ is an independent set of intervals such that its cardinality vector $C_{\mathcal{I}_x}$ is valid, but there is no valid cardinality vector $C_{\mathcal{I}'} \in U_i$ such that $C_{\mathcal{I}'}$ is larger or equal in every component than $C_{\mathcal{I}_x}$. Since U_{i-1} contained all valid cardinality vectors for the intervals in $\{I_1, \ldots, I_{i-1}\}$ we know that $C_{\mathcal{I}_x}$ is such that $I_i \in \mathcal{I}_x$. Yet, the set $U_{prev(I_i)}$ contained all valid cardinality vectors for the set of intervals $\{I_1, \ldots, I_{prev(I_i)}\}$. Since I_i has overlaps with all intervals in $\{I_{prev(I_i)+1}, \ldots, I_{i-1}\}$ and hence cannot be in any independent set with any such interval we can conclude that $C_{\mathcal{I}_x} - \hat{e}_{\gamma(I_i)} \in U_{prev(I_i)}$. Though, we also find $C_{\mathcal{I}_x} \in U_i$, a contradiction.

Next we consider the running time. The key observation is that there are at most $(f + 1)^k$ different valid cardinality vectors. Checking the validity can be done in $O(1)$ time for each new vector as only one entry changes. Computing the sets U_i can be done in time $O(k(f + 1)^k)$, by storing the cardinality vectors in lexicographic sorted order for each set. Keeping the sets in sorted order does not require any extra running time, as U_0 is clearly sorted in the beginning (it only contains one element) and we only increase the same entry for each vector in $U_{prev(I_i)}$ when forming the union, thus not changing their ordering. Hence, the set $U_{prev(I_i)}$ and U_{i-1} can be assumed to be sorted in lexicographic order. Consequently, by merging from smallest to largest element the set U_i is again lexicographically sorted after the union. Furthermore, we can easily discard double entries by comparing also against the vector we inserted last into U_i. Finally, we have to sort the intervals themselves. Using standard sorting algorithms this works in $O(n \log n)$ time. Altogether, this results in a running time of $O(n \log n + k(f + 1)^k n)$. □

3.2 An FPT Algorithm Parameterized by the Vertex Cover Number

Here we will give an alternative FPT algorithm for f-BIS, this time parameterized by the *vertex cover number* $\tau(G)$ of G, i.e., the size of a minimum vertex cover of G.

Lemma 2. *Let $G = (V, E)$ be a graph. Consider a vertex cover V_c in G and its complement $V_{ind} = V \setminus V_c$. Then any maximal independent set M of G can be constructed from V_{ind} by adding the subset $M \cap V_c$ of V_c and removing its neighborhood in V_{ind}, namely $M = (V_{ind} \cup (M \cap V_c)) \setminus N(M \cap V_c)$.*

Proof. For a fixed but arbitrary maximal independent set M, in the following, we denote the set $(V_{ind} \cup (M \cap V_c)) \setminus N(M \cap V_c)$ as M_{swap}.

We first prove the independence of M_{swap}. Note that by the definition of a vertex cover V_{ind} is an independent set. Furthermore, the set $(M \cap V_c)$, as a subset of the independent set M, is also independent. Then, in the union $V_{ind} \cup (M \cap V_c)$ of these two independent sets, any adjacent pair of vertices must contain one vertex in $M \cap V_c$ and one in V_{ind}. Hence, after removing all the neighboring vertices of $M \cap V_c$, the set M_{swap} is independent.

Next we prove that $M \subseteq M_{\text{swap}}$. Assume there exists one vertex v_m in M but not in M_{swap}. Since $v_m \in M$ it must also be in the set $V_{\text{ind}} \cup (M \cap V_c)$. With the assumption that $v_m \notin M_{\text{swap}}$, we get that v_m must be in $N(M \cap V_c)$. Consequently, v_m is in the independent set M and is at the same time a neighbor of vertices in M, a contradiction.

Finally we prove $M = M_{\text{swap}}$. We showed above that M_{swap} is an independent set and also $M \subseteq M_{\text{swap}}$. Since M is a maximal independent set by assumption we get $M = M_{\text{swap}}$. $\qquad\square$

Lemma 3. *Let $G = (V, E)$ be a graph with vertex cover number $\tau(G)$. There are $O(2^{\tau(G)})$ maximal independent sets of G.*

Proof. Consider a minimum vertex cover V_c in G and its complement $V_{\text{ind}} = V \setminus V_c$. Note that since V_c is a (minimum) vertex cover, V_{ind} is a (maximum) independent set. Furthermore, any maximal independent set M of G can be constructed from V_{ind} by adding $M \cap V_c$ and removing its neighborhood in V_{ind}, namely $M = (V_{\text{ind}} \cup (M \cap V_c)) \setminus N(M \cap V_c)$ by Lemma 2. Thus there are $O(2^{\tau(G)})$ maximal independent sets of G. $\qquad\square$

Theorem 4. *Let $G = (V, E)$ be an interval graph with a color assignment of the vertices $\gamma \colon V \to \{1, \ldots, k\}$. We can compute an f-balanced independent set of G or determine that no such set exists in $O(2^{\tau(G)} \cdot n)$ time.*

Proof. According to Lemma 3, there are $O(2^{\tau(G)})$ maximal independent sets of G. The basic idea is to enumerate all the $O(2^{\tau(G)})$ maximal independent sets and compute their maximum balanced subsets. Enumerating all maximal independent sets of an interval graph takes $O(1)$ time per output [17]. Given an arbitrary independent set of G we can compute an f-balanced independent subset in $O(n)$ time or conclude that no such subset exists. Therefore, the running time of the algorithm is $O(2^{\tau(G)} \cdot n)$. $\qquad\square$

4   Approximation Algorithms for the 1-Max-Colored Independent Set

Here we study a variation of the BIS, which asks for a maximally colorful independent set.

1-Max-Colored Independent Set (1-MCIS): Let $G = (V, E)$ be an interval graph with a color assignment of the vertices $\gamma \colon V \to \{1, \ldots, k\}$. The objective is to find a 1-max-colored independent set of G, i.e., an independent set $L \subseteq V$, whose vertices contain a maximum number of colors and L contains exactly 1 element from each color class.

We note that the NP-completeness of 1-BIS implies that 1-MCIS is an NP-hard optimization problem as well.

Fig. 3. Comparison of a solution S of the algorithm and an optimal solution O. Subset $M \subseteq O$ contains two colors (red and blue) missing from S, but each interval in M contains the right endpoint of a different interval from S. (Color figure online)

4.1   A 2-Approximation for the 1-Max-Colored Independent Set

In the following, we will show a simple sweep algorithm for 1-MCIS with approximation ratio 2.

First, we sort the intervals from left to right based on their right end-points. Then, our algorithm scans the intervals from left to right, and at each step selects greedily an interval of a distinct color such that no interval of the same color has been selected before. Moreover, we maintain a solution array S of size k to store the selected intervals.

For each interval I_i in this order, we check if the color of I_i is still missing in our solution (by checking if $S[\gamma(I_i)]$ is not yet occupied). If yes, we store I_i in $S[\gamma(i)]$ and remove all the remaining intervals overlapping I_i. Otherwise, if $S[\gamma(I_i)]$ is not empty, we remove I_i and continue scanning the intervals. This process is repeated until all intervals are processed. Then, by using a simple charging argument on the colors in an optimal solution that are missing in our greedy solution, we obtain the desired approximation factor.

Theorem 5. *Let $G = (V, E)$ be an interval graph with a color assignment of the vertices $\gamma \colon V \to \{1, \ldots, k\}$. In $O(n \log n)$ time, we can compute an independent set with at least $\lceil \frac{c}{2} \rceil$ colors, where c is the number of colors in a 1-max-colored independent set.*

Proof. It is clear from the above description that the greedy algorithm finds an independent set. We maintain a solution array S, and it is possible to check if an interval of a particular color is already available in S in constant time. Therefore, the entire algorithm runs in $O(n \log n)$ time.

In order to prove the approximation factor, we compare the solution S of our greedy algorithm with a fixed 1-max-colored independent set O (see Fig. 3). Let $M = \{I_i \in O \mid \nexists I_j \in S \text{ with } \gamma(I_j) = \gamma(I_i)\}$ be the subset of O consisting of intervals of missing colors in S. Now, consider an interval $I_m \in M$. There must be at least one interval $I_s \in S$, whose right endpoint is contained in the interval I_m. Otherwise, since there is no interval of the same color as I_m in S, the greedy algorithm would scan I_m as the interval with the leftmost right endpoint in the process and select it in S. Thus, the function ρ, which maps each interval I_m in M to an interval I_s in S such that I_s is the rightmost interval in S with its right endpoint is contained in I_m, is well-defined. Furthermore, ρ is an injective function because of the independence of the set M. Therefore, we can conclude that the cardinality of the set S is greater than or equal to the cardinality of M. Note that, $|M| + |S| \geq |O|$. Hence, S has size at least $\lceil \frac{c}{2} \rceil$.   □

4.2   A PTAS for the 1-Max-Colored Independent Set

In this section, we present a polynomial time approximation scheme (PTAS) for 1-Max-Colored Independent Set (1-MCIS). Our algorithm is based on the careful usage and analysis of the local search technique. We prove that, this algorithm is, in fact, a PTAS for 1-MCIS on interval graphs. Let $\mathscr{L}$ be the solution of the local search algorithm. We aim to bound the size of an optimal solution $\mathscr{O}$ in terms of $|\mathscr{L}|$. To this end, we construct a bipartite planar conflict graph between the subsets of $\mathscr{L}$ and $\mathscr{O}$. Then, by applying a version of the planar separator theorem [8], we obtain the desired bounds. Mustafa and Ray [16] were the first to show the usefulness of local search to obtain a PTAS for the geometric hitting set problem. Here, we use an analysis that is similar to the one used by Chan and Har-Peled for the maximum independent set problem on pseudo-disks [5].

The Algorithm. Let $G = (V, E)$ be a vertex-colored interval graph with a k-coloring $\gamma : V \rightarrow \{1, \ldots, k\}$ for some $k \in \mathbb{N}$. Furthermore, set $n = |V|$ and $m = |E|$. For two subsets $L, L' \subseteq V$, we say L and L' are b-local neighbors if their differences are bounded by some $b \in \mathbb{R}$, i.e., $|L' \setminus L| \leq b$ and $|L \setminus L'| \leq b$. Let $N(L)$ be the set of all b-local neighbors of L. Observe, that for each subset $L \subseteq V$ we find $|N(L)| \leq O(\binom{n}{2b})$. We denote with $c(L)$ the number of different colors among the vertices in L. An independent set $L \subseteq V$ is b-*locally optimal* for the 1-MCIS problem on G if for each $L' \in N(L)$ we find that either L' is not an independent set or $c(L') \leq c(L)$.

Our algorithm first computes an initial solution L by executing the algorithm described in Sect. 4.1. In case $c(L) = k$ we return L as there is no chance to improve the solution. Assume $c(L) < k$. To turn L into a b-locally optimal solution for some fixed $b \in \mathbb{R}$ we perform a local search over the b-local neighbors of L. If a b-local neighbor L' of L is an independent set for G and $c(L') > c(L)$ we set L' as the current solution and restart the local search with L'. Once the local search terminates without finding such an L' or when $c(L) = k$ we return the current solution L.

Run-Time. Clearly, checking for a set $L \subseteq V$ if it is an independent set for G can be done in $O(m)$ time. Furthermore, we can compute $c(L)$ in time $O(|L|)$. Recall, that for $L \subseteq V$, the set $N(L)$ has at most $O(\binom{n}{2b})$ elements. It remains to bound the number of times we might swap the current solution in the second step of our algorithm. Let $L \subseteq V$ be the current solution in the second step, then we swap L for some $L' \in N(L)$ only if $c(L') > c(L)$. This happens at most k times as after k such improvements we would have found an optimal solution to the 1-MCIS problem on G. Consequently, the running time of the whole algorithm is bounded by $O(k \cdot n^{2b+1})$.

Analysis. Let $\mathscr{L}$ be a $\frac{1}{\epsilon^2}$-locally optimal solution for 1-MCIS on G obtained by our local search approach for a fixed constant ϵ and $\mathscr{O}$ is a fixed but arbitrary optimal solution for the same problem on G. To ease the following analysis, we assume each solution set contains for each color at most one vertex. Let $L = \mathscr{L} \setminus \mathscr{O}$ and $O = \mathscr{O} \setminus \mathscr{L}$. Next, we construct a graph $H = (V_H, E_H)$ containing a vertex $u \in V_H$ for every interval in $L \cup O$ and there is an edge between two vertices $u, v \in V_H$ (with $u \neq v$) such that, either the corresponding intervals of u and v intersect or $\gamma(u) = \gamma(v)$. We distinguish between these two types of edges: the former edges are called *interval-edges* and the latter are called *color-edges*.

Observation 1. *Let $H = (V_H, E_H)$ be a graph constructed as above, then a vertex $u \in V_H$ is incident to at most one color-edge.*

Lemma 4. *Let graph $H = (V_H, E_H)$ be constructed as above, H is bipartite and planar.*

Proof. Let $V_H = L \cup O$ be the set as used in the definition of H. Since L and O are both independent sets in G and contain for each color at most one vertex it follows that H is bipartite.

It remains to show that H is also planar. We are going to show that H cannot contain a $K_{3,3}$ as subgraph. For the sake of contradiction, assume H did in fact contain a $K_{3,3}$ and let $V' \subseteq V_H$ be its vertices and $E' \subseteq E_H$ its edges. To make the following arguments easier we fix an arbitrary interval representation $\mathcal{I} = \{I_1, \ldots, I_n\}$ of G. Let $I_L = \{I_\ell^1, I_\ell^2, I_\ell^3\}$ be the set of three intervals corresponding to vertices in $V' \cap L$ and $I_O = \{I_o^1, I_o^2, I_o^3\}$ the set of three intervals corresponding to vertices in $V' \cap O$. Without loss of generality we assume that the intervals are ordered by their left endpoints. Since the corresponding vertices are part of the independent sets $\mathscr{L}$ and $\mathscr{O}$ we get that I_ℓ^1 is completely to the left of I_ℓ^2 which is in turn completely to the left of I_ℓ^3. The same holds for the I_o^i with $i = 1, 2, 3$.

We differentiate two cases, namely if there are nesting intervals in $I_L \cup I_O$ or not. First, assume there are no nesting intervals in $I_L \cup I_O$. Among the edges in E' at most three are color-edges by Observation 1. Hence, the other edges must be interval-edges and consequently, every interval in I_O has to intersect at least two intervals in I_L and vice versa. Furthermore, since the intervals in I_L are pairwise non-intersecting, no interval in I_O can intersect all three intervals in I_L. Consequently, every interval in I_L has to intersect two intervals in I_O and every interval in I_O has to intersect two intervals in I_L. An impossibility since no nestings are allowed. Second, assume that there are two intervals nesting and let $u \in E_H$ be the vertex corresponding to the nested interval. But then, u has degree at most two in $H[V']$. This is since the intervals in I_L and I_O are pairwise non-intersecting and by Observation 1 at most one of the edges is a color-edge.   □

Since H is planar, we can follow a similar analysis as in [5] using the following lemma. For a set $U \subseteq (O \cup L)$, let $\Gamma(U) \subseteq V_H$ be the set of neighbors of vertices in U.

Lemma 5. *([8]) There are constants c_1, c_2 and c_3, such that for any planar graph $G = (V, E)$ with n vertices, and a parameter r, one can find a set of $X \subseteq V$*

of size at most $\frac{c_1 n}{\sqrt{r}}$, and a partition of $V \setminus X$ into $\frac{n}{r}$ sets $V_1,...,V_{\frac{n}{r}}$, satisfying: (i) $|V_i| \leq c_2 r$, (ii) $\Gamma(V_i) \cap V_j = \emptyset$, for $i \neq j$, and (iii) $|\Gamma(V_i) \cap X| \leq c_3 \sqrt{r}$.

Now, we apply Lemma 5 to H with $r = \frac{1}{\epsilon^2(c_2+c_3)}$. Let $X \subseteq V_H$ be the separator set in Lemma 5 and $V_1, \ldots, V_{\frac{n}{r}}$ be the resulting vertex partition. For each $i \in \{1, \ldots, \frac{n}{r}\}$, let $L_i = V_i \cap L$, $O_i = V_i \cap O$. The following two lemmas equip us with the necessary bounds to show the result.

Lemma 6. *Let O_i be obtained from H as defined above, then $|O_i| \leq |\Gamma(O_i)|$ for every $i = 1, \ldots, \frac{n}{r}$.*

Proof. We show $|O_i| \leq |\Gamma(O_i)|$ by contradiction. First, with $r = \frac{1}{\epsilon^2(c_2+c_3)}$ we obtain that $|O_i| \leq |V_i| \leq c_2 r = \frac{c_2}{\epsilon^2(c_2+c_3)} \leq \frac{1}{\epsilon^2}$, and $|\Gamma(O_i)| \leq |V_i| + |\Gamma(V_i) \cap X| \leq c_2 r + c_3 \sqrt{r} \leq (c_2 + c_3) r = \frac{1}{\epsilon^2}$. Now, $\Gamma(O_i)$ contains exactly the intervals of L, which have the same color as or intersect with intervals in O_i. Thus, the set $L' = (L \cup O_i) \setminus \Gamma(O_i)$ is an independent set and contains each color at most once. If $|O_i| > \Gamma(O_i)$, then $|L'| > |L|$. Moreover, the sizes of O_i and $\Gamma(O_i)$ are both bounded by $\frac{1}{\epsilon^2}$. A contradiction to our assumption that $\mathscr{L}$ is a $\frac{1}{\epsilon^2}$ optimal solution and L is a subset of $\mathscr{L}$. □

Lemma 7. *Let $H = (L \cup O, E_H)$ be the graph constructed as above from sets L and O, then $|L| \geq \frac{1-O(\epsilon)}{1+O(\epsilon)}|O|$.*

Proof. Let $X \subseteq V$ be the set guaranteed to exist by Lemma 5 and the O_i for $i = 1, \ldots, \frac{n}{r}$ be constructed as above, then

$$|O| \leq \sum_i |O_i| + |X|$$

$$\leq \sum_i \Gamma(O_i) + |X| \quad \text{(by Lemma 6)}$$

$$\leq \sum_i (|L_i| + |\Gamma(O_i) \cap X|) + |X|$$

$$\leq |L| + \sum_i |\Gamma(V_i) \cap X| + |X|$$

$$\leq |L| + c_3 \sqrt{r} \cdot \frac{|O| + |L|}{r} + c_1 \cdot \frac{|O| + |L|}{\sqrt{r}}$$

$$\leq |L| + (c_1 + c_3) \cdot \frac{|O| + |L|}{\sqrt{r}}$$

$$= |L| + (c_1 + c_3)\epsilon \sqrt{c_2 + c_3}(|O| + |L|)$$

$$= |L| + O(\epsilon)(|O| + |L|).$$

Now, rearranging the final inequality gives us $|L| \geq \frac{1-O(\epsilon)}{1+O(\epsilon)}|O|$ as desired. □

Using Lemma 7 we obtain the following theorem which implies that our algorithm is indeed a PTAS for 1-MCIS on interval graphs.

Theorem 6. *Let $G = (V, E)$ be a vertex-colored interval graph with a k-coloring $\gamma \colon V \to \{1, \dots, k\}$ for some $k \in \mathbb{N}$. For a sufficiently small parameter ϵ, each $\frac{1}{\epsilon^2}$-locally optimal solution $L \subseteq V$ to the 1-MCIS problem on G contains at least $\frac{1 - O(\epsilon)}{1 + O(\epsilon)} \cdot$ opt distinct colors, where opt is the number of colors in an optimal solution to the 1-MCIS problem on G.*

Proof. From Lemma 7, $|\mathscr{L}| = |L| + |\mathscr{L} \cap \mathscr{O}| \geq \frac{1 - O(\epsilon)}{1 + O(\epsilon)} |O| + |\mathscr{L} \cap \mathscr{O}| \geq \frac{1 - O(\epsilon)}{1 + O(\epsilon)} |\mathscr{O}|.$ □

5   Conclusions

In this paper, we have studied the f-Balanced Independent and Dominating set problem for interval graphs. We proved that these problems are NP-complete and obtained algorithmic results for the f-Balanced Independent Set problem. An interesting direction is to obtain algorithmic results for f-Balanced Independent Set problem for other geometric intersection graphs, e.g., rectangle intersection graphs, unit disk graphs etc. Our results may help to tackle these problems since algorithms for computing (maximum weighted) independent sets of geometric objects in the plane often use algorithms for interval graphs as subroutines. Another interesting problem is to design approximation or parameterized algorithm for the f-Balanced Dominating Set problem for interval graphs.

Acknowledgements. This work was supported by the Austrian Science Fund (FWF) under grant P31119.

References

1. Agarwal, P.K., Van Kreveld, M.J., Suri, S.: Label placement by maximum independent set in rectangles. Comput. Geom. Theory Appl. **11**(3–4), 209–218 (1998). https://doi.org/10.1016/S0925-7721(98)00028-5
2. Balas, E., Yu, C.S.: Finding a maximum clique in an arbitrary graph. SIAM J. Comput. **15**(4), 1054–1068 (1986). https://doi.org/10.1137/0215075
3. Banerjee, S., Bhore, S.: Algorithm and hardness results on liar's dominating set and k-tuple dominating set. In: Colbourn, C.J., Grossi, R., Pisanti, N. (eds.) IWOCA 2019. LNCS, vol. 11638, pp. 48–60. Springer, Cham (2019). https://doi.org/10.1007/978-3-030-25005-8_5
4. Been, K., Nöllenburg, M., Poon, S.H., Wolff, A.: Optimizing active ranges for consistent dynamic map labeling. Comput. Geome. Theory Appl. **43**(3), 312–328 (2010). https://doi.org/10.1016/j.comgeo.2009.03.006
5. Chan, T.M., Har-Peled, S.: Approximation algorithms for maximum independent set of pseudo-disks. In: Computational Geometry (SoCG 2009), pp. 333–340. ACM, New York (2009). https://doi.org/10.1145/1542362.1542420
6. Chang, G.J.: Algorithmic aspects of domination in graphs. In: Du, D.Z., Pardalos, P.M. (eds.) Handbook of Combinatorial Optimization, pp. 1811–1877. Springer, Boston (1998). https://doi.org/10.1007/978-1-4613-0303-9_28

7. Chellali, M., Favaron, O., Hansberg, A., Volkmann, L.: k-domination and k-independence in graphs: a survey. Graphs Comb. **28**(1), 1–55 (2012). https://doi.org/10.1007/s00373-011-1040-3
8. Federickson, G.N.: Fast algorithms for shortest paths in planar graphs, with applications. SIAM J. Comput. **16**(6), 1004–1022 (1987). https://doi.org/10.1137/0216064
9. Garnero, V., Sau, I., Thilikos, D.M.: A linear kernel for planar red-blue dominating set. Discrete Appl. Math. **217**, 536–547 (2017). https://doi.org/10.1016/j.dam.2016.09.045
10. Golumbic, M.C.: Algorithmic Graph Theory and Perfect Graphs. Elsevier, Amsterdam (2004)
11. Haunert, J.H., Hermes, T.: Labeling circular focus regions based on a tractable case of maximum weight independent set of rectangles. In: ACM SIGSPATIAL Workshop on Interacting with Maps (MapInteract 2014), pp. 15–21 (2014). https://doi.org/10.1145/2677068.2677069
12. Haynes, T.W., Hedetniemi, S., Slater, P.: Fundamentals of Domination in Graphs. Pure and Applied Mathematics, vol. 208. Dekker (1998)
13. Irving, R.W.: On approximating the minimum independent dominating set. Inf. Process. Lett. **37**(4), 197–200 (1991). https://doi.org/10.1016/0020-0190(91)90188-N
14. van Kreveld, M.J., Strijk, T., Wolff, A.: Point labeling with sliding labels. Comput. Geom. Theory Appl. **13**(1), 21–47 (1999). https://doi.org/10.1016/S0925-7721(99)00005-X
15. Lekkeikerker, C., Boland, J.: Representation of a finite graph by a set of intervals on the real line. Fundam. Math. **51**(1), 45–64 (1962). https://doi.org/10.4064/fm-51-1-45-64
16. Mustafa, N.H., Ray, S.: PTAS for geometric hitting set problems via local search. In: Computational Geometry (SoCG 2009), pp. 17–22. ACM, New York (2009). https://doi.org/10.1145/1542362.1542367
17. Okamoto, Y., Uno, T., Uehara, R.: Counting the number of independent sets in chordal graphs. J. Discrete Algorithms **6**(2), 229–242 (2008). https://doi.org/10.1016/j.jda.2006.07.006
18. Pardalos, P.M., Xue, J.: The maximum clique problem. J. Global Optim. **4**(3), 301–328 (1994). https://doi.org/10.1007/BF01098364
19. Tovey, C.A.: A simplified NP-complete satisfiability problem. Discrete Appl. Math. **8**(1), 85–89 (1984). https://doi.org/10.1016/0166-218X(84)90081-7
20. Van Bevern, R., Mnich, M., Niedermeier, R., Weller, M.: Interval scheduling and colorful independent sets. J. Sched. **18**(5), 449–469 (2015). https://doi.org/10.1007/s10951-014-0398-5
21. Wagner, F., Wolff, A.: A combinatorial framework for map labeling. In: Whitesides, S.H. (ed.) GD 1998. LNCS, vol. 1547, pp. 316–331. Springer, Heidelberg (1998). https://doi.org/10.1007/3-540-37623-2_24
22. Yoshinaka, R.: Higher-order matching in the linear lambda calculus in the absence of constants is NP-complete. In: Giesl, J. (ed.) RTA 2005. LNCS, vol. 3467, pp. 235–249. Springer, Heidelberg (2005). https://doi.org/10.1007/978-3-540-32033-3_18

Bike Assisted Evacuation on a Line

Khaled Jawhar and Evangelos Kranakis$^{(\boxtimes)}$

School of Computer Science, Carleton University, Ottawa, ON, Canada
kranakis@scs.carleton.ca

Abstract. Two hikers and a bike are initially placed at the origin of an infinite line. When walking, the hikers can keep a constant speed of 1, but when riding the bike they can reach a constant speed $v > 1$ (same for both hikers). The hikers are modelled as autonomous mobile robots with communication capabilities (either in the wireless or face-to-face model) while the bike is not autonomous in that it cannot move on its own but instead it must be picked up by a hiker. An exit is placed on the line at distance d from the origin; the distance and direction of the exit from the origin is unknown to the hikers. The hikers may either walk or ride the bike however only one hiker may ride the bike at a time. The goal of the hikers is to evacuate from the exit in the minimum time possible as measured by the time it takes the last hiker to exit.

We develop algorithms for this "bike assisted" evacuation of the two hikers from an unknown exit on a line and analyze their evacuation time. In the wireless model we present three algorithms: in the first the robots move in opposite direction with max speed, in the second with a specially selected "optimal" speed, and in the third the hiker imitates the biker. We also give three algorithms in the Face-to-Face model: in the first algorithm the hiker pursues the biker, in the second the hiker and the biker use zig-zag algorithms with specially chosen expansion factors, and the third algorithm establishes a sequence a specially constructed meeting points near the exit. In either case, the optimality of these algorithms depends on $v > 1$. We also discuss lower bounds.

Keywords and Phrases: Arrival time · Bike · Evacuation · Line · Robots · Search · Speed · Optimal trajectory

1 Introduction

Search is important in theoretical computer science and recent years have witnessed an explosive growth of research studies on search from the perspective of mobile agent computing. One of the reasons is because one finds countless natural applications in distributed systems for facilitating information exchange between communicating entities. However, there are also applications in numerous other computing areas such as data mining, web crawlers, monitoring and surveillance, just to mention a few.

E. Kranakis—Research supported in part by NSERC Discovery grant.

T. Bureš et al. (Eds.): SOFSEM 2021, LNCS 12607, pp. 104–118, 2021.
https://doi.org/10.1007/978-3-030-67731-2_8

Evacuation, which is the main theme of our present investigation, is related to search in that one is also interested in searching and exploring a domain in order to find a target. However evacuation usually involves many cooperating entities forming an ensemble or group all of whose members are searching simultaneously by exchanging information; and unlike search which typically involves only one agent, it is aiming to optimize the arrival time of the last entity in the ensemble.

Our study in this paper is based on a new paradigm concerning two hikers aided by a bike and searching for an unknown exit placed somewhere on an infinite line. More specifically, in the "bike assisted evacuation" problem, the hikers and the bike all start at the origin and want to evacuate from an exit placed at an unknown distance and direction (either left or right from the origin) on the infinite line. Evacuation means that eventually both robots must find the exit by reaching its exact location (not necessarily at the same time) on the infinite line. The quality of an evacuation algorithm is measured by the time it takes the second hiker to find the exit, which is referred to as evacuation time of the ensemble.

1.1 Model and Notation

To analyze the problem proposed, first we describe details concerning mobility and communication of the hikers and describe the role that the bike will play in improving the overall evacuation time.

Mobility and Trajectories. The infinite line is the search domain. It is bidirectional in that the hikers can move in either direction without this affecting their speeds. The hikers can stop at any time and wait as long as they wish, can walk with maximum speed 1 or may ride the bike with speed $v > 1$. An evacuation algorithm is a complete description of the trajectories traced by the two hikers either waiting, walking or riding the bike until they both find the exit. Throughout this paper we are interested in evacuation algorithms.

Sharing the Bike. An interesting feature of our problem is the distinction between the hikers and the bike. On the one hand, the hikers are autonomous mobile agents that can move around on their own with speed 1 and communicate with each other. On the other hand, the bike is not autonomous and cannot move and/or communicate on its own and thus plays only the role of assistant in the search. The hiker using the bike has an advantage in that it can move with speed $v > 1$ which is of course faster than its walking speed 1. However, in our model the bike is also a limited resource in that it can be used by only one hiker at a time. This creates an interesting trade off for the evacuation time. The hikers would want to ride the bike to find the exit earlier. However, if the bike is not shared the evacuation time may get worse as the hiker not using the bike may worsen the overall evacuation time. This also implies that the hiker riding the bike has an advantage in sharing the bike with the other hiker as this will ultimately improve the overall evacuation time.

Bike Switching. An important aspect in our algorithms will be "bike switching", by which we mean changing the rider of the bike. We will assume throughout the paper that bike switching between hikers is instantaneous and at no time cost. Note that the hikers may recognize the presence of the bike when they are at the same location as the bike. From now on, to facilitate our discussions we will refer to the hiker riding the bike as the *biker*, which may be either of the two hikers.

Communication. A designated point on the infinite line is the *exit* and can be recognized as such by any of the hikers when they are at the same location as the exit. The hikers may communicate throughout the execution of the algorithms. Two types of communication will be studied, namely wireless (also known as wifi) and face-to-face. In the former, the hikers can communicate instantaneously and at any distance, while in the latter only when they are at the same location and at the same time. The fact that a hiker is riding the bike does not diminish its ability to communicate. A typical communication exchange may involve, e.g., "exit is found", "bike released", "switch bike", etc. Note that the hikers are endowed with pedometers and have computing abilities so that they can deduce the location of the other hiker and/or the bike from relevant communications exchanged and/or the protocols they execute.

Notation. Throughout the paper we will be using R_1 and R_2 to denote the two hikers and B to denote the bike. The hikers are equipped with pedometers and are identical in all their capabilities (locomotion and communication) and the subscripts $i = 1, 2$ in R_i do not imply that the hikers have identifiers. The origin of the real line will be at the point $x = 0$ on the x-axis and this will also be the starting location of the hikers and the bike. The adversary may place the exit at either of the points $\pm d$, where $d > 0$ will denote the unknown distance of the exit from the origin. In addition, $v > 1$ will denote the speed that a biker can attain when riding the bike.

1.2   Related Work

The continuous infinite line is a widely-used search domain. It is in this particular domain that the first search problems in the literature were proposed in the seminal papers [3] and [4] with a focus on stochastic search models and their analysis. Influential research for deterministic search by a single robot in the infinite line was developed in the work of [1] by proving that searching for a target has competitive ratio equal to 9, and for randomized search on the star graph by [16].

Evacuation is a form of group search in which the robots need to cooperate so that they all find the exit, It arises as a natural problem on the infinite line for the case of robots with faults (crash and/or Byzantine). The two important papers are [13] for robots with crash faults and [12] for robots with Byzantine faults. The study of evacuation in distributed computing for a unit disk is also related and was initiated in the paper [9] for both the wireless and face-to-face models. The reader can find additional related work on the continuous search domain in the survey paper [11].

The addition of an immobile token to aid in the exploration has been considered in the context of the rendezvous problem on a ring [17]. An extension of this work to mobile tokens can be found in [8]. In both of these papers the token is passive and is merely being used as a marker for the presence of the most recent "visit" of another agent. Similarly, in [7] the authors consider searching for a non-adversarial, uncooperative agent, called bus, which is moving with constant speed along the perimeter of a cycle. A different related model was investigated in [14] in which during search a robot can encounter a point or a sequence of points enabling faster and faster movement and the main goal is to adopt the route which allows a robot to reach the destination as quickly as possible.

Two related papers are [6] and its followup journal version [2]. In the former paper the authors introduce evacuation on an infinite line in the F2F model for two robots having max speed 1 and prove that 9 is a tight bound for evacuation. In the followup paper [2] tight bounds are shown for two robots with different speeds in the F2F model. In their model the robots can vary their speed between the min and max value. However, unlike our model, the slower robot is never able to move at the speed of the faster robot. As a consequence in our model a "shared" bike has the effect of averaging the speeds and improving the overall evacuation time of the ensemble. The main idea considered in the present paper of bike assisted evacuation modelled as a passive agent that can enhance the robots' evacuation time has not been considered in the relevant literature on search and evacuation before.[1]

It is also worth mentioning a different line of research that has evolved in recent years, concerning bike sharing systems in complementing traditional public transportation to reduce traffic congestion and mitigate atmospheric pollution. As a consequence bike-sharing has grown explosively everywhere [21]. This has led to extensive technical literature on different aspects of the performance of bike based transportation systems. For example, [5] addresses uncertainty in resource availability, [18] considers bike utilization conflict, [19] studies system balance maintainance, [20] investigates the efficient operation of shared mobility systems, [22] studies balancing, and [23] proposes a spatio-temporal bicycle mobility model. Finally we mention the recent paper [10] which gives a polynomial time algorithm for the Bike Sharing problem that produces an arrival-time optimal schedule for bikers to travel across the interval.

1.3   Outline and Results of the Paper

Our main results in the Wireless model are presented in Sect. 2. We give three algorithms: in the first the robots move in opposite direction with max speed, in the second with a specially selected "optimal" speed, and in the third the hiker imitates the biker. Results on the Face-to-Face model are presented in

---

[1] The present study is revised and updated from the first author's MCS Thesis [15].

Table 1. Main algorithms presented in the paper in the WiFi (top three) and F2F (bottom three) models, the theorem where the analysis, and their corresponding evacuation time as a function of the bike's speed v, where $v > 1$.

Algorithm	Theorem	Evacuation time
1 (WiFi)	1	$\max\left\{2d + \frac{d}{v}, \frac{2d}{v} + \frac{d}{2} + \frac{d}{2v^2}\right\}$
2 (WiFi)	2	$\frac{3d + 3vd + d\sqrt{v^2 + 26v + 9}}{4v}$
3 (WiFi)	3	$\frac{9d}{v} + \frac{d}{2} - \frac{d}{2v^2}$
4 (F2F)	4	$\frac{9d}{v} + d - \frac{5d}{8v^2}$
5 (F2F)	5	$\frac{3dv^3 + 63dv^2 + 15dv - 9d}{2v^2(3v+1)}$
6 (F2F)	6	$3d - \frac{5v^2 - 12v - 1}{2v(v-1)}d + \frac{5v^2 - 12v - 1}{v(v-1)(3v-1)}d$ if $1 < v \le \frac{6+\sqrt{41}}{5}$
		$3d - \frac{5v^2 - 12v - 1}{2v(v-1)}d + \frac{4(5v^2 - 12v - 1)}{v(v-1)(3v-1)}d$ if $\frac{6+\sqrt{41}}{5} \le v$

Sect. 3. We give three algorithms: in the first algorithm the hiker pursues the biker, in the second the hiker and the biker use zig-zag algorithms with specially chosen expansion factors, and in the third the algorithm establishes a sequence of specially constructed meeting points near the exit. In either communication model we conclude that the optimal algorithm depends on the speed v of the bike which we also determine. Details of the results are in Table 1. We also establish lower bounds in Sect. 4. The competitive ratio of the algorithms can be given by dividing by $\frac{v+1}{2v}d$, where d is the distance of the exit from the origin (see Theorem 7).

2   Evacuation in the Wireless (WiFi) Model

In this section we provide our main algorithms in the wireless communication model. In this model the two hikers can communicate instantaneously at any distance. Three algorithms will be considered and analyzed their evacuation time depends on the maximum speed v of the biker.

2.1   Opposite Direction with Max Speed

In Algorithm 1, the hiker and the biker move in opposite directions with their maximum speed, assuming that the biker moves with speed v. The one which finds the exit first will communicate with the other to proceed to the exit. Moreover, if it is the biker that found the exit first it returns the bike to a suitable position and shares it with the hiker. Details of the algorithm are as follows.

Algorithm 1: (OppDirectionWithMaxSpeedWiFi)

The hiker and the biker move in opposite directions. The one that finds the exit first communicates it to the other;

if *the hiker found the exit first* **then**
 | the biker moves to the exit at full speed;
end
else if *the biker found the exit first* **then**
 | it returns and drops the bike off to an appropriately chosen position x
 | and shares the bike with the hiker;
end
Stop when they both arrive at the exit;

Theorem 1. *The evacuation time for Algorithm 1 in the WiFi model is at most* $2d + \frac{d}{v}$.

2.2 Opposite Direction with Optimal Speed

Unlike Algorithm 1 in which the hiker and biker use their maximum speed, in the next Algorithm 2 the biker will not use its maximum speed v. Instead it will move with a specially chosen speed u which is less than v. The hiker or the biker which finds the exit first will communicate with the other which will then move towards the exit with its maximum speed. It turns out that the modified algorithm performs better than the previous one and it is optimal up to a certain maximum speed v. Assuming that R_1 is the hiker and R_2 is the biker, the algorithm will be as follows.

Algorithm 2: (OppDirectionWithOptimalSpeedWiFi)

R_1 moves left with unit speed;
R_2 moves right with speed $u = \frac{1}{4}(-v - 1 + \sqrt{v^2 + 26v + 9})$;
if R_1 *reaches the exit* **then**
 | Inform R_2 about the location of the exit;
 | R_2 moves toward the exit with its maximum speed v;
end
else if R_2 *reaches the exit* **then**
 | Inform R_1 about the location of the exit;
 | Drop-off the bike at distance $\frac{d}{2} + \frac{d}{2u}$;
 | R_2 heads back toward the exit;
 | R_1 reverses the direction back to the exit then picks up the bike and
 | moves to the exit with maximum speed v;
end

Theorem 2. *The evacuation time for Algorithm 2 using the WiFi model is at most* $\frac{3d + 3vd + d\sqrt{v^2 + 26v + 9}}{4v}$.

2.3 Slower Imitates Faster

In the next Algorithm 3 the robots perform a "doubling zig-zag" strategy with different parameters. The biker is using a doubling strategy to search for the exit and moves a distance 2^k during the k-th iteration. The hiker is also using a doubling strategy but since it is moving with unit speed it will try to stay as close as possible to the biker. This can be achieved by having the hiker move a distance $\frac{2^k}{v}$ during the k-th iteration, since moving any further will cause the hiker to be farther away from the biker during the $(k+1)$-st iteration. Assuming that robot R_1 is the biker and robot R_2 is the hiker, the algorithm will be as follows.

Algorithm 3: (SlowerImitateFasterWiFi)

---

for $k \leftarrow 1$ **to** ∞ **do**

    if *k is odd (resp. even)* **then**

        R_1 moves right (resp. left) a distance 2^k unless the exit is found;

        R_2 moves right (resp. left) a distance $\frac{2^k}{v}$;

        if *exit is found by R_1* **then**

            Communicate with R_2;

            R_1 moves back $\frac{d}{2} - \frac{d}{2v}$ to leave the bike for R_2 and then returns to exit;

            R_2 continues toward the exit after picking up the bike left by R_1;

            Quit;

        end

        R_1 turns; then moves left (resp. right), returns to the origin;

        R_2 turns; then moves left (resp. right), returns to the origin;

    end

end

Theorem 3. *The evacuation time for Algorithm 3 using the WiFi model is at most* $\frac{9d}{v} + \frac{d}{2} - \frac{d}{2v^2}$.

Proof. (Theorem 3) In this algorithm the biker uses a doubling strategy with maximum speed v. The hiker will follow the biker but will move $\frac{2^k}{v}$ in each iteration instead of 2^k. The biker will reach the exit first then will communicate with the hiker to proceed to the exit. The biker will go back distance $\frac{d}{2} - \frac{d}{2v}$ to drop off the bike so that the hiker can pick it up on its way to the exit. We will justify why biker R_1 needs to move $\frac{d}{2} - \frac{d}{2v}$ after reaching the exit to leave the bike for hiker R_2.

After biker R_1 reaches the exit, there is no benefit to stay at the exit with the bike since hiker R_2 which is moving with unit speed can benefit from the bike to reach the exit faster. The key to find the distance x which is the distance between the exit and the point where the bike is dropped off is to have biker R_1, drop it off at a point such that when it goes back to the exit it will reach the exit at the same time as hiker R_2. If we consider that d is the distance from the origin to the exit and x is the distance from the exit to the point where biker R_1 drops off the bike, then we have $d - x + \frac{x}{v} = \frac{d}{v} + \frac{x}{v} + x$ which leads to $x = \frac{d}{2} - \frac{d}{2v}$. This will guarantee that when the biker drops off the bike at distance x, it will reach the exit at the same time as the hiker. Hence we guarantee that the bike is not kept unnecessarily with the robot which reaches the exit first.

Assume that the exit is found during the kth iteration, then $2^{k-2} < d \leq 2^k$. We can calculate the evacuation time as follows:

$$
\begin{aligned}
T &= \frac{2 \cdot 2^0}{v} + \frac{2 \cdot 2^1}{v} + \cdots + \frac{2 \cdot 2^{k-1}}{v} + d - x + \frac{x}{v} \\
&= \frac{2(2^k - 1)}{v} + d - x + \frac{x}{v} \\
&= \frac{2^{k+1}}{v} - \frac{2}{v} + d - \frac{d}{2} + \frac{d}{2v} + \frac{d}{2v} - \frac{d}{2v^2} \\
&= \frac{2^{k+1}}{v} - \frac{2}{v} + \frac{d}{2} + \frac{d}{v} - \frac{d}{2v^2} \\
&\leq 2^3 \cdot \frac{2^{k-2}}{v} - \frac{2}{v} + \frac{d}{2} + \frac{d}{v} - \frac{d}{2v^2} \\
&\leq \frac{8d}{v} - \frac{2}{v} + \frac{d}{2} + \frac{d}{v} - \frac{d}{2v^2} \\
&\leq \frac{9d}{v} + \frac{d}{2} - \frac{d}{2v^2} - \frac{2}{v} \\
&\leq \frac{9d}{v} + \frac{d}{2} - \frac{d}{2v^2}
\end{aligned}
$$

This completes the proof of Theorem 3.   □

Figure 1 depicts and compares the performance of the three algorithms presented for the WiFi model.

3 Evacuation in the Face-to-Face (F2F) Model

In this section we provide our main algorithms in the face-to-face communication model. Recall that in this model the hikers can exchange messages only if they occupy the same location at the same time.

3.1 Slower Pursues Faster

In the first Algorithm 4, we assume that the hiker will follow the biker. Since the biker is using a "doubling zig-zag" strategy, during any iteration, let us say the k-th one, the biker will reverse the direction after reaching 2^k and will meet the hiker at some point X_k. At the meeting point the hiker will reverse its direction. We notice from this that the hiker is following a deterministic strategy specified through a sequence of points $X_1, X_2, \ldots, X_k, \ldots$ (to be defined later), where each X_k represents the meeting point for the hiker and the biker during the k-th

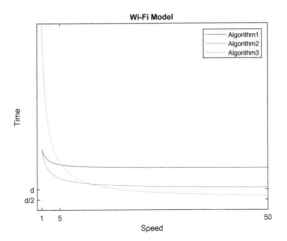

Fig. 1. Graph for the three algorithms using the wi-fi model. On high speed, the evacuation time for Algorithm 3 converges to $\frac{d}{2}$ versus $2d$ and d for Algorithm 1 and Algorithm 2, respectively

iteration. In other words, the biker will follow a doubling strategy with factor 2^k while the hiker will follow the sequence $X_1, X_2, \ldots, X_k, \ldots$ above. When the biker reaches the exit, it will go back a certain distance x, which will be determined later, to drop off the bike and then will return back walking toward the exit.

In the algorithm below we use the parameters $a := \frac{1-v}{1+v}$, $b := \frac{1}{1+v}$. Further, we assume that R_1 is the biker and R_2 is the hiker.

Algorithm 4: (SlowerPursueFasterF2F)

---

for $k \leftarrow 1$ **to** ∞ **do**
    if k *is odd(resp. even)* **then**
        R_1 moves right (resp. left) a distance 2^k unless the exit is found;
        R_2 moves right (resp. left) a distance $\frac{2b(2^k - a^k)}{2-a}$;
        if *the exit is found by R_1* **then**
            Move back distance x to drop off the bike for R_2 then switch direction toward the exit ;
            R_2 picks up bike and moves toward the exit;
            Quit;
        end
        R_1 turns; then moves left (resp. right), return to origin;
        R_2 turns; then moves left (resp. right), return to origin;
    end
end

Theorem 4. *The evacuation time for Algorithm 4 using the F2F model is at most $\frac{9d}{v} + d - \frac{5d}{8v^2}$.*

3.2   Slower Evacuation Close to Exit Without Aid

In the second Algorithm 5, the biker uses a "doubling zig-zag" strategy with its maximum speed v, while the hiker will try to be as close as possible to the biker. In order to achieve that, the hiker will use a doubling strategy as well but will use its own "expansion" factor. The factor will be determined based on the fact that both the hiker and the biker should meet at a specific point during each iteration. These meeting points will form a sequence whose k-th element during iteration k is taken to be equal to $\frac{2^{k+2}}{3v+1}$. During the last iteration, when the biker finds the exit, the hiker will eventually reach the meeting point and will not find the biker there. This will let it know that it should keep going toward the exit. Assuming that initially R_1 is the biker and R_2 is the hiker, the algorithm will be as follows:

Algorithm 5: (SlowerEvacuationCloseToExitWithoutAidF2F)

---

   for $k \leftarrow 1$ **to** ∞ **do**

      | **if** k *is odd (resp. even)* **then**

      | | R_1 moves right (resp. left) a distance 2^k unless the exit is found;

      | | R_2 moves right (resp. left) a distance $\frac{2^{k+2}}{3v+1}$;

      | | **if** $k=1$ **then**

      | | | R_2 waits for R_1;

      | | **end**

      | | **if** *exit is found by* R_1 **then**

      | | | Move back distance $\frac{d}{2} - \frac{d}{2v} + \frac{2^k(v-1)}{v(3v+1)}$ to drop off the bike for

      | | | R_2 then switch direction toward the exit;

      | | | R_2 picks up bike and moves toward exit;

      | | | Quit;

      | | **end**

      | | R_1turns; then moves left (resp. right), return to origin;

      | | R_2 turns; then moves left (resp. right), return to origin;

      | **end**

   end

Theorem 5. *The evacuation time for Algorithm 5 using the F2F model is at most* $\frac{3dv^3+63dv^2+15dv-9d}{2v^2(3v+1)}$.

Proof. (Theorem 5) The biker is using a doubling strategy and is moving 2^k during each iteration k. The hiker will use a doubling strategy as well and it will follow the biker. In order to keep the hiker as close as possible to the biker, we must find the sequence that the hiker should follow. We assume that both the hiker and the biker meet at a certain point X_k and that they are willing to meet at point X_{k+1} at the same time without waiting for one another, taking into consideration that $X_{k+1} = 2X_k$. The sequence can be calculated as follows:

$$X_k + X_{k+1} = \frac{1}{v}(X_k + 2^{k+1} + 2^{k+1} - X_{k+1})$$

$$\implies X_k + 2X_k = \frac{1}{v}(X_k + 2^{k+1} + 2^{k+1} - 2X_k)$$

$$\implies \frac{3v+1}{v}X_k = \frac{2^{k+2}}{v}$$

$$\implies X_k = \frac{2^{k+2}}{3v+1}$$

We have the sequence $\{X_0, X_1, \ldots, X_k\}$ given that $X_k = \frac{2^{k+2}}{3v+1}$ where $k \geq 1$. Each of the hiker and the biker will use its own doubling strategy. During each iteration, they will meet on both sides at specific points which are elements of the above sequence. During the kth iteration, when the biker reaches the exit, it will move back distance x to drop off the bike such that the hiker can pick it up and reach the exit at the same time as itself. The distance x can be calculated as follows: $\frac{d}{v} + \frac{1}{v} \cdot X_{k-1} + \frac{x}{v} + x = d + X_{k-1} - x + \frac{x}{v}$. Substituting X_{k-1} this becomes $\frac{d}{v} + \frac{2^{k+1}}{v(3v+1)} + \frac{x}{v} + x = d + \frac{2^{k+1}}{3v+1} - x + \frac{x}{v}$ Solving for x, the last equation yields $x = \frac{d}{2} - \frac{d}{2v} + \frac{2^k(v-1)}{v(3v+1)}$ Assuming that $2^{k-2} < d \leq 2^k$ and replacing x which was calculated above, the evacuation time T can be computed as follows:

$$T = \frac{1}{v}(2 \cdot 2^0 + 2 \cdot 2^1 + \cdots + 2 \cdot 2^{k-1}) + \frac{d}{v} + \frac{x}{v} + x$$

$$= \frac{2}{v}(2^k - 1) + \frac{d}{v} + \frac{x}{v} + x$$

$$= \frac{2^{k+1}}{v} - \frac{2}{v} + \frac{d}{v} + \frac{x}{v} + x$$

$$= \frac{2^{k+1}}{v} - \frac{2}{v} + \frac{d}{v} + \frac{d}{2v} - \frac{d}{2v^2} + \frac{2^k(v-1)}{v^2(3v+1)} + \frac{d}{2} - \frac{d}{2v} + \frac{2^k(v-1)}{v(3v+1)}$$

$$\leq \frac{16d}{2v} - \frac{2}{v} + \frac{d}{v} + \frac{d}{2} - \frac{d}{2v^2} + \frac{4d(v-1)}{v^2(3v+1)} + \frac{4d(v-1)}{v(3v+1)}$$

$$\leq \frac{18d}{2v} + \frac{d}{2} - \frac{d}{2v^2} + \frac{4d(v-1)}{v^2(3v+1)} + \frac{4d(v-1)}{v(3v+1)} - \frac{2}{v}$$

$$\leq \frac{54dv^2 + 18dv + 3dv^3 + dv^2 - 3dv - d + 8vd - 8d + 8dv^2 - 8dv}{2v^2(3v+1)} - \frac{2}{v}$$

$$\leq \frac{3dv^3 + 63dv^2 + 15dv - 9d}{2v^2(3v+1)} - \frac{2}{v}$$

$$\leq \frac{3dv^3 + 63dv^2 + 15dv - 9d}{2v^2(3v+1)}$$

This completes the proof of Theorem 5. $\qquad\qquad\qquad\qquad\qquad\qquad\qquad$ □

3.3   Nearest Meeting to Exit

In order to reduce the evacuation time, it is more suitable for the biker to search for the exit while the hiker follows a "doubling zig-zag" strategy that will keep it as close as possible to the biker and will expedite its travel time to the exit during the last iteration of the evacuation algorithm. In order to achieve that, the purpose of the next algorithm will be to find this deterministic doubling strategy that the hiker should follow. Assuming that R_1 is the biker and R_2 is the hiker, the algorithm will be as follows.

Algorithm 6: (EvacuatingWithBikeF2F)

---

for $k \leftarrow 1$ to ∞ do

  if k *is odd (resp. even)* then

    R_1 moves right (resp. left) a distance 2^k unless the exit is found;

    R_2 moves right (resp. left) a distance $\frac{2^{k+1}}{3v-1}$;

    if $k = 1$ then

       R_2 waits for R_1;

    if *exit is found by* R_1 then

      R_1 switches direction to inform R_2;

      R_1 drops off the bike at distance $\frac{x}{2}$;

      R_2 picks up the bike and continues to the exit;

      Quit;

    if *exit is found by* R_2 then

      R_2 waits till R_1 comes to the exit;

      Break;

    R_1 turns; then moves left (resp. right), return to origin;

    R_2 turns; then moves left (resp. right), return to origin;

Theorem 6. *The evacuation time for Algorithm 6 using the F2F model is upper bounded by*

$$3d - \frac{5v^2 - 12v - 1}{2v(v-1)}d + \frac{5v^2 - 12v - 1}{v(v-1)(3v-1)}d \ \text{if } 1 < v \leq \frac{6 + \sqrt{41}}{5}$$

$$3d - \frac{5v^2 - 12v - 1}{2v(v-1)}d + \frac{4(5v^2 - 12v - 1)}{v(v-1)(3v-1)}d \ \text{if } \frac{6 + \sqrt{41}}{5} \leq v$$

Figure 2 depicts and compares the performance of the three algorithms presented for the face-to-face model.

4   Lower Bounds

In this section we establish lower bounds on the competitive ratio in the WiFi and F2F models. Using bike sharing, first we prove a tight bound on the evacuation time when the robots know in which direction from the origin the exit is. Note

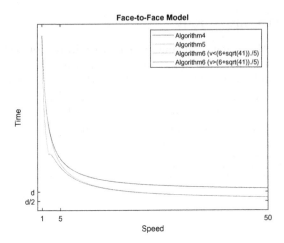

Fig. 2. Graph for the three algorithms using the face-to-face model. On high speed, the evacuation time for Algorithm 6 converges to $\frac{d}{2}$. The same is for Algorithm 5 versus d for Algorithm 4

that Theorem 7 can readily be used to compute the competitive ratio of the algorithms presented in Sects. 2 and 3.

Theorem 7. *If the direction of the exit is known to the robots then evacuation time is $\frac{v+1}{2v} \cdot d$. and this is optimal.*

Proof. (Theorem 7) Consider the algorithm whereby robot R_1 rides the bike for a distance x, releases the bike at x and continues by walking the remaining distance $d - x$, while robot R_2 walks for a distance x, picks up the bike at x and rides it for the remaining distance $d - x$. Note that robot R_1 reaches the exit at time $\frac{x}{v} + d - x$, while robot R_2 reaches the exit at time $x + \frac{d-x}{v}$. For the two robots to arrive at the same time it is required that $\frac{x}{v} + d - x = x + \frac{d-x}{v}$, which solves for $x = \frac{d}{2}$. Hence, the algorithm ensures that the two robots evacuate in time $\frac{1}{2} + \frac{1}{2v} = \frac{v+1}{2v}$.

Next we prove that the evacuation time above is optimal. If the robots never share the bike then the evacuation time will be d, which is also the arrival time of the slowest robot. So we may assume the robots share the bike. Let t_i be the termination time for robot R_i in an optimal algorithm. Let x_i be the distance that robot R_i rides the bike. Without loss of generality let R_1 be the robot that fetches the bike from the origin. Clearly, this takes time $\frac{x_1}{v} + d - x_1$. Therefore $t_1 \geq \frac{x_1}{v} + d - x_1$. Similarly, for robot R_2 we have that $t_2 \geq \frac{x_2}{v} + d - x_2$. It follows that

$$\max\{t_1, t_2\} \geq \frac{1}{2}\left(\frac{x_1}{v} + d - x_1 + \frac{x_2}{v} + d - x_2\right)$$
$$= d - \frac{x_1}{2} - \frac{x_2}{2} + \frac{x_1}{2v} + \frac{x_1}{2v}$$
$$= d - (x_1 + x_2)\frac{v-1}{2v}$$
$$\geq d - \frac{v-1}{2v} \cdot d = \frac{v+1}{2v} \cdot d,$$

where in the last inequality we used the fact that $x_1 + x_2 \leq d$, since by assumption only one robot can ride the bike at a time. This completes the proof of Theorem 7. $\qquad\square$

Using Theorem 7 we can prove the following result.

Theorem 8. *The evacuation time of any algorithm in either the WiFi or F2F model is bounded from below by* $\min\left\{\frac{d}{v} + \frac{v+1}{2v} \cdot d, d + \frac{v+1}{v} \cdot d\right\}$.

5   Conclusions

We proposed several evacuation algorithms in the wireless and face-to-face models. For each communication model we presented three algorithms which take advantage of the existence of the bike, a limited resource which can increase the search speed of the system of two robots. The resulting trajectories of the robots are specially designed so as to share the bike and ultimately reduce the overall evacuation time. We also discussed lower bounds.

Several interesting open problems remain in the context of bike assisted evacuation on the infinite line. For two robots, one could consider the problem when the speed of the bike depends on the hiker riding it. The case of multiple hikers and multiple bikes (not necessarily the same number) has never been investigated before. Additionally, one could also consider the case of faulty robots (crash or Byzantine). It would also be interesting to investigate other search domains such as stars and cycles or robots with reduced and/or enhanced capabilities.

References

1. Baeza Yates, R., Culberson, J., Rawlins, G.: Searching in the plane. Inf. Comput. **106**(2), 234–252 (1993)
2. Bampas, E., et al.: Linear search by a pair of distinct-speed robots. Algorithmica **81**(1), 317–342 (2019)
3. Beck, A.: On the linear search problem. Israel J. Math. **2**(4), 221–228 (1964)
4. Bellman, R.: An optimal search. SIAM Rev. **5**(3), 274 (1963)
5. Chen, B., Pinelli, F., Sinn, M., Botea, A., Calabrese, F.: Uncertainty in urban mobility: predicting waiting times for shared bicycles and parking lots. In: 16th International IEEE Conference on Intelligent Transportation Systems (ITSC 2013), pp. 53–58. IEEE (2013)
6. Chrobak, M., Gąsieniec, L., Gorry, T., Martin, R.: Group search on the line. In: Italiano, G.F., Margaria-Steffen, T., Pokorný, J., Quisquater, J.-J., Wattenhofer, R. (eds.) SOFSEM 2015. LNCS, vol. 8939, pp. 164–176. Springer, Heidelberg (2015). https://doi.org/10.1007/978-3-662-46078-8_14

7. Czyzowicz, J., Dobrev, S., Godon, M., Kranakis, E., Sakai, T., Urrutia, J.: Searching for a non-adversarial, uncooperative agent on a cycle. Theor. Comput. Sci. **806**, 531–542 (2020). (also Algosensors 2017)
8. Czyzowicz, J., Dobrev, S., Kranakis, E., Krizanc, D.: The power of tokens: rendezvous and symmetry detection for two mobile agents in a ring. In: Geffert, V., Karhumäki, J., Bertoni, A., Preneel, B., Návrat, P., Bieliková, M. (eds.) SOFSEM 2008. LNCS, vol. 4910, pp. 234–246. Springer, Heidelberg (2008). https://doi.org/10.1007/978-3-540-77566-9_20
9. Czyzowicz, J., Gąsieniec, L., Gorry, T., Kranakis, E., Martin, R., Pajak, D.: Evacuating robots via unknown exit in a disk. In: Kuhn, F. (ed.) DISC 2014. LNCS, vol. 8784, pp. 122–136. Springer, Heidelberg (2014). https://doi.org/10.1007/978-3-662-45174-8_9
10. Czyzowicz, J., et al.: The bike sharing problem (2020). https://arxiv.org/abs/2006.13241
11. Czyzowicz, J., Georgiou, K., Kranakis, E.: Group search and evacuation. In: Flocchini, P., Prencipe, G., Santoro, N. (eds.) Distributed Computing by Mobile Entities, Current Research in Moving and Computing, vol. 11340, pp. 335–370. Springer, Cham (2019). https://doi.org/10.1007/978-3-030-11072-7_14
12. Czyzowicz, J., et al.: Search on a line by byzantine robots. In: ISAAC, pp. 27:1–27:12 (2016)
13. Czyzowicz, J., Kranakis, E., Krizanc, D., Narayanan, L., Opatrny, J.: Search on a line with faulty robots. In: PODC, pp. 405–414. ACM (2016)
14. Gąsieniec, L., Kijima, S., Min, J.: Searching with increasing speeds. In: Izumi, T., Kuznetsov, P. (eds.) SSS 2018. LNCS, vol. 11201, pp. 126–138. Springer, Cham (2018). https://doi.org/10.1007/978-3-030-03232-6_9
15. Jawhar, K.: Bike assisted linear search and evacuation. MCS thesis, Carleton University, School of Computer Science (2020)
16. Kao, M.-Y., Reif, J.H., Tate, S.R.: Searching in an unknown environment: an optimal randomized algorithm for the cow-path problem. Inf. Comput. **131**(1), 63–79 (1996)
17. Kranakis, E., Santoro, N., Sawchuk, C., Krizanc, D.: Mobile agent rendezvous in a ring. In: Proceedings of 23rd International Conference on Distributed Computing Systems, pp. 592–599. IEEE (2003)
18. Li, Z., Zhang, J., Gan, J., Lu, P., Gao, Z., Kong, W.: Large-scale trip planning for bike-sharing systems. Pervasive Mob. Comput. **54**, 16–28 (2019)
19. O'Mahony, E., Shmoys, D.B.: Data analysis and optimization for (citi) bike sharing. In: Twenty-Ninth AAAI Conference on Artificial Intelligence (2015)
20. Pfrommer, J., Warrington, J., Schildbach, G., Morari, M.: Dynamic vehicle redistribution and online price incentives in shared mobility systems. IEEE Trans. Intell. Transp. Syst. **15**(4), 1567–1578 (2014)
21. Shaheen, S.A., Guzman, S., Zhang, H.: Bikesharing in Europe, the Americas, and Asia: past, present, and future. Transp. Res. Rec. **2143**(1), 159–167 (2010)
22. Singla, A., Santoni, M., Bartók, G., Mukerji, P., Meenen, M., Krause, A.: Incentivizing users for balancing bike sharing systems. In: Twenty-Ninth AAAI Conference on Artificial Intelligence (2015)
23. Yang, Z., Hu, J., Shu, Y., Cheng, P., Chen, J., Moscibroda, T.: Mobility modeling and prediction in bike-sharing systems. In: Proceedings of the 14th Annual International Conference on Mobile Systems, Applications, and Services, pp. 165–178 (2016)

Blocksequences of k-local Words

Pamela Fleischmann[1(✉)], Lukas Haschke[1], Florin Manea[2], Dirk Nowotka[1],
Cedric Tsatia Tsida[1], and Judith Wiedenbeck[1]

[1] Kiel University, Kiel, Germany
{fpa,dn}@informatik.uni-kiel.de,
{stu105615,stu111120,stu107029}@mail.uni-kiel.de
[2] University of Göttingen, Göttingen, Germany
florin.manea@informatik.uni-goettingen.de

Abstract. The locality of words is a relatively young structural complexity measure, introduced by Day et al. in 2017 in order to define classes of patterns with variables which can be matched in polynomial time. The main tool used to compute the locality of a word is called marking sequence: an ordering of the distinct letters occurring in the respective order. Once a marking sequence is defined, the letters of the word are marked in steps: in the ith marking step, all occurrences of the ith letter of the marking sequence are marked. As such, after each marking step, the word can be seen as a sequence of blocks of marked letters separated by blocks of non-marked letters. By keeping track of the evolution of the marked blocks of the word through the marking defined by a marking sequence, one defines the blocksequence of the respective marking sequence. We first show that the words sharing the same blocksequence are only loosely connected, so we consider the stronger notion of extended blocksequence, which stores additional information on the form of each single marked block. In this context, we present a series of combinatorial results for words sharing the extended blocksequence.

1 Introduction

The *locality* of words (also called strings) is a structural-complexity measure which has been introduced in [4]. To define the locality of a word several notions are important. Firstly, a *marking sequence* for that word is an ordering of the symbols occurring in it. For each *marking sequence*, we can mark the letters of the word in steps, as follows: in the ith marking step, all occurrences of the ith letter of the marking sequence are marked. As such, after each marking step, the word can be seen as a sequence of blocks of marked letters separated by blocks of non-marked letters. Clearly, after each new marking step of a marking sequence, more symbols become marked, so the marked blocks grow and they may unite. Observing the evolution of the marked blocks leads to the definition of *the marking number* of the respective marking sequence: the maximal number of marked blocks which occur in the word after a marking step. *The locality number of a word* (for short, *locality*) is defined as the minimal marking number over all marking sequences for that word.

© Springer Nature Switzerland AG 2021
T. Bureš et al. (Eds.): SOFSEM 2021, LNCS 12607, pp. 119–134, 2021.
https://doi.org/10.1007/978-3-030-67731-2_9

More precisely, a word is k-local if there exists a marking sequence for the respective word such that after each step of the sequence there are at most k contiguous blocks of marked symbols in the word. The *locality number* (or, for short, locality) of a word is the smallest k for which that word is k-local, or, in other words, the minimum marking number over all marking sequences. For instance, if banana is marked according to the marking sequence (b, n, a) the largest number of marked blocks we get (i.e., the marking number of the sequence) is 3. Thus, banana is 3-local. However, if we take the marking sequence (n, a, b) the largest number of blocks we get is 2 - and we cannot do better. Thus, banana has the locality number 2. The locality number of a word describes how many separated (or isolated) marked regions must at least be maintained in exploring the word w.r.t. possible marking sequences; thus, it can be interpreted as a structural complexity measure (e.g., by associating some cost per marked region).

The original motivation for the introduction of locality in [4] is the fact that patterns with variables which have a low locality can be efficiently matched. A *pattern* is a word that consists of *constant letters* (e.g., a, b, c) and *variables* (e.g., $x_1, x_2, x_3, \ldots$). A pattern is mapped to a word by uniformly replacing the variables by words with constant letters. For example, $x_1 x_1 a x_2 x_2$ can be mapped to acacacc, by replacing x_1 by ac and x_2 by c. If a pattern α can be mapped to the word w, we say that α matches w. Deciding whether a given pattern matches a given word is an important problem with applications in many areas: combinatorics on words (word equations [15, Chapters 12 and 13], unavoidable patterns [15, Chapter 3]), formal-language theory (pattern languages [1]), and learning theory (inductive inference [1], PAC-learning [14]), database theory (extended conjunctive regular path queries [2]), programming languages (the processing of extended regular expressions with backreferences [11, 12], used in programming languages like Perl, Java, Python, etc.). In general, the *matching problem* is NP-complete [1]. This is especially bad for some computational tasks on patterns which implicitly solve the matching problem: such problems become, inherently, intractable. One such example is the task of finding descriptive patterns for a set of strings [7], which is useful in the context of learning theory.

A thorough analysis of the complexity of the matching problem for patterns of variables was performed [6, 8, 9, 16] and some classes of patterns admitting polynomial time matching, usually defined by restricting structural parameters, were identified. In [4] it was shown that k-local patterns can be matched in polynomial time when k is a constant, and, based on the results of [7], that descriptive k-local patterns can be efficiently computed for a given set of strings.

Thus, the study of the locality of words and patterns seems interesting and well-motivated and the most natural problem one could identify in this area was computing the locality number of a word. The problem Loc of deciding whether the locality of a given word is upper bounded by a given number $k \in \mathbb{N}$ was shown to be NP-complete in [3]. More interestingly, in the same work, strong (and surprising) relations between the string-decision problem Loc and the graph decision problems Cutwidth (asking to decide whether the cutwidth of a graph is upper bounded by a given number) and Pathwidth (asking to decide whether the pathwidth of a graph is upper bounded by a given number) were established. These connections explained, on the one hand, all kinds of algorithmic difficulties arising in solving Loc, and, on the other hand, lead to a state-of-the-art approximation algorithm for computing the cutwidth of graphs.

Our Contribution. We extend the study of the locality of words by taking a combinatorics-on-words-centric perspective. As explained before, while marking a word with respect to a marking sequence, we obtain after each step a set of factors of the word which consist of marked letters and are bounded by unmarked letters. This set of factors provides a snapshot of the word after each marking step. In our setting the number of marked blocks from each snapshot is important. We will call the sequence of numbers of blocks occurring in these snapshots, in the order in which they occur during the marking sequence, the *blocksequence* associated to the marking sequence. Looking again at the word banana and the marking sequence $(\mathsf{b}, \mathsf{n}, \mathsf{a})$ we obtain the corresponding blocksequence $(1, 3, 1)$.

Now, if we assume that we are only given the sequence $(1, 3, 1)$, we can trivially tell that this is a blocksequence of a word over a three-letter alphabet. Taking into account that the letters may be renamed we can assume that this three-letter alphabet consists of the letters a, b, and c, and the marking sequence defining the considered blocksequence is $\sigma_\Sigma = (\mathsf{a}, \mathsf{b}, \mathsf{c})$. In other words, we can restrict ourselves to a canonical marking sequence, and our reasoning will be true up to the renaming of all letters. This leads to the question of finding the set of words having the given blocksequence when marked according to σ_Σ and understanding what these words have in common from a combinatorial point of view, e.g., w.r.t. to their locality number. As we have seen the locality of banana is 2 and not 3, so is this a characteristic of all words sharing the blocksequence $(1, 3, 1)$? We show that the blocksequence alone does not provide much information, and thus we enrich the blocksequence with more combinatorial information: we do not only store the number of marked blocks in each step, but also the *kind* of each occurrence of a letter has in the respective step, e.g., neighbour, join, or singleton. In this setting we are able to define a normal form for each class of words having the same extended blocksequence. We show how to obtain the normal form for a given word by defining three rules and we compare the locality of the normal form with the locality of the words from the same class. We finally present, in the case of words over three-letters alphabets, how the optimal marking sequence (the one determining the locality of the word) can be obtained by examining the extended block sequence.

For a full version of this work including all proofs, see [10].

2   Preliminaries and Initial Results

§ **Basic Definitions.** Let $\mathbb{N}$ be the set of natural numbers and $\mathbb{N}_0 = \mathbb{N} \cup \{0\}$. Let $[n]$ denote the set $\{1, \ldots, n\}$ and $[n]_0 = [n] \cup \{0\}$ for an $n \in \mathbb{N}$.

An alphabet is a finite set $\Sigma = \{\mathsf{a}_1, \ldots, \mathsf{a}_\ell\}$ of $\ell \in \mathbb{N}$ symbols, called *letters*. The alphabet is called *ordered* if there exists a total ordering $<$ on the letters.

We assume here Σ to be ordered with $a_i < a_{i+1}$ for all $i \in [\ell - 1]$. Σ^* denotes the set of all finite words over Σ, i.e., the free monoid over Σ. The *empty word* is denoted by ε and $\Sigma^+ = \Sigma^* \backslash \{\varepsilon\}$. The length of a word w is denoted by $|w|$. Define $\Sigma^k := \{w \in \Sigma^* \mid |w| = k\}$ for a $k \in \mathbb{N}$. The number of occurrences of a letter $a \in \Sigma$ in a word $w \in \Sigma^*$ is denoted by $|w|_a$. Define the set of letters occurring in $w \in \Sigma^*$ by $\mathrm{alph}(w) = \{a \in \Sigma \mid |w|_a > 0\}$. The ith letter of a word w is given by $w[i]$ for $i \in [|w|]$. For a given word $w \in \Sigma^n$ the *reversal* of w is defined by $w^R = w[n]w[n-1]\cdots w[2]w[1]$. The powers of $w \in \Sigma^*$ are defined recursively by $w^0 = \varepsilon$, $w^n = ww^{n-1}$ for $n \in \mathbb{N}$. A word $u \in \Sigma^*$ is a *factor* of $w \in \Sigma^*$, if $w = xuy$ holds for some words $x, y \in \Sigma^*$. Moreover, u is a *prefix* (resp., *suffix*) of w if $x = \varepsilon$ (resp., $y = \varepsilon$) holds. The factor $w[i]w[i+1]\cdots w[j]$ of w is denoted by $w[i..j]$, for $1 \le i \le j \le |w|$. Given a property $P : \Sigma \to \{0,1\}$, a factor u is a *P-block* of a word $w = xuy$ if $P(u[i]) = 1$ for all $i \in [|u|]$ and $P(x[|x|]) = P(y[1]) = 0$ (if x or y are empty the constraint does not have to be fulfilled). For the property P_a defined by $P_a(x) = 1$ iff $x = a$ for $x \in \Sigma$, the word $abaaabaabb$ has 3 P_a-blocks (or short three a-blocks).

In the following, we give the main definitions on k-locality, following [4].

Definition 1. *Let $\overline{\Sigma} = \{\overline{x} \mid x \in \Sigma\}$ be the set of* marked letters. *For a word $w \in \Sigma^*$, a* marking sequence *σ of the letters occurring in w, is an enumeration $(x_1, x_2, \ldots, x_{|\mathrm{alph}(w)|})$ of $\mathrm{alph}(w)$. Let $a_i \le_\sigma a_j$ if a_i occurs before a_j in σ, for $i, j \in [|\mathrm{alph}(w)|]$. The enumeration obeying the total order of the alphabet is called the* canonical marking sequence *σ_Σ. A letter x_i is called* marked at stage *$k \in \mathbb{N}$ if $i \le k$. Moreover, we define w_k, the marked version of w at stage k, as the word obtained from w by replacing all x_i with $i \le k$ by $\overline{x_i}$. A factor of w_k is a* marked block *if the defining property of the block is that it contains only elements from $\overline{\Sigma}$. The* locality *of a word w w.r.t. a marking sequence σ (loc$_\sigma(w)$) is the maximal number of marked blocks that occurred during the marking process.*

In the context of Definition 1, $w_{|\mathrm{alph}(w)|}$ is always completely marked. Using the idea of a marking sequence, we define the k-locality of a word.

Definition 2. *A word $w \in \Sigma^*$ is k-local for $k \in \mathbb{N}_0$ if there exists a marking sequence $(x_1, \ldots, x_{|\mathrm{alph}(w)|})$ of $\mathrm{alph}(w)$ such that, for all $i \le |\mathrm{alph}(w)|$, we have that w_i at stage i, has at most k marked blocks. A word is called* strictly k-local *if it is k-local but not $(k-1)$-local.*

Consider the word $banana \in \{a, b, n\}^*$. The marking sequence (a, b, n) leads to the sequence $w_1 = b\overline{a}n\overline{a}n\overline{a}$ (3 marked blocks), $w_2 = \overline{b}\overline{a}n\overline{a}n\overline{a}$ (3 marked blocks), and $w_3 = \overline{banana}$ (1 marked block), i.e., $banana$ is 3-local. In fact, it is strictly 2-local witnessed by the marking sequence (n, a, b) (it is not 1-local, since this would imply to start with marking b and either marking afterwards a or n leads to more than one marked block). As a second example consider the word a^3b^4. This word is 1-local since for both marking sequences (a, b) and (b, a) the blocks of letters are marked in one step. This motivates to consider the notion of the print of a word - or condensed word or simplified block letters - introduced in [3,17], and [5], respectively.

Definition 3. *For* $w = x_1^{k_1} x_2^{k_2} \ldots x_m^{k_m} \in \Sigma^*$ *with* $k_i, m \in \mathbb{N}$, $i \in [m]$, *and* $x_j \neq x_{j+1}$ *for* $j \in [m-1]$, *the* print (condensed form) *of* w *is defined by* $x_1 \ldots x_m$. *A word is called* condensed, *if it is its own print.*

§ **Initial Results.** Since in our setting the multiplicity of single letters does not affect the results (all these letters form a single marked block), we restrict the setting to condensed words implicitly, i.e., each $w \in \Sigma^*$ is implicitly meant to be condensed. Now we define the notion of the blocksequence that captures the number of marked blocks during the marking process. Moreover, we assume $\mathrm{alph}(w) = \Sigma$.

Definition 4. *Let* $w \in \Sigma^*$ *and* $\sigma = (y_1, \ldots, y_\ell)$ *be a marking sequence. The* blocksequence $\beta_\sigma(w)$ *is the sequence* $(b_1, \ldots, b_\ell)$ *over* $\mathbb{N}$ *such that in* σ's i^{th} *stage on marking* w, b_i *blocks are marked, for all* $i \in [\ell]$.

Coming back to **banana**, the marking sequence $(\mathsf{a}, \mathsf{b}, \mathsf{n})$ leads to the blocksequence $(3, 3, 1)$ and the marking sequence $(\mathsf{n}, \mathsf{a}, \mathsf{b})$ to $(2, 1, 1)$. Since $|w|_{|\mathrm{alph}(w)|}$ is one marked block, the last position in a blocksequence has to be 1 and moreover the first position is exactly $|w|_{y_1}$. Changing the perspective, n-tuples (with the last position being 1) can be seen as a blocksequence w.r.t. the canonical marking sequence given by the alphabet and its order. This point of view is inspired by the idea to group words with the same blocksequence in order to deduce information about their locality.

Definition 5. *For a given* ℓ-*tuple* $\beta = (b_1, \ldots, b_{\ell-1}, 1)$ *define the set of words that give exactly* β *on marking with* σ_Σ *by* $\mathfrak{W}_\beta = \{w \in \Sigma^* | \beta_{\sigma_\Sigma}(w) = \beta\}$.

First, we prove that the class $\mathfrak{W}_\beta$ is not empty for all $\beta = (b_1, \ldots, b_{\ell-1}, 1)$. In particular, there exists a natural number n_β for β such that: there is a word in $\mathfrak{W}_\beta$ of length n_β, and for each $n > n_\beta$ there exists at least a word w_n (not necessarily condensed) of length n with $\beta_{\sigma_\Sigma}(w_n) = \beta$, and for all $n < n_\beta$ there does not exist any word of length n having β as its blocksequence, considering the canonical marking sequence. This tight lower bound for the length results from the sum of differences two consecutive elements from β have and the hereby resulting possible positioning of the letters.

Theorem 6. *For all* $\beta = (b_1, \ldots, b_{\ell-1}, 1) \in \mathbb{N}^\ell$ *there exists* $n_\beta \in \mathbb{N}$ *such that for all* $n \geq n_\beta$ *we have that there exists at least a word* w_n *(condensed or not condensed) with* $|w_n| = n$ *and* $\beta_{\sigma_\Sigma}(w_n) = \beta$, *and for all* $m < n_\beta$ *we have that there is no word of length* m *having* β *as its blocksequence, considering the canonical marking sequence.*

In fact, one can characterise precisely the set $\Sigma^{n_\beta} \cap \mathfrak{W}_\beta$, as well as the condensed words from $\mathfrak{W}_\beta$.

A blocksequence induced by $\sigma_\Sigma = (\mathsf{a}, \mathsf{b}, \mathsf{c})$ does not determine a word uniquely witnessed by **abcba** and **abca** for the blocksequence $(2, 2, 1)$. In fact, it does not even determine a print of the words sharing the same blocksequence uniquely. Indeed, for $\beta = (3, 6, 1)$ the words $w = $ **acbcbcacbca**,

$w' = \mathtt{ababacbcbcbcbcb}$, and $w'' = \mathtt{acbcacbcacb}$ are in $\mathfrak{W}_\beta$. Moreover, when considering a different marking sequence, these words have different blocksequences. For instance, $(\mathtt{c}, \mathtt{a}, \mathtt{b})$ leads to the blocksequences $(5, 4, 1), (5, 7, 1)$, and $(5, 3, 1)$, respectively. Thus, it is to be expected that even if some words have the same blocksequence w.r.t. a marking sequence, they may have different blocksequences w.r.t. other marking sequences, and, consequently, different localities. The main difference in the above words are the different roles the letters have: in w the occurrences of $\mathtt{b}$ are between two occurrences of $\mathtt{a}$ but $\mathtt{b}$ does not join the $\mathtt{a}$-blocks whereas in w' all *gaps* between the $\mathtt{a}$s are closed by join occurrences of $\mathtt{b}$; in w'' in each *gap* between $\mathtt{a}$s is only one occurrence of $\mathtt{b}$. This observation leads to the following differentiation of occurrences of letters: when the letter is marked it may occur adjacent to exactly one marked block (neighbouring), it may join two blocks (joining), or it may not be adjacent to any marked block (singleton). Notice that different occurrences of letters may have different roles.

Definition 7. *Let $\sigma = (y_1, \ldots, y_\ell)$ be a marking sequence of $w \in \Sigma^*$. At stage $i \in [\ell]$, an occurrence of y_i is said to be a*

- *neighbour if there exist $u_1 \in \overline{\Sigma}^+$, $u_2 \in \Sigma^+$ and $v_1, v_2 \in (\Sigma \cup \overline{\Sigma})^*$ with $w_i = v_1 u_1 y_i u_2 v_2$, $w_i = v_1 u_2 y_i u_1 v_2$, $w_i = v_1 u_1 y_i$, or $w_i = y_i u_1 v_1$,*
- *join if there exist $u_1, u_2 \in \overline{\Sigma}^+$ and $v_1, v_2 \in (\Sigma \cup \overline{\Sigma})^*$ with $w_i = v_1 u_1 y_i u_2 v_2$,*
- *singleton if there exist $u_1, u_2 \in \Sigma^+$, and $v_1, v_2 \in (\Sigma \cup \overline{\Sigma})^*$ with $w_i = v_1 u_1 y_i u_2 v_2$, $w_i = v_1 u_1 y_i$, or $w_i = y_i u_2 v_2$.*

A marking sequence σ is called neighbourless *for a word $w \in \Sigma^*$ if in any stage while marking w with σ no neighbour occurrences exist. A word $w \in \Sigma^*$ is called* neighbourless *if there exists a neighbourless marking sequence σ for w.*

Another observation of w' and w'' leads to different forms of singletons: the ones occurring between previously marked letters and the ones occurring outside.

Definition 8. *Let $\sigma = (y_1, \ldots, y_\ell)$ be a marking sequence of $w \in \Sigma^*$. The* core *of w at stage $i \in [\ell] \setminus \{1\}$ is defined as $u \in \mathrm{Fact}(w_i)$ with $w_i = v_1 u v_2$, $\mathrm{alph}(v_1), \mathrm{alph}(v_2) \subseteq \{y_i, \ldots, y_\ell\}$, and $u[1], u[|u|] \in \{y_1, \ldots, y_{i-1}\}$. A singleton occurrence at stage $i \in [\ell]$ of a letter $y_i \in \Sigma$ is called* separating *(or a* separator*) if it is of the form $v_1 u_1 z_1 y_i z_2 u_2 v_2$ with $u_1, u_2 \in \overline{\Sigma}^+$, $v_1, v_2 \in (\Sigma \cup \overline{\Sigma})^*$, and $z_1, z_2 \in \Sigma^+$. A singleton occurrence that is not a separator is called a* satellite*.*

Remark 9. Separators are within the core whereas satellites are to the left or to the right of the core. For convenience we introduce for a given marking sequence $\sigma = (y_1, \ldots, y_\ell)$ of a word $w \in \Sigma^*$ the notations $\overrightarrow{y_i}$ and $\overleftarrow{y_i}$ as arbitrary elements from the sets $\{y_i x \mid x \in \{y_{i+1}, \ldots, y_\ell\}^+\}$ and $\{x y_i \mid x \in \{y_{i+1}, \ldots, y_\ell\}^+\}$ respectively, for all $i \in [\ell]$, if $\overrightarrow{y_i}$ ($\overleftarrow{y_i}$ resp.) is a factor $w[j_1 \ldots j_2]$ of w and additionally with $w[j_2 + 1] \leq_\sigma y_i$ ($w[j_1 - 1] \leq_\sigma y_i$ resp.) if $\overrightarrow{y_i}$ ($\overleftarrow{y_i}$ resp.) is not a suffix (prefix resp.) of w. By $\overrightarrow{y_i}^m$ we denote a word containing of $m \in \mathbb{N}_0$ possibly different occurrences of $\overrightarrow{y_i}$ (analogously for $\overleftarrow{y_i}$), e.g., $\mathtt{bcdbc}$ could be abbreviated by $\overrightarrow{\mathtt{b}}^2$. With this notation, the palindromic structure of k-local words already mentioned in [4] becomes clearer in this context: if c_i is the core at stage i, the word is of the form $\overrightarrow{y_\ell}^{s_\ell} \ldots \overrightarrow{y_i}^{s_i} c_i \overleftarrow{y_i}^{r_1} \ldots \overleftarrow{y_\ell}^{r_\ell}$ with $s_j, r_j \in \mathbb{N}_0$, $j \in [l]$.

As we have seen, the blocksequence does not provide much information. Therefore we refine the sets $\mathfrak{W}_\beta$ by sequences containing, as well, information on the different types of occurrences we have just introduced.

Definition 10. *Let $\sigma = (y_1, \ldots, y_\ell)$ be a marking sequence of $w \in \Sigma^*$. Define the* join-sequence *$\iota_w = (j_1, \ldots, j_{\ell-2})$ such that j_i is the number of join occurrences of y_{i+1} and the* separator-sequence *$\zeta_w = (s_1, \ldots, s_{\ell-2})$ such that s_i is the number of separating occurrences of y_{i+1}. Finally define the* extended blocksequence *(ebs) by $\gamma_w = (\beta_w, \iota_w, \zeta_w)$ w.r.t. σ.*

Consider the word $w = \text{abadbcbdacbdc}$ marked with σ_Σ. Regarding b, $w[2]$ joins the two a in stage 2 and $w[5], w[7]$ are separating the as at positions 3 and 9. The cs at position 6 and 10 join two marked blocks in stage 3 but no occurrence of c separates two marked blocks. This leads to $\beta = (3, 5, 4, 1)$. Moreover we have $\iota = (1, 2)$ and $\zeta = (2, 0)$ as join and separating sequence, resp.

Remark 11. For a blocksequence $\beta = (b_1, \ldots, b_n)$ it suffices to state $n - 2$ elements of ι and ζ explicitly. Since we only consider condensed words the first letter to be marked creates b_1 separate blocks. These occurrences are all satellites. Similarly the last letter joins all remaining gaps between the marked blocks.

Whereas by Theorem 6 for each sequence of natural numbers ending with 1 there exists a word having this sequence as a blocksequence, the same does not hold for ebs: Consider $((2, 1, 1), (0), (5))$ as an ebs for a ternary word. Thus we have two occurrences of a_1. Moreover, we know that marking a_1 and a_2 leads to one block and consequently the two a_1 need to be joined but the join-sequence dictates that we do not have a join-occurrence of a_2. So there is no word with this ebs, which leads to the introduction of the notion of valid ebs.

Definition 12. *A triple γ of sequences over natural numbers is called a* valid ebs*, if there exists a word $w \in \Sigma^*$ with $\gamma = \gamma_w$.*

Very importantly, we can exactly identify the valid ebs and thus have a validity check.

Theorem 13. *A triple $\gamma = (\beta, \iota, \zeta)$ of sequences $\beta = (b_1, \ldots, b_\ell)$, $\iota = (j_1, \ldots, j_{\ell-2})$, and $\zeta = (s_1, \ldots, s_{\ell-2})$ for $\ell \in \mathbb{N}_{\geq 2}$ is a valid ebs w.r.t. σ_Σ iff $b_\ell = 1$, $\max\{b_i - b_{i+1}, 0\} \leq j_i \leq b_i - 1$, $s_i = 0$ if $j_i = b_i - 1$, and $b_i - j_i + s_i \leq b_{i+1}$ for all $i \in [\ell - 2]$.*

Remark 14. The following observations follow from Theorem 13 for a valid ebs γ. If $b_{i+1} = b_i - j_i$, there are no separators or satellites of a_{i+1}. If $b_i = b_{i+1}$, the number of occurrences joining existing blocks and singletons (separators as well as satellites) creating new blocks of the letter a_{i+1} has to be equal and $s_i \leq j_i$. For the special case that $b_i = b_{i+1} = 1$ there is only one block before marking a_{i+1} and there cannot be any joins or separators ($j_i = s_i = 0$). Since $b_{i+1} = 1$ there can be no satellite occurrence as well and therefore a_{i+1} can only occur as a neighbour.

Definition 15. *For a valid ebs γ set $\mathfrak{V}_\gamma = \{w \in \Sigma^* | \gamma_w = \gamma\}$ and define the equivalence relation $u \sim_\gamma v$ if $\gamma_u = \gamma_v$ w.r.t. a given marking sequence σ.*

Moreover, for a valid ebs γ, we can show that all words in $\mathfrak{V}_\gamma$ have the same length (in contrast to the words of $\mathfrak{W}_\beta$, cf. Theorem 6). This will allow us to define later a normal form for each valid ebs.

Theorem 16. *For a valid ebs $\gamma = ((b_1, \ldots, b_{\ell-1}, 1), (j_1, \ldots, j_{\ell-2}), \zeta)$, all neighbourless words in $\mathfrak{V}_\gamma$ have length $b_1 + b_{\ell-1} - 1 + \sum_{i=2}^{\ell-1}(b_i - b_{i-1} + 2j_{i-1})$.*

We finish this section with a result about neighbourless marking sequences which will be of importance in the following sections.

Lemma 17. *For a given ebs γ, if all occurrences of the letters are either join-occurrences or singletons, $|w| = |w'|$ and $|w|_x = |w'|_x$ holds for all neighbourless $w, w' \in \mathfrak{V}_\gamma$ and all $x \in \Sigma$.*

3   Neighbourless Marking Sequences and a Normal Form

As seen in the previous section, adding neighbours does not change the block-sequence. For this reason, we restrict ourselves to words that are neighbourless w.r.t. σ_Σ. In this section, we firstly present some results regarding neighbourless marking sequences before we present a normal form for $\mathfrak{V}_\gamma$ for a valid ebs γ.

Theorem 18. *Given a word $w \in \Sigma^n$, a marking sequence $\sigma = (y_1, \ldots, y_\ell)$ is neighbourless for w iff $w[1] <_\sigma w[2]$, $w[n] <_\sigma w[n-1]$, and for all $i \in [\lfloor \frac{n}{2} \rfloor - 1]_{>1}$ we have $w[2i] >_\sigma w[2i+1]$ and $w[2i-1] <_\sigma w[2i]$.*

Proof. Let first σ be a neighbourless marking sequence for w. If $w[2]$ would be marked before $w[1]$ we had with $w[1]$ a neighbouring occurrence. Analogously we have $w[n] <_\sigma w[n-1]$. Suppose that there exists an $i \in [\lfloor \frac{n}{2} - 1 \rfloor]_{>1}$ with $w[2i] <_\sigma w[2i+1]$ or $w[2i-1] >_\sigma w[2i]$ (equality is excluded since w is condensed). Choose i minimal. We have to consider three cases.

Case 1: $w[2i] <_\sigma w[2i+1]$ and $w[2i-1] >_\sigma w[2i]$.
In this case the letters $w[2i-3], w[2i-2], w[2i-1], w[2i]$ are of interest. We know that $w[2i-3]$ is marked before $w[2i-2]$ by the minimality of i and $w[2i]$ is marked before $w[2i-1]$ which is marked before $w[2i-2]$ by the case-constraint. This implies that either $w[2i-2]$ is marked while $w[2i-1]$ is unmarked and thus $w[2i-2]$ is a neighbour or vice versa.

Case 2: $w[2i] <_\sigma w[2i+1]$ and $w[2i-1] <_\sigma w[2i]$
In this case $w[2i]$ is marked when $w[2i+1]$ ($w[2i-1]$) is already marked and $w[2i-1]$ ($w[2i+1]$) is still unmarked and thus $w[2i]$ is a neighbouring occurrence.

Case 3: $w[2i] \geq_\sigma w[2i+1]$ and $w[2i-1] >_\sigma w[2i]$
This case is similar to case 2.
Since we get a contradiction in all cases, the $\Rightarrow$-direction is proven.

Assume for the other direction that the constraints hold. Let $j \in [n]$. The constraints ensure that $w[j-1]$ and $w[j+1]$ are either both marked before $w[j]$ and thus $w[j]$ is join occurrence or both are marked after $w[j]$ and thus $w[j]$ is a separator. Hence, σ is neighbourless.   □

Remark 19. By Theorem 18, only words of odd length can be neighbourless.

The following two results are of algorithmic nature. We use the standard computational model RAM with logarithmic word-size (see, e.g., [13]). Following a standard assumption from stringology (see, e.g., [13]), if w is the input word for our algorithms, we can assume that $\Sigma = \mathrm{alph}(w) = \{1, 2, \dots, \ell\}$ with $\ell \leq |w|$. Since we restrict ourselves to neighbourless words and marking sequences, we show how to check in linear time whether a word is neighbourless and, if that is the case, how the ebs can be computed within the same time complexity.

Proposition 20. *We can check whether a word $w \in \Sigma^n$ is neighbourless, and compute a neighbourless marking sequence, in $O(n)$ time.*

Proof. We can assume $n = |w|$ is odd. Firstly we build a directed graph based on Theorem 18. Define $G_w = (\Sigma, E)$ with $E \subset \{(\mathsf{a}, \mathsf{b}) \mid \mathsf{a}, \mathsf{b} \in \Sigma\}$ as follows. Firstly, add the directed edges $(w[1], w[2])$ and $(w[n], w[n-1])$ to E. Then, for all $i \in [\lfloor \frac{n}{2} \rfloor - 1]_{>1}$ we add the edges $(w[2i+1], w[2i])$ and $(w[2i-1], w[2i])$. Intuitively, we have an edge (a, b) if and only if we would need to have $\mathsf{a} <_\sigma \mathsf{b}$ in any neighbourless marking sequence σ for w.

To find such a neighbourless marking sequence σ, it is enough to find the linear ordering of the vertices of V such that for every directed edge (a, b) from vertex a to vertex b, a comes before b in the respective ordering. Such a sequence can be found using a standard topological sorting algorithm based on the depth-first search (DFS). Such an algorithm produces successfully a linear ordering of the vertices of G_w (and, as such, a neighbourless marking sequence σ for w) if and only if G_w is a directed acyclic graph (DAG). The time complexity of this algorithm is $O(\ell + |E|) = O(n)$.   □

Proposition 21. *Given a word $w \in \Sigma^n$ and a neighbourless marking sequence σ for w, the ebs of w w.r.t. σ can be computed in $O(n)$ time.*

From now on, we will assume that $w \in \Sigma^n$, for $n \in \mathbb{N}$, is neighbourless w.r.t. σ_Σ. For each valid ebs γ we define a normal form $w_\gamma \in \mathfrak{V}_\gamma$ according to Theorem 13 such that w_γ is neighbourless w.r.t. σ_Σ.

Definition 22. *For a valid ebs $\gamma = (\beta, \iota, \zeta)$ with $\beta = (b_1, \dots, b_\ell)$, $\iota = (j_1, \dots, j_{\ell-2})$, and $\zeta = (s_1, \dots, s_{\ell-2})$ define w_γ by $(v_i)_{i \in [\ell]}$ with $v_\ell = w_\gamma$ with $v_1 = (\mathsf{a}_1 \bullet)^{b_1 - 1} \mathsf{a}_1$ and for $i \in [\ell-2]_{>1}$ define v_{i+1} as follows: firstly replace the first j_i occurrences of $\bullet$ by a_{i+1}, then replace the next $\bullet$ by $(\bullet \mathsf{a}_{i+1})^{s_i} \bullet$, denote the obtained word by v and set v_{i+1} to v if $b_{i+1} - (b_i - j_i + s_i) = 0$ or to $v(\bullet \mathsf{a}_{i+1})^{b_{i+1} - (b_i - j_i + s_i)}$ otherwise. For obtaining v_ℓ from $v_{\ell-1}$ replace all occurrences of $\bullet$ by a_n.*

Remark 23. For each word $w \in \Sigma^*$ which is neighbourless w.r.t. σ_Σ we have a corresponding valid **ebs** γ_w. Thus, one can define the word $w_{\gamma_w} \in \mathfrak{V}_{\gamma_w}$, as in Definition 22. This word will be called the normal form of w w.r.t. the marking sequence σ_Σ and the corresponding **ebs** γ_w.

Consider the valid **ebs** $\gamma = ((3,5,6,1),(1,2),(2,1))$ over the alphabet $\Sigma = \{\mathsf{a},\mathsf{b},\mathsf{c},\mathsf{d}\}$ ordered in the natural way. By Definition 22 we set $v_1 = \mathsf{a} \bullet \mathsf{a} \bullet \mathsf{a}$. To obtain v_2, we firstly replace the first $\bullet$ by b and the second by $\bullet\mathsf{b} \bullet \mathsf{b}\bullet$ and since $b_2 - (b_1 - j_1 s_1) = 5 - (3 - 1 + 2) = 1$ we append $\bullet\mathsf{b}$. Thus, we get $v_2 = \mathsf{aba}\bullet\mathsf{b}\bullet\mathsf{b}\bullet\mathsf{a}\bullet\mathsf{b}$. In the next step the first two $\bullet$ are replaced by c, the third $\bullet$ is replaced by $\bullet\mathsf{c}\bullet$ and we append $\bullet\mathsf{c} \bullet \mathsf{c}$ since $b_3 - (b_2 - j_2 + s_2) = 6 - (5 - 2 + 1) = 2$. This results in $v_3 = \mathsf{abacbcb} \bullet \mathsf{c} \bullet \mathsf{a} \bullet \mathsf{b} \bullet \mathsf{c} \bullet \mathsf{c}$. In the last step all $\bullet$ are replaced by d and we have the normal form belonging to γ. In the following part, we present three rules with which the normal form of a given $w \in \Sigma^*$ can be obtained.

Definition 24. *Let γ be a valid **ebs** and $i \in [\ell]_{>1}$. Define the following rules:*

Filling the Leftmost Gaps with Joins R_1: *For $w = x_1 \mathsf{a}_{k_1} u \mathsf{a}_{k_2} v \mathsf{a}_{k_3} x_2$ with $u, v \in \Sigma^+$, $k_1, k_2, k_3 < i$ and $x_1, x_2 \in (\Sigma \cup \overline{\Sigma})^*$, the application of R_1 results in $w' = x_1 \mathsf{a}_{k_1} v \mathsf{a}_{k_2} u \mathsf{a}_{k_3} x_2$ (see Fig. 1).*

All Separators in One Gap R_2: *Consider $w = x_1 z_1 u \overrightarrow{\mathsf{a}_i}^{k_1} z_2 v \overrightarrow{\mathsf{a}_i}^{k_2} z_3 x_2$ with $x_1, x_2 \in (\Sigma \cup \overline{\Sigma})^*$, $u, v \in \{\mathsf{a}_{i+1}, \ldots, \mathsf{a}_n\}^+$, $z_1, z_3 \in \{\mathsf{a}_1, \ldots, \mathsf{a}_{i-1}\}$, $z_2 \in (\Sigma \cup \overline{\Sigma})^+$ with $z_2[1], z_2[|z_2|] \in \overline{\Sigma}$ and with $\overrightarrow{\mathsf{a}_i}^{k_1} = \mathsf{a}_i t_1 \mathsf{a}_i t_2 \ldots \mathsf{a}_i t_{k_1}$ and $\overrightarrow{\mathsf{a}_i}^{k_2} = \mathsf{a}_i t'_1 \mathsf{a}_i t'_2 \ldots \mathsf{a}_i t'_{k_2}$. For an application of R_2 choose $m_1, m_2 \in \mathbb{N}$ with $m_1 + m_2 = k_1 + k_2$ and $r_1, \ldots, r_{m_1} \in \{t_1, \ldots, t_{k_1}, t'_1, \ldots, t'_{k_2}\}$ different as well as $r'_1, \ldots, r'_{m_2}$ with $\{r'_1, \ldots, r'_{m_2}\} = \{t_1, \ldots, t_{k_1}, t'_1, \ldots, t'_{k_2}\} \backslash \{r_1, \ldots, r_{m_1}\}$. Define the factors p and p' of w' by $p = \mathsf{a}_i r_1 \mathsf{a}_i r_2 \ldots \mathsf{a}_i r_{m_1}$ and $p' = \mathsf{a}_i r'_1 \mathsf{a}_i r'_2 \ldots \mathsf{a}_i r'_{m_2}$. Then the application of R_2 to w results in $w' = x_1 z_1 u p z_2 v p' z_3 x_2$ (see Fig. 1).*

Moving Satellites R_3: *For $w = x_1 \overrightarrow{\mathsf{a}_i}^r c_i \overleftarrow{\mathsf{a}_i}^s x_2$ with $r, s \in \mathbb{N}_0$, $x_1, x_2 \in (\Sigma \cup \overline{\Sigma})^*$ and the core c_i at stage i, the application of $R_3(a)$ results in $w' = x_1 (\overleftarrow{\mathsf{a}_i}^s)^R \overrightarrow{\mathsf{a}_i}^r c_i x_2$ and of $R_3(b)$ results in $w' = x_1 c_i \overleftarrow{\mathsf{a}_i}^s (\overrightarrow{\mathsf{a}_i}^r)^R x_2$ (see Fig. 1).*

Theorem 25. *For all $w \in \Sigma^*$ there exists a sequence $(r_1, \ldots, r_m)$ with $r_i \in \{R_1, R_2, R_3\}$, $i \in [m]$, $m \in \mathbb{N}_0$ such that w_{γ_w} is obtained from w w.r.t. σ_Σ.*

Proof. We construct the normal form inductively for the extended blocksequence corresponding to w marked with σ_Σ. Perform the following four steps for all $i \in [\ell]_{>1}$ (cf. Definition 7):

1. as long as w_i can be written as $x_1 \mathsf{a}_{k_1} u \mathsf{a}_{k_2} \mathsf{a}_i \mathsf{a}_{k_3} x_2$ with $u \neq \mathsf{a}_i$ apply R_1 (fill the first gaps with join occurrences),
2. if w_i can be written as $x_1 \mathsf{a}_{k_1} u \mathsf{a}_{k_2} v \mathsf{a}_{k_3} x_2$ with $v \neq \mathsf{a}_i$, $\mathsf{a}_i \in \mathrm{alph}(v)$ and $u \neq \mathsf{a}_i$, apply R_1 (move one block containing a separator occurrence to the gap immediately right to the gaps filled with joins),
3. if w_i can be written as $x_1 z_1 u \overrightarrow{\mathsf{a}_i}^{k_1} z_2 v \overrightarrow{\mathsf{a}_i}^{k_2} z_3 x_2$, apply R_2 with $m_1 = k_1 + k_2$ and $m_2 = 0$ (move all separators into the same gap),

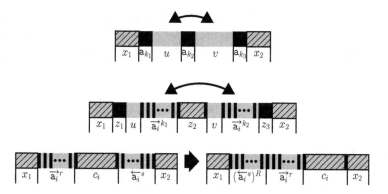

Fig. 1. Appl. of R_1, R_2, and R_3 respectively: dark is marked, light is unmarked, shaded contains both kinds.

4. if w_i can be written as $x_1\overrightarrow{\mathsf{a}_i}^r c_i \overleftarrow{\mathsf{a}_i}^s x_2$, apply $R_3(b)$ (move satellites to the right).

We prove by induction on $i \in [\ell]_{\geq 2}$ that after each application of all four steps the join occurrences of a_i are in the leftmost gaps, in the following gap are the separating occurrences of a_i, and all satellite occurrences of a_i are to the right of all a_{i-1}. Let $i = 2$. Then w_i is of the form $u_1\mathsf{a}_1 u_2 \mathsf{a}_1 u_3 \ldots u_{b_1}\mathsf{a}_1 u_{b_1+1}$ with $u_i \in (\Sigma\backslash\{\mathsf{a}_1\}))^*$ for $i \in [b_1+1]$. By γ_w we know that w_i has j_1 join occurrences of a_2 and thus there exists exactly j_1 u_i with $u_i = \mathsf{a}_2$. Since we apply R_1 as long as there exists a join-occurrence that has a factor $\mathsf{a}_1 u_k \mathsf{a}_1$ to the left in w_i, we obtain after the first step the word $u_1(\mathsf{a}_1\mathsf{a}_2)^{j_1}\mathsf{a}_1 x u_{b_1+1}$ with $x = \varepsilon$ if $j_1 = b_1 - 1$ and $x = u_{b_1-j_1-2}\mathsf{a}_1 u_{b_1-j_1-1}\ldots u_{b_1}\mathsf{a}_1$ otherwise. If $s_1 = 0$ the second step is skipped. Assume $s_1 > 0$. Thus, there exist separating occurrences of a_2 and hence at least one u_i is of the form $x_1\mathsf{a}_2 x_2$ with $\mathrm{alph}(x_1 x_2) \subseteq \Sigma\backslash\{\mathsf{a}_1,\mathsf{a}_2\}$. If this u_i is not $u_{b_1-j_1-2}$, R_1 is applied such that $u_{b_1-j_1-2}$ and u_i switch positions. This application results in the word

$$u_1(\mathsf{a}_1\mathsf{a}_2)^{j_1}\mathsf{a}_1 \cdot x_1\mathsf{a}_2 x_2 \mathsf{a}_1 u_{b_1-j_1-1}\mathsf{a}_1 \ldots \mathsf{a}_1 u_{b_1-j_1-2}\mathsf{a}_1 u_{b_1-j_1-1}\ldots u_{b_1}\mathsf{a}_1 \cdot u_{b_1+1}.$$

In the third step all other separating occurrences of a_2 are moved by rule R_2 into the same gap, i.e., if there exists another $u_{i'} = x_1'\mathsf{a}_2 x_2'$ with $\mathrm{alph}(x_1', x_2') = \Sigma\backslash\{\mathsf{a}_1,\mathsf{a}_2\}$ the application of R_2 leads to

$$u_1(\mathsf{a}_1\mathsf{a}_2)^{j_1}\mathsf{a}_1 \cdot x_1\mathsf{a}_2 x_2 \mathsf{a}_2 x_2' \mathsf{a}_1 u_{b_1-j_1-1}\ldots \mathsf{a}_1 u_{b_1-j_1-2}\mathsf{a}_1 u_{b_1-j_1-1}$$
$$\ldots \mathsf{a}_1 x_1' \mathsf{a}_1 \ldots u_{b_1}\mathsf{a}_1 \cdot u_{b_1+1}$$

and finally to

$$u_1(\mathsf{a}_1\mathsf{a}_2)^{j_1}\mathsf{a}_1 x_1 \overrightarrow{\mathsf{a}_2}^{s_1} z_1\mathsf{a}_1 z_2 \ldots z_\ell \mathsf{a}_1 z_{\ell+1}$$

for appropriate $z_i \in (\Sigma\backslash\{\mathsf{a}_1,\mathsf{a}_2\})^*$, $i \in [\ell]$, for some $\ell \in \mathbb{N}$, and $z_{\ell+1} \in (\Sigma\backslash\{\mathsf{a}_1\})^*$. After this step all separating occurrences of a_2 are between two occurrences of a_1 and especially between those a_1s such that all previous occurrences are directly joined by one occurrence of a_2. Thus only u_1 and $z_{\ell+1}$ may contain occurrences of a_2 (in the form of satellite occurrences). Set c_2 as the factor starting at $|u_1|+1$ and ending just before $z_{\ell+1}$. If w_i can be written as $x_1 \overrightarrow{a_i}^r c_1 \overleftarrow{a_i}^s x_2$ as in rule R_3 apply $R_3(b)$. After this step there is no occurrences of a_2 before the first a_1 and all satellite occurrences of a_2 are after the last a_1.

Consider now the ith stage. Then we have a word of the form

$$u_1 B_1 u_2 B_2 u_3 \ldots u_{b_{i-1}} B_{b_{i-1}} u_{b_{i-1}+1}$$

with $B_i \in \overline{\Sigma}^*$ and $u_j \in \Sigma^*$ for $i \in [b_{i-1}]$ and $j \in [b_{i-1} + 1]$. Since there exist j_{i-1} join occurrences of a_i, there exist exactly j_{i-1} occurrences of u_k which are equal to a_i. Applying j_{i-1} times rule R_1 we swap these occurrences with $u_2, \ldots, u_{j_{i-1}+1}$. In the next step we swap a separating occurrences of a_i with $u_{j_{i-1}+2}$ (if one exists). After these transformation we have with appropriate $z_1, \ldots, z_\ell$ a word of the form

$$u_1 B_1 a_i B_2 a_i \ldots a_i B_{j_{i-1}+1} z_1 B_{j_{i-1}+2} z_2 \ldots z_{\ell-1} B_{b_{i-1}} z_\ell$$

such that z_1 contains all separating occurrences of y_i. Now define c_i as the factor starting right after u_1 and ending just before z_ℓ.

Notice that u_1 and z_ℓ only may contain satellite occurrences of y_i and c_i does not contain any. With $R_3(b)$ we move these occurrences all to the right into z_ℓ. This proves that the application of the four steps results in a word where always the first gaps are filled with the join-occurrences, followed by a gap containing all separating occurrences, and that the satellite occurrences are all at the right side of the core in each marking step.

Comparing this word with the definition of w_{γ_w} leads to the claim. □

Remark 26. Notice, that by Theorem 16 an upper bound for the $m \in \mathbb{N}_0$ from Theorem 25 is given by $\sum_{i=2}^{\ell-2} b_{i+1} - b_i + 2j_i$.

Lemma 27. *For a valid* ebs *γ and $w \in \mathfrak{V}_\gamma$ applying anyone of the rules R_1, R_2, or R_3 to w, resulting in the word w', we get $w' \in \mathfrak{V}_\gamma$ as well.*

Corollary 28. *For a given valid* ebs *γ, $\mathfrak{V}_\gamma$ contains exactly one normal form and all words having this normal form are in $\mathfrak{V}_\gamma$.*

For the ebs $\gamma = ((4,4,1),(1),(1))$, we have $w_\gamma =$ abacbcaca and $\mathfrak{V}_\gamma = \{$abacacbca, abacbcaca, acabacbca, acbcabaca, acacbcaba, acbcacaba$\}$ assuming σ_Σ as marking sequence.

In the remaining part of this section we investigate the behaviour of a word in comparison to its normal form regarding the locality of the words.

Theorem 29. *Let $R_i(w)$ denote the application of R_i to w for $i \in [3]$. Then we have that $\text{loc}(R_1(w))$ differs from $\text{loc}(w)$ by at most 2 and $\text{loc}(R_2(w))$ and $\text{loc}(R_3(w))$ differ from $\text{loc}(w)$ by at most 1.*

For transforming a neighbourless word $w \in \Sigma^*$ into w_γ given the ebs γ w.r.t. σ_Σ, R_1 needs to be applied $\leq j_i + 1$ times (moving j_1 joins and one separator), $R_2 \leq s_i$ times and R_3 once (moving all satellites to the right side of the core).

Corollary 30. *For $w \in \Sigma^*$ with $|\Sigma| = \ell$ and the ebs γ_w induced by σ_Σ, we have $\mathrm{loc}(w) \leq \mathrm{loc}(w_{\gamma_w}) + \sum_{i \in [\ell]}(2j_i + s_i) + \ell.$*

In this section, we have proven that for neighbourless words (w.r.t. σ_Σ) we can always find a normal form and we showed how the locality of the word itself and its normal form differ in the worst case. This upper bound proven in Corollary 30 can only be reached if at any stage the *critical letters*, the letters adjacent to the factors moved by the rules, are all different. Since, for instance, if the rules are applied to a_2, all critical letters have to be a_1, the upper bound is not tight. The following lemma shows how the locality changes if *critical letters* are equal.

Lemma 31. *Let $w \in \Sigma^*$. Regarding R_1 we have that the locality does not change if the critical letters are identical and it changes by at most 1 if three critical letters are equal and the fourth is different or if $a_1 = a_3$ or $a_2 = a_4$. Regarding R_2 the results are similar: if the critical letters $\overrightarrow{a_i}^{k_1}[|\overrightarrow{a_i}^{k_1}|], z_2, z_4$, and $v[|v|]$ are all equal or if $\overrightarrow{a_i}^{k_1}[|\overrightarrow{a_i}^{k_1}|]$ and $z_2 = z_4$ the locality does not change. Finally regarding $R_3(b)$ the locality does not change if both $x_1[|x_1|] = x_2[1]$ and $c_i[1] = c_i \overleftarrow{a_i}^s[|c_i \overleftarrow{a_i}^s|]$ (including the case $x_1 = x_2 = \varepsilon$).*

Lemma 31 shows two peculiarities: the smaller a letter is w.r.t. the given order the less cases exist in which the locality is changed maximally; words can be categorised w.r.t. their joins and separators - the less of these occurrences appear between different critical letters the smaller is the difference between the locality of the normal form and the word itself. Moreover, the worst case does not incorporate that the worst case for one application of one rule may be the best case for another one such that the increase and decrease cancel each other out. Notice that the locality of two words $w, w' \in \mathfrak{V}_\gamma$, for a given ebs γ, differ in the sum of the locality change from each to the common normal form since the rules from Definition 24 can not only be used to compute the normal form w_γ of w but also for obtaining each word $w' \in \mathfrak{V}_\gamma$ from w_γ. We leave this investigation for general alphabets as an open problem. In the following section, we study the behaviour for alphabets of size up to 3.

4   The Case $|\Sigma| \leq 3$

In this section, we are using a, b, and c for the alphabet for better readability. For unary alphabets we have exactly one word containing of a single letter since we only consider condensed words. The binary case $\Sigma = \{a, b\}$ can also shortly be explained: blocksequences are of the form $(b_1, 1)$. Again, since the words are condensed and neighbourless, each word has to be an alternation of a and b and assuming σ_Σ the word starts and ends with a. Thus we have b_1 occurrences of a and $b_1 - 1$ join occurrences of b. This leads immediately to the fact that the only other marking sequence is better (and thus optimal) since we obtain the blocksequence $(b_1 - 1, 1)$. In the case $\Sigma = \{a, b, c\}$ ebs are of the form $\gamma = ((b_1, b_2, 1), j_1, s_1)$ (omitting some brackets for better readability) implying

$w_\gamma = (\mathsf{ab})^{j_1}\mathsf{a}(\mathsf{cb})^{s_1}(\mathsf{ca})^{b_1-j_1-1}(\mathsf{cb})^{b_2-b_1-s_1+j_1}$. Firstly, we show how the locality of w and w_γ differ. Notice that in the case $|\Sigma| = 3$ only occurrences of b may be join- or separating occurrences and all occurrences of c are joins.

Proposition 32. *Let $w \in \Sigma^*$ and $\gamma = ((b_1, b_2, 1), j_1, s_1)$ the ebs while marking with σ_Σ. Then we have $\mathrm{loc}_{\sigma_\Sigma}(w) = \mathrm{loc}_{\sigma_\Sigma}(w_\gamma)$.*

Thus, on a ternary alphabet we may assume the normal form without any restriction w.r.t. $\mathrm{loc}_{\sigma_\Sigma}$. The following proposition determines the optimal marking sequence for the normal form just by the ebs.

Theorem 33. *Given a valid ebs $\gamma = ((b_1, b_2, 1), j_1, s_1)$ and w_γ w.r.t. σ_Σ the optimal marking sequence is given by*

- *(b, a, c) if $2j_1 \geq b_1$ and $2b_1 \geq 2j_1 + b_2 + \lambda$ or $\lambda = 1$ and $2j_1 = b_1$ and $b_1 - 1 \geq b_2$,*
- *(b, c, a) if $2b_1 \geq 2j_1 + b_2 + \lambda$ and $b_2 - 1 \geq b_1 - \lambda$ or $2b_1 \leq 2j_1 + b_2 + \lambda$ and $b_1 \geq 2j_1 + 1$,*
- *(c, a, b) if $b_1 \leq 2j_1 + 1 + \lambda$ and $2b_1 \geq 2j_1 + b_2 + 2\lambda$ or $b_1 \geq 2j_1 + 1 + \lambda$ and $b_1 - \lambda \geq b_2 - 1$,*
- *(c, b, a) if $b_1 - \lambda \geq b_2 - 1$ and $2b_1 \leq 2j_1 + b_2 + \lambda$ or $b_1 + \lambda \leq b_2 - 1$ and $b_1 \leq 2j_1 + 1$,*

with $\lambda = 1$ if $b_2 - b_1 - s_1 + j_1 = 0$ and $\lambda = 0$ otherwise.

Thus, in the ternary case we are able to determine the optimal marking sequence for a neighbourless word with a constant number of arithmetic operations and comparisons if the extended marking sequence is given; notice that the normal form does not have to be computed since only the information from the extended blocksequence is needed.

5   Conclusions

In this paper, we investigated a new point of view regarding the notion of k-locality. While previous works were focussed on the locality of one single word and the connection to other domains (especially pattern matching or graph theory), we introduced the notion of blocksequence for grouping words and finding similarities of these words. We noticed that just a blocksequence does not provide enough information for a reasonable characterisation, since too many words with different locality fall into the same class. Thus, we strengthened this notion, and introduced extended blocksequences. These sequences not only count the number of marked blocks, in each step of a marking sequence, but also provide information about the roles of single letters: neighbours, joins, separators, and satellites. Further, we focused our analysis on neighbourless words. In that case, we were able to define a normal form for each class, and compute it in linear time. We have also shown an upper bound on the difference between the locality of a word and that of its normal form. It remains open to determine the exact difference between these two for a specific word over an alphabet with at least four letters. We conjecture that our upper bound is actually not tight, since the worst case for one of the applied rules can be cancelled out with the application of the next rule. Surprisingly for us, a computer programme showed that the locality of a word and that of its normal form, over a six-letter alphabet, differ by at most seven, independently of the number of satellites, joins, and separators. For a three letter alphabet we gave a full characterisation including the optimal marking sequence of a word, as determined by the extended blocksequence.

In this work, we merely started the study of this new perspective on the locality of words. Further problems, such as the computation of the normal form's locality and a deeper understanding of the locality changes between a word and its normal form, are left as future work.

References

1. Angluin, D.: Finding patterns common to a set of strings. J. Comput. Syst. Sci. **21**, 46–62 (1980)
2. Barceló, P., Libkin, L., Lin, A.W., Wood, P.T.: Expressive languages for path queries over graph-structured data. ACM Trans. Database Syst. **37**, 1–46 (2012)
3. Casel, K., Day, J.D., Fleischmann, P., Kociumaka, T., Manea, F., Schmid, M.L.: Graph and string parameters: connections between pathwidth, cutwidth and the locality number. In: Proceedings of ICALP 2019. LIPIcs, vol. 132, pp. 109:1–109:16 (2019)
4. Day, J.D., Fleischmann, P., Manea, F., Nowotka, D.: Local patterns. In: Proceedings of FSTTCS. LIPIcs, vol. 93, pp. 24:1–24:14 (2017)
5. Fernau, H.: Algorithms for learning regular expressions from positive data. Inf. Comput. **207**(4), 521–541 (2009). https://doi.org/10.1016/j.ic.2008.12.008
6. Fernau, H., Manea, F., Mercaş, R., Schmid, M.L.: Pattern matching with variables: fast algorithms and new hardness results. In: Proceedings of STACS. LIPIcs, vol. 30, pp. 302–315 (2015)
7. Fernau, H., Manea, F., Mercaş, R., Schmid, M.L.: Revisiting Shinohara's algorithm for computing descriptive patterns. Theoret. Comput. Sci. **733**, 44–54 (2016)
8. Fernau, H., Schmid, M.L.: Pattern matching with variables: a multivariate complexity analysis. Inf. Comput. **242**, 287–305 (2015)
9. Fernau, H., Schmid, M.L., Villanger, Y.: On the parameterised complexity of string morphism problems. Theory Comput. Syst. **59**(1), 24–51 (2016)
10. Fleischmann, P., Haschke, L., Manea, F., Nowotka, D., Tsatia Tsida, C., Wiedenbeck, J.: Blocksequences of k-local words. CoRR abs/2008.03516 (2020)
11. Freydenberger, D.D.: Extended regular expressions: succinctness and decidability. Theory Comput. Syst. **53**, 159–193 (2013)
12. Friedl, J.E.F.: Mastering Regular Expressions, 3rd edn. O'Reilly, Sebastopol (2006)
13. Kärkkäinen, J., Sanders, P., Burkhardt, S.: Linear work suffix array construction. J. ACM **53**(6), 918–936 (2006)
14. Kearns, M., Pitt, L.: A polynomial-time algorithm for learning k-variable pattern languages from examples. In: Proceedings of COLT, pp. 57–71 (1989)
15. Lothaire, M.: Algebraic Combinatorics on Words. Cambridge University Press, Cambridge (2002)

16. Reidenbach, D., Schmid, M.L.: Patterns with bounded treewidth. Inf. Comput. **239**, 87–99 (2014)
17. Serbanuta, V.N., Serbanuta, T.: Injectivity of the parikh matrix mappings revisited. Fundam. Inform. **73**(1–2), 265–283 (2006)

Complexity of Limit-Cycle Problems in Boolean Networks

Florian Bridoux[1], Caroline Gaze-Maillot[1], Kévin Perrot[1,2(✉)], and Sylvain Sené[1]

[1] Aix Marseille Univ., Univ. Toulon, CNRS, LIS, UMR 7020, Marseille, France
kevin.Perrot@lis-lab.fr
[2] Univ. Côte d'Azur, CNRS, I3S, UMR 7271, Sophia Antipolis, France

Abstract. Boolean networks are a general model of interacting entities, with applications to biological phenomena such as gene regulation. Attractors play a central role, and the schedule of entity updates is *a priori* unknown. This article presents results on the computational complexity of problems related to the existence of update schedules such that some limit-cycle lengths are possible or not. We first prove that given a Boolean network updated in parallel, knowing whether it has at least one limit-cycle of length k is NP-complete. Adding an existential quantification on the block-sequential update schedule does not change the complexity class of the problem, but the following alternation brings us one level above in the polynomial hierarchy: given a Boolean network, knowing whether there exists a block-sequential update schedule such that it has no limit-cycle of length k is $\mathsf{NP}^{\mathsf{NP}}$-complete.

1 Introduction

Boolean networks (BNs) were introduced by McCulloch and Pitts in the 1940s through the well known formal neural networks [15] that are specific BNs governed by a multi-dimensional threshold function. Informally, BNs are finite dynamical systems in which entities having Boolean states may interact with each other over discrete time. After their introduction, neural networks were studied in depth from the mathematical standpoint. Among the main works on them are the introduction by Kleene of finite automata and regular expressions [14], first results on the dynamical behaviors of linear feedback shift registers [12] and linear networks [7]. These researches led Kauffman and Thomas (independently) from the end of the 1960s to develop the use of BNs in the context of biological networks modeling [13,24], which has paved the way to numerous applied works at the interface between molecular biology, computer science and discrete mathematics. In parallel, theoretical developments were done in the framework of linear algebra and numerical analysis by Robert [21], and in that

The authors are thankful to project ANR-18-CE40-0002-01 "FANs", project ECOS-CONICYT C16E01, project STIC AmSud CoDANet 19-STIC-03 (Campus France 43478PD), for their funding.

T. Bureš et al. (Eds.): SOFSEM 2021, LNCS 12607, pp. 135–146, 2021.
https://doi.org/10.1007/978-3-030-67731-2_10

of dynamical system theory and computational models, which constitutes the lens through which we look at BNs in this paper.

In this context, numerous studies have already been led and have brought very important results. Considering that a BN can be defined as a collection of local Boolean functions (each of these defining the discrete evolution of one entity over time given the states of the entities that influence it), it can be represented by a directed graph at the static level, classically called the interaction digraph. Moreover, as a BN is by definition of finite size here, it is trivial to see that the trajectory of any of its configurations (or global state) ends into a cycle that can be a fixed point or a limit-cycle. The main theoretical objective in the domain is twofold: obtaining (combinatorial or algebraic) characterizations of the dynamics of such objects, through either their definition as collections of Boolean functions or their interaction graphs, and understanding the complexity of finding such characterizations.

In these lines, Robert showed that retroaction cycles between entities in the interaction graph are necessary for a BN to have a non-trivial dynamical behavior [22] and Thomas conjectured strong relations between these retroaction cycles (well known as positive and negative cycles) and the existence of multi-stationarity (several fixed points) or limit-cycles [25] which were proven later [18–20]. A notable fact about these seminal works is that they underline clearly that retroaction cycles are the engines of behavioral complexity (or dynamical richness). More recently, a real effort has been impulsed on the understanding of retroaction cycles. In particular, Demongeot et al. characterized exhaustively the behaviors of retroaction cycles and some of their intersections [6]. Furthermore, the problem of counting the number of fixed points and limit-cycles has mushroomed. Advances have been done concerning fixed points [2,4]. Nevertheless, due to the high dependence of limit-cycle appearance according to the update schedule (*i.e.* the way/order under which entities are updated over time), no general combinatorial results have been obtained, except for retroaction cycles [6]. In relation to complexity theory, the main known results based on BNs are: determining if a BN admits fixed points is NP-complete, counting fixed points is #P-complete, determining if a fixed point has a non-trivial attraction basin is NP-complete [8,16], determining if there exists another update schedule that conserves the limit-cycles of a given BN evolving in parallel is NP-hard [3]. Moreover, a recent work [5] focused on related questions on fixed point complexity by focusing on interaction digraphs and not on BNs anymore (notice that several BNs admit the same interaction digraph).

In this paper, we impregnate from these last results and transfer the problematics to limit-cycles, which constitutes to our knowledge one of the first attempts to understanding limit-cycles from the complexity theory point of view with [3,11]. More precisely, considering that the input is a BN, we prove that determining if a BN admits a limit-cycle of length k is NP-complete whatever the update schedule (in the class of block-sequential updating modes, that is updating modes defined as ordered partitions of the set of entities). Furthermore, our most important result is to show that, determining if there exists a block-sequential update schedule such that a given BN admits no limit-cycles of length k, is $\mathsf{NP}^{\mathsf{NP}}$-complete.

In what follows, Secti. 2 presents the main definitions that are used in the paper. Section 3 gives a brief state of the art of the problematic addressed. The main results of the paper are given in Sect. 4 and are followed by a conclusion developing some perspectives of this work.

2   Definitions

We denote $\mathbb{N}_+$ the set of strictly positive integers, and $[n] = \{1, \ldots, n\}$ for some $n \in \mathbb{N}_+$. For $x \in \{0,1\}^n$ and $i \in [n]$, we denote x_i the component i of x, and $x + e_i$ the vector of $\{0,1\}^n$ obtained by flipping component i of x (addition is performed modulo 2). The symbol $\oplus$ is used for the binary operator *exclusive or (xor)*.

Boolean Networks. A *Boolean network* (BN) is a function $f : \{0,1\}^n \to \{0,1\}^n$, that we see as n *local functions* $f_1, \ldots, f_n$ with $f_i : \{0,1\}^n \to \{0,1\}$ for each $i \in [n]$. The *interaction digraph* of a BN f captures the actual dependencies among its components, and is defined as $G_f = (V, A)$, with $V = [n]$ and

$$(i, j) \in A \quad \Longleftrightarrow \quad \exists x \in \{0,1\}^n : f_j(x) \neq f_j(x + e_i).$$

The arcs of the interaction digraph may be assigned signs $\sigma : A \to \{+, -, \pm\}$ as follows:

- $\sigma(i, j) = +$ when $\exists x \in \{0,1\}^n : x_i = 0 \wedge f_j(x) > f_j(x + e_i)$,
- $\sigma(i, j) = -$ when $\exists x \in \{0,1\}^n : x_i = 0 \wedge f_j(x) < f_j(x + e_i)$,
- $\sigma(i, j) = \pm$ when both conditions above hold.

For convenience, we may use various symbols to denote the components of the network, but as it will always be a finite set a bijection with $[n]$ is straightforward. The *size* of a BN is its number of components, n.

Update Schedules. The *configuration space* is $\{0,1\}^n$, and it remains to explain how components are updated. Given a BN f, a configuration x and a subset $I \subseteq [n]$, we denote[1] $f^{(I)}(x)$ the configuration obtained by updating components of I only, *i.e.*

$$\text{for any } i \in [n], \quad f^{(I)}(x)_i = \begin{cases} f_i(x) & \text{if } i \in I \\ x_i & \text{otherwise.} \end{cases}$$

Remark that $f^{([n])} = f$. A *block-sequential update schedule* is an ordered partition of $[n]$, denoted $W = (W_1, \ldots, W_t)$, and a BN f updated according to W gives the deterministic discrete dynamical system on $\{0,1\}^n$ defined as

$$f^{(W)} = f^{(W_t)} \circ \cdots \circ f^{(W_2)} \circ f^{(W_1)}.$$

The update schedule $([n])$ is called *parallel* (or *synchronous*).

---

[1] Parentheses are used to differentiate update schedules from iterations of a function.

$$f_1(x) = x_2$$
$$f_2(x) = x_1$$

$$f_1'(x) = x_3$$
$$f_2'(x) = x_1$$
$$f_3'(x) = x_2$$

Fig. 1. Two BNs and their respective interaction digraphs (all arcs are positive). Left: for $W = (\{1\}, \{2\})$ we have $\phi_2(f^{(W)}) = 0$, whereas for the parallel mode we have $\phi_2(f) = 1$. Right: for $W' = (\{1\}, \{2, 3\})$ we have $\phi_2(f'^{(W')}) = 1$ with $001 \leftrightarrow 110$, whereas for the parallel mode we have $\phi_2(f') = 0$.

Attractors. Given that the configuration space is finite and the dynamics is deterministic, the orbit of any configuration converges towards a *fixed point* (a configuration x such that $f^{(W)}(x) = x$) or a *limit-cycle* (a configuration x such that $(f^{(W)})^k(x) = x$ for some *length* $k \in \mathbb{N}_+$, and such that $(f^{(W)})^\ell(x) \neq x$ for any $\ell \in [k-1]$). A fixed point is a limit-cycle of length one, a limit-cycle is assimilated to any of its configurations, and has a unique length.

Given a BN f, an update schedule W, and $k \in \mathbb{N}_+$, we denote $\Phi_k(f^{(W)})$ the set of configurations in limit-cycles of length k, *i.e.*

$$\Phi_k(f^{(W)}) = \{x \in \{0, 1\}^n \mid (f^{(W)})^k(x) = x \text{ and } \forall \ell \in [k-1] : (f^{(W)})^\ell(x) \neq x\}$$

and $\phi_k(f^{(W)}) = \frac{|\Phi_k(f^{(W)})|}{k}$ the number of limit-cycles of length k. Remark that for a fixed k, the quantity $\phi_k(f^{(W)})$ may vary depending on W (see Fig. 1).

For retroaction cycles (such as those of Fig. 1), the dynamical behavior in terms of number of limit-cycles of size k, whatever the update schedule, is entirely characterized in [6] on the basis of [10].

Problems. We are interested in the following decision problems related to attractors in the dynamics of BNs, and especially limit-cycles.

---
k-limit-cycle problem (k-LC)
Input: a BN f updated in parallel.
Question: does $\phi_k(f) \geq 1$?

Remark 1. Note that an input BN f is encoded with its local functions as propositional formulas (see also Remark 3 at the end).

Remark 2. f updated in parallel is not a limitation here, since one can transform in polynomial time a BN f and an update schedule W into a BN f' updated in parallel such that $f' = f^{(W)}$ (simply construct local functions of f' from those of f and W), as presented in [23].

Block-sequential k-limit-cycle problem (BS k-LC)
Input: a BN f.
Question: does there exist W block-sequential such that $\phi_k(f^{(W)}) \geq 1$?

Block-sequential no k-limit-cycle problem (BS no k-LC)
Input: a BN f.
Question: does there exist W block-sequential such that $\phi_k(f^{(W)}) = 0$?

Fixed points are invariant over block-sequential update schedules [9], consequently 1-**LC** and **BS 1-LC** are identical. However, the last two problems are not complement of each other, because there exists some instance positive in both (see Fig. 1 for an example).

For the complexity lower bounds, we present a reduction from propositional formula satisfaction problems. For a formula ψ on $\{\lambda_1, \ldots, \lambda_n\}$ and a partial assignment $v : \{\lambda_1, \ldots, \lambda_s\} \rightarrow \{0, 1\}$ for some $s \in [n]$, we denote $\psi[v]$ the substitution $\psi[\lambda_1 \leftarrow v(\lambda_1), \ldots, \lambda_s \leftarrow v(\lambda_s)]$.

∃∀-**3-SAT**

Input: a 3-CNF formula ψ on $\{\lambda_1, \ldots, \lambda_n\}$ and $s \in [n]$.
Question: is there an assignment v of $\lambda_1, \ldots, \lambda_s$ such that
  all assignments of $\lambda_{s+1}, \ldots, \lambda_n$ satisfy $\psi[v]$?

∃∀-**3-SAT** is $\mathsf{NP^{NP}}$-complete [17] (one level above in the polynomial hierarchy). Also, note that $\mathsf{NP^{NP}} = \mathsf{NP^{co\text{-}NP}}$ since an oracle language or its complement are equally useful.

3   State of the Art

The k-**limit-cycle problem** is known to be NP-complete for $k = 1$ [8], and the fixed points of a BN are invariant for any block-sequential update schedule [9]. It has been proven in [1] that given a BN f, it is NP-complete to know whether there exist two block-sequential update schedules W, W' such that $f^{(W)} \neq f^{(W')}$ (that is, they differ on at least one configuration). This problem is indeed surprisingly difficult, but the proof relies on a basic construction similar to Theorem 1 for $k = 1$. Moreover, in [3], the authors study the computational complexity of limit cycle problems. Given a BN f, an update schedule W and a limit-cycle C of $f^{(W)}$, it is NP-complete to know whether there exists another update schedule W' (not equivalent to W) such that $f^{(W)}$ also has the limit-cycle C. Some variants of this problem are deduced to be NP-complete: knowing whether the sets of limit cycles are equal, and whether the sets of limit-cycles share at least one element. This work focuses on finding block-sequential update schedules sharing limit cycles. After writing this article, we learned that the PhD thesis of Gómez [11] contains results of a very close flavor: given a BN f, determining whether it is possible to find a block-sequential update schedule W such that $f^{(W)}$ has at least one limit cycle (of any length greater than two) is NP-complete, even when restricted to AND-OR networks. Moreover, the problem of finding a block-sequential W such that $f^{(W)}$ has only fixed points is NP-hard. In the sequel, we prove an analogous bound for the existence problem (Corollary 1. Our construction also has only AND-OR local functions), and a stronger tight bound for the non-existence problem (Theorems 3, 4 and Corollary 2). As a difference, in our setting the length of the limit-cycle is fixed in the problem definition. It is also proven in [11] that given a BN f and two configurations x, y, is there a W such that $f^{(W)}(x) = y$? is an NP-complete problem.

Eventually, questions on the maximum number of fixed points possible when only the interaction digraph of a BN is provided, have already let some complexity classes higher than NP appear in problems related to the attractors of BNs [5].

4   Complexity of Limit-Cycle Problems

The constructions presented in this section are gradually extended with more involved arrangements of components, to prove complexity lower bounds from formula satisfaction problems. The first result adapts a folklore proof for fixed points (case $k = 1$).

Theorem 1. k**-LC** *is* NP-*complete for any* $k \in \mathbb{N}_+$.

Proof (Sketch). The problem is obviously in NP since checking that a configuration belongs to a limit-cycle of size k is done in polynomial time.

The NP-harness reduction is from **3-SAT**. For each variable of a given formula ψ we add a component with a positive loop, which can therefore take states 0 or 1 in attractors. Then we add one component per clause of ψ with its local function implementing the clause from the states of variable components. Finally, we add one component for the whole formula (part of its local function will compute the conjunction of states from clause components), within a cycle of k components. The purpose of this cycle of k components is to create a limit-cycle of length k if and only if the formula component (ψ_1 on Fig. 2) is in state 1, which is possible if and only if all clause components are in state 1 in an attractor, which is possible if and only if the formula is satisfiable. For any assignment of states to variable components that do not satisfy the formula, after one step at least one clause component is in state 0.   □

The second result initiates the consideration of update schedules in complexity studies of the dynamics of BNs. However, with an additional existential quantification on the update schedule the problem remains NP-complete (there was already an existential quantification on configurations for the existence of a limit-cycle), and it turns out that the same construction proves it.

Corollary 1. BS k**-LC** *is* NP-*complete for any* $k \in \mathbb{N}_+$.

We have seen in Theorem 1 and Corollary 1 that with two consecutive existential quantifications (one for a block-sequential update schedule and one for a configuration of a limit-cycle) the problem remains in NP. However, **BS no** k**-LC** corresponds to an existential quantification (for a block-sequential update schedule) followed by a universal quantification (for the absence of a limit-cycle). The next results therefore jump one level above in the polynomial hierarchy.

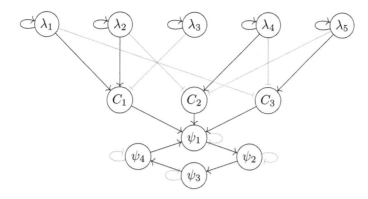

Fig. 2. Signed interaction digraph of the BN obtained for $k = 4$ and the 3-CNF formula $\psi = (\lambda_1 \vee \lambda_2 \vee \neg\lambda_3) \wedge (\neg\lambda_2 \vee \lambda_4 \vee \neg\lambda_5) \wedge (\neg\lambda_1 \vee \neg\lambda_4 \vee \lambda_5)$. Negative arcs $(-)$ are red with a flat head, positive arcs $(+)$ are black (there are no $\pm$ arcs).

Theorem 2. BS no k-LC *is in* $\mathsf{NP}^{\mathsf{NP}}$ *for any* $k \in \mathbb{N}_+$.

Proof. The problem belongs to the class $\mathsf{NP}^{\mathsf{co\text{-}NP}} = \mathsf{NP}^{\mathsf{NP}}$, as one can guess non-deterministically a block-sequential update schedule W and then check in polynomial time (in NP), using an oracle in co-NP, whether $\phi_k(f^{(W)}) = 0$. Once W is fixed this last question is indeed in co-NP, as it is the complement of **k-LC**, see Remark 2 and Theorem 1. $\qquad\qquad\square$

The hardness proof is split into three results, developing some incremental mechanisms and constructions.

Theorem 3. BS no k-LC *is* $\mathsf{NP}^{\mathsf{NP}}$*-hard for all* $k > 2$ *even.*

Proof (Sketch). This first reduction from $\exists\forall$-**3-SAT** implements an intuitive idea of having the block-sequential update schedule corresponding to an assignment of the existential variables of formula ψ (from λ_1 to λ_s), and positive loops on the universal variables (from λ_{s+1} to λ_n) so that they can be in state 0 or 1 in attractors.

To this aim, a component Ω with a negative loop flips its state at each step (hence the k even and $k > 2$), and for each existential variable we add a gadget of three components $\lambda_i, \lambda_i', \lambda_i''$ such that the state of λ_i is fixed in any attractor, but depends on the relative order of $\lambda_i, \lambda_i', \lambda_i''$ compared to Ω in the update schedule: both λ_i' and λ_i'' copy the state of Ω ($f_{\lambda_i'}(x) = f_{\lambda_i''}(x) = x_\Omega$), and

- either λ_i sees that the states of λ_i' and λ_i'' are different and goes to state 1,
- or λ_i sees that the states of λ_i' and λ_i'' are equal and goes to state 0,

which corresponds to $f_{\lambda_i}(x) = x_{\lambda_i'} \oplus x_{\lambda_i''}$. Then clause components and a formula component ψ will have the property that there exists an update schedule such that component ψ is in state 1 in all attractors, if and only if the instance of

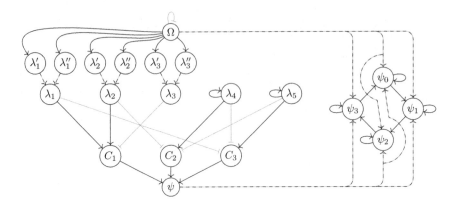

Fig. 3. Signed interaction digraph of the BN obtained for $k = 4$, the 3-CNF formula $\psi = (\lambda_1 \vee \lambda_2 \vee \neg\lambda_3) \wedge (\neg\lambda_2 \vee \lambda_4 \vee \neg\lambda_5) \wedge (\neg\lambda_1 \vee \neg\lambda_4 \vee \lambda_5)$, and $s = 3$. Negative arcs $(-)$ are red with a flat head, positive arcs $(+)$ are black, positive-negative arcs $(\pm)$ are dashed with both colors and heads. Components Ω and ψ are both connected to components ψ_0, ψ_1, ψ_2 and ψ_3 with arcs of sign $\pm$.

$\exists\forall$-**3-SAT** is positive: existential variables are set in the update schedule, and it must satisfy the formula ψ for any choice of states for the universal variables.

The last part of the construction (on the right side of Fig. 3) is a cycle of k components $\psi_0, \ldots, \psi_{k-1}$, designed to be able to implement a limit-cycle of length k if and only if component ψ is in state 0. The result follows:

- if the $\exists\forall$-**3-SAT** instance is positive then there exists an update schedule such that component ψ is in state 1 in all attractors, hence fixing the states of components $\psi_0, \ldots, \psi_{k-1}$, and leading to limit-cycles of length 2 only (because Ω is flipping);
- if the $\exists\forall$-**3-SAT** instance is negative then for any update schedule we can have component ψ in state 0 in some attractor (when the states of universal variables are set accordingly), and then a limit-cycle of length k can always take place on components $\psi_0, \ldots, \psi_{k-1}$ (Ω flipping prevents k to be odd).

This last part (ensuring that for any update schedule there exist $x_{\psi_0}, \ldots, x_{\psi_{k-1}}$ cycling around components $\psi_0, \ldots, \psi_{k-1}$ in exactly k steps) is a tricky part of the construction, with the local functions of components $\psi_0, \ldots, \psi_{k-1}$ depending non-monotonously on the states of components Ω and ψ. $\qquad\square$

In the construction above, the fact that $f_\Omega(x) = \neg x_\Omega$ imposes that any configuration converges to a limit-cycle of even length. Component Ω acts as a clock. For $k = 2$ we can adapt the construction by letting x_ψ stop this clock when the formula is satisfied, then in this case any configuration converges to a fixed point.

Corollary 2. BS no k-LC *is* $\mathsf{NP^{NP}}$-*hard for* $k = 2$.

Proof (Sketch). This is achieved by removing components $\psi_0, \ldots, \psi_{k-1}$, and replacing the local function of component Ω by $f_\Omega(x) = \neg x_\Omega \wedge \neg x_\psi$.   □

The idea presented in Corollary 2 of stopping a clock when the formula is satisfied (the clock gives a limit-cycle of length k, and stopping it leads to a fixed point), can be extended to any $k > 2$. The challenge here is to design a clock giving a limit-cycle of length k for any block-sequential update schedule.

Theorem 4. BS no k-LC *is* $\mathsf{NP^{NP}}$-*hard for any* $k > 2$.

Proof (Sketch). Now the main difficulty is to construct a clock on some components Ω_i, which could give a limit-cycle of length k for any update schedule (if it is not stopped by a specially designed $\mathtt{stop}$ component). With $k + 1$ clock components $\Omega_0, \ldots, \Omega_k$ for technical reasons, the idea to achieve this is to have a repair mechanism on $\log_2(\mathrm{BS}_{k+1})$ components ω_i with positive loops, where BS_{k+1} is the number of block-sequential update schedules on $k + 1$ components (recall that k is a constant). Then for any update schedule W, the states of components ω_i may encode the order of components Ω_i in W, which repairs the clock. Existential variables are now set in the order of λ_i', λ_i compared to Ω_0 in W, and universal variables again have positive loops (See Fig. 4).

If the instance of $\exists\forall$-**3-SAT** is positive, then there exists an update schedule W such that the clock is updated in parallel, and the states of components corresponding to existential variables encode a solution to the problem, hence $x_\psi = 1$ in all attractors. This triggers the clock stop mechanism by letting $x_{\mathtt{stop}} = 1$, and any configuration converges to a fixed point. Here the repair mechanism is carefully designed to let existential variables always take the states encoded in W, leading to $x_\psi = 1$, $x_{\mathtt{stop}} = 1$, and a fixed point.

If the instance of $\exists\forall$-**3-SAT** is negative, then for any update schedule W we can construct a configuration such that the repair mechanism in states ω_i corresponds to W, hence the clock is a limit-cycle of length k. Existential variables take the states encoded in W, which cannot solve the instance, hence there is a choice of states for the universal variables (again the positive loops let all 2^{n-s} combinations of states possible in attractors) such that formula ψ is not satisfied, giving $x_\psi = 0$ and $x_{\mathtt{stop}} = 0$. Consequently, the clock works forever, *i.e.* this attractor is a limit-cycle of length k.

The construction of the clock is not obvious. When the correct repair mechanism is encoded in the states of components ω_i, it consists in a unique state **1** moving forward at each step within the clock components $\Omega_0, \ldots, \Omega_k$, but in an order corresponding to the update schedule (not often from Ω_i to Ω_{i+1}, rather from Ω_{j_i} to $\Omega_{j_{i+1}}$ for $j_0, \ldots, j_k$ a permutation of $\{0, \ldots, k\}$ corresponding to the order of $\Omega_0, \ldots, \Omega_k$ in W). Furthermore, for any update schedule we have the property that at some step it will advance twice (hence the limit-cycle of length k), again when the correct repair mechanism is encoded. However, in the case of a positive $\exists\forall$-**3-SAT** instance, we have to consider all attractors in order to prove the absence of limit-cycle of length k, which includes wrong repair mechanisms encoded in the states of ω_i. Hopefully, when components Ω_i are updated in parallel, and we have an incorrect repair mechanism (*i.e.* the states of ω_i do not encode the parallel update schedule on $k + 1$ components), then the clock design lets it become a limit-cycle of length $k + 1$, which preserves the encoding of existential variables in the states of λ_i, and the conclusion that the stop mechanism $x_{\text{stop}} = 1$ is triggered.   □

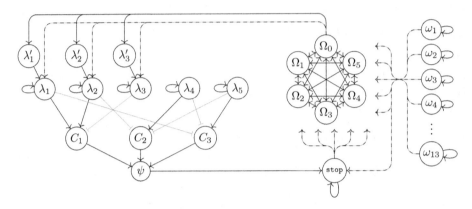

Fig. 4. Signed interaction digraph of the BN obtained for $k = 5$ ($BS_6 = 4683$), the 3-CNF formula $\psi = (\lambda_1 \vee \lambda_2 \vee \neg\lambda_3) \wedge (\neg\lambda_2 \vee \lambda_4 \vee \neg\lambda_5) \wedge (\neg\lambda_1 \vee \neg\lambda_4 \vee \lambda_5)$, and $s = 3$. Negative arcs $(-)$ are red with a flat head, positive arcs $(+)$ are black, positive-negative arcs $(\pm)$ are dashed with both colors and heads. All components stop and $\omega_1, \ldots, \omega_{13}$ are connected to all components $\Omega_0, \ldots, \Omega_5$ with arcs of sign $\pm$.

Remark 3. Encoding local function as truth tables of the components it effectively depends on (its in-neighbors in the interaction digraph) would also lead to the same complexity results, because all the constructions presented for hardness results can be adapted so that each component depends on a bounded number of components (the resulting interaction digraph has a bounded in-degree), given that k is a constant.

5   Conclusion

We have characterized precisely the computational complexity of problems related to, given a BN, the existence or not of limit-cycles of some fixed length k, with the quantifier alternation of "does there exist an update schedule such that all configurations are not in a limit-cycle of length k" bringing us to level Σ_2^P of the polynomial hierarchy.

Remark that all the constructions presented in our reductions (except for Theorem 3 which is subsumed by Theorem 4) are such that the resulting BN has either some limit-cycles of length k, or all its attractors are fixed points. Consequently, the same results directly hold for the problems where $\phi_k(f^{(W)})$ is replaced by $\phi_{\geq k}(f^{(W)}) = \sum_{\ell \geq k} \phi_\ell(f^{(W)})$, *i.e.* we consider limit-cycles of length at least k instead of exactly k. With little additional work the proofs may also be adapted to $\phi_{\leq k}(f^{(W)}) = \sum_{\ell \leq k} \phi_\ell(f^{(W)})$, *i.e.* if we consider limit-cycles of length at most k (fixed points should be transformed into limit-cycles of length larger that k).

Finally, if k is part of the input, we may ask whether there is a drastic complexity increase as observed for problems related to the number of fixed points in [5]. The complexity upper bound is not valid anymore if k is encoded in binary, and the construction presented in the proof of Theorem 4 makes heavy use of k being a constant, with the $\log_2(\mathrm{BS}_{k+1})$ components encoding the clock repair mechanism. With k encoding in binary, verifying if some configuration x is in a limit-cycle of length k naively takes an exponential time... The problem is however in PSPACE because one can try one by one the update schedules, and one by one the configurations for $k' = 1, \ldots, k$ steps, without remembering all the intermediate steps (only by counting how many steps have been performed). We conjecture that the problem would be PSPACE-complete in this case, but exploiting the parameter k seems to require completely novel ideas.

We hope that these first results on the complexity of deciding the existence of limit-cycles in Boolean networks opens a promising research direction, confronting the necessary difficulty (when the attractors under consideration are not restricted to fixed points) of comprehending the diversity of update schedules. We believe that the lens of computational complexity reveals, via the gadgets and structures of influences employed in hardness constructions, mechanisms at the heart of Boolean network's dynamical richness.

References

1. Aracena, J., Demongeot, J., Fanchon, É., Montalva, M.: On the number of different dynamics in Boolean networks with deterministic update schedules. Math. Biosci. **242**, 188–194 (2013)
2. Aracena, J., Demongeot, J., Goles, E.: Fixed points and maximal independent sets in AND-OR networks. Discr. Appl. Math. **138**, 277–288 (2004)
3. Aracena, J., Gómez, L., Salinas, L.: Limit cycles and update digraphs in Boolean networks. Disc. Appl. Math. **161**, 1–12 (2013)
4. Aracena, J., Richard, A., Salinas, L.: Number of fixed points and disjoint cycles in monotone Boolean networks. SIAM J. Discr. Math. **31**, 1702–1725 (2017)
5. Bridoux, F., Durbec, N., Perrot, K., Richard, A.: Complexity of maximum fixed point problem in Boolean networks. In: Manea, F., Martin, B., Paulusma, D., Primiero, G. (eds.) CiE 2019. LNCS, vol. 11558, pp. 132–143. Springer, Cham (2019). https://doi.org/10.1007/978-3-030-22996-2_12
6. Demongeot, J., Noual, M., Sené, S.: Combinatorics of Boolean automata circuits dynamics. Discr. Appl. Math. **160**, 398–415 (2012)
7. Elspas, B.: The theory of autonomous linear sequential networks. IRE Trans. Circuit Theory **6**, 45–60 (1959)
8. Floreen, P., Orponen, P.: On the computational complexity of analyzing Hopfield nets. Complex Syst. **3**, 577–587 (1989)
9. Goles, E., Martínez, S.: Neural and Automata Networks: Dynamical Behavior and Applications. Kluwer Academic Publishers, Dordrecht (1990)

10. Goles, E., Noual, M.: Block-sequential update schedules and Boolean automata circuits. In: Proceedings of AUTOMATA'2010, DMTCS, pp. 41–50 (2010)
11. Gómez, L.: Dynamics of discrete networks with deterministic updates schedules. Application to genetic regulatory networks. Ph.D. thesis, Univ. Concepción (2015)
12. Huffman, D.A.: Canonical forms for information-lossless finite-state logical machines. IRE Trans. Inform. Theory **5**, 41–59 (1959)
13. Kauffman, S.A.: Homeostasis and differentiation in random genetic control networks. Nature **224**, 177–178 (1969)
14. Kleene, S.C.: Representation of events in nerve nets and finite automata. Project RAND RM-704, US Air Force (1951)
15. McCulloch, W.S., Pitts, W.: A logical calculus of the ideas immanent in nervous activity. J. Math. Biophys. **5**, 115–133 (1943)
16. Orponen, P.: Neural networks and complexity theory. In: Havel, I.M., Koubek, V. (eds.) MFCS 1992. LNCS, vol. 629, pp. 50–61. Springer, Heidelberg (1992). https://doi.org/10.1007/3-540-55808-X_5
17. Papadimitriou, C.H.: Computational Complexity. Addison-Wesley, Boston (1994)
18. Remy, É., Ruet, P., Thieffry, D.: Graphic requirements for multistability and attractive cycles in a Boolean dynamical framework. Adv. Appl. Math. **41**, 335–350 (2008)
19. Richard, A.: Negative circuits and sustained oscillations in asynchronous automata networks. Adv. Appl. Math. **44**, 378–392 (2010)
20. Richard, A., Comet, J.-P.: Necessary conditions for multistationarity in discrete dynamical systems. Discr. Appl. Math. **155**, 2403–2413 (2007)
21. Robert, F.: Blocs-H-matrices et convergence des méthodes itératives classiques par blocs. Linear Algebra Appl. **2**, 223–265 (1969)
22. Robert, F.: Itérations sur des ensembles finis et automates cellulaires contractants. Linear Algebra Appl. **29**, 393–412 (1980)
23. Robert, F.: Discrete Iterations: A Metric Study. Springer, Heidelberg (1986). https://doi.org/10.1007/978-3-642-61607-5
24. Thomas, R.: Boolean formalization of genetic control circuits. J. Theor. Biol. **42**, 563–585 (1973)
25. Thomas, R.: On the relation between the logical structure of systems and their ability to generate multiple steady states or sustained oscillations. In: Della Dora, J., Demongeot, J., Lacolle, B. (eds.) Numerical Methods in the Study of Critical Phenomena, pp. 180–193. Springer, Heidelberg (1981). https://doi.org/10.1007/978-3-642-81703-8_24

Concatenation Operations and Restricted Variants of Two-Dimensional Automata

Taylor J. Smith$^{(\boxtimes)}$ and Kai Salomaa

School of Computing, Queen's University, Kingston, ON K7L 2N8, Canada
{tsmith,ksalomaa}@cs.queensu.ca

Abstract. A two-dimensional automaton operates on arrays of symbols. While a standard (four-way) two-dimensional automaton can move its input head in four directions, restricted two-dimensional automata are only permitted to move their input heads in three or two directions; these models are called three-way and two-way two-dimensional automata, respectively.

In two dimensions, we may extend the notion of concatenation in multiple ways, depending on the words to be concatenated. We may row-concatenate (resp., column-concatenate) a pair of two-dimensional words when they have the same number of columns (resp., rows). In addition, the diagonal concatenation operation combines two words at their lower-right and upper-left corners, and is not dimension-dependent.

In this paper, we investigate closure properties of restricted models of two-dimensional automata under three concatenation operations. We give non-closure results for two-way two-dimensional automata under row and column concatenation in both the deterministic and nondeterministic cases. We further give positive closure results for the same concatenation operations on unary nondeterministic two-way two-dimensional automata. Finally, we study closure properties of diagonal concatenation on both two- and three-way two-dimensional automata.

Keywords: Closure properties · Concatenation · Three-way automata · Two-dimensional automata · Two-way automata

1   Introduction

The two-dimensional automaton model, introduced by Blum and Hewitt [2], is a generalization of the well-known one-dimensional (string) finite automaton. A two-dimensional automaton takes as input an array or matrix of symbols from some alphabet Σ, and the input head of the automaton moves in four directions: upward, downward, leftward, and rightward.

If we restrict the input head movement of a two-dimensional automaton, then we obtain a variant of the model that is weaker in terms of recognition

Smith and Salomaa were supported by Natural Sciences and Engineering Research Council of Canada Grant OGP0147224.

T. Bureš et al. (Eds.): SOFSEM 2021, LNCS 12607, pp. 147–158, 2021.
https://doi.org/10.1007/978-3-030-67731-2_11

Table 1. Closure results for concatenation on two-dimensional automaton models. Closure is denoted by ✓ and nonclosure is denoted by ✗. New closure results presented in this paper are circled. Closure results marked with a † apply in the unary case.

	2DFA-4W	2NFA-4W	2DFA-3W	2NFA-3W	2DFA-2W	2NFA-2W
Row (⊖)	✗	✗	✗	✓	⊗	⊗ / ✓†
Column (⊕)	✗	✗	✗	✗	⊗	⊗ / ✓†
Diagonal (⊘)	?	?	⊗	?	⊗	✓

power, but also easier to reason about. If we prevent the input head from moving upward, then we obtain a three-way two-dimensional automaton. If we prevent both upward and leftward moves, then we obtain a two-way two-dimensional automaton. The three-way two-dimensional automaton model was introduced by Rosenfeld [9]. The two-way two-dimensional automaton model was introduced by Anselmo et al. [1] and formalized by Dong and Jin [3].

We can generalize many language operations from one dimension to two dimensions, and most of these operations have been studied in the past; for a review of previous work, see the surveys by Inoue and Takanami [5] or by the first author [10]. In this paper, we focus on the language operation of concatenation. In two dimensions, we may concatenate words either by joining rows or by joining columns. In either case, the relevant dimension of the words being concatenated must be equal (e.g., two words being concatenated column-wise must have the same number of rows).

Four-way two-dimensional automata are not closed under either row or column concatenation [6]. Three-way two-dimensional automata are not closed under column concatenation, but nondeterministic three-way two-dimensional automata are closed under row concatenation [4]. A selection of known closure results is summarized in Table 1.

In this paper, we investigate the closure of restricted two-dimensional automaton models under three concatenation operations. We give the first closure results for concatenation of languages recognized by two-way two-dimensional automata, showing that the model is not closed under row or column concatenation in the general alphabet case, while it is closed under both operations in the unary nondeterministic case. We also consider diagonal concatenation, an operation first introduced by Anselmo et al. [1], and show that nondeterministic two-way two-dimensional automata are closed under this operation, while this closure is lost in the deterministic case. Finally, we prove that deterministic three-way two-dimensional automata are also not closed under diagonal concatenation.

2   Preliminaries

A two-dimensional word consists of a finite array, or rectangle, of cells each labelled by a symbol from a finite alphabet Σ. Precisely speaking, for $m, n \geq 1$, an $m \times n$ two-dimensional word is a map from $\{1, \ldots, m\} \times \{1, \ldots, n\}$ to Σ. When a two-dimensional word is written on an input tape, the cells around the two-dimensional word are labelled with a special boundary marker $\# \notin \Sigma$; more generally, we may consider all cells outside of the bounds of an input word to contain boundary markers (see Kari and Salo [8], particularly Sects. 2 and 4).

A two-dimensional automaton has a finite state control that is capable of moving its input head in four directions within an input word: up, down, left, and right. We denote these directions by U, D, L, and R, respectively.

Definition 1 (Two-dimensional automaton). *A two-dimensional automaton is a tuple $(Q, \Sigma, \delta, q_0, q_{\text{accept}})$, where Q is a finite set of states, Σ is the input alphabet (with $\# \notin \Sigma$ acting as a boundary symbol), $\delta : (Q \setminus \{q_{\text{accept}}\}) \times (\Sigma \cup \{\#\}) \to Q \times \{U, D, L, R\}$ is the partial transition function, and $q_0, q_{\text{accept}} \in Q$ are the initial and accepting states, respectively.*

The computation of a two-dimensional automaton begins in the top-left corner (i.e., at cell $(1, 1)$) of its input word in the initial state q_0, and the automaton halts and accepts when it reaches the accepting state q_{accept}.

We can modify the deterministic model given in Definition 1 to be nondeterministic by changing the transition function to map to $2^{Q \times \{U, D, L, R\}}$ instead of $Q \times \{U, D, L, R\}$. We denote the deterministic and nondeterministic two-dimensional automaton models by 2DFA-4W and 2NFA-4W, respectively, where 4W indicates that the automaton has four directions of movement.

By restricting the movement of the input head to move in fewer than four directions, we obtain the aforementioned restricted variants of the two-dimensional automaton model. If we prohibit upward movements, then we get a three-way two-dimensional automaton. If we prohibit both upward and leftward movements, then we get a two-way two-dimensional automaton.

Definition 2 (Three-way/two-way two-dimensional automaton). *A three-way (resp., two-way) two-dimensional automaton is a tuple $(Q, \Sigma, \delta, q_0, q_{\text{accept}})$ as in Definition 1, where the transition function δ is restricted to use only the directions $\{D, L, R\}$ (resp., the directions $\{D, R\}$).*

We denote three-way two-dimensional automata by 2DFA-3W/2NFA-3W, and we denote two-way two-dimensional automata by 2DFA-2W/2NFA-2W. Note that three-way two-dimensional automata are unable to move their input head back into a word upon leaving the bottom edge of the word, while two-way two-dimensional automata are unable to do the same upon leaving either the bottom or right edge of the word. Thus, if a three-way (resp., two-way) two-dimensional automaton makes a downward (resp., downward or rightward) move and reads a boundary symbol, it can only read boundary symbols for the remainder of its computation.

3 Row and Column Concatenation

In two dimensions, we may consider the notions of row and column concatenation. The row (resp., column) concatenation of two-dimensional words w and v,

$$w \ominus v = \begin{matrix} w_{1,1} & \cdots & w_{1,n} \\ \vdots & \ddots & \vdots \\ w_{m,1} & \cdots & w_{m,n} \\ v_{1,1} & \cdots & v_{1,n} \\ \vdots & \ddots & \vdots \\ v_{m',1} & \cdots & v_{m',n} \end{matrix} \qquad w \oplus v = \begin{matrix} w_{1,1} & \cdots & w_{1,n} & v_{1,1} & \cdots & v_{1,n'} \\ \vdots & \ddots & \vdots & \vdots & \ddots & \vdots \\ w_{m,1} & \cdots & w_{m,n} & v_{m,1} & \cdots & v_{m,n'} \end{matrix}$$

Fig. 1. Row and column concatenations of two-dimensional words

denoted $w \ominus v$ (resp., $w \oplus v$), is the word produced by adjoining the last row (resp., column) of w to the first row (resp., column) of v. If w and v are of dimension $m \times n$ and $m' \times n'$ respectively, then the row and column concatenations of these words are defined only when $n = n'$ or $m = m'$, respectively.

We may similarly define the row or column concatenation of two languages A and B as $A \circ B = \{a \circ b \mid a \in A \text{ and } b \in B\}$, where $\circ \in \{\ominus, \oplus\}$.

Figure 1 illustrates the row and column concatenations of two words.

3.1 Two-Way Two-Dimensional Automata

As we noted in the introduction, basic closure results about concatenation are known for both four-way and three-way two-dimensional automata, and the only positive closure result applies to row concatenation over nondeterministic three-way two-dimensional automata. Unfortunately, for the two-way two-dimensional automaton model, we do not have closure for either row or column concatenation in the general alphabet case. Here, we state the result for the row concatenation operation on nondeterministic two-way two-dimensional automata.

Theorem 1. *Nondeterministic two-way two-dimensional automata over a general alphabet are not closed under row concatenation.*

The preceding theorem can easily be adapted to work in the deterministic case, and we can similarly prove non-closure for column concatenation over two-way two-dimensional automata.

Altogether, the previous results show that general-alphabet languages recognized by a deterministic two-way two-dimensional automaton may be concatenated either row-wise or column-wise to produce a language not recognized even by a nondeterministic two-way two-dimensional automaton.

3.2 Unary Two-Way Two-Dimensional Automata

As a consequence of the closure of nondeterministic three-way two-dimensional automata under row concatenation, we also know that unary nondeterministic three-way two-dimensional automata are closed under this operation. Aside from this fact, not much is known about closure of concatenation for unary two-dimensional automaton models. In this section, we obtain new closure results for row and column concatenation for unary nondeterministic two-way two-dimensional automata.

Remark 1. Anselmo et al. [1] previously studied properties of the two-way two-dimensional automaton model over a unary alphabet; however, their model differs from the one considered in this paper. See Sect. 4.1 for more details.

Before we proceed, we require one further definition. We say that an automaton is "immediately BR-accepting", or "IBR-accepting", if, upon reading a boundary marker on the bottom or right border of the word, the automaton immediately halts and accepts if q_{accept} is reachable from its current state.

Lemma 1. *Given a two-way two-dimensional automaton $\mathcal{M}$, there exists an equivalent IBR-accepting two-way two-dimensional automaton $\mathcal{M}'$.*

Proof. If $\mathcal{M}$ reads a boundary marker at the bottom or right border of its input word, then the input head of $\mathcal{M}$ can only read boundary markers for the remainder of its computation. After reading a boundary marker in state q_i, say, we can decide whether q_{accept} is reachable from q_i via some sequence of transitions on an arbitrary number of boundary markers. Thus, we may take $\mathcal{M}'$ to be the same as $\mathcal{M}$ apart from its transition upon reading the first boundary marker, which we modify to transition to q_{accept} in the positive case or leave undefined in the negative case. □

Using the notion of an IBR-accepting automaton, we obtain the main result of the section.

Theorem 2. *Nondeterministic two-way two-dimensional automata over a unary alphabet are closed under row concatenation.*

Proof. Let $\mathcal{A}$ and $\mathcal{B}$ be unary nondeterministic two-way two-dimensional automata recognizing languages A and B, respectively. Assume both $\mathcal{A}$ and $\mathcal{B}$ are IBR-accepting, and let the accepting computations of $\mathcal{A}$ and $\mathcal{B}$ be denoted by $C_\mathcal{A}$ and $C_\mathcal{B}$, respectively. We construct another unary nondeterministic two-way two-dimensional automaton $\mathcal{M}$ to recognize the language $A \ominus B$. The automaton $\mathcal{M}$ first makes a nondeterministic choice of which "types" of computation correspond to $C_\mathcal{A}$ and $C_\mathcal{B}$, and then interleaves both computations. The cases for each "type" of computation are as follows:

1. $C_\mathcal{A}$ accepts at the bottom border and $C_\mathcal{B}$ accepts at the right border;
2. $C_\mathcal{A}$ accepts at the right border and $C_\mathcal{B}$ accepts at the bottom border;
3. (a) $C_\mathcal{A}$ accepts at the bottom border in column i and $C_\mathcal{B}$ accepts at the bottom border in column $j < i$;
   (b) $C_\mathcal{A}$ accepts at the bottom border in column i and $C_\mathcal{B}$ accepts at the bottom border in column $k \geq i$;
4. $C_\mathcal{A}$ and $C_\mathcal{B}$ both accept at the right border.

Depending on the guessed "types" of the computations $C_\mathcal{A}$ and $C_\mathcal{B}$, the computation of $\mathcal{M}$ proceeds in one of the following ways:

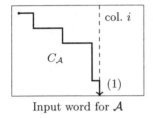 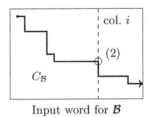

Input word for $\mathcal{A}$ Input word for $\mathcal{B}$

Fig. 2. Illustration of Case 1 computation. The simulation of $C_{\mathcal{A}}$ accepts at (1). The computation of $\mathcal{M}$ will begin its second phase at (2) in the input word consisting of the row concatenation of input words for $\mathcal{A}$ and $\mathcal{B}$.

Case 1. The computation of $\mathcal{M}$ is divided into two phases. In the first phase, $\mathcal{M}$ simulates the computations of $\mathcal{A}$ and $\mathcal{B}$ in the following order:

(i) $\mathcal{M}$ simulates all possible downward moves of $\mathcal{A}$ by moving the input head and changing the state of $\mathcal{A}$;

(ii) $\mathcal{M}$ simulates all possible downward moves of $\mathcal{B}$ by moving the input head and changing the state of $\mathcal{B}$;

(iii) when $\mathcal{A}$ and $\mathcal{B}$ both make a rightward move, $\mathcal{M}$ simulates the move and changes the state of both $\mathcal{A}$ and $\mathcal{B}$.

Note that, after completing steps (i) and (ii), at least one rightward move must occur in step (iii). After $\mathcal{M}$ completes step (iii), it continues from step (i).

When $\mathcal{M}$ simulates downward moves of the input head of $\mathcal{A}$ in step (i), it may nondeterministically guess that the input head of $\mathcal{A}$ has encountered a boundary symbol at the bottom border of the input word. If $\mathcal{A}$ is in an accepting state at that point, then $\mathcal{M}$ begins the second phase of its computation.

In the second phase, $\mathcal{M}$ simulates only the computation of $\mathcal{B}$. If $\mathcal{B}$ enters an accepting state when $\mathcal{M}$ encounters the right border, then $\mathcal{M}$ accepts.

Assume that $C_{\mathcal{A}}$ accepts at the bottom border in column i of its input word. At the point when the first phase of the computation ends, the input head of $\mathcal{M}$ will be at the position corresponding to where $C_{\mathcal{B}}$ first enters column i. (See Fig. 2.) Although $\mathcal{M}$ performs its computation on the concatenated input, $C_{\mathcal{B}}$ performs its computation only on the input word to $\mathcal{B}$.

Case 2. The first phase of the computation of $\mathcal{M}$ proceeds in the same manner as in the first phase of Case 1. However, in this case, since there may be an unknown number of rows beneath the row in which $\mathcal{A}$ accepts, the input head of $\mathcal{M}$ need not be at the bottom border when $\mathcal{B}$ accepts at the bottom border.

Thus, during step (ii), $\mathcal{M}$ may nondeterministically guess that the input head of $\mathcal{B}$ has encountered a boundary symbol at the bottom border of the input word. Since $\mathcal{B}$ is IBR-accepting, we may assume $\mathcal{B}$ transitions immediately to its accepting state. At this point, $\mathcal{M}$ begins the second phase of its computation.

In the second phase, $\mathcal{M}$ simulates only the computation of $\mathcal{A}$. If $\mathcal{A}$ enters an accepting state when $\mathcal{M}$ encounters the right border, then $\mathcal{M}$ accepts.

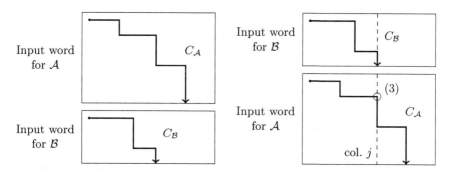

Fig. 3. Illustration of Case 3a computation. The left figure depicts the row concatenation, while the right figure depicts the "swapped" computation. When the simulation of C_B accepts, the computation of M will begin its second phase at (3).

Case 3a. We proceed in a similar manner as for Case 1, but we modify the first phase of the computation of M by swapping steps (i) and (ii). Thus, in the first phase, M simulates the computations of A and B in the following order:

(i′) M simulates all possible downward moves of B by moving the input head and changing the state of B;

(ii′) M simulates all possible downward moves of A by moving the input head and changing the state of A;

(iii′) when A and B both make a rightward move, M simulates the move and changes the state of both A and B.[1]

Since concatenation of unary words is a commutative operation, we may view this case as a simulation where the computation of B is performed before the computation of A, allowing us to swap the first two steps of the first phase.

During step (i′), M may nondeterministically guess that the input head of B has encountered a boundary symbol at the bottom border of the input word. Since B is IBR-accepting, we may assume B transitions immediately to its accepting state. At this point, M begins the second phase of its computation. (See Fig. 3.)

In the second phase, M simulates only the computation of A. If A enters an accepting state when M encounters the bottom border, then M accepts.

The logic behind determining the input head position after switching from simulating C_B to C_A is similar to the explanation given for Case 1.

Case 3b. Analogous to the proof for Case 1.

Case 4. Since both C_A and C_B accept at the right border of their input words, there may be an unknown number of rows beneath the rows in which A and B accept. Therefore, the computation of M need only verify that its input word contains a sufficient number of rows to allow simulation of C_A and C_B.

---

[1] Note that step (iii′) of Case 3a is identical to step (iii) of Case 1.

$$w \oslash v = \begin{matrix} w_{1,1} & \cdots & w_{1,n} & x_{1,1} & \cdots & x_{1,n'} \\ \vdots & & \vdots & \vdots & & \vdots \\ w_{m,1} & \cdots & w_{m,n} & x_{m,1} & \cdots & x_{m,n'} \\ y_{1,1} & \cdots & y_{1,n} & v_{1,1} & \cdots & v_{1,n'} \\ \vdots & & \vdots & \vdots & & \vdots \\ y_{m',1} & \cdots & y_{m',n} & v_{m',1} & \cdots & v_{m',n'} \end{matrix}$$

Fig. 4. Diagonal concatenation of two-dimensional words

The computation of $\mathcal{M}$ proceeds in the same order as in the first phase of Case 1. If, during step (iii), the input head of $\mathcal{M}$ encounters a boundary marker when both $\mathcal{A}$ and $\mathcal{B}$ are in accepting states, then $\mathcal{M}$ accepts.   □

Closure under column concatenation follows by interchanging downward and rightward input head moves.

Corollary 1. *Nondeterministic two-way two-dimensional automata over a unary alphabet are closed under column concatenation.*

4   Diagonal Concatenation

Anselmo et al. [1] introduced a new operation for unary two-dimensional words called "diagonal concatenation". Given unary two-dimensional words w and v of dimension $m \times n$ and $m' \times n'$ respectively, the diagonal concatenation of w and v, denoted $w \oslash v$, is a two-dimensional word of dimension $(m + m') \times (n + n')$ where w is in the top-left quadrant and v is in the bottom-right quadrant.

In this section, we extend the diagonal concatenation operation to words over a general alphabet. In this case, the diagonal concatenation of two words w and v, defined as before, produces a two-dimensional language consisting of words of dimension $(m + m') \times (n + n')$ where w is in the top-left quadrant, v is in the bottom-right quadrant, and words $x \in \Sigma^{m \times n'}$ and $y \in \Sigma^{m' \times n}$ are in the top-right and bottom-left quadrants of $w \oslash v$, respectively. The diagonal concatenation language is formed by adding to the top-right and bottom-left quadrants all possible words x and y over Σ. An example word from such a language is depicted in Fig. 4. We may define the diagonal concatenation of two languages A and B in a similar manner as for row and column concatenation: the top-left quadrant contains only words from A, and the bottom-right quadrant contains only words from B.

Remark 2. Note that an automaton recognizing $w \oslash v$ only needs to read the contents of the top-left and bottom-right quadrants to determine whether a word is in the diagonal concatenation language. Thus, we may add any symbols from Σ to the top-right and bottom-left quadrants to ensure the resulting word is a contiguous rectangle. If an automaton recognizes the diagonal concatenation language as defined earlier, where all possible words x and y are placed in the top-right and bottom-left quadrants, respectively, then it will recognize any word with w and v in the appropriate locations, as desired.

4.1   Two-Way Two-Dimensional Automata

For the two-way two-dimensional automaton model, the input head is able to recognize when it reaches the bottom or right border of its input word. However, since the input head cannot move upward or leftward, it cannot leave the border once it moves onto a boundary symbol. If the input head makes further moves upon reaching the border, it can only read boundary symbols until the automaton halts.

Anselmo et al. [1] state that their definition of a two-way two-dimensional automaton is equivalent to a two-tape one-dimensional automaton whose input heads only move rightward. This suggests that their model can detect when it has reached not only one, but both of its input word's bottom and right borders, giving it more recognition power than our model, which is only able to determine when it has reached either the bottom or right border of its input word, but not both simultaneously. In terms of boundary symbols, the model of Anselmo et al. is akin to placing a distinguished boundary symbol at the bottom-right corner of the border of the input word.

Using our two-way model, where all boundary symbols are identical, we obtain the following closure result for diagonal concatenation.

Theorem 3. *Nondeterministic two-way two-dimensional automata over a general alphabet are closed under diagonal concatenation.*

We prove the preceding theorem by constructing a nondeterministic two-way two-dimensional automaton $\mathcal{C}$ to recognize the language $A \oslash B$, where language A (resp., B) is recognized by automaton $\mathcal{A}$ (resp., $\mathcal{B}$). The automaton $\mathcal{C}$ simulates the IBR-accepting computation of $\mathcal{A}$, and then nondeterministically makes some number of moves in the input word before simulating $\mathcal{B}$. These moves allow $\mathcal{C}$ to "guess" when it has entered the lower-right quadrant of the input word; that is, when its input head is positioned at the top-left corner of the input to $\mathcal{B}$.

Evidently, then, the power of nondeterminism is crucial for the automaton $\mathcal{C}$ to recognize diagonally-concatenated words. Indeed, if we remove nondeterminism, then we also lose closure.

Theorem 4. *Deterministic two-way two-dimensional automata over a general alphabet are not closed under diagonal concatenation.*

4.2   Three-Way Two-Dimensional Automata

Given the result of Theorem 4, we should expect not to obtain a positive closure result for deterministic three-way two-dimensional automata. However, unlike Theorem 4, we are considering three directions of movement, and so we cannot assert that the input head of our automaton is incapable of reading all symbols within the input word. (Indeed, the input head of a three-way two-dimensional automaton may read all symbols via a left-to-right sweeping motion.) Thus, we require a different approach.

Under certain conditions, a two-way one-dimensional automaton $\mathcal{N}$ can simulate the computation of a three-way two-dimensional automaton $\mathcal{M}$ on a particular row of its input word. Moreover, as we will see, the number of states of $\mathcal{N}$ depends linearly on the number of states of $\mathcal{M}$.

Here, we construct a diagonal concatenation language $A \oslash B$, where A and B are languages recognized by deterministic three-way two-dimensional automata $\mathcal{A}$ and $\mathcal{B}$, and then we show that there exists no two-way one-dimensional automaton $\mathcal{C}$ with enough states to simulate the computation of $\mathcal{A}$ and $\mathcal{B}$ together on the diagonal concatenation language.

To arrive at the main result, we first require two technical lemmas.

Lemma 2. *Let $\mathcal{M}$ be a deterministic three-way two-dimensional automaton with n states working over the alphabet $\Sigma = \{0, 1\}$. Consider the computation of $\mathcal{M}$ on an input word where row i consists entirely of 0s.*

If the input head of $\mathcal{M}$ visits the first or last symbol of row i and moves downward to row $i + 1$, then this move happens at distance at most $n + 1$ from one of the boundary markers.

Proof. If $\mathcal{M}$ enters row i in the first or last column and moves downward immediately after, then the result follows. If $\mathcal{M}$ enters row i, visits the first or last symbol of the row, and makes fewer than n leftward/rightward moves before moving downward, then the result also follows.

Since $\mathcal{M}$ must visit either the first or last symbol of row i, it can make at most n moves leftward/rightward without entering a loop. If $\mathcal{M}$ does not move downward within the first n leftward/rightward moves, it will be forced to move leftward/rightward in a loop until it reaches the other end of row i.

Therefore, a downward move may only occur within distance n from the first or last symbols of the row, and thus may only occur within distance $n + 1$ from one of the boundary markers.   □

Given a deterministic three-way two-dimensional automaton $\mathcal{M}$, consider the computation of $\mathcal{M}$ on row i of its input word. We say that a two-way one-dimensional automaton $\mathcal{N}$ correctly simulates the computation of $\mathcal{M}$ on row i if, given row i as input, $\mathcal{N}$ accepts if and only if $\mathcal{M}$ moves downward from row i.

Lemma 3. *Suppose that a deterministic three-way two-dimensional automaton $\mathcal{M}$ has n states, and that $\mathcal{M}$ enters row i of its input word at distance at most $n + 1$ from one of the boundary markers. Then there exists a deterministic two-way one-dimensional automaton $\mathcal{N}$ with at most $2n + 3$ states that correctly simulates the computation of $\mathcal{M}$ on row i.*

Proof. By our assumption, $\mathcal{M}$ begins its computation at distance at most $n + 1$ from one of the boundary markers of row i. On the other hand, $\mathcal{N}$ begins its computation at the leftmost position of its input.

We require at most $n + 2$ states to move the input head of $\mathcal{N}$ to the initial position of the input head of $\mathcal{M}$ after it enters row i; $n+1$ states are used to count the number of moves made by $\mathcal{N}$, and one state is required to move the input head of $\mathcal{N}$ rightward if $\mathcal{M}$ entered row i at one of the rightmost $n+1$ positions. At this point, $\mathcal{N}$ directly simulates the computation of $\mathcal{M}$ using n states. Once $\mathcal{M}$ follows a transition with a downward move, $\mathcal{N}$ enters a designated accepting state. Altogether, this construction for $\mathcal{N}$ requires at most $2n+3$ states.   □

Kapoutsis [7] proved that, given a deterministic two-way one-dimensional automaton with n states, we may convert it to an equivalent deterministic one-way one-dimensional automaton with $h(n) = n(n^n - (n-1)^n)$ states. We will use this value $h(n)$ in the proof of the main result.

Theorem 5. *Deterministic three-way two-dimensional automata over a general alphabet are not closed under diagonal concatenation.*

Proof. Let $\Sigma = \{0,1\}$. Let A be the language of $1 \times n'$ two-dimensional words where $n' \geq 1$ and the single row consists entirely of 0s. Let B be the language of $3 \times n''$ two-dimensional words where $n'' \geq 1$ and all three rows consist entirely of 0s, apart from the top-left corner symbol of each word, which is 1.

Suppose there exists a deterministic three-way two-dimensional automaton $\mathcal{C}$ with n states recognizing the language $A \oslash B$. Each word in $A \oslash B$ consists of exactly four rows. Since $\mathcal{C}$ can remember the number of rows it visited, we may assume without loss of generality that, when $\mathcal{C}$ moves downward from row 4, it accepts. Any moves to a rejecting state are simulated by "stay-in-place" moves.

Let $k = h(2n+3) + 1$. Consider the set of two-dimensional words X where each word has dimension $4 \times 2k$, the first row of each word consists entirely of 0s, the second row is of the form $0^k 10^{k-1}$, the third row consists entirely of 0s, and the fourth row is of the form $\{0,1\}^{2k}$. Evidently, given a word $w \in X$, we also have that $w \in A \oslash B$ if and only if the last k symbols of row 4 are all 0.

Consider an accepting computation of $\mathcal{C}$ on a word $w \in X$. During this computation, $\mathcal{C}$ must visit the last symbol of the third row. Otherwise, we could change this symbol to 1, and $\mathcal{C}$ would accept a word not belonging to $A \oslash B$.

Since $\mathcal{C}$ visits the last symbol of the third row, by Lemma 2, we know that the input head must subsequently enter the fourth row at distance at most $n+1$ from one of the boundary markers. Then, by Lemma 3, there exists a deterministic two-way one-dimensional automaton $\mathcal{D}$ with $2n+3$ states that correctly simulates the computation of $\mathcal{C}$ on the fourth row. We may convert $\mathcal{D}$ to an equivalent one-way one-dimensional automaton $\mathcal{D}'$ with $h(2n+3)$ states. From here, $\mathcal{D}'$ must check that each of the rightmost $k = h(2n+3)+1$ symbols in the fourth row is 0. But, since $\mathcal{D}'$ has $k-1 = h(2n+3)$ states and the fourth row consists of $2k$ symbols, $\mathcal{D}'$ is unable to count up to the kth symbol in order to determine where the latter k symbols in that row begin.   □

5   Conclusion

In this paper, we considered closure properties of various concatenation operations on two-dimensional automata. We showed that two-way two-dimensional automata over a general alphabet are not closed under either row or column concatenation. For a unary alphabet, on the other hand, we showed that nondeterministic two-way two-dimensional automata are closed under both row and column concatenation. We further showed that nondeterministic two-way two-dimensional automata over a general alphabet are closed under diagonal concatenation, while neither deterministic two-way nor deterministic three-way two-dimensional automata are closed.

There remain some open problems related to two-dimensional concatenation. Most closure results for concatenation assume the use of a general alphabet. Studying concatenation for unary two-dimensional automaton models in particular could prove interesting. Furthermore, nothing is yet known about the closure of diagonal concatenation on four-way two-dimensional automata. Lastly, we conjecture that nondeterministic three-way two-dimensional automata over a general alphabet are not closed under diagonal concatenation. However, showing this would require essentially a different proof than that given for Theorem 5.

References

1. Anselmo, M., Giammarresi, D., Madonia, M.: New operations and regular expressions for two-dimensional languages over one-letter alphabet. Theoret. Comput. Sci. **340**(2), 408–431 (2005)
2. Blum, M., Hewitt, C.: Automata on a 2-dimensional tape. In: Miller, R.E. (ed.) SWAT 1967, pp. 155–160 (1967)
3. Dong, J., Jin, W.: Comparison of two-way two-dimensional finite automata and three-way two-dimensional finite automata. In: Yang, X. (ed.) CSSS 2012, pp. 1904–1906 (2012)
4. Inoue, K., Takanami, I.: Closure properties of three-way and four-way tape-bounded two-dimensional Turing machines. Inf. Sci. **18**(3), 247–265 (1979)
5. Inoue, K., Takanami, I.: A survey of two-dimensional automata theory. Inf. Sci. **55**(1–3), 99–121 (1991)
6. Inoue, K., Takanami, I., Nakamura, A.: A note on two-dimensional finite automata. Inf. Process. Lett. **7**(1), 49–52 (1978)
7. Kapoutsis, C.: Removing bidirectionality from nondeterministic finite automata. In: Jędrzejowicz, J., Szepietowski, A. (eds.) MFCS 2005. LNCS, vol. 3618, pp. 544–555. Springer, Heidelberg (2005). https://doi.org/10.1007/11549345_47
8. Kari, J., Salo, V.: A survey on picture-walking automata. In: Kuich, W., Rahonis, G. (eds.) Algebraic Foundations in Computer Science. LNCS, vol. 7020, pp. 183–213. Springer, Heidelberg (2011). https://doi.org/10.1007/978-3-642-24897-9_9
9. Rosenfeld, A.: Picture Languages: Formal Models for Picture Recognition. Computer Science and Applied Mathematics. Academic Press, New York (1979)
10. Smith, T.J.: Two-dimensional automata. Technical report 2019–637, Queen's University, Kingston (2019)

Distance Hedonic Games

Michele Flammini[1] , Bojana Kodric[1] , Martin Olsen[2] ,
and Giovanna Varricchio[1(✉)]

[1] Department of Computer Science, Gran Sasso Science Institute, L'Aquila, Italy
{michele.flammini,bojana.kodric,giovanna.varricchio}@gssi.it
[2] Department of Business Development and Technology, Aarhus University,
Aarhus, Denmark
martino@btech.au.dk

Abstract. In this paper we consider Distance Hedonic Games (DHGs),
a class of non-transferable utility coalition formation games that properly generalizes previously existing models, like Social Distance Games
(SDGs) and unweighted Fractional Hedonic Games (FHGs). In particular, in DHGs we assume the existence of a scoring vector α, in which the
i-th coefficient α_i expresses the extent to which an agent x contributes to
the utility of an agent y if they are at distance i. We focus on Nash stable
outcomes in the arising games, i.e., on coalition structures in which no
agent can unilaterally improve her gain by deviating.

We consider two different natural scenarios for the scoring vector,
with monotonically increasing and monotonically decreasing coefficients.
In both cases we give NP-hardness and inapproximability results on the
problems of finding a social optimum and a best Nash stable outcome.
Moreover, we characterize the topologies of coalitions that provide high
social welfare and consequently give suitable bounds on the Price of
Anarchy and on the Price of Stability.

Keywords: Coalition formation · Hedonic Games · Nash stability

1 Introduction

Hedonic Games (HGs), introduced by Dreze and Greenberg (1980) [15], model
multi-agent systems where selfish agents form coalitions and have preferences
over the coalitions they belong to and not on how the others are aggregated.
More specifically, an outcome of a HG is a partition of the set of agents into
disjoint coalitions, referred to as a *coalition structure*. One of the main goals in
HGs is to understand the nature of the stable outcomes that the selfish behavior
of the agents leads to, both from an existential and an algorithmic perspective.
In this work we focus on individual deviations and we consider the fundamental
notion defined in this setting, that is, Nash stability. A coalition structure is *Nash
stable* if no agent can improve her utility by unilaterally moving to a different
coalition. To evaluate the efficiency of Nash equilibria, we resort to the classical
measures of *price of anarchy* (PoA) [22,24] and *price of stability* (PoS) [1], being

© Springer Nature Switzerland AG 2021
T. Bureš et al. (Eds.): SOFSEM 2021, LNCS 12607, pp. 159–174, 2021.
https://doi.org/10.1007/978-3-030-67731-2_12

respectively the worst and the best case ratios between the highest achievable social welfare (i.e., the sum of the agents' utilities) of a coalition structure and that of a Nash stable one.

In many natural scenarios the relations between agents can be modeled as a graph, and the utilities that agents receive from their coalitions strongly depend on the graph structure. Classical examples are Additively Separable Hedonic games [10], Fractional Hedonic Games (FHGs) [2] and Social Distance Games (SDGs) [12]. In this work, we focus on a class of games termed *Distance Hedonic Games* (DHGs), that generalizes both unweighted FHGs and SDGs.

In particular, while in SDGs each agent x contributes to the utility of another agent y in her coalition in an inversely proportional fashion with respect to their distance, and in FHGs only if they are neighbors. In DHGs we assume the existence of a scoring vector, in which the i-th coefficient expresses the extent to which x contributes to the utility of y if they are at distance i. The scoring vector is assumed to be the same for all agents.

We focus on the most natural types of scoring vectors whose coefficients have a monotone growth and distinguish between decreasing and increasing vectors. In the case of decreasing vectors, if the distance between two agents increases, the interest of being together decreases. Thus, a decreasing vector models situations in which agents want to aggregate themselves into coalitions in which they are close together. In the case of increasing vectors, the relationships in the graph may represent competition between agents. This does not violate the hedonic nature of the game, as the graph structure does not necessarily represent the will of being together but it can represent, for example, the physical distance between agents. The idea of increasing vectors is to reach far away nodes while relying only on internal communication. In conclusion, by using our model with varying scoring vectors, one can investigate how agents aggregate in different scenarios, including both interesting new and already studied ones.

1.1   Our Contribution

We introduce and study DHGs, a natural generalization of both unweighted FHGs and SDGs, from a (game-theoretically seen) non-cooperative perspective. We give a broad picture of both the PoA and the PoS, distinguishing the following scoring vectors: general (with possibly negative coefficients), non-negative, non-negative and normalized (i.e., the first component is equal to 1), and constant. The focus of the paper, however, is set on non-negative scoring vectors with monotonically decreasing and monotonically increasing coefficients. We give refined PoS bounds for decreasing normalized scoring vectors whose second component is $\leq \frac{1}{2}$ and the underlying graph has girth ≥ 5, and for increasing normalized scoring vectors. Notice that our bound on the PoS for decreasing normalized scoring vectors is in fact a generalization of the one obtained in [4]. Indeed, when the second component α_2 of the scoring vector is $\leq \frac{1}{2}$ and the graph has girth ≥ 5, PoS $\leq n \cdot \frac{\alpha_2 + \sqrt{\alpha_2^2 + (1-\alpha_2)^2}}{1 + 2\alpha_2 \cdot (n-1)}$. On the other hand, in [4] the authors study a special case in which the second component is exactly $\frac{1}{2}$, and their bound on the

PoS is $\frac{1}{2} + \frac{1}{\sqrt{2}}$, under the assumption that the graph has girth ≥ 5. By applying $\alpha_2 = \frac{1}{2}$ to our formula we get the same result.

Table 1. Left, PoA and PoS, where m_α and M_α denote the min and the max component of the scoring vector α, respectively. By $SW(P_n)$ we denote the social welfare achieved by a path of n nodes. Right, hardness and inapproximability results for finding the optimal (MSW) and best Nash stable (MSW-S) outcomes.

Scoring Vector	PoA	PoS	MSW	MSW-S
General	∞	∞		
Non-negative	∞	$\Theta(n)$		
Non-neg. and Normalized	$\leq M_\alpha(n-1)$	$\leq \min\{\frac{M_\alpha}{m_\alpha}, \frac{n}{2} \cdot M_\alpha\}$		
Constant	1	1	MSW	MSW-S
Decreasing normalized	$n-1$	$\leq n \cdot \frac{\alpha_2 + \sqrt{\alpha_2^2 + (1-\alpha_2)^2}}{1 + 2\alpha_2 \cdot (n-1)}$ for $\alpha_2 \leq \frac{1}{2}$, girth ≥ 5	NP-hard [3],[12]	NP-hard for $\alpha_2 \leq \frac{1}{2}$
Increasing normalized	$\Theta\left(\frac{SW(P_n)}{n}\right)$	$\Theta\left(\frac{SW(P_n)}{n}\right)$	no poly-time w. approx.$< \frac{2^{n+1}}{n^2+1}$	
Increasing with $\alpha_1 = 0$	∞	$\Theta(n)$	no poly-time w. approx. > 0	no poly-time w. approx. > 0

Finally, we give NP-hardness and inapproximability results for the problems of finding a social optimum and a best Nash stable outcome (the one with the highest social welfare). Our results are summarized by Table 1.

1.2 Related Work

In the literature, HGs have been studied both with respect to individual [6,10, 17,19] and group deviations [9,18,19]. While the classical solution concept for the former is *Nash stability*, for the latter is *core stability*.

FHGs are a subclass of HGs in which the utility of an agent is given by the sum of her preferences for each member of her coalition, divided by the coalition size. The special case of agents' preferences being in $\{0,1\}$ is termed unweighted FHGs. FHGs have also been investigated with respect to group [2,3,11] and individual deviations [7,8,23]. In particular, in [8] has been shown that the existence of a stable outcome is not guaranteed if the graph has negative weights, while the grand coalition is always stable when weights also are non-negative. Moreover, the paper studies the efficiency of equilibria, providing bounds on the PoA and the PoS while considering different topologies and different assumptions on the weights. The authors focus on the complexity of computing a best Nash stable outcome and show that this problem is NP-hard both for weighted and unweighted graphs.

SDGs have been introduced in [12], where they are studied with respect to group deviations and core stability. The paper shows NP-hardness of finding a coalition structure with maximum social welfare and gives a 1/2-approximation algorithm. In [4], SDGs are investigated with respect to individual deviations,

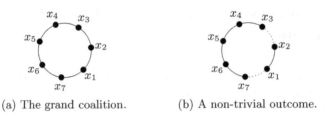

(a) The grand coalition.   (b) A non-trivial outcome.

Fig. 1. Two coalition structures on a cycle of 7 nodes. Dotted edges are in the cut between two different coalitions.

and the NP-hardness of finding a best Nash stable outcome is proven. Moreover, bounds on both the PoA and the PoS are provided, with a particular focus on graphs with girth of at least 4. Some of the bounds are improved by [21]. Finally, Pareto optimality has been considered in [5].

2   Model and Preliminaries

Given an undirected graph $G = (V, E)$, a *coalition structure* $\mathcal{C} = (C_1, \ldots, C_k)$ is a partition of V into coalitions. We denote by $\mathcal{C}(x)$ the coalition to which x belongs to. The *grand coalition* GC is a coalition structure which consists of only one coalition containing all agents and a *singleton coalition* is a coalition of size 1. Given any subset of nodes $C \subset V$, we denote by $G_C = (C, E_C)$ the *induced subgraph*, where E_C is the subset of the edges in E whose endpoints are both contained in C, i.e., $E_C = \{(x, y) \in E \mid x, y \in C\}$. The *induced distance* d_C is the one in the graph G_C, and $d_C(x, y) := \infty$ if x and y are disconnected in G_C.

Definition 1. *A* Distance Hedonic Game *(DHG) instance* $\langle G, \alpha \rangle$ *is defined by an undirected graph* $G = (V, E)$ *and a scoring vector* $\alpha \in \mathbb{R}^{n-1}$ *where: (i)* V *is a set of* n *agents and (ii) the* utility *of an agent* $x \in V$ *in a given coalition structure* $\mathcal{C}$ *is the evaluation of* x *for being in* $\mathcal{C}(x)$, *and it is given by*

$$u_x^\alpha(\mathcal{C}(x)) = \frac{1}{|\mathcal{C}(x)|} \sum_{y \in \mathcal{C}(x) \setminus \{x\}} \alpha_{d_{\mathcal{C}(x)}(x,y)}.$$

Moreover, if $d_C(x, y) = \infty$, *we define* $\alpha_\infty = 0$.

Example 1. Let the graph G be a cycle of seven nodes, $x_1, \ldots, x_7$, and let $\mathcal{C} = \{\{x_1, x_2\}, \{x_3, \ldots, x_7\}\}$, as depicted in Fig. 1b. If the scoring vector is $\alpha = (1, 2, 3, 4, \ldots)$, then the utility of agent x_3 in the coalition $\mathcal{C}(x_3)$ is $u_{x_3}^\alpha(\mathcal{C}(x_3)) = \frac{1}{5}(1 + 2 + 3 + 4) = 2$. On the other hand, in the grand coalition, as seen in Fig. 1a, the utility of each agent, so then also of agent x_3, is equal to $\frac{1}{7}(2 \cdot 1 + 2 \cdot 2 + 2 \cdot 3) = \frac{12}{7}$.

We call a scoring vector α *decreasing* if $\alpha_i \geq \alpha_{i+1}$ for each $i \in [n-2]$. Similarly, α is *increasing* if $\alpha_i \leq \alpha_{i+1}$ for each $i \in [n-2]$. We say that an increasing or decreasing scoring vector α is *normalized* if $\alpha_1 = 1$.

When α is clear from context, we simply write $u_x(\mathcal{C}(x))$. Furthermore, the social welfare of a coalition structure $\mathcal{C}$ is then given by $\mathrm{SW}(\mathcal{C}) = \sum_{x \in V} u_x(\mathcal{C}(x))$. Given a coalition $C \in \mathcal{C}$, we denote by $up(i, C)$ the number of unordered pairs that are at distance i in C, i.e., $up(i, C) = |\{\{x, y\} \mid x, y \in C \wedge d_C(x, y) = i\}|$. Thus, the social welfare of a coalition C of size k is equal to

$$\mathrm{SW}(C) = \frac{2}{k} \sum_{i=1}^{k-1} \alpha_i \cdot up(i, C). \tag{1}$$

We observe that $\sum_{i=1}^{k-1} up(i, C) = \binom{k}{2}$.

We denote by $\mathcal{C}^*$ any coalition structure that achieves the highest possible social welfare, and $\mathrm{OPT} = \mathrm{SW}(\mathcal{C}^*)$ is the *social optimum*.

We say that an agent $x \in V$ does not want to deviate in a coalition structure $\mathcal{C}$ if $u_x^\alpha(\mathcal{C}(x)) \geq u_x^\alpha(\mathcal{C}(y) \cup \{x\}), \forall y \in V$. A coalition structure $\mathcal{C}$ is *Nash stable* or a *Nash equilibrium* if no agent wants to deviate. Given a game instance $\langle G, \alpha \rangle$, we denote by $\mathsf{NS}_{\langle G,\alpha \rangle}$ the set of its Nash stable outcomes. A Nash stable outcome with maximum social welfare is said to be a *best Nash stable* outcome.

Our aim is to bound the performance of Nash stable outcomes by considering the worst/best possible ratio between the social optimum and their social welfare, called *price of anarchy* (PoA) and *price of stability* (PoS), respectively. Formally,

$$\mathrm{PoA}(\alpha) = \sup_G \max_{\mathcal{C} \in \mathsf{NS}_{\langle G,\alpha \rangle}} \frac{\mathrm{OPT}}{\mathrm{SW}(\mathcal{C})} \quad \text{and} \quad \mathrm{PoS}(\alpha) = \sup_G \min_{\mathcal{C} \in \mathsf{NS}_{\langle G,\alpha \rangle}} \frac{\mathrm{OPT}}{\mathrm{SW}(\mathcal{C})}.$$

When for some α there exists a graph G and $\mathcal{C} \in \mathsf{NS}_{\langle G,\alpha \rangle}$ such that $\mathrm{SW}(\mathcal{C}) = 0$, we say that $\mathrm{PoA}(\alpha)$ is unbounded. Similarly, if for some α there exists a graph G such that $\forall \mathcal{C} \in \mathsf{NS}_{\langle G,\alpha \rangle}, \mathrm{SW}(\mathcal{C}) = 0$, we say that $\mathrm{PoS}(\alpha)$ is unbounded.

We assume that the underlying graph G is connected, as the connected components of a graph can otherwise be considered separately for bounding the PoA and PoS. The following specific topologies will be useful for our analysis.

Stars. A k-star is a coalition of k nodes that form a tree with a diameter of at most 2. When the star is made of just two nodes, we will interchangeably refer to them as root or leaf. We denote a k-star by S_k and a coalition structure that is a star partition, i.e., in which each coalition is a star, by $\mathcal{S}$.

Given a graph G, we denote by $\Sigma(G)$ the family of all possible star partitions, where each star in the partition is of size of at least 2. For a fixed G, we can define a total order on $\Sigma(G)$ as follows: given a star partition $\mathcal{S} \in \Sigma(G)$, let $n_i(\mathcal{S})$ be the number of stars in $\mathcal{S}$ of size i. Then, for any $\mathcal{S}, \mathcal{S}' \in \Sigma(G)$ we say that $\mathcal{S}$ is co-lexicographically smaller than $\mathcal{S}'$ if $n_j(\mathcal{S}) < n_j(\mathcal{S}')$, where j is the highest index for which $n_i(\mathcal{S})$ and $n_i(\mathcal{S}')$ differ. In that case, we write $\mathcal{S} <_{colex} \mathcal{S}'$.

While in general it is possible that $\Sigma(G) = \emptyset$, when G has girth[1]>3, the existence of at least one star partition is always guaranteed. Moreover, if G has girth ≥ 5, any node of a star can be connected to at most one node of another star. In particular, if two roots are connected, then there are no further edges between the two star coalitions in the graph.

Paths. Since coalitions whose underlying subgraph is a path will be relevant to our investigation of increasing vectors, here we give some formulas for computing their social welfare. We denote by P_ℓ a path of ℓ nodes.

Lemma 1. *Given a coalition* $C \subseteq V$, *if* $C = \mathsf{P}_\ell$ *with* $\ell \geq 1$ *nodes, then* $\mathrm{SW}(\mathsf{P}_\ell) = \frac{2}{\ell} \sum_{i=1}^{\ell-1} \alpha_i(\ell - i)$. *Moreover,* $\mathrm{SW}(\mathsf{P}_{\ell+1}) - \mathrm{SW}(\mathsf{P}_\ell) = \frac{2}{\ell(\ell+1)} \sum_{i=1}^{\ell} \alpha_i \cdot i$.

Model Discussion. Both unweighted FHGs and SDGs are a subclass of DHGs, as it can be verified by setting $\alpha = (1, 0, \ldots, 0)$ and $\alpha = (1, \frac{1}{2}, \ldots, \frac{1}{n-1})$, respectively. These vectors induce utilities that are proportional to degree and harmonic centrality measures of nodes in coalitions. Further centrality measures fit into the DHG model. For instance, the Dangalchev centrality measure [13] corresponds to the i-th component of the scoring vector equaling $1/2^i$, and in its generalized version [14] the i-th component equals β^i for any fixed β in $(0, 1)$.

We observe that, both in our model and the preexisting ones, the utility of the agents depends on the distance induced by their coalitions and not on the original distance in the graph. This assumption relies not only on the hedonic character of the game, meaning that agents only care about the coalition they are involved with, but also, it is traditional in clustering settings. Furthermore, it makes our model different from general bin packing games [25], in which the utility agent i receives from being in the same coalition with agent j is a priori fixed and does not depend on other coalition members. Lastly, we set $\alpha_\infty = 0$ both for increasing and decreasing vectors, as we wish the agents to achieve positive utility only from the nodes they are connected to. In a way, this reflects the fact that a coalition should be independent from the others, with internal communication being private and not having to rely on external agents.

2.1   Preliminary Results: Quality of Equilibria

Before proceeding with our analysis we discard some classes of scoring vectors, not only because they do not represent natural scenarios, but also because of their low efficiency of Nash equilibria.

Proposition 1. *Given a scoring vector* α *that has negative components, both* $\mathrm{PoA}(\alpha)$ *and* $\mathrm{PoS}(\alpha)$ *can be unbounded.*

Proof. Let G be a star of $k > 4$ nodes and $\alpha = (-1, 1, 0, \ldots, 0)$. Then, since the root does not want to be in any coalition, every Nash stable outcome has a social welfare of 0. On the other hand, the grand coalition achieves the social

---

[1] The girth of a graph is the length of the shortest cycle contained in it.

optimum, SW(GC) $= \frac{(k-1)(k-4)}{k}$. Indeed, $up(1, V) = k - 1$ while, since the diameter of a star is 2, $up(2, V) = \frac{k(k-1)}{2} - up(1, V) = \frac{(k-1)(k-2)}{2}$. By applying Eq. 1 the computation of the SW follows. We conclude that both PoA and PoS are unbounded.   □

Proposition 2. *Given a scoring vector α such that $\alpha_j \geq 0$ for each $j \in [n-1]$, but α is not monotone, $\mathrm{PoA}(\alpha)$ can be unbounded.*

Proof. Consider a star of size $k > 2$ and $\alpha = (0, \alpha_2, 0, \ldots, 0)$, with $\alpha_2 > 0$. Every node being in its own coalition is a Nash stable outcome with a social welfare of 0, while the social optimum, achieved by the grand coalition, is $\frac{\alpha_2 \cdot (k-1)(k-2)}{k}$. □

Notice that this proof also shows that the PoA can be unbounded when $\alpha_1 = 0$. Motivated by the above arguments, and since we are interested in classes of vectors that admit bounded PoA and PoS, from now on we will only focus on non-negative scoring vectors, for which the following observation holds.

Observation 1. *Given a scoring vector α such that $\alpha_j \geq 0$ for each $j \in [n-1]$, the grand coalition is always Nash stable.*

Furthermore, we will assume that the scoring vector components are monotone, non-increasing and non-decreasing. While other scoring vector classes can still be of theoretical interest, the ones we focus on seem to be the most natural choices when edges in G represent friendship or competition. W.l.o.g. we will assume that α is normalized such that $\alpha_1 = 1$. We first provide hardness results concerning the determination of the best Nash stable outcomes, and then move to the analysis of the PoA and the PoS.

3   Hardness Results

We now present computational complexity results concerning the problem of finding good solutions. In particular, we show intractability or inapproximability results for the following two problems, considering separately the case of decreasing and increasing scoring vectors.

Definition 2. *MSW (resp. MSW-S) is the problem of computing, given a DHG instance $\langle G, \alpha \rangle$, the coalition structure $\mathcal{C}^*$ with a maximum social welfare (resp. the Nash stable coalition structure with a maximum social welfare).*

3.1   Decreasing Vectors

While for decreasing vectors the NP-hardness is already implied by the previous results on FHGs and SDGs, we now show a stronger result: the intractability holds for a large class of *fixed* scoring vectors, i.e., for any fixed α with $\alpha_2 < \frac{1}{2}$.

Theorem 1. *MSW-S problem is NP-hard when restricted to a fixed normalized decreasing vector α with $\alpha_2 < \frac{1}{2}$.*

Proof. We use a reduction from a variant of the Max-Clique Problem in which, given a graph $G = (V, E)$, a node $u \in V$, and an integer $k > \frac{2}{3}(n' + 1)$, where $n' = |N(u)|$ and $N(u)$ is the neighborhood of u, we ask whether there exists a clique in G of size $\geq k$ containing u. It is easy to see that this restriction on k does not influence the NP-hardness, as for smaller k we can easily transform the instance into the desired form by adding dummy nodes. W.l.o.g., as for any fixed $\alpha_2 < \frac{1}{2}$ one can choose k s.t. $\alpha_2 < \frac{k-3}{2(k-1)} < \frac{1}{2}$, we assume $\alpha_2 < \frac{k-3}{2(k-1)}$.

We build the reduced MSW-S instance $G' = (V', E')$ in the following way:

- u and $N(u) = \{v_1, \ldots, v_{n'}\}$ are vertices in G' and $(u, v_i) \in E', \forall i \in [n']$;
- $(v_i, v_j) \in E \implies (v_i, v_j) \in E', \forall v_i, v_j \in N(u)$;
- n' cliques $K_1, \ldots, K_{n'}$ of size $k - 1$ are added to G;
- v_i is connected to all nodes in K_i, for each $i \in [n']$.

The obtained graph G' is depicted in Fig. 2.

Our aim is to show that the following two statements are equivalent: 1) there exists a clique of size k containing u in G, and 2) in the best Nash stable outcome $\mathcal{C}$ for G', $\mathcal{C}(u)$ is a clique of size at least k.

Let us consider the following Nash stable outcomes:

a) n' coalitions where v_i is in the coalition with K_i for each $i \in [n']$, and u is in one of these coalitions and,
b) $\mathcal{C}(u)$ is a clique of size $\geq k$ and for each $v_i \notin \mathcal{C}(u)$, $\mathcal{C}(v_i) = \{v_i\} \cup K_i$.

We notice that if there exists a clique of size at least k in G then outcome b) exists and achieves a better social welfare than outcome a). Next, we show that no Nash stable outcome can achieve a social welfare better than a) and b).

We start by observing that $\forall x \in K_i$, if $\mathcal{C}$ is a Nash stable outcome, then $K_i \subseteq \mathcal{C}(x)$. Indeed, if there exist $x, y \in K_i$ such that $\mathcal{C}(x) \neq \mathcal{C}(y)$ and $u_x^\alpha(\mathcal{C}(x)) \geq u_y^\alpha(\mathcal{C}(y))$, then $u_y^\alpha(\mathcal{C}(x) \cup \{y\}) > u_y^\alpha(\mathcal{C}(y))$. Moreover, if $\mathcal{C}$ is an optimal Nash stable outcome, then K_i and K_j cannot be in the same coalition, $\forall i, j \in [n'], i \neq j$. In fact, since the vector is decreasing with $\alpha_2 < \frac{1}{2}$, and the utility is normalized by the size of the coalition, then outcome a) would achieve a better social welfare.

Let us now show that if $\mathcal{C}$ is a Nash stable outcome and $K_i \nsubseteq \mathcal{C}(u), \forall i \in [n']$, then $\mathcal{C}(u)$ is a clique of size $\geq k$. Assume otherwise, meaning that there exists at

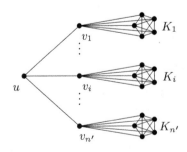

Fig. 2. Reduction from Max-Clique to MSW-S problem for decreasing vectors.

least one agent in $\mathcal{C}(u)$ which is not connected to some $v_i \in \mathcal{C}(u)$. Let m be the size of $\mathcal{C}(u)$ and j the number of agents in $\mathcal{C}(u) \setminus \{v_i\}$ which are not connected to v_i. Since $m \leq n' + 1$, the utility of v_i is $\frac{m-1-j+j \cdot \alpha_2}{m} \leq \frac{m-2+\alpha_2}{m} \leq \frac{n'-1+\alpha_2}{n'+1}$. On the other hand, v_i could deviate and become a member of a clique of size k, achieving a utility of $\frac{k-1}{k}$. Since $\alpha_2 < \frac{1}{2}$ and $k > \frac{2}{3} \cdot (n'+1)$, this implies $\frac{n'-1+\alpha_2}{n'+1} < \frac{k-1}{k}$, which contradicts the stability of $\mathcal{C}$. Moreover, $\mathcal{C}(u)$ indeed has to be a clique of size at least k. Otherwise, every $v_i \in \mathcal{C}(u)$ prefers to deviate to the coalition of K_i. Finally, the best Nash stable outcome $\mathcal{C}$ is either a) or b) (using similar arguments as above, we exclude the possibility that two or more neighbors of u form a coalition not containing u). Moreover, since $\alpha_2 < \frac{k-3}{2(k-1)}$, outcome b) achieves a better social welfare than a).

In conclusion, if there exists a clique of size at least k in G containing u, then the best Nash stable outcome is outcome b), and otherwise it is outcome a). On the other hand, if b) is the best Nash stable outcome for the instance, then there exists a clique in G of size at least k containing u. $\qquad\square$

3.2 Increasing Vectors

Even though we focus mostly on normalized vectors in this work, Theorem 2 is presented here as it gives a nice inapproximability result for general, meaning not normalized, vectors. For $\alpha_1 = 1$, we prove a slightly weaker result of the same flavour in Theorem 3. In both cases, we provide a reduction from the LONGEST INDUCED PATH (LIP) problem, which is NP-complete [20]. An instance (G, L) of the LIP problem consists of a graph G and an integer L, and the question is whether G contains an induced subgraph that is a path of length at least L.

Theorem 2. *If $NP \neq P$, there is no poly-time algorithm with approximation ratio $f(n)$ for the MSW and MSW-S problems restricted to scoring vectors with increasing $0/1$ coefficients, where f is any strictly positive function.*

Proof. We prove the theorem for MSW-S. The same reduction can be used for MSW. Assume that there is a polynomial time algorithm A for the MSW-S problem with an approximation ratio $f(n)$, where f is a strictly positive function.

We transform a LIP instance (G, L) into a MSW-S instance $\langle G', \alpha \rangle$ where α_i is 0 if $i \leq L - 1$ and 1 otherwise, and G' is the graph obtained by adding a node x to G that connects to all original nodes from G. Note that $\text{SW}(\mathcal{C}(x)) = 0$.

We now show that the following two statements are equivalent: 1) There is an induced path in G of length L, and 2) The algorithm A returns a positive value for the MSW-S instance. The direction 2) $\Rightarrow$ 1) is obvious. To prove the other direction, assume that there is an induced path in G of length L. Consider $\{C_1, C_2\}$ where C_1 is formed by the nodes on the path of length L and $C_2 = V \setminus C_1$. If this coalition structure is not stable, then there must be a member z of C_2 that will obtain a positive utility by moving to C_1. We let z move to C_1 and repeat the argument recursively. After finitely many steps, we will reach a stable coalition structure with positive social welfare (C_2 shrinks at every step). $\qquad\square$

Theorem 3. *If $NP \neq P$, there is no poly-time algorithm with approximation ratio less than $\frac{2^{n+1}}{n^2+1}$ for the MSW problem when α is increasing normalized.*

Proof. Let us assume that there is a polynomial time algorithm A for the MSW problem with an approximation ratio $\frac{2^{n+1}}{n^2+1}$. We transform a LIP instance (G, L) into a MSW instance $\langle G, \alpha \rangle$, where $\alpha_i = 1$ if $i \leq L - 1$, and $\alpha_i = 2^n$ otherwise.

We now show that the following two statements are equivalent: 1) There is an induced path in G with length L, and 2) The algorithm A returns a value strictly greater than n for the MSW instance. The direction 2) $\Rightarrow$ 1) is obvious. To prove the other direction, assume there exists an induced path in G of length L. Consider the coalition structure $\mathcal{C} = \{C_1, C_2\}$ where C_1 is made by the nodes on the path of length L and $C_2 = V \setminus C_1$. The welfare of $\mathcal{C}$ is at least $2 \cdot \frac{2^n}{n}$, already by considering the two nodes in C_1 that are the endpoints of the path of length L, implying that A will return a value greater than $2 \cdot \frac{2^n}{n} \cdot \frac{n^2+1}{2^{n+1}} > n$. $\square$

4   Price of Anarchy and Price of Stability

In the previous section we showed that the best (stable) outcomes cannot be easily computed. As the next step, we want to estimate the quality of stable outcomes providing bounds on both the PoA and the PoS.

Theorem 4. *Given a scoring vector α, $\mathrm{PoA}(\alpha) \leq M_\alpha \cdot (n-1)$ and $\mathrm{PoS}(\alpha) \leq \min\left\{\frac{M_\alpha}{m_\alpha}, \frac{n}{2} \cdot M_\alpha\right\}$, where m_α (resp. M_α) is the minimum (resp. maximum) component of α.*

Proof. For the PoS, note that the social welfare of the best Nash stable outcome can be lower bounded by $\mathrm{SW}(GC)$. A lower bound for the social welfare achieved by the grand coalition is $\mathrm{SW}(GC) \geq \frac{2}{n} \cdot \sum_{i=1}^{n-1} m_\alpha \cdot up(i, V) = m_\alpha(n-1)$. This bound is not useful when m_α is close to 0 but then we can use that $\mathrm{SW}(GC) \geq \frac{1}{n} \cdot \sum_{x \in V} \delta_x = \frac{2}{n} \cdot |E| \geq 2 \cdot \frac{n-1}{n}$, where δ_x denotes the number of neighbors of node $x \in V$. If the optimum is made by m coalitions $\{C_1, \ldots, C_m\}$ of sizes $k_1, \ldots, k_m$, respectively, then

$$\mathrm{OPT} \leq \sum_{j=1}^{m} \frac{2}{k_j} \cdot \sum_{i=1}^{k_j-1} M_\alpha \cdot up(i, C_j) \leq M_\alpha \cdot (n-1).$$

By the definition of PoS the claimed bound follows.

Regarding PoA, in any Nash stable outcome any agent achieves a utility of at least $\frac{\alpha_1}{n} = \frac{1}{n}$. Thus, the social welfare of any Nash stable outcome is at least 1. By the definition of PoA, also in this case the bound follows. $\square$

In particular, if α is the constant and normalized vector, then $\frac{M_\alpha}{m_\alpha} = 1$ and $\mathrm{PoS}(\alpha) = 1$. Moreover, in this case also $\mathrm{PoA}(\alpha)$ is equal to 1 since the grand coalition is not only the optimum but also the only Nash stable outcome.

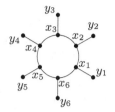

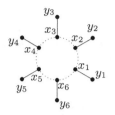

(a) Example of G_k for $k = 6$.   (b) The star partition of G_6.

Fig. 3. An example of a graph that admits no stable star partition for $\alpha_2 > \frac{1}{2}$. Dotted edges are in the cut between two different coalitions.

4.1   Decreasing Vectors

We now consider instances $\langle G, \alpha \rangle$ with α decreasing and normalized. By Theorem 4, the following bounds hold.

Corollary 1. *Given a decreasing vector α, $\mathrm{PoA}(\alpha) \leq n - 1$ and $\mathrm{PoS}(\alpha) \leq \frac{n}{2}$.*

In what follows, we explore the connection between the upper bound on the price of stability and the existence of stable star partitions in the underlying graph.

Star Partitions. A key ingredient for arriving at a lower price of stability is studying instances which allow stable star partitions. We turn our attention to star partitions, since star subgraphs provide high social welfare as shown below.

Proposition 3. *Given an instance $\langle G, \alpha \rangle$, a star partition $\mathcal{S} \in \Sigma(G)$ and α is decreasing and normalized, $\mathrm{SW}(\mathcal{S}) \geq \frac{1}{2} + \alpha_2 \cdot (n - 1)$. In particular, if $\alpha_2 \geq \frac{1}{2}$, then $\mathrm{SW}(\mathcal{S}) \geq \frac{n}{2}$.*

Proof. Let $\mathcal{S} = \{\mathsf{S}_{k_1}, \ldots, \mathsf{S}_{k_m}\}$ be a partition made of m stars of size $k_1, \ldots, k_m$. Then, $\mathrm{SW}(\mathcal{S}) = \sum_{i=1}^{m} \mathrm{SW}(\mathsf{S}_{k_i}) = \sum_{i=1}^{m} \frac{k_i - 1}{k_i} + \sum_{i=1}^{m} \frac{(k_i - 1)(1 + \alpha_2(k_i - 2))}{k_i}$. Note that $\sum_{i=1}^{m} \frac{k_i - 1}{k_i} \geq \frac{m}{2}$ while the second summation is $\geq \alpha_2 \cdot (n - m)$. By minimizing the whole expression w.r.t. m, the claim follows.   □

Not every star partition, however, is necessarily Nash stable. In what follows, we provide an analysis of stability of star partitions. We know that the existence of star partitions is guaranteed when the girth of G is ≥ 4. Unfortunately, when the girth is exactly 4, no star partition need be stable. This can be easily checked by considering the complete bipartite graph with 2 left and 3 right nodes.

Even if the girth is ≥ 5, we cannot ensure stability of star partitions for every α_2.

Proposition 4. *For any decreasing vector α with $\alpha_2 > \frac{1}{2}$ and every $k \geq 5$, there exists a graph G_k of girth k such that no star partition is Nash stable.*

Proof. For a fixed $k \geq 5$ we build $G_k = (V_k, E_k)$ where $V_k = \{x_1, \ldots, x_k\} \cup \{y_1, \ldots, y_k\}$, $x_1, \ldots, x_k$ are in a ring and $(x_i, y_i) \in E_K, \forall i \in [k]$. An example of G_k and its unique star partition are depicted in Fig. 3. The only possible star partition in G_k is $\mathcal{S} = \{\{x_i, y_i\} : i \in [k]\}$, but $\mathcal{S}$ is not stable. $\quad\square$

Next, we show that when the girth is ≥ 5 and $\alpha_2 \leq \frac{1}{2}$, a Nash stable star partition always exists (Theorem 5). Then, we provide an upper bound on OPT for girth ≥ 5 (Proposition 5). Finally, Theorem 6 establishes a better bound on the price of stability. To this aim we first state the following simple lemma.

Lemma 2. *If* $\alpha_2 \leq \frac{1}{2}$, *in any star partition* $\mathcal{S} \in \Sigma(G)$ *1) no root wants to deviate, 2) given* $S_1, S_2 \in \mathcal{S}$ *such that a leaf* x *of* S_1 *is connected to the root* $y \in S_2$, x *does not want to deviate iff* $|S_1| > |S_2| + 1$.

Proof. In this proof we consider two possible connections between stars in a star partition: root to root connection and root to leaf connection.

For each $k, h \geq 2$ the root of a k-star connected to the root of a h-star does not want to leave the coalition when $\frac{k-1}{k} \geq \frac{1+\alpha_2(h-1)}{h+1}$. This is satisfied for all $k, h \geq 2$ if and only if $\alpha_2 \leq \frac{1}{2}$. Moreover, if the root of a k-star is connected to the leaf of a h-star, then by deviating it would achieve a utility of $\frac{1+\alpha_2+\alpha_3(h-2)}{h+1}$, which is smaller than $\frac{1+\alpha_2(h-1)}{h+1}$. Thus, the claim holds.

For each $k, h \geq 2$, a leaf of the k-star does not want to leave its coalition and join the h-star when $\frac{1+\alpha_2(k-2)}{k} \geq \frac{1+\alpha_2(h-1)}{h+1}$. If $\alpha_2 \leq \frac{1}{2}$, this implies that $k \leq h - 1$. $\quad\square$

Theorem 5. *Given an instance* $\langle G, \alpha \rangle$ *where* G *has girth* ≥ 5 *and* α *is decreasing with* $\alpha_2 \leq \frac{1}{2}$, *there always exists a Nash stable star partition.*

Proof. We observe the stability of $\mathcal{S}$, the minimum star partition according to the co-lexicographic order. First, note that a star of size ≤ 3 is always stable. Now, assume that $\mathcal{S}$ is not Nash stable. By Lemma 2, this means that there exists a leaf x of a star $S_k \in \mathcal{S}$, $k > 3$, that wants to deviate to another star $S_h \in \mathcal{S}$. We distinguish two cases, depending on whether the node y to which x is connected to is the root or a leaf in S_h. 1) If y is the root of S_h, x would become a leaf by deviating, and, by Lemma 2, $k \geq h+1 > h$. Thus, the resulting partition $\mathcal{S}'$ is also a star partition s.t. $n_i(\mathcal{S}) = n_i(\mathcal{S}')$ for $i \geq k+1$ and $n_k(\mathcal{S}) < n_k(\mathcal{S}')$. This means $\mathcal{S}' <_{colex} \mathcal{S}$, contradicting the minimality of $\mathcal{S}$. 2) If y is a leaf in S_h, we can build a new star partition $\mathcal{S}'$ from $\mathcal{S}$ where x and y form a star of size 2. Also in this case, $n_i(\mathcal{S}) = n_i(\mathcal{S}')$ for $i \geq k+1$ and $n_k(\mathcal{S}) < n_k(\mathcal{S}')$. $\quad\square$

Proposition 5. *Given an instance* $\langle G, \alpha \rangle$, *where* G *has girth* ≥ 5 *and* α *is decreasing with* $\alpha_2 \leq \frac{1}{2}$, OPT $\leq \frac{n}{2} \cdot \left(\alpha_2 + \sqrt{\alpha_2^2 + (1-\alpha_2)^2} \right)$.

Proof. If $C^* = \{C_1^*, \ldots, C_m^*\}$ where $|C_i^*| = k_i$, for each $i \in [m]$, then

$$\text{OPT} \leq \sum_{i=1}^{m} \sum_{x \in C_i^*} \frac{\delta_{C_i^*}(x) + \alpha_2 \cdot (k_i - 1 - \delta_{C_i^*}(x))}{k_i} = 2(1-\alpha_2) \sum_{i=1}^{m} \frac{|E_i|}{k_i} + \alpha_2(n-m).$$

When the graph has girth ≥ 5 the number of edges is upper bounded by $\frac{n\sqrt{n-1}}{2}$ [16]. Thus, applying this bound to all the coalitions in $\mathcal{C}$, OPT $\leq 2(1 - \alpha_2) \cdot \sqrt{nm - m^2} + \alpha_2 \cdot (n - m)$. Moreover, since $m \leq \frac{n}{2}$, the previous expression is maximized when m is equal to $\frac{n}{2} \cdot \left(1 - \frac{\alpha_2}{\alpha_2^2 + (1-\alpha_2)^2} \right)$. $\qquad\square$

Theorem 6. *Given a decreasing scoring vector α with $\alpha_2 \leq \frac{1}{2}$, if we restrict our attention to graphs with girth ≥ 5, then* $\mathrm{PoS}(\alpha) \leq n \cdot \frac{\alpha_2 + \sqrt{\alpha_2^2 + (1-\alpha_2)^2}}{1 + 2\alpha_2 \cdot (n-1)}$.

Proposition 3 and 5 together with Theorem 5 imply Theorem 6. The bound provided in Theorem 6 is better than the bound of $\frac{n}{2}$ from Corollary 1 if and only if $\alpha_2 \geq \frac{\sqrt{4n^2 - 12n + 6} - n}{2((n-2)^2 - 2)} \approx \frac{1}{2n}$. We also note that this result generalizes the result for SDGs (a decreasing vector with $\alpha_2 = \frac{1}{2}$) obtained in [4].

4.2   Increasing Vectors

To complete the picture, we focus on instances $\langle G, \alpha \rangle$ with α increasing and normalized. The following theorem summarizes our contribution.

Theorem 7. *Given an instance $\langle G, \alpha \rangle$, where α is increasing and normalized,* $\mathrm{PoA}(\alpha) \leq \frac{2}{n} \cdot \mathrm{SW}(\mathsf{P}_n)$ *and* $\mathrm{PoS}(\alpha) \leq \frac{1}{n-1} \cdot \mathrm{SW}(\mathsf{P}_n)$. *Moreover, these bounds are tight.*

Proof (Sketch). Our first objective is to prove that if there are n agents, the highest possible social welfare, in any instance, is achieved by the grand coalition on a graph that is a path on n nodes. To this aim, we first show in Lemma 3 that for a fixed coalition size the underlying graph that provides the highest social welfare is a path and then conclude in Proposition 6 that any coalition structure on any underlying graph has a social welfare lower than the grand coalition on a graph that is a path on n nodes.

Lemma 3. *Given an instance $\langle G, \alpha \rangle$, where α is increasing and normalized,* $\mathrm{SW}(C) \leq \mathrm{SW}(\mathsf{P}_k)$, *for any $C \subseteq V$ of size k.*

Proof. Since the utility of any coalition C of size k is given by eq. 1, we want to prove that, when k is fixed, $\mathrm{SW}(C)$ is maximized for $C = \mathsf{P}_k$. Since we know that $\sum_{i=1}^{k-1} up(i, C) = \binom{k}{2}$, meaning that the sum of all unordered pairs at all possible distances is fixed, and α is increasing, we conclude that $\mathrm{SW}(C) \leq \mathrm{SW}(\mathsf{P}_k)$. $\qquad\square$

Proposition 6. *Given an instance $\langle G, \alpha \rangle$, where α is increasing,* $\mathrm{SW}(\mathcal{C}) \leq \mathrm{SW}(\mathsf{P}_n)$ *for any coalition structure $\mathcal{C}$.*

Proof. Given any outcome $\mathcal{C} = \{C_1, \ldots, C_m\}$, if $k_i = |C_i|$, by Lemma 3 $\mathrm{SW}(\mathcal{C}) \leq \sum_{i=1}^{m} \mathrm{SW}(\mathsf{P}_{k_i})$. Lastly, the summation is a convex function of $k_1, \ldots, k_m$. $\qquad\square$

Next, in Lemma 4 we give a lower bound of $\frac{n}{2}$ on the social welfare of any Nash stable outcome and in Lemma 5 a tighter bound of $n - 1$ for the social welfare of the grand coalition, yielding the PoA and PoS upper bounds of Theorem 7.

Lemma 4. *Given an instance* $\langle G, \alpha \rangle$, *where* α *is increasing, if* $\mathcal{C} \in \mathrm{NS}_{\langle G,\alpha \rangle}$, *then* $\mathrm{SW}(\mathcal{C}) \geq \frac{n}{2}$.

Proof. Let us assume that $\mathcal{C}$ consists of k coalitions $C_1, \ldots, C_k$ that are of sizes $i_1, \ldots, i_k$, respectively. Since α is normalized w.r.t. the first component and increasing, if x is in the coalition C_j, then $u_x(C_j) \geq \frac{i_j - 1}{i_j}$. Thus, $\mathrm{SW}(\mathcal{C}) \geq \sum_{j=1}^{k} i_j - 1 = n - k$. Moreover, if the outcome is stable, then the coalitions are made of at least 2 nodes. This implies that $\mathrm{SW}(\mathcal{C}) \geq n - \frac{n}{2} = \frac{n}{2}$. $\quad\square$

Lemma 5. *Given an instance* $\langle G, \alpha \rangle$, *where* α *is increasing and normalized,* $\mathrm{SW}(\mathrm{GC}) \geq n - 1$.

Proof. Since $\alpha_i \geq 1$ for every $i = 1, \ldots, n-1$, $u_x(\mathrm{GC}) \geq \frac{n-1}{n}$ for any $x \in V$. Thus, $\mathrm{SW}(\mathrm{GC}) \geq \sum_{x \in V} \frac{n-1}{n} = n - 1$. $\quad\square$

Finally, we show an example that guarantees the tightness (up to a constant) by considering $G = (V, E)$ where $V = \{x_1, \ldots, x_n\}$, $(x_i, x_{i+1}) \in E, \forall i \in [n-2]$ and $(x_n, x_i) \in E, \forall i \in [n-1]$. Since $\mathcal{C}^* = \{\{x_1, \ldots, x_{n-1}\}, \{x_n\}\}$, $\mathrm{OPT} = \mathrm{SW}(\mathsf{P}_{n-1})$.

Lemma 6. *In the just described graph, if* $\alpha_2 = 1 + \varepsilon$ *and* $\alpha_{i+1} - \alpha_i > \varepsilon, \forall i = 2, \ldots, n-2$, *there exists a constant* c_ε *such that* $\sup_{\mathcal{C} \in \mathrm{NS}_{\langle G, \alpha \rangle}} \mathrm{SW}(\mathcal{C}) \leq c_\varepsilon (n-1)$.

Proof. We set $\varepsilon = 2\varepsilon'$ and denote by $\mathcal{C}(x_n) = \{x_{i_1}, \ldots, x_{i_k}\}$ the coalition of x_n. Given any x_{i_j} and $x_{i_{j+1}}$ in $\mathcal{C}(x_n)$, since $\mathcal{C}$ is a Nash stable outcome, then either $i_{j+1} = i_j + 1$ or $i_{j+1} - i_j - 1 > 2$ (in a stable outcome a node cannot be isolated). Now, we want to prove that if $\mathcal{C}$ is a Nash stable outcome, then $i_{j+1} - i_j - 1 \leq \ell_{\varepsilon'}$ for some $\ell_{\varepsilon'}$. If so, $\mathrm{SW}(\mathcal{C}) \leq \alpha_{\ell_{\varepsilon'}}(n-1)$, and the claim follows. Let us assume $i_{j+1} - i_j - 1 = \ell$, meaning that there is a coalition between x_{i_j} and $x_{i_{j+1}}$ which is a path P_ℓ on ℓ nodes by the stability of $\mathcal{C}$. Since neither x_{i_j} nor $x_{i_{j+1}}$ wants to deviate if $\frac{1 + (k-2)\alpha_2}{k} \geq \frac{\sum_{i=1}^{\ell} \alpha_i}{\ell + 1}$, as $\frac{1 + (k-2)\alpha_2}{k} < \alpha_2 = 1 + 2\varepsilon'$ and $\frac{\sum_{i=1}^{\ell} \alpha_i}{\ell + 1} \geq \frac{\sum_{i=1}^{\ell} 1 + 2\varepsilon'(i-1)}{\ell+1} = \frac{\ell - 1 + \varepsilon'(\ell - 1)\ell}{\ell + 1}$, then $1 + 2\varepsilon' \geq \frac{\ell + \varepsilon'(\ell-1)\ell}{\ell+1}$. Thus, $\frac{1}{\varepsilon'} \geq \ell^2 - 3\ell - 2$ must hold. In conclusion, if the outcome is stable, then $1 < \ell < \ell_{\varepsilon'}$, where $\ell_{\varepsilon'} = \frac{3 + \sqrt{9 + 8(1 + \frac{1}{2\varepsilon'})}}{2}$. $\quad\square$

Furthermore, by altering G s.t. x_n connects only once every two nodes in the path, we can show that tightness holds even for bipartite graphs. $\quad\square$

5   Open Problems

Giving a complete picture of the classes of networks admitting low PoS, and characterizing other kinds of partitions that provide a good social welfare when star partitions are not Nash stable, are worth investigating questions. Moreover, one might further explore other relevant specific scoring vectors. Weighted graphs are another promising avenue. The aim would be to find a way to express the agents' utilities according to the weights of the graph, for instance by substituting the scoring vector with a distance scoring function. Finally, even if we focused on Nash equilibria, it would be nice to consider other relevant stability notions traditionally considered in these games, both for individual and group deviations.

References

1. Anshelevich, E., Dasgupta, A., Kleinberg, J.M., Tardos, É., Wexler, T., Roughgarden, T.: The price of stability for network design with fair cost allocation. SIAM J. Comput. **38**(4), 1602–1623 (2008)
2. Aziz, H., Brandl, F., Brandt, F., Harrenstein, P., Olsen, M., Peters, D.: Fractional hedonic games. ACM Trans. Econ. Comput. **7**(2), 6:1–6:29 (2019)
3. Aziz, H., Gaspers, S., Gudmundsson, J., Mestre, J., Täubig, H.: Welfare maximization in fractional hedonic games. In: Proceedings of the 24th International Joint Conference on Artificial Intelligence (IJCAI), pp. 461–467 (2015)
4. Balliu, A., Flammini, M., Melideo, G., Olivetti, D.: On non-cooperativeness in social distance games. J. Artif. Intell. Res. **66**, 625–653 (2019)
5. Balliu, A., Flammini, M., Olivetti, D.: On pareto optimality in social distance games. In: Proceedings of the 31st Conference on Artificial Intelligence (AAAI), pp. 349–355 (2017)
6. Banerjee, S., Konishi, H., Sönmez, T.: Core in a simple coalition formation game. Soc. Choice Welf. **18**(1), 135–153 (2001)
7. Bilò, V., Fanelli, A., Flammini, M., Monaco, G., Moscardelli, L.: On the price of stability of fractional hedonic games. In: Proceedings of the 14th Conference on Autonomous Agents and Multi-Agent Systems (AAMAS), pp. 1239–1247 (2015)
8. Bilò, V., Fanelli, A., Flammini, M., Monaco, G., Moscardelli, L.: Nash stable outcomes in fractional hedonic games: existence, efficiency and computation. J. Artif. Intell. Res. **62**, 315–371 (2018)
9. Bloch, F., Diamantoudi, E.: Noncooperative formation of coalitions in hedonic games. Int. J. Game Theory **40**(2), 263–280 (2011)
10. Bogomolnaia, A., Jackson, M.O.: The stability of hedonic coalition structures. Games Econ. Behav. **38**(2), 201–230 (2002)
11. Brandl, F., Brandt, F., Strobel, M.: Fractional hedonic games: individual and group stability. In: Proceedings of the 14th Conference on Autonomous Agents and Multi-Agent Systems (AAMAS), pp. 1219–1227 (2015)
12. Brânzei, S., Larson, K.: Social distance games. In: Proceedings of the 22nd International Joint Conference on Artificial Intelligence (IJCAI), pp. 91–96 (2011)
13. Dangalchev, C.: Residual closeness in networks. Phys. Stat. Mech. Appl. **365**(2), 556–564 (2006)
14. Dangalchev, C.: Residual closeness and generalized closeness. Int. J. Found. Comput. Sci. **22**(8), 1939–1948 (2011)
15. Dreze, J., Greenberg, J.: Hedonic coalitions: optimality and stability. Econometrica **48**(4), 987–1003 (1980)
16. Dutton, R.D., Brigham, R.C.: Edges in graphs with large girth. Graphs Comb. **7**(4), 315–321 (1991)
17. Elkind, E., Wooldridge, M.J.: Hedonic coalition nets. In: 8th International Joint Conference on Autonomous Agents and Multiagent Systems (AAMAS 2009), Budapest, Hungary, 10–15 May 2009, vol. 1, pp. 417–424 (2009)

18. Feldman, M., Lewin-Eytan, L., Naor, J.: Hedonic clustering games. TOPC **2**(1), 4:1–4:48 (2015)
19. Gairing, M., Savani, R.: Computing stable outcomes in symmetric additively separable hedonic games. Math. Oper. Res. **44**(3), 1101–1121 (2019)
20. Garey, M.R., Johnson, D.S.: Computers and Intractability: A Guide to the Theory of NP-Completeness. W. H. Freeman (1979)
21. Kaklamanis, C., Kanellopoulos, P., Patouchas, D.: On the price of stability of social distance games. In: Proceedings of the 11th International Symposium, Algorithmic Game Theory (SAGT), pp. 125–136 (2018)
22. Koutsoupias, E., Papadimitriou, C.H.: Worst-case equilibria. Comput. Sci. Rev. **3**(2), 65–69 (2009)
23. Olsen, M.: On defining and computing communities. In: Proceedings of the 18th Conference on Computing: The Australasian Theory Symposium (CATS), pp. 97–102 (2012)
24. Papadimitriou, C.H.: Algorithms, games, and the internet. In: Proceedings of the 28th International Colloquium on Automata, Languages and Programming (ICALP), pp. 1–3 (2001)
25. Wang, Z., Han, X., Dósa, G., Tuza, Z.: A general bin packing game: interest taken into account. Algorithmica **80**(5), 1534–1555 (2018)

Distributed Independent Sets in Interval and Segment Intersection Graphs

Barun Gorain[1], Kaushik Mondal[2], and Supantha Pandit[3(✉)]

[1] Indian Institute of Technology Bhilai, Raipur, Chattisgarh, India
barun@iitbhilai.ac.in
[2] Indian Institute of Technology Ropar, Rupnagar, Punjab, India
kaushik.mondal@iitrpr.ac.in
[3] Dhirubhai Ambani Institute of Information and Communication Technology,
Gandhinagar, Gujrat, India
pantha.pandit@gmail.com

Abstract. The Maximal Independent Set problem is a well-studied problem in the distributed community. We study Maximum and Maximal Independent Set problems on two geometric intersection graphs; interval graphs and axis-parallel segment intersection graphs, and present deterministic distributed algorithms in the local communication model. We compute the maximum independent set on interval graphs in $O(k)$ rounds and $O(n)$ messages, where k is the size of the maximum independent set and n is the number of nodes in the graph. We provide a matching lower bound of $\Omega(k)$ on the number of rounds whereas $\Omega(n)$ is a trivial lower bound on message complexity. Thus our algorithm is both time and message optimal. We also study the maximal independent set problem in bi-interval graphs, a special case of the interval graphs where the intervals have two different lengths. We prove that a maximal independent set can be computed in bi-interval graphs in constant rounds that is $\frac{1}{6}$-approximation. For axis-parallel segment intersection graphs, we design an algorithm that finds a maximal independent set in $O(D)$ rounds, where D is the diameter of the graph. We further show that this independent set is a $\frac{1}{2}$-approximation. The results in this paper extend the results of Molla et al. [J. Parallel Distrib. Comput. 2019].

Keywords: Maximal Independent Set · Interval graph · Segment intersection graph · Distributed algorithm · Approximation algorithm

1 Introduction

The Maximal Independent Set (MIS) is a fundamental and well-studied problem in the distributed computing. In a graph $G(V, E)$, a maximal independent set is a subset of vertices $V' \subseteq V$ such that no two vertices in V' are connected by an edge in G and the size of V' can not be increased by adding any vertex from $V \backslash V'$ to V'. A Maximum Independent Set (MaxIS) in a graph $G(V, E)$ is

© Springer Nature Switzerland AG 2021
T. Bureš et al. (Eds.): SOFSEM 2021, LNCS 12607, pp. 175–188, 2021.
https://doi.org/10.1007/978-3-030-67731-2_13

a maximum cardinality subset of vertices $V' \subseteq V$ such that no two vertices in V' are connected by an edge in G.

Study of MIS on geometric graphs is also important from both theoretical and practical perspectives. In this paper, we concentrate on some special classes of geometric graphs namely, interval graphs, bi-interval graphs, and axis-parallel segment intersection graphs, and present efficient distributed algorithms. All our algorithms are deterministic in nature and use the Local communication model [14]. In the Local model, communication proceeds in synchronous rounds and all nodes start simultaneously. In each round, each node can exchange arbitrary messages with all of its neighbors, and perform arbitrary local computations. The time complexity of an algorithm is the number of synchronous rounds executed by the nodes. The message complexity of an algorithm is the total number of messages sent by all the nodes during the execution of the algorithm. All our proposed algorithms are efficient in terms of time as well as message complexity.

For a given set of objects $\mathcal{O}$ in the plane, a geometric intersection graph $G(V, E)$ can be defined as follows. For each object $o \in O$ take a vertex $v_o \in V$ and two objects $o_1, o_2, \in O$ intersect if and only if there is an edge $e \in E$ between the two vertices v_{o_1} and v_{o_2} corresponding to the two objects o_1 and o_2 respectively. We can define various classes of geometric graphs based on the types of the objects, namely, (i) interval graphs (objects are intervals on the real line), (ii) bi-interval graphs (objects are intervals of only two different lengths on the real line), and (iii) segment intersection graphs (axis-parallel segments on the plane); see Fig. 1. Throughout the paper we use node and object (interval for interval graphs, segment for segment intersection graph) interchangeably to represent the same entity unless otherwise stated. For any two nodes u and v in G, define the *distance*, $dist(u, v)$ as the length of the shortest path between them in G.

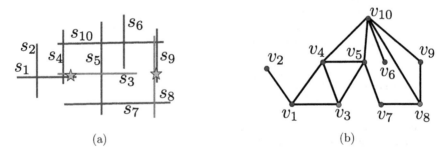

(a)   (b)

Fig. 1. (a) Given input segments. We use "star" (☆) to represent overlap between segments. (b) Intersection graph of (a).

1.1   Related Work

Most of the results on Maximal Independent Set problem are randomized. The most classical results include Luby's [11] $O(\log n)$ time randomized algorithm and Linial's [10] $\Omega(\log^* n)$ time lower bound, where n is the number of nodes of a graph. There are much faster algorithms also that are developed recently [5,6]. On the deterministic side a little progress is made for general graphs. In [9] a detailed review can be found. Notably, using network decomposition the fastest deterministic algorithm runs in $2^{O(\sqrt{\log n})}$-time [13]. The most fascinating open problem till date was to design a polylogarithmic time deterministic algorithm for the maximal independent set problem. Very recently, Rozhon and Ghaffari [15] provided a polylogarithmic time deterministic algorithm for the maximal independent set problem using network decomposition.

Researchers paying attentions in designing deterministic algorithms for special classes of graphs. For the growth bounded graphs, Kuhn et al. [8] provided a deterministic algorithm that runs in $O(\log \Delta \log^* n)$-time. This bound wa improved by Schneider and Wattenhofer [16] to an optimal $O(\log^* n)$-time for the same classes of graphs. Barenboim and Elkin [1,2] provide efficient deterministic algorithms on bounded arboricity graphs. In a recent article, Molla et al. [12] provide maximal independent sets in constant rounds in congest model for various classes of graphs; unit interval, unit square, unit disk, etc.

It is well-known that finding a maximum independent set in a graph is NP-hard. Effort is given on designing efficient approximation algorithms (see [3,4,7]). An $O(n^\epsilon)$-approximation of can be computed in $O(\frac{1}{\epsilon})$ rounds [3]. In planar graphs, an $O(1+\epsilon)$- approximation can be computed in $O(\log^* n)$ rounds [4]. In bounded independence graphs, there is an $O(\log^* n)$-time distributed algorithm to compute a maximal independent set [16]. In [12], the authors present constant factor approximation algorithms in $O(1)$ rounds for unit interval, unit square, unit disk graphs. They also present a $O(1/\epsilon)$-time algorithm to compute a $(1-\epsilon)$-approximation in unit interval graphs.

1.2   Our Contributions

➤ We design an algorithm that finds a MaxIS in interval graphs in $O(k)$ rounds, k is the size of a maximum independent set. We also propose a tight lower bound $\Omega(k)$ on number of rounds for finding MaxIS. (see Sect. 2.1)

➤ We design a constant round algorithm that finds a MIS in bi-interval graphs. Moreover, this is $\frac{1}{6}$-approximation algorithm. (see Sect. 2.2)

➤ We compute a MIS in axis-parallel segment intersection graphs in $O(D)$ rounds, where D is the diameter of the graph. We further show that this independent set is a $\frac{1}{2}$-approximation to the MaxIS of the graph. The message complexity of the proposed algorithm is $O(n+k^2)$, where n is the number of nodes in the graph and k is the size of the MaxIS. We also describe how to improve the algorithm to have message complexity $O(n + k \log k)$. (see Sect. 3).

➤ In case of axis-parallel unit segment intersection graphs, we propose a constant round algorithm for computing a MIS. (see Sect. 3).

2   Interval Graphs

We first present a distributed algorithm that finds a MaxIS in a general interval graph G in $O(k)$ rounds, k is the size of the optimal independent set in G. We also provide a matching lower bound i.e., $\Omega(k)$ on time complexity. Next we consider the bi-interval graphs and compute a MIS that is $\frac{1}{6}$-approximation.

2.1   Maximum Independent Set for Interval Graphs

Let $G(V, E)$ be an interval graph, where each node of G corresponding to an interval on the real line. Each interval has the id as (x, l) where x is the left end point and l is the length of the interval. Without loss of generality, we assume that G is connected. Otherwise, the same algorithm can compute the MaxIS simultaneously for different connected components of G.

At any round, a node can be one of the three *types*: *selected*, *normal*, and *removed*. A node is of type selected, if it has already selected itself in the MaxIS. A node is of type removed if at least one of its neighbor is a selected node. A node that is neither a selected nor a removed is called normal. At any round i, a normal node selects itself in the MaxIS and change its type to selected only if its right end point is minimum among all its normal neighbors and it has not received any message from a selected node in the previous round. It then sends a message to its neighbors. Otherwise, if it has received a message from a selected node in the previous round, then it changes its type to removed and sends a message to its neighbors. This node (after changing its type from normal to removed or from normal to selected) does not participate in the subsequent rounds of the algorithm.

Theorem 1. *Algorithm 1 correctly computes a MaxIS in an interval graph in at most 2k rounds, k is the size of the MaxIS. The message complexity is $O(n)$.*

Proof. See the full version of the paper.

The Lower Bound for Interval Graphs: We prove the following theorem (refer the full version of the paper for the description and proof).

Theorem 2. *Computing a MaxIS in an interval graph requires $\Omega(k)$ time, where k is the size of a MaxIS.*

2.2   Bi-interval Graphs

We consider the maximal independent set problem on a special class of interval graphs, namely *bi-interval graphs*. Bi-interval graphs are interval graphs where the given intervals are of at most two different lengths. We propose an algorithm that finds a maximal independent set in a bi-interval graph in constant rounds. Further, We show that the size of the MIS returned by the algorithm is not less than a factor of $\frac{1}{6}$ of the size of MaxIS of the given bi-interval graph.

Algorithm 1: $Interval\_MaxIS(v, i)$

---

1 $N''(v) = \phi$.

2 **if** $i = 1$ **then**

3 v sends $< type, id >$ to its neighbors

4   Let $N(v)$ be the set of nodes from where it got any message in round 1.

5 **else**

6   **if** v *is normal* **then**

7   **if** $i = 2$ **then**

8   Let $N(v)$ be the set of nodes from where it got any message in round 1.

9 $N''(v) \leftarrow N(v)$.

10   **if** v *received a message in round (i-1) from a node w with type selected* **then**

11 v changes its type to removed

12 v sends $< type, id >$ to all its neighbors.

13   **else**

14   Let $N'(v)$ be the set of removed nodes from where it received messages in round $i - 1$.

15 $N''(v) \leftarrow N''(v) \backslash N'(v)$

16   **if** *The right end point of v is smaller than all the nodes in $N''(v)$* **then**

17 v changes its type to selected.

18 v sends $< type, id >$ to all its neighbors.

In our algorithm, we use the constant round $\frac{1}{2}$-approximation MIS algorithm for the unit interval graphs proposed by Molla et al. [12] as a subroutine. The same algorithm and its analysis hold for l length intervals instead of unit intervals by simply taking the vertical lines at distance l apart instead of unit distance apart. For ease of our use, we denote $A(l)$ as this algorithm for l-length intervals. Then $A(1)$ represents the algorithm of [12] for unit intervals.

MIS for Bi-interval Graphs: We present an algorithm for finding a MIS in bi-interval graphs. Let G be a bi-interval graph where the lengths of the intervals in G be l_1 and l_2. Without loss of generality, assume that $l_1 > l_2$. We also assume that none of the intervals has left end point at either pl_1 or pl_2 where p is any positive integer including zero. First we draw vertical lines through each point pl_1 on the x-axis. Clearly there is no interval whose left end point is on any of these vertical lines. A vertical line whose x-coordinate is equal to pl_1 where p is even or zero, is called a $even_{l_1}$-*line*, otherwise if p is odd, the line is said to be an odd_{l_1}-*line*. We also consider vertical lines through each point pl_2 on the x-axis. Again there is no interval whose left end point is on any of these lines. A vertical line whose x-coordinate is equal to pl_2 where p is even or zero, is called a $even_{l_2}$-*line*, otherwise if p is odd, the line is called an odd_{l_2}-*line*. If a set of intervals intersects a single vertical line, they must be neighbors and at most one of them can be selected in a MIS. Let G_{l_1} and G_{l_2} be the subgraphs of G induced by intervals of length l_1 and l_2 respectively. Note that, G_{l_1} as well as G_{l_2} can be disconnected.

Algorithm: We first consider the graph G_{l_2} and run the algorithm $A(l_2)$ on it. This returns a MIS, say M_2 of size k_2 of G_{l_2}. After that, all the members of M_2 broadcast and all their neighbors in G become silent (i.e., remain idle till the end of the algorithm) till the end of the algorithm. If there is any interval that is still not silent, that must be from G_{l_1}. Call the set of these (non-silent) intervals as S and the graph spanned by S as G_S. Next, run the algorithm $A(l_1)$ on G_S (recall that all the intervals in S are of length l_1). The algorithm $A(l_1)$ returns a MIS, say M_S of size k_S of G_S. Our algorithm returns a set $M = M_2 \cup M_S$.

Analysis: We claim that in 7 rounds a MIS M is returned by our algorithm. Further, it is a $\frac{1}{6}$-approximation algorithm (see the full version of the paper for the details).

3   Axis-Parallel Segment Intersection Graph

In this section we propose an algorithm that finds a MIS in axis-parallel segment intersection graphs. First, we start with the high level idea of the algorithm. Let G be a connected graph where each of the nodes are axis-parallel line segments. Consider the subgraphs G' and G'' of G induced by the line segments parallel to the x-axis and y-axis, respectively. Note that G' as well as G'' may not be connected. Consider two nodes u and v in G' that are in the same connected component. Since both u and v are corresponding to the two lines that are parallel to the x-axis, therefore if they intersect, the left end point of v must lie on the line segment u or vice versa. To be more specific, if (x_1, y_1) is the coordinate of the left end point of a node u of length l_1 and (x_2, y_2) is the coordinate of the left end point of a node v of length l_2 with $x_1 \leqslant x_2$, then $y_1 = y_2$ and $x_2 \in [x_1, x_1 + l_1]$. This shows that each node in a connected component of G' can be realised as an interval on the real line. It is possible to find the maximum independent sets for every connected component of G' using $Interval\_MaxIS(v, i)$ (Algorithm 1) in parallel. The similar argument can apply to G'' as well.

Let M_1 (resp. M_2) be the union of the maximum independent sets, corresponding to each connected component in G' (resp. G''). Observe that M_1 and M_2 are maximum independent sets of G' and G'' respectively. Let M be $M_1 \cup M_2$. Let M' be the maximum cardinality set among M_1 and M_2. Our algorithm selects all the nodes in M' in the final MIS of G along with some other nodes as M' alone might not be maximal. For example, if M_1 is selected as M', then there might be some nodes parallel to y-axis that do not intersects with any node in M'. In that case, a subset of those nodes are added with M' and our algorithm terminates with a maximal independent set.

In order to achieve this goal in a distributed way, each node transmits a message whenever it learns a new node has selected itself in M (either in M_1 or in M_2). Whenever a node selects itself as a candidate (i.e., a possible member), it informs all its neighbors in G about its decision by transmitting a message. Hence, its neighbors learn that a new node is selected itself in M. Then they propagate this information to their neighbors and so on. Once every node learns about all the candidate nodes, the set of nodes in M_1 and M_2 are known to all the nodes in the network. If $|M_1| \leq |M_2|$, then the nodes in M_1 stay in the final MIS, else, the nodes in M_2 stay in the final MIS.

The main difficulty for a node is to understand when it completes receiving information of all the nodes in M_1 as well as M_2. Also, if each node transmits to all its neighbors whenever learns about a new node in M, the number of messages in the algorithm becomes very high. To overcome these difficulties, we use two observations.

Observation 1. *Let $u \in V(G)$ and $v \in M$, such that $dist(u,v) = d$. Let $r = \max_{w \in M} (dist(u,w))$. If $d < r$, then there must exists a node $v' \in M$ other than v such that $d < dist(u,v') \leq d + 2$.*

The above observation shows that if a node u has not learned the entire set M, and if i is the last round it has learned about a new node in M, then it must learn about at least one new node in M by round $i + 2$. Hence, in our algorithm, a node identifies it has learnt all about M if it does not receive any new node information for consecutive two rounds.

Observation 2. *Let u be a node in M_1 and u' and u'' be neighbors of u in G' whose x-coordinate of the right end point is maximum and x-coordinate of the left end point is minimum, respectively, among all other neighbors of u. Similarly, let v be a node in M_2 and v' and v'' be neighbors of v in G'' whose y-coordinate of the top end point is maximum and y-coordinate of the bottom end point is minimum, respectively, among all other neighbors of v. Then the graph induced by the set $\bigcup_{u \in M_1, v \in M_2} \{u, u', u'', v', v', v''\}$ is a connected dominating set of G.*

The above observation says that it is not necessary to transmit the information about the new nodes in MIS by all the nodes in the network. If only the nodes in the MIS and few of their carefully chosen neighbors transmit, then all the information will be successfully propagated to all the nodes in the network.

3.1   The Algorithm

We now introduce some terminologies for the description of our algorithm. For a node v, define id of v, $id(v)$ as $<x, y, \ell, d>$, where (x, y) is the coordinates of the left end point if v is parallel to the x-axis otherwise it is the coordinates of the top end point, ℓ is the length of the interval, and the third component d take a binary value where $d = 0$ indicates that the interval is parallel to the x-axis and $d = 1$ indicates that the interval is parallel to the y-axis. We define $N(v)$ as the set of all neighbors of v. Further, $N_x(v) \subseteq N(v)$ (resp. $N_y(v) \subseteq N(v)$) denotes the neighbors of v that are parallel to the x-axis (y-axis).

For any subset of nodes S of G', define $min_x(S)$ as the node in S whose x-coordinate of the right end point is minimum among all the nodes in S. Similarly, for any subset of nodes S of G'', define $min_y(S)$ as the node in S whose y-coordinate of the top end point is minimum among all the nodes in S.

For any node $v \in G'$ (resp. $v \in G''$) define $min(v)$, whose x coordinate of the left end point (resp. y-coordinate of the bottom end point) is minimum among all its neighbors including itself. Similarly, for any node $v \in G'$ (resp. $v \in G''$) define $max(v)$, whose x-coordinate of the right end point (resp. y-coordinate of the top end point) is maximum among all its neighbors including itself. In case of a tie in both of the above definitions, the node with smaller length is chosen. Note that in some cases, there may exists a node v for which $min(v)$ and $max(v)$ are same. We say that a node v *reaches* a node u by round i, if there exists a path $v = u_0, u_1, \cdots, u_p = u$ and integers $0 < t_1 < \cdots < t_p \leq i$ such that u_{i-1} transmits in round t_i, $1 \leq i \leq p$. Each node v maintains the following binary variables that are initialized to zero before the start of the algorithm.

▷ **candidate(v)**: v sets $candidate(v) = 1$, if it becomes a candidate for MIS.
▷ **mis(v)**: v sets $mis(v) = 1$, if it selects itself in the MIS.
▷ **start(v)**: For every node w that sets $candidate(w) = 1$ in some round, the node v sets $start(v) = 1$ only if $min(w) = v$.
▷ **dom(v)**: For every node v that sets $candidate(v) = 1$ in some round, the node w sets $dom(w) = 1$ only if $max(v) = w$.
▷ **rem(v)**: A node $v \in G'$ sets $rem(v) = 1$ if either $candidate(v) = 1$, or one of the nodes w in $N_x(v)$ has $candidate(w) = 1$.

Each node v also maintains the following sets which are initially empty.

▷ **$MIS_x(v)$**: At round i, $MIS_x(v)$ contains ids of the nodes w parallel to the x-axis those have set $candidate(w) = 1$ and reached node v by round $i - 1$.
▷ **$MIS_y(v)$**: At round i, $MIS_y(v)$ contains ids of all the nodes w parallel to y-axis those have set $candidate(w) = 1$ and reached v by round $i - 1$.
▷ **NEW(v)**: At round i, $NEW(v)$ contains the ids of all the nodes w with $candidate(w) = 1$ those have reached v between round $j + 1$ and $i - 1$, where j is the round where v transmitted the last message.

At any round $i \geq 1$, any message that is sent by a node v, denoted by $M(v)$ contains $id(v)$, $rem(v)$, $candidate(v)$, $mis(v)$, $start(v)$, $dom(v)$, NEW, $min(v)$, and $max(v)$.

During the execution of the algorithm, we partition the graph into the following three *types* of nodes; *normal*, *active*, and *removed*. A node v is called *normal*, if $rem(v) = 0$. A node v is called *active*, if either $candiate(v) = 1$ or $dom(v) = 1$ or $start(v) = 1$. A node v is called *removed* if it is neither normal nor active. At any round i, a node can identify its type by looking the values of its variables. We now describe the algorithm (Algorithm 2) for different types of nodes.

Initially all nodes in the network are normal. The normal nodes execute the algorithm $NORMAL(v, i)$ (Algorithm 3). In the first round of the algorithm,

---

Algorithm 2: $MIS\_INTERSECTION(v, i)$

---

1 **if** v *is a normal node* **then**
2 $\quad\lfloor\ NORMAL(v, i)$

3 **if** v *is an active node* **then**
4 $\quad\lfloor\ ACTIVE(v, i)$

5 **if** v *is a removed node* **then**
6 $\quad\lfloor\ REMOVED(v, i)$

---

every node transmits a message and therefor in round 2, every node v learns their neighborhood $N(v)$. This is the round where for the first time some node in the network selects itself as a candidate for the MIS by setting $candidate(v) = 1$. Suppose that v is parallel to the x-axis. The node v sets $candidate(v) = 1$, if the x-coordinate of the right end point of v is smallest among all its normal neighbors. This is done is Step 22 of Algorithm 3. It also set $rem(v) = 1$ and at the end of this round it becomes an active node. As v selects itself as a candidate, it includes itself in $MIS_x(v)$. Similarly, if v is parallel to the y-axis, then it compares its top end point with all its neighbors top end points and selects itself as a candidate if the y-coordinate of its top end point is the smallest among all its neighbors. In case of a tie in each of the above cases, the node with smallest length is selected.

If a neighbor w of v sets $candidate(w) = 1$ in round $i-1$ and becomes active, then v sets $rem(v) = 1$. If v has the largest x-coordinate among the right end points of all its neighbors, then $max(w) = v$ and v learns this from $M(w)$ that it receives in round $i - 1$. After learning this, v sets $dom(v) = 1$ and becomes active. Also, if $min(w) = v$, then v sets $start(v) = 1$ and become active. Else, v becomes a removed node.

A node v that is active, executes subroutine $ACTIVE(v, i)$ (Algorithm 4). At any round i, if v is an active node and v learns about a new node u in round $i - 1$ (from its active neighbors) that is selected itself as a candidate for the MIS, it updates $MIS_x(v)$, $MIS_y(v)$ and transmit the information about this new node to all its neighbors. If there are multiple such new nodes which it learns in round $i-1$ for the first time, the entire set of these new candidates are transmitted in the form of the set $NEW(v)$.

In Fig. 2, we show that a component parallel to the x-axis connected with a component parallel to the y-axis. Here red nodes are candidates nodes, blue nodes are start nodes, black nodes are removed nodes, and green nodes have dom value 1. We see that the red and green nodes with the blue nodes form a connected dominating set.

A removed node v executes the subroutine $REMOVED(v, i)$ (Algorithm 5). If it has not received any message in the last three rounds, then it execute Algorithm 6. Else, at any round i, v updates $MIS_x(v)$, $MIS_y(v)$ by adding the information of the new candidates it received from its active neighbors in round

---

Algorithm 3: $NORMAL(v, i)$

---

1 if $i = 1$ **then**

2   v transmits $M(v)$.

3 else

4   **if** $i = 2$ **then**

5   Let $N_x(v)$ be the set of neighbors from where it received any message in round 1.

6      $N_x''(v) \leftarrow N_x(v)$.

7   **if** v *is parallel to* x-*axis* **then**

8   Let $N_x'(v)$ be the set of removed neighbors parallel to x-axis from where v has received messages in round $i - 1$.

9      $N_x''(v) \leftarrow N_x''(v) \backslash N_x'(v)$

10   Let $Z(v)$ be the set of active neighbors from where v received any messages in round $i - 1$.

11      $M_1 \leftarrow \bigcup_{w \in Z(v)} NEW(w)$, where w is a node parallel to x-axis.

12      $M_2 \leftarrow \bigcup_{w \in Z(v)} NEW(w)$, where w is a node parallel to y-axis.

13      $MIS_x(v) \leftarrow MIS_x(v) \cup M_1$ and $MIS_y(v) \leftarrow MIS_y(v) \cup M_2$.

14      $NEW(v) \leftarrow NEW(v) \cup M_1 \cup M_2$.

15   **if** $Z(v)$ *contains a node* w *with* $candidate(w) = 1$ *and* w *is parallel to* x-*axis* **then**

16        $rem(v) \leftarrow 1$

17   **if** $max(w) = v$ **then**

18          $dom(v) \leftarrow 1$

19   **if** $min(w) = v$ **then**

20          $start(v) \leftarrow 1$

21   v transmits $M(v)$

22   **else**

23   **if** $min_x(N_x''(v) \cup \{v\}) = v$ **then**

24          $candiate(v) \leftarrow 1$, $rem(v) \leftarrow 1$

25          $MIS_x(v) \leftarrow MIS_x(v) \cup v$,

26          $NEW(v) \leftarrow NEW(v) \cup \{v\}$.

27   v transmits $M(v)$.

28   **if** v *is parallel to* y-*axis* **then**

29   Perform Step 8 to Step 27 exchanging x with y in everywhere.

$i - 1$. Also, if it received any message from a node w such that $candidate(w) = 1$ and $min(w) = v$, then it sets $start(v) = 1$ and become an active node.

Every active node in the network that has learned at least one candidate for the MIS, i.e., at least one of $MIS_x(v)$ or $MIS_y(v)$ is non-empty, and has not received any message in last two rounds, executes Algorithm 7. At this point, the node v already learned all the candidates for the MIS in G (by Observation 1). If the node v is parallel to the x-axis and $candidate(v) = 1$, then it sets $mis(v) = 1$ if $|MIS_x(v)| \geq |MIS_y(v)|$. Else if $|MIS_x(v)| < |MIS_y(v)|$, then it sets $mis(v) = 1$

Algorithm 4: $ACTIVE(v,i)$

---

1 **if** *v has not received any messages in last two rounds and* $candidate(v) = 1$
   then
2 | **if** $MIS_x(v) \cup MIS_y(v) \neq \Phi$ **then**
3 | | $Final(v,i)$

4 **else**
5 | Let $Z(v)$ be the set of active nodes from where v received messages in round
   | $i-1$.
6 | $M_1 \leftarrow \bigcup_{w \in Z(v)} NEW(w) \backslash MIS_x(v)$, where w is a node parallel to x-axis.
7 | $M_2 \leftarrow \bigcup_{w \in Z(v)} NEW(w) \backslash MIS_y(v)$, where w is a node parallel to y-axis.
8 | $MIS_x(v) \leftarrow MIS_x(v) \cup M_1$ and $MIS_y(v) \leftarrow MIS_y(v) \cup M_2$.
9 | $NEW(v) \leftarrow M_1 \cup M_2$.
10 | **if** $NEW(v) \neq \Phi$ **then**
11 | | The node v transmits $M(v)$

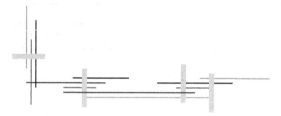

Fig. 2. Showing different types of segments: overlapping line segments are grouped using pink rectangles. (Color figure online)

only if $MIS_y(v) \cap N(v) = \varnothing$. If the node v is parallel to the y-axis, the algorithm for v is similar (by interchanging the subscripts x and y). The other active nodes (other than the candidate nodes) executes Algorithm 6 in the next round.

A node v with $candidate(v) = 0$ participates in Algorithm 2 sets $mis(v) = 1$, if none of its neighbors select themselves in the final MIS and it has the minimum x-coordinate in the right end point among all its neighbors that does not have any neighbors in the final MIS.

3.2 Analysis

We prove the following three theorems whose proofs are in the full version of the paper.

Theorem 3. *Let* $M' = \{v|\ v\ terminates\ with\ mis(v) = 1\ according\ to$ *Algorithm 2}. Then* M' *is an MIS of* G.

Theorem 4. *Let* M_{opt} *be a MaxIS of* G. *Then* $|M'| \geq \frac{1}{2}|M_{opt}|$.

Algorithm 5: $REMOVED(v, i)$

---

1 **if** *v received a message from a node w with mis(w) = 1* **then**
2 $\quad$ terminate
3 **if** *v has not received any message for last three rounds* **then**
4 $\quad$ $REVISIT(v, i)$
5 Let $Z(v)$ be the set of active nodes from where v received any message in round $i - 1$.
6 $M_1 \leftarrow \bigcup_{w \in Z(v)} NEW(w) \backslash MIS_x(v)$, where w is a node parallel to x-axis.
7 $M_2 \leftarrow \bigcup_{w \in Z(v)} NEW(w) \backslash MIS_y(v)$, where w is a node parallel to y-axis.
8 $MIS_x(v) \leftarrow MIS_x(v) \cup M_1$ and $MIS_y(v) \leftarrow MIS_y(v) \cup M_2$.
9 **if** $start(v) = 0$ *and there exists* $w \in Z(v)$ *such that* $min(w) = v$ **then**
10 $\quad$ $start(v) \leftarrow 1$.
11 $\quad$ $NEW(v) = M_1 \cup M_2$.
12 $\quad$ The node v transmits $M(v)$

Algorithm 6: $REVISIT(v, i)$

---

1 **if** *v is parallel to x-axis and* $|MIS_y(v)| > |MIS_x(v)|$ **then**
2 $\quad$ Let $T_x(v)$ be the set of neighbors of v which does not intersects with any node in $MIS_y(v)$.
3 $\quad$ **if** $min_x((T_x(v) \cup \{v\}) = v$ **then**
4 $\quad\quad$ v sets $mis(v) = 1$ and terminate
5 **if** *v is parallel to y-axis and* $|MIS_y(v)| \leqslant |MIS_x(v)|$ **then**
6 $\quad$ Let $T_y(v)$ be the set of neighbors of v which does not intersects with any node in $MIS_x(v)$.
7 $\quad$ **if** $min_y((T_y(v) \cup \{v\}) = v$ **then**
8 $\quad\quad$ v sets $mis(v) = 1$ and terminate.

Theorem 5. *The time complexity of Algorithm 2 is $O(D)$, and the message complexity is $O(n + k^2)$, where D is the diameter of the graph G and k is the size of the MaxIS.*

We improve the message complexity to $O(n + k \log k)$ by modifying the information propagation part of our above algorithm. The idea and analysis is provided in the full version of the paper. We also provide an algorithm to find MIS of axis-parallel unit segment intersection graphs in constant rounds (details are given in the full version of the paper).

Algorithm 7: $Final(v, i)$

---

1 **if** v *is parallel to x-axis* **then**
2   **if** $|MIS_x(v)| \geq |MIS_y(v)|$ **then**
3   **if** $candidate(v) = 1$ **then**
4        $mis(v) = 1$

5   **else**
6   **if** $candidate(v) = 1$ **then**
7   **if** *there does not exists any* $w \in N(v)$ *such that* $w \in MIS_y(v)$ **then**
8          $mis(v) = 1$

9   **else**
10        $REVISIT(v, i + 1)$

11 **if** v *is parallel to y-axis* **then**
12   **if** $|MIS_x(v)| < |MIS_y(v)|$ **then**
13   **if** $candidate(v) = 1$ **then**
14        $mis(v) = 1$

15   **else**
16   **if** $candidate(v) = 1$ **then**
17   **if** *there does not exists any* $w \in N(v)$ *s.t.* $w \in MIS_x(v)$ *and* $candidate(v) = 1$ **then**
18          $mis(v) = 1$

19   **else**
20        $REVISIT(v, i + 1)$

21 **if** $mis(v) = 1$ **then**
22   v transmits $M(v)$ and terminates.

---

4   Conclusion

Our proposed algorithm for computing the MaxIS in interval graphs uses $O(n)$ message exchanges. This is optimal as $\Omega(n)$ is a trivial lower bound on message complexity. On the other hand, for the segment intersection graphs, the message complexity of our proposed algorithm is $O(n + k \log k)$, where k is the size of the MaxIS. Since $k \leq n$, and $\Omega(n)$ is a trivial lower bound, this leaves a gap smaller than any polynomial in n. Therefore, designing an algorithm with optimal message complexity to fill this small gap is a natural open problem. Also, we plan to extend our results for congest communication model, where the size of every message can be of $\Theta(\log n)$ bits.

References

1. Barenboim, L., Elkin, M.: Sublogarithmic distributed MIS algorithm for sparse graphs using nash-williams decomposition. Distrib. Comput. **22**(5–6), 363–379 (2010)
2. Barenboim, L., Elkin, M.: Deterministic distributed vertex coloring in polylogarithmic time. J. ACM **58**(5), 23:1–23:25 (2011)
3. Bodlaender, M.H., Halldórsson, M.M., Konrad, C., Kuhn, F.: Brief announcement: local independent set approximation. In: PODC, pp. 93–95 (2016)
4. Czygrinow, A., Hańćkowiak, M., Wawrzyniak, W.: Fast distributed approximations in planar graphs. In: Taubenfeld, G. (ed.) DISC 2008. LNCS, vol. 5218, pp. 78–92. Springer, Heidelberg (2008). https://doi.org/10.1007/978-3-540-87779-0_6
5. Fischer, M., Noever, A.: Tight analysis of parallel randomized greedy MIS. In: SODA, pp. 2152–2160 (2018)
6. Ghaffari, M.: An improved distributed algorithm for maximal independent set. In: SODA, pp. 270–277 (2016)
7. Halldórsson, M.M., Konrad, C.: Distributed large independent sets in one round on bounded-independence graphs. In: Moses, Y. (ed.) DISC 2015. LNCS, vol. 9363, pp. 559–572. Springer, Heidelberg (2015). https://doi.org/10.1007/978-3-662-48653-5_37
8. Kuhn, F., Moscibroda, T., Nieberg, T., Wattenhofer, R.: Fast deterministic distributed maximal independent set computation on growth-bounded graphs. In: Fraigniaud, P. (ed.) DISC 2005. LNCS, vol. 3724, pp. 273–287. Springer, Heidelberg (2005). https://doi.org/10.1007/11561927_21
9. Kuhn, F., Moscibroda, T., Wattenhofer, R.: Local computation: lower and upper bounds. J. ACM **63**(2), 17:1–17:44 (2016)
10. Linial, N.: Locality in distributed graph algorithms. SIAM J. Comput. **21**(1), 193–201 (1992)
11. Luby, M.: A simple parallel algorithm for the maximal independent set problem. In: STOC, pp. 1–10 (1985)
12. Molla, A.R., Pandit, S., Roy, S.: Optimal deterministic distributed algorithms for maximal independent set in geometric graphs. J. Parallel Distrib. Comput. **132**, 36–47 (2019)
13. Panconesi, A., Srinivasan, A.: On the complexity of distributed network decomposition. J. Algorithms **20**(2), 356–374 (1996)
14. Peleg, D.: Distributed Computing: A Locality-Sensitive Approach. Society for Industrial and Applied Mathematics (2000)
15. Rozhon, V., Ghaffari, M.: Polylogarithmic-time deterministic network decomposition and distributed derandomization. CoRR abs/1907.10937 (2019)
16. Schneider, J., Wattenhofer, R.: An optimal maximal independent set algorithm for bounded-independence graphs. Distrib. Comput. **22**(5), 349–361 (2010)

Hierarchical b-Matching

Yuval Emek[1], Shay Kutten[1], Mordechai Shalom[2(✉)], and Shmuel Zaks[3,4]

[1] Department of Industrial Engineering and Management, Technion, Haifa, Israel
{yemek,kutten}@technion.ac.il
[2] Işık University, Şile, Turkey
cmshalom@gmail.com
[3] Department of Computer Science, Technion, Haifa, Israel
zaks@cs.technion.ac.il
[4] ORT Braude Academic College of Engineering, Karmiel, Israel

Abstract. A matching of a graph is a subset of edges no two of which share a common vertex, and a maximum matching is a matching of maximum cardinality. In a b-matching every vertex v has an associated bound b_v, and a maximum b-matching is a maximum set of edges, such that every vertex v appears in at most b_v of them. We study an extension of this problem, termed *Hierarchical b-Matching*. In this extension, the vertices are arranged in a hierarchical manner. At the first level the vertices are partitioned into disjoint subsets, with a given bound for each subset. At the second level the set of these subsets is again partitioned into disjoint subsets, with a given bound for each subset, and so on. We seek for a maximum set of edges, that obey all bounds (that is, no vertex v participates in more than b_v edges, then all the vertices in one subset do not participate in more that subset's bound of edges, and so on hierarchically). This is a sub-problem of the matroid matching problem which is NP-hard in general. It corresponds to the special case where the matroid is restricted to be laminar and the weights are unity. A pseudo-polynomial algorithm for the weighted laminar matroid matching problem is presented in [8]. We propose a polynomial-time algorithm for Hierarchical b-matching, i.e. the unweighted laminar matroid matching problem, and discuss how our techniques can possibly be generalized to the weighted case.

Keywords: Matching · b-matching · Matroids

1 Introduction

Background: A matching of a graph is a subset of its edges such that no two edges share a common vertex. The maximum matching problem is the problem of finding a matching of maximum cardinality in a given graph. The maximum weighted

This research was supported in part by PetaCloud - a project funded by the Israel Innovation Authority.

T. Bureš et al. (Eds.): SOFSEM 2021, LNCS 12607, pp. 189–202, 2021.
https://doi.org/10.1007/978-3-030-67731-2_14

matching problem is an extension of the problem for edge-weighted graphs in which one aims to find a matching of maximum total weight. Both problems are fundamental in graph theory and combinatorial optimization. As such, they have been extensively studied in the literature. While pioneering works focused on the non-weighted bipartite case, later work considered general graphs and weights. The general case is solved in [4] and a more efficient algorithm is proposed later in [10].

An important extension of these problems is the following maximum b-matching problem. We are given a (possibly weighted) graph and a positive integer b_v for every vertex v of the graph. A b-matching of the graph is a multiset M of its edges such that, for every vertex v, the number of edges of M incident to v does not exceed b_v. Clearly, a matching is a special case of b-matching in which $b_v = 1$ for every vertex v. The problems of finding a b-matching of maximum cardinality and of maximum weight are widely studied. The weighted version of the problem is solved in [12]. A faster algorithm is later proposed in [1]. This result is recently improved in [6]. Being a fundamental problem, the b-matching problem is considered in the literature in specific graph classes (e.g. [13]). The b-matching model is used to solve numerous problems in different areas, e.g. [14]. See [9] for flow techniques and other algorithmic techniques used to solve matching problems.

Our Work and Related Results: In this work, we consider an extension of the maximum cardinality b-matching problem and propose a polynomial-time algorithm for it. In this extension, the vertices are arranged in a hierarchical manner, such that every set is either a single vertex or the union of other sets, and with each set, there is an associated upper bound on the sum of the degrees of the vertices in it.

This problem is a sub-problem of the matroid matching problem where the weights are unity and the matroid is laminar. The weighted version of the problem is shown to be equivalent to the b-matching problem when the numbers b_v are upper-bounded by some polynomial function on the input size [8]. This clearly implies a pseudo-polynomial algorithm for the weighted case. On the other hand it is possible to describe the problem as an integer linear program such that the sum of the absolute values of the coefficients of every variable is at most 2. This class of integer linear programs are also solvable in pseudo-polynomial time [5]. We present a (fully) polynomial-time combinatorial algorithm for the case of unit weights.

Applications: This problem can arise in hierarchical structures, for instance as in the following scenario. Pairs of researchers are willing to pay mutual visits to each other. However, every researcher r has a budget that allows her to exercise at most b_r visits. The goal is to find a maximum number of such pairs (that will visit each other) without exceeding the individual budget of any researcher. This problem can be modeled as a b-matching problem. Now we extend this scenario to the hierarchical case. Some institutions assign budgets not only to individual researchers but also to research groups, departments, faculties and so on. In this case a set of pairs is feasible if the number of visits to be done by every individual researcher, every research group, every department and every faculty is within its assigned budget.

An important application comes from simultaneous scheduling of communication requests in tree networks. Consider a tree network with communication requests between pairs of nodes and capacities on the links and nodes. The goal is to find a maximum cardinality subset of the communication requests such that the number of requests served by every intermediate node/link does not exceed its capacity. This problem is exactly the maximum integral multi-commodity problem in tree networks proved to be NP-hard in [7]. If all the communication paths have a vertex in common then the problem reduces to the Hierarchical b-matching problem for which we present a polynomial-time algorithm in this work.

Outline: In Sect. 2 we introduce basic definitions, notations and the problem's statement. In Sect. 3.1 we present a pseudo polynomial algorithm for the problem, which is improved in Sect. 3.2 to a polynomial-time algorithm. We conclude with remarks and further research in Sect. 4. This includes a discussion how the techniques can be used to extend the results to the weighted case.

2 Preliminaries

Sets: For two non-negative integers n_1, n_2, denote by $[n_1, n_2]$ the set of integers that are not smaller than n_1 and not larger than n_2. $[n]$ is a shorthand for $[1, n]$, and $\uplus$ denotes the union operator of multisets, i.e., $A \uplus B$ is a multiset in which the multiplicity of an element is the sum of its multiplicities in A and B. A set system $\mathcal{L}$ over a set U of elements is *laminar* if for every two sets $L, L' \in \mathcal{L}$ one of the following holds: $L \cap L' = \emptyset$, $L \subseteq L'$, or $L' \subseteq L$. We consider laminar set systems of distinct sets and $\emptyset \notin \mathcal{L}$. In this case, at most one of the conditions may hold. Since adding U and all the singletons of U to $\mathcal{L}$ preserves laminarity, we assume without loss of generality that $U \in \mathcal{L}$ and $\{u\} \in \mathcal{L}$ for every $u \in U$.

The next Lemma summarizes well known facts about laminar set systems:

Lemma 1. *Let $\mathcal{L}$ be a laminar set system over a set U. Then*

 1 the elements of $\mathcal{L}$ can be represented as a rooted tree $T_{\mathcal{L}}$, in which the root corresponds to U and the leaves to the singletons $\{u\}$ for every $u \in U$.
 2 Every non-leaf node of $T_{\mathcal{L}}$ has at least two children.
 3 The number of sets in $\mathcal{L}$ is at most $2|U| - 1$.

Note that in this lemma: *2)* follows from the fact that we assumed that a laminar set system consists of distinct sets, *3)* follows from *2)* and holds with equality (i.e. the number of elements is exactly $2|U| - 1$) if and only if $T_{\mathcal{L}}$ is a full binary tree. See Fig. 1 for an example.

Identifying the sets of $\mathcal{L}$ with the nodes of $T_{\mathcal{L}}$, we say that a set $L \in \mathcal{L}$ is the *parent* of $L' \in \mathcal{L}$, or that L' is a *child* of L. Denote by $\mathrm{chd}(L)$ the set of all children of L.

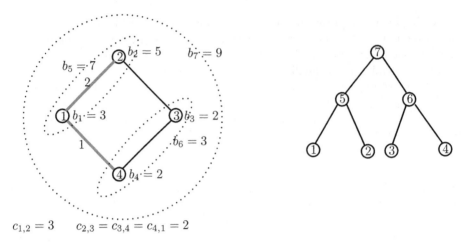

Fig. 1. An instance of MAX H-MATCHING and a solution M: Depicted on the left hand side is the graph G that is a cycle on four vertices 1, 2, 3, and 4. The set system $\mathcal{L}$ consists of the four singletons $L_i = \{i\}$ for $i \in [4]$, and the sets $L_5 = \{1, 2\}$, $L_6 = \{3, 4\}$ and $L_7 = V(G)$. The edges of M are shown as thick red lines. The numbers on these lines are the multiplicities of the corresponding edges in M. Depicted on the right hand side is the Hasse diagram of the inclusion relation on $\mathcal{L}$.

Graphs: We use standard terminology and notation for graphs, see for instance [3]. Given a simple undirected graph G, denote by $V(G)$ the set of vertices of G and by $E(G)$ the set of the edges of G. Denoting an edge between two vertices u and v as uv, we say that the edge $uv \in E(G)$ is *incident* to u and v, u and v are the endpoints of uv, and u is adjacent to v (and vice versa). For directed graphs, the arc uv is said to be from u to v. Denote by $\delta_G(v)$ the set of all edges incident to the vertex v of G, i.e., $\delta_G(v) = \{uv \in E(G)\}$. The number of these edges is the *degree* $d_G(v)$ of v in G. When there is no ambiguity, the subscript G is omitted. A *walk* of a graph (resp. directed graph) G is a sequence $u_0, e_1, u_1, e_2, \ldots, e_\ell, u_\ell$ where every u_i is a vertex of G, every e_i is an edge (resp. arc) of G, and $e_i = u_{i-1}u_i$ for every $i \in [\ell]$. A *trail* is a walk with distinct edges, i.e. $e_i \neq e_j$ whenever $i \neq j$, $i, j \in [\ell]$. A walk (resp. trail) is *closed* if $u_0 = u_\ell$ and *open* otherwise.

Hierarchical b-Matching: Let G be a graph and $L \subseteq V(G)$ a set of vertices of G and $M \subseteq E(G)$ a multiset over the edges of G where $x_{e,M} \geq 0$ denotes the multiplicity of e in M. The degree of L in M is the sum of the degrees (in M) of its vertices, i.e. $d_M(L) \overset{def}{=} \sum_{v \in L} d_M(v)$. ($d_M(v)$ is the degree of v in the graph induced by the edges of M.) Clearly, for a singleton $\{v\}$, we have $d_M(\{v\}) = d_M(v)$. Let $\mathcal{L}$ be a laminar set system over $V(G)$, c a vector of positive integers indexed by the edges of G, and b a vector of positive integers indexed by the sets in $\mathcal{L}$. A multiset $M \subseteq E(G)$ is a Hierarchical b-matching (or an H-matching for short) of $(G, \mathcal{L}, b, c)$ if the multiplicity $x_{e,M}$ of every edge e

of G is at most c_e, and $d_M(L) \leq b_L$ for every $L \in \mathcal{L}$. In this work, we consider the following problem

---
MAX H-MATCHING
Input: A quadruple $(G, \mathcal{L}, b, c)$ where
G is a graph,
$\mathcal{L}$ is a laminar set system over $V(G)$,
b is a vector of positive integers indexed by (the sets of) $\mathcal{L}$, and
c is a vector of positive integers indexed by the edges of G.
Output: An H-matching M of $(G, \mathcal{L}, b, c)$ of maximum cardinality.

Without loss of generality the vertex set of G is $[n]$, $\mathcal{L} = \{L_1, \ldots, L_m\}$ with $m > n$, $L_i = \{i\}$ for every $i \in [n]$, $L_m = [n]$ is the root of $\mathcal{L}$, $b_{L_k} = b_k$ for every $k \in [m]$, and $c_e = c_{i,j}$ for every edge $e = ij$ $(i, j \in [n])$ of G.

Assume also without loss of generality that

- $\max\{b_{L'} | L' \in \mathrm{chd}(L)\} \leq b_L \leq \sum_{L' \in \mathrm{chd}(L)} b_{L'}$ for every non-leaf $L \in \mathcal{L}$, and
- $c_{uv} \leq \min\{b_u, b_v\}$ for every edge uv of G.

In fact, if this is not the case, the vectors b and c can be modified as follows without affecting the set of feasible solutions. First process the sets $L \in \mathcal{L}$ in a preorder manner and set $b_L = b_{\mathrm{par}(L)}$ whenever $b_L > b_{\mathrm{par}(L)}$. Then process the sets $L \in \mathcal{L}$ in a postorder manner and set $b_L = sum_{L' \in \mathrm{chd}(L)}$ whenever $b_L > sum_{L' \in \mathrm{chd}(L)}$.

Given an H-matching M of $(G, \mathcal{L}, b, c)$, define the *slackness* $s_{e,M}$ of an edge e as $c_e - x_{e,M}$, and the *slackness* $s_{L,M}$ of a set $L \in \mathcal{L}$ as $b_L - d_M(L)$. Whenever no ambiguity arises, the name of the matching in the indices is omitted, and $x_e, s_e, s_L, d(v)$ is written instead of $x_{e,M}, s_{e,M}, s_{L,M}$, and $d_M(v)$, respectively. A set $L \in \mathcal{L}$ (or an edge e of G) is *tight* in M if its slackness in M is zero. A vertex v is *tight* in M if there is at least one tight set $L \in \mathcal{L}$ that contains v.

A *matching* of G is an H-matching of $(G, \mathcal{L}, b, c)$ where $\mathcal{L}$ consists of $V(G)$ and its singletons, $c_e = 1$ for every edge e of G, $b_{\{v\}} = 1$ for every vertex v of G and $b_{V(G)} = |V(G)|$. A matching M *matches* (or *saturates*) a vertex v if $d_M(v) = 1$ and it *exposes* v otherwise (i.e., $d_M(v) = 0$). M *saturates* (resp. *exposes*) a set of vertices $W \subseteq V(G)$, if M saturates (resp. exposes) all the vertices of W. Denote by $V(M)$ (resp. $\exp(M)$) the set of vertices matched (resp. exposed) by M.

3 Hierarchical b-Matching

Given a matching M of a graph G, an *M-augmenting path* of G is a path of odd length that starts with an edge that is not in M and its edges alternate between edges and non-edges of M. It is well known that a matching M is of maximum cardinality in a graph G if and only if G does not contain an M-augmenting path (Berge's Lemma [2]). Since an augmenting path can be found in polynomial time, this implies a polynomial-time algorithm that starts with any matching (e.g., the empty one) and improves it using augmenting paths until no such path is found.

Our design of the polynomial-time algorithm for MAX H-MATCHING consists of three parts. We start by proving an analogous Lemma for H-matchings. This implies a pseudo-polynomial algorithm to augment a given H-matching. Starting from an empty H-matching and applying this algorithm until an augmentation is impossible, implies a pseudo-polynomial algorithm for MAX H-MATCHING. This is done in Sect. 3.1.

We note that a pseudo-polynomial algorithm is already known for the weighted case [8]. We also note that our technique can be slightly modified to achieve the same result.

We improve the result, by first getting a polynomial-time algorithm for a single augmentation step, and then extending the technique introduced in [1] to improve the overall algorithm to run in polynomial time. This is done in Sect. 3.2.

3.1   A Pseudo-polynomial Algorithm

We now present a pseudo-polynomial algorithm for the MAX H-MATCHING problem. Our solution reduces the problem to the problem of finding a maximum cardinality matching of a graph using a pseudo-polynomial reduction.

The reader is encouraged to consult Fig. 1 and Fig. 2 for the following definition.

Definition 1. *The* representing graph *of an instance* $(G, \mathcal{L}, b, c)$ *of* MAX H-MATCHING *is the graph* $\text{repr}(G, \mathcal{L}, b, c) = (\mathcal{L}_T \cup \mathcal{L}_B \cup \mathcal{E}, E_{IN} \cup E_{UP} \cup E_E)$ *where*

- $\mathcal{L}_B = \cup_{k=1}^m L_{k,B}$, $\mathcal{L}_T = \cup_{k=1}^{m-1} L_{k,T}$, *and every set* $L_{k,B}$ *and* $L_{k,T}$ *consists of* b_k *vertices,*
- $\mathcal{E} = \cup_{ij \in E(G)} E_{i,j}$, *and every set* $E_{i,j}$ *consists of* $c_{i,j} = c_{j,i}$ *vertices,*
- E_{IN} *contains* b_k *edges for every* $k \in [m-1]$ *connecting the* b_k *vertices of* $L_{k,B}$ *with the* b_k *vertices of* $L_{k,T}$ *so that* $L_{k,T} \cup L_{k,B}$ *induces a perfect matching,*
- E_{UP} *contains* $b_k \cdot b_{k'}$ *edges between the* b_k *vertices of* $L_{k,T}$ *and the* $b_{k'}$ *vertices of* $L_{k',B}$ *so that* $L_{k,T} \cup L_{k',B}$ *induces a complete bipartite graph, whenever* $L_{k'}$ *is the parent of* L_k *in* $\mathcal{L}$. *Moreover,* E_{UP} *contains* $c_{i,j} \cdot b_i$ *edges between the* $c_{i,j}$ *vertices of* $E_{i,j}$ *and the* b_i *vertices of* $L_{i,B}$ *for every edge* ij *of* G.
- E_E *contains* $c_{i,j}$ *edges between the* $c_{i,j}$ *vertices of* $E_{i,j}$ *and the* $c_{j,i}(= c_{i,j})$ *vertices of* $E_{j,i}$ *so that* $E_{i,j} \cup E_{j,i}$ *induces a perfect matching.*

Let M *be an H-matching of* $(G, \mathcal{L}, b, c)$. *The* representing matching $\text{repr}(M)$ *of* M *is the matching* M' *of* $\text{repr}(G, \mathcal{L}, b, c)$ *constructed as follows.*

- *Start with the empty matching* M'.
- *Process the edges* e *of* G *in some predefined order, for every edge* $e = ij$ *of* G, *add to* M'
  - *the last* s_e *edges of* $E_E \cap (E_{i,j} \times E_{j,i})$, *and*
  - *the* x_e *edges connecting the first* x_e *vertices of* $E_{i,j}$ *to the first* x_e *vertices of* $L_{i,B}$ *that are yet unmatched in* M'.

Note that at this point (a) all the vertices of $\mathcal{E}$ *are matched by* M', *and (b) the number of vertices of* $L_{i,B}$ *matched by* M' *is* $d_M(i)$ *for every* $i \in [n]$.

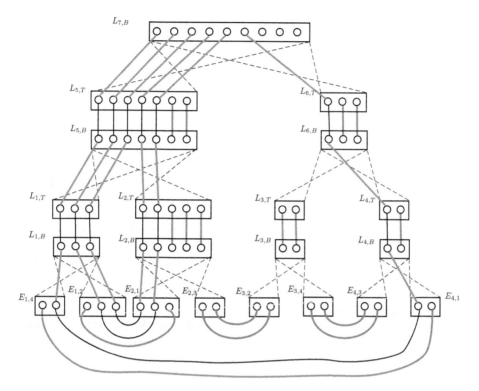

Fig. 2. The representing graph of the instance of MAX H-MATCHING depicted in Fig. 1, and the representing matching M' of its solution depicted in the same figure. The edges of M' are shown as thick red lines. Two crossing dashed lines between two sets (e.g. the lines between $L_{1,T}$ and $L_{5,B}$) indicate that these sets are complete to each other. (Color figure online)

- *Process the sets $L_i \in \mathcal{L} \setminus \{L_m\}$ in some predefined postorder traversal of $\mathcal{L}$.*
  - *Assume that the number of vertices of $L_{i,B}$ matched by M' is $d_M(i)$ at the time it is processed. As was already mentioned, this assumption holds when a leaf (i.e., a singleton) of $\mathcal{L}$ is processed.*
  - *Add to M' the perfect matching induced by the last s_{L_i} vertices of $L_{i,B}$ and the last s_{L_i} vertices of $L_{i,T}$. At this point, all the vertices of $L_{i,B}$ are matched by M' and the number of unmatched vertices of $L_{i,T}$ is $d_M(i)$.*
  - *Add to M' the $d_M(i)$ edges that connect the first $d_M(i)$ vertices of $L_{i,T}$ with the first $d_M(i)$ vertices of $L_{j,B}$ that are yet unmatched by M' where L_j is the parent of L_i. At this point all the vertices of $L_{i,B} \cup L_{i,T}$ are matched by M'.*
  - *We note that after all the children of a set L_j have been processed, the number of vertices of $L_{j,B}$ matched by M' is $\sum_{j'|L_{j'} \in \mathrm{chd}(L_j)} d_M(L_{j'}) = d_M(L_j)$, i.e. our assumption holds when L_j is processed.*

The following Lemma is implied by the above description.

Lemma 2. *Let M be an H-matching of $(G, \mathcal{L}, b, c)$, and $M' = \mathrm{repr}(M)$. Then*

(i) $|V(M') \cap L_{m,B}| = d_M(L_m) = 2\,|M|$, and
(ii) the number of edges of M' between $L_{i,B}$ and $L_{i,T}$ is equal to $s_{L_i,M}$ for every $i \in [m-1]$.

Moreover, $\exp(M') \subseteq L_{m,B}$.

Informally, Lemma 2 states that (i) the number of matched vertices in the set $L_{m,B}$ is $2|M|$, and (ii) the number of unmatched vertices of M in L_i is equal to the number of pairs matched by M' between the sets $L_{i,B}$ and $L_{i,T}$ for every i, and in addition the unmatched vertices of M' are all in the set $L_{m,B}$. In our example, the unmatched vertices are all in $L_{7,B}$, and (i) the number of matched vertices in $L_{7,B}$ is $2|M| = 6$. As for (ii), for example, the slack of $L_1 = \{1\}$ is 0, and correspondingly there are no matched pairs between $L_{1,B}$ and $L_{1,T}$; the slack of $L_2 = \{2\}$ is 3, and correspondingly there are 3 pairs of M' between $L_{1,B}$ and $L_{1,T}$; and the slack of $L_6 = \{3, 4\}$ is 2, and correspondingly there are 2 pairs of M' between $L_{6,B}$ and $L_{6,T}$.

We now prove the opposite direction. Informally it states that starting from a given matching M' of MAX H-MATCHING in which the unmatched vertices all belong to the set $L_{m,B}$, we can construct, in polynomial time, an H-matching M of $(G, \mathcal{L}, b, c)$, such that $M' = \mathrm{repr}(M)$, and M' satisfies properties (i) and (ii) of that Lemma.

Lemma 3. *Let $(G, \mathcal{L}, b, c)$ be an instance of MAX H-MATCHING, and M' be a matching of $\mathrm{repr}(G, \mathcal{L}, b, c)$ such that $\exp(M') \subseteq L_{m,B}$. Then there exists an H-matching M of $(G, \mathcal{L}, b, c)$ such that $M' = \mathrm{repr}(M)$, and it satisfies*

(i) $|V(M') \cap L_{m,B}| = 2\,|M|$,
(ii) the number of edges of M' between $L_{i,B}$ and $L_{i,T}$ is equal to $s_{L_i,M}$ for every $i \in [m-1]$.

Moreover, M can be found in time linear in the size of $\mathrm{repr}(G, \mathcal{L}, b, c)$.

Proof. Consider an edge $e = ij$ of G, and the sets $E_{i,j}, E_{j,i} \subseteq \mathcal{E}$ of vertices of $G' = \mathrm{repr}(G, \mathcal{L}, b, c)$. For every vertex w of $E_{i,j}$ let w' be its corresponding vertex in $E_{j,i}$. Then exactly one of the following holds: a) $ww' \in M'$, b) w is matched to a vertex of $L_{i,B}$ and w' is is matched to a vertex of $L_{j,B}$ by M'. Let M be the multiset of edges of G such that, for every edge $e = ij$ of G, $x_{e,M}$ equals to the number of vertices w of $E_{i,j}$ for which condition b) holds. We claim that M is an H-matching of $(G, \mathcal{L}, b, c)$.

By definition of M, the multiplicity of an edge e in M is at most c_e. For every $i \in [n]$, the number of vertices of $L_{i,B}$ matched to a vertex of $\mathcal{E}$ is $d_M(i)$. Let $z_B \in L_{i,B}$ and $z_T \in L_{i,T}$ for $i \in [m-1]$ such that $z_B z_T$ is an edge of G'. Then exactly one of the following holds: a) $z_B z_T \in M'$, b) z_B is matched to some vertex of $L_{j,T}$ and z_T is matched to some vertex of $L_{j',B}$ such that L_j is a child of L_i and $L_{j'}$ is the parent of L_i. From the above facts, it follows by induction on the structure of $\mathcal{L}$ that the number of vertices of $L_{i,B}$ matched to a vertex of $L_{j,T}$ for some j is $d_M(L_i)$. Therefore, for every $L_i \in \mathcal{L}$ we have $d_M(L_i) \le b_i$. We conclude that M is an H-matching of $(G, \mathcal{L}, b, c)$.

It follows that the number of vertices of $L_{m,B}$ matched to a vertex of $L_{j,T}$ for some j (i.e., the number of vertices of $L_{m.B}$ matched by M') is $d_M(L_m) = 2\,|M|$.

Theorem 1. FINDREPRESENTINGMATCHING *is a pseudo-polynomial algorithm for* MAX H-MATCHING.

Proof. By Lemma 2 we have $\exp(M') \subseteq L_{m.T}$. We observe that for any matching obtained by applying a sequence of augmenting paths to M', in particular for M'^* we have $\exp(M'^*) \subseteq \exp(M') \subseteq L_{m,B}$. Furthermore, $\exp(M'^*)$ is minimum. Therefore, $V(M'^*) \cap L_{m,B}$ is maximum. By Lemma 3 (i)), $|M^*|$ is maximum.

The size of G' is $\mathcal{O}\left(\sum_{e \in G} c_e + \sum_{L \in \mathcal{L}} b_L\right) = \mathcal{O}\left(\sum_{L \in \mathcal{L}} b_L\right)$. Since we want to prove pseudo-polynomial running time we assume that the values b_L are bounded by $|V(G)|^c$ for some fixed $c > 0$. Then, $\sum_{L \in \mathcal{L}} b_L \le |\mathcal{L}|\,|V(G)|^c \le 2\,|V(G)|^{c+1}$. Therefore the size of G' is $\mathcal{O}(|V(G)|^{c+1})$. Since every step of the algorithm can be performed in time polynomial to $|V(G')|$ we conclude the result.

3.2   Polynomial-Time Algorithm

In this section we improve the pseudo-polynomial algorithm of Sect. 3.1 to get a polynomial-time algorithm. We achieve this in two stages. First, we present (in Lemma 4) a polynomial-time algorithm to augment a given matching M. Then, we present (in Lemma 5) a technique to bound the number of augmentations by a polynomial in the size of the input. Combining these two lemmas we get (in Theorem 2) our polynomial-time algorithm.

Algorithm 1. FINDREPRESENTINGMATCHING

Require: An instance $(G, \mathcal{L}, b, c)$ of MAX H-MATCHING
Ensure: Return an H-matching of $(G, \mathcal{L}, b, c)$ of maximum cardinality.

1: $G' \leftarrow \mathrm{repr}(G, \mathcal{L}, b, c)$.
2: $M' \leftarrow \mathrm{repr}(\emptyset)$.
3: $M'^* \leftarrow$ a maximum matching of G' such that $\exp(M'^*) \subseteq \exp(M')$.
4: $M^* \leftarrow$ the H-matching of $(G, \mathcal{L}, b, c)$ corresponding to M'^* by Lemma 3.
5: **return** M^*.

Definition 2. *Let M be an H-matching of $(G, \mathcal{L}, b, c)$. The* augmentation graph $\mathrm{aug}(M)$ *of M is the 2-edge-colored induced subgraph of* $\mathrm{repr}(G, \mathcal{L}, b, c)$ *obtained by*

- *coloring every edge of* $\mathrm{repr}(M)$ *red, and every other edge blue,*
- *marking* $\min\{2, d_M(L_i)\}$ *blue and* $\min\{2, s_{L_i}\}$ *red edges between $L_{i,T}$ and $L_{i,B}$ for every $i \in [m-1]$,*

- marking $\min\{2, x_{e,M}\}$ blue and $\min\{2, s_{e,M}\}$ red edges between $E_{i,j}$ and $E_{j,i}$ for every edge $e = ij$ of G, and finally
- removing all vertices and edges that are not incident to any of the marked edges, except for two vertices x_1, x_2 of $L_{m,B}$ unmatched by repr(M).

In our example, the first step of coloring the edges of repr(M) red and blue is depicted in Fig. 2, where the red edges are as indicated in that figure, and all other edges are blue.

Though the above definition uses repr($G, \mathcal{L}, b, c$) in order to construct aug(M), it is easy to see that it can be constructed in time $\mathcal{O}(|E(G)|)$, without constructing repr(M) at the first place.

Lemma 4. *Let M be an H-matching of $(G, \mathcal{L}, b, c)$. Then*

(i) The only unmatched vertices in aug(M) are x_1 and x_2, and

(ii) M is not of maximum cardinality if and only if aug(M) contains an alternating (odd) path (connecting x_1 and x_2).

Proof. i) follows immediately from the construction of aug(M). We now prove ii). To show sufficiency, suppose that aug(M) contains a path P as claimed. Since aug(M) is a subgraph of repr($G, \mathcal{L}, b, c$), P is a path of repr($G, \mathcal{L}, b, c$). Moreover, since red edges are edges of repr(M) and blue edges are non-edges of it, P is a repr(M)-augmenting path. Therefore, M is not of maximum cardinality.

To show necessity, suppose that M is not of maximum cardinality. Then, $H = \text{repr}(G, \mathcal{L}, b, c)$ contains a repr(M)-augmenting path P. We color those edges of H that are in repr(M) red, and the others blue. The path P connects unmatched vertices, hence it must connect two vertices of $L_{m,B}$ and its end edges are blue. Let H' be the multigraph obtained by contracting every set $L_{i,X}$ ($i \in [m], X \in \{B, T\}$) and $E_{i,j}$ ($ij \in E(G)$) of vertices to a single vertex, and allowing parallel edges. Clearly, P corresponds to an alternating trail T' of H' starting and ending with blue edges incident to $L_{m,B}$. Note that whenever $b_k = 1$ for some $k \in [m-1]$ or $c_e = 1$ for some edge $e = ij$ of G the corresponding vertices, namely $L_{k,B}$, $L_{k,T}$, $E_{i,j}$ and $E_{j,i}$ have multiplicity of one in the multigraph. Therefore, such vertices may appear at most once in T'. Let T'' be the shortest trail of H' having these properties, and v a vertex of H'. The trail T'' does not contain even cycles, since by eliminating an even cycle one can get a shorter alternating trail. Therefore, the number of edges between any two occurrences of v in T'' must be odd. If v occurs (at least) three times in T'' then two of the occurrences must be at even distance from each other. We conclude that the number of occurrences of v in T'' is at most two. We can construct from T'' a path P'' of aug(M) by a) splitting up every two parallel edges between some $L_{i,T}$ and $L_{i,B}$ into two disjoint edges, b) splitting up every two parallel edges (that necessarily have the same color) between some $E_{i,j}$ and E_j, into two disjoint edges, and c) splitting into two non-adjacent vertices any vertex that is still traversed twice by P''. Figure 3 depicts this operation. Note that the only case that the resulting path is possibly not a path of aug(M) is the case that a vertex v is visited twice by T'' but has multiplicity of one in the multigraph. However, as already observed, such vertices appear at most once in T''.

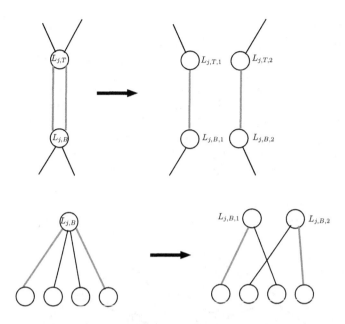

Fig. 3. The splitting of a trail T'' into a path P''.

Since aug(M) can be constructed in time $\mathcal{O}(|E(G)|)$ and an augmenting path of it can be found in time $\mathcal{O}(|E(G)|)$, Lemma 4 implies that given an H-matching M, one can find in time $\mathcal{O}(|E(G)|)$ an H-matching of cardinality $|M|+1$ or decide that M is of maximum cardinality. Therefore,

Corollary 1. *A maximum cardinality H-matching M of $(G, \mathcal{L}, b, c)$ can be found in time $|M| \cdot \mathcal{O}(|E(G)|)$.*

In the sequel we extend the technique introduced in [1] to bound the number of augmentations needed to find a maximum matching by a polynomial. This is done by finding a nearly optimal H-matching by means of a flow network.

Lemma 5. *An H-matching M of cardinality at least $|M^*| - \mathcal{O}(|V(G)|)$ can be found in time $\mathcal{O}(|V(G)| \cdot |E(G)|)$ where M^* is a maximum cardinality H-matching of $(G, \mathcal{L}, b, c)$.*

Proof. We present an algorithm that works in three stages. In the first stage we construct a flow network corresponding the instance, and compute a maximum flow of it. In the second stage we use this maximum flow to find an optimal fractional solution of the MAX H-MATCHING instance. Finally we round this fractional solution with a loss of $\mathcal{O}(|V(G)|)$.

We start by describing the construction of the flow network $F = (N, A, \kappa, s, t)$ (see Fig. 4). N is a directed graph with vertex set $[m] \cup \{i' | i \in [m]\} \cup \{s, t\}$. For every $k \in [m-1]$, there are two arcs pk and $k'p'$ with capacity $\kappa(pk) = \kappa(k'p') = b_k$ where L_p is the parent of L_k. There are two arcs sm and $m't$, with capacities

$\kappa(sm) = \kappa(m't) = b_{L_m}$. For every edge $e = ij$ of G, N contains two arcs ij' and ji' with $\kappa(ij') = \kappa(ji') = c_e$. Every H-matching M of $(G, \mathcal{L}, b, c)$ implies a feasible flow f of F by setting $f(ij') = f(ji') = x_{e,M}$ for every edge $e = ij$ of G, $f(pk) = f(k'p') = d_M(L_k)$ for every $k \in [m-1]$ such that $L_p = \mathrm{par}(L_k)$, and $f(sm) = f(m't) = d_M(L_m)$. It is easy to verify that f is a feasible $s - t$ flow and its value $|f|$ is $d_M(R) = 2|M|$. Therefore, for a maximum flow f^* and an H-matching M^* of maximum cardinality, we have $|f^*| \geq 2|M^*|$. The number of vertices of N is $2|\mathcal{L}| + 2$ which is linear in $n = |V(G)|$. The number of arcs of N is dominated by $2|E(G)|$. It is well known that, since all the capacities are integral, there is an integral maximum flow f^*. Such a flow can be found in time $\mathcal{O}(|V(G)| \cdot |E(G)|)$ [11]. If f^* is symmetric, i.e. $f^*(ij') = f^*(ji')$ for every edge ij of G then we may stop at this stage and f^* induces an optimal solution of MAX H-MATCHING.

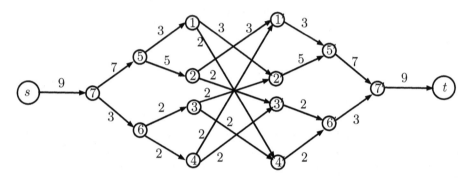

Fig. 4. The flow network instance corresponding to the instance of MAX H-MATCHING depicted in Fig. 1.

In the second stage we compute $\bar{f}_a = \frac{f^*(a) + f^*(a')}{2}$ for every pair of symmetric arcs a and a' of N. Clearly, $\bar{f}$ is symmetric and $|\bar{f}| = |f^*|$. It remains to show that $\bar{f}$ is a feasible flow. Clearly the flow on each edge is bounded by its capacity; moreover, it is easy to verify that $\bar{f}$ satisfies flow conservation at each vertex $\neq s, t$, since f^* satisfies it.

If $\bar{f}$ is integral we can assign $x_{e,M} = \bar{f}(ij') = \bar{f}(ji')$ for every edge $e = ij$ of G to get an optimal solution M of MAX H-MATCHING. Since this is not necessarily the case, this assignment leads to a half-integral fractional H-matching M' with $|M'| \geq |M^*|$.

In the last stage we round M' with a small loss, to get a feasible solution M with $|M| \geq |M'| - \mathcal{O}(|V(G)|)$. We start with $M = M'$. Let H_M be the graph induced by the edges e of G such that $x_{e,M}$ is non-integral. As far as M contains an even cycle C, we pick a matching of C consisting of half of its edges, increase $x_{e,M}$ by $1/2$ for every edge e of the matching and decrease it by $1/2$ for all the other edges of C. This modification does not affect the degrees of the vertices and thus the degrees of the sets of L, in particular it does not affect $|M|$. At this point all the cycles of H_M are odd. These cycles are vertex disjoint, since otherwise there is an even cycle in H_M. Therefore, the number of these odd cycles is at most $|V(G)|/3$. Let C be an odd cycle of H_M. We pick a maximum matching of C, increase $x_{e,M}$ by $1/2$ for every edge e of the matching and decrease it by $1/2$ for all the other edges of C. This modification does not increase the degrees of the vertices and thus the degrees of the sets of L, however it decreases $|M|$ by $1/2$. Therefore, the total loss at this stage is at most $|V(G)|/6$. At this point H_M is acyclic, i.e. a forest. If we decrease $|M|$ by $1/2$ in all the edges of the forest, $|M|$ decreases by at most $|V(G)|/2$. We conclude that $|M| \geq |M'| - \frac{2}{3}|V(G)| \geq |M^*| - \frac{2}{3}|V(G)|$.

We are now ready to prove our main theorem.

Theorem 2. *A maximum cardinality H-matching of $(G, \mathcal{L}, b, c)$ can be found in time $\mathcal{O}(|E(G)| \cdot |V(G)|)$.*

Proof. Let M^* be a maximum cardinality H-matching of $(G, \mathcal{L}, b, c)$. By Lemma 5, we can find an H-matching M of cardinality at least $|M^*| - \mathcal{O}(|V(G)|)$ in time $\mathcal{O}(|V(G)| \cdot |E(G)|)$. To get an optimal H-matching we can augment M using $\mathcal{O}(|V(G)|)$ augmentations, each of which can be done in time $\mathcal{O}(|E(G)|)$, by Lemma 4.

4   Conclusion and Open Problems

In this paper we studied the H-matching problem, which is an extension of the b-matching problem, in which the vertices are organized in a hierarchical manner (independently of the structure of the graph). At each level the vertices are partitioned into disjoint subsets, with a given bound on the sum of degrees of every subset. The optimization problem is to find a maximum set of edges, that will obey all degree bounds. This problem is applicable to many social structures, where the organization is of hierarchical nature.

We have presented a polynomial-time algorithm for this new problem, in a few stages. We first reduced it to an ordinary matching in an associated larger graph G'. The size of G' is larger than the size of the input, but polynomial in it when the values of bounds are polynomial in the input size. This resulted in a pseudo polynomial algorithm for the problem. We then improved it to a polynomial-time algorithm. This was achieved by combining results of two stages: in the first stage we presented a polynomial-time algorithm to augment a given matching. This is done by constructing a graph G'' whose size is polynomial in the input such that G' contains an augmenting path if and only if G'' contains one (Lemma 4). In the second stage we presented a technique to bound the number of augmentations by a polynomial in the size of the input.

The Weighted Case: The first open problem related to our result is weighted MAX H-MATCHING, in which every edge has an associated weight and the goal is to find an H-matching of maximum weight. We note that Lemma 4 can be extended to any subgraph of G' and any matching of this subgraph. Combining with Lemma 5, this would imply a polynomial-time algorithm to find a maximum cardinality matching of any subgraph of G'. On the other hand, weighted MAX H-MATCHING is equivalent to the problem of finding a maximum weight perfect matching of a variant of G' with appropriate weights. The maximum weighted matching problem reduces to successive invocations of the maximum cardinality matching algorithm on subgraphs of G'. Whereas, as noted above, each such invocation takes polynomial time, the number of such invocation is polynomial in the size of G'. We believe that a more careful analysis will show that the number of such invocations is polynomial in the size of G''.

Another problem to consider, is the hierarchical case where the bound on a sets is interpreted as the maximum number of edges that may connect the vertices of the set to the rest of the graph.

References

1. Anstee, R.P.: A polynomial algorithm for b-matchings: an alternative approach. Inf. Process. Lett. **24**, 153–157 (1987)
2. Berge, C.: Two theorems in graph theory. Proc. Natl. Acad. Sci. U. S. A. **43**, 842–844 (1957)
3. Diestel, R.: Graph Theory. Graduate Texts in Mathematics, vol. 173, p. 4. Springer, Heidelberg (2012)
4. Edmonds, J.: Paths, trees, and flowers. Can. J. Math. **17**, 449–467 (1965). https://doi.org/10.4153/CJM-1965-045-4
5. Edmonds, J., Johnson, E.L.: Matching: a well-solved class of integer linear programs. In: Combinatorial Optimization - Eureka, You Shrink! Papers Dedicated to Jack Edmonds, 5th International Workshop, Aussois, France, 5–9 March 2001, Revised Papers, pp. 27–30 (2001). https://doi.org/10.1007/3-540-36478-1_3
6. Gabow, H.N.: Data structures for weighted matching and extensions to b-matching and f-factors. ACM Trans. Algorithms **14**(3), 39:1–39:80 (2018). https://doi.org/10.1145/3183369. http://doi.acm.org/10.1145/3183369
7. Garg, N., Vazirani, V.V., Yannakakis, M.: Primal-dual approximation algorithms for integral flow and multicut in trees. Algorithmica **18**(1), 3–20 (1997)
8. Kaparis, K., Letchford, A.N.: On laminar matroids and b-matchings (2014). http://www.optimization-online.org/DB_FILE/2014/09/4539.pdf
9. Lawler, E.: Combinatorial Optimization: Networks and Matroids. Holt, Rinehart and Winston (1976). https://books.google.co.il/books?id=w_lQAAAAMAAJ
10. Micali, S., Vazirani, V.V.: An $o(\sqrt{|V|} \cdot |e|)$ algorithm for finding maximum matching in general graphs. In: Proceedings of the 21st Annual Symposium on Foundations of Computer Science, SFCS 1980, Washington, DC, USA, pp. 17–27. IEEE Computer Society (1980). https://doi.org/10.1109/SFCS.1980.12
11. Orlin, J.B.: Max flows in o(nm) time, or better. In: Proceedings of the Forty-fifth Annual ACM Symposium on Theory of Computing, STOC 2013, New York, NY, USA, pp. 765–774. ACM (2013). https://doi.org/10.1145/2488608.2488705
12. Pulleyblank, R.: Faces of Matching Polyhedra. Ph.D. thesis, University of Waterloo (1973)
13. Tamir, A., Mitchell, J.S.: A maximum b-matching problem arising from median location models with applications to the roommates problem. Math. Program. **80**, 171–194 (1995)
14. Tennenholtz, M.: Tractable combinatorial auctions and b-matching. Artif. Intell. **140**(1–2), 231–243 (2002). https://doi.org/10.1016/S0004-3702(02)00229-1

Improved Algorithms for Online Load Balancing

Yaxiong Liu[1,3]([✉]) [ID], Kohei Hatano[2,3] [ID], and Eiji Takimoto[1] [ID]

[1] Department of Informatics, Kyushu University, Fukuoka, Japan
{yaxiong.liu,hatano,eiji}@inf.kyushu-u.ac.jp
[2] Faculty of Arts and Science, Kyushu University, Fukuoka, Japan
[3] RIKEN AIP, Tokyo, Japan

Abstract. We consider an online load balancing problem and its extensions in the framework of repeated games. On each round, the player chooses a distribution (task allocation) over K servers, and then the environment reveals the load of each server, which determines the computation time of each server for processing the task assigned. After all rounds, the cost of the player is measured by some norm of the cumulative computation-time vector. The cost is the makespan if the norm is L_∞-norm. The goal is to minimize the regret, i.e., minimizing the player's cost relative to the cost of the best fixed distribution in hindsight. We propose algorithms for general norms and prove their regret bounds. In particular, for L_∞-norm, our regret bound matches the best known bound and the proposed algorithm runs in polynomial time per trial involving linear programming and second order programming, whereas no polynomial time algorithm was previously known to achieve the bound.

Keywords: Online learning · Blackwell approachability · Online load balancing · Makespan · Second order cone programming

1 Introduction

Online load balancing problem is an active research topic since last century. Instead of the traditional measurement of algorithm performance, competitive ratio (e.g., [2,3,5,12]), we utilize another well-known measurement as "Regret", involved by [6].

In this paper we define online load balancing problem as follows. There are K parallel servers and the protocol is defined as a game between the player and the environment. On each round $t = 1, \ldots, T$, (i) the player selects a distribution α_t over K servers, which can be viewed as an allocation of data, (ii) then the environment assigns a loaded condition $l_{t,i}$ for each server i and the loss of server i is given as $\alpha_{t,i} l_{t,i}$. The goal of the player is to minimize the makespan of the

This work was supported by JSPS KAKENHI Grant Numbers JP19H04174 and JP19H04067, respectively.

T. Bureš et al. (Eds.): SOFSEM 2021, LNCS 12607, pp. 203–217, 2021.
https://doi.org/10.1007/978-3-030-67731-2_15

cumulative loss vector of all servers after T rounds, i.e., $\max_{i=1,...,K} \sum_{t=1}^{T} \alpha_{t,i} l_{t,i}$, compared relatively to the makespan obtained by the optimal static allocation α^* in hindsight. More precisely, the goal is to minimize the regret, the difference between the player's makespan and the static optimal makespan. The makespan cost can be viewed as L_∞-norm of the vector of cumulative loss of each server (we will give a formal definition of the problem in the next section).

Even-Dar et al. [6] gave an algorithm based on the regret minimum framework by involving an extra concept, the Blackwell approachability [4] with respect to L_2-norm, to a target set, which is defined in the following section. This algorithm achieves the regret bound as $O(\sqrt{KT})$. Simultaneously another algorithm, DIFF, achieves the regret upper bound as $O((\ln K)\sqrt{T})$. Rahklin et al. [13] gave a theoretical result for the online load balancing problem, that the upper bound to regret can achieve $O(\sqrt{(\ln K)T})$, rather than $O((\ln K)\sqrt{T})$. However there is no efficient algorithm given in this paper to obtain this regret.

Then, there were some explorations about the equivalence between the Blackwell approachability and online linear optimization (OLO) [1], in addition and online convex optimization (OCO) by involving a support function [15].

These work [1,15] implied that the Blackwell approachability with respect to general norm can be guaranteed by sub-linearity of regret from OCO problem reduced by Blackwell approaching game. Moreover due to this result we give an efficient algorithm to online load balancing problem, achieving the best known regret.

More specifically speaking, we propose algorithms for online load balancing for arbitrary norms under a natural assumption. This algorithm is composed by three reductions. (i) First reduction is from load balancing problem to Blackwell approaching game in a general metric. In this reduction we extend the L_2-norm of load balancing problem in [6] to any general norm with a reasonable assumption. In this reduced Blackwell approaching game the metric is induced by the norm of load balancing problem. This reduction implies that the regret of load balancing problem can be bounded by the convergence rate of a corresponding Blackwell approaching game. (ii) Second reduction directly follows the existing work. Due to [15], we give a reduction from Blackwell approaching game to an OCO problem, by showing the existence of such reduction. Thus we can bound the regret of online load balancing with the regret of corresponding OCO problem. (iii) The last reduction is from OCO problem to two OLO problems, so that we can predict with FTRL.

Conclusively, we can predict the allocation of serves on each round in online load balancing according to the prediction of corresponding two OLO problems. Simultaneously we give the regret bound of online load balancing problem with this OLO regret.

Thus our technical contributions are the following:

- We propose a new reduction technique from online load balancing to a Blackwell approaching game. This reduction enables us to use more general norms, induced by online load balancing, in Blackwell approaching game rather than L_2-norm used in the previous work [6]. Based on this reduction we can reduce online load balancing with general norm to OLO problem, by using the reduction technique of Shimkin [15] from Blackwell games to OCO problem, further to OLO problems. In conclusion, online load balancing problem can be reduced to two OLO problems according to our reduction route. Therefore the regret bound to online load balancing problem can be optimized by the corresponding OLO regret bound.

– Especially, according to above reduction route, we give an efficient algorithm for online load balancing w.r.t. L_∞-norm, achieving the best known $O(\sqrt{T \ln K})$ regret. The algorithm involves linear programming and the second order cone programming and runs in polynomial time per trial. This is the first polynomial time algorithm achieving $O(\sqrt{T \ln K})$ regret.

2 Preliminaries

First we give some notations. We use $\|\cdot\|$ to denote a norm of a vector. Moreover, for a norm $\|\cdot\|$, $\|x\|_*$ denotes the dual norm of $\|x\|$. A norm $\|\cdot\|$ over $\mathbb{R}^d$ is monotone if $\|x\| \le \|y\|$ whenever $|x_i| \le |y_i|$ for every $1 \le i \le d$.

2.1 Online Load Balancing

Firstly we begin with a standard (offline) load balancing problem. Suppose that we have K servers to do a simple task with a large amount of data. The task can be easily parallelized in such a way that we can break down the data into K pieces and assign them to the servers, and then each server processes the subtask in time proportional to the size of data assigned. An example is to find blacklisted IP addresses in an access log data. Each server is associated with loaded condition, expressed in terms of "the computation time per unit data". The goal is to find a data assignment to the servers so as to equalize the computation time for all servers. In other words, we want to minimize the *makespan*, defined as the maximum of the computation time over all servers.

Formally, the problem is described as follows: The input is a K-dimensional vector $l = (l_1, l_2, \ldots, l_K) \in \mathbb{R}_+^K$, where each l_i represents the loaded condition of the i-th server. The output is a K-dimensional probability vector $\alpha = (\alpha_1, \alpha_2, \ldots, \alpha_K) \in \Delta(K) = \{\alpha \in [0,1]^K \mid \sum_{i=1}^K \alpha_i = 1\}$, where each α_i represents the fraction of data assigned to the i-th server. The goal is to minimize the makespan $\|\alpha \odot l\|_\infty$, where $\alpha \odot l = (\alpha_1 l_1, \alpha_2 l_2, \ldots, \alpha_K l_K)$. Note that it is clear that the optimal solution is given by $\alpha_i = l_i^{-1} / \sum_{j=1}^K l_j^{-1}$, which equalizes the computation time of every server as $C_\infty^*(l) \overset{\text{def}}{=} \min_{\alpha \in \Delta(K)} \|\alpha \odot l\|_\infty = \frac{1}{\sum_{j=1}^K 1/l_j}$.

Note also that the objective is generalized to the L_p-norm for any p in the literature.

In this paper, we consider a more general objective $\|\alpha \odot l\|$ for an arbitrary norm that satisfies certain assumptions stated below. In the general case, the optimal value is denoted by $C^*(l) \overset{\text{def}}{=} \min_{\alpha \in \Delta(K)} \|\alpha \odot l\|$.

Assumption 1. *Throughout the paper, we put the following assumptions on the norm. (i) The norm is monotone, and (ii) the function C^* is concave.*

Note that the first assumption is natural for load balancing and the both assumptions are satisfied by L_p-norm for $p > 1$.

Now we proceed to the online load balancing problem with respect to a norm $\|\cdot\|$ that satisfies Assumption 1. The problem is described as a repeated game between the learner and the environment who may behave adversarially. In each round $t = 1, 2, \ldots, T$, the learner chooses an assignment vector $\boldsymbol{\alpha}_t \in \Delta(K)$, and then receives from the environment a loaded condition vector $\boldsymbol{l}_t \in [0,1]^K$, which may vary from round to round. After the final round is over, the performance of the learner is naturally measured by $\left\| \sum_{t=1}^T \boldsymbol{\alpha}_t \odot \boldsymbol{l}_t \right\|$. We want to make the learner perform nearly as well as the performance of the best fixed assignment in hindsight (offline optimal solution), which is given by $C^*(\sum_{t=1}^T \boldsymbol{l}_t)$. To be more specific, the goal is to minimize the following *regret*:

$$\text{Regret}(T) = \left\| \sum_{t=1}^T \boldsymbol{\alpha}_t \odot \boldsymbol{l}_t \right\| - C^* \left(\sum_{t=1}^T \boldsymbol{l}_t \right).$$

2.2 Repeated Game with Vector Payoffs and Approachability

We briefly review the notion of Blackwell's approachability, which is defined for a repeated game with vector payoffs. The game is specified by a tuple $(A, B, r, S, \text{dist})$, where A and B are convex and compact sets, $r : A \times B \to \mathbb{R}^d$ is a vector-valued payoff function, $S \subseteq \mathbb{R}^d$ is a convex and closed set called the *target set*, and $\text{dist} : \mathbb{R}^d \times \mathbb{R}^d \to \mathbb{R}_+$ is a metric. The protocol proceeds in trials: In each round $t = 1, 2, \ldots, T$, the learner chooses a vector $\boldsymbol{a}_t \in A$, the environment chooses a vector $\boldsymbol{b}_t \in B$, and then the learner obtains a vector payoff $\boldsymbol{r}_t \in \mathbb{R}^d$, given by $\boldsymbol{r}_t = r(\boldsymbol{a}_t, \boldsymbol{b}_t)$. The goal of the learner is to make the average payoff vector arbitrarily close to the target set S.

Definition 1 (Approachability). *For a game $(A, B, r, S, \text{dist})$, the target set S is approachable with convergence rate $\gamma(T)$ if there exists an algorithm for the learner such that the average payoff $\bar{\boldsymbol{r}}_T = (1/T) \sum_{t=1}^T \boldsymbol{r}_t$ satisfies*

$$\text{dist}(\bar{\boldsymbol{r}}_T, S) \stackrel{\text{def}}{=} \min_{\boldsymbol{s} \in S} \text{dist}(\bar{\boldsymbol{r}}_T, \boldsymbol{s}) \leq \gamma(T)$$

against any environment. In particular, we simply say that S is approachable if it is approachable with convergence rate $o(T)$.

Blackwell characterizes the approachability in terms of the support function as stated in the proposition below.

Definition 2. *For a set $S \subseteq \mathbb{R}^d$, the support function $h_S : \mathbb{R}^d \to \mathbb{R} \cup \{\infty\}$ is defined as*

$$h_S(\boldsymbol{w}) = \sup_{\boldsymbol{s} \in S} \langle \boldsymbol{s}, \boldsymbol{w} \rangle.$$

It is clear from definition that h_S is convex whenever S is convex.

Definition 3 (Blackwell [4]). *A game $(A, B, r, S, \text{dist})$ satisfies Blackwell Condition, if and only if*

$$\forall w \in \mathbb{R}^d \left(\min_{a \in A} \min_{b \in B} \langle w, r(a, b) \rangle \leq h_S(w) \right). \tag{1}$$

Remark 1. In [4], Blackwell characterized the approachability of a target set for L_2-norm metric in terms of the Blackwell condition.

In what follows, we only consider a norm metric, i.e, $\text{dist}(r, s) = \|r - s\|$ for some norm $\|\cdot\|$ over $\mathbb{R}^d$. The following proposition is useful.

Proposition 1. *For any $w \in \mathbb{R}^d$, $s^* = \arg\max_{s \in S} \langle s, w \rangle$ is a sub-gradient of $h_S(w)$ at w.*

Proof. For any $w, u \in \mathbb{R}^d$, let $s^* = \arg\max_{s \in S} \langle s, w \rangle$ and $s^u = \arg\max_{s \in S} \langle s, u \rangle$. Since $\langle s^*, u \rangle \leq \langle s^u, u \rangle$, we have

$$h_S(w) - h_S(u) = \sup_{s \in S} \langle s, w \rangle - \sup_{s \in S} \langle s, u \rangle = \langle s^*, w \rangle - \langle s^u, u \rangle$$
$$\leq \langle s^*, w - u \rangle,$$

which implies the proposition. □

2.3 Online Convex Optimization

In this subsection we briefly review online convex optimization with some known results. See, e.g., [7,14] for more details.

An online convex optimization (OCO) problem is specified by (W, F), where $W \subseteq \mathbb{R}^d$ is a compact convex set called the decision set and $F \subseteq \{f : W \to \mathbb{R}\}$ is a set of convex functions over W called the loss function set. The OCO problem (W, F) is described by the following protocol between the learner and the adversarial environment. For each round $t = 1, 2, \ldots, T$, the learner chooses a decision vector $w_t \in W$ and then receives from the environment a loss function $f_t \in F$. In this round, the learner incurs the loss given by $f_t(w_t)$. The goal is to make the cumulative loss of the learner nearly as small as the cumulative loss of the best fixed decision. To be more specific, the goal is to minimize the following regret:

$$\text{Regret}_{(W,F)}(T) = \sum_{t=1}^{T} f_t(w_t) - \min_{w \in W} \sum_{t=1}^{T} f_t(w).$$

Here we add the subscript (W, F) to distinguish from the regret for online load balancing.

Any OCO problem can be reduced to an online linear optimization (OLO) problem, which is an OCO problem with linear loss functions. More precisely, an OLO problem is specified by (W, G), where $G \subseteq \mathbb{R}^d$ is the set of cost vectors such that the loss function at round t is $\langle g_t, \cdot \rangle$ for some cost vector $g_t \in G$. For the OLO problem (W, G), the regret of the learner is thus given by

$$\text{Regret}_{(W,G)}(T) = \sum_{t=1}^{T} \langle g_t, w_t \rangle - \min_{w \in W} \sum_{t=1}^{T} \langle g_t, w \rangle.$$

The reduction from OCO to OLO is simple. Run any algorithm for OLO (W, G) with $g_t \in \partial f_t(w_t)$, and then it achieves $\text{Regret}_{(W,F)}(T) \leq \text{Regret}_{(W,G)}(T)$, provided that G is large enough, i.e., $G \supseteq \bigcup_{f \in F, w \in W} \partial f(w)$.

A standard FTRL (follow-the-regularized-leader) strategy for the OLO problem (W, G) is to choose w_t as

$$w_t = \arg \min_{w \in W} \left(\sum_{s=1}^{t-1} \langle g_s, w \rangle + \eta_t R(w) \right), \tag{2}$$

where $R : W \to \mathbb{R}$ is a strongly convex function called the regularizer and $\eta_t \in \mathbb{R}_+$ is a parameter. Using the strategy (2) the following regret bound is known.

Proposition 2 ([14]). *Suppose that the regularizer $R : W \to \mathbb{R}$ is σ-strongly convex w.r.t. some norm $\| \cdot \|$, i.e., for any $w, u \in W$, for any $z \in \partial R(w)$, $R(u) \geq R(w) + \langle z, u - w \rangle + \frac{\sigma}{2} \|u - w\|^2$. Then, for the OLO problem (W, G), the regret of the strategy (2) satisfies*

$$\text{Regret}_{(W,G)}(T) = O(D_R L_G \sqrt{T/\sigma}),$$

where $D_R = \sqrt{\max_{w \in W} R(w)}$, $L_G = \max_{g \in G} \|g\|_*$ and $\eta_t = (L_G/D_R)\sqrt{T/\sigma}$.

Note however that the strategy does not consider the computational feasibility at all. For efficient reduction, we need an efficient algorithm that computes a sub-gradient $g \in \partial f(w)$ when given (a representation of) $f \in F$ and $w \in W$, and an efficient algorithm for solving the convex optimization problem (2).

For a particular OLO problem (W, G) with L_1 ball decision set $W = \{w \in \mathbb{R}^d \mid \|w\|_1 \leq 1\}$, an algorithm called $EG^{\pm}$ [8] finds in linear time the optimal solution of (2) with an entropic regularizer and achieves the following regret.

Theorem 2 ([9]). *For the OLO problem (W, G) with $W = \{w \in \mathbb{R}^d \mid \|w\|_1 \leq 1\}$ and $G = \{g \in \mathbb{R}^d \mid \|g\|_\infty \leq M\}$, $EG^{\pm}$ achieves*

$$\text{Regret}_{(W,G)}(T) \leq M\sqrt{2T \ln(2d)}.$$

3   Main Result

In this section, we propose a meta-algorithm for online load balancing, which is obtained by combining a reduction to two independent OLO problems and an OLO algorithm (as an oracle) for the reduced problems. Note that the reduced

OLO problems depend on the choice of norm for online load balancing, and the OLO problems are further reduced to some optimization problems defined in terms of the norm. For efficient implementation, we assume that the optimization problems are efficiently solved.

Now we consider the online load balancing problem on K servers with respect to a norm $\|\cdot\|$ defined over $\mathbb{R}^K$ that satisfies Assumption 1. The reduction we show consists of three reductions, the first reduction is to a repeated game with vector payoffs, the second one is to an OCO problem, and the last one is to two OLO problems. In the subsequent subsections, we give these reductions, respectively.

3.1   Reduction to a Vector Payoff Game

We will show that the online load balancing problem can be reduced to the following repeated game with vector payoffs, denoted by $P = (A, B, r, S, \text{dist})$, where

- $A = \Delta(K), \quad B = [0,1]^K$,
- $r : A \times B \to \mathbb{R}^K \times \mathbb{R}^K$ is the payoff function defined as $r(\boldsymbol{\alpha}, \boldsymbol{l}) = (\boldsymbol{\alpha} \odot \boldsymbol{l}, \boldsymbol{l})$,
- $S = \{(\boldsymbol{x}, \boldsymbol{y}) \in [0,1]^K \times [0,1]^K \mid \|\boldsymbol{x}\| \le C^*(\boldsymbol{y})\}$, and
- dist is the metric over $\mathbb{R}^K \times \mathbb{R}^K$ defined as $\text{dist}(\boldsymbol{r}, \boldsymbol{s}) = \|\boldsymbol{r} - \boldsymbol{s}\|^+$, where $\|\cdot\|^+$ is the norm over $\mathbb{R}^K \times \mathbb{R}^K$ defined as

$$\|(\boldsymbol{x}, \boldsymbol{y})\|^+ = \|\boldsymbol{x}\| + \|\boldsymbol{y}\|.$$

Here we use the convention that $\mathbb{R}^{2K} = \mathbb{R}^K \times \mathbb{R}^K$. Note that the target set S is convex since $\|\cdot\|$ is convex and C^* is concave by our assumption. Note also that it is easy to verify that $\|\cdot\|^+$ is a norm whenever $\|\cdot\|$ is a norm, and its dual is

$$\|(\boldsymbol{x}, \boldsymbol{y})\|^+_* = \max\{\|\boldsymbol{x}\|_*, \|\boldsymbol{y}\|_*\}. \tag{3}$$

The reduction is similar to that in [6], but they consider a fixed norm $\|\cdot\|_2$ to define the metric, no matter what norm is used for online load balancing.

Proposition 3. *Assume that we have an algorithm for the repeated game P that achieves convergence rate $\gamma(T)$. Then, the algorithm, when directly applied to the online load balancing problem, achieves*

$$\text{Regret}(T) \le T\gamma(T).$$

Proof. Let $\mathcal{A}$ denote an algorithm for the repeated game P with convergence rate $\gamma(T)$. Assume that when running $\mathcal{A}$ against the environment of online load balancing, we observe, in each round t, $\boldsymbol{\alpha}_t \in \Delta(K)$ output from $\mathcal{A}$ and $\boldsymbol{l}_t \in [0,1]^K$ output from the environment.

Let $(\boldsymbol{x}, \boldsymbol{y}) = \arg\min_{(\boldsymbol{x},\boldsymbol{y}) \in S} \|\bar{r}_T - (\boldsymbol{x}, \boldsymbol{y})\|^+$, where $\bar{r}_T = (1/T)\sum_{t=1}^T r(\boldsymbol{\alpha}_t, \boldsymbol{l}_t)$ is the average payoff. Note that by the assumption of $\mathcal{A}$, we have $\|\bar{r}_T - (\boldsymbol{x}, \boldsymbol{y})\|^+ \le \gamma(T)$. For simplicity, let $L_T^{\mathcal{A}} = (1/T)\sum_{t=1}^T \boldsymbol{\alpha}_t \odot \boldsymbol{l}_t$ and $L_T = (1/T)\sum_{t=1}^T \boldsymbol{l}_t$.

Then, we have

$$
\begin{aligned}
(1/T)\mathrm{Regret}(T) &= \left\| L_T^A \right\| - C^*(L_T)\\
&= \left[\|\boldsymbol{x}\| - C^*(\boldsymbol{y})\right] + \left[\left\| L_T^A \right\| - \|\boldsymbol{x}\|\right] + \left[C^*(\boldsymbol{y}) - C^*(L_T)\right]\\
&\le \left\| L_T^A - \boldsymbol{x} \right\| + \left[\min_{\boldsymbol{\alpha}\in\Delta(K)} \|\boldsymbol{\alpha}\odot\boldsymbol{y}\| - \min_{\boldsymbol{\alpha}\in\Delta(K)} \|\boldsymbol{\alpha}\odot L_T\|\right]\\
&\le \left\| L_T^A - \boldsymbol{x} \right\| + \max_{\boldsymbol{\alpha}\in\Delta(K)} \left[\|\boldsymbol{\alpha}\odot\boldsymbol{y}\| - \|\boldsymbol{\alpha}\odot L_T\|\right]\\
&\le \left\| L_T^A - \boldsymbol{x} \right\| + \max_{\boldsymbol{\alpha}\in\Delta(K)} \|\boldsymbol{\alpha}\odot(\boldsymbol{y} - L_T)\|\\
&\le \left\| L_T^A - \boldsymbol{x} \right\| + \|\boldsymbol{y} - L_T\|\\
&= \left\|(L_T^A, L_T) - (\boldsymbol{x},\boldsymbol{y})\right\|^+ = \left\|\bar{r}_T - (\boldsymbol{x},\boldsymbol{y})\right\|^+ \le \gamma(T),
\end{aligned}
$$

where the first inequality is from the definition of S and the triangle inequality, the third inequality is from the triangle inequality, and the fourth inequality is from the monotonicity of the norm. □

3.2   Reduction to an OCO Problem

Next we give the second sub-reduction from the repeated game P to an OCO problem. We just follow a general reduction technique of Shimkin [15] as given in the next theorem.

Theorem 3 ([15]). *Let $(A, B, r, S, \mathrm{dist})$ be a repeated game with vector payoffs, where $\mathrm{dist}(\boldsymbol{r}, \boldsymbol{s}) = \|\boldsymbol{r} - \boldsymbol{s}\|$ for some norm $\|\cdot\|$ over $\mathbb{R}^d$. Assume that we have an algorithm $\mathcal{A}$ that witnesses the Blackwell condition, i.e., when given $\boldsymbol{w} \in \mathbb{R}^d$, $\mathcal{A}$ finds $\boldsymbol{a} \in A$ such that $\langle \boldsymbol{w}, r(\boldsymbol{a}, \boldsymbol{b})\rangle \le h_S(\boldsymbol{w})$ for any $\boldsymbol{b} \in B$. Assume further that we have an algorithm $\mathcal{B}$ for the OCO problem (W, F), where $W = \{\boldsymbol{w} \in \mathbb{R}^d \mid \|\boldsymbol{w}\|_* \le 1\}$ and $F = \{f : \boldsymbol{w} \mapsto \langle -r(\boldsymbol{a}, \boldsymbol{b}), \boldsymbol{w}\rangle + h_S(\boldsymbol{w}) \mid \boldsymbol{a} \in A, \boldsymbol{b} \in B\}$. Then, we can construct an algorithm for the repeated game such that its convergence rate $\gamma(T)$ satisfies*

$$
\gamma(T) \le \frac{\mathrm{Regret}_{(W,F)}(T)}{T}.
$$

Moreover, the algorithm runs in polynomial time (per round) if $\mathcal{A}$ and $\mathcal{B}$ are polynomial time algorithms.

For completeness, the reduction algorithm(Algorithm 1) is as follow.

The rest to show in this subsection is to ensure the existence of algorithm $\mathcal{A}$ required for the reduction as stated in the theorem above. In other words, we show that the Blackwell condition holds for our game $P = (\Delta(K), [0,1]^K, r, S, \mathrm{dist})$, where $r(\boldsymbol{\alpha}, \boldsymbol{l}) = (\boldsymbol{\alpha}\odot\boldsymbol{l}, \boldsymbol{l}) \in \mathbb{R}^K \times \mathbb{R}^K$, $S = \{(\boldsymbol{x}, \boldsymbol{y}) \in [0,1]^K \times [0,1]^K \mid \|\boldsymbol{x}\| \le C^*(\boldsymbol{y})\}$, and $\mathrm{dist}(\boldsymbol{r}, \boldsymbol{s}) = \|\boldsymbol{r} - \boldsymbol{s}\|^+$.

Lemma 1. *The Blackwell condition holds for game P. That is, for any $\boldsymbol{w} \in \mathbb{R}^K \times \mathbb{R}^K$, we have*

$$
\min_{\boldsymbol{\alpha}\in\Delta(K)} \max_{\boldsymbol{l}\in[0,1]^K} \langle \boldsymbol{w}, r(\boldsymbol{\alpha}, \boldsymbol{l})\rangle \le h_S(\boldsymbol{w}).
$$

Algorithm 1. Reduction from game $(A, B, r, S, \text{dist})$ with $\text{dist}(\boldsymbol{a}, \boldsymbol{b}) = \|\boldsymbol{a} - \boldsymbol{b}\|$ to OCO [15]

Require: An algorithm $\mathcal{A}$ that, when given $\boldsymbol{w}$, finds $\boldsymbol{a} \in A$ such that $\langle \boldsymbol{w}, r(\boldsymbol{a}, \boldsymbol{b}) \rangle \leq h_S(\boldsymbol{w})$ for any $\boldsymbol{b} \in B$.

Require: An algorithm $\mathcal{B}$ for the OCO problem (W, F), where $W = \{\boldsymbol{w} \mid \|\boldsymbol{w}\|_* \leq 1\}$ and $F = \{f : \boldsymbol{w} \mapsto \langle -r(\boldsymbol{a}, \boldsymbol{b}), \boldsymbol{w} \rangle + h_S(\boldsymbol{w}) \mid \boldsymbol{a} \in A, \boldsymbol{b} \in B\}$.

for $t = 1, 2, \ldots, T$ do

    1. Obtain $\boldsymbol{w}_t \in W$ from $\mathcal{B}$.

    2. Run $\mathcal{A}(\boldsymbol{w}_t)$ and obtain $\boldsymbol{a}_t \in A$.

    3. Output $\boldsymbol{a}_t \in A$ and observe $\boldsymbol{b}_t \in B$.

    4. Construct the loss function $f_t : \boldsymbol{w} \mapsto \langle -r(\boldsymbol{a}_t, \boldsymbol{b}_t), \boldsymbol{w} \rangle + h_S(\boldsymbol{w})$ and feed it to $\mathcal{B}$.

end for

Proof (Proof of Lemma 1). Let $\boldsymbol{w} = (\boldsymbol{w}_1, \boldsymbol{w}_2) \in \mathbb{R}^K \times \mathbb{R}^K$. By the definition of r, the inner product in the Blackwell condition can be rewritten as a bilinear function

$$f(\boldsymbol{\alpha}, \boldsymbol{l}) = \langle \boldsymbol{w}, r(\boldsymbol{\alpha}, \boldsymbol{l}) \rangle = \sum_{i=1}^{K} w_{1,i} \alpha_i l_i + \sum_{i=1}^{K} w_{2,i} l_i$$

over $\Delta(K) \times [0, 1]^K$. Therefore, f meets the condition of Minimax Theorem of von Neumann. and we have

$$\min_{\boldsymbol{\alpha} \in \Delta(K)} \max_{\boldsymbol{l} \in [0,1]^K} f(\boldsymbol{\alpha}, \boldsymbol{l}) = \max_{\boldsymbol{l} \in [0,1]^K} \min_{\boldsymbol{\alpha} \in \Delta(K)} f(\boldsymbol{\alpha}, \boldsymbol{l}).$$

Let $\boldsymbol{l}^* = \arg\max_{\boldsymbol{l} \in [0,1]^K} \min_{\boldsymbol{\alpha} \in \Delta(K)} f(\boldsymbol{\alpha}, \boldsymbol{l})$ and $\boldsymbol{\alpha}^* = \arg\min_{\boldsymbol{\alpha} \in \Delta(K)} \|\boldsymbol{\alpha} \odot \boldsymbol{l}^*\|$. Note that by the definition of S, we have $(\boldsymbol{\alpha}^* \odot \boldsymbol{l}^*, \boldsymbol{l}^*) \in S$. Hence we get

$$\begin{aligned}
\min_{\boldsymbol{\alpha} \in \Delta(K)} \max_{\boldsymbol{l} \in [0,1]^K} f(\boldsymbol{\alpha}, \boldsymbol{l}) &= \max_{\boldsymbol{l} \in [0,1]^K} \min_{\boldsymbol{\alpha} \in \Delta(K)} f(\boldsymbol{\alpha}, \boldsymbol{l}) \\
&= f(\boldsymbol{\alpha}^*, \boldsymbol{l}^*) \\
&= \langle \boldsymbol{w}, ((\boldsymbol{\alpha}^* \odot \boldsymbol{l}^*), \boldsymbol{l}^*) \rangle \\
&\leq \sup_{\boldsymbol{s} \in S} \langle \boldsymbol{w}, \boldsymbol{s} \rangle \\
&= h_S(\boldsymbol{w}),
\end{aligned}$$

which completes the lemma. $\qquad\square$

The lemma ensures the existence of algorithm $\mathcal{A}$. On the other hand, for an algorithm $\mathcal{B}$ we need to consider the OCO problem (W, F), where the decision set is

$$W = \{\boldsymbol{w} \in \mathbb{R}^K \times \mathbb{R}^K \mid \|\boldsymbol{w}\|_*^+ \leq 1\}, \tag{4}$$

and the loss function set is

$$F = \{f : \boldsymbol{w} \mapsto \langle -r(\boldsymbol{\alpha}, \boldsymbol{l}), \boldsymbol{w} \rangle + h_S(\boldsymbol{w}) \mid \boldsymbol{\alpha} \in \Delta(K), \boldsymbol{l} \in [0, 1]^K\}. \tag{5}$$

Since W is a compact and convex set and F consists of convex functions, we could apply a number of existing OCO algorithms to obtain $\text{Regret}_{(W,F)}(T) = O(\sqrt{T})$.

In the next subsection, we show that the problem can be simplified to two OLO problems.

3.3   Reduction to Two OLO Problems

Consider the OCO problem (W, F) given by (4) and (5). Following the standard reduction technique from OCO to OLO stated in Sect. 2.3, we obtain an OLO problem (W, G) to cope with, where $G \subseteq \mathbb{R}^K \times \mathbb{R}^K$ is any set of cost vectors that satisfies

$$G \supseteq \bigcup_{\substack{f \in F \\ w \in W}} \partial f(\boldsymbol{w}) = \left\{ -r(\boldsymbol{\alpha}, \boldsymbol{l}) + \boldsymbol{s} \;\middle|\; \boldsymbol{\alpha} \in \Delta(K), \boldsymbol{l} \in [0,1]^K, \boldsymbol{s} \in \bigcup_{\boldsymbol{w} \in W} \partial h_S(\boldsymbol{w}) \right\}.$$
(6)

By (3), the decision set W can be rewritten as $W = B_*(K) \times B_*(K)$ where $B_*(K) = \{ \boldsymbol{w} \in \mathbb{R}^K \mid \|\boldsymbol{w}\|_* \le 1 \}$ is the K-dimensional unit ball with respect to the dual norm $\|\cdot\|_*$. By Proposition 1, any $\boldsymbol{s} \in \partial h_S(\boldsymbol{w})$ is in the target set S, which is a subset of $[0,1]^K \times [0,1]^K$. Moreover, $r(\boldsymbol{\alpha}, \boldsymbol{l}) = (\boldsymbol{\alpha} \odot \boldsymbol{l}, \boldsymbol{l}) \in [0,1]^K \times [0,1]^K$ for any $\boldsymbol{\alpha} \in \Delta(K)$ and $\boldsymbol{l} \in [0,1]^K$. Therefore, $G = [-1,1]^K \times [-1,1]^K$ satisfies (6).

Thus, $(B_*(K) \times B_*(K), [-1,1]^K \times [-1,1]^K)$ is a suitable OLO problem reduced from the OCO problem (W, F). Furthermore, we can break the OLO problem into two independent OLO problems $(B_*(K), [-1,1]^K)$ in the straightforward way: Make two copies of an OLO algorithm $\mathcal{C}$ for $(B_*(K), [-1,1]^K)$, denoted by $\mathcal{C}_1$ and $\mathcal{C}_2$, and use them for predicting the first half and second half decision vectors, respectively. More precisely, for each trial t, (1) receive predictions $\boldsymbol{w}_{t,1} \in B_*(K)$ and $\boldsymbol{w}_{t,2} \in B_*(K)$ from $\mathcal{C}_1$ and $\mathcal{C}_2$, respectively, (2) output their concatenation $\boldsymbol{w}_t = (\boldsymbol{w}_{t,1}, \boldsymbol{w}_{t,2}) \in W$, (3) receive a cost vector $\boldsymbol{g}_t = (\boldsymbol{g}_{t,1}, \boldsymbol{g}_{t,2}) \in [0,1]^K \times [0,1]^K$ from the environment, (4) feed $\boldsymbol{g}_{t,1}$ and $\boldsymbol{g}_{t,2}$ to $\mathcal{C}_1$ and $\mathcal{C}_2$, respectively, to make them proceed.

It is clear that the procedure above ensures the following lemma.

Lemma 2. *The OCO problem (W, F) defined as (4) and (5) can be reduced to the OLO problem $(B_*(K), [0,1]^K)$, and*

$$\text{Regret}_{(W,F)}(T) \le 2\text{Regret}_{(B_*(K), [0,1]^K)}(T).$$

3.4   Putting All the Pieces Together

Combining all reductions stated in the previous subsections, we get an all-in-one algorithm as described in Algorithm 2.

It is clear that combining Proposition 3, Theorem 3 and Lemma 2, we get the following regret bound of Algorithm 2.

Theorem 4. *Algorithm 2 achieves*

$$\text{Regret}(T) \le 2\text{Regret}_{(B_*(K), [-1,1]^K)}(T),$$

Algorithm 2. An OLO-based online load balancing algorithm

Require: An algorithm $\mathcal{A}$ that, when given $\boldsymbol{w}$, finds $\boldsymbol{\alpha} = \arg\min\limits_{\boldsymbol{\alpha} \in \Delta(K)} \max\limits_{\boldsymbol{l} \in [0,1]^K} \langle \boldsymbol{w}, (\boldsymbol{\alpha} \odot \boldsymbol{l}, \boldsymbol{l}) \rangle$.

Require: An algorithm $\mathcal{B}$ that, when given $\boldsymbol{w}$, finds $\boldsymbol{s} \in \partial h_S(\boldsymbol{w})$.

Require: Two copies of an algorithm, $\mathcal{C}_1$ and $\mathcal{C}_2$, for the OLO problem $(B_*(K), [-1, 1]^K)$.

   for $t = 1, 2, \ldots, T$ **do**

     1. Obtain $\boldsymbol{w}_{t,1}$ and $\boldsymbol{w}_{t,2}$ from $\mathcal{C}_1$ and $\mathcal{C}_2$, respectively, and let $\boldsymbol{w}_t = (\boldsymbol{w}_{t,1}, \boldsymbol{w}_{t,2})$.

     2. Run $\mathcal{A}(\boldsymbol{w}_t)$ and obtain $\boldsymbol{\alpha}_t \in \Delta(K)$.

     3. Output $\boldsymbol{\alpha}_t$ and observe $\boldsymbol{l}_t \in [0, 1]^K$.

     4. Run $\mathcal{B}(\boldsymbol{w}_t)$ and obtain $\boldsymbol{s}_t = (\boldsymbol{s}_{t,1}, \boldsymbol{s}_{t,2})$.

     5. Let $\boldsymbol{g}_{t,1} = -\boldsymbol{\alpha}_t \odot \boldsymbol{l}_t + \boldsymbol{s}_{t,1}$ and $\boldsymbol{g}_{t,2} = -\boldsymbol{l}_t + \boldsymbol{s}_{t,2}$.

     6. Feed $\boldsymbol{g}_{t,1}$ and $\boldsymbol{g}_{t,2}$ to $\mathcal{C}_1$ and $\mathcal{C}_2$, respectively.

   end for

---

where the regret in the right hand side is the regret of algorithm $\mathcal{C}_1$ (and $\mathcal{C}_2$ as well). Moreover, if $\mathcal{A}$, $\mathcal{B}$ and $\mathcal{C}_1$ runs in polynomial time, then Algorithm 2 runs in polynomial time (per round).

By applying the FTRL as in (2) to the OLO problem $(B_*(K), [-1, 1]^K)$ with a strongly convex regularizer R, Proposition 2 implies the following regret bound.

Corollary 1. *Assume that there exists a regularizer $R : B_*(K) \to \mathbb{R}$ that is σ-strongly convex w.r.t. L_1-norm. Then, there exists an algorithm for the online load balancing problem that achieves*

$$\mathrm{Regret}(T) = O(D_R\sqrt{T/\sigma}),$$

where $D_R = \sqrt{\max_{\boldsymbol{w} \in B_*(K)} R(\boldsymbol{w})}$.

In particular, for the OLO problem $(B_1(K), [-1, 1]^K)$, algorithm $\mathrm{EG}^{\pm}$ achieves $\sqrt{2T \ln 4K}$ regret bound as shown in Theorem 2. Thus we have $O(\sqrt{T \ln K})$ regret bound for online load balancing with respect to L_∞-norm (i.e., w.r.t. makespan), which improves the bound of [6] by a factor of $\sqrt{\ln K}$. Moreover, for L_∞-norm, it turns out that we have polynomial time algorithms for $\mathcal{A}$ and $\mathcal{B}$, which we will give in the next section. We thus obtain the following corollary.

Corollary 2. *There exists a polynomial time (per round) algorithm for the online load balancing problem with respect to L_∞-norm that achieves*

$$\mathrm{Regret}(T) \leq 2\sqrt{2T \ln 4K}.$$

4 Algorithmic Details for L_∞-norm

In this section we give details of Algorithm 2 for the makespan problem, i.e., for L_∞-norm.

4.1 Computing α_t

First, we give details of implementation of $\mathcal{A}$ in Algorithm 2. Specifically, on the round t, we need to choose α_t, which is the optimal solution of the problem in Lemma 1. That is,

$$\min_{\alpha \in \Delta(K)} \max_{l \in [0,1]^K} \langle w_1, (\alpha \odot l) \rangle + \langle w_2, l \rangle, \tag{7}$$

where we set that $w = (w_1, w_2)$ and w_1 and w_2 are K-dimensional vectors, respectively. We see that the optimization of this objective function is defined by $l_i = 0$ if $w_{1,i} \cdot \alpha_i + w_{2,i} \leq 0$, otherwise we let $l_i = 1$. Hence we can convert our problem to choose α as

$$\min_{\alpha \in \Delta(K)} \max_{l \in [0,1]^K} \langle w_1, (\alpha \odot l) \rangle + \langle w_2, l \rangle = \min_{\alpha \in \Delta(K)} \sum_{i=1}^{K} \max\{0, \alpha_i w_{1,i} + w_{2,i}\},$$

which is equivalent to

$$\min_{\alpha \in \Delta(K), \beta \geq 0} \sum_{i=1}^{K} \beta_i \quad \text{s.t. } \beta_i \geq w_{1,i}\alpha_i + w_{2,i} \quad \forall i = 1, \ldots, K.$$

The above problem is a linear program with $O(K)$ variables and $O(K)$ linear constraints. Thus, computing α_t in the problem (7) can be solved in polynomial time.

4.2 Computing Subgradients g_t for the ∞-norm

The second component of Algorithm 2 is the algorithm $\mathcal{B}$, which computes subgradients $s_t \in \partial h_S(w_t)$. By Proposition 1, we have $s_t = \arg\max_{s \in S} \langle s, w_t \rangle$. Recall that $S = \{(x, y) \in [0,1]^K \times [0,1]^K \mid \|x\|_\infty \leq C_\infty^*(y)\}$. In particular, the condition that $\|x\|_\infty \leq C_\infty^*(y)$ can be represented as

$$\max_i x_i \leq \min_{\alpha \in \Delta(K)} \|\alpha \odot y\|_\infty \iff x_i \leq \frac{1}{\sum_{j=1}^{K} \frac{1}{y_j}}, \forall i.$$

Therefore, the computation of the subgradient s_t is formulated as

$$\max_{x, y \in [0,1]^K} \langle w_1, x \rangle + \langle w_2, y \rangle \quad \text{s.t. } x_i \leq \frac{1}{\sum_j \frac{1}{y_j}}, \quad \forall i = 1, \ldots, K. \tag{8}$$

Now we show that there exists an equivalent second order cone programming (SOCP) formulation (e.g., [11]) for this problem.

First we give the definition of the second order cone programming, and then we give a proposition, which states that our optimization problem is equivalent to the second order cone programming.

Definition 4. *The standard form for the second order conic programming (SOCP) model is as follows:*

$$\min_{\boldsymbol{x}}\langle\boldsymbol{c},\boldsymbol{x}\rangle \ s.t. \ \boldsymbol{Ax}=\boldsymbol{b}, \|C_i\boldsymbol{x}+\boldsymbol{d}_i\|_2 \leq \boldsymbol{e}_i^{\top}\boldsymbol{x}+f_i \quad for \ i=1,\cdots,m,$$

where the problem parameters are $\boldsymbol{c} \in \mathbb{R}^n$, $C_i \in \mathbb{R}^{n_i \times n}$, $\boldsymbol{d}_i \in \mathbb{R}^{n_i}$, $\boldsymbol{e} \in \mathbb{R}^n$, $f_i \in \mathbb{R}$, $A \in \mathbb{R}^{p \times n}$, and $\boldsymbol{b} \in \mathbb{R}^p$. $\boldsymbol{x} \in \mathbb{R}^n$ is the optimization variable.

Then we obtain the following proposition.

Proposition 4. $\sum_{i=1}^{K} \frac{x^2}{y_i} \leq x$, $x \geq 0$ *and* $y_i \geq 0$ *is equivalent to* $x^2 \leq y_i z_i$, *where* $y_i, z_i \geq 0$ *and* $\sum_{i=1}^{K} z_i = x$.

Proof. On the direction "⇒"

From $\sum_{i=1}^{k} \frac{x^2}{y_i} \leq x$ we obtain that $\sum_{i=1}^{k} \frac{x}{y_i} \leq 1$. By setting

$$z_i = x \cdot \frac{\frac{1}{y_i}}{\sum_i \frac{1}{y_i}},$$

we can have that $x^2 \leq y_i z_i$, and $\sum_{i=1}^{k} z_i = x$.

On the other direction "⇐" Due to $x^2 \leq y_i z_i$, we have $\frac{x^2}{y_i} \leq z_i$. So we have that

$$\sum_{i=1}^{k} \frac{x^2}{y_i} \leq \sum_{i=1}^{k} z_i = x.$$

□

Again in our case we need find to the optimal vector $\boldsymbol{s} \in S$, which satisfies that $\boldsymbol{s}_t = \arg\max_{\boldsymbol{s} \in S}\langle\boldsymbol{w}_t, \boldsymbol{s}\rangle$. Then we can reduce our problem in following theorem.

Theorem 5. *The optimization problem (8) can be solved by the second order cone programming.*

Proof. To prove this theorem we only need to represent the original problem (8) as a standard form of the SOCP problem. Note that we only consider the case that $y_i \neq 0$ for all $i = 1, \ldots, K$. The case where $y_i = 0$ for some i is trivial. To see this, by definition of S, we know that for all i, $x_i = 0$. Then, the resulting problem is a linear program, which is a special case of the SOCP. Now we assume that $y_i \neq 0$ for $i = 1, \ldots, K$. For $x_i \leq \frac{1}{\sum_j \frac{1}{y_j}}$, we multiply x_i on both sides and rearrange the inequality:

$$\sum_{j=1}^{K} \frac{x_i^2}{y_j} \leq x_i.$$

By Proposition 4, this is equivalent with

$$y_j z_{i,j} \geq x_i^2, \quad y_j, z_{i,j} \geq 0, \quad \sum_{j=1}^{K} z_{i,j} = x_i.$$

By [11], we may rewrite it as follows: For each i,

$$x_i^2 \leq y_j z_{i,j}; \quad y_j, z_{i,j} \geq 0 \iff \|(2x_i, y_j - z_{i,j})\|_2 \leq y_j + z_{i,j} \quad \forall j = 1, \ldots, K. \quad (9)$$

The above equivalence is trivial. On the other hand, since $x_i \leq \frac{1}{\sum_j \frac{1}{y_j}}$, and $y_i \in [0, 1]$, naturally we have $x_i \in [0, 1]$. So we need only constrain that $y_i \in [0, 1]$. We can apply the face that if y_i is positive so $|y_i| = y_i$, and if $y_i \leq 1$, so $|y_i| \leq 1$. Therefore we may give a $(K^2 + 2K) \times (K^2 + 2K)$-matrix C_i in SOCP, and the variable vector is composed as follows:

$$\tilde{x} = (x_1, \cdots, x_K, y_1, \cdots, y_K, z_{1,1}, \cdots, z_{1,K}, \cdots, z_{K,1} \cdots, z_{K,K}), \quad (10)$$

where for $z_{i,j}$, i is corresponding to x_i.

Now we may give the second order cone programming of our target problem as follows:

$$\min_{\tilde{x}} \langle -(w_1, w_2, 0, \cdots, 0), \tilde{x} \rangle$$

$$\text{s.t.} \|C_i \tilde{x}\|_2 \leq e_i^\top \tilde{x} + d_i \quad \forall i = 1, \cdots, K^2 + 2K, \quad (11)$$

$$A\tilde{x} = b.$$

where C_i, e_i, A and b are defined as follows:

Firstly the matrix C for hyperbolic constraints are given as: For a fixed $s \in [K]$, where $[K] = \{1, \cdots, K\}$ in matrix C_i, where $i \in [(s-1)K, sK]$ we let $(C_i)_{1,s} = 2$, $(C_i)_{K+i,K+i} = 1$, $(C_i)_{2K+(s-1)K+i,2K+(s-1)K+i} = -1$, and others are 0. e_i is defined as $(e_i)_{K+i} = 1$ and $(e_i)_{2K+(s-1)K+i} = 1$, others are 0.

Next we need to constrain that y_i is less than 1. For $i \in [K^2, K^2 + K]$ we let that $(C_i)_{K+i,K+i} = 1$ and others are 0. And we let that e_i is a zero vector and $d_i = 1$. It means that $\|y_i\| \leq 1$. For $i \in [K^2 + K, K^2 + 2K]$, we set $(C_i)_{K+i,K+i} = 1$ $e_{K+i} = 1$, and $d_i = 0$.

At last we need to constrain that $\sum_{j=1}^{K} z_j = x_i$ in Eq. 9: Let $A \in \mathbb{R}^{K \times (3K + K^2)}$ for each row vector A_j, where $j \in [K]$, we have that $(A_j)_j = 1$ and $(A_j)_{2K+(j-1)j+m} = -1$, for all $m = 1, \cdots, K$. No w the matrix A is composed by the row vectors A_j. and b is a zero vector. $\qquad \square$

5   Conclusion

In this paper we give a framework for online load balancing problem by reducing it to two OLO problems. Moreover, for online load balancing problem with respect to L_∞-norm we achieve the best known regret bound in polynomial time. Firstly, we reduce online load balancing with $\| \cdot \|$ norm to a vector payoff game measured by combination norm $\| \cdot \|^+$. Next due to [15] this vector payoff game is reduced to an OCO problem. At last, we can reduce this OCO problem to two independent OLO problems. Especially, for makespan, we give an efficient algorithm, which achieves the best known regret bound $O(\sqrt{T \ln K})$, by processing linear programming and second order cone programming in each trial. Recently Kwon [10] proposed a similar reduction with other type of induced norm instead of our combination norm.

There are some open problems left in this topic. For instance, an efficient algorithm for online load balancing with respect to general norm or p-norm is still an open problem. Kwon's reduction [10] might be helpful to this discussion. Furthermore, the lower bound of online load balancing is still unknown.

References

1. Abernethy, J., Bartlett, P.L., Hazan, E.: Blackwell approachability and no-regret learning are equivalent. In: Proceedings of the 24th Annual Conference on Learning Theory, pp. 27–46 (2011)
2. Azar, Y.: On-line load balancing. In: Fiat, A., Woeginger, G.J. (eds.) Online Algorithms. LNCS, vol. 1442, pp. 178–195. Springer, Heidelberg (1998). https://doi.org/10.1007/BFb0029569
3. Azar, Y., Kalyanasundaram, B., Plotkin, S., Pruhs, K.R., Waarts, O.: Online load balancing of temporary tasks. In: Dehne, F., Sack, J.-R., Santoro, N., Whitesides, S. (eds.) WADS 1993. LNCS, vol. 709, pp. 119–130. Springer, Heidelberg (1993). https://doi.org/10.1007/3-540-57155-8_241
4. Blackwell, D., et al.: An analog of the minimax theorem for vector payoffs. Pac. J. Math. 6(1), 1–8 (1956)
5. Crescenzi, P., Gambosi, G., Nicosia, G., Penna, P., Unger, W.: On-line load balancing made simple: greedy strikes back. J. Discrete Algorithms 5(1), 162–175 (2007)
6. Even-Dar, E., Kleinberg, R., Mannor, S., Mansour, Y.: Online learning for global cost functions. In: COLT (2009)
7. Hazan, E.: Introduction to online convex optimization. Found. Trends Optim. 2(3–4), 157–325 (2016). http://ocobool.cs.prinston.edu/
8. Hoeven, D., Erven, T., Kotłowski, W.: The many faces of exponential weights in online learning. In: Conference On Learning Theory, pp. 2067–2092 (2018)
9. Kivinen, J., Warmuth, M.K.: Exponentiated gradient versus gradient descent for linear predictors. Inf. Comput. 132(1), 1–63 (1997)
10. Kwon, J.: Refined approachability algorithms and application to regret minimization with global costs. arXiv preprint arXiv:2009.03831 (2020)
11. Lobo, M.S., Vandenberghe, L., Boyd, S., Lebret, H.: Applications of second-order cone programming. Linear Algebra Appl. 284(1–3), 193–228 (1998)
12. Molinaro, M.: Online and random-order load balancing simultaneously. In: Proceedings of the Twenty-Eighth Annual ACM-SIAM Symposium on Discrete Algorithms, pp. 1638–1650. Society for Industrial and Applied Mathematics (2017)
13. Rakhlin, A., Sridharan, K., Tewari, A.: Online learning: beyond regret. In: Proceedings of the 24th Annual Conference on Learning Theory, pp. 559–594 (2011)
14. Shalev-Shwartz, S.: Online learning and online convex optimization. Found. Trends® Mach. Learn. 4(2), 107–194 (2012)
15. Shimkin, N.: An online convex optimization approach to blackwell's approachability. J. Mach. Learn. Res. 17(1), 4434–4456 (2016)

Iterated Uniform Finite-State Transducers on Unary Languages

Martin Kutrib[1], Andreas Malcher[1]([⊠]), Carlo Mereghetti[2],
and Beatrice Palano[3]

[1] Institut für Informatik, Universität Giessen, Arndtstr. 2, 35392 Giessen, Germany
{kutrib,andreas.malcher}@informatik.uni-giessen.de
[2] Dipartimento di Fisica "Aldo Pontremoli", Università degli Studi di Milano,
via Celoria 16, 20133 Milan, Italy
carlo.mereghetti@unimi.it
[3] Dipartimento di Informatica "G. degli Antoni", Università degli Studi di Milano,
via Celoria 18, 20133 Milan, Italy
palano@unimi.it

Abstract. We consider the model of an iterated uniform finite-state transducer, which executes the same length-preserving transduction in iterative sweeps. The first sweep takes place on the input string, while any subsequent sweep works on the output of the previous one. We focus on unary languages.

We show that any unary regular language can be accepted by a deterministic iterated uniform finite-state transducer with at most $\max\{2 \cdot \varrho, p\} + 1$ states, where ϱ and p are the greatest primes in the factorization of the, respectively, pre-periodic and periodic part of the language. Such a state cost cannot be improved by using nondeterminism, and it turns out to be exponentially lower in the worst case than the state costs of equivalent classical models of finite-state automata.

Next, we give a characterization of classes of unary languages accepted by non-constant sweep-bounded iterated uniform finite-state transducers in terms of time bounded one-way cellular automata. This characterization enables both to exhibit interesting families of unary non-regular languages accepted by iterated uniform finite-state transducers, and to prove the undecidability of several questions related to iterated uniform finite-state transducers accepting unary languages with an amount of sweeps that is at least logarithmic.

Keywords: Iterated transducers · Unary languages · State complexity · Cellular automata · Undecidability results

1 Introduction

The notion of an iterated uniform finite-state transducer (IUFST) has been introduced in [12]. Basically, it consists of a length-preserving finite-state transducer that works in iterative sweeps from left to right on its input tape. In the first

© Springer Nature Switzerland AG 2021
T. Bureš et al. (Eds.): SOFSEM 2021, LNCS 12607, pp. 218–232, 2021.
https://doi.org/10.1007/978-3-030-67731-2_16

sweep the input string is processed, while any further sweep operates on the output of the previous sweep. The model is uniform in that every sweep always starts from the same initial state on the leftmost tape symbol, and operates the same transduction rules at each computation step. An input string is accepted whenever the transducer halts in an accepting state at the end of a sweep.

A theoretical investigation of IUFSTs is motivated by the fact that iterated or cascade transductions show up in several fields of computer science. For example, in the context of natural language processing, cascades of finite-state transducers are used in [5] to extract information from natural language texts. In compiler design, the lexical analysis is often done by a finite-state transducer whose output is subsequently processed by a pushdown transducer implementing the syntactical analysis. Again, from a theoretical perspective, the Krohn-Rhodes decomposition theorem states that every regular language can be represented as a cascade of several finite-state transducers with a simple algebraic structure [6,7]. Finally, cascades of deterministic pushdown transducers as language accepting devices have been studied in [3]. Yet, in [1,14], iterated finite-state transducers as language generating devices have been proposed. It might be worth noticing that only this latter contribution introduces a notion of "uniformity" on iterated transduction, in the sense that always the same transducer is iteratively applied.

Deterministic and nondeterministic IUFSTs (the nondeterministic model being abbreviated as NIUFST) have been deeply studied in [12,13]. In case of a constant number of sweeps, IUFSTs and NIUFSTs characterize the class of regular languages. In case of a non-constant number of sweeps, non-regular languages can be accepted as soon as at least a logarithmic number of sweeps is provided, and infinite proper language hierarchies depending on sweep complexity are shown. Recently, in [11], IUFSTs and NIUFSTs have been enhanced with the possibility of two-way motion, implying a sweep alternation from left to right and from right to left.

In this paper, we continue our investigation on iterated transduction on unary languages. In Sect. 3, we tackle the problem of constructing state-efficient iterated transducers for general unary regular languages. We provide our construction step by step, starting from finite unary languages. We show that finite unary languages consisting of words with length up to ℓ can be accepted by an IUFST with $2 \cdot \varrho$ states, ϱ being the greatest prime in the factorization of ℓ. Next, we switch to unary periodic languages, and prove that any n-periodic unary language can be accepted by an IUFST featuring p states, p being the greatest prime in the factorization of n. By combining these two results, we show that any unary regular language can be accepted by an IUFST with at most $\max\{2 \cdot \varrho, p\} + 1$ states. We then show that these state costs cannot be improved by using nondeterminism, and that they turn out to be exponentially lower in the worst case than the state costs of equivalent classical models of finite-state automata.

In Sect. 4, we provide a tight connection between the non-constant sweep complexity of IUFSTs and the time complexity of one-way cellular automata (OCAs), when both models work on unary inputs. Precisely, we show that a unary language is accepted by an $n + r(n)$ time bounded OCA if and only if it is accepted by an $r(n) + 1$ sweep-bounded IUFST. This characterization directly brings some interesting consequences. First of all, it enables to exhibit a rich class of unary non-regular languages accepted by $\Omega(\ln n)$ sweep-bounded IUFSTs, together with some closure properties. Furthermore, it implies the undecidability of some classical problems – such as emptiness, finiteness, infiniteness, inclusion, and equivalence – for $\Omega(\ln n)$ sweep-bounded IUFSTs accepting unary languages.

2 Definitions and Preliminaries

We denote the set of positive integers and zero by $\mathbb{N}$. The Fundamental Theorem of Arithmetic establishes that any integer $n > 1$ can be univocally expressed as a product $n = p_1^{\alpha_1} \cdot \cdots \cdot p_s^{\alpha_s}$, where $p_1 < \cdots < p_s$ are primes, and $\alpha_1, \alpha_2, \ldots, \alpha_s$ are positive integers. For any $n > 1$, we let $\mathbb{Z}_n = \{0, 1, \ldots, n-1\}$. By $\ln n$ we denote the logarithm of n to base e and by $\mathrm{ld} n$ we denote the logarithm of n to base 2. Set inclusion is denoted by $\subseteq$ and strict set inclusion by $\subset$. Let Σ^* denote the set of all words over the finite alphabet Σ. The empty word is denoted by λ and $\Sigma^+ = \Sigma^* \setminus \{\lambda\}$. The length of a word w is denoted by $|w|$. A language on Σ is any set $L \subseteq \Sigma^*$.

Roughly speaking, an iterated uniform finite-state transducer is a finite-state transducer which processes the input in multiple passes (also sweeps). In the first pass, it reads the input word preceded and followed by endmarkers and emits an output word. In the following passes, it reads the output word of the previous pass and emits a new output word. It should be noted that the transducer may alter the two endmarkers as well. The number of passes taken, the *sweep complexity*, is given as a function of the length of the input. Here, we are interested in weak processing devices: we will consider length-preserving finite-state transducers, also known as Mealy machines [16], to be iterated.

Formally, we define a *nondeterministic iterated uniform finite-state transducer* (NIUFST) as a system $T = \langle Q, \Sigma, \Delta, q_0, \rhd, \lhd, \delta, F \rangle$, where Q is the set of *internal states*, Σ is the set of *input symbols*, Δ is the set of *output symbols*, $q_0 \in Q$ is the initial state, $\rhd \in \Delta \setminus \Sigma$ and $\lhd \in \Delta \setminus \Sigma$ are *left and right endmarkers*, respectively, $F \subseteq Q$ is the set of *accepting states*, and $\delta \colon Q \times (\Sigma \cup \Delta) \to 2^{Q \times \Delta}$ is the partial *transition function*. The NIUFST T *halts* whenever the transition function is undefined or T enters an accepting state at the end of a sweep. Since the transduction is applied in multiple passes, that is, in any but the initial pass it operates on an output of the previous pass, the transition function depends on input symbols from $\Sigma \cup \Delta$. We let $T(w)$ be the set of possible outputs produced by T in a complete sweep on input $w \in (\Sigma \cup \Delta)^*$. During a computation on input $w \in \Sigma^*$, the NIUFST T produces a sequence of words $w_1, \ldots, w_i, w_{i+1}, \ldots \in (\Sigma \cup \Delta)^*$, where $w_1 \in T(\rhd w \lhd)$ and $w_{i+1} \in T(w_i)$ for $i \geq 1$.

An iterated uniform finite-state transducer is said to be *deterministic* (IUFST) if and only if $|\delta(p, x)| \leq 1$, for all $p \in Q$ and $x \in (\Sigma \cup \Delta)$. In this case, we simply write $\delta(p, x) = (q, y)$ instead of $\delta(p, x) = \{(q, y)\}$ assuming that the transition function is a mapping $\delta \colon Q \times (\Sigma \cup \Delta) \to Q \times \Delta$.

Now we turn to language acceptance. With respect to nondeterministic computations and some complexity bound, in the literature several acceptance modes are considered. For example, a machine accepts a language in the *weak mode*, if for any input $w \in L$ there is an accepting computation that obeys the complexity bound. Language L is accepted in the *strong mode*, if the machine obeys the complexity bound for all computations (accepting or not) on all inputs. Here we deal with the number of sweeps as (computational) complexity measure. The weak mode seems too optimistic for this measure, while the strong mode seem too restrictive. Therefore, here we consider an intermediate mode, the so-called accept mode. A language is accepted in the *accept mode* if all accepting computations obey the complexity bound (see [17] for separation of these modes with respect to space complexity).

A computation is halting if there exists an $r \geq 1$ such that T halts on w_r, thus performing r sweeps. The input word $w \in \Sigma^*$ is *accepted* by T if at least one computation on w halts at the end of a sweep in an accepting state. Otherwise it is *rejected*. Indeed, the output of the last sweep is not used. The language accepted by T is the set $L(T) \subseteq \Sigma^*$ defined as $L(T) = \{ w \in \Sigma^* \mid w$ is accepted by $T \}$.

Given a function $s \colon \mathbb{N} \to \mathbb{N}$, an iterated uniform finite-state transducer T is said to be of *sweep complexity* $s(n)$ if for all $w \in L(T)$ all accepting computations on w halt after at most $s(|w|)$ sweeps. In this case, we add the prefix $s(n)$- to the notation of the device. It is easy to see that 1-IUFSTs (resp., 1-NIUFSTs) are essentially deterministic (resp., nondeterministic) finite-state automata (DFAs and NFAs, respectively).

Throughout the paper, two accepting devices are said to be *equivalent* if and only if they accept the same language.

A language L is said to be unary whenever it is built over a single-letter alphabet, i.e., $L \subseteq \Sigma^*$ and $|\Sigma| = 1$. In this case, we usually let $L \subseteq 0^*$ or $L \subseteq a^*$. A unary language $L \subseteq 0^*$ is n-periodic whenever there exists a set $\mathcal{R} \subseteq \mathbb{Z}_n$ such that $L = \{ 0^{c \cdot n + R} \mid c \geq 0 \text{ and } R \in \mathcal{R} \}$. We will always be assuming that n is the minimal value defining L. This is usually referred to as L being *properly n-periodic*. To emphasize periodicity and the set $\mathcal{R}$ of remainders modulo n, we will express L in the form $L_{n,\mathcal{R}}$.

By using pumping arguments, it can be shown that n states are necessary and sufficient for DFAs and NFAs to accept $L_{n,\mathcal{R}}$. In particular, the minimal DFA for $L_{n,\mathcal{R}}$ consists of a single cordless cycle of n states, with an initial state and final states settled according to $\mathcal{R}$. On the other hand, for n factorizing as $n = p_1^{\alpha_1} \cdot p_2^{\alpha_2} \cdot \cdots \cdot p_s^{\alpha_s}$, we have that any two-way DFA and NFA, or isolated cutpint probabilistic finite automaton (PFA) for $L_{n,\mathcal{R}}$ must have at least $\sum_{i=1}^{s} p_i^{\alpha_i}$ states [19, 20].

It is well known that any unary regular language can be seen as the disjoint union of a finite language and an ultimately periodic language. More precisely, it can be defined by three parameters ℓ, n, $\mathcal{R} \subseteq \mathbb{Z}_n$ as

$$L_{\ell,n,\mathcal{R}} = L_\ell \cup \{ 0^{\ell + c \cdot n + R} \mid c \geq 0 \text{ and } R \in \mathcal{R} \},$$

The language L_ℓ, called the pre-periodic part of $L_{\ell,n,\mathcal{R}}$, is a finite unary language containing strings of length less than or equal to ℓ. In addition, the set $\{\, 0^{\ell+c\cdot n+R} \mid c \geq 0 \text{ and } R \in \mathcal{R} \,\}$ is called the periodic part of $L_{\ell,n,\mathcal{R}}$. As usual, we assume that the parameters ℓ and n are the smallest possible defining $L_{\ell,n,\mathcal{R}}$.

Notice that $L_{\ell,n,\mathcal{R}}$ is accepted by a DFA whose transition digraph consists of an initial path of ℓ states joined to a cordless cycle of n states. Clearly, the above recalled state lower bound for two-way DFAs and NFAs, or isolated cut-point PFAs for $L_{n,\mathcal{R}}$ carries over to $L_{\ell,n,\mathcal{R}}$ as well. By simulation results in [2,18], if $L_{\ell,n,\mathcal{R}}$ is accepted by a b-state NFA or two-way NFA, then we can assume $\ell = O(b^2)$ and $n = e^{\Theta(\sqrt{b \cdot \ln b})}$.

3   Iterated Transduction and Unary Regular Languages

In [11], we showed that iterated transducers are more state-efficient than classical models of finite-state automata on unary inputs by focusing on a particular family of unary periodic languages. Precisely, $\Pi(p)$ being the product of all primes not exceeding a given prime p, we introduced the unary language $L_{\Pi(p)} = \{\, 0^{c \cdot \Pi(p)} \mid c \geq 0 \,\}$. We exhibited a p-state $(p/\ln p)$-IUFST for $L_{\Pi(p)}$, whereas any equivalent DFA or NFA needs not less that $\Pi(p) \sim e^p$ states.

Here, we are going to tackle the general problem of constructing state-efficient iterated transducers for *any* unary regular language. It should be mentioned that here we focus on the number of states as complexity measure disregarding, for example, the number of output symbols. To consider the descriptional complexity in its entirety, the sizes of all parameters in the definition of iterated transducers have to be combined.

For a better understanding, we will show our construction step by step, dealing one at a time with meaningful families of unary regular languages. We will start with unary periodic languages, pass through finite unary languages, and finally get to designing iterated transducers for general unary regular languages.

3.1   Unary Periodic Languages

For reader's ease of mind, we start by considering a particular family of unary periodic languages, which is actually a generalization of $L_{\Pi(p)}$ languages. For any $n \geq 1$, we let $L_n = \{\, 0^{c \cdot n} \mid c \geq 0 \,\}$.

Theorem 1. *Let $n \geq 2$ factorize as $n = p_1^{\alpha_1} \cdot \cdots \cdot p_s^{\alpha_s}$, with $\alpha_i > 0$. The language L_n can be accepted by a p_s-state r-IUFST with $r = \sum_{i=1}^{s} \alpha_i$ sweeps.*

Proof. To accept language L_n, we design the IUFST $T = \langle Q, \Sigma, \Delta, q_0, \triangleright, \triangleleft, \delta, F \rangle$, where $Q = \{q_0, q_1, \ldots, q_{p_s - 1}\}$, $\Sigma = \{0\}$, $F = \{q_0\}$, and $\Delta = \{\triangleright, 1, 2, \ldots, s\} \cup \{\, \triangleleft_j^i \mid 1 \leq i \leq s \text{ and } 1 \leq j \leq \alpha_i \,\} \cup \{\, *_j^i, \sqcup_j^i \mid 1 \leq i \leq s \text{ and } 1 \leq j \leq \alpha_i - 1 \,\}$.

Informally, the computation of T runs through s consecutive **phases**. During the ith **phase**, for $1 \leq i \leq s$, the IUFST T checks whether or not the length of the input string is divisible by $p_i^{\alpha_i}$; assume for the moment $\alpha_i > 1$. Along this

phase, α_i sweeps are performed. During the jth sweep, for $1 \leq j \leq \alpha_i$, the divisibility of the input length by $p_i{}^j$ is checked. The input string is accepted if and only if at the end of the s **phases**, all the $(\sum_{i=1}^{s} \alpha_i)$ many sweeps witness input length divisibility by prime powers, as explained.

Let us define the transition function δ by first modeling the behavior of T on the endmarkers. Since q_0 is the accepting state, the last step taking place from q_0 of all but the last sweep of the last **phase** sends T into the non accepting state q_1, to avoid premature incorrect acceptance. Whereas, if the divisibility check is positive at the end of the last sweep of the last **phase**, the last step taking place from q_0 keeps T in q_0, and so T may halt and accept:

$$\delta(q_0, \rhd) = (q_0, \rhd), \tag{1}$$

$$\delta(q_0, \lhd) = (q_1, \lhd_1^1), \tag{2}$$

$$\delta(q_0, \lhd_j^i) = (q_1, \lhd_{j+1}^i) \quad \text{for } 1 \leq i \leq s-1 \text{ and } 1 \leq j \leq \alpha_i - 1, \tag{3}$$

$$\delta(q_0, \lhd_{\alpha_i}^i) = (q_1, \lhd_1^{i+1}) \quad \text{for } 1 \leq i \leq s-1, \tag{4}$$

$$\delta(q_0, \lhd_j^s) = (q_1, \lhd_{j+1}^s) \quad \text{for } 1 \leq j \leq \alpha_s - 2, \tag{5}$$

$$\delta(q_0, \lhd_{\alpha_s-1}^s) = (q_0, \lhd_{\alpha_s}^s). \tag{6}$$

For $1 \leq i \leq s$, in the first sweep of the ith **phase**, during which phase the divisibility of the input length by $p_i^{\alpha_i}$ is to be checked, T verifies that the input length is divisible by p_i, while rewriting the input as a sequence of consecutive blocks of the form $(\sqcup_1^i)^{p_i-1} *_1^i$. Please note that at the end of the $(i-1)$st **phase** $(2 \leq i \leq s)$ every input symbol has been replaced by symbol $i-1$. The detailed transitions are defined below in (12)–(14).

$$\delta(q_k, i-1) = (q_{k+1}, \sqcup_1^i) \quad \text{for } 0 \leq k \leq p_i - 2, \tag{7}$$

$$\delta(q_{p_i-1}, i-1) = (q_0, *_1^i). \tag{8}$$

In each of the following $\alpha_i - 2$ sweeps of the ith **phase**, T verifies whether or not the number of '$*_j^i$' symbols, for $1 \leq j \leq \alpha_i - 2$, is divisible by p_i. While doing this, T rewrites the tape so that, for each group of p_i many symbols '$*_j^i$' encountered, the last is replaced by the symbol '$*_{j+1}^i$', while each of the previous $p_i - 1$ many symbols '$*_j^i$' is replaced by the symbol $\sqcup_{j+1}^i$. Moreover, all symbols $\sqcup_j^i$ are replaced by the symbol $\sqcup_{j+1}^i$. So, the last sweep of this ith **phase** is easily seen to globally check the divisibility of the length of the input string by $p_i^{\alpha_i}$, while replacing each tape symbol by the symbol 'i':

$$\delta(q_k, \sqcup_j^i) = (q_k, \sqcup_{j+1}^i) \quad \text{for } 0 \leq k \leq p_i - 1, \tag{9}$$

$$\delta(q_k, *_j^i) = (q_{k+1}, \sqcup_{j+1}^i) \quad \text{for } 0 \leq k \leq p_i - 2, \tag{10}$$

$$\delta(q_{p_i-1}, *_j^i) = (q_0, *_{j+1}^i), \tag{11}$$

$$\delta(q_k, \sqcup_{\alpha_i-1}^i) = (q_k, i) \quad \text{for } 0 \leq k \leq p_i - 1, \tag{12}$$

$$\delta(q_k, *_{\alpha_i-1}^i) = (q_{k+1}, i) \quad \text{for } 0 \leq k \leq p_i - 2, \tag{13}$$

$$\delta(q_{p_i-1}, *_{\alpha_i-1}^i) = (q_0, i). \tag{14}$$

If $\alpha_i = 1$, i.e. the ith **phase** consists of a single sweep, the instructions for δ are those here provided for the last sweep of the ith **phase** for the case $\alpha_i > 1$, the only difference being the input symbols which are now '$i - 1$'.

It is not hard to verify that T accepts if and only if the length of the input string is divisible by every $p_i^{\alpha_i}$, i.e., if and only if the input string belongs to L_n. Indeed, T features p_s states and $\sum_{i=1}^{s} \alpha_i$ sweeps.   □

The minimality – in terms of number of states – of the IUFST for L_n designed in Theorem 1 is provided in the following theorem, which also shows that non-determinism cannot help in reducing state size:

Theorem 2. *Let $n \geq 2$ factorize as $n = p_1^{\alpha_1} \cdot \cdots \cdot p_s^{\alpha_s}$, with $\alpha_i > 0$. Any IUFST and NIUFST accepting L_n must use at least p_s states, regardless of the number of performed sweeps.*

Let us now move on to a slightly different version of L_n. Precisely, for any $n \geq 1$ and a fixed remainder $R \in \mathbb{Z}_n \setminus \{0\}$, we let $L_{n,R} = \{ 0^{c \cdot n + R} \mid c \geq 0 \}$. The next theorem shows that this modification of L_n does not increase state and sweep complexity of acceptance on iterated transducers.

Theorem 3. *Let $n \geq 2$ factorize as $n = p_1^{\alpha_1} \cdot \cdots \cdot p_s^{\alpha_s}$, with $\alpha_i > 0$. The language $L_{n,R}$ can be accepted by a p_s-state r-IUFST with $r = \sum_{i=1}^{s} \alpha_i$ sweeps.*

Proof. To simplify our reasoning, we begin by considering the particular case where $n = p^\alpha$, for a prime p and a positive integer α. Thus, we consider the language $L_{p^\alpha,R} = \{ 0^{c \cdot p^\alpha + R} \mid c \geq 0 \}$, with $R \in \mathbb{Z}_{p^\alpha} \setminus \{0\}$.

In this case, we can construct a p-state α-IUFST T consisting of a single **phase** (recall from the proof of Theorem 1, a **phase** consists of a sequence of sweeps) where T checks whether the input length modulo p^α yields R. We make this single **phase** work as in Theorem 1, but now at every sweep T stores in its states a digit of the representation in base p of $R < p^\alpha$. More precisely: let $r_\alpha r_{\alpha-1} \cdots r_1$ be the representation of R in base p, with r_1 being the least significant digit. According to Theorem 1, the set of states of T is $\{q_0, q_1, \ldots, q_{p-1}\}$ and, for $1 \leq i \leq \alpha$, the digit r_i will be represented by the state q_{r_i}, which will be entered at the end of the ith sweep if and only if the input string belongs to $L_{p^\alpha,R}$.

To show this, consider the string $0^m \in L_{p^\alpha,R}$ and let q_{x_i} be the state reached by T on the ith sweep before reading the right endmarker. We are going to show that $q_{x_i} = q_{r_i}$ by induction on i. For $i = 1$, the property follows trivially. Otherwise, according to the construction in Theorem 1, it is not hard to see that, before reading the right endmarker on the ith sweep, T will represent in its states the number $m_i \bmod p$ where, for a given k, we have

$$m_i = \frac{m}{p^{i-1}} - \sum_{j=1}^{i-1} \frac{r_j}{p^{i-j}} = \frac{1}{p^{i-1}}\left(k \cdot p^i + \sum_{j=1}^{i} r_j \cdot p^{j-1}\right) - \sum_{j=1}^{i-1} \frac{r_j}{p^{i-j}}$$

$$= k \cdot p + \sum_{j=1}^{i} \frac{r_j}{p^{i-j}} - \sum_{j=1}^{i-1} \frac{r_j}{p^{i-j}} = k \cdot p + r_i.$$

So, $x_i = m_i \bmod p = r_i$, whence the result follows. This property enables us to define the transition function δ of T on the right endmarkers only in those situations where the sequence $r_\alpha r_{\alpha-1} \cdots r_1$ of remainders correctly show up along the α sweeps, eventually accepting the input string. In all the other situations, δ is suitably left undefined, thus leading to rejection.

Let us now consider the general case, where $n = p_1^{\alpha_1} \cdot \cdots \cdot p_s^{\alpha_s}$. For every $1 \leq i \leq s$, we let $R_i = R \bmod p_i^{\alpha_i}$. The Chinese Remainder Theorem states that R is the only non-negative integer less than n satisfying the system of modular equations $\{R_i = m \bmod p_i^{\alpha_i}\}_{1 \leq i \leq s}$, with m being the unknown. All the other solutions are of the form $m = c \cdot n + R$, for any $c > 0$. So, to check whether an input string 0^m belongs to $L_{n,R}$, it suffices to check whether $m \bmod p_i^{\alpha_i} = R_i$, for every $1 \leq i \leq s$. From a set theoretical point of view, this implies that

$$L_{n,R} = \bigcap_{i=1}^{s} L_{p_i^{\alpha_i}, R_i}$$

where each of the languages involved in the intersection has already been dealt with in the first part of this proof. Therefore, we can construct a p_s-state $(\sum_{i=1}^{s} \alpha_i)$-IUFST implementing the following recognition algorithm:

1: **input**(0^m);
2: **for** $i = 1$ to s **do**
3:     **if** $0^m \notin L_{p_i^{\alpha_i}, R_i}$ **then**
4:         REJECT BY UNDEFINED δ;
5:     **end if**
6: **end for**
7: ACCEPT.

The test $0^m \notin L_{p_i^{\alpha_i}, R_i}$ at line 3 is performed according to the single **phase** algorithm for the language $L_{p^\alpha, R}$ outlined at the beginning of this proof. However, for $i > 1$, the test actually takes as input the string $(i - 1)^m$ which is the output of the previous **phase**, as described in the proof of Theorem 1.   □

Finally, we come to tackle the acceptance of a general unary n-periodic language $L_{n,\mathcal{R}}$, for a fixed set $\mathcal{R} \subset \mathbb{Z}_n$: $L_{n,\mathcal{R}} = \{ 0^{c \cdot n + R} \mid c \geq 0 \text{ and } R \in \mathcal{R} \}$.

Theorem 4. *Let $n \geq 2$ factorize as $n = p_1^{\alpha_1} \cdot \cdots \cdot p_s^{\alpha_s}$, with $\alpha_i > 0$. The language $L_{n,\mathcal{R}}$ can be accepted by a p_s-state r-IUFST with $r = \sum_{i=1}^{s} \alpha_i$ sweeps.*

We conclude by observing that from Theorem 2 one may obtain that any IUFST and NIUFST accepting $L_{n,\mathcal{R}}$ must use at least p_s states, regardless the number of performed sweeps. In addition, as recalled in Sect. 2, we remark that n states are necessary and sufficient for DFAs and NFAs to accept $L_{n,\mathcal{R}}$, while $\sum_{i=1}^{s} p_i^{\alpha_i}$ states are necessary for two-way DFAs and NFAs, and one-way isolated cut point PFAs.

3.2   Unary Finite Languages

For any positive integer ℓ, let L_ℓ be any unary language whose longest word has length ℓ. In what follows, we assume $\ell \geq 2$. The case $\ell = 1$ can be trivially managed by a 2-state DFA seen as a transducer.

Theorem 5. *Let $\ell \geq 2$ factorize as $\ell = \varrho_1^{\beta_1} \cdot \cdots \cdot \varrho_r^{\beta_r}$, with $\beta_i > 0$. The language L_ℓ can be accepted by a $(2 \cdot \varrho_r)$-state t-IUFST with $t = \sum_{i=1}^{r} \beta_i$ sweeps.*

We conclude by observing that ℓ states are easily seen to be necessary on classical model of finite-state automata to accept L_ℓ. Again, a pumping argument as in Theorem 2 may be used to show that not less than ϱ_r states are needed for iterated transduction.

3.3   General Unary Regular Languages

Finally, let us put things together. As addressed in Sect. 2, a general (infinite) unary regular language consists of the disjoint union of a (possibly empty) finite pre-periodic language and a ultimately periodic language. Hence, it can be defined by three parameters ℓ, n, and $\mathcal{R} \subseteq \mathbb{Z}_n$ as

$$L_{\ell,n,\mathcal{R}} = L_\ell \cup \{ 0^{\ell + c \cdot n + R} \mid c \geq 0 \text{ and } R \in \mathcal{R} \},$$

where, with a slight abuse of notation with respect to notation in Sect. 3.2, we intend L_ℓ as a finite unary language that is accepted by an ℓ-state DFA. So, differently from Sect. 3.2, here and from now on L_ℓ does not necessarily contain the unary word of length ℓ. In the following theorem, we consider $\ell, n \geq 2$. Otherwise, we have languages that can be trivially dealt with by our constructions in this paper.

Theorem 6. *Let $\ell, n \geq 2$ factorize, respectively, as $n = p_1^{\alpha_1} \cdot \cdots \cdot p_s^{\alpha_s}$ with $\alpha_i > 0$, and $\ell = \varrho_1^{\beta_1} \cdot \cdots \cdot \varrho_r^{\beta_r}$ with $\beta_i > 0$. The unary language $L_{\ell,n,\mathcal{R}}$ can be accepted by an x-state t-IUFST, where $x = \max\{2 \cdot \varrho_r, p_s\} + \xi$, $\xi = 0$ if $\varrho_r < p_s$ and 1 otherwise, and $t = \sum_{i=1}^{s} \alpha_i + \sum_{i=1}^{r} \beta_i$.*

Proof. We use in cascade the transducer, say T', provided in Theorem 5 and the transducer, say T'', designed in Theorem 4. However, T' is slightly modified to take into the account that T'' must be activated only for inputs of length exceeding ℓ. To this aim, T':

- on input words of length less than or equal to ℓ not in L_ℓ, it now halts on the right endmarker by undefined δ,
- it accepts words in L_ℓ by the original construction,
- for words of length exceeding ℓ, it enters a "new" non-accepting state sweeping the rest of the input; such a new state can be q_{ϱ_r} whenever $\varrho_r < p_s$.

A further modification of T' is the fact that on the last sweep any input symbol is rewritten by 0, so that T'' can start working on a string of 0's, as assumed in Theorem 4. The reader may easily obtain the claimed number of states and sweeps for the transducer described so far. $\square$

Again, the pumping argument in Theorem 2 can be adapted to show that not less than $\max\{\varrho_r, p_s\}$ states can be used to accept $L_{\ell,n,\mathcal{R}}$ on iterated transducers. On the other hand, as recalled in Sect. 2, $\ell + n$ states are necessary and sufficient for a DFA to accept $L_{\ell,n,\mathcal{R}}$, whereas not less than $\sum_{i=1}^{s} p_i^{\alpha_i}$ states on two-way DFAs and NFAs, and on isolated cut-point PFAs are needed.

4   Beyond Constant Sweep Complexity

In this section, we will discuss the case of IUFSTs working on a unary input and having a non-constant sweep complexity. Since for sweep bounds of order $o(\ln n)$ deterministic and nondeterministic IUFSTs in the one-way case as well as in the two-way case accept regular languages only (see [12]), it remains to consider sweep bounds beyond $o(\ln n)$.

4.1   Characterizing Sweep Complexity by One-Way Cellular Automata Time Complexity

The purpose of this subsection is to establish a meaningful relation between the sweep complexity of a unary IUFST and the time complexity that is needed by a one-way cellular automaton beyond real time. In this way, the sweep complexity can be characterized by the time complexity of a massively parallel device.

In detail, a one-way cellular automaton (OCA) is a linear array of identical deterministic finite automata, called *cells*, where each cell except the leftmost one is connected to its left neighbor. The transition of a cell depends on its current state and the current states of its neighbor, where the leftmost cell receives information associated with a boundary symbol on its free input line. The cells work synchronously at discrete time steps. The input mode for OCA is called parallel. One can suppose that all cells fetc.h their input symbol during a pre-initial step.

More formally, an OCA is a system $M = \langle S, \#, A, \delta, F \rangle$, where $S \neq \emptyset$ is the finite set of cell states, $\# \notin S$ is the permanent boundary symbol, $A \subseteq S$ is the input alphabet, $F \subseteq S$ is the set of accepting cell states and $\delta : (S \cup \{\#\}) \times S \to S$ is the local transition function. A *configuration* of an OCA at some time step $t \geq 0$ is a mapping $c_t : \{1, 2, \ldots, n\} \to S$, for $n \geq 1$, which maps the single cells to their current states. The computation starts at time 0 in a so-called *initial configuration*, which is defined by the given input $w = x_1 x_2 \cdots x_n \in A^+$ as $c_0(i) = x_i$, for $1 \leq i \leq n$. Let c_t, $t \geq 0$, be a configuration. Then its successor configuration c_{t+1} is computed by $c_{t+1}(i) = \delta(c_t(i-1), c_t(i))$ for $i \in \{2, 3, \ldots, n\}$ and $c_{t+1}(1) = \delta(\#, c_t(1))$. An input w is *accepted* by an OCA M if at some time step during the course of its computation the rightmost cell enters an accepting state. Let $t : \mathbb{N} \to \mathbb{N}$ be a mapping. If all $w \in L(M)$ are accepted with at most $t(|w|)$ time steps, then M is said to be of time complexity t. Since in general OCA do not halt, this implies also that all $w \notin L(M)$ are not accepted, that is, rejected at time $t(|w|)$. Clearly, the identity function n is the least time complexity for non-trivial computations. So, if $t(n) = n$ acceptance is said to be in *real time* (see, for example, [9] for further information about cellular automata as language acceptors).

The next lemma shows that a non-constant number of sweeps significantly increase the computational power of IUFSTs even in the unary case. In particular, they increase the computational power in the same way as adding the same amount of time to a real-time OCA.

Lemma 7. *Let* $r : \mathbb{N} \to \mathbb{N}$ *be a mapping and* M *be an* OCA *with unary input alphabet obeying the time complexity* $n + r(n)$. *Then an equivalent* $(r(n) + 1)$-IUFST *can effectively be constructed.*

Proof. Let $M = \langle S, \#, \{a\}, \delta_M, F_M \rangle$ be an OCA. By a straightforward modification we can always achieve that M does not accept before time step n and that the input state a is never entered again.

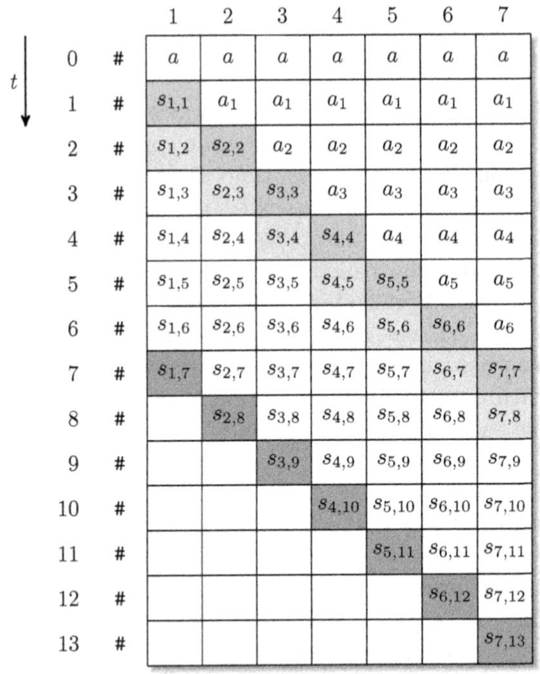

Fig. 1. Space-time diagram of a schematic computation of an OCA on input a^n with $n = 7$, that accepts at time $n + r(n) = 7 + 6$.

Considering the time-space diagram of a computation of M, one sees that all cells that did not receive any information from the left border are in the same state in any configuration (see Fig. 1). Moreover, these states can be computed as $a_1 = \delta_M(a, a)$, $a_2 = \delta_M(a_1, a_1)$, and so on. Now the basic idea of the construction of an equivalent IUFST $T = \langle Q, \{a\}, \Delta, q_0, \triangleright, \triangleleft, \delta_T, F_T \rangle$ is as follows. In a first sweep, T reads the a's and emits the first diagonal of the space-time diagram that consists of states on which the left border may had an effect (the green diagonal in Fig. 1). To this end, T enters in every step a state that is actually a pair of states of M, that is, the state on the diagonal and the state to the right of the diagonal. In subsequent sweeps, T reads the states of a diagonal and emits the states of the next diagonal. To this end, it enters the states on the diagonal. More formally, we set $Q = \{q_0, q_+\} \cup S \cup S^2$, $\Delta = \{\triangleright, \triangleleft\} \cup S$, $F_T = \{q_+\}$, and specify δ_T as follows.

$$\delta_T(q_0, \triangleright) = (q_0, \triangleright) \tag{15}$$

$$\delta_T(q_0, a) = \Big(\big(\delta_M(\#, a), \delta_M(a, a)\big), \delta_M(\#, a) \Big) \tag{16}$$

$$\delta_T((s, a'), a) = \Big(\big(\delta_M(s, a'), \delta_M(a', a')\big), \delta_M(s, a') \Big) \tag{17}$$

$$\delta_T((s, a'), \triangleleft) = (q_0, \triangleleft) \quad \text{if } s \notin F_M \tag{18}$$

$$\delta_T((s, a'), \triangleleft) = (q_+, \triangleleft) \quad \text{if } s \in F_M \tag{19}$$

$$\delta_T(q_0, s) = \big(\delta_M(\#, s), \delta_M(\#, s)\big) \tag{20}$$

$$\delta_T(s', s) = \big(\delta_M(s', s), \delta_M(s', s)\big) \tag{21}$$

$$\delta_T(s', \triangleleft) = (q_0, \triangleleft) \quad \text{if } s' \notin F_M \tag{22}$$

$$\delta_T(s', \triangleleft) = (q_+, \triangleleft) \quad \text{if } s' \in F_M \tag{23}$$

Finally, T accepts if it simulates an accepting state of M when it reads the right endmarker. In this case, the rightmost cell of M has entered an accepting state and, thus, M has accepted. If M never accepts then T will never accept. We conclude that both devices accept the same language. Moreover, the state of the rightmost cell of M at time $n + r(n)$ is simulated at the end of the $(r(n) + 1)$st sweep of T. $\qquad\Box$

Now we turn to the converse simulation of Lemma 7.

Lemma 8. *Let T be an $s(n)$-IUFST with unary input alphabet. Then an equivalent OCA obeying the time complexity $n + s(n) - 1$ can effectively be constructed.*

The previous lemmas reveal the following characterization.

Theorem 9. *Let $r : \mathbb{N} \to \mathbb{N}$ be a mapping. A unary language is accepted by an OCA obeying the time complexity $n + r(n)$ if and only if it is accepted by an IUFST with sweep complexity $r(n) + 1$.*

The characterization opens the door to a rich family of unary languages that are accepted by IUFSTs. It is known that the family of languages accepted by OCAs obeying time complexity $(1 + \varepsilon)n$, where ε is an arbitrarily small positive number, coincides with the reversals of languages accepted by two-way cellular automata in real time (see, for example, [9]). Since the reversal of a unary language is the language itself, all unary languages accepted by two-way cellular automata in real time are accepted by $(\varepsilon n + 1)$-IUFSTs. This language family is very rich. Examples are $\{\,a^{n^k} \mid n \geq 1\,\}$, for all $k \geq 1$, $\{\,a^{k^n} \mid n \geq 1\,\}$, for all $k \geq 1$, $\{\,a^{n!} \mid n \geq 1\,\}$, $\{\,a^p \mid p \text{ is prime}\,\}$, and $\{\,a^p \mid p \text{ is a Fibonacci number}\,\}$ [4,15,22,23]. Moreover, the class of these languages is closed under several operations applied to the functions that give the word lengths.

4.2   Reducing Sweeps on Unary Languages

In this subsection, we show a general result on sweep reduction for unary languages accepted by $s(n)$-IUFSTs with $s(n) \in O(n)$. In detail, it is shown that the sweep complexity can be exponentially reduced at the price of accepting a modified language. However, the modification does not change the size, i.e., the number of words in the language. This feature will be essential for the undecidability results given in the next subsection. Our main result in this subsection is the following translational lemma.

Lemma 10. *Let a unary language L be accepted by an $s(n)$-IUFST with sweep complexity $s(n) \in O(n)$. Then, the language $L' = \{\,a^{2^m} \mid a^m \in L\,\}$ is accepted by an $s'(n)$-IUFST with $s'(n) \in O(\ln n)$.*

The following lemma is then an easy observation.

Lemma 11. *Let L be a unary language and $L' = \{\,a^{2^m} \mid a^m \in L\,\}$. Then, $|L| = |L'|$ and, in particular, L is finite if and only if L' is finite.*

4.3   Undecidability Results

Concerning decidability questions it is shown in [12] that all commonly studied decidability questions such as emptiness, finiteness, infiniteness, inclusion, and equivalence are undecidable for $s(n)$-IUFSTs with $s(n) \in \Omega(\ln n)$. Obviously, these undecidability results carry over to the stronger models with nondeterministic moves and/or two-way motion. Taking a look on the proof of these results it is clear that the underlying languages used in the proof are not unary. Thus, the question arises whether the above-mentioned decidability questions become decidable in case of IUFSTs working on unary inputs. For example, it is known for one-way multi-head finite automata (see, e.g., [8]) that all above-mentioned decidability questions are undecidable in general, but become decidable in case of unary languages. However, for IUFSTs we can show in the following that the decidability questions for IUFSTs remain undecidable even if only unary inputs are considered. The way to obtain these results is to first show that the questions of emptiness, finiteness, infiniteness, inclusion, and equivalence are undecidable for OCAs working in linear time and accepting a unary input. Using the results of Subsect. 4.1 we can construct an equivalent $s(n)$-IUFST with $s(n) \in O(n)$. Using then the construction from Subsect. 4.2 we can construct an $s'(n)$-IUFST with $s'(n) \in O(\ln n)$ and translate the undecidability results for unary linear-time OCAs to undecidability results for IUFSTs having a sweep complexity in $\Omega(\ln n)$.

Theorem 12. *For linear-time* OCAs *accepting unary languages the problems of testing emptiness, finiteness, infiniteness, inclusion, and equivalence are undecidable.*

Using the results of Subsect. 4.1 and 4.2 we are able to prove undecidability results for $s(n)$-IUFSTs accepting unary languages with $s(n) \in \Omega(\ln n)$.

Theorem 13. *Let* $s(n) \in \Omega(\ln n)$. *Then for* $s(n)$-IUFSTs *accepting unary languages the problems of testing emptiness, finiteness, infiniteness, inclusion, and equivalence are undecidable.*

Proof. First, we note that owing to a speed-up result for linear-time OCAs (see, e.g., [9]) we may always assume that linear-time OCAs work in time $t(n) = 2n$. Then, due to Lemma 7 we know that for every unary linear-time OCA accepting a language L with time complexity $2n$ an equivalent $(n+1)$-IUFST can effectively be constructed. By applying Lemma 10 we can construct an $s'(n)$-IUFST T with $s'(n) \in O(\ln n)$ that accepts L'.

Let us now assume that emptiness is decidable for an $s(n)$-IUFST with $s(n) \in \Omega(\ln n)$. Then, we can decide the emptiness of T accepting L'. Hence, we can decide the emptiness of L since by Lemma 11 L' is empty if and only if L is empty. This implies the decidability of emptiness for linear-time OCAs which is a contradiction to Theorem 12.

Similarly, we can show that finiteness and infiniteness are undecidable, since by Lemma 11 L' is finite if and only if L is finite. Finally, the fact that the empty set is accepted by an $s(n)$-IUFST with $s(n) \in \Omega(\ln n)$ and the result that emptiness is undecidable imply that the questions of inclusion and equivalence are undecidable as well. $\square$

References

1. Bordihn, H., Fernau, H., Holzer, M., Manca, V., Martín-Vide, C.: Iterated sequential transducers as language generating devices. Theor. Comput. Sci. **369**(1–3), 67–81 (2006)
2. Chrobak, M.: Finite automata and unary languages. Theor. Comp. Sci. **47**, 149–158 (1986) - Corrigendum, ibid, 302, 497–498 (2003)
3. Citrini, C., Crespi-Reghizzi, S., Mandrioli, D.: On deterministic multi-pass analysis. SIAM J. Comput. **15**(3), 668–693 (1986)
4. Fischer, P.C.: Generation of primes by a one-dimensional real-time iterative array. J. ACM **12**, 388–394 (1965)
5. Friburger, N., Maurel, D.: Finite-state transducer cascades to extract named entities in texts. Theor. Comput. Sci. **313**(1), 93–104 (2004)
6. Ginzburg, A.: Algebraic Theory of Automata. Academic Press, Cambridge (1968)
7. Hartmanis, J., Stearns, R.E.: Algebraic Structure Theory of Sequential Machines. Prentice-Hall, Upper Saddle River (1966)
8. Holzer, M., Kutrib, M., Malcher, A.: Complexity of multi-head finite automata: origins and directions. Theor. Comput. Sci. **412**(1–2), 83–96 (2011)
9. Kutrib, M.: Cellular automata and language theory. In: Meyers, R. (ed.) Encyclopedia of Complexity and System Science, pp. 800–823. Springer (2009)

10. Kutrib, M., Malcher, A.: Cellular automata with limited inter-cell bandwidth. Theor. Comput. Sci. **412**(30), 3917–3931 (2011)
11. Kutrib, M., Malcher, A., Mereghetti, C., Palano, B.: Iterated uniform finite-state transducers: descriptional complexity of nondeterminism and two-way motion. In: Jiráskova, G., Pighizzini, G. (eds.) DCFS 2020. LNCS, vol. 12442, pp. 117–129. Springer, Cham (2020). https://doi.org/10.1007/978-3-030-62536-8_10
12. Kutrib, M., Malcher, A., Mereghetti, C., Palano, B.: Descriptional complexity of iterated uniform finite-state transducers. In: Hospodár, M., Jiráskova, G., Konstantinidis, S. (eds.) DCFS 2019. LNCS, vol. 11612, pp. 223–234. Springer, Cham (2019). https://doi.org/10.1007/978-3-030-23247-4_17
13. Kutrib, M., Malcher, A., Mereghetti, C., Palano, B.: Deterministic and nondeterministic iterated uniform finite-state transducers: computational and descriptional power. In: Anselmo, M., Della Vedova, G., Manea, F., Pauly, A. (eds.) CiE 2020. LNCS, vol. 12098, pp. 87–99. Springer, Cham (2020). https://doi.org/10.1007/978-3-030-51466-2_8
14. Manca, V.: On the generative power of iterated transductions. In: Words, Semigroups, and Transductions, pp. 315–327. World Scientific (2001)
15. Mazoyer, J., Terrier, V.: Signals in one-dimensional cellular automata. Theor. Comput. Sci. **217**, 53–80 (1999)
16. Mealy, G.H.: A method for synthesizing sequential circuits. Bell Syst. Tech. J. **34**, 1045–1079 (1955)
17. Mereghetti, C.: Testing the descriptional power of small Turing machines on nonregular language acceptance. Int. J. Found. Comput. Sci. **19**, 827–843 (2008)
18. Mereghetti, C., Pighizzini, G.: Optimal simulations between unary automata. SIAM J. Comput. **30**, 1976–1992 (2001)
19. Mereghetti, C., Palano, B., Pighizzini, G.: Note on the succinctness of deterministic, nondeterministic, probabilistic and quantum finite automata. Theor. Inf. Appl. **35**, 477–490 (2001)
20. Mereghetti, C., Pighizzini, G.: Two-way automata simulations and unary languages. J. Autom. Lang. Comb. **5**, 287–300 (2000)
21. Minsky, M.L.: Recursive unsolvability of Post's problem of "tag" and other topics in theory of turing machines. Ann. of Math. **2**(74), 437–455 (1961)
22. Umeo, H., Kamikawa, N.: A design of real-time non-regular sequence generation algorithms and their implementations on cellular automata with 1-bit inter-cell communications. Fundam. Inform. **52**, 257–275 (2002)
23. Umeo, H., Kamikawa, N.: Real-time generation of primes by a 1-bit-communication cellular automaton. Fundam. Inform. **58**, 421–435 (2003)

New Bounds on the Half-Duplex Communication Complexity

Yuriy Dementiev[1] , Artur Ignatiev[1] , Vyacheslav Sidelnik[1] ,
Alexander Smal[2(✉)] , and Mikhail Ushakov[1]

[1] St. Petersburg State University, St. Petersburg, Russia
[2] St. Petersburg Department of Steklov Mathematical Institute
of Russian Academy of Sciences, St. Petersburg, Russia
smal@pdmi.ras.ru

Abstract. In this work, we continue the research started in [6], where
the authors suggested to study the half-duplex communication complexity. Unlike the classical model of communication complexity introduced
by Yao, in the half-duplex model, Alice and Bob can speak or listen simultaneously, as if they were talking using a walkie-talkie. The motivation
for such a communication model comes from the study of the KRW conjecture. Following the open questions formulated in [6], we prove lower
bounds for the disjointness function in all variants of half-duplex models and an upper bound in the half-duplex model with zero, that separates disjointness from the inner product function in this setting. Next,
we prove lower and upper bounds on the half-duplex complexity of the
Karchmer-Wigderson games for the counting functions and for the recursive majority function, adapting the ideas used in the classical communication complexity. Finally, we define the non-deterministic half-duplex
complexity and establish bounds connecting it with non-deterministic
complexity in the classical model.

Keywords: Communication complexity · Half-duplex
communication · Karchmer-wigderson games

1 Introduction

1.1 Background

Communication complexity is a powerful tool with applications in algorithms,
circuit complexity, proof complexity, and many other areas of theoretical computer science. In the classical model of communication complexity introduced
by Yao [13], two players, Alice and Bob, try to compute $f(x, y)$ for some function f, where Alice only knows x and Bob only knows y. Alice and Bob can
communicate by sending bits to each other, one bit per round, and at the end
of the communication, both players must know the result $f(x, y)$. The essential
property of this classical model is that in each round of communication, one
player sends a bit, and the other receives it.

© Springer Nature Switzerland AG 2021
T. Bureš et al. (Eds.): SOFSEM 2021, LNCS 12607, pp. 233–248, 2021.
https://doi.org/10.1007/978-3-030-67731-2_17

There are many extensions of this basic two-party communication model, such as randomized communication complexity, non-deterministic communication complexity, various types of multiparty communication models, etc. In [6], the authors suggested considering a communication model where the players speak over *a half-duplex channel*. A well-known example of half-duplex communication is talking using a walkie-talkie: one has to hold a "push-to-talk" button to speak to another person, and the other has to keep it released to listen. If two persons try to speak simultaneously, then they do not hear each other. Formally speaking, every round, each player chooses one of three actions: send 0, send 1, or receive. There are three different types of rounds: a *classical round*, when one player sends some bit while the other receives, a *wasted*[1] *round*, when both players send bits (there bits get lost), and a *silent round*, when both players receive. In [6], the authors defined three variations of the half-duplex model based on what happens in silent rounds: half-duplex models with silence, with zero, and with adversary (see Sect. 2 for more information).

It turned out that the communication complexity in the half-duplex models not only differs from the classical case, but also behaves differently. For example, in the classical case, the equality function, the disjointness function, and the inner product function have complexity $n + 1$, meaning that all three are the hardest functions. In the half-duplex models with silence and with zero, these three functions are of different complexity.

The original motivation for the half-duplex communication models comes from the study of the Karchmer-Wigderson games [8]. In [12], results from the half-duplex communication complexity were used to prove a lower bound on a composition of the universal relation with the Karchmer-Wigderson game for some function. The authors suggest that a better understanding of the half-duplex communication complexity might help to achieve new bound in the study of the KRW conjecture [7] and even prove a supercubic lower bound on the De Morgan formula size of an implicit function.

We continue the research started [6], and close some open questions from it regarding the complexity of the disjointness function. We also study the complexity of the Karchmer-Wigderson games for the counting functions and for the recursive majority function. In addition, we define the non-deterministic half-duplex communication complexity and prove bounds connecting it to the classical non-deterministic communication complexity.

1.2   Overview of Results

For a communication problem R, let $\mathrm{D}_s^{hd}(R)$, $\mathrm{D}_0^{hd}(R)$, and $\mathrm{D}_a^{hd}(R)$, denote the half-duplex communication complexity of R with silence, with zero, and with adversary, respectively (see Sect. 2 for formal definitions). Table 1 contains a summary of lower and upper bounds for the communication problems considered in [6], the bounds proved in this paper are marked with $\star$.

---

[1] In the original paper, this type of rounds is called *spent*.

Table 1. Lower and upper bounds for the communication problems considered in [6].

	EQ_n	IP_n	$DISJ_n$		KW_{MOD2}	
D_s^{hd}	$\geq n/\log 5$	$\geq n/1.67$	$\geq n/\log 5$	$\star$	$\geq 1.12 \log n$	$\star$
	$\leq n/\log 5 + o(n)$		$\leq n/2 + O(1)$		$\leq 1.262 \log n$	$\star$
D_0^{hd}	$\geq n/\log 3$	$\geq n/1.234$	$\geq n/\log 3$	$\star$	$\geq 1.62 \log n$	$\star$
	$\leq n/\log 3 + o(n)$		$\leq 3n/4 + o(n)$	$\star$	$\leq 1.893 \log n$	$\star$
D_a^{hd}	$\geq n/\log 2.5$	$\geq n$	$\geq n/\log 2.5$	$\star$	$= 2 \log n$	

In addition to the bounds in Table 1, we prove the following upper bounds for special cases of the counting function, and for the recursive majority function,

$$D_s^{hd}(KW_{MOD3}) \leq 1.893 \log n, \quad D_s^{hd}(KW_{MOD5}) \leq 2.46 \log n,$$

$$D_s^{hd}(KW_{MOD11}) \leq 3.48 \log n, \quad D_s^{hd}(KW_{RecMaj}) \leq 2 \log_3 n,$$

$$D_0^{hd}(KW_{RecMaj}) \leq 2 \log_3 n.$$

For arbitrary $p \geq 7$, we prove that $D_s^{hd}(KW_{MODp}) \leq 1.16 \lceil 1 + \log_3 \frac{p}{2} \rceil \cdot \log n$. We also show that the lower bounds for KW_{MOD2} in Table 1 apply for KW_{MODp} for arbitrary p in all three models.

In Sect. 5, we introduce non-deterministic half-duplex communication complexity. Let $N_s^{hd}(f)$, $N_0^{hd}(f)$, and $N_a^{hd}(f)$ denotes the non-deterministic half-duplex communication complexity of f with silence, with zero, and with adversary, respectively. For any function $f : \{0,1\}^n \times \{0,1\}^n \rightarrow \{0,1\}$, we show that

$$N_s^{hd}(f) = N(f)/\log 5 + \Theta(\log N(f)), \quad N_0^{hd}(f) = N(f)/\log 3 + \Theta(\log N(f)),$$

$$N_a^{hd}(f) \geq N(f)/\log 3,$$

where $N(f)$ denotes the classical non-deterministic communication complexity.

Due to the page limit, we have to omit many proofs, which can be found in the full version [4].

2   Half-Duplex Communication Complexity

We expect that the reader is familiar with the standard definitions of communication complexity that can be found in [10]. It will be necessary to understand that a communication protocol can be described by a binary tree, where every node has an associated combinatorial rectangle of all input pairs (x, y) such that if the players are given x and y, then the communication goes through this node. Finally, we expect the reader to understand why the rectangles associated with the leaves of the protocol tree are monochromatic.

Let's assume that the players have some synchronizing mechanism, e.g., synchronized clocks, that allows them to understand when each round begins. In the half-duplex communication, every round, each player chooses one of three actions: send 0, send 1, or receive. So, there are three different types of rounds.

- A *classical round:* one player sends some bit and the other one receives it.
- A *wasted round:* both players send bits, and these bits get lost.
- A *silent round:* both players receive.

In [6], the authors considered three variations of this model based on what happens in silent rounds.

- *The half-duplex communication model with silence.* In a silent round, both players receive a special symbol silence, so it is possible for both players to distinguish a silent round from a classical one.
- *The half-duplex communication model with zero.* In a silent round, both players receive 0, i.e., players can not distinguish a silent round from a classical round where the other player sends 0.
- *The half-duplex communication model with adversary.* In a silent round, each player receives arbitrary bit, not necessarily the same as the other player.

In the half-duplex model with zero, there is no need to send zeros—a player can choose to receive instead and the other player will not notice the difference.

Unlike the classical case, in the half-duplex communication models a player does not always know what the other player's action was—the information about it can be "lost", i.e., in wasted rounds a player do not know what the other player's action was. It means that a player might not know what node of the protocol corresponds to the current state of communication. In the half-duplex case, a protocol is described by two trees—one for each player. The protocol trees have arity 5 in the half-duplex model with silence, arity 3 in the model with zero, and arity 4 in the model with adversary. For the formal definition of the half-duplex communication protocols see [6]. It should be noted that despite the differences, every node of a half-duplex protocol tree has an associated rectangle, and every leaf rectangle is monochomatic.

The minimal number of rounds that is enough to solve a communication problem R on all inputs defines the communication complexity of R. For the classical communication model, we denote it by $D(R)$, for the half-duplex models with silence, with zero, and with adversary, we denote it by $D_s^{hd}(R)$, $D_0^{hd}(R)$, and $D_a^{hd}(R)$, respectively.

3   Bounds for the Disjointness Function

The disjointness function $DISJ_n : \{0,1\}^n \times \{0,1\}^n \to \{0,1\}$ is defined by $DISJ_n(x,y) = 1 \iff \forall i \in [n] : x_i \neq 1 \vee y_i \neq 1$. This is one of the hardest functions in the classical communication model—it has communication complexity exactly $n+1$. In other words, the trivial protocol where Alice sends all her bits to Bob, Bob computes the result and then sends it back to Alice, is optimal. This is not the case in the half-duplex models. In [6], the authors prove an upper bound $n/2 + O(1)$ on $DISJ_n$ in the half-duplex model with silence (Theorem 16 in [6]). Note that in this model the inner product function requires a protocol of complexity at least $n/1.67$, so the disjointness is not the hardest function in this setting. In this section we prove lower bounds for DISJ_n in all three half-duplex models, and an upper bound in the model with zero showing that the disjointness is not the hardest function there as well. We start with the lower bounds.

Theorem 1. *For all* $n \in \mathbb{N}$, $\mathrm{D}_s^{hd}(\mathrm{DISJ}_n) \geq n/\log 5$, $\mathrm{D}_0^{hd}(\mathrm{DISJ}_n) \geq n/\log 3$, $\mathrm{D}_a^{hd}(\mathrm{DISJ}_n) \geq n/\log 2.5$.

To prove this theorem, we will need the following folklore property of communication protocols for DISJ_n. For a Boolean vector $x \in \{0,1\}^n$, let $\bar{x}$ denotes its complement, i.e. $x_i = 1 - \bar{x}_i$ for all $i \in [n]$.

Lemma 1 ([10]). *Let* $x, y \in \{0,1\}^n$ *and* $x \neq y$. *The pair of inputs* $(x, \bar{x})$ *and* $(y, \bar{y})$ *do not belong to the same monochromatic rectangle of* DISJ_n.

This property of DISJ_n allows us to define a sub-additive measure $\mu(R)$ that is equal to the number of pairs $(x, \bar{x})$ in rectangle R. In [6], a special framework was developed specifically for such measures. The following lemma allows to get a lower bound by showing that for every protocol the measure of the root rectangle is large while the measures of all leaf rectangles are small. We say that some rectangle of inputs R is *good* for a protocol Π if restricting the problem to R allows the players to omit the first round of Π.

Lemma 2 (Lemma 10 in [6]). *Let* μ *be some sub-additive measure on rectangles such that* $\mu(X \times Y) \geq \mu_r$ *and for any leaf rectangle* R_l, $\mu(R_l) \leq \mu_\ell$. *If for any rectangle* R *there is always a good subrectangle for function* $f \restriction R$ *of measure at least* $\alpha \cdot \mu(R)$ *then the depth of the protocol is at least* $\log_{1/\alpha} \frac{\mu_r}{\mu_\ell}$.

Now we are ready to prove Theorem 1.

Proof (Proof of Theorem 1). For the first two lower bounds it is enough to use *the fooling set method* [10]. There are 2^n pairs $(x, \bar{x})$, and hence there are at least 2^n 1-monochromatic rectangles, that gives a lower bound on the number of leaves in the protocol. It remains to note that the protocol trees in the half-duplex models with silence and with zero have arities 5 and 3, respectively.

The third lower bound requires a little bit more effort. The same argument would prove only $n/2$ lower bound which is trivial. Instead, we use *the rectangle elimination technique* introduced in [6]. We will use the fact that for any protocol solving DISJ_n on some rectangle R there is a set of five good rectangles covering each element of R twice. One of there rectangles has measure at least $2/5 \cdot \mu(R)$ and we can reduce the problem to it (see [5, Theorem 13] for more information). Application of Lemma 2 for μ and $\alpha = 2/5$ concludes the proof. □

Now we proceed to the upper bound for DISJ_n in the half-duplex model with zero. In order to show a protocol with $\frac{3}{4}n + o(n)$ rounds, we start with a less efficient protocol and then improve it. Let us remind that in the half-duplex model with zero there is no need to send zeros, so the players never do it.

Theorem 2. *For all* $n \in \mathbb{N}$, $\mathrm{D}_0^{hd}(\mathrm{DISJ}_n) \leq 5n/6 + O(\log n)$.

Table 2. The first stage of the half-duplex protocol for $DISJ_n$ with zero.

Case 1			Case 2			Case 3		
Block	Alice	Bob	Block	Alice	Bob	Block	Alice	Bob
00	receive	send(1)	00	receive	receive	00	send(1)	receive
01	send(1)	receive	01	send(1)	send(1)	01	receive	receive
10	receive	receive	10	receive	receive	10	receive	send(1)
11	receive	receive	11	receive	receive	11	receive	receive

Proof. W.l.o.g., we assume that n is even. Consider the following protocol. Alice and Bob split their input strings into blocks of size 2, so each player has $n/2$ such blocks. Let $\sharp(ab)$ denotes the number of blocks ab among the blocks of Bob. Note that one of the following cases holds:

1. $\sharp(00) \geq n/6$, then $\sharp(01) + \sharp(10) + \sharp(11) \leq n/2 - n/6 = n/3$,
2. $\sharp(01) \geq n/6$, then $\sharp(00) + \sharp(10) + \sharp(11) \leq n/2 - n/6 = n/3$,
3. $\sharp(00) + \sharp(01) < n/3$.

At the beginning Bob must check which of the cases applies and tell Alice using two bits of communication. Further communication depends on it. We will show that in all the cases the players can solve the problem using at most $5n/6 + O(\log n)$ rounds. The communication will be divided into two stages. In the first stage, Alice and Bob process their input considering one pair of corresponding blocks per round. Each round they act as it is described in Table 2. Alice and Bob need to be able to distinguish the situations when the corresponding blocks intersect, that is, to distinguish block pairs $(01,01)$, $(01,11)$, $(11,01)$, $(11,10)$, $(11,11)$, $(10,10)$, $(10,11)$ from others.

Case 1. After $n/2$ rounds, Bob tells Alice whether he ever has received 1 while processing a block 11 or 01. If he has, then the corresponding block of Alice was 01, and hence their strings intersect. This corresponds to identifying $(01,01)$ and $(01,11)$. Further, Alice tells Bob whether she ever has a silent round while processing 11. If she has, then the corresponding block of Bob was one of 01, 10 or 11, and hence their strings intersect, so the players identified block pairs $(11,01)$, $(11,10)$, and $(11,11)$. If any intersecting blocks have been found, the players stop the communication and output 0. Otherwise, they proceed to the second stage.

In the second stage, to identify the remaining two block pairs $(10,10)$ and $(10,11)$, Alice needs to distinguish zeros she received when Bob was processing 10 or 11, and zeroes she received when Bob was processing 01. Bob sequentially (starting from his first silent round on 01, 10 or 11) goes through all his blocks 01, 10, 11 corresponding to silent rounds. When he processes 10 and 11, he sends 1, and when he processes 01, he sends 0. Alice knows how many bits Bob will send her, since he sends one bit for every silent round. Alice simultaneously processes her blocks corresponding to the silent rounds. Now for every such blocks she knows whether Bob has 10 or 11, and 01. If she receives 1 having 10 then they identified $(10, 10)$ and $(10, 11)$. At the end of the protocol, Alice needs one more round to tell Bob whether she has found an intersection.

The complexity of the first stage is $n/2 + O(1)$, the complexity of the second stage is $n/3 + O(1)$, so the total complexity is $5n/6 + O(1)$.

Case 2. After $n/2$ rounds, Bob tells Alice whether he has ever received 1 while processing 11. If he has, then Alice had 01 in the corresponding block, and hence their strings intersect, so the players identified $(01, 11)$. After that, Alice tells Bob whether she has ever received 1 while processing 11. If she has, then they identified $(11, 01)$. Next, Bob tells the number of rounds in which he sent 1. Alice compares it with the number of 1 she received. If these two numbers are equal, then there were no wasted rounds in the first stage, otherwise the players identified a block pair $(01, 01)$. If any intersecting blocks have been found, the players stop the communication and output 0. Otherwise, they proceed to the second stage.

In the second stage, to identify the remaining four block pairs $(10, 10)$, $(10, 11)$, $(11, 10)$ and $(11, 11)$, Alice needs to distinguish zeroes received when Bob was processing 10 or 11 from zeros received when Bob was processing 00. Bob sequentially (starting from his first silent round on 00, 10 or 11) goes through all his blocks 00, 10, 11 corresponding to silent rounds. When he processes 10 and 11, he sends 1, and when he processes 00, he sends 0. Similarly to the previous case, if she receives 1 having 10 or 11 then they identified one of the desired pairs of blocks. At the end of the protocol Alice needs one more round to tell Bob whether she has found an intersection.

The complexity of the first stage is $n/2 + O(1)$, the complexity of the second stage is $n/3 + O(\log n)$, so the total complexity is $5n/6 + O(\log n)$.

Case 3. After $n/2$ rounds, Bob tells Alice if there was a silent round corresponding to his block 11. If there was such a round, the Alice had 01, 10 or 11 in the corresponding block, so the players identified block pairs $(01, 11)$, $(10, 11)$, and $(11, 11)$. Next, Alice tells Bob if she has ever received 1 while processing 10 or 11. If she has, then Bob had 10, and hence they identified a block $(10, 10)$ or $(11, 10)$. If any intersecting blocks have been found, the players stop the communication and output 0. Otherwise, they proceed to the second stage.

In the second stage, to identify the remaining two block pairs $(01, 01)$ and $(11, 01)$, Alice needs to distinguish zeroes received while Bob was processing a block 00 and zeroes received while Bob was processing a block 01. Bob sequentially (starting from his first silent round on 00 or 01) goes through all his blocks 00 and 01 corresponding to silent rounds. When he processes a block 01, he sends 1, and when he processes 00, he sends 0. Similarly to the previous cases, if Alice receives 1 while processing 01 or 11, she identifies one of the desired block pairs.

The complexity of the protocol in this case is $5n/6 + O(1)$.   □

The protocol proposed in Theorem 2 can be improved if we notice that reiterating over a part of the blocks that happens in the second stage can be reduced to solving disjointness problem on smaller inputs.

Theorem 3. *For all $n \in \mathbb{N}$, $D_0^{hd}(\text{DISJ}_n) \leq 3n/4 + o(n)$.*

Proof. We are going to modify the protocol from the proof of Theorem 2. In the modified protocol, the players consider the same three cases, and they have the same first stages in all cases. The second stage is different. Instead of reiterating all blocks corresponding to silent rounds, Alice and Bob reduce this problem to solving disjointness on strings of size at most $n/3$, and then run the same protocol for disjointness recursively. Thus, we get the following bound

$$D_0^{hd}(\text{DISJ}_n) \leq \sum_{i=0}^{\lceil \log_3(n) \rceil} \frac{n}{2 \cdot 3^i} + o(n) \leq \sum_{i=0}^{\infty} \frac{n}{2 \cdot 3^i} + o(n) = \frac{3n}{4} + o(n).$$

It remains to understand how the second stage works in each of the cases.

Case 1. To identify two block pairs $(10, 10)$ and $(10, 11)$, Bob writes down a string x' that has one bit for every silent rounds: 1 for a block 10 or 11, and 0 for 01. Similarly, Alice writes down a string y' that has one bit for every silent round: 1 for a block 10, and 0 for other blocks. It is not hard to see, that $\text{DISJ}(x', y') = 0$ if and only if there was a silent round corresponding to $(10, 10)$ or $(10, 11)$.

Case 2. To identify four block pairs $(10, 10)$, $(10, 11)$, $(11, 10)$ and $(11, 11)$, Bob writes down a string x' that has one bit for every silent rounds: 1 for a block 10 or 11, and 0 for 00. Similarly, Alice writes down a string y' using the same rules. It is not hard to see, that $\text{DISJ}(x', y') = 0$ if and only if there was a silent round corresponding to one of the desired block pairs.

Case 3. To identify the remaining two block pairs $(01, 01)$ and $(11, 01)$, Bob writes down a string x' that has one bit for every silent rounds: 1 for a block 01, and 0 for others (at this point, he already knows that there were no silent rounds corresponding to 11). Similarly, Alice writes down a string y' that has one bit for every silent round: 1 for a block 01 or 11, and 0 for 10. And again, it is not hard to see, that $\text{DISJ}(x', y') = 0$ if and only if there was a silent round corresponding $(01, 01)$ and $(11, 01)$. $\square$

This theorem shows that $D_0^{hd}(\text{DISJ}_n) < D_a^{hd}(\text{DISJ}_n)$. Moreover, it separates DISJ_n and IP_n in the half-duplex model with zero, $D_0^{hd}(\text{DISJ}_n) < D_0^{hd}(\text{IP}_n)$, showing that the disjointness is not the hardest function in this model.

4   Bounds on the Karchmer-Wigderson Games

The seminal work of Karchmer and Wigderson [8] established a correspondence between De Morgan formulas for non-constant Boolean function f and communication protocols for the Karchmer-Wigderson game for f. *De Morgan formula* is a Boolean formula over the De Morgan basis $\{\wedge, \vee, \neg\}$, where $\neg$ operation is only applied to input variables. *The Karchmer-Wigderson game* for Boolean function $f : \{0, 1\}^n \rightarrow \{0, 1\}$ is the following communication problem: Alice gets an input $x \in \{0,1\}^n$ such that $f(x) = 0$, and Bob gets an input $y \in \{0,1\}^n$ such that $f(y) = 1$. Their goal is to find a coordinate $i \in [n]$ such that $x_i \neq y_i$. The Karchmer-Wigderson game for f can be considered as a communication problem for *the Karchmer-Wigderson relation for f*:

$$\mathrm{KW}_f = \{(x,y,i) \mid x,y \in \{0,1\}^n, i \in [n], f(x) = 0, f(y) = 1, x_i \neq y_i\}.$$

Karchmer and Wigderson showed that the communication complexity of KW_f is exactly equal to the formula depth complexity of f. This observation allows us to use communication complexity methods for proving formula depth lower bounds.

In this section, we prove bounds on the half-duplex communication complexity of the Karchmer-Wigderson games for *the counting function* MODp : $\{0,1\}^n \rightarrow \{0,1\}$, defined by $\mathrm{MOD}p(x) = 0 \iff x_1 + \ldots + x_n = 0 \mod p$, and for *the recursive majority function* $\mathrm{RecMaj}_n : \{0,1\}^n \rightarrow \{0,1\}$, defined by

$$\mathrm{RecMaj}_n(x_1, \ldots, x_n) = \mathrm{Maj}_3(\mathrm{RecMaj}_{\frac{n}{3}}(x_1, \ldots, x_{\frac{n}{3}}),$$
$$\mathrm{RecMaj}_{\frac{n}{3}}(x_{\frac{n}{3}+1}, \ldots, x_{\frac{2n}{3}}),$$
$$\mathrm{RecMaj}_{\frac{n}{3}}(x_{\frac{2n}{3}+1}, \ldots, x_n)),$$

where $\mathrm{Maj}_3 : \{0,1\}^3 \rightarrow \{0,1\}$ is majority of three bits, and n is a power of three. This does not immediately imply any bounds for De Morgan formulas— the correspondence between formulas and protocols works only for the classical model. On the other hand, better understanding of the half-duplex model helps to prove bounds in the classical case as it was done in [12].

We start with lower bounds for MODp functions. In the classical case, a lower bound on the communication complexity of the Karchmer-Wigderson game for some function f corresponds to a lower bound on De Morgan formula depth complexity of f. For MOD2, the parity function, we have the tight bound $2 \log n$: the lower bound is due to the famous work of Khrapchenko [9], and the upper bound is straightforward by implementing binary search. The method of Khrapchenko can also be used to prove $2 \log n - O(1)$ lower bounds for MODp for arbitrary p. In [6], the authors proved $2 \log n$ lower bound for $\mathrm{KW}_{\mathrm{MOD2}_n}$ in the half-duplex model with adversary. We use the same ideas to prove general lower bounds for MODp in all the half-duplex models.

Theorem 4. *For any $p \geq 2$, $\mathrm{D}_s^{hd}(\mathrm{KW}_{\mathrm{MOD}p}) > 1.12 \log n$, $\mathrm{D}_0^{hd}(\mathrm{KW}_{\mathrm{MOD}p}) > 1.62 \log n$, $\mathrm{D}_a^{hd}(\mathrm{KW}_{\mathrm{MOD}p}) \geq 2 \log n - O(1)$.*

We prove this theorem using the information-theoretic approach from [6]. For basic definitions of information theory, we refer to [3]. We show that there is a probability distribution over the inputs of Alice and Bob, such that at the beginning of the communication each player has uncertainty roughly $\log n$ bits about the input of the other player. At the end of the communication (for this specific distribution) each player necessarily knows the input of the other player. This means that during the protocol each player learns roughly $\log n$ bits of information. For the classical communication model, this would be enough to show the $2 \log n$ lower bound, because in every round one of the players learns at most one bit of information and the other learns nothing, so there must be at least $2 \log n$ rounds. In the half-duplex communication, the situation is more complicated—in silent rounds both players might learn some information. To estimate the amount of information the players learn during half-duplex communication, we use the upper bounds proved in [6].

Proof. Let $(\mathcal{X}, \mathcal{Y})$ be a pair of jointly distributed random variables where $\mathcal{X}$ is uniformly distributed on the set $\{x \in \{0,1\}^n \mid \mathrm{MOD}p(x) = 0, n/4 < \|x\|_1 < 3n/4\}$, that corresponds to Alice's inputs of Hamming weight between $n/4$ and $3n/4$, and $\mathcal{Y}$ is obtained from $\mathcal{X}$ by flipping one 0 bit uniformly at random. Thus, $H(\mathcal{Y} \mid \mathcal{X}) \geq \log(n/4)$ and $H(\mathcal{X} \mid \mathcal{Y}) \geq \log(n/4)$. Before any communication takes place $H(\mathcal{Y} \mid \mathcal{X}) + H(\mathcal{X} \mid \mathcal{Y}) \geq 2 \log n - O(1)$. Given inputs from the distribution $(\mathcal{X}, \mathcal{Y})$ the players have to find the unique bit of difference.

Let $\mathcal{P}$ be a protocol for MODp. W.l.o.g., we assume that all the leaves of $\mathcal{P}$ are on the same depth. For any natural k, let Π_A^k and Π_B^k be the marginal distributions over Alice's and Bob's partial transcripts after running $\mathcal{P}$ for k rounds induced by $(\mathcal{X}, \mathcal{Y})$. If the protocol $\mathcal{P}$ has depth d, then $H(\mathcal{Y} \mid \mathcal{X}, \Pi_A^d) + H(\mathcal{X} \mid \mathcal{Y}, \Pi_B^d) = 0$. This means that the players have to learn $2 \log n - O(1)$ bits.

Now we apply upper bounds on the amount of information that can be learned in one round. For the half-duplex model with silence, for any distribution on the inputs the players together can learn at most 1.67 bits per round [5, Theorem 18], so we get $\mathrm{D}_s^{hd}(\mathrm{KW_{MOD}}_p) > (2 \log n)/1.67 > 1.12 \log n$. For the half-duplex model with zero, for any distribution on the inputs the players can learn at most 1.234 bits per round [5, Theorem 21], hence using the same reasoning, $\mathrm{D}_0^{hd}(\mathrm{KW_{MOD}}_p) > (2 \log n)/1.234 > 1.62 \log n$. Finally, for the half-duplex model with adversary, for any distribution on the inputs the players can learn at most one bit per round [5, Theorem 24], that concludes the proof. □

Now we proceed to the upper bounds. First, we will consider a few special cases of the counting function, and then we will prove the general upper bound for arbitrary $p \geq 7$. The following two theorems establish upper bounds for MOD2 in the half-duplex models with silence and with zero. Both protocols use the idea of ternary search but in a little bit different manner.

Theorem 5. $\mathrm{D}_s^{hd}(\mathrm{KW_{MOD2}}) \leq 2 \log_3 n + O(1) < 1.262 \log n$.

Proof. Alice and Bob split their input strings into three equal parts and compute MOD2 for the resulting substrings. There are four possible cases for each player.

- Parities of Alice's substrings: 1) 000; 2) 011; 3) 101; 4) 110.
- Parities of Bob's substrings: 1) 111; 2) 100; 3) 010; 4) 001.

Using two rounds of communication the players determine which pair of corresponding substrings have different parities, and then repeat the protocol recursively for these substrings of size $n/3$. That gives the desired bound, $\mathrm{D}_s^{hd}(\mathrm{MOD2}) \leq 2 \log_3 n + O(1)$. These two rounds are described in Table 3.

Table 3. The half-duplex protocol for KW_{MOD2} with silence.

	Round 1				Round 2	
Case	Alice	Bob		Case	Alice	Bob
1	receive	receive		1	send 0	send 1
2	receive	receive		2	send 1	send 0
3	send 0	send 1		3	receive	receive
4	send 1	send 0		4	receive	receive

If one of two rounds was silent, i.e., the players received the symbol of silence, then they know that the first substrings have different parities. Otherwise, if none of the rounds was silent, then there were no wasted rounds (if the first was wasted, then the second was necessarily silent, and vice versa, if the second was wasted, then the first was silent). In this case, the players know that they have the same parity of the first substrings, and each player have sent one bit that was received by the other player. Moreover, these bits correspond to the parities of the second substrings. So, both Alice and Bob know the parities of the first two substrings of the other player's input, hence both players know the parities of all the substrings. □

Theorem 6. $D_0^{hd}(KW_{MOD2}) \leq 3\log_3 n + O(1) < 1.893\log n$.

Proof. Similarly to the proof of Theorem 5, Alice and Bob split their input strings into three equal parts and compute MOD2 for all the resulting substrings. There are the same four possible cases for each player as in the proof of Theorem 5. The players use three rounds to determine which pair of corresponding substrings have different parities, and then repeat the protocol recursively for these substrings of size $n/3$. That gives the desired bound $D_0^{hd}(MOD2) \leq 3\log_3 n + O(1)$.

In the first round, Alice and Bob send 1 if they both have Cases 1, otherwise they receive.

- If the first round was silent then they both know that none of them has Case 1. In the second round, Alice sends 1 if her first substring is even (Case 2), otherwise she receives. Bob does the reverse, he sends 1 if his first substring is odd (Case 2), otherwise he receives. The third round is similar, Alice and Bob send 1 in their Cases 3, otherwise they receive.
- If at least one of them sent 1 in the first round, then again both know about it. Alice sends 1 if her first substring is odd, otherwise she receives. Bob does the reverse, he sends 1 if his first substring is even, otherwise he receives. In the third round, the players do the same for the second substrings.

If the second or the third rounds were silent, then, respectively, the first or the second substrings have different parities. Otherwise, the third substrings have different parities. □

The next theorem considers the MOD3 function. In the classical case, the best known upper bound for it is $2.881 \log n$ [2]. We show a simple upper bound based on the idea of ternary search.

Theorem 7. $D_s^{hd}(\mathrm{KW}_{\mathrm{MOD3}}) \leq 3 \log_3 n + O(1) \leq 1.893 \log n$.

Next, we consider the MOD5 function. The best known upper bound in the classical case is $3.475 \log n$ [2]. For this and for all the following upper bounds for MODp functions, we adapt the prefix code technique used in [2].

Theorem 8. $D_s^{hd}(\mathrm{KW}_{\mathrm{MOD5}}) \leq 2.46 \log n$.

Proof. Alice and Bob divide their inputs into two parts: the first of length εn, and the second of length $(1-\varepsilon)n$, and compute *the remainder* for every resulting substring, that is the number of ones modulo 5. During the protocol the players will narrow the search area from the current string to one of its substrings repeatedly. At the beginning of the communication, Alice sends the remainder of her first substring to Bob. Then the players speak in turns, starting with Bob, sending each other pairs (r, b), where r is a remainder and b is a bit flag. Every turn, the speaking player does the following.

- (except for the very first turn) If $b = 0$ in the previous message then the player narrows the search area to the first substring, otherwise the player narrows the search area to the second substring. The player subdivides the new search area into two parts in proportion $\varepsilon : (1 - \varepsilon)$.
- The player choose one of the substrings and narrows the search area to it. If the remainder r received in the previous message is equal to the remainder of the first substring, then the player chooses the second substring, otherwise the player chooses the first one. The player subdivides the new search area into two parts in proportion $\varepsilon : (1 - \varepsilon)$.
- The player sends message (r, b), where r is the remainder of the first substring of the current search area, and b is set to 1 if and only if the second substring was chosen in the previous step.

It remains for us to discuss, how exactly the pair (r, b) pair is encoded. The encoding is the key ingredient of this technique. We are going to use the following prefix-free code in ternary alphabet: $(0,0), \ldots, (0,4)$ are encoded with 00, 01, 0s, 10, 11, and $(1,0), \ldots, (1,4)$ are encoded with s00, s01, s0s, s10, s11, respectively. Note that "s" stands for "silence". The code is chosen such that every message with $b = 0$ has encoding of length 2, and every message with $b = 1$ has encoding of length 3. To estimate the number of rounds, we need to solve the following system of recurrent relations, where $T(n)$ stands for the number of rounds.

$$\begin{cases} T(n) = 2 + T(\varepsilon n) \\ T(n) = 3 + T((1 - \varepsilon)n) \end{cases} \implies \begin{cases} T(n) = 2 \log_{\frac{1}{\varepsilon}} n \\ T(n) = 3 \log_{\frac{1}{1-\varepsilon}} n \end{cases}$$

From $\frac{2}{3} = \frac{\log \varepsilon}{\log(1-\varepsilon)}$ we get $\varepsilon < 0.57$, and hence $T(n) < 2.466 \log n$. $\qquad \square$

Following [2], we use the same methods for the MOD11 function with the best known upper bound is $4.93 \log n$ in the classical case.

Theorem 9. $D_s^{hd}(\mathrm{KW}_{\mathrm{MOD11}}) \leq 3.48 \log n$.

To generalize the previous results, we prove the following upper bound for MODp for arbitrary $p \geq 7$.

Theorem 10. *For all* $p \geq 7$, $D_s^{hd}(\mathrm{KW}_{\mathrm{MOD}p}) \leq 1.16 \lceil 1 + \log_3 \frac{p}{2} \rceil \cdot \log n$.

Note that this upper bound is not useful for some p, e.g., for $p \in \{7, 8, 9\}$ this bound gives $3.48 \log n$, while regular binary requires only $3 \log n$. Moreover, in the classical case, the corresponding bound [2] is surpassed by the upper bound on all symmetric functions [1] starting with some p. We expect that the similar happens in the half-duplex model with silence.

To conclude this series of results, we consider the recursive majority function RecMaj. In the classical case, its communication complexity is known to be bounded between $2 \log_3 n$ and $3 \log_3 n$ [11]. The structure of this function is ideal for implementing a ternary search. So, given the fact that the half-duplex model with silence allows the players to send messages encoded in ternary, the following theorem is straightforward.

Theorem 11. $D_s^{hd}(\mathrm{KW}_{\mathrm{RecMaj}}) \leq 2 \log_3 n$.

The same upper bound holds in the half-duplex model with zero.

Theorem 12. $D_0^{hd}(\mathrm{KW}_{\mathrm{RecMaj}}) \leq 2 \log_3 n$.

5   Non-deterministic Half-Duplex Complexity

The standard definition of the non-deterministic communication complexity does not involve any communication at all, so it is applicable to the half-duplex model without any changes. Let X and Y be non-empty finite sets.

Definition 1. *We say that a function* $f : X \times Y \to \{0,1\}$ *has non-deterministic communication protocol of complexity d if there are two functions* $A : X \times \{0,1\}^d \to \{0,1\}$ *and* $B : Y \times \{0,1\}^d \to \{0,1\}$, *such that*

- $\forall (x,y) \in f^{-1}(1)\ \exists w \in \{0,1\}^d : A(x,w) = B(y,w) = 1$,
- $\forall (x,y) \in f^{-1}(0)\ \forall w \in \{0,1\}^d : A(x,w) \neq 1 \lor B(y,w) \neq 1$.

The non-deterministic communication complexity *of* f, *denoted* $N(f)$, *is the minimal complexity of a non-deterministic communication protocol for* f.

There is also an alternative definition of the non-deterministic communication complexity that uses communication between players [12].

Definition 2. *We say that a function* $f : X \times Y \to \{0,1\}$ *has privately non-deterministic communication protocol of complexity d if there is a function* $\hat{f} : (X \times \{0,1\}^d) \times (Y \times \{0,1\}^d) \to \{0,1\}$ *of (deterministic) communication complexity at most d such that*

- $\forall (x, y) \in f^{-1}(1) \; \exists w_x, w_y \in \{0, 1\}^d : \hat{f}((x, w_x), (y, w_y)) = 1,$
- $\forall (x, y) \in f^{-1}(0) \; \forall w_x, w_y \in \{0, 1\}^d : \hat{f}((x, w_x), (y, w_y)) = 0.$

The privately non-deterministic communication complexity of f *is the minimal depth of a privately non-deterministic communication protocol for f.*

This alternative definition of non-deterministic communication uses private witnesses instead of a public one, and hence the players need to communicate. In the classical case, Definition 1 and Definition 2 are equivalent (see [12] for more details). We think that this way of defining it is the right way to define *the non-deterministic half-duplex communication complexity*. So, we define it by replacing the communication model in Definition 2 with the half-duplex models. Let $N_s^{hd}(f)$, $N_0^{hd}(f)$, and $N_a^{hd}(f)$ denotes *the non-deterministic half-duplex communication complexity of f with silence, with zero, and with adversary*, respectively. We are going to prove bounds that connect the classical non-deterministic communication complexity with the non-deterministic half-duplex communication complexity.

Let's start with the lower bounds.

Theorem 13. *For any function $f : X \times Y \rightarrow \{0, 1\}$, $N_s^{hd}(f) \geq N(f)/\log 5$, $N_0^{hd}(f) \geq N(f)/\log 3$, $N_a^{hd}(f) \geq N(f)/\log 3$.*

Proof. In the half-duplex model with silence, the protocol is a pair of trees of arity 5. The following (classical) non-deterministic protocol can simulate any non-deterministic half-duplex protocol Π with silence. Alice and Bob guess a root-to-leaf path π_A in the tree of Π corresponding to Alice. Alice checks that this transcript is a valid transcript for her input. Bob checks that there exists a root-to-leaf path π_B in his tree that is a valid transcript for his input, and at the same time π_B matches π_A (in all rounds where Alice receives in π_A, Bob in π_B does the corresponding action, and in all rounds where Alice sends, Bob receives the corresponding bit or sends some bit). If Π has complexity d, then the length of the description of π_A is $\lceil d \cdot \log 5 \rceil$. This gives us the first lower bound.

Similarly, in the half-duplex model with zero, the protocol is a pair of trees of arity 3. The same reasoning shows that for any non-deterministic half-duplex protocol Π with zero of complexity d, there exists a (classical) non-deterministic protocol of complexity $\lceil d \cdot \log 3 \rceil$.

In the half-duplex model with adversary, we can consider only such transcripts where the players always receive zeroes in silent rounds. Thus, the lower bound for the half-duplex model with zero applies. □

The upper bounds are based on the upper bounds for the equality function. We don not know any non-trivial upper bounds for the equality in the half-duplex model with adversary, so we prove upper bounds for two other models only.

Theorem 14. *For any function $f : X \times Y \to \{0,1\}$,*

$$\mathrm{N}_s^{hd}(f) \le \mathrm{N}(f)/\log 5 + O(\log \mathrm{N}(f)), \quad \mathrm{N}_0^{hd}(f) \le \mathrm{N}(f)/\log 3 + O(\log \mathrm{N}(f)).$$

Proof. The proof is very straightforward. For any (classical) non-deterministic protocol Π, Alice and Bob can privately guess a public witness w and then check that they both guessed the same witness. This requires solving the equality on strings of length $\mathrm{N}(f)$. Together with the upper bounds on the equality [5, Theorems 15 and 19], this gives us the desired bounds.   □

6   Open Problems

In addition to the open questions in [6], we state the following open problems.

1. Prove new lower bound for disjointness using information-theoretic methods.
2. Prove an upper bound for the KW game for MOD_p in the model with zero.
3. Prove better upper bound for RecMaj in the model with silence.

References

1. Brodal, G.S., Husfeldt, T.: A communication complexity proof that symmetric functions have logarithmic depth. BRICS (1996). https://www.brics.dk/RS/96/1/BRICS-RS-96-1.pdf
2. Chin, A.: On the depth complexity of the counting functions. Inf. Process. Lett. **35**(6), 325–328 (1990). https://doi.org/10.1016/0020-0190(90)90036-W
3. Cover, T.M., Thomas, J.A.: Elements of Information Theory. Wiley-Interscience, New York, USA (2006)
4. Dementiev, Y., Ignatiev, A., Sidelnik, V., Smal, A., Ushakov, M.: New bounds on the half-duplex communication complexity. Electron. Colloquium Comput. Complex. **27**, 117 (2020). https://eccc.weizmann.ac.il/report/2020/117
5. Hoover, K., Impagliazzo, R., Mihajlin, I., Smal, A.: Half-duplex communication complexity. Electron. Colloquium Comput. Complex. **25**, 89 (2018). https://eccc.weizmann.ac.il/report/2018/089
6. Hoover, K., Impagliazzo, R., Mihajlin, I., Smal, A.V.: Half-duplex communication complexity. In: 29th International Symposium on Algorithms and Computation, ISAAC 2018. LIPIcs, vol. 123, pp. 10:1–10:12 (2018). https://doi.org/10.4230/LIPIcs.ISAAC.2018.10
7. Karchmer, M., Raz, R., Wigderson, A.: Super-logarithmic depth lower bounds via the direct sum in communication complexity. Comput. Complex. **5**(3/4), 191–204 (1995). https://doi.org/10.1007/BF01206317
8. Karchmer, M., Wigderson, A.: Monotone circuits for connectivity require super-logarithmic depth. In: Proceedings of the 20th Annual ACM Symposium on Theory of Computing, pp. 539–550 (1988). https://doi.org/10.1145/62212.62265
9. Khrapchenko, V.: Complexity of the realization of a linear function in the class of II-circuits. Math. Notes Acad. Sci. USSR **9**(1), 21–23 (1971)
10. Kushilevitz, E., Nisan, N.: Communication Complexity. Cambridge University Press, Cambridge (1997)

11. Laplante, S., Lee, T., Szegedy, M.: The quantum adversary method and classical formula size lower bounds. In: 20th Annual IEEE Conference on Computational Complexity (CCC 2005), pp. 76–90 (2005). https://doi.org/10.1109/CCC.2005.29
12. Mihajlin, I., Smal, A.: Toward better depth lower bounds: the XOR-KRW conjecture. Electron. Colloquium Comput. Complex. **27**, 116 (2020), https://eccc.weizmann.ac.il/report/2020/116
13. Yao, A.C.C.: Some complexity questions related to distributive computing(preliminary report). In: Proceedings of the 11h Annual ACM Symposium on Theory of Computing, pp. 209–213 (1979). https://doi.org/10.1145/800135.804414

Novel Results on the Number of Runs of the Burrows-Wheeler-Transform

Sara Giuliani[1]([⊠]), Shunsuke Inenaga[2,3], Zsuzsanna Lipták[1], Nicola Prezza[4],
Marinella Sciortino[5], and Anna Toffanello[1]

[1] Dipartimento di Informatica, University of Verona, Verona, Italy
{sara.giuliani_01,zsuzsanna.liptak}@univr.it,
anna.toffanello@studenti.univr.it
[2] Department of Informatics, Kyushu University, Fukuoka, Japan
inenaga@inf.kyushu-u.ac.jp
[3] PRESTO, Japan Science and Technology Agency, Kawaguchi, Japan
[4] Department of Business and Management, LUISS University, Rome, Italy
nprezza@luiss.it
[5] Dipartimento di Matematica e Informatica, University of Palermo, Palermo, Italy
marinella.sciortino@unipa.it

Abstract. The Burrows-Wheeler-Transform (BWT), a reversible string transformation, is one of the fundamental components of many current data structures in string processing. It is central in data compression, as well as in efficient query algorithms for sequence data, such as webpages, genomic and other biological sequences, or indeed any textual data. The BWT lends itself well to compression because its number of equal-letter-runs (usually referred to as r) is often considerably lower than that of the original string; in particular, it is well suited for strings with many repeated factors. In fact, much attention has been paid to the r parameter as measure of repetitiveness, especially to evaluate the performance in terms of both space and time of compressed indexing data structures.

In this paper, we investigate $\rho(v)$, the ratio of r and of the number of runs of the BWT of the reverse of v. Kempa and Kociumaka [FOCS 2020] gave the first non-trivial upper bound as $\rho(v) = O(\log^2(n))$, for any string v of length n. However, nothing is known about the tightness of this upper bound. We present infinite families of binary strings for which $\rho(v) = \Theta(\log n)$ holds, thus giving the first non-trivial lower bound on $\rho(n)$, the maximum over all strings of length n.

Our results suggest that r is not an ideal measure of the repetitiveness of the string, since the number of repeated factors is invariant between the string and its reverse. We believe that there is a more intricate relationship between the number of runs of the BWT and the string's combinatorial properties.

Keywords: Burrows-Wheeler-Transform · Compressed data structures · String indexing · Repetitiveness · Combinatorics on words

© Springer Nature Switzerland AG 2021
T. Bureš et al. (Eds.): SOFSEM 2021, LNCS 12607, pp. 249–262, 2021.
https://doi.org/10.1007/978-3-030-67731-2_18

1   Introduction

Since its introduction in 1994 by Michael Burrows and David J. Wheeler, the Burrows-Wheeler Transform (BWT) [6] has played a fundamental role in lossless data compression and string-processing algorithms. The BWT of a word w can be obtained by concatenating the last characters of the lexicographically-sorted conjugates (that is, rotations) of w. Among its many fundamental properties, this permutation turns out to be invertible and more compressible than the original word w. The latter property follows from the fact that sorting the conjugates of w has the effect of clustering together repeated factors; as a consequence, characters preceding those repetitions are clustered together in the BWT, and thus repetitions in w tend to generate long runs of equal characters in its BWT. The more repetitive w, the lower the number r of such runs. This fact motivated recent research on data structures whose size is bounded as a function of r: the most prominent example in this direction, the *r-index* [13], is a fully-compressed index of size $\mathcal{O}(r)$ able to locate factor occurrences in log-logarithmic time each. Other examples of recent algorithms working in runs-bounded space include index construction [14] and data compression in small working space [1,24,25].

As it turns out, r is a member of a much larger family of word-repetitiveness measures that have lately generated much interest in the research community. Examples of those measures include (but are not limited to) the number z of factors in the LZ77 factorization [21], the number g of rules in the smallest context-free grammar generating the word [17], the size b of the smallest bidirectional macro scheme [26], and the size e of the CDAWG [4]. More recently, it was shown that all those compressors are particular cases of a combinatorial object named *string attractor* [16] whose size γ lower-bounds all measures r, z, g, b, and e. In turn, in [19] it was shown that γ is lower-bounded by another measure, δ, which is linked to factor complexity (that is, to the number of distinct factors of each length) and better captures the word's repetitiveness. On the upper-bound side, the papers [16,19] provided approximation ratios of all measures but r with respect to γ. Finding an upper-bound for r remained an open problem until the recent work of Kempa and Kociumaka [15], who showed that, for any word of length n, $r = \mathcal{O}(\delta \log^2 n)$ (which in turn implies $r = \mathcal{O}(\gamma \log^2 n)$). As stated explicitly in [15], this implies the first upper bound on the ratio ρ between r and the number of runs in the BWT of the reverse of the word, namely $\rho = \mathcal{O}(\log^2 n)$.

This leaves open the interesting question of whether this bound is tight. In this paper, we give a first answer to this question by exhibiting an infinite family of binary words whose members satisfy $\rho = \Theta(\log n)$. This contrasts the experimental observation made in [2,25] that ρ appears to be constant on real repetitive text collections, and shows that r is not a strong repetitiveness measure since—unlike b, g, γ, and δ—it is not invariant under reversal.

An added value of the proof we present lies in a surprising insight into the exact structure of the BWT-matrix of the words we study: right-extensions of Fibonacci words. This insight allows us to further extend the method to a much larger family of words, giving the number of runs of the BWT for both the word and its reverse, for right-extensions of all standard words. As it turns out, the words we obtain from Fibonacci words are maximal with respect to ρ within this class. At the same time, we have verified experimentally that these words are not maximal among all words of the same length. This leaves a gap on the maximum on ρ, taken over all words of length n, between our lower bound $\Omega(\log n)$ and the upper bound of $\mathcal{O}(\log^2 n)$ of [15].

As a matter of fact, the reverse of the Fibonacci extensions allow us to prove an even more surprising result: a single character extension can increase r by a *multiplicative* factor $\Theta(\log n)$. This result is the equivalent of the "one-bit catastrophe" exhibited by Lagarde and Perifel [20] for Lempel-Ziv '78: using these compression schemes, the compression ratio of the word can change dramatically if just one bit is prepended to the input.

2   Basics

Let $\Sigma = \{a, b\}$, with $a < b$. A *binary word* (or *string*) w is a finite sequence of *characters* (or *letters*) from Σ. We denote the ith character of w by $w[i]$ and index words from 1. We denote by $|w|$ the length of w, and by $|w|_a$ resp. $|w|_b$ the number of characters a resp. b in w. The empty word ϵ is the unique word of length 0. The set of words over Σ is denoted Σ^*. We write $w^{\text{rev}} = w[n] \cdots w[1]$ for the *reverse* of a word w of length n. The word w' is a *conjugate* of the word w if $w' = w[i] \cdots w[n]w[1] \cdots w[i-1] =: \text{conj}_i(w)$ for some $i = 1, \ldots, n$ (also called the ith *rotation* of w).

If $w = uxv$, for some words $u, x, v \in \Sigma^*$, then u is called a *prefix*, v a *suffix*, and x a *factor* of w. A prefix (suffix, factor) u of w is called *proper* if $u \neq w$. A word u is a *circular factor* of w if it is the prefix of some conjugate of w. A circular factor u is called *left-special* if both au and bu occur as circular factors. For an integer $k \geq 1$, $u^k = u \cdots u$ is the kth power of u. A word w is called *primitive* if $w = u^k$ implies $k = 1$. A word w is primitive if and only if it has exactly $|w|$ distinct conjugates.

For two words v, w, the *longest common prefix* $lcp(v, w)$ is defined as the maximum length word u such that u is a prefix both of v and of w. The *lexicographic order* on Σ^* is defined by: $v < w$ if either v is a proper prefix of w, or ua is a prefix of v and ub is a prefix of w, where $u = lcp(v, w)$. A *Lyndon word* is a primitive word which is lexicographically smaller than all of its conjugates. To simplify the discussion, we will assume from now on that w is primitive (but everything can be extended also to non-primitive words).

The *Burrows-Wheeler-Transform* (BWT) [6] of a word w of length n is a permutation of the characters of w, defined as the sequence of final characters of the lexicographically ordered set of conjugates of w. More precisely, let the *BW-array* be an array of size n defined as: $BW[i] = k$ if $\text{conj}_k(w)$ is the ith conjugate of w in lexicographic order.[1] Then $bwt(w)[i] = w[BW[i] - 1]$, where we set $w[0] = w[n]$. Another way to visualize the BWT is via an $(n \times n)$-matrix containing the lexicographically sorted conjugates of w: the BWT of w equals

---

[1] Note that this is in general not the same as the suffix array SA, since here we have the conjugates and not the suffixes.

the last column of this matrix, read from top to bottom, see Fig. 1. By definition, $\text{bwt}(w) = \text{bwt}(w')$ if and only if w and w' are conjugates.

For a word w, let $\text{runs}(w)$ denote the number of maximal equal-letter runs of w, and $r(w) = \text{runs}(\text{bwt}(w))$. We are now ready for our main definition:

Definition 1. Let $w \in \{a, b\}^*$. We define the *runs-ratio* $\rho(w)$ as

$$\rho(w) = \max\left(\frac{\text{runs}(\text{bwt}(w))}{\text{runs}(\text{bwt}(w^{\text{rev}}))}, \frac{\text{runs}(\text{bwt}(w^{\text{rev}}))}{\text{runs}(\text{bwt}(w))}\right) = \max\left(\frac{r(w)}{r(w^{\text{rev}})}, \frac{r(w^{\text{rev}})}{r(w)}\right),$$

and $\rho(n) = \max\{\rho(w) : |w| = n\}$.

Note that $\rho(w) \geq 1$ holds by definition. Since $r(w) = r(w^{\text{rev}})$ for all w with $|w| \leq 6$, we have $\rho(n) = 1$ for $n < 7$. In Table 1, we give the values of $\rho(n)$ for $n = 7, \ldots, 30$ (computed with a computer program):

Table 1. The values of $\rho(n)$ for $n = 7, \ldots, 30$.

n	7	8	9	10	11	12	13	14	15	16	17	18	19	20	21	22	23	24	25	26	27	28	29	30
$\rho(n)$	1.5	1.5	2	2	2	2	2	2	2	2	2.5	2.5	2.5	2.5	3	2.5	3	3	2.67	3	3	3	3	3

We introduce *standard words* next, following [11]. Given an infinite sequence of integers $(d_0, d_1, d_2, \ldots)$, with $d_0 \geq 0, d_i > 0$ for all $i > 0$, called a *directive sequence*, define a sequence of words $(s_i)_{i \geq 0}$ of increasing length as follows: $s_0 = b, s_1 = a, s_{i+1} = s_i^{d_{i-1}} s_{i-1}$, for $i \geq 1$. The index i is referred to as the *order* of s_i. The best known example is the sequence of *Fibonacci words*, which are given by the directive sequence $(1, 1, 1, \ldots)$, and of which the first few elements are as follows:

$s_0 = b, s_1 = a, s_2 = ab, s_3 = aba, s_4 = abaab, s_5 = abaababa, s_6 = abaababaabaab,$
$s_7 = abaababaabaababaababa, s_8 = abaababaabaababaabaababaabaababaabaab, \ldots$

Note that $|s_i| = F_i$, where F_i is the Fibonacci sequence, defined by $F_0 = F_1 = 1$ and $F_{i+1} = F_i + F_{i-1}$. Moreover, $|s_i|_a = F_{i-1}$ and $|s_i|_b = F_{i-2}$, for $i \geq 2$.

Standard words are used for the construction of infinite Sturmian words, in the sense that every characteristic Sturmian word is the limit of a sequence of standard words (cf. Chapter 2 of [22]). These words have many interesting combinatorial properties and appear as extreme case in a great range of contexts [7,8,10,12,18]. A fundamental result in connection with the BWT is the following: $\text{bwt}(w) = b^q a^p$ with $\gcd(q, p) = 1$ if and only if w is a conjugate of a standard word [23].

3   Fibonacci-Plus Words Have $\rho = \Theta(\log n)$

Since for a standard word s, s^{rev} is a conjugate, we have $\rho(s) = 1$ for all standard words s. We will show in this section that adding just one character at the end of the word suffices to increase ρ from 1 to logarithmic in the length of the word.

Definition 2. A word v is called *Fibonacci-plus* if it is either of the form sb, where s is a Fibonacci word of even order $2k$, $k \geq 2$, or of the form sa, where s is a Fibonacci word of odd order $2k + 1$, $k \geq 2$. In the first case, v is *of even order*, otherwise *of odd order*.

The aim of this section is to prove the following theorem:

Theorem 1. *Let v be a Fibonacci-plus word, and let $|v| = n$. Then $\rho(v) = \Theta(\log n)$.*

We will prove the theorem by showing that, for a Fibonacci-plus word v, $r(v) = 4$ (Proposition 2) and $r(v^{\text{rev}})$ is linear in the order of the word itself (Proposition 3). The statement will then follow by an argument on the length of v.

Fibonacci words have very well-known structural and combinatorial properties [9], some of them can be deduced from more general properties that hold true for all standard words (see [3,5,11,12]). In the next proposition we summarize some of these properties, which will be useful in the following.

Proposition 1 (Some known properties of the Fibonacci words). *Let s_i be the Fibonacci word of order $i \geq 0$. The following properties hold:*

1. *for all $k \geq 1$, $s_{2k} = x_{2k}ab$ and $s_{2k+1} = x_{2k+1}ba$, where x_{2k} and x_{2k+1} are palindromes ($x_2 = \epsilon$).*
2. *for all $k \geq 2$,*
   - *$s_{2k} = x_{2k-1}bax_{2k-2}ab = x_{2k-2}abx_{2k-1}ab$*
   - *$s_{2k+1} = x_{2k}abx_{2k-1}ba = x_{2k-1}bax_{2k}ba$.*
3. *for all $i \geq 2$, ax_ib is a Lyndon word, where x_i is the palindrome from 1.*
4. *for all circular factors y, z of s_i with $|y| = |z|$, and for each $c \in \Sigma$, one has that $||y|_c - |z|_c| \leq 1$ (Balancedness Property).*

Example 1. Let us consider $s_8 = abaababaabaababaabaabababaabaabababaabaab$ the Fibonacci word of order 8 and length $F_8 = 34$.

One can verify that the prefix $x_8 = abaababaabaababaabaababaabaababaaba$ is a palindrome. Moreover $x_8 = x_7bax_6 = x_6abx_7$, where $x_7 = abaababaabaababaaba$ and $x_6 = abaababaaba$.

Proposition 2. *Let v be a Fibonacci-plus word. Then $r(v) = 4$. In particular,*

1. *if $v = s_{2k}b$, then $bwt(v) = b^{F_{2k}-2}a^{F_{2k-1}-1}ba$, and*
2. *if $v = s_{2k+1}a$, then $bwt(v) = bab^{F_{2k-1}-1}a^{F_{2k}}$.*

Proof. We give the proof for even order only. The proof for odd order is analogous.

Let us write $v = sb$, with $s = s_{2k}$, and $n = |v|$. Since Fibonacci words are standard words, it follows that $bwt(s) = b^{F_{2k-2}}a^{F_{2k-1}}$ (see Sect. 2). By Proposition 1, part 1, s can be written as $s = xab$ for a palindrome x; moreover, it follows from the specific form of x (Proposition 1, part 2) that both xab

and xba are conjugates. It is further known that the lexicographically smallest conjugate is axb and the largest is bxa [5,23].

Now consider the conjugates of $v = sb$. We will show that the conjugates of s retain their relative order after the insertion of the new b, i.e. that if $\mathrm{conj}_i(s) < \mathrm{conj}_j(s)$ then also $\mathrm{conj}_i(v) < \mathrm{conj}_j(v)$. We further show that the new conjugate $\mathrm{conj}_n(v)$ is the penultimate one in the lexicographic order of the conjugates of v. Since $\mathrm{conj}_n(v)$ ends in b, while the other conjugates $\mathrm{conj}_i(v)$ end in the same character as $\mathrm{conj}_i(s)$, for $i = 1, \ldots, n-1$, the claim follows.

Let $\mathrm{conj}_i(s) < \mathrm{conj}_j(s)$ be lexicographically consecutive conjugates of s. If $i < j$, then the new b appears earlier in $\mathrm{conj}_j(s)$ than in $\mathrm{conj}_i(s)$, therefore $\mathrm{conj}_i(v) < \mathrm{conj}_j(v)$ clearly holds. Now let $i > j$. It is known [5] that two lexicographically consecutive conjugates of s have the form $uabu'$ and $ubau'$, where $u'u = x$ is the palindrome from Proposition 1, part 2. From $s_{2k} = x_{2k-1}bax_{2k-2}ab = x_{2k-2}abx_{2k-1}ab$, it follows that $x_{2k} = x_{2k-1}bax_{2k-2} = x_{2k-2}abx_{2k-1}$, and we deduce that $x = x_{2k}$ has exactly two occurrences in s as a circular factor. Therefore, $\mathrm{conj}_i(v) = uabbu'$, and the new b appears in $\mathrm{conj}_j(v)$ within the suffix u'. This implies $u = lcp(\mathrm{conj}_i(v), \mathrm{conj}_j(v))$, and thus $\mathrm{conj}_i(v) < \mathrm{conj}_j(v)$.

Now note that $\mathrm{conj}_n(v) = \mathrm{conj}_{n-1}(s)b = bxab$. We know that $\mathrm{conj}_{n-1}(s) = bxa$ is the lexicographically largest conjugate of s; let $\mathrm{conj}_i(s)$ be the one immediately preceding it lexicographically. Then, for some u, u', we have $\mathrm{conj}_i(s) = uabu'$ and $\mathrm{conj}_{n-1}(s) = ubau'$, and therefore $\mathrm{conj}_i(v) = uabbu' < ubau'b = \mathrm{conj}_n(v)$. On the other hand, $\mathrm{conj}_n(v) < \mathrm{conj}_{n-1}(v) = bbxa$.

This completes the proof.

The next proposition gives the form of the BWT of the reverse.

Proposition 3. *Let v be a Fibonacci-plus word. Then $r(v^{rev}) = 2k$. In particular,*

1. *if v is of even order, i.e. $v = s_{2k}b$ for some $k \geq 1$, then $bwt(v^{rev}) = b^{F_{2k-2}-k+1}a^{F_0}ba^{F_2}ba^{F_4}b \cdots a^{F_{2k-4}}bba^{F_{2k-2}}$,*

2. *if v is of odd order, i.e. $v = s_{2k+1}a$ for some $k \geq 1$, then $bwt(v^{rev}) = b^{F_{2k-2}}aab^{F_{2k-4}}ab^{F_{2k-6}}a \cdots b^{F_2}ab^{F_0}a^{F_{2k}-k+1}$.*

Example 2. In Fig. 1 we display the BWT-matrices of the Fibonacci-plus word $v = s_8b$ of length 35 and of its reverse.

The rest of this section is devoted to the proof of Proposition 3. We will prove the case of even order v only; an analogous argument proves the case of odd order v. Our proof is based on a detailed analysis of the structure of the BWT-matrix of v^{rev}. We will divide the BWT-matrix, and thus the BWT, into three parts, based on the positions of three specific conjugates of v^{rev}, and analyse each of these separately.

BW array	rotations of $v =$ abaababaabaababababaabaababaabaabb	bwt(v)	BW array	rotations of $v^{rev} =$ bbaabaababaabaababababaabaababaababaaba	bwt(v^{rev})
1 21	aabaababaabaabbabaabaabaabaababaabaabb	b	1 3	aabaababaabaababababaabaababaabababb	b
2 8	aabaababaabaabaabaabaabbabaabaabab	b	2 11	aabaababaabaabaabababaababbaabaabab	b
3 29	aabaabbabaabaabaabaababaabaabaabab	b	3 24	aabaababaababbaabaababaabaabaababaabab	b
4 16	aabaababaabaabaabbabaabaabaabab	b	4 6	aabaababaababaabaabaabaababaababbaab	b
5 3	aabababaabaabababaabaabaabaabbab	b	5 19	aabaababaabaababbaababaabaababaabab	b
6 24	aabaabbabaabaabaabaababaabaabaabab	b	6 14	aabaababaabaabaababaababaabaabaabab	b
7 11	aabaabababaabaabaabaabbabaabaabab	b	7 27	aabaababaabbaabaababaabaabaababaabab	b
8 32	aabbabaabaabaabaababaabaabaabaabab	b	8 32	aabaabbaabaabaababaabaababaabaabab	b
9 19	abaababaabaabbabaabaabaabaababaabaab	b	9 9	abaababaabaabaababaabaababaababbaab	b
10 6	abaababaabaabaabaababaabaabbabaab	b	10 22	abaababaabaababbaabaabaababaababaabab	b
11 27	abaabaabbabaabaabaabaababaabaabab	b	11 4	abaababaabaabababaabaababaabababba	a
12 14	abaababaabaabaabaabbabaabaabab	b	12 17	abaababaabaababbaabaababaabaababab	b
13 1	abaababaabaabaababaabaabaabaabb	b̲	13 12	abaababaabaabaabaabaababbaabaabaaba	a
14 22	abaababaabbabaabaabaabaababaabaab	a	14 25	abaababaababbaabaababaabaabaababaaba	a
15 9	abaababaabaabaababaabaabbabaabaab	a	15 30	abaababbaabaababaabaabaababaabaabaab	b
16 30	abaabbabaabaabaabaababaabaabaabaab	a	16 7	ababaabaabaababaabaababaababbaab	a
17 17	abaababaabaabaabbabaabaabaabab	a	17 20	abaababaabaababbaabaabaababaabab	a
18 4	ababaabaabaabababaabaabaabaabbaba	a	18 15	abaababaabaabaababaababbaabaabaaba	a
19 25	abaabaabbabaabaabaabaababaabaab	a	19 28	ababababbaabaababaabaabaababaaba	a
20 12	abaabaabaabaabaabbabaabaabab	a	20 33	ababbaabaabaababaabaababaabaaba	a
21 33	abbabaabaabaabaababaabaabaabaab	a	21 35	abbaabaabaababaabaabaababaabaabb	b
22 20	baabaababaabbabaabaabaabaababaab	a	22 2	baabaababaabaababababaabaababaabab	b̲
23 7	baabaababaabaabaabaabaabbabaab	a	23 10	baabaababaabaabaababaababbaabaab	a
24 28	baabaabbabaabaabaabaababaabaab	a	24 23	baabaababaababbaabaababaabaababaab	a
25 15	baabaababaabaababaabaabbabaab	a	25 5	baabaababaabaabababaabaababaabaabba	a
26 2	baababaabaababaabaabaabaababaabb	a	26 18	baabaababaabaababbaabaababaabaab	a
27 23	baabaabbabaabaabaabaababaabaab	a	27 13	baabaababaabaababbaabaabaababaab	a
28 10	baabababaabaababaabaabaabbabaab	a	28 26	baabaababbaabaababaabaababaabaab	a
29 31	baabbabaabaabaabaababaabaabab	a	29 31	baababbaabaabaababaabaababaabaab	a
30 18	babaabaabaabaabbabaabaabaabab	a	30 8	babaabaabaababaabaababaababbaab	a
31 5	babaabaabaabaababaabaabaabbab	a	31 21	babaabaabaababbaabaababaabaabab	a
32 26	babaabbabaabaabaabaababaabaab	a	32 16	babaabaabaababaabaababbaabaabab	a
33 13	babaabaabaabaabaabbabaabaab	a	33 29	babaabbaabaabaababaabaababaabaab	a
34 35	babababaabaabaabababaabaabaabaab	b	34 34	babbaabaabaababaabaababaabaabaab	a
35 34	bbababaabaabaabababaabaabaabaab	a	35 1	bbaabaababaabaababababaabaababaababa	a

Fig. 1. BWT-matrices of the Fibonacci-plus word $v = s_8 b$ of length 35 and its reverse, underlined the added b.

Now consider the first few conjugates of v^{rev}. Since $v = s_{2k}b = x_{2k}abb$, we have $v^{rev} = bbax_{2k}$, noting that x_{2k} is a palindrome. Thus

$$\mathrm{conj}_1(v^{rev}) = bbax_{2k},$$
$$\mathrm{conj}_2(v^{rev}) = bax_{2k}b,$$
$$\mathrm{conj}_3(v^{rev}) = ax_{2k}bb,$$
$$\mathrm{conj}_4(v^{rev}) = x_{2k}bba.$$

Since Fibonacci words have no occurrence of bb, the conjugate $\mathrm{conj}_1(v^{rev}) = v^{rev}$ is the last row of the matrix. Moreover, by Proposition 1, $ax_{2k}b$ is a Lyndon word, and therefore $\mathrm{conj}_3(v^{rev})$, having only an extra b at the end, is also Lyndon, and thus can be found in the first row. The relative order of the other two conjugates is also clear, since x_{2k} begins with an a, thus we have

$$ax_{2k}bb < x_{2k}bba < bax_{2k}b < bbax_{2k}.$$

We will now subdivide the BWT-matrix into three parts, according to the positions of these conjugates, and we will call these *top part*, *middle part*, and *bottom part.* The conjugates $ax_{2k}bb$, $x_{2k}bba$ and $bax_{2k}b$ are the first row of the top part, middle part and bottom part, respectively. We use this to partition the BWT into the three corresponding parts $\mathrm{bwt}(v^{\mathrm{rev}})_{\mathrm{top}}$, $\mathrm{bwt}(v^{\mathrm{rev}})_{\mathrm{mid}}$, and $\mathrm{bwt}(v^{\mathrm{rev}})_{\mathrm{bot}}$. Thus we have

$$\mathrm{bwt}(v^{\mathrm{rev}}) = \mathrm{bwt}(v^{\mathrm{rev}})_{\mathrm{top}} \cdot \mathrm{bwt}(v^{\mathrm{rev}})_{\mathrm{mid}} \cdot \mathrm{bwt}(v^{\mathrm{rev}})_{\mathrm{bot}}.$$

We will prove the form of the BWT of v^{rev} separately for the three parts. In Fig. 2 we give a visual presentation of the proof.

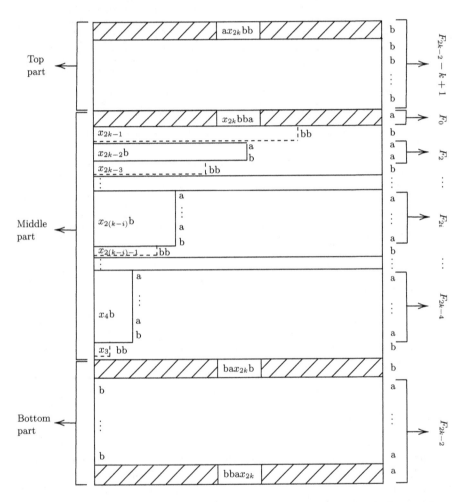

Fig. 2. A sketch of the BWT-matrix of v^{rev} where v is a Fibonacci-plus word.

3.1 Bottom Part

Proposition 4. $bwt(v^{rev})_{\mathrm{bot}} = ba^{F_{2k-2}}$.

Proof. By definition, the bottom part starts with the conjugate $\text{conj}_2(v) = bax_{2k}b$. Since $ax_{2k}bb$ is Lyndon (Proposition 1, part 3), it is smaller than all other conjugates, and therefore, $bax_{2k}b$ is smaller than all other conjugates starting with b. Thus, the bottom part consists exactly of all conjugates starting with b. The number of b's in v, and thus in v^{rev} is $F_{2k-2}+1$. Since s_{2k} has no occurrence of bb, every b in v^{rev} except the one in position 2 is preceded by an a, thus $bax_{2k}b$ is the only conjugate ending in b. This proves the claim.

3.2   Middle Part

Lemma 1. *The left-special circular factors of v^{rev} are exactly the prefixes of $x_{2k-1}b$ and the prefixes of bax_{2k-2}.*

Proof. Let u be a left-special circular factor of $v^{\text{rev}} = bbax_{2k}$. From Proposition 1 part 2, $v^{\text{rev}} = bbax_{2k-1}bax_{2k-2} = bbax_{2k-2}abx_{2k-1}$. Since bb occurs only once, u does not contain bb as factor. Moreover, from combinatorial properties of standard words (see [5]), it is known that for each $0 \leq h \leq F_{2k} - 2$, there is exactly one left-special circular factor of bax_{2k} having length h and it is a prefix of x_{2k}. Since $x_{2k-1}ba$ (that is a prefix of x_{2k}) occurs exactly once in v^{rev} and bax_{2k-2} has exactly two occurrences (one preceded by b and followed by a, the other one preceded by a and followed by b), either u is prefix of $x_{2k-1}b$ or it is prefix of bax_{2k-2}.

Lemma 2. *Let s_{2k} be a Fibonacci word of even order. Then, for all $i = 0, \ldots, k-2$, $ax_{2(k-i)}b$ and $ax_{2(k-i)-1}b$ have F_{2i} and F_{2i+1} occurrences, respectively, as circular factors of s_{2k}.*

Proof. The statement can be proved by induction on i. For $i = 0$, the statement follows from the fact that $ax_{2k}b$ and $ax_{2k-1}b$ have just $1 = F_0 = F_1$ occurrence. Let us suppose the statement is true for all $j \leq i$. Note that $ax_{2(k-i)-2}b$ appears as suffix of $ax_{2(k-i)}b$ and as suffix of $ax_{2(k-i)-1}b$. Moreover, such two occurrences are distinct because $ax_{2(k-i)-1}b$ is not a suffix of $ax_{2(k-i)}b$. This means that, by using the inductive hypothesis, the number of occurrences of $ax_{2(k-i)-2}b$ is $F_{2i} + F_{2i+1} = F_{2i+2}$. Analogously, $ax_{2(k-i)-3}b$ appears as prefix of $ax_{2(k-i)-1}b$ and as prefix of $ax_{2(k-i)-2}b$. Moreover, such two occurrences are distinct because $ax_{2(k-i)-2}b$ is not a prefix of $ax_{2(k-i)-1}b$. This means that the number of occurrences of $ax_{2(k-i)-3}b$ is $F_{2i+1} + F_{2i+2} = F_{2i+3}$.

Proposition 5. $bwt(v^{\text{rev}})_{\text{mid}} = a^{F_0}ba^{F_2}b\ldots a^{F_{2k-4}}b$.

Proof. For all $2 \leq i < j$, x_i is a prefix (and also a suffix) of x_j. This means that the rotations starting with x_ibb are lexicographically greater than x_jbb. Note that, if $k = 2$, $v = x_4abb = x_3bax_2abb$ where $x_4 = aba$, $x_3 = a$, $x_2 = \epsilon$ by Proposition 1. Therefore $bwt(v^{\text{rev}})_{\text{mid}} = a^{F_0}b$ since the rotations involved start with x_4bb and x_3bb, respectively. Let us suppose $k \geq 3$. By Proposition 1 part 2, $x_{2k-1}b$ is a prefix of $v = s_{2k}b$, as well as $x_{2t}ab$ for $2 \leq t \leq k-1$. This means that, for $1 \leq i \leq k - 2$, $x_{2(k-i)}b$ is not a prefix of $x_{2k-1}b$. Thus, by Lemma 1, $x_{2(k-i)}b$

is not left-special. Therefore, each occurrence of $x_{2(k-i)}b$ is preceded by the same character; this character must be a, since otherwise, both $bx_{2(k-i)}b$ and $ax_{2(k-i)}a$ would be factors, contradicting the fact that s_{2k}^{rev} is balanced (Proposition 1, part 4). Therefore, all occurrences of $x_{2(k-i)}b$ correspond to a run of a's in the BWT. The length of this run is F_{2i} by Lemma 2. The claim follows from the fact that each $x_{2(k-i)-1}bb$ occurs exactly once and it is preceded by b.

3.3   Top Part

Lemma 3. *Let i be such that $\text{conj}_i(v^{rev}) < x_{2k}bba$. Then the last character of $\text{conj}_i(v^{rev})$ is b.*

Proof. Let $u = lcp(\text{conj}_i(v^{\text{rev}}), x_{2k}bba)$. Then u is a proper prefix of x_{2k-1}. This is because there are only two occurrences of x_{2k-1}, one followed by ba, this is the prefix of $x_{2k}bba$, and the other followed by bb, thus greater than $x_{2k}bba$. Therefore, $u' = ua$ is a prefix of $\text{conj}_i(v^{\text{rev}})$ but not of x_{2k-1}, and thus by Lemma 1 it is not left-special. Now assume that $\text{conj}_i(v^{\text{rev}})$ ends with a. Then aua is a factor of v^{rev}, and since u does not contain bb, it is thus also a factor of s_{2k}^{rev}. On the other hand, ub is left-special, since it is a prefix of $x_{2k-1}b$ (Lemma 1), therefore both bub and aua are factors of v^{rev}, and again, of s_{2k}^{rev}. This implies that both $au^{\text{rev}}a$ and $bu^{\text{rev}}b$ are factors of s_{2k}. This is a contradiction, since s_{2k} is balanced (Proposition 1, part 4).

Proposition 6. $bwt(v^{rev})_{\text{top}} = b^{F_{2k-2}-k+1}$.

Proof. By Lemma 3, $bwt(v^{\text{rev}})_{\text{top}}$ consists of b's only. The number of b's of v is $F_{2k-2}+1$, of which we have accounted for k (since 1 is contained in $bwt(v^{\text{rev}})_{\text{bot}}$ and $k-1$ in $bwt(v^{\text{rev}})_{\text{mid}}$), there remaining exactly $F_{2k-2}-k+1$ b's.

3.4   Putting It All Together

Proof of Proposition 3: The claim for even-order Fibonacci-plus words follows from Propositions 4, 5, and 6. The claim for odd-order Fibonacci-plus words can be proved in an analogous manner.

Proof of Theorem 1: From Propositions 2 and 3, we have that $\rho(v) = 2k/4 = k/2$. On the other hand, $n = |v| = F_{2k}+1$, if v is of even order $2k$, $n = |v| = F_{2k+1}+1$ if v is of odd order $2k+1$. Thus by the properties of the Fibonacci numbers, $2k = \Theta(\log n)$, implying that $\rho(v) = k/2 = \Theta(\log n)$.

4   Standard-Plus Words Have $\rho = \mathcal{O}(\log n)$

In this section we consider other infinite families of finite words, defined from standard words. Here we assume that $d_0 \geq 1$, otherwise we could consider the word obtained by exchanging a's and b's and the results still hold true.

Definition 3. A word v is called *standard-plus* if it is either of the form sb, where s is a standard word of even order $2k$, $k \geq 2$, or of the form sa, where s is a standard word of odd order $2k + 1$, $k \geq 2$. In the first case, v is *of even order*, otherwise *of odd order*.

We show that, when a standard-plus word $v = s_{2k}b$ is considered, the exact asymptotic growth of ρ depends on the directive sequence of the word s_{2k}. Here we give the proof of the result for standard-plus words of even order, however an analogous statement can also be proved for standard-plus words of odd order.

Proposition 7. Let $v = s_{2k}b$ be a standard-plus word of even order. Then $r(v) = 4$.

The proof of Proposition 7 is analogous to that of Proposition 2.

Proposition 8. Let $v = s_{2k}b$ be a standard-plus word of even order $2k$, where s_{2k} is the standard word obtained by using the directive sequence $(d_0, d_1, \ldots, d_{2k-2})$ of length $2k - 1$, where $d_0 \geq 1$. If $d_0 = 1$, then $r(v^{rev}) = 2k$. Otherwise, $r(v^{rev}) = 2k + 2$.

Proof. (Sketch) Similar to what happens with Fibonacci's words (see Proposition 1), it is known that $s_{2k} = Cab$, where C is a palindrome, the conjugate aCb is a Lyndon word (see [3,12]). Then $v^{rev} = bbaC$ and, in order to lexicographically sort the conjugates of v^{rev}, we can consider its Lyndon rotation $aCbb$. One can verify that $C \in \{a^{d_0}b, a^{d_0+1}b\}^*$. It is possible to see that bwt(v^{rev}) ends with $ba^{|s_{2k}|_b}$, since $baCb$ is the smallest rotation starting with b. Moreover, since $t = b(a^{d_0}b)^{d_1}b$ is a suffix of $aCbb$, all rotations of v^{rev} starting with the first occurrence of a in each run a^{d_0} in t determine d_1 consecutive b's in bwt(v^{rev}). If $d_0 = 1$ such rotations are followed by the rotation $baCb$, otherwise several rotations preceded by a (including the rotations starting with the other a's of t) are in between. So, if $d_0 = 1$, the last run of b's has length $d_1 + 1$, otherwise the last two runs of b's have length d_1 and 1, respectively.

Finally, when d_i (with odd i) is used to generate standard words, a set of consecutive rotations starting with $(a^{d_0}b)^{d_1}a^{d_0+1}b$ and preceded by b is produced. This means that the other runs of b's have length $d_3, d_5, \ldots, d_{2k-3}, |s_{2k}|_b - (d_1 + d_3 + \ldots + d_{2k-3})$.

Example 3. Let us consider the standard-plus word v of order 6 constructed by using the directive sequence $(2, 3, 1, 2, 1)$ of length 5. One can verify that

$$v = aabaabaabaaabaabaabaabaaabaabaabaabaaabaabaabaaabb.$$

Moreover, bwt(v^{rev}) $= b^{10}ab^2a^3b^3a^{15}ba^{15}$ and bwt(v) $= b^{15}a^{33}ba$. Therefore, $r(v^{rev}) = 8$ and $r(v) = 4$.

Theorem 2. Let v be a standard-plus word of even order with $|v| = n$. Then $\rho(v) = \mathcal{O}(\log n)$.

Proof. By definition, $v = s_{2k}b$ where s_{2k} is a standard word of order $2k$ for some positive k. Then $|s_{2k}| \geq F_{2k}$, and by Proposition 7 and 8, $\rho(v) \leq \frac{k+1}{2} \in \mathcal{O}(\log n)$.

The following proposition states that Fibonacci-plus words are maximal w.r.t. ρ among all standard-plus words.

Proposition 9. *Let v be a Fibonacci-plus word, and v' a standard-plus word s.t. $|v| = |v'|$. Then $\rho(v) \geq \rho(v')$.*

Proof. Follows directly from Propsition 7 and 8, and from the fact that Fibonacci words have the longest directive sequence among all standard words of the same length.

5   Conclusion and Outlook

In this paper, we presented the first non-trivial lower bound on the maximum runs-ratio $\rho(n)$ of a word of length n. This shows for the first time that the widely used parameter r, the number of runs of the BWT of a word, is not an ideal measure of the repetitiveness of the word. Moreover, it proves that for BWT-based compression a parallel result holds to the "one-bit catastrophe" recently shown for LZ78-compression [20].

Several open questions remain. We saw in the previous section that Fibonacci-plus words are maximal among the class of standard-plus words with respect to the runs-ratio ρ. However, they stay strictly below $\rho(n)$, the maximum among all words of length n, even for lengths up to $n = 30$. In Table 2, we report the values of $\rho(n)$ and compare them to the maximum reached by standard-plus words. Note that this is a Fibonacci-plus word only for $n = 9, 14, 22$.

Table 2. The values of $\rho(n)$ for $n = 9, \ldots, 30$, and the maximum value of $\rho(n)$ among all standard-plus words of length n.

n	9	10	11	12	13	14	15	16	17	18	19	20	21	22	23	24	25	26	27	28	29	30
$\rho(n)$	2	2	2	2	2	2	2	2	2.5	2.5	2.5	2.5	3	2.5	3	3	2.67	3	3	3	3	3
std-plus	1	1.5	1.5	1.5	1	1.5	1.5	1.5	1.5	1.5	2	1.5	1.5	1.5	1.5	2	1.5	2	2	2	2	2

It is possible to construct binary words of arbitrary length and greater runs-ratio ρ than any standard-plus word of the same length. However, we currently do not know the asymptotic growth of the ρ value for such words. Therefore, the question of closing the gap for $\rho(n)$ between our lower bound $\Omega(\log n)$ and the upper bound $\mathcal{O}(\log^2(n))$ remains open.

It would be interesting to explore the question also for larger alphabets. Our preliminary experimental results on ternary alphabets indicate that the increase in ρ happens at smaller lengths than for the binary case. This suggests that the effect we showed in this paper, of a divergence between the string's repetitiveness and r, may be even more pronounced in real-life applications.

Acknowledgements. Zs.L. and M.S. wish to thank Dominik Kempa for getting them interested in the problem treated in this paper. We thank Gabriele Fici and Daniele Greco for interesting discussions, Akihiro Nishi for preliminary experiments, and the anonymous referees for their careful reading of the paper. Finally, we thank the Leibniz Zentrum für Informatik for the possibility of participating at Dagstuhl Seminar no. 19241 in June 2019, where some of the authors started collaborating on this problem.

References

1. Bannai, H., Gagie, T.: Online LZ77 parsing and matching statistics with RLBWTs. In: Annual Symposium on Combinatorial Pattern Matching (CPM 2018), vol. 105, pp. 7:1–7:12 (2018)
2. Belazzougui, D., Cunial, F., Gagie, T., Prezza, N., Raffinot, M.: Composite repetition-aware data structures. In: 26th Annual Symposium on Combinatorial Pattern Matching (CPM 2015), pp. 26–39 (2015)
3. Berstel, J., de Luca, A.: Sturmian words, Lyndon words and trees. Theoretical Comput. Sci. **178**(1–2), 171–203 (1997)
4. Blumer, A., Blumer, J., Haussler, D., McConnell, R.M., Ehrenfeucht, A.: Complete inverted files for efficient text retrieval and analysis. J. ACM **34**(3), 578–595 (1987)
5. Borel, J., Reutenauer, C.: On christoffel classes. RAIRO Theor. Inf. Appl. **40**(1), 15–27 (2006)
6. Burrows, M., Wheeler, D.J.: A block-sorting lossless data compression algorithm. Technical report, DIGITAL System Research Center (1994)
7. Castiglione, G., Restivo, A., Sciortino, M.: Hopcroft's algorithm and cyclic automata. In: Martín-Vide, C., Otto, F., Fernau, H. (eds.) LATA 2008. LNCS, vol. 5196, pp. 172–183. Springer, Heidelberg (2008). https://doi.org/10.1007/978-3-540-88282-4_17
8. Castiglione, G., Restivo, A., Sciortino, M.: Circular Sturmian words and Hopcroft's algorithm. Theor. Comput. Sci. **410**(43), 4372–4381 (2009)
9. de Luca, A.: A combinatorial property of the Fibonacci words. Inf. Process. Lett. **12**(4), 193–195 (1981)
10. Luca, A.: Combinatorics of standard sturmian words. In: Mycielski, J., Rozenberg, G., Salomaa, A. (eds.) Structures in Logic and Computer Science. LNCS, vol. 1261, pp. 249–267. Springer, Heidelberg (1997). https://doi.org/10.1007/3-540-63246-8_15
11. de Luca, A.: Sturmian words: structure, combinatorics, and their arithmetics. Theor. Comput. Sci. **183**(1), 45–82 (1997)
12. de Luca, A., Mignosi, F.: Some combinatorial properties of sturmian words. Theor. Comput. Sci. **136**(2), 361–385 (1994)
13. Gagie, T., Navarro, G., Prezza, N.: Fully functional suffix trees and optimal text searching in BWT-runs bounded space. J. ACM **67**(1), 1–54 (2020)
14. Kempa, D.: Optimal construction of compressed indexes for highly repetitive texts. In: Proceedings of the Thirtieth Annual ACM-SIAM Symposium on Discrete Algorithms (SODA 2019), pp. 1344–1357 (2019)
15. Kempa, D., Kociumaka, T.: Resolution of the burrows-wheeler transform conjecture. CoRR, abs/1910.10631, Accepted to the 61st Annual Symposium on Foundations of Computer Science (FOCS 2020) (2019)
16. Kempa, D., Prezza, N.: At the roots of dictionary compression: string attractors. In: Proceedings of the 50th Annual ACM SIGACT Symposium on Theory of Computing (STOC 2018), pp. 827–840 (2018)

17. Kieffer, J.C., Yang, E.: Grammar-based codes: a new class of universal lossless source codes. IEEE Trans. Inf. Theory **46**(3), 737–754 (2000)
18. Knuth, D., Morris, J., Pratt, V.: Fast pattern matching in strings. SIAM J. Comput. **6**(2), 323–350 (1977)
19. Kociumaka, T., Navarro, G., Prezza, N.: Towards a definitive measure of repetitiveness. In: Proceedings of the 14th Latin American Symposium on Theoretical Informatics (LATIN 2020) (2020)
20. Lagarde, G., Perifel, S.: Lempel-Ziv: a "one-bit catastrophe" but not a tragedy. In: Proceedings of the Twenty-Ninth Annual ACM-SIAM Symposium on Discrete Algorithms (SODA 2018), pp. 1478–1495 (2018)
21. Lempel, A., Ziv, J.: On the complexity of finite sequences. IEEE Trans. Inf. Theory **22**(1), 75–81 (1976)
22. Lothaire, M.: Algebraic Combinatorics on Words. Cambridge University Press, Cambridge (2002)
23. Mantaci, S., Restivo, A., Sciortino, M.: Burrows-wheeler transform and sturmian words. Inf. Process. Lett. **86**(5), 241–246 (2003)
24. Ohno, T., Sakai, K., Takabatake, Y., Tomohiro, I., Sakamoto, H.: A faster implementation of online RLBWT and its application to LZ77 parsing. J. Discrete Algorithms **52**, 18–28 (2018)
25. Policriti, A., Prezza, N.: From LZ77 to the run-length encoded Burrows-Wheeler transform, and back. In: 28th Annual Symposium on Combinatorial Pattern Matching (CPM 2017), vol. 78, pp. 1–10 (2017)
26. Storer, J.A., Szymanski, T.G.: Data compression via textual substitution. J. ACM **29**(4), 928–951 (1982)

On the Redundancy of D-Ary Fano Codes

Ferdinando Cicalese[1]([ID]) and Massimiliano Rossi[2]([ID])

[1] Department of Computer Science, University of Verona, Verona, Italy
ferdinando.cicalese@univr.it
[2] CISE Department, University of Florida, Florida, USA
rossi.m@ufl.edu

Abstract. We study the redundancy of D-ary Fano source codes. We show that a novel splitting criterion allows to prove a bound on the redundancy of the resulting code which sharpens the guarantee provided by Shannon's classical result for the case of an optimal code.

In particular we show that, for any $D \geq 2$ and for every source distribution $\mathbf{p} = p_1, \ldots, p_n$, there is a D-ary Fano code that satisfies the redundancy bound

$$\overline{L} - H_D(\mathbf{p}) \leq 1 - p_{\min}, \tag{1}$$

where, $\overline{L}$ denotes the average codeword length, $p_{\min} = \min_i p_i$, and $H_D(\mathbf{p}) = -\sum_{i=1}^{n} p_i \log_D(p_i)$ is the D-ary entropy of the source.

The existence of D-ary Fano codes achieving such a bound had been conjectured in [ISIT2015], where, however, the construction proposed achieves the bound only for $D = 2, 3, 4$. In [ISIT2020], a novel construction was proposed leading to the proof that the redundancy bound in (1) above also holds for $D = 5$ (and some other special cases). This result was attained by a dynamic programming based algorithm with time complexity $O(Dn)$ (per node of the codetree).

Here, besides proving that the redundancy bound in (1) can be achieved, unconditionally, for every $D > 3$, we also significantly improve the time complexity of the algorithm building a D-ary Fano code tree achieving such a bound: We show that, for every $D \geq 4$, a D-ary Fano code tree satisfying (1) can be constructed by an efficient greedy procedure that has complexity $O(D \log_2 n)$ per node of the codetree (i.e., improving from linear time to logarithmic time in n).

Keywords: D-ary Fano codes · Redundancy · D-ary aggregations

1 Introduction

A (discrete and memoryless) source of information X is defined by the discrete set $\mathcal{X} = \{x_1, \ldots, x_n\}$ of symbols emitted by X and the probability distribution $\mathbf{p} = (p_1, \ldots, p_n)$ ruling the emissions of X, i.e., $p_i = \text{Prob}\{X = x_i\}$, for each $i = 1, \ldots, n$. For a fixed integer $D \geq 2$, a D-ary code $\mathcal{C}$ for X is a mapping $\mathcal{C} : x \in \mathcal{X} \mapsto \mathcal{C}(x) \in \{0, 1, \ldots, D-1\}^*$. For each $i = 1, \ldots, n$ we say that $\mathcal{C}(x_i)$ is the codeword associated to x_i and denote by $|\mathcal{C}(x_i)|$ its length. Then, the average

© Springer Nature Switzerland AG 2021
T. Bureš et al. (Eds.): SOFSEM 2021, LNCS 12607, pp. 263–277, 2021.
https://doi.org/10.1007/978-3-030-67731-2_19

codeword length of $\mathcal{C}$ is $\overline{L}(\mathcal{C}) = \sum_{i=1}^{n} p_i |\mathcal{C}(x_i)|$. We say that $\mathcal{C}$ is a prefix code if no codeword is a prefix of any other codeword.

A D-ary prefix code corresponds to a D-ary (code) tree $\mathcal{T}$, whose leaves are associated to the source symbols; each edge stemming from each internal node is labelled with a distinct letter from $\{0, \ldots, D-1\}$ and the codeword of a source symbol is the sequence of labels on the path from the root to the corresponding leaf. Because of this correspondence we also write $\overline{L}(\mathcal{T})$ to denote the average codeword length—clearly equivalent to the average codetree height.

By the classical Shannon's source coding theorem, the average length of a D-ary code for a source X is lower bounded by the D-ary entropy of the source $H_D(X) = \sum_{i=1}^{n} p_i \log_D(\frac{1}{p_i})$. Therefore, a performance measure of a D-ary code $\mathcal{C}$ for X is the so called *redundancy* of the code, here denoted by $r(\mathcal{C})$, which measures the difference between the average code length and the D-ary entropy of the source: $r(\mathcal{C}) = \overline{L}(\mathcal{C}) - H_D(X)$.

Shannon's classical source coding theorem also says that for an (optimal) code $\mathcal{C}^*$ achieving minimum average length for a source X the redundancy is smaller than 1, i.e., $\overline{L}(\mathcal{C}^*) - H_D(X) < 1$. Huffman codes are known to be minimum average length codes, hence attaining Shannon's bound on the redundancy. In fact, the minimum redundancy of optimal (Huffman) prefix D-ary codes is well established, and tight bounds sharper than Shannon's 1 bit have been proved (see, e.g., [16,17] and references therein quoted).

Alphabetic Codes and Fano Codes. We say that a code $\mathcal{C}$ is *alphabetic* if the lexicographic ordering of the codewords respects the order of the corresponding source symbols, i.e., for each $i < j$ we have that $\mathcal{C}(x_i) \preceq_{Lex} \mathcal{C}(x_j)$. In a D-ary prefix alphabetic code tree, if we number leaves from left to right it holds that for each $i = 1, \ldots, n$, the ith source symbol is associated to the ith leaf. Alphabetic codes are a special case of binary identification procedures [5] with many important applications spanning from information retrieval to circuit testing to planning [7,15,18]. Alphabetic codes have the additional property of yielding group testing procedure with an efficient representation of the tests (which can be expressed as comparison questions), a problem that has recently attracted renewed interest [3].

The prefix code produced by the Huffman algorithm is not guaranteed to be alphabetic. For the binary case $D = 2$, algorithms for constructing optimal alphabetic codes in time $O(n \log n)$ were given by Hu and Tucker [11] and Garsia and Wachs [6] (see also [12]), improving previous constructions by Knuth [13] and Gilbert and Moore [7]. In [7] the authors also showed that an optimal alphabetic binary prefix code $\mathcal{C}_{\mathcal{A}}^*$ for a source X satisfies the redundancy bound $\overline{L}(\mathcal{C}_{\mathcal{A}}^*) - H_2(X) \leq 2$.

If the source symbols are ordered in non-increasing order of probability, i.e., $p_1 \geq p_2 \geq \cdots \geq p_n$, a binary Fano code [4] is an alphabetic prefix code with redundancy upper bounded by $1 - 2p_n$ [9]. A binary Fano codes tree is obtained by recursively splitting the probability distribution $p_1, \ldots, p_n$ into two parts $p_1, \ldots, p_k$ and $p_{k+1}, \ldots, p_n$ so that the cumulative mass of the parts are as close as possible.

In [14], the authors started the investigation of the redundancy of D-ary Fano codes. The definition of a D-ary Fano code, and its efficient construction and redundancy, critically depends on the way the idea of splitting a distribution into balanced contiguous parts is implemented. In [14], the authors employ for such a splitting operation the solution of the following subproblem: Given a probability distribution $\mathbf{p} = (p_1, p_2, \ldots, p_n)$, find a partition $\Pi = (\Pi_1, \ldots, \Pi_D)$ of $[n] = \{1, \ldots, n\}$, where each Π_i consists of consecutive elements of $[n]$, and such that the sum $\sum_{i=1}^{D} \sum_{j=1}^{D} |q_i - q_j|$, is *minimized*, where each q_j is the sum of the probabilities p_k's for all $k \in \Pi_j$.

Based on this criterion, the authors of [14] prove that for $D \in \{2, 3\}$ the resulting D-ary Fano code has average codeword length $\overline{L} \leq H_D(\mathbf{p}) + 1 - p_{\min}$, where $p_{\min}$ in the smallest component of the source probability distribution, and *conjectured* that this bound also holds for all $D \geq 4$.

However, it is not clear how to efficiently perform the optimization employed in [14], as a direct approach would result in time complexity exponential in D. On the basis of this observation, in [1], we proposed an alternative *even splitting* optimization criterion, which *can be* optimally solved via dynamic programming in time $O(n\,D)$. This approach is shown to guarantee the redundancy bound $\overline{L} - H_D(X) \leq 1 - p_{\min}$ for $D = 2, 3, 4$ and in the special case where the resulting code tree is complete, so providing a partial extension of the result of [14].

Our Results. In this paper we continue the investigation on *efficient* construction of *low redundancy* D-ary Fano codes. We significantly improve the results of [1,14] both in terms of the redundancy guarantee and the time complexity of the construction algorithm. We show that a somehow even simpler splitting criterion can be employed that can be implemented in time $O(D \log n)$. This allows to construct the whole D-ary code tree in time $O(Dn \log n)$ guaranteeing the upper bound $1 - p_{\min}$ on the redundancy for all $D \geq 4$. Remarkably the time complexity of our algorithm for D-ary Fano codes (hence for alphabetic codes when the input distribution is sorted) matches the optimal bound for the binary case and also the time complexity of D-ary Huffman coding (which are not alphabetic). In terms of redundancy of D-ary alphabetic codes, to the best of our knowledge, our result provides the first redundancy guarantee smaller than one for the case of $D > 2$.

2 D-ary Fano Codes with Nice Aggregations

We now introduce some basic terminology on code trees and on the splitting criteria used in constructing our D-ary Fano code trees. For an integer k, we denote by $[k]$ the set $\{1, \ldots, k\}$.

Definition 1. *Given an n-dimensional vector of non-negative numbers $\mathbf{p} = (p_1, \ldots, p_n)$, with $p_1 \geq p_2 \geq \cdots \geq p_n$ and a positive integer $2 \leq D \leq n$, we say that a vector $\mathbf{q} = (q_1, \ldots, q_D)$ is a contiguous D-aggregation of $\mathbf{p}$ if there exist indices $0 = i_0 < i_1 < \cdots < i_{D-1} < i_D = n$ such that for each $j \in [D]$ it holds that $q_j = \sum_{k=i_{j-1}+1}^{i_j} p_k$.*

We refer to $(i_0, i_1, \ldots, i_D)$ as the *boundaries* of the aggregation $\mathbf{q}$. For each $j \in [D]$, we refer to the subsequence of components $p_{i_{j-1}+1}, \ldots, p_{i_j}$ as the *j-th block* of the aggregation $\mathbf{q}$. We define the *size of block* j to be $i_j - i_{j-1}$, i.e., the number of components of $\mathbf{p}$ it contains. For each $j \in [D]$, we denote by $q_{j,First}$ and $q_{j,Last}$ the first and the last component of $\mathbf{p}$ in the jth block of $\mathbf{q}$, i.e., $q_{j,First} = p_{i_{j-1}+1}$ and $q_{j,Last} = p_{i_j}$.

The main tool for our definition of a D-ary Fano code is a special type of contiguous aggregation as specified in the following definition.

Definition 2. *Let* $\mathbf{p} = p_1, \ldots, p_n$ *be a probability distribution of dimension* $n \geq D$, *with* $p_i \geq p_{i+1}$ $(i \in [n-1])$. *Let* $\mathbf{q}$ *be a contiguous D-aggregation of* $\mathbf{p}$ *with boundaries* $(i_0, i_1, \ldots, i_D)$. *Let* $\mathcal{O} = \{j \in [D] \mid i_j - i_{j-1} = 1\}$ *be the set of indices of blocks of size one. Let* $\mathcal{S} = \{j \in [D] \mid 1 < i_j - i_{j-1} < D\}$ *be the set of indices of blocks of size smaller than* D *and larger than* 1 *(which we refer to as* small blocks*). Let* $\mathcal{F} = \{j \in [D] \mid i_j - i_{j-1} = D\}$ *be the set of indices of blocks of size exactly* D *(which we refer to as* full blocks*). Let* $\mathcal{L} = [D] \setminus \mathcal{O} \cup \mathcal{S} \cup \mathcal{F}$, *which is the set of indices of blocks of size* $> D$ *(which we refer to as* large blocks*). We say that* $\mathbf{q}$ *is* nice *iff the following condition holds*

$$\sum_{j \in [D] \setminus \mathcal{L}} \sum_{i=i_{j-1}+1}^{i_j} p_i \log_D \frac{1}{p_i} + \sum_{j \in \mathcal{L}} q_j \log_D \frac{1}{q_j} \geq \sum_{j \in \mathcal{S} \cup \mathcal{F}} q_j + \sum_{j \in \mathcal{L}} (q_j - p_{i_j}) + p_n \quad (2)$$

or, equivalently,

$$\sum_{j \in [D] \setminus \mathcal{L}} \sum_{i=i_{j-1}+1}^{i_j} p_i \log_D \frac{1}{p_i} + \sum_{j \in \mathcal{L}} (q_{j,Last} + q_j \log_D \frac{1}{q_j}) \geq \sum_{j \in \mathcal{S} \cup \mathcal{F}} q_j + \sum_{j \in \mathcal{L}} q_j + q_{D,Last}$$
$$(3)$$

We define a D-ary Fano code as the generalization of the original binary Fano code, where the partitioning operation is based on *nice* contiguous D-aggregations. The following definition formalizes the structure of such a code in terms of the corresponding code-tree.

Definition 3. *A D-ary Fano code tree* $\mathcal{T}$ *for a source* X *emitting symbols from* $\mathcal{X} = \{x_1, \ldots, x_n\}$ *according to the probability distribution* $\mathbf{p} = (p_i)_{i \in [n]}$—*where* $p_i = p(x_i) = \text{Prob}\{X = x_i\}$—*is produced by the following procedure:*

1. *Rearrange the symbols in order of non-increasing probability, i.e., such that* $p_1 \geq \cdots \geq p_n$.
2. *If* $n = 1$ *then* $\mathcal{T}$ *is a tree made of a sigle node* ν *(being the root and also a leaf) with assigned symbol* x_1.
3. *If* $n < D$, *then* $\mathcal{T}$ *is a tree made of a root node* ν *with* n *children* $\nu_1, \ldots, \nu_n$ *all being leaves and* ν_i *is assigned symbol* x_i.
4. *If* $n \geq D$, *let* $\mathbf{q}$ *be a nice contiguous D-aggregation of* $\mathbf{p}$ *and* $(i_0, i_1, \ldots, i_D)$ *be* $\mathbf{q}$'s *boundaries. For* $j \in [D]$ *let* X_j *be the source emitting symbols from*

$\mathcal{X}_j = \{x_{i_{j-1}+1}, \ldots, x_{i_j}\} \subseteq \mathcal{X}$ with probability $\mathbf{p}_{X_j}(x) = \frac{p(x)}{p_{X_j}}$ where $p_{X_j} = \sum_{x \in \mathcal{X}_j} p(x) = \sum_{k=i_{j-1}+1}^{i_j} p(x_k)$.

Then $\mathcal{T}$ is recursively defined as the tree with root ν with D children $\nu_1, \ldots, \nu_D$ where ν_j is the root of a D-ary Fano code tree for source X_j.

For obtaining the corresponding code $\mathcal{C}$ proceeding top-down, we first assign to each edge stemming from the same node a distinct symbol from the D-ary alphabet $\{0, 1, \ldots, D-1\}$; then we fix the encoding of each x_i to be the sequence of symbols on the edges of the unique path in $\mathcal{T}$ from the root to the leaf assigned to x_i.

Some Basic Facts on Code Trees. We now fix some notation and recall standard facts about prefix code trees (refer to, e.g., [2] for a more detailed treatment). Given a distribution $\mathbf{p} = (p_1, \ldots, p_n)$ we define $p_{\min} = \min_{i=1}^n p_i$. We use both $H_D(\mathbf{p})$ and $H_D(X)$ to denote the D-ary Shannon entropy of a source distributed according to $\mathbf{p}$, i.e., $H_D(X) = H_D(\mathbf{p}) = \sum_{i=1}^n p_i \log_D \frac{1}{p_i}$.

Let $\mathcal{T}$ be an arbitrary prefix code tree for the source X emitting symbols from $\mathcal{X} = \{x_1, \ldots, x_n\}$ according to the probability distribution $\mathbf{p} = (p(x_i))_{i \in [n]}$. Let $N(\mathcal{T})$ denote the set of internal (non-leaf) nodes of the tree $\mathcal{T}$. Assign the probabilities to leaves and nodes in $\mathcal{T}$ as follows: first, for each $i \in [n]$, assign probability $p_i = p(x_i)$ to the leaf corresponding to letter x_i; then assign to each node $\nu \in N(\mathcal{T})$ the sum of the probabilities over all the descendent leaves of ν, which we denote by p_ν. In particular, probability one is assigned to the root of $\mathcal{T}$, which is denoted by $r(\mathcal{T})$.

Let $\nu \in N(\mathcal{T})$ and $\nu_1, \ldots, \nu_k$, be its children. We define the distribution $\mathbf{q}^{(\nu)} = \left(\frac{p_{\nu_1}}{p_\nu}, \ldots, \frac{p_{\nu_k}}{p_\nu} \right)$ and we call it the *split-distribution of ν* to indicate that it records the way the probability mass of descendent leaves of ν is distributed among the subtrees rooted at the children of ν.

For any $\nu \in N(\mathcal{T})$, let $\mathcal{X}_\nu = \{x_{\nu,1}, \ldots, x_{\nu,t}\}$ be the set of symbols associated to the leaves of the subtree rooted at ν, in the order they appear from left to right. We also associate to node ν the probability distribution $\mathbf{p}^{(\nu)} = \left(\frac{p(x_{\nu,1})}{p_\nu}, \ldots, \frac{p(x_{\nu,t})}{p_\nu} \right)$ and we call it the *sub-distribution of node ν* as it gives the scaled probabilities of the symbols in $\mathcal{X}_\nu$ relative the subtree rooted at ν.

We denote by $\overline{L}(\mathcal{T})$ the average height of $\mathcal{T}$ and equivalently, the average codeword length of the code defined by $\mathcal{T}$. The following fact records known properties of any code tree $\mathcal{T}$, that are easily provable by induction on the height of $\mathcal{T}$ using the additivity of the entropy function (see [8, Chapter 3]).

Fact 1. *Using the above notation, it holds that*

$$\overline{L}(\mathcal{T}) = \sum_{\nu \in N(\mathcal{T})} p_\nu \quad and \quad H_D(\mathbf{p}) = \sum_{\nu \in N(\mathcal{T})} p_\nu H_D(\mathbf{q}^{(\nu)}).$$

The following theorem is the key tool of our main result. Its proof is in Sect. 3.

Theorem 1. *Let* $\mathbf{p} = (p_1, \ldots, p_n)$ *be a probability distribution with* $p_1 \geq p_2 \geq \cdots \geq p_n$. *For all* $3 < D < n$, *there exists a* nice *contiguous* D-*aggregation* $\mathbf{q}$ *of* $\mathbf{p}$ *which can be computed in time* $O(D \log n)$.

The implication of the above theorem on the construction of low redundancy D-ary Fano codes, is given by the following result which had been conjectured in [1] and for which we are now giving a complete proof.

Theorem 2. *Fix* $D \geq 2$, $n \geq D$ *and let* X *be an* n-*ary source, distributed according to probability* $\mathbf{p} = p_1, \ldots, p_n$. *Let* $\mathcal{T}$ *be a* D-*ary Fano code tree for* X *such that for each internal node* ν *of* $\mathcal{T}$ *with exactly* D *children* $\nu_1, \ldots, \nu_D$, *the split-distribution* $\mathbf{q}^{(\nu)}$ *is a* nice *contiguous* D-*aggregation of the sub-distribution* $\mathbf{p}^{(\nu)}$. *Then,*

$$\overline{L}(\mathcal{T}) \leq H_D(X) + 1 - p_{\min}.$$

Proof. Let $N^{(D)}$ be the set of internal nodes in $\mathcal{T}$ with exactly D children, and $N^{(<D)} = N(\mathcal{T}) \setminus N^{(D)}$.

For each $\nu \in N^{(D)}$ let us denote by $C_\nu = \{\nu_1, \ldots, \nu_D\}$ be the ordered set of ν's children, ordered from left to right. We will use $C_\nu^{(<D)}, C_\nu^{(=D)}, C_\nu^{(>D)}$, to denote the set of children of ν which are internal nodes at the root of a subtree of $\mathcal{T}$ with respectively, *less than*, *exactly*, and *more than* D leaves. We also define $C_\nu^{(\leq D)} = C_\nu^{(<D)} \cup C_\nu^{(=D)}$. Finally, we define $C_\nu^{(\ell)}$ as set of children of ν which are leaves. Note, that, by the definition of a D-ary Fano tree, for each $\rho \in C_\nu^{(\leq D)}$ the children of ρ are leaves.

With reference to the terminology introduced at the beginning of this section, we have that for each internal node ν, p_ν denotes the sum of the probabilities of the leaves in the subtree rooted at ν. Let us denote the D children of ν by $\nu_1, \ldots, \nu_D$. Then, by assumption, $\mathbf{q}^{(\nu)} = (q_1^{(\nu)}, \ldots, q_D^{(\nu)}) = (\frac{p_{\nu_1}}{p_\nu}, \ldots, \frac{p_{\nu_D}}{p_\nu})$, the split probability distribution associated to node ν, is a nice contiguous D-aggregation of the sub-distribution of ν, $\mathbf{p}^{(\nu)} = \left(\frac{p(x_a)}{p_\nu}, \frac{p(x_{a+1})}{p_\nu}, \ldots, \frac{p(x_{b-1})}{p_\nu}, \frac{p(x_b)}{p_\nu} \right)$. Here a and b are such that the leaves of the subtree rooted at ν contains the symbols from the a-th one to the b-th one, inclusively.

We denote by $p_{\nu, Last}$ the probability of the symbol in the rightmost leaf of the subtree rooted at ν, i.e., $p_{\nu, Last} = p(x_b)$. Then, we have that for each $i \in [D]$, it holds that $p_{\nu_i, Last} = q_{i, Last}^{(\nu)}$.

By Definition 2, since $\mathbf{q}^{(\nu)}$ is a *nice* contiguous D-aggregation of the sub-distribution $\mathbf{p}^{(\nu)}$ we have

$$\sum_{\rho \in C_\nu^{(\ell)}} \frac{p_\rho}{p_\nu} \log_D \frac{p_\nu}{p_\rho} + \sum_{\rho \in C_\nu^{(\leq D)}} \sum_{x \text{ is a leaf in } \mathcal{T}_\rho} \frac{p(x)}{p_\nu} \log_D \frac{p_\nu}{p(x)} + \sum_{\rho \in C_\nu^{(>D)}} \frac{p_\rho}{p_\nu} \log_D \frac{p_\nu}{p_\rho}$$

$$\geq \sum_{\rho \in C_\nu^{(\leq D)}} \frac{p_\rho}{p_\nu} + \sum_{\rho \in C_\nu^{(>D)}} \left(\frac{p_\rho}{p_\nu} - \frac{p_{\rho, Last}}{p_\nu} \right) + \frac{p_{\nu_D, Last}}{p_\nu}, \quad (4)$$

where $\mathcal{T}_\rho$ denotes the subtree rooted at ρ. We can rewrite the second summation on the left-hand side of (4) as follows

$$\sum_{\rho \in C_\nu^{(\leq D)}} \sum_{x \text{ is a leaf in } \mathcal{T}_\rho} \frac{p(x)}{p_\nu} \log_D \frac{p_\nu}{p(x)} = \sum_{\rho \in C_\nu^{(\leq D)}} \frac{p_\rho}{p_\nu} \sum_{x \text{ is a leaf in } \mathcal{T}_\rho} \frac{p_\nu}{p_\rho} \frac{p(x)}{p_\nu} \log_D \frac{p_\rho}{p(x)} \frac{p_\nu}{p_\rho}$$

$$= \sum_{\rho \in C_\nu^{(\leq D)}} \left(\frac{p_\rho}{p_\nu} H_D(\mathbf{q}^{(\rho)}) + \frac{p_\rho}{p_\nu} \log_D \frac{p_\nu}{p_\rho} \right). \tag{5}$$

We now note that first and third terms on the left-hand side of (4) and the second term on the right-hand side of (5) give the entropy of $\mathbf{q}^{(\nu)}$, i.e.,

$$\sum_{\rho \in C_\nu^{(\ell)}} \frac{p_\rho}{p_\nu} \log_D \frac{p_\nu}{p_\rho} + \sum_{\rho \in C_\nu^{(>D)}} \frac{p_\rho}{p_\nu} \log_D \frac{p_\nu}{p_\rho} + \sum_{\rho \in C_\nu^{(\leq D)}} \frac{p_\rho}{p_\nu} \log_D \frac{p_\nu}{p_\rho} = H_D(\mathbf{q}^{(\nu)}). \tag{6}$$

Then, we can rewrite (4) as follows

$$H_D(\mathbf{q}^{(\nu)}) + \sum_{\rho \in C_\nu^{(\leq D)}} \frac{p_\rho}{p_\nu} \left(H_D(\mathbf{q}^{(\rho)}) - 1 \right) \geq \sum_{\rho \in C_\nu^{(>D)}} \left(\frac{p_\rho}{p_\nu} - \frac{p_{\rho,Last}}{p_\nu} \right) + \frac{p_{\nu_D,Last}}{p_\nu}, \tag{7}$$

where we also subtracted on both sides the first term on the right-hand side of (4).

If we add and subtract $\sum_{\rho \in C_\nu^{(\ell)} \cup C_\nu^{(\leq D)}} \frac{p_\rho}{p_\nu}$ on the right-hand side of (7) we have that this term added to $\sum_{\rho \in C_\nu^{(>D)}} \frac{p_\rho}{p_\nu}$ gives 1. Then, multiplying both sides by p_ν and re-organizing terms we get

$$p_\nu \left(1 - H_D(\mathbf{q}^{(\nu)}) \right) + \sum_{\rho \in C_\nu^{(\leq D)}} p_\rho \left(1 - H_D(\mathbf{q}^{(\rho)}) \right)$$

$$\leq \sum_{\rho \in C_\nu^{(\ell)} \cup C_\nu^{(\leq D)}} p_\rho + \sum_{\rho \in C_\nu^{(>D)}} p_{\rho,Last} - p_{\nu_D,Last}. \tag{8}$$

We now prove the claim in the statement of the theorem. The proof will be a direct consequence of the following.

Claim. Let ν be an internal node of $\mathcal{T}$ and $\mathcal{T}_\nu$ be the subtree of $\mathcal{T}$ rooted at ν. Then,

$$\sum_{u \in N(\mathcal{T}_\nu)} p_u \left(1 - H_D(\mathbf{q}^{(u)}) \right) \leq p_\nu - p_{\nu,Last}.$$

We proceed by induction on the height h of the tree $\mathcal{T}_\nu$.

Induction Base: $h \leq 2$. Let ν be the root of $\mathcal{T}$ then all the children of ν have at most D children. Hence, we have

$$\sum_{u \in N(\mathcal{T}_\nu)} p_u \left(1 - H_D(\mathbf{q}^{(u)}) \right) = p_\nu \left(1 - H_D(\mathbf{q}^{(\nu)}) \right) + \sum_{\rho \in C_\nu^{(\leq D)}} p_\rho \left(1 - H_D(\mathbf{q}^{(\rho)}) \right)$$

$$\leq p_\nu - p_{\nu,Last},$$

where the last inequality follows from (8), using that $p_{\nu_D,Last} = p_{\nu,Last}$ and $C_\nu^{(>D)} = \emptyset$, yields $\sum_{\rho \in C_\nu^{(>D)}} \frac{p_{\rho,Last}}{p_\nu} = 0$.

Induction Step. Let $h > 2$ and ν be an internal node such that $\mathcal{T}_\nu$ has height h. Assume (induction hypothesis) that the claim holds for each subtree of height smaller than h.

Let $\nu_1, \ldots, \nu_D$ be the children of ν. Then,

$$
\sum_{u \in N(\mathcal{T}_\nu)} p_u \left(1 - H_D(\mathbf{q}^{(u)})\right) = \left(p_\nu \left(1 - H_D(\mathbf{q}^{(\nu)})\right) + \sum_{\rho \in C_\nu^{(\leq D)}} p_\rho \left(1 - H_D(\mathbf{q}^{(\rho)})\right) \right)
$$

$$
+ \sum_{\rho \in C_\nu^{(>D)}} \sum_{u \in N(\mathcal{T}_\rho)} p_u \left(1 - H_D(\mathbf{q}^{(u)})\right) \quad (9)
$$

$$
\leq \sum_{\rho \in C_\nu^{(\ell)} \cup C_\nu^{(\leq D)}} p_\rho + \sum_{\rho \in C_\nu^{(>D)}} p_{\rho,Last} - p_{\nu_D,Last} \quad (10)
$$

$$
+ \sum_{\rho \in C_\nu^{(>D)}} (p_\rho - p_{\rho,Last}) \quad (11)
$$

$$
= \sum_{\rho \in C_\nu^{(\ell)} \cup C_\nu^{(\leq D)} \cup C_\nu^{(>D)}} p_\rho - p_{\nu_D,Last} = p_\nu - p_{\nu,Last}, \quad (12)
$$

where in the equality in (9) we used the brackets to separate the contribution of the root ν and the subtrees rooted at the children of ν with at most D children, from the contribution of the nodes in the subtrees rooted at some vertex in $C_\nu^{(>D)}$; the first inequality follows from using (8) on the terms in brackets in right-hand side of (9) and induction hypothesis on the remaining term;

The desired result now follows by applying the claim with ν being the root of $\mathcal{T}$, and using the fact that in this case we have $p_\nu = 1$.

3   Nice Aggregations in Time $O(D \log n)$

We begin this section by showing two technical lemmas which will be used in our following analysis. Lemma 1 says that if we "reorder" the blocks of an aggregation in non-decreasing order of their sizes, keeping the same set of sizes, the resulting aggregation preserves useful bounds on the mass of the blocks.

Let $\mathbf{p} = (p_1, \ldots, p_n)$ be a probability distribution such that $p_1 \geq \cdots \geq p_n$. Let $\mathbf{q}$ be a contiguous D-aggregation of $\mathbf{p}$ with boundaries $(i_0, \ldots, i_D)$. Let $a_j = i_j - i_{j-1}$ be the size of the jth block of $\mathbf{q}$. Let $b_1, \ldots, b_D$ be the sequence of values $a_1, \ldots, a_D$ sorted in nonincreasing order. We denote by $\mathrm{sort}(\mathbf{q})$ the contiguous D-aggregation $\tilde{\mathbf{q}}$ of $\mathbf{p}$ with boundaries $(\tilde{i}_1, \ldots, \tilde{i}_D)$ such that the size of the jth block of $\tilde{\mathbf{q}}$ is b_j, in formulas $\tilde{i}_j - \tilde{i}_{j-1} = b_j$, for $j = 1, \ldots, D$.

Lemma 1. *Let $\mathbf{q}$ be a contiguous D-aggregation of $\mathbf{p}$ with boundaries $(i_0, \ldots, i_D)$. Let $\tilde{\mathbf{q}} = \mathrm{sort}(\mathbf{q})$. Then, for each $j = 1, \ldots, D - 1$, the following properties hold*

1) *if $q_j \leq \frac{1}{D}$ then we have that $\tilde{q}_j \leq \frac{1}{D}$ holds too;*
2) *if $q_j - q_{j,Last} \leq \frac{1}{D}$ then we have that $\tilde{q}_j - \tilde{q}_{j,Last} \leq \frac{1}{D}$ holds too;*

Proof. For each $j = 1, \ldots, D$, let $a_j = i_j - i_{j-1}$ be the size of the jth block of $\mathbf{q}$ and $b_j = \tilde{i}_j - \tilde{i}_{j-1}$ be the size of the jth block of $\tilde{\mathbf{q}}$. Then, by definition $b_1, \ldots, b_D$ is the sequence of values $a_1, \ldots, a_D$ sorted in nonincreasing order.

If $a_1 \leq a_2 \leq \cdots \leq a_D$, we have $\tilde{\mathbf{q}} = \mathbf{q}$ and the claim trivially holds. If the block sizes a_j are not sorted there is some $1 \leq k \leq D-1$ such that $a_k > a_{k+1}$. Let us call this an inversion. Let $\hat{\mathbf{q}}$ be the contiguous D-aggregation obtained from $\mathbf{q}$ by removing this inversion, i.e., the boundaries $(\hat{i}_0, \ldots, \hat{i}_D)$ of $\hat{\mathbf{q}}$ are defined by

$$\hat{i}_j = \begin{cases} i_j & j \neq k \\ i_{k-1} + a_{k+1} & j = k \end{cases}$$

For each $j \notin \{k, k+1\}$, we have $\hat{q}_j = q_j$ and $\hat{q}_{j,Last} = q_{j,Last}$, hence these components of $\hat{\mathbf{q}}$ satisfy both conditions in the statement of the lemma.

For $j = k$, using $a_k > a_{k+1}$, we have

$$\hat{q}_k = \sum_{\ell=i_{k-1}+1}^{i_{k-1}+a_{k+1}} p_\ell < \sum_{\ell=i_{k-1}+1}^{i_{k-1}+a_k} p_\ell \leq q_k - q_{k,Last},$$

which also implies that conditions 1) and 2) hold for $j = k$. Moreover, using $p_{i_{k-1}+1} \geq p_{i_{k-1}+2} \geq \cdots \geq p_{i_{k+1}}$ we have that for each $t = a_k - 1, a_k$

$$\sum_{\ell=i_{k-1}+a_{k+1}+1}^{i_{k-1}+a_{k+1}+t} p_\ell \leq \sum_{\ell=i_{k-1}+1}^{i_{k-1}+t} p_\ell.$$

Noting that for $t = a_k - 1$ (resp. $t = a_k$) the left-hand side of this inequality is equal to $\hat{q}_{k+1} - \hat{q}_{k+1,Last}$ (resp. $\hat{q}_{k+1}$) and the right hand side is equal to $q_k - q_{k,Last}$ (resp. q_k) we have that conditions 1) and 2) hold also for $j = k + 1$.

The following lemma says that any aggregation without blocks of size $> D$ is nice. Due to the space limitations, the proof is deferred to the extended version of the paper.

Lemma 2. *Let $\mathbf{p} = (p_1, \ldots, p_n)$ be a probability distribution such that $p_1 \geq \cdots \geq p_n$. Let $\mathbf{q}$ be a contiguous D-aggregation of $\mathbf{p}$ with boundaries $(i_0, \ldots, i_D)$ such that for each $j = 1, \ldots, D-1$, it holds that $i_j - i_{j-1} \leq i_{j+1} - i_j$. Following the notation in Definition 2, let $\mathcal{L} = \{j \mid i_j - i_{j-1} \geq D+1\}$, be the set of blocks of size larger than D. If $\mathcal{L} = \emptyset$ then $\mathbf{q}$ is nice.*

Theorem 3. *Let $D \geq 4$. Let $\mathbf{p} = (p_1, \ldots, p_n)$ be a probability distribution such that $p_1 \geq p_2 \geq \ldots \geq p_n$. Let $\mathbf{q}$ be a D-aggregation of $\mathbf{p}$ with boundaries $(i_0, i_1, \ldots, i_D)$ and such that:*

1. $i_{j+1} - i_j \geq i_j - i_{j-1}$ for each $j = 1, \ldots, D-1$,

2. *for all* $j \in \mathcal{S} \cup \mathcal{F}$, $p_{i_{j-1}+1}, \ldots, p_{i_j} \leq \frac{1}{D}$.
3. *for all* $j \in \mathcal{L}$ *such that* $j < D$, $q_j - q_{j,Last} \leq \frac{1}{D}$.
4. *either there is a block in* $\mathcal{L}$ *of mass smaller than* $1/D$ *or there exists an index* $\hat{j} \in [D-1] \setminus \mathcal{L}$ *and an index* $i_{\hat{j}-1} < k \leq i_{\hat{j}}$ *such that* $p_k \leq \frac{1}{D}$ *and* $\frac{\frac{1}{D}-p_k}{D-1} \geq q_{D,Last}$.

Then, $\mathbf{q}$ *is nice.*

Proof. If $\mathcal{L} = \emptyset$ the desired result directly follows by Lemma 2.

If $\mathcal{L} \neq \emptyset$, because of 1., we have $D \in \mathcal{L}$.

In order to show that $\mathbf{q}$ is *nice*, we show that Eq. (3) of Definition 2 holds. We consider two cases according to 4. and we first consider the case where there is $\hat{j} \in \mathcal{L}$ with $q_{\hat{j}} \leq \frac{1}{D}$. We first show that

$$\sum_{j \in [D] \setminus \mathcal{L}} \sum_{i=i_{j-1}+1}^{i_j} p_i \log_D \frac{1}{p_i} \geq \sum_{j \in \mathcal{S} \cup \mathcal{F}} \sum_{i=i_{j-1}+1}^{i_j} p_i = \sum_{j \in \mathcal{S} \cup \mathcal{F}} q_j$$

This is true since for all $j \in \mathcal{S} \cup \mathcal{F}$ $p_{i_{j-1}+1}, \ldots, p_{i_j} \leq \frac{1}{D}$, hence $\log_D \frac{1}{p_i} \geq 1$ and $p_i \log_D \frac{1}{p_i} \geq p_i$.

For the second part of the equation, we have to show that

$$\sum_{j \in \mathcal{L}} (q_{j,Last} + q_j \log_D \frac{1}{q_j}) \geq \sum_{j \in \mathcal{L}} q_j + q_{D,Last}$$

We first observe that since each block $j \in \mathcal{L}$ has size not smaller than $D+1$, and the components are in nonincreasing order, it holds that $q_{j,Last} \leq \frac{q_j - q_{j,Last}}{D} \leq \frac{1}{D^2}$. This, together with the hypothesis $q_j - q_{j,Last} \leq 1/D$, implies that $q_j \leq \frac{D+1}{D^2} \leq 1/e$ for all $D \geq 4$.

Therefore, since the function $x \log_D \frac{1}{x}$ is monotonically increasing for $x \leq 1/e$, we have that for each $j \in \mathcal{L}$, it holds that

$$q_j \log_D \frac{1}{q_j} \geq (q_j - q_{j,Last}) \log_D \frac{1}{(q_j - q_{j,Last})} \geq (q_j - q_{j,Last}). \qquad (13)$$

Therefore, we have

$$\sum_{j \in \mathcal{L}} (q_{j,Last} + q_j \log_D \frac{1}{q_j}) = q_{\hat{j},Last} + q_{\hat{j}} \log_D \frac{1}{q_{\hat{j}}} + \sum_{j \in \mathcal{L} \setminus \{\hat{j}\}} (q_{j,Last} + q_j \log_D \frac{1}{q_j}) \quad (14)$$

$$\geq q_{\hat{j},Last} + q_{\hat{j}} + \sum_{j \in \mathcal{L} \setminus \{\hat{j}\}} (q_{j,Last} + q_j \log_D \frac{1}{q_j}) \qquad (15)$$

$$\geq q_{D,Last} + q_{\hat{j}} + \sum_{j \in \mathcal{L} \setminus \{\hat{j}\}} (q_{j,Last} + (q_j - q_{j,Last})) \qquad (16)$$

$$= \sum_{j \in \mathcal{L}} q_j + q_{D,Last}, \qquad (17)$$

where (15) follows from (14) because of $q_{\hat{j}} \leq \frac{1}{D}$; and (16) follows from (15) by (13) and $q_{\hat{j},Last} \geq q_{D,Last}$.

We now consider the case where there exists an index $\hat{j} \in [D-1] \setminus \mathcal{L}$ and an index $i_{\hat{j}-1} < k \le i_{\hat{j}}$ such that $p_k \le \frac{1}{D}$ and $\frac{\frac{1}{D} - p_k}{D-1} \ge q_{D,Last}$.

If $\frac{1}{D^2} \le p_k \le \frac{1}{D}$ it holds that $p_k \log_D \frac{1}{p_k} \ge p_k + \frac{\frac{1}{D} - p_k}{D-1} \ge p_k + q_{D,Last}$, where the first inequality follows by the concavity of the function $x \log \frac{1}{x}$ and the fact that at $x = 1/D$ and $x = 1/D^2$ we have equality. On the other hand, if $p_k < \frac{1}{D^2}$ it holds that $p_k \log_D \frac{1}{p_k} \ge 2p_k \ge p_k + q_{D,Last}$. Hence,

$$\sum_{j \in [D] \setminus \mathcal{L}} \sum_{i=i_{j-1}+1}^{i_j} p_i \log_D \frac{1}{p_i} \ge p_k \log \frac{1}{p_k} + \sum_{j \in (\mathcal{S} \cup \mathcal{F}) \setminus \{\hat{j}\}} \sum_{\substack{i=i_{j-1}+1,\dots,i_j \\ i \ne k}} p_i$$

$$\ge \sum_{j \in \mathcal{S} \cup \mathcal{F}} q_j + q_{D,Last} \quad (18)$$

Using (13), we also have

$$\sum_{j \in \mathcal{L}} (q_{j,Last} + q_j \log_D \frac{1}{q_j}) \ge \sum_{j \in \mathcal{L}} (q_{j,Last} + (q_j - q_{j,Last})) = \sum_{j \in \mathcal{L}} q_j, \quad (19)$$

that together with (18) implies (3) also in this case.

3.1   The Proof of Theorem 1

We are now ready to prove Theorem 1. We will show that the procedure in Algorithm 1 constructs the desired nice contiguous D-aggregation of an input distribution $\mathbf{p}$ in time $O(D \log n)$.

Algorithm 1. An $O(D \log n)$ algorithm to construct nice D aggregations

---

NICE-D-AGGREGATION($\mathbf{p}, D, s[1..D]$)

Input: probability distribution $\mathbf{p} = p_1, \dots, p_n$, with $p_1 \ge \dots \ge p_n$, integer $3 < D < n$, array $s[1..D]$ s.t. $s[i] = \sum_{k=1}^i p_k$

Output: a nice contiguous D-aggregation of $\mathbf{p}$

1: $i_0 \leftarrow 0, j \leftarrow 1$
2: **while** $j \le D$ **do**
3:     $k^* \leftarrow \min\{k \mid k \in \{i_{j-1}+1, \dots, n-1\}, s[k] - s[i_{j-1}] \ge \frac{1}{D}\}$
4:     $i_j \leftarrow \min\{k^*, n-D+j\}$
5:     $j \leftarrow j+1$
6: $\mathbf{q} \leftarrow$ the D-aggregation with boundaries $(i_0, i_1, \dots, i_D)$
7: **return** $\tilde{\mathbf{q}} = \text{sort}(\mathbf{q})$

The pseudocode in Algorithm 1 describes a greedy strategy for constructing a D-aggregation whose components are as close as possible to the value $1/D$. The criterion followed by the algorithm corresponds to greedily setting the boundary of the jth block to the smallest value k^* such that with $i_j = k^*$ we have $q_j \geq 1/D$. We will first show that the algorithm correctly returns a contiguous D-aggregation in time $O(D \log n)$. Then, we will show that under the condition $D > 3$ the aggregation returned is guaranteed to satisfies the condition of Theorem 3, hence it is nice.

We assume that the input probability is sorted in non-increasing order and that together with the distribution also the prefix sums $s[i] = \sum_{k=1}^{i} p_k$ (for $i = 0, \ldots, D$)—with $s[0] = 0$—are given. Note that for the final purpose of building the code tree, these prefix sums need to be computed only once before the code tree construction starts. Their computation can done in $O(n)$ and this time is accounted for in the overall $O(Dn \log n)$ time for the construction of the whole code tree.

Let us first analyze the time complexity of the procedure. The **while** loop is executed D times. The computation of k^* (in line 3) can be obtained by binary search, hence we have the claimed time bound $O(D \log n)$. Finally sorting the block sizes of $\mathbf{q}$ takes $O(D \log D)$ and once the block sizes are defined computing the boundaries of the output aggregation $\tilde{\mathbf{q}}$ can be done in $O(D)$. Overall, we have a time complexity $O(D + D \log D + D \log n)$ which is $O(D \log n)$ since $D < n$.

We now show that the procedure correctly outputs a contiguous D-aggregation that satisfies the condition of Theorem niceness-0, whenever $n > D > 3$.

The invariant maintained at the beginning of each iteration j of the **while** loop is that the set $\{i_{j-1} + 1, \ldots, n\}$ contains enough components for accommodating the remaining $D - j + 1$ blocks that are still to be defined. This is clearly true at the beginning of the first iteration, since $n > D$. The idea is that in the jth iteration of the **while** loop, we try to set boundary i_j to the value $k^* \in \{i_{j-1}+1, \ldots, n\}$ such that $s[k^*] - s[i_{j-1}] \geq 1/D$ and $s[k^*-1] - s[i_{j-1}] < 1/D$ and at the same time there are enough components left for the remaining $D - j$ blocks, i.e. $|\{p_{k^*+1}, \ldots, p_n\}| > D - j$. When this is possible, $k^* \leq n - D + j$ and the boundary i_j is set to k^* in line 4.

Conversely, if $k^* > n - D + j$, it means that setting i_j to k^* would leave too few components for the remaining blocks. In this case, i_j is set to the rightmost position such that the remaining blocks all have size 1, i.e. $n - D + j$. This preserves the invariant that there is enough space to accommodate the remaining $D - j$ blocks.

Let $\mathbf{q}$ be the contiguous D-aggregation with boundaries $(i_0, \ldots, i_D)$. As direct consequence of the above analysis we have the following:

1. for each $j = 1, \ldots, D - 1$, we have

$$q_j - q_{j,Last} \leq \frac{1}{D}. \tag{20}$$

2. because of the decreasing order of the components of $\mathbf{p}$, every block of $\mathbf{q}$ of size greater than one includes components whose probability mass is not larger than $1/D$.

By Lemma 1, properties 1 and 2 above also hold for the aggregation $\tilde{\mathbf{q}}$ with boundaries $(\tilde{i}_0, \ldots, \tilde{i}_D)$, returned by the algorithm.

Note that by construction the Dth block of $\mathbf{q}$ has mass $q_D \leq 1/D$. However, it might happen that as a result of the `sort` operation the Dth block of $\tilde{\mathbf{q}}$ has mass $\tilde{q}_D > 1/D$. For our following analysis it is important to characterize the special case where, as a result of $\tilde{\mathbf{q}} = \text{sort}(\mathbf{q})$, the Dth block of $\tilde{\mathbf{q}}$ has mass $\tilde{q}_D > 1/D$ and size greater than D, i.e., it is a large block. This happens if there is a large block j in $\mathbf{q}$ of size larger than the Dth block.

Let $\tilde{j}$ be the minimum such a j. Then, in $\tilde{\mathbf{q}}$ we have that the size of the $\tilde{j}$th block is equal to the size of the Dth block of $\mathbf{q}$. If this was a large block, it means that only the large blocks have changed mass in the transformation of $\mathbf{q}$ into $\tilde{\mathbf{q}}$. Hence, since the mass of the Dth block has become larger than $1/D$ there must be some other large block in $\tilde{\mathbf{q}}$ of mass not larger than $1/D$.

Otherwise, if the Dth block of $\mathbf{q}$ was not of size larger than D, than the same holds true for the $\tilde{j}$th block of $\tilde{q}$. In this case, we have that $q_{\tilde{j},First} \leq 1/D$ and, because of $q_{\tilde{j}} - q_{\tilde{j},Last} \leq 1/D$, we have also

$$\frac{1/D - q_{\tilde{j},First}}{D-1} \geq \frac{q_{\tilde{j}} - q_{\tilde{j},Last} - q_{\tilde{j},First}}{D-1} \geq q_{\tilde{j},Last} \geq q_{D,Last},$$

where the last but first inequality follows by the "largeness" of the block $\tilde{j}$, and the last inequality by the non-increasing masses of the components of $\mathbf{p}$.

Now, let $k \in [n]$ be the index of the component of $\mathbf{p}$ coinciding with $q_{\tilde{j},First}$, hence $p_k = q_{\tilde{j},First}$. By the sorting and the minimality of $\tilde{j}$ we have that p_k will be part of a non-large block of $\tilde{\mathbf{q}}$.

Based on this consideration, the niceness of the aggregation returned by the procedure is guaranteed by Theorem 3, where condition 4 takes care of the case in which the sorting of the sizes of the blocks of $\mathbf{q}$ results in a $\tilde{\mathbf{q}}$ with a large Dth component of mass larger than $1/D$.

4 Final Remarks

The following theorem summarizes our finding.

Theorem 4. *Fix integers $n > D > 3$ and a probability distribution $\mathbf{p} = (p_1, \ldots, p_n)$, and let X be a source emitting symbols according to $\mathbf{p}$. There exists a D-ary Fano code $\mathcal{C}$ for X whose redundancy satisfies $r(\mathcal{C}) \leq 1 - p_n$. Moreover, the codetree for $\mathcal{C}$ can be constructed in time $O(nD \log n)$.*

Proof. We define $\mathcal{C}$ as the code defined by the D-ary Fano code tree using nice aggregations at each node. The bound on the redundancy follows directly by Theorem 2. The construction of such tree requires:

- rearranging symbols in order of nonincreasing probability, which can be done in $O(n \log n)$;
- the computation of the partial sums $s[i] = \sum_{j=1}^{i} p_j$ for each $i = 1, \ldots, n$, which can be done in time $O(n)$;
- the computation of a nice aggregation per interna node of the tree. By Theorem 1 this can be done in $O(nD \log n)$.

Altogether the time complexity of the above steps is $O(nD \log n)$ as desired.

A question left open by our result is about the case $D = 3$ which is not covered by our main theorem, while the case $D = 2$ is covered by the result of [9]. Two observation are in order here: We observe that Theorem 1 can also be proved based on a variant of Algorithm 1 where the assignment in line 3 is substituted with $k^* = \max\{k \mid k \in \{i_{j-1} + 1, \ldots, n - 1\}, s[k] - s[i_{j-1}] \leq \frac{1}{D}\}$. This alternative corresponds to the dual greedy choice of cutting blocks of the minimum mass not smaller than $1/D$. For the approach presented in Sect. 3 the constraint $D > 3$ is due to the magnitude of the first block of the aggregation in output; conversely, for the dual approach presented above the constraint $D > 3$ is due to extreme cases where the mass of the last block is too large. We believe that an algorithm that considers both options would always succeed also for $D = 3$. Moreover, it is possible to show that the splitting criterion used in [1] can also be adapted to guarantee nice aggregation in time $O(Dn)$ for all $D \geq 2$. This, however, leads to the overall more expensive construction of a code with redundancy $1 - p_n$ in overall $O(n^2 D)$ time.

Another question is about the possibility of attaining even sharper bounds on the redundancy.

Acknowledgments. We wish to thank the participants of the "Monday Meetings" at the University of Verona for several stimulating discussions. MR is supported by the National Science Foundation (NSF) IIS (Grant No. 1618814).

References

1. Cicalese, F., Rossi, E.: On D-ary Fano Codes. In: Proceedings of ISIT 2020 (2020)
2. Cover, T., Thomas, J.: Elements of Information Theory. Wiley-Interscience (2006)
3. Dagan, Y., Filmus, Y., Gabizon, A., Moran, S.: Twenty (short) questions. Combinatorica **39**(3), 597–626 (2019)
4. Fano, R.M.: The transmission of information, Research Laboratory of Electronics, Mass. Inst. of Techn. (MIT), Technical Report, No. 65 (1949)
5. Garey, M.R.: Optimal binary identification procedures. SIAM J. Appl. Math. **23**, 148–151 (1977)
6. Garsia, A.M., Wachs, M.L.: A new algorithm for minimal binary search trees. SIAM J. Comput. **6**, 622–642 (1977)
7. Gilbert, E.N., Moore, E.F.: Variable-length binary encodings. Bell Syst. Techn. J. **38**(4), 933–967 (1959)
8. Han, T.S., Kobayashi, K.: Mathematics of Information and Coding, Translations of Mathematical Monographs, vol. 203. American Mathematical Society (2007)

9. Horibe, Y.: An Improved bound for weight-balanced tree. Inf. Contr. **34**, 148–151 (1977)
10. Huffman, D.A.: A method for the construction of minimum-redundancy codes. Proc. Inst. Radio Eng. **40**(9), 1098–1101 (1952)
11. Hu, T.C., Tucker, A.C.: Optimal computer search trees and variable-length alphabetical codes. SIAM J. Appl. Math. **21**(4), 514–532 (1971)
12. Karpinski, M., Larmore, L.L., Rytter, W.: Correctness of constructing optimal alphabetic trees revisited. Theor. Comp. Sci. **180**, 309–324 (1997)
13. Knuth, D.E.: Optimum binary searchtrees. Acta Informatica **1**, 14 (1971)
14. Krajči, S., Liu, C.-F., Mikeš, L., Moser, S.M.: Performance analysis of Fano coding. In: Proceedings of ISIT 2015, pp. 1746–1750 (2015)
15. Lirov, Y., Yue, O.: Circuit pack troubleshooting via semantic control. I. goal selection. In: Proceedings of the International Workshop on Artificial Intelligence for Industrial Applications, pp. 118–122 (1988)
16. Mohajer, S., Pakzad, P., Kakhbod, A.: Tight bounds on the redundancy of huffman codes. IEEE Trans. IT, **58** (11), 6737–6746 (2012). IEEE Trans. Inform. Theor. **54**, 344–366 (2008)
17. Navarro, G., Brisaboa, N.: New bounds on D-ary optimal codes. Inform. Process. Lett. **96**(5), 178–184 (2005)
18. Pattipati, K.R., Alexandridis, M.G.: Application of heuristic search and information theory to sequential fault diagnosis. IEEE Trans. Syst. Man Cybern. **20**, 872–887 (1990)

On the Terminal Connection Problem

Alexsander A. de Melo[1]([⊠])(iD), Celina M. H. de Figueiredo[1](iD),
and Uéverton S. Souza[2](iD)

[1] Federal University of Rio de Janeiro, Rio de Janeiro, Brazil
{aamelo,celina}@cos.ufrj.br
[2] Fluminense Federal University, Niterói, Brazil
ueverton@ic.uff.br

Abstract. A *connection tree* of a graph G for a *terminal set* W is a
tree subgraph T of G such that leaves$(T) \subseteq W \subseteq V(T)$. A non-terminal
vertex of a connection tree T is called *linker* if its degree in T is exactly 2,
and it is called *router* if its degree in T is at least 3. The TERMINAL
CONNECTION problem (TCP) asks whether G admits a connection tree
for W with at most ℓ linkers and at most r routers, while the STEINER
TREE problem asks whether G admits a connection tree for W with at
most k non-terminal vertices. We prove that TCP is NP-complete even
when restricted to strongly chordal graphs and $r \geq 0$ is fixed. This
result separates the complexity of TCP from the complexity of STEINER
TREE, which is known to be polynomial-time solvable on strongly chordal
graphs. In contrast, when restricted to cographs, we prove that TCP
is polynomial-time solvable, agreeing with the complexity of STEINER
TREE. Finally, we prove that TCP remains NP-complete on graphs of
maximum degree 3 even if either $\ell \geq 0$ or $r \geq 0$ is fixed.

Keywords: Terminal vertices · Connection tree · Steiner tree ·
Strongly chordal graphs · Cographs · Bounded degree

1 Introduction

STEINER TREE is one of the most fundamental network design problems, proved
to be NP-complete by Karp in his seminal paper [17]. Besides being related to
several real-world applications, STEINER TREE is of great theoretical interest,
and it has been extensively studied from the perspective of graph theory [4,
8,13,25,29] and computational complexity [2,7,11,26]. Formally, the STEINER
TREE problem has as input a connected graph G, a non-empty terminal set
$W \subseteq V(G)$, and a non-negative integer k, and it asks whether there exists a
tree subgraph T of G such that $W \subseteq V(T)$ and $|V(T) \setminus W| \leq k$. In this paper,
we analyse the computational complexity of a network design problem closely
related to STEINER TREE, called TERMINAL CONNECTION.

Let G be a graph and $W \subseteq V(G)$ be a non-empty set. A *connection tree*
T of G for W is a tree subgraph of G such that leaves$(T) \subseteq W \subseteq V(T)$. In a
connection tree T for W, the vertices belonging W are called *terminal*, and the

© Springer Nature Switzerland AG 2021
T. Bureš et al. (Eds.): SOFSEM 2021, LNCS 12607, pp. 278–292, 2021.
https://doi.org/10.1007/978-3-030-67731-2_20

vertices belonging to $V(T) \setminus W$ are called *non-terminal* and are classified into two types according to their respective degrees in T, namely: the non-terminal vertices of degree exactly equal to 2 in T are called *linkers* and the non-terminal vertices of degree at least 3 in T are called *routers* cf. [9]. We remark that the vertex set of every connection tree can be partitioned into terminal vertices, linkers and routers. For each connection tree T, we let $\mathsf{L}(T)$ denote the linker set of T and $\mathsf{R}(T)$ denote the router set of T. Next, we present a formal definition for the TERMINAL CONNECTION problem.

TERMINAL CONNECTION (TCP)

Input:　　A connected graph G, a non-empty terminal set $W \subseteq V(G)$ and two non-negative integers ℓ and r.

Question:　Does there exist a connection tree T of G for W such that $|\mathsf{L}(T)| \leq \ell$ and $|\mathsf{R}(T)| \leq r$?

TCP was introduced by Dourado et al. [9], having as motivation applications in information security and network routing, and it was proved to be polynomial-time solvable when the parameters ℓ and r are both fixed [9]. Nevertheless, it was proved to be NP-complete even if either $\ell \geq 0$ or $r \geq 0$ is fixed [9]. In particular, the problem was proved to be NP-complete even if $\ell \geq 0$ is fixed and the input graph has constant maximum degree [10].

There is a straightforward Turing reduction from STEINER TREE to TCP, namely: (G, W, k) is a yes-instance of STEINER TREE if and only if (G, W, ℓ, r) is a yes-instance of TCP for some pair $\ell, r \in \{0, \dots, k\}$ such that $\ell + r = k$. An interesting aspect of this Turing reduction is the fact that it preserves the structure of the input graph. Consequently, if TCP is polynomial-time solvable on some graph class $\mathcal{G}$, then so is STEINER TREE. Analogously, if STEINER TREE is NP-complete on some graph class $\mathcal{G}$, then TCP cannot be solved in polynomial-time on $\mathcal{G}$, unless P=NP. Nevertheless, possibly STEINER TREE is polynomial-time solvable on some graph class $\mathcal{G}$ whereas TCP remains NP-complete on $\mathcal{G}$.

In this work, we confirm the existence of such a non-trivial graph class. More specifically, we prove that TCP remains NP-complete on *strongly chordal* graphs, while it is known that STEINER TREE is polynomial-time solvable on *strongly chordal* graphs [29]. On the other hand, we prove that TCP can be solved in polynomial-time on *cographs*, agreeing with the computational complexity of STEINER TREE [4]. Finally, we prove that TCP remains NP-complete on planar graphs of maximum degree 3 even if either $\ell \geq 0$ or $r \geq 0$ is fixed. It is worth mentioning that TCP can be trivially solved in polynomial-time when restricted to graphs of maximum degree 2. Thus, our result establishes an *NP-complete versus polynomial-time dichotomy* for the problem with respect to the maximum degree of the input graph. Moreover, we note that, although it is known that STEINER TREE is NP-complete on planar graphs of maximum degree 3 [19], our result cannot be seen as an immediate consequence of such a fact. Indeed, possibly TCP is polynomial-time solvable on a graph class $\mathcal{G}$ if either the parameter $\ell \geq 0$ or the parameter $r \geq 0$ is fixed, while STEINER TREE remains NP-complete on $\mathcal{G}$.

Related Works. Motivated by applications in optical networks and bandwidth consumption minimization, another variant of STEINER TREE that has been investigated is the one in which the number of *branching nodes* in the sought tree T, i.e. vertices (which not necessarily are non-terminal) of degree at least 3 in T, is bounded. In [14,27,28], the authors addressed the undirected and directed cases of this variant, for which they devised approximation and parameterized tractable algorithms, apart from obtaining some intractability results.

In addition, Dourado et al. introduced in [10] the *strict* variant of TCP, so-called S-TCP, which has the same input of TCP but further requires that the sought connection tree T satisfies leaves$(T) = W \subseteq V(T)$. It is worth mentioning that, just as TCP can be seen as a generalization of STEINER TREE, S-TCP can be seen as a generalization of FULL STEINER TREE, which is a widely studied variant of STEINER TREE [15,18,20]. Similarly to TCP, it was proved that S-TCP is polynomial-time solvable when the parameters $\ell \geq 0$ and $r \geq 0$ are both fixed [10], and that the problem is still NP-complete if $\ell \geq 0$ is fixed [10]. Nevertheless, except for the case $r \in \{0,1\}$, which was shown to be polynomial-time solvable [22], the complexity of S-TCP for fixed $r \geq 2$ has remained open. Motivated by this question, S-TCP was also investigated in [21,23]. In particular, in [23], S-TCP was proved to be NP-complete (and W[2]-hard when parameterized by r), even if $\ell \geq 0$ is constant and the input graph is restricted to split graphs. An interesting fact of this proof is that it can be easily adapted to TCP. Consequently, we obtain that TCP is also NP-complete (and W[2]-hard when parameterized by r) on split graphs. Besides this result, it was analysed in [23] the complexity of S-TCP when restricted to graphs of bounded maximum degree, and it was also proved that S-TCP is polynomial-time solvable on cographs.

Graph Notation. For any missing definition or terminology, we refer to [3]. In this work, all graphs are finite, simple and undirected. Let G be a graph. We let $V(G)$ and $E(G)$ denote the vertex set and the edge set of G, respectively. For every vertex $u \in V(G)$, we let $N_G(u)$ and $N_G[u] = N_G(u) \cup \{u\}$ denote the *(open)* *neighbourhood* and the *closed neighbourhood* of u in G, respectively; and we let $d_G(u) = |N_G(u)|$ denote the *degree* of u in G. Two distinct vertices $u, v \in V(G)$ are said to be *true twins* in G if $N_G[u] = N_G[v]$. A vertex $u \in V(G)$ is called a *universal vertex* of G if $N_G[u] = V(G)$. The *length* of a path P is defined as the number of edges of P. The *distance* between two vertices $u, v \in V(G)$ is the length of a path of G between u and v of minimum length. For every non-empty subset $S \subseteq V(G)$, we let $G[S]$ denote the *subgraph of G induced by S*.

Due to space restrictions, throughout this work, proofs of statements marked with $(\star)$ are omitted.

2   Strongly Chordal Graphs

In this section, we prove that, for each $r \geq 0$, TCP remains NP-complete when restricted to strongly chordal graphs.

A *chord* of a cycle C is an edge between any two non-consecutive vertices of C. A graph G is called *chordal* if every cycle of G of length at least 4 has a chord.

In other words, a graph G is chordal if every induced cycle of G has length 3. An *even cycle* is a cycle of even length. A chord uv of an even cycle C is called an *odd chord* if the distance between u and v in C is odd. A graph G is called *strongly chordal* if it is chordal and every even cycle of G of length at least 6 has an odd chord. A vertex u is called a *simple vertex* of a graph G if, for any two vertices $v, v' \in N_G(u)$, $N_G[v] \subseteq N_G[v']$ or $N_G[v'] \subseteq N_G[v]$. In other words, a vertex u of a graph G is simple if the collection $\{N_G[v] \mid v \in N_G(u)\}$ can be linearly ordered by set inclusion. Farber [12] proved that a graph G is strongly chordal if and only if there exists a linear order $\langle u_1, \ldots, u_n \rangle$ of the vertices of G, called *simple elimination ordering*, such that u_i is a simple vertex of $G[\{u_i, \ldots, u_n\}]$ for each $i \in \{1, \ldots, n\}$, where n denotes the number of vertices of G.

In order to prove that TCP remains NP-complete on strongly chordal graph, we present a polynomial-time reduction from the HAMILTONIAN PATH problem on strongly chordal graphs, which was shown to be NP-complete by Müller [24]. Actually, we prove in Proposition 1 that HAMILTONIAN PATH problem can be reduced in polynomial-time to st-HAMILTONIAN PATH on strongly chordal graphs, and then we present in Theorem 1 (built on Construction 2) a polynomial-time reduction from st-HAMILTONIAN PATH to TCP on strongly chordal graphs.

The HAMILTONIAN PATH problem has as input a graph G and asks whether G admits a *Hamiltonian path*, i.e. a path that contains all vertices of G; and the st-HAMILTONIAN PATH problem is the variant of HAMILTONIAN PATH which has as input a graph G and two distinct vertices s and t and asks whether G admits a st-Hamiltonian path, i.e. a Hamiltonian path between s and t.

Lemma 1. *The class of strongly chordal graphs is closed under the operation of adding universal vertices.*

Proof. Let G be a strongly chordal graph and let $\langle u_1, \ldots, u_n \rangle$ be a simple elimination ordering of G. Also, let H be the graph obtained from G by adding a universal vertex v. One can verify that $\langle u_1, \ldots, u_n, v \rangle$ is a simple elimination ordering of H. Therefore, H is strongly chordal. $\square$

Proposition 1. st-HAMILTONIAN PATH *remains* NP-*complete when restricted to strongly chordal graphs in which s and t have degree 1 each.*

Proof. Let G be a strongly chordal graph and let G' be the graph obtained from G by adding two universal vertices v and v', adding two new vertices s and t, and by adding the edges sv and $v't$. Based on Lemma 1, it is not hard to check that G' is strongly chordal. Furthermore, by construction, s and t have degree 1 in G' each. Finally, we note that $\langle u_1, \ldots, u_n \rangle$ is a Hamiltonian path of G if and only if $\langle s, v, u_1, \ldots, u_n, v', t \rangle$ is a st-Hamiltonian path of G'. $\square$

Construction 1. (Gadget H_r and Terminal Set W_r). Let r be a positive integer. We define the gadget H_r as the graph such that

$$V(H_r) = \{\rho_1, \ldots, \rho_r\} \cup \{x_1^1, x_1^2\} \cup \{x_i \mid i \in \{2, \ldots, r\}\} \text{ and}$$
$$E(H_r) = \{\rho_i \rho_{i+1} \mid i \in \{1, \ldots, r-1\}\} \cup \{x_1^1 \rho_1, x_1^2 \rho_1\} \cup \{x_i \rho_i \mid i \in \{2, \ldots, r\}\}.$$

Moreover, we let $W_r = \{x_1^1, x_1^2\} \cup \{x_2, \ldots, x_r\}$ be the terminal set of H_r.

Construction 2. (Reduction from st-HAMILTONIAN PATH to TCP). Let G be a graph and $s, t \in V(G)$ be two distinct vertices of G. Based on Proposition 1, assume without loss of generality that $d_G(s) = d_G(t) = 1$. Additionally, assume that $V(G) = \{u_1, \ldots, u_n\}$, for some positive integer n, where $u_1 = s$ and $u_n = t$. Let r be a non-negative integer. We let G' be the graph obtained from G, s, t and r as follows:

- Add all vertices and all edges of G to G';
- Add new vertices s' and t' and add the edges $s's$ and tt';
- For each vertex $u_i \in V(G) \setminus \{s, t\}$, add a true twin u_i' of u_i, in such a way that $N_{G'}[u_i'] = N_{G'}[u_i]$;
- For each vertex $u_i \in V(G) \setminus \{s, t\}$, add a new vertex w_i and add the edges $u_i w_i$ and $u_i' w_i$, where u_i' denotes the true twin of u_i added in the last step;
- If $r \geq 1$, create the gadget H_r and the terminal set W_r described in Construction 1, and add the edge $\rho_r s'$; if $r = 0$, define $W_r = \emptyset$.

Then, we let $g(G, s, t, r) = (G', W, \ell, r)$ be the instance of TCP such that $W = \{s', t'\} \cup \{w_2, \ldots, w_{n-1}\} \cup W_r$ and $\ell = 2n - 2$.

Lemma 2. *Let G be a graph and $s, t \in V(G)$ be two distinct vertices of G. Assume that s and t have degree 1 in G each. For each $r \geq 0$, G admits a st-Hamiltonian path if and only if the instance $g(G, s, t, r)$ described in Construction 2 is a yes-instance of TCP.*

Proof. Assume that $g(G, s, t, r) = (G', W, \ell, r)$. Moreover, for simplicity, consider $W_r = V(H_r) = E(H_r) = \emptyset$ if $r = 0$. First, suppose that there exists in G a st-Hamiltonian path $P = \langle s, u_{j_2}, \ldots, u_{j_{n-1}}, t \rangle$. Then, let T be the graph with vertex set $V(T) = V(H_r) \cup V(P) \cup \{s', t'\} \cup \{w_{j_2}, u_{j_2}', \ldots, w_{j_{n-1}}, u_{j_{n-1}}'\}$ and edge set

$$
\begin{aligned}
E(T) = E(H_r) &\cup \{\rho_r s'\} \cup \{s's\} \cup \{su_{j_2}\} \\
&\cup \{u_{j_2} w_{j_2}, w_{j_2} u_{j_2}', \ldots, u_{j_{n-1}} w_{j_{n-1}}, w_{j_{n-1}} u_{j_{n-1}}'\} \cup \{u_{j_{n-1}}' t\} \cup \{tt'\},
\end{aligned}
$$

where u_{j_i}' denotes the true twin of u_{j_i} added in the construction of G'. Note that T is a connection tree of G' for W with $\mathsf{L}(T) = \{s, u_{j_2}, u_{j_2}', \ldots, u_{j_{n-1}}, u_{j_{n-1}}', t\}$ and $\mathsf{R}(T) = \{\rho_1, \ldots, \rho_r\}$. Therefore, $g(G, s, t, r)$ is a yes-instance of TCP.

Conversely, suppose that $g(G, s, t, r)$ is a yes-instance of TCP. Let T be a connection tree of G' for W such that $|\mathsf{L}(T)| \leq 2n - 2$ and $|\mathsf{R}(T)| \leq r$. We note that ρ_1 is the only neighbour of the terminal vertices $x_1^1, x_1^2 \in W_r$ and, for each $i \in \{2, \ldots, r\}$, ρ_i is the only neighbour of the terminal vertex $x_i \in W_r$. As a result, T must contain all the vertices $\rho_1, \ldots, \rho_r$. More specifically, such vertices must be routers of T. Consequently, $T' = T - H_r$ cannot contain any router, and all non-terminal vertices of T' must be linkers. Moreover, by construction, s' and t' have degree 1 in T'. This implies that the vertices $s, w_2, \ldots, w_{n-1}, t$ have degree exactly 2 in T' each, otherwise T would not be connected or $W \not\subseteq V(T)$. Hence, T' consists in a path P' between s' and t' of the form

$$
P' = \langle s', s, u_{j_2}, w_{j_2}, u_{j_2}', \ldots, u_{j_{n-1}}, w_{j_{n-1}}, u_{j_{n-1}}', t, t' \rangle,
$$

where u'_{j_i} denotes the true twin of u_{j_i} added in the construction of G'. Therefore, G admits a st-Hamiltonian path. Indeed, $\langle s, u_{j_2}, \ldots, u_{j_{n-1}}, t \rangle$ is a st-Hamiltonian path of G.   □

Lemma 3. *The class of strongly chordal graphs is closed under the operation of adding true twins.*

Proof. Let G be a strongly chordal graph and let $\langle u_1, \ldots, u_n \rangle$ be a simple elimination ordering of G. Also, let v be a vertex of G and H be the graph obtained from G by adding a true twin v' of v. Suppose that $v = u_i$, for some $i \in \{1, \ldots, n\}$. One can readily verify that $\langle u_1, \ldots, u_i, v', \ldots, u_n \rangle$ is a simple elimination ordering of H. Therefore, H is strongly chordal.   □

Lemma 4. *Let G be a strongly chordal graph with two true twin vertices v and v'. The graph G' obtained from G by adding a new vertex w and adding the edges vw and $v'w$ is strongly chordal.*

Proof. Let $\langle u_1, \ldots, u_n \rangle$ be a simple elimination ordering of G. Since by construction $N_{G'}(w) = \{v, v'\}$ and $N_G[v] = N_G[v']$, it is immediate that $\langle w, u_1, \ldots, u_n \rangle$ is a simple elimination ordering of G'. Therefore, G' is strongly chordal.   □

Theorem 1 ($\star$). *For each $r \geq 0$, TCP remains NP-complete when restricted to strongly chordal graphs.*

3   Cographs

In this section, we prove that TCP is linear-time solvable when restricted to cographs. A *cograph*, also called *complement reducible graph*, is a graph that does not contain a path of length 3 as an induced subgraph. Alternatively, cographs are characterized by the following recursive definition, given by Corneil et al. [5]:

- A graph on a single vertex is a cograph;
- If $G_1, \ldots, G_k$ are cographs, then so is their *disjoint union* $G_1 \cup \cdots \cup G_k$, i.e. the graph with vertex set $V(G_1 \cup \cdots \cup G_k) = V(G_1) \uplus \cdots \uplus V(G_k)$ and edge set $E(G_1 \cup \cdots \cup G_k) = E(G_1) \uplus \cdots \uplus E(G_k)$;
- If G is a cograph, then so is its complement $\overline{G}$.

We note that, if $\overline{G}$ is a cograph on more than one vertex, then there exist $k \geq 2$ cographs $G_1, \ldots, G_k$ such that G is their *join* $G_1 \wedge \cdots \wedge G_k$, i.e. the graph with vertex set $V(G_1 \wedge \cdots \wedge G_k) = V(G_1 \cup \cdots \cup G_k)$ and edge set $E(G_1 \wedge \cdots \wedge G_k) = E(G_1 \cup \cdots \cup G_k) \uplus \{uv \mid u \in V(G_i), v \in V(G_j), i, j \in \{1, \ldots, k\}, i \neq j\}$.

An interesting property of cographs is the fact that every cograph G can be uniquely represented (up to isomorphism) by a rooted tree $\mathcal{T}_G$, called *cotree*, such that the leaves of $\mathcal{T}_G$ correspond to the vertices of G, and each internal node u of $\mathcal{T}_G$ corresponds to either the disjoint union or the join of the cographs induced by the leaves of the subtrees of $\mathcal{T}_G$ rooted at each child of u [5]. Another important property is that, given a graph G, recognising G as a cograph, as well as obtaining its respective cotree (if any), can be performed in time linear in the number of vertices and the number of edges of G [6].

Let $I = (G, W, \ell, r)$ be an instance of TCP, where G is a cograph. Since TCP can be easily solved in linear-time if $|W| < 3$ or $G[W]$ is connected, we assume throughout this section that $|W| \geq 3$ and $G[W]$ is not connected. Moreover, we assume that G is connected. Therefore, G must be the join of $k \geq 2$ cographs $G_1, \ldots, G_k$.

Lemma 5 ($\star$). *Let G be a cograph that is the join of $k \geq 2$ cographs $G_1, \ldots, G_k$, and let $W \subseteq V(G)$ be a terminal set such that $|W| \geq 3$ and $G[W]$ is not connected. Then, there exists a unique $i \in \{1, \ldots, k\}$ such that $V(G_i) \cap W \neq \emptyset$. Moreover, G admits a connection tree for W that contains exactly one router and no linker.*

Considering the input graph G as the join of $k \geq 2$ cographs $G_1, \ldots, G_k$, it follows from Lemma 5 that TCP can be trivially solved if $r \geq 1$, or $V(G_i) \cap W \neq \emptyset$ and $V(G_j) \cap W \neq \emptyset$ for some $i, j \in \{1, \ldots, k\}$, with $i \neq j$. Thus, we dedicate the remainder of this section to resolve the case in which $r = 0$ and there exists a unique $i \in \{1, \ldots, k\}$ such that $V(G_i) \cap W \neq \emptyset$.

Lemma 6. *Let G be a cograph and $W \subseteq V(G)$ be a non-empty terminal set. If T is a connection tree of G for W such that $\mathsf{R}(T) = \emptyset$ and $|\mathsf{L}(T)|$ is minimum, then $N_T(u) \subseteq W$ for each $u \in \mathsf{L}(T)$.*

Proof. Let T be a connection tree of G for W such that $\mathsf{R}(T) = \emptyset$ and $|\mathsf{L}(T)|$ is minimum. For the sake of contradiction, suppose that $N_T(u) \not\subseteq W$ for some linker $u \in \mathsf{L}(T)$. Since $\mathsf{R}(T) = \emptyset$ and leaves$(T) \subseteq W$, u belongs to a path P of T between two terminal vertices $w, w' \in W$, such that $(V(P) \setminus \{w, w'\}) \cap W = \emptyset$. Thus, it follows from the assumption $N_T(u) \not\subseteq W$ that $|V(P)| \geq 4$. Since cographs do not contain paths of length 3 as induced subgraphs, there exists a path P' of G between w and w' such that $|V(P')| \leq 3$ and $V(P') \subseteq V(P)$. Then, let T' be the graph with vertex set $V(T') = (V(T) \setminus V(P)) \cup V(P')$ and edge set $E(T') = (E(T) \setminus V(P)) \cup E(P')$. One can easily verify that T' is a connection tree of G for W such that $\mathsf{R}(T) = \emptyset$ and $\mathsf{L}(T') \subsetneq \mathsf{L}(T)$, which contradicts the minimality of $|\mathsf{L}(T)|$.   □

For each graph G, we let $\mathsf{cc}(G)$ denote the set of connected components of G, and we let $o(G) = |\mathsf{cc}(G)|$ denote the number of connected components of G.

Corollary 1 ($\star$). *Let G be a cograph, $W \subseteq V(G)$ be a non-empty terminal set, and let T be a connection tree of G for W such that $\mathsf{R}(T) = \emptyset$. If $|\mathsf{L}(T)|$ is minimum, then $|\mathsf{L}(T)| = o(G[W]) - 1$.*

Corollary 1 establishes that, whenever a cograph G admits a connection tree for a non-empty terminal set $W \subseteq V(G)$ that does not contain routers, G admits a connection tree T for W such that $\mathsf{R}(T) = \emptyset$ and $\mathsf{L}(T) = o(G[W]) - 1$. More importantly, it establishes that $o(G[W]) - 1$ is the minimum possible number of linkers that such a tree T can have. Therefore, if $I = (G, W, \ell, r)$ is an instance of TCP such that G is a cograph and $r = 0$, then ℓ must be at least $o(G[W]) - 1$, otherwise I is certainly a no-instance of the problem.

A *connection forest* of a graph G for a non-empty terminal set W is a subgraph F of G such that F is a forest and $\bigcup_{T \in \mathrm{cc}(F)} \mathrm{leaves}(T) \subseteq W \subseteq V(F)$. A connection forest F is said to be *routerless* if $\bigcup_{T \in \mathrm{cc}(F)} \mathsf{R}(T) = \emptyset$. For each graph G and each non-empty terminal $W \subseteq V(G)$, we let

$$\eta[G, W] = \min \{ o(F) \mid F \text{ is a routerless connection forest of } G \text{ for } W \}.$$

As a degenerate case, we define $\eta[G, \emptyset] = 0$. We note that $\eta[G, W] = 1$ if and only if G admits a connection tree of G for W such that $\mathsf{R}(T) = \emptyset$. In particular, for $|W| \geq 3$, $\eta[G, W] = 1$ if and only if $G[W]$ is connected.

Lemma 7 ($\star$). *Let G be a cograph and $W \subseteq V(G)$ be a terminal set. If G is the disjoint union of $k \geq 2$ cographs $G_1, \ldots, G_k$, then*

$$\eta[G, W] = \sum_{i \in \{1, \ldots, k\}} \eta[G_i, V(G_i) \cap W].$$

Lemma 8 ($\star$). *Let G be a cograph and $W \subseteq V(G)$ be a terminal set. If G is the join of $k \geq 2$ cographs $G_1, \ldots, G_k$ and there exists a unique $i \in \{1, \ldots, k\}$ such that $V(G_i) \cap W \neq \emptyset$, then*

$$\eta[G, W] = \max \{1, \eta[G_i, W] - n + n_i\},$$

where $n = |V(G)|$ and $n_i = |V(G_i)|$.

Theorem 2. *TCP is linear-time solvable on cographs.*

Proof. Let $I = (G, W, \ell, r)$ be an instance of TCP, where G is a cograph. Assume without loss of generality that $|W| \geq 3$, G is connected but $G[W]$ is not connected. Moreover, based on Lemma 5 and on Corollary 1, assume that $r = 0$ and $\ell \geq o(G[W])$, respectively. Then, let $\mathcal{T}_G$ be the cotree associated with G. Compute $\eta[G, W]$ in a bottom-up manner, according to the post-order traversal of $\mathcal{T}_G$, following the rules described below:

$$\eta[G, W] = \begin{cases} \begin{aligned} &\left[\begin{array}{l} \textbf{case 1. } |V(G)| = 1 : \\ \quad 0 \quad \text{if } V(G) \cap W = \emptyset, \\ \quad 1 \quad \text{otherwise;} \end{array}\right. \\[2ex] &\left[\begin{array}{l} \textbf{case 2. } G = G_1 \cup \cdots \cup G_k, \text{ for some } k \geq 2 : \\ \quad \sum_{i \in \{1, \ldots, k\}} \eta[G_i, V(G_i) \cap W]; \end{array}\right. \\[2ex] &\left[\begin{array}{l} \textbf{case 3. } G = G_1 \wedge \cdots \wedge G_k, \text{ for some } k \geq 2 : \\ \quad 0 \quad \text{if } \forall i \in \{1, \ldots, k\}, V(G_i) \cap W = \emptyset, \\ \quad 1 \quad \text{if } \exists i, j \in \{1, \ldots, k\}, i \neq j, V(G_i) \cap W \neq \emptyset \text{ and } V(G_j) \cap W \neq \emptyset, \\ \quad \max \{1, \eta[G_i, W] - n + n_i\} \quad \text{if } \exists! i \in \{1, \ldots, k\}, V(G_i) \cap W \neq \emptyset, \\ \quad \text{where } n = |V(G)| \text{ and } n_i = |V(G_i)|. \end{array}\right. \end{aligned} \end{cases}$$

Return that I is a yes-instance of TCP if and only if $\eta[G, W] = 1$. It is not hard to check that $\eta[G, W]$ can be computed in time linear in the number of vertices and the number of edges of G. The correctness of the rules described above follows from Lemmas 7 and 8. $\qquad\square$

4 Bounded Maximum Degree

In this section, we analyse the complexity of TCP when restricted to graphs of bounded maximum degree. More specifically, we prove that TCP remains NP-complete on graphs of maximum degree 3 even if either the parameter $\ell \geq 0$ or the parameter $r \geq 0$ is fixed. In particular, for fixed $r \geq 0$, we show that TCP is NP-complete on graphs of maximum degree 3 that are *planar*.

It is worth mentioning that, if the input graph G is connected and has maximum degree at most 2, then G is either a path or a cycle, and consequently TCP can be trivially solved in polynomial-time, regardless of ℓ or r. Thus, we obtain that our results establish an NP-*complete versus polynomial-time dichotomy* for TCP with respect to the maximum degree of the input graph.

Another interesting fact about our results is that they separate the complexity of TCP from the complexity of its strict variant, so-called S-TCP. Indeed, while we prove that, for each fixed $\ell \geq 0$, TCP is NP-complete on graphs of maximum degree 3, S-TCP was proved to be polynomial-time solvable on graphs of maximum degree 3 if $\ell \geq 0$ is fixed [23].

4.1 Fixed Number of Linkers

First, we consider the case in which the parameter $\ell \geq 0$ is fixed. To prove the NP-completeness of this particular case, we present a polynomial-time reduction from an NP-complete (cf. [24]) variant of 3-SAT called 3-SAT(3). The 3-SAT(3) problem has as input a set X of boolean variables and a set $\mathcal{C}$ of clauses over X that satisfies the following conditions: each clause in $\mathcal{C}$ has two or three distinct literals and each variable in X appears exactly twice positive and once negative in the clauses belonging to $\mathcal{C}$; and it asks whether there exists a truth assignment $\alpha \colon X \to \{false, true\}$ for the variables in X such that every clause in $\mathcal{C}$ has at least one true literal under α.

Construction 3. (Reduction from 3-SAT(3) to TCP on Graphs of Maximum Degree 3). Let $I = (X, \mathcal{C})$ be an instance of 3-SAT(3), with variable set $X = \{x_1, x_2, \ldots, x_p\}$ and clause set $\mathcal{C} = \{C_1, C_2, \ldots, C_q\}$, and let ℓ be a non-negative integer. We let G be the graph obtained from I and ℓ as follows:

- Create the vertices $u_1, u_2, \ldots, u_\ell$ and, for each $i \in \{1, 2, \ldots, \ell - 1\}$, add the edges $u_i u_{i+1}$; moreover, create the vertices w_I and v_I and add the edges $w_I u_1$ and $u_\ell v_I$, originating the path $P_I = \langle w_I, u_1, \ldots, u_\ell, v_I \rangle$;
- For each variable $x_i \in X$, create the gadget G_i such that

$$V(G_i) = \{w_i^1, w_i^2, t_i^1, t_i^2, f_i\} \text{ and } E(G_i) = \{w_i^1 t_i^1, t_i^1 t_i^2, t_i^2 w_i^2, w_i^2 f_i, f_i w_i^1\};$$

- Create a complete binary tree T_I, rooted at v_I, whose leaves are the vertices $w_1^1, \ldots, w_p^1$;
- For each clause $C_j \in \mathcal{C}$, create the vertices v_j^1, v_j^2 and v_j^3, and add the edges $v_j^1 v_j^2$, $v_j^2 v_j^3$ and $v_j^3 v_j^1$;

– For each clause $C_j \in \mathcal{C}$, add the edge $t_i^a v_j^b$ if the b-th literal belonging to C_j corresponds to the a-th occurrence in I of the positive literal x_i, for $x_i \in X$, $a \in \{1, 2\}$ and $b \in \{1, \ldots, |C_i|\}$; on the other hand, add the edge $f_i v_j^b$ if the b-th literal belonging to C_j corresponds to the (only) occurrence in I of the negative literal $\overline{x}_i$, for $x_i \in X$ and $b \in \{1, \ldots, |C_j|\}$.

We let $g(I, \ell) = (G, W, \ell, r)$ be the instance of TCP such that $W = \{w_I\} \cup V(T_I) \cup \{w_i^1, w_i^2 \mid x_i \in X\} \cup \{v_j^1, v_j^2, v_j^3 \mid C_j \in \mathcal{C}\}$ and $r = 2p$.

Lemma 9. *Let $I = (X, \mathcal{C})$ be an instance of 3-SAT(3). For each $\ell \geq 0$, I is a yes-instance of 3-SAT(3) if and only if the instance $g(I, \ell)$ described in Construction 3 is a **yes** instance of TCP.*

Proof. Assume that $X = \{x_1, x_2, \ldots, x_p\}$ and $\mathcal{C} = \{C_1, C_2, \ldots, C_q\}$. Additionally, assume that $g(I, \ell) = (G, W, \ell, r)$.

First, suppose that there exists a truth assignment $\alpha \colon X \to \{false, true\}$ for the variables in X such that every clause belonging to $\mathcal{C}$ has at least one true literal under α. Then, let S be the vertex set defined as follows

$$S = \{t_i^1, t_i^2 \mid x_i \in X, \alpha(x_i) = true\} \cup \{f_i \mid x_i \in X, \alpha(x_i) = false\}$$
$$\cup \{w_1^i, w_i^2 \mid x_i \in X\} \cup \{v_j^1, v_j^2, v_j^3 \mid C_j \in \mathcal{C}\} \cup V(P_I) \cup V(T_I),$$

and let $G[S]$ be the subgraph of G induced by S. We note that $G[S]$ is connected but may contain cycles. Thus, let T be a spanning tree subgraph of $G[S]$ that contains all edges of $G[S]$ except for possibly not containing some edges between the vertices v_j^1, v_j^2 and v_j^3, for $C_j \in \mathcal{C}$. In other words, T is a spanning tree subgraph of $G[S]$ such that $E(T) \supseteq E(G[S]) \setminus \{v_j^a v_j^b \mid a, b \in \{1, 2, 3\}, C_j \in \mathcal{C}\}$. It is not hard to check that T is a connection tree of G for W with linker set $\mathsf{L}(T) = \{u_1, \ldots, u_\ell\}$ and router set $\mathsf{R}(T) = \{t_i^1, t_i^2 \mid x_i \in X, \alpha(x_i) = true\} \cup \{f_i \mid x_i \in X, \alpha(x_i) = false\}$. Therefore, $g(I, \ell)$ is a **yes**-instance of TCP.

Conversely, suppose that $g(I, \ell)$ is a **yes**-instance of TCP, and let T be a connection tree of G for W such $|\mathsf{L}(T)| \leq \ell$ and $|\mathsf{R}(T)| \leq 2p$. We note that the path P_I must be in T, since every path of G between the terminal vertex w_I and any other terminal vertex $w \in W \setminus \{w_I\}$ contains all the vertices of P_I. Consequently, the graph $T' = T - P_I$ cannot contain any liker, and all non-terminal vertices of T' must be routers. This, along with the fact that $\Delta(G) = 3$, implies that $N_T(v) = N_G(v)$ for each $v \in V(T') \setminus W$. Hence, if $t_i^1 \in V(T)$ or $t_i^2 \in V(T)$, then $w_i^1, t_i^2 \in N_T(t_i^1)$ and $w_i^2, t_i^1 \in N_T(t_i^2)$. Analogously, if $f_i \in V(T)$, then $w_i^1, w_i^2 \in N_T(f_i)$. Thus, since T is acyclic, we have that, for each $x_i \in X$, either $t_i^1, t_i^2 \in V(T)$ and $f_i \notin V(T)$, or $t_i^1, t_i^2 \notin V(T)$ and $f_i \in V(T)$. Then, we define a truth assignment $\alpha \colon X \to \{false, true\}$ for the variables in X as follows: for each $x_i \in X$, $\alpha(x_i) = false$ if and only if $f_i \in V(T)$. We note that, for each $C_j \in \mathcal{C}$, every path of G between the terminal vertices v_j^1, v_j^2, v_j^3 and any other terminal vertex $w \in W \setminus \{v_j^1, v_j^2, v_j^3\}$ must contain one of the vertices t_i^1, t_i^2, f_i for some $x_i \in X$. Moreover, by supposition, $V(T) \supseteq W \supseteq \{v_j^1, v_j^2, v_j^3 \mid C_j \in \mathcal{C}\}$. Consequently, every clause in $\mathcal{C}$ has at least one true literal under α. Therefore, I is a **yes**-instance of 3-SAT(3). $\qquad\square$

Theorem 3 (⋆). *For each $\ell \geq 0$, TCP remains NP-complete when restricted to graphs of maximum degree 3.*

4.2   Fixed Number of Routers

Now, we consider the case in which the parameter $r \geq 0$ is fixed. To prove the NP-completeness of this particular case, we present a polynomial-time reduction from HAMILTONIAN CYCLE on graphs of maximum degree 3, which was shown to be NP-complete by Itai et al. [16]. HAMILTONIAN CYCLE has as input a graph G and asks whether G contains a *Hamiltonian cycle*, i.e. a cycle that contains all vertices of G. More precisely, our reduction is actually from the *st*-HAMILTONIAN PATH problem on planar graphs of maximum degree 3, and it is slightly similar to the one described in Construction 2 so as to prove that TCP is NP-complete on strongly chordal graphs. Thus, based on the fact that HAMILTONIAN CYCLE is NP-complete on graphs of maximum degree 3, we first prove in the next propositions that *st*-HAMILTONIAN PATH remains NP-complete if the input graph G has maximum degree 3 and s and t have degree 1 in G.

Proposition 2. HAMILTONIAN CYCLE *remains NP-complete when restricted to planar graphs of maximum degree 3 that have at least two adjacent vertices of degree 2 each.*

Proof. Itai et al. [16] proved that HAMILTONIAN CYCLE is NP-complete on planar graphs of maximum degree 3. Based on their proof (see Lemma 2.1 [16]), we can suppose without loss of generality that the input graph G has at least one vertex of degree 2. Thus, let $u \in V(G)$ be such a vertex, and let $e = uv$ be an edge that has u and v as endpoints, for some $v \in V(G) \setminus \{u\}$. Then, we define H as the graph obtained from G by *subdividing* e, i.e. by removing e, adding a new vertex u_e and adding the edges uu_e and u_ev. We note that H is a graph of maximum degree 3 that has at least two adjacent vertices, namely u and u_e, of degree 2 each. Furthermore, it is immediate that G has a Hamiltonian cycle if and only if H has a Hamiltonian cycle.

Proposition 3. *st*-HAMILTONIAN PATH *remains NP-complete when restricted to planar graphs of maximum degree 3 in which s and t have degree 1 each.*

Proof. Let G be a planar graph of maximum degree 3. Based on Proposition 2, assume without loss of generality that G contains two vertices $u, v \in V(G)$ such that $uv \in E(G)$ and $d_G(u) = d_G(v) = 2$. Then, let H be the graph obtained from G by adding two new vertices s and t, and by adding the edges su and vt. We note that H is a graph of maximum degree 3 and that s and t have degree 1 in H each. Furthermore, it is straightforward that G has a Hamiltonian cycle if and only if H has a *st*-Hamiltonian path. □

Construction 4. (Reduction from *st*-HAMILTONIAN PATH to TCP on Planar Graphs of Maximum Degree 3). Let G be a graph of maximum degree 3 and $s, t \in V(G)$ be distinct vertices of G. Based on Proposition 3, assume without loss of generality that $d_G(s) = d_G(t) = 1$. Moreover, assume that every vertex of G different from s and t has degree at least 2, otherwise G would certainly not admit a st-Hamiltonian path. Also, assume that $V(G) = \{u_1, \ldots, u_n\}$, for some positive integer n, where $s = u_1$ and $t = u_n$. Let r be a non-negative integer. For each $u_i \in V(G) \setminus \{s,t\}$, let $\alpha_i \colon N_G(u_i) \to |N_G(u_i)|$ be the bijection such that, for each two distinct vertices $u_{j_1}, u_{j_2} \in N_G(u_i)$, we have that $\alpha_i(u_{j_1}) < \alpha_i(u_{j_2})$ if and only if $j_1 < j_2$. We let G' be the graph obtained from G, s, t and r as follows:

- Add all vertices of G to G';
- For each vertex $u_i \in V(G)$ of degree 2 in G, add new vertices $v_i^1, v_i^2, u_i^1, u_i^2$ and add the edges $u_i v_i^1$, $u_i v_i^2$, $v_i^1 u_i^1$ and $v_i^2 u_i^2$ (see Fig. 1b);
- For each vertex $u_i \in V(G)$ of degree 3 in G, add new vertices $v_i^1, v_i^2, u_i^1, u_i^2, u_i^3$ and add the edges $u_i v_i^1$, $u_i v_i^2$, $v_i^1 u_i^2$, $v_i^2 u_i^2$, $v_i^1 u_i^1$ and $v_i^2 u_i^3$; (see Fig. 1a)

(a) $d_G(u_i) = 2$ (b) $d_G(u_i) = 3$

Fig. 1. (a) Case in which $d_G(u_i) = 2$: vertices $v_i^1, v_i^2, u_i^1, u_i^2$. (b) Case in which $d_G(u_i) = 3$: vertices $v_i^1, v_i^2, u_i^1, u_i^2, u_i^3$.

- For each vertex $u_i \in V(G)$ and each vertex $u_j \in N_G(u_i)$, add the edges $u_i^a u_j^b$, where $a = \alpha_i(u_j)$ and $b = \alpha_j(u_i)$;
- If $r \geq 1$, create the gadget H_r and the terminal set W_r described in Construction 1, and add the edge $\rho_r s$; if $r = 0$, define $W_r = \emptyset$.

We let $g(G, s, t, r) = (G', W, \ell, r)$ be the instance of TCP such that $W = V(G) \cup W_r$ and $\ell = 4n - 4$.

Lemma 10. *Let G be a graph of maximum degree 3 and $s, t \in V(G)$ be two distinct vertices of G. Assume that s and t have degree 1 in G each. For each $r \geq 0$, G admits a st-Hamiltonian path if and only if the instance $g(G, s, t, r)$ described in Construction 4 is a yes-instance of TCP.*

Proof. Assume that $V(G) = \{u_1, \ldots, u_n\}$, for some positive integer n, where $s = u_1$ and $t = u_n$. Additionally, assume that $g(G, s, t, r) = (G', W, \ell, r)$ and, for simplicity, consider $W_r = V(H_r) = E(H_r) = \emptyset$ if $r = 0$.

Suppose that there is in G a Hamiltonian path $P = \langle u_{j_1}, u_{j_2}, \ldots, u_{j_{n-1}}, u_{j_n} \rangle$ such that $s = u_{j_1}$ and $t = u_{j_n}$. Then, let S be the vertex set defined as follows:

$$S = V(H_r) \cup V(G) \cup \{v_i^1, v_i^2 \mid i \in \{2, \ldots, n-1\}\} \cup \{u_{j_2}^{\alpha_{j_2}(s)}, u_{j_{n-1}}^{\alpha_{j_{n-1}}(t)}\}$$
$$\cup \{u_{j_i}^a, u_{j_{i+1}}^b \mid a = \alpha_{j_i}(u_{j_{i+1}}), b = \alpha_{j_{i+1}}(u_{j_i}), i \in \{2, \ldots, n-2\}\},$$

and let $G'[S]$ be the subgraph of G' induced by S. We note that $G'[S]$ is connected but may contain cycles. More precisely, every cycle of $G'[S]$ is of the form $\langle u_i, v_i^1, u_i^2, v_i^2, u_i \rangle$, and it exists if and only if $d_G(u_i) = 3$ and either $S \supseteq \{u_i^1, u_i^2\}$ or $S \supseteq \{u_i^2, u_i^3\}$, for $u_i \in V(G) \setminus \{s, t\}$. Thus, we let T be the graph obtained from $G'[S]$ by removing, for each vertex $u_i \in V(G) \setminus \{s, t\}$ with $d_G(u_i) = 3$, the edge $v_i^1 u_i^2$ if $S \supseteq \{u_i^1, u_i^2\}$, or the edge $v_i^2 u_i^2$ if $S \supseteq \{u_i^2, u_i^3\}$. One can verify that T is a connection tree of G' for W such that $\mathsf{L}(T) = S \setminus (V(H_r) \cup V(G))$ and $\mathsf{R}(T) = \{\rho_1, \ldots, \rho_r\}$. Therefore, $g(G, s, t, r)$ is a yes-instance of TCP.

Conversely, suppose that $g(G, s, t, r)$ is a yes-instance of TCP, and let T be a connection tree of G for W such that $|\mathsf{L}(T)| \leq 4n - 4$ and $|\mathsf{R}(T)| \leq r$. We note that $\mathsf{R}(T) = \{\rho_1, \ldots, \rho_r\}$. Consequently, $T' = T - H_r$ cannot contain any router, and all non-terminal vertices of T' must be linkers. Moreover, by construction, s and t have degree 1 in T'. This implies that the vertices $u_2, \ldots, u_{n-1}$ have degree exactly 2 in T' each, otherwise T would not be connected or $W \not\subseteq V(T)$. Hence, T' consists in a path P' between s and t of the form

$$P' = \langle s, u_{j_2}^{a_2}, v_{j_2}^{c_2}, u_{j_2}, v_{j_2}^{c_2'}, u_{j_2}^{b_2}, \ldots, u_{j_{n-1}}^{a_{n-1}}, v_{j_{n-1}}^{c_{n-1}}, u_{j_{n-1}}, v_{j_{n-1}}^{c_{n-1}'}, u_{j_{n-1}}^{b_{n-1}}, t \rangle,$$

where $a_i = \alpha_{j_i}(u_{j_{i+1}})$, $b_i = \alpha_{j_{i+1}}(u_{j_i})$, and $c_i, c_i' \in \{1, 2\}$, with $c_i \neq c_i'$ for each $i \in \{2, \ldots, n-2\}$. Therefore, G admits a st-Hamiltonian path. Indeed, one can verify that $\langle s, u_{j_2}, \ldots, u_{j_{n-1}}, t \rangle$ is a st-Hamiltonian path of G. □

Theorem 4 ($\star$). *For each $r \geq 0$, TCP remains NP-complete when restricted to planar graphs of maximum degree 3.*

5   Concluding Remarks

We conclude this work by posing some open questions. As mentioned in the introduction, if STEINER TREE is NP-complete on a graph class $\mathcal{G}$, then, unless $P = NP$, TCP cannot be solved in polynomial-time on $\mathcal{G}$. Nevertheless, possibly TCP is polynomial-time solvable on a graph class $\mathcal{G}$ if either $\ell \geq 0$ or $r \geq 0$ is fixed, while STEINER TREE remains NP-complete on $\mathcal{G}$. Motivated by this, we ask for the existence of such graph classes. Another interesting question concerns the complexity of TCP when the number of terminal vertices is fixed. Even though it is well-known that STEINER TREE can be solved in polynomial-time if the number of terminal vertices is fixed [11], the complexity of TCP in this particular case has not been settled yet. Finally, we remark that, beyond cographs, STEINER TREE is also polynomial-time solvable on the superclass of permutation graphs [4] and on the superclass of graphs of constant cliquewidth [1]. However, it is unknown whether TCP admits polynomial-time algorithms when restricted to such graph classes.

Acknowledgments. The authors would like to thank anonymous reviewers for their suggestions and comments. This work was supported by the Brazilian agencies CAPES (Finance Code: 001), CNPq (Grant Numbers: CNPq/GD 140399/2017-8, 407635/2018-1, 303726/2017-2) and FAPERJ (Grant Numbers: E-26/202.793/2017 and E-26/203.272/2017).

References

1. Bergougnoux, B., Kanté, M.: Fast exact algorithms for some connectivity problems parameterized by clique-width. Theoret. Comput. Sci. **782**, 30–53 (2019)
2. Björklund, A., Husfeldt, T., Kaski, P., Koivisto, M.: Fourier meets möbius: fast subset convolution. In: Proceedings of the Thirty-Ninth Annual ACM Symposium on Theory of Computing. p. 67–74. STOC 2007, Association for Computing Machinery, New York, USA (2007)
3. Bondy, A., Murty, U.: Graph Theory. Graduate Texts in Mathematics. Springer, London (2008)
4. Colbourn, C.J., Stewart, L.K.: Permutation graphs: connected domination and Steiner trees. Discrete Math. **86**(1–3), 179–189 (1990)
5. Corneil, D.G., Lerchs, H., Burlingham, S.L.: Complement reducible graphs. Discrete Appl. Math. **3**(3), 163–174 (1981)
6. Corneil, D.G., Perl, Y., Stewart, L.K.: A linear recognition algorithm for cographs. SIAM J. Comput. **14**(4), 926–934 (1985)
7. Cygan, M., Pilipczuk, M., Pilipczuk, M., Wojtaszczyk, J.O.: Kernelization hardness of connectivity problems in d-degenerate graphs. Discrete Appl. Math. **160**(15), 2131–2141 (2012)
8. D'Atri, A., Moscarini, M.: Distance-hereditary graphs, Steiner trees, and connected domination. SIAM J. Comput. **17**(3), 521–538 (1988)
9. Dourado, M.C., Oliveira, R.A., Protti, F., Souza, U.S.: Design of connection networks with bounded number of non-terminal vertices. In: Proceedings of V Latin-American Workshop on Cliques in Graphs. Matemática Contemporânea, vol. 42, pp. 39–47. SBM, Buenos Aires (2014)
10. Dourado, M.C., Oliveira, R.A., Protti, F., Souza, U.S.: Conexão de terminais com número restrito de roteadores e elos. In: proccedings of XLVI Simpósio Brasileiro de Pesquisa Operacional. pp. 2965–2976 (2014)
11. Dreyfus, S.E., Wagner, R.A.: The Steiner problem in graphs. Networks **1**(3), 195–207 (1971)
12. Farber, M.: Characterizations of strongly chordal graphs. Discrete Math. **43**(2), 173–189 (1983)
13. Garey, M.R., Johnson, D.S.: The rectilinear Steiner tree problem is NP-complete. SIAM J. Appl. Math. **32**(4), 826–834 (1977)
14. Gargano, L., Hammar, M., Hell, P., Stacho, L., Vaccaro, U.: Spanning spiders and light-splitting switches. Discrete Math. **285**(1), 83–95 (2004)
15. Hwang, F.K., Richards, D.S., Winter, P.: The Steiner tree problem, Annals of Discrete Mathematics, vol. 53. Elsevier (1992)
16. Itai, A., Papadimitriou, C.H., Szwarcfiter, J.L.: Hamilton paths in grid graphs. SIAM J. Comput. **11**(4), 676–686 (1982)
17. Karp, R.M.: Reducibility Among Combinatorial Problems, pp. 85–103. Springer, Boston (1972). https://doi.org/10.1007/978-1-4684-2001-2_9
18. Lin, G., Xue, G.: On the terminal Steiner tree problem. Inf. Proces. Lett. **84**(2), 103–107 (2002)
19. Lozzo, G.D., Rutter, I.: Strengthening hardness results to 3-connected planar graphs (2016). https://arxiv.org/abs/1607.02346
20. Lu, C.L., Tang, C.Y., Lee, R.C.T.: The full Steiner tree problem. Theoret. Comput. Sci. **306**(1–3), 55–67 (2003)
21. Melo, A.A., Figueiredo, C.M.H., Souza, U.S.: On undirected two-commodity integral flow, disjoint paths and strict terminal connection problems. Networks (accepted for publication)

22. Melo, A.A., Figueiredo, C.M.H., Souza, U.S.: Connecting terminals using at most one router. In: proceedings of VII Latin-American Workshop on Cliques in Graphs. Matemática Contemporânea, vol. 45, pp. 49–57. SBM (2017)
23. Melo, A.A., Figueiredo, C.M.H., Souza, U.S.: A multivariate analysis of the strict terminal connection problem. J. Comput. Syst. Sci. **111**, 22–41 (2020)
24. Müller, H.: Hamiltonian circuits in chordal bipartite graphs. Discr. Math. **156**(1–3), 291–298 (1996)
25. Müller, H., Brandstädt, A.: The NP-completeness of Steiner tree and dominating set for chordal bipartite graphs. Theoret. Comput. Sci. **53**(2–3), 257–265 (1987)
26. Nederlof, J.: Fast polynomial-space algorithms using inclusion-exclusion. Algorithmica **65**(4), 868–884 (2013)
27. Watel, D., Weisser, M.-A., Bentz, C., Barth, D.: Steiner problems with limited number of branching nodes. In: Moscibroda, T., Rescigno, A.A. (eds.) SIROCCO 2013. LNCS, vol. 8179, pp. 310–321. Springer, Cham (2013). https://doi.org/10.1007/978-3-319-03578-9_26
28. Watel, D., Weisser, M.-A., Bentz, C., Barth, D.: Directed Steiner trees with diffusion costs. J. Comb. Optim. **32**(4), 1089–1106 (2015). https://doi.org/10.1007/s10878-015-9925-3
29. White, K., Farber, M., Pulleyblank, W.: Steiner trees, connected domination and strongly chordal graphs. Networks **15**(1), 109–124 (1985)

Parameterized Complexity of d-Hitting Set with Quotas

Sushmita Gupta[1]([✉]), Pallavi Jain[2], Aditya Petety[3], and Sagar Singh[3]

[1] The Institute of Mathematical Sciences (IMSc), HBNI, Jodhpur, India
sushmitagupta@imsc.res.in
[2] Indian Institute of Technology Jodhpur, Jodhpur, India
pallavi@iitj.ac.in
[3] National Institute of Science Education and Research (NISER), HBNI,
Jodhpur, India
{aditya.petety,singh.sagar}@niser.ac.in

Abstract. In this paper we study a variant of the classic d-Hitting Set problem with lower and upper capacity constraints, say A and B, respectively. The input to the problem consists of a universe U, a set family, $\mathscr{S}$, of sets over U, where each set in the family is of size at most d, a non-negative integer k; and additionally two functions $\alpha \colon \mathscr{S} \to \{1, \ldots, A\}$ and $\beta \colon \mathscr{S} \to \{1, \ldots, B\}$. The goal is to decide if there exists a hitting set of size at most k such that for every set S in the family $\mathscr{S}$, the solution contains at least $\alpha(S)$ elements and at most $\beta(S)$ elements from S. We call this the (A, B)-Multi d-Hitting Set problem. We study the problem in the realm of parameterized complexity. We show that (A, B)-Multi d-Hitting Set can be solved in $\mathcal{O}^{\star}(d^k)$ time. For the special case when $d = 3$ and $d = 4$, we have an improved bound of $\mathcal{O}^{\star}(2.2738^k)$ and $\mathcal{O}^{\star}(3.562^k)$, respectively. The former matches the running time of the classical 3-Hitting Set problem. Furthermore, we show that if we do not have an upper bound constraint and the lower bound constraint is same for all the sets in the family, say $A > 1$, then the problem can be solved even faster than d-Hitting Set.

We next investigate some graph-theoretic problems which can be thought of as an implicit d-Hitting Set problem. In particular, we study (A, B)-Multi Vertex Cover and (A, B)-Multi Feedback Vertex Set in Tournaments. In (A, B)-Multi Vertex Cover, we are given a graph G and a non-negative integer k, the goal is to find a subset $S \subseteq V(G)$ of size at most k such that for every edge in G, S contains at least A and at most B of its endpoints. Analogously, we can define (A, B)-Multi Feedback Vertex Set in Tournaments. We show that unlike Vertex Cover, which is same as $(1, 2)$-Multi Vertex Cover, $(1, 1)$-Multi Vertex Cover is polynomial-time solvable. Furthermore, unlike Feedback Vertex Set in Tournaments, (A, B)-Multi Feedback Vertex Set in Tournaments can be solved in polynomial time.

Sushmita Gupta was supported by SERB-Starting Research Grant (SRG/2019/001870).

© Springer Nature Switzerland AG 2021
T. Bureš et al. (Eds.): SOFSEM 2021, LNCS 12607, pp. 293–307, 2021.
https://doi.org/10.1007/978-3-030-67731-2_21

Keywords: Parameterized complexity · Kernelization · Multi hitting set

1   Introduction

The HITTING SET problem is a well-known combinatorial problem, in which given a universe U, a family, $\mathscr{S}$, of subsets over U, and a non-negative integer k, we have to decide the existence of a k-sized subset $X \subseteq U$ such that X contains at least one element from every set in the family $\mathscr{S}$. It is one of the Karp's 21 NP-complete problems which was shown to be NP-complete in 1971. The HITTING SET problem and its variants have drawn sustained attention from computer scientists over the decades [1,4,5,8,13,19,24,25,28]. The problem is not only interesting from the complexity and algorithmic point-of-view, it also finds applications in finding optimal drug combinations, an critical issue in the present times. Vazquez [27] found the application of HITTING SET in oncological drug therapy. We refer the reader to [7,11,17,18,21] for other interesting applications of HITTING SET in Biology.

In the HITTING SET problem when the size of every set in the given set family $\mathscr{S}$ is at most d, then the problem is known as the d-HITTING SET problem. The d-HITTING SET problem is known to be NP-complete even for $d = 2$ [16]. In this paper, we study another constrained version of the HITTING SET problem, in which every set in the family $\mathscr{S}$ has size at most d, and additionally there exist constraints on each set on the number of elements that it can have in common with the solution. The study of this problem was initiated by Mellor *et al.* [21] as an application to multiple drug selection for cancer therapy. Formally, we define our problem as follows.

(A, B)-MULTI d-HITTING SET   **Parameter:** k
Input: An instance $\mathcal{I} = (U, \mathscr{S}, k)$ of d-HITTING SET, two functions $\alpha : \mathscr{S} \to \{1, \ldots, A\}$, $\beta : \mathscr{S} \to \{1, \ldots, B\}$ such that $\alpha(S) \leq \beta(S)$ for each $S \in \mathscr{S}$.
Question: Is there a subset $X \subseteq U$ of size at most k such that for each set $S \in \mathscr{S}$, we have $\alpha(S) \leq |X \cap S| \leq \beta(S)$?

This problem is studied as the (A, B, d)-HITTING SET problem in [21]. We slightly changed the name of the problem to be consistent with other papers in the literature that have such "demand" constraints on the solution [3,6] and to make the problem definition consistent with the constrained version of graph-theoretic problems, to be defined later. We call the optimization version of this problem as the MIN (A, B)-MULTI d-HITTING SET problem, in which instead of finding a solution of size at most k, the goal is to find a minimum sized solution.

Note that the (A, B)-MULTI d-HITTING SET problem is a generalization of the d-HITTING SET problem. Thus, the NP-completeness of d-HITTING SET extends to (A, B)-MULTI d-HITTING SET as well. We study the problem in the realm of parameterized complexity. Mellor *et al.* [21] showed that the problem admits a polynomial kernel when parameterized by k. Thus, using the well-known result in parameterized complexity that a problem admits an FPT algorithm if and only if it admits a kernel, we know that (A, B)-MULTI d-HITTING SET admits an FPT algorithm. However, using Mellor et al. [21] result, we obtained an FPT algorithm that runs in $\mathcal{O}^{\star}(2^{Adk^d})^1$ time. In this paper, we give an $\mathcal{O}^{\star}(c^k)$ time algorithm, where c is a constant. In particular, we prove the following result.

Theorem 1. (A, B)-MULTI d-HITTING SET *can be solved in $\mathcal{O}^{\star}(d^k)$ time. However, when $d = 3$, it can be solved in $\mathcal{O}^{\star}(2.2738^k)$ time, and when $d = 4$, it can be solved in $\mathcal{O}^{\star}(3.562^k)$ time.*

Note that the running time of the (A, B)-MULTI d-HITTING SET problem claimed in the above theorem is same as the running time of the best known FPT algorithm for the d-HITTING SET problem when parameterized by k [29]. Further, using Theorem 1 along with the machinery of designing exact exponential-time algorithms using FPT algorithms given in [14], we obtained the following result.

Theorem 2. MIN (A, B)-MULTI d-HITTING SET *can be solved in $\mathcal{O}^{\star}((2 - \frac{1}{d})^{n+o(n)})$ time, where n is the size of the given universe. However, when $d = 3$, it can be solved in $\mathcal{O}^{\star}(1.5603^{n+o(n)})$ time, and when $d = 4$, it can be solved in $\mathcal{O}^{\star}(1.7193^{n+o(n)})$.*

We further show that if we do not have upper bound constraint, that is $\beta(S) = d$ for every set S in the family $\mathscr{S}$, and $\alpha(S)$ is same for every set S in the family, then the problem can be solved even faster than the d-HITTING SET problem for $A > 2$, as we can reduce the problem to $(d - A + 1)$-HITTING SET problem. This variant of the problem is formally defined as follows.

UNIFORM MULTI d-HITTING SET   **Parameter:** k
Input: An instance $\mathcal{I} = (U, \mathscr{S}, k)$ of d-HITTING SET, and a positive integer $2 \leq A \leq d$.
Question: Is there a subset $X \subseteq U$ of size at most k such that for each set $S \in \mathscr{S}$, we have $|X \cap S| \geq A$?

We call the minimisation version of this problem as MIN UNIFORM MULTI d-HITTING SET. Due to the reduction of UNIFORM MULTI d-HITTING SET to the $(d - A + 1)$-HITTING SET problem, we obtain the following results.

Theorem 3. UNIFORM MULTI d-HITTING SET *can be solved in $\mathcal{O}^{\star}((d - A + 0.2738)^k)$ time.*

Furthermore, using Theorem 3 along with the machinery of designing exact exponential-time algorithms using FPT algorithms given in [14], we obtain the following result.

Theorem 4. MIN UNIFORM MULTI d-HITTING SET *can be solved in $\mathcal{O}^{\star}((2 - \frac{1}{d-A+0.2738})^{n+o(n)})$ time, where n is the size of the given universe.*

---

[1] $\mathcal{O}^{\star}()$ hides factors that are polynomial in the input size.

We next extend our study of (A, B)-MULTI d-HITTING SET to some graph-theoretic problem which are implicitly d-HITTING SET problems. In particular, we study the VERTEX COVER problem and FEEDBACK VERTEX SET IN TOURNAMENTS in the presence of lower and upper bound constraints. Note that in the implicit HITTING SET problems, the family of sets is not given as an input. Thus, we can not give the functions α and β as input in an implicit HITTING SET problem. Thus, we appropriately redefine the constrained version of VERTEX COVER and FEEDBACK VERTEX SET IN TOURNAMENTS. The classical version of VERTEX COVER and FEEDBACK VERTEX SET IN TOURNAMENTS are defined as follows.

VERTEX COVER   **Parameter:** k
Input: A graph G and a non-negative integer k
Question: Is there a subset $S \subseteq V(G)$ of size at most k such that for each edge in G at least one of its endpoint is in S ?

Given an instance (G, k) of VERTEX COVER, a solution S of the problem is called as a *vertex cover* of the graph G.

Next, we define FEEDBACK VERTEX SET IN TOURNAMENTS. Towards this, we first define *tournament*. A tournament is a directed graph in which there is an arc (directed edge) between every pair of vertices.

FEEDBACK VERTEX SET IN TOURNAMENTS (FVST)   **Parameter:** k
Input: A tournament T and a non-negative integer k
Question: Is there a subset $S \subseteq V(G)$ of size at most k such that $G - S$ is acyclic?

Given an instance (T, k) of FVST, a solution S of the problem is called as a *feedback vertex set* of the tournament T.

Next, we define the variant of VERTEX COVER and FVST in which we have lower and upper bound constraints.

(A, B)-MULTI VERTEX COVER   **Parameter:** k
Input: An instance (G, k) of VERTEX COVER
Question: Is there a subset $S \subseteq V(G)$ of size at most k such that for each edge in G at least A and at most B of its endpoint are in S?

Since (A, B)-MULTI VERTEX COVER is a constrained version of VERTEX COVER, only values $A \geq 1$ and $1 \leq B \leq 2$ are of interest to us. Note that $(1, 2)$-MULTI VERTEX COVER is same as the classical VERTEX COVER problem. In the following theorem, we show that the complexity of the $(1, 1)$-MULTI VERTEX COVER problem contrasts with that of the classical VERTEX COVER problem.

Theorem 5. $(1, 1)$-MULTI VERTEX COVER *can be solved in polynomial time.*

Note that in the $(1, 1)$-MULTI VERTEX COVER problem, a vertex cover to the given graph is also an independent set in the graph. Clearly, due the the definition of VERTEX COVER, if S is a vertex cover of the given graph G, then $V(G) - S$ is an independent set in the graph G. Thus, the problem is reduced to check if the graph G is a bipartite graph in which one part is of size at most k. Clearly, this can be checked using well-known Breadth First Search (BFS) algorithm in polynomial time. Thus, we obtained Theorem 5.

We wish to mention here that $(1,1)$-MULTI VC is a restriction of the CONFLICT FREE VERTEX COVER problem, in which along with graph G and a non-negative integer k, we are also given a graph H; and the goal is to find a vertex cover of G of size at most k that induces an independent set in the graph H [19]. Jain et al. [19] showed that the CONFLICT FREE VERTEX COVER problem is NP-hard, however, due to Theorem 5, we get a polynomial-time algorithm when $H = G$.

We next define the constrained variant of FVST.

(A, B)-MULTI FVST   **Parameter:** k
Input: An instance (T, k) of FEEDBACK VERTEX SET IN TOURNAMENTS
Question: Is there a subset $S \subseteq V(T)$ of size at most k such that for each directed cycle C in T, we have $A \leq V(C) \leq B$?

The FVST problem is known to be NP-complete [26], however, we have the following result about the constrained version.

Theorem 6. (A, B)-MULTI FVST *can be solved in polynomial time.*

2 Preliminaries

Parameterized Complexity. In parameterized complexity, each problem instance is associated with an integer called the *parameter*. Formally, a *parameterized problem* Π is a subset of $\Sigma^* \times \mathbb{N}$, where Σ is a finite alphabet set. An instance of a parameterized problem is a tuple (x, k), where x is a classical problem instance and k is an integer, called the *parameter*. A central notion in parameterized complexity is *fixed-parameter tractability* (FPT, in short), which means, for a given instance (x, k), decidability in time $f(k) \cdot \mathsf{poly}(|x|)$, where $f(\cdot)$ is an arbitrary computable function and $\mathsf{poly}(\cdot)$ is a polynomial function. A *kernelization algorithm* is a polynomial-time algorithm that transforms an arbitrary instance of the problem to an equivalent instance (known as *kernel*) of the same problem, such that the size of the new instance is bounded by some computable function g of the parameter of the original instance. If g is a polynomial function, then we say that the problem admits a polynomial kernel. Kernelization typically involves applying a set of rules (called *reduction rules*) to the given instance. The rules are numbered, and each rule consists of a condition and an action. We always apply the first rule whose condition is true. A reduction rule is said to be *safe* if it is sound and complete, i.e. applying it to the given instance produces an equivalent instance. We say that a reduction rule is applicable on an instance if the output instance is different from the input instance.

Further details on parameterized algorithms and kernnelization algorithms can be found in [10,12,15].

Sets. The set of natural numbers $\{1, \ldots, n\}$ is denoted by $[n]$. For two sets A and B, their union is denoted by $A \cup B$. If A and B are two disjoint sets, then we denote their union by $A \uplus B$. A partition of a set A is a set of non-empty subsets of A such that every element in A is in exactly one of these subsets. However, in this paper we abuse the definition of partition and also allow empty set in the partition.

Graphs. Let G be a directed graph. By $V(G)$, we denote the vertex set of the graph G. A directed graph is called strongly connected if there exists a directed path between every pair of vertices. In a digraph, a Hamiltonian cycle is a directed cycle in the given graph that visits each vertex of the graph.

3 MULTI d-HITTING SET

In this section we will prove Theorem 1. Towards this, let $\mathcal{I} = (U, \mathscr{S}, k, \alpha, \beta)$ be an instance of (A, B)-MULTI d-HITTING SET. We begin with the following reduction rule, applied only once at the beginning. The significance of the rule is that we add an element in the universe and make sure that it is part of every hitting set. This will be used later to ensure that after the application of every reduction rule the α-value is greater than 0 for each set in the family, a requirement for a valid instance of the problem.

After the application of every reduction rule, we reuse the notations $U, \mathscr{S}, k, \alpha$ and β to denote the reduced universe, family of sets, solution size, and updated functions. We also reuse the notation $\mathcal{I}$ to denote the reduced instance.

Reduction Rule 1. *Let $\mathcal{I} = (U, \mathscr{S}, k, \alpha, \beta)$ be an instance of (A, B)-MULTI d-HITTING SET. Then, we output the instance $\mathcal{I}' = (U', \mathscr{S}', k', \alpha', \beta')$, where*

($\star$) *the universe $U' = U \cup \{x\}$, where $x \notin U$.*
($\star$) *the set family $\mathscr{S}' = \mathscr{S} \cup \{\{x\}\}$;*
($\star$) *the parameter $k' = k + 1$; and*
($\star$) *for each set $S \in \mathscr{S}' \setminus \{x\}$, we define $\alpha'(S) = \alpha(S)$ and $\beta'(S) = \beta(S)$, and $\alpha'(\{x\}) = \beta'(\{x\}) = 1$.*

Claim. Reduction Rule 1 is safe.

Proof. Let $\mathcal{I}$ be a **Yes**-instance of (A, B)-MULTI d-HITTING SET, and let X be one of its solution. Then, $X \cup \{x\}$ is quite clearly a solution of $\mathcal{I}'$. Conversely, if X' is a solution of $\mathcal{I}'$, then $x \in X'$ since the set $S = \{x\} \in \mathscr{S}'$ has to be "hit". Thus, $X' \setminus \{x\}$ is a solution of $\mathcal{I}$. □

We begin by using the algorithm for d-HITTING SET to compute a solution X for the instance of d-HITTING SET, $(U, \mathscr{S}, k)$ that runs in time $\mathcal{O}^*((d - 0.7262)^k)$ [29].

If X satisfies the capacity constraints of $\mathcal{I}$, i.e. for every $S \in \mathscr{S}$, $\alpha(S) \leq |S \cap X| \leq \beta(S)$, then we have nothing more to do, and we can output X as the solution. Suppose that X does not satisfy one or more capacity constraints, then we do as follows.

We compute every possible partition of X: subsets $X_+ \subseteq X$ and $X_- \subseteq X$ such that $X_+ \cup X_- = X$ and $X_+ \cap X_- = \emptyset$. The goal is to find a solution of $\mathcal{I}$, denoted by Y, such that in addition to satisfying each of the capacity constraints of $\mathcal{I}$ it also satisfies: $X_+ \subseteq Y$ and $X_- \cap Y = \emptyset$.

Thus, we want to solve DISJOINT (A, B)-MULTI d-HITTING SET, as defined below on the instance $(U, \mathscr{S}, k, \alpha, \beta, X_+, X_-)$.

DISJOINT (A, B)-MULTI d-HITTING SET   **Parameter:** k
Input: An instance $\mathcal{I} = (U, \mathscr{S}, k, \alpha, \beta)$ of (A, B)-MULTI d-HITTING SET, and disjoint subsets X_+, $X_- \subseteq U$.
Question: Is there a solution Y of the instance $\mathcal{I}$ such that $X_+ \subseteq Y$ and $X_- \cap Y = \emptyset$?

To solve this problem we use the following reduction rules, applied exhaustively, in the order of appearance.

We begin with the following rule that removes redundant sets.

Reduction Rule 2. Let $\mathcal{I} = (U, \mathscr{S}, k, \alpha, \beta, X_+, X_-)$ be an instance of DISJOINT (A, B)-MULTI d-HITTING SET. Suppose that there exists a set $S \in \mathscr{S}$ such that $\beta(S) \leq 0$. Then, we output $\mathcal{I}' = (U, \mathscr{S}' = \mathscr{S} \setminus S, k, \alpha_{\restriction \mathscr{S}'}, \beta_{\restriction \mathscr{S}'}, X_+, X_-)$, where $f_{\restriction A}$ denotes a function f restricted to the subset A in its domain.

Claim. Reduction Rule 2 is safe.

Proof. The safeness follows from the property that $\alpha(S) \leq \beta(S) \leq 0$ which implies that Y is a solution of $\mathcal{I}$ if and only if Y is a solution of $\mathcal{I}'$. □

Reduction Rule 3. Let $\mathcal{I} = (U, \mathscr{S}, k, \alpha, \beta, X_+, X_-)$ be an instance of DISJOINT (A, B)-MULTI d-HITTING SET. Suppose that there exists a set $S \in \mathscr{S}$ such that $S \subseteq X_-$ or $|S \setminus X_-| < \alpha(S)$ or $|S \cap X_+| > \beta(S)$. Then, output "no".

Claim. Reduction Rule 3 is safe.

Proof. It is sufficient to argue that $\mathcal{I}$ is a No-instance of DISJOINT (A, B)-MULTI d-HITTING SET. That follows readily from the definition of the problem. □

The next reduction rule will be applied when the above is no longer applicable. That is, for every set $S \in \mathscr{S}$ we have $S \setminus X_- \neq \emptyset$, $|S \setminus X_-| \geq \alpha(S)$ and $|S \cap X_+| \leq \beta(S)$.

Reduction Rule 4. Let $\mathcal{I} = (U, \mathscr{S}, k, \alpha, \beta, X_+, X_-)$ be an instance of DISJOINT (A, B)-MULTI d-HITTING SET. Then, for a set $\bar{S} \in \mathscr{S}$ such that $x \notin \bar{S}$ and $X_{\bar{S}} = \bar{S} \cap X_+ \neq \emptyset$, we reduce the instance as follows, where

$(\star)$ the set family $\mathscr{S}' = \mathscr{S}_1 \cup \mathscr{S}_2$, where

$$\mathscr{S}_1 = \{S \setminus (\bar{S} \cap X) : S \in \mathscr{S}, \alpha(S) > |S \cap X_{\bar{S}}|\}, \text{ and}$$
$$\mathscr{S}_2 = \{S \cup \{x\} \setminus (\bar{S} \cap X) : S \in \mathscr{S}, \alpha(S) \leq |S \cap X_{\bar{S}}|\}$$

$(\star)$ the universe $U' = \cup_{S' \in \mathscr{S}'} S'$;

$(\star)$ the parameter $k' = k - |X_{\bar{S}}|$;

$(\star)$ for a set $S' \in \mathscr{S}_1$, let $S' = S \setminus (\bar{S} \cap X)$, where $S \in \mathscr{S}$. Then, $\alpha'(S') = \alpha(S) - |S \cap X_{\bar{S}}|$ and $\beta'(S') = \beta(S) - |S \cap X_{\bar{S}}|$. For a set $S' \in \mathscr{S}_2$, let $S' = S \cup \{x\} \setminus (\bar{S} \cap X)$, where $S \in \mathscr{S}$. Then, $\alpha'(S') = 1$ and $\beta'(S') = \beta(S) - |S \cap X_{\bar{S}}| + 1$;

$(\star)$ sets $X'_+ = X_+ \setminus \bar{S}$ and $X'_- = X_-$.

We output the reduced instance $\mathcal{I}' = (U', \mathscr{S}', k', \alpha', \beta', X'_+, X'_-)$.

Claim. Reduction Rule 4 is safe.

Proof. We begin by observing that $\mathcal{I}'$ is clearly an instance of DISJOINT (A, B)-MULTI d-HITTING SET.

Suppose that $\mathcal{I}$ is a Yes-instance of DISJOINT (A, B)-MULTI d-HITTING SET. Then, there exists a subset $Y \subseteq U$ such that $|Y| \leq k$, $X_+ \subseteq Y$, $X_- \cap Y = \emptyset$, and $\alpha(S) \leq |Y \cap S| \leq \beta(S)$ for every set $S \in \mathscr{S}$. We will prove that $Y' = Y \setminus X_{\bar{S}} \subseteq U'$ is a solution for $\mathcal{I}'$, and thereby prove the forward direction of the claim.

The condition $X_+ \subseteq Y$ implies that $X'_+ \subseteq Y'$; and conditions $Y' \subseteq Y$ and $Y \cap X_- = \emptyset$ imply that $Y' \cap X'_- = \emptyset$. Moreover, since $X_{\bar{S}} \subseteq X_+ \subseteq Y$, we have $|Y'| = |Y| - |X_{\bar{S}}| \leq k - |X_{\bar{S}}| = k'$. Therefore, the only condition left to check is whether for any $S' \in \mathscr{S}'$, the set $Y' \cap S'$ satisfies the specified upper and lower bounds.

Consider an arbitrary set $S' \in \mathscr{S}_1$. Thus, there is some $S \in \mathscr{S}$, such that $S' = S \setminus (\bar{S} \cap X)$ and $\alpha(S) > |S \cap X_{\bar{S}}|$. Note that $S' = S$ is a possibility.

We observe that $Y' \cap S' = (Y \cap S) \setminus X_{\bar{S}}$, which yields the following relation due to the set identity $|(A \setminus C) \cap (B \setminus C)| = |A \cap B| - |A \cap B \cap C|$

$$|Y' \cap S'| = |Y \cap S| - |Y \cap S \cap X_{\bar{S}}| = |Y \cap S| - |X_{\bar{S}} \cap S|, \tag{I}$$

where the second equality holds because $X_{\bar{S}} \subseteq Y$. Since $\alpha(S) \leq |Y \cap S| \leq \beta(S)$, it follows that $|Y' \cap S'|$ is at least $\alpha(S) - |S \cap X_{\bar{S}}|$ and at most $\beta(S) - |S \cap X_{\bar{S}}|$, that is $\alpha'(S') \leq |Y' \cap S'| \leq \beta'(S')$.

Next, consider a set $S' \in \mathscr{S}_2$. Then, there exists a set $S \in \mathscr{S}$ such that $S' = S \cup \{x\} \setminus (\bar{S} \cap X)$, where $1 \leq \alpha(S) \leq |S \cap X_{\bar{S}}|$. Then, we have $Y' \cap S' = (Y \cap S) \setminus X_{\bar{S}}$, which yields the same relation as Eq. (I). Moreover, note that $x \in Y' \cap S'$ since $x \in Y$ but $x \notin X_{\bar{S}}$. Thus, we have $\alpha'(S') = 1 \leq |Y' \cap S'| = |Y \cap S| + 1 - |X_{\bar{S}} \cap S| \leq \beta(S) + 1 - |X_{\bar{S}} \cap S| = \beta'(S')$.

Hence, we have proved that $\mathcal{I}'$ is a Yes-instance as well. $(\Rightarrow)$

For the reverse direction, suppose that Y' is a solution for $\mathcal{I}'$. We claim that the set $Y = Y' \cup X_{\bar{S}} \subseteq U$ is a solution for the instance $\mathcal{I}$. Since $X_{\bar{S}}$ and Y' are disjoint, we have $|Y| = |Y'| + |X_{\bar{S}}| \leq k$.

Additionally, we have $X_+ \setminus \bar{S} \subseteq Y'$. For any element $u \in X_+ \cap \bar{S} = X_{\bar{S}}$, we have $u \in Y$. Therefore, $X_+ \subseteq Y$. The other condition is that $(X_- \setminus \bar{S}) \cap Y' = \emptyset$. Since $X_{\bar{S}}$ and X_- are disjoint, it follows that $(X_- \setminus \bar{S}) \cap Y = \emptyset$. For any element $u \in X_- \cap \bar{S}$, we have $u \notin X_{\bar{S}}$, and so $u \notin Y$. Therefore, $X_- \cap Y = \emptyset$.

Next, we will prove that Y satisfies the bounds, for this consider a set $S \in \mathscr{S}$. Let $S = S' \uplus (\bar{S} \cap X)$, where $S' \in \mathscr{S}_1$. Then, by definition we have $\alpha'(S') = \alpha(S) - |S \cap X_{\bar{S}}|$ and $\beta'(S') = \beta(S) - |S \cap X_{\bar{S}}|$, from the definition. Thus,

$$\alpha(S) - |S \cap X_{\bar{S}}| \leq |Y' \cap S'| = |Y \cap S| - |S \cap X_{\bar{S}}| \leq \beta(S) - |S \cap X_{\bar{S}}|$$
$$\alpha(S) \leq |Y \cap S| \leq \beta(S)$$

where the equality in the first relation holds due to the aforementioned set identity $|(A \setminus C) \cap (B \setminus C)| = |A \cap B| - |A \cap B \cap C|$, taking $A = Y$, $B = S$ and $C = X_{\bar{S}}$.

Next, suppose that $S = (S' \setminus \{x\}) \uplus (\bar{S} \cap X)$, where $S' \in \mathscr{S}_2$. Then, we note that $Y' \cap S' = (Y \setminus X_{\bar{S}}) \cap (S \cup \{x\} \setminus (X \cap \bar{S})) = Y \cap (S \cup \{x\}) \setminus X_{\bar{S}}$, since as before $X_{\bar{S}} \subseteq X \cap \bar{S}$.

Thus, we have the following derivations, the last equality due to $X_{\bar{S}} \subseteq Y$.

$$|Y' \cap S'| = |Y \cap (S \cup \{x\})| - |Y \cap (S \cup \{x\}) \cap X_{\bar{S}}| = |Y \cap (S \cup \{x\})| - |(S \cup \{x\}) \cap X_{\bar{S}}|$$

Note that the set $\{x\}$ is in the instance $\mathcal{I}'$ because $\{x\} \in \mathscr{S}_1$, since $X_{\bar{S}} \cap \{x\} = \emptyset$ (by definition of $\bar{S}$) and $\alpha(\{x\}) = 1$. Thus, $x \in Y'$ else Y' cannot be a solution of $\mathcal{I}'$. Moreover, since $Y' \subseteq Y$, we also have $x \in Y$. Therefore, $x \in Y \cap (S \cup \{x\})$ follows readily. Additionally, since $x \notin X_{\bar{S}}$ it also follows that $(S \cup \{x\}) \cap X_{\bar{S}} = S \cap X_{\bar{S}}$. Thus, we can infer that $|Y' \cap S'| = |Y \cap S| + 1 - |S \cap X_{\bar{S}}|$. From the definition of Y' we have $1 \leq |Y' \cap S'| \leq \beta(S) - |S \cap X_{\bar{S}}| + 1$. Combining these relations and reordering the terms yields $|S \cap X_{\bar{S}}| \leq |Y \cap S| \leq \beta(S)$. Recall that $\alpha(S) \leq |S \cap X_{\bar{S}}|$ (as $S' \in \mathscr{S}_2$), so $\alpha(S) \leq |Y \cap S| \leq \beta(S)$, follows readily.

Therefore, it follows that $\alpha(S) \leq |Y \cap S| \leq \beta(S)$, for every $S \in \mathscr{S}$. Hence, the reverse direction also holds and $\mathcal{I}$ is a Yes-instance. $\qquad\square$

After exhaustively applying these rules, we obtain an instance $\mathcal{I} = (U, \mathscr{S}, k, \alpha, \beta, X_+, X_-)$ of DISJOINT (A, B)-MULTI d-HITTING SET , where for every set $S \in \mathscr{S}$, we have either $S \cap X_+ = \emptyset$ or $S \cap X_+ = \{x\}$. Note that there may still be a set S such that $S \cap X_- \neq \emptyset$. However, we know that vertices from the set X_- do not belong to our solution. Therefore, we apply the following reduction rule.

Reduction Rule 5. *Let $\mathcal{I} = (U, \mathscr{S}, k, \alpha, \beta, X_+, X_-)$ be an instance of DIS-JOINT (A, B)-MULTI d-HITTING SET. Then, from a set $\bar{S} \in \mathscr{S}$, delete $\bar{S} \cap X_-$. Let $\mathscr{S}' = \{S \setminus X_- : S \in \mathscr{S}\}$, $U' = U \setminus X_-$. We output the reduced instance $\mathcal{I}' = (U', \mathscr{S}', k, \alpha, \beta, X_+, \emptyset)$.*

The safeness of Reduction Rule 5 follows from the fact that the vertices of X_- are not in the solution to $\mathcal{I}$.

The following result follows from the straightforward application of Reduction Rule 1 which adds the set $\{x\}$ in the set family and repeated applications of Reduction Rule 4 which ensures that every set in the original instance is "reduced" by removal of a subset of elements in X_+. At no point during our construction are we increasing the size of any set. Hence, the resulting instance is also an instance of DISJOINT (A, B)-MULTI d-HITTING SET . For any set $S \in \mathscr{S}$ such that $S \cap X_- \neq \emptyset$, we know that the Reduction Rule 5 ensures that S is reduced in size in the resulting instance.

Every set in the original instance of DISJOINT (A, B)-MULTI d-HITTING SET will be a candidate for $\bar{S}$ in Reduction Rule 4 if the set has non-empty intersection with X_+. It may happen that for some set $\bar{S}$ in the original instance we have $|\bar{S}| = d$, $\bar{S} \cap X_- = \emptyset$, $|\bar{S} \cap X| = 1$, and $\alpha(S) \leq 1$. During the application of the Reduction Rule 4 with respect to the set $\bar{S}$, we would remove one element from $\bar{S}$ and replace it with another, namely x, thereby creating a new set $S' = \bar{S} \cup \{x\} \setminus X_+$. But then, we have $|S'| = |S| = d$ even though $\alpha(S') = 1$ and $\beta(S') = \beta(S) \leq |S|$.

Observation 1. *After exhaustive applications of Reduction Rules 1–5 we have an instance $\mathcal{I} = (U, \mathscr{S}, k, \alpha, \beta, X_+, X_- = \emptyset)$ of* DISJOINT (A, B)-MULTI d-HITTING SET *, where set $\{x\} \in \mathscr{S}$ with $\alpha(S) = \beta(S) = 1$. Moreover, each set $S \in \mathscr{S} \setminus \{x\}$ is one of the following kinds:*

- *$x \in S$, such that $2 \leq |S| \leq d$, $\alpha(S) = 1$ and $\beta(S) \leq |S|$,*
- *$x \notin S$, such that $|S| \leq d - 1$, $1 \leq \alpha(S)$ and $\beta(S) \leq |S|$.*

Using $\mathcal{I}$, we will create an instance of ONES $(d-1)$-SAT, formally defined as follows.

ONES k-SAT   **Parameter:** t
Input: An instance ψ of CNF formula with at most k literals in each clause.
Question: Is there a satisfying assignment for ψ with t variables set to 1?

Creating Clauses: For each element $i \in U$, we create a positive literal v_i and negative literal $\neg v_i$. Using those literals and the sets $S \in \mathscr{S}$ we create two types clauses as follows, named *positive clauses* and *negative clauses*.

For any set $S = \{a_1, \ldots, a_t\}$, where $t \leq d$, we create a set of clauses, denoted by $\mathscr{C}_S$ as follows. We create $\binom{|S|}{(\alpha(S)-1)}$ number clauses each containing exactly $|S| - \alpha(S) + 1$ positive literals, where each clause corresponds to a $(|S| - \alpha(S) + 1)$-sized subset of S. Moreover, if $\beta(S) \leq |S| - 1$, then we create $\binom{|S|}{\beta(S)+1}$ number clauses each containing exactly $(\beta(S) + 1)$ negative literals, where each clause corresponds to a $(\beta(S) + 1)$-sized subset of S.

For example if $S = \{a_1, a_2, a_3\}$, and $\alpha(S) = 1$ and $\beta(S) = 2$, we have one positive clause $(v_{a_1} \vee v_{a_2} \vee v_{a_3})$, and a negative clause $(\neg v_{a_1} \vee \neg v_{a_2} \vee \neg v_{a_3})$. If $\alpha(S) = 2$ and $\beta(S) = 2$, then there are three positive clauses $(v_{a_1} \vee v_{a_2})$, $(v_{a_2} \vee v_{a_3})$, and $(v_{a_1} \vee v_{a_3})$ and one negative clause $(\neg v_{a_1} \vee \neg v_{a_2} \vee \neg v_{a_3})$.

The resulting CNF formula is denoted by ψ and the instance $\mathcal{J} = (\psi, k)$ is a valid instance of ONES d-SAT.

Claim. $\mathcal{I} = (U, \mathscr{S}, k, \alpha, \beta, X_+, X_-)$ is a **Yes**-instance of DISJOINT (A, B)-MULTI d-HITTING SET if and only if $\mathcal{J} = (\psi, k)$ is a **Yes**-instance of ONES d-SAT.

Proof. Let Y be a solution for $\mathcal{I}$. For each element in Y, we set the corresponding variable to true, and all others are set to false. This a boolean assignment for ψ. We will prove that this constitutes a solution for $\mathcal{J}$. Each clause in ψ corresponds to a set in $\mathscr{S}$, and the clause can either be a positive clause or negative. We will show that the assignment satisfies each clause in ψ.

We know that for any set $S \in \mathscr{S}$, we have $|S \setminus Y| \le |S| - \alpha(S)$. Each positive clause in ψ associated to the set S contains exactly $|S| - \alpha(S) + 1$ elements. Thus, the clause will contain at least one positive literal that corresponds to an element $u \in Y \cap S$. Thus, variable v_u is true. Consequently, we know that each positive clause associated to S will be satisfied in ψ. There are negative clauses corresponding to S if $\beta(S) \le |S| - 1$. Note that Y contains at most $\beta(S)$ elements from the set S. Each negative clause contains exactly $\beta(S) + 1$ literals, hence at least one variable in each negative clause is set to false. Thus, each negative clause corresponding to S will be satisfied. This completes the forward direction.

Conversely, suppose that A is a satisfying assignment for ψ in which at most k variables are true. We define a set $Y \subseteq U$ such that each element of Y corresponds to a variable that is true in A. We claim that Y is a solution for $\mathcal{I}$.

Clearly, $|Y| \le k$. Consider an arbitrary set $S \in \mathscr{S}$. Suppose that $|Y \cap S| < \alpha(S)$. Thus, $|S \setminus Y| \ge |S| - \alpha(S) + 1$. Consider the positive clause that contains the literals corresponding to the elements in $S \setminus Y$. That clause must be unsatisfied in ψ, a contradiction. Thus, $|Y \cap S| \ge \alpha(S)$.

Suppose that $|S \cap Y| \ge \beta(S) + 1$. Then, $|S \setminus Y| \le |S| - \beta(S) - 1$. Then, since A satisfies each of the negative clauses corresponding to S (if any), there are $\beta(S) + 1$ negative literals in any negative clause associated to S. In any of these clauses, there must exist at least one variable, denoted by v_y, that is set to false so that $\neg v_y$ appears in the negative clause and ensures that it is satisfied. Thus, at most $\beta(S)$ number of variables can be set to true in any negative clause of S. In other words, at most $\beta(S)$ elements from S can be in Y. This completes the proof of the reverse direction. □

Before we proceed with the rest of the discussion we want to point out that due to Observation 1 and our construction of ψ, it follows that there is a clause in ψ that consists of the only v_x. Hence, we may reduce the instance $\mathcal{J}$ by setting the variable v_x to true.

Let $\mathcal{J} = (\psi, k)$ be an instance of ONES d-SAT. For any clause C in ψ that contains the variable v_x be true and consequently the negated literal $\neg v_x$ to be false. The clauses that have been set to true (as a result of this) are deleted and all occurrences of the literal $\neg v_x$ are deleted from the formula. The resulting instance is $\mathcal{J}' = (\psi', k - 1)$.

Claim. $\mathcal{J} = (\psi, k)$ is Yes-instance of ONES d-SAT if and only if $\mathcal{J}' = (\psi', k - 1)$ is Yes-instance of ONES $(d - 1)$-SAT.

Proof. We will first argue that ψ' is a $(d - 1)$-SAT formula. The set of clauses in ψ corresponding to the set $S \in \mathscr{S}$ is denoted by $\mathscr{C}_S$.

We begin by observing that for each set $S \in \mathscr{S}$, where $\beta(S) \leq |S| - 1$, the clauses in $\mathscr{C}_S$ have size $|S| - \alpha(S) + 1$ or $\beta(S) + 1$. If $\beta(S) = |S|$, then the formula only has (positive) clauses of size $|S| - \alpha(S) + 1$.

Now we split into cases based on the size of S, and the last two possibilities described in Observation 1. Note that the clause containing only v_x does not exist in ψ'. Either $|S| \leq d - 1$ or $|S| = d$ and $x \in S$.

If $|S| \leq d - 1$, then we have $|S| - \alpha(S) + 1 \leq d - 1$, since $\alpha(S) \geq 1$. Thus, the positive clauses in $\mathscr{C}_S$ contain at most $d - 1$ literals. Similarly, if $\beta(S) < |S| \leq d - 1$, then the negative clauses contain at most $d - 1$ literals. If $\beta(S) = |S|$, then there are no negative clauses in $\mathscr{C}_S$. Note that these conclusions hold regardless of whether $x \in S$.

If $2 \leq |S| = d$ and $x \in S$. Then, consider an arbitrary positive clause C in $\mathscr{C}_S$ that does not contain v_x. Clause C is present in ψ', even though each of the clauses that contain v_x are not. The clause C only contains positive literals that correspond to the elements in $S \setminus \{x\}$. Thus, there can be at most $d - 1$ literals. If $\beta(S) = |S|$, then there are no negative clauses in $\mathscr{C}_S$, and our argument is complete. Suppose that $\beta(S) < |S| = d$, then negative clauses contain $\beta(S) + 1$ literals. Next, consider a negative clause in $\mathscr{C}_S$ that does not contain $\neg v_x$. This clause is present in ψ' and it only contains literals that correspond to elements in $S \setminus \{x\}$. Thus, there can only be at most $d - 1$ literals. Any negative clause in $\mathscr{C}_S$ that contains $\neg v_x$ is reduced by one literal in ψ'. Thus, this too is of size at most $d - 1$.

Thus, we have shown that ψ' is a $(d - 1)$-SAT formula. What remains to be shown is that there is a satisfying assignment $A \in \{0, 1\}^{n'}$ for ψ that sets at most k variables to true if and only if there is a satisfying assignment $A' \in \{T, F\}^{n'-1}$ for ψ' in which at most $k - 1$ variables are true.

Suppose that A is a satisfying assignment for (ψ, k). Then, A must set v_x to true, since there is a clause containing only v_x. Clearly, the assignment $A' \in \{T, F\}^{n'-1}$ obtained by restricting A to the variables in ψ' is a satisfying assignment for ψ' that sets at most $k - 1$ variables to true.

For the converse, let $A' \in \{T, F\}^{n'-1}$ be a solution for $\mathscr{J}' = (\psi', k-1)$. Then, extending A' by setting the variable v_x to true yields a satisfying assignment for ψ that sets at most k variables to true. The argument is straightforward, since the clause (v_x) in ψ will be immediately satisfied as will any other clause that contains the variable v_x. All other clauses are already satisfied by A' and that remains unchanged in ψ. $\square$

Running Time Analysis: For $d \geq 5$, we will solve ONES $(d - 1)$-SAT using $T_{d-1}(k) = (d - 1)^k$ algorithm using a simple branching algorithm mentioned in [14]. Since we try all possible subsets of X a hitting set of the instance $(U, \mathscr{S}, k)$, the running time is $\sum_{i=0}^{k+1} \binom{k+1}{i} T_{d-1}(k - i) = d^k$.

- Mishra et al. [22] gives a 1.2738^k algorithm for ONES 2-SAT, using which we can solve (A, B)-MULTI 3-HITTING SET in time $\mathcal{O}^*(2.2738^k)$.
- Kutzkov et al. [20] gives a 2.562^k algorithm for ONES 3-SAT, using which we can solve (A, B)-MULTI 4-HITTING SET in time $\mathcal{O}^*(3.562^k)$.

Thus, Theorem 1 is proved.

Proof of Theorem 3. We will give a reduction from UNIFORM MULTI d-HITTING SET to $(d-A+1)-$HITTING SET. Let $\mathcal{I} = (U, \mathscr{S}, k, A)$ be an instance of UNIFORM MULTI d-HITTING SET. We will create an instance by taking all possible $(d - A + 1)$-sized subsets of each set $S \in \mathscr{S}$, this gives the set family $\mathscr{S}'$. Thus, $\mathcal{I}' = (U, \mathscr{S}', k)$ is an instance of $(d - A + 1)$-HITTING SET.

Next, we will prove that $\mathcal{I}$ is a Yes-instance of UNIFORM MULTI d-HITTING SET if and only if $\mathcal{I}'$ is a Yes-instance of $(d-A+1)$-HITTING SET. Suppose that $\mathcal{I}$ is a Yes-instance and X is a solution for $\mathcal{I}$. Thus, for each set $S \in \mathscr{S}$, we have $|X \cap S| \geq A$. Hence, $|X \setminus S| \leq d - A$, and so for every set $S' \in \mathscr{S}'$, it follows that $|X \cap S'| \geq 1$. This proves X is also a solution for $\mathcal{I}'$.

Conversely, suppose that $\mathcal{I}'$ is a Yes-instance of $(d - A + 1)$-HITTING SET and X' is a solution. Suppose that there is a set $S \in \mathscr{S}$ such that $|S \cap X'| < A$. Then, any $(d - A + 1)$-sized subset of $S' = S \setminus X'$ has a non-empty intersection with X', a contradiction to definition of X'. Hence, for every $S \in \mathscr{S}$ we have $|S \cap X'| \geq A$. Therefore, Theorem 3 is proved.

4 MULTI FEEDBACK VERTEX SET IN TOURNAMENTS

In this section, we will prove Theorem 6. Let (T, k) be an instance of (A, B)-MULTI FEEDBACK VERTEX SET IN TOURNAMENTS. For the FEEDBACK VERTEX SET problem, without loss of generality, we can assume that the given directed graph is a strongly connected directed graph, otherwise, we can find the minimum solution in each strongly connected subgraph independently. With this observation in hand we assume that the given tournament T is a strongly connected directed graph. We next use the following well-known result about the tournament, [9,23].

Proposition 1. *A strongly connected tournament has a Hamiltonian cycle.*

Due to Proposition 1, any solution to (T, k) contains at most B vertices. Since B is fixed, the size of the solution is constant. Thus, we can try all possible subsets of $V(T)$ of size at least A and at most $\min\{B, k\}$ in polynomial time. Now, we check if a given subset is a solution to (T, k) using the following lemma.

Lemma 1. *Given an instance (T, k) of (A, B)-MULTI FEEDBACK VERTEX SET IN TOURNAMENTS, where T is a strongly connected tournament, and a subset $S \subseteq V(T)$, one can check in polynomial time if S is a solution to (T, k).*

Proof. Since T is a strongly connected tournament, due to Proposition 1, if $|S| > B$, then S is not a solution to (T, k). Next, if $|S| > k$, then also S is not a solution to (T, k). Now, we suppose that $|S| \leq \min\{B, k\}$. Next, we use a following well-known fact about tournament: A tournament has a directed cycle if and only if it has a directed triangle [2]. Note that we can enumerate all the triangle in the given tournament T in $\mathcal{O}(n^3)$ time. Clearly, if S contains less than A vertices from any triangle, then S is not a solution to (T, k). Otherwise, S contains at least A vertices from every cycle in T. Since $|S| \leq B$, S contains at most B vertices from every cycle in T.

Due to Lemma 1 and the fact that the solution size is constant, we obtain Theorem 6.

5   Conclusion

In this paper, we studied a generalisation of the d-HITTING SET problem, namely (A, B)-MULTI d-HITTING SET, in the realm of parameterized complexity, and showed that (A, B)-MULTI d-HITTING SET can be solved in $\mathcal{O}^{\star}(d^k)$ time. We identified some special cases that has running time better than d-HITTING SET. Specifically, when $d = 3$ and $d = 4$, we have an improved bound of $\mathcal{O}^{\star}(2.2738^k)$ and $\mathcal{O}^{\star}(3.562^k)$, respectively. The former matches the running time of the classical 3-HITTING SET problem.

We next extended our study to graph-theoretic problems, in particular some vertex deletion problems, in which we have d-HITTING SET implicitly. Unlike VERTEX COVER, we obtained that $(1, 1)$-MULTI VERTEX COVER can be solved in polynomial time. Even more interestingly, FEEDBACK VERTEX SET IN TOURNAMENTS is NP-complete, while (A, B)-MULTI FEEDBACK VERTEX SET IN TOURNAMENTS can be solved in polynomial time. Now, the natural question that arises here is that "what is the computational complexity of (A, B)-MULTI FEEDBACK VERTEX SET ?" Does it also become tractable? We wish to mention here that it is not clear whether (A, B)-MULTI FEEDBACK VERTEX SET is in NP. That is, we do not know if given a solution, we can check if it is a solution to the given instance of (A, B)-MULTI FEEDBACK VERTEX SET, for arbitrary values of A and B. Thus, it is an interesting question to study further.

Another natural questions that arises here is that can we give a kernel of size $\mathcal{O}(k^{d-1})$ for (A, B)-MULTI d-HITTING SET?

References

1. Abu-Khzam, F.N.: A kernelization algorithm for d-hitting set. J. Comput. Syst. Sci. **76**(7), 524–531 (2010)
2. B-Jensen, J., Gutin, G.: Digraphs: Theory, Algorithms and Applications (2001)
3. Banerjee, S., Mathew, R., Panolan, F.: 'target set selection' on graphs of bounded vertex cover number (2018)
4. Bannach, M., Skambath, M., Tantau, T.: Kernelizing the hitting set problem in linear sequential and constant parallel time. In: 17th Scandinavian Symposium and Workshops on Algorithm Theory (SWAT 2020) (2020)
5. Bannach, M., Tantau, T.: Computing hitting set kernels by ac 0-circuits. Theor. Comput. Syst. 1–26 (2019)
6. Barman, S., Fawzi, O., Ghoshal, S., Gürpınar, E.: Tight approximation bounds for maximum multi-coverage. In: Bienstock, D., Zambelli, G. (eds.) IPCO 2020. LNCS, vol. 12125, pp. 66–77. Springer, Cham (2020). https://doi.org/10.1007/978-3-030-45771-6_6
7. Berman, P., DasGupta, B., Sontag, E.: Randomized approximation algorithms for set multicover problems with applications to reverse engineering of protein and gene networks. Discrete Appl. Math. **155**(6–7), 733–749 (2007)

8. van Bevern, R., Smirnov, P.V.: Optimal-size problem kernels for d-hitting set in linear time and space. arXiv preprint arXiv:2003.04578 (2020)

9. Camion, P.: Chemins et circuits hamiltoniens des graphes complets. Comptes rendus hebdomadaires des séances de l'Académie des sciences **249**(21), 2151–2152 (1959)

10. Cygan, M., et al.: Parameterized Algorithms. Springer, Berlin (2015)

11. De Kleer, J., Mackworth, A.K., Reiter, R.: Characterizing diagnoses and systems. Artif. Intell. **56**(2–3), 197–222 (1992)

12. Downey, R.G., Fellows, M.R.: Fundamentals of Parameterized Complexity, vol. 4. Springer, Berlin (2013)

13. El Ouali, M., Fohlin, H., Srivastav, A.: A randomised approximation algorithm for the hitting set problem. Theor. Comput. Sci. **555**, 23–34 (2014)

14. Fomin, F.V., Gaspers, S., Lokshtanov, D., Saurabh, S.: Exact algorithms via monotone local search. J. ACM (JACM) **66**(2), 1–23 (2019)

15. Fomin, F.V., Lokshtanov, D., Saurabh, S., Zehavi, M.: Kernelization: Theory of Parameterized Preprocessing. Cambridge University Press, Cambridge (2019)

16. Garey, M.R., Johnson, D.S.: Computers and Intractability, vol. 174 (1979)

17. Haus, U.U., Klamt, S., Stephen, T.: Computing knock-out strategies in metabolic networks. J. Comput. Biol. **15**(3), 259–268 (2008)

18. Hvidsten, T.R., Lægreid, A., Komorowski, J.: Learning rule-based models of biological process from gene expression time profiles using gene ontology. Bioinformatics **19**(9), 1116–1123 (2003)

19. Jain, P., Kanesh, L., Misra, P.: Conflict free version of covering problems on graphs: Classical and parameterized. Theory Comput. Syst. **64**(6), 1067–1093 (2020)

20. Kutzkov, I., Scheder, D.: Computing minimum directed feedback vertex set in $o(1.9977^n)$. abs/1007.1166 (2010)

21. Mellor, D., Prieto, E., Mathieson, L., Moscato, P.: A kernelisation approach for multiple d-hitting set and its application in optimal multi-drug therapeutic combinations. PLoS One **5**(10), e13055 (2010)

22. Misra, N., Narayanaswamy, N., Raman, V., Shankar, B.S.: Solving min ones 2-sat as fast as vertex cover. Theor. Comput. Sci. **506**, 115–121 (2013)

23. Moon, J.W.: Topics on Tournaments in Graph Theory. Courier Dover Publications, United States (2015)

24. Niedermeier, R., Rossmanith, P.: An efficient fixed-parameter algorithm for 3-hitting set. J. Discrete Algorithms **1**(1), 89–102 (2003)

25. Shi, L., Cai, X.: An exact fast algorithm for minimum hitting set. In: 2010 Third International Joint Conference on Computational Science and Optimization, vol. 1, pp. 64–67 (2010)

26. Speckenmeyer, E.: On feedback problems in digraphs. In: International Workshop on Graph-Theoretic Concepts in Computer Science, pp. 218–231 (1989)

27. Vazquez, A.: Optimal drug combinations and minimal hitting sets. BMC Syst. Biol. **3**(1), 81 (2009)

28. Fernandez de la Vega, W., Paschos, V.T., Saad, R.: Average case analysis of a greedy algorithm for the minimum hitting set problem. In: Simon, I. (ed.) LATIN 1992. LNCS, vol. 583, pp. 130–138. Springer, Heidelberg (1992). https://doi.org/10.1007/BFb0023824

29. Wahlström, M.: Algorithms, measures and upper bounds for satisfiability and related problems. Ph.D. thesis, Doctoral dissertation, Department of Computer and Information Science, Linköpings universitet (2007)

Parameterizing Role Coloring on Forests

Sukanya Pandey[1]([✉]), Venkatesh Raman[2]([✉]), and Vibha Sahlot[2]([✉])

[1] Utrecht University, Utrecht, The Netherlands
s.pandey1@uu.nl
[2] The Institute of Mathematical Sciences, HBNI, Chennai, India
vraman@imsc.ac.in, sahlotvibha@gmail.com

Abstract. A role coloring of a graph is an assignment of colors to the vertices such that if any two vertices are assigned the same color, then their neighborhood are assigned the same set of colors. In k-ROLE COLORING, we want to ask whether a given graph is role colorable by using exactly k colors.

Determining whether a graph admits a k-ROLE COLORING is a notoriously hard problem even for a fixed $k \geq 2$. It is known to be NP-complete for $k \geq 2$ on general graphs. For many hereditary graph classes like chordal graphs, planar graphs and split graphs, k-ROLE COLORING is NP-complete even when k is a constant. A recent result shows that k-ROLE COLORING is NP-complete for bipartite graphs when $k \geq 3$. The only known classes of graphs for which k-role coloring is polynomial time for any fixed k, are Cographs and Proper Interval graphs.

We consider the parameterized complexity of $(n - k)$-role coloring on n vertex graphs parameterized by k. This parameterization had interesting fixed-parameter tractable algorithms for the standard proper coloring [Chor et al. WG2004] and list-coloring variants [Banik et al. IWOCA 2019, Gutin et al. STACS 2020]. As our main results, we show that this parameterization for role coloring has
  - an $n^{O(k)}$ algorithm on general graphs (putting the problem in the parameterized complexity class XP), and
  - an $f(k)n^{O(1)}$ algorithm (placing the problem in the class FPT) on forests (here f is a computable exponential function).

Keywords: Role coloring · Fpt · Forests · Trees

1   Introduction

Given a graph $G(V, E)$, a *role coloring* of G is an assignment of colors to its vertices such that if two vertices get the same color, then the set of colors assigned to their neighborhood is also the same. That is, k-role coloring is an assignment (basically an onto function) $\alpha : V \to \{1, 2, ..., k\}$ such that for all $u, v \in V$, if $\alpha(u) = \alpha(v)$ then $\alpha(N(u)) = \alpha(N(v))$ where $\alpha(S)$, for a set of vertices, is the set $\{\alpha(v) | v \in S\}$.

Role coloring of graphs was introduced by Borgatti and Everett [12] in 1991. The underlying motivation was that in a social network, individuals play the

© Springer Nature Switzerland AG 2021
T. Bureš et al. (Eds.): SOFSEM 2021, LNCS 12607, pp. 308–321, 2021.
https://doi.org/10.1007/978-3-030-67731-2_22

same role if they relate in the same way to other individuals playing counterpart roles. Similar identities in a social network have a similar relation to their counterpart identities. This idea was modeled using a vertex coloring problem on graphs, which was eventually termed "role coloring".

Role coloring was formalized initially using graph homomorphisms by White and Reitz [19] and Sailer [18]. The terms "regular equivalence" and "regular coloration" are also used for the same concept (see survey by Borgatti and Everett [6]). We formally define the problem k-ROLE COLORING (a general instance of the problem) as follows.

---

k-ROLE COLORING
Input: An undirected graph G on n vertices and an integer k.
Question: Does there exist a coloring function $\alpha : V(G) \rightarrow \{1, 2, ..., k\}$ such that for any pair $u, v \in V(G)$, if $\alpha(u) = \alpha(v)$ then $\alpha(N(u)) = \alpha(N(v))$?

For a k-role coloring α, the corresponding role graph $R(V_R, E_R)$ is defined as the graph with $V_R = \{1, 2, ..., k\}$ and $E_R = \{(\alpha(u), \alpha(v)) | (u, v) \in E(G)\}$. A related problem in terms of role graphs is as follows.

R-ROLE COLORING
Input: An undirected graph $G(V, E)$ on n vertices and $R(V_R, E_R)$.
Question: Does there exist a function (coloring) $\alpha : V \rightarrow V_R$ satisfying $\alpha(N_G(u)) = N_R(\alpha(u))$ for all $u \in V$?

This problem is equivalent to deciding if there exists a *locally surjective* homomorphism between the graphs G and R [7]. Observe that given a role graph R and a role coloring α of G, we can find in polynomial time if α agrees with R, that is if G is R-role colorable for α. Also, given a role coloring α of G, we can find whether α is a valid role coloring and obtain the corresponding role graph R, in polynomial time.

Fiala et al. [7] showed that R-ROLE COLORING is polynomial time solvable when R has no edges, or has a component isomorphic to a single loop-incident vertex, or it is simple and bipartite and has at least one component isomorphic to a K_2. For every other case, they proved that R-ROLE COLORING is NP-complete. They applied this result to show that k-ROLE COLORING is NP-complete for all $k \geq 3$. Thus for general graph class, k-ROLE COLORING is para-NP-hard parameterized by k (see Sect. 2 for definitions). Prior to their work, it was shown by Roberts and Sheng [17] that k-ROLE COLORING is NP-complete for $k = 2$. The complexity of computing role-colorings has been studied on several hereditary graph classes. For example, k-ROLE COLORING is shown to be NP-complete for chordal graphs [11], split graphs [5], planar graphs [16] and recently on bipartite graphs [15] where k is a constant. The only known classes of graphs for which k-ROLE COLORING can be decided in polynomial time are cographs [16] and proper interval graphs [10].

Chaplick et al. [3] further showed that given graphs G and H, deciding if there exists a locally surjective homomorphism from G to H takes polynomial time, provided G has bounded treewidth and either G or H has bounded maximum degree. This implies that R-ROLE COLORING can be solved in polynomial time on graphs of bounded treewidth if R has bounded degree. Purcell and Rombach [16] used this result and proposed a polynomial time algorithm to solve k-ROLE COLORING on trees on n vertices, assuming that either k or $n - k$ is a constant.

We build on the work of Purcell and Romback [16]. First, we show that their polynomial time algorithm on trees works even for general graphs, when $n - k$ is a constant. Towards that, we first define the following problem:

$(n - k)$-ROLE COLORING   **Parameter(s):** k

Input: An undirected graph $G(V, E)$ on n vertices and an integer k.
Question: Does there exist a function $\alpha : V \to \{1, 2, ..., n - k\}$ such that for any pair $u, v \in V$, if $\alpha(u) = \alpha(v)$, then $\alpha(N(u)) = \alpha(N(v))$?

Such an $(n - k)$ parameterization can be thought of as the problem of saving k colors. Such parameterization has been studied for proper coloring and list coloring variants and has given rise to interesting tools and techniques. For the standard (chromatic number) graph coloring, a linear sized kernel in k is known [4] for this parameterization using the combinatorial crown decomposition. Recently, a generalization of this for list coloring variants has also been shown to be fixed-parameter tractable [2,9] (See Sect. 2 for definitions on kernel and fixed-parameter tractability).

We show in Sect. 3, an XP ($n^{O(k)}$) algorithm for $(n - k)$-ROLE COLORING on general graphs. Then in Sect. 4, we develop our main algorithm taking $\mathcal{O}(k^{O(k)} n^2)$ time, on trees. Using the same techniques, we generalize it to an FPT (fixed parameter tractable) algorithm on forests which will be given in full version of the paper. See Sect. 2 for definitions of the terms XP and FPT.

En route, we give an FPT algorithm for the following problem.

SEMI-DEGREE-PRESERVING FOREST ON TREES   **Parameter(s):** k

Input: A tree T on n vertices, a forest H of rooted trees with k vertices.
Question: Does there exist a function $f : V(H) \to V(T)$ such that whenever $(u, v) \in E(H)$, $(f(u), f(v)) \in E(T)$ and $deg_H(v) = deg_T(f(v))$ for every vertex v of H that is not a root?

We obtain our algorithm through an adaptation of the classical *color coding* technique [1] to find subgraphs of bounded treewidth in arbitrary graphs.

2   Preliminaries

In this section, we state the graph theoretic terminology and notation used in this paper. The set of consecutive integers from 1 to n is denoted by $[n]$. All graphs considered in this paper are simple and undirected, unless specified otherwise.

The vertex set and the edge set of a graph G are denoted by $V(G)$ and $E(G)$ respectively. An edge between vertices u and v is denoted as (u, v). For a vertex $v \in V(G)$, its *neighborhood* $N_G(v)$ is the set of all vertices adjacent to it and its *closed neighborhood* $N_G[v]$ is the set $N_G(v) \cup \{v\}$. This notation is extended to subsets of vertices as $N_G[S] = \bigcup_{v \in S} N_G[v]$ and $N_G(S) = N_G[S] \setminus S$ where $S \subseteq V(G)$. The *degree* of a vertex $v \in V(G)$, denoted by $d_G(v)$, is the size of $N_G(v)$. A *pendant vertex* is a vertex $v \in V(G)$ with $d_G(v) = 1$.

In parameterized complexity, each problem instance is associated with an integer called *parameter*. XP is the class of parameterized problems that can be solved in time $\mathcal{O}(n^{f(k)})$ where k is the associated parameter, f is some computable function and n is the input size. FPT is the class of parameterized problems solvable in $g(k)n^{\mathcal{O}(1)}$ time for some computable function g of k. We refer to such a running time as FPT running time, and call such an algorithm FPT algorithm. A parameterized problem is para-NP-hard if it is NP-hard for constant values of the parameter k. A kernelization algorithm is a polytime algorithm that transforms an arbitrary instance of the problem to an equivalent instance (known as kernel) of the same problem, such that the size of the new instance is bounded by some computable function g of the parameter of the original instance. If g is a polynomial function, then we say that the problem admits a polynomial kernel.

A (n, k)-perfect hash family is a family $\mathcal{F}$ of functions $f : [n] \rightarrow [k]$ such that for any $S \subseteq [n]$, $|S| = k$, there exists a function that injectively maps S to $[k]$.

Theorem 2.1 ([13]). *There is a deterministic algorithm with running time $e^k k^{\mathcal{O}(\log k)} n \log n$ that constructs an (n, k)-perfect hash family $\mathcal{F}'$ of cardinality at most $e^k k^{\mathcal{O}(\log k)} \log n$.*

Observation 1. *If G is a connected graph that is R-role colorable with the role assignment α, then R must be connected.*

3   XP Algorithm for $(n - k)$-Role Coloring graphs

Consider the classical k'-PROPER COLORING problem where we are given a graph and we want to color its vertices with at most k' colors such that no two adjacent vertices share the same color. It is well-known that k'-PROPER COLORING is NP-hard for any fixed $k' \geq 3$ [8]. Hence, k'-PROPER COLORING is para-NP-hard, when parameterized by k'. As one aim in parameterized complexity is to identify natural parameters under which the problem becomes tractable, researchers looked at $(n - k')$-PROPER COLORING parameterized by k', where one is interested in *saving* k' colors. It has been shown that this has a polynomial kernel (and hence FPT) using a technique known as crown decomposition [4]. This motivates us to study the problem $(n - k)$-ROLE COLORING parameterized by k.

Purcell and Rombach [16] proposed a polynomial time algorithm to solve the k-ROLE COLORING problem on trees as long as k or $n - k$ is a constant. Their algorithm solves k-ROLE COLORING in $k^{\mathcal{O}(k)} n^{\mathcal{O}(1)}$ time on trees implying an

FPT algorithm for k-ROLE COLORING parameterized by k. Similarly, assuming $n - k$ to be constant, they give an $\mathcal{O}(n^{n-k})$ algorithm for k-ROLE COLORING.

We give an $O(n^{\mathcal{O}(k)})$ algorithm for $(n-k)$-ROLE COLORING on general graphs, showing that the problem is in XP. We begin the development with the assumption that $n - k > 2k$. For otherwise, $n \leq 3k$ resulting in a linear kernel for the problem which also places the problem in FPT. We call a subgraph *rainbow colored* if all the vertices of the subgraph are assigned distinct colors. If the colors assigned to the vertices of a subgraph are not shared with the vertices in the rest of the graph, then the subgraph is said to be *uniquely colored*. We start with the following observation.

Observation 2. *For any valid $(n - k)$-role coloring of a graph G, there exists a set of $2k$ vertices in G that are colored with k colors, and the remaining vertices are uniquely colored.*

Proof. Suppose that $\alpha : V(G) \longrightarrow \{1, 2, ..., n - k\}$ is an $(n - k)$-role coloring of G. Let $C \subset [n - k]$ be the set of colors that are repeated more than once. Let $|C| = c$. Thus there are $n - k - c$ colors that appear uniquely in α. So $(n - k - c) + 2c \leq n$, as $|V(G)| = n$ from which it follows that $c \leq k$, and $n - k - c \geq n - 2k$. Thus at least $n - 2k$ colors are assigned uniquely. Let V' be a set of $n - 2k$ vertices that are uniquely colored by α. Hence $|V \setminus V'| = 2k$ and $|\alpha(V \setminus V')| = k$ from which the claim follows. $\square$

Now we prove the main result of this section.

Lemma 3.1. *There exists an $n^{\mathcal{O}(k)} k^{\mathcal{O}(k)}$ running time algorithm for $(n - k)$-ROLE COLORING on general graphs.*

Proof. From Observation 2, there is a set of $2k$ vertices colored with k colors. We first guess these $2k$ vertices out of n vertices. There are total $\binom{n}{2k}$ many such guesses. For each set S in this collection, we distinctly color $V(G) \setminus S$ using colors from $\{k+1, ... n-k\}$. We try all possible k^{2k} k-Role Coloring of $G[S]$ and check whether any of these leads to a valid role coloring. If there is a valid role coloring then we return YES, else we return NO. Our algorithm runs in $n^{\mathcal{O}(k)} k^{\mathcal{O}(k)}$ time. The correctness of the algorithm is clear. $\square$

4   FPT Algorithm for $(n - k)$-Role Coloring Trees

Here, we give an FPT algorithm for $(n - k)$-ROLE COLORING, when the input is restricted to trees. We recall the problem.

$(n - k)$-ROLE COLORING TREES   **Parameter(s):** k
Input: Given a tree $T(V, E)$ on n vertices and an integer k.
Question: Does there exist a function (coloring) $\alpha : V \rightarrow \{1, 2, ..., n - k\}$ such that for all pairs $u, v \in V$, if $\alpha(u) = \alpha(v)$ then $\alpha(N(u)) = \alpha(N(v))$?

Throughout this section we assume that $n - k \geq 3k$, or else we would trivially have a kernel of size $4k$ where we need to test for k'-role coloring for some $k' \leq 3k$. This can be done in some $k^{\mathcal{O}(k)}$ time by brute-force algorithm resulting in an *FPT* algorithm. We also assume that $|V(T)| \geq 3$, otherwise the problem can be trivially solved. We start with some properties of any $(n - k)$-role coloring on trees.

Lemma 4.1 *[16]. Given a tree T and any valid role coloring α of T, the role graph R corresponding to α is a tree with at most one self loop.*

We show a stronger claim for $(n - k)$-role coloring when $(n - k) > 3k$.

Lemma 4.2. *Let $n \geq 4k$. For any valid $(n - k)$-role coloring α of a tree T on n vertices, the role graph R corresponding to α is also a tree.*

Proof. As $(n - k) \geq 3k$, R has at least $3k$ vertices. Suppose R has a self loop at a node (color) i. Let $u, v \in V(T)$ be such that $\alpha(v) = \alpha(u) = i$ and $(u, v) \in E(T)$. Consider the two connected components one containing u and the other containing v in $T \setminus (u, v)$. As R is connected and u and v are colored with color i, each of the connected components contains $|R| \geq 3k$ vertices and colors. I.e. $|R| \geq 3k$ colors are repeated in T, and so the number of distinct colors in α is at most $(n - 3k)$ which is a contradiction. $\qquad\square$

This also proves that for any valid $(n - k)$-role coloring α of a tree T, the distance between two vertices colored differently should be same as distance between their colors in a role graph. Now consider a $v \in V(T)$ such that $degree(v) > 1$ (such a vertex exists as G has at least 3 vertices.) We call a connected component of $T[V \setminus v]$ a pendant-subtree rooted at v.

Lemma 4.3. *Given any valid $(n - k)$-role coloring α of a tree T, for any vertex $v \in V(T)$, any pair of pendant-subtrees P_1, P_2 rooted at v such that $\alpha(v) \notin \alpha(P_1)$ and $\alpha(v) \notin \alpha(P_2)$, then P_1 and P_2 either share the same set of colors or do not share any color.*

Proof. Let the role graph corresponding to α is R. Hence R is a tree without self loop (by Lemma 4.2). Thus role graphs corresponding to P_1 and P_2 are also subtrees of R, say R_1 and R_2, respectively. Root the tree T at any uniquely colored vertex. Let x be the neighbor of v in P_1 and y be the neighbor of v in P_2. If $\alpha(x) = \alpha(y)$, then $R_1 = R_2$ rooted at $\alpha(x)$ which implies that $\alpha(P_1) = \alpha(P_2)$. Otherwise, R_1 and R_2 are distinct subtrees rooted at $\alpha(x)$ and $\alpha(y)$ respectively implying that $\alpha(P_1) \cap \alpha(P_2) = \emptyset$. $\qquad\square$

Lemma 4.4. *Given any valid $(n - k)$-role coloring α of a tree T, for any vertex $v \in V(T)$, any pair of pendant-subtrees P_1, P_2 rooted at v such that $\alpha(P_1) \setminus \alpha(P_2) \neq \emptyset$ and $\alpha(P_2) \setminus \alpha(P_1) \neq \emptyset$, then P_1 and P_2 do not share any color.*

Proof. Root T at any uniquely colored vertex. Let the role graph corresponding to α is R. Hence R is a tree without self loop (by Lemma 4.2). Also, the role graphs corresponding to P_1 and P_2 are subtrees of R, say R_1 and R_2, respectively. Let $a \in \alpha(P_1) \setminus \alpha(P_2)$, $b \in \alpha(P_2) \setminus \alpha(P_1)$. This means R_1 and R_2 are distinct. Suppose the Lemma is not true and $c \in \alpha(P_1) \cap \alpha(P_2)$. This is a contradiction to our intial assumption about the existence of a and b which implies that R_1 and R_2 are distinct. Hence proved.   □

Lemma 4.5. *Let α be an $(n-k)$-role coloring of T and let $O \subseteq V(T)$ such that $|O| = 2k$ and $|\alpha(O)| = k$. Then there exists a set S such that $O \subseteq S$, $|S| = 3k$, $|\alpha(S)| = 2k$ and S contains all non-uniquely colored vertices of α and their parents.*

Proof. Let us root the tree T at an uniquely colored vertex. From Observation 2, there exists a set, say O, of $2k$ vertices sharing k colors in α. Also, all non uniquely colored vertices lie in O. Let $\alpha(O) = C$. Let S contain O and the parents of all the vertices in T. Clearly $|S| \leq 4k$ and $|\alpha(S)| \leq 3k$. In what follows, we argue that $|S| \leq 3k$ and $|\alpha(S)| \leq 2k$ essentially by arguing that for many vertices of O, their parents are already in O.

Our main claim is that for vertices that are colored the same in O, among their parents, at most one of them is outside O. Suppose not. Let $\alpha(u) = \alpha(v) = i$ for some pair of vertices $u, v \in O$ such that p_u is the parent of u and p_v is the parent of v where p_u and p_v are different and are not in O. As all vertices outside O are uniquely colored, p_u and p_v are uniquely colored by α. Now consider the least common ancestor, say x, of p_u and p_v. If $x \in \{p_u, p_v\}$, this violates the validity of role coloring as an assignment of color i is adjacent to p_u while other is not. Otherwise the subtrees containing u and v in $T \setminus x$ violates the Lemma 4.4 as p_u and p_v are uniquely colored but both the subtrees contain vertices colored i, resulting in a contradiction.

So if p of the k colors in O are repeated in O, the number of parents of the vertices in O outside O is at most $p + (k - p)$ (the first term accounts for the parents of non-uniquely colored vertices, and the second for the parents of the $k - p$ uniquely colored vertices) resulting in k. This proves the Lemma.   □

While Lemma 4.5 proves the existence of a set of vertices and colors in any valid $(n-k)$-coloring of T, we stitch them to argue the existence of certain type of forest in such a coloring.

Lemma 4.6. *Let α be a valid $(n-k)$-role coloring of T. Then there exists a subgraph F of T which is a forest whose connected components are rooted trees satisfying the following:*

1. *$|V(F)| = 3k$, $|\alpha(V(F))| = 2k$,*
2. *The root of every component of F is uniquely colored among vertices in T, and these are the only uniquely colored vertices in F.*
3. *Except the root of each tree in F, all the other vertices of F have the same degree in both F and T.*
4. *α projected to vertices in F is a valid role coloring of F.*

Proof. We first root the tree T at a uniquely colored vertex. From Observation 2 and Lemma 4.5 there exist sets O and S, where:

- $O \subset S \subset V(T)$, and
- $|O| = 2k$, $|\alpha(O)| = k$ such that all non uniquely colored vertices are in O, and
- $|S| = 3k$, $|\alpha(S)| = 2k$, and S contains the parents of all non uniquely colored vertices.

We prove the existence of F such that $F = T(S, E' \subseteq E(T[S]))$. Consider the forest $T[S]$. We delete any edges (u, v) from $T[S]$ where u and v are uniquely colored in T. Let F be the resulting forest. Note that the first condition follows from the property of S.

We root the connected components of F at the uniquely colored vertices of S. Every connected component in F has a uniquely colored vertex for otherwise, all the vertices in the component would be in O. However, at least one of their parents (say the parent of the vertex in the component closest to the root) must be outside O which, by definition, is uniquely colored, and is connected to the non uniquely colored vertices of the component by an edge. Let u be such a uniquely colored vertex in the component. Now to prove the second condition of the Lemma, we need to show that no other vertex in the component is uniquely colored. Assuming the contrary, let v be another vertex in the component that is uniquely colored and is closest to u among those uniquely colored. Consider the unique path connecting u and v. This path has at least one intermediate vertex (as we have deleted edges connecting pairs of uniquely colored vertices) and all the intermediate vertices are non-uniquely colored, and hence has at most $2k$ intermediate vertices from Observation 2.

First we claim that all the occurrences of the colors of the intermediate vertices in this path should lie in this path. Suppose not. For $x, y \in T'$, let $\alpha(x) = \alpha(y)$, such that x lies in the path between u and v, but y does not. Now consider the subtrees rooted at v, one containing x and other containing y. There are following cases. In the first case we consider pendant trees rooted at u such that y belongs to a pendant tree and x and v together belong to another pendant tree. This violates the Lemma 4.3. Similarly, in the second case we have y belongs to a pendant tree and u and x together belong to another pendant tree, both rooted at v. This too violates the Lemma 4.3. Now let y, u belong to a pendant tree and v, x all belong to a pendant tree rooted at some vertex. This violates the Lemma 4.4. Similarly we can argue for the case when x, u belong to a pendant tree and v, y all belong to a pendant tree rooted at some vertex. Otherwise let u, v and y all belong to distinct pendant trees rooted at x. There can't be an edge (x, y) in T as R has no loop. Now consider the path between x and u, and, y and u in T. According to current arrangement the length of both the paths differ which violates the fact that R is a tree without self loop.

Now we claim that the path between u and v has at least three intermediate vertices. Suppose not and there is only one intermediate vertex x. This is ruled out as intermediate vertex is non uniquely colored. Two intermediate vertices between u and v are ruled out as the role graph of α does not have a loop by Lemma 4.2.

Thus the $u - v$ path has three vertices a, b, c such that $\alpha(a) = \alpha(c) \neq \alpha(b)$ and the three vertices appear in that order as we traverse the $u - v$ path. Now consider the two pendant subtrees attached to the vertex b, one containing a and the other containing c. Each of these trees has a uniquely colored vertex (u and v, respectively) and the two share a color ($\alpha(a)$), contradicting Lemma 4.4. This proves the second condition.

To show the third condition, consider a vertex $v \in V(T_1)$ that is non uniquely colored and is in a component T_1 in F with $deg_T(v) \neq deg_F(v)$. As we don't add any edges to non uniquely colored vertices while constructing F, $deg_T(v) > deg_F(v)$. So there is a vertex $x \in V(T) \setminus V(F)$ adjacent to v in T. As v is non uniquely colored, there is a vertex $u \in V(T_1)$ such that $\alpha(u) = \alpha(v)$. Recall that vertices in $V(T) \setminus V(F)$ are uniquely colored, and so to satisfy the role coloring condition, u must also be adjacent to x which is a contradiction to the fact that T is a tree.

Now to prove the last condition, we need to show that if $\alpha(u) = \alpha(v)$ for some pair of vertices in F, then $\alpha(N(u)) = \alpha(N(v))$. As the roots of the trees are colored uniquely by α, it suffices to show this for non-root vertices of F. Note that by above conditions, the non root vertices in F maintain their degree, thus their neighborhood in T. As α is a valid role coloring of T, thus for all non root vertices, if for any pair u, v, $\alpha(u) = \alpha(v)$ then $\alpha(N(u)) = \alpha(N(v))$. Hence α projected to vertices in F is a valid role coloring of F. $\qquad\square$

Let F be a forest on $3k$ vertices with each connected component of F being a rooted tree. We call a valid $(2k)$-role coloring of F a *special* role coloring if it colors only the roots of the trees uniquely, and for any color, all the vertices with that color are in one tree of F (i.e. the coloring satisfies the conditions of Lemma 4.6). Also we say that F appears in a given rooted tree T in a *degree preserving* way, if there exists a function $f : V(F) \to V(T)$ such that if $(u, v) \in F$, then $(f(u), f(v)) \in V(T)$ and for all vertices x of F that are not roots of a tree in F, $degree_F(x) = degree_T(f(x))$.

Then Lemma 4.6 says that in any $(n-k)$-role coloring of a tree on n vertices, there exists a forest F on $3k$ vertices and a special role coloring of F such that F appears in T in a degree preserving way. We show the converse in the following Lemma.

Lemma 4.7. *There exists a valid $(n-k)$-role coloring α of a tree T if and only if there is a forest F on $3k$ vertices that has a special $(2k)$-role coloring, and it appears in a degree preserving way in T.*

Proof. By Lemma 4.6, if T has a valid $(n - k)$-role coloring say α, then the forest F satisfying the conditions of Lemma 4.6, and α restricted to F satisfies the condition of the Lemma. This proves the forward direction.

Conversely suppose that there is a forest F on $3k$ vertices with a special $(2k)$-role coloring α and that appears in a degree preserving way in T. Then we extend α by giving unique colors to the vertices of $V(T) \setminus V(F)$. We claim that this extension is a valid $(n - k)$-coloring of T. We only need to worry about the neighborhood of the colors in non-root vertices of F, as all other vertices are uniquely colored. However, all these non-root vertices of F, have no neighbors in $V(T)\backslash V(F)$ due to the degree-preserving property, and α is a valid role coloring of F. So it suffices to show that the colors of non-root vertices do not appear beyond their connected components. Suppose not. For some pair $u, v \in F$, $\alpha(u) = \alpha(v)$ and u lies in T_u whereas v lies in T_v, where T_u and T_v are connected components in F. Recall that the roots of T_u and T_v are uniquely colored, say y and z, respectively. Consider the least common ancestor x in T of the roots of these two trees. Note that x could be one of the two roots (if either one of them is an ancestor of the other). If $x \in \{y, z\}$, then this violates the Lemma 4.3. If $x \notin \{y, z\}$, then $T \setminus x$ has two pendant trees, that violate the Lemma 4.4 as each subtree has a distinct uniquely colored vertex but shares the color $\alpha(u)$.   □

Now our main algorithm finds an $(n - k)$-role coloring of the given tree by enumerating all forests F on $3k$ vertices (which can be done in $\mathcal{O}(3^{\mathcal{O}(k}k^{\mathcal{O}(1)})$ time, see Lemma 4.8) and checking for

- a special $(2k)$-role coloring of F (which can be done in $O((2k)^{3k+\mathcal{O}(1)})$ time, see Lemma 4.9) and
- a degree preserving occurrence of F in T (see Lemma 4.10).

The main technical work is in finding a degree preserving occurrence of F in T (Lemma 4.10).

Lemma 4.8. *The number of $3k$ sized forests $\mathcal{F}$ is $\mathcal{O}((3k + 1)(3^{3k}))$ and they can be enumerated in $\mathcal{O}((3k + 1)3^{3k}k^{\mathcal{O}(1)})$ time.*

Proof. Consider any forest of size $3k$. We can add a vertex to this forest and add an edge from it to arbitrary vertices in each connected component of the forest, to make it a tree. Thus if we remove this vertex from the $3k + 1$ sized tree thus formed, we can retrieve the initial forest. So every forest of size $3k$ can be generated from a tree of size $3k + 1$ after removing a vertex. As there are $\mathcal{O}(3^{3k+1})$ trees of size $3k+1$, upto unlabelled isomorphism [14], so the number of forests are $\mathcal{O}((3k+1)(3^{3k}))$. The unlabelled trees of size $3k+1$ can be enumerated in time proportional to the number of trees (See for example [20]). Hence, the total time taken to enumerate all the forests is $\mathcal{O}(3^{3k+1})(3k + 1)$.   □

Lemma 4.9. *Given a forest F with rooted trees on $3k$ vertices, we can test in $\mathcal{O}((2k)^{3k+\mathcal{O}(1)})$ whether it has a special $(2k)$-role coloring.*

Proof. By arbitrarily giving any of the $2k$ colors to each of the vertices, there are $(2k)^{3k}$ coloring to be checked. Given a fixed coloring, one can check in $k^{\mathcal{O}(1)}$ time whether it is a special $(2k)$-role coloring.   □

In the next subsection, we describe our FPT algorithm to find a degree preserving forest in a tree T using color coding technique of Alon et al. [1].

4.1   Finding Degree Preserving Occurrence of F

We prove the following main Lemma in this subsection.

Lemma 4.10. *Let T be a tree on n nodes, and let F be a forest with rooted trees on $3k$ vertices. It can be determined in $2^{\mathcal{O}(k)}n^{\mathcal{O}(1)}$ time whether there is a degree preserving occurrence of F in T.*

This Lemma is proved by a series of Lemmas using the color coding technique of [1]. Let T be a tree on n vertices where each vertex is also labeled with a color from $\{1, 2, \ldots 3k\}$. We call such a tree a *color-labeled* tree. Let F be a forest on $3k$ vertices with each connected component being a rooted tree. We say that F has a colorful degree-preserving appearance in T if there exists a function $f : V(F) \to V(T)$ such that f is degree-preserving and the color labels of $f(F) = \{1, 2, \ldots 3k\}$, i.e. the color labels of the images of vertices of F in T are distinct. We first show the following.

Lemma 4.11. *Let T be a color labeled tree with $3k$ colors and n vertices, and let F be a forest on $3k$ vertices with each connected component being a rooted tree. We can determine in $2^{\mathcal{O}(k)}n^2$ time whether F has a colorful degree-preserving appearance in T.*

Proof. Let $c : V(T) \to [3k]$ be the given $3k$ coloring of tree T and f be a colorful degree-preserving mapping of F in T, if it exists. We use dynamic programming to find f.

Let F has ℓ connected components $T_1, T_2 \ldots T_\ell$ with vertex set sizes $t_1, t_2, \ldots t_\ell$, respectively. Consider R to be the set of root vertices of connected components in F and $U = V(F) \backslash R$. Consider a vertex $v \in V(T)$ and a tree (subtree) T' in F. We will try to map T' in a degree preserving way to the subtree rooted at v in T and let $S[v, T']$ capture color sets of all such mappings. Formally, let $S[v, T']$ be the set of colors assigned to all the occurrences of T' where the root $r_{T'}$ of T' (here $r_{T'}$ does not necessarily belong to R) is mapped to v and all the vertices of T' are rainbow colored in T by c. In addition, for all vertices of T' not in R, we want the mapping to preserve their degrees in T. We compute $S[v, T']$ in a bottom up fashion starting from where T' is just a vertex. If T' is just a leaf node $x \notin R$ and v is also a leaf (i.e. $deg_F(x) = deg_T(v)$), then $S[v, T'] = \{\{c(v)\}\}$.

Now we give the general recurrence to find $S[v, T']$ for a tree (or subtree) $T' \in F$ with root r_{T_i} mapped to $v \in V(T)$ satisfying the constraints.

$$S[v, T_i] = \begin{cases} \emptyset & \text{if Condition 1} \\ \{\{c(v)\}\} & \text{if Condition 2} \\ \bigcup_{u \in N(v)}\{A \cup B | A \in S[u, T_p], \ B \in S[v, T'_p] \text{ and } A \cap B = \emptyset\} & \\ & \text{if Condition 3} \end{cases}$$

$$(1)$$

Condition $1 = r_{T_i} \in U$ and $deg_F(r_{T_i}) \neq deg_T(v)$

Condition 2 = $(|V(T_i)| = 1)$ and $\left(r_{T_i} \in U \implies deg_F(r_{T_i}) = deg_T(v)\right)$
Condition 3 = $(|V(T_i)| > 1)$ and $\left(r_{T_i} \in U \implies deg_F(r_{T_i}) = deg_T(v)\right)$

where T_p and T_p' are subtrees of T_i obtained after removing an edge in T_i incident on r_{T_i}. The subtree T_p' is rooted at r_{T_i} and T_p is rooted at another endpoint of the edge removed. Here, the equality holds if the associated condition evaluates to True.

As there are 2^{3k} subsets of $3k$ colors, the number of sets in each $S[v, T']$ is bounded by 2^{3k}. The number of choices for v are n. Similarly, there are $3k - 1$ many choices for T' as F can have at most $3k - 1$ components.

We compute the entries in bottom up fashion. For any entry $S[v, T']$, we check if the root of T' is in U and the degree of v and root of T' are the same. If not, we set $S[v, T'] = \emptyset$. Finally, for each T' in F, we check if $|S[v, T']| > 0$ for some $v \in T$. If not, we return No. Otherwise, for each $i \in [\ell] \backslash 1$, we find the set S_i where $S_i = \{A \cup B | A \in \cup_{v \in T} S[v, T_i], B \in S_{i-1}, A \cap B = \emptyset\}$. Finally $S_1 = \{A | A \in \cup_{v \in T} S[v, T_1]\}$ If $S_\ell \neq \emptyset$, then we return YES, else we return No. As $|S_i| \leq 2^{\sum_{j \in [i]} t_j}$, we can check whether S_ℓ is non-empty in time $\mathcal{O}(2^{3k})$ where we can precompute $\cup_{v \in T} S[v, T_i]$ for each $i \in [\ell]$. As there are at most n choices of v and $3k$ choices for T' in the recurrence 1, hence, our algorithm takes total of $2^{\mathcal{O}(k)} n^{\mathcal{O}(1)}$ time.

Now we prove the correctness of the recurrence in our algorithm. The set $S[v, T']$ denotes the collection of the sets of colors such that each set is of size $|V(T')|$, and is assigned to some occurrence of the tree/subtree T' in F such that the root is mapped to $v \in T$ and all the vertices in $U \cap V(T_i)$ maintain their degree when mapped in T. The first condition takes care of the case when the degrees of vertices in $U \cap V(T_i)$ are not preserved. In that case all such sets are discarded. If $|T_i| = 1$, then $S[v, T_i] = \{\{c(v)\}\}$, if the degree constraint is maintained. So the only case left is when the degree constraints are maintained and $|V(T_i)| > 1$. For this we have to prove that $S[v, T_i] = \bigcup_{u \in N(v)} \{A \cup B | A \in S[u, T_p], B \in S[v, T_p']$ and $A \cap B = \emptyset\}$ where T_p and T_p' are as defined in the recurrence. Let $S[v, T_i] = X$ and $\bigcup_{u \in N(v)} \{A \cup B | A \in S[u, T_p], B \in S[v, T_p']$ and $A \cap B = \emptyset\} = Y$. Now consider the set Y. If both T_p and T_p' are disjointly and rainbow colored, then the set containing colors of both of these subtrees in the corresponding sets in $S[u, T_p]$ and $S[v, T_p']$ gives a coloring of T_i where each vertex is dijointly colored. In the set Y we are taking all such possibilities, for all $u \in N(v)$. Thus $Y \subseteq X$. Now consider the set X. Each element of this set corresponds to an occurrence of T_i in T such that it is rainbow colored. So it gives a coloring of T_p and $T_{p'}$ such that both are disjointly rainbow colored and thus such sets are contained in $S[u, T_p]$ and $S[v, T_p']$ where in the occurence of T_i in T, the root of T_p is mapped to u, for some $u \in N_T(v)$. So, $X \subseteq Y$ proving that $X = Y$. □

Lemma 4.12. *Let T be a tree on n vertices, and let F be a forest on $3k$ vertices. There is a probabilistic algorithm that can determine in $2^{\mathcal{O}(k)} n^{\mathcal{O}(1)}$ time whether F has a degree-preserving appearance in T. Specifically if F has a degree preserving appearance in T, the algorithm will find it in $2^{\mathcal{O}(k)} n^{\mathcal{O}(1)}$ time with probability at least e^{-3k}, and will return NO otherwise.*

Proof. We start with coloring the vertices of T with colors from $[3k]$ uniformly at random, and apply the algorithm of Lemma 4.11 to determine whether there is a colorful degree-preserving appearance of F in T. If such an appearance of F exists we return YES and return NO otherwise.

Suppose that there is a degree-preserving mapping f of F into T. The probability that f is colorful is the probability that the color set of $f(F) = [3k]$. As the vertices of T are colored uniformly at random, the probability that $f(F) = [3k]$ is $\frac{(3k)!}{(3k)^{3k}} \geq e^{-3k}$. Hence our algorithm will find the degree-preserving occurrence of F with this probability. $\square$

Proof of Lemma 4.10. In the proof of Lemma 4.12, instead of coloring the vertices of T randomly, we use the functions from $[n]$ to $[3k]$ from an $(n, 3k)$-perfect hash family (see Theorem 2.1 in Preliminaries) and report YES if any of the coloring functions from the family returns an YES answer. By the property of the perfect hash family, if there is a degree-preserving function f from F to T, at least one of the functions of the hash family will color all vertices of $f(F)$ in T distinctly, and our algorithm of Lemma 4.11 will determine the occurrence. Thus, our overall algorithm takes total of $(2e)^{\mathcal{O}(k)}(3k)^{\mathcal{O}(\log k)}n^{\mathcal{O}(1)}$ time. $\square$

Putting Things together

We summarise the main algorithm as a pseudocode in Algorithm 1.

Algorithm 1: $(n-k)$-ROLE COLORING TREES
---
1 **Input:** A tree T,k
  Result: Return YES if T is $(n-k)$-role colorable, else NO
2 Enumerate the family of all forests $\mathcal{F}$ on $3k$ vertices using Lemma 4.8
3   FORALL($F \in \mathcal{F}$) {
4   IF$(F$ can be mapped in T in a degree-preserving way {determined using Lemma 4.10}) AND
5   IF $(F$ has a special $2k$-role coloring {determined using Lemma 4.9})
6   { return YES } }
7 return NO

Now we the have following Theorem.

Theorem 4.1. *There exists an FPT algorithm for* $(n-k)$-ROLE COLORING TREES *with running time* $k^{\mathcal{O}(k)}n^{\mathcal{O}(1)}$.

Proof. The correctness follows from above arguments. If we have at most $4k$ sized kernel, then we may try and verify all possible colorings in $k^{\mathcal{O}(k)}n^2$ time. Else we use Algorithm 1. Step 2 can be done in $3^{\mathcal{O}(k)}$ time by Lemma 4.8 and thus the Step 3 iterates $3^{\mathcal{O}(k)}$ times. The conditions in Step 4 can be checked in $2^{\mathcal{O}(k)}k^{\mathcal{O}(\log k)}n^{\mathcal{O}(1)}$ time using Lemma 4.10 and in Step 5 can be checked in $(2k)^{\mathcal{O}(k)}$ time using Lemma 4.9 for each iteration. Thus the Algorithm 1 runs in $k^{\mathcal{O}(k)}n^{\mathcal{O}(1)}$ time. $\square$

5 Conclusions

We have shown that $(n-k)$-ROLE COLORING is in XP on general graphs and is FPT on forests. Note that our FPT algorithm for finding degree preserving forest in trees (Lemma 4.10) actually works even if the target graph is a general graph rather than a tree. So a next natural question to ask is whether $(n-k)$-ROLE COLORING is FPT on general graphs. Of course, here the role-graph can be arbitrary. Another open problem is whether $(n-k)$-ROLE COLORING admits a polynomial sized kernel on forests.

References

1. Alon, N., Yuster, R., Zwick, U.: Color-coding. J. ACM **42**(4), 844–856 (1995)
2. Banik, A., Jacob, A., Paliwal, V.K., Raman, V.: Fixed-parameter tractability of (n-k) list coloring. In: IWOCA 2019, Proceedings. pp. 61–69 (2019)
3. Chaplick, S., Fiala, J., van 't Hof, P., Paulusma, D., Tesar, M.: Locally constrained homomorphisms on graphs of bounded treewidth and bounded degree. Theor. Comput. Sci. **590**, 86–95 (2015)
4. Chor, B., Fellows, M., Juedes, D.W.: Linear kernels in linear time, or how to save k colors in o(n²) steps. In: WG 2004, Revised Papers. pp. 257–269 (2004)
5. Dourado, M.C.: Computing role assignments of split graphs. Theor. Comput. Sci. **635**, 74–84 (2016)
6. Everett, M.G., Borgatti, S.P.: Regular equivalence: general theory. J. Math. Sociol. **19**(1), 29–52 (1994)
7. Fiala, J., Paulusma, D.: A complete complexity classification of the role assignment problem. Theor. Comput. Sci. **349**(1), 67–81 (2005)
8. Garey, M.R., Johnson, D.S., Stockmeyer, L.J.: Some simplified np-complete graph problems. Theor. Comput. Sci. **1**(3), 237–267 (1976)
9. Gutin, G.Z., Majumdar, D., Ordyniak, S., Wahlström, M.: Parameterized pre-coloring extension and list coloring problems. In: STACS 2020. pp. 1–18 (2020)
10. Heggernes, P., van 't Hof, P., Paulusma, D.: Computing role assignments of proper interval graphs in polynomial time. J. Discrete Algorithms **14**, 173–188 (2012)
11. van't Hof, P., Paulusma, D., van Rooij, J.M.M.: Computing role assignments of chordal graphs. Theor. Comput. Sci. **411**(40–42), 3601–3613 (2010)
12. Martin G. Everett, S.B.: Role colouring a graph. Mathematical Social Sciences pp. 183–188 (1991)
13. Naor, M., Schulman, J.L., Srinivasan, A.: Splitters and near-optimal derandomization. In: FOCS. pp. 182–191 (1995)
14. Otter, R.: Richard otter. The Annals of Mathematics, 2nd Ser. 49(3), 583–599 (1948)
15. Pandey, S., Sahlot, V.: Role coloring bipartite graphs. Manuscript
16. Purcell, C., Rombach, M.P.: On the complexity of role colouring planar graphs, trees and cographs. J. Discrete Algorithms **35**, 1–8 (2015)
17. Roberts, F.S., Sheng, L.: How hard is it to determine if a graph has a 2-role assignment? Networks **37**, 67–73 (2001)
18. Sailer, L.D.: Structural equivalence: Meaning and definition, computation and application. Social Networks **1**(1), 73–90 (1978)
19. White, D., Reitz, K.: Graph and semigroup homomorphisms on networks of relations. Social Networks **5**(2), 193–234 (1983)
20. Wright, R.A., Richmond, L.B., Odlyzko, A.M., McKay, B.D.: Constant time generation of free trees. SIAM J. Comput. **15**, 540–548 (1986)

The Balanced Satisfactory Partition Problem

Ajinkya Gaikwad, Soumen Maity$^{(\boxtimes)}$, and Shuvam Kant Tripathi

Indian Institute of Science Education and Research, Pune 411008, India
{ajinkya.gaikwad,tripathi.shuvamkant}@students.iiserpune.ac.in,
soumen@iiserpune.ac.in

Abstract. The Satisfactory Partition problem asks whether it is possible to partition the vertex set of a given undirected graph into two parts such that each vertex has at least as many neighbours in its own part as in the other part. The Balanced Satisfactory Partition problem is a variant of the above problem where the two partite sets are required to have the same cardinality. Both problems are known to be NP-complete but its parameterized complexity remains open until now. We enhance our understanding of the problem from the viewpoint of parameterized complexity. The two main results of the paper are the following: (1) The Satisfactory Partition problem and its balanced version are fixed parameter tractable (FPT) when parametrized by neighbourhood diversity, (2) The Balanced Satisfactory Partition problem is W[1]-hard when parametrized by treewidth.

Keywords: Parameterized complexity · FPT · W[1]-hard · Treewidth · Neighbourhood diversity

1 Introduction

Gerber and Kobler [7] introduced the problem of deciding if a given graph has a vertex partition into two non-empty parts such that each vertex has at least as many neighbours in its part as in the other part. A graph satisfying this property is called *partitionable*. For example, complete graphs, star graphs, complete bipartite graphs with at least one part having odd size are not partitionable, where as some graphs are easily partitionable: cycles of length at least 4, trees that are not star graphs [4].

Given a graph $G = (V, E)$ and a subset $S \subseteq V(G)$, we denote by $d_S(v)$ the degree of a vertex $v \in V$ in $G[S]$, the subgraph of G induced by S. For $S = V$, the subscript is omitted, hence $d(v)$ stands for the degree of v in G. In this paper, we study the parameterized complexity of SATISFACTORY PARTITION and BALANCED SATISFACTORY PARTITION problems. We define these problems as follows:

S. Maity—The author's research was supported in part by the Science and Engineering Research Board (SERB), Govt. of India, under Sanction Order No. MTR/2018/001025.

T. Bureš et al. (Eds.): SOFSEM 2021, LNCS 12607, pp. 322–336, 2021.
https://doi.org/10.1007/978-3-030-67731-2_23

SATISFACTORY PARTITION
Input: A graph $G = (V, E)$.
Question: Is there a nontrivial partition (V_1, V_2) of V such that for every $v \in V$, if $v \in V_i$ then $d_{V_i}(v) \geq d_{V_{3-i}}(v)$?

A variant of this problem where the two parts have equal size is:

BALANCED SATISFACTORY PARTITION
Input: A graph $G = (V, E)$ on an even number of vertices.
Question: Is there a nontrivial partition (V_1, V_2) of V such that $|V_1| = |V_2|$ and for every $v \in V$, if $v \in V_i$ then $d_{V_i}(v) \geq d_{V_{3-i}}(v)$?

Given a partition (V_1, V_2), we say that a vertex $v \in V_i$ is *satisfied* if $d_{V_i}(v) \geq d_{V_{3-i}}(v)$, or equivalently if $d_{V_i}(v) \geq \lceil \frac{d(v)}{2} \rceil$. A graph admitting a nontrivial partition where all vertices are satisfied is called *satisfactory partitionable*, and such a partition is called *satisfactory partition*. For the standard concepts in parameterized complexity, see the recent textbook by Cygan et al. [5]. We now review the concept of a tree decomposition, introduced by Robertson and Seymour in [12].

Definition 1. A *tree decomposition* of a graph G is a pair $(T, \{X_t\}_{t \in V(T)})$, where T is a tree and each node t of the tree T is assigned a vertex subset $X_t \subseteq V(G)$, called a bag, such that the following conditions are satisfied:

1. Every vertex of G is in at least one bag.
2. For every edge $uv \in E(G)$, there exists a node $t \in T$ such that bag X_t contains both u and v.
3. For every $u \in V(G)$, the set $\{t \in V(T) \mid u \in X_t\}$ induces a connected subtree of T.

It is important to note that a graph may have several different tree decomposition. Similarly, the same tree decomposition can be valid for several different graphs. Every graph has a trivial tree decomposition for which T has only one vertex including all of V. However, this is not effective for the purpose of solving problems.

Definition 2. The *width* of a tree decomposition is defined as $width(T) = max_{t \in V(T)} |X_t| - 1$ and the treewidth $tw(G)$ of a graph G is the minimum width among all possible tree decomposition of G.

The reason for subtracting 1 in the above definition for width is so that we can define forests as having treewidth 1.

Our Results: Our main results are the following:

- The SATISFACTORY PARTITION and BALANCED SATISFACTORY PARTITION problems are fixed parameter tractable (FPT) when parameterized by neighbourhood diversity.

- The BALANCED SATISFACTORY PARTITION problem is W[1]-hard when parameterized by treewidth.

Related Work: In the first paper on this topic, Gerber and Kobler [7] considered a generalized version of this problem by introducing weights for the vertices and edges and showed that a general version of the problem is strongly NP-complete. For the unweighted version, they presented some sufficient conditions for the existence of a solution. This problem was further studied in [1,6,8]. The SATISFACTORY PARTITION problem is NP-complete and this implies that BALANCED SATISFACTORY PARTITION problem is also NP-complete via a simple reduction in which we add new dummy vertices and dummy edges to the graph [2,4]. Both problems are solvable in polynomial time for graphs with maximum degree at most 4 [4]. They also studied generalizations and variants of this problem when a partition into $k \geq 3$ nonempty parts is required. Bazgan, Tuza, and Vanderpooten [1,3] studied an "unweighted" generalization of SATISFACTORY PARTITION, where each vertex v is required to have at least $s(v)$ neighbours in its own part, for a given function s representing the degree of satisfiability. Obviously, when $s = \lceil \frac{d}{2} \rceil$, where d is the degree function, we obtain satisfactory partition. They gave a polynomial-time algorithm for graphs of bounded treewidth which decides if a graph admits a satisfactory partition, and gives such a partition if it exists.

2 FPT Algorithm Parameterized by Neighbourhood Diversity

In this section, we present an FPT algorithm for the SATISFACTORY PARTITION and BALANCED SATISFACTORY PARTITION problems parameterized by neighbourhood diversity. We say two vertices u and v in G have the same type if and only if $N_G(u) \backslash \{v\} = N_G(v) \backslash \{u\}$. The relation of having the same type is an equivalence relation. The idea of neighbourhood diversity is based on this type structure.

Definition 3 [10]. The neighbourhood diversity of a graph $G = (V, E)$, denoted by $\mathrm{nd}(G)$, is the least integer k for which we can partition the set V of vertices into k classes, such that all vertices in each class have the same type.

If neighbourhood diversity of a graph is bounded by an integer k, then there exists a partition $\{C_1, C_2, \ldots, C_k\}$ of $V(G)$ into k type classes. It is known that such a minimum partition can be found in linear time using fast modular decomposition algorithms [14]. Notice that each type class could either be a clique or an independent set by definition. For algorithmic purpose it is often useful to consider a *type graph* H of graph G, where each vertex of H is a type class in G, and two vertices C_i and C_j are adjacent iff there is complete bipartite clique between these type classes in G. It is not difficult to see that there will be either a complete bipartite clique or no edges between any two type classes. In this section, we prove the following theorem:

Theorem 1. *The* SATISFACTORY PARTITION *problem is fixed-parameter tractable when parameterized by the neighbourhood diversity.*

Let G be a connected graph such that $\text{nd}(G) = k$. Let $C_1, \ldots, C_k$ be the partition of $V(G)$ into sets of type classes. We assume $k \geq 2$ since otherwise the problem becomes trivial. We define $I_1 = \{C_i \mid C_i \subseteq V_1\}$, $I_2 = \{C_i \mid C_i \subseteq V_2\}$ and $I_3 = \{C_i \mid C_i \cap V_1 \neq \emptyset, C_i \cap V_2, \neq \emptyset\}$ where (V_1, V_2) is a satisfactory partition. We next guess if C_i belongs to I_1, I_2, or I_3. There are at most 3^k possibilities as each C_i has three options: either in I_1, I_2, or I_3. We reduce the problem of finding a satisfactory partition to an integer linear programming optimization with k variables. Since integer linear programming is fixed parameter tractable when parameterized by the number of variables [11], we conclude that our problem is FPT when parameterized by the neighbourhood diversity.

ILP Formulation: Given I_1, I_2 and I_3, our goal here is to answer if there exists a satisfactory partition (V_1, V_2) of G with all vertices of C_i are in V_1 if $C_i \in I_1$, all vertices of C_i are in V_2 if $C_i \in I_2$, and vertices of C_i are distributed amongst V_1 and V_2 if $C_i \in I_3$. For each C_i, we associate a variable x_i that indicates $|V_1 \cap C_i| = x_i$. Because the vertices in C_i have the same neighbourhood, the variables x_i determine (V_1, V_2) uniquely, up to isomorphism. We now characterize a satisfactory partition in terms of x_i. Note that $x_i = n_i = |C_i|$ if $C_i \in I_1$; $x_i = 0$ if $C_i \in I_2$.

Lemma 1. *Let C be a clique type class. Then C is either in I_1 or I_2.*

Proof. Let C be a clique type class. Let $u, v \in C$. Let us denote $N(u) \setminus \{v\} = N(v) \setminus \{u\}$ by S and let $a = |S \cap V_1|$ and let $b = |S \cap V_2|$. The satisfiability of u implies $a \geq b + 1$ and the satisfiablity of v implies $b \geq a + 1$. Clearly, u and v cannot be satisfied simultaneously, as the two inequalities imply $a \geq b+1 \geq a+2$, a contradiction. This proves the lemma.

Now we consider the following four cases:

Case 1: Suppose v belongs to a clique type class C_j in I_1. Then the number of neighbours of v in V_1, that is,

$$d_{V_1}(v) = \sum_{i:C_i \in N_H[C_j] \cap I_1} n_i + \left(\sum_{i:C_i \in N_H[C_j] \cap I_3} x_i \right) - 1.$$

The number of neighbours of v in V_2, that is,

$$d_{V_2}(v) = \sum_{i:C_i \in N_H(C_j) \cap I_2} n_i + \sum_{i:C_i \in N_H[C_j] \cap I_3} (n_i - x_i).$$

Therefore, vertex v is satisfied if and only if

$$\sum_{i:C_i \in N_H[C_j] \cap I_1} n_i + \sum_{i:C_i \in N_H[C_j] \cap I_3} 2x_i \geq 1 + \sum_{i:C_i \in N_H(C_j) \cap I_2} n_i + \sum_{i:C_i \in N_H[C_j] \cap I_3} n_i$$

$$(1)$$

Case 2: Suppose v belongs to a clique type class C_j in I_2. Then similarly, v is satisfied if and only if

$$\sum_{i:C_i \in N_H[C_j] \cap I_2} n_i + \sum_{i:C_i \in N_H[C_j] \cap I_3} n_i \geq 1 + \sum_{i:C_i \in N_H(C_j) \cap I_1} n_i + \sum_{i:C_i \in N_H[C_j] \cap I_3} 2x_i \tag{2}$$

Case 3: Suppose v belongs to an independent type class C_j in V_1, that is, $C_j \in I_1 \cup I_3$. Then the number of neighbours of v in V_1, that is,

$$d_{V_1}(v) = \sum_{i:C_i \in N_H(C_j) \cap I_1} n_i + \sum_{i:C_i \in N_H(C_j) \cap I_3} x_i.$$

Note that if $C_j \in I_3$, then only x_j vertices of C_j are in V_1 and the the remaining y_j vertices of C_j are in V_2. The number of neighbours of v in V_2, that is,

$$d_{V_2}(v) = \sum_{i:\ C_i \in N_H(C_j) \cap I_2} n_i + \sum_{i:\ C_i \in N_H(C_j) \cap I_3} (n_i - x_i).$$

Therefore, v is satisfied if and only if

$$\sum_{i:C_i \in N_H(C_j) \cap I_1} n_i + \sum_{i:C_i \in N_H(C_j) \cap I_3} 2x_i \geq \sum_{i:C_i \in N_H(C_j) \cap I_2} n_i + \sum_{i:C_i \in N_H(C_j) \cap I_3} n_i \tag{3}$$

Case 4: Suppose v belongs to an independent type class C_j in V_2, that is, $C_j \in I_2 \cup I_3$. Similarly, vertex v is satisfied if and only if

$$\sum_{i:C_i \in N_H(C_j) \cap I_2} n_i + \sum_{i:C_i \in N_H(C_j) \cap I_3} n_i \geq \sum_{i:C_i \in N_H(C_j) \cap I_1} n_i + \sum_{i:C_i \in N_H(C_j) \cap I_3} 2x_i \tag{4}$$

We now formulate ILP formulation of satisfactory partition, for given I_1, I_2 and I_3. The question is whether there exist x_j under the conditions $x_j = n_j$ if $C_j \in I_1$, $x_j = 0$ if $C_j \in I_2$, $x_j \in \{1, 2, \ldots, n_j - 1\}$ if $C_j \in I_3$ and the additional conditions described below:

- Inequality 1 for all clique type classes $C_j \in I_1$
- Inequality 2 for all clique type classes $C_j \in I_2$
- Inequality 3 for all independent type classes $C_j \in I_1$
- Inequality 4 for all independent type classes $C_j \in I_2$
-

$$\sum_{C_i \in N_H(C_j) \cap I_2} n_i + \sum_{C_i \in N_H(C_j) \cap I_3} n_i = \sum_{C_i \in N_H(C_j) \cap I_1} n_i + \sum_{C_i \in N_H(C_j) \cap I_3} 2x_i$$

for all independent type classes $C_j \in I_3$.

For BALANCED SATISFACTORY PARTITION problem, we additionally ask that

$$\sum_{i:C_i \in I_1} n_i + \sum_{i:C_i \in I_3} x_i = \sum_{i:C_i \in I_3} (n_i - x_i) + \sum_{i:C_i \in I_2} n_i.$$

Solving the ILP: Lenstra [11] showed that the feasibility version of p-ILP is FPT with running time doubly exponential in p, where p is the number of variables. Later, Kannan [9] designed an algorithm for p-ILP running in time $p^{O(p)}$.

p-VARIABLE INTEGER LINEAR PROGRAMMING FEASIBILITY (p-ILP): Let matrices $A \in Z^{m \times p}$ and $b \in Z^{p \times 1}$ be given. The question is whether there exists a vector $x \in Z^{p \times 1}$ satisfying the m inequalities, that is, $A \cdot x \leq b$. We use the following result:

Lemma 2 [9, 11]. p–ILPcan be solved using $O(p^{2.5p+o(p)} \cdot L)$ arithmetic operations and space polynomial in L. Here L is the number of bits in the input.

In the formulation for SATISFACTORY PARTITION problem, we have at most k variables. The value of any variable in the integer linear programming is bounded by n, the number of vertices in the input graph. The constraints can be represented using $O(k^2 \log n)$ bits. Lemma 2 implies that we can solve the problem with the given guess I_1, I_2 and I_3 in FPT time. There are at most 3^k choices for (I_1, I_2, I_3), and the ILP formula for a guess can be solved in FPT time. Thus Theorem 1 holds.

3   Hardness of Balanced Satisfactory Partition Parameterized by Treewidth

In this section, we prove the following theorem:

Theorem 2. The BALANCED SATISFACTORY PARTITION problem is W[1]-hard when parameterized by the treewidth of the graph.

We introduce several variants of BALANCED SATISFACTORY PARTITION that we require in our proofs. The problem BALANCED SATISFACTORY PARTITION[S] generalizes BALANCED SATISFACTORY PARTITION where some vertices are forced to be in the second part V_2. This variant can be formalized as follows:

BALANCED SATISFACTORY PARTITION[S]
Input: A graph $G = (V, E)$ on an even number of vertices, and a set $V_\square \subseteq V(G)$.
Question: Is there a balanced satisfactory partition (V_1, V_2) of V such that $V_\square \subseteq V_2$.

BALANCED SATISFACTORY PARTITION[FS] is a further generalization where some vertices are forced to be in the first part V_1 and some other vertices are forced to be in the second part V_2. This variant can be formalized as follows:

BALANCED SATISFACTORY PARTITION[FS]

Input: A graph $G = (V, E)$ on an even number of vertices, a set $V_\triangle \subseteq V(G)$, and a set $V_\square \subseteq V(G)$.

Question: Is there a balanced satisfactory partition (V_1, V_2) of V such that (i) $V_\triangle \subseteq V_1$ (ii) $V_\square \subseteq V_2$.

Finally, we introduce the generalization BALANCED SATISFACTORY PARTITION[FSC] in which we are also given a subset of "complementary pairs" of vertices and feasible solutions are only those for which neither V_1 nor V_2 contains a complementary pair.

BALANCED SATISFACTORY PARTITION[FSC]

Input: A graph $G = (V, E)$ on an even number of vertices, a set $V_\triangle \subseteq V(G)$, a set $V_\square \subseteq V(G)$, and a set $C \subseteq V(G) \times V(G)$.

Question: Is there a balanced satisfactory partition (V_1, V_2) of V such that (i) $V_\triangle \subseteq V_1$ (ii) $V_\square \subseteq V_2$, and (iii) for all $(a, b) \in C$, V_1 contains either a or b but not both?

Let $G = (V, E)$ be an undirected and edge weighted graph, where V, E, and w denote the set of nodes, the set of edges and a positive integral weight function $w : E \rightarrow Z^+$, respectively. An orientation Λ of G is an assignment of a direction to each edge $\{u, v\} \in E(G)$, that is, either (u, v) or (v, u) is contained in Λ. The weighted outdegree of u on Λ is $w^u_{out} = \sum_{(u,v)\in\Lambda} w(\{u, v\})$. We define MINIMUM MAXIMUM OUTDEGREE problem as follows:

MINIMUM MAXIMUM OUTDEGREE

Input: A graph G, an edge weighting w of G given in unary, and a positive integer r.

Question: Is there an orientation Λ of G such that $w^u_{out} \leq r$ for each $u \in V(G)$?

It is known that MINIMUM MAXIMUM OUTDEGREE is W[1]-hard when parameterized by the treewidth of the input graph [13]. To prove Theorem 2, we give a 4-step reduction. In the first step of the reduction, we reduce MINIMUM MAXIMUM OUTDEGREE to BALANCED SATISFACTORY PARTITION[FSC]. In the second step of the reduction we reduce the BALANCED SATISFACTORY PARTITION[FSC] to BALANCED SATISFACTORY PARTITION[FS]. In the third step of the reduction we reduce the BALANCED SATISFACTORY PARTITION[FS] to BALANCED SATISFACTORY PARTITION[S]. Finally we reduce BALANCED SATISFACTORY PARTITION[S] to BALANCED SATISFACTORY PARTITION. To measure the treewidth of a BALANCED SATISFACTORY PARTITION[FSC] instance, we use the following definition. Let $I = (G, V_\triangle, V_\square, C)$ be a BALANCED SATISFACTORY PARTITION[FSC] instance. The *primal graph* G' of I is defined as follows: $V(G') = V(G)$ and $E(G') = E(G) \cup C$.

Lemma 3. *The* BALANCED SATISFACTORY PARTITION^{FSC} *is W[1]-hard when parameterized by the treewidth of the primal graph.*

Proof. Let $G = (V, E, w)$ and a positive integer r be an instance of MINIMUM MAXIMUM OUTDEGREE. We construct an instance of BALANCED SATISFACTORY PARTITION^{FSC} as follows. An example is given in Figure 1. For each vertex $v \in V(G)$, we introduce a set of new vertices $H_v = \{h_1^{v\triangle}, \ldots, h_{2r}^{v\triangle}\}$. For each edge $(u, v) \in E(G)$, we introduce the set of new vertices $V_{uv} = \{u_1^v, \ldots, u_{w(u,v)}^v\}$, $V_{uv}' = \{u_1^{\prime v}, \ldots, u_{w(u,v)}^{\prime v}\}$, $V_{vu} = \{v_1^u, \ldots, v_{w(u,v)}^u\}$, $V_{vu}' = \{v_1^{\prime u}, \ldots, v_{w(u,v)}^{\prime u}\}$, $V_{uv}^{\square} = \{u_1^{v\square}, \ldots, u_{w(u,v)}^{v\square}\}$, $V_{uv}^{\prime\square} = \{u_1^{\prime v\square}, \ldots, u_{w(u,v)}^{\prime v\square}\}$, $V_{vu}^{\square} = \{v_1^{u\square}, \ldots, v_{w(u,v)}^{u\square}\}$, $V_{vu}^{\prime\square} = \{v_1^{\prime u\square}, \ldots, v_{w(u,v)}^{\prime u\square}\}$. Let $\omega = \sum_{(u,v) \in E} w(u, v)$. Finally we add a set V_0 of $8\omega + |V|(2r + 1) - 4$ isolated vertices. We now define the graph G' with

$$V(G') = V(G) \bigcup_{v \in V(G)} H_v \bigcup_{(u,v) \in E(G)} (V_{uv} \cup V_{uv}^{\square} \cup V_{vu} \cup V_{vu}^{\square})$$
$$\bigcup_{(u,v) \in E(G)} (V_{uv}' \cup V_{uv}^{\prime\square} \cup V_{vu}' \cup V_{vu}^{\prime\square}) \bigcup V_0$$

and

$$E(G') = \{(v, h) \mid v \in V(G), h \in H_v\} \bigcup \{(u, x) \mid (u, v) \in E(G), x \in V_{uv} \cup V_{uv}^{\square}\}$$
$$\bigcup \{(x, v) \mid (u, v) \in E(G), x \in V_{vu} \cup V_{vu}^{\square}\}$$
$$\bigcup \{(u_i^v, u_i^{\prime v}), (u_i^{v\square}, u_i^{\prime v\square}), (v_i^u, v_i^{\prime u}), (v_i^{u\square}, v_i^{\prime u\square}) \mid (u, v) \in E(G), 1 \le i \le w(u, v)\}.$$

The number of vertices in $V(G') \setminus V_0$ is $8\omega + |V|(2r + 1)$. We define the complementary vertex pairs

$$C = \left\{(u_i^{\prime v}, v_i^{\prime u}), (u_{i+1}^{\prime v}, v_i^{\prime u}), (u_i^v, v_i^{\prime u}), (u_i^{\prime v}, v_i^u) \mid (u, v) \in E(G), 1 \le i \le w(u, v)\right\}$$

Complementary vertex pairs are shown in dashed lines in Fig. 1. Finally we define $V_\triangle = V(G) \bigcup_{v \in V(G)} H_v$ and $V_\square = \bigcup_{(u,v) \in E(G)} (V_{uv}^{\square} \cup V_{uv}^{\prime\square} \cup V_{vu}^{\square} \cup V_{vu}^{\prime\square})$. We use I to denote $(G', V_\triangle, V_\square, C)$ which is an instance of BALANCED SATISFACTORY PARTITION^{FSC}.

Clearly, it takes polynomial time to compute I. We now prove that the treewidth of the primal graph G' of I is bounded by a function of the treewidth of G. We do so by modifying an optimal tree decomposition τ of G as follows:

- For every edge (u, v) of G, there is a node in τ whose bag B contains both u and v; add to this node a chain of nodes $1, 2, \ldots, w(u, v) - 1$ where the bag of node i is $B \cup \{u_i^v, u_i^{\prime v}, v_i^u, v_i^u, u_{i+1}^v, u_{i+1}^{\prime v}, v_{i+1}^u\}$.
- For every edge (u, v) of G, there is a node in τ whose bag B contains u; add to this node a chain of nodes $1, 2, \ldots, w(u, v)$ where the bag of node i is $B \cup \{u_i^{v\square}, u_i^{\prime v\square}\}$.

- For every edge (u, v) of G, there is a node in τ whose bag B contains v and add to this node a chain of nodes $1, 2, \ldots, w(u, v)$ where the bag of node i is $B \cup \{v_i^{u\square}, v_i'^{u\square}\}$.
- For every vertex v of G, there is a node in τ whose bag B contains v and add to this node a chain of nodes $1, 2, \ldots, 2r$ where the bag of node i is $B \cup \{h_i^{v\triangle}\}$.

Clearly, the modified tree decomposition is a valid tree decomposition of the primal graph of I and its width is at most the treewidth of G plus eight.

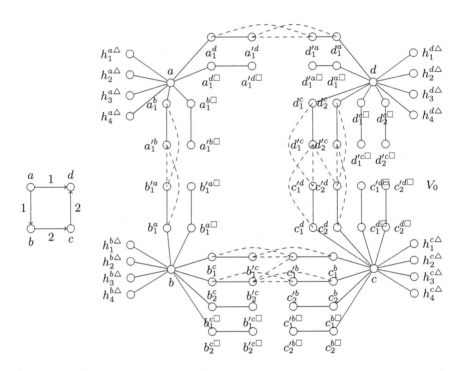

Fig. 1. Result of our reduction on a MINIMUM MAXIMUM OUTDEGREE instance G with $r = 2$. The graph G long with its orientation is shown at the left; and G' is shown at the right. Complementary vertex pairs are shown using dashed lines. The vertices in the first part of satisfactory partition (V_1, V_2) of G' are shown in red for the given orientation of G. Here $\omega = 6$ and V_0 contains 64 isolated vertices. The vertices of V_0 are distributed among V_1 and V_2 so that (V_1, V_2) becomes balanced satisfactory partition.

Let D be the directed graph obtained by an orientation of the edges of G such that for each vertex the sum of the weights of outgoing edges is at most r. Consider the partition of $G' - V_0$

$$V_1 = V_\triangle \bigcup_{(u,v) \in E(D)} (V_{vu} \cup V_{vu}') = V(G) \bigcup_{v \in V(G)} H_v \bigcup_{(u,v) \in E(D)} (V_{vu} \cup V_{vu}')$$

and
$$V_2 = \bigcup_{(u,v)\in E(D)} (V_{uv} \cup V'_{uv} \cup V^\square_{uv} \cup V'^\square_{uv}) \bigcup_{(u,v)\in E(D)} (V^\square_{vu} \cup V'^\square_{vu}).$$

To prove that (V_1, V_2) is a satisfactory partition, first we prove that $d_{V_1}(x) \geq d_{V_2}(x)$ for all $x \in V_1$. If x is a vertex in H_v or $V_{vu} \cup V'_{vu}$, then clearly all neighbours of x are in V_1, hence x is satisfied. Suppose $x \in V(G)$. Let w^x_{out} and w^x_{in} denote the sum of the weights of outgoing and incoming edges of vertex x, respectively. Hence $d_{V_1}(x) = 2r + w^x_{\text{in}}$ and $d_{V_2}(x) = 2w^x_{\text{out}} + w^x_{\text{in}}$ in G'. This shows that x is satisfied as $w^x_{\text{out}} \leq r$. Now we prove that $d_{V_2}(x) \geq d_{V_1}(x)$ for all $x \in V_2$. If x is a vertex in $V_{uv} \cup V^\square_{uv} \cup V^\square_{vu}$ then x has one neighbour in V_1 and one neighbour in V_2. If $x \in V'_{uv} \cup V'^\square_{uv} \cup V'^\square_{vu}$ then x has one neighbour in V_2 and no neighbours in V_1. Thus the vertices in V_2 are satisfied. The isolated vertices of V_0 are distributed among V_1 and V_2 so that it becomes balanced satisfactory partition for G'.

Conversely, suppose (V_1, V_2) is a balanced satisfactory partition of G'. That is $|V_1| = |V_2| = 8\omega + (2r+1)|V| - 2$. Then $V'_1 = V_1 \setminus V_0$ and $V'_2 = V_2 \setminus V_0$ form a satisfactory partition of $G' - V_0$. For every $(u,v) \in E(G)$, either $V_{uv} \cup V'_{uv} \in V'_1$ or $V_{vu} \cup V'_{vu} \in V'_1$ due to the complementary vertex pairs. We define a directed graph D by $V(D) = V(G)$ and

$$E(D) = \Big\{ (u,v) \mid V_{vu} \cup V'_{vu} \in V'_1 \Big\} \bigcup \Big\{ (v,u) \mid V_{uv} \cup V'_{uv} \in V'_1 \Big\}.$$

Suppose there is a vertex x in D for which $w^x_{\text{out}} > r$. Clearly $x \in V'_1$. We know $d_{V'_1}(x) = 2r + w^x_{\text{in}}$ and $d_{V'_2}(x) = 2w^x_{\text{out}} + w^x_{\text{in}}$. Then $d_{V'_2}(x) > d_{V'_1}(x)$, as by assumption $w^x_{\text{out}} > r$, a contradiction to the fact that (V'_1, V'_2) is a satisfactory partition of $G' - V_0$. Hence $w^x_{\text{out}} \leq r$ for all $x \in V(D)$.

Next we prove the following result which eliminates complementary pairs.

Lemma 4. *The* BALANCED SATISFACTORY PARTITION^{FS} *problem, parameterized by the treewidth of the graph, is W[1]-hard.*

Proof. Let $I = (G, V_\square, V_\triangle, C)$ be an instance of BALANCED SATISFACTORY PARTITION^{FSC}. Consider the primal graph of I, that is the graph G^p where $V(G^p) = V(G)$ and $E(G^p) = E(G) \cup C$. From this we construct an instance $I' = (G', V'_\square, V'_\triangle)$ of BALANCED SATISFACTORY PARTITION^{FS} problem. For each $(a,b) \in C$ in the primal graph G^p, we introduce two new vertices $\triangle^{ab}$ and $\square^{ab}$ and four new edges in G'. We now define the G' with $V(G') = V(G) \bigcup_{(a,b)\in C} \{\triangle^{ab}, \square^{ab}\}$ and $E(G') = E(G) \bigcup_{(a,b)\in C} \Big\{ (a,\triangle^{ab}), (a,\square^{ab}), (b,\triangle^{ab}), (b,\square^{ab}) \Big\}$. Finally, we define the sets $V'_\triangle = V_\triangle \bigcup_{(a,b)\in C} \{\triangle^{ab}\}$ and $V'_\square = V_\square \bigcup_{(a,b)\in C} \{\square^{ab}\}$. We illustrate our construction in Fig. 2. It is easy to see that we can compute I' in polynomial time and its treewidth is linear in the treewidth of I. The following holds for every solution (V'_1, V'_2) of I': V'_1 contains $\triangle^{ab}$ for every $(a,b) \in C$, so it must also contain a or b. It cannot contain both a and b for any $(a,b) \in C$, because $\square^{ab} \in V'_2$.

Restricting (V_1', V_2') to the original vertices thus is a solution to I. Conversely, for every solution (V_1, V_2) of I, the partition (V_1', V_2') where $V_1' = V_1 \bigcup_{(a,b) \in C} \{\triangle^{ab}\}$ and $V_2' = V_2 \bigcup_{(a,b) \in C} \{\square^{ab}\}$, is a solution of I'.

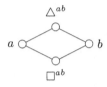

Fig. 2. Gadget for a pair of complementary vertices (a, b) in the reduction from BALANCED SATISFACTORY PARTITION^{FSC} to BALANCED SATISFACTORY PARTITION^{FS}.

Lemma 5. *The* BALANCED SATISFACTORY PARTITION^S *is W[1]-hard when parameterized by the treewidth of the graph.*

Proof. Let $I = (G, V_\triangle, V_\square)$ be a BALANCED SATISFACTORY PARTITION^{FS} instance; let n denote the number of vertices in G. First, we fix a vertex $v \in V_\square$. For every pair (u, v) of vertices where $u \in V_\triangle$, we introduce two sets of new vertices $X_{uv} = \{x_1^{uv}, x_2^{uv}, \dots, x_n^{uv}\}$ and $Y_{uv}^\square = \{y_1^{uv\square}, y_2^{uv\square}, \dots, y_n^{uv\square}\}$. Next, we define the BALANCED SATISFACTORY PARTITION^S instance $I' = (G', V_\square')$ where $V_\square' = V_\square \bigcup_{u \in V_\triangle} Y_{uv}^\square$ and G' is the graph defined by

$$V(G') = V(G) \bigcup_{u \in V_\triangle} X_{uv} \bigcup_{u \in V_\triangle} Y_{uv}^\square$$

and

$$E(G') = E(G) \bigcup_{u \in V_\triangle} \left\{ (u, x_i^{uv}), (u, y_i^{uv\square}), (x_i^{uv}, v), (y_i^{uv\square}, v) \mid i \le i \le n \right\}$$

$$\bigcup_{u \in V_\triangle} \left\{ (x_i^{uv}, y_i^{uv\square}), (x_i^{uv}, y_{i+1}^{uv\square}) \mid 1 \le i \le n-1 \right\} \cup \left\{ (x_n^{uv}, y_n^{uv\square}), (x_n^{uv}, y_1^{uv\square}) \right\}$$

$$\bigcup_{u \in V_\triangle} \left\{ (x_i^{uv}, x_{i+1}^{uv} \mid 1 \le i \le n-1 \right\} \cup \left\{ (x_n^{uv}, x_1^{uv}) \right\}$$

$$\bigcup_{u \in V_\triangle} \left\{ (y_i^{uv\square}, y_{i+1}^{uv\square}) \mid 1 \le i \le n-1 \right\} \cup \left\{ (y_n^{uv\square}, y_1^{uv\square}) \right\}$$

An example is given in Fig. 3. The treewidth of G' is equal to the treewidth of G plus 5. We now claim that I is a yes-instance if and only if I' is a yes-instance. Assume first that there exists a balanced satisfactory partition (V_1, V_2) of I such

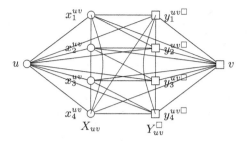

Fig. 3. Let $n = 4$. Gadget for a pair of vertices (u, v) where $u \in V_\triangle$ and v is a fixed vertex in $V_\square$ in the reduction from BALANCED SATISFACTORY PARTITION^{FS} to BALANCED SATISFACTORY PARTITION^{S}.

that $V_\triangle \in V_1$ and $V_\square \in V_2$. In this case, we will get a balanced satisfactory partition (V_1', V_2') of I' as follows:

$$V_1' = V_1 \bigcup_{u \in V_\triangle} X_{uv} \quad \text{and} \quad V_2' = V_2 \bigcup_{u \in V_\triangle} Y_{uv}^\square.$$

It is easy to see that (V_1', V_2') forms a balanced satisfactory partition of G' as all the vertices in V_1 and V_2 will remain satisfied and also the new vertices in $X_{uv} \cup Y_{uv}^\square$ for all $u \in V_\triangle$ are satisfied in their respective part as each vertex has three neighbours in its own part and three neighbors in the other part. Since we are adding equal number of vertices in the balanced partition (V_1, V_2), we again get a balanced satisfactory partition. This shows that I' is a yes-instance.

Conversely, suppose that there exists a balanced satisfactory partition (V_1', V_2') of G' such that $V_\square' \in V_2'$. We first show that all the vertices in $V_\triangle$ must lie in V_1'. Let us assume that there exists a vertex $u \in V_\triangle$ that lies in V_2'. Then each vertex in X_{uv} has at least 4 neighbors in V_2' and at most 2 neighbours in V_1'; therefore all the vertices in X_{uv} lie in V_2'. In this case, we cannot get a balanced satisfactory partition as already more than half of the vertices are in V_2'. This proves that all the vertices in $V_\triangle$ lie in V_1'. Next, we show that as $V_\triangle \subseteq V_1'$, the vertices in $\bigcup_{u \in V_\triangle} X_{uv}$ also lie in V_1'. Since $u \in V_1'$, it must be satisfied in V_1'. As the vertices in $Y_{uv}^\square$ lie in V_2', u has at least n neighbors in V_2' and since u has at most $n - 1$ neighbors in graph G, it implies that at least one vertex from X_{uv} must be in V_1'. Without loss of generality, we can assume that $x_1^{uv} \in V_1'$. Since $x_1^{uv} \in V_1'$, it must be satisfied in V_1' and this forces x_n^{uv}, x_2^{uv} to be in V_1' as well. Repetitively applying the above argument we get that all the vertices in set X_{uv} lie in V_1'. We claim that $(V_1' \cap V(G), V_2' \cap V(G))$ forms a balanced satisfactory partition of graph G. As for each vertex in $V_i' \cap V(G)$, $i = 1, 2$, we are removing equal number of neighbors from both the partitions, this implies that all the vertices are satisfied and the partition is balanced. This shows that I is a yes-instance.

Lemma 6. The BALANCED SATISFACTORY PARTITION problem, parameterized by the treewidth of the graph, is W[1]-hard.

Proof. Let $I = (G, V_\square)$ be a BALANCED SATISFACTORY PARTITION^S instance, where $V_\square = \{u_1, u_2, \ldots, u_{n'}\}$. For every vertex u_i in the set $V_\square$, we introduce two new sets of vertices $X^{u_i} = \{x_1^{u_i}, x_2^{u_i}, \ldots, x_{4n}^{u_i}\}$ and $Y^{u_i} = \{y_1^{u_i}, y_2^{u_i}, \ldots, y_{4n}^{u_i}\}$. We also introduce a clique of size 2 containing vertices $\{s, t\}$ and a set $C = \{c_1, c_2, \ldots, c_{8n}\}$ of $8n$ vertices. We add two new vertices $\{s', t'\}$ along with two sets of vertices $S' = \{s_1', s_2', \ldots, s_{4n}'\}$ and $T' = \{t_1', t_2', \ldots, t_{4n}'\}$. Now, we define the BALANCED SATISFACTORY PARTITION instance $I' = G'$ where G' is the graph defined by

$$V(G') = V(G) \cup \bigcup_{i=1}^{n'} X^{u_i} \cup \bigcup_{i=1}^{n'} Y^{u_i} \cup \{s, t, s', t'\} \cup S' \cup T' \cup C$$

and

$$E(G') = E(G) \cup \bigcup_{i=1}^{n'} \bigcup_{j=1}^{4n} \left\{ (x_j^{u_i}, u_i), (y_j^{u_i}, u_i), (y_j^{u_i}, s), (y_j^{u_i}, t) \right\} \cup \{(s, t)\}$$

$$\bigcup_{j=1}^{8n} \left\{ (c_j, s), (c_j, t) \right\} \cup \bigcup_{j=1}^{4n} \left\{ (s', s_j'), (t', t_j') \right\} \cup \left\{ (s', s)(s', t), (t', s), (t', t) \right\}.$$

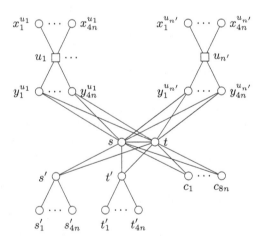

Fig. 4. An illustration of the reduction from BALANCED SATISFACTORY PARTITION^S to BALANCED SATISFACTORY PARTITION.

Now we claim that I is a yes-instance if and only if I' is a yes-instance. Assume first that there exists a balanced satisfactory partition (V_1, V_2) in the graph G such that $V_\square \subseteq V_2$. In this case, a balanced satisfactory partition (V_1', V_2') for G' is defined as follows:

$$V_1' = V_1 \cup \bigcup_{i=1}^{n'} Y^{u_i} \cup \{s, t\} \cup C \text{ and } V_2' = V_2 \cup \bigcup_{i=1}^{n'} X^{u_i} \cup \{s', t'\} \cup S' \cup T'.$$

Clearly, all the vertices are satisfied. Since we are adding equal number of vertices in both the parts, (V_1', V_2') is a balanced satisfactory partition of G'. This proves that if I is a yes-instance then I' is a yes-instance.

Conversely, suppose that there exists a balanced satisfactory partition (V_1', V_2') of G'. We first prove that all the vertices of $V_\square$ are in the same part. Since $N_{G'}[s] = N_{G'}[t]$, both s and t would be in the same part; without loss of generality suppose they lie in V_1'. For $1 \leq i \leq n'$, each vertex $y_j^{u_i}$ is adjacent to 3 vertices $\{u_i, s, t\}$ and since $\{s, t\}$ belong to V_1', it forces $y_j^{u_i}$ to be in V_1' for $1 \leq j \leq 4n$. Similarly, as $s, t \in V_1'$, each c_i would also be in V_1' for $1 \leq i \leq 4n$. For the sake of contradiction, suppose the vertices of $V_\square$ are distributed among V_1' and V_2', that is, r many vertices of $V_\square$ are in V_1' and remaining $n' - r$ vertices of $V_\square$ are in V_2'. This implies that V_1' contains at least $4n(n' + r + 2) + r + 2$ vertices and V_2' contains at most $4n(n' - r + 2) + 2 + (n - r)$. It implies that $|V_1'| > |V_2'|$, a contradiction to our assumption that (V_1', V_2') is a balanced satisfactory partition. This shows that all the vertices of $V_\square$ must go to V_2'. Therefore, for every balanced satisfactory partition of G', we have

$$\bigcup_{i=1}^{n'} \bigcup_{j=1}^{4n} \{y_j^{u_i}\} \cup \{s, t\} \cup C \subseteq V_1' \text{ and } \bigcup_{i=1}^{n'} \bigcup_{j=1}^{4n} \{x_j^{u_i}\} \cup \{s', t'\} \cup S' \cup T' \cup V_\square \subseteq V_2'.$$

We now claim that $(V_1' \cap V(G), V_2' \cap V(G))$ forms a balanced satisfactory partition of G. From the above observation, we have $V_\square \subset V_2' \cap V(G)$. All the vertices are satisfied in the new partition $(V_1' \cap V(G), V_2' \cap V(G))$ and it is a balanced partition because we are removing equal number of vertices from both parts. This shows that if I' is a yes-instance then I is also a yes-instance.

This proves Theorem 2.

4 Conclusion

In this work we proved that the SATISFACTORY PARTITION and BALANCED SATISFACTORY PARTITION problems are FPT when parameterized by neighbourhood diversity; the BALANCED SATISFACTORY PARTITION problem is W[1]-hard when parameterized by treewidth. The parameterized complexity of the SATISFACTORY PARTITION problem remains unsettle when parameterized by other important structural graph parameters like clique-width and modular width.

Acknowledgement. The first author gratefully acknowledges support from the Ministry of Human Resource Development, Government of India, under Prime Minister's Research Fellowship Scheme (No. MRF-192002-211).

References

1. Bazgan, C., Tuza, Z., Vanderpooten, D.: On the existence and determination of satisfactory partitions in a graph. In: Ibaraki, T., Katoh, N., Ono, H. (eds.) ISAAC 2003. LNCS, vol. 2906, pp. 444–453. Springer, Heidelberg (2003). https://doi.org/10.1007/978-3-540-24587-2_46

2. Bazgan, C., Tuza, Z., Vanderpooten, D.: Complexity and approximation of satisfactory partition problems. In: Wang, L. (ed.) COCOON 2005. LNCS, vol. 3595, pp. 829–838. Springer, Heidelberg (2005). https://doi.org/10.1007/11533719_84

3. Bazgan, C., Tuza, Z., Vanderpooten, D.: Degree-Constrained decompositions of graphs: bounded treewidth and planarity. Theor. Comput. Sci. **355**(3), 389–395 (2006)

4. Bazgan, C., Tuza, Z., Vanderpooten, D.: The satisfactory partition problem. Discr. Appl. Math. **154**(8), 1236–1245 (2006)

5. Cygan, M., et al.: Parameterized Algorithms. Springer, Cham (2015). https://doi.org/10.1007/978-3-319-21275-3

6. Gerber, M.U., Kobler, D.: Classes of graphs that can be partitioned to satisfy all their vertices. Australas. J. Combin. **29**, 201–214 (2004)

7. Gerber, M.U., Kobler, D.: Algorithmic approach to the satisfactory graph partitioning problem. Eur. J. Oper. Res. **125**(2), 283–291 (2000)

8. Gerber, M.U., Kobler, D.: Algorithms for vertex-partitioning problems on graphs with fixed clique-width. Theoret. Comput. Sci. **299**(1), 719–734 (2003)

9. Kannan, R.: Minkowski's convex body theorem and integer programming. Math. Oper. Res. **12**(3), 415–440 (1987)

10. Lampis, M.: Algorithmic meta-theorems for restrictions of treewidth. Algorithmica **64**, 19–37 (2012)

11. Lenstra, H.W.: Integer programming with a fixed number of variables. Math. Oper. Res. **8**(4), 538–548 (1983)

12. N. Robertson and P. Seymour. Graph minors. iii. planar tree-width. J. Combinatorial Theory, Series B, **36**(1), 49–64 (1984)

13. Szeider, S.: Not so easy problems for tree decomposable graphs. CoRR, abs/1107.1177 (2011)

14. Tedder, M., Corneil, D., Habib, M., Paul, C.: Simpler linear-time modular decomposition via recursive factorizing permutations. In: Aceto, L., Damgård, I., Goldberg, L.A., Halldórsson, M.M., Ingólfsdóttir, A., Walukiewicz, I. (eds.) ICALP 2008. LNCS, vol. 5125, pp. 634–645. Springer, Heidelberg (2008). https://doi.org/10.1007/978-3-540-70575-8_52

The Multiple Traveling Salesman Problem on Spiders

Pedro Pérez-Escalona[1], Ivan Rapaport[1,2]($\boxtimes$), José Soto[1,2], and Ian Vidal[2]

[1] Departamento de Ingeniería Matemática, Universidad de Chile, Santiago, Chile
{peperez,rapaport,jsoto}@dim.uchile.cl
[2] Centro de Modelamiento Matemático (UMI 2807 CNRS), Universidad de Chile, Santiago, Chile
ian.vidal@ing.uchile.cl

Abstract. Given (i) a set of $N + 1$ vertices, that corresponds to N *clients* and 1 *depot*, (ii) the travel time between each pair of vertices and (iii) a number m of *salespersons*, the *multiple traveling salesman problem* consists in finding m tours such that, starting from the depot, all clients are visited in such a way that some objective function is minimized. The objective function we consider in this paper is the *makespan*. More precisely, the goal is to find m tours (one for each salesperson) that minimize the time elapsed from the beginning of the operation until the last salesman comes back to the depot. We take into account *handling times*, i.e., the time spent visiting each client, which we assume to be the same for all of them. We address the problem in the particular case where the *depot-clients network* is a spider, with the depot located at its center. We show that this case is NP-hard even for 2 salespersons. We also show structural properties of the optimal solutions. These properties allow us to devise a PTAS for minimizing the makespan. More precisely, a $(1 + \varepsilon)$-approximation algorithm with running time $N^{O(m/\varepsilon)}$.

Keywords: Multiple traveling salesman problem · Salesperson routing problem · Approximation algorithms · Polynomial-time approximation schemes

1 Introduction

The *Traveling Salesman Problem* (TSP) is probably the best-known problem in combinatorial optimization [12]. It finds countless applications in different fields, ranging from logistics [13] to electronic circuit manufacturing [8].

The *Multiple Traveling Salesman Problem* (mTSP [3]) is a natural generalization of the TSP. While in the TSP there is one salesman who must visit all the clients, in the mTSP there are m salespersons, who must jointly visit all the

Additional support from ANID via FONDEF IDeA I+D ID18I10250, PIA/Apoyo a Centros Científicos y Tecnológicos de Excelencia AFB170001, Fondecyt 1170021 and Fondecyt 1181180.

T. Bureš et al. (Eds.): SOFSEM 2021, LNCS 12607, pp. 337–348, 2021.
https://doi.org/10.1007/978-3-030-67731-2_24

clients. In turn, the Vehicle Routing Problem (VRP) is a generalization of the mTSP, where the role of the salespersons is played by (capacitated) vehicles [11].

In the mTSP there are N clients, 1 depot, and m salespersons that must visit all the clients starting from the depot. The standard objective function is to minimize the sum of the length of all m tours. In this work we focus on the *min-max* version of the mTSP. More precisely, the goal is to find m tours (one for each salesperson) that minimize the makespan: the time elapsed from the beginning of the operation until the last salesperson comes back to the depot. In the literature this problem is equivalent to the Single-Depot Min-Max Cycle Cover Problem (SDMMCCP). The aim of SDMMCCP is to cover all the vertices of a weighted graph with at most m cycles, all of them passing through one particular vertex D, the depot, such that the weight of the heaviest cycle is minimized. Frederickson et al. devised a $\rho + 1$-approximation algorithms in [5], where ρ is any approximation ratio for TSP (from Christofides [4] we know that $\rho \leq 3/2$).

The mTSP is NP-complete, as it is a generalization of the TSP. One way to tackle NP-complete problems is to study subproblems and variants. In graph problems a typical approach consists in restricting the topology of the network. For instance, in [14], the authors study the mTSP in trees. They devise, for fixed values of m, a pseudo-polynomial, $(1 + \varepsilon)$-approximation algorithm running in time $O(N^{2m-1}/\varepsilon^{2k-2})$. Later, Becker and Paul develop, also for trees, a $(1+\varepsilon)$-approximation algorithm running in time $N^{O(\varepsilon^{-8})}$ [2].

In [16], Yu and Liu study the variant of mTSP with *release times*, which are times fixed by each client before which she/he cannot be visited. They study graphs as simple as paths, and they show that the problem of minimizing the makespan is polynomially solvable.

One can also take into account *handling times*, i.e., the time of visit to the clients. In fact, when each client has, together with his/her own release time, his/her own handling time, the problem is called *Multi-Vehicle Scheduling Problem* (VSP), and it is NP-complete even in a path [9,10]. The authors also give, for every fixed m, a $(1 + \varepsilon)$-approximation algorithm that runs in time $O((1 + 2/\varepsilon)m^2N^2(N + 2^{1+2/\varepsilon})(mN^3(1 + 2/\varepsilon)/\varepsilon)^{m(1+2/\varepsilon)})$. On the other hand, Gaur et al. [7] give a polynomial-time $\frac{5}{3}$-approximation algorithm.

Bao and Liu study the VSP in cycles and trees [1]. They show, for cycles, a 12/7-approximation algorithm for minimizing the makespan. In the case of trees, they give a 9/5-approximation algorithm. In [15], Xu and Xu show a $\max\{3 - 2/m, 2\}$-aproximation for VSP in arbitrary graphs.

The topology we consider in the present paper is a spider. A spider is a tree with one distinguished vertex called the center and where every non-center vertex has degree at most 2. We study the mTSP when the depot is located at the center of a spider, and we consider uniform handling times (i.e, all clients have the same handling time). We denote this problem by mTSPHT for spiders.

In this paper we prove that mTSPHT in a spider is strongly NP-hard, even in a star (the complete bipartite graph $K_{1,N}$). So we cannot hope to obtain a fully polynomial time approximation scheme (FPTAS) unless P = NP. Our main contribution, together with establishing structural properties of the optimal solutions, is to give a polynomial time approximation scheme (PTAS), more precisely, a $(1 + \varepsilon)$-approximation algorithm running in time $N^{O(m/\varepsilon)}$.

Our approach is based on an interesting structural result, namely, the existence of particular type of solutions, that we call *well-structured*. Such solutions have the following very nice property: there is always one salesperson who visits just blocks of consecutive clients located at the end of some branches; once we remove such salesperson together with the clients he/she visited, the remaining (smaller) solution is also well-structured. From this result we can compute the solution of mTSPHT in the spider through dynamic programming.

As we have already mentioned, Becker and Paul develop, for trees, a $(1+\varepsilon)$-approximation running in time $N^{O(\varepsilon^{-8})}$ [2]. In the present work, the PTAS we develop is devised for spiders (particular types of trees) and runs in time $N^{O(m/\varepsilon)}$. The result of Becker and Paul is more general than ours (although they do not consider handling times). Nevertheless, we would like to discuss a little bit the difference when we restrict the two approaches to spiders.

Our algorithm, in the case of only one branch, takes time $O(N^2)$ and finds the optimal solution, while the one of [2] takes time $N^{O(\varepsilon^{-4})}$ and gives a $(1+\varepsilon)$-approximation. In the case of spiders with more branches, our algorithm gives a $(1 + \varepsilon)$-approximation that takes time $N^{O(m/\varepsilon)}$, while the one of [2] takes time $N^{O(\varepsilon^{-8})}$. Note that, for fixed values of m, a situation which is already NP-hard for $m = 2$, our algorithm takes time $N^{O(\varepsilon^{-1})}$.

2 Definitions and Basic Results

Let $G = (V \cup \{D\}, E)$ be a simple, connected, undirected graph where V is a set of N clients and D is a depot. The number of salespersons is m. The function $t\colon E \to \mathbb{R}_+$ represents the travel time between neighboring nodes. We consider the handling time, the time spent by any salesperson visiting each client, to be a constant $t_0 \in \mathbb{R}_+$. We assume that the route taken by any salesperson between two nodes u and v is always the shortest one (in terms of time). Therefore, we will replace the function $t\colon E \to \mathbb{R}_+$ with its metric completion $t\colon \binom{V}{2} \to \mathbb{R}_+$ so that the travel time between any two nodes is well-defined. We reserve the term *distance* between two nodes to refer to the minimum number of edges in a path from one node to the other.

For any $r \in \mathbb{N}_+$, we define a *route* S of $r+1$ nodes in $V \cup \{D\}$, $(s_j)_{j=0}^r$, where $s_0 = D$. Nodes s_1 and s_r are, respectively, the first and last clients visited in S. We note by $C(S)$ the set of r clients visited in the route S (observe that $C(S)$ may be a strict subset of V). In other words, $C(S) = \{s_1, \ldots, s_r\}$. When there is no confusion we write S instead of $C(S)$. The travel time of a route $S = (s_j)_{j=0}^r$ corresponds to the value $T(S) = \sum_{j=1}^r [t(s_{j-1}, s_j) + t_0] + t(s_r, D)$.

A set of m routes $\widehat{S} = \{S^1, \ldots, S^m\}$ is feasible if $C(S^1) \dot\cup \ldots \dot\cup C(S^m) = V$. We define the makespan$(\widehat{S}) = \max_{1 \leq k \leq m} T(S^k)$. In the Multiple Traveling Salesman Problem with Handling Times (mTSPHT) the goal is to find a feasible set of m

routes that minimizes the makespan. In this work we study problem mTSPHT when the graph G is a spider with the depot D located at its center.

A branch B is a maximal path in G starting in the depot D. (Obviously, B can be seen as a particular route). We denote by $M \geq 1$ the number of branches, and we assume that they are enumerated as $B_1, \ldots, B_M$. We can encode every vertex $v \in V \setminus \{D\}$ with two positive integers: (1) the branch b where v belongs, with $1 \leq b \leq M$, and (2) the *label* $j = \text{label}(v)$ defined as the distance from D to v. We write $v = v_j^b$ to refer to the unique vertex with label j and branch b.

Let S^k be a route and let B_b be a branch of the spider G. Let $v_{k,b}$ be the farthest node of the branch B_b visited in S^k. If S^k does not include any node of branch B_b, then $v_{k,b} = D$. It is clear that the optimal solution for visiting the clients of $C(S^k)$ is to go branch by branch (the order of the branches does not matter for the makespan), visiting all the clients until the farthest one, come back to the depot, and then start with another branch. Therefore, we are going to assume that this is indeed the route S^k taken by the k-th salesperson. In other words, $T(S^k) = 2\sum_{b=1}^{M} t(D, v_{k,b}) + |S^k| t_0$.

Proposition 1. mTSPHT *for stars (and thus, also for spiders) is **strongly NP-hard**. In fact, with $m = 2$ it is still **NP-hard**.*

Proof. We show a reduction from the *Multiprocessor Scheduling Problem* (MSP) to mTSPHT. MSP is a **strongly NP-hard** problem when m is part of the input, and remains **NP-hard** even for 2 available machines [6]. MSP is defined as follows. There are N jobs $J_1, \ldots, J_N$, each job J_i requires a processing time t_i. We have to schedule these N jobs in m machines in such a way that the makespan (the largest completion time) is minimized. The reduction is as follows.

- We construct a star G with a depot D at its center and N leaves connected to D, each leaf corresponding to a job J_i.
- We define t_0, the handling time, as the shortest processing time. Therefore, $t_0 = t_z$ for some particular $1 \leq z \leq N$.
- We define the travel time associated to each edge $e = \{D, J_i\}$ as $t(e) = \frac{t_i - t_z}{2}$.
- There are m salespersons (corresponding to the m machines).

Observe that the output of any instance of MSP and the output of the corresponding instance of mTSPHT, created through the aforementioned reduction, are the same. It follows that the total processing time of machine k is exactly $T(S^k)$. Therefore, minimizing the makespan in MSP is equivalent to minimizing the makespan in mTSPHT. □

Recall that we are always assuming that any route S^k goes branch by branch, visiting all the clients until the farthest one in $C(S^k)$, comes back to the depot, and then start with another branch. We now explain how to transform any of these solutions into a more structured one, without increasing the makespan.

Let us define $S^{k,b}$ as the clients of the k-th route that are in branch b. Consider first the situation where a branch B_b is visited by only two salespersons, through routes S^i and S^j. Let n_b be the size of the branch. Assume, without loss of generality, that the farthest node of the branch is visited by the i-th salesperson. More precisely: $v_{i,b} = v_{n_b}^b \in S^{i,b}$. Now, the i-th salesperson and the j-th salesperson exchange clients (See Fig. 1) in such a way that the number of clients served by each does not change and, all the clients served by the j-th salesperson are closer to the depot than the clients served by the i-th salesperson. Since the time spent by each salesperson in the branch depends only on the number of clients visited and the distance of the farthest one, the previous modification does not increase the makespan. If there are more than two routes in a branch we do exactly the same, shifting clients between pair of routes (see Fig. 2) until the set of clients served by each salesperson on each branch is a consecutive block. We say that such type of solutions is *structured in intervals*. Therefore:

Proposition 2. mTSPHT *in the spider admits an optimal solution that is structured in intervals.*

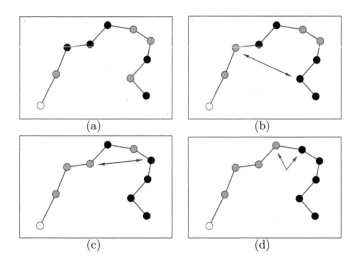

Fig. 1. Transforming an arbitrary solution of a branch into a solution structured in intervals. In this case there are two routes, one represented by grey nodes and the other by black nodes; the depot is white.

3   Canonical Solutions

We already know that there exists an optimal solution that is structured in intervals. In this section we will prove the existence of optimal solutions with even more structure. For this end we need some definitions.

Definition 3   The $\preccurlyeq$ relation. *Let B_b be a branch of a spider $G = (V, E)$. Let S^i and S^j be two routes. We say that $S^{i,b} \preccurlyeq S^{j,b}$ if the clients of $S^{i,b}$ are all closer to the depot than those of $S^{j,b}$. Formally, $\forall u \in C(S^{i,b}), \forall v \in C(S^{j,b}) :$ label$(u) <$ label(v). We also write $S^i \preccurlyeq S^j$ if $S^{i,b} \preccurlyeq S^{j,b}$ holds for every branch B_b with $1 \leq b \leq M$.*

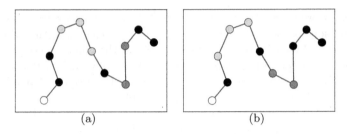

Fig. 2. In this example there are three salespersons visiting the clients of the branch. By shifting the assignment of two clients we get closer to a solution structured in intervals, without increasing the makespan.

Definition 4 *Concurrent routes.* *Let $G = (V, E)$ be a spider. Let S^i and S^j be two routes. We say that S^i and S^j are concurrent if there exists at least one branch that they both visit (see Fig. 3).*

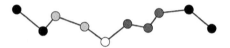

Fig. 3. There are three routes: black, dark gray and light gray. The depot is white. The black route is concurrent with the two others. But the light gray route and the dark gray route are not.

Definition 5 *Antisymmetric solutions.* *Let $G = (V, E)$ be a spider. We say that a solution (a collection of m routes) is antisymmetric if, for every two concurrent routes S^i and S^j, either $S^i \preccurlyeq S^j$ or $S^j \preccurlyeq S^i$.*

Proposition 6. *The mTSPHT problem for spiders admits an optimal solution that is antisymmetric.*

Proof. Let us suppose that there is no optimal antisymmetric solution. Let us define an obstruction as a 4-tuple (B_x, B_y, S^i, S^j) such that S^i and S^j visit both B_x and B_y, $S^{i,x} \preccurlyeq S^{j,x}$ and $S^{j,y} \preccurlyeq S^{i,y}$. Clearly, a solution is antisymmetric iff there are no obstructions. Consider an optimal solution with a minimum number of obstructions. Let (B_x, B_y, S^i, S^j) be an obstruction for such solution (in Fig. 4(a) these are the black and dark gray routes). In order to get a contradiction we perform local changes in such a way that: (1) we do not create new obstructions, (2) we do not increase the makespan, (3) (B_x, B_y, S^i, S^j) is not an obstruction anymore.

The local changes are defined as follows. First, consider the branch B_x. If $S^{i,x}$ and $S^{j,x}$ are consecutive intervals (this happens in the right branch of Fig. 4(a)), then assign the last client (the one with largest label) visited by the route $S^{i,x}$ to the route $S^{j,x}$ (right branch of Fig. 4(b)).

If $S^{i,x}$ and $S^{j,x}$ are not consecutive intervals, we shift the assignment of all nodes between $S^{i,x}$ and $S^{j,x}$ one step towards the depot. With this movement, S^i looses the farthest client visited (by the i-th salesperson) in B_x. On the other hand, one client is left unassigned: the client with smallest label in $S^{j,x}$ (because such assignment was shifted towards the depot). We simply assign this client to S^j. Now, in the branch B_x, there is one more client visited by S^j and one less client visited by S^i.

We do the same in B_y, changing the roles of S^i and S^j (see the development of the left branch in Fig. 4). We iterate these local changes until the 4-tuple (B_x, B_y, S^i, S^j) is not an obstruction anymore. This will end up happening because at every step both $|S^{i,x}|$ and $|S^{j,y}|$ decrease by one: at some point, one of them will be zero (see Fig. 4(d)).   □

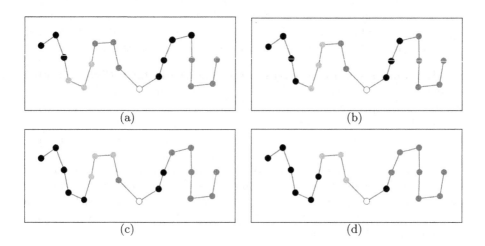

(a)   (b)

(c)   (d)

Fig. 4. Eliminating an obstruction.

Definition 7 *Transitive solutions.* *Let $G = (V, E)$ be a spider. We say that a solution (a collection of m routes) is transitive if, for every three routes S^i, S^j, S^k such that $S^i \preccurlyeq S^j$ and $S^j \preccurlyeq S^k$, it follows that, if S^i and S^k are concurrent, then $S^i \preccurlyeq S^k$.*

Definition 8 *Well-structured solutions.* *Let $G = (V, E)$ be a spider. We say that a solution (a collection of m routes) is well-structured if it is antisymmetric and transitive.*

Proposition 9. *The mTSPHT problem for spiders admits an optimal solution that is well-structured.*

Proof. The existence of an optimal antisymmetric solution has already been proven. Of these solutions, consider the one with the fewest number of 6-tuples

$(B_x, B_y, B_z, S^i, S^j, S^k)$ such that $S^i \preccurlyeq S^j$, $S^j \preccurlyeq S^k$ and $S^k \preccurlyeq S^i$, B_x is visited by (at least) S^i and S^j, B_y is visited by S^j and S^k and B_z is visited by S^i and S^k. We call these 6-tuples obstructions. Consider the following local change: if S^i and S^j are not consecutive in B_x, in the same way as we did in the proof of Proposition 6, we shift each route between $S^{i,x}$ and $S^{j,x}$ towards the depot. If there are no routes between $S^{i,x}$ and $S^{j,x}$ (they are consecutive) we just unassign the client of largest label in $S^{j,x}$. In both cases, only the last client of $S^{j,x}$ is left unassigned. We do the same in the other two branches (cyclically exchanging roles). Note that $S^{i,x}$, $S^{j,y}$ and $S^{k,z}$ all lose a client. We then assign the unassigned client of B_x to S^j, the unassigned client of B_y to S^k, and the unassigned client of B_z to S^i. The number of clients that each salesperson visits is the same and the distance from the depot to the last client of each route (in each branch) does not increase. Then, this new solution is still optimal. The idea is to repeat this local change in the 6-tuple $(B_x, B_y, B_z, S^i, S^j, S^k)$ as long as possible. The process ends since all $|S^{i,x}|, |S^{j,y}|$ and $|S^{k,z}|$ decrease by one and, at the end, an optimal antisymmetric solution is obtained with one less obstruction, a contradiction. Hence, the minimum number of obstructions is zero.   □

A Polynomial Dynamic Programming Algorithm for a Fixed Number of Branches. A well-structured solution has the following property: there is always one salesperson who visits just blocks of consecutive clients located at the end of some branches; once we remove such salesperson together with the clients he/she visited, the remaining (smaller) solution is also well-structured. Every instance $\mathcal{I}$ can be characterized by the travel time t, the handling time t_0, the number of salespersons m and the (ordered) set of M branches $\mathcal{B}$. Let $F_{\mathcal{I}}(k_1, \ldots, k_M, m')$ be the optimum makespan for the subinstance in which m' salespersons must collectively visit only the first k_i clients of branch B_i. The solution of mTSPHT, $F_{\mathcal{I}}(|B_1|, \ldots, |B_M|, m)$, can be computed by dynammic programming (DP) as follows:

- For all $m' \geq 1$ $F_{\mathcal{I}}(0, \ldots, 0, m') = 0$.
- if the k_i are not all zero, $F_{\mathcal{I}}(k_1, \ldots, k_M, 1) = \sum_{b=1}^{M}(2t(D, v_{k_b}^b) + t_0 k_b)$.
- if the k_i are not all zero and $m' > 1$, $F_{\mathcal{I}}(k_1, \ldots, k_M, m')$ is the minimum, for all possible values of $0 \leq i_1 \leq k_1, \ldots, 0 \leq i_M \leq k_M$ of

$$\max\left\{ F_{\mathcal{I}}(k_1 - i_1, \ldots, k_M - i_M, m' - 1), \sum_{b=1}^{M}(2t(D, v_{k_b}^b) + t_0 i_b)\mathbb{1}_{\{i_b > 0\}} \right\}.$$

Since the DP table has size at most mN^M, and each value is the minimum among at most N^M values, the time complexity of this DP is at most $O(mN^{2M})$.

4   PTAS for a Fixed Number m of Salespersons

We start by defining the *weight* of a branch B_b of the spider as the time it would take a single salesman to process it alone: weight$(B_b) = 2d(D, v_{|B_b|}^b) +$

$t_0|B_b|$. Also, for a set of branches $\widehat{B}$, define $\text{weight}(\widehat{B}) = \sum_{B \in \widehat{B}} \text{weight}(B_b)$.
Define $H_m = \frac{1}{m} \sum_{b=1}^{M} \text{weight}(B_b) = \frac{1}{m}(N t_0 + 2 \sum_{B \in \widehat{B}} d(D, v_{|B_b|}^b))$. Any feasible
solution $\widehat{S} = \{S^1, \ldots, S^m\}$ has to cover the distance from the depot to the
client of largest label in each branch twice, and each client has to be visited.
Therefore, $\sum_{k=1}^{m} T(S^k) \geq m H_m$ and $\text{makespan}(\widehat{S}) = \max_{k \in \{1,\ldots,m\}} T(S^k) \geq$
H_m. In particular, H_m is a lower bound for the makespan (i.e. for mTSPHT),
    Our goal is to solve mTSPHT through binary search, using the DP defined
at the end of previous section.

Theorem 10. *There exists a PTAS for problem* mTSPHT *that finds a $(1+\varepsilon)$-approximation and takes time $N^{O(m/\varepsilon)}$.*

    In what remains we prove previous theorem. We divide this proof in three
parts: the algorithm, the complexity analysis, and the proof of correctness.

4.1   The Algorithm

Consider an instance $\mathcal{I}$ and a tolerance $\varepsilon > 0$. Sort the branches according to
their weight in decreasing order, define a threshold $K = \lceil m/\varepsilon \rceil$, and build a new
instance $\mathcal{I}'$ as follows. The first K branches are not modified. The remaining
branches are grouped so that the sum of the weights on each group does not
exceed $m H_m / K$. Each of these groups is identified with a new branch consisting
of a single client. The new instance has at most $3K$ branches, and it is solved
using the DP of last section. We transform the output into a solution of the
original instance, with a small "price" to pay. Such price explains the $(1 + \varepsilon)$
term of the approximation algorithm. Formally:

1. *Initialization*
   - Compute the weight of each branch in $\mathcal{I}$ and compute H_m.
   - Sort the branches in decreasing order according to their weights.
   - Define the threshold $K = \lceil m/\varepsilon \rceil$.
2. *The Simple Case*
   - If $M \leq K$, solve $F_{\mathcal{I}}(|B_1|, \ldots, |B_M|, m)$ using the DP.
   - If $M > K$ continue with next step.
3. *Grouping the Branches*
   - From the $(K+1)$-th branch on, i.e., from B_{K+1}, group the branches in a
     greedy way so that the weight of each group is at most $m H_m / K$.
   - Replace each group of branches C by a branch with a single client v_C,
     and set $t(D, v_C) = (\text{weight}(C) - t_0)/2$.
   - Denote by $\mathcal{I}'$ the new instance with branches $B_1', \ldots, B_{M'}'$ (the K first
     ones of $\mathcal{I}$, together with the new, singleton branches).
4. *Solving the Problem for the Modified Instance*
   - Solve $F_{\mathcal{I}'}(|B_1'|, \ldots, |B_{M'}'|, m)$ through the DP.
   - Call $\widehat{R} = \{R^1, \ldots R^m\}$ the set of routes corresponding to the solution.

5. *Solving the Problem for the Original Instance*

For each branch B_b' of instance $\mathcal{I}'$ and each salesperson k:
- If $b \leq K$, then $S^{k,b} = R^{k,b}$.
- If $b > K$, then the branch is a singleton v_C. If, according to the solution $\widehat{R}$, the k-th salesperson serves v_C, then we assign to S^k all the clients of all the branches grouped in v_C.

4.2 Complexity

Computing weights and sorting the branches takes time $O(N) + O(M \log M) = O(N \log N)$. If $M \leq K$, then solving the DP takes time $O(mN^{2K})$. Since $m \leq N$, this can be written as $O(N^{2K+1})$.

If $M > K$, then we need first to group the branches. There can be at most $2K$ new groups. Therefore, since $M \leq N$, generating the modified instance takes time $O(N^2)$. Note that the new number of branches $M' \leq 3K$. Hence, solving the new instance's DP takes time $O(mN^{2(3K)}) = O(mN^{6K}) = O(N^{6K+1})$.

Finally, since there are at most $3K$ branches in the modified instance, obtaining the approximate solution in step 5 takes time $O(mN^{3K})$.

Overall, the time complexity of the whole algorithm is dominated by the term $O(N^{6K+1}) = O(N^{6(m/\varepsilon)+7}) = N^{O(m/\varepsilon)}$.

4.3 Correctness

If the number of branches M is less or equal than K we are in *The Simple Case* and the problem is solved to optimality. We may therefore assume that $M > K$, and the algorithm creates a new instance $\mathcal{I}'$ by *Grouping the Branches*. Since the branches of the original instance are sorted by weight and since the total weight is mH_m, the K-th branch (and each of the following branches) weights at most mH_m/K. This implies that at most $2K$ groups are formed. In fact, if there were $2K + 1$ groups (or more), the weight of at least two groups C_1 and C_2 should be smaller than $mH_m/2K$. This is not possible, because if we created C_1 before C_2, then the weight of any branch sorted after those in C_1 is smaller than $mH_m/2K$, and at least one could be added to C_1 without exceeding the threshold. Therefore, the number M' of branches of the modified instance is at most $K + 2K = 3K$. The travel time from the depot D to any "new" client v_C is chosen so that the weight of the new branch associated with v_C is equal to the original weight of the branches in C.

After *Grouping the branches*, we *Solve the Problem for the Modified Instance*, and we obtain the optimal solution $\widehat{R}$ of this modified instance. Finally, we *Solve the Problem for the Original Instance* in order to obtain a solution $\widehat{S}$ of the original instance.

Claim. If $\widehat{S}_{\mathrm{OPT}} = (S_{\mathrm{OPT}}^1, \ldots, S_{\mathrm{OPT}}^m)$ is an optimal solution of the original instance, then there exists a solution $\widehat{R}_{\mathrm{mod}} = (R_{\mathrm{mod}}^1, \ldots, R_{\mathrm{mod}}^m)$ of the modified instance such that, for each saleperson k, $T(R_{\mathrm{mod}}^k) \leq T(S_{\mathrm{OPT}}^k) + mH_m/K$.

Proof. Let $\widehat{B} = \{B_{K+1}, B_{K+2}, \ldots, B_M\}$ be the branches of the original instance that were grouped into new branches $\widehat{B}' = \{B'_{K+1}, \ldots, B'_{M'}\}$ of the modified instance. Let $T(S^{k,b}_{OPT}) = 2t(D, v_{k,b}) + |B_b|t_0$ be the time spent by the k-th salesperson of the optimal at B_b. Let $A_k = \sum_{b=K+1}^{M} T(S^{k,b}_{OPT})$.

Consider any partition $\mathcal{Q} = \{Q_1, \ldots, Q_m\}$ of the branches of $\widehat{B}'$ into m parts (allowing empty parts). For $k \in \{1, \ldots, m\}$ we define the utility of k as $U_{\mathcal{Q}}(k) = \left(\sum_{B' \in Q_k} \text{weight}(B') \right) - A_k$. We can use $\mathcal{Q}$ to create a solution $\widehat{R}_{\text{mod}}$ of the modified instance. In this solution, the k-th salesperson serves the clients of $\{B_1, \ldots, B_K\}$ according to $\widehat{S}_{OPT}$ and, in addition, he/she also serves all branches of Q_k. With this, the total time used by the k-th salesperson is $T(R^k_{\text{mod}}) = T(S^k_{OPT}) - A_k + \sum_{B' \in Q_k} \text{weight}(B') = T(S^k_{OPT}) + U_{\mathcal{Q}}(k)$. To conclude we prove the existence of a partition $\mathcal{Q}$ such that $U_{\mathcal{Q}}(k) \leq mH_m/K$ for all k.

Of all the possible partitions $\mathcal{Q}$ consider the one that (1) minimizes the maximum utility $\eta_{\mathcal{Q}} = \max_{k \in \{1, \ldots, m\}} U_{\mathcal{Q}}(k)$ and, subject to this, (2) minimizes the number of indexes k with maximum utility (i.e, such that $U_{\mathcal{Q}}(k) = \eta_{\mathcal{Q}}$).

Define $A := \sum_{B \in \widehat{B}} \text{weight}(B)$, and note that $A \leq \sum_{k=1}^{m} A_k$, since in the sum on the right, each edge of the branches of $\widehat{B}$ can be counted more than twice, while, in A, each edge is counted only 2 times. On the other hand, A can also be computed as $A = \sum_{k=1}^{m} \sum_{B' \in Q_k} \text{weight}(B')$.

It follows that $\sum_{k=1}^{m} U_{\mathcal{Q}}(k) = \sum_{k=1}^{m} \left(\sum_{B' \in Q_k} \text{weight}(B') \right) - A_k \leq 0$. Therefore, there is an index j such that $U_{\mathcal{Q}}(j) \leq 0$. Let us then consider an index i such that $\eta_{\mathcal{Q}} = U_{\mathcal{Q}}(i)$ and suppose, by contradiction, that $U_{\mathcal{Q}}(i) > mH_m/K$.

We could create a new partition $\mathcal{Q}'$, starting from $\mathcal{Q}$, reassigning the branch $B' \in Q_i$ of greater weight to the set Q_j. With this, the utility of i decreases by weight$(B') > 0$, and the utility of j increases by weight(B'). Recalling that weight$(B') < mH_m/K$ (in this way the branches of the modified instance were built), we conclude that either the maximum utility $\eta_{\mathcal{Q}'}$ of the new partition is less than $\eta_{\mathcal{Q}'}$, or the maximum utility remains, but in $\mathcal{Q}'$, the number of indexes of maximum utility decreases (since i does not have maximum utility anymore). In any case we come to a contradiction with the choice of $\mathcal{Q}$. □

Since R is the optimal solution of the modified instance it follows that makespan$(\widehat{R}) \leq$ makespan$(\widehat{R}_{\text{mod}})$. Therefore, using previous claim, we have that makespan$(\widehat{R}) \leq$ makespan$(\widehat{S}_{OPT}) + mH_m/K$.

But, as explained in the beginning of this section, H_m is a lower bound for the makespan of every feasible solution. Hence,

$$\text{makespan}(\widehat{R}) \leq \text{makespan}(\widehat{S}_{OPT}) \left(1 + \frac{m}{K} \right).$$

Note that, by construction, the makespan of the solution $\widehat{S}$ given by the algorithm is exactly the makespan of $\widehat{R}$. Therefore,

$$\text{makespan}(\widehat{S}) = \text{makespan}(\widehat{R}) \leq \text{makespan}(\widehat{S}_{OPT}) \left(1 + \frac{m}{K} \right).$$

By recalling that $K = \lceil \frac{m}{\varepsilon} \rceil$, we conclude that $\widehat{S}$ is indeed a $(1 + \varepsilon)$-appoximation.

References

1. Bao, X., Liu, Z.: Approximation algorithms for single vehicle scheduling problems with release and service times on a tree or cycle. Theor. Comput. Sci. **434**, 1–10 (2012)
2. Amariah, B., Alice, P.: A framework for vehicle routing approximation schemes in trees. In: Workshop on Algorithms and Data Structures, pp. 112–125. Springer (2019)
3. Bektas, T.: The multiple traveling salesman problem: an overview of formulations and solution procedures. Omega **34**(3), 209–219 (2006)
4. Nicos, C.: Worst-case analysis of a new heuristic for the travelling salesman problem. Technical report, Carnegie-Mellon University Pittsburgh Pa Management Sciences Research Group (1976)
5. Greg, N.F., Matthew, S.H., Chul, E.K.: Approximation algorithms for some routing problems. SIAM J. Comput. **7**(2), 178–193 (1978)
6. Michael, R.G., David, S.J.: Computers and Intractability; A Guide to the Theory of NP-Completeness. W. H. Freeman & Co., New York, NY, USA (1990)
7. Daya, G., Arvind, G., Ramesh, K.: A 5/3-approximation algorithm for scheduling vehicles on a path with release and handling times. Inf. Process. Lett. **86**, 87–91 (2003)
8. Grötschel, M., Jünger, M., Reinelt, G.: Optimal control of plotting and drilling machines: a case study. Zeitschrift für Oper. Res. **35**(1), 61–84 (1991)
9. Karuno, Y., Nagamochi, H.: A 2-approximation algorithm for the multi-vehicle scheduling problem on a path with release and handling times. In: auf der Heide, F.M. (ed.) ESA 2001. LNCS, vol. 2161, pp. 218–229. Springer, Heidelberg (2001). https://doi.org/10.1007/3-540-44676-1_18
10. Karuno, Y., Nagamochi, H.: An approximability result of the multi-vehicle scheduling problem on a path with release and handling times. Theor. Comput. Sci. **312**(2–3), 267–280 (2004)
11. Laporte, G.: The vehicle routing problem: An overview of exact and approximate algorithms. Euro. J. Oper. Res. **59**(3), 345–358 (1992)
12. Eugene, L.L.: The traveling salesman problem: a guided tour of combinatorial optimization. Wiley-Interscience Series in Discrete Mathematics (1985)
13. Donald Ratliff, H., Arnon, S.R.: Order-picking in a rectangular warehouse: a solvable case of the traveling salesman problem. Oper. Res. **31**(3), 507–521 (1983)
14. Liang, X., Zhou, X., Dongsheng, X.: Exact and approximation algorithms for the min-max k-traveling salesmen problem on a tree. Euro. J. Oper. Res. **227**(2), 284–292 (2013)
15. Xu, Z., Xu, L.: Approximation algorithms for min-max path cover problems with service handling time. In: Dong, Y., Du, D.-Z., Ibarra, O. (eds.) ISAAC 2009. LNCS, vol. 5878, pp. 383–392. Springer, Heidelberg (2009). https://doi.org/10.1007/978-3-642-10631-6_40
16. Wei, Y., Zhaohui, L.: Vehicle routing problems on a line-shaped network with release time constraints. Oper. Res. Lett. **37**, 85–88 (2009)

Tightness of Sensitivity and Proximity Bounds for Integer Linear Programs

Sebastian Berndt[1], Klaus Jansen[2], and Alexandra Lassota[3][✉]

[1] Institute of IT Security, University of Lübeck, Lübeck, Germany
s.berndt@uni-luebeck.de
[2] Department of Computer Science, Kiel University, Kiel, Germany
kj@informatik.uni-kiel.de
[3] Department of Computer Science, Kiel University, Kiel, Germany
ala@informatik.uni-kiel.de

Abstract. We consider Integer Linear Programs (ILPs), where each variable corresponds to an integral point within a polytope $\mathcal{P} \subseteq \mathbb{R}^d$, i. e., ILPs of the form $\min\{c^\top x \mid \sum_{p \in \mathcal{P} \cap \mathbb{Z}^d} x_p p = b, x \in \mathbb{Z}_{\geq 0}^{|\mathcal{P} \cap \mathbb{Z}^d|}\}$. The distance between an optimal fractional solution and an optimal integral solution (called the *proximity*) is an important measure. A classical result by Cook et al. (Math. Program., 1986) shows that it is at most $\Delta^{\Theta(d)}$ where $\Delta = \|\mathcal{P} \cap \mathbb{Z}^d\|_\infty$ is the largest coefficient in the constraint matrix. Another important measure studies the change in an optimal solution if the right-hand side b is replaced by another right-hand side b'. The distance between an optimal solution x w.r.t. b and an optimal solution x' w.r.t. b' (called the *sensitivity*) is similarly bounded, i. e., $\|b-b'\|_1 \cdot \Delta^{\Theta(d)}$, also shown by Cook et al. (Math. Program., 1986).

Even after more than thirty years, these bounds are essentially the best known bounds for these measures. While some lower bounds are known for these measures, they either only work for very small values of Δ, require negative entries in the constraint matrix, or have fractional right-hand sides. Hence, these lower bounds often do not correspond to instances from algorithmic problems. This work presents for each $\Delta > 0$ and each $d > 0$ ILPs of the above type with non-negative constraint matrices such that their proximity and sensitivity is at least $\Delta^{\Theta(d)}$. Furthermore, these instances are closely related to instances of the Bin Packing problem as they form a subset of columns of the *configuration ILP*. We thereby show that the results of Cook et al. are indeed tight, even for instances arising naturally from problems in combinatorial optimization.

Keywords: Sensitivity · Proximity · Lower bounds

1 Introduction

Integer (Linear) Programs are of great interest throughout computer science, both in theory and in practice. Many natural parameters were studied to describe

This work was supported by DFG project JA 612/20-1.

T. Bureš et al. (Eds.): SOFSEM 2021, LNCS 12607, pp. 349–360, 2021.
https://doi.org/10.1007/978-3-030-67731-2_25

the properties of such programs. Let $d \in \mathbb{N}_{>0}$. For a point $x \in \mathbb{R}^d$ and a set $Y \subseteq \mathbb{R}^d$, we define $\mathrm{dist}(x, Y)$ as the minimal ℓ_∞-distance of x to any point in Y, i.e., $\mathrm{dist}(x, Y) = \min_{y \in Y}\{\|x - y\|_\infty\}$. Furthermore, for two sets $X, Y \in \mathbb{R}^d$, we define $\mathrm{dist}(X, Y) = \max_{x \in X}\{\mathrm{dist}(x, Y)\}$ as the maximum over all minimal distances between any point $x \in X$ to the set Y. This work focuses on two such measures called *sensitivity* and *proximity* that frequently arise in the design of approximation and online algorithms (see e.g. [8,9,13,16,21,26,28,29]). For a given constraint matrix $A \in \mathbb{Z}^{d \times n}$, a right-hand side $b \in \mathbb{Z}^d$, and an objective function $c \in \mathbb{Z}^n$, let $\mathrm{Solint}(A, b, c) = \mathrm{argmin}\{c^\top x \mid Ax = b, x \in Z_{\geq 0}^n\}$ be the set of optimal integral solutions. Further, denote by $\mathrm{Solfrac}(A, b, c) = \mathrm{argmin}\{c^\top x \mid Ax = b, x \in Q_{\geq 0}^n\}$ the set of optimal fractional solutions, i.e., the integrality constraint $x \in \overline{\mathbb{Z}}_{\geq 0}^n$ is relaxed to $z \in \mathbb{Q}_{\geq 0}^n$. Throughout this work, we always assume that an ILP has n variables, d constraints, and is of full rank. Thus $n \geq d$ holds.

The *sensitivity* of the ILP measures the distance between two optimal integral solutions if the right-hand side changes. Formally, we define $\mathrm{sens}(A, b, b', c)$ as $\mathrm{dist}(\mathrm{Solint}(A, b, c), \mathrm{Solint}(A, b', c))$. A small sensitivity is useful when the right-hand side changes in a problem formulation as this implies that an optimal solution for the new problem is close. Thus, we do not have to change our current optimal integral solution x too much. Hence, we can just search for it exhaustively or by a dynamic program. Typical applications are online algorithms where new items arrive or leave (thus changing the right-hand side corresponding to the present items).

The *proximity* of the ILP denoted by $\mathrm{prox}(A, b, c)$ is formally defined as the term $\mathrm{dist}(\mathrm{Solfrac}(A, b, c), \mathrm{Solint}(A, b, c))$, i.e., the maximal distance between any optimal fractional solution and an optimal integral one. If the proximity is small, i.e., there exists an optimal integer solution near to any optimal fractional solution, this allows us to solve the Integer Linear Program fast: First, we compute the optimal fractional solution z, then we search for an optimal integral solution x in the small box implied by the proximity bound around z.

Cook et al. presented in [5] upper bounds for these values. In the following, Δ will always denote the largest absolute value of the entries in A, i.e., $\Delta = \|A\|_\infty$ and $\mathrm{subDet}(A)$ will be the largest determinant of any $d \times d$ submatrix of A. Note that this value bounds the determinant of any submatrix of any dimension as A is of full rank.

Proposition 1 (Theorem 1 in [5]). If $\mathrm{Solint}(A, b, c)$ is non-empty, then for each $x \in \mathrm{Solint}(A, b, c)$ we have $\mathrm{dist}(x, \mathrm{Solfrac}(A, b, c)) \leq n \cdot \mathrm{subDet}(A)$ and furthermore, for each $y \in \mathrm{Solfrac}(A, b, c)$ we have $\mathrm{dist}(y, \mathrm{Solint}(A, b, c)) \leq n \cdot \mathrm{subDet}(A)$.

Note that this implies that $\mathrm{prox}(A, b, c) \leq n \cdot \mathrm{subDet}(A)$.

Proposition 2 (Theorem 5 in [5]). If both $\mathrm{Solint}(A, b, c)$ and $\mathrm{Solint}(A, b', c)$ are non-empty, we have $\mathrm{dist}(x, \mathrm{Solint}(A, b', c)) \leq (\|b - b'\|_\infty + 2) \cdot n \cdot \mathrm{subDet}(A)$ for each $x \in \mathrm{Solint}(A, b, c)$.

Note that this implies that $\text{sens}(A, b, b', c) \leq (\|b - b'\|_\infty + 2) \cdot n \cdot \text{subDet}(A)$.

The Hadamard inequality states that the determinant of a quadratic matrix $N^{n \times n}$ with columns n_i is bounded by $\det(N) \leq \prod_{i=1}^n \|n_i\|$ [12]. This implies that $\text{subDet}(A) \leq \Delta^d \cdot d^{d/2}$. As $n \leq (2\Delta + 1)^d$ (maximum number of distinct columns), we can bound $n \cdot \text{subDet}(A)$ by $((2\Delta + 1)^d) \cdot d = \Delta^{\Theta(d)}$. Surprisingly, these bounds do not depend on the objective function c nor on the size of b (only the sensitivity depends on the distance between b and b') but only on the matrix A. We will thus often drop the objective function from our notation and write $\text{prox}(A, b)$ (resp. $\text{sens}(A, b, b')$) to reflect this.

While it is known that these bounds are tight, all known examples either have a very small value of $\Delta = 1$, use negative entries in the constraint matrix, and have a non-integral right-hand side [27].

Hence, these lower bounds often do not correspond to instances from algorithmic problems. Nevertheless, knowing the exact bounds is often helpful. For example the exponent denoted $C(A_\delta)$ in the running time of the algorithm in [21] is just an upper bound on the proximity of the underlying configuration IP. Hence, improving this upper bound would directly lead to a better running time. Another example concerning the sensitivity comes from the field of online algorithms. Often times, the requirement that decisions are not allowed to be rewinded is too strict. Hence, [26] introduced the model of the *migration factor* where a bounded amount of rewinding is allowed. The migration factor in their work and in many others (e. g. [8,9,16,28]) are simply given by the sensitivity of the underlying IPs. Again, any improvement on the general sensitivity results would directly improve these migration factors.

This work presents for each $\Delta > 0$ and each $d > 0$ ILPs of the above type with non-negative constraint matrices such that their proximitiy and sensitivity are at least $\Delta^{\Theta(d)}$. Note that $\Delta > 0$ and $d > 0$ can be chosen arbitrarily large, however, we restrict d to be odd or even depending on the case.

Theorem 1. *For each $\Delta > 0$ and each even $d > 0$, there is a non-negative matrix $A \in \mathbb{Z}_{\geq 0}^{d \times d}$, a right-hand side $b \in \mathbb{Z}_{\geq 0}^d$, and a right-hand side $b' \in \mathbb{Z}_{\geq 0}^d$ with $\|b - b'\|_1 = 1$ such that $\text{sens}(A, b, b') \geq \Delta^{\Theta(d)}$. Furthermore, the underlying ILP is polytopish.*

Theorem 2. *For each $\Delta \geq 2$ and each odd $d > 0$, there is a non-negative matrix $A \in \mathbb{Z}_{\geq 0}^{15d \times 15d+6}$ and a right-hand side $b \in \mathbb{Z}_{\geq 0}^{15d}$ such that $\text{prox}(A, b) \geq \Delta^{\Theta(d)}$. Furthermore, the underlying ILP is polytopish.*

Polytopish Integer (Linear) Programs. This work considers a special case of integer (linear) programs where each variable corresponds to an integral point within a polytope $\mathcal{P} \subseteq \mathbb{R}^d$. The corresponding Integer Linear Program is defined by

$$\min c^\top x$$

$$\sum_{p \in \mathcal{P} \cap \mathbb{Z}^d} x_p p = b$$

$$x \in \mathbb{Z}_{\geq 0}^{|\mathcal{P} \cup \mathbb{Z}^d|}.$$

We call such an ILP *polytopish*.

These ILPs often arise in the context of algorithmic applications. Probably the most famous one among such ILPs is the *configuration ILP* introduced by Gilmore and Gomory [10] and used for many packing and scheduling problems (e. g. [3,11,17–19]).

The origin of the configuration ILP lies in the Bin Packing problem. There we are given n items with sizes $s_1, \ldots, s_n \leq 1$. The objective is to pack these items into as few unit-sized bins as possible. As some sizes may be equal, i. e., $\{s_1, \ldots, s_n\} = \{s_1, \ldots, s_d\}$ for some $d < n$, we can rewrite the instance as a multiplicity vector of sizes, i. e., $(b_1, \ldots, b_d)$ where the ith item size occurs b_i times. Further we define configurations. A configuration $k = (k_1, \ldots, k_d) \in \mathbb{Z}_{\geq 0}^d$ is a multiplicity vector of item sizes such that the sum of their sizes is at most 1, i. e., $k \cdot (s_1, \ldots, s_d)^T \leq 1$, hence a feasible packing for a bin. Define the constraint matrix as the set of feasible configurations (one configuration per column). We now aim to find a set of configurations such that we cover each item, i. e., the multiplicities of the item sizes of the chosen configurations equal the occurrences of the item sizes from the input. The goal is to minimize the number of used configurations (including how often they are chosen). Note that all fractional solutions to the constraint $k \cdot (s_1, \ldots, s_d)^\top \leq 1$ describe a knapsack polytope $\mathcal{P} := \mathcal{P}_{s_1, \ldots, s_d}$. Hence, the integer linear program (i. e., the *configuration ILP*) can be written as

$$\min \|x\|_1$$
$$\sum_{p \in \mathcal{P} \cap \mathbb{Z}^d} x_p p = b$$
$$x \in \mathbb{Z}_{\geq 0}^{|\mathcal{P} \cup \mathbb{Z}^d|}.$$

We define item sizes such that the set C_1 of columns in the examples for the general ILPs are a subset of configurations for the Bin Packing problem. Then we define an objective function where all values corresponding to the configurations $k \in C_1$ get value 0 and the remaining ones value 1. To minimize this function we thus cannot take other columns than the ones in C_1. Setting the right-hand side as for the general ILPs this essentially yields the same examples. Thus the same bounds are achieved. This construction shows that in order to improve bounds on the proximity or sensitivity of the Bin Packing problem the objective function $\min \|x\|_1$ needs to be taken into account.

Related Work. Already in 1986, Cook et al. proved upper bounds regarding the proximity and sensitivity for general Integer Linear Programs [5], see Proposition 2 and Proposition 1. Still, these classical bounds are state-of-the-art. This rises the question if these bounds are tight. In this work we answer this affirmatively.

For the case of $d = 1$, Aliev et al. present a tight lower bound regarding proximity of $\|x - z\|_\infty \leq \Delta - 1$ [2]. Further settings were studied, such as separable convex objective functions [14] or mixed integer constraints [24].

Recently, another proximity bound independent of n was proven by Eisen-brand and Weismantel [7]. Using the Steinitz lemma, they show that the ℓ_1-distance of an optimal fractional solution z and its corresponding integral solution x is bounded by $\|x - z\|_1 \leq m \cdot (2m\Delta + 1)^m$. This result also holds when upper bounds for the variables are present. This result is improved to $\|x - z\|_1 < 3m^2 \log(2\sqrt{m} \cdot \Delta^{1/m}) \cdot \Delta$ using sparsity [23].

For a special sub-case of Integer Linear Programs where the constraint matrix consists of non-zero entries only in the first r rows and in blocks of size $s \times t$ in the diagonal beneath, sensitivity and proximity results were also obtained. For these so-called n-fold ILPs it holds that if x is a solution to a right-hand side b and the right-hand side changes to b' still admitting a finite, optimal solution x' then $\|x - x'\|_1 \leq \|b - b'\|_1 \cdot O(rs\Delta)^{rs}$ [20]. In turn, it was shown that the proximity is bounded by $\|x - z\|_1 \leq (rs\Delta)^{O(rs)}$ [6]. Note that both bounds are independent of the number of rows and columns of the complete constraint matrix.

2   Sensitivity of ILPs

This section provides lower bounds for the sensitivity of ILPs. First, we present an example for general ILPs. Then we show how we can use this example to prove the same bound for the ILP which arises from the Bin Packing polytope.

2.1   Sensitivity of General ILPs

This section proves the sensitivity bound for general ILPs, i.e., a lower bound on the distance between $\mathrm{Solint}(A, b)$ and $\mathrm{Solint}(A, b')$. Let d be an even number and $\Delta \in \mathbb{N}_{>0}$. We consider the following ILP (I) with an objective function $c \equiv \mathbf{0}$ (corresponding to no objective function).

$$
\underbrace{\begin{pmatrix} 1 & 0 & \cdots & 0 & 0 \\ \Delta & 1 & \cdots & 0 & 0 \\ 0 & \Delta & \cdots & 0 & 0 \\ \vdots & \vdots & \ddots & \vdots & \vdots \\ 0 & 0 & \cdots & 1 & 0 \\ 0 & 0 & \cdots & \Delta & 1 \end{pmatrix}}_{=:A} x = \begin{pmatrix} 1 \\ \Delta \\ \Delta^2 \\ \vdots \\ \Delta^{d-2} \\ \Delta^{d-1} \end{pmatrix} \tag{I}
$$

Note that ILP (I) is polytopish. To see this, let $A_1, \ldots, A_d$ be the columns of the ILP and define $\mathcal{P} = \mathrm{conv}\{A_1, \ldots, A_d\}$ as the convex hull of the columns. In the following, we prove that the integer points in $\mathcal{P}$ are exactly the columns themselves.

Claim 1. It holds that $\mathrm{conv}\{A_1, A_2, \ldots, A_d\} \cap \mathbb{Z}^d = \{A_1, A_2, \ldots, A_d\}$.

Proof. Let $x_1, \ldots, x_n$ be a convex combination of the columns where Ax is an integer point. Let i be the first column with $0 < x_i < 1$. The ith row appears with a non-zero entry only in the columns i and $i - 1$. Since x_{i-1} is not fractional, the ith entry of Ax is fractional. This is a contradiction. Hence, there are no fractional values in x and therefore exactly one is 1 and all others are 0. $\square$

Hence, the ILP is polytopish. Next we prove the main result of this section.

Theorem 1. *For each $\Delta > 0$ and each even $d > 0$, there is a non-negative matrix $A \in \mathbb{Z}_{\geq 0}^{d \times d}$, a right-hand side $b \in \mathbb{Z}_{\geq 0}^d$, and a right-hand side $b' \in \mathbb{Z}_{\geq 0}^d$ with $\|b - b'\|_1 = 1$ such that $\mathrm{sens}(A, b, b') \geq \Delta^{\Theta(d)}$. Furthermore, the underlying ILP is polytopish.*

Proof. An optimal solution to the ILP above is clearly unique (Note that we set the objective function to zero, thus optimality corresponds to feasibility.). We have only one column with a non-zero entry for the first row. Thus, the high-hand side b determines this value. By that, we have only one free, non-zero variable for the second row. Using this argument inductively we get a unique solution of form $x = (1, 0, \Delta^2, 0, \Delta^4, \ldots, \Delta^{d-2}, 0)$.

If we now change the first entry of the right-hand side to 0, we get again a unique solution for b' due to the same argument as above. The solution is of form: $x' = (0, \Delta, 0, \Delta^3, \ldots, \Delta^{d-1})$. Obviously, the difference is $\|x - x'\|_1 \geq \|b - b'\|_1 \Delta^{\Theta(d)}$ implying the statement. The ILP is polytopish due to Claim 1.

$\square$

2.2   Sensitivity of the Bin Packing ILP

Let us now construct an example where the sensitivity for the Bin Packing polytope is large. In this problem, we are given n items with d different sizes. Define these sizes as $s_i = 1/(2\Delta) + i \cdot \epsilon$ for $i = 1, \ldots, d$ and some $\epsilon > 0$ with $\epsilon \leq \frac{1}{4(d-1+\Delta d)}$. Obviously, the constraint matrix from the previous example is a subset of feasible configurations, i.e., a subset of the columns of the constraint matrix for this problem, as

$$s_i + \Delta s_{i+1} \leq s_{d-1} + \Delta s_d = 1/(2\Delta) + (d-1)\epsilon + 1/2 + \Delta d \epsilon$$
$$= 1/2 + 1/(2\Delta) + \epsilon(d - 1 + \Delta d) \underbrace{\leq}_{d \geq 2} 1/2 + 1/4 + \epsilon(d - 1 + \Delta d)$$

$$\underbrace{\leq}_{\epsilon \leq \frac{1}{4(d-1+\Delta d)}} 1/2 + 1/4 + 1/4 = 1.$$

Define by C_1 the set of these columns. Let us now define a linear objective function c which has a 0 entry for each configuration $k \in C_1$ and 1 otherwise. Thus to minimize the objective function we can only choose configurations from C_1. Setting and changing the right-hand side as in the previous example will clearly lead to the same sensitivity bound. Combining it with the result of Cook et al. we thus get:

Corollary 1. *There is an objective function c such that for the configuration ILP with constraints A and right-hand sides b and b' we have $sens(A, b, b', c) \geq \Delta^{\Theta(d)}$.*

Hence, if one aims to improve the sensitivity of the configuration ILP, the special objective function $\|x\|_1$ needs to be taken into account.

3   Proximity of ILPs

This section presents an example for general ILPs, where the optimal integer solution x differs greatly from the corresponding fractional solution z, i.e., $\|x - z\|_1 = \Delta^{\Theta(d)}$. By this, we give a lower bound on the proximity of general ILPs which meets the upper bound for ILPs shown by Cook et al. implying their tightness. Further we use this example to construct an instance of the Bin Packing problem where the same bound is met.

3.1   Proximity of General ILPs

To construct this example we make use of the Petersen graph. This graph $P = (V, E)$ has fifteen edges, ten vertices and six perfect matchings. A perfect matching M is a set of edges such that each vertex $v \in V$ is part of exactly one edge, i.e., there exists exactly one edge $e = (u, w) \in M$ satisfying $v = u$ or $v = w$. The Petersen graph has the nice property that every edge is part of exactly two perfect matchings and every two perfect matchings share exactly one edge [1]. The graph and its perfect matchings are displayed in Fig. 1.

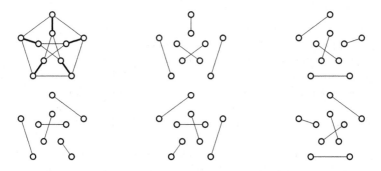

Fig. 1. The first sub-figure presents the complete Petersen graph with one perfect matching marked by thick edges. The remaining sub-figures each present one of the remaining five perfect matchings.

The Petersen graph is named after its appearance in a paper written by Petersen [25] in 1898. However, it was first mentioned as far back as 1886 [22]. This graph is often used to construct counter-examples for various conjectures due to its neat structure and nice properties. For example it was used in [4] to construct small examples where the Round-up Property for Bin Packing instances does not hold. For a survey concerning this graph and more applications we refer to [15].

We set up a constraint matrix $M \in \{0,1\}^{15 \times 6}$ where every row represents an edge in the Petersen graph and every column corresponds to the indicator vector of one of the perfect matchings. Denote by I the identity matrix of size (15×15). An identity matrix is a matrix where all entries are zero except the diagonal being 1. Further let $\Delta \geq 2$ and d be an odd number. Construct the ILP (II) as follows, where the objective function is again zero, i.e., $c \equiv \mathbf{0}$:

$$\underbrace{\begin{pmatrix} M & I & 0 & \cdots & 0 & 0 \\ 0 & \Delta \cdot I & I & \cdots & 0 & 0 \\ 0 & 0 & \Delta \cdot I & \cdots & 0 & 0 \\ \vdots & \vdots & \vdots & \ddots & \vdots & \vdots \\ 0 & 0 & 0 & \cdots & I & 0 \\ 0 & 0 & 0 & \cdots & \Delta \cdot I & I \end{pmatrix}}_{=:A} x = \begin{pmatrix} (1, \ldots, 1)^T \in \mathbb{N}^{15} \\ (\Delta, \ldots, \Delta)^T \in \mathbb{N}^{15} \\ (\Delta^2, \ldots, \Delta^2)^T \in \mathbb{N}^{15} \\ \vdots \\ (\Delta^{d-1}, \ldots, \Delta^{d-1})^T \in \mathbb{N}^{15} \\ (\Delta^d, \ldots, \Delta^d)^T \in \mathbb{N}^{15} \end{pmatrix}. \quad \text{(II)}$$

Obviously, the number of columns is $n = 6 + 15 \cdot d$. Call the first six columns corresponding to the perfect matchings *matching columns*. Further, we want a solution where $z \in [0,1]^n$ for the fractional case and $x \in \{0,1\}^n$ for the integral one. To show that the ILP is polytopish, we argue as before. First, let $A_1, \ldots, A_n$ be the columns of A and define $\mathcal{P} = \text{conv}\{A_1, \ldots, A_n\}$. Next, we argue that the integer points in $\mathcal{P}$ are again only the columns themselves.

Claim 2. It holds that $\text{conv}\{A_1, A_2, \ldots, A_n\} \cap \mathbb{Z}^{6+15d} = \{A_1, A_2, \ldots, A_n\}$.

Proof. Let $x_1, \ldots, x_n \in [0,1]$ with $\sum_{i=1}^n x_i = 1$ such that $A(x_1 \ldots, x_n)$ is integral. First suppose that $0 < x_i < 1$ for some column $1 \leq i \leq 6$ corresponding to a matching column. Then, to obtain an integral point $A(x_1, \ldots, x_n)$, we need to also choose another set of columns $J \subseteq \{1, \ldots, 21\} \setminus \{i\}$ with $x_j > 0$ for all $j \in J$. For each such j, there is a row r_j, where column j has a value 0 where columns i has value 1, as two matchings only share one edge and the identity matrix only has one non-zero entry in each column. Hence, one cannot choose the coefficients x_j for $j \in J$ such that $A(x_1, \ldots, x_n)$ is integral and $\sum_{i=1}^n x_i = 1$ holds. Hence, the coefficients of the matching columns must be integral.

Now, consider the remaining columns. Suppose there is a column $i > 6$ with $0 < x_i < 1$. If $i \leq 21$, this column corresponds to the first identity matrix. As no other column has entries in the first 15 rows, the resulting point $A(x_1, \ldots, x_n)$ cannot be integral. If $i \leq 36$, the only other columns that have non-zero entries have index ≤ 21 and can thus not be fractional. Using this argument inductively, we see that all solutions for this ILP are integral and thus the assumption holds. $\square$

Next we want to estimate the ℓ_1 norm of a (fractional) solution. Define $p = \sum_{i=1}^{(d-1)/2} \Delta^{2i-1}$ and $q = \sum_{i=1}^{(d-1)/2} \Delta^{2i-2} = \Delta \cdot \sum_{i=0}^{(d-1)/2} \Delta^{2i-1} = \Delta \cdot p$.

Claim 3. The ℓ_1-norm of any (fractional) solution x is at least $\|x\|_1 = \|y\|_1 + \|w\|_1 \geq \|y\|_1 + (15 - \|y\|_1) \cdot \Delta \cdot p + \|y\|_1 \cdot p$.

Proof. Consider a (fractional) solution $x = (y, w)$, where y corresponds to the first 6 columns, i.e., to the matching columns. Likewise, divide $A = (B, C)$ into matching and non-matching columns. The value for the right-hand side given by y covers some part of the first 15 rows, namely $0 \leq \|By\|_1 \leq 15$, as we can choose at most 3 columns (fractionally) such that edges are not overlapping. If we would choose more, edges would be overlapping and thus the right-hand side would be greater than 1 and the solution would be infeasible. Further, each column contains exactly 5 ones as each perfect matching admits exactly 5 edges. Combining this we get at most $\|y\|_1 \cdot 5 \leq 3 \cdot 5 = 15$.

Let $i \leq 15$ and $a_i := (B \cdot y)_i$, i.e., the right-hand side covered by the matching columns at position i. Thus set $x_i = 1 - a_i$ to satisfy the remaining right-hand side. Further,

$$w_{i+1 \cdot 15} = \Delta - \Delta(1 - a_i) = \Delta(1 - (1 - a_i)) = \Delta \cdot a_i,$$

as these are the only free variable to satisfy the right-hand side, which already has the value $\Delta(1 - a_i)$. In turn, this determines the next 15 variables, i.e.,

$$w_{i+2 \cdot 15} = \Delta^2 - \Delta^2(a_i) = \Delta^2(1 - a_i).$$

Proceeding with setting the only free variables for the next 15 rows to be satisfied we get $w_{i+3 \cdot 15} = \Delta^3 a_i$. The scheme proceeds like this. Therefore,

$$
\begin{aligned}
\|w\|_1 &= \sum_{i=1}^{15} \left[\sum_{j=1}^{(d+1)/2} (1 - a_i) \cdot \Delta^{2i-2} + \sum_{j=1}^{(d-1)/2} a_i \cdot \Delta^{2i-1} \right] \\
&= \sum_{i=1}^{15} (1 - a_i) \left(\sum_{j=1}^{(d+1)/2} \cdot \Delta^{2i-2} \right) + \sum_{i=1}^{15} a_i \left(\sum_{j=1}^{(d-1)/2} \cdot \Delta^{2i-1} \right) \\
&= (15 - \|a\|_1) \left(\sum_{j=1}^{(d+1)/2} \cdot \Delta^{2i-2} \right) + \|a_i\|_1 \left(\sum_{j=1}^{(d-1)/2} \cdot \Delta^{2i-1} \right) \\
&= (15 - \|a\|_1) q + \|a_i\|_1 p \geq (15 - \|y\|_1) \cdot \Delta \cdot p + \|y\|_1 \cdot p.
\end{aligned}
$$

Thus $\|x\|_1 = \|y\|_1 + \|w\|_1 = \|y\|_1 + (15 - \|y\|_1) \cdot \Delta \cdot p + \|y\|_1 \cdot p$ completing the proof. $\qquad \square$

Theorem 2. *For each $\Delta \geq 2$ and each odd $d > 0$, there is a non-negative matrix $A \in \mathbb{Z}_{\geq 0}^{15d \times 15d+6}$ and a right-hand side $b \in \mathbb{Z}_{\geq 0}^{15d}$ such that $\mathrm{prox}(A, b) \geq \Delta^{\Theta(d)}$. Furthermore, the underlying ILP is polytopish.*

Proof. An optimal fractional solution z is to take each matching column $1/2$ times, i.e., $z = $

$$(1/2, \ldots, 1/2, 0, \ldots 0, \Delta, \ldots, \Delta, 0, \ldots 0, \Delta^2, \ldots, \Delta^2, \ldots, \Delta^{d-1}, \ldots, \Delta^{d-1}, 0, \ldots 0).$$

Note that again optimality corresponds to feasibility, as we have set the objective function to zero. It is easy to verify that this solution is feasible as in the first 15 columns we have two entries in M with value 1. Taking both $1/2$ often and setting all variables of the identity matrix to zero gives the right-hand side 1. Then again the values for the remaining columns are determined as explained in Theorem 1.

In turn, an optimal integral solution would either avoid all matching columns or take some of them. In the first case this would lead to take all columns of the first identity matrix and again all other values would be determined and thus the solution looks as follows:

$$x = (0, \ldots 0, 1, \ldots, 1, 0, \ldots, 0, \Delta^2, \ldots, \Delta^2, 0, \ldots 0, \ldots, \Delta^d, \ldots, \Delta^d).$$

In the second case, at most one matching column is chosen as two would already give a too large right-hand side in the first 15 rows (every two matchings share one edge). Then the identity matrix will take the column corresponding to rows which have a zero entry in the chosen matching column. The remaining solution is then determined by the free variables and the right-hand side as explained in Claim 3.

Now let us look at the difference of the optimal fractional solution z and the optimal integral ones. It is easy to see that when the optimal solution takes no matching columns, every non-zero component in z is zero in x and vice versa. As the sum of both solutions is $\Delta^{\Theta(d)}$, their difference is $\Delta^{\Theta(d)}$. For the other case, where a matching column is used, we get that the matching columns differ in all positions leading to difference of all other positions. Thus

$$\|x - z\|_1 \geq |\|x\|_1 - \|z\|_1| \geq (1 + p + 2q) - (15 \cdot \Delta \cdot p)$$
$$= |1 + p + 2\Delta p - 15\Delta p| = |(1 - 13\Delta)p + 1| \geq 13\Delta p = \Delta^{\Theta(d)}.$$

Thus the difference between any (optimal) fractional solution z and an (optimal) integral one x is $\|x - z\|_1 \geq \Delta^{\Theta(d)}$. The ILP is polytopish due to Claim 2 completing the proof.   □

3.2   Proximity of the Bin Packing ILP

We construct an example with a huge proximity by relying on the previous construction. Recall that we are given n items with d different sizes in his problem. Define these sizes as $s_i = 1/(30\Delta) + i \cdot \epsilon$ for $i = 1, \ldots, d$ and some $\epsilon > 0$ with $\epsilon \leq \frac{57}{60(d-2+\Delta(d-1))}$. Obviously, the constraint matrix from the previous example is a subset of feasible configurations, i.e., a subset of the columns of the constraint matrix for this problem, as the value of the largest configuration is bounded by

$$s_i + \Delta s_{i+1} \leq s_{d-2} + \Delta s_{d-1} = 1/(30\Delta) + (d-2)\epsilon + 1/30 + \Delta(d-1)\epsilon$$
$$= 1/30 + 1/(30\Delta) + \epsilon(d-2+\Delta(d-1)) \underbrace{\leq}_{d\geq 2} 1/30 + 1/60 + \epsilon(d-2+\Delta(d-1))$$
$$\underbrace{\leq}_{\epsilon \leq \frac{1}{2(d-2+\Delta(d-1))}} 1/30 + 1/60 + 57/60 = 1.$$

Define by C_1 the set of these columns. Let us now define a linear objective function c, which has a 0 entry for each configuration $k \in C_1$ and 1 otherwise. Thus to minimize the objective function we can only choose these configurations. Minimize the constraint matrix accordingly. Computing a fractional optimal solution and an optimal integral one for the right-hand side of the example above will clearly lead to the same proximity. Combining it with the result of Cook et al. we thus get:

Corollary 2. *There is an objective function c such that for the configuration ILP with constraint matrix A and right-hand side b we have prox$(A, b, c) \geq \Delta^{\Theta(d)}$.*

Hence, if one aims to improve the proximity of the configuration ILP, the special objective function $\|x\|_1$ needs to be taken into account.

Acknowledgments. The authors want to thank Lars Rohwedder for enjoyable and fruitful discussions at the beginning of this project.

References

1. Akiyama, J., Kano, M.: Matchings and 1-factors. In: Factors and Factorizations of Graphs, pp. 15–67. Springer (2011). https://doi.org/10.1007/978-3-642-21919-1_2
2. Aliev, I., Henk, M., Oertel, T.: Distances to lattice points in knapsack polyhedra. Math. Program. 175–198 (2019). https://doi.org/10.1007/s10107-019-01392-1
3. Alon, N., Azar, Y., Woeginger, G.J., Yadid, T.: Approximation schemes for scheduling on parallel machines. J. Sched. **1**(1), 55–66 (1998)
4. Caprara, A., Dell'Amico, M., Díaz, J.C.D., Iori, M., Rizzi, R.: Friendly bin packing instances without integer round-up property. Math. Program. **150**(1), 5–17 (2015)
5. Cook, W.J., Gerards, A.M.H., Schrijver, A., Tardos, É.: Sensitivity theorems in integer linear programming. Math. Program. **34**(3), 251–264 (1986)
6. Cslovjecsek, J., Eisenbrand, F., Weismantel, R.: N-fold integer programming via LP rounding. CoRR abs/2002.07745 (2020)
7. Eisenbrand, F., Weismantel, R.: Proximity results and faster algorithms for integer programming using the steinitz lemma, **16**(1), 5:1–5:14. ACM (2020)
8. Epstein, L., Levin, A.: A robust APTAS for the classical bin packing problem. Math. Program. **119**(1), 33–49 (2009)
9. Epstein, L., Levin, A.: Robust approximation schemes for cube packing. SIAM J. Optim. **23**(2), 1310–1343 (2013)

10. Gilmore, P.C., Gomory, R.E.: A linear programming approach to the cutting-stock problem. Oper. Res. **9**(6), 849–859 (1961)
11. Goemans, M.X., Rothvoß, T.: Polynomiality for bin packing with a constant number of item types. In: SODA, pp. 830–839. SIAM (2014)
12. Hadamard, J.: Resolution d'une question relative aux determinants. Bull. des Sci. Math. **2**, 240–246 (1893)
13. Hochbaum, D.S.: Monotonizing linear programs with up to two nonzeroes per column. Oper. Res. Lett. **32**(1), 49–58 (2004)
14. Hochbaum, D.S., Shanthikumar, J.G.: Convex separable optimization is not much harder than linear optimization, **37**(4), 843–862. ACM (1990)
15. Holton, D.A., Sheehan, J.: The Petersen Graph. Cambridge University Press, Cambridge (1993)
16. Jansen, K., Klein, K.-M.: A robust AFPTAS for online bin packing with polynomial migration. SIAM J. Discret. Math. **33**(4), 2062–2091 (2019)
17. Jansen, K., Klein, K.-M., Maack, M., Rau, M.: Empowering the configuration-ip - new PTAS results for scheduling with setups times. In: ITCS, volume 124 of LIPIcs, pp. 44:1–44:19. Schloss Dagstuhl - Leibniz-Zentrum für Informatik (2019)
18. Jansen, K., Klein, K.-M., Verschae, J.: Closing the gap for makespan scheduling via sparsification techniques. In: ICALP, volume 55 of LIPIcs, pp. 72:1–72:13. Schloss Dagstuhl - Leibniz-Zentrum für Informatik (2016)
19. Jansen, K., Lassota, A., Maack, M.: Approximation algorithms for scheduling with class constraints. In: SPAA (in print) (2020)
20. Jansen, K., Lassota, A., Rohwedder, L.: Near-linear time algorithm for n-fold ILPS via color coding. In: ICALP, volume 132 of LIPIcs, pp. 75:1–75:13 (2019)
21. Jansen, K., Robenek, C.: Scheduling jobs on identical and uniform processors revisited. In: Solis-Oba, R., Persiano, G. (eds.) WAOA 2011. LNCS, vol. 7164, pp. 109–122. Springer, Heidelberg (2012). https://doi.org/10.1007/978-3-642-29116-6_10
22. Kempe, A.B.: A memoir in the theory of mathematical form. Philos. Trans. R. Soc. Lond. **177**, 1–70 (1886)
23. Lee, J., Paat, J., Stallknecht, I., Xu, L.: Improving proximity bounds using sparsity. CoRR abs/2001.04659 (2020)
24. Paat, J., Weismantel, R., Weltge, S.: Distances between optimal solutions of mixed-integer programs. Math. Program. 455–468 (2018). https://doi.org/10.1007/s10107-018-1323-z
25. Petersen, J.: Sur le théorèm de tait. L'Intermédiare des Mathématiciens **5**(1), 225–227 (1898)
26. Sanders, P., Sivadasan, N., Skutella, M.: Online scheduling with bounded migration. Math. Oper. Res. **34**(2), 481–498 (2009)
27. Schrijver, A.: Theory of linear and integer programming. Wiley-Interscience series in discrete mathematics and optimization. Wiley (1999)
28. Skutella, M., Verschae, J.: Robust polynomial-time approximation schemes for parallel machine scheduling with job arrivals and departures. Math. Oper. Res. **41**(3), 991–1021 (2016)
29. Subramani, K.: On deciding the non-emptiness of 2sat polytopes with respect to first order queries. Math. Log. Q. **50**(3), 281–292 (2004)

Using the Metro-Map Metaphor
for Drawing Hypergraphs

Fabian Frank[1], Michael Kaufmann[2] , Stephen Kobourov[3] ,
Tamara Mchedlidze[4] , Sergey Pupyrev[5] , Torsten Ueckerdt[1] ,
and Alexander Wolff[6(✉)]

[1] Karlsruhe Institute of Technology, Karlsruhe, Germany
`fabian-frank97@web.de, torsten.ueckerdt@kit.edu`
[2] Universität Tübingen, Tübingen, Germany
`mk@uni-tuebingen.de`
[3] University of Arizona, Tucson, USA
`kobourov@cs.arizona.edu`
[4] Utrecht University, Utrecht, Netherlands
`mched@iti.uka.de`
[5] Facebook, Menlo Park, USA
`spupyrev@gmail.com`
[6] Universität Würzburg, Würzburg, Germany
`alexander.wolff@uni-wuerzburg.de`

Abstract. For a planar graph G and a set Π of simple paths in G, we define a *metro-map embedding* to be a planar embedding of G and an ordering of the paths of Π along each edge of G. This definition of a metro-map embedding is motivated by visual representations of hypergraphs using the metro-map metaphor. In a metro-map embedding, two paths cross in a so-called *vertex crossing* if they pass through the vertex and alternate in the circular ordering around it.

We study the problem of constructing metro-map embeddings with the minimum number of *crossing vertices*, that is, vertices where paths cross. We show that the corresponding decision problem is NP-complete for general planar graphs but can be solved efficiently for trees or if the number of crossing vertices is constant. All our results hold both in a fixed and variable embedding settings.

Keywords: Metro-map metaphor · Hypergraph visualization · Crossing minimization · NP-hardness · Clustered planarity

1 Introduction

We consider a visualization style for hypergraphs that is inspired by schematic metro maps. Such maps are common for urban citizens, who all know that the stations traversed by the same colored curve belong to the same metro line. This intuitive understanding of grouping has been employed to visualize other abstract data forming hypergraphs. For example, Foo [8] turns personal memories into a metro map, Nesbitt [12] and Stott et al. [17] use the metro-map

© Springer Nature Switzerland AG 2021
T. Bureš et al. (Eds.): SOFSEM 2021, LNCS 12607, pp. 361–372, 2021.
https://doi.org/10.1007/978-3-030-67731-2_26

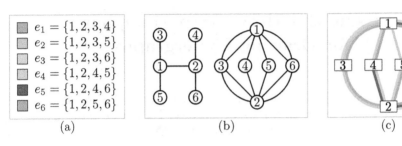

Fig. 1. (a) The hypergraph H with vertex set $\{1,\dots,6\}$ whose hyperedges are all 4-element subsets containing $\{1,2\}$, (b) two supports of H, and (c) a metro-map drawing of H.

metaphor to visualize relationships between PhD theses and items of a business plan, Sandvad et al. [15] for building Web-based guided tour systems, and Shahaf et al. [16] use it for visualizing historical events. A popular visualization shows the 250 best movies according to a vote on IMDb.com [10].

Informally, the problem of constructing such a visualization for a given hypergraph is as follows. Let $H = (V, \mathcal{E})$ be a hypergraph with vertex set V and edge set $\mathcal{E} \subseteq 2^V$. A *metro-map drawing* of H is a graphical representation where each node in V is depicted by a point in the plane and each hyperedge $e \in \mathcal{E}$ by an open continuous curve, referred to as *line*, that passes through the points corresponding to the vertices in e; see Fig. 4 below.

The problem of constructing a metro-map drawing of a hypergraph can be broken down into several algorithmically challenging steps that are each worth of independent investigation. The first step is to construct a so-called path-based hypergraph support. Given a hypergraph H, a graph G with $V(G) = V(H)$ is a *support* of H if, for each hyperedge e of H, the graph $G[e]$ induced by e is connected. A support is *path-based* if, for every hyperedge e, $G[e]$ contains a Hamiltonian path. For example, Fig. 1 shows a hypergraph H with two supports; the right one is path-based while the left one is not. The second step is to draw the path-based support. The third and final step is to route the lines along the edges of the support. All three steps strongly influence the readability of the final metro-map drawing.

Even just the first step leads to two difficult problems. Constructing a path-based support with the minimum number of edges—a natural optimization goal for obtaining a readable final result—is NP-hard [5]. Assuming that a support G is provided as part of the input, ordering the vertices within a hyperedge e is NP-hard as this task implicitly tests whether the induced subgraph $G[e]$ contains a Hamiltonian path. In this paper, we study the algorithmic complexity of the other two steps: embedding the support and routing the lines.

The input for our problem is a planar graph G (the support of H) and a set Π of simple paths in G (the hyperedges). For example consider the metro-map drawing in the right of Fig. 1. Here the path-based support is $G \cong K_{2,4}$, and the set Π contains for example the path $p_1 = [2, 3, 1, 4]$ for hyperedge

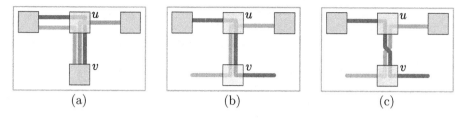

(a)   (b)   (c)

Fig. 2. The vertex crossing in (a) can be eliminated by reordering lines at v. Sometimes (but not always) a vertex crossing (b) can be turned into a line crossings (c).

$e_1 = \{1, 2, 3, 4\}$. In general, let u be a vertex of G, let $u_1, \ldots, u_k$ be the neighbors of u in clockwise order, as determined by an embedding $\mathcal{G}$ of G, and let $\Pi_i \subseteq \Pi$ be the set of paths that contain the edge (u, u_i). A *line ordering at vertex u on the edge (u, u_i)*, $\mathrm{ord}_u(u_i)$, is an ordering $p_1, \ldots, p_h$ of Π_i such that u_{i-1} precedes p_1 and p_h precedes u_{i+1} in $\mathcal{G}$. In Fig. 1 the line ordering $\mathrm{ord}_1(3)$ on edge $(1, 3)$ of G is $\langle p_1, p_4, p_3 \rangle$, where p_i denotes the path in Π for hyperedge e_i of H. Intuitively, a line ordering at vertex u on the edge (u, u_i) is an extension of the embedding $\mathcal{G}$ to the ordering of the paths passing through (u, u_i). A *line ordering at vertex u* is the concatenation $\mathrm{ord}_u(u_1) \oplus \cdots \oplus \mathrm{ord}_u(u_k)$. A *vertex crossing* at u is a pair (p, q) of paths that appear in the line ordering at u alternatingly, that is, $p...q...p...q$; see the crossing between the green line and the orange line in vertex u in Fig. 2(a,b). A *line crossing* along an edge $e = (v, w)$ is a pair (p, q) of paths that appear in the line orderings at v and at w in the same order; refer to Fig. 2(c).

Minimizing the number of line crossings has been studied extensively in the context of drawing geographic metro maps [1,2,7,13,14]. We advocate that it is also interesting to minimize vertex crossings. Graphic designers sometimes seem to prefer them over line crossings; see Fig. 3.

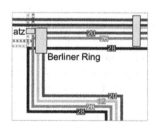

Fig. 3. A crossing vertex in a clipping of the official bus & tram map of Würzburg [18].

In this paper, we focus on vertex crossings and forbid line crossings. When representing abstract hypergraphs as metro maps, one has more freedom to place vertices; this can be used to produce drawings that avoid both types of crossings. For an example of such a drawing, see Fig. 4.

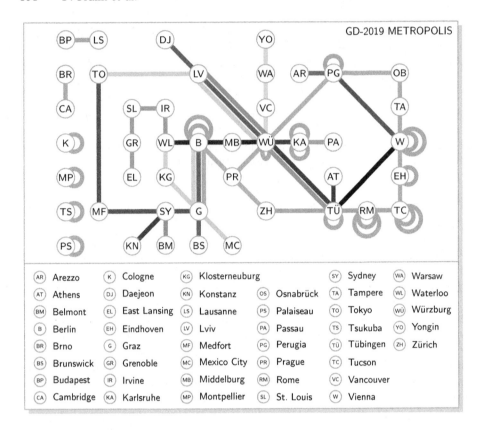

Fig. 4. A visualization of the conference GD 2019 as a metro map: the stations correspond to cities and the lines to papers. A line connects the cities where the authors of the corresponding paper are affiliated. The drawing has no vertex crossings.

We formalize our problem, which has two variants, as follows. In the *fixed-embedding* setting, an embedding $\mathcal{G}$ of G is given, and a *metro-map embedding* of $(\mathcal{G}, \Pi)$ is a set $\{\mathrm{ord}_u(v), \mathrm{ord}_v(u) : (u, v) \in E\}$ of line orderings. If the embedding of G is not part of the input—the *variable-embedding* setting—a *metro-map embedding* of (G, Π) is an embedding $\mathcal{G}$ of G and a metro-map embedding of $(\mathcal{G}, \Pi)$. We then define the problem CROSSING VERTEX MINIMIZATION: Given a pair (G, Π) or a pair $(\mathcal{G}, \Pi)$, we seek for a metro-map embedding that minimizes the *number of crossing vertices*, that is, the number of vertices containing vertex crossings—under the restriction that line crossings are not allowed.

Our contribution is as follows. We settle the complexity of CROSSING VERTEX MINIMIZATION, which turns out to be NP-hard in general, but polynomial-time solvable for trees. We also present an efficient algorithm for testing whether an instance $(\mathcal{G}, \Pi)$ or (G, Π) admits a metro-map embedding without any vertex crossings, for example as the one in Fig. 4. Table 1 gives an overview of our results.

We note that the problem of constructing a metro-map embedding in the fixed-embedding setting with a slightly different optimization goal was studied by Bast et al. [3]. The authors presented an ILP to minimize the total number of vertex crossings (as opposed to our optimization goal of minimizing the total number of crossing vertices).

Table 1. Our results for CROSSING VERTEX MINIMIZATION. Here k denotes the number of crossing vertices.

Problem type	Embedding	Graph	Result	Ref.
k Part of input	Fixed or Variable	Planar	NP-hard	Theorem 1
k Fixed	Fixed or Variable	Planar	Polynomial	Corollary 1
Optimization	Fixed or Variable	Tree	Polynomial	Theorem 3

2   Complexity

Theorem 1. CROSSING VERTEX MINIMIZATION *is NP-hard, both with fixed and variable embedding.*

Proof. We prove NP-hardness of the decision problem corresponding to CROSSING VERTEX MINIMIZATION by reducing from PLANAR VERTEX COVER, which is defined as follows. Given a planar graph $G = (V, E)$ and a number k, is there a set S of k vertices such that, for every edge (u, v) in G, it holds that $u \in S$ or $v \in S$ (or both)?

Given an instance (G, k) of PLANAR VERTEX COVER, we construct a planar graph $G' = (V', E')$ and a set Π' of paths in G' as follows (see Fig. 5):

$$V' = V \cup \{x_e^1, x_e^2 \mid e \in E\}$$
$$E' = E \cup \{(x_e^1, u), (x_e^2, u), (x_e^1, v), (x_e^2, v) \mid e = (u, v) \in E\}$$
$$\Pi' = \{P_e^1 = [x_e^1, u, v, x_e^2], P_e^2 = [x_e^2, u, v, x_e^1] \mid e = (u, v) \in E\}$$

In Fig. 5(b) and (c), vertices in V' are white, edges in E' are gray, and the two paths in Π' for the specific edge e are yellow and green. Clearly G' is planar.

We now claim that, for any embedding $\mathcal{G}'$ of G', there exists a metro-map embedding of $(\mathcal{G}', \Pi')$ with k crossing vertices if and only if G admits a vertex cover of size k. Note that this implies NP-hardness for both fixed *and* variable embeddings.

Given a metro-map embedding, for any edge $e = (u, v)$ in G, paths P_e^1 and P_e^2 necessarily cross, making at least one of u and v a crossing vertex. In other words, the set S of all crossing vertices forms a vertex cover of G.

Conversely, if S is a vertex cover of G, we can choose for each vertex $u \in V \setminus S$ and each edge $e = (u, v)$ incident to u in G the line ordering $\mathrm{ord}_u(v)$ such that P_e^1 and P_e^2 do not cross at u (but at v). For $i, j \in \{1, 2\}$ and for two different

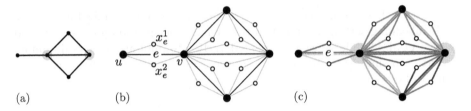

Fig. 5. Reduction from PLANAR VERTEX COVER to CROSSING VERTEX MINIMIZATION: (a) G with vertex cover (pink); (b) graph G'; (c) (G', Π) with two crossing vertices. (Color figure online)

edges $e' = (u, v')$ and $e'' = (u, v'')$ incident to u, paths $P_{e'}^i$ and $P_{e''}^j$ do not cross since, due to planarity, the triangles $[u, v', x_{e'}^i]$ and $[u, v'', x_{e''}^j]$ do not alternate along u. As crossings cannot occur at vertices in $V' \setminus V$, the resulting metro-map embedding has at most $|S| = k$ crossing vertices. □

3   Algorithms

We now turn to positive results, starting with metro-map embeddings without any vertex crossings. We formulate the corresponding decision problem as an instance of CLUSTERED PLANARITY, which was introduced by Lengauer [11] and independently by Feng et al. [6]. An instance of CLUSTERED PLANARITY consists of a planar graph H and a set $\mathcal{C}$ of subsets of vertices, called clusters. Any pair $C_1, C_2 \in \mathcal{C}$ of clusters is either disjoint or comparable by inclusion, i.e., $C_1 \cap C_2 \in \{\emptyset, C_1, C_2\}$. The task is to decide whether $(H, \mathcal{C})$ admits a clustered planar drawing, i.e., a crossing-free drawing of H together with a set of crossing-free closed Jordan curves, one for each cluster, such that each curve γ_C for cluster C contains exactly the vertices of C in its interior, and each curve crosses each edge at most once. Only very recently, Fulek and Tóth [9] showed that CLUSTERED PLANARITY can be decided efficiently. Their algorithm runs in $O(n^{16})$ time, where n is the number of vertices of the given planar graph. In the meantime, Bläsius et al. [4] came up with a simpler and faster algorithm, running in quadratic time.

For convenience, we denote the size of an instance (G, Π) for our metro-map embedding problems by $\|G, \Pi\|$ and remark that $\|G, \Pi\| = O(|V(G)| \cdot |\Pi|)$. While we state and prove the following theorem for the variable-embedding case, it is simple to adjust it to a given fixed embedding; see the discussion in Sect. 4.

Theorem 2. *Given a planar graph G and a set Π of paths in G, there is an algorithm that decides efficiently whether (G, Π) admits a metro-map embedding without vertex crossings. The algorithm runs in time $O(f(\|G, \Pi\|))$, where f denotes the time needed to decide an instance of CLUSTERED PLANARITY.*

Proof. Given (G, Π), we construct in $O(\|G, \Pi\|)$ time an equivalent instance $(H, \mathcal{C})$ of CLUSTERED PLANARITY. First, by adding single-edge paths to Π, we ensure that every edge of G lies in some path in Π. Then for each edge e of G we add a parallel[1] edge $\bar{e}$ to the graph and a new path $P(\bar{e})$ consisting just of $\bar{e}$ to the set of paths. The resulting instance $(G' = (V, E'), \Pi')$ admits a crossing-free metro-map embedding if and only if (G, Π) does.

For the graph H, we take as vertex set the incidences between vertices of G', edges of G', and paths in Π'. Formally, a vertex–edge incidence is a pair $(v, e) \in V \times E'$ with $v \in e$, a vertex–path incidence is a pair $(v, P) \in V \times \Pi'$ with $v \in V(P)$, and a vertex–edge–path incidence is a triple $(v, e, P) \in V \times E' \times \Pi'$ with $v \in e \in E(P)$. (Note that there are no more than $2|E'|$, $|V| \cdot |\Pi'|$, and $2|V| \cdot |\Pi'|$ instances of each type, respectively.) For each path $P = [v_1, \ldots, v_p]$ in Π' with $v_i \in V$ $(i = 1, \ldots, p)$, $e_i = v_i v_{i+1} \in E'$ $(i = 1, \ldots, p - 1)$ graph H contains a path $[(v_1, P), (v_1, e_1, P), (v_2, e_1, P), (v_2, e_2, P), \ldots, (v_p, e_{p-1}, P), (v_p, P)]$ on all incidences of P as they appear along the path. We call these paths the *metro-line paths*. Additionally, for each edge $e = uv$ of the original graph G with parallel edge $\bar{e}$ in G', we put two paths $[(u, e), (u, \bar{e})]$ and $[(v, e), (v, \bar{e})]$ into H, which we simply call the *additional paths*. Thus H is the vertex-disjoint union of paths.

For the clustering, we first define, for each vertex–edge incidence (v, e), a cluster $C(v, e) = \{(v, e)\} \cup \{(v, e, P) \in V(H) \mid P \in \Pi'\}$. Second, for each vertex v in G', we define an inner cluster $C_{\text{in}}(v) = \{(v, P) \in V(H) \mid P \in \Pi'\}$ and an outer cluster $C_{\text{out}}(v) = C_{\text{in}}(v) \cup \bigcup_{(v,e) \in V(H)} C(v, e)$. Let $\mathcal{C}$ be the set of all these clusters. This completes the construction of the CLUSTERED PLANARITY instance $(H, \mathcal{C})$. Clearly H is planar, and any pair of clusters in $\mathcal{C}$ is either disjoint or in inclusion-relation. Moreover we have that the size of $(H, \mathcal{C})$ is in $O(|V| \cdot |\Pi'|) = O(\|G, \Pi\|)$. See Fig. 6 for an illustration.

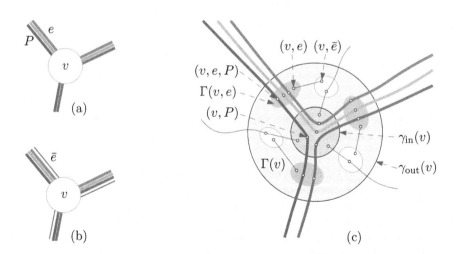

Fig. 6. Part of a crossing-free metro-map embedding of (G, Π) (a) and (G', Π') (b), and a corresponding clustered planar drawing of $(H, \mathcal{C})$ (c).

---

[1] To avoid parallel edges, paths of length two with the appropriate modifications would do equally well.

It remains to show that any clustered planar drawing of (H, C) can be transformed into a metro-map embedding of the original instance (G, Π) without crossings. (The other direction is easy; see Fig. 6.)

For any vertex v in G, we have $C_{\text{in}}(v) \subsetneq C_{\text{out}}(v)$ and hence the corresponding closed curves $\gamma_{\text{out}}(v)$ and $\gamma_{\text{in}}(v)$ define an annulus-shaped region $\Gamma(v)$ (light yellow region in Fig. 6(c) in the plane that contains the region $\Gamma(v, e)$ (one of the gray regions in Fig. 6(c) for cluster $C(v, e)$ for every incident edge e at v. For every incidence (v, e, P), the metro-line path for P enters $\Gamma(v)$ from the outside, passes through $\Gamma(v, e)$, and leaves $\Gamma(v)$ to the inside. This gives a circular ordering σ_v of the incidence (v, e, P) around v. As $\Gamma(v, e) \cap \Gamma(v, e') = \emptyset$ for any e, e' at v, it follows that all incidences (v, e, P) for the same edge e appear consecutively in σ_v. Moreover, the additional path between (v, e) and $(v, \bar{e})$ implies that in σ_v the incidence for edge $\bar{e}$ appears next to the block of incidences for edge e.

We construct a crossing-free metro-map embedding of (G, Π) by drawing each vertex v inside its curve $\gamma_{\text{in}}(v)$, drawing each edge e of G along the metro-line path for $P(\bar{e})$ connecting the ends to v inside $\gamma_{\text{in}}(v)$ in a crossing-free way, and choosing the line ordering as the subordering of σ_v on incidences (v, e, P) with $P \in \Pi' - \Pi$. The constructed embedding of G is clearly crossing-free. Moreover, we have no vertex crossing at v as the metro-line paths do not cross inside $\gamma_{\text{in}}(v)$.

It remains to show that there are no line crossings, i.e., that for each edge $e = (u, v)$ in G, the line ordering at u on e is the reverse of the line ordering at v on e. (This would not be guaranteed without the parallel edges and additional paths, see Fig. 7.)

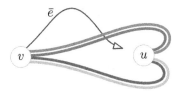

Fig. 7. Without the extra edge $\bar{e}$, a clustered planar drawing of (H, C) might give line crossings if e is a bridge.

For the edge $e = (u, v)$, the circular ordering of incidences (v, e, P) around v is the reverse of the circular ordering of incidences (u, e, P) around u since the corresponding metro-line paths in H are non-crossing. Moreover, both sets of incidences appear as a consecutive block around the respective vertices. Finally, since the metro-line path for $\bar{e}$ starts and ends between (in the cyclic ordering at the vertices) the same metro-line paths for e at vertex u and vertex v, the line orderings $\text{ord}_u(v)$ and $\text{ord}_v(u)$ are indeed reversals of each other. In particular, a situation as shown in Fig. 7 is prevented.   □

Theorem 2 implies the following.

Corollary 1. *For any fixed k, one can decide in polynomial time whether there is a metro-map embedding with at most k crossing vertices.*

Proof. We go through all $O(n^k)$ sets of k vertices for which we allow vertex crossings. Given such a set $S \subseteq V$, we split each path $P \in \Pi$ at every vertex of S. That is, consider Π_S to be the set of all inclusion-maximal subpaths of paths in Π with no inner vertex in S. By Theorem 2, we can test in polynomial time whether there is a metro-map embedding of (G, Π_S) without crossings. Clearly, such an embedding can be seen as a metro-map embedding of (G, Π) where all vertex crossings occur at vertices in S, and vice versa. As k is fixed, we obtain overall polynomial runtime. $\square$

We now improve the result above for the case of trees.

Theorem 3. *There is an algorithm that solves* CROSSING VERTEX MINIMIZATION *for trees efficiently, both for variable and fixed embedding. Given a tree T and a set Π of paths, the algorithm runs in time $O(|V(T)| \cdot f(\|T, \Pi\|))$, where f denotes the time needed to decide an instance of* CLUSTERED PLANARITY.

Proof. Let (T_0, Π_0) denote a given instance with T_0 being a tree and Π_0 a set of paths in T_0. We need to efficiently find a smallest subset S such that (T_0, Π_0) admits a metro-map embedding with every vertex crossing in S. Along with the set S, we obtain the edge-partition $\mathcal{T}(S)$ of T_0 into its inclusion-maximal subtrees with the property that each vertex of S is either a leaf in the subtree or not contained in it. To compute S, pick any vertex as the root in T_0 and process the vertices of the tree from the leaves towards the root, i.e., considering each vertex only if all its children have already been considered. On the way, we will remove vertices from tree, thereby removing or shortening some paths. We always denote by T the current tree and by Π the current set of paths.

Let T_v denote the subtree of T rooted at the currently processed vertex v and (if v is not the root) let w denote the parent of v. We consider the subtree T_v^+ of T on $T_v \cup w$, i.e., the tree T_v plus edge (w, v), and compute the set $\Pi|_{T_v^+} = \{P \cap T_v^+ \mid P \in \Pi\}$ of all paths in Π, each restricted to its maximal (possibly empty) subpath in T_v^+. We then use Theorem 2 to test in $O(f(\|T, \Pi\|))$ time whether $(T_v^+, \Pi|_{T_v^+})$ admits a metro-map embedding without any crossing. If it does, we consider v as successfully processed and continue with the next vertex. Otherwise, if $(T_v^+, \Pi|_{T_v^+})$ requires at least one vertex crossing, we add v to the set S and remove from T all vertices in T_v except for v, i.e., continue with the instance $(T_v^- = T - (T_v - v), \Pi|_{T_v^-})$. Observe that if $u_1, \ldots, u_k$ are the children of v, then T is the edge-disjoint union of $T_{u_1}^+, \ldots, T_{u_k}^+$ and T_v^-.

Once every vertex of T_0 is processed, we have computed a set $S \subseteq V(T_0)$ with corresponding edge-partition $\mathcal{T}(S)$ with the properties that

(i) for every tree $T' \in \mathcal{T}(S)$ the instance $(T', \Pi_0|_{T'})$ admits a crossing-free metro-map embedding, and

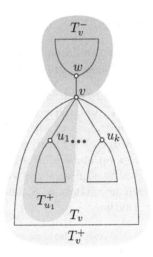

Fig. 8. Illustration of the subtrees of T for v and its children $u_1, \ldots, u_k$. Note that T is the edge-disjoint union of $T_v^- = T - (T_v - v)$ and $T_{u_1}^+, \ldots, T_{u_k}^+$.

(ii) if $T_1, \ldots, T_k \in \mathcal{T}(S)$ are the trees containing the edges of a vertex $v \in S$ with parent w (if existent) to its k children, then every metro-map embedding of $(T_v^+ = T_1 \cup \cdots \cup T_k \cup \{vw\}, \Pi_0|_{T_v^+})$ has at least one vertex crossing.

Combining the metro-map embeddings of all trees in $\mathcal{T}(S)$ given by (i) gives a metro-map embedding of (T_0, Π_0) with all vertex crossings in S, i.e., $|S|$ crossing vertices are sufficient. On the other hand, (ii) implies that every metro-map embedding of T_0 has at least one vertex crossing at a non-leaf vertex of T_v^+. As for distinct $u, v \in S$, trees T_v^+ and T_u^+ do not share non-leaf vertices, $|S|$ crossing vertices are necessary.

The runtime of our algorithm is in $O(|V(T)| \cdot f(\|T, \Pi\|))$ since it is dominated by the $|V(T)|$ calls to Theorem 2. □

4   Discussion

First, note that the algorithm in Theorem 2, and hence also those in Corollary 1 and Theorem 3, assume that G has variable embedding. Of course, we can handle the fixed-embedding setting by triangulating the given embedded graph in a preprocessing step. This also holds for the treatment of trees in Theorem 3 by doing a separate triangulation for each call of Theorem 2 therein.

Second, we leave as an open problem whether CROSSING VERTEX MINIMIZATION is fixed-parameter tractable.

Third, refer back to Fig. 1. Intuitively, the metro-map drawing on the right could be improved by switching the order of paths p_1 and p_4 on edge $(1, 4)$. However, this improvement is not reflected by objective functions considered so far since the drawing has neither vertex nor line crossings. Maybe there is a need for a more fine-grained objective?

Acknowledgments. We thank the organizers and the other participants of the 2017 Dagstuhl seminar "Scalable Set Visualization", where this work started, in particular Robert Baker, Nan Cao, and Yifan Hu.

References

1. Argyriou, E., Bekos, M.A., Kaufmann, M., Symvonis, A.: On metro-line crossing minimization. J. Graph Algorithms Appl. **14**(1), 75–96 (2010). https://doi.org/10. 7155/jgaa.00199
2. Asquith, M., Gudmundsson, J., Merrick, D.: An ILP for the metro-line crossing problem. In: Proceedings 14th Computing Australasian Theory Symposium (CATS 2008), vol. 77, pp. 49–56. CRPIT (2008). https://crpit.scem.westernsydney.edu.au/confpapers/CRPITV77Asquith.pdf
3. Bast, H., Brosi, P., Storandt., S.: Efficient generation of geographically accurate transit maps. In: Proceedings 26th ACM SIGSPATIAL International Conference on Advances in Geographic Information Systems (SIGSPATIAL 2018), pp. 13–22 (2018). https://doi.org/10.1145/3274895.3274955
4. Bläsius, T., Fink, S.D., Rutter, I.: Synchronized planarity with applications to constrained planarity problems. arXiv (2020). https://arxiv.org/abs/2007.15362
5. Brandes, U., Cornelsen, S., Pampel, B., Sallaberry, A.: Path-based supports for hypergraphs. J. Discrete Algorithms **14**, 248–261 (2012). https://doi.org/10.1016/j.jda.2011.12.009
6. Feng, Q.-W., Cohen, R.F., Eades, P.: Planarity for clustered graphs. In: Spirakis, P. (ed.) ESA 1995. LNCS, vol. 979, pp. 213–226. Springer, Heidelberg (1995). https://doi.org/10.1007/3-540-60313-1_145
7. Fink, M., Pupyrev, S., Wolff, A.: Ordering metro lines by block crossings. J. Graph Algorithms Appl. **19**(1), 111–153 (2015). https://doi.org/10.7155/jgaa.00351
8. Foo, B.: The memory underground. http://memoryunderground.com
9. Fulek, R., Tóth, C.D.: Atomic embeddability, clustered planarity, and thickenability. In: Proceedings ACM-SIAM Symposium Discrete Algorithms (SODA), pp. 2876–2895 (2020). https://doi.org/10.1137/1.9781611975994.175
10. Honnorat, D.: The best movies of all time map (2009). http://www.dyblog. fr/index.php?2009/07/20/928-une-carte-des-250-meilleurs-films-de-tous-les-temps+www.dyblog.fr/index.php?2009/07/20/928-une-carte-des-250-meilleurs-films-de-tous-les-temps+, Accessed 8 Jun 2020
11. Lengauer, T.: Hierarchical planarity testing algorithms. J. ACM **36**(3), 474–509 (1989). https://doi.org/10.1145/65950.65952
12. Nesbitt, K.V.: Getting to more abstract places using the metro map metaphor. In: Proceedings 8th International Conference Information Vision (IV 2004), pp. 488–493. IEEE (2004). https://doi.org/10.1109/IV.2004.1320189
13. Nöllenburg, M.: An improved algorithm for the metro-line crossing minimization problem. In: Eppstein, D., Gansner, E.R. (eds.) GD 2009. LNCS, vol. 5849, pp. 381–392. Springer, Heidelberg (2010). https://doi.org/10.1007/978-3-642-11805-0_36
14. Nöllenburg, M., Wolff, A.: Drawing and labeling high-quality metro maps by mixed-integer programming. IEEE Trans. Vis. Comput. Graph. **17**(5), 626–641 (2011). https://doi.org/10.1109/TVCG.2010.81

15. Sandvad, E., Grønbæk, K., Sloth, L., Knudsen, J.L.: A metro map metaphor for guided tours on the Web: the Webvise guided tour system. In: Shen, V.Y., Saito, N., Lyu, M.R., Zurko, M.E. (eds.) Proceedings 10th International World Wide Web Conference (WWW 2001), pp. 326–333. ACM (2001). https://doi.org/10.1145/371920.372079

16. Shahaf, D., Yang, J., Suen, C., Jacobs, J., Wang, H., Leskovec, J.: Information cartography: Creating zoomable, large-scale maps of information. In: Proceedings 19th ACM SIGKDD Conference. Knowledge Discovery and Data Mining (KDD), pp. 1097–1105 (2013). https://doi.org/10.1145/2487575.2487690

17. Stott, J.M., Rodgers, P., Burkhard, R.A., Meier, M., Smis, M.T.J.: Automatic layout of project plans using a metro map metaphor. In: Proceedings 9th International Conference Information Vision (IV 2005), pp. 203–206. IEEE (2005). https://doi.org/10.1109/IV.2005.26

18. Verkehrsunternehmensverbund Mainfranken. Liniennetz Würzburger Straenbahn (2019). https://www.wvv.de/de/media/downloads/downloadcenter/hauptnavigation/mobilitaet/liniennetz/2019-11-01-liniennetzplan-busse-und-strabas_a3.pdf, Accessed 8 Jun 2020

Weighted Microscopic Image Reconstruction

Amotz Bar-Noy[1], Toni Böhnlein[2,3(✉)], Zvi Lotker[2,4], David Peleg[3],
and Dror Rawitz[2]

[1] City University of New York (CUNY), New York, USA
amotz@sci.brooklyn.cuny.edu
[2] Bar Ilan University, Ramat-Gan, Israel
{toni.bohnlein,dror.rawitz}@biu.ac.il
[3] Weizmann Institute of Science, Rehovot, Israel
david.peleg@weizmann.ac.il
[4] Ben Gurion University of the Negev, Beer Sheva, Israel
zvi.lotker@gmail.com

Abstract. Assume that we inspect a specimen represented as a collection of points. The points are typically organized on a grid structure in 2D- or 3D-space, and each point has an associated physical value. The goal of the inspection is to determine these values. Yet, measuring these values directly (by *surgical probes*) may damage the specimen or is simply impossible. The alternative is to employ *aggregate* measuring techniques (e.g., CT or MRI), whereby measurements are taken over subsets of points, and the exact values at each point are subsequently extracted by computational methods. In the MINIMUM SURGICAL PROBING problem (MSP) the inspected specimen is represented by a graph G and a vector $\ell \in \mathbb{R}^n$ that assigns a value ℓ_i to each vertex i. An aggregate measurement (called *probe*) centered at vertex i captures its entire neighborhood, i.e., the outcome of a probe centered at i is $\mathcal{P}_i = \sum_{j \in N(i) \cup \{i\}} \ell_j$ where $N(i)$ is the open neighborhood of vertex i. Bar-Noy et al. [4] gave a criterion whether the vector ℓ can be recovered from the collection of probes $\mathcal{P} = \{ \mathcal{P}_v \mid v \in V(G) \}$ alone. However, there are graphs where $\mathcal{P}$ is inconclusive, i.e., there are several vectors ℓ that are consistent with $\mathcal{P}$. In these cases, we are allowed to use surgical probes. A surgical probe at vertex i returns ℓ_i. The objective of MSP is to recover ℓ from $\mathcal{P}$ and G using as few surgical probes as possible.

In this work, we introduce the WEIGHTED MINIMUM SURGICAL PROBING (WMSP) problem in which a vertex i may have an aggregation coefficient w_i, namely $\mathcal{P}_i = \sum_{j \in N(i)} \ell_j + w_i \ell_i$. We show that WMSP can be solved in polynomial time. Moreover, we analyze the number of required surgical probes depending on the weight vector w. For any graph, we give two boundaries outside of which no surgical probes are needed to recover the vector ℓ. The boundaries are connected to the *(Signless) Laplacian matrix*.

This work was supported by US-Israel BSF grant 2018043 and ARL Cooperative Grant ARL Network Science CTA W911NF-09-2-0053.

T. Bureš et al. (Eds.): SOFSEM 2021, LNCS 12607, pp. 373–386, 2021.
https://doi.org/10.1007/978-3-030-67731-2_27

In addition, we focus on the special case, where $w = \vec{0}$. We explore the range of possible behaviors of WMSP by determining the number of surgical probes necessary in certain graph families, such as trees and various grid graphs. Finally, we analyze higher dimensional grids graphs. For the hypercube, when $w = \vec{1}$, we only need surgical probes if the dimension is odd, and when $w = \vec{0}$, we only need surgical probes if the dimension is even. The number of surgical probes follows the binomial coefficients.

Keywords: Graph theory · Graph realization · Realization algorithm · Image reconstruction · Graph spectra · Grid graphs

1   Introduction

Imaging technologies are widely used in many applications that are related to medicine and engineering. In this context we consider a model in which a specimen is represented by a collection of points organized in a 2D- or 3D-space, where each point is associated with a physical value (e.g., atom density, brightness, etc.).

Learning these values at all points is necessary to generate an image of the specimen. Yet, the problem is that obtaining these values through a direct and precise inspection may be damaging to the specimen or require expensive and rare equipment. A common solution to this problem is to use *aggregate* measuring techniques (such as CT scans or MRI). The idea is to measure large areas instead of points, and subsequently calculate the values at the points from the aggregate measurements. As an example, consider a microscope with a scanning window that is used for inspecting the specimen by systematically going over it and taking an aggregate measurement, or *probing*, each window. (This is sometimes referred to as the *luminosity* of the window [14].)

The above setting was extensively studied as the DISCRETE TOMOGRAPHY RECONSTRUCTION problem (DTR) (see [18] for a survey). In this problem the specimen is represented by a 2-dimensional grid, whose points, $x = (i, j)$, for $i \in \{1, \ldots, n_1\}$ and $j \in \{1, \ldots, n_2\}$, are assigned nonnegative integer values $\ell_{i,j}$. The window of a probe is typically an entire row or column of the grid, i.e., a probe can be thought of as performed by a ray piercing the specimen from side to side. The MICROSCOPIC IMAGE RECONSTRUCTION problem (MIR) was introduced by Frosini and Nivat [14,20] as a natural extension of DTR. In MIR, it is assumed that the microscope's scanning window is a segment of the plane (e.g., a circle or a rectangle). For example, if the window corresponds to a circle of radius 1, then the input can be thought of as an $n_1 \times n_2$ integer matrix, and the output is an $n_1 \times n_2$ integer matrix (see Fig. 1a). A similar setting can be described with a square scanning window consisting of a node and its eight neighbors in the grid as illustrated in Fig. 1b.

Bar-Noy et al. [4] introduced an extended setting where the inspected object is represented by a simple undirected graph. Given a graph $G = (V, E)$, the vector $\ell \in \mathbb{R}^n$ is an assignment of a value ℓ_i to each vertex i. Probing a vertex returns an aggregate measurement of the values that are assigned to vertices

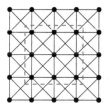

(a) Circle window and the grid graph.   (b) Square window and the King's graph.

Fig. 1. Scanning windows for the grid.

in its neighborhood. Formally, let $N(i)$ denote the open neighborhood of a vertex $i \in V$, i.e., $N(i) \triangleq \{j : (i, j) \in E\}$. The closed neighborhood of a vertex i is $N[i] \triangleq N(i) \cup \{i\}$. An *inclusive probe* at i is an operation whose outcome is $\ell(N[i])$, where $\ell(U) \triangleq \sum_{v \in U} \ell_v$, for every $U \subseteq V$. An *inclusive probe vector* $\mathcal{P}$ with respect to G and ℓ is the result of probing all vertices in G, and it is defined as $\mathcal{P}_i \triangleq \ell(N[i])$, for every $i \in V$. Bar-Noy et al. [4] give a criterion for graphs for which extended MIR can be solved by extracting the vector ℓ from the collection of probes $\mathcal{P}$. They also consider cases where a unique reconstruction is impossible, i.e., when there may be more than one vector ℓ yielding $\mathcal{P}$. As an example, consider the case where G is a single edge. Here, a probe vector $\mathcal{P}$ corresponds to any label vector (ℓ_1, ℓ_2) such that $\ell_1 + \ell_2 = \mathcal{P}_1 = \mathcal{P}_2$. A setting is introduced in which *surgical probes*, whose outcome at vertex i is the exact value of ℓ_i, are technically available (yet are expensive or risky and must be used sparingly). The goal is to find a minimum number of surgical probes necessary for a unique reconstruction, given a graph and the probe vector $\mathcal{P}$. This is referred to as the MINIMUM SURGICAL PROBING problem (MSP). Bar-Noy et al. [4] show that MSP can be solved in polynomial time. Moreover, they explore the range of possible behaviors of the MSP by determining the number of surgical probes necessary in certain specific graph families, such as trees and a variety of grid graphs.

In this paper, we generalize the above setting. Imagine that we seek to measure the temperature on a surface. More precisely, we cover the surface with a grid and seek to measure the temperature at each vertex. However, we are only able to take aggregate measurements over several vertices, e.g., a vertex and its neighborhood. That is, our measurements are not precise and are influenced by the neighboring vertices' temperature. Intuitively, the temperature at a vertex itself has a bigger contribution to the aggregate measurement than its neighbors. For our extension, we have a weight $w_i \in \mathbb{R}$ for each vertex i. Then, the *weighted probe* at vertex i is defined as

$$\mathcal{P}_i(w) \triangleq \ell(N(i)) + w_i \cdot \ell_i .$$

Note that if we can choose the grid's density, we gain control over the weights since, in a denser grid, the contribution of the central vertex is less than in a sparser grid.

Another example that falls within this weighted setting are *exclusive probes*. An exclusive probe at a vertex i is the aggregation of the values of the labels in $N(i)$. Open neighborhoods can be understood as a localized measurement where the label of a vertex itself is not taken into account (in the same sense that in a wireless network, a station must keep quiet in order to receive signals transmitted by its neighbors). Based on weighted probes, we define WEIGHTED MINIMUM SURGICAL PROBING (abbreviated WMSP) as follows: given a graph G, a weight vector w and a probe vector $\mathcal{P}(w)$, the goal is to find the vector ℓ that corresponds to $\mathcal{P}(w)$, using as few surgical probes as possible.

Our Results. In Sect. 2, we show that WMSP can be solved in polynomial time. It can be determined whether it is necessary to use surgical probes or not. If so, a minimum set of vertices to be surgically probed can be computed. The label vector can be recovered by solving a system of linear equations. The result follows from the efficient algorithm for MINIMUM SURGICAL PROBING which was given in [4]. We note that this algorithm uses linear algebra to solve the problem. More specifically, it is based on diagonalization of the matrix $\bar{A}_G(w) \triangleq A_G + \text{diag}(w)$, where A_G is the adjacency matrix of the input graph G and $\text{diag}(w)$ is a diagonal matrix with the entries of weight vector w on the diagonal. If $\bar{A}_G(w)$ is non-singular, then no surgical probes are required to recover the label vector.

In Sect. 3, we analyze the number of required surgical probes depending on the weight vector w. Intuitively, if the absolute value of all entries of w is extremely large, then $\bar{A}_G(w)$ is non-singular and WMSP can be solved without any surgical probes. We explore the boundaries of this behavior: We show that one boundary is obtained when $w = -\vec{\delta}(G)$, where $\vec{\delta}(G)$ is the degree vector of the graph G. In this case the matrix $\bar{A}_G(w)$ is equal to minus the *Laplacian matrix*, which plays a central role for the analysis of networks and in spectral graph theory (see, e.g., [16]). The other boundary is obtained when $w = \vec{\delta}(G)$. In this case, $\bar{A}_G(w)$ is the *Signless Laplacian matrix* (see, e.g., [8–10]). The degree vector $-\vec{\delta}(G)$ is a boundary in the sense that when used as a weight, we need one surgical probe to uncover a label vector, but if we reduce entries by an arbitrary small amount, we no longer require surgical probes. A similar result holds when $\vec{\delta}(G)$ is used as a weight vector and entries are increased. However, for positive weights it makes a difference whether G is bipartite or not. In the latter case, we show that weight vectors with smaller entries than $\vec{\delta}(G)$ exhibit the boundary behavior. Moreover, semidefinite programming can be used to compute weight vectors that guarantee reconstruction without surgical probes. Knowing these boundaries is essential for applications where one controls w.

In Sect. 4, we explore WMSP on special graph classes in the exclusive case, namely the case where $w = 0$. We compare the results to the inclusive case ($w = 1$) that was studied in [4]. We consider paths and cycles as well as their *Cartesian products*, namely grids, tubes and tori. The respective theorems for the tube and torus graphs can be found in the full version of the paper. Additionally, in the full version we deal with the *Strong Product* of two path graphs which is known as the King's graph (see Fig. 1b) as well as trees showing that the minimum number of surgical probes can be very high in the exclusive case while it is very low in the inclusive case, and vice versa.

Finally, we analyze the behavior of higher dimensional objects when we consider the hypercube. The d-dimensional hypercube is the Cartesian Product of d path graphs of length 2. We show that for the hypercube, in the inclusive case, we only need surgical probes if the dimension is odd, and in the exclusive case, we only need surgical probes if the dimension is even. We discover that the number of surgical probes follows the (middle) binomial coefficients. The analysis of the hypercube is only contained in the full version of the paper.

We introduce the following indicator variables to present our results: $I_b^a(n) = 1$, if $n \bmod a \equiv b$, otherwise $I_b^a(n) = 0$ and $\gcd(\cdot, \cdot)$ is the greatest common divisor of two integers. Table 1 lists the number of surgical probes that are sufficient to discover ℓ in the exclusive and inclusive cases.

Table 1. The table shows the number of surgical probes. The results for the inclusive case (except the hypercube) appeared in Bar-Noy et al. [4].

	Inclusive	Exclusive
Grid	$I_2^3(n_1)I_1^2(n_2) + I_1^2(n_1)I_2^3(n_2) + 2I_4^5(n_1)I_4^5(n_2)$	$\gcd(n_1 + 1, n_2 + 1) - 1$
Path	$I_2^3(n)$	$I_1^2(n)$
Hypercube	$I_1^2(d)\binom{d}{(d-1)/2}$	$I_0^2(d)\binom{d}{d/2}$
Tube	$2I_2^3(n_1)I_0^4(n_2) + 2I_1^2(n_1)I_0^3(n_2) + I_2^3(n_1)I_0^2(n_2) + 4I_4^5(n_1)I_0^5(n_2)$	$I_0^2(n_2) \cdot 2(\gcd(n_1 + 1, \frac{n_2}{2}) - 1) + I_1^2(n_2) \cdot (\gcd(n_1 + 1, n_2) - 1)$
Cycle	$2I_0^3(n)$	$2I_0^4(n)$
Torus	$4I_0^3(n_1)I_0^4(n_2) + 4I_0^4(n_1)I_0^3(n_2) + 2I_0^2(n_1)I_0^6(n_2) + 2I_0^6(n_1)I_0^2(n_2) + 8I_0^5(n_1)I_0^5(n_2)$	$(1 - I_1^2(n_1)I_1^2(n_2))2\gcd(n_1, n_2) - I_0^2(n_1) - I_0^2(n_2)$
King's graph	$I_2^3(n_1)n_2 + I_2^3(n_2)n_1 - I_2^3(n_1)I_2^3(n_2)$	$I_1^2(n_1)I_1^2(n_2) + 2I_4^5(n_1)I_4^5(n_2)$

Related Work. Frosini and Nivat [14,20] introduce the problem of reconstructing a binary matrix from a rectangular scan. Battaglino et al. [5] analyze the reconstruction problem where the scanning windows have different sizes and discover relations to tiling. Moreover, Frosini et al. [15] analyze a reconstruction problem with two rectangular scanning windows. They assumed that a small number of the values are known to reconstruct the unknown values. Note the similarity to surgical probes.

Alpers and Gritzmann [1] combine DTR and MRI to reconstruct a matrix from column and row sums with additional windows constraints. In [3] they studied applications to image reconstruction. Moreover, Gritzmann et al. [17] showed that determining the minimum number of prescribed values making the DTR problem unique is in general a NP-hard problem. Prescribed values are analogue to surgical probes. The hardness follows from the fact that the values in the DTR problem are integers. Alpers and Gritzmann [2] discussed uniqueness problems for a dynamic variation of DTR.

2   Solving WEIGHTED MINIMUM SURGICAL PROBING

In this section we show how to solve WMSP. We start with some preliminaries. Denote the $n \times n$ identity matrix by I_n. Given a matrix A, let rank(A) denote its rank, and let $\Lambda(A)$ denote its set of eigenvalues. For an eigenvalue $\lambda \in \Lambda(A)$, denote by $\phi(\lambda, A)$ the multiplicity of λ in $\Lambda(A)$. Given a simple graph $G = (V, E)$, let $A_G = \{a_{ij}\}$ be G's $n \times n$ adjacency matrix, i.e., $a_{ij} = 1$ if $(i, j) \in E$, and $a_{ij} = 0$ otherwise. Given a vector $w \in \mathbb{R}^n$, let diag$(w) = \{d_{ij}\}$ be the $n \times n$ diagonal matrix with the entries of w on the diagonal, i.e., $d_{ij} = w_i$ if $i = j$ and $d_{ij} = 0$ otherwise. Given a weight-vector $w \in \mathbb{R}^n$, define

$$\bar{A}_G(w) \triangleq A_G + \text{diag}(w)$$

as the adjacency matrix whose main diagonal is set to the weights w. A probe vector $\mathcal{P}(w)$ is induced by $\ell \in \mathbb{R}^n$ if the following is satisfied:

$$\bar{A}_G(w) \cdot \ell = \mathcal{P}(w). \tag{1}$$

Observation 1. *For matrix* $\bar{A}_G(w)$, *we have*

$$\phi(0, \bar{A}_G(w)) = |V| - rank(\bar{A}_G(w)) .$$

Before we state the general result, we introduce two special cases. The *inclusive* case where $w = \mathbf{1}$ was analyzed by Bar-Noy et al. [4]. As a second important case, we identify the *exclusive* case where $w = \mathbf{0}$. Note that $\bar{A}_G(\mathbf{0}) = A_G$.

The next observation shows how eigenvalues can be shifted.

Observation 2. *If* $\lambda \in \Lambda(A)$, *then* $\lambda + a \in \Lambda(A + diag(a))$, *for* $a \in \mathbb{R}$.

Observation 3. *The multiplicities of the eigenvalues* -1 *and* 0 *in the matrix* A_G *are*

(i) $\phi(-1, A_G) = |V| - rank(\bar{A}_G)$.
(ii) $\phi(0, A_G) = |V| - rank(A_G)$.

Proof. If 0 is an eigenvalue of $\bar{A}_G$, then -1 is an eigenvalue of A_G, and the multiplicity is the same. Equations (i) and (ii) follow from Observation 1.   □

We now present the result for the general case.

Theorem 1. *Consider a graph G, weights w and a probe vector* $\mathcal{P}(w)$.

1. *If the matrix* $\bar{A}_G(w)$ *has full rank, i.e.,* $rank(\bar{A}_G(w)) = |V|$, *then* ℓ *can be uncovered in polynomial time without using any surgical probes.*

2. *Otherwise, the minimum number of surgical probes needed to uncover ℓ is $s = \phi(0, \bar{A}_G(w))$. Moreover, a set of s nodes whose surgical probes uncovers ℓ can be computed in polynomial time.*

The theorem follows readily from the proof presented by Bar-Noy et al. [4] for the inclusive case ($w = \mathbf{1}$). In their proof, the system of equations given by Equation (1) is analyzed. But there is no restriction on the coefficient matrix.

In the inclusive case, the rank of $\bar{A}_G(\mathbf{1})$ can be as low as one, e.g., consider $\text{rank}(\bar{A}_{K_n}(\mathbf{1})) = 1$, where K_n is the complete graph with n vertices. Hence, to solve WMSP a maximum number of $n - 1$ surgical probes is required. Similarly in the exclusive case, the rank of A_G can be as low as two (considering only graphs that have at least one edge). For example, $\text{rank}(A_{K_{n,m}}) = 2$, where $K_{n,m}$ is a complete bipartite graph. This is the lowest possible rank for a connected graph, since a connected graph must have at least two different open neighborhoods.

Observation 1 revealed a connection to spectral graph theory, which studies the eigenvalues of matrices related to graphs (cf. Godsil and Royle [16]). We denote the spectrum of a graph G as $(\lambda_1^{\phi(\lambda_1, A_G)}, \lambda_2^{\phi(\lambda_2, A_G)}, \ldots)$. It is known that the spectrum of K_n is $(n - 1, -1^{n-1})$ and that the spectrum of $K_{n,m}$ is $(\sqrt{mn}, -\sqrt{mn}, 0^{m+n-2})$.

Observation 4. *Consider weights $w \in \mathbb{R}^n$, $\bar{A}_{K_n}(w)$ and a probe vector $\mathcal{P}(w)$.*

  (i) *If $w = \vec{1}$, then WMSP can be solved with $n - 1$ surgical probes.*
 (ii) *If $w = -\overrightarrow{(n-1)}$, then WMSP can be solved with one surgical probe.*
(iii) *Otherwise, WMSP can be solved without any surgical probe.*

Observation 5. *Consider weights $w \in \mathbb{R}^{2n}$, $\bar{A}_{K_{n,n}}(w)$ and a probe vector $\mathcal{P}(w)$.*

  (i) *If $w = \mathbf{0}$, then WMSP can be solved with $n + n - 2$ surgical probes.*
 (ii) *If $w = \pm n$, then WMSP can be solved with one surgical probe.*
(iii) *Otherwise, WMSP can be solved without any surgical probe.*

The two observations follow readily with Observation 2 and Theorem 1. Note that each vertex in K_n has degree $n - 1$ and that each vertex in $K_{n,n}$ has degree n. Hence, for K_n and $K_{n,n}$, using $w = -\vec{\delta}(G)$ produces a matrix that can be considered an extreme case. This matrix is called the Laplacian and it plays a central role in the next section.

3 Number of Surgical Probes Depending on w

To solve WMSP, we consider a system of linear equations where the coefficient matrix is $\bar{A}_G(w)$ for a weight vector $w \in \mathbb{R}^n$. In this section, we study the number of required surgical probes depending on the vector w.

Observation 4 shows that the number of surgical probes can be as large as $n - 1$ (for an n vertex graph). Intuitively, a weight vector w where all entries are "sufficiently large" causes the matrix $\bar{A}_G(w)$ to have full rank. According to Theorem 1 WMSP can be solved without any surgical probes in this case. In what follows, we quantify "sufficiently large." Formally, given a graph G, we determine two weight vectors w_G^- and w_G^+ such that $\bar{A}_G(w)$ has full rank, if either $w < w_G^-$ or $w_G^+ < w$, where $w < w'$ means that $w_i < w'_i$ for every $i \in [1,n]$. Moreover, using weight w_G^- or w_G^+ requires at least one surgical probe.

We start with some notation. Matrix A is *positive semidefinite* (denoted $A \succeq 0$) if it is symmetric and $x^t A x \geq 0$ for all vectors $x \neq 0$. Matrix A is *positive definite* $(A \succ 0)$ if the inequality is strict. *Negative (semi-)definite* matrices are defined analogously.

Observation 6. *(i) A symmetric matrix A has only positive/non-negative eigenvalues if and only if A is positive definite/semidefinite.*
(ii) If matrix A is positive/negative definite, then A has full rank.

3.1 Negative Weights and the Laplacian Matrix

First, we consider weight vectors where all entries are negative. Here, the Laplacian matrix is crucial. The *Laplacian* matrix of a graph G is defined as follows:

$$L_G \triangleq -A_G + \operatorname{diag}(\vec{\delta}(G)) .$$

For our reconstruction problem, we consider the matrix

$$L_G^- \triangleq -L_G = A_G - \operatorname{diag}(\vec{\delta}(G)) .$$

Lemma 7. *Let G be a connected graph. Then*

(i) L_G^- is negative semidefinite,
(ii) $\phi(0, L_G^-) = 1$,
(iii) $x^t L_G^- x = 0$, for $x \neq 0$, if and only if $x = a \cdot (1^n)$, for $a \in \mathbb{R}_{\neq 0}$.

Proof. For any graph G, the Laplacian matrix L_G is positive semidefinite (cf. [16]). It follows that L_G^- is negative semidefinite, proving (i). Moreover, it is known that the multiplicity of the eigenvalue 0 of L_G is equal to the number of connected components of G. Since G is connected, $\phi(0, L_G) = 1$. The eigenvalue 0 has the same multiplicity for L_G as for L_G^-, implying (ii). To show (iii), observe that

$$\begin{aligned}
x^t L_G^- x &= x^t A_G x - x^t \operatorname{diag}(\vec{\delta}(G)) x \\
&= \sum_{(i,j) \in E} 2 x_i x_j - \sum_{i \in V} \vec{\delta}_i(G) x_i^2 \\
&= - \sum_{(i,j) \in E} (x_i - x_j)^2
\end{aligned}$$

Hence if $x = a \cdot \mathbf{1}$, for $a \in \mathbb{R}_{\neq 0}$, we get that $x^t L_G^- x = 0$ and $x \neq 0$. On the other hand, assume that $x^t L_G^- x = 0$, for $x \neq 0$. It follows that $x_i = x_j$ for each edge $(i, j) \in E$. Since G is connected, each pair of vertices is connected by a path and for each vertex i on this path $x_i = a$, for $a \in \mathbb{R}_{\neq 0}$. Hence $x_i = a$ for all $i \in [1, n]$, i.e., $x = a \cdot \mathbf{1}$. Since $x \neq 0$, $a \neq 0$. $\qquad\square$

The next theorem follows readily from the previous lemma and Theorem 1.

Theorem 2. *Let G be a connected graph. If $w = -\vec{\delta}(G)$, the induced labels ℓ can be uncovered with one surgical probe.*

We show that no surgical probes are needed below the threshold $-\vec{\delta}(G)$.

Theorem 3. *Let G be a connected graph and let ε be a vector such that $\varepsilon_i \geq 0$, for every $i \in [1, n]$ and there exists $i \in [1, n]$ such that $\varepsilon_i > 0$. Then, matrix $L_G^- - diag(\varepsilon)$ has full rank, i.e., if $w = -(\vec{\delta}(G) + \varepsilon)$, the labels ℓ can be uncovered without any surgical probes.*

Proof. We show that $x^t L_G^- x - x^t \text{diag}(\varepsilon) x < 0$, for every $x \neq 0$, i.e., that $L_G^- - \text{diag}(\varepsilon)$ is negative definite. Then, the theorem follows with Observation 6.

Let $x \neq 0$. We have two cases. First, assume that $x = a \cdot (1^n)$, for $a \in \mathbb{R}_{\neq 0}$. Due to Lemma 7, $x^t L_G^- x = 0$. Moreover, $x^t \text{diag}(\varepsilon) x = a^2 \cdot \sum_{i=1}^{n} \varepsilon_i > 0$. It follows that $x^t L_G^- x - x^t \text{diag}(\varepsilon) x < 0$. Next, assume that $x \neq a \cdot (1^n)$, for $a \in \mathbb{R}_{\neq 0}$. By Lemma 7, we have $x^t L_G^- x < 0$. Moreover, $x^t \text{diag}(\varepsilon) x = \sum_{i=1}^{n} x_i^2 \cdot \varepsilon_i \geq 0$. Consequently, $x^t L_G^- x - x^t \text{diag}(\varepsilon) x < 0$. $\qquad\square$

For disconnected graphs, the above theorems can be applied to each component.

3.2   Positive Weights and the Signless Laplacian

In this section, we consider weight vectors where all entries are positive. We use the following variant of L_G (or L_G^-) which is called the *Signless Laplacian* of G:

$$L_G^+ \triangleq A_G + \text{diag}(\vec{\delta}(G)),$$

for a graph G. As shown later, the matrix L_G^+ exhibits similar properties for positive weights as the matrix L_G^- did for negative weights. However, it makes a difference whether G is bipartite or not. The next theorem summarizes known properties of the signless Laplacian (see e.g. [7]).

Theorem 4. *For a graph G, the matrix L_G^+ is positive semidefinite. Moreover, $\phi(0, L_G^+)$ is equal to the number of G's bipartite components.*

Bipartite Graphs. Analogous results for positive weights only hold for bipartite graphs.

Lemma 8. *Let $G = (A \cup B, E)$ be a connected bipartite graph. Then*

(i) $\phi(0, L_G^+) = 1$,
(ii) $x^t L_G^+ x = 0$, *for $x \neq 0$, if and only if $x = a \cdot (1^{|A|}, -1^{|B|})$, for $a \in \mathbb{R}_{\neq 0}$.*

Proof. Item *(i)* follows with Theorem 4. To show *(ii)*, let $z = (1^{|A|}, -1^{|B|})$. Since G is bipartite, if $x = a \cdot z$, for $a \in \mathbb{R}_{\neq 0}$, we have that

$$x^t L_G^+ x = x^t A_G x + x^t \mathrm{diag}(\vec{\delta}(G)))x = a^2 \sum_{(i,j) \in E} (z_i + z_j)^2 = 0.$$

For the converse, assume that $x^t L_G^+ x = \sum_{(i,j) \in E} (x_i + x_j)^2 = 0$, for a vector $x \neq 0$. Let $i \in A$ and $j \in B$. If $(i, j) \in E$, then the contribution of this edge to the above sum is $(x_i + x_j)^2 = 0$. It follows that $x_j = -x_i$. Since G is connected, there is a path with an even number of edges connecting any two vertices in A. It follows that $x_i = x_{i'}$, if i and i' are on the same side of G. Hence $x = a \cdot z$, and $a \neq 0$ since $x \neq 0$. $\square$

Theorem 5. *Let G be a connected bipartite graph. If $w = \vec{\delta}(G)$, the induced labels ℓ can be uncovered with one surgical probe.*

Theorem 5 is a direct consequence of the previous lemma and Theorem 1. The next theorem shows that $\vec{\delta}(G)$ is the threshold weight vector w_G^+ for bipartite graphs.

Theorem 6. *Let $G = (A \cup B, E)$ be a connected, bipartite graph and let ε be a vector such that, for all $i \in [1, n]$, $\varepsilon_i \geq 0$ and there exists $i \in [1, n]$ such that $\varepsilon_i > 0$. Then, matrix $L_G^+ + \mathrm{diag}(\varepsilon)$ has full rank, i.e., if $w = \vec{\delta}(G) + \varepsilon$, the induced labels ℓ can be uncovered without any surgical probes.*

Proof. We show that $x^t L_G^+ x + x^t \mathrm{diag}(\varepsilon)x > 0$, for every $x \neq 0$, i. e., that $L_G^+ + \mathrm{diag}(\varepsilon)$ is positive definite. Then, the theorem follows with Observation 6.

Let $x \neq 0$. We split the proof into two cases. First, assume that $x = a \cdot (1^{|A|}, -1^{|B|})$, for $a \in \mathbb{R}_{\neq 0}$. Due to Lemma 8, $x^t L_G^+ x = 0$. Moreover, $x^t \mathrm{diag}(\varepsilon)x = \sum_{i=1}^{n} \varepsilon_i \cdot x_i^2 = a^2 \cdot \sum_{i=1}^{n} \varepsilon_i > 0$. It follows that $x^t L_G^+ x + x^t \mathrm{diag}(\varepsilon)x > 0$. In the second case $x \neq a \cdot (1^{|A|}, -1^{|B|})$, for $a \in \mathbb{R}_{\neq 0}$. Due to Theorem 4 and Lemma 8, we have that $x^t L_G^+ x > 0$. Moreover, $x^t \mathrm{diag}(\varepsilon)x = \sum_{i=1}^{n} \varepsilon_i \cdot x_i^2 \geq 0$. Consequently, $x^t L_G^- x + x^t \mathrm{diag}(\varepsilon)x > 0$. $\square$

Non-bipartite Graphs. Recall that $\bar{A}_{K_n}(1)$ has nullity $n - 1$, but $\bar{A}_{K_n}(1 + \varepsilon)$ has full rank, for a vector $\varepsilon > 0$. Hence, the threshold case for a complete graph is already attained for $w = 1$ whereas $\vec{\delta}(K_n) = n - 1$. For non-bipartite graphs, in general, smaller weight vectors than w_G^+ can cause $\bar{A}_G(w)$ to have full rank. The next lemma formalizes this insight. It follows readily from Theorem 4 and Observation 6.

Lemma 9. *If the graph G is connected and non-bipartite, then L_G^+ is positive definite.*

To reduce the weight vector of L_G^+ when G is not bipartite, we can shift the eigenvalues based on Observation 2. Let μ be the smallest eigenvalue of L_G^+ and let $S_G^+ = L_G^+ - \mu I_n$. It follows that $\lambda - \mu \in \Lambda(S_G^+)$ if $\lambda \in \Lambda(L_G^+)$. Since G is not bipartite, $\mu > 0$ and all eigenvalues of S_G^+ are non-negative. As S_G^+ is symmetric, Observation 6 implies that it is positive semidefinite.

Theorem 7. *Let $G = (V, E)$ be a graph and let ε be a vector such that $\varepsilon_i > 0$ for all $i \in [1, n]$. Then the matrix $S_G^+ + diag(\varepsilon)$ has full rank, i.e., if $w = \vec{\delta}(G) - \mu$, the induced labels ℓ can be uncovered without any surgical probes.*

The theorem follows with Observation 6: $diag(\varepsilon)$ is positive definite and for matrices $A \succeq 0$ and $B \succ 0$, we have that $A + B \succ 0$. Recall that the spectrum of K_n is $(n - 1, -1^{n-1})$. It follows that the spectrum of $L_{K_n}^+$ is $(2n - 2, (n - 2)^{n-1})$ and that the diagonal entries of $S_{K_n}^+$ are equal to 1, i.e., $S_{K_n}^+$ corresponds to the inclusive case for complete graphs.

The smallest eigenvalue μ of L_G^+ indicates whether G is bipartite or not. Connections between the "bipartiteness" and μ are studied in the literature (cf. [11–13, 19]). The intuition is that the larger μ is the further G is away from being bipartite.

In the full version of the paper, we provide additional material showing that semidefinite programming can be used to compute a non-negative weight vector that guarantees $\bar{A}_G(w)$ to be positive semidefinite.

4   Exclusive Probes vs Inclusive Probes

In this section, we study the exclusive case and compare it to the inclusive case, which was studied in [4]. We provide closed form results regarding the number of surgical probes needed for specific graphs. We consider mesh graphs, which are Cartesian products of simpler graphs. For example, grid graphs which were studied in previous papers on discrete tomography are Cartesian products of two path graphs. In addition we consider the Cartesian product of a path and a cycle (a tube) and two cycles (a torus); these results as well as an analysis on the number of surgical probes in trees are only contained in the full version of the paper.

Graph Products. We need the following definitions and notation from [6]. Given two graphs, $G_1 = (V_1, E_1)$ and $G_2 = (V_2, E_2)$, the *Cartesian product* of G_1 and G_2, denoted $G_1 \square G_2$, is the graph $G = (V, E)$, where $V = V_1 \times V_2$ and

$$E = \left\{ ((v, u), (v', u)) : (v, v') \in E_1 \right\} \cup \left\{ ((v, u), (v, u')) : (u, u') \in E_2 \right\} .$$

Given two square matrices A and B of respective sizes n and m, the *Kronecker product* and *Kronecker sum* of A and B are defined, respectively, as $A \otimes B \triangleq [a_{ij}B]$

and $A \oplus B \triangleq (A \otimes I_m) + (I_n \otimes B)$. The Kronecker sum of the adjacency matrices of two graphs is the adjacency matrix of the Cartesian product graph, i.e., $A_{G_1 \square G_2} = (A_{G_1} \otimes I_{|V_2|}) + (I_{|V_1|} \otimes A_{G_2})$. The Kronecker sum preserves eigenvalues of its summands in the following way.

Theorem 8 ([6]). *Let G_1 and G_2 be graphs. Then, the set of eigenvalues of $A_{G_1 \square G_2}$ is the Minkowski sum of the set of eigenvalues of A_{G_1} and the set of eigenvalues of A_{G_2}, i.e., it is $\Lambda(A_{G_1 \square G_2}) = \{\lambda + \mu \mid \lambda \in \Lambda(A_{G_1}), \mu \in \Lambda(A_{G_2})\}$.*

A grid graph is the Cartesian product of two path graphs (of lengths n_1 and n_2).

Theorem 9 ([4]). *Let G be a grid graph of size $n_1 \times n_2$. In the inclusive case,*

$$I_1^2(n_1)I_2^3(n_2) + I_2^3(n_1)I_1^2(n_2) + 2I_4^5(n_1)I_4^5(n_2)$$

surgical probes are necessary and sufficient to uncover ℓ. In particular, the number of surgical probes to uncover ℓ for grid graphs of any size is at most 4.

We continue with the exclusive case.

Theorem 10. *Let G be a grid graph of size $n_1 \times n_2$. In the exclusive case,*

$$gcd(n_1 + 1, n_2 + 1) - 1$$

surgical probes are necessary and sufficient to uncover ℓ.

Proof. Let G be a grid graph which is the Cartesian product of the two path graphs P_1 and P_2, of length n_1 and n_2, resp. By Observation 3, we look for eigenvalues of A_G that are 0. By Theorem 8, we need to identify eigenvalues of A_{P_1} and A_{P_2} that add up to 0. The eigenvalues of A_P where P is a path of length n are given by $2\cos(\frac{\pi j}{n+1})$, for $j \in [1, n]$ (cf. [6]). Hence, we are looking for the number of solutions to the following equation:

$$2\cos\left(\frac{i}{n_1+1} \cdot \pi\right) + 2\cos\left(\frac{j}{n_2+1} \cdot \pi\right) = 0, \tag{2}$$

for $i \in [1, n_1], j \in [1, n_2]$. By an elementary trigonometric identity (2) is equivalent to

$$\cos\left(\frac{\pi}{2}\left(\frac{i}{n_1+1} + \frac{j}{n_2+1}\right)\right)\cos\left(\frac{\pi}{2}\left(\frac{i}{n_1+1} - \frac{j}{n_2+1}\right)\right) = 0. \tag{3}$$

One of the factors has to be zero. We have $0 < \frac{i}{n_1+1}, \frac{j}{n_2+1} < 1$. Thus, $0 < \frac{i}{n_1+1} + \frac{j}{n_2+1} < 2$ and $-1 < \frac{i}{n_1+1} - \frac{j}{n_2+1} < 1$. In these ranges, $\cos(\frac{\pi}{2}x)$ evaluates to zero if $x = 1$. Only the additive part can yield a solutions to (3). These are determined by $\frac{i}{n_1+1} + \frac{j}{n_2+1} = 1$. If $n_1 + 1$ and $n_2 + 1$ are co-prime, i.e., $gcd(n_1 + 1, n_2 + 1) = 1$, no combination of values for the i's and j's can add up to 1.

Otherwise, if $gcd(n_1 + 1, n_2 + 1) = a \neq 1$, let $n_1 + 1 = ab_1$ and $n_2 + 1 = ab_2$, where b_1 and b_2 are co-prime. Then, we have

$$\frac{i}{ab_1} + \frac{j}{ab_2} = 1. \tag{4}$$

Here, i takes the values $b_1, 2b_1, \ldots, (a-1)b_1$ and j takes the values $b_2, 2b_2, \ldots, (a-1)b_2$. Only multiples of b_1 and b_2 for values of i and j can satisfy (4), respectively. For each of these values of i there is a matching value of j that together add up to 1, e.g., $\frac{b_1}{ab_1} + \frac{(a-1)b_2}{ab_2} = 1$. Consequently, we get $(a-1)$ solutions to (2). $\qquad \square$

Theorem 11. *Let P be a path with n vertices, where $V = \{1, \ldots, n\}$. In the exclusive case, if n is odd, then a single surgical probe is needed, and it should be at a node i such that i is even. Otherwise, no surgical probes are needed. In both cases, the labels can be discovered in $O(n)$ time.*

Proof. The number of surgical probes follows from Theorem 10. To discover the labels along the path, we use the following procedures. If n is even, then start with $\ell_2 = p_1$. Iteratively, ℓ_{2i}, for $i = 2, \ldots, \frac{n}{2}$, can be discovered using $f_{2i-1} - \ell_{2i-2} = \ell_{2i}$. The odd labels can be discovered similarly from right to left. If n is odd, then even labels can be discovered as above. Probing any even i would result in discovering the rest of the even labels. See example in Fig. 2. $\square$

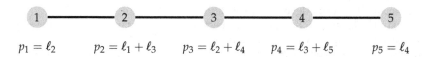

Fig. 2. A path of length $n = 5$. In the inclusive case, one surgical probe is needed, but not at $i = 3$. In the exclusive case, one surgical probe is needed in an odd location.

5   Future Directions

In our model, surgical probes have identical costs at each vertex. However, it is conceivable that parts of a specimen might be less accessible and therefore more expensive to probe surgically. It might be interesting to study a variation where a surgical probe at vertex i implies costs c_i, and the goal is to uncover the labels at minimum total costs.

Furthermore, considering directed graphs leads to a type of probes that are not symmetric. However, this implies that the adjacency matrix is no longer symmetric and Observation 3 does not longer hold (see example on page 3 of [6]). Moreover, the theory of definite matrices breaks.

Another direction is to consider additional constraints on the label vector ℓ. For example, the labels might satisfy box-constraints of the form $a_i \leq \ell_i \leq b_i$

for each vertex i. Consider the inclusive case based on K_n where labels must be non-negative. Theorem 1 says that we require $n - 1$ surgical probes. However, if there are probes $\mathcal{P}_i = 0$, then $\ell_j = 0$ for all $j \in N[i]$. Variations where the labels are integer or binary values are most likely NP-hard as the work by Gritzmann et al. [17] suggests. Yet, our results provide an upper bound on the number of required surgical probes in such cases.

References

1. Alpers, A., Gritzmann, P.: Reconstructing binary matrices under window constraints from their row and column sums. Fundamenta Informaticae 155(4), 321–340 (2017)
2. Alpers, A., Gritzmann, P.: Dynamic discrete tomography. Inv. Prob. 34(3), 034003 (2018)
3. Alpers, A., Gritzmann, P.: On double-resolution imaging and discrete tomography. SIAM J. Discrete Math. 32(2), 1369–1399 (2018)
4. Bar-Noy, A., Böhnlein, T., Lotker, Z., Peleg, D., Rawitz, D.: The generalized microscopic image reconstruction problem. In: 30th ISAAC, pp. 42:1–42:15 (2019)
5. Battaglino, D., Frosini, A., Rinaldi, S.: A decomposition theorem for homogeneous sets with respect to diamond probes. Comp. Vis. Image Underst. 117(4), 319–325 (2013)
6. Brouwer, A.E., Haemers, W.H.: Spectra of Graphs. Springer, New York (2011)
7. Cvetković, D., Rowlinson, P., Simić, S.K.: Signless Laplacians of finite graphs. Linear Algebra Appl. 423(1), 155–171 (2007)
8. Cvetković, D., Simić, S.K.: Towards a spectral theory of graphs based on the signless Laplacian. I. Publications de l'Institut Mathematique 85(99), 19–33 (2009)
9. Cvetković, D., Simić, S.K.: Towards a spectral theory of graphs based on the signless Laplacian. II. Linear Algebra Appl. 432(9), 2257–2272 (2010)
10. Cvetković, D., Simić, S.K.: Towards a spectral theory of graphs based on the signless Laplacian. III. Appl. Anal. Discrete Math. 156–166 (2010)
11. de Lima, L.S., Oliveira, C.S., de Abreu, N.M.M., Nikiforov, V.: The smallest eigenvalue of the signless Laplacian. Linear Algebra Appl. 435(10), 2570–2584 (2011)
12. Desai, M., Rao, V.: A characterization of the smallest eigenvalue of a graph. J. Graph Theory 18(2), 181–194 (1994)
13. Fallat, S., Fan, Y.-Z.: Bipartiteness and the least eigenvalue of signless Laplacian of graphs. Linear Algebra Appl. 436(9), 3254–3267 (2012)
14. Frosini, A., Nivat, M.: Binary matrices under the microscope: a tomographical problem. Theor. Comput. Sci. 370(1–3), 201–217 (2007)
15. Frosini, A., Nivat, M., Rinaldi, S.: Scanning integer matrices by means of two rectangular windows. Theoretical Comput. Sci. 406(1–2), 90–96 (2008)
16. Godsil, C., Royle, G.F.: Algebraic Graph Theory. Springer Science & Business Media, New York (2013)
17. Gritzmann, P., Langfeld, B., Wiegelmann, M.: Uniqueness in discrete tomography: three remarks and a corollary. SIAM J. Discrete Math. 25(4), 1589–1599 (2011)
18. Herman, G.T., Kuba, A.: Discrete Tomography: Foundations, Algorithms, and Applications. Springer Science & Business Media, New York (2012)
19. Kirkland, S., Paul, D.: Bipartite subgraphs and the signless Laplacian matrix. Appl. Anal. Discrete Math. 1–13 (2011)
20. Nivat, M.: Sous-ensembles homogénes de z2 et pavages du plan. Comptes Rendus Mathematique 335(1), 83–86 (2002)

Foundations of Computer Science – Short Papers

A Normal Sequence Compressed by PPM* But Not by Lempel-Ziv 78

Liam Jordon$^{(\boxtimes)}$ and Philippe Moser

Department of Computer Science, Maynooth University,
Maynooth, Co Kildare, Ireland
{liam.jordon,philippe.moser}@mu.ie

Abstract. This paper compares the difference in performance of the Prediction by Partial Matching family of compressors (PPM* and the original PPM$_k$) and the Lempel-Ziv 78 (LZ) algorithm. We construct an infinite binary sequence whose worst-case compression ratio for PPM* is 0, while PPM$_k$'s and LZ's best-case compression ratios are at least $1/2$ and 1 respectively. This sequence is normal and is an enumeration of all binary strings in order of length, i.e. all strings of length 1 followed by all strings of length 2 and so on. The sequence is built using repetitions of de Bruijn strings of increasing order.

Keywords: Lempel-Ziv · Prediction by Partial Matching · Normality

1 Introduction

A *normal* number in base 2, as defined by Borel [5], is a real number whose infinite binary expansion in that base is such that for all block lengths n, every binary string of length n occurs as a substring in the binary expansion with limiting frequency 2^{-n}.

A common question studied about normal sequences is whether or not they are compressible by certain families of compressors. Results by Schnorr and Stimm [17] and Dai, Lathrop, Lutz and Mayordomo [10] demonstrate that loss-less finite-state transducers (FSTs) cannot compress a sequence if and only if the sequence is normal (see [2] for a proof). Becher, Carton and Heiber [1] have examined the compression of normal sequences in various scenarios such as when FSTs have access to one or more counters or a stack, and what happens when the transducer is not required to run in real-time nor be deterministic. Carton and Heiber [7] showed that deterministic and non-deterministic two-way FSTs cannot compress normal sequences. Among other compression algorithms, Lathrop and Strauss [13] have shown that there exists a normal sequence such that the Lempel-Ziv 78 (LZ) algorithm can compress.

Supported by the Government of Ireland Postgraduate Scholarship Programme managed by the Irish Research Council.

© Springer Nature Switzerland AG 2021
T. Bureš et al. (Eds.): SOFSEM 2021, LNCS 12607, pp. 389–399, 2021.
https://doi.org/10.1007/978-3-030-67731-2_28

This paper focuses on the performance of the Prediction by Partial Matching (PPM) compression algorithm introduced by Cleary and Witten [9]. PPM works by building a model of its input as it reads each bit. The model keeps track of previously seen substrings of the input, known as *contexts*, and the bits that follow them. The model uses these contexts to encode the bit being read based on its frequency counts in the relevant contexts. The model is updated after each bit is encoded. This involves updating the frequency counts of the seen bit in the relevant contexts and, if needed, adding new contexts to the model. These prediction probabilities are used to encode the sequence via arithmetic encoding [18].

In the original PPM algorithm, prior to reading the input, a value $k \in \mathbb{N}$ must be provided which sets the maximum length of a context the model can store. This version of the algorithm with bound k is denoted by PPM_k. The PPM* algorithm was introduced later and sets no upper bound on the length of contexts the model can keep track of [8].

We continue the study of the performance of compressors on normal sequences by constructing a normal sequence S and compare how it is compressed by PPM*, PPM_k and LZ. PPM* can compress S with a worst-case compression ratio of 0. We also show that no matter what upper bound for k chosen, PPM_k's best-case compression ratio is at least $1/2$. Also, LZ has a best-case compression ratio of 1 on S, i.e. S cannot be compressed by LZ.

S is constructed such that it is an enumeration of all binary strings in order of length, i.e. all strings of length 1 followed by all strings of length 2 and so on. The order is which the strings are listed is chosen using de Bruijn strings to maximise repetitions of substrings. PPM* can exploit these repetitions to compress the sequence. However, such sequences cannot be compressed by LZ, which in turn means they cannot be compressed by any FST [19], i.e. S is normal.

Some proofs are omitted due to space constraints.

2   Preliminaries

$\mathbb{N}$ denotes the set of non-negative integers. In the following we let $n \in \mathbb{N}$. A *string* is an element of $\{0,1\}^*$. A *sequence* is an element of $\{0,1\}^\omega$. The length of a string x is denoted by $|x|$. λ denotes the empty string, i.e. the string of length 0. $\{0,1\}^n$ denotes the set of strings of length n. For a string (or sequence) x and $i,j \in \{0,1,\ldots,|x|-1\}$ with $i \leq j$, $x[i..j]$ denotes the ith through j^{th} bits of x with the convention that if $j < i$ then $x[i..j] = \lambda$. Similarly $x[i]$ denotes the ith bit of x. For a string x and string (sequence) y, xy (occasionally denoted by $x \cdot y$) denotes the string (sequence) of x concatenated with y. For a string x, x^n denotes x concatenated with itself n times. For strings x,y and string (sequence) z, if $w = xyz$, we say y is a *substring* of w, x is a *prefix* of w, and if z is a string, then z is a *suffix* of w. The *lexicographic* ordering of $\{0,1\}^*$ is defined by saying for two strings x,y, x is less than y if either $|x| < |y|$ or else $|x| = |y|$ with $x[n] = 0$ and $y[n] = 1$ for the smallest n such that $x[n] \neq y[n]$.

Given a sequence S and a function $T : \{0,1\}^* \to \{0,1\}^*$, the *best-case* and *worst-case compression ratios* of T on S are respectively given by

$$\rho_T(S) = \liminf_{n \to \infty} \frac{|T(S[0..n-1])|}{n} \text{ and, } R_T(S) = \limsup_{n \to \infty} \frac{|T(S[0..n-1])|}{n}.$$

Given strings x, w we use the following notation to count the number of times w occurs as a substring in x. The number of occurrences of w as a substring of x is given by

$$\operatorname{occ}(w, x) = |\{u \in \{0,1\}^* : uw = x[0..|uw| - 1]\}|.$$

The block number of occurrences of w as a substring of x is given by

$$\operatorname{occ}_b(w, x) = |\{i : x[i..i + |w| - 1] = w, i \equiv 0 \mod |w|\}|.$$

A sequence S is said to be *normal* [5] if for all $w \in \{0,1\}^*$, w occurs as a substring of S with asymptotic frequency $2^{-|w|}$.

We say that a sequence S is an *enumeration of all strings* if S can be broken into substrings $S = S_1 S_2 S_3 \ldots$, such that for each n, S_n is a concatenation of all strings of length n with each string occurring once. That is, for all $w \in \{0,1\}^n, \operatorname{occ}_b(w, S_n) = 1$. Note in such instances, $|S_n| = n2^n$.

3   Description of the PPM Algorithms

We first acknowledge that implementations of the PPM algorithm family implement what is known as the *exclusion principle* to achieve better compression ratios. We ignore this in our implementation for simplicity as even without this, the sequence we build below achieves a compression ratio of 0 via PPM*.

3.1   PPM$_k$

In the original presentation of PPM [9], a bounded version is introduced. Prior to encoding, a value $k \in \mathbb{N}$ must be provided to the encoder which sets the maximum *context* length the model can store. We refer to this version of PPM with bound k as PPM$_k$. By context, we mean previously seen substrings of the input stream contained in the model. For each context, the model records what bits have followed the context in the input stream, and the frequency each bit has occurred. These frequencies are used to build *prediction probabilities* that the encoder uses to encode the rest of the input stream. When reading the next bit of the input stream, the encoder examines the longest *relevant* context each time and encodes the current bit based on its current prediction probability in that context. By relevant context, we mean suffixes of the input stream already read by the encoder that are contained in the model. The longest relevant context available is referred to as the *current* context as it is the one the model uses to first encode the next bit seen. Once encoded, the model is updated to include new contexts if necessary, and to update the prediction probabilities of the relevant contexts to reflect the bit that has just been read.

When a bit being encoded has never occurred previously in the current context an *escape* symbol (denoted by \$) is transmitted and the next shortest relevant context becomes the new current context. If the bit has not been seen before even when the current context is λ, that is, the context where none of the previous bits are used to predict the next bit, an escape is outputted and the bit is assigned the prediction probability from the order-(-1) table. By convention, this table contains all bits in the alphabet being used and assigns each bit equal probability.

This paper uses *Method C* proposed by Moffat [15] to assign probabilities to \$ in each context. Here, \$ is given a frequency equal to the number of distinct bits predicted in the context so far. Hence in our case it will always have a count of 1 or 2.

3.2   PPM*

Like PPM_k, PPM* builds a model of contexts of its input, continuously updates the model, and encodes each bit it sees based on its frequency probability in the current context. The key difference is that there is no upper bound on the max context length stored in the model. Instead of building a context for every substring seen, a context is only extended until it is unique. Suppose PPM* has read the string x. Then for any string w with $occ(w, x) \geq 2$, the context wb must be built in the model for each b such that $occ(wb, x) \geq 1$. When examining all relevant contexts, unlike PPM_k which chooses the longest context available to be the first current context to encode the next bit, PPM* chooses the shortest *deterministic* context available. Here, a context is said to be *deterministic* if \$ has a frequency of 1. If no such context exists, the longest is chosen. We also use the *Method C* approach to compute \$ probabilities for PPM*.

The following is a full example of a model being updated. Suppose an input stream of $s = 0100110110$ has already been read. The model for this is seen in Table 1. Say the next bit read is a 0. The relevant contexts are the $\lambda, 0, 10, 110$ and 0110. The shortest deterministic context is 110. It does not predict a 0 so \$ is transmitted with probability $1/2$ and then 0 is transmitted from the context 10 with probability $1/4$. The model is then updated as follows. λ, 0 and 10 all predict a 0, so their counts are updated. 0 is added as a prediction to 110 and 0110. Furthermore, the substrings 00 and 100 are not unique in $s0$ while they were in just s. That is $occ(00, s0) \neq 1$ and $occ(100, s0) \neq 1$ while $occ(00, s) = occ(100, s) = 1$. These contexts must be extended to create new contexts 001 and 1001. This is because 1 is what follows 00 and 100 in s. These contexts both predict 1. If another 0 is read after $s0$, since both a 0 and 1 now have been seen to follow 110 and 0110, contexts for 1100 and 01100 will be created both predicting a 0, since a context has to be made for each branching path of 110 and 0110 (1101 and 01101 already exist).

3.3   Arithmetic Encoding

PPM's final output is found via arithmetic encoding [3,18]. Beginning with the interval $[0,1)$, at each stage of the encoding the interval is split into subintervals of lengths corresponding to the probabilities of the current context being examined. The subinterval corresponding to the bit or $ transmitted is then carried forward to the next stage. Once the final bit of the input is encoded, a number $c \in [a,b)$ is transmitted, where $[a,b)$ is the final interval. Note that c can be encoded in $-\lceil \log(|b-a|) \rceil$ bits. With c and the length of the original sequence to be encoded, the original sequence can be recovered.

Table 1. PPM* model for the input 0100110110

ctxt	pred	cnt	pb	ctxt	pred	cnt	pb	ctxt	pred	cnt	pb
Order $k = 5$				101	1	1	$\frac{1}{2}$	Order $k = 1$			
01101	1	1	$\frac{1}{2}$	$	1	1	$\frac{1}{2}$	0	0	1	$\frac{1}{6}$
$	1	1	$\frac{1}{2}$	110	1	1	$\frac{1}{2}$		1	3	$\frac{1}{2}$
Order $k = 4$				$	1	1	$\frac{1}{2}$		$	2	$\frac{1}{3}$
0110	1	1	$\frac{1}{2}$	Order $k = 2$				1	0	3	$\frac{3}{7}$
$	1	1	$\frac{1}{2}$	00	1	1	$\frac{1}{2}$		1	2	$\frac{2}{7}$
1101	1	1	$\frac{1}{2}$	$	1	1	$\frac{1}{2}$		$	2	$\frac{2}{7}$
$	1	1	$\frac{1}{2}$	01	0	1	$\frac{1}{5}$	Order $k = 0$			
Order $k = 3$					1	2	$\frac{2}{5}$	λ	0	5	$\frac{5}{12}$
010	0	1	$\frac{1}{2}$		$	2	$\frac{2}{5}$		1	5	$\frac{5}{12}$
$	1	1	$\frac{1}{2}$	10	0	1	$\frac{1}{4}$		$	2	$\frac{1}{6}$
011	0	2	$\frac{2}{3}$		1	1	$\frac{1}{4}$	Order $k = -1$			
$	1	1	$\frac{1}{3}$		$	2	$\frac{1}{2}$		0	1	$\frac{1}{2}$
100	1	1	$\frac{1}{2}$	11	0	2	$\frac{2}{3}$		1	1	$\frac{1}{2}$
$	1	1	$\frac{1}{2}$		$	1	$\frac{1}{3}$				

For simplicity, we assume the encoder can calculate the endpoints of the intervals with infinite precision. In reality, a fixed finite limit precision is used to represent the intervals and their endpoints and a process known as *renormalisation* occurs to prevent the intervals becoming too small to handle.

4   An Analysis of PPM*

In this section we build a sequence S that is an enumeration of all strings such that $R_{\text{PPM}^*}(S) = 0$.

4.1   de Bruijn Strings

For $n \in \mathbb{N}$, a de Bruijn string of order n is a string of length 2^n that when viewed cyclically, contains all binary strings of length n exactly once [6]. That is, for a de Bruijn string x of order n, for all $w \in \{0,1\}^n$, $occ(w, x \cdot x[0..n-2]) = 1$. For example, 00011101 and 00010111 are the de Bruijn strings of order 3.

We write $db(n)$ to denote the least lexicographic de Bruijn string of order n. Martin [14] provided the following algorithm to build this string: Write the string $x = 1^{n-1}$. While possible, append a bit (with 0 taking priority over 1) to the end of x so that substrings of length n occur only once in x. When this is no longer possible [1], remove the prefix 1^{n-1} from x. The resulting string is $db(n)$.

Remark 1. For $n \geq 3$, $db(n)[0..2n] = 0^n 10^{n-2} 11$ and $db(n)$ has 1^n as a suffix.

The first property is clear when constructing the sequence. The second property is proven by Martin when showing when his algorithm terminates.

For $0 \leq i < 2^n$, let $db_i(n)$ denote the left shift of $db(n)$ by i bits, i.e. $db_i(n) = db(n)[i..2^n - 1] \cdot db(n)[0..i-1]$. We write $db(n)$ instead of $db_0(n)$ when no shift occurs. $db_i^j(n)$ denotes $db_i(n)$ concatenated with itself j times.

4.2   Construction and Properties of S

The sequence $S = S_1 S_2 S_3 \dots$ is built such that each S_n zone is a concatenation of all strings of length n and maximises repetitions to exploit PPM*. Maximising repetitions ensures deterministic contexts are repeatedly used to predict bits in the sequence, thus resulting in compression.

For every $n \in \mathbb{N}$, n can be written in the form $n = 2^s t$, where $s, t \in \mathbb{N}$ and t is odd. We set $S_n = B_{n,0} \cdot B_{n,1} \cdots B_{n,2^s-1}$, where $B_{n,i} = db_i^t(n)$. Each $B_{n,i}$ is called the ith *block* of S_n. Note that if n is odd then $S_n = db^n(n)$, and if n is a power of 2 then $S_n = db(n) \cdot db_1(n) \cdots db_{n-1}(n)$. For example, $S_6 = db^3(6) \cdot db_1^3(6)$.

The following lemma states that S is an enumeration of all strings.

Lemma 1. *For each $n \in \mathbb{N}$, for $w \in \{0,1\}^n$, $occ_b(w, S_n) = 1$.*

Henceforth, we write $\overline{S_n}$ to denote $S_1 \cdots S_n$. Suppose the encoder has already processed $\overline{S_{n-1}}$. While the encoder's model may contain contexts of length n at this stage, the following lemma shows it will contain all possible contexts of length n after reading the first $2^n + n$ bits of S_n. The idea is that in the first $2^n + n - 1$ bits of S_n, for each $x \in \{0,1\}^{n-1}$, x occurs at least twice, and $x0$ and $x1$ occur once. Hence a context for each branching path of x must be created, i.e. contexts for $x0$ and $x1$.

Lemma 2. *Let $n \geq 2$. Once the prefix $\overline{S_{n-1}} S_n[0..2^n + n - 1]$ is processed, the encoder will contain a context for all $x \in \{0,1\}^n$.*

---

[1] Martin proves that this occurs when $|x| = 2^n + n - 1$.

For each S_n, its first $2^n + 2n$ bits are referred to as the *bad zone*. This is the section of the string where contexts often incorrectly predict bits, requiring a $ be transmitted which results in a longer output. This is the section of the string where deterministic contexts are built which will successfully predict the remaining bits of S_n.

The following lemma bounds the maximum number of bits used to encode any singular bit within an S_n zone. The proof requires a counting argument examining how many times a substring of length n and $n - 1$ occurs in $\overline{S_n}$.

Lemma 3. *For all but finitely many n, if $\overline{S_{n-1}}$ has already been read, each bit in S_n contributes at most $5\log(n)$ bits to the encoding of S.*

With Lemma 3 and knowing the size of the *bad zone*, this allows us to bound the number of bits contributed by the bad zone of S_n.

Corollary 1. *For all but finitely many n, if $\overline{S_{n-1}}$ has already been read, the bad zone of S_n contributes at most $5(2^n + 2n)\log(n)$ bits to the encoding of S.*

4.3   Main Result

In this section we prove our main result that $R_{\mathrm{PPM}^*}(S) = 0$. This compression is achieved from the repetition of the de Bruijn strings which lead to the repeated use of deterministic contexts which correctly make predictions on the encoded bit. When deterministic contexts are used, correct predictions are performed with probability $\frac{k}{k+1}$, for some $k \in \mathbb{N}$. Note that as k increases, the number of bits contributed to the encoding $(-\log(\frac{k}{k+1}))$ approaches 0.

The following lemma shows that deterministic contexts correctly predict every bit outside of the *bad zone* for infinitely many S_n zones.

Lemma 4. *For all but finitely many n, whenever n is odd or $n = 2^j$ for some j, all bits not in the bad zone of S_n are correctly predicted by deterministic contexts.*

For n-even but not a power of 2, Lemma 4 does not hold. While most bits are predicted by deterministic contexts, the shifts of the de Bruijn strings between blocks $B_{n,0}$ and $B_{n,1}$ mean that some contexts which may have been deterministic in $B_{n,0}$, soon see the opposite bit due to a shift. Consider context $1^6 0^5$. We have that $\mathrm{occ}(1^6 0^5, \overline{S_5}) = 0$, but it does occur in S_6 multiple times. The first two times it occurs it sees a 0 (as $db(6)[2^6 - 6..2^6 - 1] \cdot db(6)[0..5] = 1^6 0^6$) by Remark 1). The third time it sees a 1 due to the shift in $B_{6,1}$ (as $db(6)[2^6 - 6..2^6 - 1] \cdot db_1(6)[0..5] = 1^6 0^5 1$). Hence, $1^6 0^5$ is no longer deterministic.

The following result bounds the number of bits each S_n zone contributes to the encoding. Here $|\mathrm{PPM}^*(S_n|\overline{S_{n-1}})|$ represents the number of bits contributed to the output by S_n if the encoder has already processed $\overline{S_{n-1}}$.

Theorem 1. *For all but finitely many n,*

$$|\mathrm{PPM}^*(S_n \,|\, \overline{S_{n-1}})| \leq 5(2^n + 2n + n^2)\log(n) + \log((n - 1)^n n^{2^{n+1}}).$$

Proof. By Lemma 4, every bit outside the *bad zone* is predicted correctly by a deterministic context in S_n for all but finitely many n where n is odd or when n is a power or 2. This is not true for the remaining n as mentioned in the discussion preceding this theorem. As such, the output contributed by the case where n is even but not a power of 2 acts as an upper bound for all n.

In this case, $n = 2^s t$, for $s, t, \in \mathbb{N}$, where t is odd. Recall that $S_n = B_0 \cdot B_1 \cdots B_{2^s-1}$ where $B_i = db_i^t(n)$. Let $b_n = 2^s$, the number of blocks in S_n. Unlike in the other two cases where all contexts used to encode remained deterministic during the encoding of S_n after the *bad zone* by Lemma 4, in this case some contexts do not due to the shifts that occur within each block. If there are b_n blocks, there are $b_n - 1$ shifts. However, we can pinpoint which bits are predicted by deterministic contexts.

Following the *bad zone*, a 1 is deterministically correctly predicted by the context $010^{n-2}1$ with probability at least $1/2$. This is because $\mathrm{occ}(010^{n-2}1, \overline{S_{n-1}}) = 0$ as the only place the string 10^{n-2} occurs is in S_{n-1} where it would be preceded by 1^{n-2} and not a 0, in S_{n-2} where it would be preceded by 1^{n-3} and not a 0, or along a straddle between two prior S_i's for $i \leq n-1$, where it would be preceded by a 1 and not a 0. Hence, $010^{n-2}1$ first appears in $S_n[0..2^n - 1] = db(n)$ where it is followed by a 1 (by Remark 1), and so is deterministic.

The succeeding $2^n - n - 2$ bits are also predicted by a deterministic contexts successfully throughout the process. This is because these contexts are suffixes of extensions of $010^{n-2}1$ and see the same bits within S_n. The next time $010^{n-2}1$ is seen it predicts a 1 with probability at least $2/3$ and so on. When $010^{n-2}1$ is seen for the nth time, there are only $2^n - 2n + b_n - 1$ bits left to encode as the encoder has *fallen behind* by $b_n - 1$ bits due to the $b_n - 1$ shifts that occur. These bits are encoded with probability at least $\frac{n-1}{n}$. Excluding the *bad zone* we have accounted for $2^n n - 2^n - n^2 - n + 1 + b_n$ bits. Using that $b_n < 2^n$, these bits are encoded in at most

$$- \log\left(\left(\prod_{i=2}^{n-1} \left(\frac{i-1}{i}\right)^{2^n-n-1}\right)\left(\frac{n-1}{n}\right)^{2^n-2n+b_n-1}\right) < \log((n-1)^n n^{2^{n+1}})\dagger$$

bits.

Including the $n^2 - n - 1 - b_n$ bits not accounted for which may be impacted by the shifts that occur between blocks, by $\dagger$, Lemma 3 and Corollary 1, one can derive the desired upper bound. □

We now prove the main theorem.

Theorem 2. $R_{\mathrm{PPM}^*}(S) = 0$.

Proof. Note that the worst compression of S is achieved if the input ends with a complete bad zone, i.e. for a prefix of the form $S_n^* = \overline{S_{n-1}} S_n[0..2^n + 2n - 1]$.

Let k be such that Theorem 1 holds for all zones S_i with $i \geq k$. The prefix $\overline{S_{k-1}}$ will always be encoded in $O(1)$ bits. Hence, from the fact that

$$|\text{PPM}^*(S_n^*)| \leq 5 \sum_{j=k}^{n-1} ((2^j + 2j + j^2) \log(j) + \log((j-1)^j j^{2^{j+1}}))$$
$$+ 5(2^n + 2n) \log(n) + O(1)$$

and that the overhead contributes at most one bit, it follows that $R_{\text{PPM}^*(S)} = 0$. $\qquad\square$

4.4 Comparison with PPM$_k$

A crude counting argument shows that for any sequence S which is an enumeration of all strings, for all $k \in \mathbb{N}$, PPM$_k$'s best-case compression ratio is at least $1/2$ on S. For $n \geq k$, each context $x \in \{0,1\}^k$ predicts the same number of 0s and 1s in an S_n zone. Suppose $\text{occ}(x, S_n) = t$. The fewest amount any bit can contribute in S_n is if the first $t/2$ times x is seen it sees the same bit. The final time this bit is seen contributes the fewest amount of bits to the encoding, and if this amount is used as a lower bound for every bit in S_n, the lower bound of $1/2$ is achieved. Taking S from Theorem 2 gives the following result.[2]

Theorem 3. *There exists a sequence S which is an enumeration of all binary strings such that $R_{\text{PPM}^*}(S) = 0$ but for all $k \in \mathbb{N}$, $\rho_{\text{PPM}_k}(S) > \frac{1}{2}$.*

4.5 Comparison with Lempel-Ziv 78

The Lempel-Ziv 78 (LZ) algorithm [19] is a lossless dictionary based compression algorithm. On input x, LZ parses x into phrases $x = x_1 x_2 \ldots x_n$ such that each phrase x_i is unique in the parsing, except for maybe the last phrase, where for each phrase x_i, every prefix of x_i also appears as a phrase in the parsing. LZ encodes x by encoding each phrase as a pointer to its dictionary containing the longest proper prefix of the phrase along with the final bit of the phrase.

Sequences that are enumerations of all strings are incompressible by the LZ algorithm. As such, taking S from Theorem 2, S satisfies the following theorem.

Theorem 4. *There exists a normal sequence S such that $R_{\text{PPM}^*}(S) = 0$, and $\rho_{LZ}(S) = 1$.*

5 Remarks

Our argument for Theorem 1 relies on the string $1^n 0^n 1 0^{n-2} 1$ being a substring of $db(n)$ (when viewed cyclically), i.e $db(n)$ has prefix $0^n 1 0^{n-2} 1$ and suffix 1^n.

---

[2] We note that post submission, we developed a proof that for all k, $\rho_{\text{PPM}_k}(S) = 1$ for any normal S. This will appear in a later journal version.

Hence, any de Bruijn string satisfying this may be used to construct S_n and so an infinite family of sequences satisfy Theorem 4. We plan on extending these results to anu base k. Bounded and unbounded versions of PPM suggests the possibility to develop a notion of Bennett's logical depth [4] based on these algorithms. Depth notions based on compressors and transducers have already been introduced in [11,12].

We note that post submission we discovered that the construction we used to build S was used by Pierce and Shields in [16] to build binary sequences that are incompressible by LZ.

References

1. Becher, V., Carton, O., Heiber, P.A.: Normality and automata. J. Comput. Syst. Sci. **81**(8), 1592–1613 (2015). https://doi.org/10.1016/j.jcss.2015.04.007
2. Becher, V., Heiber, P.A.: Normal numbers and finite automata. Theor. Comput. Sci. **477**, 109–116 (2013). https://doi.org/10.1016/j.tcs.2013.01.019
3. Bell, T.C., Cleary, J.G., Witten, I.H.: Text Compression. Prentice-Hall Inc., Upper Saddle River, NJ, USA (1990)
4. Bennett, C.H.: Logical depth and physical complexity. The Universal Turing Machine, A Half-Century Survey, pp. 227–257 (1988)
5. Émile Borel, M.: Les probabilités dénombrables et leurs applications arithmétiques. Rendiconti del Circolo Matematico di Palermo (1884–1940) **27**(1), 247–271 (1909). https://doi.org/10.1007/BF03019651
6. Bruijn, N.G.D.: A combinatorial problem. Proc. Koninklijke Nederlandse Academie van Wetenschappen **49**, 758–764 (1946)
7. Carton, O., Heiber, P.A.: Normality and two-way automata. Inf. Comput. **241**, 264–276 (2015). https://doi.org/10.1016/j.ic.2015.02.001
8. Cleary, J.G., Teahan, W.J.: Unbounded length contexts for PPM. Comput. J. **40**(2/3), 67–75 (1997). https://doi.org/10.1109/DCC.1995.515495
9. Cleary, J.G., Witten, I.H.: Data compression using adaptive coding and partial string matching. IEEE Trans. Commun. **32**(4), 396–402 (1984). https://doi.org/10.1109/TCOM.1984.1096090
10. Dai, J., Lathrop, J., Lutz, J., Mayordomo, E.: Finite-state dimension. Theoretical Comput. Sci. **310**, 1–33 (2004). https://doi.org/10.1016/S0304-3975(03)00244-5
11. Doty, D., Moser, P.: Feasible depth. In: Cooper, S.B., Löwe, B., Sorbi, A. (eds.) CiE 2007. LNCS, vol. 4497, pp. 228–237. Springer, Heidelberg (2007). https://doi.org/10.1007/978-3-540-73001-9_24
12. Jordon, L., Moser, P.: On the difference between finite-state and pushdown depth. In: Chatzigeorgiou, A., et al. (eds.) SOFSEM 2020. LNCS, vol. 12011, pp. 187–198. Springer, Cham (2020). https://doi.org/10.1007/978-3-030-38919-2_16
13. Lathrop, J.I., Strauss, M.J.: A universal upper bound on the performance of the Lempel-Ziv algorithm on maliciously-constructed data. In: Proceedings of the Compression and Complexity of Sequences, vol. 1997, pp. 123–135 (1997). https://doi.org/10.1109/SEQUEN.1997.666909
14. Martin, M.H.: A problem in arrangements. Bull. Amer. Math. Soc. **40**(12), 859–864 (1934). https://doi.org/10.1090/S0002-9904-1934-05988-3
15. Moffat, A.: Implementing the PPM data compression scheme. IEEE Trans. Commun. **38**(11), 1917–1921 (1990). https://doi.org/10.1109/26.61469

16. Pierce, L.A., Shields, P.C.: Sequences incompressible by slz (lzw), yet fully compressible by ulz. In: Numbers, Information and Complexity, pp. 385–390. Springer (2000). https://doi.org/10.1007/978-1-4757-6048-4_32
17. Schnorr, C., Stimm, H.: Endliche Automaten und Zufallsfolgen. Acta Inf. **1**, 345–359 (1972). https://doi.org/10.1007/BF00289514
18. Witten, I.H., Neal, R.M., Cleary, J.G.: Arithmetic coding for data compression. Commun. ACM **30**(6), 520–540 (1987). https://doi.org/10.1145/214762.214771
19. Ziv, J., Lempel, A.: Compression of individual sequences via variable-rate coding. IEEE Trans. Inf. Theory **24**(5), 530–536 (1978). https://doi.org/10.1109/TIT.1978.1055934

Clusters of Repetition Roots: Single Chains

Szilárd Zsolt Fazekas[1(✉)] and Robert Mercaş[2]

[1] Graduate School of Engineering Science, Akita University, Akita, Japan
szilard.fazekas@ie.akita-u.ac.jp
[2] Department of Computer Science, Loughborough University, Loughborough, UK
R.G.Mercas@lboro.ac.uk

Abstract. This work proposes a new approach towards solving an over 20 years old conjecture regarding the maximum number of distinct squares that a word can contain. To this end we look at clusters of repetition roots, that is, the set of positions where the root u of a repetition u^ℓ occurs. We lay the foundation of this theory by proving basic properties of these clusters and establishing upper bounds on the number of distinct squares when their roots form a chain with respect to the prefix order.

1 Introduction

Repetitions (periodicities) in words are well-studied, due primarily to their importance in word combinatorics [19] as well as in various applications such as string matching algorithms [6], molecular biology [11], or text compression [21]. The most basic repetitive structure is xx, where x is a non-empty string. Such a string is also called, due to its form $xx = x^2$, a *square*.

A string is said to be square-free or repetition-free if it contains no squares. It was shown by Thue [22,23] that there exist square-free, respectively, cube-free, strings of infinite length over a ternary, respectively, binary, alphabet. On the other hand, it has been shown that the minimal number of distinct squares that any sufficiently long binary string must contain is three [9].

A string of length n can have $\Theta(n^2)$ occurrences of squares, by the trivial example of a unary word, and it is known that the maximum number of square occurrences xx, where x itself is not a repetition is $\Theta(n \log n)$ [6]. Repetition counting has also been investigated in other settings: when the length of the root (x for a repetition x^ℓ) has length as small or large as possible (e.g., [7,9,20]), for partial words, where words contain extra joker symbols that match every letter of the alphabet (e.g., [2,3], as well as for abelian and other types of repetitions where the consecutive factors are not identical copies but equivalent in a looser sense (e.g. [17]).

Some, quite old and well studied, problems regarding this topic refer to the maximal number of distinct repetitions that a word can have, as well as to the maximum number of maximal repetitions (runs) that a string can contain.

This Work Was Supported By JSPS KAKENHI Grant Number JP19K11815.

T. Bureš et al. (Eds.): SOFSEM 2021, LNCS 12607, pp. 400–409, 2021.
https://doi.org/10.1007/978-3-030-67731-2_29

Problems. In [10], the authors prove that the maximum number of distinct squares in a word is bounded by twice the length of the word (by looking at the start position of the last occurrence of each square) and conjecture the following:

Conjecture 1. The number of distinct squares in a length n word is less than n.

In the same paper, the authors also provide a construction for a lower bound of $n - \mathcal{O}(\sqrt{n})$. Another simple construction of a good lower bound of the same order was provided in [16], by binary words with k occurrences of b's and with a number of a's quadratic in k, which have $\frac{2k-1}{2k+2}n$ many distinct squares.

Several alternative proofs regarding the $2n$ upper bound are known, either using combinatorics on words techniques [14], or just calculus [12]. The upper bound was later improved to $2n - \Theta(\log n)$ in [15] by showing that the number of double squares is bounded. Finally, in [8] the bound was reduced to $11n/6$ by using quite technical arguments to further restrict the number of double squares.

Regarding larger exponents, in [4] the authors showed that for a fixed integer $\ell > 2$, the number of distinct ℓ-powers in a length n word is less than $\frac{n}{\ell-2}$. For cubes, i.e., $\ell = 3$ the bound was improved to $4n/5$ in [5].

The latter problem involving repetitions of a higher fixed exponent, has its inspiration in the investigation of the maximum number of runs that a word can have. A run represents a repetition whose period is less than half and which cannot be extended to either left or right in the given word, without breaking the periodicity. The bound on this number was long conjectured to be less than the word's length [18], but only recently it is was showed to be the case [1].

Theorem 1. *The number of runs in a length n word is less than n.*

This bound was improved by Holub [13] to $\approx 0.9482n$, indicating that the optimal upper bounds will differ in the cases of runs and distinct squares.

Discussion of Techniques. The technique we use here also considers the global properties of occurrences of repetitions in a word, unlike previous approaches where the bounds were derived from local properties.

The main idea behind the approach is to group the repetitions we want to count by their root and the partial order imposed on them by the prefix ordering.

A word with 7 distinct squares:
a^2, $(aa)^2$, $(aaba)^2$, $(aba)^2$, $(abaa)^2$
$(baa)^2$, $(baaa)^2$
and their rightmost occurrences

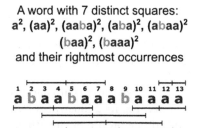

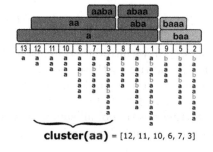

Fig. 1. Squares in *abaabaaabaaaa*   **Fig. 2.** Suffix array and cluster inclusion

All repetitions whose roots share a common prefix are in one group. Then, the aim is to show that for every element in a group there are at least a certain number of positions which are not part of the positions of another element's.

Our Contribution. In this work we pose a conjecture which would imply Conjecture 1 to be true, and prove it in the special case when the roots of repetitions considered form a chain of square roots (totally ordered set) with respect to the prefix ordering.

It is worth noting that while most of the earlier results concerning the bounds on the maximum number of distinct squares were obtained using some version of the so called Three Squares Lemma [6], the bounds concerning runs, as well as those concerning bounds on the repetitions with integer exponents higher than 2, made use of Lyndon trees and Lyndon words, and these approaches were never connected. In this work, we show the first framework which may allow a unified presentation of the bounds for distinct repetitions and runs by representing repetitions as all positions where their roots (appropriately defined for each particular type of repetition) occur.

Preliminaries. A *word* is a concatenation of letters from a *finite alphabet* Σ of size $|\Sigma|$. The *empty word* ε is the word of length 0. For a factorization $w = xyz$, we call x a *prefix* (denoted by $x \leq_p w$, or $x <_p w$ if $x \neq w$) and z a *suffix* of w, while each of x, y, z are called *factors* of w. A factor is *proper* if it is non-empty and not equal to w. If x is both a prefix and suffix of w, then x is a *border* of w. We call p a *period* of w if the letters p positions apart in w are the same. The *minimal period* is given by the smallest such p. By $|w|_x$ we denote the number of times x occurs as a factor of w (including overlaps).

A *repetition* represents consecutive catenations of the same word. An *ℓ-power* (*ℓ-repetition*) represents ℓ such repetitions of the same factor. If a word is not a repetition, then it is called *primitive*. Moreover, if $w = u^\ell$ is an ℓ-repetition we say that u is a *root* of w, and call u *the primitive root* of w when u is primitive. Finally, t^ω denotes the infinite word formed by consecutive repetitions of t.

Although unnecessary for the proofs, in order to simplify the illustrations, for all words w we consider their *suffix array* structures, which are permutations of $\{1, \ldots, |w|\}$ such that the ith entry is the starting position of the ith smallest suffix of w in the lexicographical order.

2   Clusters of Repetition Roots

In this section we introduce the clusters of repetition roots and prove some fundamental properties for these clusters in relation with clusters of other repetitions. Let us fix a word w and let its suffix array be S.

For each factor u^ℓ of w, we denote by $\mathbf{clust}_w(u)$ the *cluster* in S that contains the starting position of all suffixes having u as a prefix. Figure 2 illustrates how these clusters could be perceived (for $\ell = 2$), arranged one on top of the other.

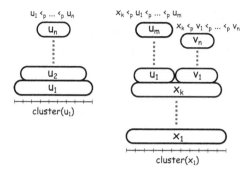

Fig. 3. Single (left) and multiple (right) chains of clusters

Observation 1. *The set of suffixes of a word sharing a common prefix are contiguous in the suffix array, forming a cluster. If an ℓ-repetition u^ℓ is a factor of a word, then the suffix array of the word contains a cluster of size at least ℓ of suffixes having the root u of the ℓ-repetition as a prefix.*

As every word, and therefore every suffix having v as prefix, also has u as prefix when $u <_p v$, the next observation is straightforward.

Observation 2. *For any two factors u and v of any word w, we have*
$$u \leq_p v \Leftrightarrow \mathbf{clust}_w(v) \subseteq \mathbf{clust}_w(u) \Leftrightarrow \mathbf{clust}_w(u) \cap \mathbf{clust}_w(v) \neq \emptyset \text{ and } |u| \leq |v|.$$

We pose the following conjecture, which, if true, would give a general upper bound for integer exponent distinct repetitions:

Conjecture 2. For any word w, any positive integer ℓ, and any set of words $S = \{u_1, u_2, \ldots, u_n\}$ such that, for all $i \in \{1, \ldots, n\}$, u_i^ℓ is a factor of w and $u_1 \leq_p u_i$, we have $|S| < \frac{1}{\ell-1} |w|_{u_1}$.

In other words, for a number n of ℓ-repetitions $u_1^\ell, \ldots, u_n^\ell$ with a common prefix x, we conjecture $n < \frac{1}{\ell-1} \cdot |\mathbf{clust}(x)|$. In this paper we approach the problem by analysing the case where $\ell = 2$ and $u_1 \leq_p \cdots \leq_p u_n$, that is, S is a set of roots of distinct squares, totally ordered by the prefix relation. We call such a collection of square roots a *(prefix) chain*. In Sect. 3 we prove a special case of Conjecture 2:

Problem 1. For a word w and a prefix chain $S = \{u_1, u_2, \ldots, u_n\}$ with $u_i \leq_p u_{i+1}$ for all $i \in \{1, \ldots, n-1\}$, we have $|S| < \frac{1}{\ell-1} |w|_{u_1}$.

Compared to any of the results in [8,10,15,16], the bound in Problem 1 is different because it is in a sense optimal, as we will argue at the end of Sect. 3. It is also important to note that while all the bounds on distinct repetition would be a direct corollary of Conjecture 2, the converse does not hold.

The next lemmas explore the situation of two equal clusters. This is a crucial issue, since when the clusters are all different, the bound easily follows: one can assign to each root a position which is in its cluster but not in the clusters of longer words. Most of the following results can be proved in general for ℓ-repetitions, but to simplify the exposition, here we usually restrict ourselves to $\ell = 2$. First recall the following well-known result about primitivity of words.

Lemma 1. *[19] A word w is primitive if and only if it occurs only twice in ww.*

In the following lemma we look at the relative positions of the rightmost occurrences of two squares whose roots have the same cluster.

Lemma 2. *For two squares u^2, v^2 with $u <_p v$, if $\mathbf{clust}_w(u) = \mathbf{clust}_w(v)$, then the rightmost occurrences of u^2 and v^2 in w cannot start on the same position.*

Proof. Let the rightmost occurrences of u^2 and v^2 start at the same position i. This means that $|u^2| > |v|$, as otherwise u^2 would occur later, at $i + |v|$. We have occurrences of u at i, $i + |u|$ and $i + |v|$. Since $\mathbf{clust}_w(u) = \mathbf{clust}_w(v)$, we also have v at $i + |u|$ and by Lemma 1, we get that v is non-primitive, and by the theorem of Fine and Wilf, the primitive roots of u and v are the same, say t. Since u is shorter than v, this gives an occurrence of u^2 at $i + |t|$, contradicting the assumption that u^2 does not occur after position i. $\square$

Next, we show that if the clusters of two words are equal and one of the words is non-primitive, then the other word has to be of a very specific form.

Lemma 3. *Consider the factors $u^2 \neq v^2$ of some word w, such that $\mathbf{clust}_w(u) = \mathbf{clust}_w(v)$ and $u <_p v$. Then the following hold:*

1. *if $u = t^m$ for some $m > 1$ and primitive t, then $v = t^m t'$ for $\varepsilon \neq t' \leq_p t$;*
2. *if $v = t^m$ for some $m > 1$ and primitive t, then $u = t^{m-1} t'$ for $\varepsilon \neq t' \leq_p t$.*

Proof. If two words have equal clusters, their rightmost occurrences start at the same position. Let us denote this position by i for u and v.

If $u = t^m$ for some primitive t and $m > 1$, and $|v| \geq 2|u|$, then we get a contradiction, because u occurs at position $i + |u|$. So, $|v| < 2|u|$, which means that $v = t^n t'$, for some $n \geq m$ and $t' \leq_p t$. If $n > m$, then we have an occurrence of u at $i + |t|$. So, $n = m$ and because $u \neq v$, we get that t' is not empty.

If $v = t^m$ for some primitive t and $m > 1$, since $u \leq_p v$ we get that $u = t^n t'$ for $n < m$ and $t' \leq_p t$. However, if $n < m - 1$ or $t' = \varepsilon$, then $\mathbf{clust}_w(u) \neq \mathbf{clust}_w(v)$, because we get an occurrence of u at $i + |t|$. $\square$

The next lemma helps establish the minimum number of non-overlapping occurrences of a word whose cluster is equal to the cluster of a longer word.

Lemma 4. *Let $u^2 \neq v^2$ be two squares in some word w with $u \leq_p v$ and $\mathbf{clust}_w(u) = \mathbf{clust}_w(v)$. If their corresponding rightmost occurrences start at positions u_s and v_s, respectively, then $|u_s - v_s| \geq |u|$.*

Proof. **Case 1:** $v_s > u_s$. Since u occurs at v_s, if $v_s - u_s < |u|$, then u occurs at v_s, between u_s and $u_s + |u|$, and by Lemma 1 u is a repetition. Furthermore, v occurs at $u_s + |u|$, between v_s and $v_s + |v|$ so by Lemma 1 v is also a repetition, which contradicts Lemma 3.

Case 2: $0 < u_s - v_s < |u|$. There are two possibilities to consider, depending on the relative position of $u_s + |u|$ and $v_s + |v|$.

If $u_s + |u| \leq v_s + |v|$, then u occurs inside v other than as a prefix, which leads to u occurring after the last occurrence of v, contradicting $\mathbf{clust}_w(u) = \mathbf{clust}_w(v)$.

If $u_s + |u| > v_s + |v|$, then there is an occurrence of u at position $v_s + |v|$, and an occurrence of v at position u_s, and by Lemma 1 we get that both u and v are non-primitive, which again contradicts Lemma 3. $\qquad\square$

Corollary 1. *Let* $u_1^2, \ldots, u_n^2$ *be squares in* w *such that* $\mathbf{clust}_w(u_1) = \cdots = \mathbf{clust}_w(u_n)$. *Then,* $|\mathbf{clust}_w(u_1)| > n$.

This means that for a chain of square roots $u_1 \leq_p \cdots \leq_p u_n$, in both extreme cases, that is, when $|\mathbf{clust}(u_1)| > \cdots > |\mathbf{clust}(u_n)|$ or when $|\mathbf{clust}(u_1)| = \cdots = |\mathbf{clust}(u_n)|$, our hypothesis for single chains holds, $|\mathbf{clust}(u_1)| > n$. In the next section we prove the hypothesis for single chains in the general case.

3 Bound for Single Chains

In this section we first prove the upper bound from Conjecture 2 in the special case of single chains. That is, we show that for a set of squares $S = \{u_1^2, \ldots, u_n^2\}$ in an arbitrary word w, with $u_1 <_p \cdots <_p u_n$, the inequality $|\mathbf{clust}_w(u_1)| > n$ holds. Afterwards we will discuss the challenge in extending the result to multiple chains, the sharpness of the bound and the existence of words $w, u_1, \ldots, u_n$ for every possibility of cluster sizes satisfying the bound.

Upper Bound. For a prefix $x \leq_p u$, we say that the x-*representative* (x-rep) of u^2 is the longest prefix of u^2 which ends in x. Note that this x-rep is of length at least $|u| + |x|$. Formally, the x-rep of u^2 is $uu'x \leq_p u^2$ such that for every y with $uyx \leq_p u^2$ we have that $|y| \leq |u'|$.

Let w be a word which contains u^2 as a factor. For the first (leftmost) occurrence in w of the x-rep $uu'x$ of square u^2, let u_s be its starting position and u_m be the start of the u' part, that is, $u_m = u_s + |u|$. We define the x-*anchor* of u^2 in w as the rightmost occurrence of a factor x in the first occurrence of the x-representative of square u^2 in w. This x-anchor is denoted by $\mathbf{\Psi}_w(u^2, x)$. If the x-rep of u^2 is $uu'x$, then $\mathbf{\Psi}_w(u^2, x) = u_s + |uu'|$. For example, in the word $w = abaabcabaabab$ we have the square $u = (aba)^2$ starting at position 7. The a-rep of u^2 is $abaaba = u^2$, first occurring at position 7, so $\mathbf{\Psi}_w(u^2, a) = 7 + 5 = 12$. The ab-rep of u^2 is $abaab$, first occurring at position 1, therefore $\mathbf{\Psi}_w(u^2, ab) = 1 + 3 = 4$.

It is one of the novel aspects of our method that we associate a position to a square, its x-anchor, which may not even be close to where the square occurs. Later, in Theorem 2 we reassign some of the squares with colliding x-anchors, further removing the close relation of earlier methods between the counted repetition and the position assigned to it, by which it was counted. This allows us to state a result which - albeit partial - is the first sharp bound on distinct repetitions of any type that we are aware of.

Lemma 5. *Let w be an arbitrary word with two square factors u^2, v^2 such that $u <_p v$, and let $x \leq_p u$ be a common prefix of theirs. If $\Psi_w(u^2, x) = \Psi_w(v^2, x)$, then $u = t^k$ for some primitive word t with $|t| < |x|$ and $k \geq 2$. Moreover, $tu'x \leq_p v$, where $u'x$ is the longest prefix of u bordered by x.*

Proof. Assume $\Psi_w(u^2, x) = \Psi_w(v^2, x)$. We distinguish three cases based on the relative positions of u_s, u_m and v_m, and derive contradictions in all of them, except when u is non-primitive with its root shorter than x. Note that $v_m \leq u_m$ always holds, since $u \leq_p v$ implies $\Psi_w(u^2, x) - u_m \leq \Psi_w(v^2, x) - v_m$.

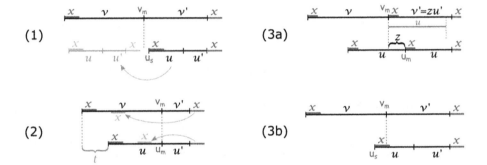

Fig. 4. Possible cases when $\Psi_w(u^2, x) = \Psi_w(v^2, x)$.

(1) If $v_m \leq u_s$ (Fig. 4(1)), then the x-rep of u^2 is a factor of v, whence it also occurs at $u_s - |v|$, contradicting that the occurrence at u_s was the first.

(2) If $v_m = u_m$ (Fig. 4(2)), then u is a suffix of v and since $|v| > |u|$, we have $v = tu$, for a non-empty word t. Let the x-rep of u^2 be $uu'x$. From $\Psi_w(u^2, x) = \Psi_w(v^2, x)$, we get that the x-rep of v^2 is $vu'x$. However, $tu'x \leq_p v$, so

$$\Psi_w(v^2, x) \geq v_s + |vtu'| > v_s + |vu'| = \Psi_w(v^2, x),$$

a contradiction.

(3) If $u_s < v_m < u_m$, then let the x-reps of u^2 and v^2 be $uu'x$ and $vzu'x$, respectively, where z is the non-empty word starting at v_m and ending at $u_m - 1$. Both $zu'x$ and u are prefixes of v, so if $|zu'x| < |u|$, then $zu'x \leq_p u$, therefore

$$\Psi_w(u^2, x) \geq u_s + |uzu'| > u_s + |uu'| = \Psi_w(u^2, x),$$

a contradiction. If $|zu'x| \geq |u|$, then since $u \leq_p v$, there is an occurrence of u at v_m, so by Lemma 1, we get that u is not primitive (see Fig. 4(3a)).

Now let $u = t^k$, with t primitive and $k \geq 2$. If $|uu'| \geq |v|$ then a conjugate of v is a prefix of uu', and synchronization, together with $u = t^k \leq_p v$, gives $v = t^m$, where $m > k$. This, in turn, means that u^2 and hence the x-rep of u^2 occurs at position v_s, so the occurrence at u_s is not the leftmost, a contradiction. We are left with the case $|uu'| < |v|$. Given that we have an occurrence of x at u_s, if that

x finishes before position v_m, then there is a copy of x located $|v|$ positions to the right in v^2, that is, $\Psi_w(v^2, x) \geq u_s + |v| > u_s + |uu'| = \Psi_w(u^2, x)$, contradicting $\Psi_w(v^2, x) = \Psi_w(u^2, x)$.

Hence, we get that $v_m - u_s < |x|$, which means $|t| < |x|$ (see Fig. 4(3b)). As x is a prefix of $u = t^k$, it has the form $x = t^\ell t'$ for some $\ell < k$ and $t' \leq_p t$. The longest prefix of $u = t^k$ bordered by x is $t^{k-1} t' = u'x$. As $u_m > v_m$, we get that $tt^{k-1}t' = tu'x \leq_p v$. $\qquad \square$

Corollary 2. *Let $u_1^2, \ldots, u_n^2$ and $v_1^2, \ldots, v_n^2$ be squares in a word w with their roots from the same chain, and x a common prefix of theirs, such that $\Psi_w(u_i^2, x) = \Psi_w(v_i^2, x)$ and $|u_i| < |v_i|$ for all $i \in \{1, \ldots, n\}$. Then, there exists a primitive word t shorter than x, such that $u_i = t^{k_i}$ with $k_i \geq 2$, for all $i \in \{1, \ldots, n\}$.*

Proof. From Lemma 5, whenever the x-anchor of some u_i^2 and v_i^2 coincide, there is some primitive t_i with $|t_i| < |x|$ such that $u_i = t_i^{k_i}$ with $k_i \geq 2$ and $t_i x$ is a prefix of v_i. Given that the roots of these squares form a prefix chain, we get that the words $t_i x$ also form a prefix chain, that is, for all $i, j \in \{1, \ldots, n\}$ either $t_i x \leq_p t_j x$ or $t_j x \leq_p t_i x$. Furthermore, since x is a common prefix of all the squares, we have $x \leq_p t_i x$, so x has period $|t_i|$, and therefore, trivially, so does $t_i x$. For any pair t_i, t_j, with $|t_i| \leq |t_j|$, we know that $t_i x \leq_p t_j x$, so $t_i x$ also has period $|t_j|$. Since $|t_i x| > |t_i| + |t_j| > |t_i| + |t_j| - \gcd(|t_i|, |t_j|)$, we can apply the theorem of Fine and Wilf and get that t_i and t_j have a common primitive root t. We already know that t_i and t_j are primitive, so $t_i = t_j = t$. $\qquad \square$

Theorem 2. *For all words w and squares $u_1^2, \ldots, u_n^2$ in w with $u_1 <_p \cdots <_p u_n$:*

$$|\mathbf{clust}_w(u_1)| \geq n + 1.$$

Proof. Our strategy consists of assigning a distinct occurrence of u_1 to each u_i^2, and finding one extra occurrence of u_1 not assigned to any square. Let $x = u_1$.

One by one, in decreasing order of length, we assign to each u_i the position $\Psi_w(u_i^2, x)$, as long as this position has not been previously assigned to a longer square. If all squares have been assigned such a unique position, we are done, because this renders n distinct occurrences of x, while the leftmost occurrence of x in w cannot be the x-anchor of any square.

Otherwise, there is some u^2 in the chain such that $\Psi_w(u^2, x)$ has been assigned to a longer square and we may assume that u^2 is the longest such square. By Lemma 5, $u = t^k$ for some primitive word t and $k \geq 2$. To all squares u_i^2, if $|u_i| > |u|$ or $u_i \notin t^+$, then assign the position $\Psi_w(u_i^2, x)$. Those are all distinct, by Corollary 2. After this, the roots of all squares which do not have an assigned position yet are powers of t with exponent at most k. Let those squares have roots $t^{k_1}, \ldots, t^{k_m}$ with $1 < k_1 < \cdots < k_m = k$. Let $x = t^\ell t'$ for some non-empty $t' \leq_p t$. We know that $|x| \leq |t^{k_1}|$, since $x = u_1$, so $k_1 > \ell$, which means $|t^{k_m}| \geq (m + \ell) \cdot |t|$. By Lemma 5, we know that $t^{k_m} t' \leq_p u_n$, so $t^{m+\ell} t' \leq_p u_n$.

Let s_i be the leftmost position where $t^i x$ occurs in w. We assign the position $p_i = s_i + i \cdot |t|$ to the square $(t^{k_i})^2$. It is easy to see that at each of these positions we have an occurrence of x starting, and that $p_i \neq p_j$ whenever $i \neq j$ (in fact, $p_i < p_{i+1}$). Therefore, what is left to show is that p_i does not coincide with any position assigned in the first phase.

Assume there exists $v \in \{u_1, \ldots, u_n\} \setminus \{t^{k_1}, \ldots, t^{k_m}\}$ such that $\boldsymbol{\Psi}_w(v^2, x) = p_i = s_i + i \cdot |t|$. From the definition of x-anchor we get that the factor preceding p_i is vv', where $v'x \leq_p v$. We derive a contradiction in all cases depending on v, which is either (1) a power of t, (2) some other prefix of a power of t or (3) neither, and as such, has ut' as a prefix:

(1) $v = t^q$. The powers of t which have been assigned a position in the first phase are longer than u, so $q \leq k$ is not possible, hence $q > k$. In this case there is a factor t^q preceding $\boldsymbol{\Psi}_w(v^2, x) = p_i$, which means that $t^k t' = t^{m+\ell} t' = t^m x$ occurs at $p_i - q \cdot |t|$, but $t^i x \leq t^m x$ and $p_i - q \cdot |t| < p_i - k \cdot |t| = s_i$, a contradiction.

(2) $v = t^j t''$, with non-empty $t'' <_p t$. In this case, $v' = t^r$ for some $r \geq 0$. If $r \geq i$, then $t^i x$ occurs at $s_i - |v|$, a contradiction. For the other case, let $t = t''t'''$. If $r < i$, then we get that $p_i - |v'|$ is immediately preceded by $t = t''t'''$, because of the definition of p_i, and it is also immediately preceded by $t'''t''$, because it is a suffix of v. Hence, $t''t''' = t'''t''$, so t is non-primitive, a contradiction.

(3) $v = t^k t' z$, for some z with $t' z \not<_p t^\omega$. Let the leftmost x-rep of v^2 start at position v_s in w. We have $\boldsymbol{\Psi}_w(v^2, x) \geq v_s + |v| > v_s + |u|$ from the definition of $\boldsymbol{\Psi}_w(v^2, x)$ and the shape of v. We know $v_s + |u| > v_s + m \cdot |t|$, because $u = t^k = t^m t^\ell$ and $\ell \geq 1$. Since $t^i x \leq_p t^k x \leq_p v$ and s_i is the leftmost position where $t^i x$ occurs we get $s_i \leq v_s$, and so $v_s + m \cdot |t| \geq s_i + m \cdot |t|$. Further, $s_i + m \cdot |t| \geq s_i + i \cdot |t|$, because $i \in \{1, \ldots, m\}$, and finally, $s_i + i \cdot |t| = p_i$ by definition the of p_i. Putting it all together we get $\boldsymbol{\Psi}_w(v^2, x) > p_i$, contradicting the assumption that they coincide.

We have assigned a distinct occurrence to each square u_i. Moreover, the leftmost x in w cannot be the x-anchor of any square and occurs no later than $s_1 (< p_1)$, and so it has not been assigned yet, therefore the theorem holds. $\qquad \square$

Now let us see why this result cannot be applied in a straightforward manner to cases when the prefix order is only a partial order on the roots of the squares. Consider the chains $x_1 <_p \cdots <_p x_k$, $u_1 <_p \cdots <_p u_m$ and $v_1 <_p \cdots <_p v_n$, where $x_k <_p u_1$ and $x_k <_p v_1$, but u_1 and v_1 are incomparable by $<_p$ (as in Fig. 3). By Theorem 2 we know that $|\mathbf{clust}(u_1)| \geq m+1$ and $|\mathbf{clust}(v_1)| \geq n+1$, so $|\mathbf{clust}(x_k)| \geq m+n+2$. Unfortunately, for the clusters of x_i, $i < k$, we cannot use the same argument as before, since $\boldsymbol{\Psi}_w(u_j^2, x_i) = \boldsymbol{\Psi}_w(v_\ell^2, x_i)$ is possible without either u_j or v_ℓ being non-primitive, a key condition in the proof of the previous theorem. Take, for example, $u_j = yzzyz$ and $v_\ell = zyz$, for some words y, z, both bordered by x_i, and incomparable by $\leq_p$. Then, in the word $w = yzzyzyzzyz$ we get $\boldsymbol{\Psi}_w((yzzyz)^2, x_i) = |w| - |x_i| + 1 = \boldsymbol{\Psi}_w((zyz)^2, x_i)$. However, as this example shows, in such a case u_j and v_ℓ have a special structure resembling the reverses of the FS double squares analyzed in [8], so a refinement of the anchor positions and the assignment algorithm might work.

References

1. Bannai, H.I.T., Inenaga, S., Nakashima, Y., Takeda, M., Tsuruta, K.: The "runs" theorem. SIAM J. Comput. **46**(5), 1501–1514 (2017)
2. Blanchet-Sadri, F., Mercaş, R., Scott, G.: Counting distinct squares in partial words. Acta Cybern. **19**(2), 465–477 (2009)
3. Blanchet-Sadri, F., Mercaş, R., Scott, G.: A generalization of Thue freeness for partial words. Theor. Comput. Sci. **410**(8–10), 793–800 (2009)
4. Crochemore, M., Fazekas, S., Iliopoulos, C., Jayasekera, I.: Number of occurrences of powers in strings. Int. J. Found. Comput. Sci. **21**(4), 535–547 (2010)
5. Crochemore, M., Iliopoulos, C., Kubica, M., Radoszewski, J., Rytter, W., Waleń, T.: The maximal number of cubic runs in a word. J. Comput. System Sci. **78**(6), 1828–1836 (2012)
6. Crochemore, M., Rytter, W.: Squares, cubes, and time-space efficient string searching. Algorithmica **13**(5), 405–425 (1995)
7. Dekking, F.: On repetitions of blocks in binary sequences. J. Combin. Theory Ser. A **20**, 292–299 (1976)
8. Deza, A., Franek, F., Thierry, A.: How many double squares can a string contain? Discrete Appl. Math. **180**, 52–69 (2015)
9. Fraenkel, A., Simpson, J.: How many squares must a binary sequence contain? Electron. J. Combin. **2**, #R2 (1995)
10. Fraenkel, A., Simpson, J.: How many squares can a string contain? J. Combin. Theory Ser. A **82**(1), 112–120 (1998)
11. Gusfield, D.: Algorithms on Strings, Trees, and Sequences - Computer Science and Computational Biology. Cambridge University Press, Cambridge (1997)
12. Hickerson, D.: Less than $2n$ distinct squares in a word of length n, communicated by Dan Gusfield (2003)
13. Holub, Š.: Prefix frequency of lost positions. Theoretical Comput. Sci. **684**, 43–52 (2017)
14. Ilie, L.: A simple proof that a word of length n has at most $2n$ distinct squares. J. Combin. Theory Ser. A **112**(1), 163–164 (2005)
15. Ilie, L.: A note on the number of squares in a word. Theoret. Comput. Sci. **380**(3), 373–376 (2007)
16. Jonoska, N., Manea, F., Seki, S.: A stronger square conjecture on binary words. In: Geffert, V., Preneel, B., Rovan, B., Štuller, J., Tjoa, A.M. (eds.) SOFSEM 2014. LNCS, vol. 8327, pp. 339–350. Springer, Cham (2014). https://doi.org/10.1007/978-3-319-04298-5_30
17. Kociumaka, T., Radoszewski, J., Rytter, W., Waleń, T.: Maximum number of distinct and nonequivalent nonstandard squares in a word. Theor. Comput. Sci. **648**(C), 84–95, October 2016
18. Kolpakov, R., Kucherov, G.: Finding maximal repetitions in a word in linear time. In: Proceedings 40th FOCS, pp. 596–604. IEEE Computer Society Press (1999)
19. Lothaire, M.: Combinatorics on Words. Cambridge University Press, Cambridge (1997)
20. Rampersad, N., Shallit, J., Wang, M.W.: Avoiding large squares in infinite binary words. Theor. Comput. Sci. **339**(1), 19–34 (2005)
21. Storer, J.A.: Data Compression: Methods and Theory. Press, Inc., Comp. Sci (1988)
22. Thue, A.: Über unendliche Zeichenreihen. Kra. Vidensk. Selsk. Skrifter. I Mat. Nat. Kl. 7 (1906)
23. Thue, A.: Über die gegenseitige Lage gleicher Teile gewisser Zeichenreihen. Kra. Vidensk. Selsk. Skrifter. I Mat. Nat. Kl. 1 (1912)

Drawing Two Posets

Guido Brückner[(✉)] [iD] and Vera Chekan

Karlsruhe Institute of Technology, Karlsruhe, Germany
brueckner@kit.edu, vera.chekan@student.kit.edu

Abstract. We investigate the problem of drawing two posets of the same ground set so that one is drawn from left to right and the other one is drawn from the bottom up. The input to this problem is a directed graph $G = (V, E)$ and two sets X, Y with $X \cup Y = E$, each of which can be interpreted as a partial order of V. The task is to find a planar drawing of G such that each directed edge in X is drawn as an x-monotone edge, and each directed edge in Y is drawn as a y-monotone edge. Such a drawing is called an *xy-planar* drawing.

Testing whether a graph admits an xy-planar drawing is NP-complete in general. We consider the case that the planar embedding of G is fixed and the subgraph of G induced by the edges in Y is a connected spanning subgraph of G whose upward embedding is fixed. For this case we present a linear-time algorithm that determines whether G admits an xy-planar drawing and, if so, produces an xy-planar polyline drawing with at most three bends per edge.

1 Introduction

A partial order $<$ over a set V can be interpreted as a directed graph G by interpreting the elements of V as the vertices of G, and interpreting the fact $u < v$ for $u, v \in V$ as a directed edge from u to v in G. In an upward drawing of G, every directed edge is drawn as an increasing y-monotone curve. Such a drawing is a bottom-up visualization of the partial order $<$. If the drawing is also planar, then it is especially easy to understand for humans [9]. Testing graphs for upward planarity is NP-hard in general [7], but feasible in linear time for graphs with a single source [3] and for graphs with a fixed underlying planar embedding [2].

More recent research has sought to extend this concept to two directions. The input to BI-MONOTONICITY is an undirected graph whose vertices have fixed coordinates and the task is to draw each edge as a curve that is both x-monotone and y-monotone while maintaining planarity. This problem is NP-hard in general [8]. In UPWARD-RIGHTWARD PLANARITY, the question is whether there exists a planar drawing of a directed graph in which each edge is x-monotone or y-monotone. Every planar directed graph has an upward-rightward straight-line drawing in polynomial area that can be computed in linear time [5]. The input to HV-RECTILINEAR PLANARITY is an undirected graph G with vertex-degree at most four where each edge is labeled either as horizontal or as vertical. The task is to find a planar drawing of G where each edge labeled as horizontal (vertical)

© Springer Nature Switzerland AG 2021
T. Bureš et al. (Eds.): SOFSEM 2021, LNCS 12607, pp. 410–420, 2021.
https://doi.org/10.1007/978-3-030-67731-2_30

is drawn as a horizontal (vertical) line segment. This problem is NP-hard in general [6]. A windrose graph consists of an undirected graph G and for each vertex v of G a partition of its neighbors into four sets that correspond to the four quadrants around v. A windrose drawing of G is a drawing such that for each vertex v of G each neighbor lies in the correct quadrant and all edges are represented by curves that are monotone with respect to each axis. Testing graphs for windrose planarity is NP-hard in general, but there exists a polynomial-time algorithm for graphs with a fixed underlying planar embedding [1].

In this paper, we investigate a new planarity variant called *xy-planarity*. Let $G = (V, E)$ be a directed graph together with two sets X, Y with $X \cup Y = E$. In an *xy-drawing* of G each directed edge in X is drawn as a strictly increasing x-monotone curve and each directed edge in Y is drawn as a strictly increasing y-monotone curve. Hence, an xy-drawing of G is a left-to-right visualization of the partial order defined by X and a bottom-up visualization of the partial order defined by Y, i.e., it is a drawing of two posets on the same ground set V. A planar xy-drawing is an *xy-planar* drawing. The study of xy-planarity has been proposed by Angelini et al. [1]. Because xy-planarity generalizes both upward planarity and windrose planarity, we immediately obtain the following.

Theorem 1. *Testing graphs for xy-planarity is NP-complete.*

We therefore consider the restricted case where the planar embedding of G is fixed, and the Y-induced subgraph of G is a connected spanning subgraph of G whose upward embedding is fixed. For this case we present a linear-time algorithm that determines whether G admits an xy-planar drawing. Our algorithm uses several structural insights. First, in Sect. 3, we provide a new, simple combinatorial characterization of windrose planar embeddings. From each xy-planar drawing of G we can derive an embedded windrose planar graph G^+. Using our combinatorial characterization of windrose planar embeddings we can simplify G^+. In Sect. 4 we show that in this simplified graph, every edge of the original graph G corresponds to one of four windrose planar gadgets. To test G for xy-planarity, we show in Sect. 5 how to determine in linear time whether there exists a choice of one gadget for each edge of G that leads to a windrose planar embedding. In the positive case our algorithm outputs an xy-planar drawing on a polynomial-size grid where each edge has at most three bends. If every windrose planar graph has a straight-line drawing (an open question), then each edge has at most one bend, which we show to be optimal. For space reasons, proofs of lemmas marked with a star ($\star$) have been omitted. They can be found in the full version [4].

2   Preliminaries

We use standard terminology concerning (upward) planar graph drawings and embeddings. Let $G = (V, E)$ be a connected graph. A *drawing* of G maps each vertex to a point in the plane and each edge to a finite polygonal chain between its two endpoints. A drawing is *planar* if distinct edges do not intersect except in common endpoints. An *embedding* of G consists of a counter-clockwise cyclic order of edges incident to each vertex of G. A planar drawing of G induces an embedding of G. An embedding $\mathcal{E}$ of G is *planar* if there exists a planar drawing of G that induces $\mathcal{E}$. For an inner face (the outer face) f of $\mathcal{E}$, define the *boundary* of f as the clockwise (counter-clockwise) cyclic walk on the edges incident to f.

Let G be a directed graph. A drawing of G is *upward* if each directed edge (u, v) is drawn as a connected series of strictly increasing y-monotone line segments. A drawing is *upward planar* if it is both upward and planar. An *upward embedding* of G consists of left-to-right orders of incoming and outgoing edges incident to each vertex of G. An upward planar drawing of G induces an upward embedding of G. An upward embedding of G is *planar* if it is induced by an upward planar drawing of G. An upward embedding induces an *underlying embedding* of G by concatenating the left-to-right order of incoming edges and the reversed left-to-right order of outgoing edges into one counter-clockwise cyclic order around each vertex. An embedding of G is *bimodal* if the incoming (outgoing) edges appear consecutively around each vertex. The underlying embedding of an upward embedding is bimodal. A vertex of G is a *sink* (*source*) if it is incident only to incoming (outgoing) edges. A vertex that is neither a source nor a sink of G is called an *inner vertex*. Consider an upward planar drawing of G and its underlying planar embedding $\mathcal{E}$ of G. For three consecutive vertices u, v, w on the boundary of a face f, the vertex v is called a *face-source* (*face-sink*) of f if the edges uv and vw are both directed away from (towards) v. Define n_f as the number of face-sources of f, which equals the number of face-sinks of f. A *sink/source assignment* $\psi : v \mapsto (e, e')$ maps each source and sink v to two edges e, e' incident to v so that e immediately precedes e' in counter-clockwise cyclic order of edges incident to v defined by $\mathcal{E}$. This corresponds to a unique face f of $\mathcal{E}$ such that e immediately precedes e' on the boundary of f. Thus, we say that ψ assigns v to f. The assignment is *upward consistent* if ψ assigns $n_f + 1$ vertices to one face, and $n_f - 1$ vertices to all other faces. The face to which $n_f + 1$ vertices are assigned is the outer face. From an embedding $\mathcal{E}$ and a sink/source assignment ψ an upward embedding of G can be obtained by splitting for each sink (source) v the counter-clockwise cyclic order of edges incident to v defined by $\mathcal{E}$ between the two edges e, e' with $\psi(v) = (e, e')$ to obtain the right-to-left (left-to-right) order of incoming (outgoing) edges. In the reverse direction, from an upward embedding of G a sink/source assignment ψ can be obtained as follows. Assign each sink v to (e, e') where e and e' are the rightmost and leftmost incoming edge incident to v, respectively. Assign each source v to (e, e') where e and e' are the leftmost and rightmost outgoing edge incident to v, respectively. Thus, upward embeddings are equivalent to planar embeddings together with a sink/source assignment. The following was observed by Bertolazzi et al. [2] for biconnected graphs, we provide a straight-forward extension to simply-connected graphs.

Lemma 1 ($\star$). *Let G be a connected directed acyclic graph together with an embedding $\mathcal{E}$. There exists an upward planar embedding of G whose underlying* *embedding is $\mathcal{E}$ if and only if $\mathcal{E}$ is planar and bimodal, and it admits an upward consistent assignment.*

3   Combinatorial View of Windrose Planarity

A *windrose graph* is a directed graph G whose edges are labeled as either north-west (NW) or north-east (NE). A *windrose drawing* of G is an upward drawing of G where all NW (NE) edges decrease (increase) monotonically along the x-axis. In this way, the neighbors of each vertex are partitioned into the four quadrants of the plane around v. An upward planar embedding of G is *windrose planar* if it is induced by a windrose planar drawing of G. Let $\mathcal{U}$ be an upward planar embedding of G and let v be a vertex of G. We say $\mathcal{U}$ is *windrose consistent* at v if (i) the NW edges precede the NE edges in the left-to-right order of outgoing edges incident to v, and (ii) the NE edges precede the NW edges in the left-to-right order of incoming edges incident to v. We say that $\mathcal{U}$ is *windrose consistent* if it is windrose consistent at all vertices of G and show the following.

Lemma 2 ($\star$). *Let G be a directed graph together with an upward planar embedding $\mathcal{U}$. Then $\mathcal{U}$ is a windrose planar embedding of G if and only if $\mathcal{U}$ is windrose consistent.*

4   From xy-Drawings to Windrose Drawings

Let $G = (V, E)$ be a directed graph together with sets X, Y such that $X \cup Y = E$. Define $G|_Y$ as the subgraph of G induced by the edges in Y. Further, let Γ denote an xy-drawing of G. Recall that edges are drawn as finite polygonal chains. Define G^+ as the graph obtained from G by subdividing the edges of G at each bend in Γ such that each directed edge (u, v) of G^+ corresponds to an upward straight-line segment from u to v (u is below v) in Γ. Label (u, v) as NW (NE) if the corresponding segment decreases (increases) along the x-axis. Then G^+ is a windrose graph together with a windrose planar drawing Γ^+. Let $\mathcal{E}^+$ denote the windrose planar embedding induced by Γ^+.

4.1   Simplifying Windrose Planar Embeddings

Each edge (u, v) of G in Y corresponds to a path $(u = y_1, y_2, \ldots, y_n = v)$ in G^+. For $1 \leq i < n$ the edge connecting y_i and y_{i+1} is oriented from y_i to y_{i+1} and is either an NE edge or an NW edge. We can simplify G^+ and $\mathcal{E}^+$. Similarly-labeled edges $(y_i, y_{i+1}), (y_j, y_{j+1})$ with $1 \leq i < j < n$ can be replaced by a single edge (y_i, y_{j+1}) with the same label. We argue that the arising embedded graph is still windrose planar. First, the order of labels around vertices y_i and y_{j+1} has not been changed, and the remaining vertices have not been affected, as a result the embedding is still windrose consistent. Second, we show that the embedding is still upward planar. This is directly implied by two facts. First, vertices $y_{i+1}, \ldots, y_j$ are neither sources nor sinks. And second, the sink/source

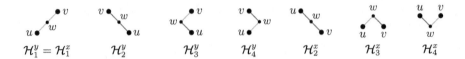

Fig. 1. The gadgets $\mathcal{H}_1^x, \ldots, \mathcal{H}_4^x$ and $\mathcal{H}_1^y, \ldots, \mathcal{H}_4^y$ that are used to represent an x-monotone edge and an y-monotone edge (u, v), respectively. NW (NE) edges are drawn in blue (green). (Color figure online)

assignment of y_i and y_{j+1} has not been changed. Thereby the number of face-sources and face-sinks and the number of sources and sinks assigned to every face also stay the same. Since $\mathcal{E}^+$ is upward consistent, then the simplified embedding is upward consistent, too. By Lemma 2, the simplified embedding admits a windrose planar drawing (it is also an xy-planar drawing of G). We can repeat this, until every edge $(u, v) \in Y$ is represented with either a single edge, or with two edges with different labels. In the following, we want that every gadget consists of exactly two edges. For this purpose, if the path from u to v consists of a single edge, we subdivide it into two edges with the same label. See Fig. 1 for the four possible gadgets $\mathcal{H}_1^y, \ldots, \mathcal{H}_4^y$.

Each edge (u, v) of G in X corresponds to a path $(u = x_1, x_2, \ldots, x_n = v)$ in G^+. For $1 \leq i < n$ the edge connecting x_i and x_{i+1} in G^+ is either a NE edge oriented from x_i to x_{i+1}, or an NW edge oriented from x_{i+1} to x_i. Again, we can simplify $\mathcal{E}^+$. For $1 < i < n$ if the edges connecting x_{i-1} and x_i, and x_i and x_{i+1} are oriented in the same direction they also are similarly labeled and the same argument as above can be used to replace x_i and its incident edges by an edge connecting x_{i-1} and x_{i+1}. Now consider the case that for $1 \leq i \leq n - 3$ the edges $e_1 = (x_i, x_{i+1})$ and $e_3 = (x_{i+2}, x_{i+3})$ are labeled as NE and the edge $e_2 = (x_{i+1}, x_{i+2})$ is labeled as NW. Because Γ is an xy-drawing, the sink/source assignment induced by $\mathcal{E}^+$ assigns x_{i+1} to (e_2, e_1) and x_{i+2} to (e_2, e_3) (in terms of upward planarity as defined in Sect. 2). Replacing the vertices x_{i+1}, x_{i+2} and their incident edges by a single edge (x_i, x_{i+3}) labeled as NE reduces the number of face-sinks by one and it reduces the number of face-sources of both incident faces by one. The number of assigned face-sinks and face-sources is also reduced by one. Thereby, the sink/source assignment is still consistent and the embedding is upward planar. Together with the arguments for edges of G in Y this shows that the simplified embedding remains a windrose planar embedding. See Fig. 1 for the four possible gadgets $\mathcal{H}_1^x, \ldots, \mathcal{H}_4^x$.

Let G^* and $\mathcal{E}^*$ denote the simplified windrose graph and windrose planar embedding. Every windrose planar drawing of G^* with embedding $\mathcal{E}^*$ induces an xy-planar drawing Γ' of G such that Γ and Γ' induce the same planar embedding of G and the same upward planar embedding of $G|_Y$. Note that G^* is obtained from G by replacing (i) each edge of G in $X \setminus Y$ with a gadget in $\mathcal{H}^x$, (ii) each edge of G in $Y \setminus X$ with a gadget in $\mathcal{H}^y$, and (iii) each edge of G in $X \cap Y$ with the (unique) gadget in $\mathcal{H}^x \cap \mathcal{H}^y$ (where $\mathcal{H}^x = \{\mathcal{H}_1^x, \mathcal{H}_2^x, \mathcal{H}_3^x, \mathcal{H}_4^x\}$ and $\mathcal{H}^y = \{\mathcal{H}_1^y, \mathcal{H}_2^y, \mathcal{H}_3^y, \mathcal{H}_4^y\}$). We say that a windrose graph obtained from G by

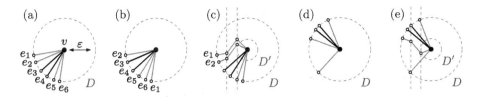

Fig. 2. Two xy-drawings that have the same cyclic order of edges around the boundary of D and assignment of line segments to quadrants, but distinct upward planar embeddings (a, b). Edges in X are drawn in red, edges in Y are drawn in black. The xy-drawing (a) can be locally modified to obtain a special xy-drawing (c) that admits no such ambiguities. Modifying a drawing where Property (2) does not hold true works symmetrically (d, e).

such a gadget replacement is *derived* from G. A windrose planar embedding of a graph derived from G induces a planar embedding of G and an upward planar embedding of $G|_Y$. We have shown the following.

Lemma 3. *Let $G = (V, E)$ be a directed graph together with sets X, Y such that $X \cup Y = E$. This graph admits an xy-planar drawing with planar embedding $\mathcal{E}$ of G and upward planar embedding $\mathcal{U}$ of $G|_Y$ if and only if there exists a derived graph G^* of G with a windrose planar embedding that induces $\mathcal{E}$ and $\mathcal{U}$.*

4.2   Special Windrose Planar Embeddings

Inspired by Lemma 3, part of the approach to test G for xy-planarity will be to use Lemma 1 to test for every edge $e \in X$ and each gadget $\mathcal{H}_i^x \in \mathcal{H}^x$ whether replacing e with $\mathcal{H}_i^x$ leads to an upward planar embedding of $G|_Y + e$. If all edges incident to e lie in the same quadrant, it is not right away possible to derive the upward planar embedding of $G|_Y + e$ just from the upward planar embedding of $G|_Y$ and the gadget choice $\mathcal{H}_i^x$. For an example, consider Fig. 2 (a, b). Even though e_1 might be replaced by the same gadget the sink assignment of $G|_Y + e_1$ in (a) is $\psi : v \mapsto (e_4, e_1)$, whereas in (b) it is $\psi : v \mapsto (e_1, e_3)$. To prevent such ambiguities, we introduce the notion of special xy-drawings.

In any xy-planar drawing Γ of G there exists some $\varepsilon > 0$ so that the disk D of radius ε centered at v does not contain any vertex other than v, intersects only edges incident to v, and does not contain any point where an edge bends. A counter-clockwise traversal of the boundary of D gives four (possibly empty) linear orders of the edges in each quadrant. We say that Γ is *special* if for each vertex v of G the following four properties hold true. (1) If v has only incoming edges in X and incoming edges in Y, then the first edge in the southwestern quadrant is in Y. (2) If v has only incoming edges in X and outgoing edges in Y, then the last edge in the northwestern quadrant is in Y. (3) If v has only outgoing edges in X and incoming edges in Y, then the last edge in the southeastern quadrant is in Y. (4) If v has only outgoing edges in X and outgoing edges in Y, then the first edge in the northeastern quadrant is in Y.

Fig. 3. An xy-planar graph that does not admit an xy-planar straight-line drawing.

If the drawing Γ is not special, then we can modify it locally around each vertex where one of the four properties does not hold to obtain a special drawing. Consider the case that v is a vertex of G that has only incoming edges in X and Y but the first edge in the southwestern quadrant is not in Y, i.e., Property (1) does not hold true for v. See Fig. 2 (a). Introduce two new bends on each edge $e_1, e_2, \ldots, e_n$ in X that precede the first edge in Y in the southwestern quadrant so that the line segments incident to v lie in the northwestern quadrant. This preserves the x-monotonicity of the drawing and ensures Property (1). See Fig. 2 (c) for the modified drawing, where Property (1) holds true (consider the smaller disk D'). The other three properties can be ensured symmetrically; see Fig. 2 (d, e) for an example of how to ensure Property (2).

Note how in the special windrose drawings in Fig. 2 (c, e) for each red edge e the upward planar embedding of $G|_Y + e$ can be derived just from the upward planar embedding of $G|_Y$ and the gadget choice $\mathcal{H}_i^x$ for e. A windrose planar embedding is *special* if it is derived from a special xy-planar drawing. Observe that simplifying the windrose planar embedding as explained in the previous section does not alter edges incident to non-subdivision vertices. Therefore, Lemma 3 can be strengthened to special windrose planar embeddings as follows.

Lemma 4. *Let $G = (V, E)$ be a directed graph together with sets X, Y such that $X \cup Y = E$. This graph admits an xy-planar drawing with planar embedding $\mathcal{E}$ of G and upward planar embedding $\mathcal{U}$ of $G|_Y$ if and only if there exists a derived graph G^* of G together with a special windrose planar embedding that induces $\mathcal{E}$ and $\mathcal{U}$.*

Because every windrose planar graph admits a polyline drawing in polynomial area with at most one bend per edge [1] we immediately obtain the following.

Corollary 1. *Every xy-planar graph admits a polyline drawing in polynomial area with at most three bends per edge.*

If every embedded windrose planar graph admitted a straight-line drawing, then every xy-planar graph would admit a polyline drawing with at most one bend per edge. Not every xy-planar graph admits an xy-planar straight-line drawing; see Fig. 3. Lemma 4 also motivates our approach of testing G for xy-planarity by testing whether there exists a replacement of the edges of G with gadgets that respects the given planar and upward planar embeddings and yields a special windrose planar embedding.

5   An xy-Planarity Testing Algorithm

Let G be a directed graph together with edge sets X, Y and let e be an edge in X. Define the *gadget candidate set* $\mathcal{H}(e)$ as the subset of $\mathcal{H}^x = \{\mathcal{H}_1^x, \mathcal{H}_2^x, \mathcal{H}_3^x, \mathcal{H}_4^x\}$ that contains each $\mathcal{H}_i^x \in \mathcal{H}^x$ so that the embedding $\mathcal{U} + \mathcal{H}_i^x$ is an upward planar embedding of $G|_Y + e$. Recall that Lemma 4 justifies that we can limit our considerations to windrose planar embeddings that are special, which lets us unambiguously derive the upward planar embedding $\mathcal{U} + \mathcal{H}_i^x$ of $G|_Y + e$ from the fixed upward planar embedding $\mathcal{U}$ of $G|_Y$ and the gadget choice $\mathcal{H}_i^x$ for e. This is needed to test for upward planarity using Lemma 1. For $e \in X$ the gadget candidate set $\mathcal{H}(e)$ can be computed by tentatively replacing e with each $\mathcal{H}_i^x$ and then running the upward planarity test for fixed upward embeddings. In fact, this can even be done in overall linear time for all edges in X.

Lemma 5 ($\star$). *The gadget candidate sets for all edges in X can be computed in linear time.*

5.1   Finding a Windrose Planar Derived Graph

For every edge e of G, add the variables $e^{\text{NE}}, e^{\text{NW}}, e^{\text{SW}}, e^{\text{SE}}$ together with a clause $\neg x \lor \neg y$ for each pair x, y of distinct variables. This means that every edge of G^* is assigned to at most one quadrant. Make sure that every edge of G^* is assigned to at least one quadrant as follows. Let (u, v) be an edge of G and let w denote the vertex of the gadget in G^* that replaces (u, v). If $(u, v) \in X$, then add the clauses $(u, w)^{\text{NE}} \lor (u, w)^{\text{SE}}$ so that (u, v) exits u in the east, and $(w, v)^{\text{NW}} \lor (w, v)^{\text{SW}}$ so that (u, v) enters v from the west. Next, if $(u, v) \in Y$, then add the clauses $(u, w)^{\text{NE}} \lor (u, w)^{\text{NW}}$ so that (u, v) exits u in the north, and $(w, v)^{\text{SW}} \lor (w, v)^{\text{SE}}$ so that (u, v) enters v from the south.

Placing the edges of G^* into quadrants induces a unique gadget that replaces each edge of G. Let $e = (u, v)$ be an edge of G. Each gadget $\mathcal{H}_i^x \notin \mathcal{H}(e)$ places the edge (u, w) in quadrant p and the edge (w, v) in quadrant q. Include the clause $\neg((u, w)^p \land (w, v)^q) = \neg(u, w)^p \lor \neg(w, v)^q$, this would prevent the gadget $\mathcal{H}_i^x$ from being induced. Because no other gadget places the edge (u, w) in quadrant p and (w, v) in q adding this clause does not prevent any other gadget from being induced. Add such a clause for each gadget $\mathcal{H}_i^x \notin \mathcal{H}(e)$.

The last step is to ensure windrose consistency at each vertex v of G^*. Use the combinatorial criterion from Lemma 2. Since we consider gadgets with a prescribed assignment at w, we implicitly ensure that the embedding is windrose consistent around such vertices (see Fig. 1). Let v be a non-subdivision vertex of G^*, i.e., v is also a vertex of G. Consider the case that v has incoming and outgoing edges in Y. Let $\sigma = e_1, e_2, \ldots, e_i, \ldots, e_n, e_1$ denote the counter-clockwise cyclic order of edges incident to v in G^* such that e_1 is a subdivision edge of an outgoing edge in Y and e_i is a subdivision edge of an incoming edge in Y. To achieve windrose consistency the edges must be labeled as NE, then NW, then SW and finally SE in the sequence $e_1, \ldots, e_i$. This can be ensured with the constraints

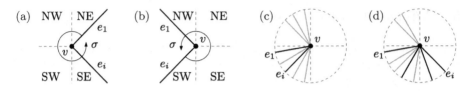

Fig. 4. The situation around a vertex v that has both an outgoing edge e_1 and an incoming edge e_i in Y (a, b). An example of a vertex v that has only incoming edges in X and Y (c, d). Here e_1 and e_i are the leftmost and rightmost edges with respect to the fixed upward embedding.

$$e_j^{NW} \implies \neg e_{j+1}^{NE}$$
$$e_j^{SW} \implies \neg e_{j+1}^{NW} \quad \text{and} \quad e_j^{SW} \implies \neg e_{j+1}^{NE}$$
$$e_j^{SE} \implies \neg e_{j+1}^{SW} \quad \text{and} \quad e_j^{SW} \implies \neg e_{j+1}^{NW} \quad \text{and} \quad e_j^{SW} \implies \neg e_{j+1}^{NE}$$

for $1 \le j < i$; see Fig. 4 (a). Similarly, in $e_i, \ldots, e_n, e_1$ edges must be labeled as SW, then SE, then NE and finally NW; see Fig. 4 (b). A symmetric argument holds for vertices of G that have both incoming and outgoing edges in X.

The remaining case consists of four subcases where v has only incoming or only outgoing edges in Y, and only incoming or only outgoing edges in X. Consider the case that v has only incoming edges in Y and only incoming edges in X (the other cases are symmetric); see Fig. 4 (c, d). Let $\sigma = e_1, e_2, \ldots, e_i, \ldots, e_n, e_1$ be the counter-clockwise cyclic order of edges incident to v in G^* such that e_1 and e_i are subdivision edges of the leftmost and rightmost incoming edges in Y in the fixed upward planar embedding of $G|_Y$. Add the constraints $e_j^{SE} \lor e_j^{SW}$ and $e_j^{SE} \implies e_{j+1}^{SE}$ for $1 \le j < i$, the constraint $e_i^{SE} \implies e_{i+1}^{NW}$, and, because we seek special embeddings, the constraints $e_j^{NW} \implies e_{j+1}^{NW}$ for $i < j < n$.

5.2 Correctness

Every windrose graph derived from G induces a solution of the 2-SAT instance. Every solution of the 2-SAT instance induces a windrose graph G^* derived from G together with a windrose planar embedding. For each edge $e \in X$ a solution to the 2-SAT instance induces a replacement gadget $\mathcal{H}_i^x$ so that $\mathcal{U} + \mathcal{H}_i^x$ is an upward planar embedding of $G|_Y + e$. The final component to our xy-planarity test is to show that even though we tested the gadget candidates individually, the fact that the 2-SAT instance is satisfiable implies that inserting for each edge in X its replacement gadget leads to an upward planar embedding of G^*.

Lemma 6. *Let $G = (V, E)$ be a directed graph together with sets X, Y such that $X \cup Y = E$. Let $\mathcal{E}$ be an embedding of G and let $\mathcal{U}$ be an upward planar embedding of $G|_Y$. If the corresponding 2-Sat instance is satisfiable, then the embedding $\mathcal{U}^*$ of the graph G^* induced by a solution of this instance is upward planar.*

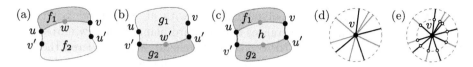

Fig. 5. Proof sketch of Lemma 6. If f, f_1, f_2, g_1, g_2 are upward planar, then so is h (a–c). The case of adjacent edges reduces to the case of independent edges (d, e).

Proof Sketch. We show that $\mathcal{U}^*$ is upward planar inductively by showing that inserting the gadgets one by one preserves upward planarity using Lemma 1. Edges that are inserted into different faces of $\mathcal{U}$ can be treated independently. Consider two independent edges $e = (u, v), e' = (u', v') \in X$ that are inserted into the same face of $\mathcal{U}$; see Fig. 5 (a–c). Inserting e into f splits f into two faces f_1, f_2. The fact that e can be inserted into f means that for $i = 1, 2$ about half of the face-sources and face-sinks on the boundary of f_i are assigned to f_i by Lemma 1. Likewise, inserting e into f splits f into two faces g_1, g_2. Again, for $i = 1, 2$ about half of the face-sources and face-sinks on the boundary of g_i are assigned to g_i. Inserting e and e' into f splits f into three faces f_1, h and g_2. We show that then about half of the face-sources and face-sinks on the boundary of h are assigned to h, so the resulting upward embedding is upward planar by Lemma 1. The case of adjacent edges reduces to the case of independent edges by subdividing for each edge $(u, v) \in X$ the edges of the gadget that replace (u, v) and treating the subdivision edges incident to u and v as edges in Y; see Fig. 5 (d, e).

Lemma 6 gives that $\mathcal{U}^*$ is upward planar. The clauses of the 2-SAT instance are designed such that (i) $\mathcal{U}^*$ is windrose consistent by Lemma 2, i.e., $\mathcal{U}^*$ is windrose planar, and (ii) $\mathcal{U}^*$ is special. Lemma 4 gives that G is xy-planar if and only if the 2-SAT instance is satisfiable. To compute an xy-planar drawing of G, use the linear-time windrose-planar drawing algorithm of Angelini et al. [1] to compute a windrose planar drawing of G^*, which induces an xy-planar drawing of G.

Theorem 2. *Let $G = (V, E)$ be a directed graph together with subsets X, Y of its edges E such that $X \cup Y = E$, a planar embedding $\mathcal{E}$ of G and an upward planar embedding $\mathcal{U}$ of $G|_Y$. It can be tested in linear time whether there exists an xy-planar drawing of G whose underlying planar embedding is $\mathcal{E}$ and whose underlying upward planar embedding restricted to $G|_Y$ is $\mathcal{U}$. In the positive case, such a drawing can be computed in linear time as well.*

6   Conclusion

We introduced and studied the concept of xy-planarity which is particularly suitable to draw two posets on the same ground set, one from bottom to top and the other from left to right. Every xy-planar drawing of a graph G induces a derived windrose planar graph G^*, which implies that every xy-planar graph admits a polyline drawing in polynomial area with at most three bends per edge. Because xy-planarity generalizes both upward planarity and windrose planarity, xy-planarity testing is NP-complete in general. We considered the case that the upward part $G|_Y$ is a connected spanning subgraph of G whose upward embedding $\mathcal{U}$ is fixed, and that the planar embedding $\mathcal{E}$ of G is fixed as well. For this case, we have given a linear-time xy-planarity testing algorithm. It uses the connection to derived windrose planar graphs, a novel combinatorial view of windrose planarity and a careful analysis of upward planar embeddings and windrose planar embeddings.

References

1. Angelini, P., et al.: Windrose planarity: embedding graphs with direction-constrained edges. ACM Trans. Algorithms, **14**(4), 54:1–54:24 (2018)
2. Bertolazzi, P., Di Battista, G., Liotta, G., Mannino, C.: Upward drawings of triconnected digraphs. Algorithmica **12**(6), 476–497 (1994)
3. Bertolazzi, P., Di Battista, G., Mannino, C., Tamassia, R.: Optimal upward planarity testing of single-source digraphs. SIAM J. Comput. **27**(1), 132–169 (1998)
4. Brückner, G., Chekan, V.: Drawing two posets. CoRR, abs/2010.12928 (2020)
5. Di Giacomo, E., Didimo, W., Kaufmann, M., Liotta, G., Montecchiani, F.: Upward-rightward planar drawings. In: Bourbakis, N.G., Tsihrintzis, G.A., Virvou, M., (eds.), 5th International Conference on Information, Intelligence, Systems and Applications, IISA 2014, Chania, Crete, Greece, 7–9 July 2014, pp. 145–150. IEEE (2014)
6. Didimo, W., Liotta, G., Patrignani, M.: Hv-planarity: algorithms and complexity. J. Comput. Syst. Sci. **99**, 72–90 (2019)
7. Garg, A., Tamassia, R.: On the computational complexity of upward and rectilinear planarity testing. SIAM J. Comput. **31**(2), 601–625 (2001)
8. Klemz, B., Rote, G.: Ordered level planarity and its relationship to geodesic planarity, bi-monotonicity, and variations of level planarity. ACM Trans. Algorithms, **15**(4), 53:1–53:25 (2019)
9. Purchase, H.: Which aesthetic has the greatest effect on human understanding? In: Di Battista, G. (ed.) GD 1997. LNCS, vol. 1353, pp. 248–261. Springer, Heidelberg (1997). https://doi.org/10.1007/3-540-63938-1_67

Fair Division Is Hard Even for Amicable Agents

Neeldhara Misra and Aditi Sethia[(✉)]

Indian Institute of Technology, Gandhinagar, India
{neeldhara.m,aditi.sethia}@iitgn.ac.in

Abstract. We consider the problem of distributing a collection of indivisible objects among agents in a manner that satisfies some desirable notions of fairness and efficiency. We allow agents to "share" goods in order to achieve efficiency and fairness goals which may be otherwise impossible to attain. In this context, our goal is to find allocations that minimize the "amount of sharing". We follow up on recent work demonstrating that finding fair allocations with minimum sharing is tractable when valuations are non-degenerate, a notion which captures scenarios that are "far from identical". This result holds for any fixed number of agents. We show that the usefulness of non-degeneracy does not scale to the setting of many agents. In particular, we demonstrate that the problem of finding fractionally Pareto optimal and envy-free allocations is NP-complete even for instances with constant degeneracy and no sharing. We also demonstrate an alterate approach to enumerating distinct consumption graphs for allocations with a small number of sharings.

Keywords: Fair division · Indivisible items · NP-completeness

1 Introduction

The task of fairly distributing indivisible goods among interested agents is challenging already for the simplest possible scenario: one object valued by two or more people. We are typically dealing with m *objects* and n *agents*. All agents specify their *value* for each of the objects, and the *utility* they derive from a set of objects is the sum of the values for the individual objects in the collection[1]. An *allocation* of m goods to n agents is a partition of the goods into n *bundles*.

A natural and well-studied notion of fairness is *envy-freeness*, which demands that every agent finds themselves no worse than any other in that they value their own bundle at least as much as any of the other bundles. Note that by itself, envy-freeness can be achieved by trivial allocations where all bundles are empty. This motivates the pursuit of some notion of efficiency—for instance, *completeness*

---

[1] This is the setting of additive utilities, which will be the focus of our discussion. In a more general setting agents might have different and unrelated utility associated with every possible subset of items.

Supported by the Indian Institute of Technology, Gandhinagar and DST-SERB.

© Springer Nature Switzerland AG 2021
T. Bureš et al. (Eds.): SOFSEM 2021, LNCS 12607, pp. 421–430, 2021.
https://doi.org/10.1007/978-3-030-67731-2_31

requires all items to be allocated, and *fractionally Pareto Optimal*(fPO), where no agent can be made better off without making another worse off. The opening example involving one good valued equally by two agents already shows that there are instances where no allocation is simultaneously complete and envy-free (EF). This has led to several notions of "workarounds": approximate envy-freeness up to one good [2,7], or any good [3], or using hidden goods [6]), subsidy [1], donating items [4]), and sharing [8,9]).

Our focus is on settings sharing goods appears to be the most reasonable of all workarounds, and the question of interest is to find allocations that meet our goals of fairness and efficiency with minimum sharing. In a recent development, Sandomirskiy and Segal-Halevi [8] propose a notion of degeneracy which captures the degree of similarity across agent valuations and argue that the intractable cases are those that have a rather high degree of similarity. In retrospect, one might argue that similar valuations signal high conflict, and this possibly contributes to making this a hard scenario. We say that a set of goods are valued similarly by two agents if the ratios of their values for all goods are the same. The degree of similarity between two agents is one less than the largest number of goods that are valued similarly by them. The degeneracy of an instance with n agents is the highest degree of similarity across all pairs of agents. In particular, the degeneracy of an instance with identical valuations is $m - 1$ and it can be as small as zero, when all agents view all goods differently.

Informally speaking, we refer to the setting of low degeneracy, the ones where agent valuations over goods are generally dissimilar, as a scenario involving *amicable agents*. Unlike the case of identical valuations, we expect such valuations to invoke relatively "less conflict". One of the key results in [8] is that while finding EF allocations remains hard even with two amicable agents, finding allocations that are both fPO and EF is tractable for a constant number of amicable agents. In particular, the time to compute such allocations was shown to be $O(3^{\frac{n(n-1)}{2}} d^m \frac{n(n-1)}{2}+2)$, where d is the degeneracy of the valuation matrix. In contrast, it was shown that the problem remains NP-hard for instances that have high degeneracy.

Our Contributions. The two results above nicely illustrate the influence of degeneracy on the complexity of finding fPO and EF allocations. We investigate the complexity from the perspective of the number of agents. For example, can this running time be improved to $(n + m)^{O(d)}$, which would increase the realm of tractability to scenarios with any number of agents and constant degeneracy, or more ambitiously, $O(2^{O(d)} \cdot (m + n)^{O(1)})$, which would make the problem tractable for instances with any number of agents and degeneracy logarithmic in $(n + m)$? Our main contribution here is to show that even the former goal is unlikely to be achievable: when the number of agents is unbounded, the problem of finding allocations that are fPO and EF remains *strongly* NP-complete for instances with degeneracy one, even for the specific question of allocations with no sharings.

Our result also has consequences for the problem of finding EF allocations. We recall that the problem of finding EF allocations is weakly NP-complete by a reduction from PARTITION [8]. It turns out that the arguments in the reverse direction of our reduction do not require the allocation in question to be fPO. Since the valuation matrix of our reduced instance happens to only have values that are bounded by a polynomial function of n and m, we obtain a stronger hardness result for the problem of finding complete EF allocations for instances with constant degeneracy.

We also revisit the algorithm for finding fPO+EF allocations from [8]. The algorithm relies on enumerating certain *consumption graphs* corresponding to fPO allocations that fix the sharing structure of a potential solution, after which the task of determining the exact proportions of sharing while respecting fairness constraints is outsourced to an ILP formulation. It is shown [8, Lemma 2.5] that there always exists a fPO allocation with at most $(n-1)$ sharings. We propose an alternate method for generating the relevant consumption graphs that takes advantage of the upper bound on the number of sharings upfront. This leads to a slightly different bound that leads to a better exponential term at the cost of a worse polynomial factor. Although the difference in the bound is not significant, we believe our approach lends additional understanding to the structure of class of graphs based on fPO allocations. The arguments regarding this are deferred to the full version of the paper.

2   Preliminaries

We use $\mathcal{A} = \{a_1, \ldots, a_n\}$ to denote a set of agents and $\mathcal{G} = \{g_1, \ldots, g_m\}$ to denote a collection of objects.

Allocations and Sharing. A *bundle* of objects is a vector $\mathbf{b} = (b_j)_{j \in [m]} \in [0, 1]^m$, where the component b_j represents the portion of g_j in the bundle. The total amount of each object is normalized to one. An *allocation* $\mathbf{z}$ is a collection of bundles $(\mathbf{z}_i)_{i \in [n]}$, one for each agent, with the condition that all the objects are fully allocated. Note that an allocation can be identified with the matrix $\mathbf{z} := (z_{i,j})_{i \in [n], j \in [m]}$ such that all $z_{i,j} \geq 0$ and $\sum_{i \in [n]} z_{i,j} = 1$ for each $j \in [m]$.

Let $j \in [m]$ be arbitrary but fixed. If for some $i \in [n]$, $z_{i,j} = 1$, then the object g_j is not shared—it is fully allocated to agent a_i. Else, object g_j is *shared* between two or more agents.

- The *number of shared objects* is given by the number of items that are shared:

$$\#s^{\dagger}(\mathbf{z}) = \big| \, \{j \in [m] \, : \, z_{i,j} \in (0, 1) \text{ for some } i \in [n]\} \, \big|.$$

- The *total number of sharings* accounts for the number of times that an object is shared, i.e:

$$\#s^{\star}(\mathbf{z}) = \sum_{j \in [m]} \big(\big| \{i \in [n] : z_{i,j} > 0\} \big| - 1 \big).$$

For allocations with no shared objects, both measures are zero, but they can differ by as much as $m(n-2)$ in general. Note that the number of sharings is at least the number of shared objects, since each shared object is shared at least once by definition. Unless mentioned otherwise, our measure for "extent of sharing" in the computational questions that we will shortly define will be the notion of the total number of sharings.

Value and Utility. For every $i \in [n], j \in [m]$, $v_{i,j}$ denotes agent a_i's *value* for the entire object g_j. In the setting of *additive* utilities, the valuations naturally lead us to a utility function over bundles defined as $u_i(\mathbf{b}) = \sum_{j \in [m]} v_{i,j} \cdot b_j$.

The matrix $\mathbf{v} = (v_{i,j})_{i \in [n], j \in [m]}$ is called the *valuation matrix*; it encodes the information about the preferences of agents and is used as the input of fair division algorithms. We use $v^\star$ to denote the largest value in a valuation matrix v. We say that a class of inputs $\mathcal{C}$ has *bounded valuations* if there exists a polynomial $p(n, m)$ such that $v^\star \leq p(n, m)$ for all instances in $\mathcal{C}$.

We recall the notion of degeneracy that was proposed in [8,9]. To this end, we say that two goods g_p, g_q are valued *similarly* by a pair of agents i, j if there exists a constant r such that $v_{i,p} \cdot v_{j,q} = v_{i,q} \cdot v_{j,p} = r$.

Any collection of goods valued identically by a pair of agents would be pairwise similar with respect to the agents in question, but this definition generalizes the notion of "identical" to, roughly speaking, "identical up to a scaling factor". Now, let us define the *similarity* between a pair of agents i and j as:

$$s_{\mathbf{v}}(i, j) = \max_{r > 0} \left| \left\{ k \in [m] \ : \ v_{i,k} = r \cdot v_{j,k} \right\} \right| - 1.$$

Note that the similarity of a pair of agents captures the notion of the largest number of goods that the agents value similarly when considered pairwise. This finally leads us the the notion of *degeneracy*, which is defined as:

$$d(\mathbf{v}) = \max_{i,j \in [n], i \neq j} s_{\mathbf{v}}(i, j).$$

Valuations for which $d(\mathbf{v}) = 0$ are called *non-degenerate*. Also, note that if any two agents have the same valuations for all goods, then $d(\mathbf{v}) = m - 1$.

Fairness and Efficiency. An allocation $\mathbf{z} = (z_i)_{i \in [n]}$ is called *envy-free (EF)* if every agent prefers her bundle to the bundles of others. Formally, for all $i, j \in [n]$: $u_i(\mathbf{z}_i) \geq u_i(\mathbf{z}_j)$. An allocation $\mathbf{z}$ is *proportional (Prop)* if each agent prefers her bundle to the equal division: $\forall i \in [n]$ $u_i(\mathbf{z}_i) \geq \frac{1}{n} \sum_{o \in [m]} v_{i,o}$. An allocation $\mathbf{z}$ is *equitable (EQ)* if any pair of agents derive equal utility from their respective bundles. Formally, for all $i, j \in [n]$: $u_i(\mathbf{z}_i) = u_j(\mathbf{z}_j)$.

An allocation $\mathbf{z}$ is Pareto-dominated by an allocation $\mathbf{y}$ if $\mathbf{y}$ gives at least the same utility to all agents and strictly more to at least one of them. An allocation $\mathbf{z}$ is *fractionally Pareto-optimal (fPO)* if no feasible $\mathbf{y}$ dominates it. If $\mathbf{y}$ is such that $y_{i,o} \in \{0, 1\}$, then $\mathbf{z}$ is called *discrete Pareto-Optimal (dPO)*. The following lemma provides a complete characterisation of fPO allocations.

Lemma 1 ([8], **Lemma 2.3**). *An allocation* **z** *is fractionally Pareto Optimal if and only if there exists a vector of weights* $\lambda = (\lambda_i)_{i \in [n]}$ *with* $\lambda_i > 0$, *such that for all agents* $i \in [n]$ *and goods* $p \in [m]$, *if* $z_{i,p} > 0$ *then for any agent* $j \in [n]$,

$$\lambda_i \cdot v_{i,p} \geq \lambda_j \cdot v_{j,p}$$

Computational Questions. Formally, for a fairness concept $\alpha \in \{\text{EF, EQ, Prop}\}$ and an efficiency concept $\beta \in \{\text{fPO, dPO}\}$, the (α, β)-MINIMAL SHARING problem is the following. Given $(\mathcal{A}, \mathcal{G}, \mathbf{v}, t \in \mathbb{N})$ as input, the question is if there exists an α, β allocation where the total number of sharings is at most t. In this paper, we focus on {EF, fPO}-minimal sharing problem.

3 Hardness for Instances of Constant Degeneracy

To prove the hardness of the minimal sharing problem, we will show a reduction from a structured version of SATISFIABILITY problem called LINEAR NEAR-EXACT SATISFIABILITY (LNES) which is known to be NP-complete [5]. An instance of LNES consists of $5p$ clauses (where $p \in \mathbb{N}$) denoted as follows:

$$\mathcal{C} = \{U_1, V_1, U_1', V_1', \cdots, U_p, V_p, U_p', V_p'\} \cup \{C_1, \cdots, C_p\}.$$

We will refer to the first $4p$ clauses as the *core* clauses, and the remaining clauses as the *auxiliary* clauses. The set of variables consists of p *main variables* $x_1, \ldots, x_p$ and $4p$ *shadow variables* $y_1, \ldots, y_{4p}$. Each core clause consists of two literals $\forall i \in [p], U_i \cap V_i = \{x_i\}$ and $U_i' \cap V_i' = \{\bar{x}_i\}$. Each main variable x_i occurs exactly twice as a positive literal and exactly twice as a negative literal. The main variables only occur in the core clauses. Each shadow variable makes two appearances: as a positive literal in an auxiliary clause and as a negative literal in a core clause. Each auxiliary clause consists of four literals, each corresponding to a positive occurrence of a shadow variable. We will use u_i, v_i, u_i', and v_i' to refer to the shadow variables in the main clauses U_i, V_i, U_i', and V_i', respectively.

The LNES problem asks whether, given a set of clauses with the aforementioned structure, there exists an assignment τ of truth values to the variables such that *exactly one* literal in every core clause and *exactly two* literals in every auxiliary clause evaluate to TRUE under τ. The main result of this section is the following, and is established by a reduction from LNES.

Theorem 1. *(EF,fPO)-*MINIMAL SHARING *is NP-hard even when restricted to inputs with bounded valuations, degeneracy one, and no sharing.*

Proof. We reduce from LNES. Let $\mathcal{C} = \{U_1, V_1, U_1', V_1', \cdots, U_p, V_p, U_p', V_p'\} \cup \{C_1, \cdots, C_p\}$ be an instance of LNES as described above.

We begin with a description of the construction of the reduced instance. We refer the reader to Fig. 1 for a high-level schematic of this construction. For each main variable x_i we introduce three agents: $\{a_i, \bar{a}_i, d_i\}$, and the goods $\{g_i, \bar{g}_i, h_i\}$.

We refer to d_i as the *dummy* agent associated with x_i and a_i and $\bar{a}_i$ as the *key* agents associated with x_i. Also, we refer to h_i as the *trigger* good and g_i and $\bar{g}_i$ as *consolation* goods. For the shadow variables u_i, v_i, u'_i, v'_i, we introduce four agents: b_i, c_i, b'_i, c'_i which we simply refer to as *shadow agents* and four goods: r_i, s_i, r'_i, s'_i, which we refer to as the *essential* goods. Finally, for each auxiliary clause C_j, we introduce the goods f_j^1 and f_j^2. These goods are called *backup* goods.

Note that our instance consists of $n = 7p$ agents and $m = 9p$ goods. Thus the size of the valuation matrix is $N := 63 \cdot p^2$. We let $L = 4000 \cdot p^5$. We will use $\mathcal{A}$ and $\mathcal{G}$ to refer to the set of agents and goods that we have defined here.

Let $\mathbf{w} = (w_{i,j})_{i \in [n], j \in [m]}$ denote the $(7p \times 9p)$ matrix whose entries are given by $w_{i,j} = (i-1) \cdot m + j$. Intuitively, we can think of these values as being small enough to be negligible, and we will obtain our final valuation matrix by starting from $\mathbf{w}$ and "overwriting" some entries to reflect the fact that certain goods are valued highly by certain agents. This is done to ensure that the final valuation matrix has low degeneracy. We now describe the specific modifications that we have to make to $\mathbf{w}$.

To this end, let us define another set of values given by $\mathbf{w}^\star = (w^\star_{i,j})_{i \in [n], j \in [m]}$. Let $\pi : \mathcal{A} \to [n]$ and $\sigma : \mathcal{G} \to [m]$ be arbitrary but fixed orderings of the agents and goods, respectively.

- For $i \in [p]$, we have that the dummy agent corresponding to the main variable x_i has a high value for the consolation goods g_i and $\bar{g}_i$.

$$w^\star_{\pi(d_i),j} = \begin{cases} L & \text{if } \sigma^{-1}(j) \in \{g_i, \bar{g}_i\}, \\ 0 & \text{otherwise.} \end{cases}$$

- For $i \in [p]$, we have that the first key agent corresponding to the main variable x_i has a somewhat high value for the consolation good g_i and the essential goods r_i and s_i, and a high value for the trigger good h_i.

$$w^\star_{\pi(a_i),j} = \begin{cases} L/3 & \text{if } \sigma^{-1}(j) \in \{g_i, r_i, s_i\}, \\ L & \text{if } \sigma^{-1}(j) = h_i, \\ 0 & \text{otherwise.} \end{cases}$$

- For $i \in [p]$, we have that the second key agent corresponding to the main variable x_i has a somewhat high value for the consolation good $\bar{g}_i$ and the essential goods r'_i and s'_i, and also has a high value for the trigger good h_i.

$$w^\star_{\pi(\bar{a}_i),j} = \begin{cases} L/3 & \text{if } \sigma^{-1}(j) \in \{\bar{g}_i, r'_i, s'_i\}, \\ L & \text{if } \sigma^{-1}(j) = h_i, \\ 0 & \text{otherwise.} \end{cases}$$

- For $i \in [p]$ the shadow agents have a high value for their associated essential goods and the backup good which represents an auxiliary clause that contains the shadow variable associated with the shadow agent. Formally, we have:

$$w^\star_{\pi(b_i),j} = \begin{cases} L & \text{if } \sigma^{-1}(j) \in \{r_i, f^1_\ell, f^2_\ell\}, \\ 0 & \text{otherwise.} \end{cases}$$

where ℓ is such that C_ℓ is the unique clause that contains the shadow variable u_i. The valuations for $w_{\pi(c_i),j}$, $w_{\pi(b'_i),j}$ and $w_{\pi(c'_i),j}$ are analogously defined, with r_i being replaced by s_i, r'_i, and s'_i, respectively, and ℓ would be such that C_ℓ is the unique clause that contains v_i, u'_i, and v'_i, respectively.

The final valuations that we will work with are obtained by taking a point-wise max of the two valuation matrices defined above with the following exceptions:

- Dummy agents value the four essential goods associated with them at zero.
- The shadow agent b_i (respectively, c_i) values the consolation good g_i and the essential good s_i (respectively, r_i) at zero.
- The shadow agent b'_i (respectively, c'_i) values the consolation good $\bar{g}_i$ and the essential good s'_i (respectively, r'_i) at zero.

In particular, we propose the final valuation matrix $\mathbf{v} = (v_{i,j})_{i\in[n],j\in[m]}$ as follows:

$$v_{i,j} = \begin{cases} \min(w_{i,j}, w^\star_{i,j}) & \text{if } \pi^{-1}(i) = d_k \text{ and } \sigma^{-1}(j) \in \{r_k, s_k, r'_k, s'_k\}, \\ & \text{or } \pi^{-1}(i) = b_k \text{ and } \sigma^{-1}(j) \in \{g_k, s_k\}, \\ & \text{or } \pi^{-1}(i) = c_k \text{ and } \sigma^{-1}(j) \in \{g_k, r_k\}, \\ & \text{or } \pi^{-1}(i) = b'_k \text{ and } \sigma^{-1}(j) \in \{\bar{g}_k, s'_k\}, \\ & \text{or } \pi^{-1}(i) = c'_k \text{ and } \sigma^{-1}(j) \in \{\bar{g}_k, r'_k\}, \\ & \text{for any } k \in [p] \\ \max(w_{i,j}, w^\star_{i,j}) & \text{otherwise.} \end{cases}$$

For convenience, we say an entry of $\mathbf{v}$ is *large* if it is at least $L/3$ and is *small* otherwise. For (i, j) which are such that $v_{i,j}$ is small, we introduce the notation $\varepsilon_{i,j}$ to denote $v_{i,j}$. We ask if this instance admits an allocation with zero sharing. We now argue the equivalence of the instances.

Forward Direction. Let τ be a boolean assignment for the variables of the LNES instance that we start with. We now propose an allocation:

- If $\tau(x_i) = 1$, then the first key agent a_i gets $\{g_i, r_i, s_i\}$, the second key agent $\bar{a}_i$ gets the trigger good h_i and the dummy agent d_i gets the consolation good $\{\bar{g}_i\}$.
- If $\tau(x_i) = 0$, then the first key agent a_i gets the trigger good $\{h_i\}$, the second key agent $\bar{a}_i$ gets $\{\bar{g}_i, r'_i, s'_i\}$ and the dummy agent gets the consolation good $\{g_i\}$.
- If $\tau(x_i) = 1$, then the shadow agents b'_i and c'_i get the essential goods that they value highly, i.e, r'_i and s'_i.

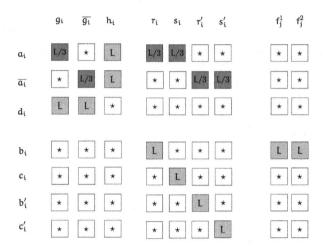

Fig. 1. The overall schematic of the construction in the proof of Theorem 1. The entries depicted by a $\star$ indicate small values

- If $\tau(x_i) = 0$, then the shadow agents b_i and c_i get the essential goods that they value highly, i.e, r_i and s_i.

Note that there are $2p$ shadow agents who have not been allocated any goods so far. It is easy to check that these shadow agents correspond exactly to shadow variables x for which $\tau(x) = 1$. Since τ is a satisfying assignment for the LNES instance, we know that each auxiliary clause C_ℓ contains exactly two shadow variables which evaluate to true under τ. Let $\mu(C_\ell)$ denote the shadow agents corresponding to these shadow variables. Then, for each $j \in [p]$, the goods f_j^1 and f_j^2 are allocated arbitrarily, one each, to the two shadow agents in $\mu(C_j)$.

We claim that this allocation is fPO and EF, and we defer the proofs of these properties to the full version.

Reverse Direction. For the discussion in the reverse direction, we say that an allocation is *valid* if it is EF and fPO and involves no sharing. Let $\mathbf{z} := (z_{i,j})_{i \in [n], j \in [m]}$ be a valid allocation. First, we argue that $\mathbf{z}$ must have a certain structure in a series of claims whose proofs are deferred to the full version.

Claim. In the allocation $\mathbf{z}$, any trigger good h_i must be allocated to one of the corresponding key agents $\{a_i, \bar{a}_i\}$.

Claim. Every consolation good g_i is allocated to either to the key agent a_i or to the dummy agent d_i. Likewise, the good $\bar{g}_i$ is allocated to either to the key agent $\bar{a}_i$ or to the dummy agent d_i.

Claim. If the consolation good g_i is allocated to a key agent a_i, then the shadow agents b_i and c_i must be allocated the backup goods.

Claim. If the consolation good $\bar{g}_i$ is allocated to a key agent $\bar{a}_i$, then the shadow agents b'_i and c'_i must be allocated the backup goods.

Now observe that the two claims above account for the allocation of $2p$ backup goods among $2p$ distinct shadow agents. Let us call these shadow agents *happy* and the remaining shadow agents *unhappy*. We claim that the bundle of every unhappy shadow agent must contain an essential good—this is because these are the only highly valued goods left in the pool and are the only way to eliminate the envy that the unhappy agents feel for the happy ones. Note that every unhappy agent values the bundle of exactly two happy shadow agents.

Based on this, we propose the following assignment of truth values:

$$\tau(x_i) = \begin{cases} 1 & z_{\pi(a_i),\sigma(g_i)} = 1, \\ 0 & \text{otherwise.} \end{cases}$$

We extend this assignment to shadow variables in the natural way: if $\tau(x_i) = 1$, then $\tau(u_i) = \tau(v_i) = 1$ and $\tau(u'_i) = \tau(v'_i) = 0$, while if $\tau(x_i) = 0$, then $\tau(u_i) = \tau(v_i) = 0$ and $\tau(u'_i) = \tau(v'_i) = 1$. We now argue that τ is a satisfying assignment for the original LNES instance.

Suppose g_i is allocated to a_i. We set $\tau(x_i) = 1$. This satisfies all the clauses containing the literal x_i, namely, U_i and V_i. Further, note that these clauses are satisfied exactly once, since we also set $\tau(u_i) = \tau(v_i) = 1$ (recall that u_i and v_i appear in these clauses with negative polarity). The other main clauses U'_i and V'_i are satisfied since we set $\tau(u'_i) = \tau(v'_i) = 0$, and these clauses are satisfied exactly once as well, since x_i appears in them with a negative polarity and we are in the case when $\tau(x_i) = 1$. The case when $\tau(x_i) = 0$ is analogous, and we see that all core clauses are satisfied exactly once by τ, as desired.

We now turn to the auxiliary clauses. Observe that $\tau(x_i) = 1$ if and only if $z_{\pi(a_i),\sigma(g_i)} = 1$, that is, the key agent a_i gets the consolation good g_i. This implies that b_i and c_i are happy agents. On the other hand, recall that we also set $\tau(u_i)$ and $\tau(v_i)$ to one. Similarly, it can be argued that if $\tau(x_i) = 0$, then b'_i and c'_i are happy agents, and in this case, we had also set $\tau(u'_i)$ and $\tau(v'_i)$ to one. So we conclude that all happy agents correspond to variables that evaluate to one under τ. Along similar lines, it is easy to check that all unhappy agents who receive essential goods as explained in the last claim correspond to variables that are set to zero under τ.

Now consider an auxiliary clause C_ℓ. Notice that f_ℓ^1 and f_ℓ^2 have been allocated to happy agents that value these goods highly, so we know that C_ℓ contains at least two variables that evaluate to true. Now suppose there is some auxiliary clause that contains more than two variables that evaluate to true. This would imply the existence of more than $2p$ happy agents, which is a contradiction. The argument for the reduced instance having constant degeneracy is deferred to the full version. □

4   Concluding Remarks

We demonstrated the hardness of finding fPO+EF and EF allocations even for instances with constant degeneracy for instances with an unbounded number of agents. We note that running times of the form $d^{O(n)} \cdot poly(m, n)$ are "weakly ruled out" because of the hardness result in [8] which is based on a reduction from PARTITION. However, all the hardness results combined so far do not rule out the possibility of an algorithm with a running time of $c^{O(d+n)} \cdot m^{O(1)}$, which would imply strongly polynomial running times for instances where $(d + n)$ is bounded by $O(\log m)$. One framework to rule out such a possibility would be parameterized complexity, where one might attempt demonstrating W-hardness in the combined parameter (n, d). On a related note, we show that instances that have bounded degeneracy and a bounded number of values in the valuation matrix are essentially bounded—we refer the reader to full version of the paper for a more detailed discussion.

References

1. Brustle, J., Dippel, J., Narayan, V.V., Suzuki, M., Vetta, A.: One dollar each eliminates envy. In: Proceedings of the 2020 ACM Conference on Economics and Computation (2019)
2. Budish, E.: The combinatorial assignment problem: approximate competitive equilibrium from equal incomes. In: Proceedings of the Behavioral and Quantitative Game Theory BQGT, p. 74:1. ACM (2010)
3. Caragiannis, I., Kurokawa, D., Moulin, H., Procaccia, A.D., Shah, N., Wang, J.: The unreasonable fairness of maximum nash welfare. ACM Trans. Econ. Comput. **7**(3), 12:1–12:32 (2019)
4. Chaudhury, B.R., Kavitha, T., Mehlhorn, K., Sgouritsa, A.: A little charity guarantees almost envy-freeness. In: Proceedings of the 2020 ACM-SIAM Symposium on Discrete Algorithms, SODA 2020, pp. 2658–2672. SIAM (2020)
5. Dayal, P., Misra, N.: Deleting to structured trees. In: Du, D.-Z., Duan, Z., Tian, C. (eds.) COCOON 2019. LNCS, vol. 11653, pp. 128–139. Springer, Cham (2019). https://doi.org/10.1007/978-3-030-26176-4_11
6. Hosseini, H., Sikdar, S., Vaish, R., Wang, J., Xia, L.: Fair division through information withholding. In: Proceedings of the Thirty-Fourth AAAI Conference on Artificial Intelligence (AAAI) (2020)
7. Lipton, R.J., Markakis, E., Mossel, E., Saberi, A.: On approximately fair allocations of indivisible goods. In: Proceedings of the 5th ACM Conference on Electronic Commerce (EC), pp. 125–131. ACM (2004)
8. Sandomirskiy, F., Segal-Halevi, E.: Fair division with minimal sharing. CoRR abs/1908.01669 (2019). http://arxiv.org/abs/1908.01669
9. Segal-Halevi, E.: Fair division with bounded sharing. CoRR abs/1912.00459 (2019). http://arxiv.org/abs/1912.00459

The Complexity of Flow Expansion
and Electrical Flow Expansion

Dorothea Wagner[ID] and Matthias Wolf[(✉)][ID]

Karlsruhe Institute of Technology, Karlsruhe, Germany
{dorothea.wagner,matthias.wolf}@kit.edu

Abstract. FLOWEXPANSION is a network design problem, in which the
input consists of a flow network and a set of candidate edges, which may
be added to the network. Adding a candidate incurs given costs. The
goal is to determine the cheapest set of candidate edges that, if added,
allow the demands to be satisfied. FLOWEXPANSION is a variant of the
MINIMUM-COST FLOW problem with non-linear edge costs.

We study FLOWEXPANSION for both graph-theoretical and electrical
flow networks. In the latter case this problem is also known as the TRANS-
MISSION NETWORK EXPANSION PLANNING problem. We give a structured
view over the complexity of the variants of FLOWEXPANSION that arise
from restricting, e.g., the graph classes, the capacities, or the number of
sources and sinks. Our goal is to determine which restrictions have a crucial impact on the computational complexity. The results in this paper
range from polynomial-time algorithms for the more restricted variants
over $\mathcal{NP}$-hardness proofs to proofs that certain variants are $\mathcal{NP}$-hard to
approximate even within a logarithmic factor of the optimal solution.

Keywords: Flow networks · Electrical flows · Expansion planning ·
Minimum cost flow

1 Introduction

Expanding flow networks is a challenging task with a wide range of applications
such as deciding where to build new roads, which regions to connect by new rail
lines, or where to build new power lines for transmitting electrical power. The
latter problem is often called TRANSMISSION NETWORK EXPANSION PLANNING
(TNEP or TEP), and a huge body of research on it exists in the electrical engineering community; see for example [9] for a recent survey. What distinguishes
TNEP from other flow expansion problems is the underlying flow model, which
needs to capture additional physical laws such as Kirchhoff's Voltage Law.

This work was funded (in part) by the Helmholtz Program Storage and Cross-linked
Infrastructures, Topic 6 Superconductivity, Networks and System Integration and by
the German Research Foundation (DFG) as part of the Research Training Group
GRK 2153: Energy Status Data – Informatics Methods for its Collection, Analysis
and Exploitation.

© Springer Nature Switzerland AG 2021
T. Bureš et al. (Eds.): SOFSEM 2021, LNCS 12607, pp. 431–441, 2021.
https://doi.org/10.1007/978-3-030-67731-2_32

In this work we take a more theoretical view on flow expansion problems and TNEP in particular. An instance of FLOWEXPANSION consists of an undirected flow network and a set of *candidate edges* with given costs. The goal is to find the cheapest subset of candidate edges to add to the network such that the resulting network admits a flow satisfying all constraints. As outlined before, the underlying flow model plays a crucial role. We consider two types of flow in this work: *(graph-theoretic) flows*, which require flow conservation at the vertices and impose a maximum flow on each edge, and *electrical flows*, where additional electrical constraints need to be satisfied. We study the computational complexity of FLOWEXPANSION under various restrictions, e.g., restricting the networks to certain graph classes or restricting the number of sources and sinks. Our goal is to understand which restrictions have a crucial impact on the complexity.

The problem of expanding electrical networks (TNEP) is well-studied [9], but the focus in most works lies on having more realistic models of the real-world transmission system or finding more efficient solution methods. From a more theoretical point of view, TNEP is known to be $\mathcal{NP}$-hard [12]. The related MAXIMUM TRANSMISSION SWITCHING FLOW problem (MTSF), where edges may be removed instead of added, is $\mathcal{NP}$-hard as well even if the underlying graph is series-parallel [4,6]. On general graphs there is no PTAS for MTSF unless $\mathcal{P} = \mathcal{NP}$ [8]. These results can easily be transferred to TNEP.

Expanding graph-theoretical (non-electrical) flow networks can be considered as a minimum-cost flow problem with non-linear cost functions. We make this connection more precise in Sect. 2. For the related problem of maximizing the flow subject to a budget constraint heuristics exist [3]. A generalization of FLOWEXPANSION is the FIXED CHARGE TRANSPORTATION PROBLEM, where the cost of each edge with non-zero flow is given by a fixed amount plus an amount proportional to the flow on the edge. It is $\mathcal{NP}$-hard as well, and there are several exact algorithms based on integer linear programming [10,13].

Contribution and Outline. We give a fine-grained view on the complexity of various variants of FLOWEXPANSION. To this end we classify the variants of FLOWEXPANSION according to the graph classes, the number of sources and sinks, variable vs. fixed production, unit vs. arbitrary capacities, unit vs. arbitrary candidate edge costs, graph-theoretic vs. electrical flow, and (for electrical flows) unit vs. arbitrary resistances. We combine existing complexity results with a variety of new results. These include proofs of the $\mathcal{NP}$-hardness of FLOWEXPANSION in trees (Lemma 2) and the $\mathcal{NP}$-hardness of approximating FLOWEXPANSION with electrical flows better than within a logarithmic factor of the optimal solution in general graphs (Theorem 4). For more restricted variants, e.g., cacti with fixed production (Lemma 8), we give polynomial-time algorithms.

We formally define FLOWEXPANSION and relate it to the MINIMUM-COST FLOW problem in Sect. 2. Sect. 3 contains the hardness proofs for FLOWEXPANSION with variable production. In contrast, having fixed productions makes the problem easier as shown in Sect. 4. In Sect. 5 we consider the variants of FLOWEXPANSION with only one source and one sink. We conclude with a short summary of the results in Sect. 6.

2   Problem Definition

In this work we consider flows in undirected graphs. For notational convenience, we assume that each edge has been given an arbitrary direction. We use uv to denote the edge between u and v with direction towards v. Let $G = (V, E)$ be a graph where the edges are directed as described above. Throughout this work we denote the number of vertices and edges by n and m, respectively. Let cap: $E \to \mathbb{N}$ be a function that describes the edge capacities. Moreover, there are two disjoint vertex sets S and T, which represent sources and sinks in the network. Each sink $t \in T$ has a given demand $d(t) \in \mathbb{N}$. For sources we distinguish two cases. Either each source $s \in S$ has a fixed production $p(s) \in \mathbb{N}$ or an upper bound $\overline{p}(s) \in \mathbb{N}$ is given. We call the tuple $(G, S, T, \mathrm{cap}, p, d)$ a *flow network with fixed productions* or an *F-network* for short, and the tuple $(G, S, T, \mathrm{cap}, \overline{p}, d)$ a *flow network with variable production* or a *V-network*.

Note that in a flow network with fixed productions there is no flow if the sum of the productions does not equal the sum of the demands. In the remainder of this work we therefore only consider networks in which these two sums are equal. Similarly, there is no flow in a flow network with variable demands if the total maximum production is less than the total demand, and we only consider flow networks where the total maximum production is at least the total demand.

A *(network) flow* in an F- or V-network is a function $f: E \to \mathbb{R}$ such that

$$|f(vw)| \le \mathrm{cap}(vw) \qquad\qquad \forall vw \in E, \qquad (1)$$

$$\sum_{u:uv\in E} f(uv) - \sum_{w:vw\in E} f(vw) = 0 \qquad\qquad \forall v \in V \setminus (S \cup T), \qquad (2)$$

$$\sum_{u:ut\in E} f(ut) - \sum_{w:tw\in E} f(tw) = d(t) \qquad\qquad \forall t \in T, \qquad (3)$$

and for F-networks, we have

$$\sum_{u:us\in E} f(us) - \sum_{w:sw\in E} f(sw) = -p(s) \qquad\qquad \forall s \in S, \qquad (4)$$

whereas for V-networks, we have

$$\sum_{u:us\in E} f(us) - \sum_{w:sw\in E} f(sw) \in [-\overline{p}(s), 0] \qquad\qquad \forall s \in S. \qquad (5)$$

In the context of electrical flows every edge e is equipped with a positive resistance $r(e)$ in addition to its capacity. We then call a tuple $(G, S, T, \mathrm{cap}, r, p, d)$ an *electrical flow network with fixed productions* (an *EF-network*). Similarly, a tuple $(G, S, T, \mathrm{cap}, r, \overline{p}, d)$ is an *electrical flow network with variable productions* (an *EV-network*). A flow f is an *electrical flow* if there are vertex potentials $\varphi: V \to \mathbb{R}$ such that for all $uv \in E$ we have $r(uv) \cdot f(uv) = \varphi(v) - \varphi(u)$. In flow networks with fixed production there is at most one electrical flow, and if the capacities are sufficiently large, there is exactly one flow [1, Ch. II]. This distinguishes electrical flows from network flows, which are not unique in general.

In the expansion problem, the edge set E is partitioned into *existing edges* E_0 and *candidate edges* E_1, and there is a cost $c(e) \in \mathbb{R}_{\geq 0}$ associated with every candidate edge $e \in E_1$. For $E' \subseteq E_1$ we call the flow network with underlying graph $H = (V, E_0 \cup E')$ an *expansion* if there is a flow in H. The sum of all candidate edge costs in an expansion H is the *total cost* of H and denoted by $\mathrm{cost}(H)$. The objective of FLOWEXPANSION is to find an expansion of minimum total cost. We specify the type of the flow (e.g., electrical flow with fixed productions) by prefixing FLOWEXPANSION with the abbreviation for the flow type (e.g., EF-FLOWEXPANSION). If we do not explicitly prefix FLOWEXPANSION in a statement, the statement is applicable to all four variants. Note that while we consider simple graphs only, parallel edges can be modeled by parallel paths.

FLOWEXPANSION for network flows can be interpreted as a minimum-cost flow problem with a step cost function. The cost for a candidate edge $e \in E_1$ is 0 if the flow on e is 0, and $c(e)$ otherwise. All existing edges have costs 0. Note that to any flow f in this resulting network there is a flow f' with only integral flow values costing at most as much as f since all edge capacities, productions, and demands are integral. The special case that all candidate edges have capacity 1 is therefore equivalent to a minimum-cost flow with linear edge costs. Hence, it can be solved in $\tilde{O}(m\sqrt{n})$ time [7]. Note that in simple graph classes, e.g., trees, faster algorithms exist. However, our focus in this work lies on distinguishing $\mathcal{NP}$-hard cases from cases solvable in polynomial time.

Lemma 1. *Finding an optimal solution for* F- *or* V-FLOWEXPANSION *with unit capacities is equivalent to solving a minimum-cost flow with linear costs.*

3   Networks with Variable Production

First, we consider FLOWEXPANSION with variable productions. We show that it is $\mathcal{NP}$-hard even in the simple case that the input network is a tree. Moreover, for general graphs, we prove that EV-FLOWEXPANSION cannot be approximated within a logarithmic factor of the optimal solution unless $\mathcal{P} = \mathcal{NP}$.

3.1 $\mathcal{NP}$-Hardness on Trees

We reduce the problem SUBSETSUM to FLOWEXPANSION with variable production. An instance (A, k) of SUBSETSUM consists of a finite set $A \subseteq \mathbb{N}$ and some $k \in \mathbb{N}$. The goal is to find a subset of A with sum k.

Lemma 2. *Finding an optimal solution to* FLOWEXPANSION *with variable production is* $\mathcal{NP}$-*hard even if the graph is a star.*

Proof. Let (A, k) be an instance of SUBSETSUM. We construct a star graph $K_{1,|A|}$, where the center u is a sink with demand k. Each leaf v_a corresponds to an element $a \in A$ and is a source with maximum production $\overline{p}(v_a) = a$. All edges are candidate edges, and the edge uv_a has capacity a and cost a.

As every leaf and consequently every edge corresponds to one element of A, there is a one-to-one correspondence between subsets of A and subsets of the edges. A subset E' of edges, which corresponds to $A' \subseteq A$, is the edge set of an expansion if and only if the sum of the edge capacities is at least k, which means $\sum_{a' \in A'} a' \geq k$, because then the demand of the source can be satisfied. As the cost of E' is $\sum_{a' \in A'} a' \geq k$ as well, any expansion costs at least k and an expansion costing exactly k corresponds to a solution of the SUBSETSUM-instance. Hence, the SUBSETSUM-instance has a solution if and only if there is an expansion costing exactly k.   □

3.2 Approximation Hardness on General Graphs

For electrical flows, the expansion problems are $\mathcal{NP}$-hard by a reduction from STEINERTREE [12, Prop. 1]. This reduction is applicable to all variants of FLOW-EXPANSION. Thus, we can transfer the inapproximability of STEINERTREE [2].

Lemma 3. FLOWEXPANSION *is $\mathcal{NP}$-hard on planar graphs, and on general graphs it is $\mathcal{NP}$-hard to approximate* FLOWEXPANSION *within a factor of* $96/95$ *even if there is only one source or only one sink.*

But for EV-flows we can give a logarithmic lower bound on the approximation factor by a reduction from MINIMUMDOMINATINGSET.

Theorem 4. *For every $\varepsilon > 0$ EV-FLOWEXPANSION with unit resistances cannot be approximated within a factor of $(1/2 - \varepsilon) \cdot \ln(|V|/3) + 1/2$ unless $\mathcal{P} = \mathcal{NP}$.*

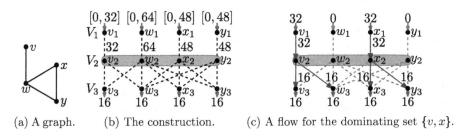

(a) A graph.   (b) The construction.   (c) A flow for the dominating set $\{v, x\}$.

Fig. 1. An example of the network constructed in the reduction from MINIMUM DOMINATING SET in the proof of Theorem 4. The candidate edges are dashed, the intermediate layer is a clique, and $n = 4$.

Proof. An instance of the MINIMUMDOMINATINGSET problem consists of an undirected graph $H = (V_H, E_H)$. The goal is to find a minimum size vertex set $D \subseteq V_H$ such that every vertex in H belongs to D or is adjacent to a vertex in D. Any set with these properties is called a *dominating set*. Given H we build an instance G of EV-FLOWEXPANSION such that expansions correspond to dominating sets in H; see Fig. 1 for an example. All edges in G have resistance 1. The graph G is organized in three layers: the *source layer* with vertex set V_1, the *intermediate layer* (V_2), and the *sink layer* (V_3). Each layer contains a copy of all vertices of H. For $v \in V_H$ we denote its copy in the source, intermediate, and sink layers by v_1, v_2, and v_3, respectively. The vertex v_1 is a source with a maximum production of $\overline{p}(v_1) = (\deg(v)+1){\cdot}n^2$, where $\deg(v)$ denotes the degree of v in H and $n = |V_H|$. The vertex v_3 is a sink with demand $d(v_3) = n^2$. The vertices in the intermediate layer form a clique of existing edges with capacity 1. Each vertex $v_1 \in V_1$ is connected to the corresponding vertex v_2 by a candidate edge with capacity $(\deg(v) + 1) \cdot n^2$ and cost n. Finally, for $v, w \in V_H$ there is the candidate edge v_2w_3 if and only if $v = w$ or v and w are adjacent in H. The capacity of these edges is n^2 and their cost is 1.

Consider any expansion of G and let φ be a potential function of an electrical flow in the expansion. Let $v_2 \in V_2$ and $w_3 \in V_3$. We show that $\varphi(v_2) < \varphi(w_3)$. The vertex w_3 is a sink with demand n^2 and incident to at most n edges. Hence, one of these edges has a flow of at least n; say the edge to $x_2 \in V_2$. This implies $\varphi(w_3) - \varphi(x_2) \geq n$. If $v_2 = x_2$, we are done. Otherwise, we note that the capacity of the edge x_2v_2 is 1, and therefore, we have $\varphi(x_2) - \varphi(v_2) \geq -1$. Adding these two inequalities gives $\varphi(w_3) - \varphi(v_2) \geq n - 1 > 0$, since $v_2 \neq x_2$ and thus $n \geq 2$. Hence, there is no positive flow from the sink layer to the intermediate layer.

Similarly, there is no positive flow from the intermediate layer to the source layer as there are no sinks in the source layer and all sources have degree 1. We claim that in every expansion every sink is connected to a source by a path of length 2. Let $G' = (V, E')$ be an expansion of G and let $v_3 \in V_3$ be a sink. As the demand of v_3 is n^2 and v_3 has at most n neighbors, there is an edge w_2v_3 with $f(w_2v_3) \geq n$. But there is no positive flow to w_2 from the sink layer, and the flow from other intermediate layer vertices is bounded by

$$\sum_{x \in V_2 \setminus \{w_2\}} f(xw_2) \leq \sum_{x \in V_2 \setminus \{w_2\}} \mathrm{cap}(xw_2) = n - 1 < n.$$

Hence, there must be positive flow from the source w_1 to w_2. Thus, the expansion contains the path $w_1w_2v_3$. As there is such a path for every $v \in V_H$, we can transform any expansion $G' = (V, E')$ to a dominating set D by setting $D = \{u \in V_H \mid u_1u_2 \in E'\}$. The existence of length-2 paths to all sinks guarantees that D dominates all vertices of H.

Conversely, from any dominating set D we can construct an expansion of G of cost $(|D| + 1) \cdot n$ as follows. The additional edges are the edge u_1u_2 for each $u \in D$ and for every $v \in V_H$ the edge w_2v_3, where $w \in D$ is an arbitrarily chosen vertex that dominates v. To see that there is a flow in the expansion, we assign $\varphi(v_2) = 0$ and $\varphi(v_3) = n^2$ for all $v \in V_H$, i.e., vertices in the intermediate layer have a potential of 0 and sinks have a potential of n^2. The production $p(v_1)$ of each source is set to n^2 times the number of neighbors of v_2 in the sink layer, and we set $\varphi(v_1) = -p(v_1)$. Note that for $w \notin D$ we have $p(w_1) = 0$. It is easy to verify that this is indeed an expansion with cost $(|D| + 1) \cdot n$.

The transformation presented above can be performed in polynomial time. It remains to show a relation between approximate solutions of FLOWEXPANSION and the transformed dominating set.

Claim. Let $c^\star$ be the cost of a cost-minimal expansion, and let $d^\star$ be the size of a minimum dominating set. If $\text{cost}(H) \leq (1 + \alpha)c^\star$ for some $\alpha > 0$, then $|D| \leq (1 + 2\alpha) \cdot d^\star$.

Proof. We first note that in any expansion each sink is incident to at least one edge, each costing 1. In total the edges between the intermediate and the sink layer cost at least n. Since each edge between the source and the intermediate layer costs n and corresponds to one vertex in the dominating set D, we have $|D| \leq (\text{cost}(H) - n)/n = \text{cost}(H)/n - 1$.

From any minimum dominating set of size $d^\star$ we can construct an expansion of cost $(d^\star + 1) \cdot n$. By the inequality above this is a cost-minimal expansion as otherwise we could construct a smaller dominating set. Hence, we have $d^\star = c^\star/n - 1$. Together with $d^\star \geq 1$ and $\text{cost}(H) \leq (1 + \alpha) \cdot c^\star$, we obtain

$$|D| \leq \frac{\text{cost}(H)}{n} - 1 \leq (1 + \alpha) \cdot \frac{c^\star}{n} - 1 = (1 + \alpha) \cdot (d^\star + 1) - 1 \leq (1 + 2\alpha) \cdot d^\star.$$

$\triangleleft$

Unless $\mathcal{P} = \mathcal{NP}$, MINIMUMDOMINATINGSET cannot be approximated within a factor of $(1 - \delta) \ln |V_H|$ for $\delta \in (0, 1)$ in polynomial time [11]. Hence, it follows from the claim that EV-FLOWEXPANSION cannot be approximated within a factor of $(1/2 - \varepsilon) \ln |V_H| + 1/2 = (1/2 - \varepsilon) \ln(|V|/3) + 1/2$ for $\varepsilon \in (0, 1/2)$. $\square$

4   Networks with Fixed Production

Consider an F- or EF-network $\mathcal{N}$. We construct an equivalent network $\mathcal{N}'$ with variable production. Recall that we assume that the sum of all productions equals the sum of all demands. We use the production in $\mathcal{N}$ as an upper bound for the production in $\mathcal{N}'$, i.e., we set $\overline{p} = p$. As all demands have to be satisfied, all possible production needs to be used. Hence, any flow in $\mathcal{N}'$ is a flow in $\mathcal{N}$. Clearly, any flow in $\mathcal{N}$ is a flow in $\mathcal{N}'$ as well. Thus, $\mathcal{N}$ and $\mathcal{N}'$ are equivalent.

Observation 5. *For any F-network (EF-network), there is an equivalent V-network (EV-network) on the same graph.*

In the other direction, a V-network $\mathcal{N}$ can be transformed into an equivalent F-network $\mathcal{N}'$. We add a super source s^* and connect it to all original sources. We set the capacity of each such edge s^*s to $\overline{p}(s)$. The capacities of the other edges stay the same. We define the new set of sources $S' = \{s^*\}$ and set $p(s^*) = \sum_{t \in T} d(t)$. Restricting any flow f' in $\mathcal{N}'$ to the original edges yields a flow in $\mathcal{N}$. Conversely, any flow in $\mathcal{N}$ can be extended to a flow in $\mathcal{N}'$.

Observation 6. *For any V-network there is an equivalent F-network with one additional vertex that is connected to all sources in the original network.*

Note that adding the super source to a graph in a certain graph class $\mathcal{C}$ may create a graph that does not belong to $\mathcal{C}$ anymore, e.g., a planar graph may become non-planar. Further, the construction does not work for electrical flow networks because it is not clear how to set the resistances of the new edges.

Applying the construction that leads to Observation 6 to the one in Lemma 2, we obtain that F-FLOWEXPANSION is $\mathcal{NP}$-hard on parallel paths. By setting the resistances of the edges such that a all paths induce the same angle difference when their edges are saturated, we further see that EF-FLOWEXPANSION is $\mathcal{NP}$-hard as well. By Observation 5 the same holds if the production is variable.

Lemma 7. FLOWEXPANSION *is $\mathcal{NP}$-hard on graphs formed by parallel paths between the only source and the only sink.*

In the remainder of this section, we make some observations that lead to an $O(n^2)$ time algorithm for F- and EF-FLOWEXPANSION on cacti, which are graphs in which two simple cycles do not share any edges. This contrasts with V- and EV-FLOWEXPANSION, which are $\mathcal{NP}$-hard on trees by Lemma 2.

Suppose e is a candidate edge and a bridge, i.e., $G - e$ contains two components. If the generation equals the demand in both components, there is a cost-minimal expansion without e. Otherwise, any expansion contains e.

Let v be a cut-vertex, i.e., the graph $G - v$ consists of $k \geq 2$ connected components $G_1, \ldots, G_k$. There is a unique way of distributing the demand or production of v to demands or productions of $H_i := G_i + v$ such that the total demand in H_i equals the total production. The graphs $H_1, \ldots, H_k$ can then be considered independently. Repeating this process, G can be split into its blocks (maximal biconnected subgraphs). With these observations we obtain quadratic time algorithms for FLOWEXPANSION with fixed productions on cacti.

Lemma 8. F- *and* EF-FLOWEXPANSION *on cacti can be solved in $O(n^2)$ time.*

Proof. All blocks can be handled independently, and blocks containing bridges can be handled as described above. All other blocks are cycles. Let C be a cycle with ℓ edges. In a cost-minimal expansion either all edges are included or at least one of the edges is missing. We check for all $\ell + 1$ cases whether there is a flow in the resulting subgraph of C and, if so, we compute the cost of the expansion ignoring the candidate edges with flow 0. The computation for C takes $O(\ell^2)$ time, and hence $O(n^2)$ time for the whole network. □

5 Single Source, Single Sink

In this section we consider the special case that there is only one source and one sink in the network. Since there is only one source, its production is determined by the demand. We may therefore consider the production as fixed.

FLOWEXPANSION is $\mathcal{NP}$-hard on graphs where the source and the sink are connected by parallel paths by Lemma 7. But for series-parallel graphs a straightforward dynamic programming on the graph structure yields a pseudo-polynomial time algorithm for F-FLOWEXPANSION, where one terminal of the graph is the only source and the other one is the only sink.

Lemma 9. *On series-parallel graphs with one source and one sink, the problem* F-FLOWEXPANSION *can be solved in $O(n^3 \cdot \min\{C^2, U^2\})$ time, where C and U are upper bounds for the edge costs and capacities, respectively.*

The analogous problem for electrical flows, EF-FLOWEXPANSION, however, is $\mathcal{NP}$-hard even if all capacities are 1 and edge costs are ignored [4]. Hence, there is no pseudo-polynomial time algorithm for this problem unless $\mathcal{P} = \mathcal{NP}$.

But we prove that there is a pseudo-polynomial time algorithm for FLOW-EXPANSION on a subclass of the series-parallel graph, namely those graphs that are formed by a series composition of blocks consisting of parallel paths. We call such graphs *sps-graphs* (for series–parallel–series).

Lemma 10. *In sps-graphs with one source and one sink,* FLOWEXPANSION *can be solved in pseudo-polynomial time.*

Proof. We note that in sps-graphs each block, which consists of parallel paths, can be considered independently. We reduce finding an optimal solution for FLOWEXPANSION on parallel paths to solving a linear number of MINKNAP-SACK instances. An instance of MINKNAPSACK consists of a set of objects A, some $k \in \mathbb{R}_{>0}$, as well as a cost $c(a)$ and a value $v(a)$ for each $a \in A$. The goal is to find a subset $A' \subseteq A$ with minimum cost such that the sum of the values is at least k. A straightforward dynamic programming approach yields a pseudo-polynomial time algorithm for MINKNAPSACK [5, Sec. 13.3.3].

We only present the reduction for EF-FLOWEXPANSION; similar approaches work for all other variants. Let $P_1, \ldots, P_k$ be the paths between the source s and the sink t, each associated with its costs $c(P_i)$, resistance $r(P_i)$, and capacity $\text{cap}(P_i)$. Let further be $\Phi(P_i) = \text{cap}(P_i) \cdot r(P_i)$, which describes the maximum potential difference induced by P_i. We assume that the paths are ordered such that $\Phi(P_i) \leq \Phi(P_j)$ for $i \leq j$. We call the paths with candidate edges *candidate paths* and the others *existing paths*.

In any expansion there is a path P_j with minimum index that is completely contained in the expansion. This path P_j restricts the potential difference between s and t to (at most) $\Phi(P_j)$. For each choice of P_j, we reduce the search for a cost-minimal expansion to an instance of MINKNAPSACK. For each path P_i with $i \geq j$ we define $F(P_i) = \Phi(P_j)/r(P_i)$. This describes the flow along P_i if the potential difference is exactly $\Phi(P_j)$. With the fixed potential difference of $\Phi(P_j)$, the remaining demand d' is the original demand $d(t)$ minus the flows $F(P_i)$ along all existing paths P_i. The goal is then to find a subset Π' of the candidate paths P_i with $i \geq j$ such that $\sum_{P \in \Pi'} F(P) \geq d'$ and $\sum_{P \in \Pi'} c(P)$ is minimal. This is exactly an instance of the MINKNAPSACK problem, which can be solved in pseudo-polynomial time. The cost-minimal expansion then corresponds to the cheapest solution of one of the MINKNAPSACK instances for $j \in \{1, \ldots, k\}$. □

6   Conclusion

FLOWEXPANSION is an optimization problem that can be seen as a variant of the MINIMUM-COST FLOW problem. It is $\mathcal{NP}$-hard even in very simple cases, e.g., if the network is a star (Lemma 2) or if there are only parallel paths between the only source and the only sink (Lemma 7). The more general variants even prove to be hard to approximate (Theorem 4). For some restricted cases, there are (pseudo-)polynomial time algorithms. Our results show that for all parameters (number of sources and sinks, capacities, edge costs, resistances, fixed vs. variable production, and the flow model) there are cases where the complexity differs. One of the most notable cases is the restriction of the capacities to 1, which reduces F- and V-FLOWEXPANSION to a standard minimum-cost flow.

This work studies the complexity of the main variants of FLOWEXPANSION, but the complexity of some special cases is still open. It may also be possible to extend the results for series-parallel graphs to graphs of bounded treewidth.

References

1. Bollobás, B.: Modern Graph Theory. Graduate Texts in Mathematics. Springer, New York (1998). https://doi.org/10.1007/978-1-4612-0619-4
2. Chlebík, M., Chlebíková, J.: The Steiner tree problem on graphs: inapproximability results. Theoret. Comput. Sci. **406**(3), 207–214 (2008). https://doi.org/10.1016/j.tcs.2008.06.046
3. Eiselt, H.A., von Frajer, H.: On the budget-restricted max flow problem. Oper. Res. Spektrum **3**(4), 225–231 (1982). https://doi.org/10.1007/BF01719791
4. Grastien, A., Rutter, I., Wagner, D., Wegner, F., Wolf, M.: The maximum transmission switching flow problem. In: Proceedings of the Ninth International Conference on Future Energy Systems, e-Energy 2018, New York, NY, USA, pp. 340–360. ACM (2018). https://doi.org/10.1145/3208903.3208910
5. Kellerer, H., Pferschy, U., Pisinger, D.: Knapsack problems. In: Du, D.Z., Pardalos, P.M. (eds.) Handbook of Combinatorial Optimization. Springer, Boston (2004). https://doi.org/10.1007/978-1-4613-0303-9_5
6. Kocuk, B., Jeon, H., Dey, S.S., Linderoth, J., Luedtke, J., Sun, X.A.: A cycle-based formulation and valid inequalities for DC power transmission problems with switching. Oper. Res. **64**(4), 922–938 (2016). https://doi.org/10.1287/opre.2015.1471
7. Lee, Y.T., Sidford, A.: Path finding II : An $\tilde{O}(m \sqrt{n})$ algorithm for the minimum cost flow problem. CoRR abs/1312.6713 (2013). https://arxiv.org/abs/1312.6713
8. Lehmann, K., Grastien, A., Hentenryck, P.V.: The complexity of DC-switching problems. CoRR abs/1411.4369 (2014). https://arxiv.org/abs/1411.4369
9. Mahdavi, M., Sabillon Antunez, C., Ajalli, M., Romero, R.: Transmission expansion planning: literature review and classification. IEEE Syst. J. **13**, 1–12 (2018). https://doi.org/10.1109/JSYST.2018.2871793
10. Mingozzi, A., Roberti, R.: An exact algorithm for the fixed charge transportation problem based on matching source and sink patterns. Transp. Sci. **52**(2), 229–238 (2018). https://doi.org/10.1287/trsc.2017.0742
11. Moshkovitz, D.: The projection games conjecture and the NP-hardness of ln n-approximating set-cover. Theory Comput. **11**(7), 221–235 (2015). https://doi.org/10.4086/toc.2015.v011a007

12. Moulin, L.S., Poss, M., Sagastizábal, C.: Transmission expansion planning with re-design. Energy Syst. **1**(2), 113–139 (2010). https://doi.org/10.1007/s12667-010-0010-9
13. Roberti, R., Bartolini, E., Mingozzi, A.: The fixed charge transportation problem: an exact algorithm based on a new integer programming formulation. Manage. Sci. **61**(6), 1275–1291 (2015). https://doi.org/10.1287/mnsc.2014.1947

... ...
... ...

Foundations of Software Engineering – Full papers

An Infrastructure
for Platform-Independent
Experimentation of Software Changes

Florian Auer[✉] and Michael Felderer[✉]

University of Innsbruck, 6020 Innsbruck, Austria
{florian.auer,michael.felderer}@uibk.ac.at

Abstract. Current experimentation platforms for online controlled experimentation focus on the technical execution of an experiment. This makes them specific to the application domain, the expected infrastructure, and the used technology. Moreover, the experiment definitions include numerous implicit assumptions about the platform's implementation. As a result, experiments are difficult to replicate or compare across platforms or even platform versions.

This paper presents an experimentation infrastructure based on platform-independent experimentation of software changes. Experiments are defined technology-independently and the experimentation platform's role is reduced to execution. The explicit definition of experiments in an independent artifact and the modular architecture of the services make experimentation replicable and the architecture open to change. Additionally, a lightweight approach to include the knowledge of past experiments is demonstrated. The infrastructure is presented by a running example experiment and its prototypical implementation.

Keywords: Online controlled experimentation · Experimentation infrastructure · Continuous experimentation · Platform-independent experimentation

1 Introduction

Controlled experimentation evolved from a research tool to a vehicle for the empirical evaluation of software changes, like failure corrections or feature ideas. Moreover, it makes modern techniques of software engineering like machine learning or artificial intelligence testable [2] and allows their optimization through automatic experimentation [13].

Experimentation platforms allow to define, execute, monitor, and systematically analyze experiments with software changes. Therefore, the platforms automate tasks like the power calculation, the segmentation, or the detection of interference between experiments. With the introduction of an experimentation platform, the number of possible experiments is expected to increase and feature teams are expected to be able to experiment independently [7]. There exist

© Springer Nature Switzerland AG 2021
T. Bureš et al. (Eds.): SOFSEM 2021, LNCS 12607, pp. 445–457, 2021.
https://doi.org/10.1007/978-3-030-67731-2_33

proprietary as well as open-source experimentation platforms that provide the necessary components to define and execute experiments. Each platform comes with its own set of features, but also with its interpretation of the experimentation process [5]. Thus, an organization introducing a platform needs to adjust its experimentation process and ideas to the platform. As a consequence, the growth of the organization's experimentation activities is constrained by the platform's capabilities. According to a recent survey among practitioners by Fabijan et al. [8], many practitioners use in-house built experimentation platforms. Compared to third-party platforms, the organization can adjust the experimentation platform to their needs and processes. For instance, a risk-averse organization may introduce extended risk assessment activities to the experimentation process and enforce them through the implementation of mandatory steps for the definition of experiments in the platform. However, developing a reliable experimentation platform is resource-intensive and error-prone [11]. Moreover, not all organizations are willing or able to raise the necessary resources to develop their own experimentation platform.

This paper aims to point out a third option to the decision between a self-built or a third-party experimentation platform. Based on the results of previous work, a prototype of a platform-independent experimentation infrastructure for online controlled experimentation is presented. It is based on the results of dedicated efforts to make experimentation more accessible, improve the overall reliability of experimentation, and to foster knowledge sharing. Therefore, the characteristics and properties necessary to define reliable experiments [5], a language to specify them [3] and an architecture that defines experiments technology-independently within an explicit software artifact [4] were developed. The proposed alternative reduces the role of experimentation platforms to the execution of experiments. All other activities and their artifacts are created and modified with adaptable services of the infrastructure. As a consequence, organizations can use third-party experimentation platforms for the execution, and adjust their experimentation process by adapting the experimentation infrastructure. In the case that a platform no longer suites the needs of an organization, the technology-independence of the experiment definition allows to change the platform without large migration costs. The experimentation process and its activities are not affected. Only the services related to the experimentation platform need to be adapted. Additionally, the increased level of detail of the definition artifact that is necessary for platform-independent experimentation increases the reproducibility and thus the reliability of the results. Finally, the explicit experiment definitions are beneficial for the construction of a knowledge base upon past experiments.

The remaining of this paper is structured as follows. Section 2 discusses related work. Next, Sect. 3 introduces the running example experiment that is used throughout the paper. Thereafter, Sect. 4 presents the experimentation environment and its architecture. Section 5 illustrates the usage of the infrastructure in each phase of experimentation by the running example. Finally, Sect. 6 concludes the paper and Sect. 7 points out future work directions.

2   Related Work

Only a few solutions are proposed in the literature for the infrastructure or tool support of controlled experimentation. Tools presented in the context of online controlled experimentation focus on experiment automation [13], multi-phase deployment strategies [15], configurable user interfaces for mobile applications [12], and experimentation in self-driving vehicles [10]. Besides, the tools presented in the literature, there are existing open-source as well as proprietary experimentation platforms available [5].

Mattos et al. [13] present an automated continuous experimentation architecture framework. A system build with the framework is supposed to control and run experiments automatically. Therefore, the proposed architecture focuses on the automation of experiment coordination, the generation of different experiment versions and their management. In contrast, the proposed experimentation infrastructure presented in this paper aims to resolve the dependency between the experiment definition and the execution of the experiment.

With Bifrost, Schermann et al. [15] provide an implementation of their proposed formal model to define multi-phase experimentation. Their prototype allows to define multi-phase release strategies (e.g. canary releases, A/B tests) in a YAML-based language and to then execute them. Similarly, the presented experimentation infrastructure in this paper uses a domain-specific language based on a data serialization language (i.e. JSON) to define experiments. However, in contrast to the Bifrost language, all aspects of an experiment are defined.

Lettner et al. [12] present an approach supporting the remote exchange of user interface as well as UI functionality in native mobile applications. A modified build process and the introduction of aspect-oriented programming reduce the complexity that is exposed to the developer. The paper discusses six experimentation platforms that were considered at the time of writing (i.e. 2013) state-of-the-art. At the time of writing of this paper (i.e. 2020) the websites of two platforms are no longer accessible[1]. Similarly, the mobile platform Windows Phone that was considered for future evaluation of the work is no longer supported with the beginning of 2020. The fast evolution of technology motivates to reduce the dependency of the experimentation infrastructure on the used technology as much as possible. As a consequence, each service has a modular architecture that can be extended to fit the currently used technology. Moreover, the experiment itself is defined without specifics of the used technology to execute the experiment. Hence, the services are designed with change in mind.

Giaimo et al. [10] present the adoption of experimentation to the automotive domain. The cyber-physical systems built into cars imply additional requirements on experimentation like increased safety constraints and hardware-related constraints like limited processing power. Similar Rissanen et al. [14] highlight requirements for online controlled experimentation in the business to business domain. Thereby, they found technical, customer-related as well as organizational challenges imposed by the domain on experimentation. Both publica-

---

[1] Convert Experiments and Pathmapp, tried to access on 2020-07-27.

tions demonstrate that each domain imposes its specific set of constraints and requirements on experimentation. Although, across all domains experimentation is based on the same fundamental theory, its concrete execution varies from domain to domain. Hence, the infrastructure proposed in this paper does not make any assumptions about the domain or infrastructure. Instead, it focuses on the fundamental activities that are part of experimentation. As a result, the experimentation infrastructure is expected to be adaptable to each domain and its requirements.

As part of a recent study, Auer et al. [5] reviewed experimentation platforms. The analyzed platforms allow to define an experiment, describe its variants and specify the intended segmentation. Additionally, some platforms allow to define a hypothesis (e.g. Optimize[2]), provide sophisticated segmentation techniques (e.g. Wasabi[3]), control the duration (e.g. Unbounce[4]) or even pause an experiment (e.g. Petri[5]). Although experimentation platforms support different sets of features, none of the analyzed platforms allowed to define all aspects [5] or support all activities of experimentation [6]. Hence, it seems that with the growing maturity of the experimentation process of an organization, third-party platforms may become insufficient to support all needs of an organization. Fabijan et al. [7] describe in their experimentation growth model the transition from no experimentation platform, over a third-party platform to an internally developed platform as part of the experimentation growing of an organization. In contrast, the infrastructure presented in this paper combines the initial advantages of third-party platforms with the adaptability of internally developed platforms, by reducing the role of the experimentation platform to experiment execution.

To conclude the proposed infrastructure differentiates itself from existing academic as well as industrial solutions by the following aspects:

- *Process-Focused*: Existing platforms are focused on the technical execution of experiments [3]. Hence, experiment definitions miss other aspects like risk assessment or even the definition of the hypothesis (e.g. Petri, Unbounce, or Wasabi). In contrast, the presented infrastructure focuses on the process of experimentation. For instance, documentation fields are part of the definition, although they are not required to execute an experiment.
- *Complete Experiment Definitions*: The used definition language allows to specify all characteristics of an experiment because it is based on a taxonomy of experiment definition characteristics [5].
- *Technology-Neutral*: The concrete used technology is transparent to the shareholder, given that the technology-specifics are delegated to the concrete implementation of the services.
- *Cross-Domain*: The experiment definition and the services are based on fundamental experimentation activities. As a consequence, they can be adapted to their concrete application domain.

---

[2] https://optimize.google.com.
[3] https://github.com/intuit/wasabi.
[4] https://unbounce.com/.
[5] https://github.com/wix/petri.

– *Adaptable*: The modular architecture of each service combined with the usage of an interpreted language (Python), ease the adaptation of the environment. Additionally, the usage of common data exchange formats, ease the extension of the infrastructure about further services.

3   Example Experiment Description

As a running example, the experimental evaluation of the introduction of a geocoding service for a parcel tracking service is considered. The tracking service provides a status page for every parcel (see Fig. 1) that gives information about the parcel itself (e.g. weight) and its current as well as past status.

(a) Without Location   (b) With Location

Fig. 1. Status page of a parcel with and without its current location.

Based on customer feedback, the organization wants to extend the status page about the current location of the parcel. The location of the parcel is determined by the continuously collected GPS coordinates of the related truck. The corresponding address of the coordinates should be displayed on the status page. To reverse geocode a position to an address, the external geocoding service Nominatim[6] that is based on data from OpenStreetMap[7] was selected. The parcel service tracks millions of parcels, which is why it would require considerable resources to continuously determine the address of each parcel. Hence, the external geocoding service should be called by the client itself for the latest position of the parcel. However, this introduces a dependency on the external service. The responsiveness of the external service and the quality of its responses are directly visible to the customer. Slow response times or confusing results of the external

---

[6] https://www.nominatim.org.

[7] https://www.openstreetmap.org.

service could considerably deteriorate the customer experience and eventually motivate customers to use another service in the future. To assess the geocoding service, an experiment should be conducted to determine whether the geocoding service provides timely responses (i.e. total page load time) and whether the integration of the service leads to increased customer interaction (i.e. page views). A traditional software test is not sufficiently in this case, because the various environmental differences encountered in practice (e.g. operating system, network stability) cannot be simulated cost-efficiently. Finally, it is unknown whether the external service can provide a description for every possible location. Thus, the number of failed requests or empty responses should be measured too.

4   Experimentation Infrastructure for Platform-Independent Experimentation

In this section the infrastructure for platform-independent experimentation is presented (see Fig. 2) by giving an overview of the environment, describing its technological stack and its characteristics.

4.1   Overview

The infrastructure is based on the architecture for platform-independent experimentation as outlined in [4] by Auer et al. Hence, the services Transformation, Execution and Verification are defined that make the experiment definition artifact convertible into required representations, executable by an experimentation platform and verifiable according to syntactic and semantic rules. Additionally, the infrastructure consists of the services Knowledge that can answer questions about past experiments and Data that provide a uniform interface to request the collected data of an experiment.

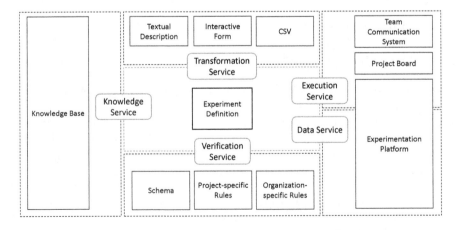

Fig. 2. Overview of the presented experimentation infrastructure.

In detail, the infrastructure comprises the following services:

- **Transformation** to convert an experiment definition into suitable representations for individual tasks. This can be, for instance, CSV for analysis software, interactive HTML forms for meetings, or textual descriptions for reports. Note that representations can be made editable by extending the service appropriately.
- **Knowledge** to answer questions about past experiments. The service can be used to execute queries (i.e. term-based search) against past experiment definitions (i.e. collection of JSON documents). It is a lightweight approach to introduce the knowledge base of past experiments into the experimentation process.
- **Verification** to ensure that an experiment is defined syntactically correct and that it follows all defined project as well as organizational rules.
- **Execution** to deploy the experiment on the experimentation platform for execution. Additionally, the service can be extended to monitor metrics (e.g. click-through rate) about their deterioration and alert or shutdown an experiment if necessary. In the running example, it is further extended to create cards on the team's project board (Trello).
- **Data** to download the data from the experimentation platform. This makes the experimentation platform transparent for the stakeholders.

4.2 Technological Stack

Concerning the used technology, the services are implemented in Python[8] following a modular architecture that allows to extend each service by necessary functionalities. The **Execution** service has three modules that apply the necessary actions on the external services to execute an experiment. In the running example, the services are Optimizely[9], Trello[10] and Discord[11]. The **Data** service uses the API of the experimentation platform to download the collected data. The **Verification** service uses a standard library to syntactically verify the experiment definition (JSON) by the provided JSON Schema. The project-, as well as organizational rules are provided in individual python files that define one rule per file. Finally, the **Knowledge** service is implemented as a full-text search on all past experiment definition artifacts. A more elaborated implementation would allow to query specific fields (e.g. start date) of the experiment definitions' artifacts (i.e. JSON documents). However, the described implementation is sufficient to cover all activities mentioned in the running example (see Sect. 5).

5 Methodology

To illustrate the usage of the tool environment, the running example is described according to the phases of the experimentation lifecycle [6], namely ideation,

---

[8] https://www.python.org.
[9] https://www.optimizely.com.
[10] https://www.trello.com.
[11] https://www.discord.com.

design, execution, analysis, and learning. In addition, it's prototypical implementation is available online[12].

5.1 Ideation

During the ideation phase, the experiment's hypothesis is formulated and necessary changes for the experiment are implemented in the software. In a meeting, the team discusses the idea to integrate the current position of the parcel in the parcel status page. The members of the team have different backgrounds of expertise (e.g. user experience, software engineering, business). Hence, a representation of the experiment definition is chosen that is accessible for every member. With the `Transformation` service, the HTML-form representation of a blank experiment is created. In the meeting, the hypothesis is formulated, the scope of the experiment is determined and the owners are nominated (see Fig. 3). Questions about past experiments are answered with the `Knowledge` service. For instance, what past experiments in the same scope were conducted? Exist similar experiments with the keywords "location", "position" or "GPS"? At the end of the meeting, the experiment definition is saved and verified with the `Verification` service. It highlights relevant problems with the experiment definition and serves as a quality gate. For example, it can verify that the definition conforms to organizational rules about the hypothesis formulation. To conclude, after the meeting an experiment definition artifact exists and is stored at a central place, like the version control repository of the software.

```
{
  "Ideation": {
    "Hypothesis": "Based on qualitative insight, we predict
      that changing the parcel status page to include the
      parcel's current location will cause increase in the
      number of views.",
    "Owners": [
      { "Name": "Bob", "Contact": "bob@parcel-service.at" }
    ],
    "Identification": {
      "ExperimentID": "487719",
      "Name": "Parcel Status Page with Current Location",
      "Created": "2020-05-08"
    },
    "Scope" : {
      "Application": "web-frontend",
      "Area": "parcel-status"
    }
```

(a) Excerpt of the Experiment Definition Artefact   (b) HTML Form

Fig. 3. The experiment definition in different representations.

Next, the changes necessary for the experiment are implemented. A feature flag is introduced to control which variant is exposed to the user. Its name and possible values are captured in the experiment definition as variants and their value expressions. The identification numbers of the related commits to the

---

[12] https://git.uibk.ac.at/c7031224/sofsem2021-prototype.

version control repository are stored in the experiment definition. This creates a relationship between the experiment and the related changes in the source code. In the case of a technical problem during an experiment, for instance, the experiment owner can quickly access the related source code changes.

5.2 Design

Next, the definition of the experiment is completed. This includes the specification of the experiment's variants, segmentation, size, and duration. Moreover, the required telemetry and alert as well as shutdown criteria are specified. Considering the later analysis of the experiment, metrics are defined to measure the impact of the experiment and to ensure the reliability of the experiment (e.g. data quality). At the end of this phase, the experiment is ready for execution. After the ideation, the experiment is designed. Its variants and the desired segmentation are defined. Next, the power calculation is conducted to determine the necessary size and duration of the experiment. Both characteristics are captured in the experiment definition. The Verification service controls that the segmentation is correct and that each variant has a segment. Besides the design of the experiment, the risk associated with the execution of the experiment is assessed. In the definition artifact, all determined risks are documented together with the decisions that were made to mitigate them. The Knowledge service can guide the team, by looking for common risks or past experiments with similar risks. Finally, the start date of the experiment is determined. Again the Knowledge service supports this step. It is used to search for experiments that possibly interfere with the planned experiment. A search for experiments that are executed in the planned time frame and affect the same scope of the application reveals possible interfering experiments. Next, the metrics measured in the experiment are defined. This includes guardrail metrics to ensure that no key aspects of the software are negatively impacted (e.g. page load time), data quality metrics to measure the quality of the collected data (e.g. ratio of data to errors) and success metrics that are expected to be impacted by the experiment (e.g. page views). Again the Knowledge service provides valuable insights into past experiments by listing used metrics of similar past experiments. After having specified the metrics involved in the experiment, the required telemetry and its trigger conditions are defined. Finally, the Verification service is called to ensure that all necessary properties are set correctly and for example, all mentioned telemetry sources are available.

5.3 Execution

In this phase, the experiment is executed. Therefore, its variants are exposed to users and data about the users' behavior is collected. During the execution, the experiment is monitored, for instance, to timely react to harmful experiments that deteriorate guardrail metrics. A final execution of Verification ensures that the experiment is ready for execution. Next, the Execution service creates the experiment at the experimentation platform according to the definition.

Therefore, it translates the defined characteristics into the related concepts of the experimentation platform and calls the necessary platform interface functions. The running example uses Optimizely as platform. Optimizely has no alert or shutdown functionality at the time of writing of this paper. Hence, the infrastructure is extended about this functionality. This is achieved by an extension of the `Execution` service that requests every hour the current data of the experiment from the experimentation platform and evaluates the alert and shutdown conditions on them. In the case that a condition applies, the experiment owner is alerted and if necessary the experiment is stopped. Additionally, the `Execution` service is extended about the functionality to create a notice for the experiment owner to keep track of the experiment and a notice for the data scientist to analyze the data after the experiment ended. The team uses Trello as a project board. Therefore, the `Execution` service connects to the team's project board and creates the appropriate notes. Recently, the team adopted the messenger Discord to improve team-wide communication. The `Execution` service could be further extended to send a message about the start of an experiment.

5.4 Analysis

Next, the experiment is analyzed. Based on the collected telemetry data, the metrics are computed and analyzed regarding statistically significant differences between the experiment's variants. The result of the analysis is used to make data-driven decisions about the evaluated software change. In the running example, the data scientist of the team executes the `Data` service to request the collected data and uses `Transformation` to obtain the experiment definition as metadata in a format appropriate for the analysis software. Hence, the experiment definition is transformed into a CSV-file and loaded with standard libraries into the statistical software R^{13}. Data scientists analyze the experimentation results about their statistical significance and may find common patterns within the data. With the metadata stored in the CSV, the data scientist is able to analyze the experiment independently of his prior knowledge about the actual experiment. Thus, it would be possible to pass the metadata and the collected data to an independent data scientist to analyze the results a second time. The phase ends with the written presentation of the experiment in a report. Again, the `Transformation` service can be used to provide an appropriate representation of the experiment. In this case, a standardized description of an experiment is generated with the `Transformation` service that can be embedded in the report.

5.5 Learning

In the last phase of an experiment, the knowledge acquired by the experiment is documented. Moreover, its results are set in relation to past experiments. This can question underlying assumptions or lead to new insights about the software

---

[13] https://www.r-project.org.

and lead to knew knowledge about the users' behavior. After the experiment is over, all relevant data is archived at a central place to be accessible for later research. The service `Knowledge` showed throughout experimentation the benefit of querying past experiments' definitions. Additionally, to the archival of an experiment definition itself, the experiment's results and its analysis should be archived too. A uniform format for the archival of an experiment and its data is beneficial for later processing (e.g. by `Knowledge`). The project structure and naming conventions proposed in the context of Open Science by Fernández et al. in [9] could serve as an initial draft for a possible structure. In the running example, the data scientist structures his work in an appropriate format for the institutional knowledge base and archives it. The `Data` as well as `Transformation` services may be used in this phase to document the raw data and to provide the experiment definition in necessary formats. Besides the archival of the experiment, the learning phase is used to reflect on the experimentation process itself. What worked well? What needs to be changed? For instance, what additional requests on past experiments by the `Knowledge` service should be supported to further improve experimentation? The adaptable architecture allows the services to grow with the experimentation process of the organization.

6   Conclusion

Online controlled experimentation is limited by the capabilities of the used experimentation platform. Building in-house platforms is a resource and time-intensive endeavor that is not realizable for every organization. To mitigate the need to develop an in-house platform, an experimentation platform-independent experimentation infrastructure and its prototypical implementation was presented. The presented experimentation infrastructure separates the experiment definition from the platform and further reduces the role of the platform to the execution of experiments. All other tasks are covered by modular, lightweight services that can be adjusted to support all requirements of an organization on experimentation. Moreover, the integration of a knowledge base of past experiments was demonstrated.

7   Future Work

An interesting future research direction is to improve the infrastructure. With service extensions that cover generic tasks of experimentation (e.g. interference detection), more and more features become platform-independent and can be shared among the experimentation community across technological boundaries. Additionally, the requirements on an experimentation platform are reduced and thus the number of platforms to choose from increase.

Another idea to pursue can be summarized by the term "experimentation container". Instead of one experimentation platform, the best-suited experimentation platform is selected to execute a specific experiment. Similar to the virtual runtime environment provided by virtualization containers, experimentation containers provide a runtime environment for the execution of an experiment.

Finally, an important future research direction is the development of techniques and methods to foster the sharing of experimentation results. Current research on online controlled experimentation is driven by researchers that have access to experimentation platforms of large organizations [1]. The adaption of technology-independent experiment definition artifacts could be the first step towards the publication of experimentation results. Research in this direction could be a catalyst for the field and improve the reliability of experimental results.

References

1. Auer, F., Felderer, M.: Current state of research on continuous experimentation: a systematic mapping study. In: 2018 44th Euromicro Conference on Software Engineering and Advanced Applications (SEAA), pp. 335–344. IEEE (2018)
2. Auer, F., Felderer, M.: Shifting quality assurance of machine learning algorithms to live systems. In: Tichy, M., Bodden, E., Kuhrmann, M., Wagner, S., Steghöfer, J.P. (eds.) Software Engineering und Software Management 2018, pp. 211–212. Gesellschaft für Informatik, Bonn (2018)
3. Auer, F., Felderer, M.: Evaluating the usefulness and ease of use of an experimentation definition language (S). In: García-Castro, R. (ed.) The 32nd International Conference on Software Engineering and Knowledge Engineering, SEKE 2020, KSIR Virtual Conference Center, USA, 9–19 July 2020, pp. 158–163. KSI Research Inc. (2020). https://doi.org/10.18293/SEKE2020-067
4. Auer, F., Felderer, M.: Platform-independent online controlled experimentation. In: Winkler, D., Biffl, S., Mendez, D., Wimmer, M., Bergsmann, J. (eds.) Software Quality: Quality Intelligence in Software and Systems Engineering - 13th International Conference, SWQD 2021. Springer, Switzerland (2021). https://doi.org/10.1007/978-3-030-65854-0
5. Auer, F., Lee, C.S., Felderer, M.: Characteristics of continuous experiment definitions. In: 2020 46th Euromicro Conference on Software Engineering and Advanced Applications (SEAA). IEEE (2020)
6. Fabijan, A., Dmitriev, P., Holmstrom Olsson, H., Bosch, J.: The online controlled experiment lifecycle. IEEE Softw. **37**(2), 60–67 (2020)
7. Fabijan, A., Dmitriev, P., Olsson, H.H., Bosch, J.: The evolution of continuous experimentation in software product development: From data to a data-driven organization at scale. In: 2017 IEEE/ACM 39th International Conference on Software Engineering (ICSE). IEEE (2017). https://doi.org/10.1109/icse.2017.76
8. Fabijan, A., Dmitriev, P., Olsson, H.H., Bosch, J.: Online controlled experimentation at scale: an empirical survey on the current state of a/b testing. In: 2018 44th Euromicro Conference on Software Engineering and Advanced Applications (SEAA), pp. 68–72. IEEE (2018)
9. Fernández, D.M., Graziotin, D., Wagner, S., Seibold, H.: Open science in software engineering. ArXiv abs/1904.06499 (2019)
10. Giaimo, F., Berger, C.: Design criteria to architect continuous experimentation for self-driving vehicles. In: 2017 IEEE International Conference on Software Architecture (ICSA), pp. 203–210. IEEE (2017)

11. Kohavi, R., Deng, A., Frasca, B., Longbotham, R., Walker, T., Xu, Y.: Trustworthy online controlled experiments: Five puzzling outcomes explained. In: Proceedings of the 18th ACM SIGKDD International Conference on Knowledge Discovery and Data Mining, pp. 786–794 (2012)
12. Lettner, F., Holzmann, C., Hutflesz, P.: Enabling A/B testing of native mobile applications by remote user interface exchange. In: Moreno-Díaz, R., Pichler, F., Quesada-Arencibia, A. (eds.) EUROCAST 2013. LNCS, vol. 8112, pp. 458–466. Springer, Heidelberg (2013). https://doi.org/10.1007/978-3-642-53862-9_58
13. Mattos, D.I., Bosch, J., Olsson, H.H.: Your system gets better every day you use it: towards automated continuous experimentation. In: 2017 43rd Euromicro Conference on Software Engineering and Advanced Applications (SEAA), pp. 256–265. IEEE (2017)
14. Rissanen, O., Münch, J.: Continuous experimentation in the B2B domain: a case study. In: 2015 IEEE/ACM 2nd International Workshop on Rapid Continuous Software Engineering, pp. 12–18. IEEE (2015)
15. Schermann, G., Schöni, D., Leitner, P., Gall, H.C.: Bifrost: supporting continuous deployment with automated enactment of multi-phase live testing strategies. In: Proceedings of the 17th International Middleware Conference, pp. 1–14 (2016)

Using Process Models to Understand Security Standards

Fabiola Moyón[1,4](✉) [ID], Daniel Méndez[2,5] [ID], Kristian Beckers[3],
and Sebastian Klepper[4]

[1] Siemens Technology, Munich, Germany
fabiola.moyon@siemens.com
[2] Blekinge Institute of Technology, Karlskrona, Sweden
daniel.mendez@bth.se
[3] Social Engineering Academy, Munich, Germany
kristian.beckers@social-engineering.academy
[4] Technical University Munich TUM, Munich, Germany
sebastian.klepper@tum.de
[5] fortiss GmbH, Munich, Germany

Abstract. Many industrial software development processes today have
to comply with security standards such as the IEC 62443-4-1. These standards, written in natural language, are ambiguous and complex to understand. This is especially true for non-security experts. Security practitioners thus invest much effort into comprehending standards and, later,
into introducing them to development teams. However, our experience in
the industry shows that development practitioners might very well also
read such standards, but nevertheless end up inviting experts for interpretation (or confirmation). Such a scenario is not in tune with current
trends and needs of increasing velocity in continuous software engineering. In this paper, we propose a tool-supported approach to make security
standards more precise and easier to understand for both non-security
as well as security experts by applying process models. This approach
emerges from a large industrial company and encompasses so far the
IEC 62443-4-1 standard. We further present a case study with 16 industry practitioners showing how the approach improves communication
between development and security compliance practitioners.

Keywords: Secure software engineering · Security standards ·
Business process modeling · Industrial control systems

1 Introduction

Industrial Automation and Control Systems (IACS) are at risk of outages caused
by vulnerabilities in information technology. Security risk could be reduced by
following a strict secure development life cycle (SDLC) [12]. For IACS such a
secure development process should be compliant with norms like the IEC 62443-
4-1 security standard (short: 4–1) [10]. The 4–1 standard provides a blueprint

© Springer Nature Switzerland AG 2021
T. Bureš et al. (Eds.): SOFSEM 2021, LNCS 12607, pp. 458–471, 2021.
https://doi.org/10.1007/978-3-030-67731-2_34

for a SDLC with the aim of reducing impact on critical infrastructure running IACS systems. This standard is based on SDLC standards such as ISO 27034, BSIMM or Secure CMMI [11,15,26].

Compliance with security standards, such as the 4–1 standard, is especially challenging for large-scale industrial companies [5,8]. While they move from traditionally plan-driven development to an agile approach, complexity increases since security standards have to be integrated by several collaborating agile teams. Development practitioners are urged on a daily basis to make decisions on system security [2,28], regardless whether these decisions are made implicitly or not. Hence, practitioners need awareness of requirements as outlined by security standards in order to implement them as early as possible in the SDLC (e.g., in every sprint). Moreover, in case of system attacks, development teams need to cooperate immediately and extensively with security experts; therefore, they need prior understanding of the aforementioned standards.

However, security standards are complex and ambiguous [4]. Development practitioners find them difficult to understand and usually require interpretation and explanations by security experts. Moreover, to accurately implement standards, security experts are essential to tailor requirements to the existent development process (see [14]).

Models are described as useful for overcoming the complexity of security concepts [3,9,13,21,25], however current contributions do not focus on modeling security standards.

In order to tackle the issue of complex and ambiguous security standards, a process-model-based representation of security standards might contribute to the understanding.

In this paper, we present an approach to improve understanding of security standards with model-based representations. Our contribution is threefold and aims at bridging current gaps between security compliance and software engineering [27].

First, we contribute *a visual description of the IEC 62443-4-1 security standard*. We present this in the form of process models, following the Business Process Model and Notation (BPMN) [29]. Our target is to present the standard in a more intuitive way and allow easier review, thus, helping development practitioners and security experts to have more focused discussions compared to just textual descriptions.

Second, we conduct a *qualitative of the IEC 62443-4-1 process models* at Siemens AG, a large industrial company. Given that the security standard is in its introductory phase (released in 2018), the evaluation is still in a preliminary form, focusing particularly on expert interviews. At the same time, we overcome current lacks in reported evidence from contemporary evaluations either having a particularly small sample or invoking students as subjects (c.f. [19]).

Third, we contribute *tool support for the 4–1 standard process models* with ARIS and Symbio [1,20]. Both tools support the visualization of the models and improve dissemination within the company. Additionally, tool support leverages change management and accuracy to BPMN notation.

Our long-term objective is to enable security compliance (including training) for continuous software engineering in industrial environments. By providing a comprehensive representation of the 4–1 standard, its integration into existing agile frameworks is possible. Besides the qualitative evaluation with practitioners (presented in this paper), we reported already on how the 4–1 process models serve as building blocks to: (a) visualize and close the security compliance gap of the Scale Agile Framework (SAFe) (c.f. [16]), a process framework used for large scale industrial software development [22], and (b) leverage security compliance assessment with framework and tool (c.f. [6,18]).

We concentrate this paper on the process models and qualitative evaluation, and we kindly refer the reader to the online material at https://doi.org/10.6084/m9.figshare.8063159 for further information on the detailed models, meta model and tools. The remainder of this paper is structured as follows: Sect. 2 presents an introduction to the standard and the modeling work. Section 3 and Sect. 4 show the study design and results. Finally, we conclude by interpreting results in Sect. 5.

2   Model Implementation of the 4–1 Standard

The 4–1 standard provides a blueprint for a SDLC considering eight practices namely: **security management** (SM), treating security activities to implement the product's life cycle; **specification of security requirements** (SR), referring to accurate eliciting IACS security capabilities; **secure design** (SD), ensuring security as basis in overall architecture; **secure implementation** (SI), guiding the use of secure coding techniques; **security verification and validation testing** (SVV), describing security plans and test types; **management of security-related issues** (DM), providing a flow to handle security issues; **security update management** (SUM), providing a delivery flow for security updates; and finally **security guidelines** (SG), describing the required guidelines to secure deploy the product.

To approach our contribution, the first step is to generate a model representation of the 4–1 standard. Models can support development and security practitioners to better understand and comprehend the norm. As basis for the modeling, we start understanding basic constructs and relationships of the 4–1, as well as the elements of a process model. This helps to determine that process models are suitable to describe the standard. To facilitate comprehension of the models, we use the Business Process Model and Notation 2.0 (BPMN) [29] since BPMN elements are easy to understand for technical and non-technical people. Hence process models include elements like: tasks (t), events (e), artifacts (a) (c.f. Meta-models file in online material). BPMN elements are enumerated and referred with the abbreviation of the 4–1 practice. Example: SR-a1 states for Security Requirements Practice artifact 1.

Subsequently, we modelled the high-level overview of the 4–1 standard to depict practices and its input/output artifacts, as well as events that trigger further practices. Figure 1 shows the first half of this view with each 4–1 practice.

Besides the overview, each practice is refined into individual models depicting inner tasks and how the input/output artifacts are generated. The model of the 4–1 practice *Security Requirements* (SR) is in Fig. 2. The complete set of process models is available online at the file *The IEC 62443-4-1 Standard Process Models*. During modeling, we continuously validated the outcomes for completeness, correctness, and consistency. Prior the evaluation study, experts on the standard checked for missing, wrong, or misplaced elements as well as connections between tasks, flows, and artifacts.

Finally, in order to improve dissemination and knowledge transfer, we provide the process models in several tool formats. As an initial approach Microsoft Visio was used, allowing easy distribution of the models as PDF files, however, with limitations in change management. This leads us to use BPMN modeling tools. Models are available in: ARIS, an intuitive visualization tool, which provides the necessary flexibility to apply changes with an acceptable learning curve [1]; and Symbio, that represents artefacts, tasks and events as rectangles with different icons and colors. Even though less flexible than ARIS, it provides more detailed views of models as matrices [20]. Excerpt of process models in the tools are available online at file *Tool Support*.

3   Evaluation Design

We evaluated our 4–1 process models via expert interviews involving 16 practitioners working at Siemens in security compliance or agile software engineering. Among these experts is an IEC committee member for 4–1.

Our overall goal is to investigate the subjective usefulness of our process models to transfer knowledge of security standards, as represented by the IEC 62443-4-1. Through the evaluation, we explore potential benefits and limitations of the models. Our evaluation is guided by good practices on empirical studies [24] and is constraint to the following question:

To what extent can models help comprehending the IEC 62443-4-1 security standard?

3.1   Subject Selection

As study environment we chose typical project settings at Siemens. There, product development projects follow the large-scale agile framework Scaled Agile Framework (SAFe) and the processes are deemed to comply with the 4–1 security standard. Most industrial projects that fit these characteristics demand direct collaboration between security experts and development teams. Moreover, development practitioners need to be more knowledgeable on security standards to accurately implement security requirements on a day-to-day basis. Therefore, we selected development practitioners working in these projects and security experts that join the projects on-demand.

The IEC 62443-4-1 Process (1 of 2)

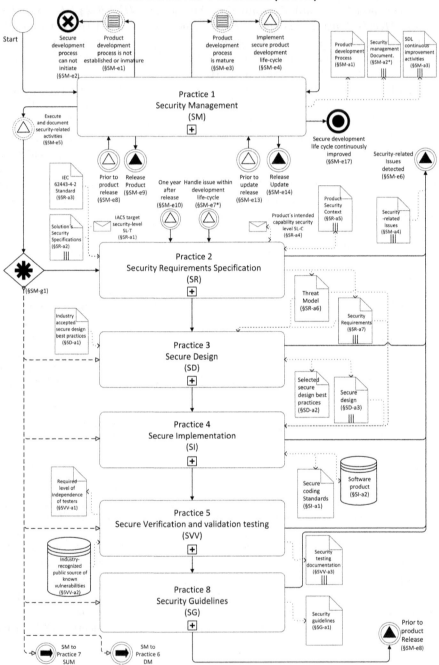

Fig. 1. The IEC 62443-4-1 security standard overview process model (Excerpt). BPMN diagram depicting the standard practices, their flow, and artifacts.

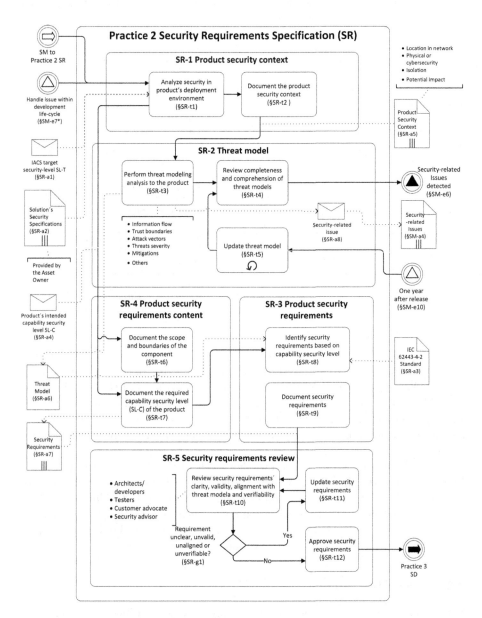

Fig. 2. The IEC 62443-4-1 practice 2 security requirements (SR) process model. BPMN diagram depicting the 4–1 standard requirements to document security capabilities in IACS.

Our selection comprises 16 experienced professionals. We defined profiles to distinguish their level of expertise according to their key role. Table 1 shows each role's background and the distribution in the interviews.

Table 1. Mapping of interviews to profile groups with background. Adapted from [17]

Profile	Sample size	Interview numbers	Background
Contributor IEC	1	13	Industrial systems life cycle standardisation
Contributor SAFe	1	12	Industrial systems agile development
Principal Expert	3	4, 5, 8	Industrial systems security standards and processes, secure design for industrial solutions
Senior Expert	4	1, 2, 6, 9	Industrial systems cloud security, security processes improvement, IT security assessments
Expert	7	3, 7, 10, 11, 14, 15, 16	Industrial systems agile development, quality compliance, design and development of access control systems, data privacy on smart cities, security design management, DevOps, security tools development, automated security testing, IT security in critical infrastructure

In this table, we distinguish between standards contributors and topic experts. We divided the 4–1 standard (*Contributor IEC*) and the contributos to the SAFe framework (*Contributor SAFe*). The topic experts are categorized into *Principle Experts* having broad knowledge and leading teams, *Senior Experts* having deep knowledge and responsible for putting specific topics into practice, and general *Experts*.

Our subjects have different knowledge levels of the 4–1 standard and SAFe. Figure 3 shows the knowledge of our subjects in different areas, depending on their category. Even though not all of them know the 4–1 standard, all except for one are aware of other security standards such as ISO/IEC 27001 or other standards of the IEC 62443 family. Similarly, not all know SAFe, but all subjects are familiar with other agile process frameworks such as Scrum.

3.2 Survey Instrument

Since our goal is to explore practitioners' opinions, we identified semi-structured interviews as the most suitable technique (see [24]). Each interview lasted 1.5 to 2 h and took place in an isolated environment with one interviewee and two interviewers. One interviewer actively followed a questionnaire and the other one documented the answers along the protocol. The questionnaire is available in the online material.

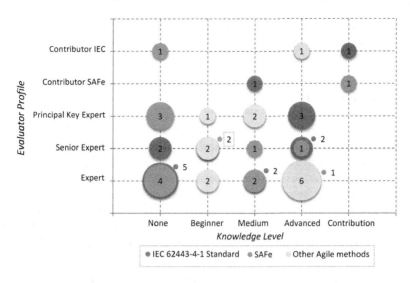

Fig. 3. Subject knowledge of IEC 62443-4-1 and SAFe or comparable process frameworks. Image adapted from [17]

Each interview deals with one 4–1 standard practice, which was chosen in advance according to the subject's background. Practices are either security requirements (SR), secure implementation (SI) or security verification and validation testing (SVV) as shown in Fig. 4.

Interview subjects intentionally received no instruction or training on the 4–1 models at all. They were first briefed about the interview flow and the purpose of the process models. Afterwards, we conducted the interviews in the following steps:

- Interviewees were introduced to our 4–1 process models as well as their hierarchy (the entire overview models (see Fig. 1) and an individual practice model).
- They analyzed one of the 4–1 practice models without time limits (e.g. practice SR shown in Fig. 2).
- They read a textual excerpt from the 4–1 standard corresponding to the practice.
- They answered the protocol questions about 4–1 (e.g. "Are process models easier to understand than the 4–1 text?").

Finally, the interviewer notes on the questionnaire were discussed with the subject for clarification.

3.3 Data Analysis

Our preliminary evaluation is based on summarizing the answers to closed questions and clustering comments and concerns according to commonalities.

We further analyzed the emphasis of answers to differentiate acceptance vs. conviction, rejection vs. repulsion, and neutrality vs. doubt. Hence, we tabulated answers according a 9-point Likert scale.

4   Evaluation Results

The evaluation shows that understanding of the 4–1 standard is increased. 14 participants have claimed to understand our models better than the 4–1 standard. All subjects felt like Activities and Flows could be more easily identified, while 14 also identified artifacts more easily. Furthermore, all interviewees except for one claimed that they require less time for reading and understanding the model, when compared to the text. Moreover, 15 participants consider the models as useful for their work. Except for the required time to read, all subjects considered the model approach in all aspects as fitting at least equally well.

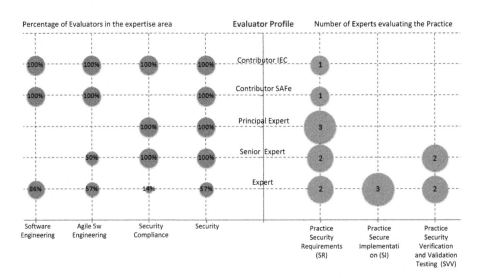

Fig. 4. Distribution of IEC 62443-4-1 practices into profile groups. Right side: number of interviewees per practice. Left side: percentage of interviewees per expertise area. Image adapted from [17]

In order to identify potential improvements, the comments provided by the subjects were clustered into categories. Table 2 summarizes common opinions on the model approach. Further outcomes of our study can be found below. For any specific participant statement, the respective interview of Table 1 is referenced:

Security Standard Models are Intuitive and Precise. Subjects read models quicker than the standard text and could also understand the global process better. Artifacts, activities, and flows are easier to identify than in text. They corroborated the criteria that the complexity could be reduced in comparison to

Table 2. Models common issues as referred by interview participants

Evaluators' opinion	Interviews	Total
Find models helpful to have good overview of the standard. models don't replace the document. Interviewees would use text and models	4, 5, 9, 11, 13, 14, 15, 16	8
Analyze the models and discuss doubts on the standard that they had beforehand	5, 8, 11, 13, 14, 15	6
Would like to understand deep the notation, analyze in deep the elements and/or provide feedback to the notation	2, 4, 8, 10, 11, 13	6
Analyze the models and ask where the standard says so. They consult the text and notice something new or another interpretation	5, 6, 8, 11, 13	5
Provide feedback on visualization (line thickness, elements location)	7, 8, 10, 13, 14	5
Have a concern on models interpretation. Suggests PM approval and refinement by competent professionals e.g. IEC Committee	4, 6, 9, 11	4
Provide feedback on nomenclature	4, 7, 8, 10	4
Have a concern about the suitable audience of the models	5, 13, 15	3
Envision issues or feedback to the standard	8, 13, 14	3
Requires to know content of artifacts, e.g. templates of documents	1, 4, 5	3
Requires a catalog of models	1, 12	2
Require clarification about the term artifact	9, 11	2

reading a standard: *"I can concentrate on specific things, that is why I like it"* (I14 - *expert* security researcher).

Security Standard Models Increase Comprehension of the Standard Without Replacing the Text. During the interviews, some respondents solved preexisting doubts while others rediscovered some statements of the standard, e.g., *"Why there is no flow here?"* (I14 *expert* product owner). Nonetheless, they recognized that a deep understanding of the standard requires to read the document, e.g., *"text provides some reasoning that cannot fit in the diagram"* (I4 security *principal expert*). Also, the *contributor IEC* (I13) appreciated the 4–1 standard models. They started skeptic but ended up rather convinced. First, it took them time to read the 4–1 global model and analyze the detailed practice in depth. They asked for the reference of some elements in the model *"Where does the standard say so?"*. Later, they discussed some model references to other members of the 62443 standard family. They agreed on some assumptions we had to make and openly discussed the accuracy of the standard referring to security requirements and its relationship to the threat model. They argued on the purpose of the corresponding text, thus, corroborating again the need of rich descriptions as a rationale. Finally, they approved our model while stating *"[The] Model helps to see relationships, text has more description. We need both."*

Security Standard Models Support Quick Understanding. Interviewees referred to different scenarios to apply models, such as (1) to report issues to the IEC committee, (12) to plan and estimate projects well, or (3) to solve issues related to knowledge transfer: *"Models will help standardization steps in a memorable way."* (I9 - security assessments *senior expert*); *"There were discussions within IEC about this reference to 4–2"* (I13 *contributor IEC*); *"I would like to use it in my lectures"* (I8 - security *principal expert*).

Proficient Review of Security Standard Models Motivates Adoption. Our models are a translation of the standard (as understood by us and validated by experts) to a visual language. Interviewees pointed out the risk of crossing the line between representation and interpretation/assumption. They would have felt more comfortable to follow the models after an accurate review and possible approval by the IEC Committee. However, the fact that the *4–1 global PM* and *practice 2* were approved by the IEC Contributor strengthens our confidence in the reliability and accuracy of our models.

Development Teams Require Derived Models. The *IEC contributor* (I13), and a security *principal expert* had concerns about confronting development teams with the 4–1 models. They thought teams would either underestimate the models or they might feel overwhelmed: *"It is intimidating at first sight"* (I5). In addition, an expert system architect (I15) was highly skeptic when looking at the models: *"My experience shows that models do not model reality, [...] I have not seen a process that is being followed"*. Even though at end of the interview, the subject (I15) describe to get more familiar with the standard, it is clear, more refinements of the models are needed for development teams. For this use case process modeling tools can be beneficial.

Artifact Instances are Needed. Interviewees asked for examples of the artifacts. They consider models as a "to-do checklist", therefore a template of the artifacts would help to estimate implementation effort. Also, it seems to be unclear what an artifact is according to the standard, e.g., *"[...] standards don't say specifically these are artifacts [...] security requirements is not an individual document"* (I5 -*principal expert*). Artifact instantiation is not trivial, for example for threat models, a main security analysis artifact, there is not yet a common agreement (c.f. [7,23]). A future work goal is to explore artifacts instantiation.

Security Standard Models Catalog is Needed. Subjects reviewed parts of the models. Some of them had interest in a comprehensive list of all models to have an idea of the size. *"To manage the catalog of flowcharts may be complicated"* (I5).

Security Standard Models Need Precise Notation for Artifacts. BPMN 2.0 provides limited elements to represent artifacts: document, data store, data message. These elements are not suitable to visually express the type artifact. We model most of our artifacts as documents, however, according to *contributor IEC* "*artifacts are not documents*" (I13). An evaluator would like to "*Update notation to reflect type of artifact*" (I4).

Security Standard Models Require Highlighting. Evaluators gave feedback on how to improve models appearance, e.g., lines position, bold titles, and subtitles; e.g., *"Change line from right to left"* (I8).

BPMN Notation is Intuitive. Except for one, subjects read the models without introduction on BPMN. All of them understood models in limited time. Based on this observation, we perceive that *BPMN is highly intuitive*. However, some elements of the last version BPMN 2.0 required clarification, e.g., event types escalation, signal, event trigger throwing and receiving. Also others were simply disregard, e.g., the collection symbol to describe a document artifact is a set, indirect flow. Some participants requested a legend for BPMN.

5   Conclusion

In this paper, we reported on our ongoing work towards using process models to implement and disseminate complex and easy to misunderstand security requirements derived from IEC 62443-4-1 standard. In scope of the paper at hand and of particular interest to us was to facilitate comprehensibility and focused discussions on the 4–1 standard for which we used BPMN process models. We evaluated this visualization by interviewing 16 industry experts.

Our results strengthen our confidence in that the models can be understood in a time-effective manner and challenge popular belief that especially agile processes are a "gateway to chaos" and, thus, not reconcilable with security and compliance concerns. The unanimous response to our work was the exact opposite: Introducing large-scale agile processes demands a culture and mindset change. Even though not our primary intention, the models seemed to have helped to convey to skeptical practitioners that both secure and agile development is feasible at scale with reasonable effort.

Our research indicates that models are an excellent way to mediate between agile practitioners and security experts. Particularly visual models allowed them to engage the challenge of continuous security compliance together. Moreover, these models pave the way for analyzing various further challenges of the research field: Do models increase the speed of adapting large organizations to secure agile processes at scale? Are models a better way of getting security norms accepted into daily software engineering activities? Can models provide guided and precise support for secure agile security governance? We are confident that our contribution supports researchers to further investigate these questions.

5.1   Relation to Existing Evidence

Our study is in tune with existing trends of empirical studies on secure software engineering [19], but extends the study population in number and profile. To the best of our knowledge, preceding studies involved up to 11 practitioners with mixed background or students as subjects and focused on valuated, yet isolated topics. An integrated view on security standard compliant scalable agile framework was not in their scope. Our contribution is aimed at this gap and involves 16 experienced professionals, partially with contributing roles to the standards or decision-making roles in the organization. We focused on the highest ranking experts available. Their opinion is the closest to certainty in a timely evaluation.

5.2   Limitations and Threats to Validity

Qualitative studies inherently carry limitations and interview research in particular has threats to validity that need discussion, the most important of which shall be discussed here.

The individual expertise of each participant might influence their attention and interpretation of security requirements as well as agile practices captured in the models. We tried to mitigate this with discussion-intensive preparation procedures but also by letting subjects interpret the models as they are without any further instruction. We were interested in potential bias towards the subject of security compliance as that reflects on the projects where those models shall be applied.

Similarly, involving experts from each respective field carries the risk of self-selection and confirmation bias. To mitigate this we selected subjects according to typical roles in the target organization environment instead of their particular interest in the topic. The same is true for which part of the 4–1 standard they reviewed (requirements, implementation, or testing). We also designed interview plan and questionnaire accordingly and allocated interviewees to models based on previously defined profiles.

References

1. AG, S.: Aris - software ag. https://www.ariscommunity.com/
2. Ahola, J., et al.: Handbook of the Secure Agile Software Development Life Cycle. University of Oulu, Finland (2014)
3. Al-Hamdani, W.A.: Three models to measure information security compliance. IJISP **3**(4), 43–67 (2009)
4. Beckers, K.: Pattern and Security Requirements. Springer, Cham (2015). https://doi.org/10.1007/978-3-319-16664-3
5. Bell, L., Brunton-Spall, M., Smith, R., Bird, J.: Agile Application Security. Enabling Security in a Continuous Delivery Pipeline. O'Reilly, Sebastopol (2017)
6. Dännart, S., Constante, F.M., Beckers, K.: An assessment model for continuous security compliance in large scale agile environments. In: Giorgini, P., Weber, B. (eds.) CAiSE 2019. LNCS, vol. 11483, pp. 529–544. Springer, Cham (2019). https://doi.org/10.1007/978-3-030-21290-2_33
7. Fernandez, E.B.: Threat modeling in cyber-physical systems. In: Proceedings (DASC/PiCom/DataCom/CyberSciTech) (2016)
8. Fitzgerald, B., Stol, K.J., O'Sullivan, R., O'Brien, D.: Scaling agile methods to regulated environments: an industry case study. In: Proceedings of ICSE, IEEE (2013)
9. Hu, J.: Idea to derive security policies from collaborative business processes. In: 2009 13th Enterprise Distributed Object Computing Conference Workshops, pp. 243–246 (September 2009)

10. IEC: 62443-4-1 security for industrial automation and control systems part 4-1 product security development life-cycle requirements (2018)
11. ISO/IEC: 27034. Information technology - Security techniques - Application security (2011)
12. Keramati, H., Mirian-Hosseinabadi, S.H.: Integrating software development security activities with agile methodologies. In: AICCSA (2008)
13. Leitner, M., Miller, M., Rinderle-Ma, S.: An analysis and evaluation of security aspects in the business process model and notation. In: 2013 International Conference on Availability, Reliability and Security, pp. 262–267 (September 2013)
14. Maidl, M., Kröselberg, D., Christ, J., Beckers, K.: A comprehensive framework for security in engineering projects - based on IEC 62443. In: 2018 IEEE ISSRE Workshops (2018)
15. McGraw, G., Migues, S., Chess, B.: Building security in maturity model, https://www.bsimm.com/about.html
16. Moyón, F., Beckers, K., Klepper, S., Lachberger, P., Bruegge, B.: Towards continuous security compliance in agile software development at scale. In: Proceedings of RCoSE, ACM (2018)
17. Moyón, F.: Towards continuous security. In: Master's Thesis: Department of Informatics. Technical University Munich (2018)
18. Moyón, F., Bayr, C., Mendez, D., Dännart, S., Beckers, K.: A light-weight tool for the self-assessment of security compliance in software development – an industry case. In: Chatzigeorgiou, A. (ed.) SOFSEM 2020. LNCS, vol. 12011, pp. 403–416. Springer, Cham (2020). https://doi.org/10.1007/978-3-030-38919-2_33
19. Othmane, L., Jaatun, M., Weippl, E.: Empirical Research for Software Security: Foundations and Experience. CRC Press, Boca Raton (2017)
20. Ploetz, Zeller: Symbio. https://www.symbioworld.com/
21. Riesner, M., Pernul, G.: Supporting compliance through enhancing internal control systems by conceptual business process security modeling. In: ACIS Proceedings (2010)
22. Scaled Agile Inc.: Safe reference guide. http://www.scaledagileframework.com/ (2017)
23. Shostack, A.: Threat Modeling: Designing for Security. Wiley, Hoboken (2014)
24. Shull, F., Singer, J., Sjøberg, D.I.: Guide to Advanced Empirical Software Engineering. Springer, New York (2007)
25. Sunkle, S., Kholkar, D., Kulkarni, V.: Model-driven regulatory compliance: A case study of "know your customer" regulations. In: 18th ACM/IEEE MODELS, pp. 436–445 (September 2015)
26. Technology, S.A.C.: Security by Design with CMMI for Development Version 1.3. CMMI Institute (2013)
27. Tøndel, I.A., Jaatun, M.G., Cruzes, D.S., Moe, N.B.: Risk centric activities in secure software development in public organisations. IJSSE 8(4), 1–30 (2017)
28. Turpe, S., Poller, A.: Managing security work in scrum: tensions and challenges. In: Proceedings of SecSE (2017)
29. White, S., Miers, D.: BPMN Modeling and Reference Guide. Future Strategies, USA (2008)

Web Test Automation: Insights from the Grey Literature

Filippo Ricca[1]([✉])[ID] and Andrea Stocco[2][ID]

[1] Università Degli Studi di Genova, Genoa, Italy
filippo.ricca@unige.it
[2] Università della Svizzera italiana, Lugano, Switzerland
andrea.stocco@usi.ch

Abstract. This paper provides the results of a survey of the grey literature concerning best practices for end-to-end web test automation. We analyzed more than 2,400 sources (e.g., blog posts, white-papers, user manuals, GitHub repositories) looking for guidelines by IT professionals on how to develop and maintain web test code. Ultimately, we filtered 142 relevant documents from which we extracted a taxonomy of guidelines divided into technical tips (i.e., concerning the development, maintenance, and execution of web tests), and business-level tips (i.e, concerning the planning and management of testing teams, design, and process). The paper concludes by distilling the ten most cited best practices for developing good quality automated web tests.

Keywords: Web test automation · Grey literature · Best practices

1 Introduction

End-to-end (E2E) web testing is one of the approaches used for assuring the correctness of web applications. In this context, the tester verifies the correct functioning of the application under test through automated test scripts. Such scripts automate the set of manual operations that the end-user would perform on the web application's graphical user interface (GUI), such as delivering events with clicks or filling in forms, and they are typically used for regression testing [41]. Thus, test cases become software artifacts that developers write resorting to specific testing frameworks. However, the development of complex test suites requires nontrivial programming skills and domain knowledge of the application under test.

An effective code development process must be driven by guidelines and best practices. To the best of our knowledge, the scientific literature has been neglecting the topic of surveying existing best practices or proposing new ones to produce high-quality test code. Instead, researchers have proposed solutions to mitigate specific issues like test fragility [26], or automated repair [40], which are based mostly on anecdotal findings.

© Springer Nature Switzerland AG 2021
T. Bureš et al. (Eds.): SOFSEM 2021, LNCS 12607, pp. 472–485, 2021.
https://doi.org/10.1007/978-3-030-67731-2_35

On the other hand, the grey literature—constituted by white-papers, magazines, online blog-posts, question-answers sites, survey results, and technical reports—is a rich source of documents in which practitioners often share their experience matured on the field, and propose best practices, guidelines, and tips related to different quality aspects of test code. Synthesizing knowledge from the grey literature is a contemporary issue in empirical software engineering research [16]. For instance, works have mined the knowledge by practitioners about how to best select the right test automation tool [34], or to highlight the factors behind the choice of what and when to automate [17].

From our experience, the grey literature is still an unexplored gold mine of guidelines for E2E web test automation. However, such insights are still hidden as practitioners lack both the time and the scientific background to distill the most relevant best practices rigorously. For this reason, we have conducted a survey to help structure, curate, and unify the grey literature in E2E web test automation, to understand what best practices are suggested by practitioners, and what are the challenges reported when they are used.

The main contribution of our work is a taxonomy of best practices for E2E web test automation, composed by a rich set of guidelines about different technical and business-level aspects of the testing and development life cycle. We distilled the set of ten most cited best practices that, according to developers, can improve the quality of automated tests. Our taxonomy can be useful to both practitioners and researchers, who can, respectively, use the most quoted best practices to guide the development of better quality test code, and foster future research in this field.

2   Background

E2E web testing is a type of black-box testing based on the concept of test scenario, i.e., a sequence of steps and actions performed by a user on the application under test's GUI. One or more test cases can be derived from a scenario by specifying the input data and the expected results. The test case execution can be automated through test scripts within specific testing frameworks [24].

Selenium is the de-facto ecosystem [14] to support different kinds of E2E web testing [7,27]. For instance, Selenium IDE is used for quick *exploratory testing* as it allows recording the actions performed by the tester on the web application, from which generated test scripts can be conveniently replayed multiple times. With Selenium WebDriver, on the other hand, test scripts are programmed in a high-level programming language using the framework's APIs. As such, developed test scripts become first-class citizens that developers design, maintain, review, and refactor the same way as the production code. For this reason, Web-Driver is used mostly to create complex and large test suites for browser-based *regression test automation*. Finally, Selenium Grid offers services that allow distributing test scripts over multiple browsers and platforms, which is convenient for performing *cross-browser and cross-platform testing*.

Even though the web testing community is highly influenced by the Selenium ecosystem, in this paper we focus on the best practices for web test code development and maintenance, regardless of the specific testing framework for which they were originally proposed.

3   Related Work

Researchers have long proposed methodologies and techniques to test web based systems, including testing classical [12,37] and modern [4–6,29,30] web apps.

In recent years, the increased popularity of tools like Selenium motivated the research community to study the challenges of E2E test automation and propose solutions to improve the quality of test code produced by such tools [24,36,39]. This literature can be broadly divided into two main categories. A first category pertains to empirical studies in web test automation such as studies on the evolution of web test scripts [21], the differences between the approaches [24], economic perspectives in test automation [33], or other secondary studies on web test automation [9,18,22,28]. A second category, instead, refers to solution-based papers that tackle a specific problem in web test automation, such as robustness of test code [26], automated test repair [8,20,25,40], or test adequacy criteria [31,32] Most of this research is built on anecdotal facts, or on knowledge acquired by studies of the first category.

We recognize two main drawbacks. First, both kinds of works are limited in providing a list of best practices for testers to produce good quality test suites. Second, existing works are either too focused on one single problem or not driven by the current state-of-the-practice.

There are works that gathered the practitioners' opinions to improve the overall quality of the testing process. Gamido and Gamido [13] provide a comparative review of open-source and commercial testing tools to help users select the appropriate software testing tool based on their needs. Rafi et al. [10] report academic and practitioner views on software test automation. While publications are biased by positive results, practitioners agreed that available test automation tools offer a poor fit for their needs and generally disagreed that automated testing can be fully replaced by manual testing. Raulamo-Jurvanen et al. [34] identify 14 different criteria for choosing the right testing tool and highlight that practitioners' judgment is highly influenced by related grey literature. Another study by Garousi [17] aims to characterize what industry wants from academia in software testing, by soliciting testers' challenges during their activities.

To the best of our knowledge, no paper provides a curated list of best practices to drive the development of high-quality *test code*, even less by taking into account the developers' perspective. This paper differs from the existing literature as it distills and summarizes best practices for E2E web test automation that can better inform researchers of the developers' desiderata thereby providing actionable feedback and more awareness when devising future testing approaches.

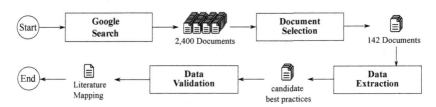

Fig. 1. Overview of the selection procedure

4 Experimental Study

Our study focuses on the *grey literature* for functional testing of web applications with the goals to understand what best practices are suggested by practitioners and, to structure, curate, and unify the grey literature. This section describes the selection procedure we carried out to obtain the relevant documents, which has been designed according to the guidelines proposed by Garousi et al. [15].

4.1 Procedure

Figure 1 graphically illustrates the overall process, which consists of four main phases: (1) Google search, (2) document selection, (3) data extraction, and (4) data validation. In the rest of the section, we provide additional details on each phase.

Google Search. To formulate the string for the Google search, the authors identified an initial set of candidate keywords starting from the goal of the study. Each tentative search string was then validated against a list of relevant documents, as suggested in the guidelines by Kitchenham and Charters [23]. This list includes documents that were already known and which were expected to be included in the search results. The process terminated when the authors were satisfied by the search results, i.e., the number of retrieved papers was manageable, all relevant documents known in advance were included, and no candidate relevant keyword was missing in the search string. The final search string is:

```
(("best practices" OR "guidelines" OR "recommendation" OR "tips")
                            AND
     ("Selenium" OR "UI" OR "end-to-end" OR "Web" )
                            AND
                         ("test"))
```

Since we are mainly interested in documents that propose testing guidelines, the first group of terms characterizes words that relate to methods or techniques that have been generally accepted as superior to any alternatives and have become a de-facto standard. The second group of terms defines specific aspects related to the testing phase in the software life cycle, along with Selenium, which is the undisputed framework for browser automation. Finally, we included the "test" keyword to focus the search on testing-related documents. All relevant documents contained an instance of each keyword from each group (AND operator), whereas keywords within the same group were ORed.

The search was performed from 20 May 2020 to 10 July 2020. For each search query, the first 15 pages of results were scraped, each having 10 documents. The first author conducted 16 queries, which accounted for 2,400 documents that were analyzed overall (150 documents for each query). No more significant documents were found after the 15th page.

Document Selection. The Google search is, by construction, very inclusive. This allowed us to collect as many documents as possible in our pool, at the price of having documents that are not directly related to the scope of this study. Accordingly, we defined a set of specific inclusion and exclusion criteria to remove documents not meeting the criteria and ensure that each collected document is in line with the scope of the study.

Inclusion Criteria. First, the document should propose guidelines to help functional test automation of web applications, i.e., such as GUI testing, or acceptance testing. Other kinds of testing such as performance, load, stress, security, or usability testing are not considered. Second, the document should apply to either capture-replay (C&R), programmable, visual, or combinations of these testing approaches. Last, tools' user manuals and presentations are included as long as they specify some guidelines.

Exclusion Criteria. We excluded papers not written in the English language, or that provided guidelines for manual testing or web development. Furthermore, we did not consider videos or books, which are quite difficult to extract information from or to retrieve, respectively. We also discarded websites that required registration for consulting the resource. We excluded sources that provided either too generic, partial guidelines related to only one specific aspect (e.g., documents only explaining the Page Object design pattern), or that were tool-specific and difficult to generalize to other toolsets. We did not consider documents explaining bad practices, even though, in principle, it is possible to infer some best practices, for instance, by the negation of such good practices.

Results of the Document Selection. The studies obtained from the database search were assessed manually by the first author and only those studies that provide direct evidence about the objective of the study were retained. The final number of selected primary documents is 142.

Data Extraction. In the data extraction step, the first author read and analyzed in detail the candidate documents, filling out an extraction form with the best practices gathered from each source [23]. A tabular data extraction form was used to keep track of the extracted information. In particular, each row of such form reports a study and each column corresponds to an individual best practice. It is important to highlight that no predefined set of best practices was provided; for each newly retrieved best practice found during the data extraction phase, a new column was added to the form incrementally (Table 1).

Table 1. Study selection process

Search query	Retrieved documents	Relevant documents
Best practices selenium test	150	46
Best practices UI test	150	32
Best practices Web test	150	12
Best practices end-to-end test	150	11
Guidelines selenium test	150	1
Guidelines UI test	150	2
Guidelines Web test	150	3
Guidelines end-to-end test	150	7
Recommendation Selenium test	150	1
Recommendation UI test	150	2
Recommendation Web test	150	1
Recommendation end-to-end test	150	2
Tips Selenium test	150	10
Tips UI test	150	7
Tips Web test	150	2
Tips end-to-end test	150	3
Total	2,400	**142**

Data Validation and Taxonomy Construction. In the data validation step, the second author independently analyzed each candidate document, with the aim of validating each individual best practice retrieved during the data extraction phase. During this task, 130/142 documents (92%) were marked with a correct and complete extraction. Only 12/142 documents were found to miss some best practices, which were added. The high agreement rate between the authors indicates overall a low degree of subjectivity in the extraction task.

After enumerating all best practices, the authors began the process of creating a taxonomy, following a systematic process [19]. For each best practice, candidate equivalence classes were identified and assigned to descriptive labels. By following a bottom-up approach, the first clustered tags that correspond to similar notions into categories. Then, they created parent categories, in which categories and their subcategories follow specialization relationships.

5   Results

Table 2 illustrates our taxonomy of E2E web test automation best practices from the grey literature. Our study grouped 706 occurrences of best practices into two main categories, namely *technical aspects* (80%) and *business-level aspects* (20%).

Table 2. E2E web test automation best practices from the grey literature.

Best Practice	#
TECHNICAL (566)	
Structural Test Script Quality	**163**
Manage the synchronization w/ the web app	67
Keep the tests atomic and short	40
Use appropriate naming and code conventions	31
Focus on reusable test code	25
Test Script Development	**67**
Remove sources of uncertainty (no flakiness)	26
Create tests that are resilient to minor GUI changes	16
Mock external services	15
Write both positive and negative test	10
Monitoring Execution of Test suites and Reporting	**67**
Produce detailed reports	36
Take/use screenshots	17
Use Continuous Integration (CI)	14
Design Patterns	**66**
Use the Page Object Pattern (also Page Factory)	52
Others	14
Locators	**65**
Create robust/proper locators/selectors	48
Preferred locators order	17
Data	**52**
Use data-driven testing	33
Use high-quality test data	19
Test Script Grouping and Ordering	**46**
Make tests independent from each other	34
Group tests, e.g., by functional area	12
Test Execution	**40**
Prioritization	19
Parallelization	14
"Green tests run" policy: All tests must pass	7
BUSINESS-LEVEL (140)	
Planning	**54**
Do not consider test automation as a replacement for manual testing	16
Choose the correct testing framework	15
Mentorships/Experts	12
Test early and test often	11
Design	**46**
Focus on key user flows or process flows or functionalities	24
Understand what test cases to actually automate	14
Test from the end-user perspective	8
Process	**40**
Do not limit to only GUI testing (the testing pyramid)	28
Implement test code review	8
Integrate exploratory testing	4

5.1 Technical Best Practices

Technical best practices refer to the development, maintenance, and execution of web tests. That is, testers are already equipped with test requirements, and their task is to translate such requirements into actual test code, with appropriate oracles, or to adapt existing test code to changes and extensions of such requirements, or applications' functionalities.

The most represented subcategory pertains to guidelines on how to achieve a high *structural quality* of the test code (29%). Particularly, the most mentioned tip is careful handling of the synchronization between the web app and the test code [2]. Modern web applications are developed using front-end technologies in which the Document Object Model (DOM) elements are loaded dynamically by the browser and may be ready for interaction at unpredictable time intervals [3]. This is a huge problem for automated testing since there is no universal mechanism to understand when a page is fully loaded and when it is possible to perform actions. As a result, test scripts may encounter exceptions like `NoSuchElementException`, `StaleElementReferenceException`, or `ElementNotVisibleException`. In Selenium WebDriver, testers can use implicit or explicit waits, which should be preferred to the more generic `Thread.sleep()`. If one fails to place appropriate wait commands in the test code, the associated risks span from having pointless lengthy delays in tests' execution, to having flaky checks due to the waits being non-deterministic. Other best practices pertain to keep the test scripts *atomic* (each test method should concern only one single test scenario), using test *naming* conventions as well as *coding rules*, and focusing on *reusable test code*.

The second most mentioned subcategories pertain to *test development* and *reporting* of the test results. Concerning the former, it is suggested to implement deterministic tests by removing uncertainties that may cause tests to pass/fail nondeterministically [11], as well as implementing GUI-resilient tests, both positive and negative tests, and mock external services to keep the testing environment under full control. Related to the latter, developers suggest providing detailed reporting, making use of screenshots to help visually assess the bugs, and of continuous integration (CI) environments.

Design patterns are suggested as an effective mechanism to isolate the code's functionalities into reusable methods (12%). Developers suggest different design patterns: most of our references mention the Page Object [39], whereas lower occurrences pertain to other patterns such as Bot Pattern, AAA Pattern, and Screenplay Pattern which do not seem yet consolidated within test development.

Other relevant categories pertain to locators (11%). *Locators* are commands that tell the testing framework that GUI elements it needs to operate on. Identification of correct GUI elements is a prerequisite to creating robust test scripts, even if accurate localization of GUI elements can be quite challenging due to the mentioned synchronization issues with the DOM being loaded dynamically. Developers suggest crafting robust locators, which, however, requires in-depth domain knowledge of the web app under test.

Finally, a test suite is cost-effective iff test data are of *high quality* (9%). In a way, a test suite is as weak as the test data it uses, which defines the overall fault-finding capability and hence cost-effectiveness of running it. Among the tips, developers suggest adopting data-driven testing techniques by parameterizing the test cases and using realistic inputs, as well as meaningful real-world combinations that the users may experience.

Other less numerous, yet representative, categories pertain to tests *ordering* (8%) and *execution* (7%). Having independent tests is also a strongly advocated best practice, as well as grouping them, for instance by functional area. Speeding up the feedback to developers by prioritizing the execution of tests that are more immediately impacted by the latest code changes [1] is also a highly suggested guideline. Then, developers care also about performance, and parallelization has been also mentioned as a preferred way to speed up the execution of tests.

5.2 Business-Level Best Practices

Business-level aspects are related to the practices of establishing a process that ensures the final quality of the software product and satisfies the customers as well as users. Also, it concerns aspects like resource optimization, communication, cost management, and team building.

The most represented subcategory pertains to *Planning* the process of test code development (39%). The main guidelines in this subcategory are: not considering automation as a replacement for manual testing, choosing the correct/right testing tool/framework for your organization and, hiring a team of experts or a skilled automation engineer.

The second most mentioned subcategory is *Design* (33%), which pertains to guidelines on how design test cases and how to transform them into test code. In this subcategory, the most mentioned tips are the following: (1) focusing on key user flows during test code development, that means to test mainly "happy paths" capturing typical use scenarios and so limit exception testing; (2) creating scenarios and test cases in advance before automating test cases, i.e., having a clear understanding of what test cases to automate, indeed diving straight into automation without a proper test design can be dangerous; (3) conducting testing from the users' perspective, e.g., by getting into the mindset of novice users.

Finally, it is also worth mentioning the best practice of not relying entirely on GUI test automation belonging to the *Process* subcategory. This is one of the main best practices a testing team should consider at first. Ideally, a test suite should be constituted by more low-level unit tests and integration tests than E2E tests running through a GUI (the practical test pyramid[1]). Another best practice that is gaining momentum concerns reviewing the test code [38], similarly to production code. Test code review aims to analyze its quality and to find mismatches or bad practices. For example, a set of tests could be fulfilling their coverage criteria, sufficiently invoking the intended code sections, but if

---

[1] https://martinfowler.com/articles/practical-test-pyramid.html.

assertions are poorly implemented, the tests will be useless in revealing faults. Lastly, exploratory testing is also suggested as a way to quickly get an intuition of the web app's main functionalities.

5.3 Findings

Based on our analysis, ten best practices emerged as essential for obtaining high-quality test code (Table 3). Nine of them are related to technical aspects, and only one to business-level best practices. This suggests that most sources of grey literature in this domain are predominantly of technological nature. Thus, our final takeaway message to practitioners is to follow, during the planning and implementation of automated tests, at least these top 10 guidelines.

Table 3. Top 10 best practices (listed in descending order of references)

Rank	Best practice	Technical	Business
1	Manage the synchronization w/ the web app	x	
2	Use the Page Object Pattern (also Page Factory)	x	
3	Create robust/proper locators/selectors	x	
4	Keep the tests atomic and short	x	
5	Produce detailed reports	x	
6	Make tests independent from each other	x	
7	Use data-driven testing	x	
8	Use appropriate naming and code conventions	x	
9	Do not limit to only GUI testing (the testing pyramid)		x
10	Remove sources of uncertainty (no flakiness)	x	

As for researchers, our taxonomy can be useful to foster future research and spot the areas deserving attention. As an example, existing work has been proposed for creating robust locators [26], automated page objects [39], test independence [4], and test minimization [6]. On the other hand, practitioners suggest removing sources of uncertainties from tests that may cause tests to pass/fail non-deterministically. However, to the best of our knowledge, in the literature, no solutions and tools have been proposed to detect and solve flaky web tests, even less to tackle the synchronization problem.

5.4 Threats to Validity

The main threat to the *internal validity* of this work is the possibility of introducing bias when selecting and classifying the surveyed documents included in our study. We may have missed relevant documents that are not captured by our list of terms. In this paper, multiple Google searches have been performed with no use of private browsing mechanisms (i.e., Google's Chrome Incognito mode) that prevent saving browsing history, cookies, and other site data. Thus, it is possible that Google's search engine provided us with the most suitable results based on our preferences, or our previous searches. We will refine our search procedure in our future work. We do not claim that our survey captures all relevant grey literature; yet, we are confident that the included documents cover the major related best practices.

Concerning the best practices, we manually classified all candidate guidelines into different categories. There is no ground-truth labeling for such a classification. To minimize classification errors, we added a data validation phase to the selection procedure. To reduce the subjectivity involved in the task, the authors followed a systematic and structured procedure, with multiple interactions.

Concerning the *external validity*, we overviewed only the documents available from Google in a specific time frame, and our taxonomy may not generalize to different documents. Also, other relevant classes of best practices might be unrepresented or underrepresented within our taxonomy. Nevertheless, we tried to mitigate this threat by selecting a diverse range of documents using different search queries.

Concerning *reproducibility*, all our results and references are available in our replication package [35].

6   Conclusions and Future Work

The increasing interest of developers and industry around web test automation has fostered a large amount of software engineering research. Novel analysis and testing techniques are being proposed every year, however, without a centralized knowledge base of best practices by professionals, it is difficult to fairly design and implement solutions, or to assess research advancements.

Towards filling this gap, in this paper, we presented a taxonomy of best practices for E2E web test automation derived from an analysis of the grey literature. We manually analyzed several hundreds of documents from which we retrieved many best practices, pertaining to different technical and business-level categories. Moreover, our taxonomy can be used to foster future research in this field, and spot the areas that merit the greatest attention.

As part of our ongoing and future work, we plan to include other sources of grey literature (e.g., arXiv) as well as conducting a thorough literature review of the academic literature that may be useful to validate and improve our taxonomy of best practices. Triangulating our results through surveys and semi-structured interviews with developers is also part of the plan to validate our findings. Moreover, we plan to rate our sources with a credibility score, so as to establish the reliability of a website prior to the data extraction phase.

References

1. Alimadadi, S., Mesbah, A., Pattabiraman, K.: Hybrid DOM-sensitive change impact analysis for JavaScript. In: Proceedings of the 29th European Conference on Object-Oriented Programming, ECOOP 2015, vol. 37, pp. 321–345 (2015)

2. Alimadadi, S., Mesbah, A., Pattabiraman, K.: Understanding asynchronous interactions in full-stack Javascript. In: Proceedings of the 38th International Conference on Software Engineering, ICSE 2016, pp. 1169–1180. ACM (2016)
3. Alimadadi, S., Sequeira, S., Mesbah, A., Pattabiraman, K.: Understanding Javascript event-based interactions. In: Proceedings of the 36th International Conference on Software Engineering, ICSE 2014, pp. 367–377. ACM (2014)
4. Biagiola, M., Stocco, A., Mesbah, A., Ricca, F., Tonella, P.: Web test dependency detection. In: Proceedings of 27th ACM Joint European Software Engineering Conference and Symposium on the Foundations of Software Engineering, ESEC/FSE 2019, p. 12. ACM (2019)
5. Biagiola, M., Stocco, A., Ricca, F., Tonella, P.: Diversity-based web test generation. In: Proceedings of 27th ACM Joint European Software Engineering Conference and Symposium on the Foundations of Software Engineering, ESEC/FSE 2019, p. 12. ACM (2019)
6. Biagiola, M., Stocco, A., Ricca, F., Tonella, P.: Dependency-aware web test generation. In: Proceedings of 13th IEEE International Conference on Software Testing, Verification and Validation, ICST 2020, p. 12. IEEE (2020)
7. Cerioli, M., Leotta, M., Ricca, F.: What 5 million job advertisements tell us about testing: a preliminary empirical investigation. In: Proceedings of the 35th Annual ACM Symposium on Applied Computing (2020)
8. Choudhary, S.R., Zhao, D., Versee, H., Orso, A.: WATER: web application TEst Repair. In: Proceedings of 1st International Workshop on End-to-End Test Script Engineering, ETSE 2011, pp. 24–29. ACM (2011)
9. Doğan, S., Betin-Can, A., Garousi, V.: Web application testing: a systematic literature review. J. Syst. Softw. **91**, 174–201 (2014)
10. Rafi, D.M., Moses, K.R.K., Petersen, K., Mäntylä, M.V.: Benefits and limitations of automated software testing: Systematic literature review and practitioner survey. In: 2012 7th International Workshop on Automation of Software Test (AST), pp. 36–42 (2012). https://doi.org/10.1109/IWAST.2012.6228988
11. Eck, M., Palomba, F., Castelluccio, M., Bacchelli, A.: Understanding flaky tests: the developer's perspective. In: Proceedings of the 2019 27th ACM Joint Meeting on European Software Engineering Conference and Symposium on the Foundations of Software Engineering, ESEC/FSE 2019, pp. 830–840. ACM (2019)
12. Elbaum, S., Karre, S., Rothermel, G.: Improving web application testing with user session data. In: Proceedings of 25th International Conference on Software Engineering, 2003, pp. 49–59 (2003)
13. Gamido, H., Gamido, M.: Comparative review of the features of automated software testing tools. Int. J. Electr. Comput. Eng. **9**, 4473–4478 (2019). 10.11591/ijece.v9i5.pp4473-4478
14. García, B., Gallego, M., Gortázar, F., Munoz-Organero, M.: A survey of the selenium ecosystem. Electronics **9**, 1067 (2020)
15. Garousi, V., Felderer, M., Mäntylä, M.V.: Guidelines for including grey literature and conducting multivocal literature reviews in software engineering. IST **106**, 101–121 (2019)
16. Garousi, V., Felderer, M., Mäntylä, M.V., Rainer, A.: Benefitting from the grey literature in software engineering research. Contemporary Empirical Methods in Software Engineering, pp. 385–413. Springer, Cham (2020). https://doi.org/10.1007/978-3-030-32489-6_14
17. Garousi, V., Mäntylä, M.V.: When and what to automate in software testing? a multi-vocal literature review. IST **76**, 92–117 (2016)

18. Garousi, V., Mesbah, A., Betin-Can, A., Mirshokraie, S.: A systematic mapping study of web application testing. IST **55**(8), 1374–1396 (2013)
19. Gyimesi, P., et al.: BugJS: a benchmark and taxonomy of javascript bugs. Software Testing, Verification And Reliability (2020)
20. Hammoudi, M., Rothermel, G., Stocco, A.: WATERFALL: an incremental approach for repairing record-replay tests of web applications. In: Proceedings of 24th ACM SIGSOFT International Symposium on Foundations of Software Engineering, FSE 2016, pp. 751–762. ACM (2016)
21. Hammoudi, M., Rothermel, G., Tonella, P.: Why do record/replay tests of web applications break? In: Proceedings of 9th International Conference on Software Testing, Verification and Validation, ICST 2016, pp. 180–190. IEEE (2016)
22. Imtiaz, J., Sherin, S., Khan, M.U., Iqbal, M.Z.: A systematic literature review of test breakage prevention and repair techniques. IST **113**, 1–19 (2019)
23. Kitchenham, B., Charters, S.: Guidelines for performing systematic literature reviews in software engineering (2007)
24. Leotta, M., Clerissi, D., Ricca, F., Tonella, P.: Approaches and tools for automated end-to-end web testing. Adv. Comput. **101**, 193–237 (2016)
25. Leotta, M., Stocco, A., Ricca, F., Tonella, P.: Using multi-locators to increase the robustness of web test cases. In: Proceedings of 8th IEEE International Conference on Software Testing, Verification and Validation, ICST 2015, pp. 1–10. IEEE (2015)
26. Leotta, M., Stocco, A., Ricca, F., Tonella, P.: Robula+: an algorithm for generating robust Xpath locators for web testing. J. Softw. Evol. Process **28**, 177–204 (2016)
27. Leotta, M., Stocco, A., Ricca, F., Tonella, P.: PESTO: automated migration of DOM-based web tests towards the visual approach. Softw. Test. Verification Reliab. **28**(4), e1665 (2018)
28. Li, Y.F., Das, P.K., Dowe, D.L.: Two decades of web application testing-a survey of recent advances. Inf. Syst. **43**, 20–54 (2014)
29. Mesbah, A., van Deursen, A., Lenselink, S.: Crawling ajax-based web applications through dynamic analysis of user interface state changes. ACM Trans. Web **6**(1), 3:1–3:30 (2012)
30. Mesbah, A., van Deursen, A., Roest, D.: Invariant-based automatic testing of modern web applications. IEEE TSE **38**(1), 35–53 (2012)
31. Mirshokraie, S., Mesbah, A., Pattabiraman, K.: Efficient javascript mutation testing. In: 2013 IEEE Sixth International Conference on Software Testing, Verification and Validation, pp. 74–83 (2013)
32. Mirzaaghaei, M., Mesbah, A.: Dom-based test adequacy criteria for web applications. In: Proceedings of the 2014 International Symposium on Software Testing and Analysis, ISSTA 2014, pp. 71–81. ACM (2014)
33. Ramler, R., Wolfmaier, K.: Economic perspectives in test automation: Balancing automated and manual testing with opportunity cost. In: Proceedings of 1st International Workshop on Automation of Software Test, AST 2006, pp. 85–91. ACM (2006)
34. Raulamo-Jurvanen, P., Mäntylä, M., Garousi, V.: Choosing the right test automation tool: a grey literature review of practitioner sources. In: Proceedings of the 21st International Conference on Evaluation and Assessment in Software Engineering, EASE 2017, pp. 21–30. ACM (2017)
35. Replication Package. https://github.com/riccaF/sofsem2021-replication-package-material/ (2020)
36. Ricca, F., Leotta, M., Stocco, A.: Three open problems in the context of e2e web testing and a vision: Neonate. In: Advances in Computers (01 2018)

37. Ricca, F., Tonella, P.: Analysis and testing of web applications. In: Proceedings of the 23rd International Conference on Software Engineering, ICSE 2001, pp. 25–34 (2001)
38. Spadini, D., Palomba, F., Baum, T., Hanenberg, S., Bruntink, M., Bacchelli, A.: Test-driven code review: an empirical study. In: 2019 IEEE/ACM 41st International Conference on Software Engineering (ICSE), pp. 1061–1072 (2019)
39. Stocco, A., Leotta, M., Ricca, F., Tonella, P.: APOGEN: automatic page object generator for web testing. Software Qual. J. **25**(3), 1007–1039 (2017)
40. Stocco, A., Yandrapally, R., Mesbah, A.: Visual web test repair. In: Proceedings of the 26th ACM Joint European Software Engineering Conference and Symposium on the Foundations of Software Engineering, ESEC/FSE 2018, pp. 503–514. ACM (2018)
41. Tonella, P., Ricca, F., Marchetto, A.: Recent advances in web testing. Adv. Comput. **93**, 1–51 (2014)

Foundations of Data Science and Engineering – Full Papers

A Pipeline for Measuring Brand Loyalty Through Social Media Mining

Hazem Samoaa[1]([✉])[iD] and Barbara Catania[2][iD]

[1] Chalmers University of Technology, Gothenburg, Sweden
samoaa@chalmers.se
[2] University of Genoa, Genoa, Italy
barbara.catania@unige.it

Abstract. Enhancing customer relationships through social media is an area of high relevance for companies. To this aim, Social Business Intelligence (SBI) plays a crucial role by supporting companies in combining corporate data with user-generated content, usually available as textual clips on social media. Unfortunately, SBI research is often constrained by the lack of publicly-available, real-world data for experimental activities. In this paper, we describe our experience in extracting social data and processing them through an enrichment pipeline for brand analysis. As a first step, we collect texts from social media and we annotate them based on predefined metrics for brand analysis, using features such as sentiment and geolocation. Annotations rely on various learning and natural language processing approaches, including deep learning and geographical ontologies. Structured data obtained from the annotation process are then stored in a distributed data warehouse for further analysis. Preliminary results, obtained from the analysis of three well known ICT brands, using data gathered from Twitter, news portals, and Amazon product reviews, show that different evaluation metrics can lead to different outcomes, indicating that no single metric is dominant for all brand analysis use cases.

1 Introduction

Improving customer relationships through social media, and using information that can be learned from social media content to further improve products, is an area of high relevance for companies. Traditionally, companies rely on their internal Customer Relationship Management (CRM) systems to measure customer satisfaction. However, existing CRM approaches are often not sufficient to analyze and understand customer behaviour. Frequently, feedback from external systems, such as social media, is crucial to truly understand a brand's image. To this end, Social Business Intelligence (SBI) combines corporate data with user-generated content (UGC) to make decision-makers aware of important brand-related trends, and to improve decision making through timely feedback [2,6]. UGC attempts to capture brand image through mining online textual clips, comprising the tastes, opinions, feedback, and actions from customers and other

© Springer Nature Switzerland AG 2021
T. Bureš et al. (Eds.): SOFSEM 2021, LNCS 12607, pp. 489–504, 2021.
https://doi.org/10.1007/978-3-030-67731-2_36

stakeholders alike. Textual clips span from messages posted on social media or articles taken from online newspapers or magazines to customer reviews collected from reviews portal such as Amazon or the Google Appstore.

Extracting useful information from textual UGC requires first crawling data sources to acquire relevant clips, followed by enrichment. Enrichment activities may entail simply identifying structured metadata (e.g., date, community, or review score), or using natural language processing (NLP) techniques to find the relevant concepts the clip mentions (e.g., the brands) and, if possible, to assign a sentiment (i.e., positive, negative, or neutral) to it [16]. SBI thus poses research challenges in many areas, including information retrieval, data mining, and NLP. Unfortunately, SBI research is often constrained by the lack of publicly-available, real-world data for experimental activities [2]. This might limit research results in this field.

In this paper, we describe our experience in extracting social data and processing them through an enrichment pipeline that produces valuable annotations for *brand loyalty analysis*.

As a first contribution, we present the system we have designed for collecting social media data and storing them in a data warehouse for further brand loyalty analysis with respect to many different dimensions. Texts are collected from different social media (Twitter, news portals, and Amazon product reviews) and annotated with features such as sentiment and geolocation. The obtained structured data are then stored, together with stock price information, in a distributed data warehouse based on the Hadoop File System (HDFS) and Spark SQL. The data warehouse has been designed for supporting brand loyalty analysis with respect to many different dimensions. The measures correspond to key performance indicators (KPIs) related to customer experience, customer satisfaction, and customer interaction.

As a second contribution, to show the flexibility of the proposed approach, we present some of the analytical results obtained from the analysis of three well known ICT brands, discussing the impact of the selected data sources on the whole process. The obtained results show that different evaluation metrics can lead to different outcomes, indicating that no single metric is dominant for all brand analysis use cases.

The remainder of this paper is organized as follows. In Sect. 2 we briefly review related work. The pipeline we propose is presented in Sect. 3 while details about the data annotation processes are described in Sect. 4. Section 5 presents the data warehouse design. Some preliminary experimental results are then discussed in Sect. 6, to show the applicability of the proposed pipeline. Finally, Sect. 7 presents some conclusions and outlines future work.

2   Related Work

SBI has been investigated in many different domains and many proposals exists to cope with social data and UGC in a business intelligence context. To just name a few, [14] proposes an SBI approach for analyzing term occurrences in documents belonging to a corpus. [22] presents textual measures as a solution to summarize textual information. In [24], a complete architecture for OLAP analysis of tweets in order to gain statistical information has been presented. In this paper, we build on these existing SBI proposals to develop a pipeline for an SBI approach to brand analysis.

UGC often comes in the form of textual clips. Tweets, news articles, and reviews are just some examples of types of clips that could be of interest for SBI platforms. A core issue is how to extract structured information, such as customer sentiment and geolocation, from textual clips. For *customer sentiment*, many NLP approaches have been proposed, e.g., [19]. Other approaches rely on deep learning techniques. One of the first works in this direction investigates the effects of quality, value, and customer satisfaction on consumer behavioral intention through various machine learning and deep learning classification algorithms [3]. A more recent work proposes a generic way to understand the behavioral intention of the customer [27]. These works tackle customer content for quite general purposes ("voice of customer") without aiming for metrics to extract measures and compare brands. On the other hand, we rely on a combination of different approaches for understanding customer opinions and measuring, through specific metrics, the strength of the relationships between the brand and the consumers.

A common intuition is that users often mention places that are near their current location. Several approaches have been presented to automatically *geolocate* non-geotagged textual clips using textual content [5,7,11,23,29]. Most of these methods rely on a training phase, during which they construct language models, in order to probabilistically infer the location of unseen messages. These types of models can very accurately geolocate microblog messages at a city level [5,11], but suffer from problems related to text noise, such as misspellings, non-textual content, or the presence of links. Moreover, during classification, the finer-grained the grid used to geolocate is (i.e., the higher the sub-city detail), the higher the number of classes which negatively affects performance. To overcome these problems, recent alternative approaches have been proposed that exploit external information sources publicly available on the web, e.g., GeoNames or OpenStreetMaps, to reach sub-city accuracy [25]. In our work, we exploit both data and knowledge-driven approaches for geolocating textual clips.

3   A Pipeline for Brand Analysis

A high-level schematic overview of the proposed pipeline is given in Fig. 1. As a first step, we crawl three different types of data sources to retrieve different types of textual clips, namely tweets from Twitter, news, and reviews from Amazon. Collected textual clips are then annotated by extracting both implicit and explicit structured information. Explicit features refer to the reference *time* and the *brand* of the clip. Time is usually explicitly associated with textual clips while brand information can be extracted through simple keyword search. Implicit features correspond to *sentiment* information (which is fundamental when mining customer opinion), and *geolocation*, when it is not explicitly provided. The

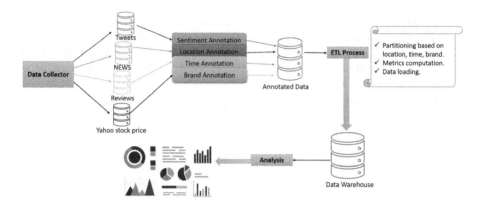

Fig. 1. SBI Pipeline for brand analysis

extraction of implicit information will be done using various techniques (see Sect. 4). The result of the annotation phase is then transformed and loaded into a data warehouse (see Sect. 5). The ETL (extraction, transformation, and loading) process includes data transformation, cleaning, and aggregation, with the ultimate aim of computing various brand analysis metrics, which can be used for further analysis.

4   Data Annotation

During the annotation phase, we start from the collected data and we annotate them with brand, time, location, and sentiment information. Brand and time information can be obtained easily through standard keyword search. On the other hand, the analytical techniques employed to generate location and sentiment annotations are often specific to the type of data, and described in the following.

Sentiment Annotation. Sentiment annotation of Amazon reviews relies on readily available ratings (1,2 is negative; 3 is neutral; 4,5 is positive). For tweets and news, we rely on both natural language processing (NLP) and machine learning approaches.

For NLP, we considered SENTIWORDNET [1], which is a sentiment analysis extension of WORDNET, associating each WORDNET synset with three numerical scores $Obj(s)$, $Pos(s)$ and $Neg(s)$, describing how objective, positive, and negative the terms contained in the synset are. As an alternative approach, we also considered Google NLP,[1] a built-in service in Google cloud, which also includes sentiment analysis. Sentiment analysis attempts to determine the overall attitude (positive or negative) expressed within the text, representing it with a score ranging between –1.0 (negative) and 1.0 (positive). This score corresponds to the overall emotional leaning of the text. Further, a magnitude value between

---

[1] http://cloud.google.com/natural-language/docs.

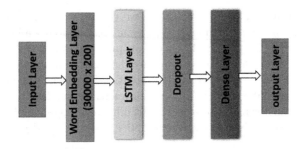

Fig. 2. Architecture of LSTM-NN

0.0 and $+\infty$ is provided, indicating the overall strength of emotion (both positive and negative) within the given text (longer texts may have greater magnitudes).

Regarding machine learning approaches, we first implemented basic classifiers, such as random forest, logistic regression, and KNN, by using SK-learn[2]. We trained the models on a corpus of tweets obtained by merging more than 5000 labeled tweets[3] together with about 1.6 million tweets[4]. To the best of our knowledge, no sentiment-based labeled news are available as ground truth. Hence, we considered only this tweet dataset as ground-truth for machine learning model training. Unfortunately, classical machine learning approaches failed to generate sufficiently accurate models in our experiments. Therefore, we decided to employ a deep learning (DL) approach for increasing the accuracy of the model. Additionally, deep learning approaches can take into account the word context, by building the meaning word after word, in an incremental way. To this aim, we rely on a Long Short Term Memory (LSTM) network, a special kind of Recurrent Neural Network, able to account for dependencies on different time scales, typical of natural language texts (see Fig. 2). We trained the model on the same dataset selected for the basic classifiers, using the Keras library[5]. The first layer (*input layer*) embeds each atomic word into a real-valued vector in a predefined vector space. Such embedding can be learned from large, unlabelled corpora using neural networks, and encode both syntactic and semantic properties of words [10]. Studies have found the learned word vectors to capture linguistic regularities and to collapse similar words into groups [17,18]. Their utility in tasks such as sentiment classification is well attested [12]. Based on these considerations, we trained Word2Vec [8] on about 30000 words from a tweets corpus (*word embedding layer*). As word embeddings alone have shown good performance in various classification tasks, we also use them in isolation, with varying dimensions, in our experiment. In the case of LSTM, a word embedding size of 300 resulted in high accuracy on the data set.

---

[2] http://scikit-learn.org/stable/.
[3] https://github.com/zfz/twitter_corpus/blob/master/full-corpus.csv.
[4] http://www.kaggle.com/kazanova/sentiment140.
[5] http://keras.io/.

To avoid the model to be over-fitted, we deactivate some nodes in LSTM, using a *dropout layer*. The fifth layer is a *dense layer* applying a linear operation, in which every input is connected to every output by a weight, followed by a non-linear activation function. In our case we use the sigmoid function to compute the probability (between 0 and 1) for a given text to be characterized by a positive sentiment. In the final *output layer*, the sentiment probability, computed by the dense layer, is transformed into a sentiment label as follows: the label is *negative* if the sentiment score s is $s \leq 0.4$, *neutral* if $0.4 < s < 0.7$, and *positive* if $s \geq 0.7$.

Location Annotation. For geolocating tweets, we rely on Geoloc [11], a recent state of the art data-driven geolocation algorithm, previously used by our group as a baseline technique for the definition of a knowledge-based geolocation app-roach [25][6]. Geoloc discretizes the Earth's surface into square cells of fixed size and models geolocation as a classification task, based on a kernel density estima-tion approach, with the aim of associating with each message a position corre-sponding to the most appropriate cell. For training this model, we considered a set of 4000 tweets, collected from and already annotated by Twitter, in addition to the training set of almost 5 million tweets provided with the model. Geoloc takes a tweet as input and provides coordinates as output. Coordinates are then enriched by considering knowledge-based information like city and country, using GeoSPARQL[7] queries on specific crowdsourced geographic ontologies, such as Geonames[8] and Open Street map (OSM)[9].

For news data, only few (and old) geolocated datasets are available (see, e.g., [13,15]). Hence, we developed our own approach for extracting geographic toponyms from the considered news dataset in two rounds. First, we extract entities cited in the text by relying on the Google entity analysis cloud service[10]. Then, based on DBPedia (an open linked dataset)[11], for each identified country, we add the capital as the city, and for each identified city, we add the correspond-ing country. If no location entity is found inside the news content, we follow the same process used for tweet annotation. Thus, we apply the Geoloc model to extract the coordinates of the text, then enrich those coordinates by applying geographic ontologies such as Geonames and OSM.

5   A Data Warehouse for Brand Loyalty Analysis

In order to analyze annotated data, we designed an ad hoc data warehouse. The data warehouse includes two data marts, one related to the *stock market*, providing stock market measures for brands at a given date, and one related to the *brand loyalty*. The resulting data warehousing schema, represented according to the Dimensional Fact Model [9], is shown in Fig. 3.

---

[6] http://code.google.com/archive/p/geoloc-kde/.

[7] http://www.geosparql.org/.

[8] http://www.geonames.org/ontology/.

[9] http://wiki.osmfoundation.org/.

[10] http://cloud.google.com/natural-language/docs/analyzing-entities.

[11] http://wiki.dbpedia.org/.

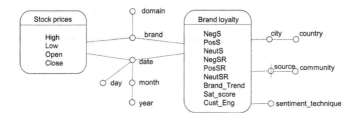

Fig. 3. Dimensional fact schema

Brand Loyalty Data Mart. Each fact in this data mart corresponds to customer opinions, computed by using a given *technique*, related to a given *brand* (generalized in the reference business *domain*), at a given *date*, in a given *city* (generalized in the reference *country*), and collected from a given *community*. The community represents the media from which texts have been collected (Amazon product reviews, Twitter, and news). Only for news, the community can be specialized into the specific data *source* (e.g., BBC, CNN news).

Each combination of the dimensional attributes leads to the identification of a set of texts, say A_i, annotated according to the considered technique. Customer opinions with respect to A_i are represented in terms of measures defined starting from metrics proposed for analyzing brand popularity and behavior in the market and, in particular, on key performance indicators (KPI) for brand analysis on social media [26], referring to the following groups: *Customer Experience (CE)*, measuring the loyalty on the sentiment basis [20, 21, 28]; *Customer Satisfaction (CS)*, focusing on how much the brand services satisfy the customers [3, 26]; *Customer Interaction (CI)*, mainly dealing with the activity level of customers in taking on responsibilities for the company (e.g., elevating the company reputation by writing positive experience about one product) [4].

For what concerns the Customer Experience (CE), we consider three metrics: (i) the number of texts characterized by an either negative ($NegS$), positive ($PosS$), or neutral ($NeutS$) sentiment; (ii) the sentiment ratio for each sentiment type, $NegSR$, $PosSR$, and $NeutSR$, with respect to the total number of texts in A_i; (iii) the Brand Trend, defined as the ratio between A_i and the total number of annotated texts. For what concerns Customer Satisfaction (CS), when A_i corresponds to reviews, we compute the satisfaction score Sat_score as the average rating values assigned by the reviews in A_i.

Finally, when A_i corresponds to tweets, Customer Interaction is measured in terms of customer engagement $Cust\_Eng$, defined as the sum of the number of quoted status, retweets, and favourite selections for each tweet t in A_i.

Stock Prices Data Mart. This data mart provides stock market measures for brands at a given date. Measures correspond to the opening, the final, the highest, the lowest stock price for a brand in a given day. The two data marts together allow the analysis of the impact of customer opinions on stock changes.

Table 1. Sentiment approach comparison per brand

Brand	DL_WordEmb_LSTM	Google NLP	WordNetLexicon
Apple	0.52	0.59	0.53
Huawei	0.58	0.51	0.53
Samsung	0.56	0.59	0.54

6 Experimental Results

In order to discuss the flexibility of the proposed approach for brand loyalty analysis, in the following we first discuss how the pipeline has been customized for the analysis of data related to three important brands in the ICT domain, then we present some preliminary results we have obtained as examples of the analysis that can be performed.

6.1 Experimental Setup

In order to demonstrate the effectiveness of the proposed pipeline, we customized it for the analysis of the loyalty with respect to three ICT brands, namely Huawei, Samsung, and Apple. To this aim, we mined data from three communities, namely, Amazon product reviews, Twitter, and news articles, in the time window between February and May 2019, filtering textual clips with respect to the selected brand names.

For the news, we relied on the News API,[12] a simple REST API for retrieving articles from across the Web. We retrieve the "Top Headlines" news (breaking news) as well as "Everything", which is a firehose of news articles published by over 30000 news sources and blogs. To avoid a too high set of neutral classifications, often generated when the annotation is applied over long and generic texts like full news, we annotated only the summary of each news (up to 250 characters, also corresponding to the limit of the free access account) and we restricted the search to the 'Technology' topic (thus, avoiding, e.g., to collect news dealing with 'apple' as a fruit instead of 'apple' as a brand).

For Amazon product reviews, we developed a custom crawler that mines reviews related to products related to the considered brands. For Twitter, we collected the reference tweets using the Streaming API[13]. Finally, stock price data have been collected using the Yahoo Finance API[14]. Table 2 summarizes the volume of data collected for each community.

Our implementation follows a typical Extraction-Transformation-Loading (ETL) approach: we extract data from the sources as described above, then annotate and transform them using the algorithms and tools discussed in Sect. 4, then compute the measures described in Sect. 5, and finally store them into the

---

[12] https://newsapi.org/.

[13] https://developer.twitter.com/en/docs/tutorials/consuming-streaming-data

[14] https://pypi.org/project/yahoo-finance/.

data warehouse implemented using HDFS, the Hadoop File System.[15] Brand loyalty analysis has then been performed by relying on Spark SQL[16] for analytical processing and Tableau[17] for data visualization.

Table 2. Brand data volume per community

Community	Apple	Huawei	Samsung
Twitter	2,371,344	1,143,697	1,247,109
Amazon	12,875	13,841	12,390
News	6,000	6,474	6,165

As a preliminary study, we compare the sentiment values generated by the three sentiment analysis approaches presented in Sect. 4 (Google's NLP service, WordNetLexicon, and the designed deep learning approach), after normalizing results in the range $[0;1]$ (indeed, the deep learning approach delivers sentiment values in $[0;1]$, with 0.5 referring to a neutral sentiment, the other two approaches deliver results in $[-1;1]$, with 0 representing a neutral sentiment). The three algorithms have been applied to Twitter and news data. For Amazon reviews, as pointed out in Sect. 4, sentiment is extracted through explicit feedback given in the rating, so we excluded this community from this experiment. Average sentiment values computed by each technique for each brand are shown in Table 1. Although there are minor differences in the resulting sentiment value, we do not observe any significant difference nor does any approach consistently judge the sentiment of any brand too positive or too negative (values are around 0.5, thus they all refer to a neutral polarity). Hence, in the following, we rely on the designed deep learning approach for further analysis.

6.2   Results

Brand Sentiment Analysis. As a first experiment, we analysed *Customer Experience* by considering, for each brand, the average number of texts that, on a daily basis, have been classified with a negative, positive, or neutral sentiment (obtained through the aggregation of *NegS*, *PosS*, and *NeutS* measures), to gain a perspective about the overall customer opinion for each brand through all communities. Table 3 shows that the sentiment value is mostly neutral for all the brands. Neutral sentiment statements indicate a quasi-objective mention of the brand, carrying neither overly positive nor negative emotion. Interestingly, there are substantially more positive expressions than negative ones for all brands. The most controversial brand in the study is Apple, for which we got an almost similar daily number of positive and negative clips. The number of positive opinions

---

[15] https://hadoop.apache.org/docs/r1.2.1/hdfs_design.html.
[16] https://spark.apache.org/sql/.
[17] http://www.tableau.com.

for Samsung is similar to that obtained from Apple, but, for the considered period, it attracts considerably less criticism overall. Table 4 refines the sentiment analysis taking into account communities. We observe that the highest sentiment values refer to Twitter for all brands. This is unsurprising, as this social media platform is often used to "vent". Another interesting observation is that there are considerably more negative sentiments about Apple in news articles than about the other two brands. This indicates that Apple might have an image problem in this specific community. Similarly, we observe that Apple has the least positive and the most negative sentiments also in Amazon reviews, indicating that some customers may be more dissatisfied with the related products than with respect to those of the competitors. These results demonstrate that it is crucial for SBI to evaluate brand opinion across multiple communities, as brand image varies, sometimes drastically, between them.

For what concerns *Customer Engagement*, Table 5 shows the average daily customer engagement on Twitter. Apple has by far the highest customer engagement across all the brands, followed by Samsung and Huawei, providing further evidence to the Apple brand being in general more polarising. However, note that Twitter is blocked in China (the homeland of Huawei). Based on the annual report of Huawei for 2018, more than 51% of their customers are from China. This might explain the relatively low Twitter engagement for this popular brand.

Finally, we compare the brands with respect to the average daily *Customer Satisfaction Score*, computed over Amazon reviews. Table 6 shows that Huawei has the highest satisfaction score, whereas customer satisfaction for Apple and Samsung is comparable.

Table 3. Customer Experience, by brand

Brand	Neutral	Avg sentiment negative	Positive
Huawei	10.36	4.12	8.31
Samsung	9.08	3.86	9.95
Apple	14.26	9.55	10.18

Geographic Analysis. Geographic information can help in further understanding *Customer Experience*. Table 7 points out the countries with the highest number of neutral, positive, and negative statements for each brand. As expected, the highest distribution of positive feedback for Apple is in the US, while the most negative sentiment is expressed in the Philippines. As for Samsung, both the most positive and neutral sentiments are expressed in Germany, while Benin (an African country) expresses the most negative sentiment about this brand.

Results about location-based *Customer Engagement* are shown in Table 8, reporting the countries with the highest Twitter engagement per brand. The results are in line with those obtained in Table 7 regarding Samsung and Apple. Thus, the highest customer engagement for Samsung is in Germany, while Apple

Table 4. Customer experience, by community and brand

Community	Brand	Neutral	Avg sentiment negative	Positive
News	Apple	1.45	2.93	2.72
News	Huawei	1.03	1.73	1.75
News	Samsung	1.03	1.83	3.37
Twitter	Apple	17.11	11.36	12.06
Twitter	Huawei	13.56	5.30	10.58
Twitter	Samsung	10.82	4.52	11.62
Amazon	Apple	0.07	0.39	0.71
Amazon	Huawei	0.08	0.20	1.00
Amazon	Samsung	0.09	0.35	1.10

Table 5. Customer engagement

Brand	Avg customer engagement
Apple	1,937,852.45
Huawei	156,962.065
Samsung	174,166.98

Table 6. Customer satisfaction

Brand	Avg customer satisfaction score
Apple	3.37
Huawei	4.049
Samsung	3.76

as the highest engagement in the US and UK. For Huawei, the highest engagement rate is in Switzerland.

Table 7. Location-based customer experience

Brand	Location-based sentiment		
	Positive	Negative	Neutral
Apple	United States	Philippines	United Kingdom
Huawei	United Kingdom	Poland	Spain
Samsung	Germany	Benin	Germany

Dashboarding. Using Tableau, we generated some SBI dashboards for brand analysis. As an example, Fig. 4 shows the most popular brands in EU countries while Fig. 5 shows brand sentiment values and changes in stock prices for all the three brands over the reference time period. We observe that for Huawei and Samsung, both metrics remained relatively stable. For Apple, the customer experience is stable over the time while the stock trend is up-wording till April then start to be stable.

Table 8. Location-based customer engagement

Brand	Countries with the highest Cust. Eng.
Apple	United States/United Kingdom
Huawei	Switzerland
Samsung	Germany

Fig. 4. Geographical brand strength

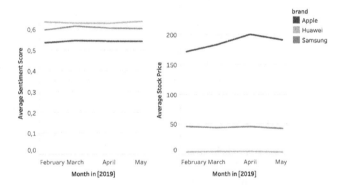

Fig. 5. Long-Term comparison of customer experience and stock prices

A second type of dashboard, comparing stock prices and customer engagement on Twitter, is shown in Fig. 6. The low direct correlation between them indicates that the effects of increasing customer engagement on stock prices may be indirect, delayed, or there may simply not be a direct impact.

Finally, Fig. 7 shows a dashboard for understanding the change of sentiment per community. The three line charts show that news sentiment is fluctuating the most (more evident for Apple and Samsung, somehow stable for Huawei). This is arguably because news coverage tends to be very sensitive to market

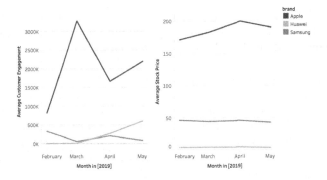

Fig. 6. Customer engagement and stock price trends

and policy events, as exemplified by the conflict between China and the USA. Twitter sentiment, on the other hand, is remarkably stable over time. Amazon reviews are rather stable for Huawei, but vary for the other brands. This indicates varying product quality for these brands.

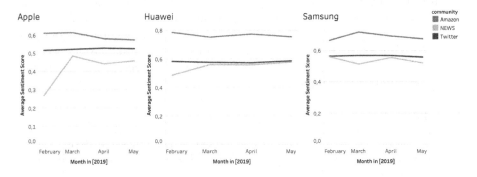

Fig. 7. Brands per community

7 Concluding Remarks

In this paper, we presented an SBI pipeline for brand analysis, relying on customer feedback gathered from social media. Data have first been collected from Twitter, news articles, and Amazon reviews, and then annotated with respect to sentiment and geolocation, relying on alternative approaches. Annotated data are then stored in a data warehouse for further analysis, through the usage of a specific set of measures tailored to brand loyalty analysis. We demonstrated the utility of the proposed pipeline through various experiments for three ICT brands (Huawei, Apple, and Samsung). The obtained (preliminary) results show the usefulness of considering a multitude of data sources and locations when analysing brand loyalty.

We remark that the presented results are just some examples of what can be obtained with the proposed pipeline and they have not to be taken as generally valid assessments about the three considered brands. For example, we investigated only three possible data source types (Twitter, Amazon reviews, and news articles). While we argue that the chosen sources are representative for common sources of brand information on the Web, this is evidently not a complete list of possible data sources. Our study makes no claims that our experiments will generalize to other sources of sentiment, such as software reviews posted on app stores or online forums such as Reddit. A similar limitation is related to the validity of the geographic analysis, due to the geographical availability of Twitter data. As already raised in Sect. 6, Twitter is currently banned in China, leading to the fact that the Huawei brand is not fairly represented in our Twitter data. Finally, we remark that different communities, locations, and policy events can impact all metrics and simple correlations are often not easy to find. Despite the issues discussed above, given that the main purpose of our experimental evaluation was to serve as an utility demonstration of our approach, we do not see these limitations as threatening the value of the conducted research as a whole: the proposed pipeline gives practitioners a framework to define their own metrics and analyse data for brands and communities of their interest.

In terms of future work, as a consequence of what stated above, additional experiments on more brands and more communities are needed to validate the proposed approach. Another important issue concerns the comparison of different KPIs with respect to their effectiveness in measuring brand loyalty, with the help of domain experts, also taking into account specific topic-related issues like, e.g., innovation and price policy.

References

1. Baccianella, S. et al.: An enhanced lexical resource for sentiment analysis and opinion mining. In: Proceedings of the International Conference on Language Resources and Evaluation, LREC (2010)
2. Castano, S., et al.: SABINE: a multi-purpose dataset of semantically-annotated social content. In: Vrandečić, D. (ed.) ISWC 2018. LNCS, vol. 11137, pp. 70–85. Springer, Cham (2018). https://doi.org/10.1007/978-3-030-00668-6_5
3. Cronin, J., et al.: Assessing the effects of quality, value, and customer satisfaction on consumer behavioral intentions in service environments. J. Retail. **76**(2), 193–218 (2000)
4. Kellogg, L.D. et al.: On the relationship between customer participation and satisfaction: Two frameworks. International Journal of Service Industry Management (1997)
5. Eisenstein, J. et al.: A latent variable model for geographic lexical variation. In: Proceedings of the 2010 Conference on Empirical Methods in Natural Language Processing, EMNLP (2010)
6. Gallinucci, E., et al.: Advanced topic modeling for social business intelligence. Inf. Syst. **53**, 87–106 (2015)
7. Gelernter, J. et al.: Automatic gazetteer enrichment with user-geocoded data. In: Proceedings of the 2nd ACM SIGSPATIAL International Workshop on Crowdsourced and Volunteered Geographic Information, GEOCROWD (2013)

8. Goldberg, Y., Levy, O.: Word2vec explained: deriving Mikolov et al'.s negative-sampling word-embedding method (2014)
9. Golfarelli, M., Rizzi, S.: Data Warehouse Design: Modern Principles and Methodologies. McGraw-Hill, New York (2009)
10. Guggilla, C. et al.: CNN-and LSTM-based claim classification in online user comments. In: Proceedings of the 26th International Conference on Computational Linguistics, COLING (2016)
11. Hulden, M. et al.: Kernel density estimation for text-based geolocation. In: Proceedings of the 29th Twenty-Ninth AAAI Conference on Artificial Intelligence, pp. 145–150 (2015)
12. Kim, Y.: Convolutional neural networks for sentence classification. In: Proceedings of the International Conference on Conference on Empirical Methods in Natural Language Processing, EMNLP, pp. 1746–1751 (2014)
13. Leidner, J.L.: An evaluation dataset for the toponym resolution task. Comput. Environ. Urban Syst. **30**(4), 400–417 (2006)
14. Lee, J., et al.: Integrating structured data and text: a multi-dimensional approach. In: Proceedings of the IEEE International Symposium on Information Technology, ITCC, pp. 264–271 (2000)
15. Lieberman, M.D., Samet, H., Sankaranarayanan, J.: Geotagging with local lexicons to build indexes for textually-specified spatial data. In: Proceedings of of the International Conference on Data Engineering, ICDE, pp. 201–212 (2010)
16. Liu, B. and Zhang, L.: A survey of opinion mining and sentiment analysis. In: Aggarwal, C.C., Zhai, C. (eds.) Mining Text Data, pp. 415–463. Springer, Boston (2012) https://doi.org/10.1007/978-1-4614-3223-4_13
17. Mikolov, T. et al.: Distributed representations of words and phrases and their compositionality. In: Proceedings of the 27th Annual Conference on Neural Information Processing Systems, pp. 3111–3119 (2013)
18. Mikolov, T. et al.: Linguistic regularities in continuous space word representations. In: Proceedings of Human Language Technologies: Conference of the North American Chapter of the Association of Computational Linguistics, pp. 746–751 (2013)
19. Mudinas, A. et al.: Combining lexicon and learning based approaches for concept-level sentiment analysis. Association for Computing Machinery (2012)
20. Parasuraman, P.A., et al.: A multiple- item scale for measuring consumer perceptions of service quality. J. Retail. **64**(1), 12 (1988)
21. Parasuraman, A., et al.: A conceptual model of service quality and its implications for future research. J. Mark. **49**(4), 41–50 (1985)
22. Ravat, F. et al.: Top_keyword: an aggregation function for textual document OLAP. In: Proceedings of the 10th International Conference on Data Warehousing and Knowledge Discovery, DaWaK, pp. 55–64 (2008)
23. Rahimi, A., Cohn, T., Baldwin, T.: Pigeo: a python geotagging tool. In: Proceedings of the ACL (System Demonstrations), pp. 127–132 (2016)
24. Rehman, N.U. et al.: Building a data warehouse for twitter stream exploration. In: Proceedings of the International Conference on Advances in Social Networks Analysis and Mining, ASONAM, pp. 1341–1348 (2012)
25. Di Rocco, L. et al.: The role of geographic knowledge in sub-city level geolocation. In: Proceedings of the 34th ACM/SIGAPP Symposium on Applied Computing, SAC, pp. 687–689 (2019)
26. Stich, V. et Al: Social media analytics in customer service: a literature overview - an overview of literature and metrics regarding social media analysis in customer service. SciTePress (2015)

27. Suresh, S., S, G.R.T., Gopinath, V.: VoC-DL: revisiting voice of customer using deep learning. In: AAAI Press (2018)
28. Verhoef, P., et al.: Customer experience creation: determinants, dynamics and management strategies. J. Retail. **85**(1), 31–41 (2009)
29. Zhang, W., Gelernter, J.: Geocoding location expressions in twitter messages: a preference learning method. J. Spat. Inf. Sci. **9**(1), 37–70 (2014)

Predicting Tennis Match Outcomes with Network Analysis and Machine Learning

Firas Bayram$^{(\boxtimes)}$ (iD), Davide Garbarino, and Annalisa Barla (iD)

DIBRIS, Università di Genova, Genova, Italy
S4712149@studenti.unige.it, davide.garbarino@edu.unige.it,
annalisa.barla@unige.it

Abstract. Singles tennis is one of the most popular individual sports in the world. Many researchers have embarked on a wide range of approaches to model a tennis match, using probabilistic modeling, or applying machine learning models to predict the outcome of matches. In this paper, we propose a novel approach based on network analysis to infer a surface-specific and time-varying score for professional tennis players and use it in addition to players' statistics of previous matches to represent tennis match data. Using the resulting features, we apply advanced machine learning paradigms such as Multi-Output Regression and Learning Using Privileged Information, and compare the results with standard machine learning approaches. The models are trained and tested on more than 83,000 men's singles tennis matches between the years 1991 and 2020. Evaluating the results shows the proposed methods provide more accurate predictions of tennis match outcome than classical approaches and outperform the existing methods in the literature and the current state-of-the-art models in tennis.

Keywords: Machine learning · Network analysis · Learning Using Privileged Information · Multi-Output Regression · Tennis outcome prediction

1 Introduction

1.1 Motivation

The sports industry is one of the most growing business sectors in the world. According to the Business Research Company, the global sports market reached a value of nearly \$488 billion in 2018, having grown at an annual growth rate of more than 4% since 2014, and is expected to reach almost \$614 billion by 2022. As we live in the age of data and analytics, this steady growth rate for the sports market size has motivated many researchers to conduct studies on sports data analytics where in sport competitions a result can convey a great deal on different aspects involved in sports like the volume of fans retention, television contracts or sponsorship deals. Essentially, sports data analytics is exploited by either the sports teams directly or by sports gambling stocks. One primary

© Springer Nature Switzerland AG 2021
T. Bureš et al. (Eds.): SOFSEM 2021, LNCS 12607, pp. 505–518, 2021.
https://doi.org/10.1007/978-3-030-67731-2_37

technique of predictive analytics is to build machine learning models to generate predictions for upcoming events and matches using historical player data and statistics.

Several leading male tennis professionals like Roger Federer, Novak Djokovic and Andy Murray have realized the importance of data analytics in tennis, so they introduced data analytics specialists into their teams to help them better prepare for tournaments. They scrutinize and analyze their opponents' key skills and tactics to make use of those insights to avail themselves of the opportunity to boost their chances of winning matches. Accurate prediction of the outcome of tennis matches has an impact on advising players of their odds so they can adjust their plans according to the forecast of the match.

1.2 Related Work

Complex network techniques have been applied to represent the network of tennis matches [9]. The majority of approaches were to rank the players in tennis history taking into account a global view of the player's performance throughout his career and compare it to the existing system that ATP is currently following, which is to rank tennis players based on the immediate past 52 weeks. The most notable work on tennis network modeling was done by Radicchi [21] where the author determined the best players on specific playing surface and proposed a ranking algorithm *Prestige Score*, that is analogous to PageRank score [6], to quantify the importance of tennis players and concluded that the prestige score is more accurate and has higher predictive power than ranking schemes adopted in professional tennis. Michieli [17] applied multiple ranking algorithms to see how active tennis players have improved their overall prestige over the recent years and compared the results of the ranking methods used with the ATP Ranking and identified *Jimmy Connros* as the best player in history up to 2017. Breznik [5] identified the best left and right-handed players in tennis history applying network analytic methods and the PageRank algorithm.

For tennis match prediction, most existing approaches to tennis prediction apply statistical models to tennis matches, starting from the hierarchical structure of the sport's scoring system under the assumption that points in tennis are independently and identically distributed or i.i.d, Klaassen and Magnus [11] show that the assumption is false but they find that deviations from i.i.d. are small and hence the i.i.d. assumption provides a reasonable approximation. O'Malley [18] and, Klaassen and Magnus [12], are illustrative examples of such models. Knottenbelt et al. [13]improved the hierarchical model that is based on the probability of winning an individual point by exploiting statistics from matches played against common opponents. In recent years, machine learning models have been utilized to predict the winner of a tennis match by representing the match and the player by a set of features instead of a single value, player's features are derived from historical match statistics. Ma et al.[16] applied logistic regression model on 16 variables representing player skills and performance, player characteristics and match characteristics. Sipko and Knottenbelt [22] have extracted more detailed set of features and applied logistic regression and artificial neural network to predict the outcome of a tennis match, their best model ANN resulted in a log loss of 0.6111. Peters and Murray [20] addressed the effects of surface type and the variation of player skills through time by using free parameters to represent the skills of players and the characteristics of court surfaces.

In this paper, we define a new method based on network analysis to extract a new feature that represent the player's skill on each surface considering the variation of his performance over time which is believed to have a big effect on the match outcome. We also make use of the match statistics directly in the prediction through applying advanced ML paradigms instead of only following the historical averaging process that was done in the literature. This project uses data obtained from the ATP official website which is the main resource for historical data of tennis matches since 1968. Each match is represented by 49 features including, for instance, player's age and ranking, the number of aces, double faults and 1st serve percentage.

2   Network Modeling and Surface-Specific Score

In this section, we describe the method followed to extract the surface-specific score.

2.1   Network of Tennis Matches

We mapped tennis matches into a weighted and directed graph: edges are directed from winner to loser and they are weighted according to the stage and type of tournament as shown in Fig. 1. The ATP has four tiers of events– Grand Slams, Masters 1000, ATP 500 and ATP 250. With the four Grand Slams awarding the most points, 2000. The numbers in each tournament category represent how many points the winner receives. For clarity, we simplified the numbers that we used to assign weights to the edges to hold the proportion between the values as follows: ATP 250/500 : 1, Masters 1000: 2, ATP Finals: 3, Grand Slams: 4. In case of multiple links of the same direction exist between the players, the weights are summed up.

Fig. 1. A single tennis match represented in a directed graph representation

2.2   Surface-Specific Score

It is evident in tennis that players' performances are affected by the court surface, Barnet and Pollard [1] showed that the type of surfaces favors those players who are best suited to this particular surface. The dataset in hand does not include any information about players' skills on each surface. Therefore, in order to quantify the latter, we subset the graph based on surface and all prior tennis matches, we compute several centrality measures for each player and, by means of PCA, we evaluate a surface-specific score. Centrality measures are a widely used analysis mechanism to reveal important elements of complex networks [8]. Note that all the used measures are normalized.

CM1 **Out-In-degree-difference Centrality:** The in-degree of a player v ($d_{in}(v)$) is the sum of the edge weights of his losing matches, while out-degree ($d_{out}(v)$) is the sum of the edge weights of his winning matches. The Out-In-degree-difference centrality measure (CM1) of each node is computed as the difference between its in-degree and out-degree.

CM2 **Hubs Centrality:** The hub score of a node estimates how many highly authoritative nodes this node is pointing to; in the tennis players network, Michieli [17] demonstrated that good hubs are often associated with successful players because they have won against a wide range of players while the authorities are modest players with long careers.

CM3 **PageRank Centrality:** PageRank centrality [19] is a spectral centrality measure. The algorithm assigns a centrality score based on its neighbors score. PageRank acknowledges that not all wins are equal, wins over strong opponents weigh more than beating mediocre players. PageRank score of player i is computed as following:

$$P_i = \frac{d}{N} + (1 - d) \sum_j P_j \left(\frac{w_{ji}}{k_j} + \frac{\delta(k_j)}{N} \right) \tag{1}$$

Where $d = 0.15$ is the damping factor, N is the number of players, w_{ji} is the edge weight between nodes i and j, k_j and P_j are the out-degree and PageRank value of the node j, respectively and δ is a function to correct the sinks (nodes with outdegree zero).

Finally, to estimate the surface-specific score, we followed Algorithm 1, based on the Principal Component Analysis (PCA) technique. We refer to the resulting first principal component scores as *surface-score*. These values can be interpreted as time-varying surface-specific scores. Table 1 and Table 2 show the top 5 scores on Clay and Hard surfaces respectively, as of June 2020.

3   Tennis Match Representation

In this section, we discuss how we processed the raw data to generate the features that, in addition to the surface-specific score, are used as input to the ML models.

Algorithm 1: Surface-specific score extraction algorithm

Input: Graph of matches on specific surface $G^{(s)}$, Centrality measure functions
 C

Output: Vector of surface-specific scores $y^{(s)}$

for i= 1 to N do   /* For each node in graph $y^{(s)}$ */
 for c= 1 to M do   /* For each function C */
  | CM(c) = C(i)   /* Calculate CM vector for node P(i) */
 end
 $y^{(s)}(i)$ = PCA(CM)   /* Apply PCA to vector CM */
end

return $(y^{(s)})$

3.1   Player's Features

There are two types of features in our dataset with respect to their availability time. Unlike some features which are available before the start of the match, such as the age and rank of the players, the statistics are only available after the end of the match. Therefore, player's skills are estimated by taking the average of the statistics of his historical matches for an upcoming match.

3.2   Labelling - Experimental Design

The raw data classifies the players as a winner and loser, whereas before the match takes place, we only have players labelled as Player 1 and Player 2. Thus, we randomly sampled the data and assigned Player 1 to be a *winner* or *loser*. The match outcome for match n can be defined as following:

$$y_n = \begin{cases} 1, & \text{if Player 1 is the winner.} \\ 0, & \text{if Player 1 is the loser.} \end{cases} \tag{2}$$

3.3   Symmetric Representation

Inspired by Sipko and Knottenbelt [22], and O'Malley [2], to achieve the symmetry of model's prediction outcome regardless of the random labeling discussed

Table 1. Top 5 scores on clay, as of June 2020

Player	Surface-score
Rafael Nadal	0.539565
Novak Djokovic	0.262964
Roger Federer	0.252947
David Ferrer	0.206311
Guillermo Vilas	0.150491

Table 2. Top 5 scores on hard, as of June 2020

Player	Surface-score
Roger Federer	0.627906
Novak Djokovic	0.566555
Rafael Nadal	0.375329
Andy Murray	0.320519
Andre Agassi	0.23004

in the previous section.We took the difference between the players' features of the same characteristic in order to obtain identical results even if we swap the labelling of Player 1 and Player 2. Also, in this way, even supposing that we reverse the labels of Player 1 and Player 2 we are going to get the same feature values but with different sign, and different target class. This would also help us avoid any bias to the same feature of both players due to assigning different weight of a feature for Player 1 than Player 2 by the model. For example, the model might give a higher weight for Player 1 rank than to Player 2 rank. Using the difference of variables to extract the features halves the number of dimensions of the dataset. The difference of the variables is calculated based on the labeling criterion defined in Equ. 2 as follows:

$$FEATURE_i = STAT_{i,p1} - STAT_{i,p2} \tag{3}$$

4   Machine Learning Methods

We think of a tennis match as a vector x_i composed of P input features. The corresponding match outcome y_i may be a *win* 1 or a *loss* 0.

As for the supervised classification methods, we resorted to four methods. Here we briefly describe the approaches and how we used them to predict the tennis match outcome.

RF **Random Forests.** Random Forests is an ensemble technique that combines bagging and random feature sub-spacing. Random Forests algorithm constructs a large collection of classification or regression ensembles of independent decision trees (forests) and aggregates their predictions by averaging [2].

LR **Logistic Regression.** Logistic regression exploits the logistic sigmoid function as loss function to estimate the probability of the sample being assigned to one of the two possible classes [10].

LUPI **Learning Using Privileged Information.** Learning Using Privileged Information, or Support Vector Machine using Privileged Information (SVM+), has been first proposed by Vapnik and Vashist [24]. LUPI is an advanced learning paradigm that uses additional (privileged) information that is available only for the training examples and not available for test examples. This additional information (prior knowledge) can be exploited to build better models and improve the results. In tennis, and sports in general, the match statistics are only available in the training examples as they are collected during the match and the final stats sheet is published after the end of the match. On the other hand, for the testing examples, we only have the match characteristics and players' profiles, thus we utilized LUPI paradigm to leverage the match statistics that are considered to be as additional information we have for the training examples to improve the performance of the learning method. In LUPI framework, we are given the training triplets:

$$\{(x_1, x_1^*, y_1), \ldots, (x_n, x_n^*, y_n)\},\ x_i \in X,\ x_i^* \in X^*,\ y_i \in \{0,1\},\ i = 1, 2, \ldots, n$$

where X is the space of match features vector x, x^* represents the match statistics vector that belongs to the correcting space X^* (the space of privileged information) and y_i is the labels vector. Supporting the learning process by incorporating the match statistics in the model can capture the complexity of the training examples by discovering hidden patterns between the players that cannot be discovered in the original features space X. There are many examples in the tennis world where Player 1 has better estimates than Player 2- this is going to be reflected by positive match features and SVM might map the match data point x to the *winning* side of the margin in space X. But still, if Player 1 struggles against Player 2 under specific conditions or due to his play style, this is going to be evident in the statistics of the matches between the two players, hence the additional information x^* that belongs to the same point x might fall in the *losing* side of the margin in space X^*. Therefore, the match statistics can facilitate the learning process by tightening or relaxing the SVM constraints to improve the predictions by including the privileged information that we have about the training matches.

MTR **Multi-Target Regression.** Multi-target regression, also known as multi-output regression [3], is an advanced machine learning paradigm that involves predicting simultaneously two or more numerical output variables given the same input features. We utilized MTR approach to predict the statistics of the players in the match and then consequently predict the winner of the match applying classification model. Figure 2 shows the workflow diagram of implementing the MTR paradigm to predict the winner of the tennis match. The workflow diagram shows that the MTR phase works as a 'black box' to the match outcome prediction since it will only help the classification model better predict the winner of the match and the MTR prediction accuracy in itself is irrelevant to the final evaluation of our learning classification task. The most common approach to deal with multi-target regression problems is *problem transformation* by transforming the multi-target problem into multiple independent single-target problems each one solved by fitting a regressor to make a single-output regression for each target. The other approach is *algorithm adaptation* methods that modify a single-output method to simultaneously support multi-output problems, this is usually done by modeling the dependencies among these targets.

We briefly describe four different approaches to MTR that we adopted in our classification pipeline:

MTSR **Multi Single-Target Regressors:** we decompose the problem to d single-target regression problems by fitting a random forest regressor to independently predict each target [3].

MTR-RC **Regressor Chains:** RC [23] is a *problem transfer* method and is built on the idea of linking chains of regressors and stacking predictions to other models of the chain as additional features. The training procedure of RC involves selecting a chain that is represented by an ordered set of target variables $C = \{y_1, y_2 \ldots y_d\}$. To predict the first

target value y_1, we trained a random forest regressor on the original input vector X of the training dataset. Then, for the subsequent
targets y_j where $j \in \{2, \ldots, d\}$ we perform transformation on the
training dataset to consist of the union of the original input vector
X and the actual value of the previous targets in the chain $y_{k<j}$ in
the original training dataset.

MTR-RF **Multi-Target Random Forest Regressor:** this method [4,14] is
an extension of the single-target random forest regressor; the only
difference is the modification of the calculation of the impurity measure of a node as the sum of squared error over the multi-target
value.

MTR-TSF **Multi-Target Regression Via Target Specific Features:** this
method, proposed by Wang et al. [25], deals with the multi-target
regression (MTR) tasks by learning target specific features (TSF).
The method assigns a cluster index to each match features vector X_i
using hierarchical clustering algorithm. The index is then added to
expand the feature space $X_{exp} = X \cup X_{index}$. Target specific features
are learned by querying a corresponding dependent similarity matrix,
generated by a classification and regression tree boosting method
(CART-boosting)[7]. The transformed training dataset for the jth
match statistics target Y_j is constructed by finding the union $\widehat{D}_J = X \cup X_{\text{index}} \cup X_{\text{TSF}}$.

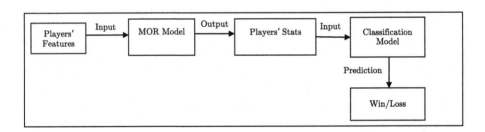

Fig. 2. Multi-output regression workflow diagram

5   Experiments

The experiments were conducted on a node hosted on DLTM[1], the node is
equipped with an Intel Xeon CPU with 27×2.3 GHz, 64 GB RAM.

---

[1] https://www.dltm.it/.

5.1   Dataset Splitting

For the standard ML models, the training dataset consists of 62,141 tennis matches between the years 1991 and 2011, and 21,083 matches between 2012 and 2020 for testing, that makes up approximately 75:25 ratio. For the advanced ML paradigms and because of their complexity, we reduced the dataset size to consist of 39,033 tennis matches between the years 2001 and 2014 for training dataset, and 13,011 matches between 2015 and 2020 for testing, that also makes up approximately 75:25 ratio. For each dataset, we used the tennis matches played in the last three years of the training set for validation.

This way of dividing the tennis dataset by complete years is widely adopted in the literature. The main reason is to maintain the temporal order of tennis matches. Shuffling the data randomly would result in testing the model on older matches than the ones used for training, which is not legitimate. For example, it would be futile to predict the winner of a tennis match played in 2006 using machine learning model trained on data that include tennis matches played in 2016. Moreover, ATP has a fixed calendar of certain tournaments played in specific weeks of the season. Splitting the matches by complete years allows us to have match samples of each tournament over the different dataset splits. In other words, we have match examples of each tournament distributed in the training, validation and test sets, which makes the learning process more feasible.

5.2   Classical Machine Learning Models Results

Before fitting our model to make the final predictions, we perform feature selection step using sequential backward selection method to select the best features of the dataset. Since the approach requires setting the number of features to be selected a priori, we tuned this parameter and evaluated the performance of the selected subset of the features using the validation set. For RF model, the optimal number of features is 6, while for LR model, the feature selection approach resulted in no improvement in the accuracy while evaluating on the validation set. Table 3 compares the results of RF and LR models when evaluated on the testing set using accuracy and log loss classification as metrics. Random forests algorithm outperformed logistic regression when implemented with feature selection step and without. When comparing the prediction results between the two algorithms using various classification metrics, random forest

Table 3. Random forests with and without feature selection (RF with FS and RF without FS respectively) and logistic regression results in terms of log-loss and accuracy.

Model	Log-loss	Accuracy
RF without FS	0.6095	0.6681
RF with FS	0.5996*	0.6729*
LR	0.6110	0.6663

with feature selection resulted in higher prediction accuracy, and also improved the uncertainty of the predictions measured by the log-loss.

To inspect the impact of the surface-score feature on the prediction results, we used the Shapley Value [15] as shown in Fig. 3. To calculate Shapley Values of each feature in the set, a model is trained with that feature present, and another model is trained with the feature withheld. Then, predictions from the two models are compared on the current input. We see that the **RANK** variable is the most important feature in making the predictions, then **SURFACE-SCORE** feature that we inferred based on network analysis.

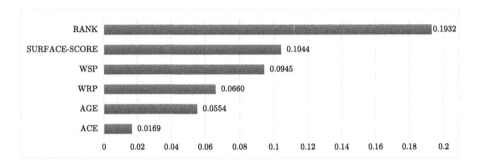

Fig. 3. Average impacts (in absolute terms) of features on model output magnitude, WSP is winning on serve percentage, WRP is winning on return percentage

5.3   SVM and SVM+ Results

Table 4 provides a summary of the accuracy results of applying SVM+ using different kernel function combinations in decision and correcting spaces. We also report the accuracy results of the classical SVM algorithm using the corresponding kernel functions. Since we have used different years range as discussed in Sect. 5.1, and for the sake of comparing, we applied the classical machine learning models on the same dataset. The standard ML models, RF and LR, are trained on the original features of the dataset without using the match statistics, named *RF-OF* and *LR-OF* respectively. We can see the improvement in the models' performance when leveraging the match statistics as privileged information to correct the decision function. Also, considering a RBF kernel has provided the highest accuracy percentage using both SVM and SVM+ models. Furthermore, the models in LUPI framework have superior predicting performance when compared to RF and LR. SVM+ improved the classification accuracy results of both models.

5.4   Multi-Output Regression Results

To predict the statistics of the match, we fitted several multi-output regression models and used the mean squared error metric to evaluate the performance of

Table 4. Accuracy results of SVM+ with different kernels. SVM, random forest and logistic regression are applied on the original features

Decision space kernel	Correcting space kernel			Original features		
	Linear	RBF	Sigmoid	SVM	RF-OF	LR-OF
RBF	0.66159	0.6612	0.6622*	0.655		
Linear	0.64822	0.64927	0.6561	0.64768	0.657	0.654
Sigmoid	0.6526	0.6503	0.6607	0.6305		

each model. Table 5 reports the predictive results for both regression and classification phases for the different models. We can notice the big impact of the output of the regression phase on the final classification predictions. Improving the mean squared error of the MTR models by 10^{-3} leads to obtain higher accuracy results by 1.5%. Comparing the performance of the different MTR approaches, we can see that the models which consider the dependency between the features have better results than the ones that neglect it. This supports the hypothesis that tennis match statistics are correlated and modeling this relationship between the features is a powerful technique that should be followed to achieve higher prediction accuracy. Specifically, multi-target regression via specific target features (MTR-TSF) has had the best regression performance. Consequently as a result, the classifier that was built on the MTR-TSF predictions as an input has the highest accuracy results compared with the other MTR models.

Table 5. Regression and classification results of multi-target regression via specific target features (MTR-TSF), multi single-target regression (MTSR), multi-target regression via regressor chain (MTR-RC), Multi-target random forest regressor(MTR-RF), random forest on the original features (RF-OF), and Logistic regression on the original feature (LR-OF)

	Regression phase						Classification phase
	Mean squared error for each target						
Approach	M-ACES	M-DFS	M-W1S	M-W2S	M-WSP	M-WSG	Accuracy
MTR-TSF	26.63	8.29	0.0191	0.0281	0.0162	0.0610	0.666*
MTSR	27.60	8.71	0.0204	0.0297	0.0173	0.0647	0.65
MTR-RC	26.39	8.34	0.020	0.0295	0.0173	0.0665	0.65
MTR-RF	27.27	8.54	0.198	0.0291	0.0168	0.0631	0.649
RF-OF	-						0.657
LR-OF	-						0.654

6   Conclusions

6.1   Contribution

In this paper, we utilized network analysis techniques and applied advanced machine learning paradigms to improve the current state-of-the-art approaches to predict the winner of a tennis match. We developed a novel method by representing the tennis matches as a network to infer a time-varying and surface-specific score that evaluate the player's performance on a specific court surface at a certain time point. We made use of the extracted score to enhance our dataset and added it to the features set that contains estimations of players' qualities based on the historical matches. We demonstrated that the extracted score has a relevant influence on the prediction results and was ranked as the second most important feature in making predictions of our classification task.

We made use of advanced machine learning paradigms (LUPI and MTR) which resulted in more accurate results when compared to the classical machine learning models. By using these advanced methods, we improved the prediction accuracy results of the classification task by 1.5%. We do emphasize that the proposed methods can outperform the current state-of-the-art models, and can be even generalized to other sports that have a similar data structure, i.e., where the match statistics are only available for training and not available for testing. The advanced paradigms leverage the match statistics directly in making predictions instead of solely using statistics estimators (for example historical average) as per usual when applying the classical machine learning models.

6.2   Limitations

Implementing the advanced machine learning paradigm is associated with additional cost and complexity. This cost in both the resources and the execution time slows down the optimization and hyperparameters tuning process to select the best model that produces the optimal performance and results. Building the kernel matrices for LUPI, and generating the dependent similarity matrix for MTR-TSF, are the most time-consuming and costly phases of the models.

6.3   Future Work

The limitations of the approaches described in the previous section prompt us to think about models that are memory and run-time efficient. Online learning would be a natural candidate. In online learning paradigm, the model is quickly updated to produce the best model as the data arrive in a sequential order. Thus, there is no need to re-train the model whenever a new data point arrives which is too expensive. Online learning is an option worth exploring in predicting tennis match outcomes as it has a rich literature.

Our dataset only includes the totals of winning points on serve and return. In fact, there is a plenty of other aspects in the game of tennis that differentiate between the players' qualities and skills. Acquiring more statistics, such as winners and unforced errors records, head-to-head results on a specific surface, or success rate in winning points at the net, can improve the models' performance. It would also be useful to model the non-numerical factors and convert them into numbers to include them in the dataset, such as the player's current form or favoring specific events which can play a part in helping predict the winner of the match.

References

1. Barnett, T., Pollard, G.: How the tennis court surface affects player performance and injuries. Med. Sci. Tennis **12**(1), 34–37 (2007)
2. Biau, G., Scornet, E.: A random forest guided tour. Test **25**(2), 197–227 (2016). https://doi.org/10.1007/s11749-016-0481-7
3. Borchani, H., Varando, G., Bielza, C., Larrañaga, P.: A survey on multi-output regression. Wiley Interdisc. Rev. Data Min. Knowl. Discovery **5**(5), 216–233 (2015)
4. Breiman, L.: Random forests. Mach. Learn. **45**(1), 5–32 (2001)
5. Breznik, K.: On the gender effects of handedness in professional tennis. J. Sports Sci. Med. **12**(2), 346 (2013)
6. Brin, S., Page, L.: The anatomy of a large-scale hypertextual web search engine (1998)
7. Chen, T., Guestrin, C.: Xgboost: a scalable tree boosting system. In: Proceedings of the 22nd ACM SIGKDD International Conference on Knowledge Discovery and Data Mining, pp. 785–794 (2016)
8. Das, K., Samanta, S., Pal, M.: Study on centrality measures in social networks: a survey. Soc. Netw. Anal. Min. **8**(1), 1–11 (2018). https://doi.org/10.1007/s13278-018-0493-2
9. Dingle, N., Knottenbelt, W., Spanias, D.: On the (Page) ranking of professional tennis players. In: Tribastone, M., Gilmore, S. (eds.) EPEW 2012. LNCS, vol. 7587, pp. 237–247. Springer, Heidelberg (2013). https://doi.org/10.1007/978-3-642-36781-6_17
10. Hastie, T., Tibshirani, R., Friedman, J.: The Elements of Statistical Learning: Data Mining, Inference, and Prediction. Springer, New York (2009)
11. Klaassen, F.J., Magnus, J.R.: Are points in tennis independent and identically distributed? evidence from a dynamic binary panel data model. J. Am. Stat. Assoc. **96**(454), 500–509 (2001)
12. Klaassen, F.J., Magnus, J.R.: Forecasting the winner of a tennis match. Eur. J. Oper. Res. **148**(2), 257–267 (2003)
13. Knottenbelt, W.J., Spanias, D., Madurska, A.M.: A common-opponent stochastic model for predicting the outcome of professional tennis matches. Comput. Math. Appl. **64**(12), 3820–3827 (2012)
14. Levatić, J., Ceci, M., Kocev, D., Džeroski, S.: Semi-supervised learning for multi-target regression. In: Appice, A., Ceci, M., Loglisci, C., Manco, G., Masciari, E., Ras, Z.W. (eds.) NFMCP 2014. LNCS (LNAI), vol. 8983, pp. 3–18. Springer, Cham (2015). https://doi.org/10.1007/978-3-319-17876-9_1
15. Lundberg, S.M., Lee, S.I.: A unified approach to interpreting model predictions. In: Advances in Neural Information Processing Systems, pp. 4765–4774 (2017)

16. Ma, S.M., Liu, C.C., Tan, Y., Ma, S.C.: Winning matches in grand slam men's singles: an analysis of player performance-related variables from 1991 to 2008. J. Sports Sci. **31**(11), 1147–1155 (2013)
17. Michieli, U.: Complex network analysis of men single atp tennis matches. arXiv preprint arXiv:1804.08138 (2018)
18. O'Malley, A.J.: Probability formulas and statistical analysis in tennis. J. Quant. Anal. Sports **4**(2), 1-23 (2008)
19. Page, L., Brin, S., Motwani, R., Winograd, T.: The pagerank citation ranking: Bringing order to the web. Technical Report, Stanford InfoLab (1999)
20. Peters, J.: Predicting the outcomes of professional tennis matches (2017)
21. Radicchi, F.: Who is the best player ever? a complex network analysis of the history of professional tennis. PLoS ONE **6**(2), e17249 (2011)
22. Sipko, M., Knottenbelt, W.: Machine learning for the prediction of professional tennis matches. MEng computing-final year project, Imperial College London (2015)
23. Spyromitros-Xioufis, E., Tsoumakas, G., Groves, W., Vlahavas, I.: Multi-label classification methods for multi-target regression. arXiv:1211.6581 (2012)
24. Vapnik, V., Vashist, A.: A new learning paradigm: learning using privileged information. Neural Netw. **22**(5–6), 544–557 (2009)
25. Wang, J., Chen, Z., Sun, K., Li, H., Deng, X.: Multi-target regression via target specific features. Knowl. Based Syst. **170**, 70–78 (2019)

Role-Based Access Control on Graph Databases

Jacques Chabin[1(✉)], Cristina D. A. Ciferri[2(✉)], Mirian Halfeld-Ferrari[1(✉)],
Carmem S. Hara[3(✉)], and Raqueline R. M. Penteado[4(✉)]

[1] Université Orléans, INSA CVL, LIFO EA, Orléans, France
{jchabin,mirian}@univ-orleans.fr
[2] Universidade de São Paulo, São Carlos, Brazil
cdac@icmc.usp.br
[3] Universidade Federal do Paraná, Curitiba, Brazil
carmem@inf.ufpr.br
[4] Universidade Estadual de Maringá, Maringá, Brazil
raque@din.uem.br

Abstract. We propose a novel access control system for graph-based models, which supports schema constraints and constraint rules to protect the data, as well as user context rules. We consider systems with huge volumes of data, where the efficient processing of aggregation operations is of paramount importance. To comply with this goal, we introduce an architecture with modules for rewriting, planning and executing queries in parallel, respecting the access constraints. Performance tests show the efficiency of our distributed query processing mechanism. Compared to a centralized approach, it reduces execution time from 25% to 68% for conjunctive queries and from 12% to 59% for queries involving aggregation.

1 Introduction

Access control is a technique based on policies or rules that restrict the access to an application or database. After being an active area of investigation for relational databases [19], it has recently attracted attention in contexts related to the Semantic Web [12,22]. There are a number of access control models proposed in the literature [14], such as: Mandatory Access Control (MAC), Discretionary Access Control (DAC), and Role Based Access Control (RBAC). They differ on how users, the entities requiring the access, can be granted or denied access to resources, which are the entities being protected. MAC is based on a classification of users and resources, and it relies on an administrator to define the access policy. In contrast, in DAC, users have authority over the resources they own and can grant access permissions to other users. In RBAC, each user is assigned to a role, and the access rights are defined on roles, instead of individual users.

RDF is the graph-based standard model for the Semantic Web. Some RDF datasets can reach the size of billions of triples [1]. Colombo and Ferrari [7] list three requirements for access control of systems with huge volumes of data: fine-grained mechanism, context-management, and efficiency for preventing non-authorized data access. Also, big data requires analysis of large volumes of data.

© Springer Nature Switzerland AG 2021
T. Bureš et al. (Eds.): SOFSEM 2021, LNCS 12607, pp. 519–534, 2021.
https://doi.org/10.1007/978-3-030-67731-2_38

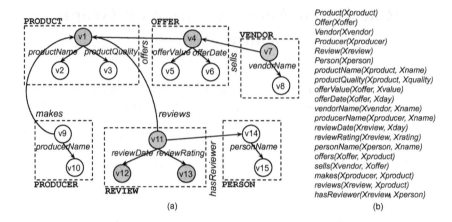

Fig. 1. Global schema (Color figure online)

$$(1) \qquad\qquad\qquad \rightarrow Vendor(ID)$$
$$(2)\ Vendor(X_{vendor}) \rightarrow (X_{vendor} = ID)$$
$$(3)\ offers(X_{offer}, X_{product}) \rightarrow sells(X_{vendor}, X_{offer})$$
$$(4)\ sells(X_{vendor}, X_{offer}),\ Vendor(Z) \rightarrow (Z = X_{vendor})$$
$$(5)\ reviews(X_{review}, X_{product}) \rightarrow offers(X_{offer}, X_{product})$$

(a) Role-based access rules

$$(6)\ reviews(X_{review}, X_{product}) \rightarrow reviewDate(X_{review}, X_{day})$$
$$(7)\ reviewDate(X_{review}, X_{day}) \rightarrow X_{day} >= \text{'01.01.2018'}$$

(b) User context rules

Fig. 2. Access constraints for the role Vendor

In this context, the query processing engine should execute aggregation operations efficiently. However, there is a gap in the literature of approaches that investigate these requirements and aggregation operations together.

In this paper, we propose an access control system for graph-based models that tackles all these requirements. Our approach combines RBAC and MAC, allowing sensitive data to have higher clearance levels than those associated to specific roles. Roles, in turn, are associated with fine-grained access rules. Each user has a single role and can define context-based rules to restrict the desired results. To support the proposed model and to deal with big data, we consider a distributed storage and a query processor that efficiently executes aggregation operations in parallel.

Example 1. Consider a database schema in the e-commerce domain based on the Berlin Benchmark and depicted in Fig. 1(a). The corresponding definition as a set of predicates is presented in Fig. 1(b). Consider the role *Vendor (V)*. We want to restrict the access of users with this role as follows. First, we want to keep the identity of the reviewers anonymous. To do so, we associate a role with a subset of predicates (those in blue in Fig. 1(b)). Users with that role are granted access only to these predicates, and we denote this as *schema constraints*.

Second, we want to restrict vendors to information on offers made by themselves, but not offers from others. We define this restriction as a set of *role-based access rules*, as presented in Fig. 2(a). Rules (1) and (2) associates X_{vendor} to ID, which is the user requesting access to the database. Other rules follow the traversal from *Vendor* to *Product* (Rule 3) and then to *Review* (Rule 5). Rule (4) requires that the vendor must be ID.

Third, each role is associated with a clearance level. For instance, if vendors are assigned a clearance of 0.8, they can only access data items with clearance less than or equal to 0.8. Here, exclusive products may be assigned higher clearance levels, such as 0.9, and they will only be available for managers.

Fourth, we allow each user to specify additional rules, which determine the context of the query results he/she expects. As an example, suppose that a specific vendor is only interested on reviews made after '01.01.2018'. It can be expressed as the set of *user context rules* presented in Fig. 2(b).

Let us exemplify how these access constraint rules are used to process user queries. Query q (Fig. 3(a)) selects data about product reviews. To ensure that only answers that consider the access constraints are retrieved, first it is checked whether the query involves only predicates that respect the schema constraints. Then, it is rewritten into a new query Q_{rw} (Fig. 3(c)), which contains the role-based and user context rules. We assume that end-users are mostly interested in performing data analysis, thus requiring queries involving aggregation. Figure 3(b) depicts an example of a query involving the *avg* function. The results of Q_{rw} are grouped by $X_{product}$ and for each group it returns the average review rating.

(a) $q(X_{product}, X_{rating}) \leftarrow$
$\quad reviews(X_{review}, X_{product}),$
$\quad reviewRating(X_{review}, X_{rating})$

(b) $q_{agg}(X_{product}, AvgRating) \leftarrow$
$\quad aggr(q(X_{product}, X_{rating}), (X_{product}),$
$\quad AvgRating = avg(X_{rating}))$

(c) $Qrw(X_{product}, X_{rating}) \leftarrow$
$\quad reviews(X_{review}, X_{product}),$
$\quad reviewRating(X_{review}, X_{rating}),$
(1) $Vendor(ID),$
(5) $offers(X_{offer}, X_{product}),$
(3) $sells(X_{vendor}, X_{offer}),$
(4) $X_{vendor} = ID,$
(6) $reviewDate(X_{review}, X_{day}),$
(7) $X_{day} >= $ '01.01.2018'

Fig. 3. (a) Conjunctive query; (b) Aggregate query; (c) Rewritten query

To carry out the rewritten query, we introduce a distributed query processing approach. Consider the aggregation query in Fig. 3(b). Each server that composes the distributed storage processes the rewritten query in parallel and execute the *sum* and *count* functions with the data locally stored, considering only those that comply with the access constraints. Then, the result is sent to a moderator. After receiving all partial values, the moderator adds them up to calculate the final *avg* query result.   □

Efficiently processing aggregate queries under access constraint rules is the goal of this paper. Example 1 shows that our approach satisfies the three requirements for access control mechanisms for big data platforms defined by [7]. First, we support fine-grained access control with our two-level mechanism: schema and role-based access rules. Second, context management is supported by allowing users to individually define the required results using user context rules. Third, we propose an efficient access control mechanism based on query-rewriting, and a distributed query processing approach that considers clearance levels and executes aggregation operations in parallel.

Paper Organisation. Section 2 reviews related work, Sects. 3 to 4 describe the system architecture and model, Sects. 5 to 7 detail the distributed query processing. Experimental study and conclusions are in Sects. 8 and 9.

2   Related Work

A survey on RDF access control mechanisms and systems can be found in [14]. XACML (eXtensible Access Control Markup Language) [2] is an OASIS standard that describes a policy and access language in XML. Although there have been some initiatives to apply XACML for graph and RDF datasets [4,13], they do not focus on the enforcement of access policies based on query rewriting, which is the goal of this paper. Among the works that adopt a query rewriting approach for access control, we refer to Pure [11] which is not an RBAC and does not deal with aggregation, and [17] whose language for expressing access constraints is less expressive than ours. Our language, on the other hand, is expressive enough to express all access constraints defined for a comparison study among Semantic Web authorization systems reported in [22][1]. Context-awareness is investigated in [8] for access control of RDF datastores for mobile devices, but it does not consider roles and fine-grained access rules. Access control based on roles and purposes is considered in [12]. But the enforcement is not based in query rewriting as our work. Likewise, this is not the approach followed by LDAP [21], which is based on the definition of views. Views may include aggregation operations, and users or roles are granted read or update operations. Their reported experimental study shows that view materialization may result in an 8 fold increase in query processing time, compared to queries with hard-coded access rules, which can be the result of query rewriting. To the best of our knowledge, there is no previous work that combines efficient distributed processing of aggregate queries under role-based access constraints with a query rewriting technique.

The query rewriting process of our current proposal extends [6,15] by considering *positive constraints with more than one atom in their bodies*, but it does not consider special cases of unification treated in [15]. Indeed, [15] proposes a detailed algorithm to deal with instantiated constraints (*e.g.* a restriction imposed only on the vendor *Bob*) or constraints having atoms with variable repetition while the repetition does not appear in the query. Both cases impose

---

[1] Definition of constraints is available at http://ws2.din.uem.br/~raque/example.

different forms of atom matching which we do not consider in our tests. Negative constraints treated in [6,15] are out of the scope of this paper as well. Notice that [6,15] only deal with conjunctive queries. In the current paper, conjunctive queries (the only ones considered in the rewriting process) are the basis of group-by queries for which we propose *an implementation method in a distributed data environment*. The query execution model extends [18] by considering parallel processing of aggregation functions, as well as the clearance level of both users and objects as integral components of query planning and processing. However, it does not consider different forms of communication, which is the main focus of [18]. In doing so, we extend some aspects of each of our previous work [6,15,18], while relaxing others, in order to propose an efficient access control mechanism based on query rewriting.

3   Architecture for Access Control on Graphs

The general architecture of our access control system for graph-based models is depicted in Fig. 4. The administrator is responsible for setting security access parameters. To this end, different tasks are performed. The first one refers to defining role-based access constraints (Fig. 4(a)), which includes the creation of *roles*, and to each role, the association of: *schema constraints*, *role-based access rules*, and a *clearance level*, as illustrated in Example 1. The second task refers to the protection of some specific portions of the data, by assigning their clearance level (Fig. 4(b)). This would allow, for instance, ordinary and exclusive products to have distinct clearance levels such as 0.5 and 0.9, respectively. The administrator is also responsible for registering a user with an existent role (Fig. 4(c)). For the sake of simplicity, we consider that each user is assigned to a single role. All information regarding the administrator tasks is stored in the metadata repository (Fig. 4(d)). Further, each data clearance level is also stored in the distributed graph database with its corresponding data (Fig. 4(e)).

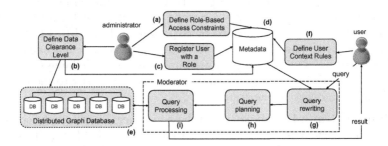

Fig. 4. General architecture of the proposed access control system.

After being registered, each user can define *context rules* (Fig. 4(f)). They restrict even more the role-based constraints, by determining a context that limit the data to be analyzed in queries. All information related to the user context rules is stored in the metadata repository (Fig. 4(d)). Regarding the users' queries, they are processed as follows. First, it is checked whether the query satisfies the schema constraints; that is, if it involves only predicates that can be manipulated by the user's role. If so, it is rewritten based on the role-based access rules and user context rules (Fig. 4(g)). The rewritten query is then used to generate a query plan, which determines the order in which the distributed graph should be traversed (Fig. 4(h)). The plan also includes the user's clearance level and how to compute the aggregate function. Regarding the query processing (Fig. 4(i)), it is responsible for sending the query plan to all servers that compose the distributed graph database, which execute it in parallel. If necessary, servers can communicate with each other without requiring interference of the moderator. After receiving the servers' results, the moderator generates the final result, which is shown to the user. The following sections detail each component of the architecture.

4   Model for Access Control

The database schema, roles and users definitions compose the system's metadata. The database instance is a set of facts. This section introduces these notions.

Metadata. Using a logical formalism, our RDF database schema is defined by a set $\mathbb{G}$ of predicate symbols. The database access is controlled through *roles*. Each role $\mathbf{r}$ is defined by a tuple $(\mathbb{R}, \mathbb{C}^{\mathbf{r}}, \tau_{\mathbf{r}})$ where $\mathbb{R}$ is a subset of predicate symbols in $\mathbb{G}$ specifying the database portion on which a user having such a role can work on, $\mathbb{C}^{\mathbf{r}}$ is a set of constraints defined by rules on $\mathbb{R}$, and $\tau_{\mathbf{r}}$ is the clearance level of the role. The set $\mathbb{C}^{\mathbf{r}}$ is composed by mandatory constraints, that all users with the role should respect. The clearance level $\tau_{\mathbf{r}}$ strengthen the control on sensitive information, establishing that any information associated to a clearance level $\tau > \tau_{\mathbf{r}}$ cannot be used to compose answers for users associated to $\mathbf{r}$. A user usr has a unique identifier ID and can be associated to one (or several) context(s) Ctx. A context Ctx $= (\mathbf{r}, \mathbb{C}^{\mathbf{u}})$ is composed by a role $\mathbf{r}$ and a set of constraints $\mathbb{C}^{\mathbf{u}}$. The latter is a set of user's self-defined constraints on $\mathbb{R}$. In Example 1, $\mathbf{r} = Vendor$ is defined by $\mathbb{R}$ (in blue in Fig. 1(b)), $\mathbb{C}^{\mathbf{r}}$ in Fig. 2(a) and $\tau_{\mathbf{r}} = 0.8$. User constraints are in $\mathbb{C}^{\mathbf{u}}$ (Fig. 2(b)). Notice that extending the model to allow users with multiple roles implies in: (*i*) re-defining Ctx, to allow a set of roles instead of a single one and (*ii*) imposing the user to choose his role before sending a query to the system.

Distributed Graph Database. A database instance $\mathbb{D}$ consists of a set of facts on $\mathbb{G}$, where unary facts are associated with a clearance level (τ). The database can be represented as a labelled graph $G_{\mathbb{D}} = (V, E)$ as follows: an unary fact $P(x)$ is mapped to a vertex x in V with an edge $(x, type, P)$ in E. We denote by $\mathbb{T}$ the set of unary predicate names in $\mathbb{G}$. A binary fact $P(x, y)$ is mapped to an edge (x, P, y) in E. An example of a database that follows the schema shown in Fig. 1 is given in Fig. 5, where *type* edges are omitted for simplicity. Likewise, a schema $\mathbb{G}$ can be represented as a graph $G_{\mathbb{G}}$, as depicted in Fig. 1.

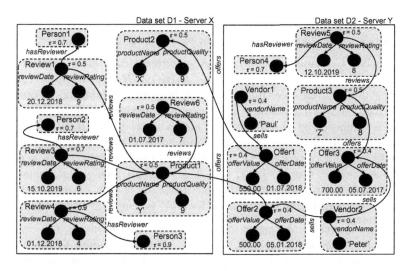

Fig. 5. Distributed graph database ($G_{\mathbb{D}}$)

5   Query Rewriting

Our querying system offers to a user $\mathsf{usr} = (ID, \mathsf{Ctx})$ a context-driven query environment. Only data that satisfy the constraints are returned as query answers. Before being evaluated, a query passes through a rewriting process (Fig. 4(h)).

Preliminaries. Queries, rules, and contexts are expressed in a logical paradigm. We consider a disjoint countably infinite sets of constants (CONST) and variables (VAR) and a finite set of predicates, each associated with its arity (PRED). A term is a constant or a variable. An *atom* has one of the forms: (*i*) $P(t_1, ..., t_n)$, where P is an n-ary predicate and $t_1, ..., t_n$ are terms; (*ii*) $\top$ (true) or $\bot$ (false); (*iii*) ($t_1 \; op \; t_2$), where t_1 and t_2 are terms and op is a comparison operator ($=$, $<$, $>$, $\leq$, $\geq$). A *fact* is an atom $P(u)$ where $u \in (\text{CONST})^n$. Let A_1 and A_2 be a set of atoms. A *homomorphism* from an atom in A_1 to an atom in A_2, both on the same predicate P, is a function h from the terms of A_1 to the terms of A_2 such that: (*i*) if $t \in$ CONST, then $h(t) = t$, and (*ii*) if $P(t_1, ..., t_n) \in A_1$, then $P(h(t_1), ..., h(t_n)) \in A_2$. This notion extends to conjunctions or sets of atoms.

Constraints. A constraint c has the form $\forall \overline{x}, \overline{y}.(\psi(\overline{x}, \overline{y}) \rightarrow \exists \overline{z}.L_2(\overline{x}, \overline{z}))$ where $\overline{x}, \overline{y}$ and $\overline{z}$ are lists of variables, $\psi(\overline{x}, \overline{y})$, refereed as *body(c)*, is a conjunction of atoms and $L_2(\overline{x}, \overline{z})$, *i.e. head(c)*, is an atom. When no confusion is possible, quantifiers are omitted. We denote by *role set-up constraint* the empty-body constraint having the form $\quad \rightarrow roleName(ID)$ where *roleName* is a unary predicate which coincides with the name of the role for $\mathsf{usr} = (ID, \mathsf{Ctx})$. This constraint is automatically imposed for each user. A set I of facts satisfies a constraint c ($I \models c$) if for every homomorphism h from the variables in *body(c)* into constants in I, we have: if $h(body(c))$ is true in I then there is an extension

h' of h such that $h'(head(c))$ is evaluated to $\top$ or is a fact in I. Given a set of constraints $\mathbb{C}$, I satisfies $\mathbb{C}$ ($I \models \mathbb{C}$) if for every $c \in \mathbb{C}$, $I \models c$ holds.

Conjunctive Connected Queries. A *(connected conjunctive) query* q over a given schema has the form $R_0(u_0) \leftarrow R_1(u_1) \ldots R_n(u_n), comp_1, \ldots, comp_m$ where $n \geq 0$ and u_i are free tuples (*i.e.* may have either variables or constants). The left hand-side of q is denoted as $head(q)$ and its right hand-side, denoted by $body(q)$, is composed by a conjunction of atoms on predicates R_i ($0 \leq i \leq n$) and comparison atoms $comp_j$ ($0 \leq j \leq m$). Conjunctive queries are range restricted, satisfiable [3], and *connected*, *i.e.* for each free tuple u_i in a query q without equality and with $\mid body(q) \mid > 1$, if u_i has variables then u_i has at least one variable which is also in $u_j \neq u_i$. Denote $ans(q, \mathbb{D})$ the set of answers (tuples) $t \in \mathrm{CONST}^n$ for which $\exists h_t$ such that $h_t(body(q))$ is true in $\mathbb{D}$ and $h_t(u_0) = t$.

Group-by Queries. A *group by query* has the form: $q_{ag}(X_1, \ldots, X_k, a_1, \ldots, a_m) \leftarrow aggr(q_1(X_1, \ldots, X_n), (X_1, \ldots, X_k), a_l = func_l(X_{k+1}, \ldots, X_n))$, where *aggr* is a second order predicate; q_1 is a connected conjunctive query with schema $X_1, \ldots, X_n$; $k \in [0, n]$; $a_1 \ldots a_m$ are new variables not existing in $\{X_1, \ldots, X_n\}$; $func_l$ is a function that returns a real value. Given $\mathsf{Ctx} = (\mathbf{r}, \mathbb{C}^{\mathbf{u}})$, let $\mathbb{C}$ be the set $\mathbb{C}^{\mathbf{r}} \cup \mathbb{C}^{\mathbf{u}}$ containing all the constraints (on $\mathbb{R}$) imposed on user's queries. The answer of q_{ag} on Ctx over a database instance $\mathbb{D}$ on $\mathbb{G}$, denoted by $ans(q_{ag}, \mathsf{Ctx}, \mathbb{D})$, is the set of tuples $t = h_u(X_1) \ldots h_u(X_k).a_1.\ldots.a_m$ (for $m \geq 0$) such that:

• $u \in ans(q_{1rw}(X_1, \ldots, X_n), \mathbb{D})$ where $q_{1rw}(X_1, \ldots, X_n) \leftarrow \phi(X_1, \ldots, X_{n_0})$ is the rewritten version of q_1 *w.r.t.* $\mathbb{C}$. Let h_u be the homomorphism used to find an answer u (respecting $\tau_{\mathbf{r}}$).
• For each real value a, we have $a = func(ans(q_2, \mathbb{D}))$ where q_2 is the query $q_2(X_{j_1}, \ldots, X_{j_{k_l}}) \leftarrow q_{1rw}(h_u(X_1), \ldots, h_u(X_k), X_{k+1}, \ldots, X_n)$, with $\{X_{j_1}, \ldots, X_{j_{k_l}}\} \subseteq \{X_{k+1}, \ldots, X_n\}$.

  Figure 3(b) illustrates a group-by query built on the connected query in Fig. 3(a).

Query Rewriting Process. Constraints are used for query rewriting, following the proposal in [6], but, here, a constraint may have more than one atom in its body. More precisely, the query rewriting process is based on the *chase* procedure, in which constraints in $\mathbb{C}$ are triggered by atoms in $body(q_1)$. For each *role set-up constraint*, we add in $body(q_1)$ the head of the constraint. For each constraint $\psi(\overline{x}, \overline{y}) \rightarrow L_2(\overline{x}, \overline{z})$, if it exists an homorphism h such that $h(\psi(\overline{x}, \overline{y})) \subseteq body(q_1)$ and $h(L_2(\overline{x}, \overline{z}))$ is not isomorphic to some atoms of $body(q_1)$, we add $h(L_2(\overline{x}, \overline{z}))$ in $body(q_1)$ where $\overline{z}$ are renamed in new variables. The next example illustrates the method.

Example 2. Let q be the query in Fig. 3(a) and $\mathbb{C} = \mathbb{C}^{\mathbf{r}} \cup \mathbb{C}^{\mathbf{u}}$ with $\mathbb{C}^{\mathbf{r}}$ in Fig. 2(a) and $\mathbb{C}^{\mathbf{u}}$ in Fig. 2(b). The first steps in the rewriting of q *w.r.t.* $\mathbb{C}$ are:
• $Vendor(ID)$ is added to $body(q)$ due to he role set-up constraint.
• Atom $reviews(X_{review}, X_{product})$ triggers constraints (5) and (6). Triggering involves a homomorphism h from atoms in the constraint's body to atoms in the query's body. For constraint (5): h is the identity because variable names

are the same. As the constraint's head has an existential variable (X_{offer}), h' extends h by assigning fresh variables to it: we can add $offers(N_1, X_{product})$ to the body of the new query being built, where N_1 is a fresh variable. Similarly, atom $reviewDate(X_{review}, N_2)$ is produced with (6).

■ At this step, the rewritten query is:

$q'(X_{product}, X_{rating}) \leftarrow reviews(X_{review}, X_{product}), reviewRating(X_{review}, X_{rating}),$
$Vendor(ID), offers(N_1, X_{product}), reviewDate(X_{review}, N_2).$

• Atom $Vendor(ID)$ in $body(q')$ triggers constraint (2). With the homomorphism $h_1(X_{vendor}) = ID$, the atom $(ID = ID)$ is generated (which, corresponds to $\top$).
• Atom $offers(N_1, X_{product},) \in body(q')$ triggers constraint (3). With the homomorphism $h_2(X_{product}) = X_{product}$ and $h_2(X_{offer}) = N_1$, atom $sells(N_3, N_1)$ is generated.
• Moreover $reviewDate(X_{review}, N_2)$ triggers constraint (7) with $h_3(X_{review}) = X_{review}$ and $h_3(X_{day}) = N_2$, generating $N_2 >= 01.01.2008$.

■ At this step, the re-written query is:

$q''(X_{pat}, X_{exam}) \leftarrow reviews(X_{review}, X_{product}), reviewRating(X_{review}, X_{rating}),$
$Vendor(ID), offers(N_1, X_{product}), reviewDate(X_{review}, N_2), (ID = ID),$
$sells(N_3, N_1), N_2 >= 01.01.2018.$

• Constraint (4) is then triggered, since we have $Vendor(ID)$ and $sells(N_3, N_1)$ in $body(q'')$. With homomorphism h_4 such that $h_4(X_{vendor}) = N_3$, $h_4(X_{offer}) = N_1$, and $h_4(Z) = ID$, the atom $(N_3 = ID)$ is generated.

■ At this step, the re-written query is:

$q'''(X_{pat}, X_{exam}) \leftarrow reviews(X_{review}, X_{product}), reviewRating(X_{review}, X_{rating}),$
$Vendor(ID), offers(N_1, X_{product}), reviewDate(X_{review}, N_2), (ID = ID),$
$sells(N_3, N_1), N_2 >= 01.01.2018, (N_3 = ID).$

The chase continues in this way until the process reaches the fix-point – there is no more new atoms added to the query's body. The complete rewritten query corresponds to Q_{rw} in Fig. 3(c) (despite variable renaming). Answers to Q_{rw} are valid answers for q w.r.t. $\mathbb{C}$. They are used by the group-by query of Fig. 3(b). □

In Example 2, note the importance of constraint (2). Suppose $\mathbb{C}_1$ built from $\mathbb{C}$ by removing constraint (2). The rewriting of $q_2(X) \leftarrow Vendor(X)$ would give $q_{2rw}(X) \leftarrow Vendor(X), Vendor(ID)$. In this situation we are not restricting the vendor to access only his own information.

Correction of Query Rewriting. We consider that the set of constraints is weakly acyclic [10] which guarantees the termination of rewriting process. The query rewriting process ensures that rewritten-query's answers respect constraints in $\mathbb{C}$. Indeed, the proof of the correction and of the termination of our rewriting process is based on the first part of the proof presented in [15] which considers the case where for atoms in the body of a constraint c there is a homomorphism h to atoms in the query's body. Cases where h does not exist but where a unification is possible are not treated in the current paper, *i.e.* although the theoretical extension exists, we have not considered its distributed data implementation counterpart yet.

Complexity of Query Rewriting. As pointed out in [9], for a fixed schema and a set of weakly acyclic constraints $\mathbb{C}$, any chase sequence terminates in polynomial time in the size of the query being chased. This fixed size assumption fits to our scenarios. Following the lines of [10] where the proof of this complexity is given, let: (*i*) p be the sum of $arity(P)$, for each predicate P in $\mathbb{C}$; (*ii*) n be the number of distinct values (*i.e.*, terms in $body(q)$ or free new variables) that can be assigned to variables appearing in constraints in $\mathbb{C}$, and (*iii*) s be the number of predicates (|PRED|). When dealing with weak acyclic constraints, the corresponding dependency graph G has no cycle on *existential* edges (refer to [10, 16] for details). Moreover, the number of *existential* edges on the incoming paths of a node in G is finite (denoted by the *rank* of a node). The proof is based on the fact that nodes in the dependency graph can be partitioned according to their rank and that the number of distinct values produced by the chase at a rank i is at most $Q_i(n)$ for a polynomial Q_i. But i is bounded by the maximum rank r which is at most p. Indeed r is not only finite but bounded by a constant. It follows that the length of any chase sequence is at most $s \times (Q(n))^p$ which is polynomial, since n, s and p are assumed to be constant.

6   Query Planning

The *Query Planning* module receives as input the user ID, his clearance level, and a rewritten query. It produces as output a query plan based on the process proposed in [18], extended to support aggregate queries and clearance level.

A query plan S is a sequence of steps used to retrieve data from $\mathbb{D}$, as illustrated in Fig. 6(a). It is composed of four parts: a clearance level, a sequence of *body steps* (s_{b1}-s_{b4}), an optional aggregation step (s_g), and a *head step* (s_h). The body steps correspond to atoms in the body of a conjunctive query, while the head step is a single projection operation with the query results. For aggregation queries, step s_g contains a sequence of *(function, group-by)* pairs.

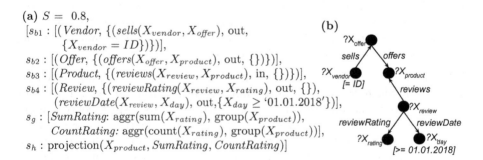

(a) $S = 0.8,$
$[s_{b1} : [(Vendor, \{(sells(X_{vendor}, X_{offer}), \text{out},$
$\{X_{vendor} = ID\})\})],$
$s_{b2} : [(Offer, \{(offers(X_{offer}, X_{product}), \text{out}, \{\})\})],$
$s_{b3} : [(Product, \{(reviews(X_{review}, X_{product}), \text{in}, \{\})\})],$
$s_{b4} : [(Review, \{(reviewRating(X_{review}, X_{rating}), \text{out}, \{\}),$
$(reviewDate(X_{review}, X_{day}), \text{out}, \{X_{day} \geq \text{'}01.01.2018\text{'}\})],$
$s_g : [SumRating:\ \text{aggr}(\text{sum}(X_{rating}), \text{group}(X_{product})),$
$CountRating:\ \text{aggr}(\text{count}(X_{rating}), \text{group}(X_{product}))],$
$s_h : \text{projection}(X_{product}, SumRating, CountRating)]$

Fig. 6. (a) Query plan; (b) Query tree

Elements in a body step have the form $(vType, eTrav)$, where $vType$ is a type in $\mathbb{T}$, and $etrav$ is a set of edge traversals of the form (r, dir, f). Here, (i) r is an atom $p(s, o)$ where either s or o is of type $vType$; (ii) dir defines the direction of the traversal, which can be in for incoming edges, or out for outgoing edges; (iii) f is a set of filters defined on s or o. We denote as *initial exploration points* the first element of the first body step. In the example of Fig. 6(b), vertices of type $Vendor$ are the initial exploration points. Query plans that involve aggregation contain an aggregate step (s_g) that assigns a variable name to each operation. For computing the average (avg), the aggregation step is generated with two operations: sum and $count$, defined over the same attributes and grouping. Aggregation variables, as well as the ones in body steps, can be used in the head step s_h. Figure 6(a) shows a projection step for an aggregate query while the query plan for the one in Fig. 3(a) consists of all the body steps of Fig. 6(a), followed by the head step: $s_h : (\text{projection}(X_{product}, X_{rating}))$.

Construction of a Query Plan. A query plan is built in two phases. The first phase is based on the graph representation of the body of a conjunctive query. An example of a graph query G_q that corresponds to the query in Fig. 3(a) is given in Fig. 6(b). In G_q each vertex is associated with a variable, and optionally with a set of filters, represented within square brackets. Given G_q, we look for subgraphs in the schema graph $G_{\mathbb{G}}$ that are homomorphic to G_q. In our running example, there exists a single subgraph, composed of nodes highlighted in gray in Fig. 1(a). A query plan is generated for each homomorphic subgraph. As a consequence, the final result is computed by combining results of all such plans. In the second phase, we have to define a graph traversal order for each homomorphic subgraph. We consider the same strategy used in [18], but with one difference concerning the choice of the initial exploration points. Access constraint rules frequently restrict a user to its own data. As seen in Sect. 5, constraints such as (2) (Fig. 2(a)) implement this restriction by setting $X = ID$ as a filter. If such a filter exists in the query, it is natural to start the graph traversal by vertices of X's type to reduce the search space of the query. This strategy was adopted to generate the query plan in Fig. 6(a).

7   Query Processing

We consider a shared-nothing master-slave architecture. The metadata is stored on the master, while the database is distributed among the slaves. The *query rewriting* and *query planning* components are executed on the master server *i.e.* , the master server receives and analyses query requisitions, generates query plans, and requires slaves in a cluster to execute the plan. All slaves start to process the same plan in parallel with their local data. When the query requires data stored on remote servers, slaves communicate with each other without the intervention of the master. The adopted architecture follows the inter-node parallelism with asynchronous BSP (Bulk Synchronous Parallel) computation model. It does not require synchronism among servers for transitions between query steps.

Distributed Graph Exploration. We assume that each slave has: (i) an index which maps types in $\mathbb{T}$ to the set of corresponding vertices that are locally stored, and (ii) an index that allows traversal to vertices in remote servers. Every slave receives the same query plan and starts its processing in parallel. The result of each body step is a set of mappings from variables to vertices in the database. In particular, mappings resulting from the first body step are the query's initial exploration points. Starting from them, each step in the plan is evaluated, and during the graph traversal, it is checked whether: (i) the vertex clearance level is less than or equal to the user's; and (ii) it satisfies the filters in the plan.

Consider the query plan in Fig. 6(a), the database in Fig. 5, and assume the user is *Vendor2*, with $\tau_\mathbf{r} = 0.8$. The initial exploration points are searched in both servers X and Y by retrieving all vertices of type *Vendor* and checking the filter $X_{vendor} = ID$. The result in server Y is $\{m_1 : \{X_{vendor} \mapsto Vendor2\}\}$, while for server X the result is empty. Thus, the graph traversal continues only on Y. When it finishes processing body step s_{b2}, the mappings are: $\{m_2 : \{X_{vendor} \mapsto Vendor2, X_{offer} \mapsto Offer2\}, m_3 : \{X_{vendor} \mapsto Vendor2, X_{offer} \mapsto Offer3\}, \}$. At this point, m_2 requires a traversal to *Product1* stored on server X. Thus, m_2 is sent to server X in order to continue the graph traversal. There, the query continues from *Product1* to *Review1*, *Review3*, *Review4*, and *Review6*. However, *Review4* is discarded because its clearance level is higher than the user's, and *Review6* is discarded because it does not satisfy filter $X_{day} \geq$ '01.01.2018'. After processing all body steps, server X produces: $\{m_4 : \{X_{vendor} \mapsto Vendor2, X_{offer} \mapsto Offer2, X_{product} \mapsto Product1, X_{review} \mapsto Review1, X_{rating} \mapsto 9\}; m_5 : X_{vendor} \mapsto Vendor2, X_{offer} \mapsto Offer2, X_{product} \mapsto Product1, X_{review} \mapsto Review3, X_{rating} \mapsto 6\}\}$, while server Y produces a single mapping: $\{m_6 : \{X_{vendor} \mapsto Vendor2, X_{offer} \mapsto Offer3, X_{product} \mapsto Product3, X_{review} \mapsto Review5, X_{rating} \mapsto 8\}\}$. Next, each server executes the aggregation step. The result from X is: $\{m_7 : \{X_{product} \mapsto Product1, sumRating \mapsto 15, countRating \mapsto 2\}\}$, and Y produces: $\{m_8 : \{X_{product} \mapsto Product3, sumRating \mapsto 8, countRating \mapsto 1\}\}$. At last, the projection step is executed by each slave and the final mappings are sent to the master server. In our example, the final result is $\{(Product1, 7.5), (Product3, 8)\}$. Observe that the query steps are computed in parallel by all slaves, and the master is responsible for gathering the results from the slaves and possibly make some additional computation, such as grouping, to produce the final query result.

8   Experimental Study

This section presents an experimental study. We compare our approach, called *distributed*, with an alternative *centralized* one. The centralized approach is based on a master-slave architecture, where the master associates each role with a subgraph (or view) on which access constraints and queries can be processed. When a user submits a query, a request to compute the view is sent to all slaves. The master is responsible for gathering all the results, filtering out those that do not satisfy the access constraints, and producing the query results.

Settings. Both the distributed and centralized approaches were implemented in Java adopting the TCP/IP communication protocol. The Berkeley DB repository was used for storage. Our experiments were executed on a cluster of three virtual machines (1 master and 2 slaves), each one with 8 GB of memory and 2.27 GHz CPUs. The database was populated using the Berlin benchmark. We generated a database with 1,811,316 triples, which correspond to the scale factor of 5,000 products. Triples were randomly distribute between the slaves, but keeping literal properties in the same server as their subject. The clearance level of the data items were randomly defined, varying from 0.6 to 1.

Role-Based Access Constraints and Query Workload. We considered four roles: senior (rfs) and junior (rfj) financial managers, and senior (rms) and junior (rmj) marketing managers. Clearance levels were set to 0.6 and 1 for junior and senior managers, respectively. In addition, two constraints were considered for junior managers: junior financial managers cannot access offers with values greater than 1,500; and junior marketing managers can only retrieve products from producers of one specific country. We considered four queries:

- $Q1$: retrieve all product offers with their vendors' name;
- $Q2$: for each producer, obtain his name and their products;
- $Q1g$: retrieve the average value of the offers for each vendor;
- $Q2g$: retrieve the number of products made by each producer.

Queries $Q1$ and $Q2$ are similar to query q in Fig. 3(a) because they encompass selections and comparisons. Also, queries $Q1g$ and $Q2g$ extend $Q1$ and $Q2$ with grouping and aggregation, similar to query q_{agg}, depicted in Fig. 3(b). $Q1$ and $Q1g$ can be used by financial managers, while $Q2$ and $Q2g$ by marketing managers. For the centralized approach, in order to minimize the volume of data sent from the slaves to the master, we consider that the view associated with each role consists only of atoms used in the queries.

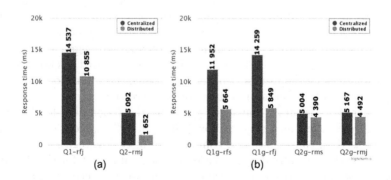

Fig. 7. Query execution time: (a) conjunctive query; (b) aggregation query

Experiments. The goal of our experiments is twofold: (a) determine the effect of the ability to rewrite queries with role-based rules and user context rules; and (b) determine the impact of our approach for computing aggregate queries under these constraints. For (a), observe that, in a distributed setting, the lack of ability to rewrite queries requires the master to either submit multiple queries to the slaves or to rely on a role view on which both constraints and query can be computed. We chose the latter for comparison purposes because it has been shown that the number of communications among servers is a key factor for query performance [20]. Moreover, experiments in [6] show that the processing time for query rewriting is negligible.

We first report on the results for queries that do not involve aggregation. The running times in this section are measured in milliseconds and consist of the average value of 15 executions. Figure 7(a) shows the processing time of $Q1$ and $Q2$, when executed by junior managers (rfj and rmj), considering the role-based constraints (clearance level and role-based rules). For the centralized approach, the master receives 100,000 subgraphs for $Q1$, while for $Q2$ the number of results is 5,000. The master applies the constraints while it receives the stream of results from the slaves. In the distributed approach, the filtering is processed on the slaves. As a result, the master receives 15,250 results for $Q1$ and 93 results for $Q2$. It shows that the query rewriting approach is effective for reducing the number of results and the query processing time. For $Q1$, the distributed approach promoted a reduction of 25%, and for $Q2$, the reduction was of 68%.

We now turn our attention to queries that involve grouping and aggregation operations. Figure 7(b) shows the execution times for both senior and junior managers. Since for senior managers the clearance level is 1, and there are no role-based rules, the difference on execution times reported for $Q1g_{rfs}$ and $Q2g_{rms}$ refers only to the different approaches for processing grouping and aggregation functions. In the centralized approach, the master processes the 100,000 results forwarded for $Q1g$ from the slaves, and 5,000 results for $Q2g$. In the distributed approach, these operations are processed on the slaves, resulting in 192 and 88 results, respectively. Observe that for $Q1g_{rfs}$ the distributed approach reduced the processing time by 53%. For $Q2g_{rms}$, the reduction was of 12%. This is because the volume of data involved in $Q2g$ is much smaller, and in the centralized approach, the master executes the grouping and aggregation functions as the slaves forward them. That is, the slaves do not wait the end of the view computation to send the results at once. Thus, when the volume of data is small, the gain of the distributed approach is not so expressive.

Consider now the junior managers. Since they have clearance level of 0.6 and role-based rules, the times reported for $Q1g_{rfj}$ and $Q2g_{rmj}$ consider both filtering data based on constraints and computation of the aggregation. The size of the views for the centralized approach remain the same, but for the distributed approach, the queries result sizes were 112 and 55, respectively. The processing time for both queries increased for the junior managers, compared to the senior managers, due to the role-based constraints processing. For the centralized approach, the increase was 11% for $Q1g$ and 3% for $Q2g$. As a consequence, the reduction in execution time of these queries were 59% and 13%, respectively.

The experiments presented in this section show that query rewriting with role-based and user context rules is effective for reducing the volume of data transmitted from the slaves to the master server. As a result, query processing time is reduced from 25% to 68%, compared to a view-based approach. Moreover, our distributed approach for processing aggregation functions on the slaves promoted a reduction from 12% to 59% when compared to the centralized approach, which computes them on the master server.

9   Conclusion

In terms of access control and quality guarantees, the contribution of our approach is threefold: (i) queries are role-oriented, limiting the access to parts of the distributed storage; (ii) answers are computed by using only data with clearance levels compatible with the user's; and (iii) query evaluation takes into account the user's context. The experimental study shows that our query rewriting and processing strategies significantly improves the execution time compared to a view-based processing approach, especially when large volumes of data are involved. Future work includes: integration with an authentication tool, the use of our model to implement extensions to the SPARQL query language or to implement the query system proposed in [5] which extends our rewriting method to recursive queries.

Acknowledgement. This work is partly developed in the context of DOING working group and CAPES-PRINT-UFPR Internationalization Program.

References

1. https://www.w3.org/wiki/LargeTripleStores
2. https://www.oasis-open.org/committees/tc_home.php?wg_abbrev=xacml
3. Abiteboul, S., Hull, R., Vianu, V.: Foundations of Databases. Addison-Wesley Reading, Boston (1995)
4. Ammar, N., Malik, Z., Bertino, E., Rezgui, A.: XACML policy evaluation with dynamic context handling. IEEE TKDE **27**(9), 2575–2588 (2015)
5. Chabin, J., Gomes Jr., L., Halfeld Ferrari, M.: A context-driven querying system for urban graph analysis. In: IDEAS, pp. 297–301. ACM (2018)
6. Chabin, J., Halfeld-Ferrari, M., Markhoff, B., Nguyen, T.B.: Validating data from semantic web providers. In: Tjoa, A.M., Bellatreche, L., Biffl, S., van Leeuwen, J., Wiedermann, J. (eds.) SOFSEM 2018. LNCS, vol. 10706, pp. 682–695. Springer, Cham (2018). https://doi.org/10.1007/978-3-319-73117-9_48
7. Colombo, P., Ferrari, E.: Access control technologies for big data management systems: literature review and future trends. Cybersecurity **2**(3), 1–13 (2019)
8. Costabello, L., Villata, S., Gandon, F.: Context-aware access control for RDF graph stores. In: Proceeding of the 20th European Conference on Artificial Intelligence (ECAI) (2012)

9. Deutsch, A., Popa, L., Tannen, V.: Query reformulation with constraints. SIGMOD Rec. **35**(1), 65–73 (2006)
10. Fagin, R., Kolaitis, P.G., Miller, R.J., Popa, L.: Data exchange: semantics and query answering. In: Database Theory - ICDT, 9th International Conference, Italy, Proceedings, pp. 207–224 (2003)
11. Goncalves, M., Vidal, M.E., Endris, K.M.: Pure: a privacy aware rule-based framework over knowledge graphs. In: Proceeding of the 30th International Conference on Database and Expert Systems Applications (DEXA), pp. 205–214 (2019)
12. Hartmann, S., Ma, H., Vechsamutvaree, P.: Providing ontology-based privacy-aware data access through web services and service composition. In: Hameurlain, A., Küng, J., Wagner, R., Schewe, K.-D., Bosa, K. (eds.) Transactions on Large-Scale Data- and Knowledge-Centered Systems XXX. LNCS, vol. 10130, pp. 109–131. Springer, Heidelberg (2016). https://doi.org/10.1007/978-3-662-54054-1_5
13. Jin, Y., Kaja, K.C.: XACML implementation based on graph database. In: Proceeding of the 34th International Conference on Computers and Their Applications, pp. 65–74 (2019)
14. Kirrane, S., Mileo, A., Decker, S.: Access control and the resource description framework: a survey. Semantic Web **8**(2), 311–352 (2017)
15. Nguyen, T.B.: L'interrogation du web de données garantissant des réponses valides par rapport à des critères donnés. (Querying the Web of Data guaranteeing valid answers with respect to given criteria). Ph.D. thesis, University of Orléans, France (2018). https://tel.archives-ouvertes.fr/tel-02426935
16. Onet, A.: The chase procedure and its applications in data exchange. In: Data Exchange, Integration, and Streams, pp. 1–37 (2013)
17. Padia, A., Finin, T., Joshi, A.: Attribute-based fine grained access control for triple stores. In: Proceeding of the Workshop on Society, Privacy and the Semantic Web - Policy and Technology (2015)
18. Penteado, R.R.M., Schroeder, R., Hara, C.S.: Exploring controlled RDF distribution. In: Proceeding of the IEEE International Conference on Cloud Computing Technology and Science (CloudCom), pp. 160–167 (2016)
19. Sandhu, R.S., Coyne, E.J., Feinstein, H.L., Youman, C.E.: Role-based access control models. IEEE Computer **29**(2), 38–47 (1996)
20. Schroeder, R., Hara, C.S.: Partitioning templates for RDF. In: Morzy, T., Valduriez, P., Bellatreche, L. (eds.) ADBIS 2015. LNCS, vol. 9282, pp. 305–319. Springer, Cham (2015). https://doi.org/10.1007/978-3-319-23135-8_21
21. Stojanov, R., Gramatikov, S., Mishkovski, I., Trajanov, D.: Linked data authorization platform. IEEE Access **6**, 1189–1213 (2018)
22. Stojanova, R., Stojanova, S., Jovanovika, M., Zdraveski, V., Trajanov, D.: Ranking semantic web authorization systems. Semantic Web **8**, 1–5 (2017)

Semi-automatic Column Type Inference for CSV Table Understanding

Sara Bonfitto[1] , Luca Cappelletti[1] , Fabrizio Trovato[2], Giorgio Valentini[1] , and Marco Mesiti[1(✉)]

[1] Department of Computer Science, Università di Milano,
Via Celoria 18, 20133 Milano, Italy
{sara.bonfitto,luca.cappelletti,giorgio.valentini,marco.mesiti}@unimi.it
[2] Area S.r.l., Via Torino 10/B, 12084 Mondovì, Italy
fabrizio.trovato@team1994.it

Abstract. Spreadsheets are often used as a simple way for representing tabular data. However, since they do not impose any restriction on their table structures and contents, their automatic processing and the integration with other information sources are particularly hard problems to solve. Many table understanding approaches have been proposed for extracting data from tables and transforming them in meaningful information. However, they require some regularities on the table contents.

Starting from CSV spreadsheets that present values of different types and errors, in this paper we introduce an approach for inferring the types of columns in CSV tables by exploiting a multi-label classification approach. By means of our approach, each column of the table can be associated with a simple datatype (such as integer, float, text), a domain-specific one (such as the name of a municipality, and address), or an "union" of types (that takes into account the frequency of the corresponding values). Since the automatically inferred types might not be accurate, graphical interfaces have been developed for supporting the user in fixing the mistakes. Experimental results are finally reported on real spreadsheets obtained by a debt collection agency.

Keywords: Table understanding · Type inference · GUI · CSVs

1 Introduction

According to [7] a great number of companies and institutions are using spreadsheets for managing, publishing and sharing their data. However, their automatic processing or transformation to other formats for storing and transmitting structured information (like relational or RDF models) are open problems because they are mainly designed for being interpreted by humans. The *Table Understanding* problem [15] consists in the extraction of meaningful information from table structured data and can be faced in 5 different steps: *localization*, i.e. identification of the position and structure of a table among all the other elements of a file; *segmentation*, i.e. extraction of all table components (cells, columns and

© Springer Nature Switzerland AG 2021
T. Bureš et al. (Eds.): SOFSEM 2021, LNCS 12607, pp. 535–549, 2021.
https://doi.org/10.1007/978-3-030-67731-2_39

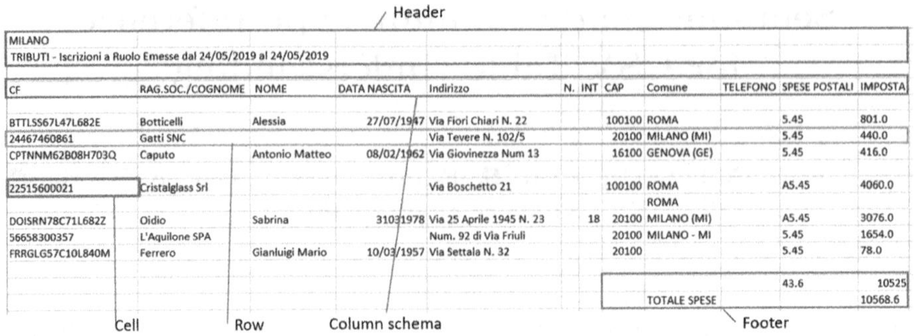

Fig. 1. Structure of a *CSV* file

rows); *functional analysis*, i.e. distinguishing between cells containing values and those containing schema information; *structural analysis*, i.e. identification of the logical organization of the table; and, *interpretation*, i.e. extraction of the meaning of the table content.

Recently we were involved in this kind of problem from a debt collection agency that receives *CSV* files from local authorities, such as municipalities, regions, tax agency and so on, containing batches of invoices to be rescued with information about the amount of debts and the debtors' personal data. These *CSV*s are heterogeneous and do not follow any standard format or notation. Some of them contain values that are organized as a relational table where column values are homogeneous, while others are highly heterogeneous and the same column contains different types of information.

An example of *CSV* file is reported in Fig. 1 (the data do not correspond to real entities but the overall organization is real). The file contains header and footer with general human readable information. A table can be identified in the central part of the spreadsheet which is formed by the *table schema* (the list of column names) and the *rows* containing values for each column. Among the rows, *blank rows* are sometimes used for aesthetic reasons while others for separating rows representing the same invoice, while *semi-blank rows* are used for reporting totals or remarks about the invoice. The CF column contains the fiscal identification codes for companies (named Partita IVA in Italy and abbreviated PIVA) and for single individuals (named codice fiscale in Italy and abbreviated codFisc). Moreover, when a PIVA value is specified in a row, the nearby column contains a company name, whereas when a codFisc value is specified, the nearby columns contain the surname and name of a person. Furthermore, the indirizzo column contains addresses but they can follow different patterns. For example, the string "Via Settala N. 32" can be decomposed according to a pattern in street name, and street number. Also the labels used as column names can be different and sometimes they do not reflect their value types (there are also situations in which the column name is not reported). We can finally remark that in many cases missing information and also errors can occur (e.g. a codFisc can be wrongly reported and might not correspond to the person or a zip code might not correspond to a city). Dealing with these kinds of heterogeneity and errors makes hard the work of the Agency's employees that usually manually develop wrappers able to extract and correct this information before the ingestion into their databases. Each time a *CSV* file containing a different structure arrives, a new wrapper needs to be developed.

In this paper we detail an approach that can be exploited in the interpretation step for identifying the data types occurring in the columns of a table. The purpose is to identify the value types of the corresponding columns and exploit them for the construction of a semantic model associated with the information extracted from the CSV. The model can be used for reasoning on the correctness of the information reported within and then for its storage and automatic processing. Moving to a semantic model also allows us to identify semantic correlations existing among values occurring in table rows (e.g. when the subject of different invoices is the same person). Our approach combines Machine learning (ML) facilities with users interfaces with the aim of supporting the user in the identification of column types through models trained on the features of the CSVs of our domain, and also graphical interfaces for easily fixing the mistakes that an automatic prediction approach can arise.

A pre-processing step is executed on the CSV file for the extraction of a table by using standard techniques. For the localization of the table, we consider the density of the information contained in the table with respect to external data. For the functional analysis of the cells, we use their position within the table and adopt dictionaries of already processed CSVs for identifying the column schema. For removing blank and semi-blank rows, predefined thresholds are used on the minimal number of non empty cells in each row w.r.t. the number of columns.

The pair $\langle S, V \rangle$ denotes an extracted table, where $S = [col_1, \ldots, col_j, \ldots, col_m]$ denotes the list of column names, and $V = \{r_1, \ldots, r_n\}$ is the set of table rows. Each row r_i, $1 \leq i \leq n$, is a list of values, $r_i = [v_{i,1}, \ldots, v_{i,j}, \ldots, v_{i,m}]$, one for each column identified in the column schema. Purpose of our work is to identify a type for each value and for each column occurring in $\langle S, V \rangle$. However, type assignment cannot be complete because of the lack of information, the occurrence of errors, and the presence of different types of information in the same column. Therefore, we model the problem as a multi-label classification approach and exploit a simple extension of decision trees with pre-defined thresholds that automatically identifies possible types that can be assigned to a column. Then, by exploiting graphical interfaces, the user is supported in the adjustment of the automated inferred types. Preliminary experiments on a set of 40 heterogeneous *CSV* files made available by the debt agency shows the feasibly of the approach.

In the reminder, Sect. 2 introduces our type system and simple type recognizers. Section 3 discusses the ML model and its application in our context. Section 4 deals with the our graphical user interfaces for fixing the inferred types. Preliminary experimental results are discussed in Sect. 5. Section 6 compares our approach with related work. Finally, Sect. 7 concludes our work.

2   Type System and Type Recognizers

Type System. Our type system $\mathcal{T}$ is formed by three kinds of types: *simple* (denoted $\mathcal{ST}$), *mixed* (denoted $\mathcal{MT}$) and *union* types (denoted $\mathcal{UT}$).

The simple types are basic domains (e.g. `integer`, `Boolean`, `decimal`, `date`) and specific domains for our application (e.g. `codFisc`, `PIVA`, `currency`, `emails`, `municipality names`, `province` or `metropolitan area` names, `region` names, `zip` codes) that can be extracted from strings. A mixed type is a record-type associated with a set of patterns for extracting the record type from a string. Formally, let m be a system/user-defined name of the mixed type, $t_1, \ldots, t_h \in \mathcal{ST}$ be simple types and $\{p_1, \ldots, p_k\}$ be a set of patterns, a mixed type is a triple $\langle m, \texttt{rec}(t_1, \ldots, t_h), \{p_1, \ldots, p_k\}\rangle$. A **pattern** is a sequence $[c_0, t_1, c_1, \ldots, t_h, c_h]$, where $c_o, c_1, \ldots, c_h$ are terminal symbols.[1] Terminal symbols are non-empty strings (with the exception of c_0 and c_h that can be empty) that are used for separating values of simple types. Thus, patterns are rules for extracting the same record-based value from heterogeneous strings expressing the same information.

Example 1. Consider the string "Via Settala N. 32" and the string "Num. 92 di via friuli" in the `Indirizzo` column in Fig. 1. The pattern $[\{\texttt{streetName}\}, $ " N. "$, \{\texttt{streetNumber}\}]$ and the pattern $[$"Num. "$, \{\texttt{streetNumber}\}, $" di "$, \{\texttt{streetName}\}]$ can be associated with them. However, they follow the same type `rec(streetName, streetNumber)`.

Union types are used for representing the occurrence of instances of different types in the same column. Formally, let $\{\bar{t}_1, \ldots, \bar{t}_l\} \subseteq \mathcal{ST} \cup \mathcal{MT}$ be a set of simple or mixed types, $union(\bar{t}_1, \ldots, \bar{t}_l)$ is a union type.

Example 2. The column `CF` contains both `codFisc` and `PIVA` values. Thus its type is `union(codFisc,PIVA)`. The column `RAG.SOC./COGNOME` contains two kinds of information, the company name and the surname of an individual. Thus its type is `union(surname,companyName)`.

Type Recognizer. For identifying the values v that adhere to the constraints of a given type, each simple type $t \in \mathcal{ST}$ is associated with a type recognizer. A *recognizer* Rec_t for a type t is a function that given a value v returns `true` when v is a valid instance of t, `false` otherwise.

Three kinds of simple types recognizers have been considered in our approach. The first one can be used when the instances of a type t are finite and enumerable. In this case, $v_{i,j}$ belongs to a type t when $v_{i,j}$ is contained in the set of valid values for t. This kind of recognizers has been applied for the types `country`, `region`, `municipality`, `zip code` (exact), `Boolean`, `gender`, `name`, `surname` and `productType`. The second one can be used when the type instances can be determined by means of regular expressions. For example, for the recognition of the Italian vehicle plates more than 20 regular expressions have been developed for the identification of the different plate variations

---

[1] To distinguish terminal symbols from types, types are delimited by brackets.

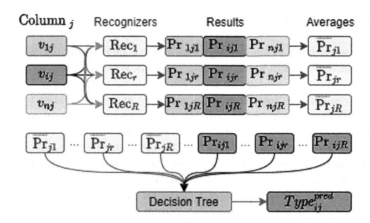

Fig. 2. Embedding of table values and execution of the decision tree. Top: Recognizers compute the features of the decision tree for each value of a column j of the table. Bottom: Using the above features the decision tree predicts the type of $v_{i,j}$. (Color figure online)

(e.g. `"^[a-zA-Z]{2}\\s?[0-9]{3}\s?[a-zA-z]{2}\$"` is one of the regular expressions that we have developed). The last one can be used when the values follow a given format and pre-defined packages are available for their recognition. Specifically, we have adopted python code for checking `emails`, `codFisc`, `PIVA`, `address`, `integer`, `decimal`, `year`, `empty` strings.

We remark that in the recognition of the type of a value $v_{i,j}$ the occurrence of a value of another type in the same row is sometimes considered and exploited for increasing the strength of the prediction. For example, for the identification of the types `name` and `surname` from a string also the `codFisc` code has been considered (when available). Indeed, the code can help in splitting the string and thus to identify the two components. Also the recognizer for the zip code uses the municipality name (when available) to check the presence of a real city.

Recognizers have been also generated for the identification of some mixed-types. For extracting name and surname from a value $v_{i,j}$, the value is split in a list of terms $[w_{i,j}^1, \ldots, w_{i,j}^s]$ by considering the blank space and some usual terminal symbols. Then, a recogniser based on sets is used by considering a collection of common names and surnames in Italy. For the recognition of the address components, we have used the *libpostal* library[2] which is frequently used in the context of Natural Language Processing and exploits the OpenStreetMap (OSM) database of location names. Finally, a recognizer has been developed that exploits a collection of patterns extracted from common strings used in our domain. A value $v_{i,j}$ is compared with each of the available patterns and whenever a single match is identified, $v_{i,j}$ is considered an instance of the mixed type associated with the pattern.

---

[2] https://github.com/openvenues/libpostal.

3   Type Inference Approach

Due to the abundance of the simple types of our type system and the errors that can occur in real data, a value $v_{i,j}$ of a table $\langle S, V \rangle$ can belong simultaneously to different types or to none of them. This requires the use of a ML approach for inferring the most probable type for a single value $v_{i,j}$ and also for the entire column. We have compared different ML models and ended up in using decision trees for the identification of the type of a single value $v_{i,j}$ and then adopting a simple multi-label classification approach for inferring the types to be associated with the column. Indeed, in our type system, a column can be associated with an union type and therefore the same column can contain values of different types. In this section we discuss the adopted model for inferring the type of each single $v_{i,j}$ and the type of the corresponding column and compare it with other ML models. Finally, we discuss the approach adopted for training the model.

The Main Model: Ensemble of Recognizers with a Decision Tree on Top. To determine the type of the single values in the table, we adopted an ensemble of binary recognizers that feed their results into a decision tree.

For each value $v_{i,j}$ in a column j, the decision tree receives as input the vector of predictions from each recognizer and the vector of average predictions of the column (shown in blue and grey in Fig. 2). More precisely R recognizers $Rec_1, Rec_2, \ldots Rec_R$ are applied to each value $v_{i,j}$ of a given column j, generating a vector of R Boolean values for each v_{ij}:

$$\mathbf{Pr}_{i,j} = \langle \mathrm{Pr}_{i,j,1}, \mathrm{Pr}_{i,j,2}, \ldots, \mathrm{Pr}_{i,j,R} \rangle \tag{1}$$

Moreover each recognizer Rec_r computes its average value $\overline{\mathrm{Pr}}_{j,r}$ across the values of a given column j:

$$\overline{\mathrm{Pr}}_{j,r} = \frac{1}{n} \sum_{i=1}^{n} \mathrm{Rec}_r (v_{i,j}) = \frac{1}{n} \sum_{i=1}^{n} \mathrm{Pr}_{i,j,r} \tag{2}$$

thus generating a vector of average values of the recognizers for the column j:

$$\overline{\mathbf{Pr}}_j = < \overline{\mathrm{Pr}}_{j,1}, \overline{\mathrm{Pr}}_{j,2}, \ldots, \overline{\mathrm{Pr}}_{j,R} > \tag{3}$$

In this way for each value $v_{i,j}$ we can construct a vector $\mathbf{Pr}_{\mathrm{conc}}^{i,j} = < \overline{\mathbf{Pr}}_j, \mathbf{Pr}_{i,j} >$ simply concatenating the vectors of Eq. 1 and 3 (the gray and blue cells on top of Fig. 2). The vector $\mathbf{Pr}_{\mathrm{conc}}^{i,j}$ is the input vector for the Decision Tree trained to predict the type of the value $v_{i,j}$ (bottom of Fig. 2).

Starting from the predicted types of the values contained in the column j, named $\mathrm{Type}_{i,j}^{\mathrm{val}}$ ($1 \leq i \leq n$), the set of potential types $PType(j)$, expressed as pairs (t, o_t), where o_t is the number of occurrences of type t in column j, includes the distinct types predicted by the Decision Tree for column j. Then, by considering a predefined threshold σ, representing the minimal allowed frequency of value types in a column, the type of the column j is determined as follows:

$$\mathrm{Type}_j^{\mathrm{col}} = \{ t | (t, o_t) \in PType(j) \wedge \frac{o_t}{\sum_{(\bar{t}, \bar{o}) \in PType(j)} \bar{o}} \geq \sigma \} \tag{4}$$

Type$_j^{\text{col}}$ can contain a single type or the members of the union type to be associated with the column j. The values whose type does not belong to this set and are not empty, are marked as errors for this column and the user can check and fix them by means of the graphical user interfaces discussed in next section.

Example 3. Consider the column 4 (DATA DI NASCITA) of the *CSV* in Fig. 1 that contains the values $\langle$ '27/07/1947', '', '08/02/1962', '', '31031978', '', '10/03/1957'$\rangle$ and suppose we wish to identify the type of $v_{1,4} = $ '27/07/1947' and $v_{5,4} = $ '31031978'. For the sake of simplicity, consider the presence of only the following type recognizers: Rec_{string}, Rec_{date}, Rec_{number}. In this case $\mathbf{Pr}_{1,4} = \langle 1, 1, 0 \rangle$ and $\mathbf{Pr}_{5,4} = \langle 1, 0, 1 \rangle$. Moreover, $\overline{\mathbf{Pr}}_4 = \langle 0.428, 0.428, 0.142 \rangle$ by taking into account that the number of rows is 7. The decision tree for $v_{1,4}$ returns date, whereas for $v_{5,4}$ returns error. The identification of the error is provided by the decision tree that has been trained on the occurrence of invalid values for this type. Consider now that the type predicted for the column 4 is the vector $\langle$ date, empty, date, empty, error, empty, date $\rangle$. Therefore, the type for column 4 is date with the presence of an error.

Simulation of Training Data. The data set made available by the debt agency are not labeled and present errors. Labeling these data would require too much time and the quantity of the data themselves would be too low for training even simple models (the available documents are around 200). For this reason, we decided to generate synthetic $\langle \bar{S}, \bar{V} \rangle$ tables similar enough to the original ones.

For creating these tables, a dataset is realized for each simple type we are interested in. Then, we generated documents with a structure similar to original ones and presenting values extracted from these datasets. The generated documents present a variable number of columns and rows for simulating real documents. Specific attention has been made to propose correlations among data as those that occur in the original tables. For example, the codFisc value occurring in a row is generated by considering the values of name, surname, date of birth occurring in the same row. For making more realistic the generated documents, also empty values and errors have been added to the synthetic tables. Empty values have been included by randomly replacing some values (e.g. "-", "_", "." and other kinds of spaces and tabs) with empty. Some of the values automatically generated are replaced with wrong values for the column type. For instance, values of type surname can be placed in a column presenting values of type ZIP. However, we avoided the introduction of errors in columns presenting too similar values (like ZIP code and integer) to avoid mis-classification. Each value is finally labeled with its type, the label empty in case of empty values, or the label error in case of error.

Alternative Models: Random Forest and Multi-layer Perceptron (MLP). With the aim of identifying the validity of the decision tree for the prediction task of this setting, we have considered also a Random forest composed of 500 decision trees, each one using the same parameters of the single decision tree, and an MLP composed of 3 dense layers (64, 32 and 1 neurons

#	CF	RAG.SOC./COGNOME	NOME	DATA NASCITA	INDIRIZZO	INT	CAP	COMUNE	SPESE POSTALI	IMPOSTA
	codFisc,... ▾	surname... ▾	name ▾	date ▾	string, m... ▾	integer ▾	ZIP ▾	municip... ▾	decimal,... ▾	decimal ▾
1	BTTLSS67L47L682E	Botticelli	Alessia	27/07/1947	Via Fiori Chiari N. 22		100100	ROMA	5.45	801
2	24467460861	Gatti SNC			Via Tevere N 102/5		20100	MILANO (MI)	5.45	440
3	CPTNNM62B08H703Q	Caputo	Antonio Matteo	08/02/1962	Via Giovinezza Num 13		16100	GENOVA (GE)	5.45	416
4	22515600021	Cristalglass Srl			Via Boschetto 21		100100	ROMA	A5.45	4060
5	DOISRN78C71L682Z	Oidio	Sabrina	310311978	Via 25 Aprile 1945 N. 23	18	20100	MILANO (MI)	A5.45	3076
6	56658300357	L'Acquilone SPA			Num. 92 di Via Friuli		20100	MILANO - MI	5.45	1654
7	FRRGLG57C10L840M	Ferrero	Gianluigi Mario	10/03/1957	Via Settala N. 32		20100		5.45	78

Fig. 3. Extracted table from the *CSV* file in Fig. 1 (Color figure online)

respectively), with activation ReLU with the exception of the last layer which uses a Sigmoid activation. The optimizer used for the MLP model was Nadam.

Python Scikit-learn [24] libraries have been used to implement DTs and random forests. Keras/TensorFlow [1] have been used for implementing MLP.

Training and Test of the Models on Synthetic Data. To train the considered models, we generated 12.000 synthetic tables randomly split 10 times in 10.000 documents for training and 2.000 for the validation set. It must be noted that since these tables are generated synthetically using a simulation, they cannot be considered independent and identically distributed, but just an approximation. The Decision Tree was trained using a maximal depth of 20, using the Gini criterion and with class imbalance aware weights. The average AUPRC and AUROC scores of the models were, respectively 0.98 and 0.995 on the validation set. The scores were then compared using a Wilcoxon signed-rank test, with p-value threshold at 0.05. The test did not display any statistically significant difference between the different compared methods. Since the decision tree is the fastest to train and the most interpretable, we have chosen to use it.

4   Visualization and Type Adjustment

Once processed by the ML approach described in the previous section, the extracted table is shown to the user for verification and adjustments.

Figure 3 shows the result obtained on our running example. The first line of the table reports the column schema and it is followed by a drop-down menu containing the inferred types for each column. When more than one type is reported, they are members of an union type and different background colors are used to distinguish their instances. The presence of mixed types is represented by using different text colors. If a column presents data of the same type, the

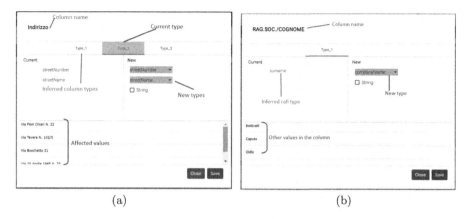

(a)   (b)

Fig. 4. Interface for altering the column types and a single cell type

background remains white, if a value is missing, the cell background color is yellow. When a value is considered an error for a column, the cell background color is red and also the column type is marked red.

Example 4. The inferred type is `union(mixed1,string)` for the `indirizzo` column, where the record type for `mixed1` is `rec(streetName,streetNumber)`. This is because the ML algorithm does not recognize the presence of an address in the strings `"Num. 92 di Via Friuli"` and `"Via Giovinezza Num. 13"` because they do not follow a recognized pattern for an Italian address.

In order to support the user to correct the inferred types, different graphical interfaces have been developed. Figure 4(a) shows the interface for altering the type associated with a column. The top part of the interface reports the column name with the list of all the inferred types (the first one is the current type). The central parts is vertically divided in two: on the left the current type is reported (or a list of type components for a mixed type), whereas on the right dropdown menu is shown (or a list of dropdown menus for a mixed type) with which the users can specify the new type/types. The user can always decide to return to the string type whenever the identified type is wrong. The bottom part of the interface contains a sample of the values of the current type for this column. The modification of a column type is propagated to all its values. Figure 4(b) illustrates the interface for changing the type of a single value. This interface is similar to the previous one. The distinctive feature is the possibility to change the type also to other values in the same column.

Example 5. Consider the value marked `error` in the CF column. By using the interface in Fig. 4(b), the user can specify that its type is `PIVA`. Whenever other values are wrong, they can be modified with few clicks directly on this interface.

The interface in Fig. 5 is used for pointing out a mixed type from string values. In the left panel, the categories of simple types are reported. Once chosen

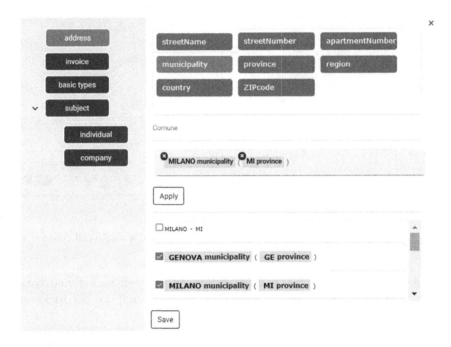

Fig. 5. Pattern definition

a category and a type *t* in the list of types reported in the top part of the interface, the user can select the substring that can be typed with *t*.

Example 6. Figure 5 shows this interface for inferring the mixed type for the value `"MILANO (MI)"` contained in the `comune` column. At the current stage, the type `municipality` of the category `address` is reported. The user can select the part of the string in the green box that should be tagged as `municipality`. Moreover, by clicking on the type `province`, the user can identify the substring containing this information. The pattern [{`municipality`}, " (", {`province`}, ")"] is thus identified. At this point, by clicking on the `apply` button, the system looks for other strings that follow the same pattern and tags them with the corresponding types. The user can decide the values to which the pattern has been correctly applied. We remark that it is not always possible to identify the same pattern and these strings should be tagged manually.

5   Experimental Results

We conducted an experiment to evaluate the type prediction capabilities of the ML algorithm. As we previously said, the ML algorithm was trained by using 12.000 synthetic tables and tested with 2.000 tables.

The trained model has been then used for inferring the type of 40 different CSV documents provided by the debt agency with at least 50 rows and between

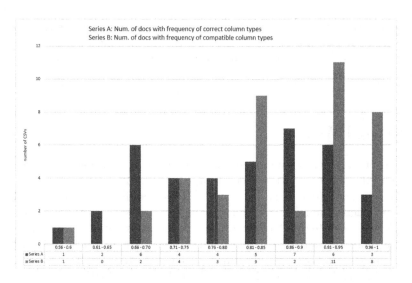

Fig. 6. Number of documents for which the frequencies of the correct columns (series A) and the correct and compatible columns (series B) with respect to the total number of columns fall in the range $[0.5, 1]$ with a step of 0.05.

8 to 70 columns. The minimum threshold for inferring union types has been set at 20%. A table is extracted from each of them and the type of values and columns inferred as described in Sect. 3.

The obtained tables have been manually checked for determining:

- **correct** columns: If the predicted type matches the content of the column;
- **compatible** columns: If the predicted type is correct but is not the most appropriate one (e.g. a street number is predicted of type integer);
- **incorrect** columns: otherwise, e.g. if the predicted type does not match the column content (e.g. the type is codFisc but it also contains PIVA).

The frequency of the "correct columns" and "correct and compatible" columns with respect to the total number of columns have been computed. We then defined ten ranges of frequencies that are used for classifying the documents. Figure 6 reports the number of documents whose frequencies ("correct columns" and "correct and compatible") fall in the range $[0.5, 1]$ with a step of 0.05.

The figure points out that for 30 documents we were able to infer correct and compatible types for more than 80% of the columns (by considering only correct types, the number of documents is 21). Moreover, for only 1 document we were able to infer correct and compatible types for less than 65% of the columns (by considering only correct types, the number of documents is 3). By looking more carefully to these last documents, the low performances are due to the high number of mixed types that are not included in our type system. Indeed, in these cases, the algorithm fails to correctly identify the correct type.

Concerning the compatibility errors, usually they occur for the streetNumber type (the values are identified as integer). All the mistakes identified in these documents have been fixed by means of the interfaces described in Sect. 4. We remark that the fixing process is quite easy and fast. Indeed, in the case of the CSV file with the highest number of errors we fixed it in less than 5 min.

6   Related Work

In the context of table understanding [15] many approaches have been proposed for table location and segmentation (e.g. [17,22,26]), for the functional and structural analysis (e.g. [9,17,28]), and for its correct interpretation by translating the extracted tables in well known data models such as the relational and RDF models (e.g. [9,10,12,18,19,23,29]). Approaches have been considered for extracting tabular data both from unstructured formats (such as ASCII files, pdf, or images) and structured formats (such as XML, HTML, CSV files, and in general spreadsheet files). These methods have been tailored for addressing specific peculiarities of spreadsheets and, at the current stage, no one of them is able to address all the issues that can arise in this domain. Moreover, many assumptions are taken on the spreadsheet layouts and on their textual content. One of the main assumption is that the values of a single column are of the same type and can be treated uniformly. Therefore, the issue of inferring the data types associated with columns is seldom considered.

Type inference refers to the task of inferring the data type of a given data column. Approaches for type inference can be classified in those that try to infer simple data types and those that try to infer concepts of a knowledge base. In the first category falls many studies, including wrangling tools [11,13,16,27,31], software libraries (e.g. [2,21,25]) and probabilistic approaches (e.g. [20,32]) that exploit validation functions and regular expressions on data samples for inferring a single type. However, these approaches are able to infer a very limited number of types and usually do not work very well when missing and anomalous data occur in the sample. In [5] the authors propose a probabilistic approach which is robust to the occurrence of missing and anomalous data. However, all these approaches can be marginally applied to our context because we need to consider also other types (like PIVA, codFisc, Municipality), the possibility to extract types from strings by means of patterns, and also the possibility to infer more than one type for a given column.

The problem of identifying a semantic description from heterogeneous data sources is at the base of data integration [8] and exchange [3]. Many approaches have been proposed for reconciling the syntactic and semantic heterogeneity of data sources by identifying logical mapping between the source schemas and a target schema by defining schema matching and schema mapping methodologies [4]. In [30], the authors propose an approach for annotating tabular data with a semantic model that describe the characteristics of table columns in terms of a Domain Ontology. The approach is equipped with a graphical tool by means of which the inferred semantic model can be checked (and eventually corrected) by the user. Other approaches (like ColNet [6] and Sherlock [14]) propose to use well known KB for inferring the semantic types of columns. By exploiting different ML approaches, they are able to associate a better description of the values contained in different kinds of tables. The work proposed in this paper started with the aim of inferring simple types and domain specific types for a column by taking into account the possibility of identifying more than one type and the presence of wrong values occurring in a column. Moreover, graphical tools have been developed for checking the predicted types and easily modifying them, when needed. In our future work we wish to exploit these types for the generation of semantic models in the same spirit of [30] and by exploiting approaches similar to those proposed in [6, 14].

7   Conclusions and Future Work

In this paper we have proposed an approach for determining the types of values and columns contained in a table extracted from a *CSV* document. This kind of activity is useful in the interpretation step of the table understanding problem when the values of a single column can assume different types and also in presence of wrong values. Due to the variability of the data that need to be handled and the lack of a big enough corpus on which a ML technique can be trained (especially for the Italian language), we have proposed an approach that combine a decision tree trained on synthetic data for inferring the type of values and columns and then the use of graphical interfaces for correcting mistakes.

The approach has been tested on a collection of documents made available from a debt collection agency that needs to handle every day this kind of documents that are highly heterogeneous and with many mistakes. Our initial experiments prove the feasibility of the approach and the utility of the developed interfaces for easily fixing the mistakes and extracting types from many columns presenting heterogeneous information. The proposed methodology is the first step of a more general system that we are developing for the entire table understanding problem. In the second step we wish to semantically labeling the column types identified in the first step with the properties of a domain ontology specifically tailored for the debt collection agency. The purpose is to provide a semantic model of the invoice contained in the CSV file and the involved people. This is the starting point for the verification "in the third step" of integrity constraints that need to be verified in this context. Once the invoices have been properly checked, they can be included in the information system of the debt collection agency.

The work discussed in this paper can be extended in several directions. By means of the graphical interfaces described in Sect. 4 it is possible to define new patterns and include them in the ML process described in Sect. 3. This is an interesting research direction in the spirit of incremental learning and thus being able to adapt the model without the entire re-training. Then, we wish to include other recognizers in our system that are approximate. They would be particularly useful for dealing with many errors. At the current stage we have considered approximate recognizers for ZIP and PIVA values that try to slightly modify these values (by padding some zeros at the beginning of the string) before checking the validity. They have been particularly useful and a systematic use can improve the performances of the type inference approach. Finally, we observe that we applied a basic multi-label approach to predict column types, and we plan to adopt more refined multi-label techniques to significantly improve predictions of union types [33].

Acknowledgements. The authors wish to thank Giovanni Mancinelli and Carlo Angelucci for working on the implementation of the tool and also the anonymous reviewers for their useful suggestions.

References

1. Abadi, M., et al.: TensorFlow: large-scale machine learning on heterogeneous systems (2015). https://www.tensorflow.org/
2. Abraham, R., Erwig, M.: Ucheck: a spreadsheet type checker for end users. J. Vis. Lang. Comput. **18**, 71–95 (2007)
3. Arenas, M., Barcelo, P., Libkin, L., Murlak, F.: Relational and XML Data Exchange. Morgan and Claypool Publishers, San Rafael (2010)
4. Bellahsene, Z., Bonifati, A., Rahm, E.: Schema Matching and Mapping. Springer, Dordrecht (2011)
5. Ceritli, T., Williams, C.K.I., Geddes, J.: ptype: probabilistic type inference. Data Mining Knowl. Discov. **34**(3), 870–904 (2020). https://doi.org/10.1007/s10618-020-00680-1
6. Chen, J., Jimenez-Ruiz, E., Horrocks, I., Sutton, C.: Colnet: embedding the semantics of web tables for column type prediction. In: Proceeding of AAAI Conference on Artificial Intelligence, vol. 33, pp. 29–36, July 2019
7. Chen, Z.: Spreadsheet property detection with rule-assisted active learning. In: Proceeding of the Conference on Information and Knowledge Management, pp. 999–1008 (2017)
8. Doan, A., Halevy, A., Ives, Z.: Principles of Data Integration. Morgan Kaufmann Publishers Inc., Waltham (2012)
9. Ermilov, I., Ngomo, A.-C.N.: Taipan: automatic property mapping for tabular data. In: Proceeding of International Conference Knowledge Engineering and Knowledge Management, pp. 163–179 (2016)
10. Fiorelli, M., et al.: Sheet2RDF: a flexible and dynamic spreadsheet import&lifting framework for RDF. In: Ali, M., Kwon, Y.S., Lee, C.-H., Kim, J., Kim, Y. (eds.) IEA/AIE 2015. LNCS (LNAI), vol. 9101, pp. 131–140. Springer, Cham (2015). https://doi.org/10.1007/978-3-319-19066-2_13
11. Fisher, K., Gruber, R.: Pads: a domain-specific language for processing ad hoc data. SIGPLAN Not. **40**(6), 295–304 (2005)
12. Galkin, M., Mouromtsev, D., Auer, S.: Identifying web tables: supporting a neglected type of content on the web. In: Proceeding of International Conference Knowledge Engineering and Semantic Web, pp. 48–62, October 2015
13. Google. Openrefine: A free, open source, powerful tool for working with messy data (2020). https://openrefine.org/
14. Hulsebos, M., et al.: Sherlock: a deep learning approach to semantic data type detection. In: Proceeding of the 25th ACM SIGKDD International Conference on Knowledge Discovery & Data Mining, pp. 1500–1508. ACM (2019)

15. Hurst, M.: The Interpretation of Tables in Texts. PhD thesis, University of Edinburgh (2000)
16. Kandel, S., Paepcke, A., Hellerstein, J., Heer, J.: Wrangler: interactive visual specification of data transformation scripts. In: ACM Human Factors in Computing Systems (CHI), pp. 3363–3372 (2011)
17. Koci, E., Thiele, M., Romero, O., Lehner, W.: A genetic-based search for adaptive table recognition in spreadsheets. In: International Conference on Document Analysis and Recognition (ICDAR), pp. 1274–1279 (2019)
18. Langegger, A., Wöß, W.: XLWrap – querying and integrating arbitrary spreadsheets with SPARQL. In: Bernstein, A., Karger, D.R., Heath, T., Feigenbaum, L., Maynard, D., Motta, E., Thirunarayan, K. (eds.) ISWC 2009. LNCS, vol. 5823, pp. 359–374. Springer, Heidelberg (2009). https://doi.org/10.1007/978-3-642-04930-9_23
19. Limaye, G., Sarawagi, S., Chakrabarti, S.: Annotating and searching web tables using entities, types and relationships. Proc. VLDB Endow. 3(1–2), 1338–1347 (2010)
20. Limaye, G., Sarawagi, S., Chakrabarti, S.: Annotating and searching web tables using entities, types and relationships. Proc. VLDB 3(1–2), 1338–1347 (2010)
21. Lindenberg, F.: Messytables python library (2020). https://messytables.readthedocs.io/
22. Milosevic, N., Gregson, C., Hernandez, R., Nenadic, G.: Disentangling the structure of tables in scientific literature. In: Proceeding of International Conference on Applications of Natural Language to Information Systems, pp. 162–174 (2016)
23. Mulwad, V., Finin, T., Joshi, A.: A domain independent framework for extracting linked semantic data from tables. In: Ceri, S., Brambilla, M. (eds.) Search Computing. LNCS, vol. 7538, pp. 16–33. Springer, Heidelberg (2012). https://doi.org/10.1007/978-3-642-34213-4_2
24. Pedregosa, F., et al.: Scikit-learn: machine learning in Python. J. Mach. Learn. Res. 12, 2825–2830 (2011)
25. Petricek, T., Guerra, G., Syme, D.: Types from data: making structured data first-class citizens in f#. In: Proceeding of 37th ACM SIGPLAN Conference on Programming Language Design and Implementation, pp. 477–490. ACM (2016)
26. Pinto, D., McCallum, A., Wei, X., Croft, W.B.: Table extraction using conditional random fields. In: Proceeding of the 26th International ACM SIGIR Conference on Research and Development in Informaion Retrieval, pp. 235–242 (2003)
27. Raman, V., Hellerstein, J.: Potter's wheel: an interactive data cleaning system. In: Proceeding of International Conference Very Large Data Bases, pp. 381–390, September 2001
28. Shigarov, A.: Table understanding using a rule engine. Expert Syst. Appl. 42, 929–937 (2015)
29. Shigarov, A., Khristyuk, V., Mikhailov, A., Paramonov, V.: TabbyXL: rule-based spreadsheet data extraction and transformation. In: Damaševičius, R., Vasiljevienė, G. (eds.) ICIST 2019. CCIS, vol. 1078, pp. 59–75. Springer, Cham (2019). https://doi.org/10.1007/978-3-030-30275-7_6
30. Taheriyan, M., Knoblock, C.A., Szekely, P., Ambite, J.L.: Learning the semantics of structured data sources. J. Web Semant. 37, 152–169 (2016)
31. Trifacta. Trifacta wrangler (2020). https://www.trifacta.com/
32. Valera, I., Ghahramani, Z.: Automatic discovery of the statistical types of variables in a dataset. Proc. Mach. Learn. Res. 70, 3521–3529 (2017)
33. Zhang, M., Zhou, Z.: A review on multi-label learning algorithms. IEEE Trans. Knowl. Data Eng. 26(8), 1819–1837 (2014)

Foundations of Data Science
and Engineering – Short Papers

Metadata Management on Data Processing in Data Lakes

Imen Megdiche[1], Franck Ravat[1], and Yan Zhao[1,2(✉)]

[1] Institut de Recherche en Informatique de Toulouse, UMR 5505, IRIT-CNRS,
Toulouse, France
{Imen.Megdiche,Franck.Ravat,Yan.Zhao}@irit.fr
[2] Centre Hospitalier Universitaire (CHU) de Toulouse, Toulouse, France

Abstract. Data Lake (DL) is known as a Big Data analysis solution. A data lake stores not only data but also the processes that were carried out on these data. It is commonly agreed that data preparation/transformation takes most of the data analyst's time. To improve the efficiency of data processing in a DL, we propose a framework which includes a metadata model and algebraic transformation operations. The metadata model ensures the findability, accessibility, interoperability and reusability of data processes as well as data lineage of processes. Moreover, each process is described through a set of coarse-grained data transforming operations which can be applied to different types of datasets. We illustrate and validate our proposal with a real medical use case implementation.

Keywords: Data lake · Data processing · Metadata management

1 Introduction

Data Lake (DL) is a Big Data analysis solution that allows users to ingest raw data, store them in their native format, process these data upon usage, ensure the availability and accessibility of data for different users and apply governance to maintain the data quality, security and data life-cycle.

Data preparation is commonly considered as the most time consuming phase when analyzing data. Transformation processes, especially those in a DL, require a lot of effort because of (i) a great amount of different types of data (structured, semi-structured and unstructured) are ingested, (ii) various transforming operators can be carried out, for instance, consolidation, join, filtering, and (iii) different users are involved, such as BI (Business Intelligence) professionals, data scientists and data analysts. Users with different profiles apply different programs to prepare data by crossing various sources in a DL, in this paper, we use *data wrangler* to refer to these users.

To better govern a DL and to facilitate data preparation, metadata management is emphasized by many authors [1, 3, 4]. The integrated metadata dedicating to data processing allow data wranglers to find, access and reuse existing data

© Springer Nature Switzerland AG 2021
T. Bureš et al. (Eds.): SOFSEM 2021, LNCS 12607, pp. 553–562, 2021.
https://doi.org/10.1007/978-3-030-67731-2_40

transforming processes easier. Moreover, the source code and execution information allow users to update or adjust programs for further usages rapidly.

Today, different DL metadata solutions have been proposed or implemented in the academic and industrial world. However, most of the current solutions only focus on dataset metadata [1–4] without referring to process metadata. Moreover, some industrial solutions apply lineage metadata by only tracing source data and result data (Zaloni, Azure), but the process metadata is not specific and adapted enough for searching different types of processes efficiently by using the involved the operation or execution information.

At the aim of improving the reusability of data processes, it is better to describe a process through a sequence of generic operations than totally through free text. Hence, we define a framework that includes a metadata model in which processes are composed of a set of transformation operations. These later can be applied to different types of data. Moreover, the operations are presented with a controlled language to make the process interrogation easier. Note that we add the operation metadata for marking the main actions of a data process instead of translating each line of the transformation code (like ETL processes). Our framework have the following advantages: (i) The storage of processes and their metadata can facilitate data preparation by improving transparency and reusability of processes. (ii) The reliability of data is ensured by lineage metadata, users can verify the provenance of data to have more confidence and understanding of the data that they will use. (iii) Process metadata help data wranglers to find more relevant datasets, for instance, datasets that are generated by the same process.

At the aim of proposing a metadata management focusing on data processing for data lakes, our paper is threefold. In Sect. 2, we introduce related work on metadata dedicated to data processing. In Sect. 3, we propose a data lake metadata model for data processes with a minimal core of transforming operations with illustrations on our motivating example. Finally, in Sect. 4, we present an implementation of our model and we validate it by technical aspects.

2 Related Work and Motivating Example

To the best of our knowledge, there are a few works [5,11] in the literature presenting metadata on data processing in the context of Big Data (contrarily to the multitude of works in the data warehousing/ETL processes [9,12])

The authors of [11] introduced a metadata system for primary care big data to control the process of transformation and analysis. The system adds six elements of metadata to the Primary Care Data Quality (PCDQ) renal program: study/audit name, queries of data extraction, data collection number, data type, repeat number and a processing suffix. As described in this approach, we observe that there is a focus on quality aspects which does not cover all the transformations and problems that we find in DL. Moreover, in this work there is not a generic metadata model presented.

The authors of [5] define a metadata schema describing data preparation tasks in the context of data mining. The system aims to automate data preparation by identifying its requirements which are classified into eight categories:

objective, output, definition, control, flow, content, composition and execution. This approach focuses on data preparation metadata for data mining and the metadata model specify all tasks of a data process. Showing all the details of data processes can facilitate the comprehension of process, but in the context of data lakes, it is too heavy for both metadata extraction and metadata searching.

Contrary to the previous work, as in DL, we pull together all type of users (BI professionals, data statisticians, data analysts, data engineers...), we need to have a generic model covering all types of transformations for each kind of data. The DL metadata system must integrate essential activities of data processing to ensure that all DL users can efficiently find and reuse existing processes.

Motivating Example. In order to exemplify our metadata model, we rely on an example throughout the paper. The motivated case is based on a feedback experience carried out on the DL of the University Teaching Hospital (CHU) of Toulouse. The purpose of this DL is to gather different types of medical data from the complex information system that contains more than 100 large or small datasets for future analysis. For the scenario, we keep only two projects in the scope of the data in order to validate our solution. The Fig. 1 shows the workflow of data processing for these projects.

EHDEN Project uses the electronic health record (EHR) dataset as the data source and creates the OMOP dataset accordingly for collaborative analysis.

- Clinical data are extracted and fed by several steps. SP1.1 extracts different subjects (e.g. patient, medical staff, diagnosis) of clinical data. During SP1.2, the extracted data are validated manually by EHR experts and doctors then stored in CSV files. SP1.3 transforms validated data to OMOP CDM. When the OMOP format clinical data are validated during SP1.4, they are used to feed the OMOP clinical tables during the SP1.5.
- Terminologies used in the EHR need to be mapped to OMOP standardized vocabularies. Firstly, during SP2.1, each terminology (e.g.. for diagnosis, medication, procedure) used in the EHR are extracted and stored in CSV files. SP2.2 aims to validate the extracted data. SP2.3 concerns to map different terminologies to OMOP standardized vocabularies. SP2.4 needs to be done by doctors to validate the mapping. When all the terminologies are mapped, relative OMOP tables are fed.

EBERS Project aims to analyze all textual medical reports stored in the CHU database using NLP (Natural Language Processing) techniques. The current database stores medical report information in different tables. Therefore, to prepare NLP, we need to firstly reconstruct medical reports with the data stored in the EHR and apply further transformations.

3   An Extended Metadata Model for Data Processing

3.1   Meta-model

To ensure the findability, accessibility, interoperability and reuability of data processing, we propose that data processing metadata include four targets:

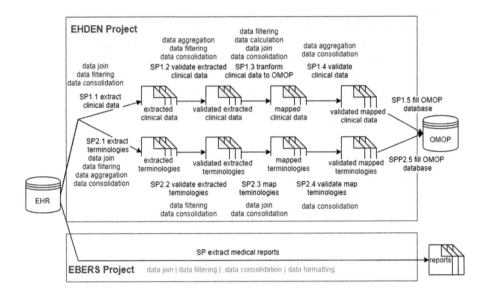

Fig. 1. Motivating example

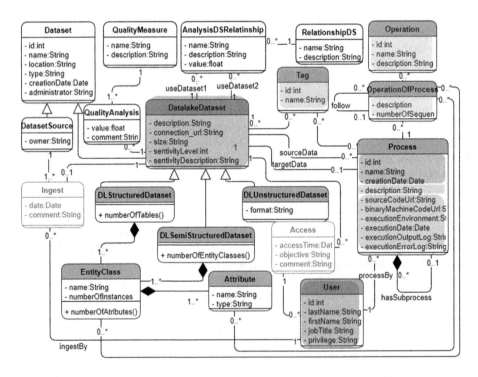

Fig. 2. Metadata conceptual model (Color figure online)

- *Process Characteristics* introduces basic information about a process. These metadata answer the question: "Who did what when".
- *Process Definition* explains why a process is created, what is the context, what is the objective. They specify the meaning of data processes.
- *Technical information* includes process code and execution information. The technical information helps users to know the deployment environment. The source code also allow users to modify, update or reuse a process.
- *Process content* concerns coarse-grained transformation operators dedicating to qualify data processing.

Firstly, we have proposed a first version of a generic and extensible metadata model that mainly focuses on datasets in [8]. In this paper, we answer the previous requirements (4 targets), so that we propose an extension of the model with detailed metadata about data processing.

From the modeling point of view (see Fig. 2), the metadata associated with the previous 4 targets are modeled through 6 object classes. (i) Process characteristics includes source and target dataset(s), name, creation date and the user who works on the process. This information is stored in 3 different classes *DatalakeDataset, Process, User* (marked in blue). (ii) Each procces is defined by a description and a set of keywords (marked in yellow). (iii) Technical information contains the source code and execution details (marked in green). And (vi) process content includes a set of coarse grained operations (marked in red).

The process content describes the data processing operations at a high level. The objective of operation metadata is not to represent all the details of the source code but to help DL users to get a glimpse the main activities of the processes. For instance, one project needs to create a dataset DS1 by using two sources DS2 and DS3. Instead of writing source code directly, the user can check if there are already some processes which use DS2 and DS3 as sources and are marked with 'merge' or 'join' operations.

3.2   Operations

To complete the meta-model and facilitate the feeding, we propose to describe data processes through a set of coarse-grained operations. Each operation is defined as $DS_{output} \leftarrow OP((DS_{input1}, [DS_{input2}...DS_{inputN}]), ARG)$, where:

- OP is the data transforming operation.
- $DS_{input1}, [DS_{input2}]...[DS_{inputN}]$ is the source dataset(s) of the operation.
- ARG is the argument of the operation, it can be a condition or a function of an operation.
- DS_{output} is the result of the operation.

In order to make the operators generically compatible with classical ETL operations [7,10,13] as well as data preparation operators for data mining [6], or specific practices like reducing data or discretizing data [14], the predefined list is $OP \in \{FL, FMT, AGGR, CALC, CNSLD, MERGE, JOIN\}$. We introduce each operation with examples from the projects in 1:

Filtering (FL) has the objective of choosing a subset of data from the data source with conditions: $FL(DS_{input}, [COND])$. The conditions concerns the selection of attributes and/or instances. ***Example***. During the SP2.1, all the diagnoses used by the CHU of Toulouse need to be extracted. However, in the EHR, different versions of diagnoses in French and German are stored. Therefore, the FL operation is needed: $Ex1 \leftarrow FL(diagtype, (cc = 'FR'))$.

Formatting (FMT) has the objective to transform a dataset from their native format into a predefined format: $(DS_{input}, [targetFormat])$. ***Example***. The medical reports in the EHR are stored in the form of relational data (title, type, reporter, text, etc.), while we need to extract reports which has a letter format, therefore, the structured data need to be transformed to unstructured: $Ex5 \leftarrow FMT(report, unstructured)$.

Aggregation (AGGR) has the objective to gather data and present the data in a summary form: $AGGR(DS_{input}, [ATTR], [FUNC])$, where ATTR is a set of attributes to group by and FUNC concerns the aggregate functions. ***Example***. To facilitate validating extracted terminologies, for instance, all the diagnoses, we need to count the diagnosed frequency of diagnoses: $Ex3 \leftarrow AGGR(JOIN((Ex2, stay\_diag), (Ex2.diagid = stay\_diag.diagid)), diagid, count(diagid))$.

Calculation (CALC) has the objective to calculate additional data with existing information: $CALC(DS_{input}, FUNC)$. FUNC may contain parameters like input attributes, output attribute and associated calculating function, for instance, mathematical, date or user defined functions. ***Example***. In the EHR, patients' birth date information is stored in the format of DD/MM/YYYY, while to count the distribution of patients' age, calculation is needed: $Ex6 \leftarrow CLAC(patient, (today() - patient.birthdate))$.

Consolidation (CNSLD) concerns converting, correcting or protecting data: $CNSLD(DS_{input}, [ATTR], [COND]$. (i) Data conversion concerns the modification of data format, the updating of data type, the splitting of data, the data combination, the data normalization and the value generator. (ii) Data correction concerns the correction of missing or incorrect data. (iii) Data protection concerns limiting the authorized access by data encryption or anonymizing data to ensure the privacy of personal data. Data protection can be applied to all the structural types of datasets. Anonymization, data pseudonymization concerns the encryption or erasure of identifiable personal information to ensure the privacy protection. ***Example***. In the EHR, the free text of medical reports is store in base64, to apply NLP processes, it needs to be decoded in UTF-8: $Ex4 \leftarrow CNSLD(report, (text), convert(UTF - 8))$.

Merging (MERGE) has the objective to combine datasets that have compatible elements: $MERGE((DS_{input1}, DS_{input2}...DS_{inputN}), [COND])$. ***Example***. three classifications are already validated and mapped to OMOP format, they need to be merged: $Ex6 \leftarrow MERGE(diag, procedure, medication)$.

Join (JOIN) has the objective to combine different data sources with common values, it can be applied on (semi-)structured data: $JOIN((DS_{input1}, DS_{input2}), [COND])$, where COND is the condition on the common value.

Example. To extract all the diagnoses in French, the tables of diagnosis and types need to be joined: $Ex2 \leftarrow JOIN((diag, diagtype), (diag.typeid = diagtype.typeid))$.

Operation	Structured DS	Semi-structured DS	Unstructured DS
Filtering	FL(DS$_{input}$, [COND]) FL(DS, n / n%) *randomly select n lines* FL(DS, (attr1, attr2...attrn)) *select attributes (projection)* FL(DS, (attrx<m)) *select by value of attributes (selection of instances)*	FL(DS$_{input}$, [COND]) FL(DS, n / n%) *randomly select n lines* FL(DS, (attr1, attr3...attrn)) *select attributes* FL(DS, (attrx<m)) *select by value of attributes*	FL(DS$_{input}$, [COND]) FL(DS, n / n%) *randomly select n parts* FL(DS, Cond) *select by UDF*
Formatting	FMT(DS$_{input}$, [targetFormat]) *targetFormat: Structured/semi-structured/unstructured*	FMT(DS$_{input}$, [targetFormat]) *targetFormat: Structured/semi-structured/unstructured*	FMT(DS$_{input}$, [targetFormat]) *targetFormat: Structured/semi-structured/unstructured*
Aggregation	AGGR(DS$_{input}$, [ATTR], [FUNC]) AGGR(DS, (attr1, attr2,...attrn), avg / count / min / max / sum / UDF (attr))	AGGR(DS$_{input}$, [ATTR], [FUNC]) AGGR(DS, (attr1, attr2,...attrn), avg / count / min / max / sum / UDF (attr))	-
Calculation	CALC(DS$_{input}$, FUNC) *function: mathematical, date, UDF*	CALC(DS$_{input}$, FUNC) *function: mathematical, date, UDF*	-
Consolidation	CNSLD(DS$_{input}$, [ATTR], [COND]) *Convert data format, Update data type, Splitting data, Combining data, Data standardization, Correct missing data, Correct incorrect data, Encrypting data, Anonymizing data, Pseudonymizing data*	CNSLD(DS$_{input}$, [ATTR], [COND]) *Convert data format, Update data type, Splitting data, Combining data, Data standardization , Correct missing data, Correct incorrect data, Encrypting data, Anonymizing data, Pseudonymizing data*	CNSLD(DS$_{input}$, [ATTR], [COND]) *Correct incorrect data, Encrypting data, Anonymizing data, Pseudonymizing data*
Merging	MERGE((DS$_{input1}$,DS$_{input2}$ ... DS$_{inputN}$), [COND]) MERGE(DS1, DS2...DSn, n% / total) *UNION in SQL*	MERGE((DS$_{input1}$,DS$_{input2}$ ... DS$_{inputN}$), [COND]) MERGE(DS1, DS2...DSn, n% / total) *Delimited text file: Adding data by rows* *NoSQL/XML/JSON: Adding data by objects/nodes*	MERGE((DS$_{input1}$,DS$_{input2}$ ... DS$_{inputN}$), [COND]) MERGE(DS1, DS2...DSn, n% / total) *Adding data by paragraphs/pages*
Join	JOIN((DS$_{input1}$, DS$_{input2}$), [COND]) JOIN((DS1, DS2), DS1.attr1 = DS2.attr1))	JOIN((DS$_{input1}$, DS$_{input2}$), [COND]) JOIN((DS1, DS2), DS1.attr1 = DS2.attr1))	-

Fig. 3. Coarse-grained operations

All these coarse grained operations can be applied to different structural types of data (see Fig. 3). FL, FMT, AGGR, CALC, CNSLD are unary operations which can be applied on a single dataset. MERGE and JOIN are binary operations which can be applied on multiple datasets, but these datasets should have the same structural type, if it is not the case, the FMT is used to convert dataset to the required structural type. The FMT is also the only operation that changes data format in our list.

3.3 Application

To better introduce the operations, we present an application of a sub-process in Fig. 1. The SP2.1 aims to extract different terminologies from the EHR database. The drug classification used at Toulouse CHU is UCD10. UCD10 is a national classification in France of all the approved drugs. To obtain the stored UCD10 and facilitate the validation phase, we extract all the drugs with their number of prescription times. The useful information is stored in 4 different tables and to respect the copy right of the database schema, we do not show the full name of tables or attributes.

$DS_{extracted\_drug} \leftarrow CNSLD(AGGR(FL(JOIN((JOIN((JOIN((JOIN((presc, medic),$

$(presc.drugid = medic.drugid))$, medpra), $(presc.drugid = medpra.drugid(+)))$, medbook), $(presc.drugid = medbook.medid))$, art), $(mdbook.artid = art.artid))$, $(presc.cancel = "))$, $(presc.drugid, medic.meducd, art.ucd, presc.drugname, medic.meddrugname, art.artdrugname)$, $COUNT(presc.drugid))$, check_missing_value(presc.drugid))$

Regarding the example, for the process $DS_{extracted\_drug}$, 7 objects of OperationOfProcess are created. Each of the objects represents one operation with its argument. And these objects are linked to 4 different objects of Operations: CNSLD, AGGR, FL and JOIN.

4   Exploitation of the Metadata

To illustrate that our metadata model of data processing can help users find the relevant processes or datasets to improve the efficiency and efficacy of data preparation, we have implemented a graph database by Neo4j. The choice of a graph database is motivated by the scalability and flexibility as well as the interconnections of this NoSql storage system. We choose the Neo4j platform for its maturity.

The implemented database of the motivate case is composed of more than 1300 nodes and 1600 relationships. There are 10 types of nodes: DLStructured-Dataset, DLSemiStructuredDataset, DLUnstructuredDataset, Process, OperationOfProcess, Operation, Keyword, User. Due to limited space, the schema of the database is presented on Github[1]. According to the schema, concerning the motivate case, different structural types of data are stored, different processes can be applied to these data and a process can have sub processes. A process is composed of a set of operation and it is carried out by a user.

We emphasize that the process metadata should at least help users on the following stages: (i) **When creating a new dataset from existing source**, data wranglers can find all other datasets created from the same source and their corresponding processes. (ii) **When working on existing dataset**, data wranglers can find the history of the different types processes that were executed on this dataset. (iii) **While manipulating process**, data wranglers need to reuse a data process or if they want to modify or update a process for further use, they can find all the source code and execution information.

To validate our implementation and present its application on data preparation, we introduce one example on searching data processing metadata in this paper (there is another example available on the Github project) : A head trauma doctor wants to analyze all the medical history of his patients to have more information and to improve the effectiveness of his medical treatment. A part of his project concerns the analysis of various medical reports. He annotated a few keywords of three types of reports (paper version): hospitalization reports, neuropsychological assessments and neuropsychological examinations. The team who works on the project needs to extract the electronic version of these reports

---

[1] https://github.com/yanzhao-irit/metadata_management_on_data_processing_in_data_lakes.

from the EHR, annotate what he marked and analyze these reports. The first step of this project is to extract the three types of reports. For the reason that the EHR database is not well documented, the team does not know where to find the corresponding data and how to restructure the reports. Therefore, they use the metadata system to check if the three types of reports are already extracted. The used query is presented below and the result is in Fig. 4.

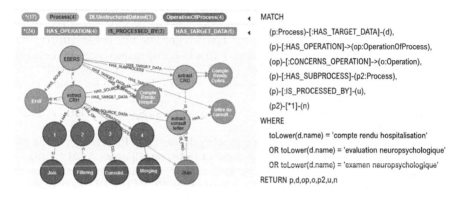

```
MATCH
    (p:Process)-[:HAS_TARGET_DATA]-(d),
    (p)-[:HAS_OPERATION]->(op:OperationOfProcess),
    (op)-[:CONCERNS_OPERATION]->(o:Operation),
    (p)-[:HAS_SUBPROCESS]-(p2:Process),
    (p)-[:IS_PROCESSED_BY]-(u),
    (p2)-[*1]-(n)
WHERE
    toLower(d.name) = 'compte rendu hospitalisation'
    OR toLower(d.name) = 'evaluation neuropsychologique'
    OR toLower(d.name) = 'examen neuropsychologique'
RETURN p,d,op,o,p2,u,n
```

Fig. 4. Query and result of example

With the result, the team discovers that hospitalization reports are already extracted for the EBERS project. Although they cannot find the other two types of reports, after studying the queries, they know that all reports data are stored in three tables. They also contact the person who worked on EBERS to request more experiences on extracting medical reports. The effectiveness of their work is much improved by the experience from the project EBERS.

5   Conclusion and Future Work

To the best of our knowledge, there is no solution which can take advantage of the existing processes in a data lake by improving the findability, accessibility, interoperability, and reusability. To better use a data lake, in this paper, we proposed a metadata model including metadata on data processing which can help users to find or even reuse certain processes to make the data transformations more efficient. The introduced process metadata contain operation metadata which are classified by coarse grain into seven categories. These operations can be described by a controlled language. We implement the metadata model in a graph database with Neo4j and validate it.

The graph database of metadata is the basic building block for a metadata management system for a data lake. For future work, we have to proceed on two fronts: (i) The automatic extraction of metadata. Although some metadata have to be entered manually, for instance, the name, description, keywords of processes, automatic metadata extraction is always essential which helps to reduce the time to metadata management and avoid possible manual entry errors; (ii) A graphical and ergonomic interface of metadata management system. There is a need to provide an interface that allows data lake users to easily search without writing complicated requests.

References

1. Alserafi, A., Abelló, A., Romero, O., Calders, T.: Towards information profiling: data lake content metadata management. In: 2016 IEEE 16th International Conference on Data Mining Workshops (ICDMW), pp. 178–185. IEEE (2016)
2. Quix, C., Hai, R., Vatov, I.: Metadata extraction and management in data lakes with gemms. Complex Syst. Inform. Model. Q. (9), 67–83, December 2016
3. Diamantini, C., Giudice, P.L., Musarella, L., Potena, D., Storti, E., Ursino, D.: An approach to extracting thematic views from highly heterogeneous sources of a data lake. In: Atti del Ventiseiesimo Convegno Nazionale su Sistemi Evoluti per Basi di Dati (SEBD 2018) (2018)
4. Halevy, A., et al.: Goods: organizing google's datasets. In: Proceedings of the 2016 International Conference on Management of Data, pp. 795–806. ACM (2016)
5. Hidalgo, M., Menasalvas, E., Eibe, S.: Definition of a metadata schema for describing data preparation tasks. In: Proceedings of the ECML/PKDD 2009 Workshop on 3rd generation Data Mining (SoKD 2009), pp. 64–75 (2009)
6. Jin, Z., Anderson, M.R., Cafarella, M., Jagadish, H.: Foofah: transforming data by example. In: Proceedings of the 2017 ACM International Conference on Management of Data, pp. 683–698. ACM (2017)
7. Poole, J.: The common warehouse metamodel as a foundation for active object models in the data warehouse environment. In: ECOOP 2000 workshop on Metadata and Active Object-Model Pattern Mining-Cannes, France (2000)
8. Ravat, F., Zhao, Y.: Metadata management for data lakes. In: Welzer, T., et al. (eds.) ADBIS 2019. CCIS, vol. 1064, pp. 37–44. Springer, Cham (2019). https://doi.org/10.1007/978-3-030-30278-8_5
9. Simitsis, A., Vassiliadis, P., Dayal, U., Karagiannis, A., Tziovara, V.: Benchmarking ETL workflows. In: Nambiar, R., Poess, M. (eds.) TPCTC 2009. LNCS, vol. 5895, pp. 199–220. Springer, Heidelberg (2009). https://doi.org/10.1007/978-3-642-10424-4_15
10. Trujillo, J., Luján-Mora, S.: A UML based approach for modeling ETL processes in data warehouses. In: Song, I.-Y., Liddle, S.W., Ling, T.-W., Scheuermann, P. (eds.) ER 2003. LNCS, vol. 2813, pp. 307–320. Springer, Heidelberg (2003). https://doi.org/10.1007/978-3-540-39648-2_25
11. VanVlymen, J., de Lusignan, S.: A system of metadata to control the process of query, aggregating, cleaning and analysing large datasets of primary care data. J. Innov. Health Inform. 13(4), 281–291 (2005)
12. Vassiliadis, P., Simitsis, A., Baikousi, E.: A taxonomy of ETL activities. In: Proceedings of the ACM 12th International Workshop on Data Warehousing and OLAP, pp. 25–32 (2009)
13. Vassiliadis, P., Simitsis, A., Skiadopoulos, S.: Conceptual modeling for ETL processes. In: Proceedings of the 5th ACM International Workshop on Data Warehousing and OLAP, pp. 14–21. ACM (2002)
14. Zhang, S., Zhang, C., Yang, Q.: Data preparation for data mining. Appl. Artif. Intell. 17(5–6), 375–381 (2003)

S2CFT: A New Approach for Paper Submission Recommendation

Dac Nguyen[1,4], Son Huynh[2,3,4], Phong Huynh[2,3,4], Cuong V. Dinh[2], and Binh T. Nguyen[2,3,4(✉)]

[1] John Von Neumann Institute, Ho Chi Minh City, Vietnam
[2] AISIA Research Lab, Ho Chi Minh City, Vietnam
ngtbinh@hcmus.edu.vn
[3] University of Science, Ho Chi Minh City, Vietnam
[4] Vietnam National University, Ho Chi Minh City, Vietnam

Abstract. There have been a massive number of conferences and journals in computer science that create a lot of difficulties for scientists, especially for early-stage researchers, to find the most suitable venue for their scientific submission. In this paper, we present a novel approach for building a paper submission recommendation system by using two different types of embedding methods, GloVe and FastText, as well as Convolutional Neural Network (CNN) and LSTM to extract useful features for a paper submission recommendation model. We consider seven combinations of initial attributes from a given submission: title, abstract, keywords, title + keyword, title + abstract, keyword + abstract, and title + keyword + abstract. We measure these approaches' performance on one dataset, presented by Wang et al., in terms of top K accuracy and compare our methods with the S2RSCS model, the state-of-the-art algorithm on this dataset. The experimental results show that CNN + FastText can outperform other approaches (CNN + GloVe, LSTM + GloVe, LSTM + FastText, S2RSCS) in term of top 1 accuracy for seven types of input data. Without using a list of keywords in the input data, CNN + GloVe/FastText can surpass other techniques. It has a bit lower performance than S2RSCS in terms of the top 3 and top 5 accuracies when using the keyword information. Finally, the combination of S2RSCS and CNN + FastText, namely S2CFT, can create a better model that bypasses all other methods by top K accuracy (K = 1,3,5,10).

Keywords: Paper submission recommendation · LSTM · CNNs

1 Introduction

Nowadays, along with the rapid development of economic and internet network systems, researchers have had many chances to access the immense knowledge source around the world much more quickly. There is an emerging number of

D. Nguyen and S. Huynh—Equal contribution.

© Springer Nature Switzerland AG 2021
T. Bureš et al. (Eds.): SOFSEM 2021, LNCS 12607, pp. 563–573, 2021.
https://doi.org/10.1007/978-3-030-67731-2_41

either fascinating journals and publication venues in different countries where various researchers can share more in-depth knowledge and give useful discussions about scientific results. However, an overwhelming number of articles and conferences/journals have created multiple challenges for many researchers (primarily for early-stage researchers) to select an appropriate scientific conference or journal to publish their works. As a result, several essential applications and studies are related to building a recommendation system that can advise the top relevant conferences or journals for a given submission and then help scientists have more time focusing on their research.

A recommendation system becomes an invaluable system in different industrial fields, especially for e-commerce, video entertainment, and social networks. Many large companies worldwide, including Youtube, Amazon, Facebook, or Xiaomi, take the advantages of recommendation systems to learn their users' behaviors for personalized experience services to maximize their profit. The recommendation system is immediately a crucial part of helping researchers find similar works and giving researchers a different perspective before deciding to submit their study to any publication venue. Especially for different scientists who want to research in a new field, those systems can give them more information and ideas for the most suitable choice. However, almost recommendation systems for conferences or journals are coming from popular publishers like Springer[1], IEEE[2], or Elsevier[3]. Given both title and abstract of submission as the input data, those systems provide a list of journals or top conferences relevant to the input topic. Other than that, there are different studies about content-based paper submission recommendation systems. One of the recent studies used TF-IDF and Chi-squared for feature selection and Logistic Regression as a classifier from Wang et al. [9]. Son and colleagues later could achieve the state-of-the-art performance of the paper submission recommendation algorithm on one dataset, proposed in [9], by constructing multilayer perceptrons as classifiers [8]. According to our knowledge, none of them apply deep learning techniques for enhancing the performance of such paper recommendation systems. Besides, both TF-IDF and Chi-squared based features are highly time-consuming in the computation during the feature selection process.

In this work, we apply deep learning methods using convolutional neural networks and LSTMs to build an efficient recommendation system for paper submission. By taking different combinations of Title, Abstract, and Keywords as the input data, we utilize the advantages of embedding models, GloVe or FastText, on the top of convolutional architectures to construct a paper submission recommendation system. The experimental results show that using the 1D CNN in the recommendation architecture can gain much better performance than using LTSM for all types of embedding methods and input data on the dataset proposed by Wang et al. [9]. Also, the list of keywords in the input data can have a significant impact on the performance of the recommendation models.

---

[1] https://journalsuggester.springer.com/.

[2] https://publication-recommender.ieee.org/home.

[3] https://journalfinder.elsevier.com/.

Without using Keywords, CNN + FastText can surpass S2RSCS in terms of top K accuracy ($K = 1, 3, 5, 10$), but S2RSCS can slightly outperform CNN + Fast-Text when using Title + Keywords for all top K accuracy ($K = 1, 3, 5, 10$) and using Keywords+ Abstract and Tittle + Keywords + Abstract for top K accuracy ($K = 3, 5, 10$). Finally, the combination of CNN + FastText and S2RSCS can surpass all other models. It is essential to emphasize that our proposed model can get better accuracy and highly less time-consuming in training and evaluating processes than existing methods.

2 Methodology

In this work, we formulate the paper submission recommendation system as a classification problem that provides top relevant publication venues from the information of a manuscript based on its title, abstract, and/or keywords. By taking title, abstract, and/or keywords as input data, we investigate seven combinations of those attributes from a given submission: title, abstract, keywords, title + keyword, title + abstract, keyword + abstract, and title + keyword + abstract. For each type of input data, we construct the most suitable classifier and measure the performance of different approaches. In experiments, we build different methods corresponding to these seven input types.

As mentioned previously, we aim to use embedding methods to enhance the paper recommendation model's performance compared to those proposed by Wang et al. [9] and Son et al. [8]. More clearly, we utilize two embedding methods, GloVe [7] and FastText [1], and combine them with one-dimensional Convolutional Neural Networks or LSTM, to design appropriate models. In our work, we study two different architectures: the GloVe/FastText + CNN as well as the GloVe/FastText + LSTM. In experiments, we use the 300-dimensional GloVe embeddings trained on Wikipedia 2014 and Gigaword 5 data for learning a paper submission recommendation model. Besides, we employ FastText sub-word vectors with 300 dimensions trained on Wikipedia news as a chosen FastText embedding technique. Like GloVe, data on Wikipedia are more related to our context (Computer Science) due to their formal writing style; by that, it could give a better result.

2.1 1D Convolutions Neural Networks

Recent years have witnessed the emergence of Convolutional Neural Networks (CNNs) [10], with unprecedented results across various application domains, including image and video recognition, recommender systems, image classification, medical image analysis, natural language processing, and financial time series [2,4–6]. In this paper, after embedding all texts from the input data, we employ one dimensional CNN (denoted by Conv 1D) to extract useful features for the problem. Figure 1 describes how we design the CNN architecture of the recommendation system. In this architecture, we use GloVe/FastText to embed a given input data of one scientific submission before passing it into a one-dimensional CNN (CNN 1D) layer. After going through the CNN layer and being flattened by the Global Max Pooling layer, we push the computed vectors to the last two fully connected layers to determine the matching score (by the probability) between the submission and each conference venue or journal. Finally, one can sort those matching scores by the descending order and select the top K relevant conference venue or journal to the initial submission. It is important to note that one of the main advantages of 1D CNNs is usually at a considerably cheaper computational cost compared to both LSTMs and RNNs.

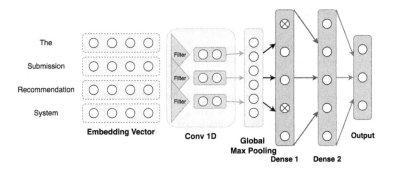

Fig. 1. The proposed CNN architecture of a paper submission recommendation model: the input data of the size n ($n = 4$ in this Figure), the Con1D layer using the activation function RELU and having the window size $c = 2$ and 1800 filters denoted by $f = 1800$. The layer "Dense 1" with the activation function RELU outputs a vector with length 1000, and the layer "Dense 2" returns a probabilistic vector for 65 categories that are 65 publication venues in the experimental datasets after using a Dropout (with the rate of 20%).

2.2 Long Short-Term Memory

Long Short-Term Memory (LSTM) networks [3] has become one of the most powerful and well known neural networks, regarded as an upgrade version of Recurrent Neural Network (RNN) and first introduced by Hochreiter et al. LSTM is primarily an artificial neural network designed to identify patterns in data sequences: sentences, documents, and numerical time-series data. Up to now, LSTM has been widely used and has become an essential part that could bypass a lot of NLP tasks, attention mechanisms, transformers, and memory networks. One can find more details at [3]. Like CNN architecture, we construct the LSTM architecture, as depicted in Fig. 2. Instead of using a combination of Conv 1D and General Mex Pooling in the previous section, we substitute it with an LSTM layer. In experiments, the best settings of LSTM networks can be estimated by fine-tunning parameters.

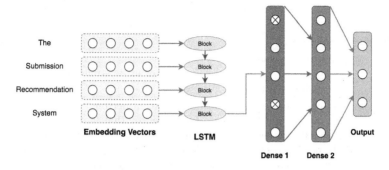

Fig. 2. Our proposed LSTM architecture can be described as follows. The input data have the size of n, and LSTM outputs the last time-step with the size 200. The layer "Dense 1" with the activation Relu outputs a vector of length 100. The layer "Dense 2" returns a probabilistic vector for 65 categories that are 65 publication venues in the experimental datasets after using a Dropout (with the rate of 20%).

2.3 Ensemble Methods

An ensemble method is a technique that combines all models to generate a new model having better predictive performance. As mentioned previously, the output vector of each proposed approach is a probabilistic vector for 65 categories. Each entry of this vector represents the matching score between the submission and each conference venue or journal. Subsequently, one can order those matching scores by the descending order and return the top K relevant conference venue or journal. In our experiments, we consider an ensemble technique, namely S2CFT, of two different models, S2RSCS and CNN + FastText, by computing a new output vector as the average of two output vectors of these two models. After that, we calculate the list of K recommended items from this new output vector.

3 Experiments

We operate all experiments on a computer with Intel(R) Core(TM) i7 2 CPUs running at 2.4 GHz with 128 GB of RAM and an Nvidia GeForce RTX 2080Ti GPU. In experiments, we choose a dataset provided by Wang et al., containing papers presented in different conferences or published in scientific journals in computer science. It is worth noting that this dataset has a total of 14012 samples among 65 different topics (categories). It has 9347 samples for training and 4665 samples for evaluation. Each sample or paper has three attributes: title, abstract, and keywords, where Son and colleagues [8] fully added a full list of keywords of these samples later. One can see Table 1 for further references.

When assessing data in this dataset, we encounter many unexpected factors, such as special symbols, numbers, punctuation marks, and hieroglyphs, that could create potential noises to recommendation models' decisions. Moreover,

Table 1. Several raw samples in the experimental dataset

Attributes	Examples
Title	"Who owns your data?" "Growing closer on facebook: changes in tie strength through social network site use"
Abstract	"Popular and professional discussions of personal data are often framed in terms of ownership – that human data subjects own the data they emit and share..." "In peer-to-peer networks (P2Ps), many autonomous peers without preexisting trust relationships share resources with each other. Due to their open environment, the P2Ps usually..."
Keywords	"Cloud computing, Bandwidth, Benchmark testing, Throughput, Virtual machining, Degradation, Computers" "online learning, click through data, diversity, multi-armed bandits, contextual bandits, regret, metric spaces"

stop words, typing errors, and different writing styles can also give wrong signals or undesirable effects on the model's evaluation. As a consequence, removing all those factors is a necessary data processing step before studying suitable models. With an abstract of a given input submission to the recommendation system, before dropping all the stop words listed by NLTK[4], we generally lower all the texts and remove any element that is not alphabet-based, as described in Table 3.

3.1   Results

Remarkable, in our proposed architectures, the first layer is an embedding layer, which automatically represents each word from the input data as an embedded vector by a provided embedding matrix (GloVe or FastText). Hence, we have two different types of embedded outputs, as illustrated in Table 4 - embedded by GloVe and Table 5 - embedded by FastText.

We employ our experiments by considering six types of recommendation models: CNN + GloVe, CNN + FastText, LSTM + GloVe, LSTM + FastText, S2RSCS, and S2CFT. It is important to note that the S2RSCS is the state-of-the-art recommendation model in the chosen dataset. Here, the notations of CNN + GloVe, CNN + FastText, LSTM + GloVe, and LSTM + FastText stand for a combination of chosen an embedding method and a model architecture, as shown in Fig. 1 and Fig. 2. We compare these recommendation models in terms of the top K accuracy ($K = 1, 3, 5, 10$), with seven types of the input data, as described in Table 2.

Table 2 shows the performance with respect to the top K accuracy ($K = 1, 3, 5, 10$) for seven types of input data and six different models. Among four

---

[4] https://www.nltk.org/.

Table 2. Top K accuracy on the experimental dataset

Types of input data	Model	Top 1	Top 3	Top 5	Top 10
Title	CNN + GloVe	0.3164	0.5510	0.6802	0.8340
	CNN + FastText	0.3249	0.5735	0.7085	0.8547
	LSTM + GloVe	0.1675	0.3360	0.4487	0.6124
	LSTM + FastText	0.1767	0.3474	0.4572	0.6281
	S2RSCS	0.3029	0.5545	0.6852	0.8426
	S2CFT	**0.3364**	**0.5895**	**0.7265**	**0.8720**
Abstract	CNN + GloVe	0.4608	0.7303	0.8287	0.9344
	CNN + FastText	0.4691	0.7460	0.8538	0.9461
	LSTM + GloVe	0.3593	0.6315	0.7604	0.8915
	LSTM + FastText	0.3645	0.6468	0.7822	0.9102
	S2RSCS	0.42378	0.6993	0.8264	0.9412
	S2CFT	**0.4844**	**0.7593**	**0.8680**	**0.9616**
Keywords	CNN + GloVe	0.5731	0.8013	0.8792	0.9517
	CNN + FastText	0.5744	0.7945	0.8794	0.9492
	LSTM + GloVe	0.4983	0.7135	0.7918	0.8895
	LSTM + FastText	0.5239	0.7314	0.8156	0.9025
	S2RSCS	0.5594	0.8212	0.9082	0.9661
	S2CFT	**0.5863**	**0.8412**	**0.9236**	**0.9742**
	CNN + GloVe	0.6005	0.8264	0.9057	0.9699
Title + Keywords	CNN + FastText	0.6010	0.8282	0.9144	0.9742
	LSTM + GloVe	0.5051	0.7382	0.8352	0.9185
	LSTM + FastText	0.4954	0.7332	0.8156	0.9070
	S2RSCS	0.6077	0.8635	0.9373	0.9802
	S2CFT	**0.6272**	**0.8706**	**0.9414**	**0.9870**
	CNN + GloVe	0.4413	0.7164	0.8356	0.9380
Title + Abstract	CNN + FastText	0.4590	0.7285	0.8495	0.9510
	LSTM + GloVe	0.3598	0.6351	0.7680	0.9025
	LSTM + FastText	0.3701	0.6459	0.7815	0.9124
	S2RSCS	0.4231	0.7024	0.8278	0.9391
	S2CFT	**0.4788**	**0.7545**	**0.8662**	**0.9596**
	CNN + GloVe	0.6510	0.8565	0.9227	0.9769
Keywords + Abstract	CNN + FastText	0.6517	0.8724	0.9351	0.9805
	LSTM + GloVe	0.5012	0.7361	0.8361	0.9230
	LSTM + FastText	0.4770	0.7159	0.8147	0.9091
	S2RSCS	0.6441	0.8947	0.9533	0.9892
	S2CFT	**0.6701**	**0.9081**	**0.9625**	**0.9921**
	CNN + GloVe	0.6131	0.8221	0.8965	0.9632
Title + Abstract + Keywords	CNN + FastText	0.6539	0.8596	0.9223	0.9748
	LSTM + GloVe	0.4900	0.7251	0.8237	0.9099
	LSTM + FastText	0.4797	0.7209	0.8253	0.9194
	S2RSCS	0.6501	0.8971	0.9567	0.9870
	S2CFT	**0.6811**	**0.9021**	**0.9593**	**0.9917**

Table 3. Samples processed after preprocessing phase

Attributes	Examples
Title	"owns data" "growing closer facebook changes tie strength social network site use"
Abstract	"popular professional discussions personal data often framed terms ownership human data subjects data emit share..." "peer peer networks pps many autonomous peers without preexisting trust relationships share resources due open environment pps usually..."
Keywords	"cloud computing bandwidth benchmark testing throughput virtual machining degradation computers" "online learning click through data diversity multi armed bandits contextual bandits regret metric spaces"

Table 4. Embedded word vectors generated by GloVe

Word	Embedded word vector
"banks"	[−0.04399, −0.14590, −032640e, −0.19623,...]
"poor"	[0.22760, 0.10096, 0.15344, −0.11363,...]
"competition"	[−0.04471, 0.44167, −0.2725, −0.28455,...]
"forward"	[0.23810, 0.06043, −0.13911, −0.63836,...]

Table 5. Embedded word vectors generated by FastText

Word	Embedded word vector
"banks"	[−0.35173e, −0.49628, 0.06561, 0.22086,...]
"poor"	[−0.09618, −0.35411, −0.23756, 0.26806,...]
"competition"	[−0.34124, 0.20422, −0.14358, −0.1084,...]
"forward"	[−0.32026, −0.15328, −0.010601, 0.4174,...]

deep learning models (CNN + GloVe, CNN + FastText, LSTM + GloVe, LSTM + FastText), using the 1D CNN in the recommendation architecture can significantly gain better performance than choosing LTSM for all experimental cases. Especially, using a list of keywords in the input data can achieve a better top K accuracy than any other combinations, where the corresponding top 1 accuracy is higher than 50%. One possible reason is that the list of keywords in each paper submission usually contains essential techniques or features used by authors. Only using the Title of each submission as the recommendation model's input data has the lowest performance for all the top K accuracy ($K = 1, 3, 5, 10$). Interestingly, all CNN models also outperform other methods

(LSTM + GloVe/FastText and S2RSCS) with the same input data in the top 1 accuracy. Notably, the CNN + FastText model surpasses all these models, about 2–5% for top 1 accuracy. Compared to CNN + GloVe, CNN + FastText has a better accuracy in terms of the top K accuracy ($K = 1, 3, 5, 10$) when using the following input data: Title, Abstract, Title + Keywords, Title + Abstract, Keywords + Abstract, and Title + Abstract + Keywords. CNN + FastText only has a slightly lower performance than CNN + GloVe in terms of the top 10 accuracy for the remaining case: Keywords. Meanwhile, LSTM + FastText only outperforms LSTM + GloVe for all the top K accuracy ($K = 1, 3, 5, 10$) with the input data as Title, Abstract, Keywords, and Title + Abstract. However, LSTM + GloVe surpasses LSTM + FastText for two types of input data: Title + Keyword and Keyword + Abstract for all the top K accuracy ($K = 1, 3, 5, 10$). When using Title + Abstract + Keywords as the input data, LSTM + GloVe gets better performance than LSTM + FastText in terms of top 1 and top 3 accuracies while having a bit lower accuracy in top 5 and top 10 accuracies. One can see that CNN + FastText obtains the best performance among our different deep learning models.

In comparison with S2RSCS, CNN + FastText gains better top K accuracy ($K = 1, 3, 5, 10$) with the following input data: Title, Abstract, and Title + Abstract. However, in the case we include Keywords in the input data, S2RSCS can outperform CNN + FastText when using Title + Keywords for all top K accuracy ($K = 1, 3, 5, 10$) as well as using Keywords+ Abstract and Tittle + Keywords + Abstract for top K accuracy ($K = 3, 5, 10$). Moreover, CNN + FastText surpasses S2RSCS in terms of top 1 accuracy when using Keywords+ Abstract and Title + Abstract + Keywords. It turns out that Keywords can be considered one of the paper submission recommendation model's key attributes. In terms of the recommendation model's complexity, it is crucial to note that computing the TF-IDF/Chi-squared features of the S2RSCS model is much time-consuming compared to extracting features by the CNN layer of our proposed architecture. In practice, there is a trade-off between accuracy and efficiency. We recommend using CNN + FastText as an efficient solution for building such a paper submission recommendation model from the experimental results above. Finally, as a combination of both CNN + FastText and S2RSCS, the S2CFT model can outperform all other models in terms of all top K accuracy for different types of input data. The best top 1 accuracy of S2CFT is 68.11% when using Title + Abstract + Keywords, and the best top 3, 5, and 10 accuracies are 90.81%, 96.25%, and 99.21% when using Keywords + Abstract, respectively.

4   Conclusion and Further Works

We have presented an efficient deep learning approach for the paper submission recommendation problem by using embedding methods, GloVe and FastText, as well as two different deep neural networks, CNNs and LSTM. The experimental results show that using the 1D CNN in the recommendation architecture can significantly achieve better performance than choosing LTSM for all types of embedding methods and input data. We have shown that the list of keywords in the input data can significantly impact the recommendation models' performance. Without using Keywords, CNN + FastText can surpass S2RSCS in terms of top K accuracy ($K = 1, 3, 5, 10$). However, S2RSCS can slightly outperform CNN + FastText when using Title + Keywords for all top K accuracy ($K = 1, 3, 5, 10$) and using Keywords+ Abstract and Tittle + Keywords + Abstract for top K accuracy ($K = 3, 5, 10$). Furthermore, CNN + FastText can better perform S2RSCS in terms of top 1 accuracy when using Keywords+ Abstract and Title + Abstract + Keywords. Notably, our proposed model gets better accuracy and less time-consuming in training and evaluating processes than existing methods due to its simplicity. We aim to continue enhancing the existent recommendation models' performance by applying other embedding methods and advanced deep learning models for the problem.

Acknowledgement. This research is funded by Vietnam National University Ho Chi Minh City (VNU-HCM) under grant number NCM2019-18-01. We want to thank the University of Science, Vietnam National University in Ho Chi Minh City and AISIA Research Lab in Vietnam for supporting us throughout this paper.

References

1. Bojanowski, P., Grave, E., Joulin, A., Mikolov, T.: Enriching word vectors with subword information. CoRR abs/1607.04606 (2016). http://arxiv.org/abs/1607.04606

2. Cao, H.K., Cao, H.K., Nguyen, B.T.: Delafo: An efficient portfolio optimization using deep neural networks. In: Lauw, H.W., Wong, R.C.W., Ntoulas, A., Lim, E.P., Ng, S.K., Pan, S.J. (eds.) Advances in Knowledge Discovery and Data Mining, pp. 623–635. Springer, Cham (2020)

3. Hochreiter, S., Schmidhuber, J.: Long short-term memory. Neural Comput. **9**(8), 1735–1780 (1997)

4. Nguyen, B.T., Nguyen, D.M., Ho, L.S.T., Dinh, V.: An active learning framework for set inversion. Knowledge-Based Systems **185**, 104917 (2019)

5. Nguyen, B.T., Nguyen, D.M., Ho, L.S.T., Dinh, V.C.: OASIS: an active framework for set inversion. In: New Trends in Intelligent Software Methodologies, Tools and Techniques - Proceedings of the 17th International Conference SoMeT_18, Granada, Spain, 26–28 September 2018. pp. 883–895 (2018)

6. Nguyen, D.M.H., Vu, H.T., Ung, H.Q., Nguyen, B.T.: 3d-brain segmentation using deep neural network and gaussian mixture model. In: 2017 IEEE Winter Conference on Applications of Computer Vision (WACV), pp. 815–824, March 2017

7. Pennington, J., Socher, R., Manning, C.: GloVe: Global vectors for word representation. In: Proceedings of the 2014 Conference on Empirical Methods in Natural Language Processing (EMNLP), pp. 1532–1543. Association for Computational Linguistics, Doha, Qatar, October 2014. https://doi.org/10.3115/v1/D14-1162, https://www.aclweb.org/anthology/D14-1162

8. Son, H., Phong, H., Dac, N., Cuong, D.V., Binh, N.T.: S2rscs: an efficient scientific submission recommendation system for computer science. In: The 33th International Conference on Industrial, Engineering & Other Applications of Applied Intelligent Systems (2020)

9. Wang, D., Liang, Y., Xu, D., Feng, X., Guan, R.: A content-based recommender system for computer science publications. Knowl. Based Syst. **157**, 1–9 (2018). https://doi.org/10.1016/j.knosys.2018.05.001, http://www.sciencedirect.com/science/article/pii/S0950705118302107
10. Zhang, X., Zhao, J.J., LeCun, Y.: Character-level convolutional networks for text classification. CoRR abs/1509.01626 (2015). http://arxiv.org/abs/1509.01626

Foundations of Algorithmic Computational Biology – Full Papers

Adding Matrix Control: Insertion-Deletion Systems with Substitutions III

Martin Vu[1](✉) and Henning Fernau[2]

[1] Universität Bremen, FB 3 – Informatik, Bremen, Germany
martin.vu@uni-bremen.de
[2] Universität Trier, FB 4 – Informatik, Trier, Germany
fernau@uni-trier.de

Abstract. We discuss substitutions as a further type of operations, added to matrix insertion-deletion systems. For such systems, we additionally discuss the effect of *appearance checking*. This way, we obtain new characterizations of the families of context-sensitive and the family of recursively enumerable languages. To reach computational completeness, not much context is needed for systems with appearance checking.

Keywords: Computational completeness · Matrix control · Insertions · Deletions · Substitutions

1 Introduction

Insertion-deletion systems, or ins-del systems for short, are well-established as computational devices and as a research topic within Formal Languages throughout the past nearly 30 years, starting off with the PhD thesis of Lila Kari [9].

Corresponding to the mismatched annealing of DNA sequences, both the insertion and deletion operation have a strong biological background which led to their study in the molecular computing framework (cf. [11]). Insertion rules add a substring to a string, given a specified left and right context, while deletion rules remove a substring from a string given a specified left and right context. Studies about the context dependency of ins-del systems revolve around the question how much context information is (in-)sufficient for an ins-del system to reach computational completeness, given the ability to add a substring of length n and to delete a substring of length p.

Ins-del systems can be extended with some form of control to further reduce their context dependency. Matrix insertion-deletion systems, or matrix ins-del systems for short, were introduced in [14,15]. These systems group insertion and deletion rules in sequences, called *matrices*; either the whole sequence is applied consecutively, or no rule is applied at all, thus resembling traditional *matrix grammars*, originally introduced with a linguistic motivation [1]. From the perspective of biocomputing, matrices correspond to small program fragments without jumps that are easier to implement than longer and more involved ones.

© Springer Nature Switzerland AG 2021
T. Bureš et al. (Eds.): SOFSEM 2021, LNCS 12607, pp. 577–592, 2021.
https://doi.org/10.1007/978-3-030-67731-2_42

The replacement of single letters (possibly within some context) by other letters by an operation called *substitution* is discussed in [4,10], again from a biocomputing background. Interestingly, all theoretical studies on grammatical mechanisms involving insertions and deletions omitted including the substitution operation in their studies. We started out a project stepping into this gap in [17–19]. Here, we are studying the context dependency of matrix ins-del systems with substitutions, or matrix ins-del-sub systems for short. Additionally, we discuss *appearance checking* in this context. In the case of matrix grammars, it is known that allowing certain rules of a matrix to be skipped if not applicable increases the computational power [5].

In this paper, we investigate the effect of appearance checking on matrix ins-del-sub systems. We show that the context dependency of ins-del systems can be greatly reduced if matrices, appearance checking, and substitution rules are allowed. For instance it is shown that a matrix ins-del-sub system which only allows context-free single letter insertions and two-letter deletions in addition to contex-free substitution is sufficient to generate any recursively enumerable language. Additionally, we show that a 'normal form' for matrix ins-del-sub systems exists in which only matrices of size at most 2 occur.

2   Definitions

We assume the reader to be familiar with the standard notations in formal language theory. By λ we denote the empty string. Let w be an arbitrary string. We denote by w^R the *reversal* or *mirror image* of w. By L^R and $\mathcal{L}^R$ we denote the *reversal* of a language L and a language family $\mathcal{L}$, respectively. We denote by RE, CS, CF and REG the families of recursively enumerable, context-sensitive, context-free and regular languages, respectively. We are interested in computational completeness results, i.e., in describing RE with matrix ins-del-sub systems with little resources as formally explained next.

A *matrix grammar* is a tuple $G = (N, T, M, S)$ where N, T and S are the finite set of nonterminals, the finite set of terminals and the start symbol, respectively. M is a finite set of sequences of the form $m = [r_1, r_2, \ldots, r_n]$, $n \geq 1$, with rewriting rules $r_i = \alpha_i \to \beta_i$ with $\alpha_i \in (N \cup T)^* N (N \cup T)^*$ and $\beta_i \in (N \cup T)^*$. Such a sequence m is called a matrix [5]. The relation $\Rightarrow$ induced by G is defined as follows. For words $w_1, w_2 \in (N \cup T)^*$, $w_1 \Rightarrow w_2$ holds if a matrix $m = [r_1, r_2, \ldots, r_n]$ and $w_0', w_n' \in (N \cup T)^*$ with $w_0' = w_1$ and $w_n' = w_2$ exist such that $w_j' \Rightarrow_{r_{j+1}} w_{j+1}'$ holds for all $0 \leq j < n$. The language generated by G is $\mathcal{L}(G) = \{w \in T^* \mid S \Rightarrow^* w\}$. We denote by $\mathcal{L}(\text{M}, \text{CF})$ the language family generated by matrix grammars with context-free rewriting rules [5]. A *matrix grammar with appearance checking* is a tuple $G_{ac} = (N, T, M, S, F)$, where N, T, M and S are defined as in usual matrix grammars. F is a set of rewriting rules occurring in matrices of M. All rules in F may be skipped in a transition of G_{ac}, if not applicable. Thus, the absence of symbols can be checked.

An *insertion-deletion system* (*ins-del system* for short) is a 5-tuple $ID = (V, T, A, I, D)$, consisting of two alphabets V and T with $T \subseteq V$, a finite language

A over V, a set of *insertion* rules I and a set of *deletion* rules D. Both sets of rules are formally defined as sets of triples of the form (u, a, v) with $u, v \in V^*$ and $a \in V^+$. We call elements occurring in T *terminal* symbols, while referring to elements of $V \setminus T$ as *nonterminals*. Elements of A are called *axioms*.

Let $w_1 uvw_2$ and $w_1 uavw_2$, with $w_1, u, v, w_2 \in V^*$, $a \in V^+$, be strings. The application of an insertion rule $(u, a, v) \in I$ (also written $(u, a, v)_{\text{ins}}$) to $w_1 uvw_2$ corresponds to inserting the string $a \in V^*$ between u and v, which results in the string $w_1 uavw_2$. The application of a deletion rule $(u, a, v) \in D$ (also written $(u, a, v)_{\text{del}}$) to $w_1 uavw_2$ results in the removal of a substring a from the context (u, v), resulting in the string $w_1 uvw_2$. The relation $\Longrightarrow$ is defined as follows: Let $x, y \in V^*$. Then we write $x \Longrightarrow y$ iff y is the result of applying an insertion or deletion rule to x. We write $\Longrightarrow_{\text{ins}}/\Longrightarrow_{\text{del}}$ if y is obtained via an insertion/ a deletion rule. We denote by $\Longrightarrow^+$ and $\Longrightarrow^*$ the transitive and the reflexive and transitive closure, respectively. The language generated by ID is defined by $L(ID) = \{w \in T^* \mid \exists \alpha \in A : \alpha \Longrightarrow^* w\}$. Consider $(u, a, v)_{\text{ins}}$ or $(u, a, v)_{\text{del}}$. We refer to u as the left context and v as the right context of $(u, a, v)_{\text{ins}}/(u, a, v)_{\text{del}}$. A *sentential form* of ID is a string over V. The *size* of ID describes its complexity and is defined by a vector $(n, m, m'; p, q, q')$, where $n = \max\{|a| \mid (u, a, v) \in I\}$, $p = \max\{|a| \mid (u, a, v) \in D\}$, $m = \max\{|u| \mid (u, a, v) \in I\}$, $q = \max\{|u| \mid (u, a, v) \in D\}$, $m' = \max\{|v| \mid (u, a, v) \in I\}$ and $q' = \max\{|v| \mid (u, a, v) \in D\}$. By $\text{INS}_n^{m,m'}\text{DEL}_p^{q,q'}$ we denote the family of all insertion-deletion systems of size $(n, m, m'; p, q, q')$ [2,16]. Depending on the context, we also denote the family of languages that can be generated by insertion-deletion systems of size $(n, m, m'; p, q, q')$ by $\text{INS}_n^{m,m'}\text{DEL}_p^{q,q'}$.

The idea of regulating ins-del systems with matrix control goes back to [13, 15]. A *matrix ins-del system* [15] is a construct $MID = (V, T, A, M)$ where V, T and A are defined as in usual ins-del systems. $M = \{m_1, \ldots, m_t\}$, $t \geq 1$, is a finite set of sequences, called matrices, of the form $m_i = [r_{i,1}, \ldots, r_{i,k_i}]$, where $k_i \geq 1$. $r_{i,j}$, with $1 \leq i \leq t$, $1 \leq j \leq k_i$, is either an insertion or a deletion rule. A sentential form of MID is a string $w \in V^*$. Consider a matrix $m_i = [r_{i,1}, \ldots, r_{i,k_i}]$. A transition $w \Longrightarrow_{m_i} w'$ is performed if there exist strings $w_1, \ldots, w_{k_i+1} \in V^*$ such that $w_j \Longrightarrow_{r_{i,j}} w_{j+1}$ with $w_1 = w$ and $w_{k_i+1} = w'$. Let $\Longrightarrow := \bigcup_{m \in M} \Longrightarrow_m$. The language generated by MID is defined as $L(MID) = \{w \in T^* \mid \exists \alpha \in A : \alpha \Longrightarrow^* w\}$.

We say that MID has *matrices of size* k if $k = \max_{1 \leq i \leq t} k_i$. If MID is an ins-del systems of size $(n, m, m'; p, q, q')$ with matrices of size k, we also say that MID is of size $(k; n, m, m'; p, q, q')$. We denote by $\text{MAT}_k \text{INS}_n^{m,m'}\text{DEL}_p^{q,q'}$ either the family of languages generated by ins-del systems of size $(k; n, m, m'; p, q, q')$ or the family of ins-del systems of size $(k; n, m, m'; p, q, q')$, depending on the context. Denote by $\text{MAT}_* \text{INS}_n^{m,m'}\text{DEL}_p^{q,q'}\text{SUB}^{r,r'}$ the family of matrix ins-del-sub systems with matrices of arbitrary size and insertion rules and deletion rules, of size (n, m, m') and (p, q, q'), respectively. The following matrix ins-del systems describe RE: $\text{MAT}_3 \text{INS}_1^{1,1}\text{DEL}_1^{0,0}$, $\text{MAT}_3 \text{INS}_1^{0,0}\text{DEL}_1^{1,1}$ [6], $\text{MAT}_3 \text{INS}_1^{0,0}\text{DEL}_1^{2,0}$, $\text{MAT}_3 \text{INS}_1^{2,0}\text{DEL}_1^{0,0}$, $\text{MAT}_2 \text{INS}_1^{1,0}\text{DEL}_1^{1,0}$ [7], $\text{MAT}_3 \text{INS}_1^{1,0}\text{DEL}_1^{0,1}$, $\text{MAT}_2 \text{INS}_1^{1,0}\text{DEL}_2^{0,0}$, $\text{MAT}_2 \text{INS}_2^{0,0}\text{DEL}_1^{1,0}$, [15]. Incompleteness results for matrix ins-del sub systems include $\mathrm{MAT}_*\mathrm{INS}_2^{0,0}\mathrm{DEL}_2^{0,0}$, for instance.[1] More precisely, the following theorem holds.

Theorem 1. $REG \setminus MAT_*INS_2^{0,0}DEL_2^{0,0} \neq \emptyset$, testified by a^*b.

This result follows from [12] as stated in the conclusion of [15].

With substitution rules, we now introduce the central notion of this paper. We define substitution rules to be of the form $(u, a \to b, v)$; $u, v \in V^*$; $a, b \in V$. Let $w_1 u a v w_2$; $w_1, w_2 \in V^*$ be a string over V. Then applying the substitution rule $(u, a \to b, v)$ allows us to substitute a single letter a with another letter b in the context of u and v, resulting in the string $w_1 u b v w_2$.

Formally, we define an ins-del-sub system rules to be a 6-tuple $ID_\varsigma = (V, T, A, I, D, S)$, where V, T, A, I and D are defined as in the case of usual ins-del systems and S is a set of substitution rules.

Let $x = w_1 u a v w_2$ and $y = w_1 u b v w_2$ be strings over V. Substitution rules define a relation $\Longrightarrow_{\mathrm{sub}}$ as follows: $x \Longrightarrow_{\mathrm{sub}} y$ if there is a substitution rule $(u, a \to b, v)$. In the context of ins-del-sub systems, we write $\hat{\Longrightarrow}$ to denote any of the relations $\Longrightarrow_{\mathrm{ins}}$, $\Longrightarrow_{\mathrm{del}}$ or $\Longrightarrow_{\mathrm{sub}}$. We define $\hat{\Longrightarrow}^*$ and $\hat{\Longrightarrow}^+$ as usual.

The language generated by an ins-del-sub system ID_ς is defined as $L(ID_\varsigma) = \{w \in T^* \mid \alpha \hat{\Longrightarrow}^* w, \ \alpha \in A\}$. As with usual ins-del system, we measure the complexity of an ins-del-sub system $ID_\varsigma = (V, T, A, I, D, S)$ via its *size*, that is, an 8-tuple $(n, m, m'; p, q, q'; r, r')$, where n, m, m', p, q and q' are defined as in the case of usual ins-del systems and r and r' limit the maximal length of the left and right context of a substitution rule, respectively, i.e., $r = max\{|u| \mid (u, a \to b, v) \in S\}$, $r' = max\{|v| \mid (u, a \to b, v) \in S\}$. $\mathrm{INS}_n^{m,m'}\mathrm{DEL}_p^{q,q'}\mathrm{SUB}^{r,r'}$ denotes the family of all ins-del-sub systems of size $(n, m, m'; p, q, q'; r, r')$.[2] Depending on the context, we also refer to the family of languages generated by ins-del-sub system of size $(n, m, m'; p, q, q'; r, r')$ by $\mathrm{INS}_n^{m,m'}\mathrm{DEL}_p^{q,q'}\mathrm{SUB}^{r,r'}$.

As with ins-del systems, ins-del-sub systems can be regulated with matrix control as well, introducing *matrix ins-del-sub systems*. A *matrix ins-del-sub systems* is a construct $MID_\varsigma = (V, T, A, M_\varsigma)$ where V, T and A are defined as in usual ins-del systems. $M_\varsigma = \{m_1, \dots, m_t\}$, $t \geq 1$, is a finite set of sequences, called matrices, of the form $m_i = [r_{i,1}, \dots, r_{i,k_i}]$, where $k_i \geq 1$. $r_{i,j}$, with $1 \leq i \leq t$, $1 \leq j \leq k_i$, is either an insertion, a deletion or a substitution rule.

We define the relation between the strings w and w' over V $w \hat{\Longrightarrow}_{m_i} w'$, as well as the generated language of MID_ς, analogously to the case without substitution rules. We say that a matrix ins-del-sub systems which has insertion rules, deletion rules, substitution rules and matrices of size $(n, m, m'), (p, q, q'), (r, r')$ and k, respectively, is of size $(k; n, m, m'; p, q, q'; r, r')$. By $\mathrm{MAT}_k\mathrm{INS}_n^{m,m'}\mathrm{DEL}_p^{q,q'}\mathrm{SUB}^{r,r'}$, denote the family of matrix ins-del-sub systems of size $(k; n, m, m'; p, q, q'; r, r')$, as well as the family of languages generated by such systems, depending on the context. Consider a language family $\mathrm{MAT}_k\mathrm{INS}_n^{m,m'}\mathrm{DEL}_p^{q,q'}\mathrm{SUB}^{r,r'}$. Concerning the reversal operator, the following lemma holds.

---

[1] Cf. the conclusion of [15], based on a result for insertion-deletion P systems [12].

[2] As only one letter is replaced by any substitution rule, there is no subscript at SUB.

Lemma 1. *Let $\mathcal{L}$ be a family of languages that is closed under reversal. Then:*

1. $\mathcal{L} = MAT_k INS_n^{m,m'} DEL_p^{q,q'} SUB^{r,r'}$ *iff* $\mathcal{L} = MAT_k INS_n^{m',m} DEL_p^{q',q} SUB^{r',r}$.
2. $\mathcal{L} \subseteq MAT_k INS_n^{m,m'} DEL_p^{q,q'} SUB^{r,r'}$ *iff* $\mathcal{L} \subseteq MAT_k INS_n^{m',m} DEL_p^{q',q} SUB^{r',r}$.
3. $MAT_k INS_n^{m,m'} DEL_p^{q,q'} SUB^{r,r'} \subseteq \mathcal{L}$ *iff* $MAT_k INS_n^{m',m} DEL_p^{q',q} SUB^{r',r} \subseteq \mathcal{L}$.

Proof. These claims follow analogously to [7].

By definition, it is clear that the following lemma holds.

Lemma 2. $MAT_k INS_n^{m,m'} DEL_p^{q,q'} \subseteq MAT_k INS_n^{m,m'} DEL_p^{q,q'} SUB^{r,r'}$.

It is known that matrix grammars with context-free production are not computationally complete, but can reach computational completeness if used with *appearance checking*. Transferring this idea to matrix ins-del-sub systems, we introduce matrix ins-del-sub systems with appearance checking and show that, similar to the matrix grammar case, formerly computationally incomplete matrix ins-del-sub systems can reach computational completeness if used in conjunction with appearance checking. We begin by defining matrix ins-del-sub systems and appearance checking. A matrix ins-del-sub systems and appearance checking is a tuple $MID_{\varsigma,ac} = (V, T, A, M_\varsigma, F)$, where V, T, A and M_ς are defined as in usual matrix ins-del-sub systems. F is a subset of all rules occurring in M_ς.

Let $w_1, w_2 \in V^*$ and z be an arbitrary rule occurring in M_ς. We define the relation $\overset{ac}{\Longrightarrow}_z$ as follows: $w_1 \overset{ac}{\Longrightarrow}_z w_2$ if one of the following conditions hold: (a) the rule z is applicable to w_1 such that $w_1 \Longrightarrow_z w_2$ or (b) the rule z is not applicable to w_1, $z \in F$ and $w_1 = w_2$. Basically, this means that if some rule in F is not applicable, we can skip that rule. Let $m = [r_1, \ldots, r_n] \in M_\varsigma$ and $x, y \in V^*$. Then $x \overset{ac}{\Longrightarrow}_m y$ iff $x = w_0 \overset{ac}{\Longrightarrow}_{r_1} w_1 \overset{ac}{\Longrightarrow}_{r_2} \ldots \overset{ac}{\Longrightarrow}_{r_n} w_n = y$. The language generated by $MID_{\varsigma,ac}$ is defined as $L(MID_{\varsigma,ac}) = \{w \in T^* \mid \exists\, m_1, \ldots, m_n \in M_\varsigma, \alpha \in A : \alpha = x_0 \overset{ac}{\Longrightarrow}_{m_1} x_1 \overset{ac}{\Longrightarrow}_{m_2} \ldots \overset{ac}{\Longrightarrow}_{m_n} x_n = w\}$. We define the *size* of $MID_{\varsigma,ac}$ analogously to matrix ins-del-sub systems without appearance checking. We denote the language family generated by matrix ins-del-sub systems with appearance checking of size $(k; n, m, m'; p, q, q'; r, r')$ by the term $MAT_k^{ac} INS_n^{m,m'} DEL_p^{q,q'} SUB^{r,r'}$.

Example 1. Consider the matrix ins-del-sub systems with appearance checking $MID_{\varsigma,ac} = (V, T, A, M_\varsigma, F)$ of size $(3; 1, 0, 0; 2, 0, 0; 0, 0)$ with $V = \{X, a, b\}$, $T = \{a, b\}$, $A = \{b\}$, $M_\varsigma = \{[(\lambda, X, \lambda)_{ins}, (\lambda, bX, \lambda)_{del}, (\lambda, X \to a, \lambda)]\}$ and $F = \{(\lambda, bX, \lambda)_{del}\}$. The language generated by $MID_{\varsigma,ac}$ is a^*b. This can be shown as follows. Let $m = [(\lambda, X, \lambda)_{ins}, (\lambda, bX, \lambda)_{del}, (\lambda, X \to a, \lambda)]$, $w_1 \in a^*b$ and $w_2 \in \{a, b\}^*$ such that $w_1 \overset{ac}{\Longrightarrow}_m w_2$.

Assume that during the application of m the nonterminal X is inserted right of b. Then clearly the deletion rule (λ, bX, λ) is applicable after the insertion and we delete X along with b. However, now the substitution rule $(\lambda, X \to a, \lambda)$ cannot be applied any more and, as $(\lambda, X \to a, \lambda) \notin F$, this means that the matrix as a whole cannot be applied.

Assume that during the application of m the nonterminal X is inserted somewhere left of b. Clearly $(\lambda, bX, \lambda)_{del}$ is not applicable and, as $(\lambda, bX, \lambda)_{del} \in F$, we skip this rule and proceed with the application of $(\lambda, X \rightarrow a, \lambda)$. Applying m in this way effectively inserts a somewhere left of b and therefore $w_2 \in a^*b$.

Using the above argument inductively yields our claim. We remark that for any word w derived from the axiom b $|w|_{\{X\}} = 0$ holds, as any X introduced during the application of m is resolved at the end of m.

The example above clarifies that appearance checking can result in an increase in computational power, as $a^*b \notin \mathrm{MAT}_*\mathrm{INS}_2^{0,0}\mathrm{DEL}_2^{0,0}\mathrm{SUB}^{0,0}$ is known (Theorem 1).

3   Computational (In-)Completeness Results

In this section, we present the main results of our research. We begin by introducing a (binary) normal form for matrix ins-del-sub systems similar to the 2-normal form for matrix grammars [5, Def. 1.2.1].

A matrix ins-del-sub systems $MID_\varsigma = (V, T, A, M_\varsigma)$ is said to be in *normal form* if all matrices are either of the form $[r, (\lambda, A \rightarrow B, \lambda)]$ or $[r, (\lambda, A, \lambda)_{\mathrm{del}}]$, where r is some insertion, deletion or substitution rule and $A, B \in V$. Clearly all matrix ins-del-sub systems in normal form are included in $\mathrm{MAT}_2\mathrm{INS}_n^{m,m'}\mathrm{DEL}_p^{q,q'}\mathrm{SUB}^{r,r'}$. We show that for every matrix ins-del-sub system, there is a matrix ins-del-sub system in normal form which generates the same language.

Theorem 2. *For every* $MID_\varsigma \in \mathrm{MAT}_k\mathrm{INS}_n^{m,m'}\mathrm{DEL}_p^{q,q'}\mathrm{SUB}^{r,r'}$, $p > 0$, *there is a system* $MID_\varsigma' \in \mathrm{MAT}_2\mathrm{INS}_n^{m,m'}\mathrm{DEL}_p^{q,q'}\mathrm{SUB}^{r,r'}$, *such that* $L(MID_\varsigma) = L(MID_\varsigma')$.

Proof. Let $MID_\varsigma = (V, T, A, M_\varsigma)$ and all matrices of MID_ς be labelled in a one-to-one manner, i.e., a bijection from M_ς to a set of labels exists. Then we define $MID_\varsigma' = (V', T, A', M_\varsigma')$, where $V' = V \cup \{(i,j) \mid i$ is the label of a matrix of MID_ς and $j \leq k\}$ and $A' = \{\alpha(i,1) \mid \alpha \in A$ and i is the label of a matrix of $MID_\varsigma\} \cup \{\alpha \mid \alpha \in A \cap T^*\}$. Without loss of generality we assume $V \cap \{(i,j) \mid i$ is the label of a matrix of MID_ς and $j \leq k\} = \emptyset$. For every matrix $m = [r_1, r_2, \ldots, r_n]$ of MID_ς, where r_j, with $j = 1, \ldots, n$, is some insertion, deletion or substitution rule and i is the label of m, we add the following matrices $[r_1, (\lambda, (i,1) \rightarrow (i,2), \lambda)]$, $[r_2, (\lambda, (i,2) \rightarrow (i,3), \lambda)]$, $\ldots$, $[r_{n-1}, (\lambda, (i, n-1) \rightarrow (i,n), \lambda)]$ and $[r_n, (\lambda, (i,n), \lambda)_{\mathrm{del}}]$ to MID_ς'. For every label i' of some matrix of MID_ς and every matrix $m = [r_1, r_2, \ldots, r_n]$ of MID_ς, we add a matrix $[r_n, (\lambda, (i,n) \rightarrow (i',1), \lambda)]$ to MID_ς'. By definition, the second component of every matrix of MID_ς' is either a context-free deletion rule of the form $(\lambda, (i,j), \lambda)_{\mathrm{del}}$ or a context-free substitution rule of the form $(\lambda, (i,j) \rightarrow (i',j'), \lambda)$, where i and i' are the labels of some matrices of MID_ς and $j, j' \leq k$. Furthermore, the first rule of any matrix of MID_ς' does not involve any nonterminals in $V' \setminus V$.

Consider a sentential form $w_1(i,j)w_2$ with $w_1, w_2 \in V^*$. It can be shown that all sentential forms of MID_ς' are either of this form or of the form $w \in V^*$. The basic idea is that the nonterminal (i, j) serves as an indicator which matrix is to be applied next. For instance, the occurrence of (i, j) in $w_1(i, j)w_2$ signifies that the next rule to be applied is either $(r_j, (\lambda, (i, j) \rightarrow (i, j+1), \lambda))$ if the length of the matrix of MID_ς labelled by i is greater than j or $(r_j, (\lambda, (i, j) \rightarrow (i', 1), \lambda))$ / $(r_j, (\lambda, (i, j), \lambda)_{\text{del}})$, otherwise. We note that in every derivation of MID'_ς, a matrix of the form $(r_j, (\lambda, (i, j), \lambda)_{\text{del}})$ is applied at most once. Furthermore, we remark that if a sentential form $w \in V^*$ occurs during a derivation of MID'_ς, the derivation cannot proceed as the second rule of any matrix cannot be applied. We prove the correctness of the construction, i.e., $L(MID_\varsigma) = L(MID'_\varsigma)$.

'$\supseteq$': Consider the derivation $w_1(i, j)w_2 \Longrightarrow_{[r, (\lambda, (i,j) \rightarrow (i', j'), \lambda)]} w'_1(i', j')w'_2$ where r is some insertion, deletion or substitution rule and $w_1, w_2 \in V^*$. As r does not involve any nonterminals in $V' \setminus V$, clearly $w_1 w_2 \Longrightarrow_r w'_1 w'_2$ holds. We now extend this result. Consider a matrix $m = [r_1, \ldots, r_n]$ labelled by i. Then clearly

$$w_1(i, 1)w_2 \underset{[r_1, (\lambda, (i,1) \rightarrow (i,2), \lambda)]}{\Longrightarrow} \cdots \underset{[r_{n-1}, (\lambda, (i,n-1) \rightarrow (i,n), \lambda)]}{\Longrightarrow} w'_1(i, n)w'_2$$
$$\underset{[r_n, (\lambda, (i,n) \rightarrow (i',1), \lambda)]}{\Longrightarrow} w''_1(i', 1)w''_2$$

or

$$w_1(i, 1)w_2 \underset{[r_1, (\lambda, (i,1) \rightarrow (i,2), \lambda)]}{\Longrightarrow} \cdots \underset{[r_{n-1}, (\lambda, (i,n-1) \rightarrow (i,n), \lambda)]}{\Longrightarrow} w'_1(i, n)w'_2 \underset{[r_n, (\lambda, (i,n), \lambda)_{\text{del}}]}{\Longrightarrow} w''_1 w''_2$$

implies $w_1 w_2 \Longrightarrow_{[r_1, \ldots, r_n]} w''_1 w''_2$.

'$\subseteq$': Conversely it can be shown that $w \Longrightarrow_{[r_1, \ldots, r_n]} w''$ implies

$$w(i, 1) \underset{[r_1, (\lambda, (i,1) \rightarrow (i,2), \lambda)]}{\Longrightarrow} \cdots \underset{[r_{n-1}, (\lambda, (i,n-1) \rightarrow (i,n), \lambda)]}{\Longrightarrow} w'(i, n) \underset{[r_n, (\lambda, (i,n) \rightarrow (i',1), \lambda)]}{\Longrightarrow} w''(i', 1)$$

and

$$w(i, 1) \underset{[r_1, (\lambda, (i,1) \rightarrow (i,2), \lambda)]}{\Longrightarrow} \cdots \underset{[r_{n-1}, (\lambda, (i,n-1) \rightarrow (i,n), \lambda)]}{\Longrightarrow} w'(i, n) \underset{[r_n, (\lambda, (i,n), \lambda)_{\text{del}}]}{\Longrightarrow} w''$$

We remark that, in the simulation of the application a matrix of MID_ς, we can assume that the leftmost symbol of any sentential form of a derivation of MID'_ς is of a nonterminal $(i, j) \in V' \setminus V$ (unless a matrix of the form $[r_n, (\lambda, (i, n), \lambda)_{\text{del}}]$ is applied). □

Similarly, for every matrix ins-del-sub system $MID_\varsigma \in \text{MAT}_k\text{INS}_n^{m,m'}\text{DEL}_0^{0,0}$ $\text{SUB}^{r,r'}$, one can construct $MID'_\varsigma \in \text{MAT}_2\text{INS}_n^{m,m'}\text{DEL}_0^{0,0}\text{SUB}^{r,r'}$ in normal form such that $L(MID'_\varsigma) = L(MID_\varsigma)$.

As a consequence of the previously introduced normal form for matrix ins-del-sub systems, we obtain the following result:

Corollary 1. *The following statements hold.*

1. $MAT_2INS_1^{0,0}DEL_1^{1,1}SUB^{0,0} = RE.$
2. $MAT_2INS_1^{1,1}DEL_1^{0,0}SUB^{0,0} = RE.$

This follows easily with Theorem 2, as computational completeness has been shown for $\text{MAT}_3\text{INS}_1^{1,1}\text{DEL}_1^{0,0}$ and for $\text{MAT}_3\text{INS}_1^{0,0}\text{DEL}_1^{1,1}$, see [6].

As $\text{MAT}_2\text{INS}_1^{1,0}\text{DEL}_1^{1,0} = RE$ has been shown in [7] (and hence the equality $\text{MAT}_2\text{INS}_1^{1,0}\text{DEL}_1^{1,0}\text{SUB}^{0,0} = RE$ is obvious), we now consider matrix ins-del-sub systems of size $(*; 1, 1, 0; 1, 0, 0; 0, 0)$.

Theorem 3. $L \in \mathcal{L}(M, CF)$ *if and only if there is a matrix ins-del-sub systems* MID_ς *of size* $(*; 1, 1, 0; 1, 0, 0; 0, 0)$, *such that* $L(MID_\varsigma) = L$.

As matrix grammars with context-free production are not computationally complete [8], matrix ins-del-sub system of size $(*; 1, 1, 0; 1, 0, 0; 0, 0)$ are not computationally complete, either. It is known that $\mathcal{L}(M, CF)$ is closed under reversal. With Lemma 1 we conclude:

Corollary 2. $MAT_2 INS_1^{1,0} DEL_1^{0,0} SUB^{0,0} \cup MAT_2 INS_1^{0,1} DEL_1^{0,0} SUB^{0,0} \subset RE.$

We now show that $MAT_* INS_1^{0,0} DEL_1^{1,0} SUB^{0,0}$ is not computationally complete. Consequently, this means that $MAT_* INS_1^{0,0} DEL_1^{1,0}$ is not complete, either.

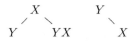

Fig. 1. Tree group corresponding to a sentential form $w = XY$

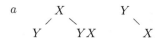

Fig. 2. Tree group following the application of $(\lambda, a, \lambda)_{\text{ins}}$

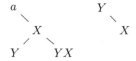

Fig. 3. Tree group following the application of $(a, X, \lambda)_{\text{del}}$

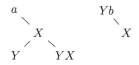

Fig. 4. Tree group following the application of $(\lambda, Y \to b, \lambda)$

Consider the following construction for the proof. For each derivation of a matrix ins-del-sub system $MID_\varsigma = (V, T, A, M_\varsigma)$ of size $(1, 0, 0; 1, 1, 0; 0, 0)$, we construct a group of trees which represents the structure of the derivation. Each tree node is labeled by a string over V such that reading the rightmost symbols of all root labels of the corresponding group of trees from left to right yields w (cf. Fig. 1).

If an insertion rule (λ, a, λ) adds the letter a at some position of the sentential form, we add a new tree with a single node labelled a at the corresponding position in the group of trees (see Fig. 2).

Applying a deletion rule (a, X, λ) has the following effect on the group of trees: The node corresponding to X becomes the rightmost child of the node corresponding to a (see Fig. 3).

Let w_Y be the string of the node corresponding to a letter Y. If a substitution rule $(\lambda, Y \to b, \lambda)$ is applied, we concatenate b right of w_Y (see Fig. 4).

Let the axiom of the derivation be $\alpha_1 \ldots \alpha_n$. Then the group of trees consists initially of n trees with single nodes, each labelled by a symbol of the axiom such that reading the labels of the respective roots from left to right yields $\alpha_1 \ldots \alpha_n$. Each root node corresponds to a letter of the current sentential form.

By construction, it is clear that only (the rightmost letter of) root labels contribute letters to the final word, i.e., each tree contributes at most one letter to the final word. Furthermore, it is clear that there is no interaction between letters of two different trees, i.e., a letter belonging to certain tree is not a context for some operation on a letter of another tree.

Example 2. Consider a matrix ins-del-sub system MID_ς of size $(1, 0, 0; 1, 1, 0; 0, 0)$, which has the axiom $X_1 X_2$. Let

$$m_1 = [(\lambda, b, \lambda)_{\text{ins}}, (b, X_1, \lambda)_{\text{del}}, (\lambda, a, \lambda)_{\text{ins}}]$$
$$m_2 = [(\lambda, b, \lambda)_{\text{ins}}, (b, X_2, \lambda)_{\text{del}}, (\lambda, X_a, \lambda)_{\text{ins}}]$$
$$m_3 = [(\lambda, X_a \to a, \lambda), (\lambda, a, \lambda)_{\text{ins}}, (a, X_3, \lambda)_{\text{del}}]$$

be matrices of MID_ς. Clearly $X_1 X_2 \overset{\wedge}{\Longrightarrow}_{m_1 m_2 m_3} bab$ holds and the corresponding group of trees is Note that all letters corresponding to the eventual b-

$$
\begin{array}{ccc}
b & X_a a & b \\
\backslash & \mid & \backslash \\
X_1 & X_3 & X_2.
\end{array}
$$

tree originate from context-free insertions. Furthermore, as there is no interaction between letters of two different trees, inserting all letters of the eventual b-tree (in the order specified by the b-tree) left or right of all letters belonging to eventual a-trees does not affect the a-trees. Thus $X_1 X_2 \overset{\wedge}{\Longrightarrow}_{m_1 m_2 m_3} abb$ and $X_1 X_2 \overset{\wedge}{\Longrightarrow}_{m_1 m_2 m_3} bba$ hold as well.

Theorem 4. $REG \setminus MAT_* INS_1^{0,0} DEL_1^{1,0} SUB^{0,0} \neq \emptyset$.

Proof. We show by contradiction that there is no matrix ins-del-sub system of size $(1, 0, 0; 1, 1, 0; 0, 0)$ generating the regular language $a^+ b^+$. Assume that $MID_\varsigma = (V, T, A, M_\varsigma)$ generates $a^+ b^+$. Then, MID_ς generates the word $a^n b^n$, $n > \gamma$, as well, where γ is the length of the longest axiom of MID_ς. Consider the group of trees corresponding to a derivation of $a^n b^n$ starting from the axiom α. As $n > \gamma$, there exists a tree t with the following properties: (1) the tree contributes a letter a to $a^n b^n$ and (2) all nodes of the tree originate from the application of some insertion rule. Consider the derivation from α to $a^n b^n$. Then, MID_ς generates $a^{n-1} b^n a$ as well. The string $a^{n-1} b^n a$ is generated by applying the same matrices used in the derivation from α to $a^n b^n$ in the same order. All insertion rules corresponding to nodes of the tree t specified above are applied right of all letters belonging to (eventual) b-trees. As there is no interaction between letters of two different trees, none of the letters corresponding to nodes of t are used as context to delete symbols not affiliated with nodes of t. Thus, inserting these letters right of all letters belonging to (eventual) b-trees changes nothing for the other trees. Note that the tree t specifies position of the inserted letters in relation to each other as well as how the rest of the rules concerning symbols of t are applied.   □

Interestingly, while neither $MAT_*INS_1^{1,0}DEL_1^{0,0}SUB^{0,0}$ nor $MAT_*INS_1^{0,0}DEL_1^{1,0}SUB^{0,0}$ are computationally complete, at least the context-free languages are included in $MAT_*INS_1^{1,0}DEL_1^{0,0}SUB^{0,0}$ (Theorem 3). $MAT_*INS_1^{0,0}DEL_1^{1,0}SUB^{0,0}$ does not even include all regular languages. Consequently, we can also state:

Corollary 3. $REG \setminus MAT_*INS_1^{0,0}DEL_1^{1,0} \neq \emptyset$.

We remark that Corollary 2 and Theorem 4 show that the result of Corollary 1 is optimal, i.e., the context dependency cannot be reduced any further without losing computational power.

We now show that extending context-free matrix ins-del systems with context-free substitution rules does not result in an increase in computational power.

Theorem 5. $MAT_*INS_n^{0,0}DEL_p^{0,0}SUB^{0,0} = MAT_*INS_n^{0,0}DEL_p^{0,0}$ with $n, p \geq 2$.

Proof. As $MAT_*INS_n^{0,0}DEL_p^{0,0} \subseteq MAT_*INS_n^{0,0}DEL_p^{0,0}SUB^{0,0}$ holds by definition, we only prove the converse.

Let $MID_\varsigma = (V, T, A, M_\varsigma)$ be of size $(*; n, 0, 0; p, 0, 0; 0, 0)$. Then there exists a system $MID = (V \cup \{X\}, T, A, M')$ of size $(*; n, 0, 0; p, 0, 0)$ where X is a new symbol not in V which simulates MID_ς. It is sufficient to prove that context-free substitution rules can be simulated by MID. Let $(\lambda, a \to b, \lambda)$ be a context-free substitution rule. Consider the sequence $(\lambda, Xb, \lambda)_{ins}$, $(\lambda, aX, \lambda)_{del}$. Applying this sequence to w_1aw_2, $w_1, w_2 \in V^*$, is equivalent to applying the substitution rule $(\lambda, a \to b, \lambda)$, i.e., $w_1aw_2 \Longrightarrow w_1aXbw_2 \Longrightarrow w_1bw_2$. Note that the string Xb has to be inserted directly right of a letter a, as otherwise $(\lambda, aX, \lambda)_{del}$ cannot be applied.

The set M' is therefore constructed as follows: Let $m \in M$ then we replace all occurrences of substitution rules $(\lambda, a \to b, \lambda)$ in m with the sequence $(\lambda, Xb, \lambda)_{ins}$, $(\lambda, aX, \lambda)_{del}$. The resulting matrix is added to M'. This procedure is applied to all $m \in M$.   □

By Theorem 1, we deduce that matrix ins-del systems of size $(*; 2, 0, 0; 2, 0, 0; 0, 0)$ are not computationally complete.

Corollary 4. $MAT_*INS_2^{0,0}DEL_2^{0,0}SUB^{0,0} \subsetneq RE$.

We now consider matrix ins-del systems with one-sided substitution rules. The families of systems discussed in detail now are $MAT_2INS_1^{0,0}DEL_1^{0,0}SUB^{1,0}$ and $MAT_2INS_1^{0,0}DEL_0^{0,0}SUB^{1,0}$.

Theorem 6. $MAT_*INS_1^{1,0}DEL_1^{1,0} \subseteq MAT_*INS_1^{0,0}DEL_1^{0,0}SUB^{1,0}$.

Proof. Let $MID = (V, T, A, M) \in \mathrm{MAT}_* \mathrm{INS}_1^{1,0} \mathrm{DEL}_1^{1,0}$. Then, we define $MID_\varsigma = (V', T, A, M')$ as follows: Let $V' := V \cup \{X\}$. Without loss of generality, we assume $V \cap \{X\} = \emptyset$.

The following procedure is applied to all matrices of MID. Consider an arbitrary matrix m of MID. We replace every occurrence of an insertion rule of the form (a, b, λ) with an insertion rule (λ, X, λ) and a substitution rule $(a, X \to b, \lambda)$. Additionally, any deletion rule of the form (a, b, λ) is replaced with a substitution rule $(a, b \to X, \lambda)$ and a deletion rule (λ, X, λ). The matrix obtained by these replacements is added to M'.

Clearly, $MID_\varsigma \in \mathrm{MAT}_* \mathrm{INS}_1^{0,0} \mathrm{DEL}_1^{0,0} \mathrm{SUB}^{1,0}$. The basic idea of this proof is that the nonterminal X is resolved immediately after being introduced. It is easy to see that applying the substitution rule $(a, b \to X, \lambda)$ immediately after the insertion rule (λ, X, λ) is essentially the same as applying a rule of the form (a, b, λ). Likewise, applying the deletion rule (λ, X, λ) immediately after the substitution rule $(a, b \to X, \lambda)$ is basically the same as applying the deletion rule (a, b, λ).

Therefore, clearly $L(MID) = L(MID_\varsigma)$.   □

It has been shown in [15] that $\mathrm{MAT}_3 \mathrm{INS}_1^{1,0} \mathrm{DEL}_1^{1,0} = \mathrm{RE}$ holds. Hence, $\mathrm{RE} = \mathrm{MAT}_* \mathrm{INS}_1^{0,0} \mathrm{DEL}_1^{0,0} \mathrm{SUB}^{1,0}$. We can improve this result by using the result presented in Theorem 2. Together with Lemma 1, the next corollary follows.

Corollary 5. $RE = MAT_2 INS_1^{0,0} DEL_1^{0,0} SUB^{1,0} = MAT_2 INS_1^{0,0} DEL_1^{0,0} SUB^{0,1}$.

It can be shown that omitting deletion rules in the systems mentioned above yields a characterization of context-sensitive languages, which is quite rare with ins-del systems. More specifically, with Lemma 1, we can state the following result.

Theorem 7. $CS = MAT_2 INS_1^{0,0} DEL_0^{0,0} SUB^{0,1} = MAT_2 INS_1^{0,0} DEL_0^{0,0} SUB^{1,0}$.

The proof is rather immediate.

We have previously shown that there are even regular languages not included in $\mathrm{MAT}_* \mathrm{INS}_2^{0,0} \mathrm{DEL}_2^{0,0} \mathrm{SUB}^{0,0}$. We now show that expanding these systems with *appearance checking* yields computational completeness. More precisely, we show that the expanded systems can simulate type-0 grammars in Penttonen normal form, which means that all production rules are of the form

$$AB \to AC \text{ or}$$
$$A \to BC \text{ or}$$
$$A \to a \text{ or}$$
$$A \to \lambda,$$

where A, B, C are nonterminal symbols and a is a terminal symbol.

Theorem 8. $MAT_*^{ac} INS_1^{0,0} DEL_2^{0,0} SUB^{0,0} = RE$.

Proof. As the inclusion $\mathrm{MAT}_*^{ac}\mathrm{INS}_2^{0,0}\mathrm{DEL}_2^{0,0}\mathrm{SUB}^{0,0} \subseteq \mathrm{RE}$ is clear, we now proceed to prove the converse by simulating a type-0 grammar $G = (N, T, P, S)$ in Penttonen normal form. The matrix ins-del-sub systems with appearance checking simulating G is defined as $MID_{\varsigma,ac} = (V, T, \{\$S\}, M_\varsigma, F)$, with $V = N \cup T \cup \{X, X_1, X_2, \$, \$'\}$ and $(N \cup T) \cap \{X, X_1, X_2, \$, \$'\} = \emptyset$. The nonterminal $\$$ is an auxiliary symbol which marks the beginning of a sentential form and is eventually deleted by the matrix $[(\lambda, \$, \lambda)_{\mathrm{del}}]$. We now describe how the rules of G are simulated.

For every rule of G of the form $A \to a$ we add a matrix $[(\lambda, A \to a, \lambda)]$ to M_ς and for every rule $A \to \lambda$, we add the matrix $[(\lambda, A, \lambda)_{\mathrm{del}}]$ to M_ς. We remark that the following matrices introduced to M_ς require the sentential form to have $\$$ as the leftmost symbol. Hence, these rules cannot be applied if $\$$ is absent. For every rule of the form $AB \to AC$, to M_ς we add a matrix $[(\lambda, \$ \to \$', \lambda), (\lambda, B \to X, \lambda), (\lambda, A_1X, \lambda)_{\mathrm{del}}, \ldots, (\lambda, A_nX, \lambda)_{\mathrm{del}}, (\lambda, X \to C, \lambda), (\lambda, \$' \to \$, \lambda)]$ with $V \setminus \{A\} = \{A_1, \ldots, A_n\}$. Add $\{(\lambda, A_1X, \lambda)_{\mathrm{del}}, \ldots, (\lambda, A_nX, \lambda)_{\mathrm{del}}\}$ to F. These deletion rules are used to check whether the left context of the B which is substituted by X has been A. The basic idea is as follows: Consider the application of the matrix above to $\$w$, where w is a string over $V \setminus \{X, X_1, X_2, \$, \$'\}$. It is clear that the letter B which is substituted by X must have some symbol as its left context, i.e., this B cannot be the leftmost symbol. Furthermore, if the matrix above has been successfully applied, neither of the deletion rules in F has been applicable, as otherwise the substitution rule $(\lambda, X \to C, \lambda)$ could not have been applied. Therefore, the application of these deletion rules has been skipped during the processing of the matrix above. As the letter B (which is eventually substituted by X) must have some left context, but neither of the deletion rules from F has been applicable, this means that the left context of this B could not have been a letter from $\{A_1, \ldots, A_n\} = V \setminus \{A\}$. Hence, the left context of this B has been A. It is therefore easy to see that the matrix above correctly simulates $AB \to AC$.

For every production rule of the form $A \to BC$, we add a matrix $[(\lambda, \$ \to \$', \lambda), (\lambda, A \to X_1, \lambda), (\lambda, X_2, \lambda)_{\mathrm{ins}}, (\lambda, A_1'X_2, \lambda)_{\mathrm{del}}, \ldots, (\lambda, A_n'X_2, \lambda)_{\mathrm{del}}, (\lambda, X_2\$', \lambda)_{\mathrm{del}}, (\lambda, X_1 \to B, \lambda), (\lambda, X_2 \to C, \lambda), (\lambda, \$' \to \$, \lambda)]$ with $\{A_1', \ldots, A_n'\} = V \setminus \{X_1\}$ to M_ς. The deletion rules $(\lambda, A_1X_1, \lambda), \ldots, (\lambda, A_nX_1, \lambda)$ and $(\lambda, X_2\$', \lambda)$ are added to F. Consider a string w over $V \setminus \{X, X_1, X_2, \$, \$'\}$. Let the matrix above be applied to the string $\$w$. Using the same argumentation as before, $(\lambda, A_1X_2, \lambda), \ldots, (\lambda, A_nX_2, \lambda)$ in F ensure that the left context of the inserted X_2 is not an element of $\{A_1', \ldots, A_n'\} = V \setminus \{X_1\}$. Additionally, if the matrix above has been successfully applied, the deletion rule $(\lambda, X_2\$', \lambda)_{\mathrm{del}}$ could not have been applicable, as otherwise the substitution rule $(\lambda, X_2 \to C, \lambda)$ could not have been be applied. This in turn means that the string X_1X_2 has not been inserted left of $\$'$, which means that X_2 has left context. It is clear that this left context is X_1 and therefore it is clear that the above matrix simulates $A \to BC$.

We remark that applying any of the matrices, which simulate a production rule of G, to a sentential form of $MID_{\varsigma,ac}$, whose leftmost symbol is $\$$, results in a string whose leftmost symbol remains \$. By induction we can show that $S \Rightarrow_G^* w$ iff $\$S \overset{\frown}{\Longrightarrow}^{ac*} \$w$. □

Additionally, we can show that $MAT_*^{ac}INS_1^{0,0}DEL_1^{1,0}SUB^{0,0}$ is computationally complete, as well.

Theorem 9. $MAT_*^{ac}INS_1^{0,0}DEL_1^{1,0}SUB^{0,0} = RE$.

Proof. The idea is the same as in Theorem 8. Replacing all deletion rules of the form (λ, ab, λ) in the matrices of the system constructed in Theorem 8 with deletion rules of the form (a, b, λ) yields our claim. □

This result shows that *appearance checking* is indeed powerful as we have previously seen that $MAT_*INS_1^{0,0}DEL_1^{1,0}SUB^{0,0}$ does not even include all regular languages. Furthermore, we can conclude the following from this result.

Theorem 10. $MAT_*^{ac}INS_2^{0,0}DEL_2^{0,0} = RE$.

Proof. All substitution rules occurring in matrices of the construction in Theorem 8 can be replaced as specified in the proof of Theorem 5. □

Additionally, the following can be derived from [3], based on ideas on P systems.

An insertion-deletion P system is a construct $\Pi = (O, T, \mu, M_1, \ldots, M_n, R_1, \ldots, R_n)$ where

- O is a finite alphabet,
- $T \subseteq O$ is the terminal alphabet,
- μ is the tree structure of the system which has n nodes,
- M_i, $1 \leq i \leq n$, is a finite language associated to the membrane i,
- R_i, $1 \leq i \leq n$, is a set of insertion and deletion rules with target indicators of the node i. Rules are of the form: $(u, x, v; \text{tar})$, where (u, x, v) is an insertion rule or a deletion rule, and $\text{tar} \in \{\text{here}, \text{in}_j, \text{out} \mid 1 \leq j \leq n\}$.

A configuration of Π is an n-tuple $(N_1, \ldots, N_n)$ of finite languages over O. The transition between two configurations consists in applying rules in parallel to all possible strings, non-deterministically with respect to the target indications associated with the rules. A sequence of transitions between configurations of a given insertion-deletion P system Π starting from the initial configuration is called a computation with respect to Π. The result of Π's computations $L(\Pi)$ consists of all strings over T sent out of the root node during its computations.

An insertion-deletion P system has priority of deletion rules over insertion rules if a rule $(u_1, x_1, v_1; \text{tar}_1)$, where (u_1, x_1, v_1) is an insertion rule, is only allowed to be applied if no rule $(u_2, x_2, v_2; \text{tar}_2)$, where (u_2, x_2, v_2) is a deletion rule, is applicable.

Theorem 11. $MAT_*^{ac}INS_1^{0,1}DEL_1^{0,0} = RE$.

Proof. Consider an insertion-deletion P system with priority of deletion rules over insertion rules. It is known that such systems with insertion rules of size $(1, 0, 1)$ and deletion rules of size $(1, 0, 0)$ are computationally complete, see [3]. We now show that such an insertion-deletion P system with priority of deletion rules over insertion rules can be simulated by an matrix ins-del system with appearance checking of size $(*; 1, 0, 1; 1, 0, 0)$.

Let $\Pi = (O, T, \mu, M_1, \ldots, M_n, R_1, \ldots, R_n)$ be such a system. An equivalent matrix ins-del system with appearance checking $MID_\varsigma = (O \cup \{1, \ldots, n\} \cup \{X\}, T, A, M_\varsigma, F)$, where X is a trap symbol, is constructed as follows. We define $A = \{wi \mid w \in M_i\}$. For every deletion rule $(\lambda, x, \lambda; \mathrm{tar}) \in R_i$ we add a matrix $[(\lambda, i, \lambda)_{\mathrm{del}}, (\lambda, x, \lambda), (\lambda, k, \lambda)_{\mathrm{ins}}]$ to M_ς, where $k = i$ if $\mathrm{tar} = \mathrm{here}$, $k = j$ if $\mathrm{tar} = \mathrm{in}_j$ and $k = i'$ if $\mathrm{tar} = \mathrm{out}$ and i' is the parent node of i. Furthermore, if the node i has no parent node and if the deletion rule $(\lambda, x, \lambda; \mathrm{out})$ is in R_i, then we add the matrix $[(\lambda, i, \lambda)_{\mathrm{del}}, (\lambda, x, \lambda)]$ to M_ς.

Let $K_i = \{(\lambda, x_1, \lambda), \ldots, (\lambda, x_m, \lambda)\}$ denote the set of all deletion rules, such that $(\lambda, x_\tau, \lambda; \mathrm{tar}) \in R_i$ iff $(\lambda, x_\tau, \lambda) \in K_i$. For every insertion rule $(\lambda, x, v; \mathrm{tar}) \in R_i$ we add the matrix

$$[(\lambda, i, \lambda)_{\mathrm{del}}, (\lambda, X, x_1)_{\mathrm{ins}}, \ldots, (\lambda, X, x_m)_{\mathrm{ins}}, (\lambda, x, v), (\lambda, k, \lambda)_{\mathrm{ins}}]$$

to M_ς, where $k = i$ if $\mathrm{tar} = \mathrm{here}$, $k = j$ if $\mathrm{tar} = \mathrm{in}_j$ and $k = i'$ if $\mathrm{tar} = \mathrm{out}$ and i' is the parent node of i. In case the node i has no parent node we add

$$[(\lambda, i, \lambda)_{\mathrm{del}}, (\lambda, X, x_1)_{\mathrm{ins}}, \ldots, (\lambda, X, x_m)_{\mathrm{ins}}, (\lambda, x, v), (\lambda, k, \lambda)_{\mathrm{ins}}]$$

to M_ς. All insertion rules, which introduce the trap symbol X are added to F. The basic is as follows. By definition of Π an insertion rule $(\lambda, x, v; \mathrm{tar}) \in R_i$ can only be applied if no deletion rule $(\lambda, x_\tau, \lambda; \mathrm{out}) \in R_i$ is applicable. In other words, $(\lambda, x, v; \mathrm{tar})$ can only be applied if the current sentential form does not have any occurrence of $x_1, \ldots, x_m$. This is simulated via the insertion rules $(\lambda, X, x_1)_{\mathrm{ins}}, \ldots, (\lambda, X, x_m)_{\mathrm{ins}}$ in our matrices. Clearly if any of these rules is applicable a trap symbol is introduced.

As the language generated by Π consist of all words over T sent outside of the system during the computation, it can be shown, that $L(\Pi) = L(MID_\varsigma)$. $\square$

4   Conclusion

We have shown that matrix ins-del systems do not need much context to reach computational completeness if substitution rules *and* appearance checking are used. For instance, we have shown that in this setting no context other than single symbol context for deletion rules is necessary for computational completeness. In the case of no context other than single symbol context for insertion rules, we have shown that appearance checking is a necessary and sufficient feature to ensure computational completeness.

References

1. Ábrahám, S.: Some questions of phrase-structure grammars. I. Comput. Linguist. **4**, 61–70 (1965)
2. Alhazov, A., Krassovitskiy, A., Rogozhin, Y., Verlan, S.: Small size insertion and deletion systems. In: Martin-Vide, C. (ed.) Applications of Language Methods, Imperial College Press, pp. 459–515 (2010)
3. Alhazov, A., Krassovitskiy, A., Rogozhin, Y., Verlan, S.: P systems with minimal insertion and deletion. Theor. Comput. Sci. **412**(1–2), 136–144 (2011)
4. Beaver, D.: Computing with DNA. J. Comput. Biol. **2**(1), 1–7 (1995)
5. Dassow, J., Păun, Gh.: Regulated Rewriting in Formal Language Theory. EATCS Monographs in Theoretical Computer Science, vol. 18. Springer Publishing Company, Incorporated (1989)
6. Fernau, H., Kuppusamy, L., Raman, I.: Investigations on the power of matrix insertion-deletion systems with small sizes. Nat. Comput. **17**(2), 249–269 (2017). https://doi.org/10.1007/s11047-017-9656-8
7. Fernau, H., Kuppusamy, L., Raman, I.: On matrix ins-del systems of small sumnorm. In: Catania, B., Královič, R., Nawrocki, J., Pighizzini, G. (eds.) SOFSEM 2019. LNCS, vol. 11376, pp. 192–205. Springer, Cham (2019). https://doi.org/10.1007/978-3-030-10801-4_16
8. Hauschildt, D., Jantzen, M.: Petri net algorithms in the theory of matrix grammars. Acta Informatica **31**, 719–728 (1994)
9. Kari, L.: On insertions and deletions in formal languages. Ph.D. thesis, University of Turku, Finland (1991)
10. Karl, L.: DNA computing: arrival of biological mathematics. Math. Intelligencer **19**(2), 9–22 (1997). https://doi.org/10.1007/BF03024425
11. Kari, L., Păun, Gh., Thierrin, G., Yu, S.: At the crossroads of DNA computing and formal languages: characterizing recursively enumerable languages using insertion-deletion systems. In: Rubin, H., Wood, D.H. (eds.) DNA Based Computers III, DIMACS Series in Discrete Mathematics and Theretical Computer Science, vol. 48, pp. 329–338 (1999)
12. Krassovitskiy, A., Rogozhin, Y., Verlan, S.: Computational power of insertion-deletion (P) systems with rules of size two. Nat. Comput. **10**, 835–852 (2011)
13. Kuppusamy, L., Mahendran, A., Krishna, S.N.: Matrix insertion-deletion systems for bio-molecular structures. In: Natarajan, R., Ojo, A. (eds.) ICDCIT 2011. LNCS, vol. 6536, pp. 301–312. Springer, Heidelberg (2011). https://doi.org/10.1007/978-3-642-19056-8_23
14. Kuppusamy, L., Mahendran, A., Krishna, S.N.: On representing natural languages and bio-molecular structures using matrix insertion-deletion systems and its computational completeness. In: Bel-Enguix, G., Dahl, V., de la Puente, A.O. (eds.) Proceedings of the 1st International Workshop on AI Methods for Interdisciplinary Research in Language and Biology (ICAART 2011). Science and Technology Publications, pp. 47–56 (2011)
15. Petre, I., Verlan, S.: Matrix insertion-deletion systems. Theor. Comput. Sci. **456**, 80–88 (2012)
16. Verlan, S.: Recent developments on insertion-deletion systems. Comput. Sci. J. Moldova **18**(2), 210–245 (2010)
17. Vu, M.: On insertion-deletion systems with substitution rules. Master's thesis, Informatikwissenschaften, Universität Trier, Germany (2019)

18. Vu, M., Fernau, H.: Insertion-deletion systems with substitutions I. In: Anselmo, M., Della Vedova, G., Manea, F., Pauly, A. (eds.) CiE 2020. LNCS, vol. 12098, pp. 366–378. Springer, Cham (2020). https://doi.org/10.1007/978-3-030-51466-2_33
19. Vu, M., Fernau, H.: Insertion-deletion with substitutions II. In: Jirásková, G., Pighizzini, G. (eds.) DCFS 2020. LNCS, vol. 12442, pp. 231–243. Springer, Cham (2020). https://doi.org/10.1007/978-3-030-62536-8_19

Sorting by Multi-cut Rearrangements

Laurent Bulteau[1], Guillaume Fertin[2](✉) [ID], Géraldine Jean[2][ID],
and Christian Komusiewicz[3][ID]

[1] LIGM, CNRS, Univ Gustave Eiffel, ESIEE Paris, 77454 Marne-la-Vallée, France
`laurent.bulteau@univ-eiffel.fr`
[2] Université de Nantes, CNRS, LS2N, 44000 Nantes, France
`guillaume.fertin@univ-nantes.fr, geraldine.jean@univ-nantes.fr`
[3] Fachbereich für Mathematik und Informatik, Philipps-Universität Marburg,
Marburg, Germany
`komusiewicz@informatik.uni-marburg.de`

Abstract. Let S be a string built on some alphabet Σ. A *multi-cut rearrangement* of S is a string S' obtained from S by an operation called *k-cut rearrangement*, that consists in (1) cutting S at a given number k of places in S, making S the concatenated string $X_1 \cdot X_2 \cdot X_3 \ldots X_k \cdot X_{k+1}$, where X_1 and X_{k+1} are possibly empty, and (2) rearranging the X_is so as to obtain $S' = X_{\pi(1)} \cdot X_{\pi(2)} \cdot X_{\pi(3)} \ldots X_{\pi(k+1)}$, π being a permutation on $1, 2 \ldots k + 1$ satisfying $\pi(1) = 1$ and $\pi(k + 1) = k + 1$. Given two strings S and T built on the same multiset of characters from Σ, the SORTING BY MULTI-CUT REARRANGEMENTS (SMCR) problem asks whether a given number ℓ of k-cut rearrangements suffices to transform S into T. The SMCR problem generalizes and thus encompasses several classical genomic rearrangements problems, such as SORTING BY TRANSPOSITIONS and SORTING BY BLOCK INTERCHANGES. It may also model *chromoanagenesis*, a recently discovered phenomenon consisting in massive simultaneous rearrangements. In this paper, we study the SMCR problem from an algorithmic complexity viewpoint, and provide, depending on the respective values of k and ℓ, polynomial-time algorithms as well as NP-hardness, FPT-algorithms, W[1]-hardness and approximation results, either in the general case or when S and T are permutations.

1 Introduction

Genome rearrangements refer to large-scale evolutionary events that affect the genome of a species. They include among others reversals [1], transpositions [2], and block interchanges [5]; see also [9] for a full description. Compared to small-scale evolutionary events such as insertion, deletion or substitution of single DNA nucleotides, they are considered to be rare and, until recently, were assumed to happen one after the other. In the recent literature, however, a new type of event,

GF was partially supported by the PHC Procope program 17746PC
GJ was partially supported by the PHC Procope program 17746PC
CK was partially supported by the DAAD Procope program 57317050.

© Springer Nature Switzerland AG 2021
T. Bureš et al. (Eds.): SOFSEM 2021, LNCS 12607, pp. 593–607, 2021.
https://doi.org/10.1007/978-3-030-67731-2_43

called *chromoanagenesis*, has been shown to occur in genomes [12,13]. The term chromoanagenesis subsumes different types of rearrangements (namely, chromothripsis, chromoanasynthesis and chromoplexy) whose common ground is the following: in a single event, the genome is cut into many blocks, and then rearranged. As stated by Pellestor and Gatinois [12], these are "massive chromosomal rearrangements arising during single chaotic cellular events". Chromoanagenesis, and notably chromothripsis, is suspected to play a role in cancer and congenital diseases [13]. In this paper, we introduce a new model for genome rearrangements that is general enough to encompass most of the previously described genome rearrangements [9] as well as chromoanagenesis. Our goal here is to study its properties in terms of computational complexity.

Notation. Given an alphabet Σ, we say that two strings $S \in \Sigma^*$ and $T \in \Sigma^*$ are *balanced* if S and T are built on the same multiset of characters—in other words, each character in S also appears in T in the same number of occurrences. We denote by $|S|$ the length of a string S. Unless otherwise stated, we assume that $|S| = |T| = n$. We denote by S_i, $1 \le i \le n$, the i-th character of S. Given a string S in Σ^*, we denote by d the maximum number of occurrences of any character of Σ in S. In the specific case where $d = 1$ (i.e. when S and T are permutations), and for any $0 \le i \le n$, we say that there is a *breakpoint* at position i in S (or, equivalently, that (S_i, S_{i+1}) is a breakpoint) if the two consecutive characters S_i and S_{i+1} are not consecutive in T. For the specific cases $i = 0$ and $i = n$, we artificially set $S_0 = T_0 = \alpha_0$ and $S_{n+1} = T_{n+1} = \alpha_{n+1}$ where $\alpha_0 \notin \Sigma$ and $\alpha_{n+1} \notin \Sigma$. Thus, there is a breakpoint at position 0 (resp. n) in S whenever $S_1 \ne T_1$ ($S_n \ne T_n$). We also denote by $b(S,T)$ the number of *breakpoints* in S with respect to T. If (S_i, S_{i+1}) is not a breakpoint, we say that it is an *adjacency*.

Definition 1. *Given a string $S \in \Sigma^*$ and an integer k, a k-cut rearrangement of S is an operation consisting in the two following steps: (1) cut S at k locations (thus S can be written as the concatenation of $k + 1$ strings, i.e. $S = X_1 \cdot X_2 \cdot X_3 \ldots X_{k+1}$, where each X_i is possibly empty, and where a cut occurs between X_i and X_{i+1}, $1 \le i \le k$) and (2) rearrange (i.e., permute) the X_is so as to obtain $S' = X_{\pi(1)} \cdot X_{\pi(2)} \cdot X_{\pi(3)} \ldots X_{\pi(k+1)}$, π being a permutation on the elements $1, 2 \ldots k+1$ such that $\pi(1) = 1$ and $\pi(k+1) = k+1$. Each of the X_is considered in a given k-cut rearrangement will be called a* block.

Note that, although a k-cut rearrangement has been defined as a cut along the string at k locations, it is always possible, if necessary, to perform only $k' \le k$ cuts at a given step—thus mimicking a k-cut rearrangement while actually realizing a k'-cut rearrangement—by cutting several times at the same location. The case where X_1 (resp. X_{k+1}) is empty corresponds to the case where the leftmost (resp. rightmost) block of S is moved to obtain S', otherwise X_1 (resp. X_{k+1}) remains unmoved in S'. Note that, in this model, each of the blocks X_is can only be permuted, thus no reversal of an X_i is allowed, and therefore the strings we consider are always unsigned. In this paper, we study the following problem.

SORTING BY MULTI-CUT REARRANGEMENTS (SMCR)
Instance: Two balanced strings S and T, two integers ℓ and k.
Question: Is there a sequence of at most ℓ many k-cut rearrangements that transforms S into T?

For convenience, we may also refer to the SMCR problem with parameters k and ℓ as the (k, ℓ)–SMCR problem. Our goal in this paper is to provide algorithmic results regarding SMCR. The computational complexity of SMCR highly depends on whether we set bounds on k and ℓ: depending on applications, they can either be fixed constants (and in that case algorithms running in e.g. $O(n^k)$ are acceptable), parameters (unbounded, but far smaller than n, then algorithms in $f(k) \cdot \text{poly}(n)$—that is, Fixed-Parameter Tractable (or FPT) algorithms [7,8] —would be relevant even for fast-growing functions f), or parts of the input (i.e. unbounded, and in that case only polynomial-time algorithms on n and k are relevant). Hence, we will consider each of these cases for both ℓ and k. For this study, we will consider separately the case of strings (i.e., $d > 1$ both in S and T) from the case of permutations (i.e., $d = 1$ both in S and T), in Sects. 2 and 3, respectively.

Basic Observations. Both in permutations and strings, the cases $k = 1$ and $k = 2$ are trivial, since they do not allow to move any block, and thus we are in presence of a YES-instance iff $S = T$.

Additionally, the SMCR problem is a natural generalization and extension of a certain number of problems that have already been defined and studied in the literature before, as described hereafter.

When $k = 3$, each k-cut rearrangement is necessarily a transposition of blocks X_2 and X_3. Thus SMCR in that case is equivalent to the SORTING BY TRANSPOSITIONS problem [2], for which we know it is NP-hard, even if S and T are permutations [3].

When $k = 4$, each k-cut rearrangement allows to move two blocks among X_2, X_3 and X_4, which exactly corresponds to the SORTING BY BLOCK INTER-CHANGE problem. This problem is known to be in P for permutations [5] and NP-hard for strings (an NP-hardness proof for binary strings is given in [6], Theorem 5.7.2).

When $\ell = 1$, the SMCR problem comes down to deciding whether k cuts are sufficient to rearrange S into T in one atomic move (i.e., one k-cut rear-rangement). In permutations, the problem is trivially solved by counting the number $b(S, T)$ of breakpoints between S and T, since we have a YES-instance iff $b(S, T) \leq k$. In strings, the SMCR problem resembles the MINIMUM COMMON STRING PARTITION problem [11], as will be discussed in Theorems 3 and 4.

When ℓ and k are constant, SMCR is trivially polynomial-time solvable, since a brute-force algorithm, exhaustively testing all possible k-cut rearrangements at each of the ℓ authorized moves, has a running time of $O(n^{k\ell+1})$—the additional n factor being needed to verify that the result corresponds to string T.

It is also natural to wonder whether (k, ℓ)-SMCR and $(k\ell, 1)$-SMCR are equivalent. It can be easily seen that a YES-instance for (k, ℓ)-SMCR is also a YES-instance for $(k\ell, 1)$-SMCR: it suffices for this to aggregate all cuts from the (k, ℓ)-SMCR solution (of which there are at most $k\ell$), and rearrange accordingly. However, the reverse (i.e. from $(k\ell, 1)$-SMCR to (k, ℓ)-SMCR) is not always true. For example, take $S = \mathtt{afedcbg}$, $T = \mathtt{abcdefg}$, $k = 3$, and $\ell = 2$: this is a YES-instance for $(6, 1)$-SMCR, whereas it is a NO-instance for $(3, 2)$-SMCR. Indeed, in this instance the number $b(S, T)$ of breakpoints is equal to 6. Thus, in the former case, the 6 following cuts (symbolized as vertical segments) in $S = \mathtt{a|f|e|d|c|b|g}$ suffice to obtain T after a single 6-cut rearrangement. In the latter case, every 3-cut rearrangement is a transposition, and in this instance no transposition can decrease $b(S, T)$ by 3. Thus at least three 3-cut rearrangements are necessary to transform S into T.

2   Sorting by Multi-cut Rearrangements in Strings

In this section, we provide algorithmic results concerning the SORTING BY MULTI-CUT REARRANGEMENTS problem, in the general case where S and T are strings. Our results are summarized in Table 1.

Table 1. Summary of the results for SORTING BY MULTI-CUT REARRANGEMENTS in strings. d is the maximum number of occurrences of a character in the input string S.

ℓ \ k	$O(1)$	parameter	part of the input
1	P	FPT(Thm 4)	NP-hard:
$O(1)$			for $\ell = 1$ even when $d = 2$ (Thm 3)
parameter		?	for any fixed $\ell \geq 1$ (Thm 2)
part of the input		for any $k \geq 5$ even in k-ary strings (Thm 1)	
		for $k = 3, 4$ even in binary strings [3,6]	

As mentioned in the previous section, we know that SMCR is NP-hard in binary strings for $k = 3, 4$. In the following theorem, we extend this result to any value of k, however in larger alphabet strings.

Theorem 1. SMCR *is NP-hard for any fixed $k \geq 5$, even in k-ary strings.*

Proof. We reduce the NP-hard 3-PARTITION problem in which the input is a set $\mathcal{A}$ of integers and an integer B, and the question is whether $\mathcal{A}$ can be partitioned into triples such that the integers of each triple sum up to B. Given an instance of 3-PARTITION $(\mathcal{A}, B)$ with $\mathcal{A} = \{a_1, a_2, \ldots, a_{3m}\}$ and $mB = \sum_{i=1}^{3m} a_i$, we construct an instance of SMCR for any fixed $k \geq 5$ as follows. For ease of presentation, we assume that each a_i is a multiple of $4m$ and that $\frac{B}{4} < a_i < \frac{B}{2}$, so that we have the following property: If for some subset I of $\{1, \ldots, 3m\}$ and some δ with $0 \leq \delta \leq 4\,m$ we have $\sum_{i \in I} a_i + \delta = B + 4$, then $\sum_{i \in I} a_i = B$, $\delta = 4$, and $|I| = 3$. We use a size-k alphabet $\{0, 1, \ldots, k-1\}$, we denote by X the string $k-1 \cdot k-2 \cdot \ldots 3$, and by X' the reverse of X, i.e. $3 \cdot 4 \cdot \ldots \cdot k-1$ (note that X and X' have length $k - 3 \geq 2$). We define $S := 10^{a_1} 10^{a_2} \ldots 10^{a_{3m}} 1(20X0X0X0)^m 2$ and $T := (1X')^{3m} 1(20^{B+4})^m 2$, and set $\ell = 3\,m$. This completes the construction. Before proving its correctness, we group the adjacencies of the strings S and T based on whether the adjacencies of the two involved characters are in excess in S, in T, or equal in both strings.

- *Group 1* contains the adjacencies $(0, 1), (1, 0), (0, k-1), (k-1, k-2), \ldots, (4, 3)$, and $(3, 0)$ which each occur $3\,m$ times in S and which do not occur in T.
- *Group 2* contains the adjacencies $(0, 0)$, which occur $Bm - 3\,m$ times in S and $Bm + 3\,m$ times in T, and the adjacencies $(1, 3), (3, 4), \ldots, (k-2, k-1), (k-, 1)$ which do not occur in S, and occur $3\,m$ times each in T.
- *Group 3* contains the adjacencies $(0, 2)$ and $(2, 0)$ which each occur m times in S and in T.

There are no further adjacencies in S or T. To show the correctness of the reduction we show that $(\mathcal{A}, B)$ is a Yes-instance of 3-Partition iff there exists a sequence of at most $\ell = 3\,m$ many k-cut rearrangements transforming S into T.

($\Rightarrow$) Pick a solution of 3-Partition. For each triple (a_i, a_j, a_p) of the solution, choose a unique substring $20X0X0X0$ of S and perform the following three k-cut rearrangements: First, cut S around 0^{a_i} and around the first copy of X in the chosen subsequence, and cut at every position inside X. Observe that the number of cuts is exactly k. Now reverse X into X' and exchange 0^{a_i} and X'. Perform a similar k-cut rearrangement with a_j and the second occurrence of X and with a_p and the third occurrence of X in the selected substring. The selected substring is transformed into $200^{a_i} 00^{a_j} 00^{a_k} 0 = 20^{B+4}$ and since each string 0^{a_i} is replaced by X', the first part of the string is $(1X')^{3m}$. Hence, the string obtained by the $3\,m$ many k-cut rearrangements described above is T.

($\Leftarrow$) There are altogether $6\,m + (k-2)3\,m = 3\,km$ adjacencies in Group 1 which are in excess in S, and $3\,km$ adjacencies in Group 2 which are in excess in T. Since $\ell = 3\,m$, each k-cut rearrangement cuts k adjacencies in Group 1 (and no adjacency in Group 2 or 3). In particular, no 00 adjacency may be cut in a feasible solution, so each subsequence 0^{B+4} in T is obtained by concatenating a number of strips of the form 0^{a_i} as well as some number δ of 0 singletons. Since S has $4\,m$ of these singleton 0s, we have $0 \leq \delta \leq 4\,m$. By the constraint on the values of a_i, each subsequence 0^{B+4} in T contains four singletons from S and three substrings 0^{a_i} of S whose lengths sum to B. Thus, the m substrings 0^{B+4} in T correspond to a partition of $\mathcal{A}$ into m sets of three integers whose values sum up to B. □

Theorem 2. SMCR *is NP-hard for any fixed* ℓ.

Proof. The reduction being very similar to the one of Theorem 1, we only highlight the differences to have a fixed ℓ instead of fixed k. First assume that m is a multiple of ℓ (add up to ℓ triples of dummy elements otherwise), and let $k = \frac{15m}{\ell}$. Note that k is a multiple of 5. The reduction is the same as above with a size-5 alphabet. In other words, we have $X = 43$ and $X' = 34$.

In the forward direction, use the described scenario using 5-cut rearrangements, but combine a series of $k/5$ such rearrangements into a single k-cut rearrangement, as described at the end of Sect. 1. This gives a total of $\frac{3m}{k/5} = \ell$ many k-cut rearrangements sorting S into T. In the reverse direction, the same breakpoint count holds, namely $3\,\text{k'm}$ adjacencies need to be broken using ℓ k-cut rearrangements, with $\ell k = 3\,\text{k'm}$. So again no 00 adjacency may be broken, and by the same argument, we obtain a valid 3-partition of $\mathcal{A}$. ☐

The previous theorem shows NP-hardness of SMCR for any fixed ℓ. However, a stronger result can be obtained in the specific case $\ell = 1$.

Theorem 3. SMCR *is NP-hard when* $\ell = 1$, *even when* $d = 2$.

Proof. The proof is obtained by reduction from the MINIMUM COMMON STRING PARTITION problem, which has been proved to be NP-hard in strings, even when $d = 2$ [11]. Recall that the decision version of MCSP asks, given two balanced strings S and T, and an integer p, whether S can be written as the concatenation of p blocks $S = X_1 \cdot X_2 \ldots X_{p-1} \cdot X_p$ and T can be written as $T = X_{\pi(1)} \cdot X_{\pi(2)} \ldots X_{\pi(p-1)} \cdot X_{\pi(p)}$, where π is a permutation of $1, 2 \ldots p$. Note that here we may have $\pi(1) = 1$ and/or $\pi(p) = p$.

Given an instance (S, T, p) of MCSP, we build an instance (S', T', k, ℓ) of SMCRby setting $S' = x \cdot S$, $T' = T \cdot x$ (with $x \notin \Sigma$), $k = p + 2$ and $\ell = 1$. Clearly, if (S, T, p) is a YES-instance for MCSP, then $(S', T', p + 2, 1)$ is a YES-instance for SMCR: the MCSP solution uses $p - 1$ cuts, to which we add one before x, one after x, and one after S_n for solving SMCR. Conversely, if SMCR is a YES-instance for SMCR, and since x occurs only once in S', then $S'_1 = x$, and thus 2 cuts are used to "isolate" x from S'. Besides, since T' ends with x, there must exist a cut after the last character of S'. Hence, since $S' = x \cdot S$, at most $k - 3 = p - 1$ cuts are used strictly within S, which in turns means that S has been decomposed in p blocks, which can be rearranged so as to obtain T since $\ell = 1$. Thus, (S, T, p) is a YES-instance for MCSP. ☐

Note that MCSP has been proved to be in FPT with respect to the size of the solution [4]. It can be seen that this result can be adapted for the SMCR problem in the case $\ell = 1$.

Theorem 4. *When* $\ell = 1$, SMCR *is FPT with respect to parameter* k.

Proof. Assuming $S \neq T$, let A (resp. B) be the length of the longest common prefix (resp. suffix) of S and T. For $0 \leq a \leq A$ and $0 \leq b \leq B$, let $S_{a,b}, T_{a,b}$ be the strings obtained from S, T by removing the first a and last b characters. Then T can be obtained from S by one k-cut rearrangement if and only if, for some pair (a, b), $S_{a,b}$ and $T_{a,b}$ admit a common string partition into $k - 1$ blocks. Indeed, this is easy to verify by matching the limits of the blocks in MCSP (including at the end of the strings) with the cuts of the rearrangement. So SMCR when $\ell = 1$ can be solved using $O(n^2)$ calls to MCSP with parameter $k - 1$, each with a different pair (a, b), which itself is FPT for k [4].   □

Note that it is not sufficient to check only with the longest common prefix and suffix (i.e. $S_{A,B}$ and $T_{A,B}$), as can be seen in the following example, where S can be transformed into T via one 3-cut rearrangement, $A = B = 2$, but only $S_{1,1}$ and $T_{1,1}$ have a common partition into 2 blocks: $S = $ a acb adb b and $T = $ a adb acb b.

3   Sorting by Multi-cut Rearrangements in Permutations

In this section, we provide algorithmic results concerning the SORTING BY MULTI-CUT REARRANGEMENTS problem, in the specific case where S and T are permutations. Our results are summarized in Table 2.

Table 2. Summary of the results for SORTING BY MULTI-CUT REARRANGEMENTS in permutations. *existence of a 2-approximation algorithm for OPT-SMCR (Theorem 8).

ℓ \ k	3	4	$O(1)$	parameter	part of the input
1 $O(1)$		P			
parameter	FPT (Thm 5)		FPT (Thm 5)	W[1]-hard (Thm 6)	
part of the input	NP-hard [3]		NP-hard (Thm 7) *		

Theorem 5. SMCR *in permutations is* FPT *with respect to parameter* $\ell + k$.

Proof. We obtain the fixed-parameter tractability result by using the following reduction rule: If there is a common adjacency (a, b) in S and T, then remove b from S and T. Before we show the correctness, observe that exhaustive application of the rule indeed gives the desired result: Any YES-instance that is reduced exhaustively with respect to the above rule has $O(k\ell)$ letters: We must cut between every adjacency in S. Overall, we may create at most $2k\ell$ cuts via ℓ many k-cut rearrangements. Hence, if S has more than $2k\ell$ adjacencies, then (S, T) is a NO-instance. Thus, after applying the rule exhaustively, we either know that the instance is a NO-instance or we may solve it in $f(k, \ell)$ time by using a brute-force algorithm. Thus it remains to show correctness of the rule. Consider an instance consisting of the permutations S and T to which the rule is applied and let S' and T' denote the resulting instance. We show that (S, T) is a YES-instance if and only if (S', T') is a YES-instance.

($\Rightarrow$) If (S, T) is a YES-instance, then there is a sequence of $\ell + 1$ permutations $(S = S_1, S_2, \ldots, S_{\ell+1} = T)$ such that S_{i+1} can be obtained from S_i via one

k-cut rearrangement. Removing b from S_i gives a sequence $(S_1', S_2', \ldots, S_{\ell+1}' = T)$ such that S_{i+1}' can be obtained from S_i' via one k-cut rearrangement.

($\Leftarrow$) If (S', T') is a YES-instance, then there is a sequence of $\ell + 1$ permutations $(S' = S_1', S_2', \ldots, S_{\ell+1}' = T')$ such that S_{i+1}' can be obtained from S_i' via one k-cut rearrangement. Replacing a by ab in each permutation S_i' gives a sequence $(S = S_1, S_2, \ldots, S_{\ell+1} = T)$ such that S_{i+1}' can be obtained from S_i' via one k-cut rearrangement. □

Theorem 6. SMCR *in permutations is W[1]-hard parameterized by* ℓ.

Proof. The proof is by reduction from UNARY BIN PACKING, whose instance is a multiset $\mathcal{A} = \{a_1, a_2, \ldots, a_n\}$ of integers encoded in unary, and two integers b and C. The goal is to decide whether one can partition $\mathcal{A}$ into b multisets $A_1, \ldots, A_b$, such that $\sum_{a_j \in A_i} a_j \leq C$, for each $1 \leq i \leq b$. This problem has been shown to be W[1]-hard [10] with respect to the number of multisets b, even when the sum of the elements $\sum_{i=1}^{n} a_i$ is equal to bC.

Take an instance I of UNARY BIN PACKING such that $\sum_{i=1}^{n} a_i = bC$. From I, we construct, in polynomial time, the following instance I^* of SMCR. We first define S as the following permutation of $[bC + 1]$:

$$S \quad := \quad 1\, X^1\, (\mathbf{a_1} + 1)\, X^2\, (\mathbf{a_1} + \mathbf{a_2} + 1)\, \ldots\, (\textstyle\sum_{i=1}^{n-1} \mathbf{a_i} + 1)\, X^n\, (\sum_{i=1}^{n} \mathbf{a_i} + 1),$$

where each X^i is the length-$(a_i - 1)$ decreasing sequence over $\{\sum_{j=1}^{i-1} a_j + 2, \ldots, \sum_{j=1}^{i} a_j\}$, that is, $X^i[k] := (\sum_{j=1}^{i} a_j) - (k - 1)$ for $1 \leq k \leq a_i - 1$. We set T to be the identity over the same alphabet $[bC + 1]$.

An element at position i in S is called an *anchor* if $S_i = i$ (in bold above). Since we want to transform S into the identity permutation, the anchors correspond to fixed points that are already well located. For any $1 \leq i \leq n$, the reversed sequence X^i is delimited by two anchors. We finally set $\ell = b$ and $k = C$. Each X^i has exactly a_i breakpoints: two at its extremities with the anchors and $a_i - 2$ internal ones. Since $\sum_{i=1}^{n} a_i = bC$, it can be seen that S contains exactly ℓk breakpoints. Since a k-cut rearrangement can remove at most k breakpoints, then at least ℓ such rearrangements are necessary to sort S. We now show that I is a YES-instance for UNARY BIN PACKING problem iff I^* is a YES-instance for SMCR.

($\Rightarrow$) Suppose I is a YES-instance for UNARY BIN PACKING. Thus there exists a partition $A_1 \ldots A_b$ of the multiset $\mathcal{A}$. To sort S, the k-cut rearrangements we apply consist in reversing the S^is. Note that in order to reverse a complete S^i corresponding to a given a_i, $1 \leq i \leq n$, we need exactly a_i cuts, e.g. to transform $\sigma = \ldots \mathbf{p+1}|p + a_i|p + a_i - 1|\ldots|p + 2|\mathbf{p + a_i + 1} \ldots$ into $\rho = \ldots (\mathbf{p+1})$ $(p + 2) \ldots (p + a_i - 1)(p + a_i)(\mathbf{p + a_i + 1}) \ldots$ (where $p = \sum_{k=1}^{i-1} a_k$).

For any $1 \leq i \leq b$, we have $\sum_{a_j \in A_i} a_j = C$ and since $C = k$, we can define a k-cut rearrangement that consists in reversing the $X^{j_1}, X^{j_2}, \ldots, X^{j_p}$ corresponding to elements $a_{j_1}, a_{j_2}, \ldots, a_{j_p}$ of A_i. Since there are b such multisets and since $b = \ell$, ℓ such k-cut rearrangements are sufficient to sort S.

($\Leftarrow$) Suppose I^* is a YES-instance for SMCR. Since $b(S, T) = \ell k$, using ℓ k-cut rearrangements to sort π means that each rearrangement removes exactly

k breakpoints. It is only feasible if each X^i is reversed at once (i.e., during a single k-cut rearrangement) using exactly a_i cuts. Indeed, if we cut at $c_i < a_i$ places in X^i, we will be able to fix strictly less than c_i breakpoints and so the k-cut rearrangement in which the c_i cuts take place will not remove k breakpoints as expected. By following the moves during the sorting of S, it suffices to see which X^is are reversed within the same k-cut rearrangement. In that case, the sum of the corresponding a_is is equal to $k = C$ and, using $\ell = b$, such multisets of a_is provide a solution to UNARY BIN PACKING. □

Theorem 7. *For any $k \geq 5$, SMCR in permutations is NP-hard.*

This hardness proof is by reduction from SORTING BY TRANSPOSITIONS on 3-cyclic permutations [3]. Intuitively, in such permutations, it is straightforward to identify triples of breakpoints, called 3-cycles, that should be solved together in a transposition, however the difficulty arises in selecting a correct order in which those 3-cycles should be solved. Our approach consists in extending these 3-cycles into k-cycles, such that any k-cut rearrangement solving the original cycle must solve all k breakpoints together, and still performs a simple transposition on the rest of the sequence (to this end, $k-3$ dummy elements are created in order to consume the extra blocks in k-cut rearrangements). We first recall the necessary definitions and properties for breakpoints and cyclic permutations, then show how to extend a single cycle by only two or three elements, and finally successively apply this method to extend *all* cycles to *any* size $k \geq 5$.

Breakpoints and Cycle Graph. For a permutation S of length n, we assume the alphabet of S is $\{1, \ldots, n\}$. We further write $S_0 = 0$ and $S_{n+1} = n + 1$. For a rearrangement r transforming S into S', we write $r(S) = S'$ and $r(S, T) = (S', T)$. The *cycle graph* $\mathcal{C}(S, T)$ of strings S and T is the graph over $n + 1$ vertices $\{0, \ldots n\}$ with arcs $T_j \to S_i$ if $T_{j+1} = S_{i+1}$. Every vertex has in-degree and out-degree 1, so the graph is a disjoint union of cycles. Self-loops are called *trivial cycles* (when seen as a cycle) or *adjacencies* (when seen as an arc), other arcs are *breakpoints*. An element (or vertex) x is an adjacency (resp. breakpoint) according to its outgoing arc (we use transparently the bijection between a vertex and its outgoing arc). A *k-cycle* is a cycle of length k. The *next breakpoint* of breakpoint $x \to y$ in $\mathcal{C}(S, T)$ is y (or equivalently, the outgoing arc of y). We write $\mathcal{C}_x(S, T)$ for the cycle of $\mathcal{C}(S, T)$ containing element x. A cycle graph is *k-cyclic* (and, by extension, a pair of sequences generating this cycle graph) if it contains only adjacencies and k-cycles. A rearrangement r applied to a permutation S *cuts* an element x, $0 \leq x \leq n$, if it cuts between $x = S_i$ and S_{i+1}. Furthermore, it *solves breakpoint* x if r cuts x and x is an adjacency in $r(S)$. It *solves a cycle* if it solves all breakpoints in it. We write $d_b(S, T)$ for the number of breakpoints of $\mathcal{C}(S, T)$. A k-cut rearrangement is *efficient* if it solves k breakpoints. A pair (S, T) is *k-efficiently sortable* if there exists a sequence of efficient k-cut rearrangements transforming S into T. The following is a trivial generalization of a well-known lower bound for the transposition distance.

Proposition 1. *A k-cut rearrangement may not solve more than k breakpoints, so S needs at least $\frac{d_b(S,T)}{k}$ k-cut rearrangements to be transformed into T. Furthermore, the bound is reached if and only if (S,T) is k-efficiently sortable.*

Proposition 2. *If r solves a breakpoint, it cuts the next breakpoint in the cycle graph.*

Proof. Let $x \to y$ be an arc of the cycle graph, and let x' be the successor of x in T as well as the successor of y in S. If r solves x, then r joins a block ending in x with a block starting in x', so x' is the first element of some block of r. Thus, y is the last element of some block of r, and r cuts the breakpoint y in $\mathcal{C}(S,T)$.   □

Proposition 3. *If r is efficient, it solves a cycle iff it solves any breakpoint in it. Furthermore r solves all breakpoints in a union of cycles of total size k.*

Proof. If r is efficient, then it solves all breakpoints that it cuts (since it may not solve a breakpoint without cutting them, and it solves and cuts k breakpoints). By Proposition 2, if r solves a breakpoint in a cycle, then it must solve all subsequent arcs in the same cycle. Hence, r either solves all breakpoints of a cycle or none at all. The size constraint follows from the fact that all cycles are disjoint.   □

Cycle C_1 is *tied* to another cycle C_2 through the pair of breakpoints (x,y) if x is in C_1, y is in C_2, the permutation S has $S_i = y$ and $S_{i+1} = x$ for some i, and T has $T_j = x$ and $T_j j + 1 = y$ for some y. A breakpoint is *without ties* if no cycle is tied to the cycle containing it.

Proposition 4. *If C_1 is tied to C_2, then any efficient rearrangement solving C_1 must also solve C_2.*

Proof. Let r be an efficient rearrangement solving C_1 and, in particular, x. Then r must place y after x in $r(S)$, although y is before x in S, so r must have a cut somewhere between y and x, i.e. just after y. So r cuts breakpoint y, and solves cycle C_2.   □

One-cycle Extensions. Let (S,T) be a pair of permutations. Let x be a vertex of $\mathcal{C}(S,T)$ with the following properties (we say that x is *safe*): x is either an adjacency or a breakpoint without ties in a cycle of length $k_x \geq 3$, and all 2-cycles in $\mathcal{C}(S,T)$ are tied. The *p-extension* of (S,T) on x, with $p \in \{2,3\}$, denoted $\phi_x^p(S,T)$ is the pair (S',T') such that:

- For $p = 2$:
  $$S' = (S_1, \ldots, S_i = x, n+2, S_{i+1}, \ldots, S_n, n+1) \qquad \text{if } x \text{ is an adjacency}$$
  $$S' = (S_1, \ldots, S_n, n+1, n+2) \qquad \text{if } x \text{ is a breakpoint}$$
  $$T' = (T_1, \ldots, T_j = x, n+2, T_{j+1} = S_{i+1}, \ldots T_n, n+1)$$
- For $p = 3$:
  $$S' = (S_1, \ldots, S_i = x, n+3, n+2, S_{i+1}, \ldots, S_n, n+1) \quad \text{if } x \text{ is an adjacency}$$
  $$S' = (S_1, \ldots, S_n, n+1, n+2, n+3) \qquad \text{if } x \text{ is a breakpoint}$$
  $$T' = (T_1, \ldots, T_j = x, n+3, n+2, T_{j+1} = S_{i+1}, \ldots T_n, n+1)$$

Lemma 1. *A p-extension on x has the following effects on the cycle graph:*

- *If x is an adjacency, it adds p trivial cycles.*
- *If x is a breakpoint and $p = 2$, it adds $n+1$ and $n+2$ to the cycle containing x.*
- *If x is a breakpoint and $p = 3$, it adds $n + 2$ to the cycle containing x and a 2-cycle $(n + 1, n + 3)$ tied to the one containing x.*

Other arcs and tied cycles are unchanged.

Proof. If x is an adjacency, the p-extension inserts elements $n+1$ to $n+p$ in both strings in the same order after x, and they are followed by the same element in both strings since x is an adjacency, so only trivial cycles are added.

Assume now that x is a breakpoint. Consider first an arc $T_j \to S_i$ with $T_j \neq x$ in $\mathcal{C}(S, T)$. Since no element is inserted after T_j or S_i, $T_j \to S_i$ also appears in $\mathcal{C}(S', T')$ (the case $i = j = n$ is particular, as $n + 1$ is explicitly introduced in both sequences, but it also yields the arc $T_j \to S_j$ in $\mathcal{C}(S', T')$). If a cycle is tied to another one through a pair (x, y) in S and (y, x) in T, these factors cannot be broken by the p-extension (since x is safe, no cycle can be tied to $\mathcal{C}_x(S, T)$), so it is still tied after the extension. Similarly, a non-tied cycle cannot become tied because of the extension.

It remains to describe arcs going out from $\{x, n+1, \ldots, n+p\}$. Let y be the head of the outgoing arc from x.

For j such that $T'_j = x$, we have $T'_{j+1} = n + p = S'_{n+p}$, so there exists an arc $x \to S'_{n+p-1} = n + p - 1$ in $\mathcal{C}(S', T')$ (note in particular that y no longer has its incoming arc $x \to y$).

For j such that $T'_j = n + 1$, we have $T'_{j+1} = n + p + 1 = S'_{n+p+1}$, so there exists an arc $n + 1 \to S'_{n+p} = n + p$ in $\mathcal{C}(S', T')$.

For $p = 3$ and j such that $T'_j = n+3$, we have $T'_{j+1} = n+2 = S'_{n+2}$, so there exists an arc $n + 3 \to S'_{n+1} = n + 1$ in $\mathcal{C}(S', T')$.

At this point, the out-going arcs for all vertices except $n + 2$ have been described, as well as in-coming arcs for all vertices except y, so the last remaining arc is $n + 2 \to y$.

Overall, for $p = 2$, arc $x \to y$ is replaced with the path $x \to n+1 \to n+2 \to y$. For $p = 3$, arc $x \to y$ is replaced with $x \to n+2 \to y$ and a 2-cycle $n+1 \leftrightarrow n+3$ is created. Note that this 2-cycle is tied to $\mathcal{C}_x(S', T')$ through $(n + 2, n + 3)$. $\quad\square$

We now show how efficient rearrangements can be adapted through extensions. Let r be a k-cut rearrangement of (S, T). We write $r' = \psi_x^p(r)$ for the k'-cut rearrangement of $(S', T') = \phi_x^p(S, T)$ defined as follows:

- If r does not cut x, then $k' = k$, r' cuts the same elements as r, and rearranges the blocks in the same order.
- If r cuts x, then $k' = k + p$, r' cuts the same elements as r as well as $n + 1$, $n + 2$ and $n + 3$ (when $p = 3$), and rearranges the blocks in the same way as r, with elements $n + 3$ (when $p = 3$) and $n + 2$ inserted after x.

The following two lemmas show how efficient rearrangements of (S, T) and those of $\phi_x(S, T)$ are related through ψ_x^p.

Lemma 2. *If r is an efficient k-cut rearrangement of (S,T), then $r' = \psi_x(r)$ is an efficient k'-rearrangement of $(S',T') = \phi_x^p(S,T)$. Furthermore $r'(S',T') = \phi_x^p(r(S,T))$.*

Proof. If r does not cut x, then $k' = k$ and r' solves in (S',T') exactly the same breakpoints as r, so it is efficient. Furthermore, all elements in $r'(S',T')$ and $\phi_x^p(r(S,T))$ are in the same order as in $r(S,T)$, except for $n+1, \ldots, n+p$ which are inserted, in both case, at the end of S and in T as in T' (since r and r' do not edit the second string).

If r cuts x, r' furthermore solves breakpoints $n+1, \ldots, n+p$, since it rearranges these elements in the same order as in T'. So it is an efficient rearrangement as well. Finally, all elements in $r'(S',T')$ and $\phi_x^p(r(S,T))$ are in the same order as in $r(S,T)$, except for $n+p, \ldots, n+2$ (which are inserted after x in both strings) and $n+1$ (which is inserted as a last element). □

Lemma 3. *If r' is an efficient k'-rearrangement of $(S',T') = \phi_x^p(S,T)$ with $k' \in \{k_x, k_x + p\}$, then there exists an efficient k-cut rearrangement r of (S,T) such that $r' = \psi_x(r)$, where $k = k' - p = k_x$ if r' cuts x and $k = k'$ otherwise. Furthermore, $r'(S',T') = \phi_x^p(r(S,T))$.*

Proof. We build r from r' using the converse operations of Lemma 2: mimicking the cuts and reordering of r', but ignoring cuts after $n+1, \ldots, n+p$ if r' cuts x. The relation between k and k' and the efficiency of r follow from the fact that r' solves either all of x, $n+1, \ldots n+p$, or none at all, as proven in the claim below. The 'furthermore' part follows from Lemma 2, applied to r.

Claim. Either r' solves all breakpoints in $\{x, n+1, \ldots, n+p\}$, or none at all.

Proof. For $p = 2$, this is a direct application of Proposition 3 since elements x, $n+1$ and $n+2$ are in the same cycle of $\mathcal{C}(S',T')$.

For $p = 3$, by Lemma 1, $C_x = C_x(S',T')$ is a $(k_x + 1)$-cycle containing x and $n+2$, and $\mathcal{C}(S',T')$ also contains a cycle denoted C_y with elements $n+1$ and $n+3$. By Proposition 3, r' solves any element in C_x (resp. C_y) iff it solves all elements in the same cycle (in particular, $k' \geq k_x + 1$ if r' cuts x, so $k' = k+p$). Furthermore C_y is tied to C_x, so if r' solves C_y it must also solve C_x (by Proposition 4). It remains to check the last direction: if r' solves C_x, then it also solves C_y. Indeed, C_x is a $k_x + 1$-cycle and r' solves a total of $k_x + 3$ breakpoints, so it must also solve some 2-cycle C_y'. Aiming at a contradiction, assume that $C_y' \neq C_y$. Then C_y' is already a 2-cycle of $\mathcal{C}(S,T)$, and it is tied to some other cycle C_x' (both in $\mathcal{C}(S,T)$ and $\mathcal{C}(S',T')$), so r' also solves C_x'. Since C_x' may not be equal to C_x (x was chosen without ties), r' solves at least $|C_x| + |C_y'| + |C_x'| > k_x + 3$ breakpoints, which yields a contradiction for a $k_x + 3$-rearrangement.

□

Extending all Cycles. We use the natural order over integers as an arbitrary total order over the nodes. The *representative* of a cycle is its minimum node.

We assume (S, T) to be k-cyclic for some k. A *sample* for (S, T), where (S, T) is k-cyclic is a list X containing the representative from each k-cycle, and an arbitrary number of adjacencies. The p-extensions of (S, T) for sample $X = (x_1, \ldots, x_\ell)$ and of a rearrangement r of (S, T) are, respectively, $\Phi_X^p(S, T) = \phi_{x_\ell}^p(\ldots \phi_{x_2}^p(\phi_{x_1}^p(S, T)) \ldots)$ and $\Psi_X^p(r) = \psi_{x_\ell}^p(\ldots \psi_{x_2}^p(\psi_{x_1}^p(r)) \ldots)$.

For x_i in the sample, we write $n_{x_i} = |S| + p \cdot (i - 1)$, i.e. n_{x_i} is the size of the strings on which $\phi_{x_i}^p$ is applied. Note that the above definition requires each x_i to be safe in $\phi_{x_{i-1}}^p(\ldots \phi_{x_1}^p(S, T) \ldots)$. This is indeed the case by Lemma 1: either $p = 2$, there are no 2-cycles, and all breakpoints are without ties, or $p = 3$, all 2-cycles are tied to a single cycle $C_{x_j}(S, T)$ with $j < i$, which are all different from $C_{x_i}(S, T)$ (since X is a sample and contains at most one element per cycle).

Proposition 5. *If (S, T) is k-cyclic, then $\Phi_X^2(S, T)$ is $(k + 2)$-cyclic.*

Proof. This follows from Lemma 1, since the 2-extension adds 2 elements to each k-cycle, so $\Phi_X^2(S, T)$ is $(k + 2)$-cyclic. $\square$

Lemma 4. *If r is an efficient k-cut rearrangement of (S, T) then $r' = \Psi_X^p(r)$ is an efficient $k + p$ rearrangement of $(S', T') = \Phi_X^p(S, T)$. Moreover, in this case, $r(S, T)$ is k-cyclic with sample X, and $\Phi_X^p(r(S, T)) = r'(\Phi_X^p(S, T))$.*

Conversely, any efficient $k + p$ rearrangement r' of $(S', T') = \Phi_X^p(S, T)$ can be written as $r' = \Psi_X^p(r)$ where r is an efficient k-cut rearrangement of (S, T).

Proof. Given a k-cut rearrangement r, let

$$(S^0, T^0) = (S, T) \quad (S^j, T^j) = \phi_{x_j}^p(S^{j-1}, Tj - 1) \text{ for all } 0 < j \leq \ell$$

$$r_0 = r \quad (r_j, r_j) = \psi_{x_j}^p(r_{j-1}) \text{ for all } 0 < j \leq \ell \text{(Forward direction)}$$

Assuming that r is an efficient k-cut rearrangement of (S, T), since (S, T) is k-cyclic, by Proposition 3 r must solve a single cycle of $\mathcal{C}(S, T)$. Let x be the representative of this cycle: x is the only breakpoint of X cut by r, and $x = x_i$ for some i. Furthermore, $\mathcal{C}(r(S, T))$ is also k-cyclic with sample X (with one cycle less than $\mathcal{C}(S, T)$).

By Lemma 2 we have that r_j is an efficient k_j-cut rearrangement of (S^j, T^j) for each j, where $k_j = k_{j-1}$ if r_{j-1} does not cut x (i.e. $j \neq i$) and $k_j = k_{j-1} + p$ otherwise. So overall $r' = r_\ell$ is a an efficient $(k + p)$-cut rearrangement of $\Phi_X^p(S, T)$. The relationship $\Phi_X^p(r(S, T)) = r'(\Phi_X^p(S, T))$ also follows from Lemma 2.

The converse direction is proven similarly using Lemma 3, with a specific attention given to the size of the rearrangements: starting from r' (with $k + p$ cuts), the number of cuts remains constant, except for $\psi_{x_j}^p$ where it drops to k and then remains constant again (so the condition $k' \in \{k, k + p\}$ in Lemma 3 is indeed satisfied). $\square$

Lemma 5. *If (S, T) is k-cyclic with sample X, then (S, T) is k-efficiently sortable if and only if $\Phi_X^p(S, T)$ is k-efficiently sortable.*

Proof. This is a direct application of Lemma 4: a sequence of efficient k-cut rearrangements of (S, T) translates into a sequence of efficient $(k + p)$-cut rearrangements of $\Phi_X(S, T)$ through function Ψ_X (note that X remains a sample of (S, T) throughout the sequence of rearrangements).   □

Lemma 6. *For any odd $k \geq 5$, deciding whether a k-cyclic pair (S, T) is k-efficiently sortable is NP-hard. For any even $k \geq 6$, deciding whether a pair (S, T) is k-efficiently sortable is NP-hard.*

Proof. By induction on k. Deciding if a 3-cyclic pair (S, T) is efficiently sortable is NP-hard (cf. [3], where it is shown that deciding if a permutation can be sorted with $\frac{d_b(S,T)}{3}$ transpositions is NP-hard). For any $k \geq 5$, take $p = 2$ if k is odd and $p = 3$ otherwise, and consider a $(k - p)$-cyclic instance (S, T) and a sample X for (S, T) (note that one always exists): (S, T) is $(k - p)$-efficiently sortable iff $\Phi_X^p(S, T)$ is k-efficiently sortable by Lemma 5, and $\Phi_X^p(S, T)$ is k-cyclic for $p = 2$ by Proposition 5. This gives a polynomial reduction proving hardness for k (even when restricted to k-cyclic permutations when k is odd).   □

Theorem 7 is a corollary of Lemma 6, since a k-cyclic pair (S, T) is k-efficiently sortable iff S can be rearranged into T with no more than $\frac{d_b(S,T)}{k}$ k-cut rearrangements (Proposition 1).

Let OPT-SMCR be the optimisation version of SMCR, where we look for the smallest ℓ that is necessary to obtain T from S by k-cut rearrangements.

Theorem 8. OPT-SMCR *in permutations is 2-approximable.*

Proof. Let $I = (S, T, k)$ be an instance of OPT-SMCR. We first rewrite S and T into S' and T' in such a way that $T' = id_n$. Let $k' = \lfloor \frac{k}{2} \rfloor$. The algorithm consists in iterating the following three steps, starting from S': (a) rewrite S' by contracting adjacencies so as to obtain a permutation without fixed point, (b) cut around (i.e., right before and right after) the first k' elements $1, 2, 3 \ldots k'$ of that permutation, and (c) rearrange it so as to obtain $id_{k'}$ followed by the rest of the permutation. Steps (b) and (c) above actually correspond to the case where k is even. If k is odd, (b) and (c) are slightly modified, since we are left with an unused cut: (b') do as (b) and additionally cut to the left of $k' + 1$, (c') do as (c) but rearrange in such a way that k' and $k' + 1$ are consecutive.

Clearly, the optimal value ℓ for OPT-SMCR satisfies $\ell \geq \frac{b(S,T)}{k}$. Our algorithm removes at least k' (at least $k' + 1$) breakpoints at each iteration when k is even (when k is odd), and thus requires $\ell' \leq \frac{b(S,T)}{k'}$ ($\ell' \leq \frac{b(S,T)}{k'+1}$) many k-cut rearrangements. Altogether we have $\ell' \leq \frac{\ell k}{k'}$ if k is even and $\ell' \leq \frac{\ell k}{k'+1}$ if k is odd. Since $k' = \lfloor \frac{k}{2} \rfloor$, we conclude that $\ell' \leq 2\ell$.   □

4   Conclusion

We introduced SORTING BY MULTI-CUT REARRANGEMENTS, a generalization of usual genome rearrangement problems that do not incorporate reversals.

We discussed its classical computational complexity (P vs. NP-hard) and its membership in FPT with respect to the parameters ℓ and k. For this, we distinguished the case where S (and thus T) is a permutation from the case where it is a string.

The obvious remaining open problems are the ones indicated with a question mark in Tables 1 and 2, namely (a) the FPT status of SMCR with respect to parameter $\ell + k$ in strings, and (b) the computational complexity for constant ℓ and k part of the input in permutations. Extensions or variants of SMCR could also be studied, notably the one allowing reversals (and thus applicable to signed strings/permutations), or the one where T is the lexicographically ordered string derived from S. Finally, it would also be interesting to better understand the comparative roles of ℓ and k in SMCR, for instance by studying the following question: assuming k is increased by some constant c, what impact does it have on the optimal distance?

References

1. Bafna, V., Pevzner, P.A.: Genome rearrangements and sorting by reversals. SIAM J. Comput. **25**(2), 272–289 (1996)
2. Bafna, V., Pevzner, P.A.: Sorting by transpositions. SIAM J. Discret. Math. **11**(2), 224–240 (1998)
3. Bulteau, L., Fertin, G., Rusu, I.: Sorting by transpositions is difficult. SIAM J. Discrete Math. **26**(3), 1148–1180 (2012)
4. Bulteau, L., Komusiewicz, C.: Minimum common string partition parameterized by partition size is fixed-parameter tractable. In: Chekuri, C. (ed.) Proceedings of the Twenty-Fifth Annual ACM-SIAM Symposium on Discrete Algorithms, SODA 2014, Portland, Oregon, USA, January 5–7, 2014, pp. 102–121. SIAM (2014)
5. Christie, D.A.: Sorting permutations by block-interchanges. Inf. Process. Lett. **60**(4), 165–169 (1996)
6. Christie, D.A.: Genome rearrangement problems. Ph.D. thesis, University of Glasgow (1998)
7. Cygan, M., et al.: Parameterized Algorithms. Springer, Cham (2015). https://doi.org/10.1007/978-3-319-21275-3
8. Downey, R.G., Fellows, M.R.: Fundamentals of Parameterized Complexity. TCS. Springer, London (2013). https://doi.org/10.1007/978-1-4471-5559-1
9. Fertin, G., Labarre, A., Rusu, I., Tannier, E., Vialette, S.: Combinatorics of Genome Rearrangements. MIT Press, Computational molecular biology (2009)
10. Jansen, K., Kratsch, S., Marx, D., Schlotter, I.: Bin packing with fixed number of bins revisited. J. Comput. Syst. Sci. **79**(1), 39–49 (2013)
11. Goldstein, A., Kolman, P., Zheng, J.: Minimum common string partition problem: hardness and approximations. In: Fleischer, R., Trippen, G. (eds.) ISAAC 2004. LNCS, vol. 3341, pp. 484–495. Springer, Heidelberg (2004). https://doi.org/10.1007/978-3-540-30551-4_43
12. Pellestor, F., Gatinois, V.: Chromoanagenesis: a piece of the macroevolution scenario. Mol. Cytogenet. **13**(3) (2020). https://doi.org/10.1186/s13039-020-0470-0
13. Stephens, P.J., et al.: Massive genomic rearrangement acquired in a single catastrophic event during cancer development. Cell **144**, 27–40 (2011)

Graphs Cannot Be Indexed in Polynomial Time for Sub-quadratic Time String Matching, Unless SETH Fails

Massimo Equi$^{(\boxtimes)}$ (ID), Veli Mäkinen (ID), and Alexandru I. Tomescu (ID)

Department of Computer Science, University of Helsinki, Helsinki, Finland
{massimo.equi,veli.makinen,alexandru.tomescu}@helsinki.fi

Abstract. The string matching problem on a node-labeled graph $G = (V, E)$ asks whether a given pattern string P has an occurrence in G, in the form of a path whose concatenation of node labels equals P. This is a basic primitive in various problems in bioinformatics, graph databases, or networks, but only recently proven to have a $O(|E||P|)$-time lower bound, under the Orthogonal Vectors Hypothesis (OVH). We consider here its *indexed* version, in which we can index the graph in order to support time-efficient string queries.

We show that, under OVH, no polynomial-time indexing scheme of the graph can support querying P in time $O(|P| + |E|^\delta |P|^\beta)$, with either $\delta < 1$ or $\beta < 1$. As a side-contribution, we introduce the notion of *linear independent-components (lic) reduction* , allowing for a simple proof of our result. As another illustration that hardness of indexing follows as a corollary of a *lic* reduction, we also translate the quadratic conditional lower bound of Backurs and Indyk (STOC 2015) for the problem of matching a query string inside a text, under edit distance. We obtain an analogous *tight* quadratic lower bound for its indexed version, improving the recent result of Cohen-Addad, Feuilloley and Starikovskaya (SODA 2019), but with a slightly different boundary condition.

Keywords: Exact pattern matching · Indexing · Orthogonal vectors · Complexity theory · Reductions · Lower bounds · Edit distance · Graph query

1 Introduction

1.1 Background

The *String Matching in Labeled Graphs (SMLG)* problem is defined as follows.

Problem 1 (SMLG).

This work was partially funded by the European Research Council (ERC) under the European Union's Horizon 2020 research and innovation programme (grant agreement No. 851093, SAFEBIO) and by the Academy of Finland (grants No. 309048, 322595, 328877).

© Springer Nature Switzerland AG 2021
T. Bureš et al. (Eds.): SOFSEM 2021, LNCS 12607, pp. 608–622, 2021.
https://doi.org/10.1007/978-3-030-67731-2_44

INPUT: A directed graph $G = (V, E, \ell)$, where $\ell : V \to \Sigma$ is a function assigning to every node $v \in V$ a label $\ell(v)$ over an alphabet Σ, and a pattern string $P \in \Sigma^+$.

OUTPUT: *True* if and only if there is a path[1] $(v_1, v_2, \ldots, v_{|P|})$ in G such that $P[i] = \ell(v_i)$ holds for all $1 \leq i \leq |P|$.

This is a natural generalization of the problem of matching a string inside a text, and it is a primitive in various problems in computational biology, graph databases, and graph mining (see references in Equi et al. [19]). In genome research, the very first step of many standard analysis pipelines of high-throughput sequencing data is nowadays to align sequenced fragments of DNA on a labeled graph (a so-called *pangenome*) that encodes all genomes of a population [17, 25, 34, 40].

The SMLG problem can be solved in time $O(|V|+|E||P|)$ [7] in the comparison model. On acyclic graphs, bitparallelism can be used for improving the time to $O(|V| + |E|\lceil|P|/w\rceil)$ [39] in the RAM model with word size $w = \Theta(\log|E|)$. It remained an open question whether a truly sub-quadratic time algorithm for it exists. However, the recent conditional lower bounds by Backurs and Indyk [10] for regular expression matching imply that the SMLG problem cannot be solved in sub-quadratic time, unless the so-called *Orthogonal Vectors Hypothesis (OVH)* is false. This result was strengthened by Equi et al. [19] by showing that the problem remains quadratic under OVH even for directed acyclic graphs (DAGs) that are *deterministic*, in the sense that for every node, the labels of its out-neighbors are all distinct.

As mentioned above, in real-world applications one usually considers the *indexed* version of the SMLG problem. Namely, we are allowed to index the labeled graph so that we can query for pattern strings in possibly sub-quadratic time. This setting is motivated by the fact that typically the large input graph is static (e.g. a pangenome graph), while new query patterns are produced continuously (e.g. genome fragments from sequencing).

In the case when the graph is just a labeled (directed) path, then the problem asks about indexing a text string, which is a fundamental problem in string matching. There exists a variety of indexes constructable in *linear time* supporting *linear-time* queries [18]. The same holds also when the graph is a tree [23]. A trivial indexing scheme for arbitrary graphs is to enumerate all the possibly exponentially many paths of the graph and index those as strings. So a natural question is whether we can at least index the graph in polynomial time to support sub-quadratic time queries. Note that the conditional lower bound for the online problem naturally refutes the possibility of an index constructable in linear time to support sub-quadratic time queries. Even before the OVH-based reductions, another weak lower bound was known to hold conditioned on the *Set Intersection Conjecture (SIC)* [12, 29, 38] (see also Table 1). Recent results [28] also underlined the link between OV and SIC, and presented an index for

---

[1] Notice that if we further require that the path repeats no node (i.e. is a *simple* path) then SMLG becomes NP-hard, since the Hamiltonian path problem can be easily reduced to it, see e.g. [19].

Table 1. Upper bounds (first four rows) and conditional lower bounds for indexed SMLG on a graph $G = (V, E)$ and a pattern P. In this table, W is the maximum length of a node label, $f(\cdot)$ is an arbitrary function, N is the total length of an elastic degenerate string and n is the number of degenerate symbols. Recall that it is NP-complete to decide whether a given graph is a Wheeler graph, while for all the other graph types recognition is not harder than indexing.

Graph	Indexing time	Query time	Reference, Year
Path	$O(|E|)$	$O(|P|)$	Classical [18]
Tree	$O(|E|)$	$O(|P|)$	[23], 2009
Wheeler graph	$O(|E|)$	$O(|P|)$	[24,42], 2014
Segment repeat-free founder block graph	$O(W|E|)$	$O(|P|)$	[35], 2020
DAG	$O(|E|^\alpha), \alpha < 2$	$f(|P|)$ impossible under SIC	[12], 2013
Arbitrary graph	$O(|E|)$	$O(|P| + |E|^\delta|P|^\beta), \delta + \beta < 2$ impossible under OVH	[10], 2016
Deterministic DAG	$O(|E|)$	$O(|P| + |E|^\delta|P|^\beta), \delta + \beta < 2$ impossible under OVH	[19], 2019
Elastic degenerate string	$O(N^\alpha)$	$O(n^\delta|P|^\beta), \delta < 1$ or $\beta < 1$ impossible under OVH	[26], 2020
Deterministic DAG	$O(|E|^\alpha)$	$O(|P| + |E|^\delta|P|^\beta), \delta + \beta < 2$ impossible under OVH	Theorem 2
Arbitrary graph	$O(|E|^\alpha)$	$O(|P| + |E|^\delta|P|^\beta), \delta < 1$ or $\beta < 1$ impossible under OVH	Theorem 3

OV which is polynomial in the number of the vectors, but exponential in their length.

The connections to SIC and to OVH constrain the possible construction and query time tradeoffs for SMLG, but they are yet not strong enough to prove the impossibility of building an index in polynomial time such that queries could be sub-quadratic, or even take time say $O(|P| + |E|^{1/2}|P|^2)$. This would be a significant result. In fact, given the wide applicability of this problem, there have been many attempts to obtain such indexing schemes. Sirén, Välimäki, and Mäkinen [42] proposed an extension of the *Burrows-Wheeler transform* [15] for prefix-sorted graphs. Standard indexing techniques [22,30,37] can be applied on such generalized Burrows-Wheeler transform to support linear-time pattern search, but the size of the transform can be exponential in the worst case. There have been some advances in making the approach more practical [25,34,41], but the exponential bottleneck has remained.

The concept of prefix-sorted graphs was later formalized into a more general concept of *Wheeler graphs* [24]: Conceptually these are a class of graphs that admit a generalization of the Burrows-Wheeler transform, and thus a linear size index in the size of the graph supporting string search in linear time in the size of the query pattern. Gibney and Thankachan showed that Wheeler graph recognition problem is NP-complete [27]. Alanko et al. [5] gave polynomial time solutions on some special cases and improved the prefix-sorting algorithm to work in near-optimal time in the size of the output. Another special type of DAGs, called *Degenerate String*, [6,31] and its *Elastic* variant [32], have recently received more attention due to improvements on the online approaches [8,11] for performing string matching. They might be thought of being a promising candidate for indexing thanks to their relatively constrained structure. Nevertheless, this type of DAGs has been proved to be hard to index [26], as we discuss below in more detail.

Mäkinen et al. [35] recently showed that another special graph class, *segment repeat-free founder block graphs*, not directly characterized by the Wheeler property, can be indexed in linear time for linear-time queries. Without these special conditions on graphs, the indexing problem is still widely open.

In this paper we refute the existence of a polynomial indexing scheme for graphs able to provide sub-quadratic [before it said "linear"] time queries, under OVH. Our result holds even for deterministic DAGs with labels from a binary alphabet.

We should note that the results of this paper, via the preprint version of this work [20], have already been used by Gibney [26] while the current paper was under review. In particular, Gibney proved that no index built in polynomial time can provide subquadratic-time queries for elastic degenerate strings, by using our Theorem 5 as [26, Lemma 1]. Even if an elastic degenerate string can be represented as a labeled DAG, our direct approach implies a stronger hardness result on DAGs. Namely, hardness holds also for DAGs labeled using a *binary* alphabet, and in which the total degree[2] is at most 3.

Table 1 and Fig. 1 summarize the complexity landscape of indexed SMLG.

1.2   Results

In the Orthogonal Vectors (OV) problem we are given two sets $X, Y \subseteq \{0,1\}^d$ such that $|X| = |Y| = N$ and $d = \omega(\log N)$, and we need to decide whether there exists $x \in X$ and $y \in Y$ such that x and y are orthogonal, namely, $x \cdot y = 0$. OVH states that for any constant $\epsilon > 0$, no algorithm can solve OV in time $O(N^{2-\epsilon}\text{poly}(d))$.

Notice that OVH [43] is implied by the better known *Strong Exponential Time Hypothesis* (SETH) [33], which states that for any constant $\epsilon > 0$, no algorithm can solve CNF-SAT in time $O(2^{(1-\epsilon)n})$, where n is the number of Boolean variables. Hence, all our lower bounds hold also under SETH.

Our results are obtained using a technique used for example in the field of dynamic algorithms, see e.g. [2,4]. Recall the reduction from k-SAT to OV from [43]: the n variables of the formula ϕ are split into two groups of $n/2$

---

[2] The total degree is the sum of in-degree and out-degree of a node.

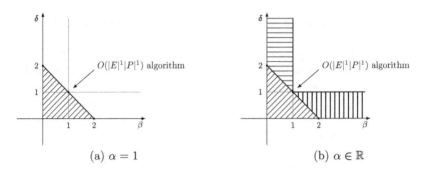

Fig. 1. The dashed areas of the plots represent the forbidden values of δ and β for $O(|P| + |E|^\delta |P|^\beta)$-time queries, under OVH. Figure 1a shows the lower bound that follows from the online case [10,19], and holds for $\alpha = 1$. Figure 1b depicts our lower bound (tight, thanks to the online $O(|E||P|)$-time algorithm from [7]) from Theorem 3. In addition, these hold for any value of α.

variables each, all partial $2^{n/2}$ Boolean assignments are generated for each group, and these induce two sets X and Y of size $N = 2^{n/2}$ each, such that OV returns 'yes' on X and Y if and only if ϕ is satisfiable. Suppose one could index X in polynomial time to support $O(M^{2-\epsilon}\text{poly}(d))$-time queries for any set Y of M vectors, for some $\epsilon > 0$. One now can adjust the splitting of the variables based on the hypothetical ϵ: the first part (corresponding to X) has $n\delta_\epsilon$ variables, and the other part (corresponding to Y) has $n(1 - \delta_\epsilon)$ variables. We can choose a δ_ϵ depending on ϵ such that querying each vector in Y against the index on X takes overall time $O(2^{n(1-\gamma)})$, for some $\gamma > 0$, contradicting SETH.

In this paper, instead of employing this technique inside the reduction for indexed SMLG (as done in previous applications of this technique), we formalize the reason why it works through the notion of a *linear independent-component reduction (lic)*. Such a reduction allows to immediately argue that if a problem A is hard to index, and we have a *lic* reduction from A to B, then also B is hard to index (Lemma 1). Since OV is hard to index, it follows simply as a corollary that any problem to which OV reduces is hard to index. In order to get the best possible result for SMLG, we also show that a generalized version of OV is hard to index (Theorem 5). Thus, we upgrade the idea of an "adjustable splitting" of the variables from a technique to a directly transferable result, once a *lic* reduction is shown to exist.

Examples of problems to which a *lic* reduction could be applied are those that arise from computing a distance between two elements. Popular examples are edit distance, dynamic time warping distance (DTWD), Frechet distance, longest common subsequence. All these problems have been shown to require quadratic time to be solved under OVH. The reductions proving these lower bounds for DTWD [1,14] and Frechet distance [13] are *lic* reductions, hence these problems automatically obtain a lower bound also for their indexed version.

On the other hand, the reductions for edit distance [9] and longest common subsequence [1,14] would need to be slightly tweaked to make the definition of *lic* reduction apply. Nevertheless, the features that are preventing these reductions from being *lic* concern only the size of the gadgets used and not their structural properties. Hence, we are confident that the modifications needed to such gadgets require only a marginal effort.

Moreover, the common indexed variation of the edit distance asks to build a data structure for a long string T such that one can decide if a given query string P is within edit distance κ from a substring of T. It suffices to observe that, in the reduction of Backurs and Indyk [9] from OV to edit distance, this problem is utilized as an intermidiate step, and up to this point their reduction is indeed a *lic* reduction (Sect. 2.2). Hence, we immediately obtain the following result.

Theorem 1. *For any $\alpha, \beta, \delta > 0$ such that $\beta + \delta < 2$, there is no algorithm preprocessing a string T in time $O(|T|^\alpha)$, such that for any pattern string P we can find a substring of T at minimum edit distance with P, in time $O(|P| + |T|^\delta |P|^\beta)$, unless OVH is false.*

For $\delta = 1$ and $\beta = 1$ this lower bound is tight because there exists a matching online algorithm [36]. Theorem 1 also complements the recent result of Cohen-Addad, Feuilloley and Starikovskaya [16], stating that an index built in polynomial time cannot support queries for approximate string matching in $O(|T|^\delta)$ time, for any $\delta < 1$, unless SETH is false. However, the boundary condition is different, since in their case $\kappa = O(\log |T|)$, while in our case $\kappa = \Theta(|P|)$.

Our approach for the SMLG problem is similar. In Sect. 3 we revisit the reduction from [19] and observe that it is a *lic* reduction. As such, we can immediately obtain the following result.

Theorem 2. *For any $\alpha, \beta, \delta > 0$ such that $\beta + \delta < 2$, there is no algorithm preprocessing a labeled graph $G = (V, E, \ell)$ in time $O(|E|^\alpha)$ such that for any pattern string P we can solve the SMLG problem on G and P in time $O(|P| + |E|^\delta |P|^\beta)$, unless OVH is false. This holds even if restricted to a binary alphabet, and to deterministic DAGs in which the sum of out-degree and in-degree of any node is at most three.*[3]

For $\delta = 1$ and $\beta = 1$ this lower bound is tight because there exists a matching online algorithm [7]. However, this bound does not disprove a hypothetical polynomial indexing algorithm with query time $O(|P| + |E|^\delta |P|^2)$, for some $0 < \delta < 1$. Since graphs in practical applications are much larger than the pattern, such an algorithm would be quite significant. However, when the graph is allowed to have cycles, we also show that this is impossible under OVH.

---

[3] We implicitly assumed here that the graph G is the part of the input to be indexed. By exchanging G and P it trivially holds that we also cannot polynomially index a pattern string P to support fast queries in the form of a labeled graph.

Theorem 3. *For any $\alpha, \beta, \delta > 0$, with either $\beta < 1$ or $\delta < 1$, there is no algorithm preprocessing a labeled graph $G = (V, E, \ell)$ in time $O(|E|^\alpha)$ such that for any pattern string P we can solve the SMLG problem on G and P in time $O(|P| + |E|^\delta |P|^\beta)$, unless OVH is false.*

We obtain Theorem 3 by slightly modifying the reduction of [19] with the introduction of certain cycles, that allow for query patterns of length longer than the graph size. The theorem statement could be made slightly stronger by retaining some of the constrain on the graph that we had in Theorem 2, but we leave these details for the extended version of this work. See Sect. 3 for a brief discussion. We leave as open question whether the lower bound from Theorem 3 holds also for DAGs. See Sect. 3 for technical details on the difficulties of this special case.

Open Problem 1 *Does there exist $\alpha, \beta, \delta > 0$, with $\beta < 1$ or $\delta < 1$, and an algorithm preprocessing a labeled (deterministic) DAG $G = (V, E, \ell)$ in time $O(|E|^\alpha)$ such that for any pattern string P we can solve the SMLG problem on G and P in time $O(|P| + |E|^\delta |P|^\beta)$?*

2 Formalizing the Technique

2.1 Linear Independent-Components Reductions

All problems considered in this paper are such that their input is naturally partitioned in two. For a problem P, we will denote by $P_X \times P_Y$ the set of all possible inputs for P. For a particular input $(p_x, p_y) \in P_X \times P_Y$, we will denote by $|p_x|$ and $|p_y|$ the length of each of p_x and p_y, respectively. Intuitively, p_x represents what we want to build the index on, while p_y is what we want to query for. We start by formalizing the concept of *indexability*.

Definition 1 (Indexability). *Problem P is (I,Q)-indexable if for every $p_x \in P_X$ we can preprocess p_x in time $I(|p_x|)$ such that for every $p_y \in P_Y$ we can solve P on (p_x, p_y) in time $Q(|p_x|, |p_y|)$.*

We further refine this notion into that of *polynomial indexability*, by specifying the degree of the polynomial costs of building the index and of performing the queries.

Definition 2 (Polynomial indexability). *Problem P is (α, δ, β)-polynomially indexable with parameter k if P is (I,Q)-indexable and $I(|p_x|) = O(k^{O(1)}|p_x|^\alpha)$ and $Q(|p_x|, |p_y|) = O(k^{O(1)}(|p_y| + |p_x|^\delta |p_y|^\beta))$. If this holds only when $k = O(1)$, then we say that P is (α, δ, β)-polynomially indexable.*

The introduction of parameter k is needed to be consistent with OVH, since when proving a lower bound conditioned on OVH, the reduction is allowed to be polynomial in the vector dimension d. As we will see, we will set $k = d$.

We now introduce linear independent-components reductions, which we show below in Lemma 1 to maintain (α, δ, β)-polynomial indexability.

Definition 3 (*lic* reduction). *Problem A has a* linear independent-components *(lic) reduction with parameter k to problem B, indicated as $A \leq_{lic}^{k} B$, if
the following two properties hold:*

  i) **Correctness:** *There exists a reduction from A to B modeled by functions
  r_x, r_y and s. That is, for any input (a_x, a_y) for A, we have $r_x(a_x) = b_x$,
  $r_y(a_y) = b_y$, (b_x, b_y) is a valid input for B, and s solves A given the output
  $B(b_x, b_y)$ of an oracle to B, namely $s(B(r(a_x), r(a_y))) = A(a_x, a_y)$.*
  ii) **Parameterized linearity:** *Functions r_x, r_y and s can be computed in linear
  time in the size of their input, multiplied by $k^{O(1)}$.*

Lemma 1. *Given problems A and B and constants $\alpha, \beta, \delta > 0$, if $A \leq_{lic}^{k} B$
holds, and B is (α, δ, β)-polynomially indexable, then A is (α, δ, β)-polynomially
indexable with parameter k.*

Proof. Let $a_x \in A_X$ be the first input of problem A. The linear independent-
components reduction computes the first input of problem B as $b_x = r_x(a_x)$
in time $O(k^{O(1)}|a_x|)$. This means that $|b_x| = O(k^{O(1)}|a_x|)$, since the size of the
data structure that we build with the reduction cannot be greater than the time
spent for performing the reduction itself. Problem B is (α, δ, β)-polynomially
indexable, hence we can build an index on b_x in time $O(|b_x|^\alpha)$ in such a way
that we can perform queries for every b_y in time $O(|b_x|^\delta |b_y|^\beta)$. Now given any
input a_y for A we can compute its corresponding $b_y = r_y(a_y)$ via the reduc-
tion in time $O(k^{O(1)}|a_y|)$ and answer a query for it using the index that we
built on b_x. Again, notice that $|b_y| = O(k^{O(1)}|a_y|)$. The cost for such a query is
$O(k^{O(1)}|a_y| + |b_x|^\delta |b_y|^\beta) = O(k^{O(1)}|a_y| + k^{O(1)}|a_x|^\delta |a_y|^\beta)$. Notice that the index-
ing time is $O(|b_x|^\alpha) = O(k^{O(1)}|a_x|^\alpha)$. Hence A is (α, δ, β)-polynomially indexable
with parameter k.   □

2.2   Conditional Indexing Lower Bounds

We begin by stating, with our formalism, a known strengthening of the hardness
of indexing reduction presented at the beginning of Sect. 1.2 (note that it also
follows as a special case of Theorem 5 below).

Theorem 4 (Folklore). *If OV is (α, δ, β)-polynomially indexable with parameter d, and $\beta + \delta < 2$, then OVH fails.*

The value of a parameterized *lic* reduction can now be apprehended: once a
parameterized *lic* reduction is found, the indexing lower bound follows directly.

Corollary 1. *Any problem P such that $OV \leq_{lic}^{d} P$ holds is not (α, δ, β)-
polynomially indexable, for any $\alpha, \beta, \delta > 0$, with $\beta + \delta < 2$, unless OVH is
false.*

Proof. Assume by contradiction that P is (α, δ, β)-polynomially indexable.
Apply Lemma 1 to prove that OV is (α, δ, β)-polynomially indexable with parameter d, and $\beta + \delta < 2$; this contradicts Theorem 4.   □

For a simple and concrete application of Corollary 1, consider the following problem, where $ed(S_1, S_2)$ denotes the edit distance between string S_1 and S_2.

Problem 2 (PATTERN).

INPUT: Two strings T and P.
OUTPUT: $\min\limits_{S \text{ substring of } T} ed(S, P)$.

Backurs and Indyk [9] reduce OV to PATTERN by constructing a string T based solely on the first input X to OV and a string P based solely on the second input Y to OV, such that if there are two orthogonal vectors then the answer to PATTERN on T and P is below a certain value, and if there are not, then the answer is equal to another specific value. Each of T and P can be constructed in time $O(d^{O(1)}N) = O(d^{O(1)}(dN))$. This is a *lic* reduction with parameter d. Directly applying Corollary 1, we obtain Theorem 1.

2.3   Indexing Generalized Orthogonal Vectors

Corollary 1 will suffice to prove Theorem 2. However, to prove that no query time $O(|E|^\delta |P|^\beta)$ is possible for any $\delta < 1$, we need a strengthening of Theorem 4. As such, we introduce the generalized (N, M)-*Orthogonal Vectors* problem:

Problem 3 ((N, M)-OV).

INPUT: Two sets $X, Y \subseteq \{0,1\}^d$, such that $|X| = N$ and $|Y| = M$.
OUTPUT: *True* if and only if there exists $(x, y) \in X \times Y$ such that $x \cdot y = 0$.

The theorem below is the desired generalization of Theorem 4, since it implies, for example, that we cannot have $O(N^{1/2}M^2)$-time queries after polynomial-time indexing. To the best of our efforts, we could not find a proof of this result in the literature, and hence we give one here. It is based on the same idea of an "adjustable splitting" of the vectors, a part of which is indexed, while the other part is queried. However, some technical subtleties arise from the combination of all parameters α, δ, β. Moreover, we care to take into account also the case $\alpha \leq 1$. In this way we rule out special cases like, for instance, $\delta < \alpha \leq 1$, which would leave the door open for efficient algorithms when $|E| \gg |P|$.

Theorem 5. *If (N, M)-OV is (α, δ, β)-polynomially indexable with parameter d, and either $\delta < 1$ or $\beta < 1$, then OVH fails. That is, under OVH, we cannot support $O(N^\delta M^\beta)$-time queries for (N, M)-OV, for either $\delta < 1$ or $\beta < 1$, even after polynomial-time preprocessing.*

Proof. Let X and Y be the input for OV and assume that their size is n. We partition set X into subsets of N vectors each, and set Y into subsets of M vectors each. Each pair of vector sets (X_i, Y_j) in which X_i is such a subset of X and Y_j is such a subset of Y constitutes an instance of (N, M)-OV. Solving all the (X_i, Y_j) instances clearly solves the original problem.[4] Given a pair (X_i, Y_j), since we are assuming that (N, M)-OV is (α, δ, β)-polynomially indexable with parameter d, we can build an index on X_i in $O(d^{O(1)}(dN^\alpha))$ time and answer a query for Y_j in $O(d^{O(1)}(dN)^\delta(dM)^\beta)$ time. Hence, by building a new index for every X_i and querying every Y_j we can cover all the pairs. Since we build $\lceil \frac{n}{N} \rceil$ indexes and we perform $\lceil \frac{n}{N} \rceil \lceil \frac{n}{M} \rceil$ queries, one for each pair (X_i, Y_j), the total cost for solving the original OV problem is:

$$O\left(d^{O(1)}\left((dN)^\alpha \frac{n}{N} + (dN)^\delta(dM)^\beta \frac{n}{N}\frac{n}{M}\right)\right) \tag{1}$$

$$=O\left(d^{O(1)}\left(N^{\alpha-1}n + N^{\delta-1}M^{\beta-1}n^2\right)\right). \tag{2}$$

In order to achieve a contradiction with OVH, we need such time complexity to be subquadratic in the original OV instance. Namely, it should be $O(d^{O(1)}(n^{2-\epsilon'} + n^{2-\epsilon}))$, for some $\epsilon, \epsilon' > 0$. Clearly, it must also hold $1 \le N \le n$ and $1 \le M \le n$, and N and M should be integers. Putting all together, we want that for every $n \in \mathbb{N}, \alpha, \delta, \beta > 0$ such that either $\delta < 1$ or $\beta < 1$ there exists $\epsilon', \epsilon > 0, N$ and M such that:

(a) $N^{\alpha-1}n = O(n^{2-\epsilon'})$ (b) $N^{\delta-1}M^{\beta-1}n^2 = O(n^{2-\epsilon})$
(c) $N \in \mathbb{N}, M \in \mathbb{N}$ (d) $1 \le N \le n, 1 \le M \le n$

The solutions to this system differ depending on the values of α, δ and β. In Table 2 we present an exhaustive list of solutions for any choice of these parameters. The complete analysis on how to find the range of possible solutions to the system is presented in preprint version of this work [21].

Table 2. The solutions to the system for any given value of α, δ and β.

α	β	δ	N	M	ϵ'	ϵ
$\alpha < 2$	$\beta < 1$	Any δ	1	n	1	$1 - \beta$
	$\beta \ge 1$	$\delta < 1$	n	1	$2 - \alpha$	$1 - \delta$
$\alpha \ge 2$	$\beta < 1$	Any δ	1	n	1	$1 - \beta$
	$\beta \ge 1$	$\delta < 1$	$\lceil n^{\frac{1}{2(\alpha-1)}} \rceil$	1	$\frac{1}{2}$	$\frac{1-\delta}{2(\alpha-1)}$

We conclude that depending on α, δ and β we find ourselves into one of the listed cases and thus we can always find valid values for ϵ, ϵ', N and M that lead to an algorithm for OV running in time $O(n^{2-\epsilon} + n^{2-\epsilon'})$, contradicting OVH. $\square$

Corollary 2. *Any problem P such that (N, M)-OV $\le_{lic}^d P$ holds is not (α, δ, β)-polynomially indexable, for any $\alpha, \beta, \delta > 0$, with either $\beta < 1$ or $\delta < 1$, unless OVH is false.*

---

[4] The idea of splitting the two sets into smaller groups was also used in [3] to obtain a fast randomized algorithm for OV, based on the polynomial method, and therein the groups always had equal size.

3   Indexing Labeled Graphs for String Matching

We are now left to prove Theorem 2 and Theorem 3. While the former can be obtained solely applying the concept of *lic* reduction, the latter requires more attention.

Recall the following conditional lower bound for SMLG from Equi et al. [19].

Theorem 6 ([19]). *For any $\epsilon > 0$, SMLG on labeled deterministic DAGs cannot be solved in either $O(|E|^{1-\epsilon}|P|)$ or $O(|E||P|^{1-\epsilon})$ time unless OVH fails. This holds even if restricted to a binary alphabet, and to deterministic DAGs in which the sum of out-degree and in-degree of any node is at most three.*

In order to prove Theorem 2 it is enough to check the structure of the reduction used to prove Theorem 6 in [19].

Proof (Theorem 2). Given an OV instance with sets X and Y, the reduction from [19] builds a graph G using solely X, and a pattern P using solely Y, both in linear time $O(dN)$, such that P has a match in G if and only if there exists a pair of orthogonal vectors. [5] This shows that the two conditions of the linear independent-components reduction property hold, thus OV $\leq_{lic}^d$ SMLG. We conclude the proof by directly applying Corollary 1.   □

Next, we show that constraint $\beta + \delta < 2$ can be dropped from Theorem 2 when we are indexing non-deterministic graphs with cycles. The idea is that if we allow (N, M)-OV instances with $M > N$, then the reduction from [19] no longer holds, because the pattern P is too large to fit inside the DAG G. As such, we need to make a minor adjustment to G.

Proof (Theorem 3). Given an (N, M)-OV instance with sets X and Y, we first show how it is possible to modify the reduction form [19] to fit an arbitrarily long pattern into the graph. The desired lower bound will then follow by applying the *lic* reduction.

The pattern that we use is the same pattern P of the original reduction, which is built over alphabet $\Sigma = \{\mathsf{b}, \mathsf{e}, 0, 1\}$, has length $|P| = O(dM)$, and can be built in $O(dM)$ time from the second set of vectors $Y = \{y_1, \ldots, y_M\}$. Namely, we define $P = \mathsf{bb}P_{y_1}\mathsf{e}\,\mathsf{b}P_{y_2}\mathsf{e}\ldots\mathsf{b}P_{y_M}\mathsf{ee}$, where P_{y_i} is a string of length d that is associated with each $y_i \in Y$, for $1 \leq i \leq M$. The h-th symbol of P_{y_i} is either 0 or 1, for each $h \in \{1, \ldots, d\}$, such that $P_{y_i}[h] = 1$ if and only if $y_i[h] = 1$.

The graph G' that we need to make our new reduction work is depicted in Fig. 2 and we now discuss how it can be built. Starting from the first set of vectors X, we define the directed graph $G_W = (V_W, E_W, L_W)$, which can be built in $O(dN)$ time and consists of N connected components $G_W^{(j)}$, one for each vector $x_j \in X$. Each component $G_W^{(j)}$ can be constructed so that the following holds.

---

[5] Originally [19] P and G were built on X and Y, respectively. Since it is immaterial for correctness, we assumed the opposite here to keep in line with the notation.

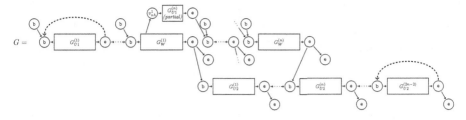

Fig. 2. Non-deterministic graph G'. We add the dashed thick edges, absent in the acyclic graph from [19], to handle (N, M)-OV instances with $M > N$.

Lemma 2 ([19]). *Subpattern* $\mathsf{b}P_{y_i}\mathsf{e}$ *has a match in* G_W *if and only if there exist* $x_j \in X$ *such that* $x_i \cdot y_j = 0$.

In addition, we need a universal gadget $G_U = (V_U, E_U, L_U)$ of $2N - 2$ components $G_U^{(k)}$. We build such components in the same way as in [19], and for the correctness of the current proof it suffices to know that each component can match any subpattern P_{y_i}. Let us now build the same final graph G as in [19] by using two instances G_{U1} and G_{U2} of G_U and merging the first one of these with G_W. The resulting graph G has total size $O(dN)$ and corresponds to the one shown in Fig. 2 without the dashed edges. Note that every path from a pair of consecutive b-nodes to a pair of consecutive e-nodes passes through a $G_W^{(j)}$ component. Indeed, this graph satisfies the following property.

Lemma 3 ([19]). *Pattern* P *has a match in* G *if and only if a subpattern* $\mathsf{b}P_{x_i}\mathsf{e}$ *of* P *has a match in the underlying subgraph* G_W *of* G_{U1W}.

From graph G we then build final graph G' with the addition of an edge from the e-node to the right of $G_{U1}^{(1)}$ back to the b-node to the left of $G_{U1}^{(1)}$, and likewise from the e-node to the right of $G_{U2}^{(2N-2)}$ back to the b-node to the left of $G_{U2}^{(2N-2)}$. This final graph G' is the one of Fig. 2.

The intuition on how the reduction works is that a prefix of P is handled by the "top" universal gadgets G_{U1}, a possible matching a subpattern P_{y_i} of P by one of the "middle" gadgets $G_W^{(j)}$, and a suffix of P by the "bottom" universal gadgets, because P has a bb prefix and an ee suffix. Our new edges allow to accommodate (N, M)-OV instances with $M > N$.

Formally, we need to prove that Lemma 3 holds also if considering G' and the case $N \neq M$.

Proof (Lemma 3 for G', $N \neq M$). For the ($\Rightarrow$) implication, we follow the same logic as in [19] and we observe that pattern P needs to start a match only by using a pair of consecutive b-nodes and such a match can be completed only by using a pair of consecutive e-nodes after having matched a $G_W^{(j)}$ component. Hence we can use Lemma 2 to ensure that there exists a pair of orthogonal vectors. The ($\Leftarrow$) implication is easier: if a subpattern $\mathsf{b}P_{x_i}\mathsf{e}$ of P has a match in the underlying subgraph G_W then we can match the prefix of P preceding

$\mathsf{b}P_{x_i}\mathsf{e}$ in G_U since every subpattern $\mathsf{b}P_{x_{i'}}\mathsf{e}$, $1 \leq i' < i$, can be matched in the $G_{U1}^{(i)}$ components. Observe that if $N < M$ then there might not be enough such components to match all the subpatterns of $|P|$. In that case, our newly added backward edges can be used to match the component $G_{U1}^{(1)}$ multiple times. The $N > M$ case poses no problem. The same reasoning applies to the subpatterns $\mathsf{b}P_{x_{i''}}\mathsf{e}$, $i < i'' \leq M$, constituting the suffix of $|P|$. Such subpatterns can be matched in G_{U2} possibly exploiting our backward edge.	□

Since Lemma 3 still holds, we conclude that the reduction using graph G' works for any value of N and M. Hence, applying Corollary 2, we obtain Theorem 3.	□

As a final note, we informally describe how some of the features of Theorem 2 could be kept also in Theorem 3. We leave a more detailed and formal discussion for the extended version of this work.

Remark 1. The statement of Theorem 3 holds even if restricted to a binary alphabet, and to DAGs in which the sum of out-degree and in-degree of any node is at most three. Hence, with respect to Theorem 2, we have to drop only determinism. Indeed, the two additional edges that we added to build our final graph G' respect the degree constraint. Moreover, applying the same transformation as in [19], the theorem holds even when we are restricted to use a binary alphabet.

References

1. Abboud, A., Backurs, A., Williams, V.V.: Tight hardness results for LCS and other sequence similarity measures. In: FOCS 2015, Berkeley, CA, USA, pp. 59–78 (2015)
2. Abboud, A., Rubinstein, A., Williams, R.R.: Distributed PCP theorems for hardness of approximation in P. In: IEEE 58th Annual Symposium on Foundations of Computer Science (FOCS), Berkeley, CA, USA, pp. 25–36. IEEE (2017)
3. Abboud, A., Williams, R., Yu, H.: More applications of the polynomial method to algorithm design. In: Proceedings of the Twenty-Sixth Annual ACM-SIAM Symposium on Discrete Algorithms, San Diego, California, pp. 218–230 (2015)
4. Abboud, A., Williams, V.V.: Popular conjectures imply strong lower bounds for dynamic problems. In: IEEE 55th Annual Symposium on Foundations of Computer Science, Philadelphia, PA, USA, pp. 434–443 (2014)
5. Alanko, J., D'Agostino, G., Policriti, A., Prezza, N.: Regular languages meet prefix sorting. In: Proceedings of the Fourteenth Annual ACM-SIAM Symposium on Discrete Algorithms, Salt Lake City, UT, USA, pp. 911–930 (2020)
6. Alzamel, M., et al.: Degenerate string comparison and applications. In: Parida, L., Ukkonen, E. (eds.) 18th International Workshop on Algorithms in Bioinformatics (WABI 2018). Leibniz International Proceedings in Informatics (LIPIcs), vol. 113, pp. 21:1–21:14. Schloss Dagstuhl-Leibniz-Zentrum fuer Informatik, Dagstuhl, Germany (2018)
7. Amir, A., Lewenstein, M., Lewenstein, N.: Pattern matching in hypertext. In: Dehne, F., Rau-Chaplin, A., Sack, J.-R., Tamassia, R. (eds.) WADS 1997. LNCS, vol. 1272, pp. 160–173. Springer, Heidelberg (1997). https://doi.org/10.1007/3-540-63307-3_56

8. Aoyama, K., et al.: Faster online elastic degenerate string matching. In: Annual Symposium on Combinatorial Pattern Matching (CPM 2018), Schloss Dagstuhl-Leibniz-Zentrum fuer Informatik (2018)

9. Backurs, A., Indyk, P.: Edit Distance Cannot Be Computed in Strongly Subquadratic Time (Unless SETH is False). In: Proceedings of the Forty-Seventh Annual ACM Symposium on Theory of Computing, New York, USA, pp. 51–58 (2015)

10. Backurs, A., Indyk, P.: Which regular expression patterns are hard to match? In: IEEE 57th Annual Symposium on Foundations of Computer Science (FOCS), New Brunswick, NJ, USA, pp. 457–466. IEEE (2016)

11. Bernardini, G., Gawrychowski, P., Pisanti, N., Pissis, S.P., Rosone, G.: Even faster elastic-degenerate string matching via fast matrix multiplication. In: Baier, C., Chatzigiannakis, I., Flocchini, P., Leonardi, S. (eds.) 46th International Colloquium on Automata, Languages, and Programming, ICALP 2019, July 9–12, 2019, Patras, Greece. LIPIcs, vol. 132, pp. 21:1–21:15. Schloss Dagstuhl - Leibniz-Zentrum fuer Informatik (2019)

12. Bille, P.: Personal Communication at Dagstuhl Seminar on Indexes and Computation over Compressed Structured Data (2013)

13. Bringmann, K.: Why walking the dog takes time: frechet distance has no strongly subquadratic algorithms unless seth fails. In: IEEE 55th Annual Symposium on Foundations of Computer Science, pp. 661–670. IEEE (2014)

14. Bringmann, K., Kunnemann, M.: Quadratic conditional lower bounds for string problems and dynamic time warping. In: IEEE 56th Annual Symposium on Foundations of Computer Science, Washington, USA, pp. 79–97. IEEE (2015)

15. Burrows, M., Wheeler, D.: A block sorting lossless data compression algorithm. Tech. Rep. 124, Digital Equipment Corporation (1994)

16. Cohen-Addad, V., Feuilloley, L., Starikovskaya, T.: Lower bounds for text indexing with mismatches and differences. In: Proceedings of the Thirtieth Annual ACM-SIAM Symposium on Discrete Algorithms, San Diego, USA, pp. 1146–1164 (2019)

17. Consortium, T.C.P.G.: Computational pan-genomics: status, promises and challenges. Briefings in Bioinform. **19**(1), 118–135 (2018)

18. Crochemore, M., Rytter, W.: Jewels of Stringology. World Scientific (2002)

19. Equi, M., Grossi, R., Mäkinen, V., Tomescu, A.I.: On the complexity of string matching for graphs. In: 46th International Colloquium on Automata, Languages, and Programming (ICALP 2019), Patras, Greece, pp. 55:1–55:15 (2019)

20. Equi, M., Grossi, R., Tomescu, A.I., Mäkinen, V.: On the complexity of exact pattern matching in graphs: determinism and zig-zag matching. arXiv e-prints arXiv:1902.03560 (2019)

21. Equi, M., Mäkinen, V., Tomescu, A.I.: Graphs cannot be indexed in polynomial time for sub-quadratic time string matching, unless seth fails. arXiv e-prints arXiv:2002.00629 (2020)

22. Ferragina, P., Manzini, G.: Indexing compressed texts. J. ACM **52**(4), 552–581 (2005)

23. Ferragina, P., Luccio, F., Manzini, G., Muthukrishnan, S.: Compressing and indexing labeled trees, with applications. J. ACM **57**(1), 4:1–4:33 (2009)

24. Gagie, T., Manzini, G., Sirén, J.: Wheeler graphs: a framework for BWT-based data structures. Theor. Comput. Sci. **698**, 67–78 (2017)

25. Garrison, E., et al.: Variation graph toolkit improves read mapping by representing genetic variation in the reference. Nat. Biotechnol. **36**, 875 (2018)

26. Gibney, D.: An efficient elastic-degenerate text index? not likely. In: Boucher, C., Thankachan, S.V. (eds.) SPIRE 2020. LNCS, vol. 12303, pp. 76–88. Springer, Cham (2020). https://doi.org/10.1007/978-3-030-59212-7_6

27. Gibney, D., Thankachan, S.V.: On the hardness and inapproximability of recognizing Wheeler graphs. In: ESA 2019, Munich/Garching, Germany, pp. 51:1–51:16 (2019)

28. Goldstein, I., Lewenstein, M., Porat, E.: Orthogonal vectors indexing. In: ISAAC 2017, Dagstuhl, Germany, pp. 40:1–40:12 (2017)

29. Goldstein, I., Lewenstein, M., Porat, E.: On the hardness of set disjointness and set intersection with bounded universe. In: ISAAC 2019, Shanghai, China. LIPIcs, vol. 149, pp. 7:1–7:22 (2019)

30. Grossi, R., Vitter, J.: Compressed suffix arrays and suffix trees with applications to text indexing and string matching. SIAM J. Comput. **35**(2), 378–407 (2006)

31. Grossi, R., et al.: On-line pattern matching on similar texts. In: CPM 2017. vol. 78, p. 1. Schloss Dagstuhl-Leibniz-Zentrum für Informatik GmbH (2017)

32. Iliopoulos, C.S., Kundu, R., Pissis, S.P.: Efficient pattern matching in elastic-degenerate texts. In: Drewes, F., Martín-Vide, C., Truthe, B. (eds.) LATA 2017. LNCS, vol. 10168, pp. 131–142. Springer, Cham (2017). https://doi.org/10.1007/978-3-319-53733-7_9

33. Impagliazzo, R., Paturi, R.: On the complexity of k-SAT. J. Comput. Syst. Sci. **62**(2), 367–375 (2001)

34. Kim, D., Paggi, J.M., Park, C., Bennett, C., Salzberg, S.L.: Graph-based genome alignment and genotyping with HISAT2 and HISAT-genotype. Nat. Biotechnol. **37**(8), 907–915 (2019)

35. Mäkinen, V., Cazaux, B., Equi, M., Norri, T., Tomescu, A.I.: Linear time construction of indexable founder block graphs. In: WABI 2020, Pisa, Italy. LIPIcs, vol. 172, pp. 7:1–7:18 (2020). https://doi.org/10.4230/LIPIcs.WABI.2020.7

36. Masek, W.J., Paterson, M.S.: A faster algorithm computing string edit distances. J. Comput. Syst. Sci. **20**(1), 18–31 (1980)

37. Navarro, G., Mäkinen, V.: Compressed full-text indexes. ACM Comput. Surv. **39**(1), 2 (2007)

38. Patrascu, M., Roditty, L.: Distance oracles beyond the Thorup-Zwick bound. SIAM J. Comput. **43**(1), 300–311 (2014)

39. Rautiainen, M., Mäkinen, V., Marschall, T.: Bit-parallel sequence-to-graph alignment. Bioinformatics **35**(19), 3599–3607 (2019)

40. Schneeberger, K., et al.: Simultaneous alignment of short reads against multiple genomes. Genome Biol. **10**, R98 (2009)

41. Sirén, J.: Indexing variation graphs. In: ALENEX 2017, Barcelona, Spain, pp. 13–27 (2017)

42. Sirén, J., Välimäki, N., Mäkinen, V.: Indexing graphs for path queries with applications in genome research. IEEE/ACM Trans. Comput. Biol. Bioinform. **11**(2), 375–388 (2014)

43. Williams, R.: A new algorithm for optimal 2-constraint satisfaction and its implications. Theor. Comput. Sci. **348**(2–3), 357–365 (2005)

Author Index

Printed in the United States
By Bookmasters